WRITER'S
HANDBOOK
2005

Barry Turner has worked on both sides of publishing, as an editor and marketing director and as an author. He started his career as a journalist with *The Observer* before moving on to television and radio. He has written over twenty books including *A Place in the Country*, which inspired a television series, and a best selling biography of the actor, Richard Burton.

His recent work includes a radio play, travel articles, serialising books for *The Times*, editing the magazine *Country* and writing a one-man show based on the life of the legendary theatre critic, James Agate. He has just published *Countdown to Victory*, a book about the last months of World War II. Barry has been editor of *The Writer's Handbook* for eighteen years and editor of *The Statesman's Yearbook* for seven.

Also edited by Barry Turner in The Writer's Handbook *series*

THE WRITER'S HANDBOOK GUIDE TO WRITING FOR CHILDREN

Featuring articles and interviews with established authors and experts in the trade, this book explores the key to success in writing for children and offers all the necessary advice for newcomers to this expanding market.

ISBN: 1405001011

THE WRITER'S HANDBOOK GUIDE TO TRAVEL WRITING

From newspaper features to armchair travellers' memoirs, this highly informative guide offers all the essential information needed by any budding travel writer looking to break into this increasingly popular genre.

ISBN 1405041781

THE WRITER'S HANDBOOK GUIDE TO CRIME WRITING

Drawing on a wide range of expertise, including top crime writers, agents, publishers and booksellers, this book looks at how to write a successful crime novel and get it published.

ISBN: 1405000996

THE WRITER'S HANDBOOK GUIDE TO WRITING FOR STAGE AND SCREEN

There are increasing opportunities for new writers of plays, be it for stage, screen or radio – but also increasing demands. This highly practical and informative book looks at how to get started, and how to become a successful playwright in any area.

ISBN: 1405000988

All Pan Macmillan titles are available from www.panmacmillan.com or from Bookpost by telephoning 01624 677237

THE
WRITER'S
HANDBOOK
2005

EDITOR

BARRY TURNER

MACMILLAN

First published 2004 by Macmillan
an imprint of Pan Macmillan Ltd
Pan Macmillan, 20 New Wharf Road,
London N1 9RR
Basingstoke and Oxford
Associated companies throughout the world
www.panmacmillan.com

ISBN 1 4050 4153 6

9 8 7 6 5 4 3 2 1

A CIP catalogue record for this book is available from
the British Library

Credits

Editor *Barry Turner*
Editorial Assistants *Jill Fenner, Jeni Giffen, Kenneth Hadley, Daniel Smith*
Poetry Editor *Peter Finch*
Contributors *Katharine Davies*
            David Hooper
            Kate Pool
            Kate Rowland
Tax and Finance Adviser *Ian Spring*

Typeset by Heronwood Press, Medstead, Hants
Printed and bound in Great Britain by Mackays of Chatham plc, Kent

Contents

Authors Look to the Bottom Line

Barry Turner

A long time ago, when I and the world were young my dears, it was said of books that they sold themselves. Asked to define marketing, a gentleman publisher (they were all gentlemen) was liable to think first of the man at the end of his mews who sold flowers off a barrow. Books were not like other goods. They appeared, as if by some strange literary osmosis, on the shelves of a high street store where each volume was clearly marked with a price set by the publisher. A discount, typically 15–20 per cent, was the predetermined profit for the retailer. Known as the Net Book Agreement, this cosy arrangement was jealously protected by its proponents who argued that to do away with the NBA would result in dearer books, fewer titles on offer and the demise of the small independent bookshop. The counter argument relied on the appeal of the free market. Abolishing retail price maintenance on books, as it had been on every other consumer item, would, it was claimed, lead to a more competitive environment. Publishers and booksellers would be forced off their butts to do some real selling instead of leaning back to wait for the reviewers and word of mouth recommendations to bring in the orders. More titles, cheaper books and a wider choice of retailer were predicted.

When, at last, in 1995, the NBA went the way of other price fixing deals, the proof of the pudding was much to the taste of the abolitionists. The book trade had a rush of energy that brought it into the brave new world of aggressive retailing. Loss leaders and three for the price of two promotions became commonplace along with attractive window displays and customer friendly stores that made book browsing a popular pastime. The number of titles published each year continued to increase (at the last count it was 125,390) and total sales enjoyed a year on year rise to £1.98 billion in 2002. There is, of course, a downside. The elevation of marketing to senior director level in all the mainline publishers has raised the stakes on identifying titles that can justify heavyweight promotion and the ever-increasing share of turnover demanded by retailers to pay for it. This emphasis on bestsellers is said to mitigate against risk taking. The tendency is to push money at those authors who have a strong track record and thus are already familiar names to the public or at writers who are promotable by virtue of their fame in sport, politics, show business or some other area where the book of the life promises a sensationalist read. It doesn't always work, but so far no one has come up with a more certain way of making money from general publishing.

Those who lose out are the mid-list authors, who used to justify their publication by sales to the libraries (with a welcome additional income from PLR) as much as by a modest take-up in the shops. Now, library budgets are tighter and so too is shelf space. The squeeze has put paid to some routine authors whose demise might be deemed a merciful release but there is a worry that new writers who need time to develop might now have fewer opportunities to get started. Philip Pullman and Ian Rankin have been mentioned as writers who did not find bestseller success until well into their careers.

But this is to assume that the big publishers have lost all capacity to identify promising newcomers, which is simply not true. Editors are only too happy to discover a bestseller writer in the making – that is how they measure their own career prospects. Agents too are heavily into the business of nurturing the literary lion cubs. For writers who are trying to make their names, the frustration comes in finding that competition is tough, the more so because publishers and agents need a lot of persuading that the books they take on really do have a chance breaking the sales barrier. A consolation is in knowing that publishing is led but not dominated by the conglomerates. One of the encouraging features of the contemporary book scene is the success of smaller publishers such as Profile, Fourth Estate, Mainstream and Serpent's Tail in discovering and advancing talent.

Every established author can recall the hard times with a collection of rejection slips; some even boast enough of them to paper a wall. No one ever claimed that making a living from writing is an easy option What has to be kept in mind is that, despite all the moans and groans, the breakthrough is no harder to achieve now than it was before we were all caught up in the marketing revolution.

The other big worry of authors about the way books are sold is that before long publishers will ask for changes in the system of paying royalties. As a hangover from the NBA, most books still have a recommended retail price printed on their jackets. This is the benchmark for the royalty share, traditionally 10 per cent on the first 2,500 copies sold, 12.5 per cent on the next 2,500 and 15 per cent thereafter. Paperbacks typically come with a royalty tag of 7.5 per cent. So far, so relatively simple. Booksellers are free to cut prices if they see this as a strategy for increasing sales while authors' income is protected by being tied to the RRP. The catch, for the bookseller, is in not being able to increase prices on some items to compensate for the loss leaders. That is how supermarkets maximise turnover and the book chains would dearly like to follow their example.

Publishers would almost certainly agree to remove printed prices from covers, thus allowing booksellers, who presumably know their market, to decide their own terms of trade, on one important condition: that authors would drop their claim to royalties in return for getting a percentage of net receipts. The proposal, still at a kite flying stage, has been greeted by authors, their agents and other representatives with a howl of anger that would do credit to the sound effects for Harry Potter. But unless the principle is accepted that any change in marketing is bound to work against the writer, it is hard to see what the fuss is all about.

There are those who worry that putting up the price of some books would make them unsaleable which is another way of saying that the bookseller is incapable of knowing his own best interest – an unlikely proposition. Others believe that the figures for net receipts would be massaged by less reputable publishers to the detriment of authors. Possibly so, but surely no one is suggesting that royalty statements are immune to light-fingered manipulation? Percentage deals already apply to book clubs and to overseas sales. There is no reason to think that thereby authors are treated unfairly any more than there is reason to suppose that sums earned from percentages and royalties could not be equated by simple mathematics.

The objective of booksellers is to sell more books which has to be to the advantage of everyone, including authors. If taking prices off books helps towards that end, then we should applaud the move. However, there is another factor worth more than passing consideration. Publishing is all about risk – more so than most other businesses – but it is a risk that is shared unevenly. Books go into the shops on a sale or return basis. If they hang about on the shelves for more than a few weeks, back they go to the publishers' warehouses. If booksellers want more commercial freedom it is surely time for them to take on more responsibility. Firm sales, starting with front-list books, would bring them closer in line to the supermarkets they seek to emulate. Such a change in the terms of trade would be more radical than taking prices off books but the smaller concession may accelerate the momentum for change. Moreover, if authors were to receive a percentage of net receipts instead of a royalty on a fixed price, it would be easier for publishers to negotiate firm deals on longer print runs.

The book trade has a long way to go before it reaches its optimum size but growth needs energy and energy needs incentive. Opinion formers among authors seem unable to recognise this. This is a pity because they should be leading the way, not following sulkily behind the van.

UK Publishers

AA Publishing
The Automobile Association, Fanum House, Basingstoke RG21 4EA
☎01256 491573 Fax 01256 491974
✉ rupert.mitchell@theAA.com
www.theAA.com

Managing Director *Stephen Mesquita*
Manager, Publishing *Rupert Mitchell*

Publishes maps, atlases and guidebooks, motoring, travel and leisure. About 100 titles a year.

Abacus
See **Time Warner Books UK**

ABC–Clio
26 Beaumont Street, Oxford OX1 2NP
☎01865 517222 Fax 01865 517228
✉ salesuk@abc-clio.com
www.abc-clio.com

Acquisitions Editor *Simon Mason*

Formerly Clio Press Ltd. Publishes academic and general reference works, social sciences and humanities. Markets, outside North America, the Web, CD-ROM publications and reference books of the American parent company.
ROYALTIES twice-yearly.

Absolute Press
Scarborough House, 29 James Street West, Bath BA1 2BT
☎01225 316013 Fax 01225 445836
✉ sales@absolutepress.demon.co.uk
www.absolutepress.demon.co.uk

Managing/Editorial Director *Jon Croft*

Founded 1979. Publishes food and wine-related subjects as well as travel guides. SERIES *Outlines* Monographs on gay and lesbian creative artists. About 10 titles a year. No unsolicited mss. Synopses and ideas for books welcome.
ROYALTIES twice-yearly.

Abson Books London
5 Sidney Square, London E1 2EY
☎020 7790 4737 Fax 020 7790 7346
✉ absonbooks@aol.com

Publisher *M.J. Ellison*

Founded 1971 in Bristol. Publishes language glossaries and curiosities. TITLES *Rude Rhyming*

Slang; Hip Hop English. No unsolicited mss; synopses and ideas for books welcome.
ROYALTIES twice-yearly.

Academic Press
See **Elsevier Ltd**

Acair Ltd
Unit 7, 7 James Street, Stornoway, Isle of Lewis HS1 2QN
☎01851 703020 Fax 01851 703294
✉ acair@sol.co.uk

Specialising in matters pertaining to the Gaidhealtachd, Acair publishes books in Gaelic and English on Scottish history, culture and the Gaelic language. 75% of their children's books are targeted at primary school usage and are published exclusively in Gaelic.
ROYALTIES twice-yearly.

Actinic Press
See **Cressrelles Publishing Co. Ltd**

Acumen Publishing Limited
15A Lewins Yard, East Street, Chesham HP5 1HQ
☎01494 794398 Fax 01494 784850
✉ steven.gerrard@acumenpublishing.co.uk
www.acumenpublishing.co.uk

Managing Director *Steven Gerrard*

Founded in 1998 as an independent publisher for the higher education market. Publishes academic books on philosophy, history and politics. 15 titles in 2003. No unsolicited mss. Synopses and ideas for books welcome; send written proposal as per Acumen guidelines.
ROYALTIES annually.

Addison Wesley Longman
See **Pearson Education**

Adlard Coles Nautical
See **A.&C. Black Publishers Ltd**

Advance Publishing
2 Northumbria Close, Haddenham, Ely CB6 3HT
☎01353 7494904
✉ editors@advance-publishing.co.uk

www.advance-publishing.co.uk
Senior Editor *Julie Underwood*
Editor *Margaret Burrows*
Founded 2002. Publishes non-ficton, fiction, biography, autobiography, history, humour, science fiction, travel, war and crime. Unsolicited mss and synopses considered if accompanied by return postage.
ROYALTIES twice-yearly.

Authors' Rating Authors may be asked to contribute towards production costs.

African Books Collective
The Jam Factory, 27 Park End Street, Oxford OX1 1HU
☎01865 726686 Fax 01865 793298
✉ abc@africanbookscollective.com
www.africanbookscollective.com

Founded 1990. Collectively owned by its 17 founder publishers. Exclusive distribution in N. America, UK, Europe and Commonwealth countries outside Africa for 80 African participating publishers. Concentration is on scholarly/academic, literature and children's books. Mainly concerned with the promotion and dissemination of African-published material outside Africa. Supplies African-published books to African libraries and organisations and publishes resource books on African publishing. TITLES *The African Writers' Handbook; African Publishers Networking Directory; Women in Publishing and the Book Trade in Africa; The Electronic African Bookworm: A Web Navigator; Courage and Consequence: Women Publishing in Africa.*

Age Concern Books
1268 London Road, London SW16 4ER
☎020 8765 7200 Fax 020 8765 7211
✉ books@ace.org.uk
www.ageconcern.org.uk
Approx. Annual Turnover £400,000

Publishing arm of Age Concern England. Publishes related non-fiction only. No fiction. About 18 titles a year. Synopses and ideas welcome for new practical handbooks.

Airlife Publishing
See **The Crowood Press Ltd**

Ian Allan Publishing Ltd
Riverdene Business Park, Molesey Road, Hersham KT12 4RG
☎01932 266600 Fax 01932 266601
✉ info@ianallanpub.co.uk

www.ianallanpublishing.com
Chairman *David Allan*
Managing Director *Tony Saunders*

Specialist transport publisher – atlases, maps, railway, aviation, road transport, military, maritime, reference. Manages distribution and sales for third party publishers. IMPRINTS **Midland Publishing** (see entry); **Classic Publications**; **OPC** Railway titles. About 80 titles a year. Send sample chapter and synopsis with s.a.e

J.A. Allen & Co.
An imprint of Robert Hale Ltd, Clerkenwell House, 45–47 Clerkenwell Green, London EC1R 0HT
☎020 7251 2661 Fax 020 7490 4958
✉ allen@halebooks.com
Publisher *Caroline Burt*
Marketing Director *Martin Kendall*
Approx. Annual Turnover £750,000

Founded 1926 as part of J.A. Allen & Co. (The Horseman's Bookshop) Ltd. Bought by **Robert Hale Ltd** in 1999. Publishes equine and equestrian non-fiction. About 20 titles a year. Mostly commissioned but willing to consider unsolicited mss of technical/instructional material related to all aspects of horses and horsemanship.
ROYALTIES twice-yearly.

Allen Lane
See **Penguin Group (UK)**

Allison & Busby
Suite 111, Bon Marche Centre, 241 Ferndale Road, London SW9 8BJ
☎020 7738 7888 Fax 020 7733 4344
✉ all@allisonbusby.co.uk
www.allisonandbusby.ltd.uk
Publishing Director *David Shelley*

Founded 1967. Publishes literary fiction, crime fiction, biography and writers' guides. TITLES *The Best British Mysteries* ed. Maxim Jakubowski; *Bushwhacked: Life in George W. Bush's America* Molly Ivins; *Blue Angel* Francine Prose. About 40 titles a year. Send synopses with two sample chapters, not full mss. No replies without s.a.e.

Authors' Rating 'A testament to the ability of smaller publishers to survive in the retail jungle' (*Publishing News*), A&B is putting its effort into marketing a streamlined list.

Alpha Press
See **Sussex Academic Press**

Alton Douglas Books
See **Brewin Books Ltd**

Amber Lane Press Ltd
Cheorl House, Church Street, Charlbury
OX7 3PR
☎01608 810024 Fax 01608 810024
✉ info@amberlanepress.co.uk
www.amberlanepress.co.uk
Chairman *Brian Clark*
Managing Director/Editorial Head *Judith Scott*
Founded 1979 to publish modern play texts.
Publishes plays and books on the theatre.
TITLES *Vampire* Snoo Wilson; *The Business of
Murder* Richard Harris; *I Thought I Heard a
Rustling* Alan Plater (play texts); *Portrait of Ellen
Terry* David Cheshire. About 4 titles a year.
'Expressly *not* interested in poetry.' No un-
solicited mss. Synopses and ideas welcome.
    ROYALTIES twice-yearly.

Amsco
See **Omnibus Press**

Andersen Press Ltd
20 Vauxhall Bridge Road, London
SW1V 2SA
☎020 7840 8703/8700 Fax 020 7233 6263
✉ andersenpress@randomhouse.co.uk
www.andersenpress.co.uk
Managing Director/Publisher *Klaus Flugge*
Editorial Director *Janice Thomson*
Editor, Fiction *Audrey Adams*
Founded 1976 by Klaus Flugge and named
after Hans Christian Andersen. Publishes chil-
dren's high-quality picture books and fiction
sold in association with **Random House
Children's Books**. Seventy per cent of the
books are sold as co-productions abroad.
TITLES *Elmer* David McKee; *I Want My Potty*
Tony Ross; *Badger's Parting Gifts* Susan Varley;
little.com Ralph Steadman; *Cat in the Manger*
Michael Foreman; *Preston Pig Books* Colin
McNaughton; *Junk* Melvin Burgess; *You*
Sandra Glover; *I Love You, Blue Kangaroo*
Emma Chichester Clark. Unsolicited mss welcome for picture books; synopsis in the first
instance for books for young readers up to age
12. No poetry or short stories.
    ROYALTIES twice-yearly.

Authors' Rating The secret of Andersen's success is publishing children's books that are
loved by adults. That and a wicked sense of fun
that has been known to upset the education
establishment – and hooray for that.

Chris Andrews Publications
15 Curtis Yard, North Hinksey Lane, Oxford
OX2 0LX
☎01865 723404 Fax 01865 725294
✉ chris.andrews1@btclick.com
www.cap-ox.co.uk
Managing Director *Chris Andrews*
Founded 1982. Publishes coffee table scenic
travel guides. Also calendars, diaries, cards and
posters. TITLES *Romance of Oxford*; *Romance of
the Cotswolds*; *Romance of the Thames & Chilterns*.
Also owns the **Oxford Picture Library** (see
entry under **Picture Libraries**). Unsolicited
synopses and ideas for travel/guide books will
be considered; phone in the first instance.

Andromeda Children's Books
See **Pinwheel Limited**

The Angels' Share
See **Neil Wilson Publishing Ltd**

Anness Publishing Ltd
Hermes House, 88–89 Blackfriars Road,
London SE1 8HA
☎020 7401 2077 Fax 020 7633 9499
✉ info@anness.com
www.aquamarinebooks.com
www.lorenzbooks.com
www.southwaterbooks.com
Chairman/Managing Director *Paul Anness*
Publisher/Partner *Joanna Lorenz*
Founded 1989. Publishes highly illustrated co-
edition titles: general non-fiction – cookery,
crafts, interior design, gardening, photography,
decorating, lifestyle and children's. IMPRINTS
Lorenz Books; **Aquamarine**; **Hermes
House**; **Peony Press**; **Southwater**. About
600 titles a year.

Anthem Press
See **Wimbledon Publishing Company**

Antique Collectors' Club
Sandy Lane, Old Martlesham, Woodbridge
IP12 4SD
☎01394 389950 Fax 01394 389999
✉ sales@antique-acc.com
www.antique-acc.com
Managing Director *Diana Steel*
Sales Director *Mark Eastment*
Founded 1966. Publishes specialist books on
antiques and collecting, the decorative arts,
architecture and gardening. The price guide

series was introduced in 1968 with the first edition of *The Price Guide to Antique Furniture*. Recently published the first six titles in a 'Starting to Collect' series. Subject areas include furniture, silver and gold, metalwork, jewellery, glass, textiles, art reference, ceramics, horology. TITLES *Understanding Jewellery* David Bennett and Daniela Mascetti; *Herbert Draper – A Life Study* Simon Toll; *Art Deco and Other Figures* Bryan Catley. Also publishes subscription-only magazine, *Antique Collecting*, published 10 times a year. Unsolicited synopses and ideas for books welcome; no mss.

ROYALTIES twice-yearly as a rule, but can vary.

Anvil Press Poetry Ltd

Neptune House, 70 Royal Hill, London SE10 8RF
☎020 8469 3033 Fax 020 8469 3363
✉ anvil@anvilpresspoetry.com
www.anvilpresspoetry.com

Editorial Director *Peter Jay*

Founded 1968 to promote English-language and foreign poetry, both classic and contemporary, in translation. English list includes Peter Levi, Dick Davis, Dennis O'Driscoll and Carol Ann Duffy. Translated books include Bei Dao, Celan, Dante, Lalic, Baudelaire, Lorca and Neruda. Preliminary enquiry required for translations. Unsolicited book-length collections of poems are welcome from writers whose work has appeared in poetry magazines. Please enclose adequate return postage.

Authors' Rating With a little help from the Arts Council, Anvil has become one of the foremost publishers of living poets.

Apollos

See **Inter-Varsity Press**

Apple

See **Quarto Publishing** under *UK Packagers*

Appletree Press Ltd

The Old Potato Station, 14 Howard Street South, Belfast BT7 1AP
☎028 9024 3074 Fax 028 9024 6756
✉ reception@appletree.ie
www.appletree.ie

Managing Director *John Murphy*

Founded 1974. Publishes cookery and other small-format gift books, plus general non-fiction of Irish and Scottish interest. TITLES *Little Cookbook* series (about 40 titles); *Ireland: The Complete Guide*. No unsolicited mss; send initial letter or synopsis.

ROYALTIES twice-yearly in the first year, annually thereafter.

Aquamarine

See **Anness Publishing Ltd**

Arc Publications

Nanholme Mill, Shaw Wood Road, Todmorden OL14 6DA
☎01706 812338 Fax 01706 818948
✉ arc.publications@btconnect.com
www.arcpublications.co.uk

Publishers *Rosemary Jones, Angela Jarman*
General Editor *Tony Ward*
Associate Editors *John Kinsella* (International), *Jo Shapcott* (UK), *Jean Boase-Beier* (Translations), *Angela Jarman* (Music)

Founded in 1969 to specialise in the publication of contemporary poetry from new and established writers both in the UK and abroad. AUTHORS John Kinsella and Alison Croggan (Australia), Donald Atkinson, Mila Haugova (Slovakia), Yannis Kondos (Greece), Tony Curtis (Ireland), Alamgir Hashmi (Pakistan), C.K. Stead (New Zealand), Jackie Wills, Julia Darling and Herbert Lomas (UK).

IMPRINT **Arc Music** specialises in profiles of contemporary composers (particularly where none have existed hitherto) and symposia which take a 'new approach' to well-visited territory. Commissioned work only. About 20 titles a year. Authors submitting material should ensure that it is compatible with the current list, include a history of published works and enclose an s.a.e. if they wish mss to be returned. Electronic submissions are not accepted.

ROYALTIES as per contracts.

Arcadia Books

15–16 Nassau Street, London W1W 7AB
☎020 7436 9898 Fax 020 7436 9898
✉ info@arcadiabooks.co.uk
www.arcadiabooks.co.uk

Managing Director *Gary Pulsifer*
Publishing Director *Daniela de Groote*

Small, independent publishing house, founded in 1996, specialising in translated fiction from around the world. Winner of the **Sunday Times Small Publisher of the Year Award** 2002–03. Publishes literary fiction, gay fiction, biography, autobiography, gender studies, travel writing. TITLE *The Nick of Time* Francis

King (long-listed for the 2003 **Man Booker Prize**). Does not welcome unsolicited material. ROYALTIES twice-yearly.

Authors' Rating A quality publisher that has great success with translated fiction.

Architectural Press
See **Elsevier Ltd**

Argentum
See **Aurum Press Ltd**

Aris & Phillips
See **Oxbow Books**

Arnold
See **Hodder Headline Ltd**

Arrow
See **The Random House Group Ltd**

Artech House
46 Gillingham Street, London SW1V 1AH
☎020 7596 8750   Fax 020 7630 0166
✉ jlancashire@artechhouse.co.uk
www.artech-uk@artechhouse.com

Managing Director (USA) *William M. Bazzy*
Senior Commissioning Editor *Dr Julie Lancashire*

Founded 1969. European office of Artech House Inc., Boston. Publishes electronic engineering, especially telecommunications, computer communications, computing, optoelectronics, signal processing, digital audio and video, intelligent transportation systems and technology management (books, software and videos). 60–70 titles a year. Unsolicited mss and synopses in the specialised areas listed are considered.
ROYALTIES twice-yearly.

Ashgate Publishing Ltd
Gower House, Croft Road, Aldershot
GU11 3HR
☎01252 331551   Fax 01252 317446
(Ashgate)/344405 (Gower)/
020 7837 6322 (Lund Humphries)
✉ info@ashgatepublishing.com
www.ashgate.com
www.gowerpub.com

Chairman *Nigel Farrow*

Founded 1967. Publishes business and professional titles under the Gower imprint and humanities, social sciences, law and legal studies under the Ashgate imprint. In December 1999 acquired Lund Humphries, publisher of art books and exhibition catalogues.

DIVISIONS **Ashgate** *Sarah Davies* Social sciences; *John Smedley* History/Variorum collected studies; *Heidi May* Music; *Erika Gaffney* Literary studies; *Tom Gray* History; *Sarah Lloyd* Theology and religious studies; *Paul Coulam* Philosophy; *John Hindley* Aviation studies. **Gower** *Jo Burges, Jonathan Norman* Business, management and training; *John Irwin* Law and legal studies. **Lund Humphries** *Lucy Myers*. Access the websites for information on submission of material.

Ashgrove Publishing
55 Richmond Avenue, London N1 0LX
☎020 7831 5013   Fax 020 7831 5011
✉ gmo73@dial.pipex.com
www.ashgrovepublishing.com

Chairman/Managing Director *Brad Thompson*

Acquired by Hollydata Publishers in 1999, Ashgrove has been publishing for over 20 years. Publishes mind, body, spirit, health, cookery, sports. 4 titles in 2003. No unsolicited mss; approach with letter and outline in the first instance.
ROYALTIES twice-yearly.

Ashmolean Museum Publications
Ashmolean Museum, Beaumont Street,
Oxford OX1 2PH
☎01865 278010   Fax 01865 278018
✉ publications@ashmus.ox.ac.uk
www.ashmol.ox.ac.uk

Contact *Declan McCarthy*

The Ashmolean Museum, which is wholly owned by Oxford University, was founded in 1683. The first publication appeared in 1890 but publishing did not really start in earnest until the 1960s. Publishes European and Oriental fine and applied arts, European archaeology and ancient history, Egyptology and numismatics, for both adult and children's markets. No fiction, American/African art, ethnography, modern art or post-medieval history. Most publications are based on and illustrated from the Museum's collections. About 8 titles a year. No unsolicited mss.
ROYALTIES annually.

Atlantic Books
26–27 Boswell Street, London WC1N 3JZ
☎020 7269 1617   Fax 020 7430 0916
✉ enquiries@groveatlantic.co.uk
www.groveatlantic.co.uk

Chairman *Morgan Entrekin*
Managing Director/Publisher *Toby Mundy*

Founded 2000. A subsidiary of **Grove/Atlantic Inc.** (see entry under *US Publishers*), New York. Publishes literary fiction, history, current affairs, autobiography, biography, politics and reference books. IMPRINT **Guardian/Observer Books** Editorial Head *Alice Hunt* TITLES *Guardian Media Directory*; *Guardian University Guide* (both annual). 70 titles in 2003. No unsolicited material.

ROYALTIES twice-yearly.

Authors' Rating The offshoot of US Grove/Atlantic has a reputation for punching above its weight. Clever marketing has a lot to do with it but it is marketing based on an instinct for what sells - still not the most common attribute in trade publishing.

Atlantic Europe Publishing Co. Ltd

Greys Court Farm, Greys Court, Nr Henley on Thames RG9 4PG
☎01491 628188 Fax 01491 628189
✉ writers@atlanticeurope.com
www.AtlanticEurope.com
www.curriculumVisions.com

Directors *Dr B.J. Knapp, D.L.R. McCrae*

Closely associated, since 1990, with Earthscape Editions packaging operation. Publishes full-colour, highly illustrated children's non-fiction in hardback for international co-editions and text books. Not interested in any other material. Main focus is on National Curriculum titles, especially in the fields of mathematics, science, technology, social history and geography. About 50 titles a year. Unsolicited synopses and ideas for non-fiction curriculum-based books welcome by e-mail only – does not accept material sent by post.

FEES paid.

Atom

See **Time Warner Books UK**

Aurum Press Ltd

25 Bedford Avenue, London WC1B 3AT
☎020 7637 3225 Fax 020 7580 2469
✉ editorial@aurumpress.co.uk

Managing Director *Bill McCreadie*
Editorial Director *Piers Burnett*
Approx. Annual Turnover £3 million

Founded 1976. Committed to producing high-quality, illustrated/non-illustrated adult non-fiction in the areas of general human interest, art and craft, lifestyle, sport and travel. IMPRINTS **Argentum** Practical photography

books; **Jacqui Small** High-quality lifestyle books. About 60 titles a year.

ROYALTIES twice-yearly.

Authentic Media

PO Box 300, Kingstown Broadway, Carlisle CA3 0QS
☎01228 554320 Fax 01228 593388
www.paternoster-publishing.com

Publishing Director *Mark Finnie*
Approx. Annual Turnover £2 million

A division of STL Ltd. IMPRINTS **Paternoster Press** Founded 1936. Editorial Coordinator *Lucy Atherton* Publishes academic, religion and learned/church/life-related journals. TITLES *Relational Leadership*; *Religion & Culture* series. **Authentic Lifestyle** Founded 1966. Editorial Coordinator *Charlotte Hubback* Publishes Christian books on evangelism, discipleship and mission for Evangelical Alliance, Christianity Explored, Icthus, Spring Harvest, Operation Christmas Child. Over 40 titles a year. Unsolicited mss, synopses and ideas for books welcome.

ROYALTIES twice-yearly.

AuthorsOnline

40 Castle Street, Hertford SG14 1HR
☎0870 7500544 Fax 0870 7500544
✉ theeditor@authorsonline.co.uk
www.authorsonline.co.uk

Submissions: Wayside, Downs Road, East Studdal CT15 5BZ
☎01304 374762

Owner *AuthorsOnLine Ltd*.
Managing Director *Richard Ovenden*
Editor *Richard Fitt*
Submissions Editor *Mrs W.A. Lake*
Approx. Annual Turnover £250,000

Founded 1998. A service for authors wishing to self-publish. Publishes new and reverted rights work in both electronic format via their website and traditional hard-copy. All genres welcome. Submit mss by e-mail or post (disk or CD-ROM) to the Submissions Editor at the East Studdal address above.

Autumn Publishing Ltd

Appledram Barns, Birdham Road, Chichester PO20 7EQ
☎01243 531660 Fax 01243 774433
✉ autumn@autumnpublishing.co.uk
www.autumnpublishing.co.uk

Managing Director *Michael Herridge*
Editorial Director *Ingrid Goldsmid*

Founded 1976, part of the Bonnier Group.

Publishes baby and toddler books, children's activity, sticker and early learning books. About 200 titles a year. No responsibility accepted for the return of unsolicited mss.

Authors' Rating The leading small publisher (along with **Little Tiger Press**) of children's books.

Award Publications Limited
1st Floor, 27 Longford Street, London NW1 3DZ
☎020 7388 7800 Fax 020 7388 7887
✉ info@awardpublications.co.uk
Founded 1958. Publishes children's books, both fiction and reference. IMPRINT **Horus Editions**. No unsolicited mss, synopses or ideas.

Azure
See **Society for Promoting Christian Knowledge**

Baillière Tindall
See **Elsevier Ltd**

Duncan Baird Publishers
Castle House, 75–76 Wells Street, London W1T 3QH
☎020 7323 2229 Fax 020 7580 5692
✉ becky@dbairdpub.co.uk
Managing Director *Duncan Baird*
Editorial Director *Bob Saxton*
Approx. Annual Turnover £5 million
Founded in 1992 to publish and package co-editions overseas and went on to launch its own publishing operation in 1998. Publishes illustrated cultural reference, world religions, health, mind, body and spirit, lifestyle, graphic design. 45 titles in 2003. No unsolicited mss. Synopses and ideas welcome; approach in writing in the first instance with s.a.e. No fiction or UK-only subjects.
ROYALTIES twice-yearly.

Bantam/Bantam Press
See **Transworld Publishers**

Barefoot Books Ltd
124 Walcot Street, Bath BA1 5BG
☎01225 322400 Fax 01225 322499
✉ sales@barefootbooks.com
www.barefootbooks.com
Publisher *Tessa Strickland*
UK Editor *Natasha Carr*
Founded in 1993. Publishes high-quality children's picture books, particularly new and traditional stories from a wide range of cultures. 32 titles in 2003. No unsolicited mss. See website for submission guidelines.
ROYALTIES twice-yearly.

Authors' Rating Writers of children's books would do well to keep track of Barefoot which, from small beginnings, is building a quality list that must be the envy of bigger publishers.

Baring & Rogerson
See **Eland Publishing Ltd**

Barny Books
Hough on the Hill, Near Grantham NG32 2BB
☎01400 250246/01522 790009
Fax 01400 251737
Managing Director/Editorial Head *Molly Burkett*
Business Manager *Tom Cann*
Approx. Annual Turnover £10,000
Founded with the aim of encouraging new writers and illustrators. Publishes mainly children's books but also adult fiction and non-fiction. Offers schools' projects where students help to produce books. TITLES *Iron Jim* Andy Howarth; *Once Upon a Wartime* (series); *Hell, Fire and Damnation* Mario Martinez; *Trusty the Traitor* Ben Bartlett; *The Boy From Donington –* Matthew Flinders* Molly Burkett and the students of Donington School; *Sutton Hoo, Bloody Mary & The Martyrs* Jenny Webb and students at Suffolk Schools. Too small a concern to have the staff/resources to deal with unsolicited mss. Writers with strong ideas should approach Molly Burkett by letter in the first instance. Also runs a readership and advisory service for new writers (£10 fee for short stories or illustrations; £25 fee for full-length stories).
ROYALTIES Division of profits 50/50.

Authors' Rating A gutsy small publisher with a sense of fun which appeals to youngsters.

Barrington Stoke
Sandeman House, Trunk's Close, 55 High Street, Edinburgh EH1 1SR
☎0131 557 2020 Fax 0131 557 6060
✉ info@barringtonstoke co.uk
www.barringtonstoke.co.uk
Chairman *David Croom*
Managing Director *Sonia Raphael*
Editorial Head *Anna Gibbons*
Approx. Annual Turnover £400,000
Founded in 1998 to publish books for 'reluc-

tant, disenchanted and under-confident' young readers. Produces a series of audio books and issues teachers' notes to acccompany teenage fiction titles. DIVISIONS **4u2read.OK** for children aged 8–13 with a reading age below 8; **Fiction** for 8–13-year olds TITLES *Living With Vampires; Tod in Biker City.* **Teenage Fiction** TITLES *Runaway Teacher; No Stone Unturned.* Books commissioned via literary agents only. *No* unsolicited material.

ROYALTIES twice-yearly.

B.T. Batsford
See **Chrysalis Books Group**

BBC Books
Room A2049, BBC Worldwide Ltd,
80 Wood Lane, London W12 0TT
☎020 8433 2000 Fax 020 8433 3707
www.bbcworldwide.com

Managing Director *Chris Weller*

Publishes TV tie-in and some stand-alone titles, including books which, though linked with BBC television or radio, may not simply be the 'book of the series'. Also TV tie-in titles for children. TITLES *Delia's Vegetarian Collection; Rick Stein's Food Heroes*; tie-in script book to *The Office; How to Be a Gardener* Alan Titchmarsh; *A History of Britain* Simon Schama; and autobiographies – Terry Wogan, Sam Torrance, David Attenborough. 100 titles a year. Unsolicited mss (which come in at the rate of about 40 weekly) are rarely accepted. However, strong ideas well expressed will always be considered, and promising letters stand a chance of further scrutiny.

ROYALTIES twice-yearly.

Authors' Rating BBC Worldwide continues to grow. The biggest expansion is in children's books where there is now a joint venture deal with Penguin to publish up to 80 titles a year using characters licensed from the BBC. The BBC archive is a treasure trove still waiting to be fully exploited. But BBC Audiobooks is already well on the way to dominating the market.

Bedford Square Press
See **NCVO Publications**

Beeline
See **Blackstaff Press Ltd**

Belair
See **Folens Limited**

Berg Publishers
1st Floor, Angel Court, 81 St Clements Street,
Oxford OX4 1AW
☎01865 245104 Fax 01865 791165
✉ enquiry@bergpublishers.com
www.bergpublishers.com

Editorial & Managing Director *Kathryn Earle*
Production Manager *Ken Bruce*

Publishes scholarly books in the fields of history, fashion, cultural studies, social sciences and humanities. TITLES *Nudity: A Cultural Anatomy* Ruth Barcan; *The Auditory Culture Reader* eds. Michael Bull and Les Back; *Fashioning London* Christopher Breward; *Al-Qaida's Jihad in Europe* Evan F. Kohlmann. IMPRINT **Oswald Wolff Books**. About 65 titles a year plus three journals, *Fashion Theory, Home Cultures* and *Textile: The Journal of Cloth and Culture.* No unsolicited mss. Synopses and ideas for books welcome.

ROYALTIES annually.

Berghahn Books
3 Newtec Place, Magdalen Road, Oxford
OX4 1RE
☎01865 250011 Fax 01865 250056
✉ publisher@berghahnbooks.com
www.berghahnbooks.com

Chairman/Managing Director *Marion Berghahn*
Approx. Annual Turnover £700,000

Founded 1994. Academic publisher of books and journals. TITLES *The History of the Armenian Genocide; Western Historical Thinking; Conservation and Mobile Indigenous Peoples.* OVERSEAS ASSOCIATE Berghahn Books Inc., New York. About 65 titles a year. No unsolicited mss; will consider synopses and ideas. Approach by e-mail in the first instance. No fiction or trade books.

ROYALTIES annually.

Berkswell Publishing Co. Ltd
PO Box 420, Warminster BA12 9XB
☎01985 840189 Fax 01985 840243

Managing Director *John Stidolph*

Founded 1974. Publishes books for churchwardens. No fiction. About 4 titles a year. Unsolicited mss, synopses and ideas for books welcome.

ROYALTIES according to contract.

Berlitz Publishing
58 Borough High Stret, London SE1 1XF
☎020 7403 0284 Fax 020 7403 0290
✉ publishing@berlitz.co.uk
www.berlitz.com

Managing Director *Jeremy Westwood*

Founded 1970. Acquired by the Langenscheidt Publishing Group in February 2002. Publishes travel and language-learning products only: visual travel guides, phrasebooks and language courses. SERIES *Pocket Guides*; *Berlitz Complete Guide to Cruising and Cruise Ships*; *Phrase Books*; *Pocket Dictionaries*; *Business Phrase Books*; *Self-teach: Rush Hour Commuter Cassettes*; *Think & Talk*; *Berlitz Kids*. No unsolicited mss.

BeWrite Books

See entry under *Electronic Publishing and Other Services*

BFI Publishing

British Film Institute, 21 Stephen Street, London W1T 1LN
☎020 7255 1444 Fax 020 7636 2516
www.bfi.org.uk
Head of Publishing *Jonathan Tilston*
Approx. Annual Turnover £600,000

Founded 1980. Part of the **British Film Institute**. Publishes academic, schools and general film/television-related books and resources. TITLES *Film Classics* (series); *Modern Classics* (series); *World Directors* (series); *The Cinema Book*, revised edition, eds. Pam Cook and Mieke Bernink; *BFI Film & Television Handbook* (annual) Eddie Dyja. About 34 titles a year. E-mail submissions preferred.
ROYALTIES annually.

BFP Books

Focus House, 497 Green Lanes, London N13 4BP
☎020 8882 3315 Fax 020 8886 5174
✉ mail@thebfp.com
Chief Executive *John Tracy*
Commissioning Editor *Stewart Gibson*

Founded 1982. The publishing arm of the Bureau of Freelance Photographers. Publishes illustrated books on photography, mainly aspects of freelancing and marketing pictures. No unsolicited mss but ideas welcome.

Clive Bingley Books

See **Facet Publishing**

BIOS Scientific Publishers

See **Taylor & Francis Group plc**

Birlinn Ltd

West Newington House, 10 Newington Road, Edinburgh EH9 1QS
☎0131 668 4371 Fax 0131 668 4466
✉ info@birlinn.co.uk
www.birlinn.co.uk
Managing Editor *Hugh Andrew*

Founded 1992. Acquired **John Donald Publishers** in 1999 (see entry). Publishes local and military history, Gaelic, humour, Highland history, adventure, Scottish reference, guidebooks and folklore. Acquired **Polygon** in 2002 (see entry). 90 titles in 2003. No unsolicited mss; synopses and ideas welcome.
ROYALTIES paid.

Bite

See **Hodder Headline Ltd**

Black & White Publishing Ltd

99 Giles Street, Edinburgh EH6 6BZ
☎0131 625 4500 Fax 0131 625 4501
✉ mail@blackandwhitepublishing.com
www.blackandwhitepublishing.com
Director *Campbell Brown*

Founded 1990. Publishes general fiction and non-fiction, including memoirs, sport, cookery, humour and guidebooks. IMPRINT **Itchy Coo** Scots language resources for use in schools. Text only submissions via website, or synopsis and sample chapter by post with s.a.e. or return postage.
ROYALTIES twice-yearly.

A.&C. Black Publishers Ltd

Alderman House, 37 Soho Square, London W1D 3QZ
☎020 7758 0200 Fax 020 7758 0222
✉ enquiries@acblack.com
www.acblack.com
Chairman *Nigel Newton*
Managing Director *Jill Coleman*
Publishing Director, Reference *Jonathan Glasspool*
Approx. Annual Turnover £10.5 million

Publishes children's and educational books, including music, for 3–15-year-olds, arts and crafts, ceramics, fishing, ornithology, nautical, reference, sport, theatre and travel. Acquisitions brought the Herbert Press' art, design and general books, Adlard Coles' and Thomas Reed's sailing lists, plus *Reed's Nautical Almanac*, Christopher Helm, Pica Press and T&AD Poyser's natural history and ornithology lists into A.&C. Black's stable. Bought by **Bloomsbury Publishing** in May 2000. Owns *Whitaker's Almanack* and children's publisher Andrew Brodie Publications.
IMPRINTS **Adlard Coles Nautical**; **Christopher Helm**; **The Herbert Press**; **Pica Press**. TITLES *New Mermaid* drama series;

Who's Who; Writers' & Artists' Yearbook; Know the Game sports series; Blue Guides travel series; Rockets and Black Cats children's series. Initial enquiry appreciated before submission of mss.
ROYALTIES Payment varies according to contract.

Black Ace Books
PO Box 6557, Forfar DD8 2YS
☎01307 465096 Fax 01307 465494
www.blackacebooks.com
Managing Director Hunter Steele
Founded 1991. Publishes new fiction, Scottish and general; some non-fiction including biography, history, philosophy and psychology. IMPRINTS Black Ace Books; Black Ace Paperbacks TITLES Succeeding at Sex and Scotland, Or the Case of Louis Morel Hunter Steele; La Tendresse Ken Strauss MD; Count Dracula (The Authorized Version) Hagen Slawkberg; Caryddwen's Cauldron Paul Hilton; The Sinister Cabaret John Herdman. No children's, poetry, cookery, DIY, religion. 36 titles in print. 'No submissions at all, please, without first checking our website for details of current requirements and submission guidelines.'
ROYALTIES twice-yearly.

Black Dagger
See BBC Audiobooks under Audio Books

Black Lace
See Virgin Books Ltd

Black Spring Press Ltd
Burbage House, 83–85 Curtain Road, London EC2A 3BS
☎020 7613 3066 Fax 020 7613 0028
✉ general@blackspringpress.co.uk
Directors Robert Hastings, Alexander Hastings
Founded 1986. Publishes fiction and non-fiction, literary criticism, biography. TITLES The Lost Weekend Charles Jackson; The Big Brass Ring Orson Welles; The Tenant Roland Topor; The Terrible News collection of Russian short stories by Zamyatin, Babel, Kharms, et al. About 5 titles a year. No unsolicited mss.
ROYALTIES annually.

Black Swan
See Transworld Publishers

Blackstaff Press Ltd
4C Heron Wharf, Sydenham Business Park, Belfast BT3 9LE
☎028 9045 5006 Fax 028 9046 6237
✉ info@blackstaffpress.com
www.blackstaffpress.com
Managing Editor Patsy Horton
Founded 1971. Publishes mainly, but not exclusively, Irish interest books, fiction, poetry, history, sport, politics, illustrated editions, natural history and humour. IMPRINT Beeline Lively popular fiction in small paperback format. About 25 titles a year. Unsolicited mss considered, but preliminary submission of synopsis plus short sample of writing preferred. Return postage must be enclosed.
ROYALTIES twice-yearly.

Authors' Rating Regional and proud of it, this Belfast publisher is noted for bringing on young talent and for 'wonderfully well-presented catalogues and promotional material'.

Blackwell Publishing
9600 Garsington Road, Oxford OX4 2DQ
☎01865 776868 Fax 01865 714591
www.blackwellpublishing.com
Also at: 108 Cowley Road, Oxford OX4 1JF
☎01865 791100
Fax 01865 791347
Chief Executive René Olivieri
President Robert Campbell
Chairman Nigel Blackwell
Blackwell Publishing was formed by merging Blackwell Science (founded 1939) and Blackwell Publishers (founded 1926). Publishes around 700 books a year and 674 journals in medicine, veterinary medicine, dentistry (IMPRINT Blackwell Munksgaard), nursing and allied health, science (particularly biology, chemistry and geology), social sciences, business and humanities. Journals are delivered online through Blackwell Synergy. Acquired BMJ Books in 2004.
ROYALTIES annually.

Authors' Rating Turnover has increased with the expanded list of learned journals.

John Blake Publishing Ltd
3 Bramber Court, 2 Bramber Road, London W14 9PB
☎020 7381 0666 Fax 020 7381 6868
✉ words@blake.co.uk
Managing Director John Blake
Deputy Managing Director Rosie Ries
Founded 1991 and expanding rapidly. Bought the assets of Smith Gryphon Ltd in 1997 and acquired Metro Publishing in 2001. Publishes mass-market non-fiction. No fiction, children's, specialist or non-commercial. About 100 titles a

year. No unsolicited mss; synopses and ideas welcome. Please enclose s.a.e.

ROYALTIES twice-yearly.

Authors' Rating One of the three top small publishers in terms of sales and revenue, John Blake specialises in sensational titles linked to the famous and infamous.

Blandford Press
See **Octopus Publishing Group**

Bloodaxe Books Ltd
Highgreen, Tarset NE48 1RP
☎01434 240500 Fax 01434 240505
✉ editor@bloodaxebooks.co.uk
www.bloodaxebooks.com
Managing/Editorial Director *Neil Astley*

Publishes poetry, literature and criticism, and related titles by British, Irish, European, Commonwealth and American writers. 95 per cent of the list is poetry. TITLES include three major anthologies, *Staying Alive; real poems for unreal times* ed. Neil Astley; *The Bloodaxe Book of 20th Century Poetry* ed. Edna Longley; *The New Poetry* eds. Hulse, Kennedy and Morley; *Sixty Women Poets* ed. Linda France; *Poems* J.H. Prynne; *Poems 1960–2000* Fleur Adcock; recent collections by Selima Hill, Helen Dunmore and Peter Reading. About 30 titles a year. Unsolicited poetry mss welcome; send a sample of no more than 10 poems with s.a.e., 'but if you don't read contemporary poetry, don't bother'. No e-mail sbmissions of any kind.

ROYALTIES annually.

Authors' Rating Assisted by regional Arts Council funding, Bloodaxe is one of the liveliest and most innovative of poetry publishers with a list that takes in some of the best of the younger poets.

Bloodlines
See **The Do-Not Press**

Bloomsbury Publishing Plc
38 Soho Square, London W1D 3HB
☎020 7494 2111 Fax 020 7434 0151
www.bloomsburymagazine.com
Chairman/Chief Executive *Nigel Newton*
Publishing Directors *Alexandra Pringle,*
  Liz Calder, Kathy Rooney, Sarah Odedina,
  Arzu Tahsin
Approx. Annual Turnover £61 million+

Founded in 1986 by Nigel Newton, David Reynolds, Alan Wherry and Liz Calder. Over the following years Bloomsbury titles were to appear regularly on *The Sunday Times* bestseller list and many of its authors have gone on to win prestigious literary prizes. In 1991 Nadine Gordimer won the **Nobel Prize for Literature**; Michael Ondaatje's *The English Patient* won the 1992 **Booker Prize**; in 1997 Anne Michaels' *Fugitive Pieces* won both the **Orange Prize for Fiction** and the Guardian Fiction Prize. J.K. Rowling's *Harry Potter and the Philosopher's Stone, Harry Potter and the Chamber of Secrets* and *Harry Potter and the Prisoner of Azkaban* won the **Nestlé Smarties Book Prize** in 1997, 1998 and 1999 respectively. Margaret Atwood's *The Blind Assassin* won the **Booker Prize** in 2000.

Published *The Encarta World English Dictionary* in 1999. Started Bloomsbury USA in 1998. Acquired **A.&C. Black Publishers Ltd** in May 2000, **Peter Collin Publishing Ltd** in September 2002 and Berlin Verlag in 2003. Publishes literary fiction and non-fiction, including general reference; also audiobooks. AUTHORS include Margaret Atwood, T.C. Boyle, Sophie Dahl, Jeffrey Eugenides, Neil Gaiman, Daniel Goleman, David Guterson, Ethan Hawke, John Irving, Jay McInerney, Tim Pears, Celia Rees, J.K. Rowling, Will Self, Donna Tartt, Rupert Thomson, Barbara Trapido, Joanna Trollope and Benjamin Zephaniah. Unsolicited mss and synopses for adult titles only; no poetry.

ROYALTIES twice-yearly.

Authors' Rating With Harry Potter's cash pile building up at an enviable rate, Bloomsbury is the first call for agents in pursuit of big money. The problem for new writers, of course, is finding a way through the crowd of other hopefuls besieging the Soho offices. Have a go by all means but don't expect a quick response.

BMJ Books
See **Blackwell Publishing**

BMM
See **SportsBooks Limited**

Boatswain Press
See **Kenneth Mason Publications Ltd**

Bobcat
See **Omnibus Press**

The Bodley Head
See **The Random House Group Ltd**

The Book Guild Ltd

Temple House, 25 High Street, Lewes
BN7 2LU
☎01273 472534 Fax 01273 476472
✉ info@bookguild.co.uk
www.bookguild.co.uk

Chairman *George M. Nissen, CBE*
Managing Director *Carol Biss*

Founded 1982. Publishes fiction, human interest,
media, children's fiction, academic, natural his-
tory, naval and military, biography, art.
Expanding mainstream list plus developing the
human interest/media genre. DIVISIONS
Human Interest TITLES *Never Take No for an
Answer* Marilyn Hawes; *Let the Children Sing*
Leonora Langley. **Biography** TITLES *The Man
Who Would Be Bing – The Life Story of Michael
Holliday* Ken Crossland; *Over the Airways* Trevor
Hill. **Fiction** TITLES *Riding on a Dangerous Wind*
Caroline Jay; *The Sodbury Crucifix* Julian Fane.
Mind, Body, Spirit TITLE *The Magic in Tea
Leaves* Amber McCarroll and The Tea Council.
Children's Fiction TITLE *Frostavia* Robin
Cousins. About 80 titles a year. Unsolicited mss,
ideas and synopses welcome.
ROYALTIES twice-yearly.

Authors' Rating An increasing proportion of
the Book Guild list is straightforward publishing but some authors may be asked to cover
their own production costs. In the latter case,
the Book Guild is unusual in not making unre-
alistic promises.

Book House

See **Salariya Book Company Ltd** under *UK
Packagers*

Border Lines Biographies

See **Seren**

Boulevard Books &
The Babel Guides

71 Lytton Road, Oxford OX4 3NY
☎01865 712931 Fax 01865 712931
✉ raybabel@dircon.co.uk
www.babelguides.com

Managing Director *Ray Keenoy*

Specialises in contemporary world fiction by
young writers in English translation. Existing or
forthcoming series of fiction from Brazil, Italy,
Latin America, Low Countries, Greece, and
elsewhere. The Babel Guides series of popular
guides to fiction in translation started in 1995.
DIVISONS **Latin American** *Ray Keenoy* TITLE
Hotel Atlantico J.G. Noll. **Italian** *Fiorenza Conte*
TITLE *The Toy Catalogue* Sandra Petrignani.
Brazil *Dr David Treece* TITLE *The Jaguar.* **Low
Countries** *Prof. Theo Hermans.* **Greece** *Marina
Coriolano-Likourezos.* **Babel Guides to Fiction
in Translation** Series Editor *Ray Keenoy* TITLES
*Babel Guide to Italian Fiction in Translation; Babel
Guide to the Fiction of Portugal, Brazil & Africa in
Translation; Babel Guide to French Fiction in English
Translation; Babel Guide to Jewish Fiction; Babel
Guide to Scandinavian Fiction.* Suggestions and
proposals for translations of contemporary fiction
welcome. Also seeking contributors to forth-
coming Babel Guides (all literatures).
ROYALTIES annually.

Bound Biographies Limited

21 Heyford Park House, Heyford Park,
Bicester OX25 5HD
☎01869 232911 Fax 01869 232766
✉ boundbiographies@aol.com
www.boundbiographies.com

Managing Director *Michael Oke*
Editorial Head *Dr A.J. Gray*
Approx. Annual Turnover £150,000

Founded in 1992 to assist in the writing and production of low numbers of private life stories.
Print-on-demand facilities to provide short runs
of paper or hardback books to complement the
Bound Biographies leather-bound range. Publishes autobiographies predominantly although
novels, poetry and special interest books are considered. TITLES *Out of the Shadows* J.V. Moloney;
Message From the Colonel David Spencer. 20 titles
in 2003. Unsolicited material welcome;
approach by post, telephone or e-mail.
ROYALTIES annually.

Bounty

See **Octopus Publishing Group**

Bowker (UK) Ltd

3rd Floor, Farringdon House, Wood Street,
East Grinstead RH19 1UZ
☎01342 310450 Fax 01342 310486
✉ sales@bowker.co.uk
www.bowker.co.uk

Managing Director *Doug McMillan*
Publishers *Geraldine Turpi, Michael Cairns*

Part of the Cambridge Information Group
(CIG), based in Maryland in the USA. Publishes
library reference, bibliography, biography, business and professional directories. TITLES *Books In
Print; Ulrich's Periodicals Directory; Children's Books
in Print; Ulrich's Serials Analysis System.* Unsolicited material will not be read.
ROYALTIES annually.

Boxtree
See **Macmillan Publishers Ltd**

Marion Boyars Publishers Ltd
24 Lacy Road, London SW15 1NL
☎020 8788 9522 Fax 020 8789 8122
✉ rebecca@marionboyars.com
www.marionboyars.co.uk

Editor *Rebecca Gillieron*
Editor, Non-fiction *Claus von Bohlen*

Founded 1975, formerly Calder and Boyars. Publishes biography and autobiography, fiction, literature and criticism, music, philosophy, psychology, sociology and anthropology, theatre and drama, film and cinema, women's studies. AUTHORS include Georges Bataille, Ingmar Bergman, Heinrich Böll, Hortense Calisher, Jean Cocteau, Carlo Gébler, Julian Green, Ivan Illich, Pauline Kael, Ken Kesey, Toby Litt, Kenzaburo Oe, Hubert Selby, Igor Stravinsky, Frederic Tuten, Eudora Welty, Judith Williamson, Tom Wiseman, Hong Ying. About 30 titles a year. Unsolicited mss not welcome for fiction or poetry; submissions from agents only. Unsolicited synopses and ideas welcome for non-fiction. OVERSEAS ASSOCIATES Marion Boyars Publishers Inc.
ROYALTIES annually.

Boydell & Brewer Ltd
PO Box 9, Woodbridge IP12 3DF
☎01394 412900

Publishes non-fiction only, principally medieval studies. All books commissioned. No unsolicited material.

Bradt Travel Guides
19 High Street, Chalfont St Peter SL9 9QE
☎01753 893444 Fax 01753 892333
✉ info@bradt-travelguides.com
www.bradt-travelguides.com

Managing Director *Hilary Bradt*
Editorial Head *Tricia Hayne*
Approx. Annual Turnover £550,000

Founded in 1974 by Hilary Bradt. Specialises in travel guides to off-beat places. SERIES country guides and island guides (Azores, Falklands, St Helena); wildlife guides (Galapagos, Arctic, Antarctica, Southern Africa); mini guides to cities (Kabul, Baghdad, Lille) and the 'Eccentric' series (Britain, London, France, America). 10 titles in 2003. No unsolicited mss; synopses and ideas for travel guidebooks (not travelogues) welcome.
ROYALTIES twice-yearly.

Brassey's
See **Chrysalis Books Group**

Nicholas Brealey Publishing
3–5 Spafield Street, London EC1R 4QB
☎020 7239 0360 Fax 020 7239 0370
✉ rights@nbrealey-books.com
www.nbrealey-books.com

Managing Director *Nicholas Brealey*

Founded 1992. Independent publishing group focusing on innovative trade/professional books covering business and finance, intelligent self-help, popular psychology and the increasingly active fields of crossing cultures and travel writing. The group now includes Intercultural Press Inc and has a global reach. TITLES *Shackleton's Way*; *Almost French*; *Money for Nothing*; *Authentic Happiness*; *The 80/20 Principle*. No fiction, poetry or leisure titles. 30 titles a year. No unsolicited mss; synopses and ideas welcome.
ROYALTIES twice-yearly.

Authors' Rating Looks to be succeeding in breaking away from the usual computer-speak business manuals to publish information and literate texts. Lead titles have a distinct trans-Atlantic feel.

The Breedon Books Publishing Co. Ltd
Breedon House, 3 Parker Centre, Derby DE21 4SZ
☎01332 384235 Fax 01332 364063
✉ steve.caron@breedonpublishing.co.uk

Editorial Director *Steve Caron*
Approx. Annual Turnover £1 million

Founded 1983. Publishes football and sport, local history, old photographs, heritage. About 50 titles a year. Unsolicited mss, synopses and ideas welcome if accompanied by s.a.e. No poetry or fiction.
ROYALTIES annually.

Breese Books Ltd
10 Hanover Crescent, Brighton BN2 9SB
☎01273 687 555
✉ MBreese999@aol.com
www.sherlockholmes.co.uk
www.abracadabra.co.uk

Chairman/Managing Director *Martin Ranicar-Breese*

Founded in 1975 to produce specialist conjuring books and then went on to become a leading publisher of Sherlock Holmes pastiches. No unsolicited submissions; Breese Books works with a regular team of authors.

Brewin Books Ltd

Doric House, 56 Alcester Road, Studley
B80 7LG
☎01527 854228 Fax 01527 852746
✉ admin@brewinbooks.com
www.brewinbooks.com

Chairman/Managing Director *Alan Brewin*
Company Secretary *Julie Brewin*

Founded 1976. Publishes books on all aspects of Midland life and history including social, hospital, police, military and family histories as well as biographies and contemporary fiction. TITLES *An Oasis of Delight: The history of the Birmingham Botanical Gardens* Phillada Ballard; *Please Stay To the Adjournment* John Taylor MP; *Hold the Line Please* Sally Southall. IMPRINTS **Alton Douglas Books**; **History Into Print**; **Brewin Books**. About 25 titles a year. Not interested in children's, poetry, short stories or novels. Approach by letter, but do not send full mss. Unsolicited synopses and ideas welcome with s.a.e.
ROYALTIES twice-yearly.

Bristol Classical Press

See **Gerald Duckworth & Co. Ltd**

British Academic Press

See **I.B. Tauris & Co. Ltd**

The British Academy

10 Carlton House Terrace, London
SW1Y 5AH
☎020 7969 5200 Fax 020 7969 5300
✉ secretary@britac.ac.uk
www.britac.ac.uk

Publications Officer *James Rivington*
Assistant Publications Officer *Janet English*
Publications Assistant *Vicky Baldwin*

Founded 1902. The primary body for promoting scholarship in the humanities and social sciences, the Academy publishes many series stemming from its own long-standing research projects, or series of lectures and conference proceedings. Main subjects include history, philosophy and archaeology. SERIES *Auctores Britannici Medii Aevi*; *Early English Church Music*; *Fontes Historiae Africanae*; *Records of Social and Economic History*. About 20 titles a year. Proposals for these series are welcome and are forwarded to the relevant project committees. The British Academy is a registered charity and does not publish for profit.
ROYALTIES only when titles have covered their costs.

The British Computer Society

1 Sanford Street, Swindon SN1 1HJ
☎01793 417417 Fax 01793 480270
✉ bcshq@hq.bcs.org.uk
www.bcs.org.uk

Chief Executive *David Clarke*
Head of Publishing & Information Products
    Elain Boyes
Approx. Annual Turnover £15 million
    (Society)

Founded 1957. BCS is the leading professional and learned society in the field of computers and information systems. Publishes books which support the professional, academic and practical needs of the IT community. TITLES *E-Commerce: Doing Business Electronically*; *A Manager's Guide to IT Law*. 2 titles in 2003. Unsolicited material welcome; submissions form and guide on website page: www.bcs.org/author
ROYALTIES annually.

The British Library

96 Euston Road, London NW1 2DB
☎020 7412 7704 Fax 020 7412 7768
✉ blpublications@bl.uk

Publishing Manager *David Way*
Approx. Annual Turnover £950,000

Founded 1979 as the publishing arm of The British Library to publish works based on the historic collections and related subjects. Publishes bibliographical reference, manuscript studies, illustrated books based on the Library's collections, and book arts. TITLES *The British Library Guide to Calligraphy, Illumination and Heraldry*; *The British Library Writers' Lives Series*; *Encyclopedia of Ephemera*; *Medieval Herbals*. About 50 titles a year. Unsolicited mss, synopses and ideas welcome if related to the history of the book, book arts or bibliography. No fiction or general non-fiction.
ROYALTIES annually.

The British Museum Press

46 Bloomsbury Street, London WC1B 3QQ
☎020 7323 1234 Fax 020 7436 7315
www.britishmuseum.co.uk

Managing Director *Andrew Thatcher*
Director of Publishing *Alasdair Macleod*

The book publishing division of The British Museum Company Ltd. Founded 1973 as British Museum Publications Ltd; relaunched 1991 as British Museum Press. Publishes ancient history, archaeology, ethnography, art history, exhibition catalogues, guides, children's books, and all official publications of the British

Museum. TITLES *How to Read Egyptian Hieroglyphs*; *The British Museum Book of Haiku*; *Enlightenment: Discovering the World in the 18th Century*; *Bacchus: A Biography*; *The British Museum Dictionary of Ancient Egypt*. About 50 titles a year. Synopses and ideas for books welcome.
ROYALTIES twice-yearly.

Brockhampton Press Ltd
See **Caxton Publishing Group**

Andrew Brodie Publications
See **A.&C. Black Publishers Ltd**

John Brown Citrus Publishing
The New Boathouse, 136–142 Bramley Road, London W10 6SR
☎020 7565 3000   Fax 020 7565 3060
✉ john.brown@jbcp.co.uk
www.jbcp.co.uk
Chairman *John Brown*
Chief Executive *Andrew Hirsch*
Managing Director *Dean Fitzpatrick*

Founded 1987. Contract magazine publisher. TITLES include the *Sky Magazine*, *Waitrose Food Illustrated* and *The Oldie*.

Brown Skin Books
PO Box 46504, London N1 3YA
☎020 7226 4789
✉ info@brownskinbooks.co.uk
www.brownskinbooks.co.uk
Chairman *Dr John Lake*
Managing Director *Vastiana Belfon*

Founded 2002. Publishes 'quality, intelligent erotic fiction by black women around the world'. TITLES *Body and Soul* Jade Williams; *Personal Business* Isabel Baptiste. 2 titles in 2003. No unsolicited mss; synopses and ideas welcome. Send by e-mail or post. No poetry.
ROYALTIES annually.

Brown, Son & Ferguson, Ltd
4–10 Darnley Street, Glasgow G41 2SD
☎0141 429 1234   Fax 0141 420 1694
✉ info@skipper.co.uk
www.skipper.co.uk
Chairman/Joint Managing Director *T. Nigel Brown*

Founded 1850. Specializes in nautical textbooks, both technical and non-technical. Also Scottish one-act/three-act plays. Unsolicited mss, synopses and ideas for books welcome.
ROYALTIES annually.

Brunner-Routledge
See **Routledge**

Bryntirion Press
Bryntirion, Bridgend CF31 4DX
☎01656 655886   Fax 01656 665919
✉ office@emw.org.uk
Press Manager *Huw Kinsey*

Owned by the Evangelical Movement of Wales. Publishes Christian books in English and Welsh. TITLES *Singing to the Lord*; *In the Shadow of Aran*. No unsolicited mss; synopses and ideas welcome.
ROYALTIES annually.

Burns & Oates
See **The Continuum International Publishing Group Limited**

Business Education Publishers Ltd
The Teleport, Doxford International, Sunderland SR3 3XD
☎0191 525 2410
✉ info@bepl.com
www.bepl.com
Managing Director *Mrs A. Murphy*
Approx. Annual Turnover £400,000

Founded 1981. Publishes business education, economics and law for BTEC and GNVQ reading. Currently expanding into further and higher education, computing, IT, business, travel and tourism, occasional papers for institutions and local government administration. Unsolicited mss and synopses welcome.
ROYALTIES annually.

Buster Books
See **Michael O'Mara Books Ltd**

Butterworth Heinemann
See **Elsevier Ltd**

C&B (Collins & Brown)
See **Chrysalis Books Group**

Cadogan Guides
Highlands House, 165 The Broadway, Wimbledon, London SW19 1NE
☎020 8544 8051   Fax 020 8544 8081
✉ info@cadoganguides.co.uk
www.cadoganguides.com
Managing Director *Jenny Calcutt*
Managing Editor *Natalie Pomier*

Founded 1982. Travel publisher: country, regional and city guides; parent travel guides

(*Take the Kids*); guides to living, working and buying property abroad. Also publishes some travel literature. Most titles are commissioned. No unsolicited material.

Authors' Rating A tougher market for guides has prompted a move into the broader spaces of travel literature.

Calder Publications Ltd
51 The Cut, London SE1 8LF
☎020 7633 0599 Fax 020 7928 5930
✉ info@calderpublications.com
www.calderpublications.com
Chairman/Managing Director/Editorial Head
  John Calder

Formerly John Calder (Publishers) Ltd. A publishing company which has grown around the tastes and contacts of John Calder, the iconoclast of the literary establishment. The list has a reputation for controversial and opinion-forming publications; Samuel Beckett is perhaps the most prestigious name. The list includes all of Beckett's prose and poetry. Publishes autobiography, biography, drama, literary fiction, literary criticism, music, opera, poetry, politics, sociology, ENO opera guides. SERIES *Thought Bites* Short polemical texts on current political and social issues. AUTHORS Antonin Artaud, Marguerite Duras, Martin Esslin, Erich Fried, P.J. Kavanagh, Robert Menasse, Robert Pinget, Luigi Pirandello, Alain Robbe-Grillet, Nathalie Sarraute, L.F. Celine, Eva Figes, Claude Simon, Howard Barker (plays). No new material accepted.
  ROYALTIES annually.

Authors' Rating Known for his patronage of eccentric talents, John Calder is one of the few publishers to carry the flag for the English language '... which is in great danger of disappearing under the American vernacular'.

California University Press
See **University Presses of California, Columbia & Princeton Ltd**

Cambridge University Press
The Edinburgh Building, Shaftesbury Road, Cambridge CB2 2RU
☎01223 312393 Fax 01223 315052
www.cambridge.org
Chief Executive *Stephen R.R. Bourne*

The oldest printer and publisher in the world with long-established branches in the USA and Australia and more recently established branches in Spain, Africa, South America and East Asia, and offices and agents around the world. Cambridge's books are sold in more than 200 countries. Publishing includes major ELT courses; tertiary textbooks and monographs; scientific and medical reference; professional lists in law and management; educational coursebooks for the National Curriculum; and e-learning materials for schools. Publishes academic/educational, ELT and reference books for markets worldwide, at all levels from primary school to postgraduate and professional. Also Bibles and some 180 academic journals. Around 25,000 authors in 116 countries and between 1500 and 2000 new titles a year.

PUBLISHING GROUPS
Bibles *C.J. Wright*; **ELT** *A.C. Gilfillan*; **Humanities and Social Sciences** *R.K. Fisher*; **STM** *R.W.A. Barling*; **Education** *J.G.Tuttle*; **Journals** *C. Guettler*. Synopses and ideas for books are welcome (and preferable to the submission of unsolicited mss). No fiction or poetry.
  ROYALTIES twice-yearly.

Authors' Rating With its traditional strength in the academic market CUP is well placed to create such intellectual blockbusters as the three volume *Economic History of Modern Britain*. An increasing number of titles reach out to the general reader.

Camden Large Print
See **BBC Audiobooks** under *Audio Books*

Camden Press Ltd
43 Camden Passage, London N1 8EA
☎020 7226 4673
Chairman *Bob Borzello*

Founded 1985. Publishes social issues; all books are launched in connection with major national conferences. DIVISION **Publishing for Change** *Bob Borzello* TITLE *Living with the Legacy of Abuse*. IMPRINT **Mindfield** TITLES *Hate Thy Neighbour: The Race Issue; Therapy on the Couch*. No unsolicited material. Approach by telephone in the first instance.
  ROYALTIES annually.

Campbell Books
See **Macmillan Publishers Ltd**

Canongate Books Ltd
14 High Street, Edinburgh EH1 1TE
☎0131 557 5111 Fax 0131 557 5211
✉ info@canongate.co.uk
www.canongate.net
Publisher *Jamie Byng*
Managing Director *David Graham*

Submissions Editor *Francis Bickmore*
Approx. Annual Turnover £4.5 million

Founded 1973. Won 'Publisher of he Year' (2002) at the British Book Awards. Publishes a wide range of literary fiction and non-fiction. Historically there is a strong Scottish slant to the list but its output is increasingly international and Canongate has a growing reputation for originating unusual projects (typified by the *Pocket Canons Bible* series). Key AUTHORS include Michel Faber, Robert Sabbag, Laura Hird, Charles Bukowski, Anthony Bourdain, John Fante, Richard Brautigan, Dorit Rabinyan, Martin Strong, Will Ferguson, Jennifer Clement, Knut Hamsun, Chester Himes, Iceberg Slim, Yann Martel, Dan Rhodes, Alasdair Gray and Toni Davidson. IMPRINTS **Canongate Classics** Adult paperback series dedicated solely to important works of Scottish literature; **Canongate International** Fiction in translation.
ROYALTIES twice-yearly.

Authors' Rating Helped along by strong sales for *Life of Pi* and other literary fiction, Canongate has achieved a six-fold increase in turnover in four years. The plan is to originate around 35 titles a year for the UK and up to 12 for the US, where Canongate has found itself a profitable niche. *Esquire* magazine is certainly impressed. It has named publisher Jamie Byng as the most influential man under 40 in UK literature.

Canterbury Press
See **SCM – Canterbury Press Ltd**

Capall Bann Publishing
Auton Farm, Milverton TA4 1NE
☎01823 401528   Fax 01823 401529
✉ enquiries@capallbann.co.uk
www.capallbann.co.uk

Chairman *Julia Day*
Editorial Head *Jon Day*

Founded 1993 with three titles and now have well over 200 in print. Family-owned and -run company which publishes British traditions, folklore, computing, boating, animals, alternative healing, environmental, Celtic lore, mind, body and spirit. TITLES *Tarot Therapy*; *How to Talk with Fairies*; *Spiritual Journey*; *Crystals Folklore & Healing*; *Return of Yesterday's People*. About 40 titles a year. Unsolicited proposals for books welcome. No fiction or poetry.
ROYALTIES twice-yearly.

Jonathan Cape Ltd
See **The Random House Group Ltd**

Capstone Publishing Ltd
8 Newtec Place, Magdalen Road, Oxford OX4 1RE
☎01865 798623   Fax 01865 240941
✉ info@wiley-capstone.co.uk
www.capstoneideas.com

Joint Managing Directors *Mark Allin, Richard Burton*

Founded 1997. Part of **John Wiley & Sons, Inc**. Publishes business books.

Carcanet Press Ltd
4th Floor, Alliance House, 30 Cross Street, Manchester M2 7AQ
☎0161 834 8730   Fax 0161 832 0084
✉ pnr@carcanet.u-net.com
www.carcanet.co.uk

Chairman *Kate Gavron*
Managing Director/Editorial Director *Michael Schmidt*

In the last 30 years Carcanet has grown from an undergraduate hobby into a substantial venture. Robert Gavron bought the company in 1983 and it has established strong European, Commonwealth and American links. Winner of the **Sunday Times Small Publisher of the Year** award in 2000, it took over the Oxford Poets list from **Oxford University Press** in 1999, which it now publishes as a distinct imprint. Primarily a poetry publisher but also publishes academic, literary biography, fiction in translation and translations. AUTHORS Homero Aridjis, John Ashbery, Eavan Boland, Joseph Brodsky, Donald Davie, Natalia Ginzburg, Robert Graves, Elizabeth Jennings, Edwin Morgan, Les Murray, Frederic Raphael, Leonardo Sciascia, Iain Crichton Smith, Pedro Tamen, Charles Tomlinson. About 60 titles a year, including the *PN Review* (six issues yearly). Poetry submissions (hard copy only): 6–10 poems with covering letter and return postage if the material is to be sent back. Prospective writers should familiarise themselves with the Carcanet list.
ROYALTIES annually.

Authors' Rating Ever in the forefront of imaginative publishing, Carcanet has taken a step closer to the source of its literary creativity by setting up a postgraduate Writing School at Manchester Metropolitan University. (See entry under **Writers' Courses**.)

Cardiff Academic Press
St Fagans Road, Fairwater, Cardiff CF5 3AE
☎029 2056 0333   Fax 029 2055 4909

✉ cap@drakeed.com
www.drakeed.com/cap

Managing Director *R.G. Drake*

Academic publishers.

Carfax Publishing
See **Taylor & Francis Group plc**

Carlton Publishing Group
20 Mortimer Street, London W1T 3JW
☎020 7612 0400 Fax 020 7612 0401
✉ enquiries@carltonbooks.co.uk

Managing Director *Jonathan Goodman*
Editorial Director *Piers Murray Hill*
Approx. Annual Turnover £11 million

Founded 1992. Owned by Carlton Communications. Has two main divisions: **Carlton Books** publishes illustrated leisure and entertainment books aimed at the mass market. Subjects include TV tie-ins, health, popular science, design, history, music, sport and puzzles. **André Deutsch** and **Prion** publishes autobiography, biography, history, current affairs, the arts, drink and humour. DIVISIONS **Carlton Books**; **André Deutsch** and **Prion Books**; **Granada Media**; **Manchester United Books**. No unsolicited mss; synopses and ideas welcome. No novels, science fiction, poetry or children's fiction.

Authors' Rating Carlton Books has built a reputation on co-editions for the international market and television tie-ins. Noted for speed of taking a book from first idea to publication.

Carroll & Brown Publishers Limited
20 Lonsdale Road, London NW6 6RD
☎020 7372 0900 Fax 020 7372 0460
✉ mail@carrollandbrown.co.uk

Managing Director *Amy Carroll*
Approx. Annual Turnover £4 million

Founded in 1989 as a packaging operation and commenced publishing in 2000. Publishes practical parenting, health, fitness, lifestyle, mind, body and spirit. TITLES *Are You Smarter Than You Think?*; *Caesarean Recovery*; *Your Pregnancy Bible*. Synopses and ideas for illustrated books welcome; approach in writing in the first instance. No fiction
PAYMENT Fees or royalties paid.

Frank Cass
See **Taylor & Francis Group plc**

Cassell Illustrated
See **Octopus Publishing Group**

Cassell Military/Cassell Reference
See **The Orion Publishing Group Limited**

Castle Publications
See **Nottingham University Press**

Kyle Cathie Ltd
122 Arlington Road, London NW1 7HP
☎020 7692 7215 Fax 020 7692 7260
✉ general.enquiries@kyle-cathie.com
www.kylecathie.co.uk

Founded 1990 to publish and promote 'books we have personal enthusiasm for'. Publishes non-fiction: cookery, food and drink, health and beauty, mind, body & spirit, gardening, homes and interiors, reference and occasional books of classic poetry. TITLES *Healthy Eating for Diabetes* Anthony Worrall-Thompson; *Green & Black's Chocolate Recipes* Caroline Jeremy; *Run for Life* Sam Murphy; *Gardeners' Question Time Plant Chooser* Matthew Biggs, John Cushnie, Bob Flowerdew and Bunny Guinness. About 25 titles a year. No unsolicited mss. 'Synopses and ideas are considered in the fields in which we publish.'
ROYALTIES twice-yearly.

Catholic Truth Society (CTS)
40–46 Harleyford Road, London SE11 5AY
☎020 7640 0042 Fax 020 7640 0046
✉ f.martin@cts-online.org.uk
www.cts-online.org.uk

Chairman *Most Rev. Peter Smith*
General Secretary *Fergal Martin*

Founded originally in 1868 and re-founded in 1884. Publishes religious books – Roman Catholic; a variety of doctrinal, moral, biographical, devotional and liturgical publications, including a large body of Vatican documents and sources. Unsolicited mss, synopses and ideas welcome if appropriate to their list.
ROYALTIES annually.

Causeway Press Ltd
PO Box 13, 129 New Court Way, Ormskirk L39 5HP
☎01695 576048 Fax 01695 570714

Chairman/Managing Director *M. Haralambos*
Approx. Annual Turnover £2 million

Founded in 1982. Publishes educational textbooks only. TITLES *Mathematics for AQA*; *Mathematics for Edexcel*; *Psychology in Focus*; *Business Accounting*; *Business Studies*; *Economics*; *Business Studies for GCSE*; *Sociology in Focus*; *Politics in Focus*; *GCSE Applied Business*. 20 titles in 2003. Unsolicited mss, synopses and ideas welcome.

ROYALTIES annually.

Cavendish Publishing Limited

The Glass House, Wharton Street, London WC1X 9PX

☎020 7278 8000 Fax 020 7278 8080

✉ info@cavendishpublishing.com

www.cavendishpublishing.com

Executive Chairman *Sonny Leong*

Founded 1990. Publishes academic law books. OVERSEAS ASSOCIATE Cavendish Publishing (Australia) Pty Ltd. 160 titles in 2003. No unsolicited mss; send synopsis accompanied by a letter in the first instance.

ROYALTIES twice-yearly.

Caxton Publishing Group

20 Bloomsbury Street, London WC1B 3JH

☎020 7636 7171 Fax 020 7636 1922

✉ office@caxtonpublishing.com

www.caxtonpublishing.com

Chairman *Stephen Hill*

Managing Director *John Maxwell*

Approx. Annual Turnover £4 million

Founded 1999. Specialises in reprinting out-of-print works for the 'value' market world-wide and commissioning new general non-fiction publications in reference, cookery, gardening and children's. DIVISIONS/IMPRINTS **Brockhampton Press Ltd** Children's fiction and non-fiction. **Caxton Editions Ltd** General non-fiction, reference and military. **Knight Paperbacks Ltd** Fiction. 200 titles a year. No unsolicited mss; synopses and ideas welcome; send letter in the first instance.

ROYALTIES twice-yearly.

CBA Publishing

Bowes Morrell House, 111 Walmgate, York YO1 9WA

☎01904 671417 Fax 01904 671384

www.britarch.ac.uk

Publications Officer *Jane Thorniley-Walker*

British Archaeology Editor *Mike Pitts*

Young Archaeologists' Club Coordinator *Alison Bodley*

Approx. Annual Turnover £80,000

Publishing arm of the **Council for British Archaeology**. Publishes academic archaeology reports, practical handbooks, yearbook, *British Archaeology* (bi-monthly magazine), *Young Archaeologist* (Young Archaeologists' Club magazine), monographs, archaeology and education. TITLES *Thomas Telford's Holyhead Road*; *Archaeology in Northumberland National Park*; *Leather and Leatherworking in Anglo-Scandinavian and Medieval York*; *Historic Landscape Analysis Practical Handbook*. Please contact by telephone before submitting mss and proposals.

ROYALTIES paid for hardback and commercial publications.

CBD Research Ltd

Chancery House, 15 Wickham Road, Beckenham BR3 5JS

☎020 8650 7745 Fax 020 8650 0768

✉ cbd@cbdresearch.com

www.cbdresearch.com

Managing Director *S.P.A. Henderson*

Approx. Annual Turnover £500,000

Founded 1961. Publishes directories and other reference guides to sources of information. No fiction. IMPRINT **Chancery House Press** Non-fiction of an esoteric/specialist nature for 'serious researchers and the dedicated hobbyist'. About 6 titles a year.

ROYALTIES quarterly.

Centaur Press

See **Open Gate Press**

Century

See **The Random House Group Ltd**

Chadwyck-Healey

See **ProQuest Information and Learning Ltd**

Chambers Harrap Publishers Ltd

7 Hopetoun Crescent, Edinburgh EH7 4AY

☎0131 556 5929 Fax 0131 556 5313

✉ admin@chambersharrap.com

www.chambersharrap.com

Managing Director *Maurice Shepherd*

Administrator *Stephanie Divens*

Publishes dictionaries and reference. The imprint was founded in the early 1800s to publish self-education books, but soon diversified into dictionaries and other reference works. The acquisition of Harrap Publishing Group's core business strengthened its position in the dictionary market, adding bilingual titles, covering almost all the major European languages, to its English-language dictionaries. About 25 titles a year. Send synopsis with accompanying letter rather than completed mss.

Chancery House Press

See **CBD Research Ltd**

Paul Chapman Publishing Ltd
See **Sage Publications**

Chapman Publishing
4 Broughton Place, Edinburgh EH1 3RX
☎0131 557 2207 Fax 0131 556 9565
✉ chapman-pub@blueyonder.co.uk
www.chapman-pub.co.uk
Managing Editor *Joy Hendry*

A venture devoted to publishing works by the best of Scottish writers, both up-and-coming and established, published in *Chapman*, Scotland's leading literary magazine. Has expanded publishing activities considerably over the last three years and is now publishing a wider range of works though the broad policy stands. Publishes poetry, drama, short stories, books of contemporary importance in 20th-century Scotland. TITLES *Ye Cannae Win* Janet Paisley; *Clan MacHine* Ian McDonough; *Wild Women Series – Wild Women of a Certain Age* Magi Gibson. About 4 titles a year. No unsolicited mss; synopses and ideas for books welcome.
ROYALTIES annually.

Chapmans Publishers
See **The Orion Publishing Group Ltd**

Charnwood
See **F.A. Thorpe (Publishing)**

Chartered Institute of Personnel and Development
CIPD House, Camp Road, London
SW19 4UX
☎020 8971 9000 Fax 020 8263 3333
✉ publish@cipd.co.uk
www.cipd.co.uk/bookstore
Publishing Manager *Sarah Brown*

Part of CIPD Enterprises Limited. Publishes people management and training titles. A list of over 200 titles. TITLES *Employment Law for People Managers*; *International HRM*; *Competencies Handbook*; *Developing Effective Training Skills*. Unsolicited mss, synopses and ideas welcome.
ROYALTIES annually.

Chatto & Windus
See **The Random House Group Ltd**

Cherrytree Books
See **Evans Brothers Ltd**

Chicken House Publishing
2 Palmer Street, Frome BA11 1DS
☎01373 454488 Fax 01373 454499
✉ doublecluck.com
Chairman/Managing Director *Barry Cunningham*

Children's publishing house founded in 2000. Publishes books 'that are aimed at real children' – fiction, original picture books, gift books and fun non-fiction. Aiming to publish about 25 titles a year. 'We are always on the lookout for new talent.' Unsolicited material welcome; send letter with synopsis and sample chapters.
ROYALTIES twice-yearly.

Authors' Rating A new kid on the street, Chicken House, according to its founder, Barry Cunningham, is a 'small, creative company which has made strategic alliances around the world'. These alliances certainly give new authors a strong international profile – just the thing in an ever more competitive market.

Child's Play (International) Ltd
Ashworth Road, Bridgemead, Swindon
SN5 7YD
☎01793 616286 Fax 01793 512795
✉ allday@childs-play.com
www.childs-play.com
Chief Executive *Neil Burden*

Founded in 1972, Child's Play is an independent publisher specialising in learning through play, whole child development, life-skills and values. Publishes books, games and A-V materials. TITLES *Big Hungry Bear, There Was an Old Lady; Our Cat Cuddles; Royston Knapper; Children of the Sun; Ten Beads Tall; Pocket Pals; Sliders; Roly Poly Books; Animal Lullabies; Monkey's Clever Tale; What's the Time, Mr Wolf?; Sign and Sing-Along; Arithmetic Lotto*. Unsolicited mss welcome. Send s.a.e. for return or response. Expect to wait two months for a reply.
ROYALTIES Outright or royalty payments are subject to negotiation.

Chimera
See **Pegasus Elliot Mackenzie Publishers Ltd**

Chivers
See **BBC Audiobooks** under *Audio Books*

Christian Focus Publications
Geanies House, Fearn, Tain IV20 1TW
☎01862 871011 Fax 01862 871699
✉ info@christianfocus.com
www.christianfocus.com
Chairman *R.W.M. Mackenzie*
Managing Director *William Mackenzie*

Editorial Manager *Willie Mackenzie*
Children's Editor *Catherine Mackenzie*

Founded 1979 to produce children's books for the co-edition market. Now a major producer of Christian books. Publishes adult and children's books, including some fiction for children but not adults. No poetry. Publishes for all English-speaking markets, as well as the UK. IMPRINTS **Christian Focus** General books; **Mentor** Study books; **Christian Heritage** Classic reprints. About 80 titles a year. Unsolicited mss, synopses and ideas welcome from Christian writers. See website for submission criteria.
ROYALTIES annually.

Christian Heritage
See **Christian Focus Publications**

Christian Publishing
See **First Century Ltd**

Chrome Dreams
See entry under *Audio Books*

Chrysalis Books Group
The Chrysalis Building, Bramley Road,
London W10 6SP
☎020 7314 1400
✉ firstinitialsurname@chrysalisbooks.co.uk
www.chrysalisbooks.co.uk

CEO *Marcus Leaver*
Director of Publications *Roger Huggins*
Approx. Annual Turnover £33.9 million

Chrysalis Books Group, owned by Chrysalis Group Plc, specialises in illustrated non-fiction, publishing under the IMPRINTS **B.T. Batsford**; **Brassey's**; **C&B (Collins & Brown)**; **Conway Maritime Press**; **Paper Tiger**; **Pavilion**; **Putnam Aeronautical Books**; **Robson Books**; **Salamander**.

IMPRINTS
B.T. Batsford Publisher *To be appointed* Founded in 1843 as a bookseller, and began publishing in 1874. Acquired by Chrysalis in 1999. A world leader in books on chess, arts and craft. Publishes non-fiction, architecture, heritage, bridge and chess, film and entertainment, fashion, crafts and hobbies. About 100 titles a year. ROYALTIES paid twice in the first year, annually thereafter.

Brassey's Publisher *John Lee* Acquired by Chrysalis in 1999. Publishes military history and technology. ROYALTIES paid annually.

C&B (Collins & Brown) Publisher *Will Steeds* Publishes a range of lifestyle categories

especially in the areas of practical art, photography and needlecrafts.

Conway Maritime Press Publisher *John Lee* Publishes naval history, maritime culture and ship modelling. ROYALTIES paid annually.

Paper Tiger Publisher *Will Steeds* Acquired by Chrysalis in 2001 (part of C&B). Publishes science fiction and fantasy art.

Pavilion Books Editorial Director *Kate Oldfield* Acquired by Chrysalis in 2001. Publishes illustrated books in biography, cookery, gardening, humour, art, interiors, music, sport and travel. Unsolicited mss not welcome. Ideas and synopses for non-fiction titles considered. ROYALTIES paid twice-yearly.

Putnam Aeronautical Books Publisher *John Lee* Publishes classic aeronautical histories, technical and reference.

Robson Books Publisher *Jeremy Robson* Founded 1973. Acquired by Chrysalis in 1998. Publishes general non-fiction including biography, cookery, gardening, sport and travel. About 90 titles a year. Unsolicited synopses and ideas for books welcome (s.a.e. essential for reply). ROYALTIES paid twice-yearly.

Salamander Publisher *Jo Messham* Founded 1973. Publishes colour illustrated books on collecting, cookery, interiors, gardening, music, crafts, military, aviation, sport and transport. Also a wide range of books on American interest subjects. No unsolicited mss but synopses and ideas for the above subjects welcome. ROYALTIES Outright fee paid instead of royalties.

Authors' Rating Having grown rapidly by acquisitions, Chrysalis publishes up to 700 titles a year covering just about every area of general non-fiction. But recent staff cutbacks suggest a greater concentration on core markets with a corresponding contraction of the publishing programme. US co-editions account for half the company's sales.

Chrysalis Children's Books
The Chrysalis Building, Bramley Road,
London W10 6SP
☎020 7314 1400 Fax 020 7314 1598
✉ firstinitialsurname@chrysalisbooks.co.uk
www.chrysalisbooks.com

Publisher *Sarah Fabiny*

Part of the **Chrysalis Books Group**. Publishes all kinds of children's books from fun books to illustrated classics and educational books under the following DIVISIONS: **Education** Editorial Manager *Joyce Bentley* Publishes children's non-fiction in all curriculum areas. TITLES *Start*

Writing; *Art for All*; *Speaking and Listening*; *Art Revolutions*; *Strange Histories*; *Talking About*. No unsolicited mss. Synopses and ideas for books welcome from experienced children's writers. **Pre-School and Fiction** Editorial Manager *Liz Flanagan* Publishes children's picture, novelty and gift books for ages 0 to 10. TITLES *War Boy*; *The Story of the Litle Mole Who Knew It Was None of His Business*; *Elephant Elements*; *Fairy Tales and Fantastic Stories*. No unsolicited mss. **Trade Non-Fiction** Editorial Head *Honor Head* Publishes innovative and interactive children's books including novelty books, popular non-fiction, licensed characters. No unsolicited mss.

Authors' Rating Chrysalis has cut back on new titles in favour of pushing its backlist and publishing more series-based titles.

Churchill Livingstone
See **Elsevier Ltd**

Churchwarden Publications Ltd
PO Box 420, Warminster BA12 9XB
☎01985 840189 Fax 01985 840243
Managing Director *John Stidolph*
Founded 1974. Publishes books and stationery for churchwardens and church administrators including *The Churchwarden's Yearbook*. About 2 titles a year. Unsolicited mss, synopses and ideas for books welcome.
  ROYALTIES paid according to contract.

Cicerone Press
2 Police Square, Milnthorpe LA7 7PY
☎01539 562069 Fax 01539 563417
✉ info@cicerone.co.uk
www.cicerone.co.uk
Managing/Editorial Director *Jonathan Williams*
Founded 1969. Guidebook publisher for outdoor enthusiasts. No fiction or poetry. TITLES *Hillwalker's Guide to Mountaineering*; *Tour of Mont Blanc*; *Coast to Coast Trail*. SERIES include *Alpine Walking*; *International Walking*; *British Long-Distance Trails*, *Cycling* and *Winter Activities*. About 20 titles a year. No unsolicited mss; synopses and ideas considered.
  ROYALTIES twice-yearly.

Cico Books
1st Floor, 32 Great Sutton Street, London EC1V 0NB
☎020 7253 7960 Fax 020 7253 7967
✉ mail@cicobooks.co.uk
Managing Director *Mark Collins*

Publisher *Cindy Richards*
Founded in 1999 by Mark Collins and Cindy Richards (both formerly with **Collins & Brown**) 'to offer flexibility by being small, selling co-edition rights to overseas publishers'. Publishes lifestyle and interiors, mind, body and spirit. About 15 titles a year. No unsolicited mss, synopses or ideas.
  ROYALTIES twice-yearly.

Clairview Books
See **Temple Lodge Publishing Ltd**

Clarion
See **Elliot Right Way Books**

T&T Clark International
See **The Continuum International Publishing Group Ltd**

James Clarke & Co.
PO Box 60, Cambridge CB1 2NT
☎01223 350865 Fax 01223 366951
✉ publishing@jamesclarke.co.uk
www.jamesclarke.co.uk
Managing Director *Adrian Brink*
Parent company of **The Lutterworth Press** (see entry). Publishes scholarly and academic works, mainly theological, directory and reference titles. TITLES *Libraries Directory* (book and CD-ROM versions); *Encyclopedia of the Middle Ages*; *Henry VIII's Bishops*; *Nonconformity*; *Enlightenment Prelate*. Approach in writing with ideas in the first instance.

Classic Publications
See **Ian Allan Publishing Ltd**

Peter Collin Publishing Ltd
See **Bloomsbury Publishing Plc**

Collins
See **HarperCollins Publishers Ltd**

Collins & Brown
See **Chrysalis Books Group**

Colonsay Books
See **House of Lochar**

Colourpoint Books
Colourpoint House, Jubilee Business Park, 21 Jubilee Road, Newtownards BT23 4YH
☎028 9182 0505 Fax 028 9182 1900
✉ info@colourpoint.co.uk
www.colourpoint.co.uk

Partners *Sheila M. Johnston, Norman Johnston, Malcolm Johnston, Wesley Johnston*

Founded 1993. Publishes school textbooks and transport (covering the whole of the British Isles), plus books of Irish and general interest. No fiction. About 25 titles a year. Unsolicited material accepted but approach in writing in the first instance; include return postage, please.

ROYALTIES twice-yearly.

Columbia University Press
See **University Presses of California, Columbia & Princeton Ltd**

Compendium Publishing Ltd
43 Frith Street, London W1D 4SA
☎020 7287 4570 Fax 020 7494 0583
✉ compendiumpub@aol.com
Managing Director *Alan Greene*
Editorial Director *Simon Forty*

Founded 1996. Publishes and packages for international publishing companies – general non-fiction: history, reference, hobbies, children's and educational transport and militaria. No unsolicited mss; synopses and ideas preferred.

ROYALTIES twice-yearly.

Condor
See **Souvenir Press Ltd**

Conran Octopus
See **Octopus Publishing Group**

Constable & Robinson Ltd
3 The Lanchesters, 162 Fulham Palace Road, London W6 9ER
☎020 8741 3663 Fax 020 8748 7562
✉ enquiries@constablerobinson.com
www.constablerobinson.com
Non-Executive Chairman *Benjamin Glazebrook*
Managing Director *Nick Robinson*
Directors *Jan Chamier, Nova Jayne Heath, Adrian Andrews*

Constable & Co Founded in 1890 by Archibald Constable, a grandson of Walter Scott's publisher. Robinson Publishing Ltd founded in 1983 by Nick Robinson. In December 1999 Constable and Robinson combined their individual shareholdings into a single company, Constable & Robinson Ltd. IMPRINTS **Constable** (Hardbacks) Editorial Director *Carol O'Brien* Publishes biography and autobiography, crime fiction, general and military history, psychology, travel, climbing, landscape photography and outdoor pursuits guidebooks. **Robinson** (Paperbacks) Senior Commissioning Editor *Krystyna Green* Publishes crime, science fiction, *Daily Telegraph* health books, the Mammoth series, psychology, true crime, military history and *Smarties* children's books. Unsolicited sample chapters, synopses and ideas for books welcome. No mss; no e-mail submissions. Enclose return postage.

Authors' Rating With an excellent result from a Society of Authors' survey of author/publisher relations, Constable & Robinson is one of the three top small publishers for sales and revenue.

Consultants Bureau
See **Kluwer Academic/Plenum Publishers**

The Continuum International Publishing Group Limited
The Tower Building, 11 York Road, London SE1 7NX
☎020 7922 0880 Fax 020 7922 0881
www.continuumbooks.com
Chairman & Chief Executive *Philip Sturrock*
Approx. Annual Turnover £16 million

Founded in 1999 by a buy-out of the academic and religious publishing of Cassell and the acquisition of Continuum New York. Publishes academic, religious and general books.

DIVISIONS
Academic Humanities Publishing Director *Anthony Haynes* Publishes education, social sciences, literature, film and music, philosophy (including the **Thoemmes** imprint), linguistics. TITLES *Getting the Buggers into Languages*; *What Philosophy Is*; *Collected Works of M.A.H. Halliday*; *Contemporary British Novel*; *Tony Benn*. **Religious Academic** Publisher *Philip Law* Publishes under **T&T Clark International** Biblical studies, theology. TITLES *Karl Barth Church Dogmatics*; *Journals for the Study of Old/New Testament*. **General Trade & Continuum Religion** Publishing Director *Robin Baird-Smith* Publishes under **Continuum**; **Burns & Oates** (R.C. books); **Morehouse** (Anglican titles). TITLES *Pride and Perjury*; *Cathechism of the Catholic Church*; *Churchwarden's Handbook*.

IMPRINTS
Continuum; **T&T Clark International**; **Thoemmes**; **Burns & Oates**; **Morehouse**.

500 titles in 2003. Unsolicited synopses and ideas within the subject areas listed above welcome; approach in writing in the first instance. OVERSEAS SUBSIDIARIES The Continuum International Publishing Group Inc., New York and Harrisburg, PA.

ROYALTIES twice-yearly.

Authors' Rating Expanding religious and academic list takes in controversial ideas and original thinking.

Conway Maritime Press
See **Chrysalis Books Group**

Thomas Cook Publishing
PO Box 227, Peterborough PE3 8XX
☎01733 417352 Fax 01733 416688

Head of Publishing *Donald Greig*
Approx. Annual Turnover £4 million

Part of the Thomas Cook Group Ltd, publishing commenced in 1873 with the first issue of *Cook's Continental Timetable*. Publishes guidebooks, maps and timetables. About 20 titles a year. No unsolicited mss; synopses and ideas welcome as long as they are travel-related.

ROYALTIES annually.

Leo Cooper
See **Pen & Sword Books Ltd**

Corgi
See **Transworld Publishers**

Coronet
See **Hodder Headline Ltd**

Countryside Books
2 Highfield Avenue, Newbury RG14 5DS
☎01635 43816 Fax 01635 551004
✉ info@countrysidebooks.co.uk
www.countrysidebooks.co.uk

Publisher *Nicholas Battle*

Founded 1976. Publishes local interest paperbacks on regional subjects, generally by English county. Local history, dialects, genealogy, walking and photographic, aviation and military, some transport. Over 400 titles available. Unsolicited mss and synopses welcome but no fiction, poetry, natural history or personal memories.

ROYALTIES twice-yearly.

CRC Press
See **Taylor & Francis Group plc**

Crescent Books
See **Mercat Press Ltd**

Cressrelles Publishing Co. Ltd
10 Station Road Industrial Estate, Colwall,
Malvern WR13 6RN
☎01684 540154 Fax 01684 540154
✉ simonsmith@cressrelles4drama.
     fsbusiness.co.uk

Managing Director *Leslie Smith*

Publishes a range of local interest books, drama and chiropody titles. IMPRINTS **Actinic Press** Specialises in chiropody; **J. Garnet Miller** Plays and theatre texts; **Kenyon-Deane** Plays and drama textbooks. Submissions welcome.

Croom Helm
See **Routledge**

Crossway
See **Inter-Varsity Press**

The Crowood Press Ltd
The Stable Block, Crowood Lane, Ramsbury,
Marlborough SN8 2HR
☎01672 520320 Fax 01672 520280
✉ enquiries@crowood.com
www.crowood.com

Chairman *John Dennis*
Managing Director *Ken Hathaway*

Publishes sport and leisure titles, including animal and land husbandry, climbing and walking, maritime, country sports, equestrian, fishing and shooting; also chess and bridge, crafts, dogs, gardening, natural history, aviation, military history and motoring. IMPRINT **Airlife Publishing** Specialist aviation titles for pilots, historians and enthusiasts. Also twentieth century naval and military history. About 70 titles a year. Preliminary letter preferred in all cases.

ROYALTIES annually.

James Currey Publishers
73 Botley Road, Oxford OX2 0BS
☎01865 244111 Fax 01865 246454
✉ editorial@jamescurrey.co.uk
www.jamescurrey.co.uk

Chairman *James Currey*
Managing Director/Editorial Director *Douglas H. Johnson*

Founded 1985. A specialist publisher. Publishes academic paperback books on Africa, the Caribbean and Third World: history, anthropology, economics, sociology, politics and literary criticism. Approach in writing by post with synopsis if material is 'relevant to our needs'.

ROYALTIES annually.

Curzon Press
See **Routledge**

Custom Publishing
See **The Orion Publishing Group Limited**

Dalesman Publishing Co. Ltd
Stable Courtyard, Broughton Hall, Skipton
BD23 3AZ
☎01756 701381 Fax 01756 701326
✉ editorial@dalesman.co.uk
www.dalesman.co.uk

Editor *Terry Fletcher*

Publishers of *Dalesman*, *Cumbria and Lake District* and *Peak District* magazines, and regional books covering Yorkshire, the Lake District and the Peak District. Subjects include crafts and hobbies, geography and geology, guidebooks, history and antiquarian, humour, travel and topography. About 20 titles a year. Will consider mss on subjects listed above.
ROYALTIES annually.

Terence Dalton Ltd
Water Street, Lavenham, Sudbury CO10 9RN
☎01787 249291 Fax 01787 248267
www.lavenhamgroup.co.uk

Director/Editorial Head *Elisabeth Whitehair*

Founded 1967. Part of the Lavenham Group Plc, a family company. No unsolicited mss; send synopsis with two or three sample chapters. Ideas welcome.
ROYALTIES annually.

C.W. Daniel
See **The Random House Group Ltd**

Darton, Longman & Todd Ltd
1 Spencer Court, 140–142 Wandsworth High Street, London SW18 4JJ
☎020 8875 0155 Fax 020 8875 0133
✉ tradesales@darton-longman-todd.co.uk
www.darton-longman-todd.co.uk

Editorial Director *Brendan Walsh*
Editor/Rights Officer *Rachel Davis*
Approx. Annual Turnover £1 million

Founded 1959. In July 1990 DLT became a common ownership company, owned and run by staff members. A leading ecumenical, predominantly Christian, publisher, with a strong emphasis on spirituality, theology and the ministry and mission of the Church. TITLES *Jerusalem Bible*; *New Jerusalem Bible*; *The Return of the Prodigal Son*; *Resurrection*. About 50 titles a year. Sample material for books on theological or spiritual subjects considered.
ROYALTIES twice-yearly.

David & Charles Publishers
Brunel House, Forde Close, Newton Abbot TQ12 4PU
☎01626 323200 Fax 01626 323317
✉ mail@davidandcharles.co.uk
www.davidandcharles.co.uk

Managing Director *Budge Wallis*

Founded 1960, owned by F.&W. Publications. Publishes illustrated non-fiction for international markets, specialising in needlecraft, crafts, art techniques, practical photography, military history, equestrian and gardening. No fiction, poetry or memoirs. TITLES *Cross Stitch Angels*; *Quick & Clever Handmade Cards*; *100 Ways to take Better Photographs*; *Painting in Watercolour*; *The Horse Behaviour Handbook*; *Voices from D-Day*. About 200 titles a year. Unsolicited mss will be considered if return postage is included; synopses and ideas welcome for the subjects listed above.
ROYALTIES twice-yearly or flat fees.

Christopher Davies Publishers Ltd
PO Box 403, Swansea SA1 4YF
☎01792 648825 Fax 01792 648825
✉ editor@cdaviesbookswales.com

Managing Director/Editorial Head *Christopher T. Davies*
Approx. Annual Turnover £50,000

Founded 1949 to promote and expand Welsh-language publications. Publishes biography, cookery, history, sport and literature of Welsh interest. TITLES *An A–Z of Wales and the Welsh*; *Welsh Birthplaces*; *Carwyn: A Personal Memoir*; *Who's Who in Welsh History*. About 3 titles a year. No unsolicited mss. Synopses and ideas for books welcome.
ROYALTIES twice-yearly.

Authors' Rating A favourite for Celtic readers and writers.

Giles de la Mare Publishers Ltd
PO Box 25351, London NW5 1ZT
☎020 7485 2533 Fax 020 7485 2534
✉ gilesdelamare@dial.pipex.com
www.gilesdelamare.co.uk

Chairman/Managing Director *Giles de la Mare*
Approx. Annual Turnover £30,000

Founded 1995 and commenced publishing in April 1996. Publishes mainly non-fiction, especially art and architecture, biography, history, music. TITLES *Married to the Amadeus* Muriel Nissel; *Venice: An Anthology Guide* Milton Grundy; *History at War* Noble Frankland; *Flint Architecture of East Anglia* Stephen Hart; *19th Century British Painting* Luke Herrmann; *Short Stories*, Vols I & II Walter de la Mare; *Handsworth Revolution* David Winkley; *The Life of Henry Moore* Roger Berthoud; *Becoming an Orchestral Musician* Richard Davis. Unsolicited mss, synopses and ideas welcome after initial telephone call.

ROYALTIES twice-yearly.

Debrett's Ltd

Brunel House, 55–57 North Wharf Road, London W2 1LA
☎020 7915 9633 Fax 020 7753 4212
✉ people@debretts.co.uk
www.debretts.co.uk

Chairman *Christopher Haines*

Founded 1769. The company's main activity (in conjunction with **Macmillan**) is the three-yearly *Debrett's Peerage and Baronetage* (published 2003) and annual *Debrett's People of Today* (also available on CD-ROM and online). Debrett's general books are published under licence through **Headline**.

ROYALTIES twice-yearly.

Dedalus Ltd

Langford Lodge, St Judith's Lane, Sawtry PE28 5XE
☎01487 832382 Fax 01487 832382
✉ DedalusLimited@compuserve.com
www.dedalusbooks.com

Chairman *Juri Gabriel*
Managing Director *Eric Lane*
Approx. Annual Turnover £200,000

Founded 1983. Publishes contemporary European fiction and classics and original literary fiction. TITLES *The Dedalus Book of the Occult*; *The Arabian Nightmare* Robert Irwin; *Memoirs of a Gnostic Dwarf* David Madsen; *The Double Life of Daniel Glick* Maurice Caldera; *Music in a Foreign Language* Andrew Crumey (winner of the **Saltire Best First Book Award** in 1994).

DIVISIONS/IMPRINTS **Original Fiction in Paperback**; **Contemporary European Fiction 1992–2004**; **Dedalus European Classics**; **Literary Concept Books**. Welcomes submissions for original fiction and books suitable for its list but 'most people sending work in have no idea what kind of books Dedalus publishes and merely waste their efforts'. Author guidelines on website. Particularly interested in intellectually clever and unusual fiction. A letter about the author should always accompany any submission. No replies without s.a.e.

ROYALTIES annually.

Authors' Rating A small, quality publisher which actually recognises that good books can come from foreign language writers.

Marcel Dekker

See **Taylor & Francis Group plc**

JM Dent

See **The Orion Publishing Group Ltd**

André Deutsch Ltd

See **Carlton Publishing Group**

Digital Octopus

See **Octopus Publishing Group**

Digital Press

See **Elsevier Ltd**

Dinas

See **Y Lolfa Cyf**

Diva Books

See **Millivres Prowler Limited**

The Do-Not Press

16 Woodlands, London SE13 6TY
☎020 8698 7833 Fax 020 8698 7834
✉ wh@thedonotpress.com
www.thedonotpress.com

Managing Director *Jim Driver*
Approx. Annual Turnover £150,000

Founded 1994. Publishes general fiction and non-fiction. IMPRINT **Bloodlines** Editorial Head *Carol de Salivate* TITLES *Judas Pig*; *Down and Out in Shoreditch and Hoxton*; *Einstein*. 18 titles in 2003. No unsolicited mss, synopses or ideas.

ROYALTIES annually.

John Donald Publishers Ltd

West Newington House, 10 Newington Road, Edinburgh EH9 1QS
☎0131 668 4371 Fax 0131 668 4466
www.birlinn.co.uk

Managing Director *Hugh Andrew*

Bought by **Birlinn Ltd** in 1999. Publishes academic and scholarly, archaeology, architecture, textbooks, guidebooks, local, and social history. New books are published as an imprint of Birlinn Ltd. About 20 titles a year.

ROYALTIES annually.

Donhead Publishing Ltd

Lower Coombe, Donhead St Mary,
Shaftesbury SP7 9LY
☎01747 828422 Fax 01747 828522
✉ jillpearce@donhead.com
www.donhead.com

Contact *Jill Pearce*

Founded 1990 to specialise in publishing how-
to books for building practitioners; particularly
interested in architectural conservation material.
Publishes building, architecture and heritage
only. TITLES *Preserving Post-War Heritage*; *Stone
Cleaning*; *Architecture 1900*; *Encyclopaedia of
Architectural Terms*; *Cleaning Historic Buildings*;
Brickwork; *Practical Stone Masonry*; *Conservation of
Timber Buildings*; *Surveying Historic Buildings*;
English Heritage Directory of Building Limes;
Heritage, Sands and Aggregates; *Journal of
Architectural Conservation* (3 issues yearly). 6 titles
a year. Unsolicited mss, synopses and ideas wel-
come.

Dorling Kindersley Ltd

Part of the Penguin Group, 80 Strand,
London WC2R 0RL
☎020 7010 3000 Fax 020 7010 6060
www.dk.com

Chief Executive *Anthony Forbes Watson*
Managing Director *Andrew Welham*
Publisher *Christopher Davis*

Founded 1974. Packager and publisher of illustrated non-fiction: cookery, crafts, gardening,
health, travel guides, atlases, natural history and
children's information and fiction. Launched a
US imprint in 1991 and an Australian imprint
in 1997. Acquired Henderson Publishing in
1995 and was purchased by Pearson plc for
£311 million in 2000.

DIVISIONS Adult: **Travel/Reference** Publisher *Douglas Amrine*; **General/Lifestyle** Publisher *John Roberts*. Children's: **Reference**
Publisher *Miriam Farby*; **PreSchool/Primary**
Publisher *Sophie Mitchell*.

IMPRINTS **Ladybird**; **Ladybird Audio**;
Funfax; **Eyewitness Guides**; **Eyewitness
Travel Guides**. TITLES *BMA Complete Family
Health Encyclopedia*; *RHS A–Z Encyclopedia of
Garden Plants*; *Children's Illustrated Encyclopedia*;
The Way Things Work. Unsolicited synopses/
ideas for books welcome.

Authors' Rating The focus is on 'soft learning'
products for the trade and education markets.
Most titles are team efforts with writers and
illustrators working closely with an in-house
editor.

Doubleday

See **Transworld Publishers**

Doubleday Picture Books

See **The Random House Group Ltd**

Drake Educational Associates

St Fagans Road, Fairwater, Cardiff CF5 3AE
☎029 2956 0333 Fax 029 2956 0313

Managing Director *R.G. Drake*

Literacy, phonics and language development
games and activities. Ideas and scripts in these
fields welcome. Also resources for subject areas
in the primary school and modern languages at
KS2.

Dref Wen

28 Church Road, Whitchurch CF14 2EA
☎029 2061 7860 Fax 029 2061 0507
✉ gwilym@drefwen.com

Chairman *R. Boore*
Managing Director *G. Boore*

Founded 1970. Publishes Welsh language and
bilingual children's books, Welsh and English
educational books for Welsh learners.
ROYALTIES annually.

Duckbacks

See **Gerald Duckworth & Co. Ltd**

Gerald Duckworth & Co. Ltd

First Floor, 90–93 Cowcross Street, London
EC1M 6BF
☎020 7490 7300 Fax 020 7490 0080
✉ info@duckworth-publishers.co.uk
www.ducknet.co.uk

Chief Operations Officer *Gillian Hawkins*
Approx. Annual Turnover £2 million

Founded 1898 by Gerald Duckworth. Original
publishers of Virginia Woolf. Other early authors
include Hilaire Belloc, John Galsworthy, D.H.
Lawrence and George Orwell. Duckworth is a
general trade publisher with eminent authors
such as Beryl Bainbridge, D.J. Taylor and John
Bayley in addition to a strong academic division.
Acquired by **Penguin** in 2003.

IMPRINTS/DIVISIONS **Bristol Classical Press**
Classical texts and modern languages;
Duckworth Academic; **Duckworth General**;
Duckbacks. No fiction. No unsolicited mss;
synopses and sample chapters only. Enclose s.a.e.
or return postage for response/return.

ROYALTIES twice-yearly at first, annually
thereafter.

Authors' Rating With the bankers knocking at

the door, Duckworth was put up for auction. The successful bidder was Peter Mayer, famous for rejuvenating Penguin in the 1980s. Better news for a much loved but not always well run publisher it is hard to imagine. The new owner promises to capitalise on the strengths of the backlist while searching for new titles that larger publishers overlook.

Duncan Petersen Publishing Limited

31 Ceylon Road, London W14 0PY
☎020 7371 2356 Fax 020 7371 2507
✉ dp@macunlimited.net

Director *Andrew Duncan*

Founded 1986. Publisher and packager of childcare, business, antiques, birds, nature, atlases, walking and travel books. IMPRINT **Duncan Petersen** SERIES *Charming Small Hotel Guides*; *Charming Restaurant Guides*; *On Foot* (city walking guides). Unsolicited synopses and ideas for books welcome.

FEES paid.

Dunedin Academic Press Ltd

Hudson House, 8 Albany Street, Edinburgh EH1 3QB
☎0131 473 2397 Fax 01250 870920
✉ mail@dunedinacademicpress.co.uk
www.dunedinacademicpress.co.uk

Managing Director *Anthony Kinahan*

Founded 2001. Publishes academic and general non-fiction. Considerable experience in academic and professional publishing. 12 titles in 2003. Not interested in science (other than earth sciences), fiction or children's. No unsolicited mss. Synopses and ideas welcome. Approach first in writing outlining proposal and identifying market.

ROYALTIES annually.

Martin Dunitz Ltd

Taylor & Francis Group plc, 11 New Fetter Lane, London EC4P 4EE
☎020 7842 2001 Fax 020 7842 2300
www.dunitz.co.uk

Managing Director *Christopher Chesher*
Production Manager *Susan Grant*

Acquired by the **Taylor & Francis Group plc** in 1999. Publishes specialist medical and dentistry atlases, texts, pocketbooks, slide atlases and CD-ROMs aimed at an international market. Particular areas of focus are psychiatry, neurology, cardiology, orthopaedics, dermatology, oncology and bone metabolism. The company won the Queen's

Award for Export Achievement in 1991. 90–100 titles a year. Unsolicited synopses and ideas welcome but no mss.

ROYALTIES twice-yearly.

Earthscan Publications

See **Kogan Page Ltd**

Ebury Press

See **The Random House Group Ltd**

Economist Books

See **Profile Books**

Eden

See **Transworld Publishers**

Edinburgh University Press

22 George Square, Edinburgh EH8 9LF
☎0131 650 4218 Fax 0131 662 0053
www.eup.ed.ac.uk

Chairman *Timothy Rix*
Managing Director *Timothy Wright*
Editorial Director *Jackie Jones*
Senior Editor *Nicola Carr*

Publishes academic and scholarly books (and journals): gender studies, geography, history – ancient, classical, medieval and modern, Islamic studies, linguistics, literary criticism, media and cultural studies, sociology and social theory, philosophy, politics, Scottish studies, theology and religious studies. About 100 titles a year.

ROYALTIES annually.

Egmont Books Limited

239 Kensington High Street, London W8 6SA
☎020 7761 3500 Fax 020 7761 3510
✉ firstname.lastname@ecb.egmont.com
www.egmont.co.uk

Managing Director *Fiona Clarke*
Publishing Director *David Riley*
Fiction & Picture Books *Cally Poplak*

Part of the Egmont Group (Copenhagen), Egmont Books publishes children's picture books, fiction, non-fiction, licensed characters, baby and toddler books and home learning. TITLES *Thomas the Tank Engine*; *Winnie-the-Pooh*; *A Series of Unfortunate Events*; *The Wind on Fire* trilogy. About 500 titles a year. Synopses and sample chapters welcome; approach in writing with s.a.e. marked for the attention of 'The Reader'. 'We regret that we are unable to return unsolicited material without s.a.e.'

ROYALTIES twice-yearly.

Authors' Rating Egmont has refined its list to focus on fiction and picture books but with dependence on supermarket and direct sales, the market can get bumpy.

Eland Publishing Ltd

Third Floor, 61 Exmouth Market, London EC1R 4QL
☎020 7833 0762 Fax 020 7833 4434
✉ info@travelbooks.co.uk
www.travelbooks.co.uk

Directors *Rose Baring, John Hatt, Barnaby Rogerson*
Approx. Annual Turnover £250,000

Travel re-print specialist, first established by travel writer and editor John Hatt in 1982. Backlist of 60 titles of classic world travel literature. TITLES *Naples '44* Norman Lewis; *Travels with Myself and Another* Martha Gelhorn. IMPRINTS **Sickle Moon** Explorer narratives, history and anthropology. TITLES *Turkish Letters* Busbecq; *The Tuareg* Jeremy Keenan. **Baring & Rogerson** *Poetry of Place* pocket books. No unsolicited mss. Postcards and e-mails welcome.
ROYALTIES annually.

Element

See **HarperCollins Publishers Ltd**

11:9

See **Neil Wilson Publishing Ltd**

Edward Elgar Publishing Ltd

Glensanda House, Montpellier Parade, Cheltenham GL50 1UA
☎01242 226934 Fax 01242 262111
✉ info@e-elgar.co.uk
www.e-elgar.com

Managing Director *Edward Elgar*

Founded 1986. International publisher in economics, the environment, public policy, business and management. TITLES *Who's Who in Economics* (3rd ed.); *Handbook of Environmental and Resource Economics*; *Who's Who in the Management Sciences*. 277 titles in 2003. No unsolicited mss; synopses and ideas in the subject areas listed above welcome. Approach by letter or e-mail; no telephone inquiries.
ROYALTIES annually.

Elliot Right Way Books

Kingswood Buildings, Lower Kingswood, Tadworth KT20 6TD
☎01737 832202 Fax 01737 830311
✉ info@right-way.co.uk
www.right-way.co.uk

Managing Directors *A. Clive Elliot, Malcolm G. Elliot*

Founded 1946 by Andrew G. Elliot. Publishes paperback how-to and educative titles on an unlimited variety of home reference, indoor and outdoor leisure pursuits, careers and business. Subjects include cookery, family financial and legal matters, public speaking, weddings, jokes, parenting, etiquette, English skills, driving, fishing, horse riding, drawing, music, puzzles, crosswords and quizzes, job seeking, running your own company.
IMPRINTS **Right Way** Instructional paperbacks in B format for the most popular subjects; **Right Way Plus** Larger C format for more specialised subjects; **Clarion** B format for promotional/ultra low-price range. Unsolicited mss, synopses and ideas for books welcome.
ROYALTIES annually.

Elliott & Thompson

27 John Street, London WC1N 2BX
☎020 7831 5013 Fax 020 7831 5011

Publishers *David Elliott, Brad Thompson*
Approx. Annual Turnover £92,000

Founded 2002. Publishes literary fiction, biography, belles lettres, reprints of classic male writers. 8 titles in 2003. New proposals welcome (send synopsis and sample pages initially) but s.a.e. essential.

Aidan Ellis Publishing

Whinfield, Herbert Road, Salcombe TQ8 8HN
☎01548 842755 Fax 01548 844356
✉ mail@aidanellispublishing.co.uk
www.aepub.demon.co.uk

Partners/Editorial Heads *Aidan Ellis, Lucinda Ellis*

Founded in 1971. Specialises in general trade books and non-fiction. TITLES *Eternity Regained* Marguerite Yourcenar; *The Royal Gardens in Windsor Great Park* Charles Lyte; *Trees For Your Garden* Roy Lancaster; *Pesca* Ian B. Hart; *Presumed Dead* Eunice Chapman; *That's Rich!* Craig Rich; *The Bird Table Book* Tony Soper. Ideas and synopses welcome (return postage, please).
ROYALTIES twice-yearly.

Elm Publications/Training

(wholly owned subsidiary of **Elm Consulting Ltd**)
Seaton House, Kings Ripton, Huntingdon PE28 2NJ
☎01487 773254
✉ sritchie@elm-training.co.uk
www.elm-training.co.uk

Managing Director *Sheila Ritchie*

Founded 1977. Publishes textbooks, teaching aids, educational resources and educational software in the fields of business and management for adult learners. Books and teaching/training resources are generally commissioned to meet specific business, management and other syllabuses. 'We are actively seeking good training materials for business/management, especially tested and proven. About 30 titles a year. Ideas are welcome; initial approach by post or e-mail with outline, or by a brief telephone call.

ROYALTIES annually.

Elsevier Ltd

The Boulevard, Langford Lane, Kidlington, Oxford OX5 1GB
☎01865 843000 Fax 01865 843010
www.elsevier.com

Chief Operating Officer *Gavin Howe*
CEO, Science & Technology (Books & Journals) *Arie Jongejan*

Parent company Reed Elsevier, Amsterdam. Now incorporates Pergamon Press and Harcourt Publishers International. Publishes academic and professional reference books, scientific, technical and medical books, journals, CD-ROMs and magazines. IMPRINTS **Academic Press**; **Architectural Press**; **Butterworth Heinemann**; **Digital Press**; **Elsevier**; **Elsevier Advanced Technology**; **Focal Press**; **Gulf Professional Press**; **JAI**; **Made Simple Books**; **Morgan Kauffman**; **Newnes**; **North-Holland**. DIVISION **Elsevier (Health Sciences)** 32 Jamestown Road, London NW1 7BY ☎020 7424 4200 Fax 020 7483 2293 Website www.elsevier-health.com CEO Health Sciences (Books & Journals) *Brian Nairn*, Managing Director *Dominic Vaughan* Publishes scientific, technical, medical books and journals. IMPRINTS **Baillière Tindall**; **Churchill Livingstone**; **Mosby**; **Pergamon**; **Saunders**. No unsolicited mss, but synopses and project proposals welcome.

ROYALTIES annually.

Emissary Publishing

PO Box 33, Bicester OX26 4ZZ
☎01869 323447 Fax 01869 324096

Editorial Director *Val Miller*

Founded 1992. Publishes mainly humorous paperback books including the complete set of Peter Pook novels; no poetry or children's. No unsolicited mss or synopses.

ROYALTIES twice-yearly.

Emma Treehouse Ltd

2nd Floor, The Old Brewhouse, Lower Charlton Trading Estate, Shepton Mallet BA4 5QE
☎01749 330529 Fax 01749 330544
✉ richard.powell4@virgin.net
www.emmatreehouse.com

Co-Directors *Richard Powell, David Bailey*
Approx. Annual Turnover £1 million

Founded 1992. Publishes children's pre-school novelty books. No mss. Illustrations, synopses and ideas for books welcome; write in the first instance.

FEES paid; no royalties.

Empiricus Books

See **Janus Publishing Company Ltd**

English Heritage (Publishing)

Kemble Drive, Swindon SN2 2GZ
☎01793 414497 Fax 01793 414769
✉ val.horsler@english-heritage.org.uk
www.english-heritage.org.uk

Head of Publishing *Val Horsler*

Founded 1984 to publish English Heritage guidebooks and a range of academic material related directly to the work of the organisation, together with a growing range of commercial publications, most published directly but some published in partnership. No unsolicited material.

Enitharmon Press

26B Caversham Road, London NW5 2DU
☎020 7482 5967 Fax 020 7284 1787
✉ books@enitharmon.co.uk
www.enitharmon.co.uk

Director *Stephen Stuart-Smith*

Founded 1967. An independent company with an enterprising editorial policy, Enitharmon has established itself as one of Britain's leading literary presses. Patron of 'the new and the neglected', Enitharmon also prides itself on the success of its collaborations between writers and artists, now published by its associate company, **Enitharmon Editions**. Publishes poetry, literary criticism, fiction, art and photography. TITLES *Book of Haikus* Jack Kerouac; *The Men Around Her Bed* Alan Brownjohn; *The House I Once Called Home* Duane Michals; *The Testament of Cresseid* Seamus Heaney; *Duck and Sally on the Inside* Jeremy Reed. No unsolicited mss.

ROYALTIES according to contract.

Epworth Press

c/o Methodist Publishing House, 4 John Wesley Road, Werrington, Peterborough PE4 6ZP

☎01733 325002 Fax 01733 384180

Chairman *Dr John A. Newton, CBE*
Commissioning Editor *Dr Natalie K. Watson*

Publishes Christian books only: philosophy, theology, biblical studies, pastoralia and social concern. No fiction, poetry or children's. A series based on the text of the *Revised Common Lectionary*, entitled *Companion to the RCL*, was launched in 1998 and the new series *Exploring Methodism* and *Thinking Things Through* continue. About 10 titles a year. Unsolicited mss, synopses and ideas welcome; send sample chapter and contents with covering letter.

ROYALTIES annually.

Euromonitor

60–61 Britton Street, London EC1M 5UX
☎020 7251 8024 Fax 020 7608 3149
www.euromonitor.com

Chairman *R.N. Senior*
Managing Director *T.J. Fenwick*
Approx. Annual Turnover £17 million

Founded 1972. International business information publisher specialising in library and professional reference books, market reports, electronic databases, journals and CD-ROMs. Publishes business reference, market analysis and information directories only.

DIVISIONS **Market Analysis** *T. Kitchin, S. Holmes*; **Reference Books & Directories** *S. Hunter*. TITLES *Credit & Charge Cards: The International Market*; *European Directory of Trade and Business Associations*; *World Retail Directory and Sourcebook*. About 200 titles a year.

PAYMENT is generally by flat fee.

Europa Publications Ltd

See **Taylor & Francis Group plc**

Evans Brothers Ltd

2A Portman Mansions, Chiltern Street, London W1U 6NR
☎020 7487 0920 Fax 020 7487 0921
✉ sales@evansbrothers.co.uk
www.evansbooks.co.uk

Managing Director *Stephen Pawley*
International Publishing Director *Brian Jones*
UK Publisher *Su Swallow*
Approx. Annual Turnover £4.5 million

Founded 1908 by Robert and Edward Evans. Originally published educational journals, books for primary schools and teacher education. After rapid expansion into popular fiction and drama, both were sacrificed to a major programme of educational books for schools in East and West Africa. A UK programme was launched in 1986 followed by the acquisition of Hamish Hamilton's non-fiction list for children in 1990. Acquired interests in Cherrytree Books and Zero to Ten in 1999. Publishes UK children's and educational books, and educational books for Africa, the Caribbean and Latin America. IMPRINTS **Cherrytree Books**; **Zero to Ten** trade under Zero to Ten Ltd at the Evans address above. OVERSEAS ASSOCIATES in Kenya, Cameroon, Sierra Leone; Evans Bros (Nigeria Publishers) Ltd. About 120 titles a year. Unsolicited mss, synopses and ideas for books welcome.

ROYALTIES annually.

Everyman

See **The Orion Publishing Group Ltd**

Everyman's Library

Northburgh House, 10 Northburgh Street, London EC1V 0AT
☎020 7566 6350 Fax 020 7490 3708
✉ katy@everyman.uk.com

Publisher *David Campbell*
Approx. Annual Turnover £3.5 million

ESTABLISHED 1906. Publishes hardback classics of world literature, pocket poetry anthologies, children's books and travel guides. Publishes no new titles apart from poetry anthologies; only classics (no new authors). AUTHORS include Bulgakov, Bellow, Borges, Heller, Marquez, Nabokov, Naipaul, Orwell, Rushdie, Updike, Waugh and Wodehouse. No unsolicited mss.

ROYALTIES annually.

The Exeter Press (formerly University of Exeter Press)

Reed Hall, Streatham Drive, Exeter EX4 4QR
☎01392 263066 Fax 01392 263064
✉ uep@exeter.ac.uk
www.ex.ac.uk/uep/

Publisher *Simon Baker*

Founded 1956. Publishes academic books: archaeology, classical studies, history, maritime studies, English literature (especially medieval), linguistics, European studies, modern languages and literature, film history, performance studies, Arabic studies and books on Exeter and the South West. About 30 titles a year. Proposals welcomed in the above subject areas.

ROYALTIES annually.

Exley Publications Ltd
16 Chalk Hill, Watford WD19 4BG
☎01923 248328 Fax 01923 800440
✉ editorial@exleypublications.co.uk
www.helenexleygiftbooks.com
Editorial Director *Helen Exley*
Founded 1976. Independent family company. Publishes giftbooks, quotation anthologies and humour. Only series ideas needed – no individual titles. No rhyming poetry, please. About 35 titles a year.

Expert Books
See **Transworld Publishers**

Eyewitness Travel Guides
See **Dorling Kindersley Ltd**

Faber & Faber Ltd
3 Queen Square, London WC1N 3AU
☎020 7465 0045 Fax 020 7465 0034
www.faber.co.uk
Chief Executive *Stephen Page*
Approx. Annual Turnover £13 million

Geoffrey Faber founded the company in the 1920s, with T.S. Eliot as an early recruit to the board. The original list was based on contemporary poetry and plays (the distinguished backlist includes Eliot, Auden and MacNeice). Publishes poetry and drama, children's, fiction, film, music, politics, biography.

DIVISIONS
Fiction Editor-in-Chief *Jon Riley* AUTHORS P.D. James, Peter Carey, Giles Foden, Michael Frayn, Kazuo Ishiguro, Barbara Kingsolver, Milan Kundera, Hanif Kureishi, John Lanchester, Patrick McCabe, John McGahern, Rohinton Mistry, Andrew O'Hagan, Jane Smiley; **Children's** *Suzy Jenvey, Julia Wells* AUTHORS Philip Ardagh, Terry Deary, Russell Stannard, G.P. Taylor; **Film** *Walter Donohue* and **Plays** *Dinah Wood* AUTHORS Samuel Beckett, Alan Bennett, David Hare, Brian Friel, Patrick Marber, Harold Pinter, Tom Stoppard, Woody Allen, John Boorman, Joel and Ethan Coen, John Hodge, Martin Scorsese, Quentin Tarantino; **Music** *Belinda Matthews* AUTHORS Alfred Brendel, Humphrey Burton, Nicholas Kenyon, Richard Morrison, Harvey Sachs, Elizabeth Wilson; **Poetry** *Paul Keegan* AUTHORS Simon Armitage, Douglas Dunn, Seamus Heaney, Ted Hughes, Paul Muldoon, Tom Paulin; **Non-fiction** *Neil Belton, Julian Loose* AUTHORS John Carey, Simon Garfield, John

Gray, Jan Morris, Francis Spufford, Frances Stonor Saunders, Jenny Uglow.
ROYALTIES twice-yearly.

Authors' Rating A slimmed-down list has given greater prominence to general non-fiction and children's books. Poetry, theatre, film and music remain the core subjects.

Facet Publishing
7 Ridgmount Street, London WC1E 7AE
☎020 7255 0590/0505 (text phone)
Fax 020 7255 0591
✉ info@facetpublishing.co.uk
www.facetpublishing.co.uk
Managing Director *Janet Liebster*

Publishing arm of **CILIP: The Chartered Institute of Library and Information Professionals** (formerly the Library Association). Publishes library and information science, monographs, reference, IT training materials and bibliography aimed at library and information professionals. IMPRINTS **Library Association Publishing**; **Clive Bingley Books**; **Facet Publishing**. Over 200 titles in print, including *Walford's Guide to Reference Material* and *AACR2*. 25–30 titles a year. Unsolicited mss, synopses and ideas welcome provided material falls firmly within the company's specialist subject areas.
ROYALTIES annually.

Falmer Press
See **Taylor & Francis Group plc**

Fernhurst Books
Duke's Path, High Street, Arundel BN18 9AJ
☎01903 882277 Fax 01903 882715
✉ sales@fernhurstbooks.co.uk
www.fernhurstbooks.co.uk
Chairman/Managing Director *Tim Davison*
Founded 1979. For people who love watersports. Publishes practical, highly-illustrated handbooks on sailing and watersports. TITLES *Knot Know-How*; *Understanding the Rules of the Road*; *New Crew's Companion*; *Understanding Yacht Design*; *GPS Afloat*. No unsolicited mss; synopses and ideas welcome.
ROYALTIES twice-yearly.

David Fickling Books
See **The Random House Group Ltd**

Findhorn Press Ltd
305A The Park, Findhorn IV36 3TE
☎01309 690582 Fax 01309 690036
✉ info@findhornpress.com
www.findhornpress.com

Directors *Karin Bogliolo, Thierry Bogliolo*
Founded 1971. Publishes mind, body, spirit, New Age and healing. 20 titles in 2003. Unsolicited synopses and ideas welcome if they come within their subject areas. No children's books, fiction or poetry.
ROYALTIES twice-yearly.

Firefly Publishing
See **Helter Skelter Publishing**

First & Best in Education Ltd
Unit K, Earlstrees Court, Earlstrees Road, Corby NN17 4HH
☎01536 399004 Fax 01536 399012
✉ editorial@firstandbest.co.uk
www.firstandbest.co.uk
Publisher *Tony Attwood*
Editor *Anne Cockburn*

Publishers of over 1000 educational books of all types for all ages of children and for parents and teachers. All books are published as being suitable for photocopying and/or as electronic books. 'Looking for new authors of educational books all the time. No fiction, please.' TITLES *Raising Grades Through Study Skills*; *Business Sponsorship of Secondary Schools*; *Policy Documents for Day Nurseries and Nursery Units*; *Citizenship Through Assembly*. IMPRINT **School Improvement Reports**. In the first instance check the website or send s.a.e. for details of requirements and current projects to *Anne Cockburn*, Editorial Dept. at the address above.
ROYALTIES twice-yearly.

First Authors
See **Vista House Ltd**

First Century Ltd
27 Greenhead Road, Huddersfield HD1 4EN
☎01484 545123
✉ editorial@first-century.co.uk
www.first-century.co.uk
Managing Director *Reggie Sharp*

IMPRINTS **First Century** Fiction and non-fiction in all areas; **Christian Publishing** Fiction, non-fiction and poetry with a Christian under-pinning. Submission guidelines on the website.
ROYALTIES annually.

Authors' Rating Formerly into shared costs with authors for putting manuscripts into print, First Century is now operating conventionally although a linked company, Vista House's First Authors, does still trawl for author contribution to costs.

Fitzgerald Publishing
89 Ermine Road, Ladywell, London SE13 5JJ
☎020 8690 0597
✉ fitzgeraldbooks@yahoo.co.uk
Managing Editor *Tim Fitzgerald*
General Editor *Andrew Smith*

Founded 1974. Specialises in scientific studies of insects and spiders. TITLES *The Tarantula*; *Keeping Spiders and Insects in Captivity*; *Tarantulas of the USA*; *Scorpions of Medical Importance* (books) and *Earth Tigers – Tarantulas of Borneo*; *Desert Tarantulas* (TV/video documentaries). 1–2 titles a year. Unsolicited mss, synopses and ideas for books welcome. Also considers video scripts for video documentaries.

Fitzjames Press
See **Motor Racing Publications**

Fitzroy Dearborn
See **Taylor & Francis Group plc**

Fitzwarren Publishing
2 Orchard Drive, Aston Clinton, Aylesbury HP22 5HR
☎01296 632627
✉ pen2paper@btopenworld.com
Contact *Julie Stretton*

Publishes two or three books a year, mainly layman's handbooks on legal matters. All books published so far have followed a rigid 128-page format. TITLES *The E-Commerce Handbook*; *Landlord & Tenants Handbook*; *The Election Handbook*; *Licensing Handbook*; *Employment Handbook*. Welcomes written approaches and synopses from prospective authors who, though not necessarily legally qualified, are expected to know their subject as well as a lawyer would.
ROYALTIES twice-yearly.

Five Star
See **Serpent's Tail**

Flame
See **Hodder Headline Ltd**

Flicks Books
29 Bradford Road, Trowbridge BA14 9AN
☎01225 767728
✉ flicks.books@dial.pipex.com
Publishing Director *Matthew Stevens*

Founded 1986. Devoted solely to publishing books on the cinema and related media. TITLES *Queen of the 'B's: Ida Lupino Behind the Camera* ed. Annette Kuhn; *By Angels Driven: The Films of Derek Jarman* ed. Chris Lippard. Unsolicited

mss, synopses and ideas within the subject area are welcome.
ROYALTIES annually or twice-yearly.

Floris Books
15 Harrison Gardens, Edinburgh EH11 1SH
☎0131 337 2372 Fax 0131 347 9919
✉ floris@florisbooks.co.uk
www.florisbooks.co.uk

Managing Director *Christian Maclean*
Editors *Christopher Moore, Gale Winskill*
Approx. Annual Turnover £350,000

Founded 1977. Publishes books related to the Steiner movement, including The Christian Community, as well as arts & crafts, children's (including fiction with a Scottish theme), history, religious, science, social questions and Celtic studies. No unsolicited mss. Synopses and ideas for books welcome.
ROYALTIES annually.

Focal Press
See **Elsevier Ltd**

Fodor's
See **The Random House Group Ltd**

Folens Limited
Apex Business Centre, Boscombe Road, Dunstable LU5 4RL
☎0870 609 1237 Fax 0870 609 1236
✉ folens@folens.com
www.folens.com

Chairman *Dirk Folens*
Managing Director *Malcolm Watson*

Founded 1987. Leading educational publisher. IMPRINTS **Folens**; **Belair**. About 150 titles a year. Unsolicited mss, synopses and ideas for educational books welcome.
ROYALTIES annually.

Foulsham Publishers
The Publishing House, Bennetts Close, Slough SL1 5AP
☎01753 526769 Fax 01753 535003

Chairman/Managing Director *B.A.R. Belasco*
Approx. Annual Turnover £2.5 million

Founded 1819 and now one of the few remaining independent family companies to survive takeover. Publishes non-fiction on most subjects including lifestyle, travel guides, family reference, cookery, diet, health, DIY, business, self improvement, self development, astrology, dreams, MBS. No fiction. IMPRINT **Quantum** Mind, body and spirit titles. TITLES *Classic 1000 Cocktails; A Brit's Guide to Orlando*

and Walt Disney World 2002; Old Moore's Almanack; Raphael's Astrological Ephemeris. Around 60 titles a year. Unsolicited mss, synopses and ideas welcome.
ROYALTIES twice-yearly.

Foundery Press
See **Methodist Publishing House**

Fountain Press
Newpro UK Ltd., Old Sawmills Road, Faringdon SN7 7DS
☎01367 242411 Fax 01367 241124
✉ sales@newprouk.co.uk

Publisher *C.J. Coleman*
Approx. Annual Turnover £800,000

Founded 1923 when it was part of the Rowntree Trust Social Service. Owned by the British Electric Traction Group until 1982 when it was bought out by H.M. Ricketts. Acquired by Newpro UK Ltd in July 2000. Publishes mainly photography and natural history. TITLES *Photography and Digital 'Workshop'; Antique and Collectable Cameras; Camera Manual* (series). About 10 titles a year. Unsolicited mss and synopses welcome.
ROYALTIES twice-yearly.

Authors' Rating Highly regarded for production values, Fountain has the reputation for involving authors in every stage of the publishing process.

Fourth Estate Ltd
77–85 Fulham Palace Road, London W6 8JB
☎020 8741 4414 Fax 020 8307 4466
✉ general@4thestate.co.uk
www.4thestate.co.uk

Publishing Director *Nick Pearson*
Editorial Director *Courtney Hodell*
Approx. Annual Turnover £17 million

Founded 1984. Acquired by **HarperCollins** in July 2000, Fourth Estate has a strong reputation for literary fiction and up-to-the-minute non-fiction. Publishes fiction, current affairs, popular science, biography, humour, travel, reference. DIVISIONS **Literary Fiction/Non-fiction**; **General Fiction/Non-Fiction** TITLES *That Old Ace in the Hole* Annie Proulx; *The Speckled People* Hugo Hamilton; *The Lucky Ones* Rachel Cusk; *Nature via Nurture* Matt Ridley; *The Essential Spike Milligan* Alex Games; *Seven Wonders of the Industrial World* Deborah Cadbury; *Toast* Nigel Slater; *Isaac Newton* James Gleick. About 100 titles a year. No unsolicited mss.
ROYALTIES twice-yearly.

Free Association Books Ltd

57 Warren Street, London W1T 5NR
☎020 7388 3182 Fax 020 8906 0006
✉ info@fabooks.com
www.fabooks.com

Managing Director/Publisher *T.E. Brown*

Publishes psychoanalysis and psychotherapy, psychology, cultural studies, sexuality and gender, women's studies, applied social sciences. TITLES *Reaching the Young Autistic Child* S. Janert; *Judo With Words* B. Berchan; *Psychoanalytic Psychotherapy Trainings – A Guide* R.M. Jones; *A Compendium of Lacanian Terms* Marks, Murphy and Glowinski. Send a letter in the first instance accompanied by a book outline. OVERSEAS ASSOCIATES ISBS, USA; Astam, Australia.

ROYALTIES twice-yearly.

The Free Press

See **Simon & Schuster UK Ltd**

W.H. Freeman

Palgrave, Houndsmill, Basingstoke RG21 6XS
☎01256 329242 Fax 01256 330688

President *Elizabeth Widdicombe* (New York)
Sales & Marketing Director *Margaret Hewinson*

Following integration into the BFW (Bedford, Freeman, Worth) College Group, USA, Freeman now *publishes* academic educational and textbooks in biochemistry, biology and zoology, chemistry, geography and geology, mathematics and statistics, medical, natural history, neuroscience, palaeontology, physics. Freeman's editorial office is in New York (Basingstoke is a sales and marketing office only) but unsolicited mss can go through Basingstoke. Those which are obviously unsuitable will be sifted out; the rest will be forwarded to New York.

ROYALTIES annually.

Samuel French Ltd

52 Fitzroy Street, London W1T 5JR
☎020 7387 9373 Fax 020 7387 2161
✉ theatre@samuelfrench-london.co.uk
www.samuelfrench-london.co.uk

Chairman *Charles R. Van Nostrand*
Managing Director *Vivien Goodwin*

Founded 1830 with the object of acquiring acting rights and publishing plays. Publishes plays only. About 50 titles a year. Unsolicited mss considered only after initial submission of synopsis and specimen scene. Such material should be addressed to the Performing Rights Department.

ROYALTIES twice-yearly for books; performing royalties monthly, subject to a minimum amount.

Authors' Rating Thrives on the amateur dramatic societies who are forever in need of play texts. Editorial advisers give serious attention to new material but a high proportion of the list is staged before it goes into print. New writers are advised to try one-act plays, much in demand by the amateur dramatic societies but rarely turned out by established playwrights.

David Fulton (Publishers) Ltd

The Chiswick Centre, 414 Chiswick High Road, London W4 5TF
☎020 8996 3610 Fax 020 8996 3622
✉ mail@fultonpublishers.co.uk
www.fultonpublishers.co.uk

Publishing Director *Christopher Glennie*
Senior Commissioning Editors *Nina Stibbe, Helen Fairlie, Margaret Marriott, Linda Evans, Tracey Alcock*

Approx. Annual Turnover £2.4 million

Founded 1987. Publishes non-fiction: books for teachers and teacher training at B.Ed and PGCE levels for early years, primary, secondary and virtually all aspects of special education. Special educational needs books cross over into other aspects of health and social care, especially educational psychology and speech and language therapy. Currently developing a range of curriculum materials (in book form, packs, on CD-ROM and/or disk) for use by teachers in the classroom. Also expanding into Early Years (pre-school) provision. About 100 titles a year. No unsolicited mss; synopses and ideas for books welcome.

ROYALTIES twice-yearly.

Funfax

See **Dorling Kindersley Ltd**

Gaia Books

See **Octopus Publishing Group**

Galaxy Children's Print

See **BBC Audiobooks** under *Audio Books*

J. Garnet Miller

See **Cressrelles Publishing Co. Ltd**

Garnet Publishing Ltd

8 Southern Court, South Street, Reading RG1 4QS
☎0118 959 7847 Fax 0118 959 7356
✉ emma@garnet-ithaca.demon.co.uk

www.garnet-ithaca.co.uk

Editorial Manager *Emma G. Hawker*

Founded 1992 and purchased Ithaca Press in the same year. Publishes art, architecture, photography, archive photography, cookery, travel classics, travel, comparative religion, Islamic culture and history, foreign fiction in translation. Core subjects are Middle Eastern but list is rapidly expanding to be more general.

IMPRINTS **Garnet Publishing** TITLES *The Story of Islamic Architecture*; *Traditional Greek Cooking*. **Ithaca Press** specialises in post-graduate academic works on the Middle East, political science and international relations TITLES *The Making of the Modern Gulf States*; *The Palestinian Exodus*; *French Imperialism in Syria*; *Philby of Arabia*. About 20 titles a year. Unsolicited mss not welcome – write with outline and ideas first plus current c.v. SISTER COMPANIES: All Prints, Beirut; Garnet France, Paris.

ROYALTIES twice-yearly.

Gay Men's Press
See **Millivres Prowler Limited**

Geddes & Grosset
David Dale House, New Lanark ML11 9DJ
☎01555 665000 Fax 01555 665694

Publishers *Ron Grosset, R. Michael Miller*

Approx. Annual Turnover £3 million

Founded 1989. Publisher of children's and reference books. Unsolicited mss, synopses and ideas welcome. No adult fiction.

Geological Society Publishing House
Unit 7, Brassmill Enterprise Centre, Brassmill Lane, Bath BA1 3JN
☎01225 445046 Fax 01225 442836
✉ sales@geolsoc.org.uk *or* enquiries@geolsoc.org.uk
www.bookshop.geolsoc.org.uk

Commissioning Editor *Angharad Hills*

Publishing arm of the Geological Society which was founded in 1807. Publishes postgraduate texts in the earth sciences. 25 titles a year. Unsolicited synopses and ideas welcome.

Stanley Gibbons Publications
7 Parkside, Christchurch Road, Ringwood BH24 3SH
☎01425 472363 Fax 01425 470247
www.stanleygibbons.com

Chairman *P. Fraser*

Editorial Head *H. Jefferies*

Long-established force in the philatelic world with almost 150 years in the business. Publishes philatelic reference catalogues and handbooks. Reference works relating to other areas of collecting may be considered. TITLES *Stanley Gibbons British Commonwealth Stamp Catalogue*; *Stamps of the World*. Foreign catalogues include Japan and Korea, Portugal and Spain, Germany, Middle East, Balkans, China. Monthly publication: *Gibbons Stamp Monthly* (see entry under *Magazines*). www.collectorcafe.com – internet site covering full range of collectables – editorial input always considered. About 20 titles a year. Unsolicited mss, synopses and ideas welcome.

ROYALTIES by negotiation.

Robert Gibson and Sons (Glasgow)
See **Hodder Gibson**

Gibson Square Books Ltd
15 Gibson Square, London N1 0RD
☎020 7689 4790 Fax 020 7689 7395
✉ publicity@gibsonsquare.com
www.gibsonsquare.com

Chairman *Martin Rynja*

Founded 2001. Publishes books with a strong biographical element based in some relevant way on personal experience. Must have high publicity value. IMPRINTS **Gibson Square** TITLES *Preachers of Hate* Angus Roxburgh; *Who's a Dandy?* George Walden. **New Editions** TITLES *South from Ephesus* Brian Sewell; *Hilaire Belloc* A.N. Wilson; *Descent of Man* Charles Darwin. Welcomes unsolicited mss, synopses and ideas. Send self-addressed, franked, return envelope. No fiction.

ROYALTIES twice-yearly.

Ginn & Co
See **Harcourt Education**

GMP (Gay Men's Press)
See **Millivres Prowler Limited**

Godsfield Press
See **Octopus Publishing Group**

Gollancz
See **The Orion Publishing Group Limited**

Gomer
Llandysul SA44 4JL
☎01559 362371 Fax 01559 363758
✉ gwasg@gomer.co.uk
www.gomer.co.uk

Chairman/Managing Director *J.E. Lewis*

Founded 1892. Publishes adult fiction and non-fiction, children's fiction and educational material in English and Welsh.

IMPRINTS **Gomer** *Bethan Mair, Bruan James* (Welsh editors), *Ceri Wyn Jones* (English). **Pont Books** *Sioned Lleinau, Helen Evans, Morys Rhys, Mairwen Prys Jones* (Welsh children's editors). About 120 titles a year (80 Welsh; 40 English). No unsolicited mss, synopses or ideas. No English books for children.

ROYALTIES twice-yearly.

The Good Web Guide Ltd
65 Bromfelde Road, London SW4 6PP
☎020 7720 8919 Fax 020 7738 5717
✉ marketing@thegoodwebguide.com
www.thegoodwebguide.com

Chairman *David Teale*
Managing Director *Sarah Mahaffy*
Marketing Director *Nicky Granville*

Founded 1999. Publishes guides to the best sites on the Internet, both as books and online. Subscription available giving full access to the website where reviews are updated and added to. 5 titles in 2003. No unsolicited mss; send synopsis/idea by post or e-mail. No fiction or children's books.

ROYALTIES twice-yearly.

Gordon & Breach
See **Taylor & Francis Group plc**

Gower
See **Ashgate Publishing Ltd**

GPC Books
See **University of Wales Press**

Graham & Whiteside Ltd
See **Gale** under *US Publishers*

Graham-Cameron Publishing & Illustration
The Studio, 23 Holt Road, Sheringham NR26 8NB
☎01263 821333 Fax 01263 821334
✉ firstname@graham-cameron-illustration.com

Also at: 59 Redvers Road, Brighton BN2 4BF
☎01273 385890

Editorial Director *Mike Graham-Cameron*
Art Director *Helen Graham-Cameron*

Founded 1984 as a packaging operation. Publishes illustrated books for children and adults for institutions and business. TITLES *Up From the Country*; *In All Directions*; *The Holywell Story*; *Let's Look at Dairying*. Has 37 contracted book illustrators concentrating on educational and children's books. *Absolutely no* unsolicited mss.

ROYALTIES annually.

Granada Media
See **Carlton Publishing Group**

Granta Books
2–3 Hanover Yard, Noel Road, London N1 8BE
☎020 7704 9776 Fax 020 7354 3469
www.granta.com

Publisher *Gail Lynch*
Editorial Director *George Miller*

Founded 1979. Publishes literary fiction and general non-fiction. About 35 titles a year. No unsolicited mss; synopses and sample chapters welcome.

ROYALTIES twice-yearly.

W. Green (Scotland)
See **Sweet & Maxwell Group**

Green Books
Foxhole, Dartington, Totnes TQ9 6EB
☎01803 863260 Fax 01803 863843
✉ edit@greenbooks.co.uk
www.greenbooks.co.uk

Chairman *Satish Kumar*
Publisher *John Elford*
Approx. Annual Turnover £300,000

Founded in 1987 with the support of a number of Green organisations. Closely associated with *Resurgence* magazine. Publishes high-quality books on a wide range of Green issues, including economics, politics and the practical application of Green thinking. No fiction or books for children. TITLES *Forest Gardening* Robert A. de J. Hart; *Eco-Renovation* Edward Harland; *The Growth Illusion* Richard Douthwaite; *The Green Lanes of England* Valerie Belsey; *The Organic Directory* ed. Clive Litchfield. No unsolicited mss. Synopses and ideas welcome.

ROYALTIES twice-yearly.

Green Print
See **The Merlin Press Ltd**

Greenhill Books/ Lionel Leventhal Ltd
Park House, 1 Russell Gardens, London NW11 9NN
☎020 8458 6314 Fax 020 8905 5245
✉ L.Leventhal@greenhillbooks.com
www.greenhillbooks.com

Managing Director *Lionel Leventhal*

Founded 1984 by Lionel Leventhal (ex-Arms & Armour Press). Publishes aviation, military and naval books, and its Napoleonic Library series. Synopses and ideas for books welcome. No unsolicited mss.

ROYALTIES twice-yearly.

Gresham Books Ltd

46 Victoria Road, Summertown, Oxford OX2 7QD

☎01865 513582 Fax 01865 512718

✉ info@gresham-books.co.uk

www.gresham-books.co.uk

Managing Director *Paul A. Lewis*

Approx. Annual Turnover £350,000

A small specialist publishing house. Publishes hymn and service books for schools and churches, school histories, also craftbound choir and orchestral folders and Records of Achievement. TITLES include music and melody editions of *Hymns for Church and School*; *The School Hymnal*; *Praise and Thanksgiving*. No unsolicited material but ideas welcome.

Grisewood & Dempsey

See **Kingfisher Publications Plc**

Grub Street

4 Rainham Close, London SW11 6SS

☎020 7924 3966/7738 1008

Fax 020 7738 1009

✉ post@grubstreet.co.uk

www.grubstreet.co.uk

Managing Director *John Davies*

Founded 1982. Publishes cookery, food and wine, health, military and aviation history books. About 20 titles a year. Unsolicited mss and synopses welcome in the above categories but please enclose return postage.

ROYALTIES twice-yearly.

Guardian/Observer Books

See **Atlantic Books**

Guild of Master Craftsman Publications Ltd

166 High Street, Lewes BN7 1XU

☎01273 477374 Fax 01273 478606

✉ pubs@thegmcgroup.com

Joint Managing Directors *J.A.J. Phillips, J.A.B. Phillips*

Approx. Annual Turnover £2 million

Founded 1974. Part of G.M.C. Services Ltd. Publishes woodworking, craft, photography and gardening books, magazines and videos; also books on dolls' houses and miniatures. IMPRINT **Photographers' Institute Press (PIP)** launched in 2004. 44 titles in 2003. Unsolicited mss, synopses and ideas for books welcome. No fiction.

ROYALTIES twice-yearly.

Guinness World Records Ltd

338 Euston Road, London NW1 3BD

☎020 7891 4567 Fax 020 7891 4501

✉ info@guinnessrecords.com

www.guinnessworldrecords.com

Chief Operations Officer *Alistair Richards*

Founded in 1954 to publish *The Guinness Book of Records*, published in 35 languages and the highest-selling copyright book in the world. The company's television shows have gained a global audience of more than 100 million and are broadcast in over 30 countries. In addition to *Guinness World Records* the company publishes the annual industry-standard volume *British Hit Singles*. In October 2002 Guinness World Records became part of HIT Entertainment Plc. Contact from prospective researchers, editors and designers welcome.

Gulf Professional Press

See **Elsevier Ltd**

Gullane Children's Books

See **Pinwheel Limited**

Gunsmoke Westerns

See **BBC Audiobooks** under *Audio Books*

Gwasg Carreg Gwalch

12 Iard yr Orsaf, Llanrwst LL26 0EH

☎01492 642031 Fax 01492 641502

✉ books@carreg-gwalch.co.uk

www.carreg-gwalch.co.uk

Managing Editor *Myrddin ap Dafydd*

Founded in 1980. Publishes Welsh language; English books of Welsh interest – history, folklore, guides and walks. About 90 titles a year. Unsolicited mss, synopses and ideas welcome if of Welsh interest.

ROYALTIES paid.

Gwasg Prifysgol Cymru

See **University of Wales Press**

Hachette-Livre

French publishing conglomerate which embraces **Orion Publishing Group**, **Octopus Publishing Group** and **Watts Publishing**

Group. For further information, see entry under *European Publishers*.

Authors' Rating Almost unnoticed, at least by British pundits, French publisher Hachette has joined the league of UK conglomerates. With Orion, Octopus and Watts, the share of the illustrated market claimed by Hachette is over 25 per cent.

Peter Halban Publishers
22 Golden Square, London W1F 9JW
☎020 7437 9300 Fax 020 7437 9512
✉ books@halbanpublishers.com
www.halbanpublishers.com

Directors *Peter Halban, Martine Halban*

Founded 1986. Independent publisher. Publishes biography, autobiography and memoirs, history, philosophy, theology, politics, literature and criticism, Judaica and world affairs. 6–8 titles a year. No unsolicited material. Approach by letter in first instance.

ROYALTIES twice-yearly for first two years, thereafter annually in December.

Robert Hale Ltd
Clerkenwell House, 45–47 Clerkenwell Green, London EC1R 0HT
☎020 7251 2661 Fax 020 7490 4958
✉ enquire@halebooks.com

Chairman/Managing Director *John Hale*

Founded 1936. Family-owned company. Publishes adult fiction (but not interested in category romance or science fiction) and non-fiction. No specialist material (education, law, medical or scientific). Acquired **NAG Press Ltd** in 1993 with its list of horological, gemmological, jewellery and metalwork titles, and **J.A. Allen & Co.** in 1999 with its extensive list of horse and dog books (see entry). TITLES Non-fiction: *New Age Encyclopaedia* Belinda Whitworth; *Andrea Bocelli* Antonia Felix; *F.M. Halford and the Dry Fly Revolution* Tony Hayter; *Field Archery* Michael Hamlett-Wood; *Roger Moore: His Films and Career* Gareth Owen and Oliver Bayan. Fiction: *Methuselah's Children* Robert A. Heinlein; *The Silent Voyage* James Pattinson; *The Curious Conspiracy* Michael Gilbert. Over 250 titles a year. Unsolicited mss, synopses and ideas for books welcome. ROYALTIES twice-yearly.

Authors' Rating Smiled upon in a Society of Authors' survey on author relations, Robert Hale has carved out a profitable niche for popular non-fiction.

Halsgrove
Halsgrove House, Tiverton Business Park, Lower Moor Way, Tiverton EX16 6SS
☎01884 243242 Fax 01884 243325
✉ sales@halsgrove.com
www.halsgrove.com

Publisher *Simon Butler*

Founded in 1990 and now the region's largest publishing and distribution group, specialising in books, video and audio tapes. Core interests remain in the South but now publishes books of regional interest throughout the UK. Publishes local history (including the *Community History* series), cookery, biography and art, mainly in hardback. Also established a series of local interest magazines in southern England. No fiction or poetry. 150 titles in 2003. Unsolicited mss, synopses and ideas for books of regional interest welcome.
ROYALTIES annually.

Hambledon and London
102 Gloucester Avenue, London NW1 8HX
☎020 7586 0817 Fax 020 7586 9970
✉ office@hambledon.co.uk

Editorial Director *Martin Sheppard*
Commissioning Director *Tony Morris*

Founded 1980 as The Hambledon Press. Winner of the **Sunday Times Award for Small Publishers** in 2001. Publishes history and biography. TITLES *Churchill: A Study in Greatness* Geoffrey Best; *The Ambassadors' Secret* John North; *Brunel: the Life and Times of Isambard Kingdom Brunel* Angus Buchanan; *Family Names and Family History* David Hey. No unsolicited mss; send preliminary letter. Synopses and ideas welcome. OVERSEAS DISTRIBUTOR Palgrave-Macmillan (USA and Canada).
ROYALTIES twice-yearly.

Hamish Hamilton
See **Penguin Group (UK)**

Hamlyn Octopus
See **Octopus Publishing Group**

Harcourt Education
Halley Court, Jordan Hill, Oxford OX2 8EJ
☎01865 311366 Fax 01865 314641
www.harcourteducation.co.uk

President/CEO *Christopher Jones*

A member of the **Reed Elsevier Group plc**, Harcourt Education incorporates Heinemann Educational and Ginn in the UK; Greenwood Heinemann in the USA; Rigby Heinemann in

Australia. **Heinemann Educational** Fax 01865 314140 Managing Director *Paul Shuter*, Primary *Kath Donovan*, Secondary *Kay Symons*. Textbooks, literature and other educational resources for primary and secondary school and further education. Mss, synopses and ideas welcome. **Ginn & Co** Fax 01865 314189 Managing Director *Paul Shuter*. Textbook and other educational resources for primary and secondary schools.

ROYALTIES twice-yearly/annually, according to contract in all divisions.

Harlequin Mills & Boon Ltd

Eton House, 18–24 Paradise Road, Richmond TW9 1SR
☎020 8288 2800 Fax 020 8288 2899
www.eharlequin.com
www.millsandboon.co.uk

Managing Director *Pam Laycock*
Approx. Annual Turnover £22 million

Founded 1908. Owned by the Canadian-based Torstar Group. Publishes a wide range of women's fiction including romantic novels.

IMPRINTS
Mills & Boon Modern Romance *Tessa Shapcott* (50–55,000 words) Alpha males and attractive women swept up in intense emotions set against a backdrop of international locations, luxury and wealth; passion is guaranteed. **Mills & Boon Tender Romance** *Bryony Green* (50–55,000 words) Contemporary emotional feel-good romance, focusing on the heroine's experiences. **Mills & Boon Medical Romance** *Sheila Hodgson* (50–55,000 words) Modern medical practice provides a unique background to love stories. **Mills & Boon Historical Romance** *Linda Fildew* (75–90,000 words) Historical romances covering a wide range of British and European historical periods from ancient civilisations up to and including the Second World War. **MIRA** *Sam Bell* (minimum 110,000 words) General women's fiction. **Red Dress Ink** *Sam Bell* (90–110,000 words) Contemporary women's fiction. **Mills & Boon Sensual Romance**, **Mills & Boon Blaze** and **Silhouette Superromance** titles are acquired through the Canadian office. **Silhouette Desire**, **Special Edition**, **Sensation** and **Intrigue** imprints are handled by US-based **Silhouette Books** (see entry under *US Publishers*). Tip sheets and guidelines for the Mills & Boon series available from the Mills & Boon website or Harlequin Mills & Boon Editorial Dept. (please send s.a.e.). For other lines see the Mills & Boon and eHarlequin websites. Over 600 titles a year.

ROYALTIES twice-yearly.

Authors' Rating Sex has overtaken romance at M&B where the new Blaze imprint allows writers' erotic imagination to run riot. But the staple M&B romance is still going strong providing a good income for writers who can adapt to the clearly defined M&B formula. Just think, M&B has a network of 12,000 authors worldwide and every title scores six-figure sales. But be warned. M&B gets 2000 unsolicited manuscripts a year.

Harley Books

Martins, Great Horkesley, Colchester CO6 4AH
☎01206 271216 Fax 01206 271182
✉ harley@keme.co.uk
www.harleybooks.com

Managing Director *Basil Harley*

Founded 1983. Natural history publishers specialising in entomological and botanical books. Mostly definitive, high-quality illustrated reference works. TITLES *The Moths and Butterflies of Great Britain and Ireland*; *Dragonflies of Europe*; *The Aurelian Legacy: British Butterflies and their Collectors*; *The Liverwort Flora of the British Isles*; *Maggots, Murder and Men: Memories and Reflections of a Forensic Entomologist*.

ROYALTIES twice-yearly in the first year, annually thereafter.

HarperCollins Publishers Ltd

77–85 Fulham Palace Road, London W6 8JB
☎020 8741 7070 Fax 020 8307 4440
www.harpercollins.co.uk

Also at: Westerhill Road, Bishopbriggs, Glasgow G64 2QT
☎0141 772 3200 Fax 0141 306 3119

CEO/Publisher *Victoria Barnsley*

HarperCollins is one of the top three book publishers in the UK, with a wider range of books than any other publisher; from cutting-edge contemporary fiction to block-busting thrillers, from fantasy literature and children's stories to enduring classics. The wholly-owned division of News Corporation also publishes a wide selection of non-fiction including history, celebrity memoirs, biography, popular science, mind, body and spirit, dictionaries, maps and reference books. HarperCollins is also the third largest education publisher in the UK. Authors include many award-winning and international bestsellers such as Paulo Coelho, Josephine

Cox, Michael Crichton, Barbara Erskine, Jonathan Franzen, Judith Kerr, Doris Lessing, Frank McCourt, Tony Parsons, Carol Shields. About 1500 titles a year.

GENERAL BOOKS DIVISION
Managing Director *Amanda Ridout*
Harper Fiction Publisher *Lynne Drew* IMPRINTS **HarperCollins** General trade and women's fiction; **Collins Crime** Publishing Director *Julia Wisdom*; **Voyager** Publishing Director *Jane Johnson* Science fiction/fantasy. **Harper Press** Managing Director/Publisher *Caroline Michel*, Associate Publisher/Editor-in-Chief *Christopher Potter* IMPRINTS **Fourth Estate** Publishing Director Nick Pearson (see entry); **HarperCollins Non-Fiction** Publishing Director *Michael Fishwick* General trade non-fiction; **HarperPerennial** Publisher *Venetia Butterfield* Paperback imprint for all HarperPress titles.

HARPERENTERTAINMENT
Managing Director/Publisher *Trevor Dolby*
IMPRINTS **HarperCollins Entertainment** Media-related books from film companions to autobiographies and TV tie-ins. **Collins Willow** Publishing Director *Michael Doggart* Sporting autobiographies; **HarperCollins Audio** Publishing Director *Rosalie George* (see entry under *Audio Books*); **Estates** Publishing Director *David Brawn* Authors include Agatha Christie, J.R.R. Tolkien, C.S. Lewis. IMPRINT **Tolkien**.
   Thorsons/Element (division & imprint) Managing Director *Belinda Budge*, Publishing Director *Wanda Whiteley* Mind, body and spirit.
   HarperCollins Children's Division Managing Director *Sally Gritten*; Publishing Directors *Gillie Russell* (Fiction), *Venetia Davie* (Properties), *Sue Buswell* (Picture Books) Quality picture books and book and tape sets for under-7s; fiction for age 6 up to young adult. IMPRINTS **Lions**; **Collins Picture Books**; **Collins Jet**; **Collins Teacher**.

COLLINS
Managing Director *Thomas Webster*
Collins Reference Division Publishing Director *Sarah Bailey* Reference, including guides and handbooks, phrase books and manuals on popular reference, art instruction, illustrated, cookery and wine, crafts, DIY, gardening, military, natural history, pet care, pastimes. IMPRINTS **Collins**; **Collins Gem**; **Collins New Naturalist Library**; **Times Books**; **Jane's**.
   Collins/Times Maps and Atlases (division & imprint) Publishing Directors *Juliet Lawler* (international titles); *Mike Cottingham*

(UK titles) Maps, atlases, street plans and leisure guides.
   Collins Dictionaries/COBUILD (division & imprint) Publishing Director *Lorna Sinclair Knight* Bilingual and English dictionaries, English dictionaries for foreign learners.
   Collins Education Division Managing Director *Jim Green* Books, CD-ROMs and online material for UK schools and colleges.

Authors' Rating 'We are determined to be the publisher of choice for new and established authors,' says Caroline Michel of HarperPress, and that goes for the other divisions of this front runner among UK publishers. But don't be misled by stories of massive advances. These are for the big names only. The further down the scale, the tighter the purse strings.

Harrap
See **Chambers Harrap Publishers Ltd**

Harvard University Press
Fitzroy House, 11 Chenies Street, London WC1E 7EY
☎020 7306 0603   Fax 020 7306 0604
✉ info@HUP-MITpress.co.uk
www.hup.harvard.edu

Director *William Sisler*
General Manager *Ann Sexsmith*

European office of **Harvard University Press**, USA. Publishes academic and scholarly works in history, politics, philosophy, economics, literary criticism, psychology, sociology, anthropology, women's studies, biological sciences, classics, history of science, art, music, film, reference. All mss go to the American office: 79 Garden Street, Cambridge, MA 02138 (see entry under *US Publishers*).

Harvill Secker
See **The Random House Group Ltd**

Haynes Publishing
Sparkford, Near Yeovil BA22 7JJ
☎01963 440635   Fax 01963 440825
✉ info@haynes.co.uk
www.haynes.co.uk

Chairman *John H. Haynes, OBE*
Approx. Annual Turnover £19.9 million

Founded in 1960 by John H. Haynes. Listed public company with majority family ownership. The mainstay of its programme has been the *Owners' Workshop Manual*, first published in the mid 1960s and still running off the presses today. Indeed the company maintains a strong bias towards motoring and transport titles.

Acquired Sutton Publishing Ltd in March 2000. Publishes DIY service and repair manuals for cars, motorbikes and leisure plus other related topics under the Haynes imprint and a broad range of general non-fiction under the Sutton imprint.

AUTOMOTIVE DIVISION IMPRINT **Haynes** Editorial Director *Matthew Minter* Service and repair manuals; Editorial Director *Mark Hughes* Motoring, motor sport, cars, motorcycles, home, DIY and leisure titles.

GENERAL PUBLISHING DIVISION IMPRINT **Sutton Publishing Ltd** (see entry). Unsolicited submissions welcome if they come within the subject areas covered. OVERSEAS SUBSIDIARIES Haynes Manuals Inc., California, USA, Editions Haynes S.A., France, Haynes Publishing Nordiska AB, Sweden.

ROYALTIES twice-yearly.

Hazleton Publishing

5th Floor, Mermaid House, Puddle Dock, London EC4V 3DS
☎020 7332 2000 Fax 020 7332 2003
✉ info@hazletonpublishing.com
www.hazletonpublishing.com

Publisher of the leading motorsport annuals: *Autocourse*; *Rallycourse*; *Motocourse* as well as Open Golf and Wimbledon Tennis annuals. About 13 titles a year. No unsolicited mss; synopses and ideas welcome. Interested in all motor sport titles.

ROYALTIES Payment varies.

Headline

See **Hodder Headline Ltd**

William Heinemann

See **The Random House Group Ltd**

Heinemann Educational

See **Harcourt Education**

Helicon Publishing

RM plc, New Mill House, 183 Milton Park, Abingdon OX14 4SE
☎01235 826000 Fax 01235 823222
✉ helicon@rm.com
www.helicon.co.uk

General Manager *Michael Holyoke*

A division of Research Machines plc. Helicon is a general reference database publisher for the UK, US and Australian markets. Licenses quality reference content for online, print and CD-ROM publications. TITLES include the flagship single volume *Hutchinson 2005 Encyclopedia*

published under license from **Hodder Headline**. CD-ROM TITLES include *The Hutchinson Encyclopedia*; *The Hutchinson Science Reference Suite*; *The Hutchinson History Reference Suite*; *The Hutchinson Music Reference Suite*.

Christopher Helm

See **A.&C. Black Publishers Ltd**

Helm Information Ltd

The Banks, Mountfield, Nr Robertsbridge TN32 5JY
☎01580 880561 Fax 01580 880541
✉ amandahelm@helm-information.co.uk
www.helm-information.co.uk

Directors *Amanda Helm, Christopher Helm*

Founded 1990. Publishes academic books for students and university libraries. SERIES *The Critical Assessments of Writers in English* (collected criticism); *Literary Sources & Documents* (primary source material on various themes/events/cultural/aesthetic movements ranging from the American Civil War to the Gothic Revival); *Sources & Documents in Art History* (literary sources of various movements in art); *The Dickens Companions*; and a new series, *Icons*, which exposes the processes by which a figure, historical or fictional, achieves iconic status, e.g. Faust, Robin Hood. Will consider ideas and proposals provided they are relevant to the series listed above.

ROYALTIES annually.

Helter Skelter Publishing

South Bank House, Black Prince Road, London SE1 7SJ
☎020 7463 2204 Fax 020 7463 2295
✉ info@helterskelterbooks.com
www.helterskelterbooks.com

Contact *Sean Body*

Founded 1995. Publishes music and film books only. IMPRINTS **Helter Skelter Publishing**; **Firefly Publishing**. 15 titles a year. Unsolicited mss, synopses and ideas welcome.

Henderson Publishing

See **Dorling Kindersley Ltd**

Ian Henry Publications Ltd

20 Park Drive, Romford RM1 4LH
☎01708 749119 Fax 01708 736213

Managing Director *Ian Wilkes*

Founded 1976. Publishes local history, transport history and Sherlockian pastiches. TITLES *Lost Castles of Essex*; *The Story of Stock and Buttsbury*; *News from Newmarket*. 8–10 titles a

year. No unsolicited mss. Synopses and ideas for books welcome.
ROYALTIES twice-yearly.

The Herbert Press
See **A.&C. Black Publishers Ltd**

Hermes House
See **Anness Publishing Ltd**

Nick Hern Books
The Glasshouse, 49a Goldhawk Road, London W12 8QP
☎020 8749 4953   Fax 020 8735 0250
✉ info@nickhernbooks.demon.co.uk
www.nickhernbooks.co.uk

Chairman/Managing Director *Nick Hern*

Founded 1988. Fully independent since 1992. Publishes books on theatre and film: from how-to and biography to plays and screenplays. About 30 titles a year. No unsolicited playscripts. Synopses, ideas and proposals for other theatre material welcome. Not interested in material unrelated to the theatre or cinema.

University of Hertfordshire Press
Learning and Information Services, Hatfield Campus Learning Resources Centre, College Lane, Hatfield AL10 9AB
☎01707 284681   Fax 01707 284666
✉ W.A.Forster@herts.ac.uk
www.herts.ac.uk/UHPress

Contact *Bill Forster*

Founded 1992. Publishes academic books on Gypsies, literature, regional and local history, parapsychology. IMPRINTS **Interface Collection**; **Hertfordshire Publications**; **University of Hertfordshire Press**. TITLES *We Are The Romany People* Ian Hancock; *Convict Theatres of Early Australia: 1788–1840* Robert Jordan; *Textual Shakespeare: Writing and the Word* Graham Holderness. 12 titles in 2003.

Hesperus Press Limited
4 Rickett Street, London SW6 1RU
☎020 7610 3331   Fax 020 7610 3217
www.hesperuspress.com

Managing Director/Publisher *Alessandro Gallenzi*

Founded 2001. Publishes lesser-known works by classical authors, both in English and in translation. TITLES *Carlyle's House* Virginia Woolf; *The Rich Boy* Francis Scott Fitzgerald; *Arctic Summer* E.M. Forster; *Hadji Murat* Lev Tolstoy. *Modern Classics* series to be launched in 2005; literary fiction list in 2006. 40 titles in

2004, including 5 poetry titles. Does not accept unsolicited mss.
ROYALTIES annually.

High Stakes
See **Oldcastle Books Ltd**

Hippo
See **Scholastic Ltd**

History Into Print
See **Brewin Books Ltd**

HMSO
See **TSO**

Hobsons Plc
Challenger House, 42 Adler Street, London E1 1EE
☎020 7958 5000   Fax 020 7958 5001
www.hobsons.com

Chairman *Martin Morgan*
Group Managing Director *Christopher Letcher*

Founded 1974. A division of Harmsworth Publishing Ltd, part of the Daily Mail & General Trust. Publishes course and career guides, under exclusive licence and royalty agreements for CRAC (Careers Research and Advisory Bureau); computer software; directories and specialist titles for employers, government departments and professional associations. TITLES *Graduate Employment and Training*; *Degree Course Guides*; *The Which Degree Series*; *Which University* (CD-ROM); *The POSTGRAD Series: The Directory of Graduate Studies*; *The Directory of Further Education*; *Hobson's Directory*; *Industry Guides* series.

Hodder & Stoughton
See **Hodder Headline Ltd**

Hodder Gibson
2a Christie Street, Paisley PA1 1NB
☎0141 848 1609   Fax 0141 889 6315
✉ hoddergibson@hodder.co.uk
www.madaboutbooks.com

Managing Director *John Mitchell*

Part of the **Hodder Headline Group**. Publishes educational books specifically for Scotland. Combines the former **Robert Gibson and Sons (Glasgow)** with the Scottish branch of **Hodder Murray** (a merger of **John Murray** and **Hodder Stoughton Educational**). About 50 titles a year. Synopses/ideas preferred to unsolicited mss.
ROYALTIES annually.

Hodder Headline Ltd

338 Euston Road, London NW1 3BH
☎020 7873 6000   Fax 020 7873 6024
www.hodderheadline.co.uk

Group Chief Executive *Tim Hely Hutchinson*
Approx. Annual Turnover £130 million

Formed in June 1993 through the merger of Headline Book Publishing and Hodder & Stoughton. Headline was formed in 1986 and had grown dramatically, whereas Hodder & Stoughton was 125 years old with a diverse range of publishing. The company was acquired by WHSmith plc in 1999. Purchased **John Murray (Publishers) Ltd** in 2002 (see entry). About 2000 titles a year.

DIVISIONS
Headline Book Publishing Managing Director *Martin Neild*, Deputy Managing Director *Kerr MacRae*, Director of Non-fiction *Val Hudson*, Director of Fiction *Jane Morpeth* Publishes commercial and literary fiction (hardback and paperback) and popular non-fiction including autobiography, biography, food and wine, gardening, history, popular science, sport and TV tie-ins. IMPRINTS **Headline**; **Review**. AUTHORS Kate Adie, Catherine Alliott, Lyn Andrews, Emily Barr, Colin Bateman, Martina Cole, Janet Evanovich, Sophie Grigson, Wendy Holden, Matthew Jukes, Faye and Jonathan Kellerman, Jill Mansell, Maggie O'Farrell, Sheila O'Flanagan, James Patterson, Pamela Stephenson.

Hodder & Stoughton General Managing Director *Jamie Hodder-Williams*; **Non-fiction** *Rowena Webb*; **Sceptre** *Carole Welch*; **Fiction** *Carolyn Mays*; **Audio** (See entry under *Audio Books*). Publishes commercial and literary fiction; biography, autobiography, history, self-help, humour, travel and other general interest non-fiction; audio. IMPRINTS **Hodder & Stoughton**; **Lir**; **Coronet**; **Flame**; **New English Library**; **Sceptre**; **Mobius**. AUTHORS Melvyn Bragg, John le Carré, Andrew Miller, Alex Ferguson, Charles Frazier, Elizabeth George, Amy Jenkins, Thomas Keneally, Stephen King, David Mitchell, Fiona Walker, Rosamunde Pilcher, Mary Stewart, Bill Cullen, Pete McCarthy.

Hodder Children's Books Managing Director *Charles Nettleton* IMPRINTS **Hodder Children's Books**; **Signature**; **Bite**; **Wayland**. AUTHORS David Almond, Enid Blyton, Lucy Daniels, Mick Inkpen, Emma Thomson, Hilary McKay, David Melling, Jenny Oldfield, David Lee Stone.

Hodder & Stoughton Religious Managing Director *Charles Nettleton*, Publishing Director *Judith Longman*, Bibles & Hodder Christian Books *David Moloney*. Publishes NIV Bibles, Christian books, autobiography, TV-tie-ins, gift books, self-help. IMPRINTS **Hodder & Stoughton**; **Hodder Christian Books**; **Help Yourself**.

Hodder Education Managing Director *Philip Walters* Publishes in the following areas: **Schoolbooks** *Lis Tribe*; **Consumer Education** *Katie Roden*; **Further Education/Higher Education Textbooks** *Mary Attree*; **Health Sciences** *Georgina Bentliff*; **Journals/Reference Books** *Mary Attree*. IMPRINTS **Hodder Murray**; **Teach Yourself**; **Hodder Arnold** *John Murray* (Educational).

Hodder Gibson (see entry).

John Murray (Publishers) Ltd (see entry).

Authors' Rating Despite strenuous denials from the top, rumours persist of WHSmith selling off its highly profitable publishing wing. The French publishing group Lagadère, which already owns **Octopus** and **Orion**, has been named as the suitor most likely to win the hand in marriage. Much depends on whether WHSmith itself succumbs to a takeover bid. Meanwhile, Hodder Headline thrives as the UK's fourth largest trade publisher with a reputation for doing well by its authors.

Honeyglen Publishing Ltd

56 Durrels House, Warwick Gardens, London W14 8QB
☎020 7602 2876   Fax 020 7602 2876

Directors *N.S. Poderegin, J. Poderegin*

Founded 1983. A small publishing house whose output is 'extremely limited'. Publishes history, philosophy of history, biography and selective fiction. No children's or science fiction. TITLES *The Soul of China*; *The Soul of India*; *Woman and Power in History*; *Lost World – Tibet*; *A Child of the Century* all by Amaury de Riencourt; *With Duncan Grant in South Turkey* Paul Roche; *Vladimir, The Russian Viking* Vladimir Volkoff; *The Dawning* Milka Bajic-Poderegin; *Quicksand* Louise Hide. Unsolicited mss welcome.

Honno Welsh Women's Press

c/o Canolfan Merched y Wawr, Vulcan Street, Aberystwyth SY23 1JH
☎01970 623150   Fax 01970 623150
✉ post@honno.co.uk
www.honno.co.uk

Editor *Lindsay Ashford*

Founded in 1986 by a group of women who wanted to create more opportunities for women in publishing. A co-operative operation which publishes fiction (adult and teenage) and children's books, all with a Welsh connection. Also publishes poetry, short story and auto-biographical anthologies. About 6 titles a year. Welcomes mss and ideas for books from women only. All material must have a Welsh connection and be sent as hard copy, not by e-mail.

ROYALTIES annually.

Horus Editions
See **Award Publications Limited**

House of Lochar
Isle of Colonsay PA61 7YR
☎01951 200232 Fax 01951 200232
✉ Lochar@colonsay.org.uk
www.houseoflochar.com

Chairman *Kevin Byrne*
Managing Director *Georgina Hobhouse*
Approx. Annual Turnover £95,000

Founded 1995 on a tiny island, taking advantage of new technology and mains electricity and taking over some 20 titles from Thomas and Lochar. Publishes mostly Scottish – history, topography, transport and fiction. IMPRINTS **House of Lochar** TITLES *The Clyde in Pictures; Alexander III; Ancient Scotland; The Clyde Puffer.* AUTHORS Neil Munro, Neill Gunn, John McPhee, Marion Campbell, Ronald Williams. **Colonsay Books** TITLE *Summer in the Hebrides.* **West Highland Series** Mini walking guides. No poetry or books unrelated to Scotland or Celtic theme. About 10 titles a year. Unsolicited mss, synopses and ideas welcome if relevant to subjects covered.

ROYALTIES annually.

House of Stratus
Thirsk Industrial Park, Thirsk YO7 3BX
☎01845 527700 Fax 01845 527711
✉ info@houseofstratus.com
www.houseofstratus.com

CEO *David Lane*

Founded 1999. Publishes fiction and non-fiction. Backlist of over 1500 titles including C.P. Snow, Brian Aldiss, Nevil Shute and G.K. Chesterton. About 30 titles annually.

ROYALTIES twice-yearly.

How To Books Ltd
3 Newtec Place, Magdalen Road, Oxford OX4 1RE
☎01865 793806 Fax 01865 248780

✉ info@howtobooks.co.uk
www.howtobooks.co.uk

Publisher/Managing Director *Giles Lewis*
Commissioning Editorial Director *Nikki Read*

An independent publishing house, founded in 1991. Publishes non-fiction, self-help reference books. How To titles are practical, accessible books that enable their readers to achieve their goals in life and work. How To authors must have first-hand experience of the subject about which they are writing. Subjects covered include management, leisure learning, career choices & career development, living & working abroad, small business & self employment, study skills & student guides, creative writing and property.

Human Horizons
See **Souvenir Press Ltd**

Human Science Press
See **Kluwer Academic/Plenum Publishers**

Hunt & Thorpe
See **John Hunt Publishing Ltd**

John Hunt Publishing Ltd
46a West Street, New Alresford SO24 9AU
☎01962 736880 Fax 01962 736881
✉ maria@johnhunt-publishing.com
www.johnhunt-publishing.com
www.o-books.net

Approx. Annual Turnover £1.5 million

Publishes children's and world religions as well as mind, body & spirit titles. About 25 a year. IMPRINTS **Hunt & Thorpe**; **John Hunt Publishing**; **Arthur James**; **O Books**. Unsolicited material welcome.

C. Hurst & Co.
38 King Street, London WC2E 8JZ
☎020 7240 2666 Fax 020 7240 2667
✉ hurst@atlas.co.uk
www.hurstpub.co.uk

Chairman/Managing Director *Christopher Hurst*
Editorial Heads *Christopher Hurst, Michael Dwyer*

Founded 1967. An independent company concerned with literacy, detail and visual aspects. Publishes contemporary history, politics, religion (not theology) and sociology. TITLES *The Hungarians* Paul Lendvai; *Greece: The Modern Sequel; Serbia: the History behind the Name; Iceland's 1100 Years; Inside Al Qaeda: Global Network of Terror.* About 25 titles a year. No unsolicited mss. Synopses and ideas welcome.

ROYALTIES annually.

Hutchinson
See **The Random House Group Ltd**

Hymns Ancient & Modern Ltd
St Mary's Works, St Mary's Plain, Norwich NR3 3BH
☎01603 612914 Fax 01603 624483
✉ admin@scm-canterburypress.co.uk
www.scm-canterburypress.co.uk
Chairman *Patrick Coldstream, CBE*
Chief Executive *G.A. Knights*
Publisher, SCM Press and Canterbury Press *Christine Smith*
Publisher, RMEP *Mary Mears*
Approx. Annual Turnover £4.4 million

Publishes hymn books for churches, schools and other institutions. All types of liturgical and general religious books and material for religious and social education. Owns SCM-Canterbury Press Ltd (see entry) controlling the IMPRINTS **SCM Press**; **Canterbury Press**; **Religious and Moral Education Press (RMEP)** Religious, social and moral books for primary and secondary schools, assembly material and books for teachers and administrators. **G.J. Palmer & Sons Ltd** TITLES *Church Times* (see entry under *Magazines*); *The Sign* and *Home Words* – two monthly nationwide parish magazine inserts; *Crucible* – quarterly magazine. Ideas welcome; no unsolicited mss.
ROYALTIES annually.

Icon Books Ltd
Grange Road, Duxford CB2 4QF
☎01763 208008 Fax 01763 208080
✉ info@iconbooks.co.uk
www.iconbooks.co.uk
Managing Director *Peter Pugh*
Editorial Director *Richard Appignanesi*
Publishing Director *Jeremy Cox*

Founded 1992. SERIES *Introducing* Graphic introductions to key figures and ideas in the history of science, philosophy, psychology, religion and the arts. TITLE *Introducing Quantum Theory*. Publishes 'provocative and intelligent' non-fiction in science, politics and philosophy. TITLE *Why do People Hate America?* IMPRINT **Wizard Books** Children's fiction and non-fiction including SERIES *Fighting Fantasy* (adventure gamebooks). Submit synopsis only. OVERSEAS ASSOCIATE Totem Books, USA, distributed by National Book Network.
ROYALTIES twice yearly.

I.M.P. Fiction Ltd
PO Box 14691, London SE1 2ZA

☎01440 788561 Fax 01440 788562
✉ info@impbooks.com
www.impbooks.com
Managing Director *Kaye Roach*

Founded 1998. Publishes 'quality new fiction'. No crime, science fiction, horror or fantasy. 2 titles in 2003. Mss only accepted from recognised agents; no unsolicited mss.
ROYALTIES twice-yearly.

The In Pinn
See **Neil Wilson Publishing Ltd**

Independent Music Press
PO Box 14691, London SE1 2ZA
☎01440 788561 Fax 01440 788562
✉ info@impbooks.com
www.impbooks.com
Managing Director *Martin Roach*

Founded 1992. Publishes music biography and youth culture. No jazz or classical. TITLES include biographies of Dave Grohl, Stereophonics, Oasis, Prodigy as well as subculture classics such as *Scooter Boys* and Ian Hunter's *Diary of a Rock 'n' Roll Star*. Approach by letter or e-mail, enclosing biography, synopsis, first three chapters and s.a.e. if return of work required. Material will not be returned if postage and packing not provided.
ROYALTIES twice-yearly.

Independent Voices
See **Souvenir Press Ltd**

Infinite Ideas
Belsyre Court, 57 Woodstock Road, Oxford OX2 6JH
☎01865 292045 Fax 01865 292001
✉ richard@infideas.com
www.infideas.com
Chairman *Jesse Norman*
Joint Managing Directors *David Grant, Richard Burton*
Approx. Annual Turnover £500,000

Founded 2004. Publishes inspirational self-help. SERIES **52 Brilliant Ideas** *Richard Burton* TITLES *Parenting; Cool Careers; Home Decoration; Wine; Beating Back Pain; Relationships*. No fiction, illustrated or children's books. 20 titles in 2004. No unsolicited mss. Synopses and ideas welcome; initial contact by e-mail or letter.
Flat FEES paid.

Authors' Rating Combining trade publishing with content licensing, this new company will build up an archive of 'inspirational 100-word ideas' on lifestyle subjects. The ideas may generate books but are just as likely to be adopted for other media interests. Could this be the future of publishing?

Informa

Informa House, 30–32 Mortimer Street, London W1W 7RE
☎020 7017 4600

Managing Director *Fotini Liontou*
Publishing Director *Wendy Gill*

Part of LLP Professional Publishing, a trading division of Informa Publishing Group Ltd. Publishes a range of maritime, commercial, insurance, banking, intellectual property, academic newsletters, reports, books and magazines aimed at senior management and professional practices.

Inter-Varsity Press

38 De Montfort Street, Leicester LE1 7GP
☎0116 255 1754 Fax 0116 254 2044
✉ ivp@uccf.org.uk
www.ivpbooks.com

Chairman *Ralph Evershed*
Chief Executive *Brian Wilson*

Founded mid-1930s as the publishing arm of Universities and Colleges Christian Fellowship, it has expanded to wider Christian markets worldwide. Publishes Christian belief and lifestyle, reference and bible commentaries. No secular material or anything which fails to empathise with orthodox Protestant Christianity. IMPRINTS **IVP**; **Apollos**; **Crossway** TITLES *The Bible Speaks Today*; *God's Big Picture* Vaughan Roberts; *Why I Am a Christian* John Stott. About 50 titles a year. Synopses and ideas welcome.
    ROYALTIES twice-yearly.

Interface Collection

See **University of Hertfordshire Press**

International Thomson Publishing

See **Thomson Learning**

Intrigue

See **Harlequin Mills & Boon Ltd**

Isis Publishing

7 Centremead, Osney Mead OX2 0ES
☎01865 250333 Fax 01865 790358
www.isis-publishing.co.uk

Part of the Ulverscroft Group Ltd. Publishes large-print books – fiction and non-fiction – and unabridged audio books. Together with **Soundings** (see entry under *Audio Books*)

produces around 4000 titles on audio tape and CD. AUTHORS Catherine Cookson, Stephen King, Terry Pratchett, Willy Russell. No unsolicited mss as Isis undertakes no original publishing.
    ROYALTIES twice-yearly.

Itchy Coo

See **Black & White Publishing Ltd**

Ithaca Press

See **Garnet Publishing Ltd**

IVP

See **Inter-Varsity Press**

Jacqui Small

See **Aurum Press Ltd**

JAI

See **Elsevier Ltd**

Arthur James

See **John Hunt Publishing Ltd**

Jane's Information Group

Sentinel House, 163 Brighton Road, Coulsdon CR5 2YH
☎020 8700 3700 Fax 020 8763 1006
✉ info.uk@janes.com
www.janes.com

Managing Director *Alfred Rolington*

Founded 1898 by Fred T. Jane with the publication of *All The World's Fighting Ships*. Now part of the Woodbridge Company Limited. In recent years management has been focusing on growth opportunities in its core business and in enhancing the performance of initiatives like Jane's information available online and on CD-ROM. Publishes Web journals, magazines and yearbooks on defence, aerospace, security and transport topics, with details of equipment and systems; plus directories and strategic studies. Also *Jane's Defence Weekly* (see under *Magazines*).
    DIVISIONS **Magazines** Sean Howe TITLES *Jane's Defence Weekly*; *Jane's International Defense Review*; *Jane's Airport Review*; *Jane's Navy International*; *Jane's Islamic Affairs Analyst*; *Jane's Missiles and Rockets*. **Publishing for Defence, Aerospace, Transport** Ian Kay TITLES *Defence, Aerospace Yearbooks*. **Transport** TITLES *Transportation Yearbooks*. **Security** Sean Howe TITLES *Jane's Intelligence Review*; *Foreign Report*; *Jane's Sentinel* (regional security assessment); *Police Review*. CD-ROM and electronic development and publication. Unsolicited mss, synopses and ideas for reference/yearbooks welcome.

OVERSEAS ASSOCIATES Jane's Information Group Inc., USA.
ROYALTIES twice-yearly.

Janus Publishing Company Ltd
105–107 Gloucester Place, London W1U 6BY
☎020 7580 7664 Fax 020 7636 5756
✉ publisher@januspublishing.co.uk

Managing Director *Sandy Leung*

Publishes fiction, human interest, memoirs, philosophy, mind, body and spirit, religion and theology, social questions, popular science, history, spiritualism and the paranormal, poetry and young adults. About 400 titles in print. IMPRINTS **Janus Books** Subsidy publishing; **Empiricus Books** Non-subsidy publishing. TITLES *The Anarchists in the Spanish Civil War; Nature of the Self; Politics and Human Nature; Napoleon 1813; King David; Chameleon Candidate; Love Emporium; Digby.* 'Two of our authors were short-listed for the European Literary Award in 2002.' Unsolicited mss welcome. Agents in the USA, Europe and Asia.
ROYALTIES twice-yearly.

Authors' Rating Authors may be asked to cover their own productions costs but Janus seems to be moving into conventional publishing with its Empiricus imprint.

Jarrold Publishing
Whitefriars, Norwich NR3 1JR
☎01603 763300 Fax 01603 662748
✉ info@jarrold-publishing.co.uk
www.jarrold-publishing.co.uk

Managing Director *Margot Russell-King*

Part of Jarrold & Sons Ltd, the printing and publishing company founded in 1770. Publishes UK tourism, travel, leisure, history and calendars. Material tends to be of a high pictorial content. IMPRINTS **Pitkin**; **Unichrome**. About 30 titles a year. Unsolicited mss, synopses and ideas welcome but before submitting anything, approach in writing to the editorial department.

Michael Joseph
See **Penguin Group (UK)**

Judith Handbooks
See **Studymates Limited**

Kahn & Averill
9 Harrington Road, London SW7 3ES
☎020 8743 3278 Fax 020 8743 3278
✉ kahn@averill23.freeserve.co.uk

Managing Director *Mr M. Kahn*

Founded 1967 to publish children's titles but now specialises in music titles. A small independent publishing house. Publishes music and general non-fiction. No unsolicited mss; synopses and ideas for books considered.
ROYALTIES twice-yearly.

Karnak House
300 Westbourne Park Road, London W11 1EH
☎020 7243 3620 Fax 020 7243 3620
✉ karnakhouse@aol.com

Managing Director *Amon Saba Saakana*

Founded 1979. Specialises in African and Caribbean studies. Publishes anthropology, education, Egyptology, history, language and linguistics, literary criticism, music, prehistory. No poetry, humour or sport. About 17 titles a year. No unsolicited mss; send introduction or synopsis with one sample chapter. Synopses and ideas welcome. OVERSEAS SUBSIDIARIES The Intef Institute, and Karnak House, Illinois, USA.
ROYALTIES annually.

Kenilworth Press Ltd
Addington, Buckingham MK18 2JR
☎01296 715101 Fax 01296 715148
✉ editorial@kenilworthpress.co.uk
www.kenilworthpress.co.uk

Chairman/Managing Director *David Blunt*
Approx. Annual Turnover £500,000

Founded in 1989 with the acquisition of Threshhold Books. The UK's principal instructional equestrian publisher, producing the official books of the British Horse Society, the famous *Threshold Picture Guides* and a range of authoritative titles sold around the world. IMPRINT **Kenilworth Press** TITLES *British Horse Society Manuals; Real Riding; Ride With Your Mind Essentials; Navicular Syndrome Explained; Threshold Picture Guides 1–48.* About 10 titles a year. Unsolicited mss, synopses and ideas welcome but only for titles concerned with the care or riding of horses or ponies.
ROYALTIES twice-yearly.

Kenyon-Deane
See **Cressrelles Publishing Co. Ltd**

Laurence King Publishing Ltd
71 Great Russell Street, London WC1B 3BP
☎020 7430 8850 Fax 020 7430 8880
✉ enquiries@laurenceking.co.uk
www.laurenceking.co.uk

Chairman *Robin Hyman*

Managing Director *Laurence King*
Approx. Annual Turnover £5 million

Founded in 1976 as a book packager under the name Calman & King Ltd, the Laurence King publishing division commenced operations in 1991. College and trade divisions were united in 2002 under Laurence King Publishing Ltd. Publishes illustrated books on art, architecture, graphic design, interior design, the decorative arts, film and religion. DIVISIONS **Professional & Trade** *Philip Cooper* TITLES *Atlas of World Art*; *No More Rules: Graphic Design and Postmodernism.* **College & Fine Art** *Lee Ripley-Greenfield* TITLES *A World History of Art*; *History of Modern Design.* About 40 titles a year. Unsolicited material welcome; send synopsis by post.
ROYALTIES twice-yearly.

Kingfisher Publications Plc

New Penderel House, 283–288 High Holborn, London WC1V 7HZ
☎020 7903 9999 Fax 020 7242 4979
✉ sales@kingfisherpub.com

Managing Director *John Richards*

Formerly Larousse plc until 1997 when the company name changed to Kingfisher Publications Plc. Founded 1994 when owners, Groupe de la Cité (also publishers of the Larousse dictionaries in France), merged their UK operations of Grisewood & Dempsey and **Chambers Harrap Publishers Ltd** (see entry). In 2002, Kingfisher officially became an imprint of **Houghton Mifflin Company** (see entry under *US Publishers*).

DIVISION **Kingfisher** Non-fiction Publishing Director *Gill Denton* Founded in 1973 by Grisewood & Dempsey Ltd. Publishes children's fiction and non-fiction in hardback and paperback: story books, rhymes and picture books, fiction and poetry anthologies, young non-fiction, activity books, general series and reference. No unsolicited mss accepted.
ROYALTIES twice-yearly where applicable.

Jessica Kingsley Publishers Ltd

116 Pentonville Road, London N1 9JB
☎020 7833 2307 Fax 020 7837 2917
✉ post@jkp.com
www.jkp.com

Managing Director and Publisher *Jessica Kingsley*
Editorial Director *Amy Lankester-Owen*

Founded 1987. Independent publisher of books for professionals and academics on social and behavioural sciences, including special needs, arts therapies, child psychology, psychotherapy (including forensic psychotherapy), practical theology and social work. International publisher of books on autism or parents, professionals and researchers. Over 100 titles a year. 'We are actively publishing and commissioning in all these areas. We welcome suggestions for books and proposals from prospective authors. Proposals should consist of an outline of the book, a contents list, assessment of the market and author's c.v., and should be addressed to *Jessica Kingsley* or *Amy Lankester-Owen.* Complete manuscript should not be sent.'
ROYALTIES twice-yearly.

Kluwer Academic/ Plenum Publishers

100 Borough High Street, London SE1 1LB
☎020 7863 3000 Fax 020 7863 3314
✉ mail@plenum.co.uk
www.wkap.nl

Publishing Director *Dr Ken Derham*
Senior Publishing Editor (Life Sciences) *Joanna Lawrence*
Senior Publishing Editor (Chemistry) *Emma Roberts*

Founded 1966. A division of **Kluwer Academic/Plenum Publishing**, New York. The London office is the editorial base for the company's UK and European operations. Publishes postgraduate, professional and research-level scientific, technical and medical textbooks, monographs, conference proceedings and reference books. IMPRINTS **Consultants Bureau**; **Kluwer Academic/Plenum Publishers**; **Plenum Press**; **Human Science Press**. Proposals for new publications will be considered, and should be sent to the editor. About 200 titles (worldwide) a year.
ROYALTIES annually.

Kluwer Law International

145 London Road, Kingston-upon-Thames KT2 6SR
☎020 8247 1611 Fax 020 8247 1607

Publisher *Sian O'Neill*

Founded 1995. Parent company: Wolters Kluwer Group. Publishes international law. About 200 titles a year. Unsolicited synopses and ideas for books on law at an international level welcome.
ROYALTIES annually.

Knight Paperbacks Ltd
See **Caxton Publishing Group**

Kogan Page Ltd
120 Pentonville Road, London N1 9JN
☎020 7278 0433 Fax 020 7837 3768/6348
✉ kpinfo@kogan-page.co.uk
www.kogan-page.co.uk
Managing Director *Philip Kogan*
Approx. Annual Turnover £6 million

Founded 1967 by Philip Kogan to publish *The Industrial Training Yearbook*. In 1992 acquired Earthscan Publications. Publishes business and management reference books and monographs, careers, marketing, personal finance, personnel, small business, training and industrial relations, transport, plus journals. Further expansion is planned, particularly in the finance and high-tech, EC publications areas, yearbooks and directories, and international business reference. Has initiated a number of electronic publishing projects and provision of EP content. DIVISIONS **Kogan Page** *Pauline Goodwin, Philip Mudd, Peter Chadwick*. **Kogan Page Science** Publishes hi-tech engineering science monographs. About 50 titles a year.
ROYALTIES twice-yearly.

Authors' Rating The doyen of business books publishers, Philip Kogan is moving into science in a big way and expanding the electronic publishing programme.

Ladybird
See **Dorling Kindersley Ltd**

Landmark Publishing Ltd
Ashbourne Hall, Cokayne Avenue, Ashbourne DE6 1EJ
☎01335 347349 Fax 01335 347303
✉ landmark@clara.net
www.landmarkpublishing.co.uk
Chairman *Mr R. Cork*
Managing Director *Mr C.L.M. Porter*
Approx. Annual Turnover £450,000

Founded in 1996. Publishes itinerary-based travel guides, regional, industrial and local history. 45 titles in 2003. No unsolicited mss; telephone in the first instance.
ROYALTIES annually.

Larousse Plc
See **Kingfisher Publications Plc**

Lawrence & Wishart Ltd
99A Wallis Road, London E9 5LN
☎020 8533 2506 Fax 020 8533 7369
✉ lw@lwbooks.co.uk
www.lwbooks.co.uk

Managing Director/Editor *Sally Davison*

Founded 1936. An independent publisher with a substantial backlist. Publishes current affairs, cultural politics, economics, history, politics and education. TITLES *A New Modernity; Liberty or Death; The Struggle for Democracy in Britain 1780–1830; Rosa Luxemburg: An Intimate Portrait.* 10 titles a year.
ROYALTIES annually, unless by arrangement.

The Learning Institute
Honeycombe House, Bagley, Wedmore BS28 4TD
☎01934 713563 Fax 01934 713492
✉ courses@inst.org
www.inst.org
Managing Director *Kit Sadgrove*

Founded 1994 to publish home-study courses in vocational subjects such as garden design, writing and computing. Publishes subjects that show the reader how to work from home, gain a new skill or enter a new career. Interests include self-improvement, interior design, hobbies, parenting, health, careers, music and investment. TITLES *Diploma in Interior Design; Become a Garden Designer.* Author's guidelines sent on receipt of s.a.e. No unsolicited mss; send synopses and ideas only.
ROYALTIES quarterly.

Lennard Associates Ltd
Windmill Cottage, Mackerye End, Harpenden AL5 5DR
☎01582 715866 Fax 01582 715866
✉ stephenson@lennardqap.co.uk
Chairman/Managing Director *Adrian Stephenson*

Founded 1979. Publisher of sporting yearbooks; sponsored and commissioned projects only. YEARBOOKS *The Cricketers' Who's Who; PFA Footballers' Who's Who; Wooden Spoon Rugby World.* IMPRINTS **Lennard Publishing; Queen Anne Press.** Acquired the latter and most of its assets in 1992. No unsolicited mss.
PAYMENT Both fees and royalties by arrangement.

Charles Letts
See **New Holland Publishers (UK) Ltd**

Lionel Leventhal Ltd
See **Greenhill Books**

Dewi Lewis Publishing
8 Broomfield Road, Heaton Moor, Stockport SK4 4ND
☎0161 442 9450 Fax 0161 442 9450

✉ mail@dewilewispublishing.com
www.dewilewispublishing.com

Contacts *Dewi Lewis, Caroline Warhurst*
Approx. Annual Turnover £260,000

Founded 1994. Publishes fiction, photography and visual arts. TITLES *Industry of Souls* Martin Booth (**Booker Prize** shortlist, 1998); *Wolfy and the Strudelbakers* Zvi Jagendorf (**Booker Prize** longlist, 2001; **Sagittarius Prize**, 2002); *Common Sense* Martin Parr; *New York 1954–5* William Klein. 20 titles in 2003. Submissions: check website.

ROYALTIES twice-yearly.

LexisNexis
See **Reed Elsevier Group plc**

John Libbey Publishing
PO Box 276, Eastleigh SO50 5YS
☎01342 315440 Fax 023 8065 0259
✉ johnlibbey@aol.com
www.johnlibbey.com

Publisher *John Libbey*

Founded 1979. Publishes books and journals on cinema, animation and media. Now the publisher of the media series from University of Luton Press. Synopses and ideas welcome. OVERSEAS SUBSIDIARY John Libbey Eurotext Ltd, France (medical publishers).

Librapharm Ltd
29 Venture West, New Greenham Park, Newbury RG19 6HX
☎01635 522651 Fax 01635 36294
www.librapharm.com

Chairman *Mr M.W. Frost*
Managing Director *Dr P.L. Clarke*
Approx. Annual Turnover £1.5 million

Founded 1995 as a partial buyout from Kluwer Academic Publishers (UK) academic list. Publishes medical and scientific books and periodicals. IMPRINT **Petroc Press**. TITLES *The Inner Consultation; Emergencies in General Practice; Thinking About Patients.* Journals: *Primary Care Psychiatry; Current Medical Research and Opinion; Paediatric and Perinatal Drug Therapy; Headache Care; Transpharma.* Unsolicited mss, synopses and ideas for medical books welcome.

ROYALTIES twice-yearly.

Library Association Publishing
See **Facet Publishing**

Frances Lincoln Ltd
4 Torriano Mews, Torriano Avenue, London
☎020 7284 4009 Fax 020 7267 5249

✉ firstname and initial of surname@
frances-lincoln.com
www.franceslincoln.com

Managing Director *John Nicoll*

Founded 1977. Publishes highly illustrated non-fiction: gardening, art and interiors, health, crafts, children's picture and information books; and stationery. DIVISIONS **Adult Non-fiction** *Jo Christian* TITLES *Chatsworth* Duchess of Devonshire; *Grow Your Own Vegetables* Joy Larkom; **Children's General Fiction and Non-fiction** *Janetta Otter-Barry* TITLE *The Wanderings of Odysseus* Rosemary Sutcliffe, illus. Alan Lee; **Stationery** *Anne Fraser* TITLES *RHS Diary and Address Book; British Library Diary.* About 60 titles a year. Synopses and ideas for books considered.

ROYALTIES twice-yearly.

Linden Press
See **Open Gate Press**

Linford Romance/Linford Mystery/Linford Western
See **F.A. Thorpe (Publishing)**

Lion Publishing
Mayfield House, 256 Banbury Road, Oxford OX2 7DH
☎01865 302750 Fax 01865 302757
✉ enquiry@lion-publishing.co.uk
www.lion-publishing.co.uk

Managing Director *Paul Clifford*
Approx. Annual Turnover £6.77 million

Founded 1971. A Christian book publisher, strong on illustrated books for a popular international readership, with rights sold in over 100 languages worldwide. Publishes a diverse list with Christian viewpoint the common denominator. All ages, from board books for children to multi-contributor adult reference, educational, paperbacks and colour co-editions and gift books. DIVISIONS **Adult** *Laura Derico*; **Children's and Giftlines** *Catherine Giddings*. Unsolicited mss accepted provided they have a positive Christian viewpoint intended for a wide general and international readership.

ROYALTIES twice-yearly.

Lions
See **HaperCollins Publishers Ltd**

Lir
See **Hodder Headline Ltd**

Little Tiger Press

An imprint of Magi Publications, 1 The Coda Centre, 189 Munster Road, London SW6 6AW

☎020 7385 6333 Fax 020 7385 7333

✉ info@littletiger.co.uk

www.littletigerpress.com

Publisher *Monty Bhatia*

Editor *Jude Evans*

Approx. Annual Turnover £4.5 million

Publishes children's picture and novelty books for ages 0–7. No texts over 750 words. About 24 titles a year. Unsolicited mss, synopses and new ideas welcome. See website for submission guidelines.

ROYALTIES annually.

Authors' Rating The leading small publisher (along with **Autumn Publishing**) of children's books.

Little, Brown

See **Time Warner Books UK**

Liverpool University Press

4 Cambridge Street, Liverpool L69 7ZU

☎0151 794 2233 Fax 0151 794 2235

✉ robblo@liv.ac.uk

www.liverpool-unipress.co.uk

Managing Director/Editorial Head *Robin Bloxsidge*

LUP's primary activity is the publication of academic and scholarly books and journals but it also has a limited number of trade titles. Its principal focus is on the arts and social sciences, in which it is active in a variety of disciplines. TITLES *The Cannibal Hymn; Excavations on St Patrick's Isle; Peel; Isle of Man; Urban Visions; Public Sculpture of Warwickshire; Public Sculpture of the City of London; The Long Road to Peace in Northern Ireland; Knowledge and Learning in the Andes; Identity Parades; Northern Irish Culture and Dissident Subjects; HIV Stories; Breeding Superman; The Business of Music; Claude Simon: A Retrospective.* 30–40 titles a year.

ROYALTIES annually.

Livewire Books for Teenagers

See **The Women's Press**

Lonely Planet Publications Ltd

72–82 Rosebery Avenue, London EC1R 4RW

☎020 7841 9000 Fax 020 7841 9001

✉ go@lonelyplanet.co.uk

www.lonelyplanet.com

Owner *Lonely Planet (Australia)*

Editorial Head *Katharine Leck*

Approx. Annual Turnover £30 million

Founded in 1973 by Tony and Maureen Wheeler to document a journey from London across Asia to Australia. Since then, Lonely Planet has grown into a global operation with headquarters in Melbourne and offices in Paris, California and London. Publishes travel guidebooks, phrasebooks, travel literature, pictorial books, city maps, regional atlases, diving and snorkelling, walking, cycling, wildlife, health, and pre-departure guidebooks. Also operates a commercial travel slide library called **Lonely Planet Images** (www.lonelyplanetimages.com). No unsolicited mss; synopses and ideas welcome.

Lorenz Books

See **Anness Publishing Ltd**

Lund Humphries

See **Ashgate Publishing Ltd**

The Lutterworth Press

PO Box 60, Cambridge CB1 2NT

☎01223 350865 Fax 01223 366951

✉ publishing@lutterworth.com

www.lutterworth.com

Managing Director *Adrian Brink*

The Lutterworth Press dates back to the 18th century when it was founded by the Religious Tract Society. In the 19th century it was best known for its children's books and magazines, both religious and secular, including *The Boys' Own Paper*. Since 1984 it has been an imprint of **James Clarke & Co** (see entry). Publishes religious books for adults and children, adult non-fiction, children's fiction and non-fiction. TITLES *Whatever Happened to Religious Education?; Burn, Holy Fire!; The Germans We Trusted; Joanna Southcott's Box of Sealed Prophecies.* Approach in writing with ideas in the first instance.

ROYALTIES annually.

Macdonald & Co.

See **Time Warner Books UK**

McGraw Hill Education

McGraw-Hill House, Shoppenhangers Road, Maidenhead SL6 2QL

☎01628 502500 Fax 01628 770224

www.mcgraw-hill.co.uk

Editorial Director *Melissa A. Rosati*

Owned by US parent company, founded in 1888. Began publishing in Maidenhead in

1965, having had an office in the UK since 1899. Publishes business, economics, finance, accounting, computing science, social sciences and engineering for the academic, student and professional markets. Acquired **Open University Press** in 2002 (see entry). Around 100 titles a year. See website for author's guide and how to submit new book proposals.
ROYALTIES twice-yearly.

Macmillan Publishers Ltd
The Macmillan Building, 4 Crinan Street, London N1 9XW
☎020 7833 4000 Fax 020 7843 4640
www.macmillan.com
Chief Executive *Richard Charkin*
Approx. Annual Turnover £300 million
  (Book Publishing Group)
Founded 1843. Macmillan is one of the largest publishing houses in Britain, publishing around 1400 titles a year. In 1995, Verlagsgruppe Georg von Holtzbrinck, a major German publisher, acquired a majority stake in the Macmillan Group and in 1999 purchased the remaining shares. In 1996, Macmillan bought Boxtree, the successful media tie-in publisher and, in 1997, it purchased the Heinemann English language teaching list from Reed Elsevier. In 2004 the educational publishing division was strengthened by the acquisition of the Mexican list, Ediciones Castillo. No unsolicited material.

DIVISIONS
Palgrave Macmillan Brunel Road, Houndmills, Basingstoke, Hampshire RG21 6XS
☎01256 329242 Fax 01256 479476 Managing Director *Dominic Knight*; **College** *Frances Arnold*; **Scholarly & Reference** *Sam Burridge*; **Journals** *David Bull*. Publishes textbooks, monographs and journals in academic and professional subjects. Publications in both hard copy and electronic format.
  Macmillan Education Macmillan Oxford, 4 Between Towns Road, Oxford OX4 3PP
☎01865 405700 Fax 01865 405701 ✉ info@macmillan.com www.macmillaneducation.com
Executive Chairman *Christopher Paterson*; Managing Director *Chris Harrison*; Publishing Directors *Sue Bale* (ELT), *Alison Hubert* (Education), *Ian Johnstone* (Internet). Publishes a wide range of ELT titles and educational materials for the international education market from Oxford and through 30 subsidiaries worldwide.
  Pan Macmillan 20 New Wharf Road, London N1 9RR ☎020 7014 6000 Fax 020 7014 6001 www.panmacmillan.com Managing

Director *David North*. IMPRINTS **Macmillan**, **Pan**, **Picador**, **Sidgwick & Jackson**, **Boxtree**, **Macmillan Children's Books**, **Campbell Books**.
IMPRINTS
Macmillan (founded 1843) Fiction: Publishing Director *Maria Rejt*, Editorial Director *Imogen Taylor* Publishes hardback commercial and literary fiction including genre fiction, romantic, crime and thrillers. IMPRINT **Tor** (founded 2003) Editorial Director *Peter Lavery* Publishes science fiction, fantasy and thrillers. Non-Fiction: Publisher *Richard Milner*, Editorial Director *Georgina Morley* Publishes serious and general non-fiction: autobiography, biography, economics, history, philosophy, politics and world affairs, psychology, popular science, trade reference titles.
  Pan (founded 1947) Paperback imprint for Pan Macmillan.
  Picador (founded 1972) Publisher *Andrew Kidd*, Senior Editorial Director *Ursula Doyle*. Publishes literary international fiction and non-fiction.
  Sidgwick & Jackson (founded 1908) Publishes popular non-fiction in hardback and trade paperback with strong personality or marketable identity, from celebrity and showbusiness to music and sport. Also military history list.
  Boxtree (founded 1986) Publishes brand and media tie-in titles, including TV, film, music and Internet, plus entertainment licences, pop culture, humour and event-related books. TITLES *Dilbert*; *James Bond*; *Purple Ronnie*; *Viz*; *Wallace & Gromit*; *The Onion*; *Crap Towns*.
  Macmillan Children's Books (New Wharf Road address) Managing Director *Kate Wilson*; **Fiction, Non-Fiction, Poetry** *Sarah Davies*; **Picture Books and Gift Books** *Suzanne Carnell*; **Campbell Books** *Camilla Reid*. IMPRINTS **Macmillan**, **Pan**, **Campbell Books**, **Young Picador**. Publishes novels, board books, picture books, non-fiction (illustrated and non-illustrated), poetry and novelty books in paperback and hardback.
  ROYALTIES annually or twice-yearly depending on contract.

Authors' Rating With a strong front list of bestsellers Pan Macmillan has cut back on its middle list. The aim is to raise new authors to stardom. The children's list continues to do well. A new science imprint will focus on stories of pioneering research, aimed at the general reader.

Made Simple Books
See **Elsevier Ltd**

Mainstream Publishing Co. (Edinburgh) Ltd

7 Albany Street, Edinburgh EH1 3UG
☎0131 557 2959 Fax 0131 556 8720
✉ editorial@mainstreampublishing.com
www.mainstreampublishing.com

Directors *Bill Campbell, Peter MacKenzie*
Approx. Annual Turnover £2.75 million

Publishes art, autobiography/biography, current affairs, health, sport, history, illustrated and fine editions, photography, politics and world affairs, popular paperbacks. TITLES *Soldier Five* Mike Coburn; *The Real Nureyev* Carolyn Soutar; *Woodward's England* Mick Collins. Over 80 titles a year. Ideas for books considered, but they should be preceded by a letter, synopsis and s.a.e. or return postage.
ROYALTIES twice-yearly.

Authors' Rating Strong on originality, Mainstream makes an impact far beyond the Scottish border. Keen on finding authors who 'can develop with us'.

Management Books 2000 Ltd

Forge House, Limes Road, Kemble,
Cirencester GL7 6AD
☎01285 771441 Fax 01285 771055
✉ m.b.2000@virgin.net
www.mb2000.com

Publisher *James Alexander*
Approx. Annual Turnover £500,000

Founded 1993 to develop a range of books for executives and managers working in the modern world of business. 'Essentially, the books are working books for working managers, practical and effective.' Publishes business, management, self-development and allied topics as well as sponsored titles. Launched the *In Ninety Minutes* series of compact guide books for managers in 2004, offering advice, ideas and practical help across a range of highly relevant business topics in an hour and a half of study. New ideas for this series are welcome. About 30 titles a year. Unsolicited mss, synopses and ideas for books welcome.

Manchester United Books

See **Carlton Publishing Group**

Manchester University Press

Oxford Road, Manchester M13 9NR
☎0161 275 2310 Fax 0161 274 3346
✉ mup@man.ac.uk
www.manchesteruniversitypress.co.uk

Publisher/Chief Executive *David Rodgers*

Head of Editorial *Matthew Frost*
Approx. Annual Turnover £2 million

Founded 1904. MUP is Britain's third largest university press, with a list marketed and sold worldwide. Remit consists of occasional trade publications but mainly A-level and undergraduate textbooks and research monographs. Publishes in the areas of: literature, TV, film, theatre and media, history and history of art, design, politics, economics and international law. DIVISIONS **Humanities** *Matthew Frost*; **History/Art History** *Alison Welsby*; **Politics and Law** *Tony Mason*. About 120 titles a year. Unsolicited mss welcome.
ROYALTIES annually.

George Mann Books

PO Box 22, Maidstone ME14 1AH
☎01622 759591 Fax 01622 209193

Chairman/Managing Director *George Mann*

Founded 1972. Publishes original non-fiction and selected reprints. Not considering new fiction for publication. 'Will only consider and respond to authors who, in the present publishing climate, are prepared to support *some of the costs* of publication on a shared venture basis. Unsolicited material not accompanied by return postage will neither be read nor returned.'
ROYALTIES annually.

Manson Publishing Ltd

73 Corringham Road, London NW11 7DL
☎020 8905 5150 Fax 020 8201 9233
✉ manson@mansonpublishing.com
www.mansonpublishing.com

Chairman/Managing Director *Michael Manson*

Founded 1992. Publishes scientific, medical and veterinary. TITLES *Clinical Medicine of the Dog and Cat*; *Clinical Bacteriology*; *A Colour Handbook of Biological Control in Plant Protection*; *Biology at a Glance*, 2nd ed. About 10 titles a year. No unsolicited mss; synopses and ideas will be considered.
ROYALTIES twice-yearly.

Marston House

Marston House, Marston Magna, Yeovil
BA22 8DH
☎01935 851331 Fax 01935 851372
✉ alphaimage@marstonhouse.ndo.co.uk

Managing Director/Editorial Head *Anthony Birks-Hay*

Founded 1989. Publishing imprint of book packager Alphabet & Image Ltd. Publishes fine art, architecture, ceramics. 4 titles a year.

ROYALTIES twice-yearly, or flat fee in lieu of royalties.

Martin Books
See **Simon & Schuster UK Ltd**

Kenneth Mason Publications Ltd
The Book Barn, Westbourne, Emsworth PO10 8RS
☎01243 377977 Fax 01243 379136
✉ info@whitechimney.com
www.researchdisclosure.com

Chairman *Kenneth Mason*
Managing Director *Piers Mason*

Founded 1958. Publishes diet, health, fitness, nutrition and nautical. No fiction. IMPRINTS **Boatswain Press**; **Research Disclosure**. About 15 titles a year. Initial approach by letter with synopsis only.

ROYALTIES twice-yearly in first year, annually thereafter.

Kevin Mayhew Publishers
Buxhall, Stowmarket IP14 3BW
☎01449 737978 Fax 01449 737834
✉ info@kevinmayhewltd.com
www.kevinmayhewltd.com

Chairman *Kevin Mayhew*
Managing Director *Gordon Carter*
Commissioning Editors *Kevin Mayhew, Jonathan Bugden*

Founded in 1976. One of the leading sacred music and Christian book publishers in the UK. Publishes religious titles – liturgy, sacramental, devotional, also children's books and school resources. IMPRINT **Palm Tree Press** Worldwide worship. Unsolicited synopses and mss welcome; telephone prior to sending material, please.

ROYALTIES annually.

Meadowside Children's Books
185 Fleet Street, London EC4A 2HS
☎020 7400 1087 Fax 020 7400 1037
✉ info@meadowsidebooks.com
www.meadowsidebooks.com

Chairman *Mark Battles*
Managing Director *Simon Rosenheim*
Editorial Manager *Alison Maloney*
Approx. Annual Turnover £1.4 million

Founded in September 2003 by D.C. Thomson. Publishes pre-school picture, novelty and early learning books. Over 100 titles a year. Unsolicited mss, synopses and ideas welcome. Send to the Editorial Department by mail or e-mail.

Melrose Press Ltd
St Thomas Place, Ely CB7 4GG
☎01353 646600 Fax 01353 646601
✉ tradesales@melrosepress.co.uk
www.melrosepress.co.uk

Chairman *Richard A. Kay*
Managing Director *Nicholas S. Law*
Approx. Annual Turnover £2 million

Founded 1960. Took on its present name in 1969. Publishes biographical who's who reference only (not including *Who's Who*, which is published by **A.&C. Black**).

Mentor
See **Christian Focus Publications**

Mercat Press Ltd
10 Coates Crescent, Edinburgh EH3 7AL
☎0131 225 5324 Fax 0131 226 6632
✉ enquiries@mercatpress.com
www.mercatpress.com

Directors *Seán Costello, Tom Johnstone*

Established as a stand-alone company in 2002 in a management buy-out following the collapse of parent firm James Thin. The Press was founded in 1971 as an adjunct to the former Scottish bookselling chain. It began by publishing reprints of classic Scottish literature but now produces a wide range of new non-fiction titles. In 1992 the company acquired the bulk of the stock of Aberdeen University Press and the backlist expanded greatly as a result. In 1999 it took over some 60 titles from the Stationery Office's Scottish heritage list. New titles are added regularly. Publishes fiction and non-fiction of Scottish interest. This includes walking guides and historical and literary books. IMPRINT **Crescent Books** Adult fiction. TITLES *A Sense of Belonging to Scotland* Andy Hall; *The Three One* Paul Reed; *West Highland Way, Official Guide* Bob Aitken and Roger Smith; *25 Walks* series; *Jessie's Journey: Autobiography of a Traveller Girl* Jess Smith; *The Silent Traveller in Edinburgh* Chiang Yee. Unsolicited synopses of Scottish interest books, preferably with sample chapters, are welcome. No new poetry.

ROYALTIES annually.

The Merlin Press Ltd
PO Box 30705, London WC2E 8QD
☎020 7836 3020 Fax 020 7497 0309
✉ info@merlinpress.co.uk
www.merlinpress.co.uk

Managing Director *Anthony W. Zurbrugg*

Founded 1956. Publishes economics, history, philosophy, left-wing politics. No fiction. IMPRINTS **Merlin Press**; **Green Print**. TITLES *Socialist Register* (annual); *Ralph Miliband and the Politics of the New Left*; *Pit Women*. About 10 titles a year.
ROYALTIES twice-yearly.

Merrell Publishers Ltd
Head office: 42 Southwark Street, London SE1 1UN
☎020 7403 2047 Fax 020 7407 1333
✉ mail@merrellpublishers.com
www.merrellpublishers.com
US office: 49 West 24th Street, 8th Floor, New York, NY 10010 ☎001 212 929 8344
Fax 001 212 929 8346
Managing Director *Hugh Merrell*
Editorial Director *Julian Honer*
US Director *Joan Brookbank*
Approx. Annual Turnover £1.8 million

Founded 1993. Publishes art, architecture, design and photography. 24 titles in 2003. Unsolicited synopses and ideas for books welcome. Send c.v. and synopsis giving details of the book's target markets and funding of illustrations.
ROYALTIES annually.

Methodist Publishing House
4 John Wesley Road, Werrington, Peterborough PE4 6ZP
☎01733 325002 Fax 01733 384180
www.mph.org.uk
Chair *Dudley Coates*
Chief Executive *Martin Stone*
Commissioning Editor *Natalie Watson*
Approx. Annual Turnover £2 million

Founded 1800. Owned by the Methodist Church. Publishes a wide range of books, magazines and resources which are sold to Christians in the UK and overseas. Also *Flame* bi-monthly magazine. IMPRINTS **Epworth Press** (see entry); **Foundery Press**; **Methodist Publishing House**. Approx 20 titles a year. Unsolicited mss, synopses and ideas welcome; send sample chapter and contents with covering letter.
ROYALTIES annually.

Methuen Publishing Ltd
215 Vauxhall Bridge Road, London SW1V 1EJ
☎020 7798 1600 Fax 020 7233 9827
✉ name@methuen.co.uk
www.methuen.co.uk

Managing Director *Peter Tummons*
Publishing Consultant (Methuen) *Max Eilenberg*
Publishing Consultant (Politico's) *Sean Magee*
Founded 1889. Methuen was owned by Reed International until it was bought by Random House in 1997. Purchased by a management buy-out team in 1998. Acquired **Politico's Publishing** in 2003 (see entry). Publishes fiction and non-fiction; travel, sport, drama, film, performing arts, humour. DIVISIONS **General**; **Drama**; **Film**; **Theatre**; **Politics**; **Current Affairs**. No unsolicited mss; synopses and ideas welcome. Prefers to be approached via agents or a letter of inquiry. No first novels, cookery books, personal memoirs.
ROYALTIES twice-yearly.

Metro Publishing
See **John Blake Publishing Ltd**

Michelin Travel Publications
Hannay House, 39 Clarendon Road, Watford WD17 1JA
☎01923 205240 Fax 01923 205241
www.Viamichelin.co.uk

Founded 1900 as a travel publisher. Publishes travel guides, maps and atlases. Travel-related synopses and ideas welcome; no mss.

Midland Publishing
An imprint of Ian Allan Publishing Ltd, 4 Watling Drive, Hinckley LE10 3EY
☎01455 255490 Fax 01455 255495
✉ midlandbooks@compuserve.com
Publisher *N.P. Lewis*

Publishes aviation, military and railways. No wartime memoirs. No unsolicited mss; synopses and ideas welcome.
ROYALTIES quarterly.

Milet Publishing Limited
6 North End Parade, London W14 0SJ
☎020 7603 5477 Fax 020 7610 5475
✉ info@milet.com
www.milet.com
Managing Directors *Sedat Turhan, Patricia Billings*

Founded 1995. Publishes children's picture books in English and dual language; world literature for adults and language books. DIVISIONS **Children's, English**; **Children's, Dual Language** *Patricia Billings* TITLES *Pink Lemon*; *A Whole World*; *How Bees Be*. **World Literature**; **Language Books** *Sedat Turhan* TITLES *Milet Picture Dictionary*; *Milet Mini*

Picture Dictionary. Welcomes synopses and ideas for books. Send proposal, outline or synopsis with sample text and/or artwork, by post only. 'Please review submission guidelines and existing titles on our website before submitting. We like bold, original stories and artwork, universal and/or multicultural.'

ROYALTIES twice-yearly.

Miller's
See **Octopus Publishing Group**

Millivres Prowler Limited
Unit M, Spectrum House, 32–34 Gordon House Road, London NW5 1LP
☎020 7424 7400 Fax 020 7424 7401
www.gaymenspress.co.uk
www.divamag.co.uk

Publisher (Books) *Kathleen Bryson*

Publishes about 12 titles of lesbian or gay interest each year as well as *Gay Times* and *Diva* magazines. IMPRINTS **Diva Books** Literary and genre fiction and non-fiction with a lesbian slant. TITLES *The Woman in Beige* V.G. Lee; *Necrologue* ed. Helen Sandler. Send first three chapters and synopsis with covering letter and s.a.e. No e-mail submissions. **GMP (Gay Men's Press)** TITLES *Adam* Anthony McDonald; *Death Comes Easy* ed. Peter Burton. Submission details as for Diva Books. **Zipper Books**; **Red Hot Diva** Explicit gay and lesbian erotica, respectively. TITLES *The Palace of Varieties* James Lear; *The Fox Tales* Astrid Fox. Contact Publisher for guidelines before sending material.

Mills & Boon
See **Harlequin Mills & Boon Ltd**

Mindfield
See **Camden Press Ltd**

MIRA
See **Harlequin Mills & Boon Ltd**

Mitchell Beazley
See **Octopus Publishing Group**

Mobius
See **Hodder Headline Ltd**

Monarch Books
Lion Hudson plc, Mayfield House, 256 Banbury Road, Oxford OX2 7DH
☎01865 302750 Fax 01865 302757
✉ monarch@lionhudson.com

Editorial Director *Tony Collins*

An imprint of Lion Hudson plc. Publishes an independent list of Christian books across a wide range of concerns. IMPRINT **Monarch** Upmarket paperback list with Christian basis and strong social concern agenda including psychology, future studies, politics, mission, theology, leadership and spirituality. About 40 titles a year. Unsolicited mss, synopses and ideas welcome.

Morehouse
See **The Continuum International Publishing Group Limited**

Morgan Kauffman
See **Elsevier Ltd**

Mosby
See **Elsevier Ltd**

Motor Racing Publications
PO Box 1318, Croydon CR9 5YP
☎020 8654 2711 Fax 020 8407 0339
✉ mrp.books@virgin.net
www.motorracingpublications.co.uk

Chairman/Editorial Head *John Blunsden*

Founded soon after the end of World War II to concentrate on motor-racing titles. Fairly dormant in the mid 1960s but was reactivated in 1968 by a new shareholding structure. John Blunsden later acquired a majority share and major expansion followed in the 1970s. Publishes motor-sport history, classic and performance car collection and restoration, race track and off-road driving and related subjects. IMPRINTS **Fitzjames Press**; **Motor Racing Publications** About 6–8 titles a year. No unsolicited mss. Send synopses and ideas in specified subject areas in the first instance.

ROYALTIES twice-yearly.

Multi-Sensory Learning Ltd
Highgate House, Groom's Lane, Creaton NN6 8NN
☎01604 505000 Fax 01604 505001
✉ info@msl-online.net
www.msl-online.net

Senior Editor *Philippa Chudley*

Publishes materials and books related to dyslexia; the multi-sensory learning course for dyslexic pupils needing literacy skills development, plus numerous other items on assessment, reading, maths, music, etc. for dyslexics. Keen to locate authors able to write materials for dyslexic people and for teachers of dyslexics.

Murdoch Books UK Ltd

Erico House, 6th Floor North, 93–99 Upper Richmond Road, London SW15 2TG
☎020 8785 5995 Fax 020 8785 5985

CEO *Juliet Rogers*
Publisher *Kay Scarlett*

Owned by Australian media group Murdoch Magazines Pty Ltd. Publishes full-colour non-fiction: homes and interiors, gardening, cookery, craft, cake decorating and DIY. About 50 titles a year.

John Murray (Publishers) Ltd

338 Euston Road, London NW1 3BH
☎020 7873 6000 Fax 020 7873 6446
www.madaboutbooks.com

Managing Director *Roland Philipps*

Founded 1768. Acquired by **Hodder Headline** in May 2002. Publishes general trade books. **Non-fiction** *Gordon Wise*; **Fiction** *Anya Serota*. No unsolicited material; send preliminary letter.
ROYALTIES twice-yearly.

Authors' Rating Benefiting from the administrative and marketing backup from its new owners, Murray remains loyal to the editorial policy of turning out quality general non-fiction.

Muse Publishing Limited

26 Mill Road, Salisbury SP2 7RZ
☎01722 414568
✉ info@musepublishing.com
www.musepublishing.com

Managing Director *Guy Nicholls*
Editorial Head *Paul Greatorex*

Founded 1998. Publishes fiction only: novels in English about the Far East. 1 title in 2003. No unsolicited material; initial enquiry by telephone or e-mail.
ROYALTIES annually.

NAG Press Ltd

See **Robert Hale Ltd**

The National Archives

The National Archives, Kew TW9 4DU
☎020 8392 5289 Fax 020 8392 5266
✉ jane.crompton@nationalarchives.gov.uk
www.nationalarchives.gov.uk

Publishing Manager *Jane Crompton*

Publishes books, guides and document packs relating to the thousand years of historical records held in The National Archives. Specialist areas: family history, military history

and general history. TITLES *English Monarchs – Treasures from The National Archives*; *The Genealogists Internet* Peter Christian; *Lord Haw Haw* Peter Martland; *Shot Down & On the Run* Graham Pitchfork; *Elizabeth I: The Golden Age of Glorianna* David Loades. Also publishes *Ancestors*, a full-colour family history magazine.

National Trust Publications

36 Queen Anne's Gate, London SW1H 9AS
☎020 7222 9251 Fax 020 7222 5097
www.nationaltrust.org.uk

Chairman *Sir William Proby*
Director-General *Fiona Reynolds*
Publisher *Margaret Willes*

Publishing arm of The National Trust, founded in 1895 by Robert Hunter, Octavia Hill and Hardwicke Rawnsley to protect and conserve places of historic interest and beauty. Publishes gardening, cookery, handbooks, social history, architecture, general interest and children's books. TITLES *History and Landscape*; *The Art of Dress*; *Farmhouse Cookery*; *World in a Garden*. No unsolicited material.
ROYALTIES twice-yearly.

Nautical Data Ltd

The Book Barn, Westbourne, Emsworth PO10 8RS
☎01243 389352 Fax 01243 379136
✉ info@nauticaldata.com
www.nauticaldata.com

Managing Director *Piers Mason*

Founded 1999. Publishes nautical almanacs, pilots and nautical reference. 23 titles in 2003. No unsolicited mss; synopses and ideas welcome. No fiction or non-nautical themes.
ROYALTIES twice-yearly.

NCVO Publications

Regent's Wharf, 8 All Saints Street, London N1 9RL
☎020 7713 6161 Fax 020 7713 6300
www.ncvo-vol.org.uk/publications

Publications and Promotions Coordinator
Josephine Finn
Approx. Annual Turnover £140,000

Founded 1928. Publishing imprint of the National Council for Voluntary Organisations, embracing former Bedford Square Press titles and NCVO's many other publications. The list reflects NCVO's role as the representative body for the voluntary sector. Publishes directories, good practice information on management and trustee development, finance and employment titles and information of primary interest to the voluntary sector. TITLES *The Voluntary Agencies Directory*; *The Good Trustee Guide*; *The Good Campaigns Guide*; *The Good Financial Management Guide*; *The Good Employment Guide*; *The Good Management Guide*; *The Good Governance Action Plan and The UK Voluntary Sector Almanac*. No unsolicited mss as all projects are commissioned in-house.

Thomas Nelson & Sons Ltd
See **Nelson Thornes Limited**

Nelson Thornes Limited
Delta Place, 27 Bath Road, Cheltenham
GL53 7TH
☎01242 267100 Fax 01242 221914
✉ cservices@nelsonthornes.com
www.nelsonthornes.com

Managing Director *Fred Grainger*

Founded in 2000 following the merger of Stanley Thornes (Publishers) Ltd and Thomas Nelson & Sons Ltd. Part of the Wolters Kluwer Group of companies. Educational publisher of printed and electronic product, from pre-school to Higher Education. Unsolicited mss, synopses and ideas for books welcome if appropriate to specialised lists.
ROYALTIES annually.

Authors' Rating The second largest education publisher in the UK after Pearson, Nelson Thornes does best in health and science where it is helped by the dominant position in the market of its parent company, Wolters Kluwer.

New Beacon Books Ltd
76 Stroud Green Road, London N4 3EN
☎020 7272 4889 Fax 020 7281 4662

Chairman *John La Rose*
Managing Director *Sarah White*
Approx. Annual Turnover £120,000

Founded 1966. Publishes fiction, history, politics, poetry and language, all concerning black people. No unsolicited material.
ROYALTIES annually.

New Editions
See **Gibson Square Books Ltd**

New English Library
See **Hodder Headline Ltd**

New Holland Publishers (UK) Ltd
Garfield House, 86–88 Edgware Road,
London W2 2EA
☎020 7724 7773
Fax 020 7258 1293 (editorial)

✉ postmaster@nhpub.co.uk
www.newhollandpublishers.com

Managing Director *John Beaufoy*
Publishing Managers *Rosemary Wilkinson, Jo Hemmings*
Approx. Annual Turnover £6 million

Founded 1956. Relaunched in 1987 as a publisher of illustrated books for the international market. In 1993, NH acquired Charles Letts Publishing Division list and four years later the then parent company (New Holland Struik Group, South Africa) acquired Southern Book Publishers, while their sister company (New Holland Australia) acquired the natural history and lifestyle divisions of Reed Australia. With its HQ in London, New Holland Publishers (UK) Ltd has now become the International Publishing Division of Johnnic Communications, one of Africa's leading publishing groups. NHP also has offices in Australia and New Zealand. Publishes non-fiction, practical and inspirational books in categories including cookery and food, crafts, DIY, fishing, gardening, interior design, mind, body and spirit, natural history, indoor and outdoor sports, travel, travel guides and general books. TITLES *The Dating Game*; *How to Mix and Use Colour*; *Top Adventure Treks*; *Container Topiary*; *One Hit Wonders*. No unsolicited mss; synopses and ideas welcome.

Newnes
See **Elsevier Ltd**

Nexus
See **Virgin Books Ltd**

nferNELSON Publishing Co. Ltd
The Chiswick Centre, 414 Chiswick High Road, London W4 5TF
☎020 8996 8444 Fax 020 8996 3660
www.nfer-nelson.co.uk

General Manager *Tim Cornford*

Founded 1981. Part of Granada Learning Ltd. Publishes educational and psychological tests and training materials. Main interest is in educational, clinical and occupational assessment and training material. Unsolicited mss welcome.
ROYALTIES vary according to each contract.

Nia
See **The X Press**

Nielsen BookData
Globe House, 1 Chertsey Road, Twickenham
TW1 1LR

☎0870 777 8710 Fax 0870 777 8711
www.nielsenbookdata.com

Chief Executive *Jonathan Nowell*

Provides a range of services for the book trade including the **ISBN Agency**, BookBank, SourceData, Teleordering and Book Scan. Also Web services: LibWeb (for libraries); PubWeb (for publishers) and WhitakerWeb (for booksellers). Publishes bibliographic reference products. TITLE *Directory of Publishers (The Red Book)*.

Nightingale Books
See **Pegasus Elliot Mackenzie Publishers Ltd**

James Nisbet & Co. Ltd
Pirton Court, Prior's Hill, Pirton, Hitchin SG5 3QA
☎01462 713444 Fax 01462 713444

Chairman *E.M. Mackenzie-Wood*

Founded 1810 as a religious publisher and expanded into more general areas from around 1850 onwards. The first educational list appeared in 1926 but the company now concentrates on business studies with the education discontinued. No fiction, leisure or religion. About 5 titles a year. No unsolicited mss; synopses and ideas welcome.

ROYALTIES twice-yearly.

NMS Enterprises Limited – Publishing
National Museums of Scotland, Chambers Street, Edinburgh EH1 1JF
☎0131 247 4026 Fax 0131 247 4012
✉ l.taylor@nms.ac.uk
www.nms.ac.uk

Director *Lesley A. Taylor*
Approx. Annual Turnover £250,000

Founded 1987 to publish non-fiction related to the National Museums of Scotland collections: academic and general; children's; archaeology, history, decorative arts worldwide, history of science, technology, natural history and geology, poetry. TITLES *Qianlong, A Great Emperor from the Forbidden City; Renaissance Decorative Painting in Scotland; Minerals of Scotland; William Spiers Bruce, Scottish Naturalist and Polar Explorer; Twa Tribes, Scots Among the Native Americans; Audubon in Edinburgh*. No unsolicited mss; only interested in synopses and ideas for books which are genuinely related to NMS collections and to Scotland in general.

ROYALTIES twice-yearly.

No Exit Press
See **Oldcastle Books Ltd**

North Holland
See **Elsevier Ltd**

Northcote House Publishers Ltd
Horndon House, Horndon, Tavistock PL19 9NQ
☎01822 810066 Fax 01822 810034
✉ northcote.house@virgin.net
www.northcotehouse.com

Managing Director *Brian Hulme*

Founded 1985. Publishes a series of literary critical studies, in association with the British Council, *Writers and their Work*; education management, literary criticism, educational dance and drama. A new series of study aids for A-level students and undergraduates in English literature is in preparation. 20 titles in 2003. 'Well-thought-out proposals, including contents and sample chapter(s), with strong marketing arguments welcome.'

ROYALTIES annually.

W.W. Norton & Company Ltd
Castle House, 75–76 Wells Street, London W1T 3QT
☎020 7323 1579 Fax 020 7436 4553
✉ office@wwnorton.co.uk

Managing Director *Alan Cameron*

Subsidiary of the US parent company founded in 1923. Publishes non-fiction and academic books.

Nottingham University Press
Manor Farm, Main Street, Thrumpton NG11 0AX
☎0115 983 1011 Fax 0115 983 1003
✉ editor@nup.com
www.nup.com

Managing Editor *Dr D.J.A. Cole*

Initially concentrated on agricultural and food sciences titles but has now branched into new areas including engineering, lifesciences, medicine and law. TITLES *Global 2050; Lung Function Tests; Diet, Lipoproteins and Coronary Heart Disease; Nutrition of Sows and Boars; Writing and Presenting Scientific Papers.* **Castle Publications** TITLES *The Cricket Coach's Guide to Man Management; The Games Guide.*

ROYALTIES twice-yearly.

NWP
See **Neil Wilson Publishing Ltd**

O Books
See **John Hunt Publishing Ltd**

Oak
See **Omnibus Press**

Oberon Books
521 Caledonian Road, London N7 9RH
☎020 7607 3637 Fax 020 7607 3629
✉ oberon.books@btinternet.com
www.oberonbooks.com

Publishing Director *James Hogan*
Managing Director *Charles D. Glanville*
Editor *Stephen Watson*

A leading theatre publisher, Oberon publishes play texts (usually in conjunction with a production), and books on theatre and dance. Specialises in contemporary plays and translations of European classics. IMPRINTS **Oberon Modern Plays**; **Oberon Classics**. Publishes for The National Theatre, The Royal Opera House, The Royal Court, The English Touring Theatre, LAMDA, The Gate Theatre, The Bush Theatre, The West Yorkshire Playhouse, The Chichester Festival Theatre, The Salisbury Playhouse and many other London and regional theatre companies. Publishes over 300 writers and translators including Rodney Ackland, Tariq Ali, Howard Barker, John Barton, Ranjit Bolt, Robert Bolt, Howard Brenton, Ken Campbell, Pam Gems, Christopher Hampton, Bernard Kops, Adrian Mitchell, Sir John Mortimer. An extensive classics list includes performance (edited) versions of Shakespeare including *King Lear, A Midsummer Night's Dream; Romeo and Juliet* and *Twelfth Night*, as well as new translations of plays by Chekhov, Molière, Strindberg and others. About 80 titles a year.

Authors' Rating Now the publisher for the Royal Opera and the Royal Ballet, Oberon is aiming for the top slot in its chosen niche.

Octagon Press Ltd
PO Box 227, London N6 4EW
☎020 8348 9392 Fax 020 8341 5971
✉ octagon@schredds.demon.co.uk
www.octagonpress.com

Managing Director *George R. Schrager*
Approx. Annual Turnover £100,000

Founded 1972. Publishes philosophy, psychology, travel, Eastern religion, translations of Eastern classics and research monographs in series. 4–5 titles a year. Unsolicited material not accepted. Enquiries in writing only.
ROYALTIES annually.

Octopus Publishing Group
2–4 Heron Quays, London E14 4JP
☎020 7531 8400 Fax 020 7531 8650
www.octopus-publishing.co.uk

Chief Executive *Derek Freeman*
Approx. Annual Turnover £45 million
(Group)

Formed following a management buyout of Reed Consumer Books from Reed Elsevier plc in 1998. Bought by French publishers Hachette-Livre in 2001 and acquired Cassell Illustrated and the lists of Ward Lock and Blandford Press; also, Gaia Books acquired in March 2004.

Conran Octopus Fax 020 7531 8627 ✉ info-co@conran-octopus.co.uk www.conran-octopus.co.uk Managing Director *Jane Aspden* Quality illustrated lifestyle books, particularly interiors, design, cookery, gardening and crafts TITLES *The Essential House Book* Terence Conran; *Fork to Fork* Monty Don; *Passion for Seafood* Gordon Ramsay; *New Retail* Rasshied Din.

Hamlyn Octopus Fax 020 7531 8562 ✉ info-ho@hamlyn.co.uk www.hamlyn.co.uk Managing Director *Alison Goff* Popular non-fiction, particularly cookery, gardening, craft, sport, health, film and music TITLES *Larousse Gastronomique; Hamlyn All Colour Cookbook; Hamlyn Book of Gardening; Hamlyn Book of DIY & Decorating.*

Mitchell Beazley/Miller's Fax 020 7537 0773 ✉ info-mb@mitchell-beazley.co.uk www.mitchell-beazley.co.uk Publisher/Managing Director *Jane Aspden* Quality illustrated reference books, particularly food and wine, gardening, interior design and architecture, antiques, general reference TITLES *Hugh Johnson's Pocket Wine Book; The New Joy of Sex; Miller's Antiques and Collectibles Price Guides.*

Philip's Fax 020 7531 8460 ✉ george.philip@philips-maps.co.uk www.philips-maps.co.uk Managing Director *John Gaisford* World atlases, globes, astronomy, road atlases, encyclopaedias, thematic reference TITLES *Philip's Atlas of the World; Philip's Modern School Atlas; Philip's Guide to the Stars and Planets; Ordnance Survey Street Atlas.*

Bounty ✉ bountybooksinfo-bp@bountybooks.co.uk Fax 020 7531 8607 Managing Director *Alison Goff* Bargain and promotional books. New, repackaged and re-issued titles.

Cassell Illustrated Fax 020 731 8624 Publishing Director *Gabrielle Mander* Serious non-fiction covering a wide range of topics from history and cookery to fitness and art.

Digital Octopus Fax 020 7531 8650 Contact *Derek Freeman* Digitally-formatted titles.
Octopus TV Fax 020 7531 8650 Contact *Derek Freeman* Television programmes from Octopus publications.
Godsfield Press Fax 020 7531 8562 enquiries@godsfieldpress.com   Publisher/ Managing Director *Alison Goff* Mind body and spirit encompassing original psychology, health and gift books.
Gaia Books Publisher/Managing Director *Alison Goff* Mind body and spirit and natural/eco titles.
ROYALTIES twice-yearly/annually, according to contract in all divisions.

Oldcastle Books Ltd

PO Box 394, Harpenden AL5 1XJ
☎01582 761264 Fax 01582 761264
www.noexit.co.uk
www.pocketessentials.com
www.highstakes.co.uk

Managing Director *Ion Mills*

Founded 1985. Publishes crime/noir fiction, gambling non-fiction and 96pp mini-reference titles on film, ideas, history, music, etc. IMPRINTS **No Exit Press** TITLES *Villa Incognito* Tom Robbins; *In the Hand of Dante* Nick Tosches; **High Stakes** TITLES *Fast Company* Jon Bradshaw; *Betting to Win* Prof Leighton V. Williams; **Pocketessentials** TITLES *Alfred Hitchcock; Vampire Films; Conspiracy Theories. No unsolicited mss.* Send synopses and ideas.
ROYALTIES annually.

Michael O'Mara Books Ltd

9 Lion Yard, Tremadoc Road, London SW4 7NQ
☎020 7720 8643 Fax 020 7627 8953
✉ firstname.lastname@
    michaelomarabooks.com
www.mombooks.com

Chairman *Michael O'Mara*
Managing Director *Lesley O'Mara*
Editorial Director (Commissioning) *Lindsay Davies*

Approx. Annual Turnover £5 million

Founded 1985. Independent publisher. Publishes general non-fiction, royalty, history, humour, children's novelties, anthologies and reference. TITLES *Diana: Her True Story* Andrew Morton; *Ozzy: Unauthorized* Sue Crawford; the 'Little Book' series, including *WAN2TLK?* IMPRINT **Buster Books** Children's titles. Unsolicited mss, synopses and ideas for books welcome.
ROYALTIES twice-yearly.

Authors' Rating With 16 titles among the year's top 5000 selling books, O'Mara is one of the leading small publishers with a knack for spotting market trends.

Omnibus Press

Music Sales Ltd, 8–9 Frith Street, London W1D 3JB
☎020 7434 0066 Fax 020 7734 2246
✉ chris.charlesworth@musicsales.co.uk
www.omnibuspress.com

Editorial Head *Chris Charlesworth*

Founded 1971. Independent publisher of music books, rock and pop biographies, song sheets, educational tutors, cassettes, videos and software. A Division of the Music Sales Group of Companies. IMPRINTS **Amsco; Bobcat; Oak; Omnibus; Wise Publications.** Unsolicited mss, synopses and ideas for music-related titles welcome.
ROYALTIES twice-yearly.

Oneworld Publications

185 Banbury Road, Oxford OX2 7AR
☎01865 310597 Fax 01865 310598
✉ info@oneworld-publications.com
www.oneworld-publications.com

Editorial Director *Juliet Mabey*

Founded 1986. Publishes adult non-fiction across a range of subjects from world religions to psychology and philosophy and popular science. SERIES include one on world religions (with authors such as Geoffrey Parrinder, Keith Ward, Klaus Klostermaier and John Hick), concise encyclopedias on world religions and a series of short histories of countries. **Oneworld Philosophers** series was launched in 2001. TITLES *God: A Guide for the Perplexed* Keith Ward; *Palestine – Israeli Conflict: A Beginner's Guide.* About 30 titles a year. No unsolicited mss; synopses and ideas welcome, but should be accompanied by s.a.e. for return of material and/or notification of receipt. No autobiographies, fiction, poetry or children's.
ROYALTIES annually.

Onlywomen Press Ltd

40 St Lawrence Terrace, London W10 5ST
☎020 8354 0796 Fax 020 8960 2817
✉ onlywomenpress@aol.com
www.onlywomenpress.com

Editorial Director *Lilian Mohin*

Founded 1974. Publishes feminist lesbian literature: fiction, poetry, literary criticism and political theory. Unsolicited mss and proposals welcome. Submissions must be accompanied by s.a.e. and explanatory letter.

OPC
See **Ian Allan Publishing Ltd**

Open Gate Press (incorporating Centaur Press 1954)
51 Achilles Road, London NW6 1DZ
☎020 7431 4391 Fax 020 7431 5129
✉ books@opengatepress.co.uk

Managing Directors *Jeannie Cohen, Elisabeth Petersdorff*

Founded in 1989 to provide a forum for psychoanalytic social and cultural studies. Publishes psychoanalysis, philosophy, social sciences, politics, literature, religion, animal rights, environment. SERIES *Psychoanalysis and Society*. Also publishes a journal of psychoanalytic social studies, *New Analysis*. IMPRINTS **Open Gate Press**; **Centaur Press**; **Linden Press**. Since the acquisition of Centaur Press, Open Gate Press is continuing its work, in particular the *Kinship Library* – a series on the philosophy, politics and application of humane education. No unsolicited mss.
ROYALTIES twice-yearly.

Open University Press
McGraw-Hill House, Shoppenhangers Road, Maidenhead SL6 2QL
☎01628 502500 Fax 01628 770224
✉ enquiries@openup.co.uk
www.openup.co.uk

Managing Director *Simon Allen*

Founded 1977 as an imprint independent of the Open University's course materials. Acquired by **McGraw Hill Education** in 2002. Publishes academic and professional books in the fields of education, sociology, health, psychology, women's studies, counselling, Higher Education. No economics or anthropology. Not interested in anything outside the social sciences. About 100 titles a year. No unsolicited mss; enquiries/proposals only.
ROYALTIES annually.

Orbit
See **Time Warner Books UK**

Orchard Books
See **The Watts Publishing Group Ltd**

The Orion Publishing Group Limited
Orion House, 5 Upper St Martin's Lane, London WC2H 9EA
☎020 7240 3444 Fax 020 7240 4822
www.orionbooks.co.uk/pub/index.htm

Chairman *Arnaud Nourry*
Chief Executive *Peter Roche*
Deputy Chief Executive *Malcolm Edwards*
Approx. Annual Turnover £70 million

Founded 1992 by Anthony Cheetham, Rosemary Cheetham and Peter Roche. Incorporates Weidenfeld & Nicolson, JM Dent, Chapmans Publishers and Cassell.

DIVISIONS
Orion Managing Director *Malcolm Edwards* IMPRINTS **Orion Fiction** Publishing Director *Jane Wood* Hardcover fiction; **Orion Media** Publishing Director *Alan Samson* Hardcover non-fiction; **Orion Children's** Publisher *Fiona Kennedy* Children's fiction/non-fiction; **Gollancz** Editorial Directors *Simon Spanton, Jo Fletcher* Science fiction and fantasy.

Weidenfeld & Nicolson Managing Director *Adrian Bourne* IMPRINTS **Weidenfeld Illustrated** Editor-in-Chief *Michael Dover* Illustrated non-fiction; **Weidenfeld General** Publishing Director *Richard Milner* General non-fiction and literary fiction; **Phoenix Press** Publishing Director *Ben Buchan* History; **Cassell Reference** Publishing Director *Richard Milbank* General reference; **Cassell Military** Publishing Director *Ian Drury* Military non-fiction; **Custom Publishing** Managing Director *Mark Smith*.

Paperback Division Managing Director *Susan Lamb* IMPRINTS **Orion**; **Phoenix**; **Everyman**.

Authors' Rating Strong marketing and imaginative publishing with fiction and children's books doing particularly well.

Osprey Publishing Ltd
Elms Court, Chapel Way, Botley, Oxford OX2 9LP
☎01865 727022 Fax 01865 727017/727019
✉ info@ospreypublishing.com
www.ospreypublishing.com

Managing Director *William Shepherd*
Editor, Military History *Rebecca Cullen*
Editor, Aviation *Tony Holmes*

Publishes illustrated, military history and aviation from around the world as well as some general publishing. Founded 1969, Osprey became independent from **Reed Elsevier** in February 1998. MILITARY SERIES *Men-at-Arms*; *New Vanguard*; *Warrior*; *Fortress*; *Essential Histories*; *Elite*; *Campaign*; *Osprey Modelling*. AVIATION SERIES *Aircraft of the Aces*; *Combat Aircraft*; *Aviation Pioneers*; *Aviation Elite Units*. About 150 titles a year. No unsolicited mss; synopses and ideas welcome.

ROYALTIES twice-yearly.

Peter Owen Ltd
73 Kenway Road, London SW5 0RE
☎020 7373 5628/7370 6093
Fax 020 7373 6760
✉ admin@peterowen.com
www.peterowen.com

Chairman *Peter Owen*
Editorial Director *Antonia Owen*

Founded 1951. Publishes biography, general non-fiction, English-language literary fiction and translations, history, literary criticism, the arts. 'No genre or children's fiction; the company only rarely takes on first novels.' AUTHORS Jane Bowles, Paul Bowles, Yuri Druzhnikov, Shusaku Endo, Anna Kavan, Jean Giono, Anaïs Nin, Jeremy Reed, Stevie Smith. 35–40 titles a year. Unsolicited synopses welcome for non-fiction material; no highly illustrated books. Please call in advance to admit fiction. Mss should be preceded by a descriptive letter and synopsis with s.a.e. OVERSEAS ASSOCIATES worldwide.

ROYALTIES twice-yearly.

Authors' Rating Peter Owen has been described as 'a publisher of the old and idiosyncratic school'. He has seven Nobel prizewinners on his list to prove it.

Oxbow Books
Park End Place OX1 1HN
☎01865 241249   Fax 01865 794449
✉ editorial@oxbowbooks.com
www.oxbowbooks.com

Editorial Director *David Brown*

Founded 1983. Publishes academic archaeology, Egyptology, ancient and medieval history. IMPRINT **Aris & Phillips** Greek, Latin and Hispanic texts and translations. About 40 titles a year.

Oxford University Press
Great Clarendon Street, Oxford OX2 6DP
☎01865 556767   Fax 01865 556646
✉ enquiry@oup.com
www.oup.com

Chief Executive *Henry Reece*
Approx. Annual Turnover £392 million

A department of Oxford University, OUP started as the university's printing business and developed into a major publishing operation in the 19th century. Publishes academic works in all formats (print and online): dictionaries, lexical and non-lexical reference, scholarly journals, student texts, schoolbooks, ELT materials, music, bibles, paperbacks, and children's books. Around 6000 titles a year.

DIVISIONS

Academic *T.M. Barton* Academic and higher education titles in major disciplines, dictionaries (acquired *The Grove Dictionary of Music* in 2003), non-lexical reference, journals and trade books. OUP welcomes first-class academic material in the form of proposals or accepted theses.

Education *K. Harris* National Curriculum courses and support materials as well as children's literature.

ELT *P.R.C. Marshall* ELT courses and dictionaries for all levels.

OVERSEAS BRANCHES/SUBSIDIARIES Sister company in USA with branches or subsidiaries in Argentina, Australia, Brazil, Canada, China, East Africa, India, Japan, Malaysia, Mexico, Pakistan, Southern Africa, Spain and Turkey. Offices in France, Greece, Italy, Poland, Taiwan, Thailand.

ROYALTIES twice-yearly.

Authors' Rating Increased investment in new publishing includes the *New Dictionary of National Biography*, one of the biggest projects of its kind in contemporary publishing and, latterly, the *Grove Dictionary of Music* and the *Grove Dictionary of Art*, bought from Macmillan. Following the acquisition of Blackstone Press, OUP now rivals Butterworths and Sweet & Maxwell as a leading law book publisher.

Palgrave Macmillan
See **Macmillan Publishers Ltd**

Palm Tree Press
See **Kevin Mayhew Publishers**

G.J. Palmer & Sons Ltd
See **Hymns Ancient & Modern Ltd**

Pan
See **Macmillan Publishers Ltd**

Paper Tiger
See **Chrysalis Books Group**

Paragon Large Print
See **BBC Audiobooks** under *Audio Books*

Parthian
The Old Surgery, Napier Street, Aberteifi (Cardigan) SA43 1ED
☎01239 612059   Fax 01239 612059
✉ parthianbooks@yahoo.co.uk

www.parthianbooks.co.uk
Publisher *Richard Davies*
Fiction Editor *Gwen Davies*
Poetry Editor *Richard Gwyn*

Founded 1993. Publishes contemporary Welsh writing in English including novels, poetry and drama, also translations from Welsh. Its list includes many young writers. TITLES *In and Out of the Goldfish Bowl* Rachel Trezise (Winner of the Orange Futures Award); *bbboing! & Associated Weirdness* Lloyd Robson; *Work, Sex and Rugby* Lewis Davies (World Book Day 'We Are What We Read' Award); *Welsh Boys Too* John Sam Jones (Winner of the American Library Association Gay and Lesbian Honor Book Award); *The Pterodactyl's Wing* (poetry anthology) ed. Richard Gwyn. Synopsis with first three sample chapters welcome. 'An idea of what we do is always an advantage.'
ROYALTIES annually.

Paternoster Press
See **Authentic Media**

Pavilion Books
See **Chrysalis Books Group**

Pearson Education
Edinburgh Gate, Harlow CM20 2JE
☎01279 623623 Fax 01279 431059
www.pearsoned.com

The world's largest educational publisher was created by the merger of Addison Wesley Longman, Financial Times Management and **Simon & Schuster**'s educational list. Publishes across a wide range of curriculum subjects from primary students to professional practictioners. OVERSEAS ASSOCIATES worldwide. Unsolicited mss should be addressed to the appropriate department: **ELT** *Sue Parker;* **Schools** *Carol Hayward;* **University and Professional Level** *Lisa Reading.*
ROYALTIES twice-yearly.

Pegasus Elliot Mackenzie Publishers Ltd
Sheraton House, Castle Park, Cambridge CB3 0AX
☎01223 370012 Fax 01223 370040
✉ editors@pegasuspublishers.com
www.pegasuspublishers.com
Senior Editor *D.W. Stern*
Editor *R. Sabir*

Publishes fiction and non-fiction, general interest, biography, autobiography, children's, history, humour, science fiction, poetry, travel, war, memoirs, crime and erotica, also Internet and e-books. IMPRINTS **Vanguard Press**; **Nightingale Books**; **Chimera** TITLES *Family Bites* Lisa Williams; *Bullying – What Have I Ever Done to You?* Robert Higgs; *Breaking Up* Malcolm McKay. Unsolicited mss, synopses and ideas considered if accompanied by return postage.
ROYALTIES twice-yearly.

Authors' Rating Liable to ask authors to contribute to production costs.

Pen & Sword Books Ltd
47 Church Street, Barnsley S70 2AS
☎01226 734734 Fax 01226 734438
✉ charles@pen-and-sword.co.uk
www.pen-and-sword.co.uk
Managing Director *Charles Hewitt*
Imprint Manager *Henry Wilson*

One of the leading military history publishers in the UK. Publishes non-fiction only, specialising in naval and aviation history, WW1, WW2, Napoleonic, autobiography and biography. Also publishes *Battleground* series for battlefield tourists. IMPRINTS **Leo Cooper**; **Pen & Sword Aviation**; **Pen & Sword Maritime**; **Wharncliffe Books** (see entry). About 100 titles a year. Unsolicited synopses and ideas welcome; no unsolicited mss.
ROYALTIES twice-yearly.

Penguin Group (UK)
A Pearson Company, 80 Strand, London WC2R 0RL
☎020 7010 3000 Fax 020 7010 6060
www.penguin.co.uk
Group Chairman & Chief Executive *John Makinson*
CEO: Penguin UK, Dorling Kindersley Ltd *Anthony Forbes Watson*
Managing Director: Penguin *Helen Fraser*
Approx. Annual Turnover £121 million

Owned by Pearson plc. The world's best known book brand and for more than 60 years a leading publisher whose adult and children's lists include fiction, non-fiction, poetry, drama, classics, reference and special interest areas. Reprints and new work.

DIVISIONS
Penguin General Books Managing Director *Tom Weldon* Adult fiction and non-fiction is published in hardback under Michael Joseph, Viking and Hamish Hamilton imprints. Paperbacks come under the Penguin imprint.

IMPRINTS **Viking/Penguin** Publisher *Juliet Annan* Publishing Director *Tony Lacey*; **Hamish Hamilton** Publishing Director *Simon Prosser*; **Michael Joseph/Penguin** Publishing Director *Louise Moore* Does not accept unsolicited mss.

Penguin Press Managing Director *Stefan McGrath* Publishing Directors *Stuart Proffitt, Simon Winder* Academic adult non-fiction, reference, specialist and classics. IMPRINTS **Allen Lane**; **Penguin Reference** Publishing Director *Nigel Wilcockson* No unsolicited mss.

Dorling Kindersley Ltd (see entry).

Frederick Warne Managing Director *Sally Floyer* Classic children's publishing and merchandising including *Beatrix Potter*(tm); *Flower Fairies*; *Orlando*. **Ventura** Publisher *Sally Floyer* Producer and packager of *Spot* titles by Eric Hill.

Ladybird (see **Dorling Kindersley Ltd**).

BBC Children's Books *Sally Floyer* New imprint launched in 2004.

Puffin Managing Director *Francesca Dow* (poetry and picture books) Publishers *Rebecca McNally* (fiction), *To be appointed* (media and popular non-fiction) Leading children's paperback list, publishing in virtually all fields including fiction, non-fiction, poetry, picture books, media-related titles. No unsolicited mss; synopses and ideas welcome.

Penguin Audiobooks (see entry under *Audio Books*).

ePenguin Commissioning Editor *Jeremy Ettinghausen* e-books list launched in 2001. OVERSEAS ASSOCIATES worldwide.

ROYALTIES twice-yearly.

Authors' Rating One of the world's biggest trade book publishers with an enviable list of bestsellers, Penguin has now set up a television division to create programmes linked to literary output. Some two-thirds of Penguin revenue derives from the US.

Peony Press
See **Anness Publishing Ltd**

Pergamon
See **Elsevier Ltd**

Persephone Books
59 Lamb's Conduit Street, London WC1N 3NB
☎020 7242 9292 Fax 020 7242 9272
✉ sales@persephonebooks.co.uk
www.persephonebooks.co.uk

Managing Director *Nicola Beauman*

Founded 1999. Publishes reprint fiction and non-fiction, mostly 'by women, for women and about women'. TITLES *Miss Pettigrew Lives for a Day* Winifred Watson; *Kitchen Essays* Agnes Jekyll; *The Far Cry* Emma Smith; *The Priory* Dorothy Whipple. 8 titles a year. No unsolicited material.

ROYALTIES twice-yearly.

Petroc Press
See **Librapharm Ltd**

Phaidon Press Limited
Regent's Wharf, All Saints Street, London N1 9PA
☎020 7843 1000 Fax 020 7843 1010
✉ name@phaidon.com
www.phaidon.com

Chairman/Publisher *Richard Schlagman*
Managing Director *Andrew Price*
Deputy Publisher *Amanda Renshaw*
Editorial Director (New York) *Karen Stein*
Approx. Annual Turnover £20 million

Publishes quality books on the visual arts, including fine art, art history, architecture, design, photography, decorative arts, music and performing arts. Also produces videos. DIVISIONS/SERIES (with Editorial Heads) **Architecture and Design** *Emilia Terragni*; **Contemporary Art** *Gilda Williams*; **Photography** *Noel Daniel*; **Art and Academic** *Bernard Dod/David Anfan*. About 100 titles a year. Unsolicited mss welcome but 'only a small amount of unsolicited material gets published'.

ROYALTIES twice-yearly.

Authors' Rating Ah, those seductive art books. The quality of illustrations is superb and since language is a minor barrier to sales, Phaidon is doing well with subsidiaries in France and Germany.

Philip's
See **Octopus Publishing Group**

Phillimore & Co. Ltd
Shopwyke Manor Barn, Chichester PO20 2BG
☎01243 787636 Fax 01243 787639
✉ bookshop@phillimore.co.uk
www.phillimore.co.uk

Chairman *Philip Harris*
Managing Director *Noel Osborne*
Approx. Annual Turnover £1.3 million

Founded in 1897 by W.P.W. Phillimore, Victorian campaigner for local archive conservation in Chancery Lane, London. Became the country's leading publisher of historical source material and local histories. Somewhat dormant in the 1960s, it was revived by Philip Harris in 1968. Publishes British local and family history, including histories of institutions, buildings, villages, towns and counties, plus guides to research and writing in these fields. IMPRINT **Phillimore** *Noel Osborne* TITLES *Domesday Book; Channel Island Churches; Bolton Past; Warwickshire Country Houses; The Haberdashers' Company.* About 70 titles a year. No unsolicited mss; synopses/ideas welcome for local or family histories.

ROYALTIES annually.

Phoenix Press
See **The Orion Publishing Group Ltd**

Photographers' Institute Press (PIP)
See **Guild of Master Craftsman Publications Ltd**

Piatkus Books
5 Windmill Street, London W1T 2JA
☎020 7631 0710   Fax 020 7436 7137
✉ info@piatkus.co.uk
www.piatkus.co.uk
Managing Director *Judy Piatkus*
Approx. Annual Turnover £5.8 million

Founded 1979 by Judy Piatkus. The company is customer-led and is committed to publishing fiction, both commercial and literary, and a wide range of non-fiction. Specialises in publishing books and authors 'who we feel enthusiastic and committed to as we like to build for long-term success as well as short-term!' Publishes fiction, biography and autobiography, history, popular culture, health, mind, body and spirit, popular psychology, self-help, history, science, business and management, cookery 'and other books that tempt us'. In 1996 launched a list of mass-market non-fiction and fiction titles. IMPRINT **Portrait** Non-fiction general books TITLES *Moving on* Simon Weston; *Life and Limb* Jamie Andrews; *Rod Stewart* Tim Ewbank and Stafford Hildred. DIVISIONS **Non-fiction** *Judy Piatkus* TITLES *Optimum Nutrition for the Mind* Patrick Holford; *One Last Time* John Edwards; *10 Day MBA* Steven Silbiger; *How to Make Money from Your Property* Fiona Fullerton. **Fiction** *Gillian Green* TITLES *Birthright* Nora Roberts; *Cry No More* Linda Howard; *The Third Child* Marge Piercy; *Tricky Business* Dave Barry; *No Escape* Hilary Norman. About 150 titles a year (70 of which are fiction). Piatkus is expanding its range of books and welcomes synopses and first three chapters.

ROYALTIES twice-yearly.

Authors' Rating A thriving independent publisher takes another leap forward with Portrait, a new non-fiction list for 'popular culture, history, memoirs and sport'. Also strong on women's fiction.

Pica Press
See **A.&C. Black Publishers Ltd**

Picador/Young Picador
See **Macmillan Publishers Ltd**

Piccadilly Press
5 Castle Road, London NW1 8PR
☎020 7267 4492   Fax 020 7267 4493
✉ books@piccadillypress.co.uk
www.piccadillypress.co.uk
Publisher/Managing Director *Brenda Gardner*
Approx. Annual Turnover £1.4 million

Founded 1983. Independent publisher of children's and parental books. 28 titles in 2003. Welcomes approaches from authors 'but we would like them to know the sort of books we do. It is frustrating to get inappropriate material. They should check in their local libraries, bookshops or look at our website. We will send a catalogue (please enclose s.a.e.).' No adult or cartoon-type material.

ROYALTIES twice-yearly.

Pictorial Presentations
See **Souvenir Press Ltd**

Pimlico
See **The Random House Group Ltd**

Pinwheel Limited
Winchester House, 259–269 Old Marylebone Road, London NW1 5XJ
☎020 7616 7200   Fax 020 7616 7201
Managing Director *Andrew Flatt*

Children's non-fiction, picture books and novelty titles. IMPRINTS **Andromeda Children's Books** Publishing/Creative Director *Linda Cole* Illustrated non-fiction for children from 3–12 years; **Gullane Children's Books** Creative Director *Paula Burgess* Picture books for children from 0–8 years; **Pinwheel Children's Books** Publishing/Creative Director *Linda Cole* Cloth and novelty books for children from 0–5 years. Unsolicited mss will not be returned.

Pitkin
See **Jarrold Publishing**

Plenum Publishers/Plenum Press
See **Kluwer Academic/Plenum Publishers**

Pluto Press Ltd
345 Archway Road, London N6 5AA
☎020 8348 2724 Fax 020 8348 9133
✉ pluto@plutobooks.com
www.plutobooks.com

Managing Director *Roger Van Zwanenberg*
Publishing Director *Anne Beech*

Founded 1970. Has developed a reputation for innovatory publishing in the field of non-fiction. Publishes academic and scholarly books across a range of subjects including cultural studies, politics and world affairs and more general titles on key aspects of currrent affairs. About 80 titles a year. Prospective authors are encouraged to consult the website for guidelines on submitting proposals.

Pocket Books
See **Simon & Schuster UK Limited**

Pocketessentials
See **Oldcastle Books Ltd**

Point
See **Scholastic Ltd**

The Policy Press
Fourth Floor, Beacon House, Queen's Road, Bristol BS8 1QU
☎0117 331 4054 Fax 0117 331 4093
✉ tpp-info@bristol.ac.uk
www.policypress.org.uk

Managing Director *Alison Shaw*

Publishes social welfare and policy work for students, academics, practitioners, professionals and policy-makers.

Politico's Publishing
215 Vauxhall Bridge Road, London SW1V 1EJ
☎020 7798 1600 Fax 020 7828 2098
✉ publishing@politicos.co.uk
www.politicos.co.uk/publishing

Chairman/Managing Director *Peter Tummons*
Publishing Director *Sean Magee*
Approx. Annual Turnover £325,000

Founded 1998. Acquired by **Methuen Publishing Ltd** in April 2003. Publishes political books. TITLES *In My Own Time* Jeremy Thorpe; *Cherie Blair* Linda McDougall; *Brief Encounters* Gyles Brandreth. 30 titles in 2003.

Unsolicited mss, synopses and ideas welcome; telephone in the first instance.
ROYALTIES annually.

Polity Press
65 Bridge Street, Cambridge CB2 1UR
☎01223 324315 Fax 01223 461385
www.polity.co.uk

Founded 1984. Publishes archaeology and anthropology, criminology, economics, feminism, general interest, history, human geography, literature, media and cultural studies, medicine and society, philosophy, politics, psychology, religion and theology, social and political theory, sociology. Unsolicited synopses and ideas for books welcome.
ROYALTIES annually.

Polygon
West Newington House, 10 Newington Road, Edinburgh EH9 1QS
☎0131 668 4371 Fax 0131 668 4466
✉ info@birlinn.co.uk
www.birlinn.co.uk

Managing Director *Hugh Andrew*

Bought by **Birlinn Ltd** in 2002. Publishes literary fiction and poetry. About 10–15 titles a year. Unsolicited mss, synopses and ideas welcome.

Pont Books
See **Gomer Press**

Pop Universal
See **Souvenir Press Ltd**

Portland Press Ltd
59 Portland Place, London W1B 1QW
☎020 7637 5873 Fax 020 7323 1136
✉ editorial@portlandpress.com
www.portlandpress.com

Chairman *Professor A.J. Turner*
Managing Director *Rhonda Oliver*
Managing Editor *Pauline Starley*
Approx. Annual Turnover £2.5 million

Founded 1990 to expand the publishing activities of the Biochemical Society (1911). Publishes biochemisty and medicine for graduate, postgraduate and research students. Expanding the list to include schools and general readership. TITLES *Programmed Cell Death*; *Proteases and the Regulation of Biological Processes*; *Excellence in Higher Education*. 4 titles in 2003. Unsolicited mss, synopses and ideas welcome. No fiction.
ROYALTIES twice-yearly.

Portrait
See **Piatkus Books**

T&AD Poyser
See **A.&C. Black Publishers Ltd**

Prestel Publishing Limited
4 Bloomsbury Place, London WC1A 2QA
☎020 7323 5004 Fax 020 7636 8004
✉ sales@prestel-uk.co.uk
www.prestel.com

Chairman *Jürgen Tesch*

Founded 1924. Publishes art, architecture, photography, children's and general illustrated books. No fiction. Unsolicited mss, synopses and ideas welcome. Approach by post or e-mail.

Princeton University Press
See **University Presses of California, Columbia & Princeton Ltd**

Prion Books
See **Carlton Publishing Group**

Profile Books
58A Hatton Gardens, London EC1N 8LX
☎020 7404 3001 Fax 020 7404 3003
✉ info@profilebooks.co.uk
www.profilebooks.co.uk

Managing Director *Andrew Franklin*
Approx. Annual Turnover £4 million

Founded 1996. Publishes interesting non-fiction including current affairs, history, politics, psychology, cultural criticism, business management and economics. Winner of the **Sunday Times Small Publisher of the Year Award** 1999/2000 and published the No.1 Christmas 2003 bestseller, *Eats, Shoots and Leaves* by Lynne Truss. AUTHORS include Alan Bennett, J.M. Coetzee, Francis Fukuyama and Peter Nichols. IMPRINTS **Profile Books** *Andrew Franklin*; **Economist Books** *Stephen Brough*. No unsolicited mss.
ROYALTIES twice-yearly.

Authors' Rating Named 'Small Publisher of the Year' in the British Book Awards, Profile has had its just reward with Lynne Truss' super-seller, *Eats, Shoots and Leaves*. Noted for author-friendly relations.

ProQuest Information and Learning Ltd
The Quorum, Barnwell Road, Cambridge CB5 8SW

☎01223 215512 Fax 01223 215513
www.proquest.co.uk

General Manager *Steven Hall*

Part of US company, ProQuest Information and Learning, the new name for Bell & Howell. Publishes humanities and literary databases on the Web, CD-ROM and microform. IMPRINT **Chadwyck-Healey** TITLES *KnowUK*; *Literature Online*; *The English Poetry Database*; *Periodicals Contents Index*; *KnowEurope*. No unsolicited mss. Synopses and ideas welcome for reference works only.
ROYALTIES annually.

Psychology Press
See **Taylor & Francis Group plc**

Publishing House
Trinity Place, Barnstaple EX32 9HJ
☎01271 328892 Fax 01271 328768
✉ publishinghouse@vernoncoleman.com
www.vernoncoleman.com

Managing Director *Vernon Coleman*
Publishing Director *Sue Ward*
Approx. Annual Turnover £750,000

Founded 1989. Self-publisher of fiction, health, humour, animals, politics. Over 90 books published. TITLES *Mrs Caldicot's Cabbage War*; *England our England*; *Bodypower*; *Bilbury Chronicles*; *Second Innings*; *It's Never Too Late*; *How to Publish Your Own Book*; *Alice's Diary*; *Rogue Nation*; *Food for Thought*, all by Vernon Coleman. No submissions.

Puffin
See **Penguin Group (UK)**

Pushkin Press Ltd
12 Chester Terrace, London NW1 4ND
☎020 7266 9136 Fax 01474 533424
✉ sasha@pushkinpress.com
www.pushkinpress.com

Chairman *Melissa Ulfane*
Editorial Head *Sasha Lillie*
Approx. Annual Turnover £250,000

Publishes novels and essays in translation drawn from the best of classic and contemporary European literature.
ROYALTIES twice-yearly.

Authors' Rating English language writers who are short on ideas might do worse than raid this select list of translated European works for something fresh to say. A bold and imaginative venture.

Putnam Aeronautical Books
See **Chrysalis Books Group**

Quadrille Publishing Ltd
Alhambra House, 27–31 Charing Cross Road,
London WC2H 0LS
☎020 7839 7117 Fax 020 7839 7118

Chairman *Sir David Cooksey*
Managing Director *Alison Cathie*
Editorial Director *Jane O'Shea*

Founded in 1994 by four ex-directors of
Conran Octopus, with a view to producing a
small list of top-quality illustrated books.
Publishes non-fiction, including cookery, gardening, interior design and decoration, craft,
health. TITLES *Trisha Guild's Passions*; *Indian
Essence* Atul Kochhar; *Fat Girl Slim* Ruth
Watson. 44 titles in 2004. Synopses and ideas
for books welcome. No fiction or children's
books.
ROYALTIES twice-yearly.

Quantum
See **Foulsham Publishers**

Quartet Books
27 Goodge Street, London W1T 2LD
☎020 7636 3992 Fax 020 7637 1866

Chairman *Naim Attallah*
Managing Director *Jeremy Beale*
Publishing Director *Stella Kane*

Founded 1972. Independent publisher. Publishes contemporary literary fiction including
translations, popular culture, biography, music,
history, politics and some photographic books.
Unsolicited sample chapters with return
postage welcome; no poetry, romance or science fiction. Submissions by disk or e-mail are
not accepted.
ROYALTIES twice-yearly.

Queen Anne Press
See **Lennard Associates Ltd**

Quiller Press
(An imprint of Quiller Publishing Ltd),
Wykey House, Wykey, Shrewsbury SY4 1JA
☎01939 261616 Fax 01939 261606
✉ info@quillerbooks.com

Managing Director *Andrew Johnston*

Specialises in sponsored books and publications
sold through non-book trade channels as well
as bookshops. Publishes architecture, biography, business and industry, collecting, cookery,
DIY, gardening, guidebooks, humour, refer-

ence, sports, travel, wine and spirits. TITLES
Camper and Nicholson Ian Dear; *Great British
Food* Heather Hay Ffrench; *The Dunlop
Slazenger Story* Brian Simpson. IMPRINT **The
Sportsman's Press** (see entry). About 10 titles
a year. Most ideas originate in-house; unso-
licited mss only if the author sees some poten-
tial for sponsorship or guaranteed sales.
ROYALTIES twice-yearly.

Radcliffe Medical Press Ltd
18 Marcham Road, Abingdon OX14 1AA
☎01235 528820 Fax 01235 528830
✉ contact.us@radcliffemed.com
www.radcliffe-oxford.com

Managing Director *Andrew Bax*
Editorial Director *Gillian Nineham*
Approx. Annual Turnover £1.5 million

Founded 1987. Medical publishers which
began by specialising in books for general practice and health service management. Publishes
clinical, management, health policy books,
training materials and CD-ROMs. 80 titles in
2003. Unsolicited mss, synopses and ideas welcome. No non-medical or medical books
aimed at lay audience.
ROYALTIES twice-yearly.

Radcliffe Press
See **I.B. Tauris & Co. Ltd**

The Ramsay Head Press
9 Glenisla Gardens, Edinburgh EH9 2HR
☎0131 662 1915
✉ conradkwilson@aol.com

Managing Director *Conrad Wilson*

Founded 1968 by Norman Wilson, OBE. A
small independent family publisher. Publishes
biography, cookery, Scottish fiction and non-
fiction, plus the literary magazine *InScotland*.
TITLES *When It Works It Feels Like Play* Tessa
Ransford; *Interesting Times, Poetry by David
Simpson*. About 3–4 titles a year. Synopses and
ideas for books of Scottish interest welcome.
ROYALTIES twice-yearly.

The Random House Group Ltd
Random House, 20 Vauxhall Bridge Road,
London SW1V 2SA
☎020 7840 8400 Fax 020 7233 6058
✉ enquiries@randomhouse.co.uk
www.randomhouse.co.uk

Chief Executive/Chairman *Gail Rebuck*
Deputy Chairman *Simon Master*
Managing Director *Ian Hudson*

The Random House Group is the UK's leading trade publisher comprising 31 diverse imprints in four separate substantially autonomous divisions: the Random House Division, Ebury Press, **Transworld** (see entry) and Random House Children's Books. Acquired The Harvill Press in 2002 and C.W. Daniel in March 2004.

RANDOM HOUSE DIVISION
IMPRINTS **Jonathan Cape Ltd** ☎020 7840 8576 Fax 020 7233 6117 Publishing Director *Dan Franklin* Biography and memoirs, current affairs, fiction, history, photography, poetry, politics and travel.

Yellow Jersey Press ☎020 7840 8637 Fax 020 7223 6117 Editorial Director *Tristan Jones* Narrative sports books.

Harvill Secker ☎020 7840 8649 Fax 020 7233 6117 Publishing Director *Geoff Mulligan* Principally literary fiction with some non-fiction. Literature in translation, English literature, quality thrillers.

Chatto & Windus ☎020 7840 8522 Fax 020 7233 6117 Publishing Director *Alison Samuel* Memoirs, current affairs, essays, literary fiction, history, poetry, politics, philosophy and translations. No unsolicited mss.

Pimlico ☎020 7840 8784 Fax 020 7233 6117 Publisher *Will Sulkin* Quality non-fiction paperbacks, specialising in history, biography, popular culture and the arts.

Vintage ☎020 7840 8573 Fax 020 7233 6117 Publisher *Rachel Cugnoni* Quality paperback fiction and non-fiction. Founded in 1990, Vintage has been described as one of the 'greatest literary success stories in recent British publishing'.

Century ☎020 7840 8554 Fax 020 7233 6127 Publishing Director *Mark Booth* General fiction and non-fiction including commercial fiction, autobiography, biography, history and self-help.

William Heinemann ☎020 7840 8400 Fax 020 7233 6127 Publishing Director *Ravi Mirchandani* General non-fiction and fiction, especially history, literary fiction, crime, science, thrillers and women's fiction.

Hutchinson ☎020 7840 8564 Fax 020 7233 7870 Publishing Director *Sue Freestone* General fiction and non-fiction including notably belles-lettres, current affairs, politics, travel and history.

Random House Business Books ☎020 7840 8550 Fax 020 7233 6127 Publisher *Clare Smith*.

Arrow ☎020 7840 8557 Fax 020 7840 6127 Publishing Director *Kate Elton* Mass-market paperback fiction and non-fiction.

EBURY PRESS DIVISION
☎020 7840 8400 Fax 020 7840 8406 Publisher *Fiona MacIntyre* IMPRINTS **Ebury Press**; **Vermilion**; **Rider**; **Fodors** Antiques, biography, Buddhism, cookery, gardening, health and beauty, homes and interiors, personal development, spirituality, travel and guides, sport, TV tie-ins.

RANDOM HOUSE CHILDREN'S BOOKS
(at Transworld Publishers, 61–63 Uxbridge Road, London W5 5SA ☎020 8231 6800 Fax 020 8231 6767) Managing Director *Philippa Dickinson* IMPRINTS **Hutchinson** Publishing Director *Caroline Roberts*; **Jonathan Cape**; **The Bodley Head**; **Doubleday Picture Books** Publisher *Penny Walker*; **David Fickling Books** Publishing Director *David Fickling*, Fiction Publisher *Annie Eaton*; **Corgi**; **Red Fox**. Unsolicited mss, synopses and ideas for books welcome.

ROYALTIES twice-yearly for the most part.

Authors' Rating Way out in front as the UK's leading trade publisher, Random has a reputation for promoting new talent. Author relations are good according to a Society of Authors' survey. Synopses and manuscripts may be passed on to freelance readers, but there is reasonable assurance that they are at least read.

Ransom Publishing Ltd
Rose Cottage, Howe Hill, Watlington
OX49 5HB
☎01491 613711 Fax 01491 613733
✉ jenny@ransom.co.uk
www.ransom.co.uk

Managing Director *Jenny Ertle*

Founded 1995 by ex-McGraw-Hill publisher. Partnerships formed with, among others, Channel 4 and the ICL. Publishes educational and consumer multimedia, study packs and children's books. TITLES include *The Early Learning* and *The Little Monsters* series; *Living Phonics*; *Rainbow Readers*. Over 40 CD-ROMs, most with educational support packs and 20 books. Unlikely to take new submissions this year though may consider storybooks and grammar books for primary education. Ransom is looking for banks of questions for primary and secondary geography and science.

Reader's Digest Association Ltd
11 Westferry Circus, Canary Wharf, London
E14 4HE
☎020 7715 8000 Fax 020 7715 8181

✉ gbeditorial@readersdigest.co.uk
www.readersdigest.co.uk

Managing Director *Andrew Lynam-Smith*
Editorial Head *Cortina Butler*

Editorial office in the USA (see entry under *US Publishers*). Publishes gardening, natural history, cookery, history, DIY, travel and word books. About 20 titles a year.

Reaktion Books

79 Farringdon Road, London EC1M 3JU
☎020 7404 9930 Fax 020 7404 9931
✉ info@reaktionbooks.co.uk
www.reaktionbooks.co.uk

Managing Director *Michael R. Leaman*

Founded in Edinburgh in 1985 and moved to London in 1987. Publishes art history, architecture, Asian studies, cultural studies, design, film, geography, history, photography and travel writing (*not* travel guides). TITLES *An Encyclopedia of Stupidity* Matthijs van Boxsel; *Forever Young: A Cultural History of Longevity* Lucian Boia; *Last Landscapes: the architecture of the cemetery in the West* Ken Worpole. About 30 titles a year.
ROYALTIES twice-yearly.

Reardon Publishing

56 Upper Norwood Street, Leckhampton, Cheltenham GL53 0DU
☎01242 231800
✉ reardon@bigfoot.com
www.reardon.co.uk
www.cotswoldbookshop.com

Managing Editor *Nicholas Reardon*

Founded in the mid-1970s. Family-run publishing house specialising in local interest and tourism in the Cotswold area. Member of the **Outdoor Writers Guild**. Publishes walking and driving guides, and family history for societies. TITLES *The Cotswold Way* (video); *The Cotswold Way Map*; *Cotswold Walkabout*; *Cotswold Driveabout*; *The Donnington Way*; *The Haunted Cotswolds*. Also distributes for other publishers such as Ordnance Survey. 10 titles a year. Unsolicited mss, synopses and ideas welcome with return postage only.
ROYALTIES twice-yearly.

Red Dress Ink

See **Harlequin Mills & Boon Ltd**

Red Fox

See **The Random House Group Ltd**

Red Hot Diva

See **Millivres Prowler Limited**

Thomas Reed

See **A.&C. Black Publishers Ltd**

William Reed Directories

Broadfield Park, Crawley RH11 9RT
☎01293 613400 Fax 01293 610322
✉ directories@william-reed.co.uk
www.william-reed.co.uk

Head of Content *Daniel Verrells*

William Reed Directories, a division of William Reed Publishing, was established in 1990. Its portfolio includes 13 titles covering the food, drink, non-food, catering, retail and export industries. The titles are produced as directories, market research reports, exhibition catalogues and electronic publishing.

Reed Elsevier Group plc

1–3 Strand, London WC2N 5JR
☎020 7930 7077
www.reedelsevier.com

Also at: 125 Park Avenue, 23rd Floor, New York, NY 10017, USA
☎001 212 309 5498 Fax 001 212 309 5480

Sara Burgerhartstraat 25, 1055 KV Amsterdam, The Netherlands ☎00 31 20 485 2434

Chief Executive Officer (UK) *Crispin Davis*

Reed Elsevier Group plc is a world-leading publisher and information provider, operating in four core segments: science and medical, legal, education, business. No trade books.

DIVISIONS **Harcourt Education** (see entry); **Elsevier** (see entry); **LexisNexis** (formerly Butterworths) Halsbury House, 35 Chancery Lane, London WC2A 1EL ☎020 7400 2500 Fax 020 7400 2842 Publishes legal and accountancy textbooks, journals, law reports, CD-ROMs and online services; **Harcourt School Publishers** (see entry under *US Publishers*); **Reed Business** Quadrant House, The Quadrant, Sutton SM2 5AS ☎020 8652 3500. No unsolicited material.

Regency House Publishing Limited

Niall House, 24–26 Boulton Road, Stevenage SG1 4QX
☎01438 314488 Fax 01438 311303
✉ regencyhouse@btclick.com

Chairman *Brian Trodd*
Managing Director *Nicolette Trodd*

Founded 1991. Publisher and packager of

mass-market non-fiction. No fiction. No unsolicited material.

Reinhardt Books Ltd
Flat 2, 43 Onslow Square, London SW7 3LR
☎020 7589 3751

Directors *Joan Reinhardt, Veronica Reinhardt*

Founded in 1887 as H.F.L. (Publishers), it was acquired by Max Reinhardt in 1947, changing its name to the present one in 1987. First publication under the new name was Graham Greene's *The Captain and the Enemy*.

Religious & Moral Educational Press (RMEP)
See **Hymns Ancient & Modern Ltd**

Research Disclosure
See **Kenneth Mason Publications Ltd**

Review
See **Hodder Headline Ltd**

Richmond House Publishing Company Ltd
70 – 76 Bell Street, Marylebone, London NW1 6SP
☎020 7224 9666 Fax 020 7224 9688
✉ sales@rhpco.co.uk
www.rhpco.co.uk

Managing Directors *Gloria Gordon, Spencer Block*

Publishes directories for the theatre and entertainment industries. TITLES *British Theatre Directory 2003*; *Artistes and Agents 2003*; *London Seating Plan Guide*. Synopses and ideas welcome.

Rider
See **The Random House Group Ltd**

Right Way/Right Way Plus
See **Elliot Right Way Books**

Robinson
See **Constable & Robinson Ltd**

Robson Books
See **Chrysalis Books Group**

RotoVision
Sheridan House, 112/116A Western Road, Hove BN3 1DD
☎01273 727268 Fax 01273 727269
www.rotovision.com

Managing Director *Ken Fund*

Publisher *Aidan Walker*

Founded 1996. Rapidly-expanding visual arts publishers with a strong emphasis on education and inspiration. Publishes graphic design, photography, web design, advertising, film, architecture, lighting design, interiors, product design, packaging design. TITLES *World's Top Photographers: Wildlife*; *What Is Graphic Design?*; *The Total Beauty of Sustainable Products*; *Materials for Inspirational Design: Plastic*; *The Designer and the Grid*; *Screencraft: Directing*; *Up Against the Wall: International Poster Design*; *Stretch: The Art of Panoramic Photography*. No unsolicited mss; written synopses and ideas welcome. No phone calls, please. No academic or fiction.
FLAT FEE paid.

Roundhouse Publishing Group
Millstone, Limers Lane, Northam EX39 2RG
☎01237 474474 Fax 01237 474774
✉ roundhouse.group@ukgateway.net

Editorial Head *Alan Goodworth*

Founded 1991. Publishes cinema and media-related titles. TITLES *The Bent Lens: A World Guide to Gay & Lesbian Films*; *Cinema of Oliver Stone*; *Cinema of Martin Scorsese*. Represents and distributes a broad range of non-fiction publishing houses throughout the UK and Europe. No unsolicited mss.
ROYALTIES twice-yearly.

Routledge (Imprint of **Taylor & Francis Group plc**)
11 New Fetter Lane, London EC4P 4EE
☎020 7583 9855 Fax 020 7842 2298
www.routledge.com

Managing Director *Roger Horton*
Publishing Directors *Claire L'Enfant, Alan Jarvis*
Approx. Annual Turnover £35.5 million (Group)

Routledge was formed in 1987 through an amalgamation of Routledge & Kegan Paul, Methuen & Co., Tavistock Publications, and Croom Helm. Subsequent acquisitions include the Unwin Hyman academic list from **HarperCollins** (1991), *Who's Who* and historical atlases from Dent/Orion (1994), archaeology and ancient history titles from Batsford (1996) and the E & FN Spon imprint from ITP Science (1997). In 1998, Routledge became a subsidiary of **Taylor & Francis Group plc** (see entry). In 2001 Curzon Press combined with the imprint to form **Routledge Curzon** for Asian studies. Also, education imprint, **Routledge Falmer** and clinical psychology imprint, **Brunner-Routledge**.

Publishes academic and professional books and journals in the social sciences, humanities, health sciences and the built environment for the international market. Subjects: addiction, anthropology, archaeology, architecture, Asian studies, biblical studies, the built environment, business and management, civil engineering, classics, heritage, construction, counselling, criminology, development and environment, dictionaries, economics, education, environmental engineering, geography, health, history, Japanese studies, journals, language, leisure studies and leisure management, linguistics, literary criticism, media and culture, Middle East, nursing, philosophy, politics, political economy, psychiatry, psychology, reference, social administration, social studies and sociology, therapy, theatre and performance studies, women's studies. No poetry, fiction, travel or astrology. About 900 titles a year. Send synopses with sample chapter and c.v. rather than complete mss.

ROYALTIES annually and twice-yearly, according to contract.

Ryland Peters and Small Limited
Kirkman House, 12–14 Whitfield Street, London W1T 2RP
☎020 7436 9090 Fax 020 7436 9790
✉ info@rps.co.uk
www.rylandpeters.com
Managing Director *David Peters*
Publishing Director *Alison Starling*

Founded 1996. Publishes highly illustrated lifestyle books aimed at an international market, covering gardening, cookery, interior design and mind, body, spirit. No fiction. No unsolicited mss; synopses and ideas welcome.

ROYALTIES twice-yearly.

Sage Publications
1 Oliver's Yard, 55 City Road, London EC1Y 1SP
☎020 7324 8500 Fax 020 7324 8600
✉ info@sagepub.co.uk
www.sagepub.co.uk
Managing Director *Stephen Barr*
Editorial Director *Ziyad Marar*

Founded 1971. Publishes academic books and journals in humanities and the social sciences. Bought academic and professional books publisher Paul Chapman Publishing Ltd in 1998.

ROYALTIES twice-yearly.

Saint Andrew Press
Church of Scotland, 121 George Street, Edinburgh EH2 4YN
☎0131 225 5722 Fax 0131 220 3113
✉ standrewpress@cofscotland.org.uk
www.standrewpress.com
www.williambarclay.org
Head of Publishing *Ann Crawford*
Approx. Annual Turnover £225,000

Founded in 1954. Owned by the Church of Scotland. Publishes religious, general reference and children's books aimed at the Christian trade and retail market in the UK and internationally. Lead TITLES in 2003 included BBC Scotland's *The Sword & the Cross*, *Root of All Evil?* by Antonia Swinson and the *Notes On* series of titles about the great composers by Conrad Wilson. About 20 titles a year. 'Saint Andrew Press is expanding and is actively seeking high-quality writing that is thought-provoking and, above all, helps readers to wrestle with the complexities of life today.' No unsolicited mss but proposals very welcome in synopsis form; approach in writing.

ROYALTIES annually.

St Pauls Publishing
187 Battersea Bridge Road, London SW11 3AS
☎020 7978 4300 Fax 020 7978 4370
✉ editions@stpauls.org.uk
Publisher *Andrew Pudussery*

Publishing division of the Society of St Paul. Began publishing in 1914 but activities were fairly limited until around 1948. Publishes religious material mainly: theology, scripture, catechetics, prayer books and biography. About 30 titles a year. Unsolicited mss, synopses and ideas welcome.

Salamander Books
See **Chrysalis Books Group**

Sangam Books Ltd
57 London Fruit Exchange, Brushfield Street, London E1 6EP
☎020 7377 6399 Fax 020 7375 1230
✉ sangambks@aol.com
Executive Director *Anthony de Souza*

Traditionally an educational publisher of school and college level textbooks. Also publishes art, India, medicine, science, technology, social sciences, religion, plus some fiction in paperback.

Saqi Books
26 Westbourne Grove, London W2 5RH
☎020 7221 9347 Fax 020 7229 7492
✉ enquiries@saqibooks.com

www.saqibooks.com
Chairman/Managing Director *André Gaspard*
Founded 1981, initially as a specialist publisher of books on the Middle East and Arab world but now includes Central Asia, South Asia and European fiction. Publishes fiction and non-fiction – academic and illustrated. About 20 titles a year. Welcomes unsolicited material; approach by post or e-mail.
ROYALTIES annually.

Authors' Rating A blunt warning from the managing editor that unsolicited manuscripts are not returned. Saqi is not alone in this. Authors should retain copies of everything they send out.

W.B. Saunders
See **Elsevier Ltd**

Savitri Books Ltd
See entry under *UK Packagers*

SB Publications
19 Grove Road, Seaford BN25 1TP
☎01323 893498   Fax 01323 893860
✉ sbpublications@tiscali.co.uk
www.sbpublications.co.uk
Owner *Mrs Lindsay Woods*
Founded 1987. Specialises in local history, including themes illustrated by old picture postcards and photographs; also travel, guides (town, walking) and railways. TITLES *Dorset As She Wus Spoke*; *The Neat and Nippy Guide to Brighton*; *Pre-Raphaelite Trail in Sussex*. Also provides marketing and distribution services for local authors. 20 titles a year.
ROYALTIES annually.

Sceptre
See **Hodder Headline Ltd**

Scholastic Ltd
Villiers House, Clarendon Avenue,
Leamington Spa CV32 5PR
☎01926 887799   Fax 01926 883331
www.scholastic.co.uk
Chairman *M.R. Robinson*
Managing Director *To be appointed*
Approx. Annual Turnover £42 million
Founded 1964. Owned by US parent company. Publishes children's fiction and non-fiction and education for primary schools.

DIVISIONS
Scholastic Children's Books *Richard Scrivener* Commonwealth House, 1–19 New

Oxford Street, London WC1A 1NU ☎020 7421 9000 Fax 020 7421 9001 IMPRINTS **Scholastic Press** (hardbacks); **Hippo** (paperbacks); **Point** (paperbacks) TITLES *Horrible Histories*; *Goosebumps*; *Point Horror*; *His Dark Materials* trilogy by Philip Pullman.
Educational Publishing *Max Adam* (Villiers House address) Professional books and classroom materials for primary teachers, plus magazines such as *Child Education, Junior Education, Junior Focus, Infant Projects, Nursery Education; Literacy Time*.
Scholastic Book Clubs *Miles Stevens Hoare* Windrush Park, Witney, Oxford OX29 0YT ☎01993 893456 Fax 01993 776813 SBC is the UK's number one Schools Book Club. Offering five age specific clubs, it provides 'the best books at great prices and supports teachers in the process'.
School Book Fairs *Miles Stevens-Hoare* The Book Fair Division sells directly to children, parents and teachers in schools through 27,000 week-long book events held in schools throughout the UK.
ROYALTIES twice-yearly.

Authors' Rating Another beneficiary of the Harry Potter phenomenon (via its children's book clubs), Scholastic also leads the intellectual sector of children's publishing with Philip Pullman who, by any literary standards, takes some beating. Fiction for 8 to 12-year-olds is seen as a growth sector. Noted for its author-friendly skills.

SCM – Canterbury Press Ltd Ltd
9–17 St Albans Place, London N1 0NX
☎020 7359 8033   Fax 020 7359 0049
✉ admin@scm-canterburypress.co.uk
www.scm-canterburypress.co.uk
Publishing Director *Christine Smith*
Approx. Annual Turnover £1.3 million
Part of **Hymns Ancient & Modern Ltd**. Has two publishing imprints: **SCM Press** Publishes text and reference books for the study of theology, philosophy of religion, ethics and religious studies; **Canterbury Press** Publishes religious titles for the general market, liturgy, spirituality and church resources. AUTHORS include Rowan Williams, Ronald Blythe, Libby Purves. Refer to website for guidelines on submitting proposals.
ROYALTIES annually.

Authors' Rating Leading publisher of religious ideas with well-deserved reputation for fresh thinking. At SCM, 'questioning theology is the norm'.

Scottish Cultural Press/ Scottish Children's Press

Unit 6, Newbattle Abbey Business Park,
Newbattle Road, Dalkeith EH22 3LJ
☎0131 660 6366 Fax 0131 660 4666
✉ info@scottishbooks.com
www.scottishbooks.com

Directors *Avril Gray, Brian Pugh*

Founded 1992. Publishes Scottish interest
titles, including cultural literature, poetry,
archaeology, local history. DIVISION **S.C.P.
Children's Ltd** (trading as **Scottish
Children's Press**) Children's fiction and non-
fiction. Unsolicited mss, synopses and ideas
accepted provided return postage is included,
but *always* telephone before sending material,
please. 'Mss sent without advance telephone
call and return postage will be destroyed.'
ROYALTIES paid.

Scribner

See **Simon & Schuster UK Limited**

Seafarer Books

102 Redwald Road, Rendlesham,
Woodbridge IP12 2TE
☎01394 420789 Fax 01394 461314
✉ info@seafarerbooks.com
www.seafarerbooks.com

Sole Proprietor *Patricia M. Eve*

Founded 1968. Publishes sailing titles, with an
emphasis on the traditional. AUTHORS Erskine
Childers, Cecily Gould, Bjorn Larsson, John
Leather, Jack London, Frank Mulville, Bob
Roberts, Adrian Seligman. No unsolicited mss;
preliminary letter essential before making any
type of submission.
ROYALTIES twice-yearly.

Search Press Ltd

Wellwood, North Farm Road, Tunbridge
Wells TN2 3DR
☎01892 510850 Fax 01892 515903
✉ searchpress@searchpress.com
www.searchpress.com

Managing Director *Martin de la Bédoyère*
Commissioning Editor *Rosalind Dace*

Founded 1970. Publishes full-colour art, craft,
needlecrafts – papermaking and papercrafts,
painting on silk, art techniques and embroidery. No unsolicited mss; synopsis with sample
chapter welcome.
ROYALTIES annually.

Seren

First Floor, 38–40 Nolton Street, Bridgend
CF31 3BN
☎01656 663018 Fax 01656 649226
✉ seren@seren-books.com
www.seren-books.com

Chairman *Cary Archard*
Managing Director *Mick Felton*
Approx. Annual Turnover £150,000

Founded 1981 as a specialist poetry publisher
but has now moved into general literary pub-
lishing with an emphasis on Wales. Publishes
poetry, fiction, literary criticism, drama, biog-
raphy, art, history and translations of fiction.
DIVISIONS **Poetry** *Amy Wack* AUTHORS
Owen Sheers, Tony Curtis, Sheenagh Pugh,
Duncan Bush, Deryn Rees-Jones. **Drama** *Amy
Wack* AUTHORS Edward Thomas, Charles Way,
Lucinda Coxon. **Fiction** *Will Atkins*; **Art,
Literary Criticism, History, Translations**
Mick Felton AUTHORS Christopher Meredith,
Leslie Norris, Richard John Evans. IMPRINT
Border Lines Biographies TITLES *Bruce
Chatwin; Dennis Potter; Mary Webb; Wilfred Owen;
Raymond Williams*. About 25 titles a year.
Unsolicited mss, synopses and ideas for books
welcome.
ROYALTIES twice yearly.

Serpent's Tail

4 Blackstock Mews, London N4 2BT
☎020 7354 1949 Fax 020 7704 6467
✉ info@serpentstail.com
www.serpentstail.com

Contact *Ben Cooper*
Approx. Annual Turnover £650,000

Founded 1986. Winner of the **Sunday Times
Small Publisher of the Year Award** (1989)
and the Ralph Lewis Award for new fiction
(1992). Serpent's Tail has introduced to British
audiences a number of major internationally
known writers. Noted for its strong emphasis
on design and an eye for the unusual. Publishes
contemporary fiction, contemporary gay fiction and non-fiction, including works in translation, crime, popular culture and biography.
No poetry, romance or fantasy.
IMPRINTS **Serpent's Tail** TITLES *Fearless Jones*
Walter Mosley; *Whatever* Michel Houellebecq;
This is Serbia Calling Matthew Collin; *Pornocopia*
Laurence O'Toole. **Five Star** TITLES *Nineteen
Seventy Four* David Peace; *Always Outnumbered,
Always Outgunned* Walter Mosley; *Beneath the
Blonde* Stella Duffy. About 40 titles a year. Send
preliminary letter outlining proposal with a sam-
ple chapter and s.a.e. No unsolicited mss.

Prospective authors unfamiliar with Serpent's Tail are advised to study the list before submitting anything.

ROYALTIES annually.

Authors' Rating A publisher noted for originality which means doing what the conglomerates are unwilling or unable to do. An exciting fiction list much praised by its own and other publishers' authors.

Severn House Publishers

9–15 High Street, Sutton SM1 1DF
☎020 8770 3930 Fax 020 8770 3850
✉ info@severnhouse.com
www.severnhouse.com

Chairman *Edwin Buckhalter*
Editorial *Amanda Stewart*

Founded 1974. A leader in library fiction publishing. Publishes hardback fiction: romance science fiction, horror, fantasy, crime. About 140 titles a year. No unsolicited material. Synopses/proposals preferred through *bona fide* literary agents only. OVERSEAS ASSOCIATE Severn House Publishers Inc., New York.

ROYALTIES twice-yearly.

Sheldon Press

See **Society for Promoting Christian Knowledge**

Sheldrake Press

188 Cavendish Road, London SW12 0DA
☎020 8675 1767 Fax 020 8675 7736
✉ mail@sheldrakepress.demon.co.uk
www.sheldrakepress.demon.co.uk

Publisher *Simon Rigge*

Founded in 1979 as a book packager and commenced publishing under its own imprint in 1991. Publishes illustrated non-fiction: history, travel, style, cookery and stationery. TITLES *The Victorian House Book*; *The Shorter Mrs Beeton*; *The Power of Steam*; *The Railway Heritage of Britain*; *Wild Britain*; *Wild France*; *Wild Spain*; *Wild Italy*; *Wild Ireland*; *Amsterdam: Portrait of a City* and Kate Greenaway stationery books. Synopses and ideas for books welcome, but not interested in fiction.

Shepheard-Walwyn (Publishers) Ltd

Suite 604, The Chandlery, 50 Westminster Bridge Road, London SE1 7QY
☎020 7721 7666 Fax 020 7721 7667
✉ books@shepheard-walwyn.co.uk
www.shepheard-walwyn.co.uk

Managing Director *Anthony Werner*
Approx. Annual Turnover £150,000

Founded 1972. 'We regard books as food for the mind and want to offer a wholesome diet of original ideas and fresh approaches to old subjects.' Publishes general non-fiction in three main areas: Scottish interest; gift books in calligraphy and/or illustrated; history, political economy, perennial philosophy. About 5 titles a year. Synopses and ideas for books welcome.

ROYALTIES twice-yearly.

The Shetland Times Ltd

Gremista, Lerwick ZE1 0PX
☎01595 693622 Fax 01595 694637
✉ publishing@shetland-times.co.uk
www.shetland-books.co.uk

Managing Director *Robert Wishart*
Publications Manager *Charlotte Black*

Founded 1872 as publishers of the local newspaper. Book publishing followed thereafter plus publication of monthly magazine, *Shetland Life*. Publishes anything with Shetland connections – local and natural history, music, crafts, maritime. Prefers material with a Shetland theme/connection.

ROYALTIES annually.

Shire Publications Ltd

Cromwell House, Church Street, Princes Risborough HP27 9AA
☎01844 344301 Fax 01844 347080
✉ shire@shirebooks.co.uk
www.shirebooks.co.uk

General Manager *Sue Ross*

Founded 1962. Publishes original non-fiction paperbacks. About 25 titles a year. No unsolicited material; send introductory letter with detailed outline of idea.

ROYALTIES annually.

Authors' Rating You don't have to live in the country to write books for Shire but it helps. With titles like *Church Fonts, Haunted Inns* and *Discovering Preserved Railways* there is a distinct rural feel to the list. Another way of putting it, to quote owner John Rotheroe, Shire specialises in 'small books on all manner of obscure subjects'.

Short Books

15 Highbury Terrace, London N5 1UP
☎020 7226 1607 Fax 020 7226 4169
✉ mark@shortbooks.biz
www.theshortbookco.com

Contacts *Rebecca Nicolson, Aurea Carpenter*

Founded 2001. Publishes informative, entertaining non-fiction (30–80,000 words), mainly biography and journalism; authors include Francis Wheen, Nicci Gerrard, Ferdinand Mount and Simon Barnes. Children's books (15–20,000 words): lively biographies of famous figures from the past. No fiction as yet but always open to new ideas. 21 titles in 2003. 'All prospective authors will be informed by e-mail of how their proposal has been received. Mss will not be returned.'

Sickle Moon
See **Eland Publishing Ltd**

Sidgwick & Jackson
See **Macmillan Publishers Ltd**

Sigma Press
5 Alton Road, Wilmslow SK9 5DY
☎01625 531035 Fax 01625 531035
✉ info@sigma.press
www.sigmapress.co.uk

Chairman/Managing Director *Graham Beech*

Founded in 1980 as a publisher of technical books, Sigma Press now publishes mainly in the leisure area. Publishes outdoor, local heritage, adventure and bioraphy. DIVISION **Sigma Leisure** TITLES *Holiday Walks in the Loire Valley*; *Leap into Legend* (biography); *Lonesome Rhodes* (biography); *Northumbria Church Walks*; *Discovering Manchester*. 15 titles in 2003. No unsolicited mss; synopses and ideas welcome. No poetry or novels required.

ROYALTIES twice-yearly.

Signature
See **Hodder Headline Ltd**

Silhouette
See **Harlequin Mills & Boon Ltd**

Simon & Schuster UK Limited
Africa House, 64–78 Kingsway, London WC2B 6AH
☎020 7316 1900 Fax 020 7316 0331

CEO/Managing Director *Ian S. Chapman*
Publishing Director *Suzanne Baboneau*
Publisher, Non-fiction *Andrew Gordon* (also The Free Press)
Publishers, Fiction *Suzanne Baboneau, Ben Ball, Kate Lyall-Grant*
Scribner *Tim Binding, Ben Ball*

Founded 1986. Sister company of the leading American company. Publishes hardback (**Simon & Schuster**) and paperback (**Pocket Books**) commercial and literary fiction and non-fiction, including autobiography, biography, sport, mind, body & spirit, humour, travel and other general interest non-fiction. **The Free Press** publishes serious non-fiction, including popular science, politics, history and current business. Literary international fiction and non-fiction is published under the **Scribner** imprint.

DIVISION **Martin Books** Director *Janet Copleston* Specialises in bespoke publishing and branded editions, and the Simon & Schuster UK cookery list.

ROYALTIES twice-yearly.

Authors' Rating Editorially independent of its American counterpart, Simon & Schuster continues to grow in reputation as a powerhouse for new work.

Skoob Russell Square
10 Brunswick Centre, off Bernard Street, London WC1N 1AE
☎020 7278 8760 Fax 020 7278 3137
✉ books@skoob.com
www.skoob.com

Editorial *M. Lovell*

Publishes literary guides, cultural studies, esoterica/occult, poetry, new writing from the Orient. TITLES *Skoob Directory of Secondhand Bookshops*; *Perspectives on Post-Colonial Literature* D.C.R.A. Goonetilleke; *The Space of City Trees* Arthur Yap. No unsolicited mss, synopses or ideas.

Smith Gryphon Ltd
See **John Blake Publishing Ltd**

Colin Smythe Ltd
PO Box 6, Gerrards Cross SL9 8XA
☎01753 886000 Fax 01753 886469
✉ sales@colinsmythe.co.uk
www.colinsmythe.co.uk

Managing Director *Colin Smythe*
Approx. Annual Turnover £2.7 million

Founded 1966. Publishes Anglo-Irish literature, drama; criticism and Irish history. About 10 titles a year. No unsolicited mss. Also acts as literary agent for a small list of authors including Terry Pratchett.

ROYALTIES annually/twice-yearly.

Snowbooks Ltd
239 Old Street, London EC1V 9Ey
☎020 7553 4473 Fax 020 7251 3130
✉ editor@snowbooks.com
www.snowbooks.com

Managing Director *Emma Cahill*
Approx. Annual Turnover £200,000

Founded 2003. Publishes fiction mainly (both contemporay and classic) but also considers fiction and poetry, non-fiction, humour, children's, business, crime, mystery, travel, general interest, biography and autobiography. No romance, science fiction, mind body and spirit, religious books. TITLES *Dance Me On the Table* R. Muir; *Adept* Robert Finn; *The London Scene* Virginia Woolf. 5 titles in 2003. Unsolicited synopses and ideas for books welcome provided a sample of writing is attached. Approach by e-mail in the first instance.

ROYALTIES vary according to contract.

Society for Promoting Christian Knowledge (SPCK)

Holy Trinity Church, Marylebone Road, London NW1 4DU
☎020 7643 0382 Fax 020 7643 0391
www.spck.org.uk

Director of Publishing *Simon Kingston*

Founded 1698, SPCK is the third oldest publisher in the country. IMPRINTS **SPCK** Editorial Director *Joanna Moriarty* Theology, academic, liturgy, prayer, spirituality, biblical studies, educational resources, mission, pastoral care, gospel and culture, worldwide. **Sheldon Press** Editor *Liz Marsh* Popular medicine, health, self-help, psychology. **Azure** Senior Editor *Alison Barr* General spirituality.

ROYALTIES annually.

Authors' Rating Religion with a strong social edge.

Sophia Books

See **Rudolf Steiner Press**

Southwater

See **Anness Publishing Ltd**

Souvenir Press Ltd

43 Great Russell Street, London WC1B 3PA
☎020 7580 9307/8 & 7637 5711/2/3
Fax 020 7580 5064
✉ souvenirpress@ukonline.co.uk

Chairman/Managing Director *Ernest Hecht*

Independent publishing house. Founded 1951. Publishes academic and scholarly, animal care and breeding, antiques and collecting, archaeology, autobiography and biography, business and industry, children's, cookery, crafts and hobbies, crime, educational, fiction, gardening, health and beauty, history and antiquarian,

humour, illustrated and fine editions, magic and the occult, medical, military, music, natural history, philosophy, poetry, psychology, religious, sociology, sports, theatre and women's studies. Souvenir's Human Horizons series for the disabled and their carers is one of the most preeminent in its field and recently celebrated 28 years of publishing for the disabled.

IMPRINTS/SERIES **Condor; Independent Voices; Human Horizons; Pictorial Presentations; Pop Universal; The Story-Tellers.** TITLES *Child Soldiers* China Keitetsi; *The Van Gogh File* Ken Wilkie; *The Sleep Book for Tired Parents* Rebecca Huntley; *Journeys Out of the Body* Robert A. Monroe; *Solutions for Writers* Sol Stein. About 55 titles a year. Unsolicited mss considered but initial letter of enquiry and outline always required in the first instance.

ROYALTIES twice-yearly.

Authors' Rating Still wonderfully dotty after all these years, the Souvenir list continues to offer the best evidence that you don't have to be in the mega league to be a publishing legend.

SPCK

See **Society for Promoting Christian Knowledge**

Special Interest Model Books

Stanley House, 3 Fleets Lane, Poole BH15 3AJ
☎01202 649930 Fax 01202 649950
✉ chrlloyd@globalnet.co.uk
www.specialinterestmodelbooks.co.uk

Contact *Chris Lloyd*

Publishes aviation, engineering, leisure and hobbies, modelling, electronics, health, craft, wine and beer making, woodwork. Send synopses rather than completed mss.

ROYALTIES twice-yearly.

Speechmark Publishing Ltd

Telford Road, Bicester OX26 4LQ
☎01869 244644 Fax 01869 320040
✉ info@speechmark.net
www.speechmark.net

Chairman and Managing Director *Ian Franklin*
Publishing Manager *Sarah Miles*
Approx. Annual Turnover £1.5 million

Founded 1979. Formerly known as Winslow Publishing, Speechmark publishes practical books and *ColorCards* for health, education and special needs practitioners and students. Unsolicited mss, synopses and ideas welcome. Approach by letter or e-mail.

ROYALTIES annually.

Spellmount Ltd

The Village Centre, Staplehurst TN12 0BJ
☎01580 893730 Fax 01580 893731
✉ enquiries@spellmount.com
www.spellmount.com

Managing Director *Jamie Wilson*
Approx. Annual Turnover £500,000

Founded 1983. Publishes history and military history. About 30 titles a year. Synopses/ideas for books in these specialist fields welcome but no personal memoirs. Enclose return postage.

ROYALTIES biannually for two years, then annually.

Spiro Press

17 – 19 Rochester Row, London SW1P 1LA
☎0870 164 8900 Fax 0870 165 8989
www.spiropress.com

Publisher *Susannah Lear*
Approx. Annual Turnover (Publishing Division) £1.6 million

Spiro Press, formerly The Industrial Society Publishing, is part of the Capita Group and has been publishing for over 20 years. Specialises in business, management, self-development, human resources – books, manuals and special reports. TITLES *Inspirational Leadership – Henry V and the Muse of Fire*; *Business 2010*; *Why Innovation Fails*. SERIES *Your Personal Trainer*. Unsolicited mss, synopses and ideas welcome. No fiction or illustrated non-fiction.

ROYALTIES twice-yearly.

E & FN Spon

See **Routledge**

SportsBooks Limited

PO Box 422, Cheltenham GL50 2YN
☎0870 071 3965 Fax 0870 075 0888
✉ randall@sportsbooks.ltd.uk
www.sportsbooks.ltd.uk

Chairman & Managing Director *Randall Northam*
Approx. Annual Turnover £100,000

Founded 1995. Publishes sports books including biographies, statistical and practical. TITLES *Phil Tufnell's A to Z of Cricket*; *Raich Carter – The Biography*; *The Complete Record of the FA Cup*. IMPRINT **BMM** *Editorial Head* Mark Jones. 6 titles in 2004. No unsolicited mss. Synopses and ideas welcome. Approach by letter or e-mail.

The Sportsman's Press

(An imprint of Quiller Publishing Ltd),
Wykey House, Wykey, Shrewsbury SY4 1JA
☎01939 261616 Fax 01939 261606
✉ info@quillerbooks.com

Managing Director *Andrew Johnson*

Specialises in books on all country subjects and general sports including fishing, fencing, shooting, equestrian, cookery, gunmaking and wildlife art. About 10 titles a year.

ROYALTIES twice-yearly.

Springer-Verlag London Limited

Sweetapple House, Catteshall Road,
Godalming GU7 3DJ
☎01483 418800 Fax 01483 415144
✉ postmaster@svl.co.uk
www.springeronline.com
www.springer-sbm.de

Managing Director *John Watson*
Editorial Director *Beverley Ford*
Approx. Annual Turnover £5 million

The UK subsidiary of Springer Science & Business Media. Publishes science, technical and medical books and journals. Specialises in computing, engineering, medicine, mathematics, statistics, astronomy. All UK published books are sold through Springer's German and US companies as well as in the UK. About 150 titles a year, plus journals. Not interested in social sciences, fiction or school books but academic and professional science and amateur astronomy mss or synopses welcome.

ROYALTIES annually.

Stainer & Bell Ltd

PO Box 110, 23 Gruneisen Road, London N3 1DZ
☎020 8343 3303 Fax 020 8343 3024
✉ post@stainer.co.uk
www.stainer.co.uk

Managing Directors *Carol Y. Wakefield*,
  Keith M. Wakefield
Publishing Director *Nicholas Williams*
Approx. Annual Turnover £790,000

Founded 1907 to publish sheet music. Publishes music and religious subjects related to hymnody. Unsolicited synopses/ideas for books welcome. Send letter enclosing brief précis.

ROYALTIES annually.

The Stationery Office

See **TSO**

Rudolf Steiner Press

Hillside House, The Square, Forest Row RH18 5ES
☎01342 824433

office@rudolfsteinerpress.com
www.rudolfsteinerpress.com

Chairman *Mr P. Martin*
Managing Director *Mr S. Gulbekian*
Approx. Annual Turnover £150,000

Founded in 1925 to publish the work of Rudolf Steiner and related materials. Publishes non-fiction: spirituality and philosophy. IMPRINT **Sophia Books** *S. Gulbekian* TITLES *From Stress to Serenity*; *Homemaking as a Social Art*. 15 titles in 2003. No unsolicited material.
    ROYALTIES annually.

The Story-Tellers
See **Souvenir Press Ltd**

Straightline Publishing Ltd
29 Main Street, Bothwell G71 8RD
☎01698 853000 Fax 01698 854208

Director *Patrick Bellew*
Editor *Colin Calder*

Founded 1989. Publishes magazines and directories – trade and technical – books of local interest. TITLES *Cabletalk*; *enterprisingglasgow*. No unsolicited material.
    ROYALTIES annually.

Studymates Publishing Limited
PO Box 2, Bishops Lydeard TA4 3YE
☎01823 432002 Fax 01823 430097
info@studymates.co.uk
www.studymates.co.uk
www.mr.educator.com
www.poemstoliveby.com

Managing Editor *Graham Lawler, MA*

Founded 1998 as part of International Briefings Ltd and taken over by education expert Graham Lawler in July 2000. Studymates are academic titles for students at university or college. Two new lists were launched in 2002 – **Studymates Professional**, for the professional person to improve their knowledge in the workplace and **Judith Handbooks**, problem-solving books for women that deal with emotional and day-to-day practical issues. TITLES *Troubleshoot Your Problems*; *Troubleshoot Your Man's Health*. Ideas first in writing; authors are asked to follow the layout of the author kit available on the website.

Summersdale Publishers Ltd
46 West Street, Chichester PO19 1RP
☎01243 771107 Fax 01243 786300
submissions@summersdale.com
www.summersdale.com

Directors *Stewart Ferris, Alastair Williams*

Commissioning Editor *Sadie Mayne*
Approx. Annual Turnover £1 million

Founded 1990. Publishes travel literature, martial arts, self-help, cookery, humour and gift books. TITLES *Greece on my Wheels* Edward Enfield; *Viva Mallorca* Peter Kerr; *UK on a G-String* Justin Brown. 50–60 titles a year. No unsolicited mss; synopses and ideas welcome by e-mail.
    ROYALTIES paid.

Sussex Academic Press
PO Box 2950, Brighton BN2 5SP
☎01273 699533 Fax 01273 621262
edit@sussex-academic.co.uk
www.sussex-academic.co.uk

Managing Director *Anthony Grahame*
Approx. Annual Turnover £225,000

Founded 1994. Academic publisher. DIVISION/IMPRINT **Sussex Academic** TITLES *Art, Crime & Madness*; *Dugald Stewart – The Pride and Ornament of Scotland*; *Human Rights & Religion*. **Alpha Press** TITLE *First and Last Editions – England's Second-Hand Bookshops*. 40 titles in 2003. No unsolicited material; send letter of inquiry in the first instance.
    ROYALTIES annually.

Sutton Publishing Ltd
Phoenix Mill, Thrupp, Stroud GL5 2BU
☎01453 731114 Fax 01453 731117
publishing@sutton-publishing.co.uk

Managing Director *Jeremy Yates-Round*
Senior Commissioning Editors *Jaqueline Mitchell* (biography), *Christopher Feeney* (general history), *Jonathan Falconer* (military), *Simon Fletcher* (local history)

Founded 1978. Acquired by **Haynes Publishing** in March 2000. Publishes academic, archaeology, biography, countryside, history, military, aviation, regional interest, local history. About 200 titles a year. Send synopses rather than complete mss.
    ROYALTIES twice-yearly.

Authors' Rating Having started as a regional publisher, Sutton has branched out into general non-fiction. Strong on popular history.

Swan Hill Press
(An imprint of Quiller Publishing Ltd),
Wykey House, Wykey, Shrewsbury SY4 1JA
☎01939 261616 Fax 01939 261606
info@quillerbooks.com

Managing Director *Andrew Johnston*

Specialises in practical books on all country and

field sports activities. Publishes books on fishing, shooting, gundog training, falconry, equestrian, deer, cookery. About 15 titles a year. Unsolicited mss must include s.a.e.

ROYALTIES twice-yearly.

Sweet & Maxwell Group

100 Avenue Road, London NW3 3PF
☎020 7393 7000 Fax 020 7393 7010
✉ customerservices@sweetandmaxwell.co.uk
www.sweetandmaxwell.co.uk

Managing Director *Peter Lake*

Founded 1799. Part of the Thomson Corporation. Publishes materials in all media; looseleaf works, journals, law reports, CD-ROMs and online. Not interested in non-legal material. The legal and professional list is varied and contains academic titles as well as treatises and reference works in the legal and related professional fields.

IMPRINTS **Sweet & Maxwell**; **W. Green (Scotland)**; **Thomson Round Hall (Ireland)**. Over 1100 products, including 180 looseleafs, 80 periodicals, more than 40 digital products and online information services and 200 new titles each year. Ideas welcome. Writers with legal/professional projects in mind are advised to contact the Legal Business Unit at the earliest possible stage in order to lay the groundwork for best design, production and marketing of a project.

ROYALTIES and fees according to contract.

Tango Books Ltd

3D West Point, 36–37 Warple Way, London W3 0RG
☎020 8996 9970 Fax 020 8996 9977
✉ sales@tangobooks.co.uk

Directors *David Fielder, Sheri Safran*

Founded 1981. Children's books publisher with international co-edition potential: pop-ups, three-dimensional, novelty, picture and board books, 1000 words maximum. About 30 titles a year. Approach with preliminary letter and sample material in the first instance.

ROYALTIES based on a per-copy-sold rate and paid in stages; or fee payment.

Taschen UK

13 Old Burlington Street, London W1S 3AJ
☎020 7437 4350 Fax 020 7437 4360
www.taschen.com

UK office of the German photographic, art and architecture publisher. Editorial office in Cologne (see entry under *European Publishers*).

I.B.Tauris & Co. Ltd

6 Salem Road, London W2 4BU
☎020 7243 1225 Fax 020 7243 1226
✉ mail@ibtauris.com
www.ibtauris.com

Chairman/Publisher *Iradj Bagherzade*
Managing Director *Jonathan McDonnell*

Founded 1984. Independent publisher. Publishes general non-fiction and academic in the fields of international relations, religion, current affairs, history, politics, cultural, media and film studies, Middle East studies. Joint projects with Cambridge University Centre for Middle Eastern Studies, Institute for Latin American Studies and Institute of Ismaili Studies.

Distributes Philip Wilson Publishers worldwide. IMPRINTS **Tauris Parke Books** Illustrated books on architecture, travel, design and culture. **Tauris Parke Paperbacks** Trade titles, including art and art history. **British Academic Press** Academic monographs. **Radcliffe Press** Colonial history and biography. Unsolicited synopses and book proposals welcome.

ROYALTIES twice-yearly.

Authors' Rating Imprint Radcliffe Press may require authors to contribute towards costs of publication.

Tavistock Publications
See **Routledge**

Taylor & Francis Group plc

11 New Fetter Lane, London EC4P 4EE
☎020 7583 9855 Fax 020 7842 2298
www.tandf.co.uk

Chairman *Robert Kiernan*
Chief Executive *David Smith*
Approx. Annual Turnover £150 million

Founded 1798 with the launch of *Philosophical Magazine*, which has been in publication ever since (now a solid-state physics journal). The Group is now a public company but with strong academic connections among the major shareholders. Falmer Press joined the group in 1979 and it doubled its size in the late 1980s with the acquisition of Crane Russak in 1986 and Hemisphere Publishing Co in 1988. In 1995, acquired Lawrence Erlbaum Associates Ltd, renamed Psychology Press, and Brunner/Mazel in 1997, adding to the growing list of psychology publications. In 1997, Garland Publishing Inc., New York, and in 1998 Routledge Publishing Holdings Ltd, including Carfax Publishing and E&FN Spon were acquired. Europa Publications Ltd, the reference book publisher covering international affairs, politics and economics and **Martin Dunitz Ltd** (see entry) were added in 1999. Acquired the international journals division of Scandinavian University Press in 2000, adding over 60 academic journals, followed in 2001 by Gordon & Breach and Curzon Press (see **Routledge**). Most recently acquired Fitzroy Dearborn in 2002, BIOS Scientific Publishers in January 2003, CRC Press including Parthenon in March 2003 followed by Frank Cass and Marcel Dekker plus the books and journals of SWETS.

Publishes scientific, technical, education titles at university, research and professional levels. About 2000 titles a year. Unsolicited mss, synopses and ideas welcome. OVERSEAS OFFICES Taylor & Francis Inc., Philadelphia, PA and New York; Taylor & Francis Asia Pacific, Singapore; Taylor & Francis AS, Norway and Sweden.

ROYALTIES yearly.

Authors' Rating One of those companies that barely registers with authors until they look at some of the famous imprints that are gathered under the corporate umbrella. Very much into higher education and reference, further expansion is predicted. Recent restructuring reflects the growing importance of the US market. Among recent deals is an agreement to be publisher for the International Institute of Strategic Studies. Still to be confirmed at the time of writing is a merger with **Informa** which specialises in business conferences.

Teach Yourself
See **Hodder Headline Ltd**

Telegraph Books
1 Canada Square, Canary Wharf, London E14 5DT
☎020 7538 6826 Fax 020 7538 6064
www.telegraphbooksdirect.co.uk

Owner *Telegraph Group Ltd*
Publisher *Morven Knowles*
Approx. Annual Turnover £3 million

Concentrates on Telegraph branded books in association/collaboration with other publishers. Also runs Telegraph Books Direct, a direct mail, phone-line bookselling service and off-the-page sales for other publishers' books. Publishes general non-fiction: reference, personal finance, health, gardening, guides, sport, humour, puzzles and games. Mainly interested in books if a Telegraph link exists. About 50 titles a year. No unsolicited material.

ROYALTIES twice-yearly.

Temple Lodge Publishing Ltd
Hillside House, The Square, Forest Row RH18 5ES
☎01342 824000
✉ office@templelodge.com
www.templelodge.com
www.clairviewbooks.com

Chairman *Mr R. Pauli*
Managing Director *Mr S. Gulbekian*
Approx. Annual Turnover £150,000

Founded in 1990 to develop the work of Rudolf Steiner (see also **Rudolf Steiner Press**). Publishes non-fiction: mind, body & spirit, current affairs, health and therapy. IMPRINT **Clairview Books** *Mr S. Gulbekian* General books challenging conventional thinking TITLES *Dreaming War* Gore Vidal; *Foodwise* Wendy Cook; *My Descent Into Death* Howard Storm. 15 titles in 2003. No unsolicited material; send initial letter of enquiry. No poetry or fiction.

ROYALTIES annually.

Texere
See **Thomson Learning**

Thames and Hudson Ltd
181A High Holborn, London WC1V 7QX
☎020 7845 5000 Fax 020 7845 5050
✉ mail@thameshudson.co.uk
www.thamesandhudson.com

Managing Director *Thomas Neurath*
Editorial Head *Jamie Camplin*
Approx. Annual Turnover £25 million

Publishes art, archaeology, architecture and design, biography, fashion, garden and landscape design, graphics, history, illustrated and fine editions, mythology, photography, popular culture, style, travel and topography. SERIES *World of Art*; *New Horizons*; *Most Beautiful Villages*; *Earth From the Air.* TITLES *Germaine Greer's The Boy*; *Manolo Blahnik Drawings*; *David Hockney: Secret Knowledge*; *Sensation*; *The Shock of the New*; *The Book of Kells*; *Brick: A World History*; *The Way We Live*; *The Mind in the Cave*; *The Eco-Design Handbook*; *The Seventy Mysteries of Ancient Egypt*; *The Complete Roman Army*; *The Mediterranean in History.* 200 titles a year. Send preliminary letter and outline before mss.

ROYALTIES twice-yearly.

Authors' Rating Quality illustrated books on art and design. The World of Art series, a huge range of modestly priced, scholarly books, is probably the best of its kind. Financial success rests on producing the sort of books that easily carry over to other languages.

Thoemmes
See **The Continuum International Publishing Group Limited**

Thomson Learning
High Holborn House, 50–51 Bedford Row, London WC1R 4LR
☎020 7067 2500 Fax 020 7067 2600
www.thomson.com

CEO (Worldwide) *Ron Schlosser*
CEO (Thomson Learning EMEA) *Charles Iossi*
Publishing Director (Thomson Learning EMEA) *John Yates*

Founded 1993. Formerly International Thomson Publishing, part of the Thomson Corporation and as such has offices worldwide with the UK office being reported to by Copenhagen (for Europe), Turkey (Middle East) and South Africa. Acquired Texere in 2003. Publishes education. TITLES *Management and Cost Accounting* Drury; *Strategy – Process, Content, Contact* DeWit and Meyer. Unsolicited material aimed at students is welcome but telephone in the first instance to check out the idea.
ROYALTIES vary according to contract.

Thomson Round Hall (Ireland)
See **Sweet & Maxwell Group**

Stanley Thornes (Publishers) Ltd
See **Nelson Thornes Ltd**

F.A. Thorpe (Publishing)
The Green, Bradgate Road, Anstey LE7 7FU
☎0116 236 4325 Fax 0116 234 0205

Group Chief Executive *Robert Thirlby*
Approx. Annual Turnover £6 million

Founded in 1964 to supply large print books to libraries. Part of the Ulverscroft Group Ltd. Publishes fiction and non-fiction large print books. No educational, gardening or books that would not be suitable for large print. DIVISIONS **Charnwood**; **Ulverscroft**. IMPRINTS **Linford Romance**; **Linford Mystery**; **Linford Western**. 456 titles in 2003. No unsolicited material.

Thorsons/Element
See **HarperCollins Publishers Ltd**

Time Warner Books UK
Brettenham House, Lancaster Place, London WC2E 7EN
☎020 7911 8000 Fax 020 7911 8100
✉ uk@twbg.co.uk
www.TimeWarnerBooks.co.uk

Chief Executive *David Young*
Publisher *Ursula Mackenzie*
Approx. Annual Turnover £40 million

Founded 1988 as Little, Brown & Co. (UK). Part of Time Warner. Began by importing its US parent company's titles and in 1990 launched its own illustrated non-fiction list. Two years later the company took over former Macdonald & Co. Publishes hardback and paperback fiction, literary fiction, crime, science fiction and fantasy; and general non-fiction including true crime, biography and autobiography, cinema, gardening, history, humour, popular science, travel, reference, cookery, wines and spirits.

IMPRINTS **Little, Brown** *Ursula Mackenzie, Richard Beswick, Barbara Daniel, Hilary Hale, Tara Lawrence* Hardback fiction and general non-fiction; **Abacus** *Richard Beswick* Literary fiction and non-fiction paperbacks; **Atom** *Darren Nash* Young adult/teen paperbacks; **Orbit** *Tim Holman* Science fiction and fantasy; **Time Warner** *Tara Lawrence, Barbara Daniel, Hilary Hale* Mass-market fiction and non-fiction hardbacks and paperbacks; **X Libris** *Sarah Shrubb* Women's erotica; **Virago Press** (see entry). Approach in writing in the first instance. No unsolicited mss.
ROYALTIES twice-yearly.

Authors' Rating After a difficult year in which the books side of Time Warner was put up for sale and then taken off the market, causing confusion all round, this quality publisher seems to be back on track.

Times Books
See **HarperCollins Publishers Ltd**

Titan Books
144 Southwark Street, London SE1 0UP
☎020 7620 0200 Fax 020 7620 0032
✉ editorial@titanmail.com
www.titanbooks.com

Managing Director *Nick Landau*
Editorial Director *Katy Wild*

Founded 1981. Now a leader in the publication of graphic novels and film and television tie-ins. Publishes comic books/graphic novels, film and television titles. IMPRINT **Titan Books** TITLES *Batman*; *Buffy the Vampire Slayer*; *Don't Panic: Douglas Adams & The Hitchhiker's Guide to the Galaxy*; *The Simpsons*; *Stargate SG-1 Seasons 5 & 6 Companion*; *Star Wars*; *Superman*; *Tales From Development Hell*; *Transformers*; *2000 AD*; *Wallace & Gromit*. About 200 titles a year. No unsolicited fiction or children's books. Ideas for film and TV titles considered; send synopsis/outline with sample chapter. No e-mail submissions. Author guidelines available.

ROYALTIES twice-yearly.

Tor
See **Macmillan Publishers Ltd**

Transworld Publishers, A division of the Random House Group Ltd
61–63 Uxbridge Road, London W5 5SA
☎020 8579 2652 Fax 020 8579 5479
✉ info@transworld-publishers.co.uk
www.booksattransworld.co.uk

Managing Director *Larry Finlay*
Publisher *Patrick Janson-Smith*
Deputy Publisher *Bill Scott-Kerr*
Senior Publishing Director *Francesca Liversidge*
Approx. Annual Turnover £72 million

Founded 1950. A subsidiary of **Random House, Inc.**, New York, which in turn is a wholly-owned subsidiary of **Bertelsmann AG**, Germany. Publishes general fiction and non-fiction, gardening, sports and leisure. IMPRINTS **Bantam** *Francesca Liversidge*; **Bantam Press** *Sally Gaminara*; **Corgi & Black Swan** *Bill Scott-Kerr*, **Doubleday** *Marianne Velmans*; **Eden** *Katrina Whone*; **Expert Books** *Gareth Pottle*. AUTHORS Monica Ali, Kate Atkinson, Charlotte Bingham, Dan Brown, Bill Bryson, Lee Child, Catherine Cookson, Jilly Cooper, Ben Elton, Nicholas Evans, Frederick Forsyth, Tess Gerritsen, Robert Goddard, Germaine Greer, Joanne Harris, Stephen Hawking, D.G. Hessayon, John Irving, Sophie Kinsella, Anne McCaffrey, Andy McNab, John O'Farrell, Terry Pratchett, Gerald Seymour, Danielle Steel, Joanna Trollope. No unsolicited mss. OVERSEAS ASSOCIATES Random House Australia Pty Ltd; Random House New Zealand; Random House (Pty) Ltd (South Africa).

ROYALTIES twice-yearly.

Authors' Rating Brings quality to the mass market.

Travel Publishing Ltd
7A Apollo House, Calleva Park, Aldermaston RG7 8TN
☎0118 981 7777 Fax 0118 982 0077
✉ info:travelpublishing.co.uk
www.travelpublishing.co.uk

Directors *Peter Robinson, Chris Day*

Founded in 1997 by two former directors of **Reed Elsevier plc**. Publishes travel, accommodation, food, drink and specialist shops guides to Britain and Ireland. SERIES *Hidden Places*; *Hidden Inns*; *Country Living Rural Guides* (in conjunction with *Country Living* magazine); *Golfers Guides*; *Off the Motorway*. Over 40 titles in print. Welcomes unsolicited material; send letter in the first instance.

ROYALTIES twice-yearly.

Trentham Books Ltd
Westview House, 734 London Road, Stoke-on-Trent ST4 5NP
☎01782 745567/844699 Fax 01782 745553
www.trentham-books.co.uk

Directors *Dr Gillian Klein, Barbara Wiggins*
Approx. Annual Turnover £1 million

Publishes education (nursery, school to higher), social sciences, intercultural studies, gender studies and law for professional readers *not* for children and parents. Also academic and professional journals. No fiction, biography or poetry. Over 30 titles a year. Unsolicited mss, synopses and ideas welcome if relevant to their interests. Material only returned if adequate s.a.e. sent.

ROYALTIES annually.

Trident Press Ltd
Empire House, 175 Piccadilly, London W1J 9TB
☎020 7491 8770 Fax 020 7491 8664
✉ admin@tridentpress.com
www.tridentpress.com

Managing Director *Peter Vine*
Approx. Annual Turnover £550,000

Founded 1997. Publishes TV tie-ins, natural history, travel, geography, underwater/marine life, history, archaeology, culture and fiction. DIVISIONS **Fiction/General Publishing** *Paula Vine;* **Natural History** Peter Vine. TITLES *Red Sea Sharks; The Elysium Testament; BBC Wildlife Specials; UAE in Focus*. No unsolicited mss; synopses and ideas welcome, particularly TV tie-ins. Approach in writing or *brief* communications by e-mail, fax or telephone.

ROYALTIES annually.

Trotman & Co. Ltd
2 The Green, Richmond TW9 1PL
☎020 8486 1150 Fax 020 8486 1161
www.trotmanpublishing.co.uk

Managing Director *Toby Trotman*
Editorial Director *Mina Patria*
Approx. Annual Turnover £3 million

Publishes general careers books, higher education guides, teaching support material, employment and training resources. TITLES *Degree Course Offers; The Student Book; UCAS/Trotman*

Complete Guides; Students' Money Matters; CRAC Degree Course Guides; Real Life Guides; Newscheck journal for careers professionals; *Trotman/ Channel 4 Creative Careers* series. About 80 titles a year. Unsolicited material welcome. Also active in the educational resources market, producing recruitment brochures.

ROYALTIES twice-yearly.

TSO (The Stationery Office)
St Crispins, Duke Street, Norwich NR3 1PD
☎01603 622211
Fax 01603 694313 (Editorial)
www.tso.co.uk

Chief Executive *Tim Hailstone*
Approx. Annual Turnover £250 million

Formerly HMSO, which was founded 1786. Became part of the private sector in October 1996. Publisher of material sponsored by Parliament, government departments and other official bodies. Also commercial publishing in the following broad categories: business and professional, environment, transport, education and law. 11,000 new titles each year with 50,000 titles in print.

Twenty First Century Publishers Ltd
Braunton Barn, Kiln Lane, Isfield TN22 5UE
☎01892 522802
✉ TFCP@btinternet.com
www.twentyfirstcenturypublishers.com

Chairman *Fred Piechoczek*

Founded 2002. Publishes general fiction, financial thrillers and crime. Welcomes submissions by e-mail: manuscripts@connectfree.co.uk (contact *Fred Piechoczek*). Send brief synopsis in the body of the e-mail with extracts from the book in a file attachment (two to three chapters from anywhere in the book). No non-fiction or children's.

ROYALTIES twice-yearly.

20/20
See **The X Press**

Ulverscroft
See **F.A. Thorpe (Publishing)**

Unichrome
See **Jarrold Publishing**

University Presses of California, Columbia & Princeton Ltd
1 Oldlands Way, Bognor Regis PO22 9SA
☎01243 842165 Fax 01243 842167

✉ lois@upccp.demon.co.uk

Publishes academic titles only. US-based editorial offices. Enquiries only. Over 200 titles a year.

Usborne Publishing Ltd
83–85 Saffron Hill, London EC1N 8RT
☎020 7430 2800 Fax 020 7430 1562
✉ mail@usborne.co.uk
www.usborne.com

Managing Director *Peter Usborne*
Publishing Director *Jenny Tyler*
Approx. Annual Turnover £20 million

Founded 1973. Publishes non-fiction, fiction, art and activity books, puzzle books and music for children, young adults and pre-school. Some titles for parents. Up to 250 titles a year. Non-fiction books are written in-house to a specific format and therefore unsolicited mss are not normally welcome. Ideas which may be developed in-house are sometimes considered. Fiction for children will be considered. Keen to hear from new illustrators and designers.

ROYALTIES twice-yearly.

Authors' Rating A children's publisher that finds favour with parents who can learn a thing or two from an imaginative non-fiction list. But fiction too is growing – up to 30 titles a year.

Vanguard Press
See **Pegasus Elliot Mackenzie Publishers Ltd**

Ventura
See **Penguin Group (UK)**

Vermilion
See **The Random House Group Ltd**

Verso
6 Meard Street, London W1F 0EG
☎020 7437 3546 Fax 020 7734 0059
www.versobooks.com

Managing Director *Guy Bentham*
Approx. Annual Turnover £2 million

Formerly New Left Books which grew out of the *New Left Review*. Publishes politics, history, sociology, economics, philosophy, cultural studies, feminism. TITLES *The Prophet Armed: Trotsky 1879–1921* Isaac Deutscher; *The Trial of Henry Kissinger* Christopher Hitchens; *The New Rulers of the World* John Pilger; *An Act of State: The Execution of Martin Luther King* William Pepper; *The Assassination of Lumumba*

Ludo de Witte; *The Clash of Fundamentalism* Tariq Ali; *Innocent in the House* Andy McSmith; *The Holocaust Industry* Norman Finkelstein. No unsolicited mss; synopses and ideas for books welcome. OVERSEAS OFFICE in New York.

ROYALTIES annually.

Authors' Rating Dubbed by the *Bookseller* as 'one of the most successful small independent publishers'.

Viking
See **Penguin Group (UK)**

Vintage
See **The Random House Group Ltd**

Virago Press
Time Warner Books UK, Brettenham House, Lancaster Place, London WC2E 7EN
☎020 7911 8000 Fax 020 7911 8100
www.virago.co.uk

Publisher *Lennie Goodings*
Senior Editor *Antonia Hodgson*
Editor, Virago Modern Classics *Jill Foulston*

An imprint of **Time Warner Books UK**. Founded in 1973 by Carmen Callil, Virago publishes women's literature, both fiction and non-fiction. IMPRINTS **Virago Modern Classics** 19th and 20th-century fiction reprints by writers such as Daphne du Maurier, Angela Carter and Edith Wharton. **Virago** AUTHORS include Margaret Atwood, Maya Angelou, Jennifer Belle, Waris Dirie, Sarah Dunant, Germaine Greer, Michèle Roberts, Gillian Slovo, Talitha Stevenson, Natasha Walter, Sarah Waters. 50 titles a year.

ROYALTIES twice-yearly.

Authors' Rating Just past its thirtieth anniversary, the first name in women's publishing has gained marketing strength from its association with Time Warner. A team of young editors favour young writers with something new to say.

Virgin Books Ltd
Thames Wharf Studios, Rainville Road, London W6 9HT
☎020 7386 3300 Fax 020 7386 3360
✉ info@virgin-books.co.uk
www.virgin.com/books

Managing Director *K.T. Forster*
Approx. Annual Turnover £10 million

The Virgin Group's book publishing company. Publishes non-fiction, reference and large-format illustrated books on lifestyle, health, music, sport, biography, crime, film, TV and current affairs. No poetry, short stories, individual novels, children's books.

DIVISIONS **Non-fiction** IMPRINT **Virgin** Editorial Director *Caroline Thorne*; Editorial Director (sports) *Vanessa Daubney*; Commissioning Editor/Scout (esp. music) *Stuart Slater*; Commissioning Editor *Kirstie Addis*. **Fiction** IMPRINTS **Virgin**; **Black Lace** Senior Editor *Kerri Sharp* erotic fiction 'written by women for women'; **Nexus** Editor *Paul Coppenwaite* erotic fiction.

ROYALTIES twice-yearly.

Vista House Ltd
Vista House, 27 Greenhead Road, Huddersfield HD1 4EN
☎01484 427200
✉ editorial@vistahouse.co.uk
www.vistahouse.co.uk

Publishing Director *H.L. Byram*

Founded 1998. IMPRINTS **Vista House** Fiction and non-fiction; biography and memoirs; **Vista Originals** Subjects away from the beaten track; **Vista Africa** Books and textbooks about and for Africa south of the Sahara; **Vista House Summaries** Educational series or secondary and tertiary education; **First Authors** See www.first-authors.co.uk. Submission guidelines on website.

ROYALTIES annually.

Authors' Rating Formerly into sharing publication costs with authors, Vista House now operates conventionally.

The Vital Spark
See **Neil Wilson Publishing Ltd**

Voyager
See **HarperCollins Publishers Ltd**

University of Wales Press
10 Columbus Walk, Brigantine Place, Cardiff CF10 4UP
☎029 2049 6899 Fax 029 2049 6108
✉ press@press.wales.ac.uk
www.wales.ac.uk/press

Director *Ashley Drake*
Deputy Director *Richard Houdmont*
Approx. Annual Turnover £500,000

Founded 1922. Publishes academic and scholarly books in English and Welsh in four core areas: history, Welsh and Celtic Studies, European Studies, religion and philosophy. IMPRINTS **GPC**

Books; **Gwasg Prifysgol Cymru; University of Wales Press** TITLES *Twentieth-century Writing and the British Working Class* John Kirk; *Medieval Visions* Peter Lord; *Delineating Wales* Richard Rawlings; *Monstrous Middle Ages* eds. Bettina Bildhauer and Robert Mills; *Echoes to the Amen: Essays After R.S. Thomas* ed. Damian Walford Davies. Unsolicited mss considered. See website for further guidance.
ROYALTIES annually.

Walker Books Ltd
87 Vauxhall Walk, London SE11 5HJ
☎020 7793 0909 Fax 020 7587 1123
✉ editorial@walker.co.uk
www.walkerbooks.co.uk

Publisher *Jane Winterbotham*
Editorial Director *Gill Evans*
Editors *Deirdre McDermott* (picture books), *Caroline Royds* (fiction, non-fiction and gift books), *Denise Johnstone-Burt* (picture books, board and novelty), *Lorraine Taylor* (character, audio, stationery and merchandising)
Approx. Annual Turnover £31.7 million

Founded 1979. Publishes illustrated children's books, children's fiction and non-fiction. TITLES *Maisy* Lucy Cousins; *Where's Wally?* Martin Handford; *Five Minutes' Peace* Jill Murphy; *Can't You Sleep, Little Bear?* Martin Waddell and Barbara Firth; *Guess How Much I Love You* Sam McBratney and Anita Jeram; *Eagle Strike* Anthony Horowitz. About 300 titles a year.
ROYALTIES twice-yearly.

Authors' Rating Ever into innovative marketing, Walker is expanding its online activities with teenagers as the main target. Author loyalty is strong.

Wallflower Press
4th Floor, 26 Shacklewell Lane, London E8 2EZ
☎020 7690 0115 Fax 020 7690 4333
✉ info@wallflowerpress.co.uk
www.wallflowerpress.co.uk

Editorial Director *Yoram Allon*
Chief Editor *Del Cullen*
Approx. Annual Turnover £150,000

Founded 1999. Publishes academic and popular film studies and related media and cultural studies. SERIES *Short Cuts* Introductory undergraduate books; *Director's Cuts* Studies on significant international film-makers. Over 20 titles a year. Unsolicited mss, synopses and proposals welcome. No fiction or academic material not related to the moving image.
ROYALTIES annually.

Ward Lock
See **Octopus Publishing Group**

Ward Lock Educational Co. Ltd
BIC Ling Kee House, 1 Christopher Road, East Grinstead RH19 3BT
☎01342 318980 Fax 01342 410980
✉ wle@lingkee.com
www.wardlockeducational.com

Owner *Ling Kee (UK) Ltd*

Founded 1952. Publishes educational books (primary, middle, secondary, teaching manuals) for all subjects, specialising in maths, science, geography, reading and English and currently focusing on Key Stages 1 and 2.

Frederick Warne
See **Penguin Group (UK)**

Franklin Watts
See **The Watts Publishing Group Ltd**

The Watts Publishing Group Ltd
96 Leonard Street, London EC2A 4XD
☎020 7739 2929 Fax 020 7739 2318
✉ gm@wattspub.co.uk
www.wattspublishing.co.uk

Managing Director *Marlene Johnson*

Part of Groupe Lagardère. Publishes children's non-fiction, reference, information, gift, fiction, picture and novelty books and audio books. IMPRINTS **Franklin Watts** *Philippa Stewart* Non-fiction and information; **Orchard Books** *Ann-Janine Murtagh* Fiction, picture and novelty books.
About 500 titles a year. Unsolicited material is not considered other than by referral or recommendation. OVERSEAS ASSOCIATES in Australia and New Zealand.
ROYALTIES twice-yearly.

Wayland
See **Hodder Headline Ltd**

Weidenfeld & Nicolson
See **The Orion Publishing Group Ltd**

West Highland Series
See **House of Lochar**

Wharncliffe Books
47 Church Street, Barnsley S70 2AS
☎01226 734222 Fax 01226 734438
✉ enquiries@wharncliffebooks.co.uk
www.wharncliffebooks.co.uk

Managing Director *Charles Hewitt*

Imprint Manager *Barbara Bramall*

An imprint of **Pen & Sword Books Ltd**. Wharncliffe is the book and magazine publishing arm of an old-established, independently owned newspaper publishing and printing house. Publishes local history throughout the UK, focusing on nostalgia and old photographs. SERIES *Aspects*. No unsolicited mss; synopses and ideas welcome.
ROYALTIES twice-yearly.

Which? Books
2 Marylebone Road, London NW1 4DF
☎020 7770 6000 Fax 020 7770 7660
www.which.net
Editorial Director *Helen Parker*
Head of Which? Books *Robert Gray*

Founded 1957. Publishing arm of the Consumers' Association, a registered charity. Publishes non-fiction: information and reference on food, health, consumer markets personal finance, property, technology, consumer law, careers and lifestage events. All titles offer direct value to the consumer. IMPRINT **Which? Books** TITLES *The Good Food Guide*; *The Good Skiing and Snowboarding Guide*; *The Which? Guide to Good Hotels*; *Which? Medicine*; *Wills and Probate*; *Be Your Own Financial Adviser*. 25–30 titles a year. No unsolicited mss; send synopses and ideas only.
ROYALTIES if applicable, twice-yearly.

Whitaker Information Services
See **Nielsen BookData**

Whittet Books Ltd
Hill Farm, Stonham Road, Cotton, Stowmarket IP14 4RQ
☎01449 781877 Fax 01449 781898
✉ annabel@whittet.dircon.co.uk
www.whittetbooks.com
Managing Director *Annabel Whittet*

Publishes natural history, pets, poultry, horses, domestic livestock, horticulture, rural interest. Unsolicited mss, synopses and ideas for books welcome.
ROYALTIES twice-yearly.

Whurr Publishers Ltd
19B Compton Terrace, London N1 2UN
☎020 7359 5979 Fax 020 7226 5290
✉ info@whurr.co.uk
www.whurr.co.uk
Chairman/Managing Director *Colin Whurr*

Approx. Annual Turnover £1 million
Founded in 1987. Publishes speech and language therapy, nursing, psychology, psychotherapy, audiology, special education including dyslexia, ADHD, autism and Downs syndrome. No fiction and general trade books. 60 titles in 2003. Unsolicited mss, synopses and ideas welcome within their specialist fields only. 'Whurr Publishers believes authors can be best served by a small, specialised company combining old-fashioned service with the latest publishing technology.'
ROYALTIES twice-yearly.

Whydown Books Limited
Sedlescombe TN33 0RN
☎01424 870875 Fax 01424 870083
✉ readerspost@whydownbooks.com
www.whydownbooks.com
Chairman *Dick Nesbitt-Dufort*
Managing & Finance Director *Chris Martin*
Editorial Head *Pamela Richards*

Founded 2002. Publishes biography, fiction, general interest with a slant towards writers with first-hand experience of distant places and profound events. TITLES *Spies and Lovers* Adrian Hill; *Black Lysander* John Nesbitt-Dufort; *The Apothecary's Gift* Bradley Bernarde; *Chinnery's Hotel* Jaysinh Birje. No academic, children's or poetry at present. No unsolicited mss. Synopses and ideas welcome. Approach by letter or e-mail with idea and writing history.
ROYALTIES twice-yearly.

Wild Goose Publications
Iona Community, 4th Floor, The Savoy Centre, 140 Sauchiehall Street, Glasgow G2 3DH
☎0141 332 6292 Fax 0141 332 1090
✉ admin@ionabooks.com
www.ionabooks.com
Editorial Head *Sandra Kramer*
Approx. Annual Turnover £200,000

The publishing house of the Iona Community, established in the Celtic Christian tradition of St Columba, publishes books, tapes and CDs on holistic spirituality, social justice, political and peace issues, healing, innovative approaches to worship, song and material for meditation and reflection.

Wiley Europe Ltd
The Atrium, Southern Gate, Chichester PO19 8SQ
☎01243 779777 Fax 01243 775878

www.wileyeurope.com

Managing Director *Dr John Jarvis*
Publishing Directors *Mike Davis, Stephen Smith*
Approx. Annual Turnover £87 million

Founded 1807. US parent company. Publishes professional, reference trade and text books, scientific, technical and biomedical.

DIVISIONS **Architecture** *Vivien Ward*; **Business** *Sarah Stevens*; **Business/Management** *Steve Hardman*; **Chemistry & Earth Sciences** *Sally Wilkinson*; **Computing** *Gaynor Redvers-Mutton*; **Finance** *Samantha Whittaker*; **General Interest** *Sally Smith*; **Management/ Marketing** *Claire Plimmer*; **Psychology** *Vivien Ward*; **Major Reference Works** *David Hughes*; **Medicine & Life Sciences** *Deborah Dixion*; **Technology & Engineering** *Ann-Marie Halligan*.
ROYALTIES annually.

Authors' Rating With an ever growing list of scientific, technical and medical books, Wiley is among the top educational and professional publishers. Academic authors are attracted by the American connection. Online publishing is set to increase.

Wiley-Academy

John Wiley & Sons, 4th Floor, International House, 7 High Street, Ealing Broadway, London W5 5DB
☎020 8326 3800 Fax 020 8326 3801
Chairman *John Jarvis*
Commissioning Editor *Helen Castle*

Founded 1969. Became part of the **John Wiley & Sons, Inc.** group in 1997. Publishes architecture and design. Welcomes unsolicited mss, synopses and ideas.
ROYALTIES annually.

Neil Wilson Publishing Ltd

Suite 303, The Pentagon Centre, 36 Washington Street, Glasgow G3 8AZ
☎0141 221 1117 Fax 0141 221 5363
✉ info@nwp.co.uk
www.nwp.co.uk
www.11-9.co.uk

Managing Director/Editorial Director *Neil Wilson*
Editorial Administrator *Sallie Moffat*
Approx. Annual Turnover £250,000

Founded 1992. Publishes Scottish interest and history, biography, humour and hillwalking, whisky; also cookery. IMPRINTS **The In Pinn** Outdoor pursuits; **The Angels' Share** Whisky, drink and food-related subjects; **The Vital Spark** Humour; **NWP** History, biography, reference, true crme; **11:9** Scottish fiction. About 10–15 titles a year. Unsolicited mss, synopses and ideas welcome. No politics, academic or technical.
ROYALTIES twice-yearly.

Philip Wilson Publishers Ltd

7 Deane House, 27 Greenwood Place, London NW5 1LB
☎020 7284 3088 Fax 020 7284 3099
✉ pwilson@philip-wilson.co.uk
www.philip-wilson.co.uk

Chairman *Philip Wilson*

Founded 1976. Publishes art, art history, antiques and collectables. About 15 titles a year.

Wimbledon Publishing Company

75–76 Blackfriars Road, London SE1 8HA
☎020 7401 4200 Fax 020 7401 4201
✉ editor@wpcpress.com
www.wpcpress.com

Managing Director *Kamaljit Sood*
General Manager *Noel McPherson*

Founded in 1992 as a publisher of school texts, going on to launch Anthem Press, an academic and general interest imprint focusing on history, politics, economics, international affairs, literature and culture. IMPRINTS **Anthem Press** *Tom Penn, Caroline Broughton*; **WPC Education** *K. Sood*. Welcomes mss, synopses and ideas for books. PARTNER ORGANISATION Stylus Publishing LLC, Sterling, VA, US.
ROYALTIES annually.

Windhorse Publications

11 Park Road, Moseley B13 8AB
☎0121 449 9696 Fax 0121 449 9191
✉ jnanasiddhi@windhorsepublications.com
www.windhorsepublications.com

Chairman/Editorial Head *Jnanasiddhi*
Approx. Annual Turnover £250,000

Founded 1977. Publishes meditation and Buddhism. Associated with the FWBO, a worldwide Buddhist movement. Publishes across the Buddhist traditions. TITLES *Female Deities in Buddhism*; *Wildmind: A Step by Step Guide to Meditation*; *Verses of Inspiration*. 9 titles in 2003. Unsolicited mss, synopses and ideas welcome; approach by letter or e-mail in the first instance.
ROYALTIES quarterly.

Windsor Large Print

See **BBC Audiobooks** under *Audio Books*

Wise Publications
See **Omnibus Press**

WIT Press
Ashurst Lodge, Ashurst, Southampton
SO40 7AA
☎023 8029 3223   Fax 023 8029 2853
✉ marketing@witpress.com
www.witpress.com

Owner *Computational Mechanics International Ltd, Southampton*
Chairman/Managing Director/Editorial Head *Professor C.A. Brebbia*

Founded in 1980 as Computational Mechanics Publications to publish engineering analysis titles. Changed to WIT Press to reflect the increased range of publications. Publishes scientific and technical, mainly at postgraduate level and above, including architecture, environmental engineering, bioengineering. TITLES *The Sustainable City; Handling Missing Data; Human Exposure to Electromagnetic Fields; Computational Ballistics*. 50 titles in 2003. Unsolicited mss, synopses and ideas welcome; approach by post or e-mail. No non-scientific or technical material or lower level (school- and college-level texts). OVERSEAS SUBSIDIARY Computational Mechanics, Inc., Billerica, USA.
ROYALTIES annually.

Wizard Books
See **Icon Books Ltd**

Oswald Wolff Books
See **Berg Publishers**

The Women's Press
27 Goodge Street, London W1T 2LD
☎020 7636 3992   Fax 020 7637 1866
www.the-womens-press.com

Managing Director *Stella Kane*
Approx. Annual Turnover £1 million

Part of the Namara Group. First title published in 1978. Publishes women only: quality fiction and non-fiction. Fiction usually has a female protagonist and a woman-centred theme. International writers and subject matter encouraged. Non-fiction: books for and about women generally; gender politics, race politics, disability, feminist theory, health and psychology, literary criticism. IMPRINTS **Women's Press Classics**; **Livewire Books for Teenagers** Fiction and non-fiction series for young adults. About 50 titles a year. Synopses and ideas for books welcome. No mss without previous letter, synopsis and sample material.
ROYALTIES twice-yearly.

Authors' Rating Though the Women's Press has been up for sale since late 2000, its current owner is pledged to keep going until an attractive suitor comes along. The call is out for new talent.

Woodhead Publishing Ltd
Abington Hall, Abington, Cambridge
CB1 6AH
☎01223 891358   Fax 01223 893694
✉ wp@woodhead-publishing.com
www.woodhead-publishing.com
www.WoodheadFoodNet.com

Chairman *Alan Jessup*
Managing Director *Martin Woodhead*
Approx. Annual Turnover £1.5 million

Founded 1989. Publishes engineering, materials technology, textile technology, finance and investment, food technology, environmental science. TITLES *Welding International* (journal); *Reinforced Plastics Durability*; *Meat Science 6e*; *Base Metals Handbook*; *Foreign Exchange Options*. The website www.WoodheadFoodNet.com was launched in 2002. Contains 50 e-books on food science, technology and nutrition. DIVISION **Woodhead Publishing** *Martin Woodhead*. About 50 titles a year. Unsolicited material welcome.
ROYALTIES annually.

Wordsworth Editions Ltd
8B East Street, Ware SG12 9HG
☎01920 465167   Fax 01920 462267
✉ enquiries@wordsworth-editions.com *or* dennis.hart@wordsworth-editions.com (editorial)
www.wordsworth-editions.co.uk

Directors *M.C.W. Trayler, E.G. Trayler, D.R. Hart*
Approx. Annual Turnover £4 million

Founded 1987. Publishes classics of English and world literature, reference books, poetry, children's classics, military history and special editions. About 75 titles a year. No unsolicited mss.

WPC Education
See **Wimbledon Publishing Company**

X Libris
See **Time Warner Books UK**

The X Press
PO Box 25694, London N17 6FP
☎020 8801 2100 Fax 020 8885 1322
✉ vibes@xpress.co.uk
Editorial Director *Dotun Adebayo*
Publisher *Steve Pope*

Launched in 1992 with the cult bestseller *Yardie*, The X Press is the leading publisher of Black-interest fiction in the UK. Also publishes general fiction and children's fiction. IMPRINTS **The X Press**; **Nia**; **20/20**. About 26 titles a year. Send mss rather than synopses or ideas (enclose s.a.e.). No poetry.

Authors' Rating A small company that has done an inestimable service by introducing Black writers to the publishing mainstream. Popular fiction is the mainstay but the list also covers reprints of classic Black fiction.

Y Lolfa Cyf
Talybont, Ceredigion SY24 5AP
☎01970 832304 Fax 01970 832782
✉ ylolfa@ylolfa.com
www.ylolfa.com/
Managing Director *Garmon Gruffudd*
General Editor *Lefi Gruffudd*
Approx. Annual Turnover £800,000

Founded 1967. Small company which publishes mainly in Welsh; has its own four-colour printing and binding facilities. Publishes Welsh language publications; Celtic language tutors; English language books for the Welsh and Celtic tourist trade. Expanding slowly. TITLES *My Kingdom of Books* Richard Booth; *The Welsh Learner's Dictionary* Heini Gruffudd; *The Fight for Welsh Freedom* Gwynfor Evans; *Celtic Vision* John Merion Morris. IMPRINT **Dinas** Part-author-subsidised imprint for non-mainstream books of Welsh interest in English and Welsh. About 50 titles a year. Write first with synopses or ideas.
ROYALTIES twice-yearly.

Yale University Press (London)
47 Bedford Square, London WC1B 3DP
☎020 7079 4900 Fax 020 7079 4901

Founded 1961. Owned by US parent company. Publishes academic and humanities. About 200 titles (worldwide) a year. Unsolicited mss and synopses welcome if in specialised subject areas.
ROYALTIES annually.

Authors' Rating A publisher with a marvellous talent for turning out scholarly books which appeal to the general reader. Academic writers who want to reach a wider audience take note.

Yellow Jersey Press
See **The Random House Group Ltd**

Zambezi Publishing
PO Box 221, Plymouth PL2 2YJ
☎01752 367300 Fax 01752 350453
✉ info@zampub.com
www.zampub.com
Chair *Sasha Fenton*
Managing Director *Jan Budkowski*

Founded 1999. Publishes non-fiction: mind, body and spirit, self-help, finance and business. IMPRINT **Zambezi Publishing** TITLES *How to be Psychic*; *Tarot Mysteries*; *Modern Palmistry*; *The Money Book*. Send synopsis and sample chapter by mail. Brief e-mail communication acceptable but *no* attachments, please.
ROYALTIES twice-yearly.

Zastrugi Books
PO Box 2963, Brighton BN1 6AW
☎01273 566369 Fax 01273 566369/562720
Chairman *Ken Singleton*

Founded 1997. Publishes English-language teaching books only. No unsolicited mss; synopses and ideas for books welcome.
ROYALTIES twice-yearly.

Zed Books Ltd
7 Cynthia Street, London N1 9JF
☎020 7837 4014 Fax 020 7833 3960
✉ hosie@zedbooks.demon.co.uk
www.zedbooks.co.uk
Approx. Annual Turnover £1.4 million

Founded 1976. Publishes international and Third World affairs, development studies, women's studies, environmental studies, cultural studies, human rights and specific area studies. No fiction, children's or poetry.

DIVISIONS **Development & Environment** *Robert Molteno, Dr Anna Hardman*; **Women's Studies, Cultural Studies**. TITLES *Rogue State: A Guide to the World's Only Superpower* William Blum; *Staying Alive* Vandana Shiva; *The Autobiography of Nawal* Nawal El Saadawi. About 60 titles a year. No unsolicited mss; synopses and ideas welcome though.
ROYALTIES annually.

Zero to Ten
See **Evans Brothers Ltd**

Zipper Books
See **Millivres Prowler Limited**

A Writer's Diary

Katharine Davies records a year in the life of A Good Voyage

January 2003

I've written a novel! Even if it never gets published, the fact that I've written 66,000 words is an achievement in itself. Although I'd love something to happen with *A Good Voyage*, which is inspired by Shakespeare's *Twelfth Night*, I remind myself that it's my first book. Real authors often admit to producing an earlier unpublished book before their 'first' novel, so I'm concentrating on ideas for a second book, which I hope to write with the help of a Welsh Arts Council bursary.

I wrote *A Good Voyage*, during the second year of a part-time creative writing MA at Middlesex University. Without the encouragement of my tutor, Sue Gee, and her belief in my writing, I would probably have given up the course in the first term. But halfway through 2002, *A Good Voyage* had gathered momentum. The final assignment of the MA required me to submit the first 20,000 words by early December, but I had set myself a personal deadline: to get the whole book done and to show it to an agent by Christmas. Taking a term out of teaching, I went to stay on the Welsh borders and worked on it flat out until, in late October, I surprised even myself by experimentally typing 'THE END'. Although I was not actually sure that I had done anything more than finish yet another draft, by this time I needed to make contact with the outside world; having got Sue's approval of the idea, I sent the opening and a synopsis to a select few agents.

'Start with the best in the business,' a publishing friend had advised me, mentioning one or two names. And so I had.

But now it's January, I'm back teaching in London with no time to write, and I'm wondering if I should ask her for some more names. There had been a great flurry of excitement when one very well-known agent had rung within days of receiving the opening to ask for the whole novel, but that was weeks ago. Now I'm kicking myself for being so impatient. I should have put it in a drawer and redrafted it after Christmas with a fresh eye. Or been like D.H. Lawrence and rewritten it from scratch. I realise, too late, that just when I sent in my manuscript, the agents would have been swept up in a whirl of Christmas parties, and probably been snowed under by blizzards of submissions.

February

A miracle. Simon Trewin of PFD has sent me an e-mail in which he has said some amazingly nice things about *A Good Voyage*! I'd sent him the whole manuscript at his request and now he has read it. His e-mail couldn't be kinder or more encouraging. He even apologises for not getting back to me sooner, saying he is 'drowning' in paper. He's going to recommend it 'in glowing terms' to one of his colleagues, Caroline Dawnay! I read the e-mail slowly several times. I look up the entry for PFD in *The Writer's Handbook* and see Caroline Dawnay's name. My publishing friend is very impressed.

March

It's three weeks since I was in touch with Simon Trewin, and Caroline Dawnay has not made contact. Full of trepidation, I send her an e-mail asking whether she has had time to read my manuscript and if she liked it. She replies straight away and says she has read it and she does really like it, in fact she says she is 'struck' by it, but she has been 'swamped' with work and doesn't want to mislead me about how much space she has. Would I like to come in for a talk anyway, without either of us making any commitments? I agree at once and decide that she is going to give me some much-needed advice. Perhaps she'll tell me how I could alter it to re-submit or suggest someone else I could send it to. Another agent, who had heard me read at the Middlesex University Literary Festival, had requested I make some changes before she'd consider taking me on, but I had not been able to see how to make them. Now, I tell myself, a total rewrite is a must. But do I have the time and resources for such an undertaking? Or should I just abandon ship and move on to novel number two?

I re-read the critical introduction from my MA in preparation for my meeting with Caroline. The critical introduction had been hard work at the time, but now I'm glad I had thought seriously about my ideas and inspiration.

April

April 2nd. My visit to PFD. Caroline greets me and leads me to her office and we talk about *A Good Voyage*. Just when I'm feeling that I'm not doing a very good job of explaining the quotation from *Twelfth Night* I've used at the beginning as an epigraph, she says that she wants to try to find me a publisher. I am in a state of shock as she takes me to meet her assistant, Alex, and Simon Trewin, without whom none of this would have happened at all. As we say goodbye, Caroline tells me she takes on very few new writers a year and that she's as thrilled as I am. I float down the street. Caroline Dawnay is my agent. My agent is Caroline Dawnay!

Later, when I am slightly calmer, I send Caroline a note on my use of *Twelfth Night*, which she wants to put as an afterword for publishers. Again, I am grateful that I had crystallised my thoughts during my MA.

In a few days, Caroline lets me know the afterword is just right and that she has re-read *A Good Voyage* and found it 'exhilarating'! I agree to use Katharine Davies, not Kathy Davies, as my *nom de plume*.

May

No news from any publishers so far. I have also heard that I have not got the writer's bursary from the Arts Council of Wales, which can only mean more teaching and no time to write. But first I am going to the Hay Festival to be a volunteer steward so I can hear lots of writers talking about their books while I'm doing 'front of house' (or tent) and hopefully pick up a few tips.

May 22nd. A call from Caroline. CHATTO & WINDUS WANT TO PUBLISH MY BOOK! I'm staying with my parents en route to the festival and I dance jubilantly around the kitchen with my mum and dad, so glad I'm with them to share the news. I go to the bookshelves and see that some of my favourite authors are published by Chatto & Windus, and by Vintage, who will publish the paperback. I fall in love with the Chatto cherubs. At Hay, in my fluorescent jerkin that says STEWARD on the back, I tentatively start to think of myself as a writer in disguise. I am in a strange state of limbo – I haven't 'gone public' about my book to any friends because I'm terrified that Chatto will change their minds before I can sign the contract. At Hay, I am surprised to bump into Caroline and I wonder what she will think of me in my guise as a steward and if it's the sort of thing writers do. A few days later, I am bowled over by congratulatory e-mails from Alison Samuel and Poppy Hampson and Ali Reynolds all welcoming me to Chatto and to Vintage.

June

I am a bona fide writer: I have joined the British Library to do my research and, when I have to send an author biography to Alex at PFD, I spend two days writing two lines, experiencing my first true case of writer's block. A photographer friend takes some pictures for the jacket on a blisteringly hot day when the sun is so bright I can hardly open my eyes – although he reassures me he's got the shots he wants. I am invited to Chatto & Windus to meet the team. I've noticed the Random House building on Vauxhall Bridge Road often enough (I used to teach just around the corner) but never thought I would have a reason to go inside. During the meeting I am plied with cups of tea and eat lots of biscuits as Alison and Poppy tell me they don't want me to change anything very much about my book - except for one scene, which we all agree needs some work, and one or two other small changes overall. I am very relieved. Everyone is beaming, but I am beaming more than anyone else.

I visit Barry Turner in search of temping work and he suggests the idea of the Writer's Diary.

July

I'm off to Wales for the summer to research my second book. I feel I've hardly had a minute to think about it. I yearn for the peace I had last year. I realise that in deciding to be a writer I have embarked on a difficult course, although I can't imagine being happy doing anything else.

Before leaving London I visit some photo libraries. I've been asked for some suggestions for the jacket of the book and I'm looking for images of the same garden in winter and in summer to have as the back and front of the book, but these prove hard to find. Poppy sends me the manuscript with some comments on it but says in her letter that Alison and she think it's 'very polished' – which I know is not only the result of hours of solitude in Wales, but also of the process of doing my MA. My job now is to go through and make any small alterations on screen. I am also working separately on the scene we agreed needed changing and thinking about the blurb for the Random House catalogue and the jacket. Because I'm in Wales again, we go through things in long phone conversations and, later in the month, we meet up in London. I feel reassured by how much in sympathy with the book Poppy is and how well she knows it.

August
August 7th THE JOY HARRIS LITERARY AGENCY IN THE US HAS TAKEN ME ON! I hadn't even considered this as a possibility, but Caroline must have been working behind the scenes. The American agent, Alexia Paul, gets in touch by e-mail, but when I get back from a two-week holiday, I find that she didn't get my reply because of the blackout in New York. I send her another e-mail - panicking that she might have changed her mind in the meantime. By the end of the month, the manuscript of *A Good Voyage* goes to the copy-editor.

September
I hope I've finally sorted out the copyright for the poetry and songs I've quoted. The copy-edited version comes back for me to check and I go through the finest of fine details with Poppy. I am starting to weary of the editorial process and just want everything to be over, even though I'm the one raising questions about every tiny thing I can think of through sheer anxiety.

Meanwhile, *A Good Voyage* is being seen by publishers in the US.

October
I start teaching evening classes in creative writing at City University.

ALEXIA CALLS ME FROM NEW YORK TO TELL ME 'LITTLE RANDOM' HAs OFFERED ME A TWO-BOOK DEAL IN THE US! A few days later, I am speaking nervously to my American editor, Danielle Durkin, on the phone. My life begins to take on an air of unreality. Everyone in America agrees on one thing: over there, the book will need a different title.

November
An interesting-sounding quarterly about books is starting called *Slightly Foxed* and I get the chance to work in their office with one day off a week to write.

There have been a lot of discussions about the artwork for the jacket and I'm adjusting my ideas to the latest design concept when Poppy sends me a completely new design. It's a beautiful tinted photograph of a girl with red hair and the title is done in copperplate with a silver swirl. She and Alison have fallen in love with it already and now so do I. Seeing the jacket with my name on it makes everything very real. I receive the final page proofs to check. I read them twice, even though a proofreader is simultaneously checking them. I have lost all ability to judge the content of the book and am alarmed to realise I know it off by heart. The title for *A Good Voyage* for the American market will be *The Madness of Love*, which makes sense when I come to think about it.

December
Poppy sends me an early Christmas present of a proof of the jacket and a bound proof of the book itself. I wrap the jacket round, even though it doesn't quite fit – because the bound proof is a little bigger than the published book will be - and put it on my bookshelf, as I would a real book written by a real author.

A Good Voyage *is published by Chatto & Windus and will be published as a Vintage paperback in July 2005. Middlesex University MA Writing Programme website www. mdx.ac.uk/subjects/emc/mawrit.htm*

Irish Publishers

International Reply Coupons (IRCs) For return postage, IRCs are required (*not* UK postage stamps). These are available from post offices: letters, 60 pence; mss according to weight. For current postal rates from the Republic of Ireland to the UK go to www.letterpost.ie and click on 'Letterpost Services'.

An Gúm

Cúirt Fhreidric, Sr. Fhreidric Thuaidh, Baile Átha Cliath 1
☎00 353 1 889 2800 Fax 00 353 1 873 1140
✉ angum@forasnagaeilge.ie

Senior Editor *Seosamh Ó Murchú*
Editors *Antain Mag Shamhráin, Máire Nic Mhaoláin*

Founded 1926. Formerly the Irish language publications branch of the Department of Education and Science. Has now become part of the North/South Language Body, Foras na Gaeilge. Publishes educational, children's, young adult, music, lexicography and general. Little adult fiction or poetry. About 50 titles a year. Unsolicited mss, synopses and ideas for books welcome. Also welcomes reading copies of first and second level school textbooks with a view to translating them into the Irish language.
ROYALTIES annually.

Anvil Books

45 Palmerston Road, Dublin 6
☎00 353 1 497 3628 Fax 00 353 1 496 8263

Managing Director *Rena Dardis*

Founded 1964 with emphasis on Irish history and biography. IMPRINT **The Children's Press**. Publishes Irish history, biography (particularly 1916–22), folklore and children's fiction. No adult fiction, poetry, fantasy, short stories or full-colour books for children. About 7 titles a year. 'Because of promotional requirements, only books by Irish-based authors considered and only books of Irish interest.' Send synopsis only with IRCs (no UK stamps); unsolicited mss not returned.
ROYALTIES annually.

Ashfield Press

30 Linden Grove, Blackrock Co. Dublin
☎00 353 1 288 9808
✉ suswaine@gofree.indigo.ie

Managing Director *Susan Waine*

An imprint of **Blackhall Publishing**. Publishes Irish-interest books, both fiction and non-fiction. TITLES *Whist for Your Life*; *That's Treason*; *Recollections of a Long Life*. Unsolicited mss and synopses welcome.
ROYALTIES annually.

Atrium

See **Attic Press Ltd**

Attic Press Ltd

c/o Cork University Press, Crawford Business Park, Crosses Green, Cork
☎00 353 21 432 1725
Fax 00 353 21 431 5329
✉ corkunip@ucc.ie
www.corkuniversitypress.com

Publisher *Mike Collins*

Founded 1988. An imprint of **Cork University Press**. Began life in 1984 as a forum for information on the Irish feminist movement. Publishes non-fiction (history, women's studies, politics, biography). IMPRINT **Atrium** General Interest. About 5 titles a year. Does not accept unsolicited proposals in adult fiction.
ROYALTIES annually.

Blackhall Publishing

27 Carysfort Avenue, Blackrock Co. Dublin
☎00 353 1 278 5090 Fax 00 353 1 278 4446
✉ blackhall@eircom.net
www.blackhallpublishing.com

Managing Director *Gerard O'Connor*
Commissioning Editor *Ruth Garvey*

Publishes business, management and living books. Main subject areas include accounting, finance, management, HRM and law books aimed at both students and professionals in the industry. TITLES *Managing Cross-Cultural Business Relations*; *Managing People in the Workplace*; *Talking the Talk*; *Law of Childcare*; *European Work Equipment Legislation*; *Bullying in the Workplace, Home and School*; *Making the Most of Redundancy*. IMPRINT **Ashfield Press** (see entry). Unsolicited mss and synopses welcome.
ROYALTIES annually.

Blackwater Press

c/o Folens Publishers, Hibernian Industrial Estate, Greenhills Road, Tallaght, Dublin 24
☎00 353 1 413 7200 Fax 00 353 1 413 7280
✉ john.o'connor@folens.ie

Chief Executive *Dirk Folens*
Managing Director *John O'Connor*

Part of Folens Publishers. Publishes political, sports, fiction (*Margaret Burns*) and children's (*Deidre Whelan*).

Bradshaw Books

Tigh Filí, Thompson House, MacCurtain Street, Cork
☎00 353 21 450 9274
Fax 00 353 21 455 1617
✉ admin@cwpc.ie
www.tighfili.com

Managing Director *Maire Bradshaw*

Founded 1985. Publishes poetry, short stories, women's issues, spiritual, children's books. Organisers of the annual Cork Literary Review poetry manuscript competition. SERIES *Cork Literary Review*. Submit letter, synopsis, sample chapters and s.a.e.
ROYALTIES not generally paid.

Brandon/Mount Eagle

Dingle, Co. Kerry
☎00 353 66 915 1463
Fax 00 353 66 915 1234
www.brandonbooks.com

Publisher *Steve MacDonogh*
Approx. Annual Turnover €500,000

Founded in 1997. Publishes Irish fiction, biography, memoirs and other non-fiction. About 15 titles a year. Not seeking unsolicited mss.

Brookside
See **New Island**

Edmund Burke Publisher

Cloonagashel, 27 Priory Drive, Blackrock, Co. Dublin
☎00 353 1 288 2159 Fax 00 353 1 283 4080
✉ deburca@indigo.ie
www.deburcararebooks.com

Managing Director *Eamonn De Búrca*
Approx. Annual Turnover €320,000

Small family-run business publishing historical and topographical and fine limited-edition books relating to Ireland. TITLES *The Great Book of Irish Genealogies*, 5 vols; *The Annals of the Four Masters*, 7 vols; *Flowers of May* (illus. Wendy Walsh); *O'Curry's Manners and Customs of the Ancient Irish*; *Joyce's Irish Names of Places*. Unsolicited mss welcome. No synopses or ideas.
ROYALTIES annually.

Butterworth Ireland Ltd
See **LexisNexis**

The Children's Press
See **Anvil Books**

Cló Iar-Chonnachta

Indreabhán, Connemara, Galway
☎00 353 91 593307 Fax 00 353 91 593362
✉ cic@iol.ie
www.cic.ie

Chairman/Director *Micheál Ó Conghaile*
Editor *Róisin Ní Mhianáin*
Approx. Annual Turnover €400,000

Founded 1985. Publishes fiction, poetry, plays, teenage fiction and children's, mostly in Irish, including translations. Also publishes cassettes of writers reading from their own works. TITLES *Máire Mhic Ghiolla Íosa: Beathaisnéis* Ray Mac Mánais; *Fardoras* Michael Davitt; *An Fear nach nDéanann Gáire* Micheál Ó Conghaile; *Ólann mo Mhiúíl as an nGainséies* Gabriel Rosenstock. 12 titles in 2003.
ROYALTIES annually.

The Columba Press

55A Spruce Avenue, Stillorgan Industrial Park, Blackrock, Co. Dublin
☎00 353 1 294 2556 Fax 00 353 1 294 2564
✉ sean@columba.ie (editorial) *or*
   info@columba.ie (general)
www.columba.ie

Chairman *Neil Kluepfel*
Managing Director *Seán O'Boyle*
Approx. Annual Turnover €1.02 million

Founded 1985. Small company committed to growth. Publishes religious and counselling titles. TITLES *Prism of Love* Donal O'Leary; *That Could Never Be* Kevin Dalton. IMPRINT **Currach Press** Publisher *Brian Lynch* (brian@columba.ie) Secular books TITLE *The Harcourt Street Line* Brian Mac Aongusa. 40 titles in 2003. Backlist of 235 titles. Unsolicited ideas and synopses rather than full mss preferred.
ROYALTIES twice-yearly.

Cork University Press

Crawford Business Park, Crosses Green, Cork
☎00 353 21 490 2980
Fax 00 353 21 431 5329
✉ corkunip@ucc.ie
www.corkuniversitypress.com

Publisher *Mike Collins*

Founded 1925. Relaunched in 1992, the Press publishes academic and some trade titles. TITLES *The Field Day Anthology of Irish Writing – Volumes IV & V*; *Newgrange and the Bend of the Boyne*; *Landscape Design in 18th Century Ireland*. Also a biannual journal, *The Irish Review*, an interdisciplinary cultural review. No fiction. IMPRINTS **Attic Press** (see entry) **Atrium**. 15 titles in 2003. Unsolicited synopses and ideas welcome for textbooks, academic monographs, belles lettres, illustrated histories and journals.

ROYALTIES annually.

Currach Press
See **The Columba Press**

Flyleaf Press
4 Spencer Villas, Glenageary, Co. Dublin
☎00 353 1 284 5906   Fax 00 353 1 280 6231
✉ Flyleaf@indigo.ie
www.flyleaf.ie

Managing Director *Dr James Ryan*

Founded 1981. Concentrates on family history and Irish history as a background to family history. No fiction. TITLES *Irish Records*; *Longford and its People*; *Tracing Your Kerry Ancestors*; *Tracing Your Limerick Ancestors*. Unsolicited mss, synopses and ideas for books welcome.

ROYALTIES twice-yearly.

Four Courts Press Ltd
7 Malpas Street, Dublin 8
☎00 353 1 453 4668   Fax 00 353 1 453 4672
✉ info@four-courts-press.ie
www.four-courts-press.ie

Chairman/Managing Director *Michael Adams*
Director *Martin Healy*

Founded 1972. Publishes mainly scholarly books in the humanities. About 60 titles a year. Synopses and ideas for books welcome.

ROYALTIES annually.

Gateway
See **Gill & Macmillan**

Gill & Macmillan
10 Hume Avenue, Park West, Dublin 12
☎00 353 1 500 9500   Fax 00 353 1 500 9599
www.gillmacmillan.ie

Managing Director *M.H. Gill*
Approx. Annual Turnover €11.5 million

Founded 1968 when M.H. Gill & Son Ltd and Macmillan Ltd formed a jointly owned publishing company. Publishes biography/auto-biography, history, current affairs, literary criticism (all mainly of Irish interest), guidebooks, cookery, popular fiction. Also educational textbooks for secondary and tertiary levels. Contacts: *Hubert Mahony* (Educational); *Fergal Tobin* (General). IMPRINTS **Tivoli** *Alison Walsh* Popular fiction; **Newleaf**; **Gateway** Popular health, psychology, mind, body and spirit. About 80 titles a year. Unsolicited synopses and ideas welcome.

ROYALTIES subject to contract.

Institute of Public Administration
57–61 Lansdowne Road, Dublin 4
☎00 353 1 240 3600   Fax 00 353 1 269 8644
✉ Sales@ipa.ie
www.ipa.ie

Chairman *Stiofán de Búrca*
Director-General *John Cullen*
Publisher *Declan McDonagh*
Approx. Annual Turnover €1 million

Founded 1957 by a group of public servants, the Institute of Public Administration is the Irish public sector management development agency. The publishing arm of the organisation is one of its major activities. Publishes academic and professional books and periodicals: history, law, politics, economics and Irish public administration for students and practitioners. TITLES *Local Government in Ireland*; *E-Government and the Decentralisation of Service Delivery*; *Governance and Policy in Ireland*; *Cross-Departmental Challenges: A Whole of Government Approach for the 21st Century*; *Sanctuary in Ireland: Perspectives on Asylum Law and Policy*. 15 titles in 2003. No unsolicited mss; synopses and ideas welcome. No fiction or children's publishing.

ROYALTIES annually.

Irish Academic Press Ltd
44 Northumberland Road, Ballsbridge, Dublin 4
☎00 353 1 668 8244   Fax 00 353 1 660 1610
✉ info@iap.ie
www.iap.ie

Chairman *Frank Cass (London)*
Managing Editor *Mike Milotte*

Founded 1974. Publishes academic monographs and humanities. 17 titles in 2003. Unsolicited mss, synopses and ideas welcome.

ROYALTIES annually.

Irish Management Institute (IMI)
Sandyford Road, Dublin 16
☎00 353 1 207 8400   Fax 00 353 1 295 5150
✉ bill.carroll@imi.ie

www.imi.ie
Chief Executive *Barry Kenny*
Approx. Annual Turnover €15 million

Founded 1952. The IMI, owned by its members, both corporate and individual, works to improve the practice of management. Offers managers a wide range of management development services. Publishes a quarterly newsletter, *Management Focus*, distributed to members, featuring latest IMI research, case studies and management theory. Other publications include *Executive Salaries in Ireland* – annual publication that reviews managerial salaries and fringe benefits. Mss, synopses and ideas relevant to Irish management practice welcome.
ROYALTIES annually.

LexisNexis (formerly Butterworth Ireland Ltd)

26 Upper Ormond Quay, Dublin 7
☎00 353 1 872 8514 (Law)/8524 (Tax)
Fax 00 353 1 873 1378
www.butterworths.ie

Chairman *Helen Mumford* (UK)
Publishing Manager *Louise Leavy*
Commissioning Editor *Amy Hayes*

Subsidiary of LexisNexis UK (**Reed Elsevier** is the holding company). Leading publisher of Irish law and tax titles. Publishes solely law and tax books and electronic products. TITLES include *Kelly: The Irish Constitution*, 4th ed. Hogan & Whyte; *Butterworths Irish Companies Acts* MacCann et al; *Irish Planning Law Direct* (online); *The Law and Taxation of Trusts* Wylie and Keogan. Unsolicited mss, synopses and ideas welcome for titles within the broadest parameters of tax and law.
ROYALTIES twice-yearly.

The Lilliput Press

62–63 Sitric Road, Arbour Hill, Dublin 7
☎00 353 1 671 1647 Fax 00 353 1 671 1233
✉ info@lilliputpress.ie
www.lilliputpress.ie

Chairman *Vincent Hurley*
Managing Director *Antony Farrell*
Approx. Annual Turnover €255,000

Founded 1984. Publishes non-fiction: literature, history, autobiography and biography, ecology, essays; criticism; fiction and poetry. TITLES *Images of Dublin*; *An Aran Keening*; *The Beautiful Changes*; *Lady Gregory's Toothbrush*; *Cats and Their Poets: Selected Prose of Patrick Kavanagh*; *Shackleton: An Irishman in Anatartica*. About 20 titles a year. Unsolicited mss, synopses and ideas welcome. No children's or sport titles.
ROYALTIES annually.

Marino Books
See **Mercier Press Ltd**

Mercier Press Ltd

Douglas Village, Cork
☎00 353 21 489 9858
Fax 00 353 21 489 9887
✉ books@mercierpress.ie
www.mercierpress.ie

Chairman *George Eaton*
Managing Director *John F. Spillane*

Founded 1944. One of Ireland's largest publishers with a list of approx 250 Irish interest titles. IMPRINTS **Mercier Press**; **Marino Books** Editorial Director *Mary Feehan* Children's, politics, history, folklore, biography, mind, body and spirit, current affairs, women's interest. TITLES *The Course of Irish History*; all of John B. Keane's works; *Beyond Prozac*; *It's a Long Way from Penny Apples*; *Ireland's Master Storyteller*. Unsolicited synopses and ideas welcome.
ROYALTIES annually.

Merlin Publishing

16 Upper Pembroke Street, Dublin 2
☎00 353 1 676 4373 Fax 00 353 1 676 4368
www.merlin-publishing.com

Managing Director *Chenile Keogh*
Managing Editor *Aoife Barrett*

Founded 2000. Member of **Clé**. Publishes film, music, art, biography, general non-fiction, history, photography, literature and gift books. IMPRINT **Wolfhound Press** Founded 1974. Non-fiction. TITLES *Famine*; *Eyewitness Bloody Sunday*; *Father Browne's Titanic Album*. About 20 titles a year (mainly Irish interest). Sample chapters of unsolicited mss (with synopses and s.a.e.) welcome but by post only. See Merlin website for submission guidelines and proposal form.

Mount Eagle
See **Brandon/Mount Eagle**

New Island

2 Brookside, Dundrum Road, Dundrum, Dublin 14
☎00 353 1 298 9937/298 3411
Fax 00 353 1 298 2783
✉ staff@newisland.ie
www.newisland.ie

Managing Director/Editorial Head *Edwin Higel*

Editorial Manager *Emma Dunne*

Founded 1990. Publishes fiction, Irish non-fiction, poetry and drama. Branching out into popular fiction and memoirs. IMPRINT **Brookside**. 25 titles in 2003. Unsolicited mss, synopses and ideas welcome. Send three chapters and synopsis by post.

ROYALTIES twice-yearly

Newleaf

See **Gill & Macmillan**

The O'Brien Press Ltd

20 Victoria Road, Rathgar, Dublin 6

☎00 353 1 492 3333   Fax 00 353 1 492 2777

✉ books@obrien.ie

www.obrien.ie

Managing Director/Publisher *Michael O'Brien*
Editorial Director *Íde Ní Laoghaire*

Founded 1974. Publishes business, true crime, biography, music, travel, sport, Celtic subjects, food and drink, history, humour, politics, reference. Children's publishing – mainly fiction for every age from tiny tots to teenage. Illustrated fiction SERIES *Solos* (3 years+); *Pandas* (5 years+); *Flyers* (6 years+); *Red Flag* (8 years+). Novels (10 years+) – contemporary, historical, fantasy. Some non-fiction – mainly historical, and art and craft, resource books for teachers. No poetry, adult fiction or academic. Unsolicited mss (sample chapters only), synopses and ideas for books welcome. No e-mail submissions. Submissions will not be returned.

ROYALTIES annually.

Oak Tree Press

19 Rutland Street, Cork

☎00 353 21 431 3855

Fax 00 353 21 431 3496

✉ info@oaktreepress.com

www.oaktreepress.com

Managing Director *Brian O'Kane*

Founded 1992. Specialist publisher of business and professional books with a focus on small business start-up and development. Unsolicited mss and synopses welcome; address to the managing director.

ROYALTIES annually.

On Stream Publications Ltd

Currabaha, Cloghroe, Co. Cork

☎00 353 21 438 5798

Fax 00 353 21 438 5798

✉ info@onstream.ie

www.onstream.ie

Chairman/Managing Director *Roz Crowley*
Approx. Annual Turnover €255,000

Founded 1992. Formerly Forum Publications. Publishes academic, cookery, wine, general health and fitness, local history, railways, photography and practical guides. TITLES *Keeping Resources Human – A Practical Guide to Retaining Staff*; *The Book of Scarves: 100 Ideas*; *Dealing With Chronic Pain*; *Stirmixmash – A Cookbook for Young People*. About 3 titles a year. Synopses and ideas welcome. No children's books.

ROYALTIES annually.

Poolbeg Press Ltd

123 Grange Hill, Baldoyle, Dublin 13

☎00 353 1 832 1477   Fax 00 353 1 832 1430

✉ poolbeg@poolbeg.com

www.poolbeg.com

Managing Director *Kieran Devlin*
Publisher *Paula Campbell*

Founded 1976 to publish the Irish short story and has since diversified to include all areas of fiction (literary and popular), children's fiction and non-fiction, and adult non-fiction: history, biography and topics of public interest. AUTHORS discovered and first published by Poolbeg include Marian Keyes, Sheila O'Flanagan, Cathy Kelly and Patricia Scanlan. 'Our slogan is Poolbeg.com – the Irish for Bestsellers!' IMPRINTS **Poolbeg** (paperback and hardback); **Poolbeg For Children**. About 70 titles a year. Unsolicited mss, synopses and ideas welcome (mss preferred). No drama.

ROYALTIES twice-yearly.

Royal Dublin Society

Science Section, Ballsbridge, Dublin 4

☎00 353 1 668 0866   Fax 00 353 1 660 4014

✉ annette.mcdonnell@rds.ie

www.rds.ie

President *Michael Jacob*

Founded 1731 for the promotion of agriculture, science and the arts, and throughout its history has published books and journals towards this end. Publishes conference proceedings, biology and the history of Irish science. TITLES *Agricultural Development for the 21st Century*; *The Right Trees in the Right Places*; *Agriculture & the Environment*; *Water of Life*; *Science, Technology & Realism*; *Science Centres for Ireland*; *Blueprint for a National Irish Science Centre*; *Science Education in Crisis*; *Science in the Service of the Fishing Industry*; occasional papers in *Irish Science & Technology* series.

ROYALTIES not generally paid.

Royal Irish Academy
19 Dawson Street, Dublin 2
☎00 353 1 676 2570   Fax 00 353 1 676 2346
✉ r.mcnicholl@ria.ie
www.ria.ie
Executive Secretary *Patrick Buckley*
Editor of Publications *Rachel McNicholl*
Founded in 1785, the Academy has been publishing since 1787. Core publications are journals but more books published in last 15 years. Publishes academic, Irish interest and Irish language. About 7 titles a year. Welcomes mss, synopses and ideas of an academic standard.

Simon & Schuster/Town House
See **Town House Dublin**

Sitric Books
62–63 Sitric Road, Arbour Hill, Dublin 7
☎00 353 1 671 1682   Fax 00 353 1 671 1233
www.sitric.com
Chair *Vivienne Guinness*
Managing Director *Antony Farrell*
Founded 2000. Publishes current affairs, biography and fiction. TITLES *Mirror, Mirror: Confessions of a Plastic Surgery Addict; Eight Ball Boogie; The State of Grace; Overnight to Innsbruck.* About 5 titles a year. Unsolicited mss, synopses and ideas welcome. No children's or sports titles.
ROYALTIES annually.

Swordpoint Intercontinental Limited
'Solas Tobann', Ballyhillion, Malin Head, Co. Donegal
☎00 353 74 937 0278
Fax 00 353 74 937 0279
✉ writer@swordpoint.com
www.swordpoint.com
Chairman/Managing Director *Joseph A. Greenleaf*
Swordpoint was established in 1995 as a media company and branched out into books in 2003. Publishes fiction, children's, non-fiction, historical, travel, technical, Irish, poetry, plays, business, management, law, biography, fantasy, teenage fiction. Publication on cassettes and CDs as well as e-books. 15 titles in 2004. Unsolicited mss, synopses and ideas wlcome by post with return postage.
ROYALTIES twice-yearly.

Tír Eolas
Newtownlynch, Doorus, Kinvara, Co. Galway
☎00 353 91 637452   Fax 00 353 91 637452
✉ info@tireolas.com
www.tireolas.com
Publisher/Managing Director *Anne Korff*
Founded 1987. Publishes books and guides on ecology, archaeology, folklore and culture. TITLES *The Book of the Burren; The Shannon Floodlands; Not a Word of a Lie; The Book of Aran; Women of Ireland, A Biographic Dictionary; Kinvara, A Seaport Town on Galway Bay; A Burren Journal.* Unsolicited mss, synopses and ideas for books welcome. No specialist scientific and technical, fiction, plays, school textbooks or philosophy.
ROYALTIES annually.

Tivoli
See **Gill & Macmillan**

Town House Dublin
Trinity House, Charleston Road, Ranelagh, Dublin 6
☎00 353 1 497 2399   Fax 00 353 1 497 0927
✉ books@townhouse.ie
Managing Director *Treasa Coady*
Founded 1980. Publishes commercial and literary fiction, art and archaeology, sport, biography and environment. TITLES *Full Time* Paul Kimmage; *Laptop Dancing and the Nanny Goat Mambo* Tom Humphries; *Irish Girls About Town* various authors; *Gardening the Soul* Sister Stan; *John McCormack The Great Irish Tenor* Gordon T. Ledbetter. IMPRINT **Simon & Schuster/TownHouse** Founded 2001. Fiction and non-fiction. About 20 titles a year. Unsolicited mss, synopses and ideas welcome. No children's books.
ROYALTIES twice-yearly.

Veritas Publications
7–8 Lower Abbey Street, Dublin 1
☎00 353 1 878 8177   Fax 00 353 1 878 6507
✉ publications@veritas.ie
www.veritas.ie
Director *Maura Hyland*
Managing Editor *Toner Quinn*
Founded 1969 to supply religious textbooks to schools and later introduced a wide-ranging general list. Part of the Catholic Communications Institute. Publishes books on religious, ethical, moral, societal and social issues. 30 titles a year. Unsolicited mss, synopses and ideas for books welcome.
ROYALTIES annually.

Wolfhound Press
See **Merlin Publishing**

Irish Literary Agents

The Book Bureau Literary Agency

7 Duncairn Avenue, Bray, Co. Wicklow
☎00 353 1 276 4996 Fax 00 353 1 276 4834
✉ thebookbureau@oceanfree.net

Contact *Geraldine Nichol*

Handles general and literary fiction. Special interest in women's fiction, crime and thrillers. Will suggest revision. Send preliminary letter, synopsis and first three chapters; return postage essential. No reading fee. COMMISSION Home 10%; Overseas 20%. Works with foreign associates.

Marianne Gunn O'Connor Literary Agency

(G.M.M.) Morrison Chambers, Suite 17, 32 Nassau St, Dublin 2
✉ mariannegmm@eircom.net
Contact *Marianne Gunn O'Connor*

Founded 1996. Handles literary and commercial fiction, non-fiction, biography, mind, body and spirit, health and children's fiction. CLIENTS include Niall Williams, Patrick McCabe, Morag Prunty, Cecelia Ahern, Claudia Carroll, Noelle Harrison, Andrew Proctor, Chris Binchy, Anita Notaro, Claire Kilroy, Vikram A. Chandra (one of India's leading political broadcasters), Julie Dam, Paddy McMahon. Send preliminary letter plus half page synopsis and first 50 pages. No reading fee. COMMISSION Home 10%; UK 15%; US & Translation 20%; Film & TV 20%. Translation rights handled by Vicki Satlow Literary Agency, Milan.

The Lisa Richards Agency

46 Upper Baggot Street, Dublin 4
☎00 353 1 660 3534 Fax 00 353 1 660 3545
✉ info@lisarichards.ie

Contact *Faith O'Grady*

Founded 1998. Handles fiction and general non-fiction. Approach with proposal and sample chapter for non-fiction, and 3–4 chapters and synopsis for fiction (s.a.e. essential). CLIENTS include June Considine, Judi Curtin, Denise Deegan, Christin Dwyer Hickey, Tara Heavey, Arlene Hunt, Roisin Meaney, Pauline McLynn, Sarah O'Brien. COMMISSION Home 10%; UK 15%; US & Translation 20%; Film & TV 15%. OVERSEAS ASSOCIATE **The Marsh Agency** for translation rights.

Jonathan Williams Literary Agency

Rosney Mews, Upper Glenageary Road, Glenageary, Co. Dublin
☎00 353 1 280 3482
Fax 00 353 1 280 3482

Contact *Jonathan Williams*

Founded 1980. Handles general trade books: fiction, auto/biography, travel, politics, history, music, literature and criticism, gardening, cookery, sport and leisure, humour, reference, social questions, photography. Some poetry, business and children's, but less of a speciality. No plays, science fiction, mind, body and spirit, computer books, theology, multimedia, motoring, aviation. No reading fee 'unless the author wants a very fast opinion'. Initial approach by phone or letter. *Commission* Home 10%; US 20%; Translation 15%. OVERSEAS ASSOCIATES Piergiorgio Nicolazzini Literary Agency, Italy; Lora Fountain & Associates Agency, France; Löcher & Lawrence, Germany; Antonia Kerrigan Literary Agency, Spain; Tuttle-Mori Agency Inc., Japan.

Audio Books

Assembled Stories
PO Box 5212, Grantham NG33 5SR
☎01476 571333 Fax 01476 571333
✉ peter@assembledstories.com *or*
michael@assembledstories.com
www.assembledstories.com

Managing Directors *Peter Joyce, Michael Joyce*

Founded 1992. Publishes classic fiction on cassette and CD with all books read by Peter Joyce. TITLES *Idle Thoughts of an Idle Fellow* Jerome K. Jerome; *The Monkey's Paw* W.W. Jacobs; *The Beloved Vagabond* W.J. Locke; *Uncle Silas* J. Sheridan LeFanu; *The Sowers* H. Seton Merriman. 6 titles in 2003. Ideas for titles welcome.

AudioBooksForFree.Com Limited
25 Green Lane, Amersham HP6 6AS
☎01494 431119 Fax 01494 583417
✉ ToUs@AudioBooksForFree.Com
www.AudioBooksForFree.Com

Managing Director *Ruslan G. Fedorovsky*

Founded 2000. Publishes fiction: thrillers, crime, science fiction only. AUTHORS Michael Hartland, James Herlihy, Jon Schiller, Patrick Walsh. 200 titles in 2003.

BBC Audiobooks
St James House, The Square, Lower Bristol Road, Bath BA2 3BH
☎01225 878000 Fax 01225 310771
✉ info@bbcaudiobooks.com

Also at: Windsor Bridge Road, Bath BA2 3AX
☎01225 878000 Fax 01225 422585

Owner *BBC Worldwide Ltd*
Managing Director *Paul Dempsey*

BBC Audiobooks consists of **Cover to Cover Cassettes Ltd** incorporating *Harry Potter* and **Cover to Cover Classics**. Unabridged readings of classic or literary fiction. IMPRINTS **BBC Cover to Cover** Unabridged readings of classic and contemporary children's titles. Unsolicited work not accepted. **BBC Radio Collection** Established 1988. BBC Radio Collection releases material associated with BBC Radio and Television. Almost all releases sourced from BBC Radio and Television. Unsolicited work not accepted. TITLES *BBC Radio Shakespeare*;

Alan Bennett; *This Sceptred Isle*; *Hancock*; *Steptoe*; *Round the Horne*; *Agatha Christie*; *Sherlock Holmes*.

BBC Audiobooks also publishes for the library market; large print books, reprints and audio books under the **Chivers** name. Material published includes contemporary and classic fiction, non-ficton, biography and autobiography, children's books, crime, westerns. No unsolicited material. **Chivers** Audio & Book IMPRINTS **Windsor Hardcover Large Print**; **Paragon Softcover Large Print**; **Chivers Hardcover Large Print**; **Camden Softcover Large Print**; **Galaxy Children's Large Print**; **Gunsmoke Westerns**; **Black Dagger**; **Chivers Audio Books**; **Chivers Children's Audio Books**.

Bloomsbury Publishing
See entry under **UK Publishers**

Bolinda Publishing Ltd
2 Ivanhoe Road, London SE5 8DH
☎020 7733 1088
✉ bolinda@marisa.fsbusiness.co.uk
www.bolinda.com

Publisher *Marisa McGreevy*

London office of Bolinda Publishing Pty, Ltd, Australia opened in 2002 and became a company in its own right in the spring of 2004. Produces fiction titles (adult, children's and young adult); all genres. TITLES *Mates, Dates and Inflatable Bras* Cathy Hopkins; *Troy* Adele Geras; *Gould's Book of Fish* Richard Flanagan; *Temple* Matthew Reilly; *Dirt Music* Tim Winton. 12 titles in 2003.

Chivers Audio Books/
Chivers Children's Audio Books
See **BBC Audiobooks**

Chrome Dreams
12 Seaforth Avenue, New Malden KT3 6JP
☎020 8715 9781 Fax 020 8241 1426
✉ mail@chromedreams.co.uk
www.chromedreams.co.uk

Managing Director *Rob Johnstone*

A small record company and publisher founded 1998 to produce audio-biographies of current rock and pop artists and legendary performers on CD and, more recently, books on the same subjects. Ideas for biographies welcome.

Corgi Audio

Transworld Publishers, A division of the Random House Group Ltd, 61–63 Uxbridge Road, London W5 5SA

☎020 8579 2652 Fax 020 8231 6666

Managing Director *Larry Finlay*

Publishes fiction, autobiography and humour. TITLES *Discworld Series* Terry Pratchett; *Down Under* Bill Bryson and other travel writing.

Cover to Cover Cassettes Ltd

See **BBC Audiobooks**

CSA Word

6a Archway Mews, 241a Putney Bridge Road, London SW15 2PE

☎020 8871 0220 Fax 020 8877 0712

✉ info@csaword.co.uk

www.csaword.co.uk

Managing Director *Clive Stanhope*

Audio Director *Victoria Williams*

Founded 1989. Publishes fiction, children's, short stories, poetry, travel, biographies. Over 100 titles to-date on cassette and CD. Tends to favour quality/classic/nostalgic/timeless literature. TITLES *Carry on Jeeves* P.G. Wodehouse; *Alfie* Bill Naughton; *The Ordeal of Gilbert Penfold* Evelyn Waugh; *Just William – Home for the Holidays* Richmal Crompton; *Sons and Lovers* D.H. Lawrence; *Room at the Top* John Braine; *Midwich Cuckoos* John Wyndham; *I Capture the Castle* Dodie Smith; *The Statement* Brian Moore; *Billy Bunter's Banknote* Frank Richards.

CYP Children's Audio

The Fairway, Bush Fair, Harlow CM18 6LY

☎01279 444707 Fax 01279 445570

✉ enquiries@cypmusic.co.uk

www.kidsmusic.co.uk

Managing Director *Mike Kitson*

Founded 1978. Publishes children's audio material for those under 10 years of age; educational, entertainment, licensed characters (*Mr Men*; *Little Miss*; *Wheels On the Bus*). Ideas for cassettes welcome. TV music and soundtrack production service available.

Faber.Penguin Audiobooks

80 Strand, London WC2R 0RL

☎020 7010 3000 Fax 020 7010 6060

✉ audio@penguin.co.uk

www.penguin.co.uk

3 Queen Square, London WC1N 3AU

☎020 7465 0045 Fax 020 7465 0108

Head of Audio Publishing *Jeremy Ettinghausen*

A joint venture between **Penguin Books** and **Faber & Faber**. AUTHORS include Ted Hughes, Garrison Keillor, Sylvia Plath, T.S. Eliot, William Golding, Peter Carey, Alex Garland, D.B.C. Pierre, Philip Ardagh. Publishes up to 5 titles per year, drawing on the strength of Faber's authors.

57 Productions

See entry under *Organisations of Interest to Poets*

Halsgrove

See entry under *UK Publishers*

HarperCollins AudioBooks

77–85 Fulham Palace Road, London W6 8JB

☎020 8741 7070 Fax 020 8307 4517

www.harpercollins.co.uk

Managing Director *Amanda Ridout*

The HarperCollins audio list was launched in 1990. ADULT Publisher *Rosalie George*. Publishes a wide range including popular and classic fiction, non-fiction, Shakespeare and poetry on cassette and CD. 60 titles in 2003. CHILDREN'S DIVISION Divisional Publishing Director *Sally Gritten*, Publisher *Rosalie George*. Publishes picture books/cassettes and story books/cassettes as well as single and double tapes and CDs for children aged 2–13 years. Fiction, songs, early learning, poetry, etc. 30 titles in 2003. AUTHORS C.S. Lewis, Roald Dahl, Dr Seuss, Lemony Snicket, J.R.R. Tolkien, Enid Blyton, Robin Jarvis, Ian Whybrow, Nick Butterworth, Judith Kerr.

Hodder Headline Audio Books

338 Euston Road, London NW1 3BH

☎020 7873 6000 Fax 020 7873 6024

www.madaboutbooks.co.uk

Publisher *Rupert Lancaster*

Launched 1994. Publishes fiction and non-fiction. AUTHORS Tony Benn, Dickie Bird, Mevyn Bragg, John LeCarré, Alex Ferguson, Ranulph Fiennes, Joanne Harris, Stephen King, Ellis Peters, Rosamunde Pilcher, Mary Wesley. About 30 titles a year.

Isis Audio Books

See **Soundings**

Ladybird Audio

See **Dorling Kindersley Ltd** under *UK Publishers*

Laughing Stock Productions

81 Charlotte Street, London W1T 4PP
☎020 7637 7943 Fax 020 7436 1666

Managing Director *Colin Collino*

Founded 1991. Issues a wide range of comedy cassettes from family humour to alternative comedy. TITLES *Red Dwarf*; *Shirley Valentine* (read by Willy Russell); *Rory Bremner, Peter Cook Anthology*; *Sean Hughes*; *John Bird and John Fortune*; *Eddie Izzard*. 12–16 titles per year.

Macmillan Audio Books

20 New Wharf Road, London N1 9RR
☎020 7014 6040 Fax 020 7014 6141
✉ a.muirden@macmillan.co.uk
www.panmacmillan.co.uk

Owner *Macmillan Publishers Ltd*
Audio Publisher *Alison Muirden*

Founded 1995. Publishes adult fiction, non-fiction and autobiography, focusing mainly on lead book titles and releasing audio simultaneously with hard or paperback publication. Also publishes children's audio titles. Won Audio Publisher of the Year at the 2003 **Spoken Word Awards**.

Naxos AudioBooks

18 High Street, Welwyn AL6 9EQ
☎01438 717808 Fax 01438 717809
✉ Naxos_Audiobooks@compuserve.com
www.naxosaudiobooks.com

Owner *HNH International, Hong Kong/
Nicolas Soames*
Managing Director *Nicolas Soames*

Founded 1994. Part of Naxos, the classical budget CD company. Publisher of the Year in the 2001 **Spoken Word Awards**. Publishes classic and modern fiction, non-fiction, children's and junior classics, drama and poetry. TITLES *Ulysses* Joyce; *King Lear* Shakespeare; *History of the Musical* Fawkes; *Just So Stories* Kipling.

Orion Audio Books (Division of the Orion Publishing Group Ltd)

Orion House, 5 Upper St Martin's Lane, London WC2H 9EA
☎020 7520 4425 Fax 020 7379 6518
✉ pandora.white@orionbooks.co.uk
www.orionbooks.co.uk

Publisher *Pandora White*

Orion Audio has released over 200 titles since it was founded in 1998. Publishes fiction, non-fiction, humour, children's, poetry, science,
crime and thrillers. AUTHORS Penny Vincenzi, Maeve Binchy, Ian Rankin, Robert Crais, Michael Connelly, Francesca Simon (*Horrid Henry* series), the Dave Pelzer trilogy, Vikram Seth, Kevin Crossley-Holland, Anita Shreve. Ideas for cassettes/CDs welcome.

Penguin Audiobooks

80 Strand, London WC2R 0RL
☎020 7010 3000 Fax 020 7010 6695
✉ audio@penguin.co.uk
www.penguin.co.uk

Head of Audio Publishing *Jeremy Ettinghausen*

Launched in November 1993 and has rapidly expanded since then to reflect the diversity of Penguin Books' list. Publishes mostly fiction, both classical and contemporary, non-fiction, autobiography and an increasing range of children's titles under the **Puffin Audiobooks** imprint. Contemporary AUTHORS include: Zadie Smith, Anne Fine, Eoin Colfer, John Mortimer, Roald Dahl, Sue Townsend, Nicci French, Michael Moore, Jonathan Coe. About 70 titles a year.

Puffin Audiobooks

See **Penguin Audiobooks**

Random House Audiobooks

20 Vauxhall Bridge Road, London SW1V 2SA
☎020 7840 8400 Fax 020 7233 6127

Owner *The Random House Group Ltd.*
Managing Director *Richard Cable*
Manager *Georgia Marnham*
Audiobooks Assistant *Louisa Gibbs*

The audiobooks division of Random House started early in 1991. Acquired the Reed Audio list in 1997. Publishes fiction, non-fiction and self help. AUTHORS include Sebastian Faulks, John Grisham, Mark Haddon, Robert Harris, Thomas Harris, Tony Hawks, Andy McNab, Alison Pearson, Ruth Rendell, Kathy Reichs, Chris Ryan. 25 titles in 2003.

Rickshaw Productions

Suite 125, 99 Warwick Street, Leamington Spa CV32 4RB
☎0780 3553214 Fax 01926 402490
✉ rickprod@aol.com
www.rickshawaudiobooks.co.uk

Executive Producer *Ms L.J. Fairgrieve*

Founded 1998. Publishes adult fiction and non-fiction. Looking for unpublished writers of any genre, particularly short stories and novellas. TITLES *The Halfway-House Hotel* by

Richard James (Peter Mimmack); *The Tailor of Salisbury* (Martin Jarvis); *The First Line of Defence – The Kent Castles* produced in association with English Heritage (Elizabeth Ryder); *Wednesdays and Other Stories* (writtten and read by Betty Smith); *Poems and Music Vol. One* (written, composed and read by Mark Yakes). Submissions by snail-mail *only*. Two sample chapters, one-page synopsis and s.a.e. to cover return by Recorded Delivey.

Simon & Schuster Audio

Africa House, 64–78 Kingsway, London WC2B 6AH
☎020 7316 1900 Fax 020 7316 0332
✉ rumana.haider@simonandschuster.co.uk
www.simonsays.co.uk

Audio Manager *Rumana Haider*

Simon & Schuster Audio began by distributing their American parent company's audio products. Moved on to repackaging products specifically for the UK market and in 1994 became more firmly established in this market with a huge rise in turnover. Publishes adult fiction, self help and business titles. TITLES *Only Dad* Alan Titchmarsh; *The 7 Habits of Highly Effective People* Stephen R. Covey; *Hollywood Divorces* Jackie Collins; *Dead Sexy* Kathy Lette; *Point of Departure* Robin Cook; *Kate Remembered* A. Scott Berg.

SmartPass Ltd

15 Park Road, Rottingdean, Brighton BN2 7HL
☎01273 300742
✉ jools@smartpass.co.uk
www.smartpass.co.uk

Managing Director *Phil Viner*

Founded 1999. Family-run business. Publishes audio study guides, drama and analysis for English Literature set texts – novels, plays and poetry. TITLES include *Animal Farm* George Orwell; *A Kestrel for a Knave* Barry Hines; *Pride and Prejudice* Jane Austen; *Great Expectations* Charles Dickens; *The Mayor of Casterbridge* Thomas Hardy; *Macbeth*; *Twelfth Night*; *Romeo and Juliet*; *Shakespeare: the works*; *War Poetry*. IMPRINT **SPAudiobooks** Full-cast unabridged dramas. TITLE *The Antipope* Robert Rankin. Welcomes ideas from authors who are teachers and from agents who represent the authors of studied texts.

Smith/Doorstop Cassettes

The Poetry Business, The Studio, Byram Arcade, Huddersfield HD1 1ND
☎01484 434840 Fax 01484 426566
✉ edit@poetrybusiness.co.uk
www.poetrybusiness.co.uk

Co-directors *Peter Sansom, Janet Fisher*

Publishes poetry, read and introduced by the writer. AUTHORS Carol Ann Duffy, Simon Armitage, Les Murray, Ian McMillan, Sujata Bhatt.

Soundings

Isis House, Kings Drive, Whitley Bay NE26 2JT
☎0191 253 4155 Fax 0191 251 0662
www.isis-publishing.co.uk

Founded in 1982. Part of the Ulverscroft Group Ltd. Together with **Isis Publishing** publishes fiction and non-fiction; crime, romance. AUTHORS include Lyn Andrews, Rita Bradshaw, Lee Child, Catherine Cookson, Alexander Fullerton, Joanne Harris, Anna Jacobs, Robert Ludlum, Patrick O'Brian, Pamela Oldfield, Susan Sallis, Judith Saxton, Mary Jane Staples, Sally Worboyes. About 190 titles a year. Many also available on CD.

SPAudiobooks
See **SmartPass Ltd**

The Watts Publishing Group Ltd
See entry under *UK Publishers*

Poetry – Too Much of a Good Thing?

Peter Finch

Poetry is not what it used to be. And as Dylan Thomas might have said, I'll drink to that. After decades of growth the whole business appears to have turned on its head. During National Poetry Day last year verse received unprecedented media attention. Poetry was showered into the broadcaster's schedules. The Forward Prize, poetry's Booker, was announced in an explosion of publicity. Blake's *Jerusalem* was rewritten. Bestsellers, *The Nation's Favourite Poems,* hit their tenth anthology with *Poetry of Remembrance.* Across the UK there were events in schools, pubs, clubs, community centres and public places. The Poetry Society set out to discover the UK's principal poetry landmarks. Roger McGough spent a day online in virtual residence. Newsreaders were heard to quote bits of verse as they tidied their papers. This, the tenth National Day, was time for poetry's pre-eminence. And what happened to sales of poetry books that week? They went down.

The signs that this was coming have long been signalled. Several years back the Arts Council of England looked into how the audience for poetry might be increased. They concluded that books of verse by single authors were no longer the future. The recent Poetry Book Society report on declining book sales bears this out. Without the support of the bookselling chains the slim volume was destined for further fall. The value and purpose of poetry was in crisis. New readers were failing to breach the barriers created by the poetry world itself. Verse was badly presented, branded itself as overly academic and took more notice if its creators than it did of its consumers. Despite apparent popularity in some quarters, poetry had become a private art amongst consenting adults.

Powered by state subsidy verse has suffered from twenty years of overproduction. In 1981 620 new verse titles hit the market. By 2001 that figure had risen to 2846. That's almost nine new books a day. Who was bothering with them? Not your average reader, certainly. Have a look at the poetry shelves at WH Smiths and Waterstones. Poetry there is almost as sparse as it was in the seventies. Some hope, however, has arrived in the shape of Neil Astley and Daisy Goodwin. Both have recently edited thematic anthologies where it is the subject matter that is in the driving seat rather than the names of the poets. Astley's *Staying Alive: Real Poems For Unreal Times*, a collection of 500 accessible and purpose-filled verses, rose encouragingly up the bestseller list. Goodwin's *101 Poems That Could Save Your Life: An Anthology of Emotional First Aid*, backed by a BBC TV series, did the same. Auden's oft quoted 'poetry makes nothing happen' proved wrong. In times of crisis – private or public – poetry is often where the nation first turns. Good news for verse. But is it enough?

Astley, who as MD of one of Britain's two leading poetry publishers, Bloodaxe Books, has taken his success to the battle lines. Poetry's feelgood factor has been compromised by out-of-touch critics, he claims, women have been excluded, and in academic circles popular success has been sneered at. At Bloodaxe's main rival, Carcanet Press, MD Michael Schmidt insists that popularity should not be the only yardstick. Poetry is not an extension of the entertainment industry; language, its precise use, and the way it echoes in the privacy of the reader's head is equally important. Poetry, of course, thrives on such battles. Left *vs* right. In your face *vs* material that only works if you read it on your own. At the *Poetry Review*, the UK's oldest and still best-selling poetry journal, the new editors have once more opened the Modern and Post-Modern debate. Poetry might not be selling shed loads in the market place but it does remain an arena for muscular intellect.

What future, then, for the average verse writer? Plenty. There are more readings, performances, writing classes; poems on buses, in doctor's surgeries, on tubes, in public places, in the mouths of advertisers and soap stars, than ever before. At the popular-end poetry has a contemporary currency that it completely lacked twenty years ago. Amongst the cognoscenti the schools of the Post-Modernists and those of the line that runs from Hardy through Larkin to Andrew Motion continue to rub against each other and create sparks. For individual collections look to the pamphleteers and the Internet. The high street is not everything. In poetry there is still plenty going on.

What should you read?

The way in is first to discover what poetry actually is. To do this means putting some time in. Be as open and catholic as you can in your selection. Ensure you check out the whole scene – the past, the present, mainstream English literature along with work in translation, the obvious poets you find you like as well as those you find difficult. Appreciation will not come without effort. Stay the course.

Start with a recent anthology of contemporary verse. You'll be spoilt for choice here, the new Millennium has rushed a whole crop of century definers into print. To get a broad view of what's going on, not only should you read Simon Armitage and Robert Crawford's Penguin *British and Irish Poetry Since the War;* Sean O'Brien's *The Firebox* (Picador); Michael Schmidt's *The Harvill Book of Twentieth-Century Poetry In English* (Harvill); the latest annual *Forward Book of Poetry* (Faber), and Richard Caddel and Peter Quartermain's *Other: British and Irish Poetry since 1970* (Wesleyan); but also Keith Tuma's *Anthology of Twentieth-Century British & Irish* Poetry (OUP); Neil Astley's *Staying Alive* (Bloodaxe), Jeni Couzyn's *The Bloodaxe Book of Contemporary Women Poets; Poems for the Millennium (two vols)* edited by Jerome Rothenberg and Pierre Joris (California) and *Postmodern American Poetry,* a really splendid selection edited by Paul Hoover (Norton). This last title might be harder to find but will be worth the effort. Fill in with a standard overview of poetry in English since Chaucer. John Gallas's *The Song Atlas: A Book of World Poetry* (Carcanet) is a good scattergun.

Progress to the literary magazine. Write off to a number of the magazine addresses which follow this article and ask the price of sample copies. Check the websites listed. It is important that poets read not only to familiarise themselves with what is currently fashionable and to increase their own facility for self-criticism, but to help support the activity in which they wish to participate. Buy – this is vital for little mags, it is the only way in which they are going to survive.

Ok, I'm well read. What next?

Take a look at your own material. Are you personally convinced that it's ready? If you are uncertain, then most likely that will be the view of everyone else. Check your text for glips and blips. Rework it. Root out any clichés or archaic poetry expressions such as O, doeth, bewilld'd and the like. Drop any of what Peter Sansom calls 'spirit of the age' poetry words. Do without shards, lozenges, lambent patina, and stippled seagulls. Try and avoid shopping trolleys or tramps. If you work with rhyme attempt to avoid the obvious. Check that any meter you may be using actually works. Try not to clank. If by this time your writing still sounds okay, then go ahead.

Internet

Although some would still love it to be, the Internet is not a diversion. For the poet, or for that rare beast, the non-contributing poetry consumer, the Web is now pre-eminent. No longer a simple extension of conventional print it is now an actual substitute which you ignore at your peril. With the advent of cheap access, always-on, lightning-fast Broadband and complimentary Web space an increasing number of poetry enthusiasts, organisations and publishers have set up sites. Some have abandoned conventional print to operate solely online; others have launched without ever having known ink and paper. Cyberspace – the place where it all happens – is a mirror of the conventional world. The electronic replicates the real. Here are online books, magazines, historical and contemporary archives, reference works, creative tools, recordings, discussion forums and news round-ups. Many dedicate themselves entirely to poetry. Some of our national institutions, notably the BBC and *The Guardian*, have discovered that poetry makes for ideal Web content and dedicate significant sections of their sites to verse. On the Internet poetry is a consumer staple.

Journals
Online magazines range from those which mirror their print based cousins (and in some cases are simply direct copies) to completely innovative, interactive

compilations which mix sound and action with the text. The Net is no static place. Some mags offer playable recordings of their poets performing, others give space for readers to add criticism. More and more run forums where readers can exchange views. The difference between online and print-based magazines becomes more apparent when you discover that what you get when you call them up is not simply an enhanced version of the current issue but access to the entire back catalogue. All searchable, storable and, best of all, free.

Geography dissolves online. America is no further and no more costly to access than Britain. One of the great mags, John Tranter's *Jacket,* is based in Australia. It's just as easy to read as George Simmers' UK *Snakeskin,* Ethan Paquan's US *Slope* or Rick Lupert's Los Angeles *Poetry Super Highway.* In fact, half the time, the user has no idea precisely where the site being accessed is physically based. Place ceases to matter, language takes over. Online journals can range from the terrible to the terrific. For my money the aforementioned *Jacket, nthposition,* Joan Houlihan's *Perihelion,* Neil Rollinson's *Boomerang,* Rupert Loydell's *Stride,* and Jennifer Ley's *Riding the Meridian* are some of the world's best.

How do you contribute? Read first. Will you fit in? If you think so then send your poems by e-mail. More than likely you'll get an instant answer. No more waiting around for six weeks before your poems return, rejected and dog-eared. Online can be lightening fast.

Cyberspace is huge. Some of the sites which list online journals, such as *Peter Howard's Poetry Contacts,* or *Patrick Martin's Poetry Resource* seem to go on for days. On the Web it is easy to put up more, so in terms of quality of content that often means less. As in the real world not everything is even. Check the site's design. If thought has gone into it then it's likely that consideration has been given to the content as well.

Home pages

If you tire of contributing to the websites of others then why not start your own. Putting a whole collection of verse online isn't that hard. Most Internet Service Providers (ISPs) offer an amount of free Web space to users. Building your own *Home Page* is not beyond anyone capable of using a word processor. Many ISPs also provide free page creation software. If you'd like to see the kind of thing that's possible have a look at the site of poets Matthew Francis and Attila the Stockbroker, or Tom Leonard's site which includes his amazing reading of *The Six O'clock News.* You might also care to look at my own, *The Peter Finch Archive.* If you are reticent get a fan to set up a site devoted to your works. This has happened to David Gascoyne, to J.H. Prynne, Maya Angelou, Ivor Cutler, Benjamin Zephaniah and others. Most of us, however, seem to prefer the idea of self build.

Hypertext

Naturally the Web has developed its own verse forms. Most of these straddle the boundaries between verse, sound and image, much in the way that concrete poetry did fifty years ago. Many critics dismiss the new work as simply moving graphic art but protagonists see the world very differently. The subject is large and developing. Check the Flash-driven examples on the BBC's poetry site as well as those by Peter Howard.

Groups
To reduce the poet's traditional feeling of isolation the Net presents a number of opportunities. E-mail provides one vehicle. Here bands of poets circulate their work, their criticisms and their views of world literature. Join a group (no cost, just ask) and you'll find a daily delivery of e-mails in your in-box. Some groups are moderated which means that contributions are filtered by a controlling individual although most are free-for-alls. Discussion can range from the moronic to the stimulating. *The British and Irish Poets Group* and *Poetryetc* are two worth trying.

A variant on e-mail discussion groups are Usenet Newsgroups. Newsgroups run through their own dedicated software and are open to contributions from anyone anywhere. Articles are delivered to your browser for consumption. If you want to contribute then type it up and it's done. The principle poetry newsgroups, *rec.arts.poems* and *alt.arts.poetry.comments*, offer pretty varied fare. By their worldwide nature they tend to be American dominated and standards of contribution are not always that high. There are also masterclasses out there with established poets offering online advice. The BBC and the Poetry Society are some of the organisations which have offered virtual residencies with well-known bards.

Tools and resources
The Net offers a multitude of these. There are online spell-checkers (in many languages), thesauri, an anagram creator, Shakespeare concordances, a rhyming dictionary. The archives of universities (particularly in America) offer the great poetry of the past in comprehensive quantity. Download facsimile editions of *The Germ* (the first ever poetry magazine from 1850) or hear Seamus Heaney recite. Read the complete works of Blake, find out what powered the Beat generation, discover how Hardy worked, check the roots of modern verse. See where it's all going at the Electronic Poetry Centre at Buffalo. Not only can you find the texts themselves but entire critical apparatuses, historical contexts, biographies, bibliographies, portraits, shoe sizes and names of lovers for most of the greats. You can access information on poetry readings locally and world-wide. Former UK journalist Martin Blyth offers a stimulating range of poetry reviews and opinion. Bill Griffith's *Lollipop* tells you all you need to know about the small presses. Interested in a particular style? Haiku? Visual poetry? Traditional forms? They've all got their sites.

E-commerce
Shopping on the Net is now the preferred method for buying specialist material. The big Internet bookshop, Amazon, offers the hunter for that difficult to obtain poetry title searchable lists. Buying online is generally safe and swift although, as with all mail order, only as perfect as the van that brings the package to your door.

How to find it all

Use the search engine. The big ones – Google and Yahoo - can return enormous lists in response to keying in the word poetry. I got 10,500,500 results out of *Google,* which does sound like verse is taking over the world. Much easier is to log on to poetry resource sites which run clickable lists of relevant pages. The UK Poetry Society, The Poetry Library and Peter Howard's *Poems and Poetry Resources* are worth consulting. Ted Slade's *Poetry Kit* provides a large amount of poetry information, competition lists, and resources.

Some Web addresses for poets:

Attila The Stockbroker	www.attilathestockbroker.com/
BBC	www.bbc.co.uk/arts/poetry/index.shtml
Martin Blyth	www.martinblyth.co.uk
Boomerang	www.boomeranguk.com/
British Poets e-mail list	www.jiscmail.ac.uk/lists/british-poets.html
Electronic Poetry Centre	www.wings.buffalo.edu/epc
Matthew Francis	www.7greenhill.freeserve.co.uk/
Jacket (magazine)	www.jacketmagazine.com
Tom Leonard	www.tomleonard.co.uk/
Lollipop (List of Little Press Publications)	www.indigogroup.co.uk/llpp/
Patrick Martin's Poetry Resource	www.pmpoetry.com/
Nth Position (magazine)	www.nthposition.com/
Perihelion (magazine)	www.webdelsol.com/Perihelion/
Peter Finch Archive	www.peterfinch.co.uk
Peter Howard's Poetry Page	www.hphoward.demon.co.uk/poetry
Poetry Super Highway (magazine)	www.poetrysuperhighway.com/ PoetLinks.html
Poetry Kit (magazine)	www.poetrykit.org/
The Poetry Library	www.poetrylibrary.org.uk/poetry/index.html
The Poetry Society (UK)	www.poetrysociety.org.uk/
Poetryetc	www.jiscmail.ac.uk/lists/poetryetc.html
Riding The Meridian (magazine)	www.heelstone.com/meridian/
Slope (magazine)	www.slope.org
Snakeskin (magazine)	homepages.nildram.co.uk/~simmers/
Stride	www.stridemagazine.co.uk

Commercial publishers

It may come as a surprise to many but the number of commercial publishers who deal in poetry is actually extremely small. Despite the apparent acceptability of verse, profit is easier turned elsewhere. Where once there was a multitude of mainstream poetry imprints there are now only three or four. Poetry is a commercial risk. If it appears on a list then it's there for decoration.

The obvious exception to this approach is long-term market leader and envy of the whole business **Faber & Faber**. Here editor Paul Keegan presides over a list which continues to be as important to the firm as when T.S. Eliot inaugurated it more than seventy years ago. This is the imprint most poets would like to join. The greats of the twentieth century are here - Pound, Eliot, Plath, Hughes, Larkin. Seamus Heaney sold half-a-million copies when he won the Nobel prize. The imprint is built on distinctively designed class and the roster of contemporary poets are some of the best we have – Simon Armitage, Derek Walcott, Don Paterson, Andrew Motion, Jo Shapcott, Hugo Williams, Paul Muldoon, Douglas Dunn. The press publishes 40 or so poetry titles each year although new editions to the list are rare. If you fancy your chances then send a brief covering letter and a sample of your writing (between six and ten poems) not forgetting s.a.e.

A commercial editor with excellent taste is **Cape**'s Robin Robertson. His list is by no means all things to all people. John Burnside, Anne Carson, Michael Longley, Sharon Olds, and Matthew Sweeney are typical. Roberston produces four or five titles annually – all books, no anthologies. Worth trying? Yes, but potential contributors should never waste anyone's time by not looking at the list first. Poetry output at fellow Random House imprint **Chatto & Windus** is slightly lower than that at Cape and has recently included Bernard O'Donoghue, Ruth Padel and John Fuller. Anthologies are an increasing speciality. Worth trying? No, unless supported by a strong recommendation from an established fellow practitioner, Chatto does not want to see unsolicited manuscripts.

Cannongate recycles Robbie Burns and publishes new work from Lemn Sissay, Alan Spence, Gil Scott-Heron, and Gillian Ferguson.

Among the other commercial houses activity appears to be limited to nominal titles, anthologies or back-list obligations. **HarperCollins** makes money from Daisy Goodwin's anthologies. **Hutchinson** sticks with Dannie Abse. **Methuen** sells John Hegley. **Women's Press** with Alice Walker. **Duckworth** rolls on with William McGonagall. **BBC worldwide** churns and churns and Nation's Favourites. **Cassell** anthologises the poems from the London Underground. **Virgin** re-issues Charles Bukowski. **Peter Owen** illustrates Stevie Smith. **Hamish Hamilton** does John Updike. **John Murray** recycles Betjeman and prints anthologies of old chestnuts. **Everyman** concentrates on work that's out of copyright, Dylan and R.S. Thomas. **Boxtree** presents Purple Ronnie. Some specialist interests are dealt with at **Lion** (Christian verse) and **Windhorse Publications** (Buddhist) – but it isn't a lot.

The smaller operators

Not all commercial publishing is vast and conglomerate. A few independents still exist and on their lists poetry occasionally occurs. Poet Jeremy Robson's **Robson** imprint publishes Vernon Scannell and Dannie Abse. Northern Ireland general publisher, **The Blackstaff Press**, brings out one or two poetry titles annually, including Patrick Crotty's excellent *Modern Irish Poetry*. Welsh family firm **Gwasg Gomer** produces neat editions of Gillian Clarke, John Barnie, Nigel Jenkins and others. Check Gomer at www.gomer.co.uk **Polygon** (which is an imprint of **Birlinn Ltd**) continues to mix Gaelic with English. The press lists at least half a dozen poets including Roddy Gorman, Liz Lochhead and W.N.Herbert. At the **Onlywomen Press** editor Lilian Mohin publishes around three poetry titles annually. Marilyn Hacker, Elana Dykewomon, Paula Jennings and Suniti Namjoshi are typical. Check their anthology *Not for the Academy: Lesbian Poets*.

Universities

With the transfer of **OUP**'s contemporary list to Carcanet, interest activity among other university presses is sparse. Reprints and literary studies at **Cambridge**, the same at **Manchester**. At the **University of Wales Press**, who publishes a splendid series of collected works from Welsh poets, you need to be dead. American university presses such as **Nebraska**, **Princeton**, **Louisiana**, **Wisconsin**, **Chicago**, **Harvard**, **Michigan**, North Carolina, **Washington**, **Alabama** and **California** along with **W.W. Norton** do an increasing amount of verse but exclusively by Americans. King's College, London has **MPT Books** which publishes modern poetry in translation. Wolfgang Görtschacher's **Poetry Salzburg** is an independent Anglophone operation run from the University of Salzburg in Austria. They publish six or so titles annually concentrating on translations from European minorities and collections from neglected UK poets. Their magazine is *Poetry Salzburg*. Their website is at www.poetrysalzburg.com

The mass-market paperback

The popular end is where many poets imagine the best starting place to be. Paperback houses were founded to publish inexpensive reprints of hard-covered originals and, despite years of innovation, to a large extent still fulfil this role. Being neither cheap nor (in sales terms) that popular poetry does not really fit in. Among the carousels at airports you do not see it. Check the empires of **Arrow**, **Bantam**, **Corgi**, **Headline** and **Mills & Boon**. If you discount the inspirational, you won't find a book of verse between them. But there are exceptions. At **Penguin**, where things are always different, poetry has a significant role. With its unfailing commercial ear the company has correctly assessed the market for contemporary and traditional verse and successfully filled it. Reprinting important volumes pioneered by less commercial poetry presses, originating historic and thematic anthologies, reviving classic authors and producing translations en route, Penguin continues to provide an almost unrivalled introduction to the world of verse. But appearances aside, this is most certainly no place for the beginner. 'We publish almost no new or unknown poets. In fact we publish very little new poetry beyond a small circle of established poets. We concentrate on selecteds and general anthologies' publishing director Tony Lacey told me. The company focuses on sure sellers such as James Fenton, Michael Rosen, Geoffrey Hill, Tony Harrison and Roger McGough. The main thrust remains the re-packaging of Derek Mahon, Carol Ann Duffy and U.A. Fanthorpe, a good range of modern poets in translation along with larger collections from the likes of William Empson, Allen Ginsberg and John Ashbery. The company's poetry overview anthologies, the Simon Armitage and Robert Crawford edited *British and Irish Poetry Since the War*, Peter Forbes' *Scanning the Century* and Paul Keegan's *New Penguin Book of English Poetry* are musts. Despite these obvious winners Lacey sees the whole market for verse as small, despite the hype.

Penguin's nearest rival, **Picador,** the literary paperbacker from **Pan Macmillan**, is now exhibiting considerable vigour and is widely regarded as one of the country's leading poetry publishers. Under the commanding eye of successful and non-metropolitan poet Don Paterson it has moved into high gear putting out a stream of successful collections both from new poets such as Jacob Polley and Yusef Komunyaaka along with established names such as Kathleen Jamie, Peter Porter, Carol Ann Duffy, Kate Clanchy, Michael Donaghy, American poet laureate Billy Collins and Sean O'Brien. With its reliable content Picador is a UK reference point. Paterson will bring out at least six new titles annually as well as an anthology. A recent example is Carol Ann Duffy's anthology of love poems *Hand in Hand*. Worth trying here? 'Certainly: 10 poems better than a full length ms, but establish some track record in the reputable journals first,' advises Paterson.

The specialists

Despite a clear lack of success in the commercial marketplace poetry still gets published in quantity. But by whom? By the specialist independents. These are the small army of semi-commercial operations scattered across the country. They are run by poetry enthusiasts whose prime concern starts not with money but with the furtherance of their art. Most (but not all) receive grant aid, without which their publishing programmes would be sunk. They are models of what poetry publishing should be – active, involving, alert and exciting. They promote their lists through readings, tours, websites and broadcasts and they involve their authors in the production and sales of their books. Never before have new poets been faced with so many publishing opportunities. And if there is any criticism then this is it. Too many books jamming the market. Just how does the reader see through the flood? By reputation I guess. Two specialist publishers have emerged well ahead of the pack – **Carcanet** and **Bloodaxe**. Along with Faber these two now dominate British poetry publishing.

Taking them alphabetically, Neil Astley's acclaimed **Bloodaxe Books** publishes 30 titles annually. Although doing fewer new titles than it once did, still brings out more poetry books than any other British imprint. Based in Northumberland and begun in Newcastle in the late '70s, the press is unhindered by a past catalogue of classical wonders or an overly regional concern. It relentlessly pursues the new. Astley presents the complete service from thematic anthologies, world greats and selecteds to slim volumes by total newcomers. Bloodaxe has its own range of excellent handbooks to the scene including *Getting Into Poetry* and *Writing Poems* along with an increasing range of critical volumes. Best poetry sellers are their anthologies: Neil Astley's own *Staying Alive: Real Poems For Unreal Times*, Edna Longley's *Bloodaxe Book of 20th Century Poetry* and their decade-framing anthology *The New Poetry*. Bloodaxe relishes the chance to publish work from outside the standard English mainstream – Ireland, Scotland and Wales are all well represented (with R.S Thomas's *Collected Later Poems* well to the forefront) – as are more traditional UK outsiders such as J.H. Prynne. Typical poets include Fleur Adcock, David Constantine, Helen Dunmore, Selima Hill, Jackie Kay and Peter Reading. Bloodaxe will not go rusty with age. Check their site, one of the best on the Web, at www.bloodaxe.com

Carcanet Press, has been the consistent recipient of critical accolades – publishing four Nobel Prize-winning authors and four Pulitzers helps. Although it is no longer exclusively a publisher of verse the press still gives poetry pre-eminence. Carcanet currently has over 900 titles in print, reps in 42 countries and pursues a programme that brings out 40 or so poetry titles annually. Managing Director Michael Schmidt agrees with Auden's observation that most people who read verse read it for some reason other than the poetry. He fights the tide with his own mainstream journal *PN Review*. Carcanet has a policy of serious quality. 'I am strongly aware of the anti-modernist slant in a lot of poetry publishing, and publish to balance this,' he comments. 'Most submissions we receive come from people ignorant of the list to which they are submitting. Nothing is more disheartening than to receive a telephone call asking whether Carcanet publishes poetry.' The press has a four-part editorial programme: to publish new writing, to dust down substantial but neglected figures of this and earlier centuries, to encourage the translation of poetry, and to publish poets' prose and work relating to modern poetry. Typical of their list are Ian McMillan, John Ashbery, Gillian Clarke, Edwin Morgan, Les Murray, Jorie Graham, Sophie Hannah, Mimi Khalvati, Iain Bamforth, John Gallas, Peter Robinson and bestseller, Elizabeth Jennings. Carcanet has an air of purpose about it. 'We avoid the Technicolour and pyrotechnic media razzmatazz,' says Schmidt. Have a look at their website – www.carcanet.co.uk New poets are welcome to submit. Send six to ten pages of work and expect to wait six weeks for a reply. Carcanet's *New Poetries* and *Oxford Poets* series of anthologies give an idea where the taste of the press is going next.

Production standards among other specialists can be equally as good as Carcanet and Bloodaxe although annual output is substantially less. And with the recent loss of **Leviathan** things are not quite what they were.

Anvil Press Poetry, founded by Peter Jay in 1968, is now England's longest-standing independent poetry publisher. Marketing director Hamish Ironside reports that Anvil's sales are steady. They publish the best of the new English language poets including Greta Stoddart, Julian Turner, and A.B. Jackson. In addition they've a deserved reputation for publishing the best of poetry in translation from around the world – Tagore, Seferis, Bei Dao, Lorca, Hikmet and others. Output is a dozen new books a year. For those who wish to familiarise themselves with the flavour of the Anvil list, Jay's acclaimed anthology *The Spaces of Hope* gives a perfect starting point. Their informative website is at www.anvilpresspoetry.com **Enitharmon Press** represents quality, cares about presentation and operates 'at the unfashionable end' of the poetry publishing spectrum. Its books are produced to the highest of standards. Enitharmon has little interest in fashion. The press is 'dedicated to a poetry of the human spirit in an age of rampant commercialism' (Anne Stevenson). Owner Stephen Stuart-Smith continues a policy of publishing new, established and unjustly neglected poets with output now up to sixteen volumes annually. Typical of the list are David Gascoyne, Ruth Pitter, Vernon Scannell and Alan Brownjohn. The future looks bright and includes Isaac Rosenberg, Jack Kerouac, Seamus Heaney and Jeremy Reed. Visit www.enitharmon.co.uk for more information and samples of some of its poets reading

Tony Ward's **Arc Publications**, based in Lancashire, brings out around twenty poetry titles annually. 'We publish work that we believe important, innovative, and of outstanding quality,' Ward told me. The imprint has Jean Boase-Beier, Jo Shapcott and John Kinsella on the Board and maintains a back-list of in excess of 150 titles. Ivor Cutler, Katherine Gallagher, John Tranter and Jackie Willis are top sellers. Arc's policy is to publish the best in contemporary poetry, in a reader-friendly medium without in any way compromising the standards of quality. The Arc website is at www.arcpublications.co.uk Submissions from unpublished authors are not accepted. Poets should familiarise themselves with the list before sending anything and, unless accompanied by a publishing history and s.a.e. will not be considered. 'We do not wish to put writers off or dampen enthusiasm, but we have never yet accepted an unpublished author', is the official line. You have been warned.

Ward has an excellent reputation as a printer to the poetry press community and does a splendid job also for David Tipton's **Redbeck Press**. Tipton, who came up the pamphlet route used by many a small press has now driven Redbeck into the top echelon. He publishes everything from Nick Toczek's performance pieces to *Katkist*, Jane Ramsden's anthology of poetry about cats. His star title of recent times has been Debjani Chatterjee's 200-page *Redbeck Anthology of British South Asian Poetry*. Other Redbeck poets include John Freeman, Jim Burns, Barry Tebb, Kim Taplin, Martin Hayes, Tulio Mora, Jenny Swann and Alan Dent. Non-centralist and politically incorrect to the core.

Seren Books is a Welsh-based literary house publishing novels, art books, short fiction, biographies and critical texts. The imprint has a solid interest in verse and publishes at least six new single author volumes annually. Poetry editor Amy Wack reads *everything* submitted but admits that she has only ever accepted one unsolicited manuscript in her entire tenure. Poets should read more, she says. Editions are quality productions with plenty of attention paid to design inside and out. Typical recent poets include Graham Mort, Zoe Skoulding, bestseller Owen Sheers, Samantha Rhydderch and Sheenagh Pugh. Their major best-seller is Dannie Abse's *Twentieth Century Anglo-Welsh Poetry*. A good press sampler is their anthology *Oxygen – New Poets from Wales*.

Rupert Loydell's **Stride** has gathered a good reputation for catholic taste and running risks. After thirty-three issues in hard-copy his eponymous magazine is now available on the Web at www.stridemagazine.co.uk This is an excellent sample of Stride's taste with an eclectic mix of verse, criticism and features. Based in the southwest output, at six titles annually, is less than it used to be. The back list runs to more than 200 titles ranging from the totally unknown to the famous. Stride perfectly fills the gap between the avant-garde and the user-friendly. Recent successes include Peter Redgrove, David Morley, Geoffrey Godbert and Martin Stannard. Plans for the future are either world domination or retirement. Visit their website at www.stridebooks.com for up to date information. Their anthology, *Ladder to the Next Floor*, offers a sampler of how the press got where it is.

Peterloo Poets, based in Cornwall, represents poetry without frills, without fuss, and most definitely without the avant-garde. Run by Harry Chambers the press aims to publish quality work by new and neglected poets, some of them late starters; to co-publish with other reputable presses; and to establish a Peterloo list of succeeding volumes by a core of poets of proven worth. Heaney described Chambers as one of the 'great hearers and hearteners of the work being done in British and Irish Poetry'. Peterloo, which represents many people's idea of what poetry is, runs an active backlist of nearly two hundred titles. Bestsellers include U.A.Fanthorpe, Elma Mitchell and Dana Gioia. Poets central to the list are William Scammell, David Sutton, Ann Drysdale, John Mole and John Whitworth. Recent additions include Brian Bartlett, Kate Scott, Christine Webb and R.V. Bailey. Peterloo, now in its 28th year, runs its own £2000 poetry competition, and insists that prospective contributors to the press have had at least six poems in reputable magazines. Send a full ms accompanied by a stamped envelope large enough to carry your work back to you. Chambers currently takes a couple of months to reply and is full to the year 2005. Peterloo are at www.peterloopoets.co.uk

John Kinsella and Chris Hamilton-Emery have now established a Cambridge base for the international Australian-born **Salt**. Both the press and the journal of the same name have solid left-field leanings and an interest in contemporary poetics. Sales from their booming catalogue are rising. The press has a contemporary modernist back list which includes Douglas Oliver, Jeff Nuttall, John Wilkinson, Peter Jaeger, Peter Larkin and Drew Milne. Bestsellers include Todd Swift's *100 Poets Against the War* anthology, Michael Hulse and John Tranter. Their website is at www.saltpublishing.com – 'no boundaries, just great writing'. Critic Andrew Duncan's *The Failure of Conservatism in Modern British Poetry* is a roadmap. Expect more titles, more collections and more criticism. An innovator to watch.

There are other presses with less prodigious outputs but whose editions are still up there with the best of them. In Northumberland, Margaret and Peter Lewis's **Flambard Press** has stuck the course and publishes around four or five or so titles annually. The press is interested in new and neglected poets especially from the north and the Borders. Josephine Dickinson, Desmond Graham, Gladys Mary Coles, Joolz and Amanda White are typical poets. Check www.flambardpress.co.uk Gladys Mary Coles has developed her **Headland Publications** into a regular Peterloo clone and is now producing an increasing number of fine books including an exciting range of anthologies. Her interest centres on North West England and Wales. Typical poets include John Barnie, Richard Poole, Brian Wake and Alison Chisholm. Ken Edwards' **Reality Street Editions** specialises in 'linguistically innovative writing by women and men on both sides of the Atlantic'. Publishing a small number of single author volumes, translations and anthologies the press takes the new poetry seriously. Typical authors include Maggie O'Sullivan, Cris Cheek, Allen Fisher and Denise Riley. Currently, Reality Street is not accepting new manuscripts. Nicholas Johnson's **Etruscan Books** carries the flame for UK avant-garde poetry and performance with a series of readers, chapbooks and multi-contributor volumes along with a first class anthology of contemporary material, *Foil.*If anyone is pushing the edge out then Johnson is, and he's doing it with style. His poets include Bob Cobbing, Ed Dorn, Maurice Scully, Wendy Mulford, Sean Rafferty, Carl Rakosi, Bill Griffiths and Tom Pickard.

Paul Beasley's poetry agency (see *Organisations of Interest to Poets*) **57 Productions**, represents performance poetry heartland and, realising that most of his material works better on audio, has concentrated on editions on cassette and CD. Recent successes include *The Poetry Jukebox*, John Cooper Clark, R.S Thomas and Christopher Logue.

In Huddersfield, Janet Fisher and Peter Sansom run **Smith/Doorstop** the poetry imprint of their enterprising **Poetry Business** (see **Organisations of Interest to Poets**). The press produces five books and six pamphlets annually. Steve Waling, Kate Bass, Andrew Wilson and Catherine Smith are recent authors. Smith/Doorstop also runs an annual poetry pamphlet competition as well as producing poetry on cassette. Their *Contemporary Poems* edited by Peter Sansom and Lesley Jeffries offers a good critical introduction to the scene. Their magazine is *The North*. On the Web they are at www.poetrybusiness.co.uk

With north American connections Jessie Lendennie runs **Salmon Publishing** from the Cliffs of Moher, Co. Clare, in Ireland. The press has been in the business for 21 years and publishes some of the best designed titles in the West. An Irish connection is pretty useful when trying here although Salmon do look at material from further afield. Typical poets include Adrienne Rich, Rita Ann Higgins, Marvin Bell, Linda McCarriston, James Simmons and Mary O'Malley. Salmon has a good website at www.salmonpoetry.com which includes discussion, advice, events listings, sound files and a complete bookshop. And if the poetry is not flowing you can always book in to a Salmon Creative Writing Workshop.

Peepal Tree is the largest independent publisher of Caribbean and black British poetry. Founded in 1986 they now produce around twelve poetry titles annually. Typical poets include Kwame Dawes, Dorothea Smartt, Raman Mundair, David Dabydeen and Anthony Kellman. Editor Jeremy Poynting and assistant Emma Smith read over 1000 submissions annually and are not known for their speedy responses. You can view the Peepal Tree catalogue at www.peepaltreepress.com

Edward Mackinnon's Nottingham-based **Shoestring Press**, an outgrowth from an episode of self-publishing, brings out the unfashionable. Recent books include JC. Hall, Barbara Hardy, Evan Gwyn Williams and Ian Caws. Check Shoestring's website at www.shoestringpress.co.uk Peter Fallon's **Gallery Press** in Co Meath continues to produce substantial collections from the likes of Frank Orsmby, Paul Muldoon, Sean Dunne, Derek Mahon, Medbh McGuckian, Richard Murphy and everyone who is anyone on the Irish scene. Edinburgh's **Luath Press**, from the heart of Burns country, has spawned an increasing poetry roster which includes Alistair Findlay, Gerry Cambridge, Des Dillon and Tom Atkinson's splendid anthology of *Poems To Be Read Out Loud*. Their website it at www.luath.co.uk

In Wales, Lewis Davies's **Parthian Books** under poetry editor Richard Gwyn continues to publish poets who resist categorisation and challenge notions of what poetry might be. Typical poets include Landeg White, David Greenslade, Rhian Saadat and their bestseller Ifor Thomas. Their anthology *The Pterodactyl's Wing* collects the best of Welsh world poetry.

Tony Fraser's *Shearsman* magazine and press publish chapbooks and solid volumes from the edges – Lee Harwood, Anne-Marie Albiarch, Robert Sheppard and more.

As technology continues to make life easier for publishers it becomes harder to draw the line between the poetry specialists and the classic small presses. Maybe by now such a division does not exist at all.

The regional anthologies

Running in parallel with the high ground literary approach of much of the poetry world are empires largely unknown to the taste-makers and ignored by the critics. The biggest, Ian and Tracy Walton's Forward Press in Peterborough, now turns over 2.2 million pounds annually, has produced approximately 15,000 titles in 14 years, and reckons to account for the highest proportion of all *new* verse published in the UK. Depressed with '20 years of not being able to enjoy poetry' because it was inevitably obscure, the couple have moved from back kitchen to three-storey offices block in the service of 800,000 active British verse scribblers. Forward Press targets contributors who find much contemporary poetry 'over complex and difficult to understand'.

For over 14 years the Press has enthusiastically promoted an 'accessible, sincere poetry which everyone can relate to'. Although they have printed the likes of Carol Ann Duffy and Simon Armitage the higher realms are not for them. Publishing under a number of imprints including Poetry Now, Anchor Books,

Young Writers and Triumph House, the operation receives thousands of contributions annually. 'It is a bit like amateur dramatics', Ian told me, 'anyone can take part.'

Forward's Press' outstanding success is built on its approachability. Their team of editors includes as many as two hundred poems in each anthology. No entry fee is asked, nor are there purchase requirements. Submissions under 30 lines are preferred. Until recently, if you wanted to see your work in print, and for most contributors this is the whole *raison d'être* for writing, then you had to buy a copy of the book. This is no longer the case, but for many poets this will be their first appearance in book form and chances are they will purchase more than a single copy. This is not a traditional vanity operation: no one is actually being ripped off, nor are the publishers raking in exorbitant profits. Page for page their titles are not much more expensive than those of Cape or Faber and are cheaper than the output of some little presses. All published poets are entered for free into the Top 100 Poets of the Year Award with an annual prize fund of £10,000. First prize is £3000. Critics claim that quality at Forward Press is being neglected in exchange for quantity. Dumb down your criteria for inclusion, cram the poems in, sell more copies. Undoubtedly the genuine literary achievement of appearing in one of Forward's Press' books is questionable. In mitigation it must be said that for some writers this will be their much-needed beginning (check Angela Macnab and Sally Spedding) but for others the only success they are ever going to get.

In addition to their schools and regional collections Forward Press runs a typesetting, print and design service for self-publishers; a bi-monthly journal, **Poetry Now Magazine**, which has been established for over eleven years; **New Fiction**, an imprint for short story writers; and **Spotlight Poets** – a joint publishing venture which showcases a dozen new poets a time. Their **Writers' Bookshop** imprint publishes a most useful series of reference books including subject and genre guides, directories and handbooks. Forward Press offers the complete poetry life. If *A Treasured Moment, Perceptions of Life, A Primrose Promise, In High Spirits, Message from Within* and *From A Distance* sound like your scene send for the group's information pack (Remus House, Peterborough, PE2 9JX), ring them on 01733 898105, fax them on 01733 313524, check their interactive website, www.forwardpress.co.uk, or e-mail your request (info@ forwardpress.co.uk). You'll find no dubious accommodation address dealing here, but on the other hand, few literary giants either.

Envious of Forward's success at catching the hearts and minds of most of the UK's poetry hobbyists a good number of rival empire builders have risen in their wake. Regional poetry anthologies, Best of Britain collections, compendiums of English, Scottish, Irish and Welsh verse abound. Contributions are sourced through notices on library walls, local free-sheets, local radio and through direct mail. These operations vary from the glossy to a number of pathetically produced and, one hopes, short-lived incarnations based in the non-metropolitan sticks. No actual rip-off occurs and contributors get in whether they purchase or not. But if you want to see your work then you must buy and the books can cost upwards of thirty pounds. Before agreeing to contribute check the press's output. Do not submit blindly, research their back list. It is what Faber would demand of you. The rule applies to the whole poetry scene.

The small press and the little magazine

Small publishing ventures have been with us since the dawn of print. And today, from a technical point of view, things are easier to manage than ever. Costs are down. Technology scores. For the past decade small press and little magazine publishing has seen a golden age. But there are signs of change. In the face of so-simple Internet publishing could print-only little mags be running out of steam? Closures outnumber start-ups. Recently *Links, Leviathan Quarterly, Thumbscrew, Tabla, Terrible Work, Gentle Reader, Upstart!, Epoch, Pause, As Well As, The Burning Bush, Still, Breathe, Konfluence, JuJu* and others have all gone. Closed, or moved online. Replacements have been scarce. Why bother with print? On the Web there are no distribution difficulties and size just doesn't matter. But the small mag isn't dead, not yet.

Statistically, the small presses and the little magazines are the largest UK publishers of new poetry both in terms of range and circulation. They operate in a bewildering blur of shapes and sizes everywhere from Brighton to Birmingham and Aberystwyth to Aberdeen. For up to the moment data have a look at the address list maintained by the Poetry Library at www.poetrylibrary.org.uk/poetry/enquiry/magset.html

This country's best poetry magazines all began as classic littles. Between them *PN Review, Ambit, Orbis* (now releaunched under the editorship of Carole Baldock), *Poetry Review*, Craig Raine's *Arete, The Rialto, Acumen, The North, Smiths Knoll, The Paper* and *Envoi*, do not come up to even half the circulation of journals like *Shooting Times* and *Practical Fishkeeping* – which says a lot about the way society values its poetry. Nonetheless, taken as a group, they will get to almost everyone who matters. They represent poetry as a whole. Read these and you will get some idea of where the cutting edge is. In the second division in terms of kudos lie the regional or genre specialists such as *Raw Edge* (new writing from the west Midlands), *The New Welsh Review, Poetry Wales, Poetry Ireland, Chapman* (Scotland's quality literary magazine), *Krax* (humorous verse), *The Liver Bards* (Liverpool verse), *Poetry Scotland, Mslexia* (for women who write), *Poetry Church* and *Haiku Quarterly*. All these magazines are well produced, sometimes with the help of grants, and all represent a specific point of view. In Wales there is *Barddas* for poets using the strict meters and in Scotland *Lallans* for poets working in Lowland Scots. The vast majority of small magazines, however, owe no allegiance. They range from quality round ups like Dublin's *Stinging Fly, Smoke, Tears in the Fence, Oxford Poetry, Poetry Nottingham International*, former Rialto editor John Wakeman's splendid *SHOp*, translation specialist *The Journal*, the Usk Valley's *Scintilla*, the enormously long-lived *Iota*,

Barry Tebb's notorious *Leeds Poetry Weekly* and *Obsessed With Pipework* (to surprise and delight), general literary magazines such as *The Reader,* and annuals, such as *Tremblestone*, to irregulars like *The Yellow Crane* (interesting new poems), *Roundyhouse* (bards from both sides of the border), *Moodswing* (a pocket broadsheet), *Poetry Life* (Britain's sharpest), *Anon* (your work judged by what it says rather than your name), *The Interpreter's House* (the best prose and verse that the editor can get), *HQ* (not just Haiku) and *Skald* (the innovative and experimental). Some like *The Penniless Press* are for the poor of pocket and the rich of mind, *Fire* goes for length and the otherwise unpublishable. If you can't find a magazine that suits you and your style then you can't be writing poetry. On the other hand if you are really sure you are then start your own.

Among the small presses there is a similar diversity, although these days slightly less choice than there once was. Brian Wake and Tony Dash's enormously long-lived **Driftwood Publications** extends the Liverpool vision with Jim Mangnall, Peggy Poole, and Henry Graham. David Perman's **Rockingham Press** manages three or four new books annually and has an online catalogue at www.rockingham-press.co.uk The Leeds-based **Sixties Press** does Barry Tebb, Brenda Williams, Niall McGrath and others. **Feather Books** publishes Christian verse. Alan Halsey's **West House Books** publishes the innovative Geraldine Monk, David Annwn, Kelvin Corcoran, David Kennedy and others. **Five Leaves Publications** anthologises British socialist poetry and has Peter Mortimer, Michael Rosen, Marge Piercy and other biggies on their list. **Katabasis** publishes Latin America. Andrea Brady and Keston Sutherland's **Barque Press** publishes post-language poets including John Tranter, Peter Manson, Andrew Duncan and Tom Jones. Janet Murch and Bob Mee's **Ragged Raven Press** follows the middle classes. With aid from Northern Arts **Biscuit Publishing** publishes some excellent Tynesiders, as does fellow Independent Northern Publishers member **Arrowhead Books**. **Y Lolfa** publishes Welsh-based unofficial bards. For the new writer these kinds of presses are the obvious place to try first. Indeed it is where many have. Who put out T.S.Eliot's first? A small publisher. Dannie Abse, Peter Redgrove, James Fenton and Dylan Thomas, the same. R.S.Thomas, Ezra Pound and Edgar Allen Poe didn't even go that far – they published themselves.

Cash

Being a poet is not really much of an occupation. You get better wages delivering papers. There will be the odd twenty pounds from the better heeled magazine, perhaps even as much as £60 or so from those periodicals lucky enough to be in receipt of a grant, but generally it will be free copies of the issues concerned, thank you letters and little more. Those with collections published by a subsidised, specialist publisher can expect a couple of hundred as an advance on royalties. Those using the small presses can look forward to complimentary copies. On the Internet published poets usually get nothing at all. The truth is that poetry itself is undervalued. You can earn money writing about it, reviewing it, lecturing on it, teaching it or, certainly, by giving public performances (£150 standard here, £1000 plus if you are Roger McGough, much more if you are Seamus Heaney). But at bottom, most things in the poetry business will earn better money than the verse itself. This isn't capitalism, this is art.

Readings

Since the great Beat Generation, Albert Hall reading of 1964, there has been an ever-expanding phenomenon of poets on platforms, reading or reciting their stuff to an audience that can be anywhere between raptly attentive and fast asleep. Begin by attending and see how others manage. Watch out for events advertised at your library, ring your local arts council, (in Wales look at www.academi.org). Poets with heavy reputations can often turn out to be lousy performers while many an amateur can really crack it out. Don't expect to catch every image as you listen. Readings are not places for total comprehension but rather for glancing blows. Treat it as fun and it will be. If you are trying things yourself for the first time, make sure you've brought your books along to sell, stand upright, drop the shoulders, gaze at a spot at the back of the hall and blow.

Competitions and Awards

Poetry competitions have been the vogue for decades now with the most unlikely organisations sponsoring them. The notion here is that anonymity ensures fairness. Entries are made under pseudonyms so that if your name does happen to be Andrew Motion, then this won't help you much. Results seem to bear this out too. The big competitions run biennially by the **Arvon Foundation** with the help of commercial sponsors, the **Academi's** *Cardiff International* and the **Poetry Society's** *National* attract an enormous entry and usually throw up quite a number of complete unknowns among the winners. And why do people bother? Cash prizes can be large – thousands – but it costs at least a few pounds a poem to enter, and often much more than that. And there has been a trend for winners to come from places like Cape Girardeau, Missouri and Tibooburra, Australia. The odds are getting longer. Who won the last Arvon? I don't remember. But if you do fancy a try then it is a pretty innocent activity. You tie up a poem for a few months and you spend a little money. Winners' tips include reading the work of the judges to see how they do it, submitting non-controversial middle-of-the-road smiling things, and doing this just before the closing date so you won't have to wait too long. Try two or three of your best. Huge wodges are costly and will only convince the judges of your insecurity. Have a look at *The Ring Of Words* (Sutton Publishing), an excellent historical anthology of Arvon winners and runners-up. For contests to enter watch the small mags, write to your regional arts council, check out *The New Writer, Poetry London* or *Writer's News*, look on the notice board at your local library, or write for the regularly updated list from **The Poetry Library** in London (see *Organisations of Interest to Poets*).

Poetry Awards are slightly different. These are usually made for published books and convention generally requires your publisher to make the nomination rather than yourself. These glittering prizes are increasing both in value and impact. Both the annual T.S. Eliot and Forward Prizes are now worth £10,000 a time with the poetry section of the Whitbread Book Award not far behind. To win one of these your book needs to be pretty hot.

Radio and TV

Poetry on the box has never been much of a success. Verse is rarely visual. On TV, when it appears at all, it is usually Great Stuff read by actors whose over-trained voices relentlessly drive home the brightness, the melancholy or the laughter of their lines. Opportunities for the newcomer, even among the digital dross of Sky's outer reaches, are rare.

On radio, however, things can be very different. In enlightened mode both Radio 3 and Radio 4 give over whole half-hours to verse and use a fair smattering of contemporary voices. What is usually important here are the poets themselves. Listen out for *The Verb* on Radio 3, and elsewhere for programmes produced by Sue Roberts, Sara Davies, Viv Beeby, Fiona Mclean, Julian May and others.

The BBC's website (www.bbc.co.uk/arts/poetry/index.shtml) collects a great deal of information on the Corporation's poetry interests.

Easy to get on board? Poetry on Radio is a large but difficult market. The BBC are pretty definite about having no remit to use 'unpublished or amateur verse'. Ideas should always be directed to a programme-making department at the BBC rather than to Radio 4 or Radio 3 themselves. If you are determined to put your verse on air then local and regional radio offer better possibilities. Try sending in self-produced readings on cassette (if you are any good at it) or topical poetry which regional magazine programmes could readily use. Don't expect to be paid much.

Starting up

Probably the best place will be locally. Find out through the library, your regional arts council or check the Internet to find which writers groups gather in your area and attend. There you will meet others of a like mind, encounter whatever locally produced magazines there might be and get a little direct feedback on your work. 'How am I doing?' is a big question for the emerging poet and although criticism is not all that hard to come by, do not expect it from all sources. Magazine editors, for example, will rarely have the time to offer advice. It is also reasonable to be suspicious of that offered by friends and relations – they will no doubt be only trying to please. Writers groups present the best chance for poets to engage in honest mutual criticism. But if you'd prefer a more detached, written analysis of your efforts and are willing to pay a small sum, then you could apply to *Prescription,* the service operated nationally by the Poetry Society (22 Betterton Street, London WC2H 9BU), to the service run by The Academi in Wales (see **Organisations of Interest to Poets**) or to those run on an area basis by your regional arts council. There are also a number of non-subsidised critical services which you will find advertised in writers' magazines.

Read; if it's all a mystery to you, try Tony Curtis' *How to Study Modern Poetry* (Macmillan); Matthew Sweeney and John Hartley Williams' *Teach Yourself Writing Poetry* (Teach Yourself) , John Whitworth's *Writing Poetry* (A&C Black) or my own *The Poetry Business* (Seren). How real poets actually work can be discovered by reading C.B. McCully's the *Poet's Voice and Craft* (Carcanet) or *How Poets Work* (Seren). After all this, if you still think it's appropriate, try sending in.

How to do it

Increase your chances of acceptance by following simple, standard procedure:

- Type or print on a single side of the paper, A4 size, single-spacing with double between stanzas, exactly as you'd wish your poem to appear when printed.
- Give the poem a title, clip multi-page works together, include your name and address at the foot of the final sheet. Avoid files, plastic covers, stiffeners and fancy clips of any sort.
- Keep a copy, make a record of what you send where and when, leave a space to note reaction.
- Send in small batches – six is a good number – with a brief covering letter saying who you are. Leave justification, apology and explanation for your writers group.
- Include a self-addressed, stamped envelope of sufficient size for reply and/or return of your work.
- Be prepared to wait some weeks for a response. Don't pester. Be patient. Most magazines will reply in the end.
- Never send the same poem to two places at the same time (and this includes e-zine vs. hard copy. The jury is still out on whether or not the inclusion of a poem on your own personal website actually counts as publication). If you've entered the poem for a competition then make sure you never simultaneously send it elsewhere.
- If you are thinking of sending your submission electronically *check* first. Many of the journals and publishers in the *Writer's Handbook* survey refuse to accept materials sent this way.

■ Send your best. Work which fails to fully satisfy even the author is unlikely to impress anyone else.

Where?

Try the list which follows. This is by no means the whole UK small press scene but only those where potential contributors might stand a chance. Even here do not expect unrelenting positive responses: magazines get overstocked, editors change, addresses shift, policy alters, operators run out of steam. Be prepared to hunt around and for a lot of your work to come back. You can help improve things by buying copies. Send in an s.a.e. asking how much. The total market is vast and if you want to go further then you could consult *Light's List of Literary Magazines* which contains both UK and US addresses (John Light, Photon Press, The Lighthouse, 37 The Meadows, Berwick upon Tweed TD15 1NY) or Bill Griffiths' Internet list at *Lollipop* (www.indigogroup.co.uk/llpp/).

The next step

Once you have placed a few poems you may like to consider publishing a booklet. There are as many small presses around as there are magazines. Start with the upmarket professionals by all means but be prepared for compromise. The specialists and the small presses are swifter and more open to new work.

If all else fails you could do it yourself. Blake did, so did Walt Whitman. Modern technology puts the process within the reach of us all and if you can put up a shelf, there is a fair chance you will be able to produce a book to go on it. Read my *How to Publish Yourself* (Allison & Busby). Remember that publishing the book may be as hard as writing it but marketing and selling it is quite something else. Check Alison Baverstock's *Marketing Your Book: An Author's Guide* (A&C Black) if you really want to get ahead.

The listings

None of the lists of addresses in the following poetry sections are exhaustive. Publishers come and go with amazing frequency. For up-to-the-minute information check with some of the **Organisations of Interest to Poets** (see page 156). Poetry has a huge market. It pays to keep your ear to the ground. The magazines and presses listed here have all been active during the past eighteen months and most (although be warned, *not all*) have indicated a willingness to look at new work. Those with a positive disinterest in receiving unsolicited work have been excluded. In all cases check before sending. Ask to see a catalogue or a sample copy. Good luck.

Poetry Presses

Abbey Press
Newry Office, Courtney Hill, Newry
BT34 2ED
☎028 3026 3142
✉ molly71freeman@aol.com
www.geocities.com/abbeypress

Poetry, anthologies and works of literary criticism.

Agenda Editions
The Wheelwrights, Fletching Street, Mayfield
TN20 6TL
✉ agendapoetry@lycos.co.uk

Contact *Patricia McCarthy*

See also **Agenda** magazine.

Akira Press
5 Blackhorse Lane, London E17 6DS
☎08700 503161
✉ info@akirapress.co.uk
www.akirapress.co.uk

Contact *Beverley Jones-Joseph*

Hip Hop Rappers and Dancehall Reggae DJs.

Anarcho Press
7 Portland Terrace, Nairn IV12 4AS
☎01667 452476
✉ stanley5@aol.com

Contact *Stan Trevor*

Literature for a rational society.

Anvil Press Poetry Ltd
Neptune House, 70 Royal Hill, London
SE10 8RF
☎020 8469 3033   Fax 020 8469 3363
✉ anvil@anvilpresspoetry.com
www.anvilpresspoetry.com

Contact *Peter Jay*

Contemporary British poetry and poetry in translation. See entry under **UK Publishers**.

Arc Publications
Nanholme Mill, Shaw Wood Road,
Todmorden OL14 6DA
☎01706 812338   Fax 01706 818948
✉ arc.publications@btconnect.com
www.arcpublications.co.uk

Contact *Tony Ward*

Contemporary poetry from new and established writers both in the UK and abroad. See entry under **UK Publishers**.

Arrowhead Press
70 Clifton Road, Darlington DL1 5DX
✉ editor@arrowheadpress.co.uk
www.arrowheadpress.co.uk

Quality books and pamphlets of contemporary poetry.

Astrapost
7 The Towers, Stevenage SG1 1HE
✉ chessmaster@ntlworld.com

Contact *Eric Ratcliffe*

Free ranging non-materialist poetry, non-profit, charity. See also **Four Quarters Press**.

Au Quai
33 Cherry Orchard, Staines TW18 2DE
✉ vennel@hotmail.com
www.indigogroup.co.uk/llpp/vennel.html

Contact *Leona Carpenter*

Modern Scottish poetry; poetry in translation; poetry that takes its bearings from modernism. See also **Vennel Press** and **Southfields** presses.

Barque
13 Heathfield Park, Flat 2, London NW2 5JE
✉ info@barquepress.com
www.barquepress.com

Contact *Keston Sutherland*

See also **Quid** magazine.

BB Books
Spring Bank, Longsight Road, Copster Green,
Blackburn BB1 9EU
☎01254 249128

Contact *Dave Cunliffe*

Post-Beat poetics and counterculture theoretic. Iconoclastic rants and anarchic psycho-cultural tracts. See also **Global Tapestry Journal**.

Between the Lines
9 Woodstock Road, London N4 3ET
☎020 8374 5526   Fax 020 8374 5736
✉ btluk@aol.com

www.interviews-with-poets.com

Contacts *Peter Dale & Others*

Interviews with leading contemporary poets.

Big Little Poem Books
3 Park Avenue, Melton Mowbray LE13 0JB

Contact *Robert Richardson*

Effective contemporary approaches to the lyric and epigram. See also **Door-To-Everywhere** press.

Biscuit Publishing
Box 123, Washington, Newcastle upon Tyne NE37 2YE

☎0191 416 9751 Fax 0191 431 1263

✉ brian@biscuitpublishing.com

www.biscuitpublishing.com

Contact *Brian Lister*

Publishers of fiction, non-fiction and poetry.

Black Arts Alliance
PO Box 86, Manchester M21 7BA

☎0161 832 7622 Fax 0161 832 2276

✉ baa@blackartists.org

www.blackartists.org.uk

Blackwater Press
PO Box 5115, Leicester LE2 8ZD

Contemporary poetry from news and established writers.

Bloodaxe Books Ltd
Highgreen, Tarset NE48 1RP

☎01434 240500 Fax 01434 240505

✉ editor@bloodaxebooks.co.uk

www.bloodaxebooks.com

Contact *Neil Astley*

Britain's leading publisher of new poetry. No submissions by e-mail attachments. See entry under **UK Publishers**.

Bradshaw Books
Tigh Filí, Thompson House, Maccurtain Street, Cork, Republic of Ireland

☎00 353 21 450 9274 Fax 00 353 21 455 1617

✉ admin@cwpc.ie

www.tighfili.com

Contact *M. Bradshaw*

Canna Press
10 Severn Road, Canton, Cardiff CF11 9NB

✉ canna@care4free.net

Contact *Phil Maillard*

Works of Chris Torrance.

Carcanet Press
4th Floor, Alliance House, 28–34 Cross Street, Manchester M2 7AQ

☎0161 834 8730 Fax 0161 832 0084

✉ pnr@carcanet.u-net.com

www.carcanet.co.uk

Contact *Michael Schmidt*

Major poetry publisher (see entry under **UK Publishers**). See also **PN Review** magazine.

Chapman Publishing
4 Broughton Place, Edinburgh EH1 3RX

☎0131 557 2207 Fax 0131 556 9565

✉ chapman-pub@blueyonder.co.uk

www.chapman-pub.co.uk

Contact *Joy Hendry*

Scottish writing. See entry under **UK Publishers**.

Cherry on the Top Press
29 Vickers Road, Firth Park, Sheffield S5 6UY

☎0114 244 1202 Fax 0114 244 1202

✉ dgk-cvk@email.msn.com

Contact *David Kennedy*

Cherrybite Publications
Linden Cottage, 45 Burton Road, Little Neston L64 4AE

☎0151 353 0967

Contact *Shelagh Nugent*

Cinnamon Press
Meirion House, Glanyrafon, Tanygrisiau, Blaenau Festiniog LL4 3SU

☎01766 832112

✉ jan@coffeehousepoetry.co.uk

www.coffeehousepoetry.co.uk

Contact *Dr Jan Fortune-Wood*

Contemporary poems of edge and depth from new voices and established writers. See also **Coffee House Poetry** magazine.

The Collective Press
c/o Penlanlas Farm, Llantilio Pertholey, Y-fenni NP7 7HN

☎01873 856350 Fax 01873 859559

✉ jj@jojowales.co.uk

www.welshwriters.com

Contacts *John Jones & Frank Olding*

Non-profit promoter and publisher of contemporary poetry.

Conybeare Publishing
48 Heol-y-bryn, Rhiwbina, Cardiff CF14 6HY

☎029 2038 4682 Fax 029 2040 5411

✉ conybeare.publishing@breathemail.net

Contact *Jonathan A. Jones*

Poetry, drama and art/architecture in Wales.

Crystal Serenades Publications Ltd
PO Box 17, Treorchy, Rhondda Cynon Taff
CF42 6YL
☎07730 899698
✉ admin@crystalserenades.co.uk
www.crystalserenades.co.uk

Bilingual publishing company interested in novels, stories, poetry and art, particularly from first time writers.

Cyhoeddiadau Barddas
Pen Rhiw, 71 Ffordd Pentrepoeth, Treforys
SA6 6AE
☎01792 792829

Contact *Alan Llwyd*

Barddoniaeth Gymreig – Welsh language poetry. See also **Barddas** magazine.

Dagger Press
1 Portland Street, Diglis, Worcester WR1 2NL
☎07986 792443
✉ dagger.press@tiscali.co.uk

Contact *Brian Morse*

Poetry pamphlets, new and established poets.

Dangaroo Press
PO Box 20, Mytholmroyd, Hebden Bridge
HX7 5UZ
☎01422 885936

Contact *Susan Burns*

Day Dream Press
39 Exmouth Street, Swindon SN1 3PU
☎01793 523927

Contact *Kevin Bailey*

See also **HQ, Haiku Quarterly**.

Dial 174 Collections
21 Mill Road, Watlington, King's Lynn
PE33 0HH
☎01553 811949

Contact *Joseph Hemmings*

Poetry. See also **Dial 174** magazine.

Diamond Twig
5 Bentinck Road, Newcastle upon Tyne
NE4 6UT
☎0191 273 5326
✉ diamond.twig@virgin.net
www.diamondtwig.co.uk

Contacts *Ellen Phethean & Others*

New writing by women in the north of England – no non-fiction or children's writing.

Dionysia Press
20a Montgomery Street, Edinburgh EH7 4JS
☎0131 478 0680 Fax 0131 478 0680

Contact *Denise Smith*

Collections of poetry, words, translations. See also **Understanding** magazine.

Donut Press
118 Napier Road, London E11 3JZ
✉ donutcops@yahoo.co.uk

Door-To-Everywhere
3 Park Avenue, Melton Mowbray LE13 0JB

Contact *Robert Richardson*

Poem card series – imagination first! See also **Big Little Poem Books** press.

Driftwood Publications
5 Timms Lane, Freshfield L37 7DW
☎01704 833911 Fax 0151 524 0216
✉ janet.speedy@btinternet.com

Contact *Brian Wake*

New work by new and established poets more suited to the page than the stage.

Enitharmon Press
26B Caversham Road, London NW5 2DU
☎020 7482 5967 Fax 020 7284 1787
✉ books@enitharmon.co.uk
www.enitharmon.co.uk

Contact *Stephen Stuart-Smith*

Poetry and criticism. See entry under **UK Publishers**.

Erran Publishing
43 Willow Road, Carlton NG4 3BH
✉ erranpublishing@hotmail.com
www.poetichours.homestead.com

Contact *Nick Clark*

Non-profit supporter of Third World charities. See also **Poetic Hours** magazine.

Essence Press
8 Craiglea Drive, Edinburgh EH10 5PA
✉ jaj@essencepress.co.uk
www.essencepress.co.uk

Contact *Julie Johnstone*

Handbound editions of poetry, poetry postcards – interest in concrete poetry and nature. See also **Island** magazine.

Etruscan Books
28 Fowler's Court, Fore Street, Buckfastleigh
TQ11 0AA
☎01364 643128   Fax 01364 643054
Contact *Nicholas Johnson*

Modernist, sound, visual poetry, Gaelic, lyric
poetry, US/UK poets.

Feather Books
PO Box 438, Shrewsbury SY3 0WN
☎01743 872177   Fax 01743 872177
✉ john@waddysweb.freeuk.com
www.waddysweb.freeuk.com
Contact *Rev. J. Waddington-Feather*

Quarterly magazine of Christian poetry and
prayers. See entry under *Small Presses*; also
The Poetry Church magazine and.

57 Productions
57 Effingham Road, Lee Green, London
SE12 8NT
Contact *Paul Beasley*

Performance poetry on cassette and CD.

Five Leaves Publications
PO Box 81, Nottingham NG5 4ER
☎0115 969 3597
✉ info@fiveleaves.co.uk
www.fiveleaves.co.uk
Contact *Ross Bradshaw*

Fiction and non-fiction, especially Jewish
interest.

Flambard
Stable Cottage, East Fourstones, Hexham
NE47 5DX
☎01434 674360   Fax 01434 674178
www.flambardpress.co.uk
Contact *Peter Elfed Lewis*

Concentrates on poetry but also publishes literary fiction.

Flarestack Publishing
41 Buckley's Green, Alvechurch, Birmingham
B48 7NG
☎0121 445 2110
Contact *Charles Johnson*

Considers first collections for A5 stapled pamphlet publication. See also **Obsessed With
Pipework** magazine.

Forward Press
Remus House, Coltsfoot Drive, Woodston,
Peterborough PE2 9JX
☎01733 898105   Fax 01733 313524
✉ info@forwardpress.co.uk
www.forwardpress.co.uk
Contact *Kerrie Pateman*

General poetry and short fiction anthologies.
See also **Triumph House** press and **Poetry
Now** magazine.

Four Quarters Press
7 The Towers, Stevenage SG1 1HE
✉ chessmaster@ntlworld.com
Contact *Eric Ratcliffe*

Free ranging non-materialist poetry, non-
profit, charity. See also **Astrapost** press.

The Gallery Press
Loughcrew, Oldcastle, Co. Meath, Republic
of Ireland
☎00 353 49 854 1779
Fax 00 353 49 854 1779
✉ gallery@indigo.ie
www.gallerypress.com
Contact *Peter Fallon*

Poems, plays and prose by contemporary Irish
writers.

Gomer Press/Gwasg Gomer
Llandysul SA44 4JN
☎01559 362371   Fax 01559 363758
Contact *Sue Davies*

Welsh interest. See entry under *UK Publishers*.

Green Arrow Publishing
2 Chambers Cottages, Underlyn Lane,
Marden, Tonbridge TN12 9BD
☎07967 315270
✉ mail@johndench.demon.co.uk
Contact *John Dench*

Collaborative publishing scheme and other services for writers. See also **Scriptor** magazine.

Gwasg Pantycelyn
Lon Ddewi, Caernarfon LL55 1ER
☎01286 672018   Fax 01286 677823
✉ gwasgpantycelyn@ukonline.co.uk
Contact *R.M. Thomas*

Headland Publications
Ty Coch, Galltegfa, Ruthin LL15 2AR
☎0151 625 9128   Fax 0151 625 9128
Contact *Gladys Mary Coles*

Fine editions of poetry; anthologies.

Hippopotamus Press

22 Whitewell Road, Frome BA11 4EL
☎01373 466653 Fax 01373 466653
✉ rjhippopress@aol.com

Contact *Roland John*

First collections of verse from those with a track record in the magazines. See also **Outposts** magazine.

Honno

Canolfan Merched Y Wawr, Vulcan Street, Aberystwyth SY23 1JH
☎01970 623150 Fax 01970 623150
✉ post@honno.co.uk
www.honno.co.uk

Contact *Lindsay Ashford*

The Welsh women's press – novels, childrens fiction, short stories, poetry and autobiographical anthologies. Must have a Welsh connection. See entry under **UK Publishers**.

I*D Books

Connah's Quay Library, Wepre Drive, Connah's Quay, Deeside
☎0161 226 3419

Poetry, short fiction, local history.

Katabasis

10 St Martin's Close, London NW1 0HR
☎020 7485 3830 Fax 020 7485 3830
✉ katabasis@katabasis.co.uk
www.katabasis.co.uk

Contact *Dinah Livingstone*

Down-to-earth and Utopian poetry and prose from home an abroad – English and Latin American.

The King's England Press

Cambertown House, Commercial Road, Goldthorpe S63 9BL
☎01709 270258 Fax 01709 897787
✉ steve@kingsengland.com
www.kingsengland.com

Contact *Steve Rudd*

History, folklore, children's poetry.

Klinker Zoundz

10 Malvern House, Stamford Hill Estate, London N16 6RR

Cassettes, records, music, poetry.

KT Publications

16 Fane Close, Stamford PE9 1HG
☎01780 754193

Contact *Kevin Troop*

Still looking for 'the perfect work'. See also **Colours** and **The Third Half** magazines.

Laurel Books

282 The Common, Holt BA14 6QJ
☎01225 782874
www.laurelbooks.co.uk

Edward Thomas, Harold Monro and more.

Leviathan

Bears Hay Farm, Brookhay Lane, Fradley WS13 8RG
☎01543 411161 Fax 01543 410679
✉ claire.brodmann@btinternet.com

Contact *Michael Hulse*

Poetry, prose classics.

Luath Press Ltd

543/2 Castlehill, The Royal Mile, Edinburgh EH1 2ND
☎0131 225 4326 Fax 0131 225 4324
✉ gavin.macdougall@luath.co.uk
www.luath.co.uk

Contact *Gavin MacDougall*

Publishers of Scottish books of all kinds.

Malfunction Press

Rose Cottage, 3 Tram Lane, Buckley CH7 3JB
☎01244 543820
✉ rosecot@presford.freeserve.co.uk

Contact *Peter E. Presford*

Mainly dedicated to fiction, fantasy, light horror.

Mandrake Poetry

PO Box 250, Oxford OX1 1AP
☎01865 243671
✉ mandrake@mandrake.uk.net

Contact *Mogg Morgan*

New edge publishers specialising in magic and the occult.

Mariscat Press

10 Bell Place, Edinburgh EH3 5HT
☎0131 343 1070
✉ mariscatpress@hotmail.com

Contacts *Hamish Whyte & Diana Hendry*

Currently publishing poetry pamphlets only.

Masque Publishing

PO Box 4194, Worthing BN11 2GT
✉ masque_pub@tiscali.co.uk
myweb.tiscali.co.uk/masquepublishing

Contact *Lisa Stewart*

For self-publishers. See also **Decanto** magazine.

The Moving Finger
PO Box 4867, Birmingham B3 3HD
Contact *Dave Reeves*

See also **Raw Edge** magazine.

New Departures
PO Box 9819, London W11 2GQ
Contact *Michael Horovitz*

See also **New Departures/Poetry Olympics** magazine.

New Hope International
20 Werneth Avenue, Gee Cross, Hyde
SK14 5NL
✉ nhi@clara.net
www.nhi.clara.net/nhihome.htm

Contact *Gerald England*

Poetry booklet publisher. No longer considering unsolicited mss.

Oasis Books
12 Stevenage Road, London SW6 6ES
☎020 7736 5059

Contact *Ian Robinson*

Pamphlets of poetry and prose. Contact before submitting material. See also **Oasis** magazine.

Odyssey Poets
Coleridge Cottage, Nether Stowey,
Bridgwater TA5 1NQ
☎01278 732662
✉ pqrrev@aol.com

Contact *Derrick Woolf*

Poetry/prose; first collections; interim booklets; full collections. See also **PQR – Poetry Quarterly Review** magazine.

The Old Stile Press
Catchmays Court,, Llandogo, Nr Monmouth
NP25 4TN
☎01291 689226
✉ oldstile@dircon.co.uk
www.oldstilepress.com

Contacts *Frances & Nicolas McDowall*

Fine, hand-printed books with text and images.

The One Time Press
Model Farm, Linstead Magna, Halesworth
IP19 0DT
☎01986 785422
✉ pw@onetimepress.com

www.onetimepress.com

Contact *Peter Wells*

Poetry of the 40s in limited editions. Illustrated.

Orchard House
Criccieth LL52 0AH

Original Plus
Flat 3, 18 Oxford Grove, Ilfracombe
EX34 9HQ
☎01271 862708
✉ smithsssj@aol.com
members.aol.com/smithsssj/index.html

Contact *Sam Smith*

Requires something extra – another language or markedly original. See also **The Journal** magazine.

Oversteps Books
Oversteps, Froude Road, Salcombe
TQ8 8LH
☎01548 843713   Fax 01548 844384
✉ anne@oversteps.fsnet.co.uk

Contact *Anne Born*

Small poetry press publishing a couple of books a year.

Parthian Books
The Old Surgery, Napier Street, Cardigan
SA43 1ED
☎01239 612059   Fax 01239 612059
✉ parthianbooks@yahoo.co.uk
www.parthianbooks.co.uk

Contact *Richard Gwyn*

New Welsh writing.

Partners
289 Elmwood Avenue, Feltham TW13 7QB
✉ partners_writing_group@hotmail.com
www.partners_writing_group_homestead.com

Contact *Ian Deal*

Competitions and poetry pamphlets. See also **A Bard Hair Day**, **Imagenation** and **Poet Tree** magazines.

Peepal Tree Press Ltd
17 King's Avenue, Leeds LS1 1QS
☎0113 245 1703
✉ hannah@peepal.demon.co.uk
www.peepaltreepress.com

Contact *Jeremy Poynting*

Best in Caribbean and south Asian writing from around the world. See entry under **Small Presses**.

Pen & Inc Press

School of English & American Studies,
University of East Anglia, Norwich NR4 7TJ
☎01603 592783
✉ info@penandinc.co.uk
www.penandinc.co.uk

Contact *Katri Skala*

A small press supported by Arts Council
England. See also **Pretext** magazine and
Reactions press.

Pennine Pens

32 Windsor Road, Hebden Bridge HX7 8LF
✉ 100342.3424@compuserve.com
www.eclipse.co.uk/pens

Contact *Chris Ratcliffe*

Peterloo Poets

The Old Chapel, Sand Lane, Calstock
PL18 9QX
☎01822 833473 Fax 01822 833989
✉ poets@peterloo.fsnet.co.uk
www.peterloopoets.co.uk

Contact *Harry Chambers*

Contemporary English poetry.

Picture Poems

114 Broadway, Herne Bay CT6 8HA
☎01227 360525
✉ picturepoems@hbaykent.freeserve.co.uk

Contact *Barbara Dordi*

Publishers of original artwork with poetry/
prose. See also **Equinox** magazine.

Pigasus Press

13 Hazely Combe, Arreton, Isle of Wight
PO30 3AJ
☎01983 865668
✉ pigasus.press@virgin.net
freespace.virgin.net/pigasus.press/index.htm

Contact *Tony Lee*

Science fiction poetry in irregular themed
anthologies.

Pikestaff Press

Ellon House, Harpford, Sidmouth EX10 0NH
☎01395 568941

Contact *Robert Roberts*

Contemporary poetry belonging to the English
tradition, mainly 24–page pamphlets.

Pipers' Ash Ltd

Pipers Ash, Church Road, Christian Malford,
Chippenham SN15 4BW

☎01249 720563 Fax 0870 056 8916
✉ pipersash@supamasu.com
www.supamasu.com

Contact *Mr A. Tyson*

See entry under **Small Presses**.

Planet

PO Box 44, Aberystwyth SY23 3ZZ
☎01970 611255 Fax 01970 611197
✉ planet.enquiries@planetmagazine.org.uk
www.planetmagazine.org.uk

Contact *John Barnie*

Fiction, poetry, current affairs, arts and environment. See also **Planet** magazine and entry
under **Small Presses**.

Plas Gwyn Books

10 Farrell Road, Wootton MK43 9DU
☎01234 766579

Contact *Merryn Williams*

Private press. See also **The Interpreter's
House** magazine.

Poems in the Waiting Room

PO Box 488, Richmond TW9 4SW
✉ pitwr@blueyonder.co.uk

Contact *Michael Lee*

Pamphlets for medical waiting rooms.

Poetry Monthly Press

39 Cavendish Road, Long Eaton, Nottingham
NG10 4HY
☎0115 946 1267
✉ martin.holroyd2@btinternet.com

Contact *Martin Holroyd*

See also **Poetry Monthly** magazine.

Poetry Now

Remus House, Coltsfoot Drive, Woodston,
Peterborough PE2 8JX
☎01733 8998101 Fax 01733 313524
✉ poetrynow@forwardpress.co.uk
www.forwardpress.co.uk

Contact *Heather Killingray*

Lively, personal and contemporary; also deals
with womenswords. See also **Poetry Now**
magazine.

Poetry Now Young Writers

Remus House, Coltsfoot Drive, Woodston,
Peterborough PE2 9JX
☎01733 890066 Fax 01733 313524
✉ forward_press@compuserve.com
www.forwardpress.co.uk

Contact *Steve Twelvetree*

Publishers of children's poetry. See also **Scribbler!** and **Wordsmith** magazines.

Poetry Salzburg
Dept of English and American Studies,
University of Salzburg, Akademiestr. 24,
A–5020 Salzburg, Austria
✉ wolfgang.goertschacher@sbg.ac.at
www.poetrysaltzburg.com

Contact *Wolfgang Görtschacher*

See also **Poetry Salzburg Review** magazine.

Poetry Wednesbury
25 Griffiths Road, West Bromwich
B71 2EH
☎07950 591455
www.poetrywednesbury.co.uk

Contact *Geoff Stevens*

See also **The Firing Squad** and **Purple Patch** magazines.

PS Avalon
Box 1865, Glastonbury BA6 8YR
✉ info@psavalon
www.psavalon.com

Contact *Will Parfitt*

Quality books of contemplative, inspirational and ecstatic poetry.

QQ Press
York House, 15 Argyle Terrace, Rothesay,
Isle of Bute PA20 0BD

Contact *Alan Carter*

Collections of poetry plus poetry anthologies. See also **Quantum Leap** magazine.

Ragged Raven Press
1 Lodge Farm, Snitterfield, Stratford upon Avon CV37 0LR
☎01789 730358 Fax 01789 730320
✉ raggedravenpress@aol.com
www.raggedraven.co.uk

Contacts *Bob Mee & Janet Murch*

Poetry. See also **Iota** magazine.

Raunchland Publications
18 Canon Lynch Court, Dunfermline
KY12 8AU
✉ raunchland@hotmail.com
www.raunchland.co.uk

Contact *John Mingay*

Limited edition poetry/graphics booklets and online publications.

Reactions
School of English & American Studies,
University of East Anglia, Norwich NR4 7TJ
☎01603 592783
✉ info@penandinc.co.uk
www.penandinc.co.uk

Contact *Katri Skala*

Annual poetry anthology – welcomes submissions from poets at first collection stage. See also **Pretext** magazine and **Pen & Inc Press**.

Reality Street Editions
4 Howard Court, London SE15 3PH
☎020 7639 7297
✉ reality.street@virgin.net
freespace.virgin.net/reality.street

Contact *Ken Edwards*

New poetry from Britain, Europe and America.

Red Candle Press
Rose Cottage, Threeholes Bridge, Wisbech
PE14 9JR
✉ rep@poetry7.fsnet.co.uk
www.members.tripod.com/redcandlepress
Contact *M.L. McCarthy*

Traditionalist press. See also **Candelabrum Poetry Magazine**.

Redbeck Press
24 Aireville Road, Frizinghall, Bradford
BD9 4HH
☎01274 498135

Contact *David Tipton*

Contemporary poetry and some short fiction.

Rive Gauche Publishing
69 Lower Redland Road, Bristol BS6 6SP
☎0117 974 5106
✉ twinset1969@hotmail.com
Contact *P.V.T. West*

Poetry by women writing and performing in Bristol.

Rockingham Press
11 Musley Lane, Ware SG12 7EN
✉ info@rockpress.freeserve.co.uk
www.rockingham-press.co.uk

Contact *David Penman*

New British poetry and poetry in translation.

Route Publishing
PO Box 167, Pontefract WF8 4WW
☎01977 603028 Fax 01977 512819
✉ info@route-online.com

www.route-online.com

Contact *Ian Daley*

Novels, short fiction and poetry.

Rumney Publishing Co
10 South View Drive, Rumney, Cardiff
CF3 8LY

Contact *Graham Jones*

Salmon Poetry Ltd
Knockeven, Cliffs of Moher, Co Clare,
Republic of Ireland
☎00 353 65 708 1941
Fax 00 353 65 708 1621
✉ siobhan@salmonpoetry.com
www.salmonpoetry.com

Contact *Jessie Lendennie*

Salt Publishing
PO Box 937, Great Wilbraham, Cambridge
CB1 5JX
✉ cemery@saltpublishing.com
www.saltpublishing.com

Contact *Chris Hamilton-Emery*

International poetry and poetics. See also **Salt**
magazine.

Seren
1st & 2nd Floors, 38–40 Nolton Street,
Bridgend CF31 3BN
☎01656 663018 Fax 01656 649226
✉ seren@seren-books.com
www.seren-books.com

Contact *Mick Felton*

Poetry, fiction, lit crit, biography, essays. See
entry under **UK Publishers**; also **Poetry Wales**
magazine.

Shearsman Books
Lark Rise, Fore Street, Kentisbeare,
Cullompton EX15 2AD
☎01884 266174 Fax 01884 266174
✉ editor@shearsman.com
www.shearsman.com

Contact *Tony Frazer*

Publishes poetry almost exclusively. Contact
editor before submitting. See also **Shearsman**
magazine.

Shoestring Press
19 Devonshire Avenue, Beeston, Nottingham
NG9 1BS
☎0115 925 1827 Fax 0115 925 1827
www.shoestringpress.co.uk

Contact *John Lucas*

Chapbooks and full collections of original
poetry, Greek poetry in translation and some
fiction.

Sixties Press
89 Connaught Road, Sutton SM1 3RJ
☎020 8286 0419

Contact *Barry Tebb*

Small press concentrating on poetry and novellas. See also **Leeds Poetry Weekly** and
Literature and Psychoanalysis magazines.

Smith/Doorstop Books
The Studio, Byram Arcade, Westgate,
Huddersfield HD1 1ND
☎01484 434840 Fax 01484 426566
✉ edit@poetrybusiness.co.uk
www.poetrybusiness.co.uk

Contacts *Peter Sansom & Janet Fisher*

Contemporary poetry books, pamphlets and
audio cassettes (see entry under **Audio Books**).
See also **The North** magazine.

Southfields
33 Cherry Orchard, Staines TW18 2DE
✉ vennel@hotmail.com
www.indigogroup.co.uk/llpp/vennel.html

Contact *Leona Carpenter*

Modern Scottish poetry that takes its bearings
from modernism. See also **Vennel** and **Au Quai**
presses.

Spectacular Diseases
83b London Road, Peterborough PE2 9BS

Contact *Paul Green*

Innovative poetry and some prose; translations
of both.

Starborn Books
Glanrhydwilym, Llandissilio, Clinderwen
SA66 7QH
☎01437 563562 Fax 01239 613754
✉ sales@starbornbooks.co.uk
www.starbornbooks.co.uk

Contact *Phil Forder*

Educational books, novels, poetry, biography
with a Welsh slant.

Stride Publications
11 Sylvan Road, Exeter EX4 6EW
✉ editor@stridebooks.co.uk
www.stridebooks.co.uk

Contact *Rupert Loydell*

Innovative poetry, criticism and music, essays and interviews. See entry under **Small Presses**.

Summer Palace Press
Cladnageeragh, Kilbeg, Kilcar, Republic of Ireland
☎00 353 733 8448   Fax 00 353 733 8448
Contacts *Kate & Joan Newman*

First collections of poetry, 64 pages, beautiful books.

Survivors' Press
45–49 King Street, Glasgow G1 5RA
☎0141 552 6111

For survivors of the mental health system. See entry under **Organisations of Interest to Poets**.

Swansea Poetry Workshop
124 Overland Road, Mumbles, Swansea SA3 4EU
Contact *Nigel Jenkins*

Tabor
2 Holyhead Road, Llanerchymedd, Ynys Mon LL71 7AB
Contact *M.A. Duxbury-Hibbert*

Poetry and prose booklets. No unsolicited mss, please.

Talking Pen
12 Derby Crescent, Moorside, Consett DH8 8DZ
☎01207 505724
Contact *Steve Urwin*

See also **Moodswing** magazine.

Triumph House
Remus House, Coltsfoot Drive, Woodston, Peterborough PE2 9JX
☎01733 898102   Fax 01733 313524
✉ triumphhouse@forwardpress.co.uk
www.forwardpress.co.uk
Contact *Kerrie Pateman*

A Christian poetry imprint publishing many anthologies annually.

Tuba Press
Tunley Cottage, Tunley, Near Cirencester GL7 6LW

☎01285 760424
Contact *Charles Graham*

Vennel Press
33 Cherry Orchard, Staines TW18 2DE
✉ vennel@hotmail.com
www.indigogroup.co.uk/llpp/vennel.html
Contact *Leona Carpenter*

Modern Scottish poetry; poetry that takes its bearings from modernism. See also **Au Quai** and **Southfields** presses.

Waterloo Press
51 Waterloo Street, Hove BN3 1AN
☎01273 202876
✉ dr.jenner@virgin.net
Contact *Simon Jenner*

Poetry and periodical publisher. Please phone for submissions. See also **Eratica** magazine.

Waywiser Press
9 Woodstock Road, London N4 3ET
☎020 8374 5526   Fax 020 8374 5736
✉ waywiserpress@aol.com
www.waywiser-press.com
Contact *Philip Hoy*

Specialises in modern poetry in English. See entry under **Small Presses**.

Wendy Webb Books
9 Walnut Close, Tavernham, Norwich NR8 6YN
✉ wwbuk@yahoo.co.uk
www.webbw.freeserve.co.uk
Contact *Wendy Webb*

Poetry anthologies selected from competition entries. See also **Norfolk Poets and Writers** magazine.

West House Books
40 Crescent Road, Nether Edge, Sheffield S7 1HN
☎0114 258 6035
✉ alan@nethedge.demon.co.uk
Contact *Alan Halsey*

Contemporary poetry, poets' prose and related work.

Poetry Magazines

Acumen
6 The Mount, Higher Furzeham, Brixham
TQ5 8QY
☎01803 851098 Fax 01803 851098
Contact *Patricia Oxley*

Good poetry, intelligent articles and wide-ranging reviews.

Agenda
The Wheelwrights, Fletching Street, Mayfield
TN20 6TL
✉ agendapoetry@lycos.co.uk
Contact *Patricia McCarthy*

Quarterly poetry magazine, founded 1959.

Ambit
17 Priory Gardens, London N6 5QY
☎020 8340 3566
www.ambitmagazine.co.uk
Contact *Martin Bax*

Poetry, fiction, art, reviews – established and emerging writers.

The Amsterdam Review
Columbusplein 19-111, 1057 TT Amsterdam,
The Netherlands
www.amsterdamreview.nl
Contacts *Duncan Bush & P.C. Evans*

Magazine for European literature.

Anon
67 Learmouth Grove, Edinburgh EH4 1BL
☎0131 332 2398
✉ mike@volta1.fsworld.co.uk
www.blanko.org.uk/anon
Contact *Mike Stocks*

Poems selected anonymously; for submission guidelines see website or send s.a.e.

Aquarius
Flat 4, Room B, 116 Sutherland Avenue,
London W9 2QP
Contact *Eddie S. Linden*

Literary magazine – prose and poetry.

Areopagus
48 Cornwood Road, Plympton, Plymouth
PL7 1AL Fax 0870 134 6384
✉ areopagus@churchnet.org.uk
www.churchnet.org.uk/areopagus/index.html
Contact *Julian Barritt*

A Christian-based arena for creative writers.

Arete
8 New College Lane, Oxford OX1 3BN
☎01865 289193 Fax 01895 289194
✉ craig.raine@new.ox.ac.uk
www.aretemagazine.com
Contact *Craig Raine*

Fiction, poetry, reportage, reviews.

Awen
38 Pierrot Steps, 71 Kursaal Way, Southend
on Sea SS1 2UY
Contact *David John Tyrer*

Poetry and vignette-length fiction of any style/genre. See also **Monomyth** and **Garbaj** magazines.

A Bard Hair Day
289 Elmwood Avenue, Feltham
TW13 7QB
✉ partners_writing_group@hotmail.com
www.homestead.com/partners_writing_group
Contact *Ian Deal*

General poetry magazine. See also **Partners** press, **Imagenation** and **Poet Tree** magazines.

Barddas
Pen Rhiw, 71 Fford Pentrepoeth, Treforys,
Swansea SA6 6AE
☎01792 792829 Fax 01792 792829
✉ alanllwyd@barddas.freeserve.co.uk
Contact *Alan Llwyd*

A magazine dedicated to Welsh language poetry.

Blithe Spirit
Longholm, East Bank, Wingland, Sutton
Bridge PE12 9YS
☎01547 528542 Fax 01547 520685
✉ alison.williams@hotmail.com
www.britishhaikusociety.org
Contact *Colin Blindell*

Journal of the British Haiku Society – haiku and related forms.

Braquemard
48 Clifton Street, Hull HU2 9AP
✉ braquemard@hotmail.com
www.braquemard.fsnet.co.uk
Contact *David Allenby*

Fifty-two pages of excellent poetry, prose and artwork.

Brittle Star
32b Gloucester Drive, London N4 2LN
☎020 8802 1507
✉ brittlestar@versify.co.uk
Contact *Jo Homan*

Poetry, short stories and articles on contemporary poetry.

Buzz Words
Calvers Farm, Thelveton, Diss IP21 4NG
✉ zoeking@calversfarm.fsnet.co.uk
www.buzzwordsmagazine.co.uk
Contact *Zoe King*

Small magazine with an international flavour – new and established writers of fiction and poetry.

Candelabrum Poetry Magazine
Rose Cottage, Threeholes Bridge, Wisbech PE14 9JR
✉ rep@poetry7.fsnet.co.uk
www.members.tripod.com/redcandlepress
Contact *M.L. McCarthy*

Formalist poetry mag for people who like poetry rhythmic and shapely. See also **Red Candle Press**.

Chanticleer Magazine
6/1 Jamaica Mews, Edinburgh EH3 6HN
☎0131 225 8883
✉ richard@livermore8304.freeserve.co.uk
Contact *Richad Livermore*

Ideas and poetry – aims to explore issues in poetry that other magazines rarely deal wth.

Chapman
4 Broughton Place, Edinburgh EH1 3RX
☎0131 557 2207 Fax 0131 556 9565
✉ chapman-pub@blueyonder.co.uk
www.chapman-pub.co.uk
Contact *Joy M. Hendry*

The best in Scottish and international writing, well-established writers and the up-and-coming. See entries under **UK Publishers** and **Magazines**.

Coffee House Poetry
Meirion House, Glanyrafon, Tanygrisiau, Blaenau Festiniog LL4 3SU
☎01766 832112
✉ jan@coffeehousepoetry.co.uk
www.coffeehousepoetry.co.uk
Contact *Dr Jan Fortune-Wood*

Contemporary poems of edge and depth from new voices and established writers. See also **Cinnamon Press**.

The Coffee House
Charnwood Arts, Loughborough Library, 31 Granby Street, Loughborough LE11 3DU
☎01509 822558 Fax 01509 822559
✉ charnwood-arts@ndirect.co.uk
www.charnwood-arts.org.uk
Contact *Deborah Tyler-Bennett*

A meeting place for the arts, poetry, prose and visual artwork.

Colours
16 Fane Close, Stamford PE9 1HG
☎01780 754193
Contact *Kevin Troop*

See also **KT Publications** press and **The Third Half** magazine.

Connections
4 Shiprights Lee, Island Wall, Whitstable CT5 1EW
☎01227 277773
✉ janehardy@fsnet.co.uk
Contact *Jane Hardy*

Emphasis on stimulating poetry, short fiction, features, reviews and artwork. Small payment.

Current Accounts
16–18 Mill Lane, Horwich, Bolton BL6 6AT
✉ rodriesco@aol.com
hometown.ao.co.uk/bswscribe/myhomepage/
  writing.html
Contact *Rod Riesco*

Poetry, short fiction, articles – magazine of the Bank Street Writers' Group.

Cyphers
3 Selskar Terrace, Ranelagh, Dublin 6, Republic of Ireland Fax 00 353 1 497 8866
Contact *Eilean Ní Chuilleanain*

Irish literary magazine: poetry, prose, reviews.

Dandelion Arts Magazine
24 Frosty Hollow, East Hunsbury NN4 0SY

☎01604 701730 Fax 01604 701730

Contact *Jacqueline Gonzalez-Marina*

International arts magazine – modern poetry, articles, stories and interviews.

The Dark Horse

3b Blantyre Mill Road, Bothwell
G71 8DD
✉ gjctdh@freename.co.uk

Contact *Gerry Cambridge*

The David Jones Journal

The David Jones Society, 48 Sylvan Way, Sketty, Swansea SA2 9JB
☎01792 206144 Fax 01792 205305
✉ anne.price-owen@sihe.ac.uk
www.sihe.ac.uk/davidjones

Contact *Anne Price-Owen*

Articles, poetry, information, reviews and inspired works.

Decanto

PO Box 4194, Worthing BN11 2GT
✉ masque_pub@tiscali.co.uk
myweb.tiscali.co.uk/masquepublishing

Contact *Lisa Stewart*

Non-conformist poetry magazine – any style considered, not just contemporary. See also **Masque Publishing** press.

Dial 174

21 Mill Road, Watlington, King's Lynn PE33 0HH
☎01553 811949

Contact *Joseph Hemmings*

Poetry, short storie, articles, travelogues, artwork, etc.

Dreamcatcher

7 Fairfield Street, Lincoln LN2 5NE
✉ editor@dreamcatcher-arts.co.uk
www.dreamcatcher-arts.co.uk

Contact *Paul Sutherland*

Poetry, prose, b&w photographs, from national & international contributors.

The Dublin Review

PO Box 7948, Dublin 1, Republic of Ireland

Contact *Brendan Barrington*

Earthlove

PO Box 11219, Paisley PA1 2WH
homepage.ntlworld.com/earth.love/
   earthlove.htm

Contact *Tracy Patrick*

Poetry magazine for the environment.

Eastern Rainbow

17 Farrow Road, Whaplode Drove, Spalding PE12 0TS
✉ p_rance@yahoo.co.uk

Contact *Paul Rance*

Focuses on 20th century culture via poetry, prose and art. See also **Peace and Freedom** magazine.

Echoes of Gilgamesh

18 Craighead Way, Barrhead, Glasgow G78 2RS
☎0141 881 9065
✉ paul@mcdonagh18.freeserve.co.uk
www.gilgamesh.fsworld.co.uk

Contact *Paul McDonagh*

Quarterly long poem magazine.

Eclipse Poetry Magazine

Linden Cottage, 45 Burton Road, Little Neston CH64 4AE
☎0151 353 0967
✉ helicon@globalnet.co.uk

Contact *Elizabeth Boyd*

Bi-monthly poetry mag which welcomes new poets. See also **Cherrybite Publications** press.

The Engine

3 Ardgreenan Drive, Belfast BT4 3FQ
☎028 9065 9866 Fax 028 9032 2767
✉ clitophon@yahoo.com
www.theengine.net

Contact *Paul Murphy*

'Zine of poetry, reviews and short stories.

Envoi

44 Rudyard Road, Biddulph Moor, Stoke-on Trent ST8 7JN
☎01782 517892

Contact *Roger Elkin*

Poetry, sequences, features, reviews, competitions.

Equinox

134b Joy Lane, Whitstable CT5 4ES

Contact *Barbara Dordi*

Twice-yearly journal of contemporary poetry illustrated with original artwork in colour. See also **Picture Poems** press.

Eratica

51 Waterloo Street, Hove BN3 1AN
☎01273 202876
✉ dr.jenner@virgin.net

Contact *Simon Jenner*

Annual journal with colour plates – focus on poetry, strong on music and art. See also **Waterloo Press**.

Fire

Field Cottage, Old Whitehill, Tackley, Kidlington OX5 3AB
www.poetical.org

Contact *Jeremy Hilton*

Poetry: alternative, unfashionable, experimental, spiritual, demotic; occasional experimental prose.

The Firing Squad

25 Griffiths Road, West Bromwich B71 2EH
☎07950 591455

Contact *Geoff Stevens*

Protest poetry broadsheet. See also **Purple Patch** magazine and **Poetry Wednesbury** press.

First Offense

Syringa, The Street, Stodmarsh, Canterbury CT3 4BA
✉ enquiries@firstoffense.co.uk
www.firstoffense.co.uk

Contact *Tim Fletcher*

Biannual magazine for contemporary poetry. Modernism, language-based texts.

First Time

The Snoring Cat, 16 Marianne Park, Dudley Road, Hastings TN35 5PU
☎01424 423105 Fax 01424 428855
✉ josephine.poetry@btopenworld.com
www.josephineaustin.co.uk

Contact *Josephine Austin*

Biannual magazine designed to encourage first-time poets.

Flaming Arrows

Sligo-Leitrim Arts, V E C, Riverside, Sligo, Republic of Ireland
☎00 353 71 914 7304
Fax 00 353 71 914 3093

Contact *Leo Regan*

Poetry of the spirit: mystical, metaphysical, grounded in the senses. Worldwide.

The Frogmore Papers

18 Nevill Road, Lewes BN7 1PF
www.frogmorepress.co.uk

Contact *Jeremy Page*

Founded 1983. Biannual. Poetry, prose and artwork.

Gabriel

27 Headingley Court, North Grange Road, Leeds LS6 2QU

Contact *Thelma Laycock*

Annual Christian poetry magazine.

Garbaj

38 Pierrot Steps, 71 Kursaal Way, Southend on Sea SS1 2UY

Contact *D.S. Davidson*

Humourous/non-pc poetry, vignette-length fiction, fake news, etc. See also **Awen** and **Monomyth** magazines.

Global Tapestry Journal

Spring Bank, Longsight Road, Copster Green, Blackburn BB1 9EU
☎01254 249128

Contact *Dave Cunliffe*

Global Bohemia, post-Beat and counterculture orientation. See also **BB Books** press.

The Green Door

The Dolls House, 103 Lincoln Street, Wakefield WF2 0ED
✉ masonharding@msn.com

Contact *Rebecca Mason-Harding*

Green Queen

BM Box 5700, London WC1N 3XX
Contact *Elsa Wallace*

Occasional magazine, Green issues, lesbian & gay fiction, articles, poetry.

Handshake

5 Cross Farm, Station Road North, Fearnhead, Warrington WA2 0QC

Contact *John Francis Haines*

Newsletter of **The Eight Hand Gang**, an association of UK sci-fi poets.

How Do I Love Thee?

1 Blue Ball Corner, Water Lane, Winchester SO23 0ER
☎01962 842621
✉ adrian.abishop@virgin.net
freespace.virgin.net/poetry.life

Contact *Adrian Bishop*

The magazine for love poetry. See also **Poetry Life** magazine.

HQ Poetry Magazine (Haiku Quarterly)
39 Exmouth Street, Swindon SN1 3PU
☎01793 523927

Contact *Kevin Bailey*

General poetry mag with slight bias towards imagistic/haikuesque work. See also **Day Dream Press**.

HU – The Honest Ulsterman
49 Main Street, Greyabbey BT22 2NF

Contact *Tom Clyde*

Ireland's premier journal for new poems, prose, articles.

Imagenation
289 Elmwood Avenue, Feltham TW13 7QB
✉ partners_writing_group@hotmail.com
www.homestead.com/partners_writing_group

Contact *Ian Deal*

Poetry and artwork magazine. See also **Partners** press, **A Bard Hair Day**, **Poet Tree** magazines.

Imagine
The Enterprise Park, Barrack Street, Tallow, Republic of Ireland
✉ tallowwriter@eircom.net

Contact *Anthony Healey*

Tallow writers.

Inclement
White Rose House, 8 Newmarket Road, Fordham, Ely CB7 5LL
✉ inclement_poetry_magazine@hotmail.com

Contact *Michelle Foster*

All forms and styles of poetry.

The Interpreter's House
10 Farrell Road, Wootton MK43 9DU

Contact *Merryn Williams*

Poems and stories up to 2500 words; new and established writers. See also **Plas Gwyn Books** press.

Iota
1 Lodge Farm, Snitterfield, Stratford upon Avon CV37 0LR
☎01789 730358   Fax 01789 730320

✉ iotapoetry@aol.com
www.iotapoetry.co.uk

Contacts *Bob Mee & Janet Murch*

Poetry, reviews; long and short poems welcome. No epics. See also **Ragged Raven Press**.

Irish Pages
The Linen Hall Library, 17 Donegall Square North, Belfast BT1 5GB
✉ irishpages@yahoo.com

Contact *Chris Agee*

Outstanding writing from Ireland and overseas: poetry, short fiction, essays, nature-writing, etc.

Island
8 Craiglea Drive, Edinburgh EH10 5PA
✉ jaj@essencepress.co.uk
www.essencepress.co.uk

Contact *Julie Johnstone*

A distinctive space for writing inspired by nature and exploring our place within the natural world. See also **Essence Press**.

The Journal
Flat 3, 18 Oxford Grove, Ilfracombe EX34 9HQ
☎01271 862708
✉ smithsssj@aol.com

Contact *Sam Smith*

Poems in translation alongside poetry written in English. See also **Original Plus** press.

Knightvision
4 Pedley Close, Westfield, Sheffield S20 8EY

Contact *Richard Middlebrook*

Sheffield's nationally acclaimed poetry and art magazine.

Krax
63 Dixon Lane, Wortley, Leeds LS12 4RR

Contact *Andy Robson*

Light-hearted, contemporary poetry, short fiction and graphics.

Lallans
Scots Language Society, A K Bell Library, York Place, Perth PH2 8AP
☎01738 440199
✉ johnmacphaillaw@aol.com
www.lallans.co.uk

Contact *John Law*

Scots language journalism and creative writing, twice-yearly.

Lantern Review
17 Sea Road, Galway, Republic of Ireland

Contact *Pat Jourdan*

Leeds Poetry Weekly
89 Connaught Road, Sutton SM1 3RJ
☎020 8286 0419

Contact *Barry Tebb*

New poems, reviews, articles on literary and psychoanalytic matters. See also **Literature and Psychoanalysis** magazine and **Sixties Press**.

Linkway
The Shieling, The Links, Burry Port SA16 0HU
☎01554 834486   Fax 01554 834486

Contact *Fay C. Davies*

A publication for writers and friends – a general interest magazine for the whole family.

Literature and Psychoanalysis
89 Connaught Road, Sutton SM1 3RJ
☎020 8286 0419

Contact *Barry Tebb*

New poems, reviews, articles on literary and psychoanalytical matters. See also **Leeds Poetry Weekly** magazine and **Sixties Press**.

Liver Bards
Flat 5, 28 Ullet Road, Liverpool L8 3SR
✉ thebrodiepress@hotmail.com

London Magazine
32 Addison Grove, London W4 1ER
☎020 8400 5882   Fax 020 8994 1713
✉ editorial@londonmagazine.ukf.net
www.londonmagazine.ukf.net

Contact *Sebastian Barker*

A review of literature and the arts. See entry under *Magazines*.

Magma
43 Keslake Road, London NW6 6DH
✉ magmapoems@aol.com
www.magmapoetry.com

Contact *David Boll*

New poetry plus poetry reviews and interviews.

Metre
Box 8745, Glenageary, Republic of Ireland

Contact *David Wheatley*

International poetry and critical prose.

Modern Poetry in Translation
The Queen's College, Oxford OX1 4AW
☎01865 244701   Fax 020 7848 2145
✉ helen-constantine@ip3.com
www.kcl.ac.uk/mpt

Contacts *David & Helen Constantine*

Publishes and promotes poetry in English translation.

Monkey Kettle
PO Box 4616, Kiln Farm, Milton Keynes MK12 6XZ
✉ monkeykettle@hotmail.com
www.monkeykettle.co.uk

Contact *Matthew Taylor*

Quarterly poetry, prose, photos, articles in Milton Keynes and further afield.

Monomyth
38 Pierrot Steps, 71 Kursaal Way, Southend on Sea SS1 2UY

Contact *David John Tyrer*

Poetry, prose and articles; all genres, styles and lengths considered. New writers welcome. See also **Awen** and **Garbaj** magazines.

Moodswing
12 Derby Crescent, Moorside, Consett DH8 8DZ
☎01207 505724

Contact *Steve Urwin*

Short poems, short prose, light/dark psychologically charged. See also **Talking Pen** press.

Mslexia
PO Box 656, Newcastle upon Tyne NE99 1PZ
☎0191 261 6656   Fax 0191 261 6636
✉ postbag@mslexia.demon.co.uk
www.mslexia.co.uk

Contact *Debbie Taylor*

National quarterly magazine for women who write. Advice, inspiration, news, reviews, interviews, etc. See entry under *Magazines*.

Multi-Storey
PO Box 62, Levenshulme, Manchester M19 1TH
✉ stuff@multistorey.co.uk
www.multistorey.co.uk

Contact *Finella Davenport*

Biannual literary magazine.

Neon Highway

35 Glebe Road, Skelmersdale WN8 9JP
✉ poetshideout@yahoo.com
www.geocities.com/poetshideout/neon.html

Contact *Alice Lenkiewicz*

Innovative and experimental poetry/arts magazine.

The New Cauldron

19 The Sandhills, Wirral CH46 3ST
☎0151 678 1105 Fax 0151 678 1965
✉ luna.cantos@virgin.net
www.thenewcauldron.co.uk

Contact *Anita Luna-Cantos*

Short stories, articles, poetry, competitions, letters, special features.

New Departures/ Poetry Olympics

PO Box 9819, London W11 2GC
☎020 7229 7850 Fax 020 7229 7850

Contact *Mike Horovitz*

Poetry journal of the Poetry Olympics. See also **New Departures** press.

New Welsh Review

PO Box 170, Aberystwyth SY23 1WZ
☎01970 626230
✉ nwr@welshnet.co.uk

Contact *Francesca Rhydderch*

Vibrant literary which showcases the best new writing from Wales – also includes features and reviews. See entry under *Magazines*.

Norfolk Poets and Writers

9 Walnut Close, Taverham, Norwich NR8 6YN
☎0798 917 4076
✉ wwbuk@yahoo.co.uk
www.webbw.freeserve.co.uk

Contact *Wendy Webb*

Postcard newsletter, brief poetry forms, mini stories, tips, etc.

The North

The Studio, Byram Arcade, Huddersfield HD1 1ND
☎01484 434840 Fax 01484 426566
✉ edit@poetrybusiness.co.uk
www.poetrybusiness.co.uk

Contacts *Peter Sansom & Janet Fisher*

Contemporary poetry and articles, extensive reviews.

Oasis

12 Stevenage Road, London SW6 6ES
☎020 7736 5059

Contact *Ian Robinson*

Poetry, short fiction, essays, reviews, etc. See also **Oasis Books** press.

Obsessed With Pipework

41 Buckley's Green, Alvechurch, Birmingham B48 7NG
☎0121 445 2110
www.poetrymagazines.org.uk

Contact *Charles Johnson*

Quarterly magazine of new poetry to surprise and delight. See also **Flarestack Publishing** press.

The Once Orange Badge Poetry Supplement

PO Box 184, South Ockendon RM15 5WT
☎01708 852827

Contact *D. M. Heath*

Free biannual poetry mag for those whose life has been touched by disability.

Orbis

17 Greenhow Avenue, West Kirby CH48 5EL
☎0151 625 1446
✉ carolebaldock@hotmail.com

Contact *Carole Baldock*

An independent international quarterly of poetry and prose with many reader-friendly features.

Other Poetry

29 Western Hill, Durham DH1 4RL
☎0191 386 4058
www.otherpoetry.com

Contact *Michael Standen & Others*

Thrice-yearly 60 – 70 poems per issue. Process of selection involves all four editors. Token payment.

Outlaw

212 Caerleon Road, Newport NP19 7CG
☎01633 666993

Contact *Bryn Fortey*

Irregular poetry magazine – beat, post-beat, underground, jazz.

Outposts

22 Whitewell Road, Frome BA11 4EL
☎01373 466653 Fax 01373 466653

Contact *Roland John*

Longest-surviving independent poetry magazine in the UK. See also **Hippopotamus Press**.

Oxford Poetry
Magdalen College, Oxford OX1 4AU
✉ editors@oxfordpoetry.co.uk
www.gnelson.demon.co.uk/oxpoetry
Contact *Graham Nelson*

Poems, interviews, critical features.

Panda
46 First Avenue, Clase, Swansea SA6 7LL
☎01792 414837   Fax 01792 414837
✉ esmond.j@ntlworld
www.geocities.com/slap_dash/
   Quarterly_poetry.html
Contact *Esmond Jones*

Poetry and prose.

The Paper
29 Vickers Road, Firth Park, Sheffield S5 6UY
☎0114 241 1202
✉ dgk@kennedyd.fsworld.co.uk
Contact *David Kennedy*

See also **Cherry on the Top** press.

Peace and Freedom
17 Farrow Road, Whaplode Drove, Spalding PE12 0TS
☎01406 330242
✉ p_rance@yahoo.co.uk
uk.vgeocities.com/p_rance/pandf.htm
Contact *Paul Rance*

Poetry, prose, art mag – humanitarian, environmental, animal welfare. See also **Eastern Rainbow** magazine.

Peer Poetry International
26 (wh) Arlington House, Bath Street BA1 1QN
☎01225 445298
✉ peerpoetryintl@tiny.com.uk
www.publish-your-poetry.com
Contact *Paul Amphlett*

All kinds and lengths of poetry.

The Penniless Press
100 Waterloo Road, Ashton, Preston PR2 1EP
☎01772 736421
Contact *Alan Dent*

Quarterly for the poor pocket and the rich mind. Poetry, fiction, essays, reviews.

Pennine Ink Magazine
The Gallery, Mid-Pennine Arts, Yorke Street, Burnley BB11 1HD
☎01282 703657
✉ sheridans@casanostra.p3online.net
Contact *Laura Sheridan*

Quality poetry reflecting traditional and modern trends.

Pennine Platform
Frizinghall, Frizinghall Road, Bradford BD9 4LD
☎01274 541015
Contact *Nicholas Bielby*

Poetry with reviews and critical articles.

Planet
PO Box 44, Aberystwyth SY23 3ZZ
☎01970 611255   Fax 01970 611197
✉ planet.enquiries@planetmagazine.org.uk
www.planetmagazine.org.uk
Contact *John Barnie*

The Welsh Internationalist – current affairs, arts, environment. See also **Planet** press.

PN Review
The Writing School, Manchester Metropolitan University, Geoffrey Manton Building, Rosamond Street West, Manchester M15 6LL
☎0161 834 8730   Fax 0161 832 0084
✉ pnr@carcanet.u-net.com
www.carcanet.co.uk
Contact *Michael Schmidt*

See **Carcanet Press** under *UK Publishers*.

Poet in the Round
18 Blackbridge Lane, Horsham RH12 1RP
Surrounded by talent.

Poet Tree
289 Elmwood Avenue, Feltham TW13 7QB
Contact *Ian Deal*

General poetry and short story magazine. See also **Partners** press, **A Bard Hair Day** and **Imagenation** magazines.

Poetic Hours
43 Willow Road, Carlton NG4 3BH
✉ erranpublishing@hotmail.com
www.poetichours.homestead.com
Contact *Nick Clark*

Non-profit supporter of Third World charities. See also **Erran Publishing**.

The Poetry Church

Feather Books, PO Box 438, Shrewsbury
SY3 0WN
☎01743 872177 Fax 01743 872177
✉ john@waddysweb.freeuk.com
www.waddysweb.freeuk.com
Contact *Rev. J. Waddington-Feather*

Quarterly magazine of Christian poetry and prayers. See **Feather Books** under *Small Presses*.

Poetry Cornwall/ Bardhonyeth Kernow

1 Station Hill, Redruth TR15 2PP
✉ les.merton@tesco.net
www.poetrycornwall.freeserve.com
Contact *Les Merton*

Poetry from Cornwall including poems in Kernewek and dialect.

Poetry Express

Diorama Arts Centre, 34 Osnaburgh Street, London NW1 3ND
☎020 7916 5317
✉ survivor@survivorspoetry.org.uk
Contact *James Ferguson*

Quarterly newsletter from **Survivors' Poetry** (entry under *Organisations of Interest to Poets*).

Poetry Ireland News

120 St Stephen's Green, Dublin 2, Republic of Ireland
☎00 353 1 478 9974 Fax 00 353 1 478 0205
✉ publications@poetryireland.ie
www.poetryireland.ie
Contact *Paul Lenehan*

Bi-monthly newsletter. See also **Poetry Ireland Review** magazine.

Poetry Ireland Review/ Eigse Eireann

120 St Stephen's Green, Dublin 2, Republic of Ireland
☎00 353 1 478 9974 Fax 00 353 1 478 0205
✉ poetry@iol.ie
www.poetryireland.ie
Contact *Peter Sirr*

Quarterly journal of poetry and reviews.

Poetry Life

1 Blue Bell Corner, Water Lane, Winchester SO23 0ER
☎01962 842621
✉ adrian.abishop@virgin.net
freespace.virgin.net/poetry.life

Contact *Adrian Bishop*

Publishing the best of modern poetry. See also **How Do I Love Thee?** magazine.

Poetry London

1a Jewel Road, London E17 4QU
✉ editors@poetrylondon.co.uk
www.poetrylondon.co.uk
Contact *Pascale Petit*

Poetry, listings, reviews, features and information. (Formerly *Poetry London Newsletter*.)

Poetry Monthly

39 Cavendish Road, Long Eaton, Nottingham NG10 4HY
☎0115 946 1267
✉ martin.holroyd@btinternet.com
Contact *Martin Holroyd*

A gallery of contemporary poetry and graphics. See also **Poetry Monthly Press**.

Poetry Nottingham International

11 Orkney Close, Stenson Fields, Derby DE24 3LW
☎01322 270590
Contact *Adrian Buckner*

Poetry, articles, reviews, published quarterly.

Poetry Now

Remus House, Coltsfoot Drive, Woodston, Peterborough PE2 9JX
☎01733 898101 Fax 01733 313524
✉ poetrynow@forwardpress.co.uk
www.forwardpress.co.uk
Contact *Kerrie Pateman*

Incorporating *Rhyme Arrival* magazine – communicating across the barriers. See also **Poetry Now** press.

Poetry Review

Poetry Society, 22 Betterton Street, London WC2H 9BU
☎020 7420 9883 Fax 020 7240 4818
✉ poetryreview@poetrysoc.com
www.poetrysoc.com
Contacts *Robert Potts & David Herd*

A quarterly forum on the state of poetry.

Poetry Salzburg Review

Dept of English and American Studies, University of Salzburg, Akademiestr. 24, A–5020 Salzburg, Austria
✉ wolfgang.goertschacher@sbg.ac.uk
www.poetrysalzburg.com

Contact *Wolfgang Görtschacher*

Poetry magazine, formerly *The Poet's Voice*. Published with the University of Salzburg.

Poetry Scotland
3 Spittal Street, Edinburgh EH3 9DY
☎0131 229 7252
www.poetryscotland.co.uk
Contact *Sally Evans*

All-poetry broadsheet with Scottish emphasis.

Poetry Wales
1st & 2nd Floors, 38–40 Nolton Street, Bridgend CF31 3BN
☎01656 663018   Fax 01656 649226
✉ poetrywales@seren.books.com
www.poetrywales.co.uk
Contact *Robert Minhinnick*

An international magazine with a reputation for fine writing and criticism. See also **Seren** under *UK Publishers*.

PQR – Poetry Quarterly Review
Coleridge Cottage, Nether Stowey, Bridgwater TA5 1NQ
☎01278 732662
✉ pqrrev@aol.com
Contacts *Derrick Woolf & Tilla Brading*

In-depth reviews of mainstream/small-press poetry – no unrequested poetry, please. See also **Odyssey Poets** press.

Praxis
Community Arts Workshop, Community Art Gallery, Avenue Road, Leamington Spa CV31 3PP
☎01926 888333
✉ community_arts_workshop@hotmail.com
Contact *Paul Lockwood*

Midlands magazine featuring poetry, short articles, illustrations. See also **Recovery** magazine.

Premonitions
13 Hazely Combe, Arreton, Isle of Wight PO30 3AJ
☎01983 865668
✉ pigasus.press@virgin.net
Contact *Tony Lee*

Magazine of sf-horror stories and horror stories, with genre poetry and art. See also **Pigasus Press**.

Presence
12 Grovehall Avenue, Leeds LS11 7EX
✉ alison.williams@virgin.net

freespace.virgin.net/haiku.presence
Contact *Martin Lucas*

Haiku, senryu, tanka, renku and related poetry in English.

Pretext
School of English & American Studies, University of East Anglia, Norwich NR4 7TJ
☎01603 592783
✉ info@penandinc.co.uk
www.penandinc.co.uk
Contact *Katri Skala*

New fiction and non-fiction. See also **Reactions** and **Pen&Inc** presses.

Pulsar
34 Lineacre Close, Grange Park, Swindon SN5 6DA
☎01793 875941
✉ ed@btopenworld.com
www.pulsarpoetry.com
Contact *David Pike*

Hard hitting/inspirational poetry – quarterly.

Purple Patch
25 Griffiths Road, West Bromwich B71 2EH
☎07950 591455
✉ ppatch66@hotmail.com
www.poetrywednesbury.co.uk
Contact *Geoff Stevens*

Poetry mag founded 1976 – includes reviews and gossip column. See also **The Firing Squad** magazine and **Poetry Wednesbury** press.

Quantum Leap
York House, 15 Argyle Terrace, Rothesay, Isle of Bute PA20 0BD
Contact *Alan Carter*

User-friendly magazine – encourages new writers – all types of poetry. See also **QQ Press**.

Quid
13 Heathfield Park, Flat 2, London NW2 5JE
✉ info@barquepress.com
www.barquepress.com
Contact *Keston Sutherland*

See also **Barque** press.

Raw Edge
PO Box 4867, Birmingham B3 3HD
Contact *Dave Reeves*

New writing, free from outlets in the West

Midlands Arts area. Writers with a regional connection only. See also **The Moving Finger** press.

Read the Music
20 Wharfedale Street, Wednesbury
WS10 9AG
☎07970 441110
✉ mooncrow@tiscali.co.uk
www.poetrywednesbury.co.uk
Contact *Brendan Hawthorne*

Original poetry based on music and its influences.

The Reader
University of Liverpool, 19 Abercromby Square, Liverpool L69 7ZR
✉ readers@thereader.co.uk
www.thereader.co.uk
Contact *Jane Davis*

Literary magazine, new fiction, poetry, essays, book recommendations and reviews. See entry under *Magazines*.

Recovery
Community Arts Workshop, Community Art Gallery, Avenue Road, Leamington Spa CV31 3PP
☎01926 888333
✉ community_arts_workshop.hotmail.com

Contact *Paul Lockwood*

Expressions of people recovering from, or living with, mental health problems. See also **Praxis** magazine.

Reveal
PO Box 184, South Ockendon RM15 5WT
Contact *D.M. Heath*

The more sensuous and heartfelt pen.

The Rialto
PO Box 309, Aylsham, Norwich NR11 6LN
www.therialto.co.uk
Contact *Michael Mackmin*

Excellent poetry in a clear environment.

Riposte
28 Emmet Road, Dublin 8, Republic of Ireland

Roundyhouse
3 Crown Street, Port Talbot SA13 1BG
✉ srjones@alunbooks.co.uk

Contact *Sally R. Jones*

Poems and articles on poetry. Reviews. Eclectic approach.

Sable
PO Box 33504, London E9 7YE
✉ hotspotwriters@compuserve.com

Contact *Kadija Sesay*

Literary magazine for writers of African, Caribbean, Asian descent – poetry, prose, memoirs, travel, etc.

Salt
PO Box 937, Great Wilbraham, Cambridge CB1 5JX
✉ cemery@saltpublishing.com
www.saltpublishing.com

Contact *John Kinsella & Others*

International journal of poetry and poetics. See also **Salt Publishing** press.

Sand
PO Box 1091, Sunderland SR2 8DW
✉ sandpoems@aol.com
www.sandwriting.co.uk

Contact *Kevin Cadwallender*

Probably the most accessible literary magazine ever.

Scintilla
Little Wentwood Farm, Llantrisant, Usk NP5 1ND
☎01291 673797
Contact *Anne Cluysenaar*

Journal of the Usk Valley Vaughan Association.

Scribbler!
Remus House, Coltsfoot Drive, Woodston, Peterborough PE2 9JX
☎01733 890066 Fax 01733 313524
✉ scribbler@forwardpress.co.uk
www.youngwriters.co.uk
Contact *Lynsey Hawkins*

Poetry, stories, guest authors, features, quarterly magazine for 7–11-year-olds. See also **Poetry Now Young Writers** press.

Scriptor
2 Chambers Cottages, Underlyn Lane, Marden, Tonbridge TN12 9BD
☎07967 315270
✉ mail@johndench.demon.co.uk
Contact *John Dench*

Poetry, short stories, essays from the UK. See also **Green Arrow Publishing** press.

Scryfa
Halwinnick Cottage, Linkinhorne, Callington
PL17 7NS

Contact *Simon Parker*

Seam
10 Collingwood Road, South Woodham
Ferrers, Chelmsford CM3 5YB
☎01245 323604
✉ fd@libertascapital.com

Contact *Frank Dullaghan*

New poetry by established and new poets. It's
the quality that counts.

Shearsman
58 Velwell Road, Exeter EX4 4LD
☎01392 434511 Fax 01392 434511
✉ editor@shearsman.com
www.shearsman.com

Contact *Tony Frazer*

Mainly poetry, some prose, some reviews.
Poetry in the modernist tradition. No fiction.
See also **Shearsman Books** press.

The Shop: A Magazine of Poetry
Skeagh, Schull, Republic of Ireland
✉ wakeman@iol.ie (not for submissions)

Contact *John Wakeman*

International but with emphasis on Irish
poetry.

Skald
2 Greenfield Terrace, Hill Street, Menai
Bridge LL59 5AY
☎01248 716343
✉ submissions@skald.co.uk
www.skald.co.uk

Contact *Zoe Skoulding*

Poetry and artwork, English and Welsh.

Smiths Knoll
49 Church Road, Little Glemham,
Woodbridge IP13 0BJ
✉ royblackman@ukonline.co.uk

Contacts *Roy Blackman & Michael Laskey*

Surprising, honest, well-crafted poems. No
e-mail submissions.

Smoke
The Windows Project, 96 Bold Street,
Liverpool L1 4HY
☎0151 709 3688

Contact *Dave Ward*

Poetry, graphics, short prose – 24pp – biannual.

South
PO Box 5369, Poole BH14 0XN
✉ south@martinblyth.co.uk
www.martinblyth.co.uk

Poetry magazine from the southern counties of
England that welcomes poets from across the
world.

Spiked
6 Whitwell Road, Norwich NR1 4HB
☎01603 629899
✉ editors@spiked-magazine.co.uk
www.spiked-magazine.co.uk

Contacts *Thea Abbott & Pamela Mulloy*

Ideas, literature and the arts for Norfolk.

Splizz
4 St Mary's Rise, Burry Port SA16 0SH
✉ amanda@stmarys4.freeserve.co.uk
www.stmarys4.freeserve.co.uk/Splizz.htm

Contact *Amanda Morgan*

Poetry and music alongside the more established.

Spoon
☎0151 733 3133
✉ spooneditor@hotmail.com

Prose, poetry, articles, photography and graphic
art.

Springboard
Corrimbla, Ballina, Co. Mayo, Republic of
Ireland
✉ bobgroom@eircom.net

Contact *Robert Groom*

Founded 1990. Quarterly mag of short fiction,
poetry and articles, competitions, news and
markets. Unsolicited material not accepted.

Stand
School of English, University of Leeds, Leeds
LS2 9JT
☎0113 233 4794 Fax 0113 233 4791
✉ stand@leeds.ac.uk
saturn.vcu.edu/~dlatane/stand.html

Contact *Jon Glover*

Quarterly magazine of poetry, fiction, reviews
and cultural criticism.

Staple
35 Carr Road, Walkley, Sheffield S6 2WY
✉ e.barrett@shu.ac.uk
Contact *Elizabeth Barrett*

Poetry, short fiction, articles. Three issues a
year.

The Stinging Fly
PO Box 6016, Dublin 8, Republic of Ireland
✉ stingingfly@hotmail.com
www.stingingfly.org
Contact *Declan Meade*

Dublin's literary magazine. New Irish and international writing. Poetry, short fiction, author interviews and book reviews.

Sub Voicive Poetry
32 Downside Road, Sutton SM2 5HP
Contact *Lawrence Upton*

Taliesin
Academi, 3rd Floor, Mount Stuart House, Mount Stuart Square, Cardiff CV10 5FQ
☎029 2047 2266 Fax 029 2049 2930
✉ taliesin@academi.org
www.academi.org
Contact *Manon Rhys*

Wales' leading Welsh language literary journal.

Tears in the Fence
38 Hod View, Stourpaine, Nr Blandford Forum DT11 8TN
☎01258 456803 Fax 01258 454026
✉ esp@euphony.net
www.wanderingdog.co.uk
Contact *David Caddy*

A magazine looking for the unusual, perceptive, risk-taking, lived and visionary literature.

10th Muse
33 Hartington Road, Southampton SO14 0EW
✉ andyj@noplace.screaming.net
Contact *Andrew Jordan*

Poetry, prose and graphics, ideally combining lyricism and pastoral.

The Third Half
16 Fane Close, Stamford PE9 1HG
☎01780 754193
Contact *Kevin Troop*

Searches for good poetry and fiction. See also **KT Publications** press and **Colours** magazine.

Time Haiku
105 Basho-an, Kings Head Hill, London E4 7JG
☎020 8529 6478
Contact *Dr Erica Facey*

Haiku magazine aimed at experts and beginners.

Understanding
20a Montgomery Street, Edinburgh EH7 5JS
☎0131 478 0680 Fax 0131 478 2572
Contact *Denise Smith*

Original poetry, short stories, parts of plays, reviews and articles. See also **Dionysia Press**.

Urthona
9a Auckland Road, Cambridge CB2 8DW
☎01223 309470
✉ urthona.mag@virgin.net
www.urthona.com
Contact *Shantigarbha*

Buddhism and the arts. Builds bridges between Buddhism and world culture.

Wasafiri
Dept of English, Queen Mary College, University of London, Mile End Road, London E1 4SN
☎020 7882 3120 Fax 020 7882 3120
✉ wasafiri@qmul.ac.uk
www.wasafiri.org
Contact *Susheila Nasta*

Literary journal of African, Asian, Caribbean and black British writing. See entry under *Magazines*.

Wordsmith
Remus House, Coltsfoot Drive, Woodston, Peterborough PE2 9JX
☎01733 890066 Fax 01733 313524
✉ wordsmith@forwardpress.co.uk
www.forward-press.co.uk
Contact *Allison Oowse*

Poetry, stories, guest authors, features in a quarterly magazine for 11–16-year-olds.

The Yellow Crane
20 Princes Court, The Walk, Roath, Cardiff CF23 3AU
Contact *J. Brookes*

Interesting new poems from S. Wales and beyond.

The Yoke
37 Thornaby Lawns, Howth, Republic of Ireland
Contact *Serena Davis*

Organisations of Interest to Poets

A survey of some of the societies, groups and other bodies which may be of interest to practising poets. Organisations not listed should send details to the Editor for inclusion in future editions.

Academi – The Welsh National Literature Promotion Agency and Society for Writers

3rd Floor, Mount Stuart House, Mount Stuart Square, Cardiff Bay CF10 5FQ
☎029 2047 2266 Fax 029 2049 2930
✉ post@academi.org
www.academi.org

North Wales Office: Ty Newydd, Llanystumdwy, Cricieth, Gwynedd LL52 0LW

West Wales Office: Dylan Thomas Centre, Somerset Place, Swansea SA1 1RR

Chief Executive *Peter Finch*

The writers' organisation of Wales with special responsibility for literary activity, writers' residencies, writers on tour, festivals, writers' groups, readings, tours, exchanges and other development work. Academi awards financial bursaries annually, runs a criticism service and organises the **Welsh Book of the Year Awards**. **Yr Academi Gymreig/The Welsh Academy** operates the Arts Council of Wales franchise for Wales-wide literature development. It has offices in Cardiff and fieldworkers based in North West, North East and West Wales. Publisher of the Lottery-funded *Encyclopedia of Wales*, the Welsh-medium literary magazine *Taliesin*, the *Academi English-Welsh Dictionary*, co-publisher of *The New Welsh Review* along with a number of other projects. The Academi sponsors a range of annual contests including the John Tripp Award For Spoken Poetry and the prestigious **Cardiff International Poetry Competition**. Publishes *A470* a bi-monthly literary information magazine.

Apples & Snakes

Battersea Arts Centre, Lavender Hill, London SW11 5TN
☎020 7924 3410 Fax 020 7924 3763
✉ info@applesandsnakes.org
www.applesandsnakes.org

Director *Geraldine Collinge*

Set up in 1982 as a platform for poetry which would be popular, relevant, cross-cultural and accessible to the widest possible range of people, A&S aims to stretch the boundaries of Poetry in Education and performance. Currently undergoing an extensive programme of expansion, bringing performance poetry to new places and new audiences across England.

The Arvon Foundation

See entry under *UK Writers' Courses*

The British Haiku Society

Lenacre Ford, Woolhope HR1 4RF
☎01432 860328
www.britishhaikusociety.org

General Secretary *David Walker*

Formed in 1990. Promotes the appreciation and writing within the British Isles of haiku, senyru, tanka, haibun and renga by way of tutorials, workshops, exchange of poems, critical comment and information. The Society runs a haiku library and administers the annual James W. Hackett Award, the prestigious **Sasakawa** prize and the Nobuyuki Yuasa International Haibun in English Contest. Organises twice-yearly 'haiku gatherings'. Details from *Brian Tasker*, The Annexe, 65 Nunney Road, Frome BA11 4LE (briantasker@hotmail.com). Publishes *The Haiku Kit* teaching pack and the quarterly journal, *Blithe Spirit*.

The Eight Hand Gang

5 Cross Farm, Station Road, North Fearnhead, Warrington WA2 0QG
Secretary *John F. Haines*

An association of SF poets. Publishes *Handshake*, a single-sheet newsletter of SF poetry and information available free in exchange for an s.a.e.

57 Productions

57 Effingham Road, Lee Green SE12 8NT
☎020 8463 0866 Fax 020 8463 0866
✉ paul57prods@yahoo.co.uk
www.57productions.com

Contact *Paul Beasley*

Specialises in the promotion of poetry and its production through an agency service, a programme of events and a series of audio publications. Services are available to event promoters, festivals, education institutions and the media. Poets represented include Jean 'Binta' Breeze, Adrian Mitchell, John Cooper Clarke and Lemn Sissay. 57 Productions' series of audio cassettes, CDs and Poetry in Performance compilations offer access to some of the most exciting poets working in Britain today.

The Football Poets
4 The Retreat, Butterow, Stroud
☎01453 757376
✉ crispin@ctmuk.freeserve.co.uk *and* dave@footballpoets.org
www.footballpoets.org
Performance *Crispin Thomas*
Secretary *Dave Cockcroft*

The Football Poets exist to promote and encourage the writing and performing of football poetry. Formed in 1995, they appear regularly at festivals and venues around the country. They also provide comprehensive and entertaining football poetry workshops in schools and communities. Their website is a fast and entertaining mix of literature and soccer poetry from around the world. Anyone may contribute.

The Poet's House/Teach na hÉigse
Clonbarra, Falcarragh, Republic of Ireland
☎00 353 749 165470
✉ poetshouse@eircom.net
Directors *Janice Fitzpatrick Simmons, Greagoir O Duill*

Set in mountain country in the Donegal Gaeltacht, the centre offers a year-long residential MA in the writing of poetry and runs two ten-day summer courses. In each summer session three American poets are in residence and six Irish and British poets each lead a day. Participating poets have recently included Ralph Angel and Richard Tillinghast, Paul Durcan, Anthony Cronin, Michael Longley, Menna Elfyn, Frank Ormsby and Medbh McGuckian.

The Poetry Archive
Ball's Green House, Minchinhampton
GL6 9AR
☎01453 832090 Fax 01453 836450
✉ info@poetryarchive.org
Directors *Richard Carrington, Andrew Motion*

A permanent archive of audio recordings of work by poets who write in English. New recordings will be made for the Archive by a wide-ranging list of poets and substantial extracts from those recordings will soon be available online. The full-length recordings will be sold by mail order on CDs and audiocassettes.

The Poetry Book Society
Book House, 45 East Hill, London SW18 2QZ
☎020 8870 8403 Fax 020 8870 0865
✉ info@poetrybooks.co.uk
www.poetrybooks.co.uk
Director *Chris Holifield*

For readers, writers, students and teachers of poetry. Founded in 1953 by T.S. Eliot and funded by the Arts Council, the PBS is a unique membership organisation and book club providing up-to-date and comprehensive information about poetry from publishers in the UK and Ireland. Members receive the quarterly *PBS Bulletin* packed with articles by poets, poems, news, listings and access to discounts of at least 25% off featured titles. These range from modern classics to contemporary works. The transactional website has over 1000 titles available at discount to members. There are three membership packages – two of which include a number of new books specially selected by the Society's panel of experts along with, at both primary and secondary levels, a special package for teachers. Subscriptions start at £10. The PBS also runs the annual **T.S. Eliot Prize** for the best collection of new poetry.

The Poetry Business
The Studio, Byram Arcade, Westgate, Huddersfield HD1 1ND
☎01484 434840 Fax 01484 426566
✉ edit@poetrybusiness.co.uk
www.poetrybusiness.co.uk
Directors *Peter Sansom, Janet Fisher*

Founded in 1986, the Business publishes *The North* magazine and books, pamphlets and cassettes under the **Smith/Doorstop** imprint. It runs an annual competition and organises monthly writing Saturdays. Send an s.a.e. for full details.

Poetry Can
Unit 11, Kuumba Project, 20–23 Hepburn Road, Bristol BS2 8UD
☎0117 942 6976 Fax 0117 944 1478
✉ lucy@poetrycan.demon.co.uk
www.poetrycan.demon.co.uk
Founded in 1995, Poetry Can is a poetry development agency working across the Bristol

and Bath areas It organises events and projects, supports the creative and professional development of poets and publishes a bi-monthly bulletin of poetry news and activity.

Poetry Ireland/Eigse Eireann

Bermingham Tower, Upper Yard, Dublin Castle, Dublin, Republic of Ireland
☎00 353 1 671 4632 Fax 00 353 1 671 4634
✉ poetry@iol.ie
www.poetryireland.ie

Education ☎00 353 671 4216 Writers in Schools scheme ☎00 353 1 475 8601

Director *Joseph Woods*

The national organisation for poetry in Ireland, with its four core activities being readings, publications, education and an information and resource service. Organises readings by Irish and international poets countrywide. Through its website, telephone, post and public enquiries, Poetry Ireland operates as a clearing house for everything pertaining to poetry in Ireland. Operates the Writers in Schools scheme. *Publishes Poetry Ireland News*, a bimonthly newsletter containing information on events, competitions and opportunities. *Poetry Ireland Review* is published quarterly and is the journal of record for poetry in Ireland; current editor: *Peter Sirr*. The organisation also produces occasional publications, most recently, *Watching the River Flow, a Century in Irish Poetry*.

The Poetry Library

Royal Festival Hall, Level 5, London SE1 8XX
☎020 7921 0943/0664 Fax 020 7921 0939
✉ info@poetrylibrary.org.uk
www.poetrylibrary.org.uk

Librarian *Simon Smith*

Founded by the Arts Council in 1953. A collection of 45,000 titles of modern poetry since 1912, from Georgian to Rap, representing all English-speaking countries and including translations into English by contemporary poets. Two copies of each title are held, one for loan and one for reference. A wide range of poetry magazines and ephemera from all over the world are kept along with casettes, records and videos for consultation, with many available for loan. There is a children's poetry section with teacher's resource collection.

An information service compiles lists of poetry magazines, competitions, publishers, groups and workshops which are available from the Library on receipt of a large s.a.e. or direct from the website. It also has a noticeboard for lost quotations through which it tries to identify lines or fragments of poetry which have been sent in by other readers.

General enquiry service available. Membership is free but proof of identity and address are essential to join. Open 11.00 am to 8.00 pm, Tuesday to Sunday. The Library's website is one of the best poetry resources on the Net.

Beside the Library is *The Voice Box*, a performance space especially for literature. For details of current programme ring 020 7921 0971.

Poetry London

1a Jewel Road, London E17 4QU
✉ editors@poetrylondon.co.uk
www.poetrylondon.co.uk

Contacts *Kathryn Maris* (listings), *Pascale Petit* (poetry editor), *Scott Verner* (reviews)

Published three times a year, *Poetry London* includes poetry by new and established writers, reviews of recent collections and anthologies, articles on issues relating to poetry, and an encyclopædic listings section of virtually everything to do with poetry in the capital and elsewhere in the UK.

The Poetry School

1a Jewel Road, London E17 4QU
☎020 8223 0401 Fax 020 8223 0401
✉ programme@poetryschool.com
www.poetryschool.com

Administrator *Jacqueline Gabbitas*

Funded by London Arts, the School offers a wide range of courses and workshops on writing and reading poetry and is open to anyone regardless of experience or formal qualifications. Tutors include Graham Fawcett, Stephen Knight, Selima Hill, Carole Satyamurti, Myra Schneider and Mimi Khalvati. The School provides a forum for practitioners to share experiences, develop skills and extend appreciation of the traditional and innovative aspects of their art. There are masterclasses with visiting poets such as Marilyn Hacker, Jorie Graham, Sean O'Brien and Don Paterson.

The Poetry Society

22 Betterton Street, London WC2H 9BX
☎020 7240 9881 Fax 020 7240 4818
✉ info@poetrysociety.org.uk
www.poetrysociety.org.uk

Director *Jules Mann*

Founded in 1909 which ought to make it venerable, the Society exists to help poets and poetry thrive in Britain. In the past decade it has undergone a renaissance, reaching out from its Covent Garden base to promote the national health of poetry in a range of imaginative ways. Membership costs £35 for individuals. *Poetry News* membership is £15. Current activities include:

- Quarterly magazine of new verse, views and criticism, *Poetry Review*.
- Quarterly newsletter, *Poetry News*, with lively relevant articles for members.
- Promotions, events and cooperation with Britain's many literature festivals, poetry venues and poetry publishers.
- Competitions and awards, including the annual **National Poetry Competition** with a £5000 first prize.
- A manuscript diagnosis service, *The Poetry Prescription*, which gives detailed reports on submissions. Reduced rates for members.
- Seminars, fact sheets, training courses, ideas packs.
- Provides information and advice, publishes books, posters and resources for schools and libraries. Education membership costs £50 (secondary) or £30 (primary) which includes free poetry anthologies, lesson plans and a subscription to Poems on the Underground. Publications include *The Poetry Book For Primary Schools* and *Jumpstart Poetry for the Secondary School*, colourful poetry posters for Keystages 1, 2, 3 and 4. Many of Britain's most popular poets – including Michael Rosen, Roger McGough and Jackie Kay – contribute, offering advice and inspiration.
- The Society's online poetry classroom is at www.poetryclass.net
- The Poetry Café serving snacks and drinks to members, friends and guests, part of The Poetry Place, a venue for many poetry activities – readings, workshops and poetry launches. This space is available for bookings (☎020 7420 9887).
- *Poetry Landmarks of Britain*, a free resource on the Society's website, updated for every National Poetry Day in October, invites the public to nominate their favourite 'poetry landmark'.

Point
Ithaca, Apdo. 125, E–03590 Altea, Spain
☎00 34 96 584 2350 Fax 00 34 96 688 2767
✉ elpoeta@point-editions.com
www.point-editions.com
Also at: Schapenstraat 157, B–1750 Lennik, Belgium
Director *Germain Droogenbroodt*
Founded as POetry INTernational in 1984, Point is based in Spain and Belgium. A multilingual publisher of contemporary verse from

established poets, the organisation has brought out more than 70 titles in at least eight languages, including English. Editions run the original work alongside a verse translation into Dutch made in cooperation with the poet. The organisation's website features the world's best-known and unknown poets in English, Spanish and Dutch. Point also co-organises an annual international poetry festival.

Scottish Poetry Library
5 Crichton's Close, Canongate, Edinburgh EH8 8DT
☎0131 557 2876
✉ inquiries@spl.org.uk
www.spl.org.uk
Director *Robyn Marsack*
A comprehensive reference and lending collection of work by Scottish poets in Gaelic, Scots and English, plus the work of British and international poets. Stock includes books, tapes, videos, news cuttings and magazines. Borrowing is free to all. Services include a postal lending scheme, for which there is a small fee, a mobile library that can visit schools and other centres by arrangement, exhibitions, bibliographies, publications, information and promotion in the field of poetry. Also available is an online catalogue and computer index to poetry and poetry periodicals. The membership scheme costs £20 annually. Members receive a newsletter and other benefits and support the library.

Second Light
9 Greendale Close, London SE22 8TG
✉ dilyswood@tiscali.co.uk
Director *Dilys Wood*
A network of over 350 women poets, established and lesser known, aged from late thirties upwards. Aims to develop and promote women's poetry especially among those who began writing or publishing poetry late. Publishes a newsletter, runs an annual poetry competition, holds residential workshops, readings and cooperates with established poetry publishers to produce anthologies of women's work.

Spiel Unlimited (formerly Slam! Productions)
20 Coxwell Street, Cirencester GL7 2BH
☎01285 640470
✉ spiel@scarum.freeserve.co.uk
www.author.co.uk/spiel
Directors *Marcus Moore, Sara-Jane Arbury*
'Spoken word, written word, anywhere, everywhere' with two writers who put a posi-

tive charge in live literature by organising quirky and original events such as Slam!Fests!, Spontaneity Days and Living Room Poetry performances, hosting UK poetry slams and running *word* shops for schools and adults. Also produce *SPIEL*, a monthly e-mail newsletter. Specialists in breathing new life into literature.

Survivors' Poetry

Diorama Arts Centre, 34 Osnaburgh Street, London NW1 3ND
☎020 7916 5317   Fax 020 7916 0830
✉ survivors@survivorspoetry.org.uk

A unique national literature organisation promoting poetry by survivors of mental distress through workshops, readings and performances to audiences all over the UK. It was founded in 1991 by four poets with first-hand experience of the mental health system. Survivors' community outreach work provides training and performance workshops and publishing projects. *Survivors* work with those who have survived mental distress and those who empathise with their experience.

Tŷ Newydd

Llanystumdwy, Cricieth LL52 0LW
☎01766 522811   Fax 01766 523095
✉ tynewydd@dial.pipex.com
www.tynewydd.org
Director *Sally Baker*

Run by the Taliesin Trust, an independent, Arvon-style residential writers centre established in the one-time home of Lloyd George in North Wales. The programme (in both Welsh and English) has a regular poetry content. (See also *UK Writers' Courses*.) Fees start at £100 for weekends and £345 for week-long courses. Among the many tutors to-date have been: Gillian Clarke, U.A. Fanthorpe, Roger McGough, Carol Ann Duffy, Liz Lochhead, Peter Finch and Paul Henry. Send for the centre's descriptive leaflets and programme of courses.

The Virtual Writing School

Manchester Metropolitan University, Dept. of English, The Virtual Writing School, Geoffrey Manton Building, Rosamond Str, Manchester M15 6LL
☎0161 247 1735
✉ h.watson@mmu.ac.uk
www.mmu.ac.uk/h-ss/eng

Contact *Heather Watson*

Manchester Metropolitan University's creative writing courses under Michael Schmidt (see also *UK Writers' Courses*) offer a virtual poetry strand with tutors Sophie Hannah, Michael Schmidt, Jeffrey Wainwright and others. The qualification is a MA/PgDip. Enquire early as places are strictly limited. The school also offers virtual novel writing.

Small Presses

Aard Press

c/o Aardverx, 31 Mountearl Gardens, London SW16 2NL

Managing Editors *D. Jarvis, Dawn Redwood*

Founded 1971. Publishes artists' bookworks, experimental/visual poetry, 'zines, eonist literature, topographics, ephemera and international mail-art documentation. Very small editions. No unsolicited material or proposals.

ROYALTIES not paid. No sale-or-return deals.

Abbey Press

Abbey Grammar School, Courtenay Hill, Newry BT34 2ED
☎028 3026 3142 Fax 028 3026 2514

Also at: 12 The Pines, Jordanstown, Newtonabbey, Co. Antrim BT37 0SE
☎028 9086 0230

Editor *Adrian Rice*
Administrator *Mel McMahon*

Founded in 1997, Abbey Press is a fast growing literary publisher with a strong poetry list. Also publishes biography, memoirs, fiction, history, politics, Irish language, academic and art. Lists currently full.

Akros Publications

33 Lady Nairn Avenue, Kirkcaldy KY1 2AW
☎01592 651522

Publisher *Duncan Glen*

Founded 1965. Publishes poetry collections, pamphlets and anthologies; literary essays and studies; local histories. Also publishes *Z20* poetry magazine. About 10 titles a year. No unsolicited mss. No fiction.

ROYALTIES twice-yearly.

Allardyce, Barnett, Publishers

14 Mount Street, Lewes BN7 1HL
☎01273 479393 Fax 01273 479393
www.abar.net

Publisher *Fiona Allardyce*
Managing Editor *Anthony Barnett*

Founded 1981. Publishes art, literature and music. IMPRINT **Allardyce Book**. About 3 titles a year. Unsolicited mss and synopses cannot be considered.

Alphard Press

See **ignotus press**

Anglo-Saxon Books

Frithgarth, Thetford Forest Park, Hockwold cum Wilton IP26 4NQ
☎01842 828430 Fax 01842 828332
✉ tony@asbooks.co.uk
www.asbooks.co.uk

Managing Editor *Tony Linsell*

Founded 1990 to promote a greater awareness of and interest in early English history, language and culture. Publishes Anglo-Saxon history, culture, language. Please phone before sending mss. About 5 titles a year.

ROYALTIES at standard rate.

Apex Publishing Ltd

PO Box 7445, Colchester CO4 9UA
☎0870 242 0938 Fax 0870 046 6536
✉ enquiry@apexpublishing.co.uk
www.apexpublishing.co.uk

Managing Editor *Susan Kidby*

Founded 2002. Subsidy publishing company for unknown and established authors. Publishes poetry, self-help, non-fiction, fiction, sci-fi, history, humour, fine art, art history, education and textbooks, economics, crime, children's books, biography, autobiography, academic, women's interests, medical and philosophy. 12 titles in 2003. Welcomes unsolicited mss, synopses and ideas for books. Approach in writing to the address above.

ROYALTIES paid.

Athelney

1 Providence Street, King's Lynn PE30 5ET
Fax 01842 828332
Managing Editor *John Cooper*

Founded 2000. Publishes nationalism in general; English nationalism in particular. 'We are interested in contemporary England and the English; e.g. culture, language, politics.' Unsolicited outlines/contents page/first chapter welcome. Please enclose return postage.

ROYALTIES at standard rate.

M.&M. Baldwin
24 High Street, Cleobury Mortimer, Kidderminster DY14 8BY
☎01299 270110 Fax 01299 270110
✉ mb@mbaldwin.free-online.co.uk

Managing Editor *Dr Mark Baldwin*

Founded 1978. Publishes local interest/history, WW2 codebreaking and inland waterways books. Up to 5 titles a year. Unsolicited mss, synopses and ideas for books welcome (not general fiction).

ROYALTIES paid.

BB Books
See entry under *Poetry Presses*

The Better Book Company Ltd
Warblington Lodge, The Gardens, Warblington, Havant PO9 2XH
☎023 9248 1160 Fax 023 9249 2819
✉ editors@better-book.co.uk
www.better-book.co.uk

Managing Editor *James Jude Garvey*

Founded 1996. Offers a complete editorial, design, printing and marketing service to authors wishing to self-publish their work in all genre. Marketing and distribution services available to all authors. Produces fiction, histories, memoirs, poetry, religious, scientific, company histories. A free booklet, *A Complete Guide to Self-Publishing*, is available on request. 80 titles in 2003.

Between the Lines
9 Woodstock Road, London N4 3ET
☎020 8374 5526 Fax 020 8374 5736
✉ btluk@aol.com
www.interviews-with-poets.com

Editorial Board *Peter Dale, Philip Hoy, J.D. McClatchy*

Founded 1998. Publishes in book form extended interviews with leading contemporary poets. Twelve volumes currently in print, featuring John Ashbery, Charles Simic, Ian Hamilton, Donald Justice, Seamus Heaney, Richard Wilbur, Thom Gunn, Donald Hall, Anthony Hecht, Anthony Thwaite, Michael Hamburger and W.D. Snodgrass. Each volume includes a career sketch, a comprehensive bibliography and a representative selection of quotations from the poets' critics and reviewers. A new series featuring several younger poets to a volume was launched in 2004.

The Bewildered Publishing Company Ltd
Argoed Hall, Tregaron SY25 6JR
☎01974 298070 Fax 01974 298708
✉ john@bewildered.co.uk

Publisher *John Wilson*

Founded in 1999 'to provide a direct route to the book market for authors with an unconventional approach to writing and publishing'. Publishes humorous paperbacks. No unsolicited material; initial inquiry by telephone, e-mail or letter.

ROYALTIES not paid.

Black Cat Books
See **Neil Miller Publications**

BlackAmber Books Ltd
3 Queen Square, London WC1N 3AU
☎020 7278 2488 Fax 020 7278 8864
✉ information@blackamber.com
www.blackamber.com

Publisher *Rosemarie Hudson*

Founded 1998. A collection point for the creative voice of European writers, in particular Black and Asian. Literary fiction and non-fiction and works in translation. Send one-page synopsis with first three chapters and s.a.e; for non-fiction send detailed outline with accompanying material plus a one-page c.v. and s.a.e.

The Book Castle
12 Church Street, Dunstable LU5 4RU
☎01582 605670 Fax 01582 662431
✉ bc@book-castle.co.uk
www.book-castle.co.uk

Managing Editor *Paul Bowes*

Founded 1986. Publishes non-fiction of local interest (Bedfordshire, Hertfordshire, Buckinghamshire, Oxfordshire, the Chilterns). About 100 titles in print. 12 titles a year. Unsolicited mss, synopses and ideas for books welcome.

ROYALTIES paid.

Bookmarque Publishing
26 Cotswold Close, Minster Lovell OX29 0SX
☎01993 775179
✉ john@bookmarque.fsbusiness.co.uk

Managing Editor *John Rose*

Founded 1987. Publishing business with aim of filling gaps in motoring history of which it is said 'there are many'. Publishes motoring history, motor sport and some 'general' titles. All design and typesetting of books done in-house.

About 8 titles a year. Unsolicited mss and synopses welcome on motoring titles. S.a.e. required for reply or return of material or for advice on publishing your work.

ROYALTIES paid.

Brilliant Publications
1 Church View, Sparrow Hall Farm, Edlesborough, Dunstable LU6 2ES
☎01525 229720 Fax 01525 229725
✉ sales@brilliantpublications.co.uk
www.brilliantpublications.co.uk
Publisher *Priscilla Hannaford*

Founded 1993. Publishes resource books for teachers, parents and others working with 0–13-year-olds. SERIES *How to Dazzle at ...* (9–13-year-olds with special needs); *How to be Brilliant at ...* (7–11-year-olds); *How to Sparkle at ...* (5–7-year-olds); *Activities* (3–5-year-olds). About 10–15 titles a year. Submit synopsis and sample pages in the first instance. All the books have black and white insides and many can be photocopied. Potential authors are strongly advised to look at the format of existing books before submitting synopses.

ROYALTIES twice-yearly.

The Brodie Press
✉ thebrodiepress@hotmail.com
www.thebrodiepress.co.uk
Managing Editors *Tom Sperlinger, Hannah Sheppard, James Bainbridge, Rhiannon Davies*

Founded 2002. Publishes poetry, literary fiction and anthologies. SERIES *The Brodie Poets*, launched in 2003, including Julie-ann Rowell, Poetry Book Society Pamphlet Choice, Winter 2003. Send synopses and proposals by e-mail in the first instance.

Charlewood Press
7 Weavers Place, Chandlers Ford SO53 1TU
☎023 8026 1192
✉ gponting@clara.net
www.home.clara.net/gponting/index-page11.html
Managing Editors *Gerald Ponting, Anthony Light*

Founded 1987. Publishes local history books and walks booklets on Hampshire and adjacent counties, especially around the Fordingbridge area. Mss in this field considered.

Chrysalis Press
7 Lower Ladyes Hills, Kenilworth CV8 2GN
☎01926 855223
✉ editor@margaretbuckley.com
www.margaretbuckley.com

Managing Editor *Brian Boyd*

Founded 1994. Publishes fiction, literary criticism and biography. No unsolicited mss.
ROYALTIES paid.

CK Publishing
151 Brookfield Road, Cheadle SK8 1EY
☎0161 491 6074
✉ editor@ckpublishing.co.uk
www.ckpublishing.co.uk
Managing Editor *Calum Kerr*

Publishes novels. Unsolicited mss welcome; no synopses or ideas. S.a.e. essential.
ROYALTIES paid.

CNP Publications
See **Lyfrow Trelyspen**

Columbia Publishing Wales Limited
Glen More, 6 Cwrt y Camden, Brecon LD3 7RR
☎01874 625270 Fax 01874 625270
✉ dng@columbiawales.fsnet.co.uk
www.columbiapublishing.co.uk
Managing Editor *Dafydd Gittins*

Founded 2000. Publishes fiction and non-fiction – books, film and music (mainly pop and rock). Subjects suitable for film or television. 2 titles in 2003. No unsolicited mss. Synopses and ideas welcome; approach by letter or e-mail in the first instance.
ROYALTIES paid.

Contact Publishing Ltd
Unit 346, 176 Finchley Road, London NW3 6BT
☎020 7794 1999 Fax 020 7794 1999
✉ info@contact-publishing.com
www.contact-publishing.com
Managing Director *Anne Kontoyannis*

Founded 2003. Publishes general fiction, non-fiction, self help and New Age. No children's, political, sports or westerns. 2 titles in 2003. 'Interested in seeing mss by new authors with original angles and new ideas.' See website for author guidelines. Send synopsis, three sample chapters and outline in the first instance.
ROYALTIES twice-yearly.

Copperfield Books
Hillbrook House, Lyncombe Vale Road, Bath BA2 4LS
☎01225 442835 Fax 01225 319755
✉ sales@www.darcybook.com
www.darcybook.com

Director *Jean Brushfield*

Publishes paperback fiction and general non-fiction. No unsolicited mss; 'we only commission books to our own specification'.

The Cosmic Elk

68 Elsham Crescent, Lincoln LN6 3YS
☎01522 820922
✉ cosmicelk@zoom.co.uk
www.cosmicelk.co.uk

Contact *Heather Hobden*

Founded 1988. Publishes easily updated books on science, history and the history of science. Websites designed and maintained, with or without associated printed books. 'Authors and books always welcome.' Check the website first for information and contacts.

Creme de la Crime

PO Box 445, Abingdon OX13 6YQ
☎01865 391768
✉ info@cremedelacrime.com
www.cremedelacrime.com

Managing Editors *Iain Pattison, Lynne Patrick*

Founded in 2003 to discover and publish crime fiction by new authors. 3 titles in 2004. Authors are urged to purchase detailed guidelines; send £2.50 with A4 envelope and two first-class stamps. One-off administration fee of £15 is charged. 'No further financial outlay is required from authors.' All submissions must be accompanied by s.a.e.

Crescent Moon Publishing and Joe's Press

PO Box 393, Maidstone ME14 5XU
☎01622 729593
✉ jrobinson@crescentmoon.org.uk
www.crescentmoon.org.uk

Managing Editor *Jeremy Robinson*

Founded 1988 to publish critical studies of figures such as D.H. Lawrence, Thomas Hardy, André Gide, Walt Disney, Rilke, Leonardo da Vinci, Mark Rothko, C.P. Cavafy and Hélène Cixous. Publishes literature, criticism, media, art, feminism, painting, poetry, travel, guidebooks, cinema and some fiction. Literary magazine, *Passion*, launched February 1994. Quarterly. *Pagan America*, twice-yearly anthology of American poetry. About 15–20 titles per year. Unsolicited synopses and ideas welcome but approach in writing first and send an s.a.e. Do not send whole mss.

ROYALTIES negotiable.

Critical Vision

See **Headpress**

Crossbridge Books

345 Old Birmingham Road, Bromsgrove B60 1NX
☎0121 447 7897   Fax 0121 445 1063
✉ crossbridgebooks@btinternet.com
www.crossbridgebooks.com

Managing Director *Eileen Mohr*

Founded 1995. Publishes Christian books for adults and children. IMPRINT **Mohr Books**. 1–2 titles a year including Trevor Dearing's latest books. No unsolicited mss; telephone in the first instance. No New Age or books not biblically Christian.

ROYALTIES twice-yearly.

Crown House Publishing

Crown Buildings, Bancyfelin, Carmarthen SA33 5ND
☎01267 211345   Fax 01267 211882
✉ books@crownhouse.co.uk
www.crownhouse.co.uk

Managing Director *David Bowman*
Acquisitions Editor *Helen Kinsey*

Founded 1998. Publishes titles in the areas of psychology, education, business training and development, mind body spirit. The aim of the list is to both demystify the latest psychological advances, particularly in the fields of Neuro-Linguistic Programming (NLP) and hypnosis. Crown House provides professional therapists, consultants and trainers with books detailing the latest cutting-edge developments in their field. About 20 titles a year.

ROYALTIES twice-yearly.

Culva House Publications

10 The Carrs, Sleights, Whitby YO21 1RR
☎01947 810819
✉ alan@culvahouse.co.uk
www.culvahouse.co.uk

Managing Editor *Alan Whitworth*

Founded in 1986 as a part-time self-publishing venture and grew into a full-time business in 2000. Publishes architecture and local history; biography. Unsolicited material welcome; approach by letter or e-mail.

ROYALTIES paid.

Day Books

Orchard Piece, Crawborough, Charlbury OX7 3TX
☎01608 811196   Fax 01608 811196
✉ diaries@day-books.com

www.day-books.com

Managing Editor *James Sanderson*

Founded in 1997 to publish a series of great diaries from around the world, one of the most recent being *Inside Stalin's Russia*. Unsolicited mss, synopses and ideas welcome. Include return postage if return of material is required.

Delancey Press Ltd

4 Delancey Passage, London NW1 7NN
☎020 7387 3544 Fax 020 7383 5314
✉ delanceypress@aol.com
www.delanceypress.com

Managing Editor *Tatiana von Saxe Wilson*

Founded 2000. Publishes fiction, children's and humour. Not interested in academic books. Overseas subsidiaries in association with **The Book Guild Ltd**. Accepts unsolicited mss sent by mail with s.a.e.

ROYALTIES twice-yearly.

Diagonal

See **Headpress**

The Dragonby Press

15 High Street, Dragonby, Scunthorpe DN15 0BE
☎01724 840645
✉ rich@rah2williams.freeserve.co.uk
freespace.virgin.net/rah.williams

Managing Editor *Richard Williams*

Founded 1987 to publish affordable bibliography for reader, collector and dealer. About 3 titles a year. Unsolicited mss, synopses and ideas welcome for bibliographical projects only.

ROYALTIES paid.

Dramatic Lines

PO Box 201, Twickenham TW2 5RQ
☎020 8296 9502 Fax 020 8296 9503
✉ mail@dramaticlinespublishers.co.uk
www.dramaticlines.co.uk

Managing Editor *John Nicholas*

Founded to promote drama for young people. Publications with a wide variety of theatrical applications including classroom use and school assemblies, drama examinations, auditions, festivals, theatre group performance and musicals. Unsolicited drama-related mss, proposals and synopses welcome; enclose s.a.e.

ROYALTIES paid.

DreamStar Books

Lasyard House, Underhill Street, Bridgnorth WV16 4BB
☎0870 777 3339 Fax 01746 765354
✉ enquiries@dreamstarbooks.com
www.dreamstarbooks.com

Owner *Corvedale Publishing Ltd*
Managing Director *Mark Horton-Oliver*

Founded 2002. Assists new and unpublished authors gain recognition for their work by offering low cost self-publishing/printing. 'No royalty tie-ins; authors are free to pursue traditional publishing deal.' Mss, synopses and ideas welcome.

Educational Heretics Press

113 Arundel Drive, Bramcote Hills, Nottingham NG9 3FQ
☎0115 925 7261 Fax 0115 925 7261
www.edheretics.gn.apc.org

Directors *Janet & Roland Meighan*

Non-profit venture which aims to question the dogmas of schooling in particular and education in general, and establish the logistics of the next learning system. No unsolicited material. Enquiries only.

ROYALTIES not paid but under review.

Enable Enterprises

PO Box 1974, Coventry CV3 1YF
☎0800 358 8484 Fax 0870 133 23347
✉ writers@enableenterprises.com
www.enableenterprises.com

Managing Director *Simon Stevens*

Enable Enterprises provides a wide range of accessibilty and disability services including publications on relevant issues. It welcomes unsolicited material related to accessibility and disability issues.

Fand Music Press

The Barony, 16 Sandringham Road, Petersfield GU32 2AA
☎01730 267341 Fax 01730 267341
✉ Paul@fandmusic.com
www.fandmusic.com

Managing Editor *Peter Thompson*

Founded in 1989 as a sheet music publisher, Fand Music Press has expanded its range to include CD recordings and books on music. Recently started publishing poetry and short stories. 10 titles a year. No unsolicited mss. Write with ideas in the first instance.

Feather Books

PO Box 438, Shrewsbury SY3 0WN
☎01743 872177 Fax 01743 872177
✉ john@waddysweb.freeuk.com

www.waddysweb.freeuk.com
Managing Director *Rev. John Waddington-Feather*
Directors *David Grundy, Tony Reavill, Paul Evans*

Founded 1980 to publish writers' group work. All material has a strong Christian ethos. Publishes poetry (mainly, but not exclusively, religious); Christian mystery novels (the Revd. D.I. Blake Hartley series); Christian children's novels; seasonal poetry collections and *The Poetry Church* quarterly magazine. Produces poetry, drama and music CD/cassettes. 20 titles a year. No unsolicited mss, synopses or ideas. All correspondence to include s.a.e., please.

Fern House
19 High Street, Haddenham, Ely CB6 3XA
☎01353 740222
✉ info@fernhouse.com
www.fernhouse.com
Managing Editor *Rodney Dale*

Founded 1995. Publishes non-fiction with a bias towards biography, reference and technology. Unsolicited synopses and ideas 'are unlikely to strike a chord'. Please avoid sending large e-mail attachments.
ROYALTIES paid.

Five Leaves Publications
PO Box 81, Nottingham NG5 4ER
☎0115 969 3597
✉ info@fiveleaves.co.uk
www.fiveleaves.co.uk
Contact *Ross Bradshaw*

Founded 1995 (taking over the publishing programme of Mushroom Bookshop). Publishes fiction, poetry, social history, politics and Jewish interest. Titles normally commissioned. About 6–8 titles a year.
ROYALTIES paid.

Flambard
Stable Cottage, East Fourstones, Hexham NE47 5DX
☎01434 674360 Fax 01434 674178
www.flambardpress.co.uk
Managing Editor *Peter Lewis*

Founded 1990. Publishes poetry and literary fiction. 6 titles in 2003. Welcomes unsolicited mss but essential to send preliminary letter with details of author and either a sample of 10 poems or a synopsis plus 2–3 chapters and s.a.e.
ROYALTIES paid.

Forth Naturalist & Historian
University of Stirling, Stirling FK9 4LA
☎01259 215091 Fax 01786 464994
✉ lindsay.corbett@stir.ac.uk
www.fnh.stir.ac.uk
Also at : 30 Dunmar Drive, Alloa, Clackmannanshire FK10 2EH
Honorary Secretary *Lindsay Corbett*

Founded 1975 by the collaboration of Stirling University members and the Central Regional Council to promote interests and publications on central Scotland. Aims to provide a 'valuable local studies educational resource for mid-Scotland schools, libraries and people'. Runs an annual symposium: Man and the Landscape. Publishes naturalist, historical and environmental studies. Over 20 selected papers from the annual *The Forth Naturalist & Historian* (Vol. 26 in 2003) are published in pamphlet form. Welcomes papers, mss and ideas relevant to central Scotland.
ROYALTIES not paid.

Foxbury Press
15 St Michael's Road, Winchester SO23 9JE
☎01962 864037
Managing Editor *Robert Cross*

Founded 2000. 4 titles published.

Frontier Publishing
Windetts, Kirstead NR15 1EG
☎01508 558174
✉ frontier.pub@macunlimited.net
www.frontierpublishing.co.uk
Managing Editor *John Black*

Founded 1983. Publishes travel, photography, sculptural history and literature. 2–3 titles a year. No unsolicited mss; synopses and ideas welcome.
ROYALTIES paid.

Galactic Central Publications
Imladris, 25A Copgrove Road, Leeds LS8 2SP
✉ philsp@compuserve.com
www.philsp.com
Managing Editor *Phil Stephensen-Payne*

Founded 1982 in the US. Publishes science fiction bibliographies. All new publications originate in the UK. About 4 titles a year. Unsolicited mss, synopses and ideas welcome.

Glosa Education Organisation
PO Box 18, Richmond TW9 2GE
www.glosa.org
Managing Editor *Wendy Ashby*

Founded 1981. Publishes textbooks, dictionaries and translations for the teaching, speaking and promotion of Glosa (an international, auxiliary language); also a newsletter, *Plu Glosa Nota*, and journal, *PGN*. Unsolicited mss and ideas for Glosa books welcome.

Grant Books

The Coach House, New Road, Cutnall Green, Droitwich WR9 0PQ
☎01299 851588 Fax 01299 851446
✉ golf@grantbooks.co.uk
www.grantbooks.co.uk
Managing Editor *H.R.J. Grant*

Founded 1978. Publishes golf-related titles only: course architecture, history, biography, etc., but no instructional material. New titles and old, plus limited editions. About 6 titles a year. Mss, synopses and ideas welcome.

ROYALTIES paid.

Great Northern Publishing

PO Box 202, Scarborough YO11 3GE
☎01723 581329 Fax 01723 581329
✉ books@greatnorthernpublishing.co.uk
www.greatnorthernpublishing.co.uk

Production Manager *Mark Marsay*
Senior Editor *Diane Crowther*

Small, independent, award-winning, family-owned company founded in 1999. Publishers of paperback books, magazines and journals. Also provides full book, magazine and print production services to individuals, businesses, charities, museums and other small publishers. Publishes non-fiction (mainly military), adult erotic material and occasionally fiction in most genres. No romance, religious, political, feminist, New Age, medical or children's books. Publishers of bi-monthly magazines, *The Great War (1914-1919)* and *Jade* (intenational erotic art and literature) magazines. Mail order and Internet-based bookshop stocking selected titles (mainly history and adult) alongside its own. Website provides submission guidelines and current publishing requirements. No unsolicited mss; send letter or text-only e-mail in the first instance.

ROYALTIES twice-yearly.

Grevatt & Grevatt

9 Rectory Drive, Newcastle upon Tyne NE3 1XT
☎0191 285 8053
✉ grevatt@softhome.net
grevatt-grevatt.freeservers.com/index.htm
Chairman/Editorial Head *Dr S.Y. Killingley*

Founded 1981. Alternative publisher of works not normally commercially viable. Three books have appeared with financial backing from professional bodies. Publishes academic titles and conference reports, particularly language, linguistics and religious studies. Some poetry also. No unsolicited mss. Synopses and ideas should be accompanied by s.a.e. Offers typesetting, editing and other services; s.a.e. with enquiries.

ROYALTIES annually (after first 500 copies).

GSSE

11 Malford Grove, Gilwern, Abergavenny NP7 0RN
☎01873 830872
✉ GSSE@zoo.co.uk
www.gsse.org.uk
Owner/Manager *David P. Bosworth*

Publishes books and booklets describing classroom practice (at all levels of education and training). Ideas welcome – particularly from practising teachers, lecturers and trainers describing how they use technology in their teaching.

ROYALTIES by arrangement.

Happy House

3b Castledown Avenue, Hastings TN34 3RJ
☎01424 434778
✉ vibezone@excite.com

Founded 1992 as a self-publishing venture for a Dave Arnold/Martin Honeysett collaboration of poetry and cartoons.

Haunted Library

Flat 1, 36 Hamilton Street, Hoole, Chester CH2 3JQ
☎01244 313685 Fax 01244 313685
✉ pardos@globalnet.co.uk
www.users.globalnet.co.uk/~pardos/GS.html
Managing Editor *Rosemary Pardoe*

Founded 1979. Publishes the *Ghosts and Scholars M.R. James Newsletter* two or three times a year, featuring articles, news and reviews (no fiction).

ROYALTIES not paid.

Headpress

40 Rossall Avenue, Radcliffe M26 1JD
☎0161 796 1935 Fax 0161 796 2032
✉ info.headpress@zen.co.uk
www.headpress.com
Managing Editor *David Kerekes*

Founded 1991. Publishes *Headpress* journal, devoted to the strange and esoteric, and *Creeping Flesh*, a journal devoted to horror and fantasy cinema. No fiction or poetry. IMPRINTS **Critical**

Vision; **Diagonal**. Unsolicited material welcome; send letter and outline in the first instance.
ROYALTIES AND FLAT FEES: paid.

Heart of Albion Press
2 Cross Hill Close, Wymeswold,
Loughborough LE12 6UJ
☎01509 880725 Fax 01509 881715
✉ albion@indigogroup.co.uk
www.hoap.co.uk

Managing Editor *R.N. Trubshaw*

Founded 1990 to publish local history. Publishes folklore, local history and mythology. Synopses relating to these subjects welcome.
ROYALTIES negotiable.

Hilmarton Manor Press
Calne SN11 8SB
☎01249 760208 Fax 01249 760379
✉ mailorder@hilmartonpress.co.uk

Chairman/Managing Director *Charles Baile de Laperriere*

Publisher of fine art dictionaries and art reference only. Editor and publisher of *Who's Who In Art* (31st edition).
ROYALTIES paid.

ignotus press
BCM-Writer, London WC1N 3XX
☎01530 831916 Fax 01530 831916
✉ ignotuspress@aol.com
www.ignotuspress.com

Publisher *Suzanne Ruthven*

Founded 1944. 'We are looking for positive, forward-looking material (fiction and non-fiction) on all aspects of British-based ritual magic, mysteries, spiritual development, traditional and hereditary witchcraft and other paths which demonstrate the writer's grasp of both traditional and contemporary esoteric practice. No New Age idealism, fantasy, pseudo-spirituality or neo-Hammer House of Horror fiction.' IMPRINTS **Moonraker Books** (fiction); **Alphard Press** (self-help and lifestyle). 'We are looking to extend these areas with the addition of compatible fiction and life-style titles).' About 20 titles a year. Send s.a.e. for authors' guidelines before submitting material for consideration.
ROYALTIES paid.

Immanion Press
8 Rowley Grove, Stafford ST17 9BJ
☎01785 613299
✉ info@immanionpress.wox.org
www.immanionpress.wox.org

Managing Editor *Storm Constantine*

Founded 2003. Publishes genre fiction (science fiction, fantasy, horror), slipstream fiction; esoteric non-fiction. Submissions by e-mail or post (enclose s.a.e.). Website gives full submission details.
ROYALTIES paid.

Infinity Junction
PO Box 64, Neston DO CH64 0WB
✉ infin-info@infinityjunction.com
www.infinityjunction.com

Managing Editor *Neil Gee*

Established originally as a self-publishing, self-help organisation in 1991, Infinity Junction became a publisher in 2001. Currently offers a variety of services to authors, including advice, free web display space and full commercial publication. Authors are strongly advised to read the detailed information on the website before making contacting. E-mail communication preferred. 'We cannot undertake to read unsolicited whole mss.'

Inner Sanctum Publications
75 Greenleaf Gardens, Polegate BN26 6PQ
☎01323 484058
✉ innersanctum@clara.co.uk
www.innersanctumpublications.com

Managing Editor *Mary Hession*

Founded in 1999 to publish spiritual books. Unsolicited mss, synopses and ideas welcome; approach in writing in the first instance.
ROYALTIES not paid.

Intellect
PO Box 862, Bristol BS99 1DE
☎0117 958 9910 Fax 0117 958 9911
✉ info@intellectbooks.com
www.intellectbooks.com

Chairman *Masoud Yazdani*

A multidisciplinary publisher of books and journals for both individual and institutional readers. Tracks newest developments in digital creative media – art, film, television, theatre design, etc. – and examines distinct theories in education, language, gender study and international culture through scholarly articles.
ROYALTIES paid.

Iolo
38 Chaucer Road, Bedford MK40 2AJ
☎01234 301718/07909 934866
Fax 01234 301718
✉ newplays@dedwyddjones.screaming.net

Managing Director *Dedwydd Jones*

Publishes Welsh theatre-related material and

campaigns for a Welsh National Theatre. Ideas on Welsh themes welcome; approach in writing.

Ivy Publications
72 Hyperion House, Somers Road, London SW2 1HZ
☎020 8671 6872

Proprietor *Ian Bruton-Simmonds*

Founded 1989. Publishes educational, science, fiction, philosophy, children's, travel, literary criticism, history, film scripts. No unsolicited mss; send two pages, one from the beginning and one from the body of the book, together with synopsis (one paragraph) and s.a.e. No cookery, gardening or science fiction.
ROYALTIES annually.

The Jupiter Press
The Coach House, Gatacre, Claverley, Nr Wolverhampton WV5 7AW
☎01746 710694 Fax 01746 710158
✉ gordon@jupiterpress.fsnet.co.uk
www.jupiter-press.com

Managing Editor *Gordon Thomas Drury*

Founded 1995. Looking for niche market and information publications, also quiz and game subjects. Interested in holistic, clairvoyance and esoteric subjects. Synopses and ideas for books welcome. Send idea and sample chapter. Unsolicited mss welcome 'but may request a reader's fee'. Currently seeking books for series entitled *How To Make Money At* ....
ROYALTIES paid.

Kittiwake
3 Glantwymyn Village Workshops, Cemmaes Road, Nr Machynlleth SY20 8LY
☎01650 511314 Fax 01650 511602
✉ kittiwake@perrocarto.co.uk
www.kittiwake-books.com

Managing Editor *David Perrott*

Founded 1986. Publishes guidebooks only, with an emphasis on careful design/production. Specialist research, writing, cartographic and electronic publishing services available. Unsolicited mss, synopses and ideas for guidebooks welcome.
ROYALTIES paid.

The Lindsey Press
Unitarian Headquarters, 1–6 Essex Street, Strand, London WC2R 3HY
☎020 7240 2384 Fax 020 7240 3089
✉ ga@unitarian.org.uk

Convenor *Kate Taylor*

Established at the end of the 18th century as a vehicle for disseminating liberal religion. Adopted the name of The Lindsey Press at the beginning of the 20th century (after Theophilus Lindsey, the great Unitarian Theologian). Publishes books reflecting liberal religious thought or Unitarian denominational history. Also worship material – hymn books, collections of prayers, etc. No unsolicited mss; synopses and ideas welcome.
ROYALTIES not paid.

Logaston Press
Logaston, Woonton, Almeley HR3 6QH
☎01544 327344
www.logastonpress.co.uk

Managing Editors *Andy Johnson, Ron Shoesmith*

Founded 1985. Publishes guides, archaeology, social history, rural issues and local history for Wales, the Welsh Border and West Midlands. 10–15 titles a year. Unsolicited mss, synopses and ideas welcome. Return postage appreciated.
ROYALTIES paid.

Luath Press Ltd
543/2 Castlehill, The Royal Mile, Edinburgh EH1 2ND
☎0131 225 4326 Fax 0131 225 4324
✉ gavin.macdougall@luath.co.uk
www.luath.co.uk

Managing Editor *G.H. MacDougall*

Founded 1981. Publishes mainly books with a Scottish connection. Current list includes guidebooks, walking and outdoor, history, folklore, politics and global issues, cartoons, fiction, poetry, biography, food and drink, environment, music and dance, sport and *On the Trail Of* and *The Quest For* SERIES. About 20–30 titles a year. Unsolicited mss, synopses and ideas welcome; 'committed to publishing well-written books worth reading'.
ROYALTIES paid.

Lyfrow Trelyspen
The Roseland Institute, Gorran, St Austell
☎01726 843501 Fax 01726 843501
✉ trelispen@care4free.net

Managing Editor *Dr James Whetter*

Founded 1975. Publishes works on Cornish history, biography, essays, etc. Also **CNP Publications** which publishes the quarterly journal *The Cornish Banner/An Baner Kernewek*. 1–2 titles a year. Unsolicited mss, synopses and ideas welcome.
ROYALTIES not paid.

The Maia Press
82 Forest Road, London E8 3BG
☎020 7249 3711/3718
✉ info@maiapress.com
www.maiapress.com
Contacts *Maggie Hamand, Jane Havell*
Founded 2002. Publishes fiction by known and
new writers. 6 titles a year. No unsolicted mss,
write with c.v. and synopsis only. S.a.e. essential.
ROYALTIES twice-yearly.

Maypole Editions
65 Mayfair Avenue, Ilford IG1 3DQ
☎020 8252 3937
www.maypoleeditions.co.uk
Contact *Barry Taylor*
Publisher of plays and poetry in the main.
Catalogue available on the website. 2–3 titles a
year. Unsolicited mss welcome provided return
postage is included. Poetry always welcome for
collected anthologies and should be approximately 30 lines of tight verse, broadly covering
social concerns, ethnic minority issues, feminist
incident, romance generally, travel and lyric
rhyming verse. No politics except evenly comparative. The biannual collected anthology is
designed as a small press platform for first-time
poets who might not otherwise get into print,
and a permanent showcase for those already
published who want to break into the mainstream. Submissions must include A5 s.a.e.
'Please be patient when sending work because
of the huge volume of submissions.' Exempt
Charity Status.

Meadow Books
35 Stonefield Way, Burgess Hill RH15 8DW
☎01444 239044
✉ meadowbooks@hotmail.com
Managing Director *C. O'Neill*
Founded 1990. Publisher of nursing history
books and nursing picture archive. No unsolicited mss although always interested in quality *published* nursing books to sell on (send sample copy
for attention of R. O'Neill, Sales Director).

Mercia Cinema Society
19 Pinder's Grove, Wakefield WF1 4AH
☎01924 372748
✉ mervyn.gould@virgin.net
Managing Editor *Paul Smith*
Founded 1980 to foster research into the history
of picture houses. Publishes books and booklets
on the subject, including cinema circuits and
chains. Books are often tied in with specific geo-

graphical areas. Unsolicited mss, synopses and
ideas.
ROYALTIES not paid.

Meridian Books
40 Hadzor Road, Oldbury B68 9LA
☎0121 429 4397
✉ meridian.books@btopenworld.com
Managing Editor *Peter Groves*
Founded 1985 as a small home-based enterprise
following the acquisition of titles from Tetradon
Publications Ltd. Publishes walking and regional
guides. 4–5 titles a year. Unsolicited mss, synopses and ideas welcome if relevant. Send s.a.e. if
mss to be returned.
ROYALTIES paid.

Mermaid Turbulence
Annaghmaconway, Cloone, Republic of
Ireland
☎00 353 71 96 36134
Fax 00 353 71 96 36134
www.mermaidturbulence.com
Managing Director *Mari-aymone Djeribi*
Founded in 1993 with the first issue of *element*
– an international literary journal. Publishes
artists' books. 5 titles in 2004. Approach in
writing, enclosing international reply coupon.
Mss will not be returned (recycled) unless an
s.a.e. with Irish stamps is provided.
ROYALTIES annually.

Merton Priory Press Ltd
67 Merthyr Road, Whitchurch, Cardiff
CF14 1DD
☎029 2052 1956 Fax 029 2062 3599
✉ merton@dircon.co.uk
www.merton.dircon.co.uk
Managing Director *Philip Riden*
Founded 1993. Publishes academic and mid-
market history, especially local, industrial and
transport history; also memoirs and autobiographies. Full catalogue available. About 6 titles a
year.
ROYALTIES twice-yearly.

Neil Miller Publications
Ormonde House, 49 Ormonde Road, Hythe
CT21 6DW
✉ neilmillerspublications@supanet.com
www.webspawner.com/users/neilmillerpubs
Also at: 4 Rue D'Equiire Bergueneuse, Pas de
Calais, France 62134
Managing Editor *Neil Miller*
Founded 1994. Publishes novels and collec-

tions of short stories on any subject: adventure mystery, horror, detective, romance, fantasy, comedy and tales with a twist. IMPRINT **Black Cat Books** Non-fiction: war memoirs, true tales, biographies, history and comedy. Interested in working with new and published writers. Evaluation and critique service available. Send for details, or send two chapters or two short stories; readers fee: £15. 'No unrequested tales, please.'

Millers Dale Publications
7 Weavers Place, Chandlers Ford, Eastleigh SO53 1TU
☎023 8026 1192
✉ gponting@clara.net
www.home.clara.net/gponting/
  index-page10.html

Managing Editor *Gerald Ponting*

Founded 1990. Publishes books on local history related to central Hampshire. Also books related to slide presentations by Gerald Ponting. Ideas for local history books on Hampshire considered.

Mohr Books
See **Crossbridge Books**

Moonraker Books
See **ignotus press**

Natzler Enterprises (Entertainments)
1 Wakeford Cottages, Selden Lane, Worthing BN11 2LQ
☎01903 211785 Fax 01903 211519
✉ natzler@btinternet.com
www.natzler.com
www.paulgordon.net

Managing Editor *Paul Gordon*

Founded 1993. Publishes magic (entertainment) books only. No unsolicited mss; send synopses and ideas by post.

Need2Know
Remus House, Coltsfoot Drive, Woodston PE2 9JX
☎01733 898105 Fax 01733 313524
✉ info@forwardpress.co.uk
www.forwardpress.co.uk

Founded 1995 'to fill a gap in the market for self-help books'. Publishes contemporary health and lifestyle issues. Need2Know is an imprint of **Forward Press** (see under *Poetry Presses*). No unsolicited mss. Telephone in the first instance.
ROYALTIES Advance plus 15% royalties.

Norvik Press Ltd
School of Language, Linguistics & Translation Studies, University of East Anglia, Norwich NR4 7TJ
☎01603 593356 Fax 01603 250599
✉ norvik.press@uea.ac.uk
www.uea.ac.uk/llt/norvik_press

Managing Editors *Janet Garton, Michael Robinson, C. Claire Thomson*

Small academic press. Publishes the journals *Scandinavica* and *Swedish Book Review* and books related to Scandinavian literature. About 4 titles a year. Interested in synopses and ideas for books within its *Literary History and Criticism* series. No unsolicited mss.
ROYALTIES paid.

The Nostalgia Collection
Silver Link Publishing Ltd, The Trundle, Ringstead Road, Great Addington, Kettering NN14 4BW
☎01536 330588 Fax 01536 330588
✉ sales@nostalgiacollection.com
www.nostalgiacollection.com

Managing Editor *Peter Townsend*

Founded 1985 in Lancashire, changed hands in 1990 and now based in Northamptonshire. Small independent company specialising in nostalgia titles including illustrated books on towns and cities, villages and rural life, rivers and inland waterways, industrial heritage, railways, trams, ships and other transport subjects. Publishes post-war nostalgia on all aspects of social history under the **Past and Present Publishing** imprint.
FEES paid.

Nyala Publishing
4 Christian Fields, London SW16 3JZ
☎020 8764 6292
Fax 020 8764 6292/0115 981 9418
✉ nyala.publish@geo-group.co.uk
www.geo-group.co.uk

Editorial Head *J.F.J. Douglas*

Founded 1996. Publishing arm of Geo Group. Publishes biography, travel and general non-fiction. Also offers a wide range of printing and publishing services. 'Quality low-cost printing a speciality.' No unsolicited mss; synopses and ideas considered.
ROYALTIES annually.

Orpheus Publishing House
4 Dunsborough Park, Ripley Green, Ripley, Guildford GU23 6AL
☎01483 225777 Fax 01483 225776

✉ orpheuspubl.ho@btinternet.com
Managing Editor *J.S. Gordon*
Founded 1996. Publishes 'well-researched and properly argued' books in the fields of occult science, esotericism and comparative philosophy/religion. 'Keen to encourage good (but sensible) new authors.' In the first instance, send maximum 3-page synopsis with s.a.e.
ROYALTIES by agreement.

Packard Publishing Limited
Forum House, Stirling Road, Chichester PO19 7DN
☎01243 537977 Fax 01243 537977
✉ info@packardpublishing.co.uk
www.packardpublishing.com
Chairman/Managing Director *Michael Packard*
Founded in 1977 to distribute overseas publishers' lists in biology, biochemistry and ecology. Publishes academic & professional: school/university interface, postgraduate – mainly in land management and applied ecology; agriculture, forestry, nature conservation, rural studies, landscape architecture and garden design; some languages (French, Arabic). SERIES Instructional books on garden and landscape design, and monographs or critical biographies in garden and landscape design and history. No unsolicited mss. Synopses and ideas in relevant areas welcome. Telephone first.
ROYALTIES twice-yearly in first year, then annually.

Palladour Books
23 Eldon Street, Southsea PO5 4BS
☎02392 826935 Fax 02392 826395
✉ palladour@powellj33.freeserve.co.uk
Managing Editors *Jeremy Powell, Anne Powell*
Founded 1986. Started with a twice-yearly issue of catalogues on the literature and poetry of World War I. Occasional catalogues on World War II poetry have also been issued. No unsolicited mss.
ROYALTIES not paid.

Panacea Press Limited
86 North Gate, Prince Albert Road, London NW8 7EJ
☎020 7722 8464 Fax 020 7586 8187
✉ ebrecher@panaceapress.net
Managing Editor *Erwin Brecher, PhD*
Founded as a self-publisher but now open for non-fiction from other authors. Material of academic value considered provided it commands a wide general market. No unsolicited

mss; synopses and ideas welcome. Approach by fax or letter. No telephone calls.
ROYALTIES annually.

Paradise Press
80 College Road, Isleworth TW7 5DS
☎020 8568 3777
✉ prdsprss@netscape.net
Founded 1995. Considers only high quality lesbian and gay fiction workshopped through **Gay Authors Workshop**.

Parapress Ltd
The Basement, 9 Frant Road, Tunbridge Wells TN2 5SD
☎01892 512118 Fax 01892 512118
✉ office@parapress.co.uk
www.parapress.co.uk
Managing Editor *Elizabeth Imlay*
Founded 1993. Publishes animals, autobiography, biography, history, literary criticism, military and naval, music, self-help. Some self-publishing. About 4 titles a year.

Partnership Publishing Ltd
2 Crown Street, Wellington, Telford TF1 1LP
☎01952 415334 Fax 01952 245077
✉ steve.rooney@busandcoach.com
Managing Director *Steve Rooney*
TITLES *Bus and Coach Professional*; *Professional Recovery*; *MOT Professional*; *Oakengates & District News*; *Wellington News*; *Dawley, Madeley, Broseley News*; *Vehicle Salvage Professional*. Offers full magazine publication services, including design and production, editorial and advertising sales service.

Past and Present Publishing
See **The Nostalgia Collection**

Paupers' Press
37 Quayside Close, Turney's Quay, Trent Bridge, Nottingham NG2 3BP
☎0115 986 3334 Fax 0115 986 3334
✉ books@pauperspress.com
www.pauperspress.com
Managing Editor *Colin Stanley*
Founded 1983. Publishes extended essays in booklet form (about 15,000 words) on literary criticism and philosophy. 'Sometimes we stray from these criteria and produce full-length books, but only to accommodate an exceptional ms.' Limited hardback editions of bestselling titles. 'About 6 titles a year. No unsolicited mss but synopses and ideas for books welcome.
ROYALTIES paid.

Peepal Tree Press Ltd
17 King's Avenue, Leeds LS6 1QS
☎0113 245 1703
✉ info@peepaltreepress.com
www.peepaltreepress.com
Managing Editor *Jeremy Poynting*
Founded 1985. Publishes fiction, poetry, drama and academic studies. Specialises in Caribbean, Black British and south Asian writing. In-house printing and finishing facilities. AUTHORS include **Forward Poetry Prize**-winner Kwame Dawes. About 18 titles a year. 'Please send an A5 s.a.e. with a 42p stamp for a copy of our submission guidelines.' Write or phone for a free catalogue.
ROYALTIES paid.

Pen Press Publishers Ltd
The Old School, 39 Chesham Road, Brighton BN2 1NB
☎0845 108 0530   Fax 01273 261434
✉ penpressltd@aol.com
www.penpress.net
Managing Editor *Lynn Ashman*
Founded 1996. Publishing across a wide range of categories, Pen Press helps new authors to self-publish. Promotion and marketing included in self-publishing deal. Write, phone or e-mail for submission form and full details. Return form with full ms (digital or hard copy).
ROYALTIES 45%, payable twice-yearly.

Pipers' Ash Ltd
'Pipers' Ash', Church Road, Christian Malford, Chippenham SN15 4BW
☎01249 720563   Fax 0870 0568916
✉ pipersash@supamasu.com
www.supamasu.com
Managing Editor *Mr A. Tyson*
Founded 1976. The company's publishing activities include individual collections of contemporary short stories, science fiction short stories, poetry, plays, short novels, local histories, children's fiction, philosophy, biographies, translations and general non-fiction. 12 titles a year. Synopses and ideas welcome; 'new authors with potential will be actively encouraged'. Offices in New Zealand and Australia.
ROYALTIES annually.

Planet
PO Box 44, Aberystwyth SY23 3ZZ
☎01970 611255   Fax 01970 611197
✉ planet.enquiries@planetmagazine.org.uk
www.planetmagazine.org.uk

Managing Editor *John Barnie*
Founded 1970 and relaunched in 1985 as publisher of the arts and current affairs magazine *Planet: The Welsh Internationalist* and branched out into book publishing in 1995. All books so far have been commissioned. Unsolicited synopses and ideas welcome.
ROYALTIES paid.

Playwrights Publishing Co.
70 Nottingham Road, Burton Joyce NG14 5AL
☎0115 931 3356
✉ playwrightspublishingco@yahoo.com
geocities.com/playwrightspublishingco
Managing Editors *Liz Breeze, Tony Breeze*
Founded 1990. Publishes one-act and full-length plays. Unsolicited scripts welcome. No synopses or ideas. Reading fees: £15 one act; £30 full length (waived if evidence of professional performance).
ROYALTIES paid.

Pomegranate Press
Dolphin House, 51 St Nicholas Lane, Lewes BN7 2JZ
☎01273 470100   Fax 01273 470100
✉ pomegranatepress@aol.com
Managing Editor *David Arscott*
Founded in 1992 by writer/broadcaster David Arscott, who also administers the **Sussex Book Club**. Specialises in books about Sussex. IMPRINT **Pomegranate Practicals** How-to books.
ROYALTIES twice-yearly.

David Porteous Editions
PO Box 5, Chudleigh, Newton Abbot TQ13 0YZ
☎01626 853310   Fax 01626 853663
✉ editorial@davidporteous.com
www.davidporteous.com
Publisher *David Porteous*
Founded 1992 to produce high quality colour illustrated books on hobbies and leisure for the UK and international markets. Publishes crafts, hobbies, art techniques and needlecrafts. No poetry or fiction. 3–4 titles a year. Unsolicited mss, synopses and ideas welcome if return postage included.
ROYALTIES twice-yearly.

Praxis Books
Crossways Cottage, Walterstone HR2 0DX
☎01873 890695
✉ author@rebeccatope.fsnet.co.uk

www.rebeccatope.com
Proprietor *Rebecca Smith*

Founded 1992. Publishes reissues of the works of Sabine Baring-Gould, memoirs, diaries and local interest. 20 titles to date. Unsolicited mss accepted with s.a.e. No fiction. Editing service available. Funding negotiable. 'I am most likely to accept work with a clearly identifiable market.'

Primrose Hill Press Ltd

Stratton Audley Park, Bicester OX27 9AB
☎01869 278000 Fax 01869 277820
✉ info@primrosehillpress.co.uk
www.primrosehillpress.co.uk

Managing Director *W.E. Butler*

Founded in 1997, having taken over the stock and projects in progress of Silent Books Ltd. Publishes general art titles, wood engraving, book studies, books on bookplates, bibliography, book design and books for the gift market, 'all high quality productions'. No fiction. About 12 titles a year. Unsolicited mss, synopses and ideas welcome.

QueenSpark Books

49 Grand Parade, Brighton BN2 9QA
☎01273 571710 Fax 01273 571710
✉ info@queensparkbooks.org.uk
www.queensparkbooks.org.uk

A community writing and publishing group run mainly by volunteers who work together to write and produce books. Since the early 1970s they have published 70 titles, mainly –featuring the lives of local people. No fiction or poetry. Writing workshops and groups held on a regular basis. New members welcome. No unsolicited mss, please.

Radikal Phase Publishing House Ltd

Willow Court, Cordy Lane, Underwood NG16 5FD
☎01773 764288 Fax 01773 764282
✉ sales@radikalbooks.com
www.radikalbooks.com

Joint Managing Directors *Philip Gardiner, Kevin Marks*

Founded 2001. Publishes radical revelation and technical electrical books. IMPRINTS **William Ernest** *Kevin Marks*; **Radikal Phase** *Philip Gardiner*. Welcomes unsolicited material; approach in writing in the first instance.
ROYALTIES twice-yearly.

The Riverside Press

PO Box 388A, Surbiton KT7 0ZT
☎020 8339 0945 Fax 020 8339 0945
✉ mruswords@aol.com
www.good-writing-matters.co.uk

Managing Editor *Michael Russell*

Founded 1998 to publish short-run titles from new writers. Mainly fiction but also special interest non-fiction. No poetry or film. Editorial support service provided. No unsolicited mss. Send synopses and three chapters only with covering letter.

The Robinswood Press

30 South Avenue, Stourbridge DY8 3XY
☎01384 397475 Fax 01384 440443
✉ info@robinswoodpress.com
www.robinswoodpress.com

Managing Editor *Christopher J. Marshall*

Founded 1985. Publishes education, particularly teacher resources, SEN, including the Spotlight and Lifeboat Read and Spell ranges. Also collaborative publishing, e.g. with Camphill Foundation. About 12–15 titles a year. Unsolicited mss, synopses and ideas welcome.
ROYALTIES paid.

Romer Publications

PO Box 10120, NL–1001 EC Amsterdam, The Netherlands
☎00 31 20 676 9442
Fax 00 31 20 676 9442
✉ harrymelkman@hotmail.com

Managing Editor *Hubert de Brouwer*

Founded 1986. Publishes critical reflection on origins and legitimacy of established institutions; law and history. Assessment of unsolicited material is suspended until further notice.
ROYALTIES paid.

St James Publishing

Suite 213 Parkway House, Sheen Lane, East Sheen, London SW14 8LS
☎0870 870 8797 Fax 0870 870 8798

Managing Editors *Linda Smith, David Smith*

Founded 1995 to provide teaching materials with spiritual substance for St James Independent Schools: 'Good Books for Fine Minds'. Also many workbooks and texbooks for the study of English and mathematics. No unsolicited mss, synopses or ideas.

Serendipity

Suite 530, 14 Tottenham Court Road, London W1T 1JY

☎0845 130 2434   Fax 0845 130 2434
Managing Director *Kimberley Wheatley*
Founded 2001. Publishes fiction, academic, memoirs, poetry, children's and religion. About 40 titles a year. Unsolicited mss and synopses welcome.
ROYALTIES twice-yearly.

Serif
47 Strahan Road, London E3 5DA
☎020 8981 3990   Fax 020 8981 3990
✉ stephen@serif.demon.co.uk
Managing Editor *Stephen Hayward*
Founded 1993. Publishes cookery, Irish and African studies, travel writing and modern history; no fiction. Ideas and synopses welcome; no unsolicited mss.
ROYALTIES paid.

Sherlock Publications
6 Bramham Moor, Hill Head, Fareham PO14 3RU
☎01329 667325
✉ sales@sherlockpublications.biz
Managing Editor *Philip Weller*
Founded to supply publishing support to a number of Sherlock Holmes societies. Publishes Sherlock Holmes and other Conan Doyle studies only. About 10 titles a year. No unsolicited mss; synopses and ideas welcome.
ROYALTIES not paid.

Shield Publications
PO Box 5, Low Fell, Gateshead NE9 7YS
☎0191 4823222
Managing Director *Norman L. Middlemiss*
Founded 1977. Publishes nautical books only – the *Merchant Fleet* series (44 vols.). Unsolicited mss and fleet lists welcome.
ROYALTIES paid.

SINAP
See **Skrev Press**

Skrev Press
15 Pwllhai, Cardigan SA43 1DB
☎01239 613683
✉ editor@skrev-press.com
www.skrev-press.com
Managing Editor *Daithidh MacEochaidh*
Founded 2002. Publishes *Texts' Bones*, a journal of avant garde short fiction (four issues a year). Special interest: Eastern Europe. IMPRINT **SINAP** publishes collections of short stories,

novellas and novels under 80,000 words. Skrev also runs an annual themed short story competition with hard publication offered as the prize. Welcomes unsolicited mss, synopses and ideas. Initial approach by e-mail or letter with description. See website for further details.

Spacelink Books
115 Hollybush Lane, Hampton TW12 2QY
☎020 8979 3148
www.spacelink.fsworld.co.uk
Managing Director *Lionel Beer*
Founded 1967. Named after a UFO magazine published in the 1960/70s. Publishes non-fiction titles connected with UFOs, Fortean phenomena and paranormal events. Publishers of *TEMS News* for the Travel and Earth Mysteries Society and *MWB Railway Society News Brief* newsletters. Distributors of a wide range of related titles and magazines. No unsolicited mss; send synopses and ideas.
ROYALTIES AND FEES according to contract.

Stenlake Publishing Limited
54–58 Mill Square, Catrine KA5 6RD
☎01290 552233
www.stenlake.co.uk
Publishes illustrated local history, railways, shipping, aviation and industrial. 51 titles in 2003. Unsolicited mss, synopses and ideas welcome if accompanied by s.a.e. Freelance writers with experience in above fields also sought for specific commissions.
ROYALTIES OR FIXED FEE paid.

Stone Flower Limited
PO Box 1513, Ilford IG1 3QU
✉ stoneflower10622@aol.com
Managing Editor *L.G. Norman*
Founded 1989. Publishes biography, humour and general fiction. Will consider mss, synopses and ideas only if sent with s.a.e. or IRC. Approach in writing in the first instance. 'No anthropomorphism, please.'

Stride
11 Sylvan Road, Exeter EX4 6EW
✉ editor@stridebooks.co.uk
www.stridebooks.co.uk
Managing Editor *Rupert Loydell*
Founded in 1982 as a magazine and booklet series. Since the mid-1980s, the press has published paperback editions of imaginative new writing. Publishes poetry, prose-poems, criti-

cism, reviews, interviews, arts (particularly experimental music). No unsolicited submissions required at this time.

ROYALTIES sometimes paid; free copies usually.

Superscript
404 Robin Square, Newtown SY16 1HP
☎01588 650452
✉ drjbford@yahoo.co.uk

Editor *Julie Ford*
Secretary *Ray Pahl*

Founded 2002. 'The fastest publisher in the West' – topical titles can be on the market within 6–8 weeks of perfect typescript. Publishes literary, philosophical and political fiction, autobiography and wartime memoirs, humanities and social sciences. 5 titles in 2004. All suitable ideas, synopses or mss are submitted to the Editorial Board who are looking for 'well-crafted material that exposes injustice, challenges stereotypes and promotes human dignity'. Will also consider new editions of out-of-print titles at author's request. Initial enquiries by letter, telephone or e-mail to the Editor.

ROYALTIES vary with each contract.

Tamarind Ltd
PO Box 52, Northwood HA6 1UN
☎020 8866 8808 Fax 020 8866 5627
✉ info@tamarindbooks.co.uk
www.tamarindbooks.co.uk

Managing Editor *Verna Wilkins*

Founded 1987 to publish picture books which give a high, positive profile to Black children. They feature regularly on the SATs List for National Curriculum, on BBC Words and Pictures, CBBC and 'Balamory'. Regularly chosen among the Best Books of the Year. All titles sold into both trade and educational markets. Age range: 2–12.

Tarquin Publications
Stradbroke, Diss IP21 5JP
☎01379 384218 Fax 01379 384289
✉ enquiries@tarquin-books.demon.co.uk
www.tarquin-books.demon.co.uk

Managing Editor *Gerald Jenkins*

Founded 1970 as a hobby which gradually grew and now publishes mathematical, cut-out models, teaching and pop-up books. Other topics covered if they involve some kind of paper cutting or pop-up scenes. 5 titles in 2003. No unsolicited mss; letter with 1–2 page synopses welcome.

ROYALTIES paid.

Tartarus Press
Coverley House, Carlton-in-Coverdale,
Leyburn DL8 4AY
☎01969 640399 Fax 01969 640399
✉ tartarus@pavilion.co.uk
www.tartaruspress.com

Proprietor *Raymond Russell*
Editor *Rosalie Parker*

Founded 1987. Publishes fiction, short stories, reprinted classic supernatural fiction and reference books. About 12 titles a year. 'Please do not send submissions. We cater to a small, collectable market and commission the fiction we publish.'

Tindal Street Press Ltd
217 The Custard Factory, Gibb Street,
Birmingham B9 4AA
☎0121 773 8157 Fax 0121 693 5525
✉ emma@tindalstreet.co.uk
www.tindalstreet.co.uk

Managing Editor *Emma Hargrave*

Founded in 1998 to publish contemporary original fiction from the English regions. Publishes original fiction only – novels and short story anthologies. No local history, memoirs or poetry. Published *Astonishing Splashes of Colour* by Clare Morrall, shortlisted for the 2003 **Man Booker Prize for Fiction**. 6 titles in 2003. Approach with a letter, synopsis and three chapters and include s.a.e. for return of ms.

ROYALTIES paid.

Tournesol Books
BP14, Lauzerte 82110 France
✉ editor@tournesolbooks.com
www.tournesolbooks.com

Managing Editors *Paul M. Muller, PhD, Sara Gill Costello, BA Hons*

Founded 2004, initially to publish the works of Paul Muller, Tournesol Books provides pre-publication services, including editing, to self-publishing authors accepted by **Sunflower Literary Agency** (see **UK Literary Agents**), as an imprint of **Pen Press Publishers Ltd** (see entry). All contact must be via Sunflower Literary Agency only; see entry for contact point and types of work sought.

Tuckwell Press Ltd
The Mill House, Phantassie, East Linton
EH40 3DG
☎01620 860164 Fax 01620 860164
✉ tuckwellpress@sol.co.uk
www.tuckwellpress.co.uk

Managing Director *John Tuckwell*

Founded 1995. Publishes history, archaeology, literature, ethnology, biography, architecture, gardening history, genealogy, palaeography, with a bias towards Scottish and academic texts, also north of England. 200 titles in print. No unsolicited mss but synopses and ideas welcome if relevant to subjects covered.

ROYALTIES annually.

Wakefield Historical Publications
19 Pinder's Grove, Wakefield WF1 4AH
☎01924 372748
✉ kate@airtime.co.uk

Managing Editor *Kate Taylor*

Founded 1977 by the Wakefield Historical Society to publish well-researched, scholarly works of regional (namely West Riding) historical significance. 1–2 titles a year. Unsolicited mss, synopses and ideas for books welcome.

ROYALTIES not paid.

Watling Street Publishing Ltd
The Glen, Southrop, Nr Lechlade GL7 3NY
☎01367 850558
✉ watlingst@btinternet.com

Managing Director *John Monk*
Editorial Head *Christine Kidney*

Founded 2001. Publishes non-fiction titles on London and its history; children's and adult. 14 titles in 2004. No unsolicited mss. Ideas and synopses welcome. Approach in writing or by e-mail with a one-page proposal. 'Not interested in anything not related to London.'

Waywiser Press
9 Woodstock Road, London N4 3ET
☎020 8374 5526   Fax 020 8374 5736
✉ waywiserpress@aol.com
www.waywiser-press.com

Editor *Philip Hoy*

Founded 2002. Specialises in modern poetry in English, publishing work by established authors such as Al Alvarez, Peter Dale and Richard Wilbur as well as less well-known figures such as Timothy Murphy, Daniel Rifenburgh and Deborah Warren. Waywiser poetry competition was launched in 2004. Occasionally publishes books of other genres. Submissions and proposals welcome; follow guidelines on website.

ROYALTIES paid.

Whitchurch Books Ltd
67 Merthyr Road, Whitchurch, Cardiff CF14 1DD
☎029 2052 1956   Fax 029 2062 3599
✉ whitchurchbooks@btopenworld.com

Managing Director *Gale Canvin*

Founded 1994. Publishes local interest, particularly local history. Welcomes unsolicited mss, synopses and ideas on relevant subjects. Approach first by phone or in writing.

ROYALTIES twice-yearly.

White Ladder Press
Great Ambrook, Near Ipplepen TQ12 5UL
☎01803 813343   Fax 01803 813928
✉ enquiries@whiteladderpress.com
www.whiteladderpress.com

Publishers *Roni Jay, Richard Craze*

Founded 2002. Publishes non-fiction books which present a new angle on everyday living. Welcomes synopses and ideas by mail or e-mail. No fiction or children's titles.

ROYALTIES quarterly.

Whittles Publishing
Roseleigh House, Latheronwheel KW5 6DW
☎01593 741240   Fax 01593 741360
✉ info@whittlespublishing.com
www.whittlespublishing.com

Managing Editor *Dr Keith Whittles*

Publisher in civil and structural engineering and geomatics disciplines plus maritime, nature writing and selected fiction. Unsolicited mss, synopses and ideas welcome on appropriate themes.

ROYALTIES annually.

William Ernest
See **Radikal Phase Publishing House Ltd**

Witan Books
Cherry Tree House, 8 Nelson Crescent, Cotes Heath, via Stafford ST21 6ST
☎01782 791673

Managing Editor *Jeff Kent*

Founded in 1980 for self-publishing and commenced publishing other writers in 1991. Publishes general books, including biography, education, environment, geography, history, politics, popular music and sport. 1 or 2 titles a year. Unsolicited mss, synopses and ideas welcome (include s.a.e.)

ROYALTIES paid.

Worple Press
PO Box 328, Tonbridge TN9 1WR
☎01732 368958
✉ worplepress@aol.com

Managing Editors *Peter Carpenter, Amanda Knight*

Founded 1997. Independent publisher specialising in poetry, art and alternative titles. Write or phone for catalogue and flyers. 4 titles a year.
ROYALTIES paid.

Writers' Bookshop

Remus House, Coltsfoot Drive, Woodston, Peterborough PE2 9JX
☎01733 898105   Fax 01733 313524
✉ info@forwardpress.co.uk
www.forwardpress.com

Writers' Bookshop is an imprint of **Forward Press** (see entry under *Poetry Presses*). Publishes writers' aids in the form of directories and how-to guides. Best-known annual title is the *Small Press Guide*.

Zymurgy Publishing

Hoults Estate, Walker Road, Newcastle upon Tyne NE6 2HL
☎0191 276 2425   Fax 0191 276 2425
✉ martin.ellis@alibris.com
zymurgypublishing.com

Chairman *Martin Ellis*

Founded 2000. Publishes adult non-fiction, ranging from full colour illustrated hardbacks to mass market paperbacks. Synopses and ideas for books welcome but no unsolicited mss. Contact by telephone or e-mail.
ROYALTIES twice-yearly.

Electronic Publishing and Other Services

ABCtales
PO Box 34203, London NW5 1FX
☎020 7209 2607 Fax 020 7209 2594
✉ markbrown@abctales.com
www.abctales.com

Owner *Burgeon Creative Ideas Ltd*
Editor *Mark Brown*

Founded by A. John Bird, MBE, co-founder of the *Big Issue* magazine, Tony Cook and Gordon Roddick. ABCtales is a free website dedicated to publishing and developing new writing. Content is predominantly short stories and poetry but includes interviews and lifestyle features, photo essays, reviews (games, websites, film, music) and competitions. Anyone can upload creative writing to the website.

Authors OnLine
See entry under *UK Publishers*

BeWrite Books
32 Bryn Road South, Wigan WN4 8QR
☎00 334 9335 9531 (editorial base in France)
Fax 00 334 9341 3509
✉ info@bewrite.net
www.bewrite.net

Managing Director *Cait Myers*
Editorial Director *Neil Marr*

A multi-genre publishing house founded in 1999 and especially geared toward the encouragement and publication in electronic and print formats of first-time authors. Unsolicited mss and synopses welcome (e-mail only). 'All offers promptly acknowledged and draft manuscript-to-publication time shorter than most other publishing houses.'

ROYALTIES quarterly (no advance).

Books 4 Publishing
Lasyard House, Underhill Street, Bridgnorth WV16 4BB
☎0870 777 3339 Fax 01746 761298
✉ editor@books4publishing.com
www.books4publishing.com

Owner *Corvedale Publishing Ltd*
Managing Director *Mark Horton-Oliver*

Founded 2000. Specialises in helping new and unpublished authors gain recognition for their work by displaying synopses and up to 5000 words on the Books 4 Publishing website and promoting to publishers and agents. Mss, synopses and ideas welcome; initial enquiries by e-mail or post.

Chameleon HH Publishing
The Quarry House, East End, Witney OX29 6QA
☎01993 880223 Fax 01993 880236
✉ marion@chameleonhh.co.uk *and*
david@chameleonhh.co.uk
www.chameleonhh.co.uk

Directors *David Hall, Marion Hazzledine*

Founded 1997. CD-ROM and Web publishers on behalf of commercial publishers, institutes, associations and government bodies. Produces web-updateable CDs – CD and DVD duplication, plus all artwork undertaken. Also digitisation of videos. Files prepared for print-on-demand. Consulting and advice on CD-ROM and Web publishing. Welcomes unsolicited mss for electronic publishing from self-publishers and print-on-demand. 'Small runs particularly catered for, whether book or CD.'

Claritybooks.com
Colt Farm, Bromley Green Road, Ashford TN26 2EQ
✉ ed@claritybooks.com
www.claritybooks.com

Internet e-book publisher and distributor. Has proprietary e-book technology which simplifies the process of downloading and reading of purchased works for the reader while still providing authors with copyright protection/ encryption. Available to individual authors or joint venture with print publishers wishing to simplify their Internet distribution of authors' works using claritybook's technology and facilities. Self-publishing option also available to authors who would rather pay an annual fee and retain their electronic publishing rights instead of receiving royalties.

Mss or synopses welcomed from new or published authors. No charges to authors. Will consider all works of a good standard which may be of interest to target market of 'the intelligent, the busy or the bored' reading on PDAs/laptops or desktop PCs (website is optimised for viewing on Pocket PC devices and roving Wifi users). E-mail communication preferred. If paper submission, please include s.a.e.

Context Limited

Grand Union House, 20 Kentish Town Road, London NW1 9NR
☎020 7267 8989   Fax 020 7267 1133
✉ tenders@context.co.uk
www.context.co.uk

Founded 1986. Electronic publisher of UK and European legal and offical information on CD-ROM, online and the Internet.

Deunant Books

PO Box 25, Denbigh LL16 5ZQ
☎01745 870259   Fax 01745 870259
✉ mail@deunantbooks.com
www.deunantbooks.com
Managing Director *Les Broad*

Founded 2001. Internet e-book publisher in English and Welsh of art, biography, children's, comedy, fiction, philosophy, poetry, science fiction, short story compendia, theology, travel. 64 titles in 2003. Welcomes written works incorporating video, sound or animation; interactive books, technical manuals.
ROYALTIES twice-yearly.

Fledgling Press Limited

7 Lennox Street, Edinburgh EH4 1QB
☎0131 332 6867
✉ info@fledglingpress.co.uk
www.fledglingpress.co.uk
Director *Zander Wedderburn*

Founded 2000. Internet publisher, aiming to be 'a launching pad for new authors. Special interest in authentic writing about the human condition, including autobiography, diaries, poetry and fictionalised variations on these.' Monthly online competition (www.canyouwrite.com) with small prizes for short pieces. Also free books and reports in the areas of shiftwork and working time. Send mss and other details by e-mail from the website or by post. Links into short-run book production.

The Good Web Guide Ltd

See entry under *UK Publishers*

The Male Alliance

✉ info@themalealliance.org.uk
www.themalealliance.org.uk

Contact *Group Contributions*

Founded 2001. Non-profit Internet-based campaign devoted to serious gay male issues: politics, debate, law, support, information, protest and male rights. Articles should promote positive images of gay men, challenge ignorance and stereotypical concepts of homosexual males. Sensible unsolicited material from gay men will be considered for publication on the website as a free contribution. No payment unless work is commissioned.

New Authors Showcase

See **Barrie James Literary Agency** under *UK Literary Agents*

NoSpine.com

26 Sunningdale Way, Bletchley MK3 7SB
✉ info@nospine.com
www.nospine.com
Managing Director *Andrew Gardner*

Founded 2000. An electronic self-publishing venture 'designed by authors for authors'. NoSpine accepts electronic mss and arranges sales and distribution in return for a commission on each sale. Authors retain complete control over their work, full copyright, and set their own sale prices of which they retain 80%. 'We are not a vanity publisher, nor a subsidy publisher. No author ever pays us a penny: in effect we are a writers' cooperative.' All new submissions are refereed by the founding authors to screen out unacceptable or illegal material.

Online Originals

Priory Cottage, Wordsworth Place, London NW5 4HG
☎020 7267 4244
✉ editor@onlineoriginals.com
www.onlineoriginals.com
Managing Director *David Gettman*
Commissioning Editor *Dr Christopher Macann*

Publishes book-length works on the Internet and as print-on-demand. Acquires global electronic rights (including print-on-demand) in literary fiction, intellectual non-fiction, drama and fiction for young readers (ages 8–16). No poetry, fantasy, how-to, self-help, picture books, cookery, hobbies, crafts or local interest. TITLES *Johanna's Refrain* Mak Gamon; *Floating Stones* Ann Lingard; *Quintet* Frederick Forsyth. 8 titles in 2003. Unsolicited mss, synopses and ideas for books welcome. *All* authors must have Internet access. Unique peer-review, automated submissions system, accessed via the website address above. Submissions or enquiries on paper or disk will be discarded.

ROYALTIES paid annually (50% royalties on standard price of £6 or £9).

StoryZone Ltd
Ryman's Cottages, Little Tew OX7 4JJ
☎0845 458 8408
✉ contact@storyzone.co.uk
www.storyzone.co.uk

Online children's story library. The website makes available new and published stories by professional writers aimed at children between the ages of 4 and 10. Maximum length 1000 words, with illustrations. Minimum subscription: £5 for 5 stories.

Triple Hitter
See entry under *Useful Websites*.

WritersServices
See entry under *Useful Websites*.

www.50connect.co.uk
Nell Gwynn's House, 5 Church Street, Windsor SL4 1PE
☎01753 850606   Fax 01753 857174
✉ admin@50connect.com
www.50connect.co.uk

Owner *Phil Cooper*
Editor *Rachael Hannan*

Launched in 2000, www.50connect.co.uk is an over-50's web portal with a large community section. Daily updates. Check the website for topics covered. Approach with ideas by e-mail in the first instance.

Useful Websites

Many of these and other useful websites for writers can be found in *The Internet for Writers* by Nick Daws (ISBN 1-84025-308-8), one of a series of books published by Internet Handbooks; *The Incredibly Indispensable Web Directory* by Clive and Bettina Zietman, published by Kogan Page (ISBN 0-7494-3617-4); *thegoodwebguide for writers* by Paul Chronnell, published by The Good Web Guide Limited (ISBN 1-903282-38-1).

AbeBooks
www.abebooks.co.uk
Second-hand, rare and antiquarian online bookshop Includes 'BookSleuth' pages for tracking down 'long-lost' books.

Academi (Welsh Academy/ Yr Academi Gymreig)
www.academi.org
News of events, publications and funding for Welsh-based literary events. (See entry under *Professional Associations*.)

Alibris
www.alibris.com
Over 35 million used, new and hard-to-find books online.

Alliance of Literary Societies
www.sndc.demon.co.uk/als.htm
Details of societies and events. (See entry under *Professional Associations*.)

Amazon Bookshop
www.amazon.co.uk
The leading online shop for books, music, videos and DVDs, electronics, toys and games, travel, and home and kitchen-ware. Access to more than 1.5 million UK published titles.

Ancestry
www.ancestry.com
Family history information - databases, articles and other sources of genealogical data.

Arvon Foundation
www.arvonfoundation.org
Information on the four Arvon centres in the UK. (See entry under *UK Writers' Courses*.)

Association for Scottish Literary Studies
www.asls.org.uk
The educational charity promoting the languages and literature of Scotland. (See entry under *Professional Associations*.)

Association of Authors' Agents (AAA)
www.agentsassoc.co.uk
UK agents' organisation including list of current members. (See entry under *Professional Associations*.)

Association of Authors' Representatives (AAR)
www.aar-online.org
US agents' organisation including list of current members. (See entry under *Professional Associations*.)

Authorbank
www.authorbank.com
Registration for a fee enables authors to present book ideas to publishers online. 'Your presentation will be able to be seen by targeted publishers with confidentiality and security.'

Authors' Licensing and Collecting Society (ALCS)
www.alcs.co.uk
Details of membership, news, publications, legal issues and rights, plus links to related sites. (See entry under *Professional Associations*.)

Author-Network
www.author-network.com
Writers' resource site run by Karen Scott and Diana Hayden.

Author-Publisher Network
www.author.co.uk
Services for writers, information network, newsletter and online magazine.

Bartleby.com
www.bartleby.com
An ever-expanding list of great books published online for reference, free of charge.

BBC
www.bbc.co.uk
Access to all BBC departments and services.

bibliofind
www.bibliofind.com
Over 20 million second-hand and rare books, periodicals and ephemera for sale online via Amazon.com.

BOL
www.bol.com
Internet shopping, including books and music; a database of over 1.5 million titles.

BookSleuth See **AbeBooks**

Book2Book
www.book2book.co.uk
Established by a group of publishers, booksellers, website developers and trade journalists to provide up-to-date news, features and useful information for the book trade.

Booktrust
www.booktrust.org.uk
Book information service, guide to prizes and awards, links to other book organisations, factsheets for writers. (See entry under *Professional Associations*.)

British Association of Picture Libraries and Agencies (BAPLA)
www.bapla.org.uk
Free telephone referrals available from the BAPLA database through this website. (See entry under *Professional Associations*.)

British Centre for Literary Translation
www.literarytranslation.com
A joint website with the British Council containing workshops by leading translators, contacts and networks, and listings of translation conferences, seminars and events.

British Council
www.britishcouncil.org
Information on the Council's English Language services, education programmes, science and health links, and information exchange. (See entry under *Professional Associations*.)

British Film Institute (bfi)
www.bfi.org.uk
Information on the services offered by the Institute. (See entry under *Professional Associations*.)

British Library
www.bl.uk
Reader service enquiries, access to main catalogues, information on collections, links to the various Reading Rooms and exhibitions. (See related entries under *Library Services*.)

Children's Writing Resource Center
www.write4kids.com
US website for children's writers', whether published or beginners. Includes special reports, advice, chat links, news on the latest bestsellers and links to related sites.

CILIP
www.cilip.org.uk
The professional body for librarians and information professionals. (See entry under *Professional Associations*.)

Complete Works of William Shakespeare
www-tech.mit.edu/Shakespeare/works.html
Access to the text of the complete works with search facility, quotations and discussion pages.

Copyright Licensing Agency Ltd (CLA)
www.cla.co.uk
Copyright information, customer support and information on CLA services. (See entry under *Professional Associations*.)

Crime Writers' Association (CWA)
www.thecwa.co.uk
Website of the professional crime writers' association. (See entry under *Professional Associations*.)

Daily Mirror
www.mirror.co.uk
The *Daily Mirror* newspaper online.

Dictionary of Slang
dictionaryofslang.co.uk
A guide to slang 'from a British perspective'. Research information; search facility.

The Dramatic Exchange
www.dramex.org
Script exchange site; over 400 unpublished

plays online for producers and readers to search through.

The Eclectic Writer
www.eclectics.com/writing/writing.html
US website offering a selection of articles on advice for writers on topics such as 'Proper Manuscript Format', 'Electronic Publishing', 'How to Write a Synopsis' and 'Motivation' Also a Character Chart for fiction writers and an online discussion board.

Electronic Telegraph
www.telegraph.co.uk
The *Daily Telegraph* online – one of the first UK national newspapers to establish itself on the web.

Encyclopædia Britannica
www.eb.com
A subscription access to the entire Encyclopædia Britannica database as well as Merriam-Webster's Collegiate Dictionary and the Britannica Book of the Year. (A 72-hour free trial is available.) EB online also gives links to more than 130,000 sites selected, rated and reviewed by Britannica editors.

The Arts Council of England
www.artscouncil.org.uk
Includes information on funding applications, publications and the National Lottery. (See entry under *Arts Councils and Regional Offices*.)

The English Association
www.le.ac.uk/engassoc
News, publications, conference and membership information. (See entry under *Professional Associations*.)

Federation of Worker Writers and Community Publishers (FWWCP)
myweb.tiscali.co.uk/thefwwcp/Info.htm
Links to members of the FWWCP, the Federation magazine, information on membership. (See entry under *Professional Associations*.)

Film Angel
www.filmangel.co.uk
Established in 2000 by Hammerwood Films to create a shop window for writers and would-be film angels alike. Writers submit a short synopsis which can be displayed for a pre-determined period, for a fee, while would-be angels are invited to finance a production of their choice.

Filmmaker Store
www.filmmakerstore.com
Scriptwriting resources, listings and advice.

Financial Times
www.ft.com
Financial Times online.

Frankfurt Book Fair
www.frankfurt-book-fair.com/en/portal.html
Provides latest news and market analysis of the book business plus information on the Book Fair.

The Guardian
www.guardian.co.uk
Website of *The Guardian* and the *Observer* newspapers online.

Guide to Grammar and Style
www.andromeda.rutgers.edu/~jlynch/Writing
A guide to grammar and style which is organised alphabetically, plus articles and links to other grammatical reference sites.

Hansard
www.parliament.the-stationery-office.
    co.uk/pa/cm/cmhansrd.htm
The official record of debates and written answers in the House of Commons. The transcript of each day's business appears at noon on the following weekday.

House of Commons Research Library
www.parliament.uk/parliamentary_
    publications_and_archives/research_paperscfm
Gives access to the text of research reports prepared for MPs on a wide range of current issues.

HTML Writers Guild
www.hwg.org
US organisation offering resources, support, representation and education for web authors. (See entry under *Professional Associations*.)

The Independent
www.independent.co.uk
The Independent newspaper online.

Ingenta
www.ingenta.com
Established in 1998, Ingenta is the largest online academic research service in the UK. Formed through a public/private partnership with the University of Bath, the site offers 'free searching of millions of academic and professional articles from thousands of journals online'.

Institute of Linguists
www.iol.org.uk
Discussion forum, news on regional societies, job opportunities, 'Find a Linguist' service, and The Linguist magazine. (See entry under *Professional Associations*.)

Institute of Translation and Interpreting (ITI)
www.iti.org.uk
Website of the professional association of translators and interpreters, with the ITI Directory, publications, training and membership information. (See entry under *Professional Associations*.)

Internet Movie Database (IMDb)
www.imdb.com
Essential resource for film buffs and researchers with search engine for cast lists, screenwriters, directors and producers; film and television news, awards, film preview information, video releases.

Internet Classics Archive
classics.mit.edu
Includes 441 works of classical literature by 59 different authors. Mostly Greek and Roman works with some Chinese and Persian. All are in English translation

The Irish Arts Council/ An Chomhairle Ealaíon
www.artscouncil.ie
Monthly e-mail newsletter available giving latest information on grants and awards, news and events, etc. (See entry under *Arts Councils and Regional Offices*.)

Journalism UK
www.journalismuk.co.uk
A website for UK-based journalists who write for text-based publications. Includes links to newspapers, magazines, e-zines, news sources plus information on jobs, training and organisations.

The Library Association See CILIP

Location Register of 20th-Century English Literary Manuscripts and Letters
www.library.rdg.ac.uk/colls/projects/locreg.html
Reference source for the study of English literature. Information about the manuscript holdings of repositories of all sizes, from the British Library to small-town museums, of literary authors – from major poets to minor science fiction writers.

Mr William Shakespeare and the Internet
daphne.palomar.edu/Shakespeare
Guide to scholarly Shakespeare resources on the Internet.

National Union of Journalists (NUJ)
www.nuj.org.uk
Represents those journalists who work in all sectors of publishing, print and broadcasting. (See entry under *Professional Associations*.)

New Writers Consultancy
www.new-writers-consultancy.com
Advice for writers and critiques, offered by Diana Hayden and Karen Scott.

New Writing North
www.newwritingnorth.com
Essentially for writers based in the north of England but also a useful source of advice and guidelines.

Arts Council of Northern Ireland
www.artscouncil-ni.org
Includes the 'Infodesk', an enquiry service based in Belfast and Dublin with access to a database of international arts contacts, information on funding, etc. (See entry under *Arts Councils and Regional Offices*.)

Novel Advice Newsletter
www.noveladvice.com
A free US journal aimed at the fiction writer; full text of current and past issues online.

PEN
www.pen.org.uk
Website of the English Centre of International PEN. News of events, membership details. (See entry under *Professional Associations*.)

PlaysOnTheNet
www.playsonthenet.com
Information and help for new playwrights. Launched in association with Oneword Radio in 2002, the site offers the chance to get involved, whether as a writer or someone who enjoys reading and listening to new plays. The site features new works that can be downloaded.

Poets and Writers Online
www.pw.org

A US site containing publishing advice, a directory of writers, online bookstore, literary links, news, articles on aspects of writing, grants and awards.

Producers Alliance for Cinema and Television (PACT)
www.pact.co.uk
Publications, jobs in the industry, production companies, membership details. (See entry under *Professional Associations*.)

Publishers Association
www.publishers.org.uk
Information about the Association and careers in publishing; also 'Getting Published' pages. (See entry under *Professional Associations*.)

RefDesk.com
refdesk.com
Facts and statistics on every country in the world plus charts and maps, illustrations and related sources.

Relax With a Book
www.relaxwithabook.com
Reviews, author interviews and competitions online.

Royal Society of Literature
www.rslit.org
Information on lectures, discussions and readings; membership details and prizes. (See entry under *Professional Associations*.)

Save Our Short Story Campaign
www.saveourshortstory.org.uk
The aims of this Arts Council England campaign are to increase the number and visibility of high quality outlets for short fiction; give the short story form more prestige and a higher profile; enable writers to specialise in the short story form; and encourage and promote exciting short fiction.

Science Fiction Foundation Collection
www.liv.ac.uk/~asawyer/sffchome.html
The research library of the Science Fiction Foundation, based at the University of Liverpool. Includes links to the Foundation, the John Wyndham archive, the Foundation's journal and other SF collections and associations. (See entry under *Library Services*.)

Scottish Arts Council
www.sac.org.uk

Information on funding and events; 'Image of the Month' and 'Poem of the Month'. (See entry under **Arts Councils and Regional Offices**.)

Scottish Book Trust
www.scottishbooktrust.com
Information on the Trust's activities and a link to their Book Information Service. (See entry under *Professional Associations*.)

Scottish Library Association (SLAINTE: Information & Libraries Scotland)
www.slainte.org.uk
Links to various services and major Scottish websites and information on people, organisations, libraries, events and resources of Scottish interest. (See entry under *Professional Associations*.)

Scottish Publishers Association
www.scottishbooks.org
Links to websites of members of the Association, information on activities and publications. (See entry under *Professional Associations*.)

Screenwriters Online
screenwriter.com/insider/news.html
Described as the 'only professional screenwriter's site run by major screenwriters who get their scripts and screenplays made into movies'. Contains screenplay analysis, expert articles and The Insider Report.

Shots Magazine
www.shotsmag.co.uk
Electronic magazine of crime and mystery fiction.

Society for Freelance Editors and Proofreaders (SFEP)
www.sfep.org.uk
Basic information about the Society. (See entry under *Professional Associations*.)

Society of Authors
www.societyofauthors.org
Includes FAQs for new writers, diary of events, membership details, links to publishers' and other societies' websites. (See entry under *Professional Associations*.)

Society of Indexers
www.socind.demon.co.uk
Indexing information for publishers and authors, 'Electronic Indexers Available' pages.

Membership information. (See entry under *Professional Associations*.)

South Bank Centre, London
www.sbc.org.uk
Links to the Royal Festival Hall, the Hayward Gallery and Poetry Library; news of literature events.

The Sun
www.thesun.co.uk
Website of *The Sun* newspaper.

The Times
www.thetimes.co.uk
Website of *The Times* newspaper.

trAce Online Writing Centre
www.trace.ntu.ac.uk
Based at Nottingham Trent University, trAce is an online centre for writers and readers worldwide to share and critique their work, discuss favourite books and talk. Also holds occasional (live) conferences and workshops. Links to a wide range of sites for writers.

Triple Hitter
www.triplehitter.net
Website dedicated to 'aiding aspiring writers in obtaining their big break' by showcasing their work free of charge. Includes various interviews, links and helpful hints.

UK Children's Books Directory
www.ukchildrensbooks.co.uk
A directory of the online world of children's books.

The Arts Council of Wales
www.ccc-acw.org.uk
Information on publications, council meetings, the arts in Wales. Links to other arts websites. (See entry under *Arts Councils and Regional Offices*.)

Webster Dictionary/Thesaurus
www.m-w.com/home.htm
Merriam-Webster Online. Includes a search facility for words in the Webster Dictionary or Webster Thesaurus; word games, 'Word of the Day' and Language Info Zone.

Welsh Academy – See Academi

Welsh Books Council (Cyngor Llyfrau Cymru)
www.cllc.org.uk and www.gwales.com

Information about books from Wales, editorial and design services, 'Wales Book Day'. (See entry under *Professional Associations*.)

The Word Pool
www.wordpool.co.uk
Children's book review site with information on writing for children and a thriving discussion group for children's writers.

Word Pool Design
www.wordpooldesign.co.uk
Web design for writers, illustrators and publishers. 'Friendly advice and help from people who understand the world of books.'

WordCounter
www.wordcounter.com
Highlights the most frequently used words in a given text. Use as a guide to see what words are overused.

Writers' Guild of Great Britain
www.writersguild.org.uk
A wide range of information including rates of pay, articles on topics such as copyright, news, writers' resources and industry regulations. (See entry under *Professional Associations*.)

Writers, Artists and their Copyright Holders (WATCH)
www.watch-file.com
Database of copyright holders in the UK and North America. (See entry under *Professional Associations*.)

Writers' Circles
www.writers-circles.com
Offers free pages to writers' circles. Listings and information.

Writernet
www.writernet.org.uk
Formerly New Playwrights Trust. Information, advice and guidance for writers on all aspects of the live and recorded performance.

WritersNet
www.writers.net
A directory of writers, editors, publishers and literary agents.

WritersServices
www.WritersServices.com
Established in March 2000 by Chris Holifield, former deputy managing director and publisher at Cassell. Offers factsheets, book reviews,

advice, links and other resources for writers including editorial services, contract vetting and self-publishing. (Enquiries to: info@ writersservices.com)

Writing-World.com
writing-world.com
'A world of writing tips ... for writers around the world.'

UK Packagers

Aladdin Books Ltd
28 Percy Street, London W1T 2BZ
☎020 7323 3319 Fax 020 7323 4829

Managing Director *Charles Nicholas*

Founded in 1979 as a packaging company but with joint publishing ventures in the UK and USA. Commissions children's fully illustrated, non-fiction reference books. IMPRINTS **Aladdin Books** *Bibby Whittaker* Children's reference; **Nicholas Enterprises** *Charles Nicholas* Adult non-fiction; **The Learning Factory** *Charles Nicholas* Early learning concepts 0–4 years. TITLES *World Issues*; *Science Readers*; *The Atlas of Animals*. About 40 titles a year. Will consider synopses and ideas for children's non-fiction with international sales potential only. No fiction.

FEES usually paid instead of royalties.

The Albion Press Ltd
Spring Hill, Idbury OX7 6RU
☎01993 831094 Fax 01993 831982

Chairman/Managing Director *Emma Bradford*

Founded 1984. Commissions illustrated trade titles, particularly children's. TITLES *From a Distance* Jane Ray and Julie Gold; *The Little Mermaid and Other Fairy Stories* Isabelle Brent. About 4 titles a year. Unsolicited synopses and ideas for books not welcome.

ROYALTIES paid; fees paid for introductions and partial contributions.

Alphabet & Image Ltd
See **Marston House** under *UK Publishers*

Amber Books Ltd
Bradleys Close, 74–77 White Lion Street, London N1 9PF
☎020 7520 7600 Fax 020 7520 7606/7
✉ enquiries@amberbooks.co.uk
www.amberbooks.co.uk

Managing Director *Stasz Gnych*
Rights Director *Sara Ballard*
Publishing Manager *Charles Catton*

Founded 1989. Commissions military, aviation, transport, sport, combat, survival and fitness, cookery, lifestyle, naval history, crime and general reference. No fiction. IMPRINT **Brown Books**. 120 titles in 2003. No unsolicited material.

FEES paid.

Archival Facsimiles
See **Erskine Press**

AS Publishing
73 Montpelier Rise, London NW11 9DU
☎020 8458 3552 Fax 020 8458 0618

Managing Director *Angela Sheehan*

Founded 1987. Commissions children's illustrated non-fiction. No unsolicited synopses or ideas for books, but approaches welcome from experienced authors, editors and illustrators in this field.

FEES paid.

BCS Publishing Ltd
2nd Floor, Temple Court, 109 Oxford Road, Cowley OX4 2ER
☎01865 770099 Fax 01865 770050
✉ bcs-publishing@dsl.pipex.com

Managing Director *Steve McCurdy*
Approx. Annual Turnover £200,000

Commissions general interest non-fiction for the international co-edition market.

Bender Richardson White
PO Box 266, Uxbridge UB9 5BD
☎01895 832444 Fax 01895 835213
✉ brw@brw.co.uk

Partners *Lionel Bender, Kim Richardson, Ben White*

Founded 1990 to produce illustrated non-fiction for children, adults and family reference for publishers in the UK and abroad. 40 titles in 2003. Unsolicited material not welcome.

FEES paid.

Book House
See **Salariya Book Company Ltd**

Book Packaging and Marketing
1 Church Street, Blakesley, Towcester NN12 8RA
☎01327 861300 Fax 01327 861300
✉ martin@marixevans.freeserve.co.uk

Contact *Martin F. Marix Evans*

Founded 1989. Essentially a project management service, handling books demanding close designer/editor teamwork or complicated multi-contributor administration, for publishers, business 'or anyone who needs one'. Mainly illustrated adult non-fiction including military, travel, historical, home reference and coffee-table books. No fiction or poetry. Proposals considered but rarely come to fruition; most books are bespoke by publishers. Additional writers are sometimes required for projects in development. TITLES *The Fall of France 1940*; *Contemporary Photographers*, 3rd ed.; *The Vital Guide to Major Battles of World War II*; *Encyclopedia of the Boer War*; *The Military Heritage of Britain and Ireland*; *Beagle*; *Guide to South Georgia*; *American Voices of World War I*. 5–8 titles a year.

PAYMENT Authors contract direct with client publishers; fees paid on first print usually and royalties on reprint but this depends on publisher.

Breslich & Foss Ltd
Unit 2A, Union Court, 20–22 Union Road, Clapham, London SW4 6JP
✉ sales@breslichfoss.com
Directors *Paula Breslich, K.B. Dunning*
Approx. Annual Turnover £650,000

Packagers of adult non-fiction titles, including interior design, crafts, gardening, health and children's non-fiction and picturebooks. Unsolicited mss welcome but synopses preferred. Include s.a.e. with all submissions.

ROYALTIES paid twice-yearly.

Brown Books
See **Amber Books Ltd**

Brown Wells and Jacobs Ltd
Forresters Hall, 25–27 Westow Street, London SE19 3RY
☎020 8771 5115 Fax 020 8771 9994
✉ postmaster@popking.demon.co.uk
www.bwj.org
Managing Director *Graham Brown*

Founded 1979. Commissions non-fiction, novelty, pre-school and first readers, natural history and science. About 40 titles a year. Unsolicited synopses and ideas for books welcome.

FEES paid.

Cameron & Hollis
PO Box 1, Moffat DG10 9SU
☎01683 220808 Fax 01683 220012
✉ info@cameronbooks.co.uk
www.cameronbooks.co.uk
Directors *Ian A. Cameron, Jill Hollis*
Approx. Annual Turnover £400,000

Commissions contemporary art, film (serious critical works only), design, collectors' reference, decorative arts, architecture and children's non-fiction About 6 titles a year.

PAYMENT varies with each contract.

Compendium Publishing Ltd
See entry under *UK Publishers*

Roger Coote Publishing
Gissing's Farm, Fressingfield, Eye IP21 5SH
☎01379 588044 Fax 01379 588055
✉ rgc@ndirect.co.uk
Director *Roger Goddard-Coote*

Founded 1993. Packager of children's and adult non-fiction for trade, school and library markets. No fiction. About 40 titles a year. Include s.a.e. for return.

FEES paid; no royalties.

Diagram Visual Information Ltd
195 Kentish Town Road, London NW5 2JU
☎020 7482 3633 Fax 020 7482 4932
✉ brucerobertson@diagramgroup.com
Managing Director *Bruce Robertson*

Founded 1967. Producer of library, school, academic and trade reference books. About 10 titles a year. Unsolicited synopses and ideas for books welcome.

FEES paid; no payment for sample material/submissions for consideration.

Duncan Petersen Publishing Limited
See entry under *UK Publishers*

Eddison Sadd Editions
St Chad's House, 148 King's Cross Road, London WC1X 9DH
☎020 7837 1968 Fax 020 7837 2025
✉ reception@eddisonsadd.co.uk
Managing Director *Nick Eddison*
Editorial Director *Ian Jackson*
Approx. Annual Turnover £2.5 million

Founded 1982. Produces a wide range of popular illustrated non-fiction – mind, body, spirit and complementary therapies are particular strengths – with books published in 30 countries. Ideas and synopses are welcome but titles must have international appeal.

ROYALTIES paid twice yearly; flat fees paid when appropriate.

Erskine Press

The Old Bakery, Banham, Norwich
NR16 2HW
☎01953 887277 Fax 01953 888361
✉ erskpres@aol.com
www.erskine-press.com

Chief Executive *Crispin de Boos*

Founded 1986. Specialist publisher of books on Antarctic exploration – facsimiles, diaries, previously unpublished works and first English translations of European expeditions of the late 19th and early 20th centuries. Publisher of general interest autobiographies with special reference to Norfolk and medical-related 'Patient's Guides' (*Hip & Knee Replacement; Chronic Fatigue Syndrome*). Recent publications include three Second World War related subjects (*Living With Heroes; The Story of the Dam Busters*). **Archival Facsimiles**, the parent company, produces scholarly reprints and limited edition publications for academic/business organisations ranging from period print reproductions to facsimiles of rare and important books no longer available. No unsolicited mss. Ideas welcome.

ROYALTIES paid twice-yearly.

Expert Publications Ltd

Sloe House, Halstead CO9 1PA
☎01787 474744 Fax 01787 474700
✉ expert@lineone.net

Chairman *Dr. D.G. Hessayon*

Founded 1993. Produces the *Expert* series of books by Dr. D.G. Hessayon. Currently 24 titles in the series, including *The Flower Expert; The Evergreen Expert; The Vegetable & Herb Expert; The Flowering Shrub Expert; The Container Expert*. No unsolicited material.

Haldane Mason Ltd

PO Box 34196, London NW10 3YB
☎020 8459 2131 Fax 020 8728 1216
✉ info@haldane.mason.com

Founded 1994. Commissions adult and children's illustrated non-fiction and some young children's fiction. Children's books are published under the **Red Kite Books** imprint. Adult list consists mainly of mind, body and spirit plus alternative health books under the Neals' Yard Remedies banner; children's age range 0–11. 15 titles in 2003. Unsolicited synopses and ideas welcome; approach in writing in the first instance. No adult fiction.

FEES paid.

The Ilex Press Limited

The Old Candlemakers, West Street, Lewes
BN7 2NZ
☎01273 487440 Fax 01273 487441
✉ surname@ilex-press.com

Managing Director *Sophie Collins*

Founded 1999. Sister company of **The Ivy Press Limited**. Commissions titles on digital art, design and photography as well as on all aspects of website design and graphics software. No fiction. Unsolicited synopses and ideas welcome; send a *brief* idea outline (3 or 4 pages) and a letter.

FEES paid.

The Ivy Press Limited

The Old Candlemakers, West Street, Lewes
BN7 2NZ
☎01273 487440 Fax 01273 487441
✉ surname@ivypress.co.uk

Managing Director *Sophie Collins*

Founded 1996. Sister company of **The Ilex Press Limited**. Commissions illustrated non-fiction books covering subjects such as art, health, self-help, mind, body and spirit, and general reference. No fiction. Unsolicited synopses and ideas welcome; send a *brief* idea outline (3 or 4 pages) and a letter.

FEES paid.

The Learning Factory

See **Aladdin Books Ltd**

Lexus Ltd

60 Brook Street, Glasgow G40 2AB
☎0141 556 0440 Fax 0141 556 2202
✉ peterterrell@lexusforlanguages.co.uk
www.lexusforlanguages.co.uk

Managing/Editorial Director *P.M. Terrell*

Founded 1980. Compiles bilingual reference, language and phrase books. TITLES Hugo and Rough Guide Phrasebooks; *Harrap Study Aids*; Langenscheidt Dictionaries; *Impact Specialist Bilingual Glossaries; HarperCollins English–Chinese; Oxford Italian Pocket Dictionary*. Own series of *Travelmates* published in 2004. About 5 titles a year. No unsolicited material. Books are mostly commissioned. Freelance contributors employed for a wide range of languages.

PAYMENT Generally flat fee.

Lionheart Books

10 Chelmsford Square, London NW10 3AR
☎020 8459 0453 Fax 020 8451 3681
✉ Lionheart.Brw@btinternet.com

Senior Partner *Lionel Bender*
Partner *Madeleine Samuel*

A design/editorial packaging team. Titles are primarily commissioned from publishers. Highly illustrated non-fiction for children aged 8–14, mostly natural history, history and general science. About 20 titles a year.

PAYMENT Generally flat fee.

M&M Publishing Services

33 Warner Road, Ware SG12 9JL
☎01920 466003
✉ Mike.Moran@moran19.fsnet.co.uk
www.mikemoranphotography.co.uk

Proprietors *Mike Moran, Maggie Copeland*

Project managers, production and editorial, packagers and publishers. TITLES *MM Publisher Database; MM Printer Database* (available in UK, European and international editions).

Market House Books Ltd

2 Market House, Market Square, Aylesbury HP20 1TN
☎01296 484911 Fax 01296 437073
✉ books@mhbref.com
www.mhbref.com

Directors *Dr Alan Isaacs, Dr John Daintith, Peter Sapsed*

Founded 1970. Formerly Laurence Urdang Associates. Compiles dictionaries, encyclopedias and reference. TITLES *Bloomsbury Thesaurus; Collins English Dictionary*; Facts on File dictionaries; *Grolier Bibliographical Encyclopedia of Scientists* (10 vols); *Larousse Thematica* (6 vols); *The Macmillan Encyclopedia*; Macmillan dictionaries; Oxford dictionaries of *Business, Science,* etc; *Penguin Dictionary of Electronics; Penguin Rhyming Dictionary; New Penguin Dictionary of the Theatre; .* About 15 titles a year. Unsolicited material not welcome as most books are compiled in-house.

FEES paid.

Marshall Editions Ltd

See **Quarto Publishing**

Monkey Puzzle Media Ltd

Gissing's Farm, Fressingfield, Eye IP21 5SH
☎01379 588044 Fax 01379 588055
✉ rgc@ndirect.co.uk

Chairman/Managing Director *Roger Goddard-Coote*
Editorial Director *Edwina Conner*

Founded 1998. Packager of adult and children's non-fiction for trade, school, library and mass markets. No fiction or textbooks. About 80 titles a year. Synopses and ideas welcome. Include s.a.e. for return.

FEES paid; no royalties.

Nicholas Enterprises

See **Aladdin Books Ltd**

Orpheus Books Limited

2 Church Green, Witney OX28 4AW
☎01993 774949 Fax 01993 700330
✉ info@orpheusbooks.com
www.orpheusbooks.com

Chairman *Nicholas Harris*

Founded 1993. Commissions children's non-fiction. 12 titles in 2003. No unsolicited material.

FEES paid.

Playne Books Limited

Chapel House, Trefin, Haverfordwest SA62 5AU
☎01348 837073 Fax 01348 837063
✉ playne.books@virgin.net

Editorial Director *Gill Davies*
Design & Production *David Playne*

Founded 1987. Commissions early learning titles for young children – fun ideas with an educational slant and novelty books. Also highly illustrated and practical books on any subject. Synopses and ideas by prior arrangement only. Vanity publications considered.

ROYALTIES paid 'on payment from publishers'. Fees sometimes paid instead of royalties.

PRC Publishing Ltd

The Chrysalis Building, Bramley Road, London W10 6SP
☎020 7314 1400 Fax 020 7314 1596
✉ jmessham@chrysalisbooks.co.uk *or* fhopkinson@chrysalisbooks.co.uk
www.chrysalisbooks.co.uk

Head of Contract Division *Joanne Messham*
Senior Commissioning Editor *Frank Hopkinson*

PRC Publishing is an imprint within the packaging division of **Chrysalis Books** (see entry under **UK Publishers**). Publishes a wide array of subjects including architecture, history and natural history, lifestyle, art, hobbies and crafts, welfare and transport. Up to 50 new titles worldwide.

Mathew Price Ltd

The Old Glove Factory, Bristol Road, Sherborne DT9 4HP
☎01935 816010 Fax 01935 816310

✉ mathewp@mathewprice.com

Chairman/Managing Director *Mathew Price*

Approx. Annual Turnover £500,000

Commissions full-colour novelty picture books and fiction for young children plus children's non-fiction for all ages. TITLES *Magnificent Mazes*; *Creepies*; *Tractor Factory*; *Join-In Stories for the Very Young*; *Treasure Hunt*. Mss should be double-spaced, typed on one side of paper. Enclose s.a.e. with submission and keep a copy of everything that is sent.

FEES sometimes paid instead of royalties.

Quarto Publishing

The Old Brewery, 6 Blundell Street, London N7 9BH

☎020 7700 6700   Fax 020 7700 4191

www.quarto.com

Chairman *Laurence Orbach*

Founded 1976. Britain's largest book packager. Acquired Marshall Editions in 2002. Commissions illustrated non-fiction, including painting, graphic design, how-to, lifestyle, visual arts, history, cookery, gardening, crafts. Publishes under the Apple imprint. Unsolicited synopses/ideas for books welcome.

PAYMENT Flat fees paid.

Red Kite Books

See **Haldane Mason Ltd**

Regency House Publishing Limited

See **entry under** *UK Publishers*

Salariya Book Company Ltd

25 Marlborough Place, Brighton BN1 1UB

☎01273 603306   Fax 01273 693857

✉ salariya@salariya.com

www.salariya.com

www.book-house.co.uk

Managing Director *David Salariya*

Founded 1989. Children's information books – fiction, history, art, music, science, architecture, education and picture books. Publishes under its IMPRINT **Book House** Publisher *David Salariya* Highly illustrated non-fiction in all subjects for children, from pre-school to teenage.

PAYMENT by arrangement.

Savitri Books Ltd

25 Lisle Lane, Ely CB7 4AS

☎01353 654327   Fax 01353 654327

✉ munni@savitribooks.demon.co.uk

Managing Director *Mrinalini S. Srivastava*

Approx. Annual Turnover £200,000

Founded 1983 and since 1998, Savitri Books has also become a publisher in its own right (textile crafts). Keen to work 'very closely with authors/illustrators and try to establish long-term relationships with them, doing more books with the same team of people'. Commissions illustrated non-fiction: biography, history, travel. About 7 titles a year. Unsolicited synopses and ideas for books 'very welcome'.

Small Packages

20 Carisbrooke Road, London E17 7EF

☎020 8520 6073   Fax 020 8926 4585

✉ mail@smallpackage.co.uk

www.smallpackage.co.uk

Partners *Adam Hibbert, Clare Hibbert*

Founded 2002. Packages children's illustrated non-fiction for trade, school and library markets, UK and co-editions. A mix of project management commissions and packaging. No unsolicited mss.

FLAT FEES paid.

Stonecastle Graphics Ltd/ Touchstone

Battle Cross Studio, Comp Lane, Offham, West Malling ME19 5PP

☎01732 220064   Fax 01732 220112

✉ paul@stonecastle-graphics.co.uk *or* sue@stonecastle-graphics.co.uk

www.stonecastle-graphics.co.uk

www.touchstone-books.com

Partner *Paul Turner*

Editorial Head *Sue Pressley*

Approx. Annual Turnover £300,000

Founded 1976. Formed additional design/packaging partnership, Touchstone, in 1983. Commissions illustrated non-fiction general books – motoring, health, sport, leisure, lifestyle and children's non-fiction. TITLES *The Ultimate History of Aston Martin*; *History of Motorbikes*; *The Sports Car*; *Teach Yourself Guitar*; *Flowers*; *The Art of Bonsai*; *Spirit of the Horse*; *Sleepover Party*; *The Children's Party Book*. 20 titles in 2003. Unsolicited synopses and ideas for books welcome

FEES paid.

Templar Publishing

Pippbrook Mill, London Road, Dorking RH4 1JE

☎01306 876361   Fax 01306 889097

✉ editorial@templarco.co.uk

www.templarco.co.uk

Managing Director/Editorial Head *Amanda Wood*

Approx. Annual Turnover £10 million

Founded 1981. A division of The Templar Company plc. Commissions quality novelty and gift books, picture books and children's illustrated non-fiction. 100 titles a year. Synopses and ideas for books welcome. 'We are particularly interested in picture book mss and ideas for new novelty concepts.'

ROYALTIES by arrangement.

Toucan Books Ltd

Third Floor, 89 Charterhouse Street, London EC1M 6HR

☎020 7250 3388   Fax 020 7250 3123

Managing Director *Ellen Dupont*

Approx. Annual Turnover £1.2 million

Founded 1985. Specialises in international co-editions and fee-based editorial, design and production services. Commissions illustrated non-fiction for children and adults. No fiction or non-illustrated titles. About 5–10 titles a year.

ROYALTIES paid twice-yearly; fees paid in addition to or instead of royalties.

Touchstone

See **Stonecastle Graphics Ltd**

David West Children's Books

7 Princeton Court, 55 Felsham Road, London SW15 1AZ

☎020 8780 3836   Fax 020 8780 9313

✉ dww@btinternet.com

www.davidwestchildrensbooks.com

Founded 1992. Commissions children's illustrated reference books. No fiction or adult books. 70 titles in 2003. Unsolicited ideas and synopses welcome; approach in writing in the first instance

FEES AND ROYALTIES paid annually.

Wordwright Publishing

8 St Johns Road, Saxmundham IP17 1BE

☎01728 604204   Fax 01728 604029

✉ wordwright@clara.co.uk

Contact *Charles Perkins*

Founded by ex-editorial people 'so good writing always has a chance with us'. Commissions illustrated non-fiction: social history and comment, military history, women's issues, sport. Specialises in military and social history, natural history, science, art, cookery, and gardening. About 6–8 titles a year. Unsolicited synopses/ideas (a paragraph or so) welcome for illustrated non-fiction. .

PAYMENT usually fees but royalties (twice-yearly) paid for sales above a specified number of copies

Working Partners Ltd

1 Albion Place, London W6 0QT

☎020 8748 7477   Fax 020 8748 7450

✉ enquiries@workingpartnersltd.co.uk

www.workingpartnersltd.co.uk

Chairman *Ben Baglio*

Managing Director *Chris Snowdon*

Creative Director *Rod Ritchie*

Editorial Director *Deborah Smith*

Specialises in quality mass-market fiction for leading children's publishers including Bloomsbury, HarperCollins, Hodder, Macmillan, Orchard, OUP, Random House and Scholastic. First chapter books to young adult. No picture books. Welcomes approaches from interested writers. Contact *Deborah Smith* on deborahsmith@workingpartnersltd.co.uk

PAYMENT Both fees and royalties by arrangement.

Zoë Books Ltd

15 Worthy Lane, Winchester SO23 7AB

☎01962 851318

✉ enquiries@zoebooks.co.uk

www.zoebooks.co.uk

Managing Director *Imogen Dawson*

Founded 1990. Specialises in full-colour information and reference books for schools and libraries worldwide. Does *not* publish picture books or fiction. No freelance work available. Unsolicited material not considered.

FEES paid.

Book Clubs

David Arscott's Sussex Book Club
Dolphin House, 51 St Nicholas Lane, Lewes BN7 2JZ
☎01273 470100 Fax 01273 470100
✉ sussexbooks@aol.com
Founded January 1998. Specialises in books about the county of Sussex. Represents all the major publishers of Sussex books and offers a wide range of titles. Free membership without obligation to buy.

Artists' Choice
PO Box 3, Huntingdon PE28 0QX
☎01832 710201 Fax 01832 710488
www.artists-choice.co.uk
Specialises in books for the amateur artist at all levels of ability.

Baker Books
Manfield Park, Cranleigh GU6 8NU
☎01483 267888 Fax 01483 267409
✉ bakerbooks@dial.pipex.com
www.bakerbooks.co.uk
Book clubs for schools: Funfare for ages 3–8 and Bookzone, ages 8–13. Four issues per year operated in the UK and overseas.

BCA (Book Club Associates)
Greater London House, Hampstead Road, London NW1 7TZ
☎020 7760 6500 Fax 020 7760 6505
With two million members, BCA is Britain's largest book club organisation. Consists of over 20 book and software clubs as well as bol.com. These include: Ancient & Medieval History Book Club, The Arts Guild, The Book Club of Ireland, Books For Children, Computer Books Direct, Discovery, The English Book Club, Escape (female fiction), Fantasy Science Fiction, History Guild, Home Software World, Just Good Books, Mango, Military and Aviation Book Society, Mind, Body & Spirit, Mystery and Thriller Club, Quality Paperbacks Direct, Railway Book Club, Taste, TSP, World Books.

Bibliophile Books
5 Thomas Road, London E14 7BN
☎020 7515 9222 Fax 020 7538 4115
✉ orders@bibliophilebooks.com
www.bibliophilebooks.com
New books covering a wide range of subjects at discount prices. Write, phone or fax for free catalogue issued 10 times a year.

Cygnus Books
PO Box 15, Llandeilo SA19 6YX
☎01550 777701 Fax 01550 777569
✉ enquiries@cygnus-books.co.uk
www.cygnus-books.co.uk
'Bookseller offering books for your next step in spirituality and complementary health care. See website for over 1000 hand-picked titles.' Publishes *The Cygnus Review* magazine which features 50–60 reviews on new mind, body and spirit titles each month.

The Folio Society
44 Eagle Street, London WC1R 4FS
☎020 7400 4222 Fax 020 7400 4242
✉ enquiries@foliosoc.co.uk
www.foliosoc.co.uk
Fine editions of classic fiction, history and memoirs; also some children's classics.

Letterbox Library
71–73 Allen Road, London N16 8RY
☎020 7503 4801 Fax 020 7503 4800
✉ info@letterboxlibrary.com
www.letterboxlibrary.com
Children's book cooperative. Hard and soft-cover, non-sexist and multi-cultural books for children from one to teenage.

Poetry Book Society
See entry under **Organisations of Interest to Poets**

Readers' Union Ltd
Brunel House, Forde Close, Newton Abbot TQ12 4PU
☎01626 323200 Fax 01626 323318
www.writersnews.co.uk
Eight book clubs, all dealing with specific

interests: Country Review, The Craft Club, Craftsman Society, Equestrian Society, The Gardeners Society, Needlecrafts with Cross Stitch, Focal Point, Puzzles Plus.

Scholastic Book Clubs
See **Scholastic Ltd** under *UK Publishers*

Writers' News Bookshelf
First Floor, Victoria House,
143–145 The Headrow, Leeds LS1 5RL
☎0113 200 2929 Fax 0113 200 2928
✉ janet.davison@writersnews.co.uk
www.writersnews.co.uk

Specialises in books for writers.

UK Literary Agents

✓ OK
✓✓ EXCELLENT
✓✓✓ Particularly good first novels

★ = Members of the **Association of Authors' Agents**

Aaron, Goldberg & Rothschild Literary Agency ✓

28 Cochrane House, Cowley Road, Uxbridge UB8 2DA
☎0870 199 7573 Fax 0870 199 7573
Contact *Don A. Williams*

Founded 2002. Handles literary fiction and non-fiction; science fiction, crime, horror, fantasy, biography, lifestyle, self-help. Philosophy and esoteric material also considered as well as drama, comedy and documentary scripts for film, TV and radio. No children's, cookery, crafts, hobbies, gardening or poetry. COMMISSION Home 15%; US & Translation 20%. ASSOCIATES Cheeks Media (USA); Docurama (UK). Prefers authors to have some form of previous publication but will consider those who do not. Synopsis and first three chapters welcome; send letter with personal background, publication history and proposal for material submitted. S.a.e. essential. No reading fee.

Sheila Ableman Literary Agency

122 Arlington Road, London NW1 7HP
☎020 7485 3409 Fax 020 7485 3409
✉ sheila@ableman.freeserve.co.uk
Contact *Sheila Ableman*

Founded 1999. Handles non-fiction including history, science, biography and autobiography. Specialises in TV tie-ins and celebrity ghost writing. No poetry, children's, cookery, gardening or sport. COMMISSION Home 15%; US & Translation 20%. Unsolicited mss welcome. Approach in writing with publishing history, c.v., synopsis, three chapters and s.a.e. for return. No reading fee.

The Agency (London) Ltd★

24 Pottery Lane, London W11 4LZ
☎020 7727 1346 Fax 020 7727 9037
✉ info@theagency.co.uk
Contacts *Stephen Durbridge, Leah Schmidt, Sebastian Born, Julia Kreitman, Bethan Evans, Hilary Delamere, Katie Haines, Ligeia Marsh, Faye Webber, Nick Quinn*

Founded 1995. Handles writers and rights for TV, film, theatre, radio scripts and children's fiction. Only existing clients for adult fiction or non-fiction. COMMISSION Home 10%; US by arrangement. Send letter with s.a.e. No unsolicited mss. No reading fee.

Gillon Aitken Associates Ltd★ ✓

18–21 Cavaye Place, London SW10 9PT
☎020 7373 8672 Fax 020 7373 6002
✉ recep@gillonaitken.co.uk
Contacts *Gillon Aitken, Clare Alexander, Lesley Shaw* (also film/TV)
Associated Agents *Anthony Sheil, Mary Pachnos*

Founded 1977. Handles fiction and non-fiction. No plays, scripts or children's fiction unless by existing clients. CLIENTS Caroline Alexander, John Banville, Pat Barker, Nicholas Blincoe, Gordon Burn, John Cornwell, Josephine Cox, Sarah Dunant, Susan Elderkin, Sebastian Faulks, Helen Fielding, John Fowles, Germaine Greer, Mark Haddon, Susan Howatch, Liz Jensen, John Keegan, Pete McCarthy, V.S. Naipaul, Jonathan Raban, Piers Paul Read, Michèle Roberts, Nicholas Shakespeare, Gillian Slovo, Matt Thorne, Colin Thubron, Sally Vickers, A.N. Wilson, Robert Wilson. COMMISSION Home 10%; US & Translation 20%; Film/TV 10%. Send preliminary letter, with half-page synopsis and first 30pp of sample material, and adequate return postage, in the first instance. No reading fee.

Michael Alcock Management★

See **Johnson & Alcock Ltd**

The Ampersand Agency ✓✓

Ryman's Cottages, Little Tew OX7 4JJ
☎01608 683677 Fax 01608 683449
✉ peter@theampersandagency.co.uk
www.theampersandagency.co.uk
Contact *Peter Buckman*

Founded 2003. Handles literary and commercial fiction and non-fiction; contemporary and historical novels, crime, thrillers, biography, women's fiction, romance, fantasy, history, cookery, pet psychology. No scripts unless by existing clients. No poetry, science fiction or illustrated children's books. CLIENTS Georgette Heyer estate, Barbara Else, Beryl Kingston, Naomi Shepherd, Rita Piper, Philip Purser, Justin Elliott, Vikas Swarup, Kirby Wright.

COMMISSION Home 10–15%; US 15–20%; Translation 20%. Translation rights handled by The Buckman Agency. Unsolicited mss, synopses and ideas welcome; send sample chapters and synopsis by e-mail or post (s.a.e. required if material is to be returned). No reading fee.

Darley Anderson Literary, TV & Film Agency*

Estelle House, 11 Eustace Road, London SW6 1JB
☎020 7385 6652 Fax 020 7386 5571
✉ enquiries@darleyanderson.com
www.darleyanderson.com

Contacts *Darley Anderson, Lucie Whitehouse* (foreign rights), *Elizabeth Wright* (women's fiction and crime), *Julia Churchill* (children's fiction/non-fiction), *Rosi Bridge* (finance)

Run by an ex-publisher with a sympathetic touch and a knack for spotting talent and making great deals – many for six and seven figure advances. Handles commercial fiction and non-fiction; children's fiction. No academic books or poetry. Special fiction interests: all types of thrillers and crime (American/hard boiled/cosy/historical); women's fiction (sagas, chick-lit, love stories, 'tear jerkers', women in jeopardy) and all types of American and Irish novels. Also comic fiction. Special non-fiction interests: investigative books, revelatory history and science TV tie-ins, celebrity autobiographies, true life women in jeopardy, diet, beauty, health, cookery, popular psychology, self-improvement, inspirational, popular religion and supernatural. CLIENTS Liz Allen, Richard Asplin, Anne Baker, Catherine Barry, Paul Carson, Caroline Carver, Cathy Cassidy, Lee Child, Kira Cochrane, Martina Cole, John Connolly, Margaret Dickinson, Joan Jonker, Astrid Longhurst, Rani Manicka, Carole Matthews, Lesley Pearse, Lynda Page, Adrian Plass, Sheila Quigley, Carmen Reid, Rebecca Shaw, Peter Sheridan, Kwong Kuen Shan, Linda Taylor, Elizabeth Waite. COMMISSION Home 15%; US & Translation 20%; Film/TV/Radio 20%. OVERSEAS ASSOCIATES APA Talent and Literary Agency (LA/Hollywood); Liza Dawson Literary Agency (New York); and leading foreign agents throughout the world. Send letter, synopsis and first three chapters; return postage/s.a.e. essential. Disk and e-mailed submissions cannot be considered.

Anubis Literary Agency

6 Birdhaven Close, Lighthorne Heath CV35 0BE
☎01926 642588 Fax 01926 642588

Contacts *Steve Calcutt, Maggie Heavey*

Founded 1994. Handles genre fiction in the following categories: science fiction, fantasy, horror thrillers and crime. No other material considered. CLIENTS include Lesley Asquith, Anthea Ingham, Tim Lebbon, Adam Roberts, Steve Savile, Brett A. Savory, Zoe Sharp. COMMISSION Home 15%; US & Translation 20%. Works with the Marsh Agency on translation rights. In the first instance send 50 pages with a one-page synopsis (s.a.e. essential). No telephone calls. No reading fee.

Artellus Limited

30 Dorset House, Gloucester Place, London NW1 5AD
☎020 7935 6972 Fax 020 7487 5957

Chairman *Gabriele Pantucci*
Director *Leslie Gardner*

Founded 1986. Full-length and short mss. Handles crime, science fiction, historical, contemporary and literary fiction; non-fiction: art history, current affairs, biography, general history, science. Charges reading fee for 'selective readers' services'. Works directly in the USA and with agencies in Europe, Japan and Russia. COMMISSION Home 10%; Overseas 12½–20%. No reading fee. Will suggest revision. Return postage essential.

Author Literary Agents

53 Talbot Road, London N6 4QX
☎020 8341 0442/07989 318245 (mobile)
Fax 020 8341 0442
✉ agile@authors.co.uk

Contact *John Havergal*

Founded 1997. Thought-through game, toy, animation, picture, graphics and children's concepts for book and screen; also marketed. COMMISSION Writing: Home 15%; Overseas & Translation 25%; Non-writing media: publishing or production 25%; advertising one-third. VAT extra. Send a half to one-page outline plus first chapter/scene/section only for initial appraisal. S.a.e. essential for reply. No reading fee.

The Bell Lomax Agency

James House, 1 Babmaes Street, London SW1Y 6HF
☎020 7930 4447 Fax 020 7925 0118
✉ agency@bell-lomax.co.uk

Executives *Eddie Bell, Pat Lomax, Paul Moreton, June Bell*

Established 2002. Handles quality fiction and non-fiction, biography, children's, business and sport. No unsolicited mss without preliminary letter. No scripts. No reading fee.

Lorella Belli Literary Agency (LBLA)★

54 Hartford House, 35 Tavistock Crescent, Notting Hill, London W11 1AY
☎020 7727 8547 Fax 0870 787 4194
✉ info@lorellabelliagency.com
www.lorellabelliagency.com

Contact *Lorella Belli*

Founded 2002. Handles full length fiction (from literary to genre) and general non-fiction. Particularly interested in first novelists, journalists, multi-cultural and international writing, books on or about Italy and/or in Italian. No children's, fantasy, science fiction, poetry, plays or academic books. CLIENTS Sean Bidder, Zöe Brân, Scott Capurro, Annalisa Coppolaro-Nowell, Sean Coughlan, Nino Filastò, Dario Fo (winner of the 1997 Nobel Prize for Literature), Jacopo Fo, Emily Giffin, Paul Martin, Nisha Minhas, Rupert Steiner, Marcello Vannucci, Diana Winston. COMMISSION Home 15%; US & Translation 20%. Works in conjunction with leading associate agencies in most countries. REPRESENTS The Imprint Agency (New York), Studio Nabu Literary Agency (Italy) and Norris Literary Agency, LLC (Seattle). Welcomes approaches from new authors. Send outline plus two chapters for non-fiction, and short synopsis plus first three chapters for fiction. S.a.e. essential. No reading fee. Revision suggested where appropriate.

Blake Friedmann Literary Agency Ltd★

122 Arlington Road, London NW1 7HP
☎020 7284 0408 Fax 020 7284 0442
✉ firstname@blakefriedmann.co.uk
www.blakefriedmann.co.uk

Contacts *Carole Blake* (books), *Julian Friedmann* (film/TV), *Conrad Williams* (original scripts/ radio), *Isobel Dixon* (books)

Founded 1977. Handles all kinds of fiction from genre to literary; a varied range of specialised and general non-fiction, plus scripts for TV, radio and film. No poetry, science fiction or short stories (unless from existing clients). Special interests: commercial women's fiction, literary fiction, upmarket non-fiction. CLIENTS include Jane Asher, Edward Carey, Elizabeth Chadwick, Barbara Erskine, Maeve Haran, Ken Hom, Billy Hopkins, Paul Johnston, Glenn Meade, Lawrence Norfolk, Gregory Norminton, Joseph O'Connor, Siân Rees,

Michael Ridpath. COMMISSION Books: Home 15%; US & Translation 20%. Radio/TV/Film: 15%. OVERSEAS ASSOCIATES worldwide. Unsolicited mss welcome but initial letter with synopsis and first two chapters preferred. Letters should contain as much information as possible on previous writing experience, aims for the future, etc. No reading fee.

David Bolt Associates

12 Heath Drive, Send GU23 7EP
☎01483 721118 Fax 01483 721118

Contact *David Bolt*

Founded 1983. Handles fiction and general non-fiction. No books for small children or verse (except in special circumstances). No scripts. Special interests: fiction, African writers, biography, history, military, theology. CLIENTS include Chinua Achebe, David Bret, Joseph Rhymer, Colin Wilson. COMMISSION Home 10%; US & Translation 19%. Preliminary letter with s.a.e. essential. Reading fee for unpublished writers. Terms on application.

BookBlast Ltd

PO Box 20184, London W10 5AU
☎020 8968 3089 Fax 020 8932 4087
www.bookblast.com

Contact *Address material to the Company*

Handles fiction and non-fiction. No scripts, horror, crime, children's, science fiction, fantasy, poetry, health, cookery, gardening, short stories, academic or articles. COMMISSION Home 12%; US & Translation 20%; TV & Radio 15%; Film 20%. No unsolicited approaches at present. No new authors taken on except by recommendation. Film, TV and radio rights mainly sold in works by existing clients. No reading fee.

Alan Brodie Representation Ltd

211 Piccadilly, London W1J 9HF
☎020 7917 2871 Fax 020 7917 2872
✉ info@alanbrodie.com
www.alanbrodie.com

Contacts *Alan Brodie, Sarah McNair, Lisa Foster*

Founded 1989. Handles theatre, film and TV scripts. No books. COMMISSION Home 10%; Overseas 15%. Preliminary letter plus professional recommendation and c.v. essential. No reading fee but s.a.e. required.

Rosemary Bromley Literary Agency

Avington, Near Winchester SO21 1DB
☎01962 779656 Fax 01962 779656

juvenilia@clara.co.uk

Contact *Rosemary Bromley*

Founded 1981. Handles non-fiction. Scripts for TV and radio by existing clients only. No poetry or short stories. Special interests: natural history, leisure, biography and cookery. CLIENTS include Elisabeth Beresford, Linda Birch, Teresa Collard, estate of Fanny Cradock, Glenn Hamilton, Cathy Hopkins, Keith West, John Wingate. COMMISSION Home 10%; US 15%; Translation 20%. No unsolicited mss. Client list is currently full. No fax, telephone or e-mail enquiries. Send preliminary letter with full details. Enquiries unaccompanied by return postage will not be answered.

Jenny Brown Associates

42 The Causeway, Edinburgh EH15 3PZ
☎0131 620 1556 Fax 0131 620 1556
jenny-brown@blueyonder.co.uk
www.jennybrownassociates.com

Contact *Jenny Brown*

Founded 2002. Handles literary fiction, non-fiction and women''s fiction. Not interested in science fiction, fantasy or academic. CLIENTS include Des Dillon, Jenny Erdal, Diana Hendry, Anne Macleod, Laura Marney, Janet Morgan, Tom Pow, Suhayl Saadi, Christopher Whyte. COMMISSION Home 10%; US & Translation 20%. Works with The Marsh Agency. Approach in writing with letter, synopsis and first two chapters. Include c.v. and s.a.e.

Felicity Bryan★

2A North Parade, Banbury Road, Oxford OX2 6LX
☎01865 513816 Fax 01865 310055

Agents *Felicity Bryan, Catherine Clarke*
Contact *Michele Topham*

Founded 1988. Handles fiction of various types and non-fiction with emphasis on history, biography, science and current affairs. No scripts for TV, radio or theatre. No crafts, how-to, science fiction or light romance. CLIENTS include Karen Armstrong, Simon Blackburn, Michael Buerk, Humphrey Carpenter, Artemis Cooper, Isla Dewar, A.C. Grayling, Julie Hearn, Angela Huth, Liz Kessler, Diarmaid MacCulloch, Sue MacGregor, James Naughtie, John Julius Norwich, Gemma O'Connor, Iain Pears, Robin Pilcher, Rosamunde Pilcher, Matt Ridley, Miriam Stoppard, Roy Strong, John Sulston, Eleanor Updale. COMMISSION Home 10%; US & Translation 20%. OVERSEAS ASSOCIATES

Andrew Nurnberg, Europe; several agencies in US. No unsolicited mss. Best approach by letter. No reading fee.

The Buckman Agency

Ryman's Cottages, Little Tew OX7 4JJ
☎01608 683677 Fax 01608 683449
r.buckman@talk21.com *or*
j.buckman@talk21.com

Partners *Rosie Buckman, Jessica Buckman*

Founded in the early 1970s, the agency specialises in foreign rights and represents leading authors and agents from the UK and US. COMMISSON 20% (including sub-agent's commission). No unsolicited mss.

Brie Burkeman★

14 Neville Court, Abbey Road, London NW8 9DD
☎0709 223 9113 Fax 0709 223 9111
brie.burkeman@mail.com

Contact *Brie Burkeman*

Founded 2000. Handles commercial and literary full-length fiction and non-fiction. Film and theatre scripts. No academic, text, poetry, short stories, musicals or short films. Also associated with Serafina Clarke Ltd and independent film/TV consultant to literary agents. CLIENTS include Richard Askwith, Alexandra Crew, Kitty Ferguson, Joanne Harris, Shaun Hutson, David Savage, Gerald Wilson. COMMISSION Home 15%; Overseas 20%. Unsolicited e-mail attachments will be deleted without opening. No reading fee but return postage essential.

Juliet Burton Literary Agency

2 Clifton Avenue, London W12 9DR
☎020 8762 0148 Fax 020 8743 8765
julietburton@virgin.net

Contact *Juliet Burton*

Founded 1999. Handles fiction and non-fiction. Special interests crime and women's fiction. No plays, film scripts, articles, poetry or academic material. COMMISSION Home 10%; US & Translation 20%. Approach in writing in the first instance; send synopsis and two sample chapters with s.a.e. No e-mail submissions. No unsolicited mss. No reading fee.

Campbell Thomson & McLaughlin Ltd★

1 King's Mews, London WC1N 2JA
☎020 7242 0958 Fax 020 7242 2408

Contacts *John McLaughlin, Charlotte Bruton*

Founded 1931. Handles fiction and general non-fiction, excluding children's. No plays, film/TV scripts, articles, short stories or poetry. OVERSEAS ASSOCIATES Fox Chase Agency, Pennsylvania; Raines & Raines, New York. No unsolicited mss or synopses. Preliminary letter with s.a.e. essential. No reading fee.

Capel & Land Ltd*

29 Wardour Street, London W1D 6PS
☎020 7734 2414 Fax 020 7734 8101
✉ robert@capelland.co.uk

Contact *Georgina Capel*

Handles fiction and non-fiction. Also film, TV, theatre and radio scripts. CLIENTS Kunal Basu, Julie Burchill, John Gimlette, Andrew Greig, Dr Tristram Hunt, Henry Porter, Andrew Roberts, Simon Sebag Montefiore, Diana Souhami, Louis Theroux, Lucy Wadham. COMMISSION Home, US & Translation 15%. Send sample chapters and synopsis with covering letter in the first instance. No reading fee.

Casarotto Ramsay and Associates Ltd

National House, 60–66 Wardour Street, London W1V 3HP
☎020 7287 4450 Fax 020 7287 9128
✉ agents@casarotto.uk.com
www.casarotto.uk.com

Film/TV/Radio *Jenne Casarotto, Tracey Hyde, Charlotte Kelly, Jodi Shields, Chris Cope, Elinor Burns, Miriam James*
Stage *Tom Erhardt, Mel Kenyon*

Handles scripts for TV, theatre, film and radio. CLIENTS include: **Theatre** Alan Ayckbourn, Caryl Churchill, Christopher Hampton, David Hare, Sarah Kane estate, Mark Ravenhill. **Film** Laura Jones, Neil Jordan, Nick Hornby, Shane Meadows, Purvis & Wade, Lynne Ramsay. **TV** Paul Abbott, Howard Brenton, Amy Jenkins, Susan Nickson, Jessica Stevenson. COMMISSION Home 10%. OVERSEAS ASSOCIATES worldwide. No unsolicited material without preliminary letter.

Celia Catchpole

56 Gilpin Avenue, London SW14 8QY
☎020 8255 7200 Fax 020 8288 0653

Contact *Celia Catchpole*

Founded 1996. Handles children's books – artists and writers. No TV, film, radio or theatre scripts. No poetry. COMMISSION Home 10% (writers) 15% (artists); US & Translation 20%. Works with associate agents abroad. No unsolicited mss.

Chapman & Vincent*

The Mount, Sun Hill, Royston SG8 9AT
☎01763 245005 Fax 01763 243033
✉ info@chapmanvincent.co.uk

Contacts *Jennifer Chapman, Gilly Vincent*

A small agency whose clients come mainly from personal recommendation. The agency looks after only a limited number of predominantly non-fiction writers and is not actively seeking clients but happy to consider really original work. Does not handle poetry, thrillers, adventure, children's books or genre fiction. CLIENTS include George Carter, Leslie Geddes-Brown, Sara George, Rowley Leigh. COMMISSION Home 15%; US & Europe 20%. Please do not telephone or submit by fax or e-mail. Write with two sample chapters and enclose s.a.e.

Mic Cheetham Literary Agency

11–12 Dover Street, London W1S 4LJ
☎020 7495 2002 Fax 020 7495 5777
www.miccheetham.com

Contacts *Mic Cheetham, Simon Kavanagh*

Established 1994. Handles general and literary fiction, crime and science fiction, and some specific non-fiction. No film/TV scripts apart from existing clients. No children's, illustrated books or poetry. CLIENTS include Iain Banks, Carol Birch, Anita Burgh, Laurie Graham, M. John Harrison, Toby Litt, Ken MacLeod, China Miéville, Antony Sher, Janette Turner Hospital. COMMISSION Home 10–15%; US & Translation 20%. Works with The Marsh Agency for all translation rights. No unsolicited mss. Approach in writing with publishing history, first two chapters and return postage. No reading fee.

Judith Chilcote Agency*

8 Wentworth Mansions, Keats Grove, London NW3 2RL
☎020 7794 3717
✉ judybks@aol.com

Contact *Judith Chilcote*

Founded 1990. Handles commercial fiction, TV tie-ins, health and nutrition, self-help, popular psychology, biography and celebrity autobiography and current affairs. COMMISSION Home 15%; Overseas 20–25%. *No* academic, science fiction, children's, short stories, film scripts or poetry. *No approaches by e-mail.* Send letter with c.v., synopsis, three chapters and s.a.e. for return. No reading fee.

Teresa Chris Literary Agency Ltd★

43 Musard Road, London W6 8NR
☎020 7386 0633

Contact *Teresa Chris*

Founded 1989. Handles crime, general, women's, commercial and literary fiction, and non-fiction: history, biography, health, cookery, lifestyle, sport and fitness, gardening, etc. Specialises in crime fiction and commercial women's fiction. No scripts. Film and TV rights handled by co-agent. No poetry, short stories, fantasy, science fiction or horror. CLIENTS include Stephen Booth, Susan Clark, Tamara McKinley, Marquerite Patten, Danuta Reah, Kate Tremayne. COMMISSION Home 10%; US 15%; Translation 20%. OVERSEAS ASSOCIATES Thompson & Chris Literary Agency, USA; representatives in most other countries. Unsolicited mss welcome. Send query letter with first two chapters plus two-page synopsis (s.a.e. *essential*) in first instance. No reading fee.

Mary Clemmey Literary Agency★

6 Dunollie Road, London NW5 2XP
☎020 7267 1290 Fax 020 7267 1290

Contact *Mary Clemmey*

Founded 1992. Handles fiction and non-fiction – high-quality work with an international market. No science fiction, fantasy or children's books. TV, film, radio and theatre scripts from existing clients only. US clients: Frederick Hill Bonnie Nadell Inc., Lynn C. Franklin Associates Ltd, The Miller Agency, Roslyn Targ, Weingel-Fidel Agency Inc. COMMISSION Home 10%; US & Translation 20%. OVERSEAS ASSOCIATE Elaine Markson Literary Agency, New York. No unsolicited mss. Approach by letter only in the first instance giving a description of the work (include s.a.e.). No reading fee.

Clissitt Michie Agency Ltd

22 Shinfield Street, London W12 0HN
☎020 8932 5629 Fax 020 8932 5629
✉ info@cmagency.co.uk
www.cmagency.co.uk

Contacts *Sappho Clissitt* (books), *Annie Michie* (scripts)

Founded 2002. Handles general fiction and non-fiction, film and TV scripts. No theatre or radio scripts, no popular science, science fiction, technical or business books. CLIENTS include film scriptwriters Louis Mellis and David Scinto. COMMISSION Home (books) 15%, (film) 10%; US (books) 20%, (film) 13%; Translation 20% Unsolicited mss welcome.

Send covering letter, synopsis, approx first 50 pages and s.a.e.

Jonathan Clowes Ltd★

10 Iron Bridge House, Bridge Approach, London NW1 8BD
☎020 7722 7674 Fax 020 7722 7677

Contacts *Ann Evans, Lisa Whadcock*

Founded 1960. Pronounced 'clewes'. Now one of the biggest fish in the pond, and not really for the untried unless they are true high-flyers. Fiction and non-fiction, plus scripts. No textbooks or children's. Special interests: situation comedy, film and television rights. CLIENTS include David Bellamy, Bill Dare, Len Deighton, Elizabeth Jane Howard, David Lawrence, Doris Lessing, David Nobbs, Gillian White and the estate of Kingsley Amis. COMMISSION Home & US 15%; Translation 19%. OVERSEAS ASSOCIATES Andrew Nurnberg Associates; Sane Töregard Agency. No unsolicited mss; authors come by recommendation or by successful follow-ups to preliminary letters.

Elspeth Cochrane Personal Management

14/2 Second Floor, South Bank Commercial Centre, 140 Battersea Park Road, London SW11 4NB
☎020 7622 0314 Fax 020 7622 5815
✉ info@ecpma.com

Contact *Elspeth Cochrane*

Founded 1960. Handles fiction, non-fiction, biographies, screenplays and plays. No children's fiction. CLIENTS include Alex Jones, Dominic Leyton, Royce Ryton, F.E. Smith, Robert Tanitch, Gerald Vaughn-Hughes. COMMISSION 12½%. No unsolicited mss. Preliminary letter, synopsis and s.a.e. in the first instance. No reading fee.

Rosica Colin Ltd

1 Clareville Grove Mews, London SW7 5AH
☎020 7370 1080 Fax 020 7244 6441

Contact *Joanna Marston*

Founded 1949. Handles all full-length mss, plus theatre, film, television and sound broadcasting but few new writers being accepted. COMMISSION Home 10%; US 15%; Translation 20%. Preliminary letter with return postage essential; writers should outline their writing credits and whether their mss have previously been submitted elsewhere. May take 3–4 months to consider full mss; synopsis preferred in the first instance. No reading fee.

Conville & Walsh Limited★

2 Ganton Street, London W1F 7QL
☎020 7287 3030 Fax 020 7287 4545
✉ firstname@convilleandwalsh.com

Directors *Clare Conville, Patrick Walsh* (book rights), *Sam North* (film/TV rights), *Peter Tallack* (popular science)

Established in 2000 by Clare Conville (ex-A.P. Watt) and Patrick Walsh (ex-Christopher Little Literary Agency). Handles literary and commercial fiction plus serious and narrative non-fiction. Clare Conville also represents many successful children's authors. Particularly interested in scientists, historians and journalists. CLIENTS John Burningham, Kate Cann, Helen Castor, Tom Conran, Michael Cordy, Mike Dash, Professor John Emsley, Steve Erikson, Katy Gardner, Sarah Hall, Christopher Hart, Dermot Healy, James Holland, Tom Holland, Sebastian Horsley, David Huggins, Guy Kennaway, Daren King, Manjit Kumar, P.J. Lynch, Hector Macdonald, Mark Mason, Harland Miller, Joshua Mowll, Jacqui Murhall, Ruth Padel, D.B.C. Pierre, Rebecca Ray, Patrick Redmond, Candace Robb, Mark Sanderson, Saira Shah, Tahir Shah, Nicky Singer, Simon Singh, Doron Swade, Dr Richard Wiseman, Adam Wishart, Isabel Wolff and the estate of Francis Bacon. COMMISSION Home 15%; US & Translation 20%.

Jane Conway-Gordon Ltd★

1 Old Compton Street, London W1D 5JA
☎020 7494 0148 Fax 020 7287 9264

Contact Jane Conway-Gordon

Founded 1982. Works in association with Andrew Mann Ltd. Handles fiction and general non-fiction. No poetry or science fiction. COMMISSION Home 15%; US & Translation 20%. OVERSEAS ASSOCIATES McIntosh & Otis, Inc., New York; plus agencies throughout Europe and Japan. Unsolicited mss welcome; preliminary letter and return postage essential. No reading fee.

Rupert Crew Ltd★

1A King's Mews, London WC1N 2JA
☎020 7242 8586 Fax 020 7831 7914
✉ rupertcrew@compuserve.com *(correspondence only)*

Contacts Doreen Montgomery, Caroline Montgomery

Founded 1927. International representation, handling volume and subsidiary rights in fiction and non-fiction properties. No plays or poetry, journalism or short stories, science fiction or fantasy. COMMISSION Home 15%; Elsewhere 20%. Preliminary letter and return postage essential. No reading fee.

Curtis Brown Group Ltd★

Haymarket House, 28/29 Haymarket, London SW1Y 4SP
☎020 7393 4400 Fax 020 7393 4401
✉ cb@curtisbrown.co.uk

Group Managing Director *Jonathan Lloyd*
Financial Director *Mark Collingbourne*
Australia: Managing Director *Fiona Inglis*
Books, London *Jonny Geller, Peter Robinson* (Joint MDs, Books Division), *Jonathan Lloyd, Ali Gunn, Camilla Hornby, Anthea Morton-Saner, Jonathan Pegg, John Saddler, Vivienne Schuster, Janie Swanson, Euan Thorneycroft*
Foreign Rights *Kate Cooper, Carol Jackson, Diana Mackay*
Film/TV/Theatre *Nick Marston* (MD, Media Division), *Ben Hall, Joe Phillips, Tally Garner*
Actors/Presenters *Jacquie Drewe, Maxine Hoffman, Sarah MacCormick, Sarah Spears, Claire Stannard, Catherine Tapsell-Jenkin, Frances Williams*

Founded 1899. Agents for the negotiation in all markets of novels, general non-fiction, children's books and associated rights (including multimedia) as well as film, theatre, TV and radio scripts. COMMISSION Home 15%; Overseas 20%. OVERSEAS ASSOCIATES in Australia, Canada and the US. Outline for non-fiction and short synopsis for fiction with two – three sample chapters and autobiographical note. No reading fee. Return postage essential. Also represents playwrights, film and TV writers and directors, theatre directors and designers, TV and radio presenters and actors.

Judy Daish Associates Ltd

2 St Charles Place, London W10 6EG
☎020 8964 8811 Fax 020 8964 8966

Contacts Judy Daish, Sara Stroud, Tracey Elliston

Founded 1978. Theatrical literary agent. Handles scripts for film, TV, theatre and radio. No books. Preliminary letter essential. No unsolicited mss.

Caroline Davidson Literary Agency

5 Queen Anne's Gardens, London W4 1TU
☎020 8995 5768 Fax 020 8994 2770

Contact Caroline Davidson

Founded 1988. Handles fiction and non-fiction, including archaeology, architecture, art, astronomy, biography, design, gardening, health, history, medicine, natural history, reference, science. CLIENTS Peter Barham, Nigel Barlow, Andrew Dalby, Emma Donoghue, Cindy Engel, Chris Greenhalgh, Tom Jaine, Huon Mallalieu, Brÿ Sharma, Linda Sonntag. COMMISSION US, Home, Commonwealth & Translation 12½%; 20% if sub-agents are involved. Finished, polished first novels positively welcomed. No occult, short stories, children's, plays or poetry. Writers should send an initial letter giving details of their project and/or book proposal, including the first 50 pages of their novel if a fiction writer, together with c.v. and s.a.e. Submissions without the latter are not considered or returned.

Merric Davidson Literary Agency

12 Priors Heath, Goudhurst, Cranbrook TN17 2RE
☎01580 212041 Fax 01580 212041
✉ authors@mdla.co.uk

Contacts *Merric Davidson, Wendy Suffield*

Founded 1990. Handles fiction. No scripts. No academic, short stories or articles. CLIENTS include Alys Clare, Francesca Clementis, Murray Davies, Alison Habens, Frankie Park, Simon Scarrow. COMMISSION Home 10%; US 15%; Translation 20%. No unsolicited mss. Send preliminary letter with synopsis and biographical details. S.a.e. essential for response. No reading fee.

Felix de Wolfe

Garden Offices, 51 Maida Vale, London W9 1SD
☎020 7289 5770 Fax 020 7289 5731
✉ info@felixdewolfe.com

Contact *Felix de Wolfe*

Founded 1938. Handles quality fiction only, and scripts. No non-fiction or children's. CLIENTS include Jan Butlin, Robert Cogo-Fawcett, Jeff Dowson, Carolina Giametta, Brian Glover, Sheila Goff, Aileen Gonsalves, John Kershaw, Bill MacIlwraith, Angus Mackay, Gerard McLarnon, Braham Murray, Julian Slade, Malcolm Taylor, David Thompson, Paul Todd, Dolores Walshe. COMMISSION Home 12½%; US 20%. No unsolicited mss. No reading fee.

The Dench Arnold Agency

10 Newburgh Street, London W1F 7RN
☎020 7437 4551 Fax 020 7439 1355
www.dencharnold.co.uk

Contacts *Elizabeth Dench, Michelle Arnold*

Founded 1972. Handles scripts for TV and film. CLIENTS include Peter Chelsom. COMMISSION Home 10–15%. OVERSEAS ASSOCIATES include: William Morris/Sanford Gross and C.A.A., Los Angeles. Unsolicited mss will be read, but a letter with sample of work and c.v. (plus s.a.e.) is preferred.

Dorian Literary Agency (DLA)★

Upper Thornehill, 27 Church Road, St Marychurch, Torquay TQ1 4QY
☎01803 312095 Fax 01803 312095

Contact *Dorothy Lumley*

Founded 1986. Handles general fiction for adults, specialising in popular fiction: women's (from romance, historicals to contemporary); crime (from historical to noir and thrillers); science fiction, fantasy (but cautious about humorous/soft fantasy, i.e. unicorns), dark fantasy and horror. CLIENTS include Gillian Bradshaw, Stephen Jones, Brian Lumley, Amy Myers, Rosemary Rowe, Lyndon Stacey. COMMISSION Home 10–12½% for new clients; US 15%; Translation 20–25%. Works with agents in most countries for translation. 'Reading only very selectively.' No poetry, drama, short stories or autobiography. Introductory letter with outline and 1–3 chapters (with return postage/s.a.e.) only, please. No enquiries or submissions by fax or e-mail. No reading fee.

Toby Eady Associates Ltd

9 Orme Court, London W2 4RL
☎020 7792 0092 Fax 020 7792 0879
✉ toby@tobyeady.demon.co.uk *or*
jessica@tobyeady.demon.co.uk
www.tobyeadyassociates.co.uk

Contacts *Toby Eady, Jessica Woollard*

Handles fiction, and non-fiction. Special interests: China, Middle East, Africa, India. CLIENTS include Nada Awar Jarrar, Julia Blackburn, Mark Burnell, Robert Carter, Bernard Cornwell, Rana Dasgupta, Fadia Faqir, Xiaolu Guo, Liu Hong, Wei Hui, Francesca Marciano, Rachel Seiffert, Ann Wroe, John Carey, Kuki Gallmann, Julia Lovell, Robert Macfarlane, Kanan Makiya, Linda Polman, Fiammetta Rocco, Deborah Scroggins, Samia Serageldin, Xinran Xue. COMMISSION Home 15%; Elsewhere 20%. OVERSEAS ASSOCIATES France: La Nouvelle Agence; Holland: Jan Michael; Italy, Spain, Portugal and Scandinavia: The Buckman Agency; China: Joanne Wang; Eastern Europe/Russia: Prava I Prevodi; Czech

Republic: Kristin Olson; Hungary: Katai & Bolza; Greeve: JLM. Approach by personal recommendation. No film/TV scripts or poetry.

Eddison Pearson Ltd
10 Corinne Road, London N19 5EY
☎020 7700 7763 Fax 020 7700 7866
✉ info@eddisonpearson.com

Contact *Clare Pearson*

Founded 1995. Handles children's books and scripts, literary fiction and non-fiction, poetry. COMMISSION Home 10%; US & Translation 15%. Please enquire in writing, enclosing s.a.e. E-mail enquiries also welcome. In the first instance a brief writing sample rather than complete ms is preferred. No reading fee.

Edwards Fuglewicz★
49 Great Ormond Street, London WC1N 3HZ
☎020 7405 6725 Fax 020 7405 6726

Contacts *Ros Edwards, Helenka Fuglewicz, Julia Forrest*

Founded 1996. Handles literary and commercial fiction (not children's, science fiction, horror or fantasy); non-fiction: biography, history, popular culture. COMMISSION Home 15%; US & Translation 20%. No unsolicited mss or e-mail submissions.

Faith Evans Associates★
27 Park Avenue North, London N8 7RU
☎020 8340 9920 Fax 020 8340 9410

Founded 1987. Small agency. Handles fiction and non-fiction. No scripts. CLIENTS Melissa Benn, Shyam Bhatia, Cherie Booth, Eleanor Bron, Carolyn Cassady, Caroline Conran, Helen Falconer, Alicia Foster, Midge Gillies, Ed Glinert, Cate Haste, Jim Kelly, Helena Kennedy, Seumas Milne, Tom Paulin, Sheila Rowbotham, the estate of Lorna Sage, Rebecca Stott, Harriet Walter, Elizabeth Wilson. COMMISSION Home 15%; US & Translation 20%. OVERSEAS ASSOCIATES worldwide. New clients by personal recommendation only; no unsolicited mss or phone calls, please.

Lisa Eveleigh Literary Agency★
3rd Floor, 11/12 Dover Street, London W1S 4LJ
☎020 7399 2803 Fax 020 7399 2801
✉ Eveleigh@dial.pipex.com

Contact *Lisa Eveleigh*

Founded 1996. Handles literary and commercial fiction and non-fiction. No plays, scripts or poetry, science fiction or horror. CLIENTS include Christina Balit, Philip Casey, Paul Heiney, Lisa Kopper, Irma Kurtz, Jonathan Meres, Libby Purves, Lori Reid, Grace Wynne-Jones. COMMISSION Home 15%; US & Translation 20%. Send synopsis with covering letter and c.v. rather than full mss. No reading fee but return postage essential. Please restrict e-mail contact to preliminary letter only.

John Farquharson★
See **Curtis Brown Group Ltd**

Film Rights Ltd
See **Laurence Fitch Ltd**

Laurence Fitch Ltd
Mezzanine, Quadrant House, 80–82 Regent Street, London W1B 5AU
☎020 7734 9911
✉ information@laurencefitch.com
www.laurencefitch.com

Contact *Brendan Davis*

Founded 1952, incorporating the London Play Company (1922) and in association with Film Rights Ltd (1932). Handles children's and horror books, scripts for theatre, film, TV and radio only. CLIENTS include Carlo Ardito, Hindi Brooks, John Chapman & Ray Cooney, Dave Freeman, John Graham, Robin Hawdon, Glyn Robbins, Lawrence Roman, John Rooney, Gene Stone, the estate of Dodie Smith, Edward Taylor. COMMISSION UK 10%; Overseas 15%. OVERSEAS ASSOCIATES worldwide. No unsolicited mss. Send synopsis with sample scene(s) in the first instance. No reading fee.

Jill Foster Ltd
9 Barb Mews, Brook Green, London W6 7PA
☎020 7602 1263 Fax 020 7602 9336
✉ agents@jflagency.com

Contacts *Jill Foster, Alison Finch, Simon Williamson, Dominic Lord, Gary Wild*

Founded 1976. Handles scripts for TV, drama and comedy. No fiction, short stories or poetry. CLIENTS include Ian Brown, Jan Etherington and Gavin Petrie, Phil Ford, Nev Fountain and Tom Jaimeson, Rob Gittins, Jenny Lecoat, Jim Pullin and Fraser Steele, Pete Sinclair, Peter Tilbury, Susan Wilkins. COMMISSION Home 12½%; Books, US & Translation 15%. No unsolicited mss; approach by letter in the first instance. No approaches by e-mail. No reading fee.

Fox & Howard Literary Agency

4 Bramerton Street, London SW3 5JX
☎020 7352 8691 Fax 020 7352 8691
Contacts *Chelsey Fox, Charlotte Howard*

Founded 1992. A small agency, specialising in non-fiction, that prides itself on 'working closely with its authors'. Handles biography, history and popular culture, reference, business, mind, body and spirit, health and fitness. COMMISSION Home 15%; US & Translation 20%. No unsolicited mss; send letter and synopsis with s.a.e. for response. No reading fee.

Fraser Ross Associates

6 Wellington Street, Edinburgh EH6 7EQ
☎0131 553 2759/657 4412
✉ lindsey.fraser@tiscali.co.uk *and* kjross@tiscali.co.uk
Contact *Lindsey Fraser, Kathryn Ross*

Founded 2002. Handles children's books, adult literary and mainstream fiction. No poetry, short stories, adult fantasy and science fiction, academic, scripts. CLIENTS Alison Bartlett, Chris Fisher, Vivian French, Magi Gibson, Julie Lacome, Michaela Morgan, Shoo Rayner, Dee Shulman. COMMISSION Home 10%; USA & Translation 20%. Unsolicited material welcome; send preliminary letter, first three chapters or equivalent, c.v. and s.a.e. No reading fee.

Futerman, Rose & Associates★

Heston Court Business Estate, 19 Camp Road, London SW19 4UW
☎020 8947 0188 Fax 020 8605 2162
✉ guy@futermanrose.co.uk
www.futermanrose.co.uk
Contact *Guy Rose*

Founded 1984. Handles scripts for film and TV. Commercial fiction and non-fiction with film potential; biography and show business, teenage fiction. No science fiction or fantasy. CLIENTS include Iain Duncan Smith, Royston Ellis, Adam Hamdy, Pal Hendy, Russell Warren Howe, Rev. Joanna Jepson, Sue Lenier, Eric MacInnes, Tony Prince, Gordon Thomas, Simon Woodham, Michael Walker, Paul Rattigan, Mark White, Allen Zeleski. COMMISSION 15–20%. OVERSEAS ASSOCIATES worldwide. No unsolicited mss. Send preliminary letter with a brief resumé, detailed synopsis and s.a.e.

Jüri Gabriel

35 Camberwell Grove, London SE5 8JA
☎020 7703 6186 Fax 020 7703 6186
Contact *Jüri Gabriel*

Handles quality fiction and non-fiction and (almost exclusively for existing clients) film, TV and radio rights. Jüri Gabriel worked in television, wrote books for 20 years and is chairman of Dedalus publishers. No short stories, articles, verse or books for children. CLIENTS include Maurice Caldera, Diana Constance, Miriam Dunne, Pat Gray, Mikka Haugaard, Robert Irwin, John Lucas, David Madsen, Richard Mankiewicz, David Miller, Andy Oakes, John Outram, Philip Roberts, Dr Stefan Szymanski, Frances Treanor, Dr Terence White, Chris Wilkins, Dr Robert Youngson. COMMISSION Home 10%; US & Translation 20%. Unsolicited mss ('two-page synopsis and three sample chapters in first instance, please') welcome if accompanied by return postage and letter giving sufficient information about author's writing experience, aims, etc.

Eric Glass Ltd

25 Ladbroke Crescent, London W11 1PS
☎020 7229 9500 Fax 020 7229 6220
✉ eglassltd@aol.com
Contact *Janet Glass*

Founded 1934. Handles fiction, non-fiction and scripts for publication or production in all media. No poetry, short stories or children's works. CLIENTS include Pierre Chesnot, Charles Dyer, Henry Fleet, Tudor Gates, Ronald Millar, and the estates of Rodney Ackland, Marc Camoletti, Jean Cocteau, Wawick Deeping, William Douglas Home, Philip King, Robin Maugham, Beverley Nichols, Jack Popplewell, Jean-Paul Sartre. COMMISSION Home 15%; US & Translation 20%. OVERSEAS ASSOCIATES in the US, Australia, France, Germany, Greece, Holland, Italy, Japan, Poland, Scandinavia, South Africa, Spain. No unsolicited mss. Return postage required. No reading fee.

David Godwin Associates

55 Monmouth Street, London WC2H 9DG
☎020 7240 9992 Fax 020 7395 6110
✉ assistant@davidgodwinassociates.co.uk
www.davidgodwinassociates.co.uk
Contact *David Godwin*

Founded 1996. Handles literary and general fiction, non-fiction, biography. No scripts, science fiction or children's. No reading fee. COMMISSION Home 10%; Overseas 20%. Send covering letter with first three chapters and s.a.e. for response.

Annette Green Authors' Agency★

1 East Cliff Road, Tunbridge Wells TN4 9AD
☎01892 514275 Fax 01892 518124
✉ annettekgreen@aol.com
www.annettegreenagency.co.uk

Contact *Address material to the Agency*

Founded 1998. Handles literary and general fiction and non-fiction, popular culture and current affairs, science, music, film, history, biography, children's and teenage fiction. No dramatic scripts or poetry. CLIENTS Andrew Baker, Nick Barlay, Bill Broady, Terry Darlington, Bernie Gaughan, Fiona Gibson, Emma Gold, Justin Hill, Maria McCann, Adam Macqueen, Ian Marchant, Professor Charles Pasternak, Owen Sheers, Elizabeth Woodcraft. COMMISSION Home 15%; US & Translation 20%. Letter, synopsis, sample chapters and s.a.e. essential. No reading fee.

Christine Green Authors' Agent★

6 Whitehorse Mews, Westminster Bridge Road, London SE1 7QD
☎020 7401 8844 Fax 020 7401 8860
✉ christine@christinegreen.co.uk
www.christinegreen.co.uk

Contact *Christine Green*

Founded 1984. Handles fiction (general and literary) and general non-fiction. No scripts, poetry or children's. COMMISSION Home 10%; US & Translation 20%. No unsolicited mss; initial letter and synopsis preferred. No reading fee but return postage essential.

Louise Greenberg Books Ltd★

The End House, Church Crescent, London N3 1BG
☎020 8349 1179 Fax 020 8343 4559
✉ louisegreenberg@msn.com

Contact *Louise Greenberg*

Founded 1997. Handles full-length literary fiction and serious non-fiction only. COMMISSION Home 15%; US & Translation 20%. DRAMATIC ASSOCIATE Micheline Steinberg Associates; CHILDREN'S ASSOCIATE Sarah Mason Literary Agent. No telephone approaches. No reading fee. S.a.e. essential.

Greene & Heaton Ltd★

37 Goldhawk Road, London W12 8QQ
☎020 8749 0315 Fax 020 8749 0318
www.greeneheaton.co.uk

Contacts *Carol Heaton, Judith Murray, Antony Topping, Linda Davis* (children's)

A medium-sized agency with a broad range of clients. Handles all types of fiction and non-fiction. No original scripts for theatre, film or TV. CLIENTS include Mark Barrowcliffe, Bill Bryson, Jan Dalley, Marcus du Sautoy, Hugh Fearnley-Whittingstall, Michael Frayn, P.D. James, William Leith, Mary Morrissy, C.J. Sansom, William Shawcross, Sarah Waters. COMMISSION Home 10–15%; US & Translation 20%. OVERSEAS ASSOCIATES worldwide. No reply to unsolicited submissions without s.a.e. and/or return postage.

Gregory & Company, Authors' Agents★ (formerly Gregory & Radice)

3 Barb Mews, London W6 7PA
☎020 7610 4676 Fax 020 7610 4686
✉ info@gregoryandcompany.co.uk
www.gregoryandcompany.co.uk

Contact *Jane Gregory*
Editorial *Anna Valdinger*
Rights Manager *Claire Morris*

Founded 1987. Handles all kinds of fiction and general non-fiction. Special interest fiction – literary, commercial, women's fiction, crime, suspense and thrillers. 'We are particularly interested in books which will also sell to publishers abroad.' No original plays, film or TV scripts (only published books are sold to film and TV). No science fiction, fantasy, poetry, academic or children's books. No reading fee. Editorial advice given to own authors. COMMISSION Home 15%; US, Translation, Radio/TV/Film 20%. Is well represented throughout Europe, Asia and US. No unsolicited mss; send a preliminary letter with c.v., synopsis, first three chapters and future writing plans (plus return postage). Short submissions by fax or e-mail in the first instance (max. five pages).

David Grossman Literary Agency Ltd

118b Holland Park Avenue, London W11 4UA
☎020 7221 2770 Fax 020 7221 1445

Contact *Submissions Dept.*

Founded 1976. Handles full-length fiction and general non-fiction – good writing of all kinds and anything healthily controversial. No verse or technical books for students. No original screenplays or teleplays (only works existing in volume form are sold for performance rights). Generally works with published writers of fiction only but 'truly original, well-written novels from beginners' will be considered.

...ON Rates vary for different markets. ...ASSOCIATES throughout Europe, ...zil and the US. Best approach by pre-...letter giving full description of the work and, in the case of fiction, with the first 50 pages. All material must be accompanied by return postage. No approaches or submissions by fax or e-mail. No unsolicited mss. No reading fee.

The Rod Hall Agency Limited
3 Charlotte Mews, London W1T 4DZ
☎020 7637 0706 Fax 020 7637 0807
✉ office@rodhallagency.com
www.rodhallagency.com

Contact *Charlotte Mann*

Founded 1997. Handles drama for film, TV and theatre and writers-directors. Does not represent writers of episodes for TV series where the format is provided but represents originators of series. CLIENTS include Simon Beaufoy (*The Full Monty*), Jeremy Brock (*Mrs Brown*), Liz Lochhead (*Perfect Days*), Martin McDonagh (*The Pillowman*), Simon Nye (*Men Behaving Badly*). COMMISSION Home 10%; US 15%; Translation 20%. No reading fee.

Margaret Hanbury Literary Agency★
27 Walcot Square, London SE11 4UB
☎020 7735 7680 Fax 020 7793 0316
✉ maggie@mhanbury.demon.co.uk

Contact *Margaret Hanbury*

Personally run agency representing quality fiction and non-fiction. No plays, scripts, poetry, children's books, fantasy, horror. CLIENTS include J.G. Ballard, Simon Callow, George Alagiah, Judith Lennox, Jane Glover, Jordan. COMMISSION Home 15%; Overseas 20%. No unsolicited approaches at present.

Roger Hancock Ltd
4 Water Lane, London NW1 8NZ
☎020 7267 4418 Fax 020 7267 0705
✉ info@rogerhancock.com

Material should be addressed to the Company

Founded 1960. Special interests: comedy drama and light entertainment. Scripts only. No books. COMMISSION Home 10%; Overseas 15%. Unsolicited mss not welcome. Initial phone call required. No reading fee.

Antony Harwood Limited
103 Walton Street, Oxford OX2 6EB
☎01865 559615 Fax 01865 310660
✉ mail@antonyharwood.com

Contacts *Antony Harwood, James Macdonald Lockhart*

Founded 2000. Handles fiction and non-fiction. CLIENTS Amanda Craig, Peter F. Hamilton, Alan Hollinghurst, A.L. Kennedy, Douglas Kennedy, Chris Manby, George Monbiot, Tim Parks. COMMISSION Home 15%; US & Translation 20%. Send letter and synopsis with return postage in the first instance. No reading fee.

A.M. Heath & Co. Ltd★
79 St Martin's Lane, London WC2N 4RE
☎020 7836 4271 Fax 020 7497 2561
www.amheath.com

Contacts *Bill Hamilton, Sara Fisher, Sarah Molloy, Victoria Hobbs*

Founded 1919. Handles fiction, general non-fiction and children's. No dramatic scripts, poetry or short stories. CLIENTS include Christopher Andrew, Bella Bathurst, Anita Brookner, Helen Cresswell, Patricia Duncker, Geoff Dyer, Katie Fforde, Lesley Glaister, Graham Hancock, Conn Iggulden, Hilary Mantel, Hilary Norman, Susan Price, John Sutherland, Adam Thorpe, Barbara Trapido. COMMISSION Home 10–15%; US & Translation 20%; Film & TV 15%. OVERSEAS ASSOCIATES in the US, Europe, South America, Japan and the Far East. Preliminary letter and synopsis essential. No reading fee.

Rupert Heath Literary Agency
The Beeches, Furzedown Lane, Amport SP11 8BW
☎01264 771899 Fax 020 7691 9331
✉ enquiries@rupertheath.com

Contact *Rupert Heath*

Founded 2000. Handles literary and general fiction and non-fiction, including history, biography and autobiography, current affairs, popular science, the arts and some popular culture. No scripts or poetry. COMMISSION Home 15%; US & Translation 20%. OVERSEAS ASSOCIATES worldwide. Approach with e-mail or letter (sample chapter and s.a.e.). E-mail submission preferred. No reading fee.

Henser Literary Agency
174 Pennant Road, Llanelli SA14 8HN
☎01554 753520
✉ henserliteraryagency@btopenworld.com

Contact *Steve Henser*

Founded 2002. Handles mystery, mainstream, literary fiction, fantasy, science fiction. Also film, TV, radio and theatre scripts. No horror. Specialises in translations from Japanese into English – especially literary fiction. CLIENTS include John Campbell, Mary Matsumoto. COMMISSION Home 15%; Foreign & Translation 20%. No unsolicited mss, synopses or ideas as not looking for additional clients at this time.

David Higham Associates Ltd★

5–8 Lower John Street, Golden Square, London W1F 9HA
☎020 7434 5900 Fax 020 7437 1072
✉ dha@davidhigham.co.uk
www.davidhigham.co.uk

Scripts *Nicky Lund, Georgina Ruffhead, Gemma Hirst*
Books *Anthony Goff, Bruce Hunter, Jacqueline Korn, Veronique Baxter, Caroline Walsh* (children's)

Founded 1935. Handles fiction, general non-fiction (biography, history, current affairs, etc.) and children's books. Also scripts. CLIENTS include John le Carré, Jonathan Dimbleby, Stephen Fry, Jane Green, James Herbert, Alexander McCall Smith, Jacqueline Wilson. COMMISSION Home 15%; US & Translation 20%. Preliminary letter with synopsis essential in first instance. No reading fee.

Vanessa Holt Ltd★

59 Crescent Road, Leigh-on-Sea SS9 2PF
☎01702 473787 Fax 01702 471890
✉ vanessa@holtlimited.freeserve.co.uk

Contact *Vanessa Holt*

Founded 1989. Handles general fiction, non-fiction and non-illustrated children's books. No scripts, poetry, academic or technical. Specialises in crime fiction, commercial and literary fiction, and particularly interested in books with potential for sales abroad and/or to TV. COMMISSION Home 15%; US & Translation 20%; Radio/TV/Film 15%. Represented in all foreign markets. No unsolicited mss. Approach by letter in first instance; s.a.e. essential. No reading fee.

Kate Hordern Literary Agency

18 Mortimer Road, Clifton, Bristol BS8 4EY
☎0117 923 9368 Fax 0117 973 1941
✉ katehordern@blueyonder.co.uk

Contact *Kate Hordern*

Founded 1999. Handles quality literary and commercial fiction including women's, suspense and genre fiction; also general non-fiction. CLIENTS Richard Bassett, Jeff Dawson, James Gray, Will Randall. COMMISSION Home 15%;

US & Translation 20%. OVERSEAS ASSOCIATES Carmen Balcells Agency, Spain; Synopsis Agency, Russia and various agencies in Asia. Approach in writing in the first instance with details of project. New clients taken on very selectively. Synopsis required for fiction; proposal/chapter breakdown for non-fiction. Sample chapters on request only. S.a.e. essential. No reading fee.

Valerie Hoskins Associates

20 Charlotte Street, London W1T 2NA
☎020 7637 4490 Fax 020 7637 4493
✉ vha@vhassociates.co.uk

Contacts *Valerie Hoskins, Rebecca Watson*

Founded 1983. Handles scripts for film, TV and radio. Special interests feature films, animation and TV. COMMISSION Home 12½%; US 20% (maximum). No unsolicited scripts; preliminary letter of introduction essential. No reading fee.

Tanja Howarth Literary Agency★

19 New Row, London WC2N 4LA
☎020 7240 5553 Fax 020 7379 0969
✉ tanja.howarth@virgin.net

Contact *Tanja Howarth*

Founded 1970. Interested in taking on both fiction and non-fiction from British writers. No children's books, plays or poetry, but all other subjects considered providing the treatment is intelligent. Also an established agent for foreign literature, particularly from the German language. COMMISSION Home 15%; Translation 20%. *No unsolicited mss.*

ICM

Oxford House, 76 Oxford Street, London W1D 1BS
☎020 7636 6565 Fax 020 7323 0101
✉ admin@icmlondon.co.uk

Contacts *Sue Rodgers, Jessica Sykes, Cathy King, Greg Hunt, Hugo Young, Michael McCoy, Duncan Heath, Paul Lyon-Maris*

Founded 1973. Specialises in scripts for film, theatre, TV and radio. No reading fee. COMMISSION 10%. OVERSEAS ASSOCIATES ICM, New York/Los Angeles.

ICM Books

International Creative Management Ltd, 4–6 Soho Square, London W1D 3PZ
☎020 7432 0800 Fax 020 7432 0808

Contact *Kate Jones*

Handles fiction and non-fiction; no plays or

scripts. OVERSEAS ASSOCIATE International Creative Management Inc., 40 West 57th Street, New York, NY 10019, USA. Send letter and sample chapters only in the first instance. No reading fee.

IMG Literary UK
The Pier House, Strand on the Green, London W4 3NN
☎020 8233 5000 Fax 020 8233 5001

IMG Literary US, 825 Seventh Avenue, Ninth Floor, New York, NY 10009
☎001 212 489 5400 Fax 001 212 246 1118

Agents *Sarah Wooldridge* (UK), *Bev Norwood*, *Lisa Queen* (US)

Handles celebrity books, commercial fiction, non-fiction, sports-related and how-to business books. No theatre, children's, poetry or academic books. COMMISSION Home 15%; US & Elsewhere 20%.

The Inspira Group
5 Bradley Road, Enfield EN3 6ES
☎020 8292 5163 Fax 0870 139 3057
✉ darin@theinspiragroup.com
www.theinspiragroup.com

Managing Director *Darin Jewell*

Founded 2001. Handles children's books, fiction, humour, lifestyle/relationships, science fiction/fantasy. No scripts. CLIENTS Paul Rogan, Jasmine Birtles, Mike Anderiesz. COMMISSION Home & US 15%. Unsolicited mss and synopses welcome; approach by e-mail or telephone. No reading fee.

Intercontinental Literary Agency*
33 Bedford Street, London WC2E 9ED
☎020 7379 6611 Fax 020 7379 6790
✉ ila@ila-agency.co.uk

Contacts *Nicki Kennedy, Sam Edenborough*

Founded 1965. Handles translation rights only for, among others, the authors of PFD, London; PFD, New York; LAW Ltd, London; Harold Matson Co. Inc., New York.

International Literary Representation & Management LLC
186 Bickenhall Mansions, Bickenhall Street, London W1U 6BX
☎020 7224 1748 Fax 020 7224 1802
✉ info@yesitive.com
www.yesitive.com

Vice President for Europe *Peter Cox*

European office of US agency. Represents authors with major international potential.

CLIENTS Martin Bell, OBE, Brian Clegg, Brian Cruver, Jeff Einstein, Senator Orrin Hatch, Commodore Scott Jones, USN, Josh McHugh, Michael J. Nelson, David Soul, Michelle Paver, Saxon Roach. COMMISSION by agreement. Submissions considered only if the guidelines given on the website have been followed. Do not send unsolicited mss by post. No radio or theatre scripts. No reading fee.

International Literary Rights & Management
18 Mill View Close, Ewell KT17 2DW
☎07866 713512
✉ MariaWhite2001@aol.com

Contact *Maria White*

Founded 2004. Small agency handling commercial and literary fiction and general non-fiction including history, biography, sports, popular science, popular culture, current affairs, cookery, narrative non-fiction, humour, health, fitness, self-help, mind/body/spirit, children's books. Illustrated and non-illustrated books considered. No science fiction, horror, poetry, short stories or plays. COMMISSION Home 15%; US & Translation 20%. Write in first instance with covering letter giving brief c.v., a synopsis and first three chapters together with s.a.e. No disks or e-mail submissions. No reading fee.

International Scripts
1A Kidbrooke Park Road, London SE3 0LR
☎020 8319 8666 Fax 020 8319 0801

Contacts *Bob Tanner, Pat Hornsey, Jill Lawson*

Founded 1979 by Bob Tanner. Handles most types of books (non-fiction and fiction) and scripts for most media. No poetry, articles or short stories. CLIENTS include Jane Adams, Zita Adamson, Ashleigh Bingham, Simon Clark, Dr James Fleming, Ed Gorman, Julie Harris, Robert A. Heinlein, Anna Jacobs, Anne Jones, Richard Laymon, Nick Oldham, Chris Pascoe, Christine Poulson, Mary Ryan, John and Anne Spencer, Janet Woods. COMMISSION Home 15%; US & Translation 20%. OVERSEAS ASSOCIATES include Ralph Vicinanza, USA; Thomas Schlück, Germany; Eliane Benisti, France. Preliminary letter plus s.a.e. required. An editorial contribution plus return postage may be requested for reading mss.

Barrie James Literary Agency (Including New Authors Showcase)
Rivendell, Kingsgate Close, Torquay TQ2 8QA
☎01803 326617

✉ mail@newauthors.org.uk
www.newauthors.org.uk

Contact *Barrie James*

Founded 1997. No unsolicited mss. First approach should be made by sending s.a.e. or e-mail. No reading fee but small charge is made for display on the Internet.

Janklow & Nesbit (UK) Ltd

29 Adam & Eve Mews, London W8 6UG
☎020 7376 2733 Fax 020 7376 2915
✉ queries@janklow.co.uk

Contacts *Tif Loehnis, Claire Paterson*

Founded 2000. Handles fiction and non-fiction; commercial and literary. (See also Janklow & Nesbit Associates, New York, under US Agents.) No unsolicited mss. Send full outline (non-fiction), synopsis and three sample chapters (fiction) plus informative covering letter and return postage.

Johnson & Alcock★

Clerkenwell House, 45–47 Clerkenwell Green, London EC1R 0HT
☎020 7251 0125 Fax 020 7251 2172
✉ info@johnsonandalcock.co.uk

Contacts *Michael Alcock, Andrew Hewson, Anna Power, Merel Reinink*

Founded 1956. Handles literary and commercial fiction, children's fiction; general non-fiction including current affairs, biography and memoirs, history, lifestyle, health and personal development. No poetry, screenplays, science fiction, technical or academic material. COMMISSION Home 15%; US & Translation 20%. No unsolicited mss; approach by letter in the first instance giving details of writing and other media experience, plus synopsis. For fiction send one-page synopsis and first three chaptes. S.a.e. essential for response. No reading fee.

Jane Judd Literary Agency★

18 Belitha Villas, London N1 1PD
☎020 7607 0273 Fax 020 7607 0623

Contact *Jane Judd*

Founded 1986. Handles general fiction and non-fiction: women's fiction, crime, thrillers, literary fiction, humour, biography, investigative journalism, health, women's interests and travel. 'Looking for good contemporary women's fiction but not Mills & Boon-type.' No scripts, academic, gardening, short stories or DIY. CLIENTS include Andy Dougan, Cliff Goodwin, Jill Mansell, Jonathon Porritt, Rosie Rushton, Manda Scott, David Winner.

COMMISSION Home 10%; US & Translation 20%. Approach with letter, including synopsis, first chapter and s.a.e. Initial telephone call helpful in the case of non-fiction.

Juvenilia

Avington, Near Winchester SO21 1DB
☎01962 779656 Fax 01962 779656
✉ juvenilia@clara.co.uk

Contact *Rosemary Bromley*

Founded 1973. Handles young/teen fiction and picture books; non-fiction and scripts for TV and radio by existing clients only. No poetry or short stories unless part of a collection or picture book material. CLIENTS include Paul Aston, Elisabeth Beresford, Linda Birch, Denis Bond, Terry Deary, Ann Evans, Gaye Hicyilmaz, Tony Maddox, Phil McMylor, Anna Perara, Elizabeth Pewsey, Fran and John Pickering, Saviour Pirotta, Eira Reeves, Kelvin Reynolds, James Riordan, Peter Riley, Susan Rollings, Malcolm Rose, Cathy Simpson, Keith West. COMMISSION Home 10%; US 15%; Translation 20%. No unsolicited mss. 'Client list is currently full.' Enquiries by phone, fax or e-mail will not be answered.

Tamar Karet Literary Agency

56 Priory Road, London N8 7EX
☎020 8340 6460 Fax 020 8348 8638
✉ tamar.karet.agent@btinternet.com

Contact *Tamar Karet*

Specialises in fiction, travel, leisure, health, cookery, biography, history, social affairs and politics. No academic, children's, poetry, science fiction, horror, militaria or scripts. COMMISSION Home 15%; US & Translation 20%. No unsolicited mss; no submissions by e-mail. Send synopsis and sample with s.a.e.

Michelle Kass Associates★

36–38 Glasshouse Street, London W1B 5DL
☎020 7439 1624 Fax 020 7734 3394

Contacts *Michelle Kass, Resham Naqvi*

Founded 1991. Handles literary fiction and film primarily. COMMISSION Home 10%; US & Translation 15–20%. Approach by telephone call in the first instance. No reading fee.

Frances Kelly★

111 Clifton Road, Kingston upon Thames KT2 6PL
☎020 8549 7830 Fax 020 8547 0051

Contact *Frances Kelly*

Founded 1978. Handles non-fiction, including

illustrated: biography, history, art, self-help, food & wine, complementary medicine and therapies, finance and business books; and academic non-fiction in all disciplines. No scripts except for existing clients. COMMISSION Home 10%; US & Translation 20%. No unsolicited mss. Approach by letter with brief description of work or synopsis, together with c.v. and return postage.

Knight Features
20 Crescent Grove, London SW4 7AH
☎020 7622 1467 Fax 020 7622 1522
✉ peter@knightfeatures.co.uk

Contacts *Peter Knight, Samantha Ferris, Gaby Martin, Andrew Knight*

Founded 1985. Handles motor sports, cartoon books, puzzles, business, history, factual and biographical material. No poetry, science fiction or cookery. CLIENTS include Frank Dickens, Gray Jolliffe, Angus McGill, Chris Maslanka, Barbara Minto. COMMISSION dependent upon authors and territories. OVERSEAS ASSOCIATES United Media, US; Auspac Media, Australia; Puzzle Co., New Zealand. No unsolicited mss and no e-mail submissions. Send letter accompanied by c.v. and s.a.e. with synopsis of proposed work.

LAW★
14 Vernon Street, London W14 0RJ
✉ firstname@lawagency.co.uk

Contacts *Mark Lucas, Julian Alexander, Araminta Whitley, Alice Saunders, Celia Hayley, Lucinda Cook, Peta Nightingale, Hannah Bellamy, Philippa Milnes-Smith* (children's), *Helen Mulligan* (children's)

Founded 1996. Handles full-length commercial and literary fiction, non-fiction and children's books. No fantasy (except children's), plays, poetry or textbooks. Film and TV scripts handled for established clients only. COMMISSION Home 15%; US & Translation 20%. OVERSEAS ASSOCIATES worldwide. Unsolicited mss considered; send brief covering letter, short synopsis and two sample chapters. S.a.e. essential. No e-mailed or disk submissions.

Cat Ledger Literary Agency★
20–21 Newman Street, London W1T 1PG
☎020 7861 8226 Fax 020 7861 8001

Contact *Cat Ledger*

Founded 1996. Handles non-fiction: popular culture – film, music, sport, travel, humour, biography, politics; investigative journalism;

fiction (non-genre). No scripts. No children's, poetry, fantasy, science fiction, romance. COMMISSION Home 10%; US & Translation 20%. No unsolicited mss; approach with preliminary letter, synopsis and s.a.e. No reading fee.

Barbara Levy Literary Agency★
64 Greenhill, Hampstead High Street, London NW3 5TZ
☎020 7435 9046 Fax 020 7431 2063

Contacts *Barbara Levy, John Selby*

Founded 1986. Handles general fiction, non-fiction, and film and TV rights. COMMISSION Home 10%; US 20%; Translation by arrangement, in conjunction with The Marsh Agency. US ASSOCIATE Arcadia Ltd, New York. No unsolicited mss. Send detailed preliminary letter in the first instance. No reading fee.

Limelight Management★
33 Newman Street, London W1T 1PY
☎020 7637 2529 Fax 020 7637 2538
✉ limelight.management@virgin.net
www.limelightmanagement.com

Contacts *Fiona Lindsay, Linda Shanks*

Founded 1991. Handles general non-fiction: cookery, gardening, antiques, interior design, wine, art and crafts and health. No fiction, TV, film, radio or theatre. Specialises in illustrated books. COMMISSION Home 15%; US & Translation 20%. Unsolicited mss welcome; send preliminary letter (s.a.e. essential). No reading fee.

The Christopher Little Literary Agency★
10 Eel Brook Studios, 125 Moore Park Road, London SW6 4PS
☎020 7736 4455 Fax 020 7736 4490
✉ christopher@christopherlittle.net or firstname@christopherlittle.net
www.christopherlittle.net

Contacts *Christopher Little, Kellee Nunley, Emma Schlesinger, Neil Blair* (legal)

Founded 1979. Handles commercial and literary full-length fiction and non-fiction. No poetry, plays, science fiction, fantasy, textbooks, illustrated children's or short stories. Film scripts for established clients only. AUTHORS include Steve Barlow and Steve Skidmore, Paul Bajoria, Andrew Butcher, Will Daws, Janet Gleeson, Carol Hughes, Alastair MacNeill, Robert Mawson, Haydn Middleton,

A.J. Quinnell, Robert Radcliffe, J.K. Rowling, Darren Shan, Wladyslaw Szpilman, John Watson. COMMISSION Home 15%; US, Canada, Translation, Audio & Motion Picture 20%. Send detailed preliminary letter in the first instance with synopsis, first 2–3 chapters and s.a.e. No reading fee.

London Independent Books

26 Chalcot Crescent, London NW1 8YD
☎020 7706 0486 Fax 020 7724 3122

Proprietor *Carolyn Whitaker*

Founded 1971. A self-styled 'small and idiosyncratic' agency. Handles fiction and non-fiction reflecting the tastes of the proprietor. All subjects considered (except computer books and young children's), providing the treatment is strong and saleable. Scripts handled only if by existing clients. Special interests: boats, travel, travelogues, commercial fiction, science fiction and fantasy. COMMISSION Home 15%; US & Translation 20%. No unsolicited mss; letter, synopsis and first two chapters with return postage the best approach. No reading fee.

The Andrew Lownie Literary Agency★

17 Sutherland Street, London SW1V 4JU
☎020 7828 1274 Fax 020 7828 7608
✉ lownie@globalnet.co.uk
www.andrewlownie.co.uk

Contact *Andrew Lownie*

Founded 1988. Specialises in non-fiction, especially history, biography, current affairs, military history, UFOs, reference and packaging celebrities and journalists for the book market. No poetry, short stories or science fiction. Formerly a journalist, publisher and himself the author of 12 non-fiction books, Andrew Lownie's CLIENTS include Richard Aldrich, Juliet Barker, the Joyce Cary estate, Tom Devine, Peter Evans, Jonathan Fryer, Laurence Gardner, Timothy Good, Robert Holden, Gloria Hunniford, Lawrence James, Robert Jobson, Leo McKinstry, Julian Maclaren-Ross estate, Patrick MacNee, Norma Major, Sir John Mills, Tom Pocock, Nick Pope, John Rae, Richard Rudgley, Desmond Seward, David Stafford, Alan Whicker, Lawrence James, editors of the *Oxford Classical Dictionary* and *Cambridge Guide to Literature in English*. Translation rights handled by The Marsh Agency. COMMISSION Worldwide 15%. Approach with letter, synopsis, sample chapter and s.a.e.

Lucas Alexander Whitley

See **LAW**

Lutyens and Rubinstein★

231 Westbourne Park Road, London W11 1EB
☎020 7792 4855 Fax 020 7792 4833

Partners *Sarah Lutyens, Felicity Rubinstein*
Submissions *Susannah Godman*

Founded 1993. Handles adult fiction and non-fiction books. No TV, film, radio or theatre scripts. COMMISSION Home 15%; US & Translation 20%. Unsolicited mss accepted; send introductory letter, c.v., two chapters and return postage for all material submitted. No reading fee.

Duncan McAra

28 Beresford Gardens, Edinburgh EH5 3ES
☎0131 552 1558 Fax 0131 552 1558
✉ duncanmcara@hotmail.com

Contact *Duncan McAra*

Founded 1988. Handles fiction (literary fiction) and non-fiction, including art, architecture, archaeology, biography, military, travel and books of Scottish interest. COMMISSION Home 10%; Overseas 20%. Preliminary letter, synopsis and sample chapter (including return postage) essential. No reading fee.

Bill McLean Personal Management Ltd

23B Deodar Road, London SW15 2NP
☎020 8789 8191

Contact *Bill McLean*

Founded 1972. Handles scripts for all media. No books. CLIENTS include Dwynwen Berry, Graham Carlisle, Pat Cumper, Jane Galletly, Patrick Jones, Tony Jordan, Bill Lyons, John Maynard, Michael McStay, Les Miller, Ian Rowlands, Jeffrey Segal, Richard Shannon, Ronnie Smith, Barry Thomas, Garry Tyler, Frank Vickery, Laura Watson, Mark Wheatley. COMMISSION Home 10%. No unsolicited mss. Phone call or introductory letter essential. No reading fee.

Eunice McMullen Children's Literary Agent Ltd

Low Ibbotsholme Cottage, Off Bridge Lane, Troutbeck Bridge, Windermere LA23 1HU
☎01539 448551 Fax 01539 442289
✉ eunicemcmullen@totalise.co.uk

Contact *Eunice McMullen*

Founded 1992. Handles all types of children's

material in particular picture books. Has 'an excellent' list of picture book authors and illustrators. CLIENTS include Wayne Anderson, Sam Childs, Caroline Jayne Church, Jason Cockcroft, Ross Collins, Siobhan Dodds, Charles Fuge, Susie Jenkin-Pearce, Angela McAllister, David Melling, Sue Porter, Susan Winter, David Wood. COMMISSION Home 10%; US 15%; Translation 20%. *No unsolicited scripts.* Telephone enquiries only.

Andrew Mann Ltd★
1 Old Compton Street, London W1D 5JA
☎020 7734 4751 Fax 020 7287 9264
✉ manscript@onetel.net.uk

Contacts *Anne Dewe, Tina Betts, Sacha Elliot*

Founded 1975. Handles fiction, general non-fiction, children's and film, TV, theatre, radio scripts. COMMISSION Home 15%; US & Translation 20%. OVERSEAS ASSOCIATES various. No unsolicited mss. Preliminary letter, synopsis and s.a.e. essential. E-mail submissions for synopses only. No reading fee.

Sarah Manson Literary Agent
6 Totnes Walk, London N2 0AD
☎020 88442 0396
✉ info@smliteraryagent.com

Contact *Sarah Manson*

Founded 2002. Handles quality fiction for children and young adults. COMMISSION Home 10%; Overseas & Translation 20%. Brief e-mail enquiry or preliminary letter with s.a.e. No reading fee.

Marjacq Scripts Ltd
34 Devonshire Place, London W1G 6JW
☎020 7935 9499 Fax 020 7935 9115
✉ subs@marjacq.com
www.marjacq.com

Contact *Philip Patterson* (books), *Luke Speed* (film/TV)

Handles fiction and non-fiction, literary and commercial as well as film, TV, radio scripts. No poetry. COMMISSION Home 10%; Overseas 20%. New work welcome; send brief letter, synopsis and approx. first 50 pages plus s.a.e. No reading fee.

The Marsh Agency Ltd★
11/12 Dover Street, London W1S 4LJ
☎020 7399 2800 Fax 020 7399 2801
✉ enquiries@marsh-agency.co.uk
www.marsh-agency.co.uk

Contacts *Paul Marsh, Chris Van Raaijen, Camilla Perrier*

Founded 1994. International rights specialists selling English and foreign language writing. No TV, film, radio or theatre. CLIENTS include several British and American agencies and publishers, and some individual authors. See also Paterson Marsh Ltd. Submissions by e-mail preferred, synopsis and sample chapters.

Martinez Literary Agency
60 Oakwood Avenue, Southgate, London N14 6QL
☎020 8886 5829

Contacts *Mary Martinez, Francoise Budd*

Founded 1988. Handles high-quality fiction, children's books, arts and crafts, interior design, autobiography, biography, popular music, sport and memorabilia books. COMMISSION Home 15%; US, Overseas & Translation 20%; Performance Rights 20%. Not accepting any new writers.

MBA Literary Agents Ltd★
62 Grafton Way, London W1T 5DW
☎020 7387 2076 Fax 020 7387 2042
✉ firstname@mbalit.co.uk

Contacts *Diana Tyler, John Richard Parker, Meg Davis, Laura Longrigg, David Riding*

Founded 1971. Handles fiction and non-fiction, TV, film, radio and theatre scripts. Works in conjunction with agents in most countries. Also UK representative for Writers House, Inc, the Donald Maass Agency, Frances Collin Literary Agency, Martha Millard Literary Agency, Montreal–Contacts/the Rights Agency and the JABberwocky Agency. COMMISSION Home 15%; Overseas 20%; Theatre/TV/Radio 10%; Film 10–20%. No unsolicited mss.

Christy Moore Ltd
See **Sheil Land Associates Ltd**

William Morris Agency (UK) Ltd★
52/53 Poland Street, London W1F 7LX
☎020 7534 6800 Fax 020 7534 6900
www.wma.com

Managing Director *Stephanie Cabot*

London office founded 1965. Worldwide theatrical and literary agency with offices in New York, Beverly Hills and Nashville and associates in Sydney. Handles fiction, general non-fiction, TV and film scripts. COMMISSION TV 10%; UK Books 15%; US Books & Translation 20%. Mss for books including s.a.e. with preliminary letter to Book Department. No reading fee.

Michael Motley Ltd

The Old Vicarage, Tredington, Tewkesbury GL20 7BP
☎01684 276390 Fax 01684 297355

Contact *Michael Motley*

Founded 1973. Handles only full-length mss (i.e. 60,000+). No short stories or journalism. No science fiction, horror, poetry or original dramatic material. COMMISSION Home 10%; US 15%; Translation 20%. OVERSEAS ASSOCIATES in all publishing centres. New clients by referral only: no unsolicited material considered. No reading fee.

Judith Murdoch Literary Agency★

19 Chalcot Square, London NW1 8YA
☎020 7722 4197

Contact *Judith Murdoch*

Founded 1993. Handles full-length fiction only, especially accessible literary and commercial women's fiction. No thrillers, science fiction/ fantasy, children's, poetry or short stories. CLIENTS include Meg Hutchinson, Lisa Jewell, Pamela Jooste. Translation rights handled by The Marsh Agency. COMMISSION Home 15%; US & Translation 20%. No unsolicited mss; approach in writing only enclosing first two chapters and brief synopsis. Return postage/s.a.e. essential. Editorial advice given. No reading fee.

The Narrow Road Company

182 Brighton Road, Coulsdon CR5 2NF
☎020 8763 9895 Fax 020 8763 9329
✉ coulsdon@narrowroad.co.uk

Contacts *Richard Ireson, James Ireson*

Founded 1986. Part of the Narrow Road Group. Theatrical literary agency. Handles scripts for TV, theatre, film and radio. No novels or poetry. CLIENTS include Helen Blizard, Vanessa Brooks, Steve Gooch, David Halliwell, Ian Kershaw, Lara Moon, Marty Ross, Andy Smith. No unsolicited mss; approach by letter with c.v. Interested in writers with some experience and original ideas.

William Neill-Hall Ltd

Old Oak Cottage, Ropewalk, Mount Hawke, Truro TR4 8DW
☎01209 891427 Fax 01209 891427
✉ wneill-hall@msn.com

Contact *William Neill-Hall*

Founded 1995. Handles general non-fiction,

religion. No TV, film, theatre or radio scripts; no fiction or poetry. Specialises in religion. CLIENTS Mary Batchelor, George Carey, Richard Foster, Selwyn Hughes, Juliet Janvrin, Jennifer Rees Larcombe, Eugene Peterson, David Pytches, Mary Pytches, Philip Yancey. COMMISSION Home 10%; US 15%; Translation 20%. No unsolicited mss. Approach by phone or letter. Enclose return postage. No reading fee.

The Maggie Noach Literary Agency★

22 Dorville Crescent, London W6 0HJ
☎020 8748 2926 Fax 020 8748 8057
✉ m-noach@dircon.co.uk

Contact *Maggie Noach*

Founded 1982. Pronounced 'no-ack'. Handles a wide range of well-written books including general non-fiction, especially biography, commercial fiction and non-illustrated children's books for ages 7–12. No scientific, academic or specialist non-fiction. No poetry, plays, short stories or books for the very young. Recommended for promising young writers but *very* few new clients taken on as it is considered vital to give individual attention to each author's work. COMMISSION Home 15%; US & Translation 20%. Unsolicited mss not welcome. Approach by letter (*not by telephone or e-mail*), giving a brief description of the book and enclosing a few sample pages. Return postage essential. No reading fee.

Andrew Nurnberg Associates Ltd★

Clerkenwell House, 45–47 Clerkenwell Green, London EC1R 0QX
☎020 7417 8800 Fax 020 7417 8812
✉ all@nurnberg.co.uk

Directors *Andrew Nurnberg, Sarah Nundy, D. Roger Seaton, Vicky Mark*

Founded in the mid-1970s. Specialises in foreign rights, representing leading authors and agents. Branches in Moscow, Budapest, Prague, Sofia, Warsaw, Riga, Beijing, Shanghai and Taipei. COMMISSION Home 15%; US & Translation 20%.

Alexandra Nye

'Craigower', 6 Kinnoull Avenue, Dunblane FK15 9JG
☎01786 825114

Contact *Alexandra Nye*

Founded 1991. Handles fiction and topical non-fiction. Special interests: literary fiction and history. CLIENTS include Dr Tom Gallagher, Harry Mehta, Robin Jenkins. COMMISSION Home 10%; US 20%; Translation 15%. Unsolicited mss welcome (s.a.e. essential for return). No phone calls. Preliminary approach by letter, with synopsis, preferred, Reading fee for supply of detailed report.

David O'Leary Literary Agents
10 Lansdowne Court, Lansdowne Rise, London W11 2NR
☎020 7229 1623 Fax 020 7229 1623
✉ d.o'leary@virgin.net

Contact *David O'Leary*

Founded 1988. Handles fiction, both popular and literary, and non-fiction. Areas of interest include thrillers, history, popular science, Russia and Ireland (history and fiction). No poetry or science fiction. CLIENTS David Crackanthorpe, James Kennedy, Nick Kochan, Jim Lusby, Derek Malcolm, Ken Russell. COMMISSION Home & US 10%. OVERSEAS ASSOCIATES Lennart Sane, Scandinavia/Spain/ South America; Tuttle Mori, Japan. No unsolicited mss but happy to discuss a proposal. Ring or write in the first instance. No reading fee.

Deborah Owen Ltd★
78 Narrow Street, Limehouse, London E14 8BP
☎020 7987 5119/5441 Fax 020 7538 4004

Contacts *Deborah Owen*

Founded 1971. Small agency specialising in representing authors direct around the world. Handles international fiction and non-fiction (books which can be translated into a number of languages). No new authors. CLIENTS Amos Oz and Delia Smith. COMMISSION Home 10%; US & Translation 15%.

Owen Robinson Literary Agents
20 Tolbury Mill, Bruton BA10 0DY
☎01749 812836 Fax 01749 812008
✉ jpr@owenrobinson.supanet.com *(enquiries only)*

Contact *Justin Robinson*

Founded 1998. Handles crime fiction and general non-fiction. No plays, film scripts, poetry or short stories. CLIENTS include Sarah Lawson, Chrissie Loveday, Roger Nichols, Alistair Owen, Dr Thomasz Witkowski, Rich Zubaty. COMMISSION Home 10%; US & Translation 15–20%. Works with agents overseas. No unsolicited mss. Approach by e-mail in the first instance. No reading fee.

Paterson Marsh Ltd★
11/12 Dover Street, London W1S 4LJ
☎020 7399 2800 Fax 020 7399 2801
✉ steph@patersonmarsh.co.uk
www.patersonmarsh.co.uk

Contacts *Mark Paterson* (☎01206 825433; ✉ mark@patersonmarsh.co.uk), *Paul Marsh, Stephanie Ebdon*

Formerly Mark Paterson & Associates, founded 1961. World rights representatives of authors and publishers handling many subjects, with specialisation in psychoanalysis and psychotherapy. CLIENTS range from Balint, Bion, Casement and Ferenczi, through to Freud and Winnicott; plus Hugh Brogan, Peter Moss and the estates of Sir Arthur Evans, Hugh Schonfield and Dorothy Richardson. No fiction, scripts, poetry, children's, articles, short stories or 'unsaleable mediocrity'. COMMISSION 20% (including sub-agent's commission). No unsolicited mss, but preliminary letter and synopsis with s.a.e. welcome.

John Pawsey
60 High Street, Tarring, Worthing BN14 7NR
☎01903 205167 Fax 01903 205167

Contact *John Pawsey*

Founded 1981. Experience in the publishing business has helped to attract some top names here, but the door remains open for bright, new ideas. Handles non-fiction: biography, politics, current affairs, popular culture, travel, sport, business; also fiction: crime, thrillers, suspense but not science fiction, fantasy or horror. Special interests: sport and biography. No children's, drama scripts, poetry, short stories, journalism or academic. CLIENTS include David Rayvern Allen, David Ashforth, Jennie Bond, Elwyn Hartley Edwards, William Fotheringham, Don Hale, Patricia Hall, Dr David Lewis, Anne Mustoe. COMMISSION Home 12½%; US & Translation 19–25%. OVERSEAS ASSOCIATES in the US, Japan, South America and throughout Europe. Preliminary letter with s.a.e. essential. No reading fee.

Maggie Pearlstine Associates Ltd★
31 Ashley Gardens, Ambrosden Avenue, London SW1P 1QE
☎020 7828 4212 Fax 020 7834 5546
✉ post@pearlstine.co.uk

Contact *Maggie Pearlstine*

Founded 1989. Small, selective agency. Handles general non-fiction and fiction. Special interests: history, current affairs, biography and health. No children's, poetry, horror, science fiction, short stories or scripts. Seldom takes on new authors. CLIENTS Debbie Beckerman, John Biffen, Matthew Baylis, Kate Bingham, Menzies Campbell, Robin Cook, Frank Dobson, Kim Fletcher, Toby Green, Roy Hattersley, Rachel Holmes, Charles Kennedy, Mark Leonard, Eleanor Mills, Claire Macdonald, Dr Raj Persaud, Prof. Lesley Regan, Hugo Rifkind, Winifred Robinson, Henrietta Spencer-Churchill, Prof. Alan Stewart, Prof. Robert Winston. Translation rights handled by Gillon Aitken Associates Ltd. COMMISSION Home 12½% (fiction), 10% (non-fiction); US & Translation 20%; TV, Film & Journalism 20%. Prospective clients should write an explanatory letter and enclose s.a.e. and the first chapter only. No submissions accepted by fax, e-mail or from abroad. No reading fee.

Peters Fraser & Dunlop Group Ltd
See **PFD**

PFD★
Drury House, 34–43 Russell Street, London WC2B 5HA
☎020 7344 1000
Fax 020 7836 9539/7836 9541
✉ postmaster@pfd.co.uk
www.pfd.co.uk
Joint Chairmen *Anthony Jones, Tim Corrie*
Managing Director *Anthony Baring*
Books *Caroline Dawnay, Michael Sissons, Pat Kavanagh, Charles Walker, Rosemary Canter, Robert Kirby, Simon Trewin, James Gill*
Serial *Pat Kavanagh, Carol MacArthur*
Film/TV *Anthony Jones, Tim Corrie, Norman North, Charles Walker, St. John Donald, Rosemary Scoular, Natasha Galloway, Jago Irwin, Louisa Thompson, Lynda Mamy*
Actors *Maureen Vincent, Dallas Smith, Lindy King, Ruth Young, Lucy Brazier, Kathryn Fleming*
Theatre *Kenneth Ewing, St John Donald, Nicki Stoddart, Rosie Cobbe*
Children's *Rosemary Canter*
Multimedia *Rosemary Scoular*

Founded 1988 as a result of the merger of A. D. Peters & Co. Ltd and Fraser & Dunlop, and was later joined by the June Hall Literary Agency. Handles all sorts of books including fiction and children's, plus scripts for film, theatre, radio and TV material. CLIENTS include Julian Barnes, Alan Bennett, Alain de Botton, A.S. Byatt, estate of C.S. Forester, Nicci Gerrard, Robert Harris, Nick Hornby, Clive James, Russell Miller, estate of Nancy Mitford, John Mortimer, Andrew Motion, Douglas Reeman, Ruth Rendell,

Anthony Sampson, Gerald Seymour, Tom Stoppard, Emma Thompson, Joanna Trollope, estate of Evelyn Waugh. COMMISSION Home 10%; US & Translation 20%. Prospective clients should write 'a full letter, with an account of what he/she has done and wants to do and enclose, when possible, a detailed outline and sample chapters'. Screenplays and TV scripts should be addressed to the 'Film & Script Dept.' Enclose s.a.e. No reading fee. The Children's Dept. accepts unsolicited written material in the form of a covering letter, brief plot summary and one paragraph only of text; submissions from illustrators also welcome

Pollinger Limited★
9 Staple Inn, London WC1V 7QH
☎020 7404 0342 Fax 020 7242 5737
✉ info@pollingerltd.com *and* Permissions: permissions@pollingerltd.com
www.pollingerltd.com
Chairman *Paul Woolf*
Managing Director *Lesley Pollinger*
Agents *Lesley Pollinger, Joanna Devereux*
Rights Manager *Katy Loffman*
Consultants *Leigh Pollinger, Joan Deitch*

Founded 2002. A successor of Laurence Pollinger Limited (founded 1958) and Pearn, Pollinger & Higham. Handles all types of general trade adult and children's fiction and non-fiction books; intellectual property development, illustrators/photographers. CLIENTS include Derry Brabbs, Michael Coleman, Teresa Driscoll, Catherine Fisher, Philip Gross, Catherine Johnson, Gary Latham, Gary Paulsen, Nicholas Rhea and Sue Welford. Also the estates of H.E. Bates, Vera Chapman, Louis Bromfield, Erskine Caldwell, D.H. Lawrence, John Masters, W.H. Robinson, Eric Frank Russell, Clifford D. Simak and other notables. COMMISSION Home 15%; Translation 20%. Overseas theatrical, and media associates. No unsolicited material.

Shelley Power Literary Agency Ltd★
13 rue du Pré Saint Gervais, 75019 Paris, France
☎00 33 1 42 38 36 49
Fax 00 33 1 40 40 70 08
✉ shelley.power@wanadoo.fr
Contact *Shelley Power*

Founded 1976. Shelley Power works between London and Paris. This is an English agency with London-based administration/accounts office and the editorial office in Paris. Handles general commercial fiction, quality fiction, business books, self-help, true crime, investigative exposés, film and entertainment. No scripts, short stories, children's or poetry. COMMISSION Home 10%; US & Translation 19%. Preliminary letter with brief outline of project (plus return postage as from UK or France) essential. 'We do not consider submissions by e-mail.' No reading fee.

Elizabeth Puttick
Literary Agency★
46 Brookfield Mansions, Highgate Hill West, London N6 6AT
☎020 8340 6383 Fax 0870 751 8098
✉ agency@puttick.com
www.puttick.com
Contact *Liz Puttick*

Founded 1995. Handles general non-fiction (including illustrated books) with special interest in self-help, mind-body-spirit, health and fitness, lifestyle, business. Also interested in narrative non-fiction, biography, history, philosophy, science, humour, and popular culture. No fiction, poetry, scripts, drama or children's books. CLIENTS include William Bloom, Cornel Chin, Mike Fisher, Ann-Marie Gallagher, Ross Heaven, Nirmala Heriza, Martin Lewis, Steve Nobel, Emma Restall Orr, Ed and Deb Shapiro. COMMISSION Home 15%; US & Translation 20%. Works with associates in the US and with The Marsh Agency for translation rights. Preliminary enquiries and c.v. by post or e-mail. No reading fee, but s.a.e. essential.

PVA Management Limited
Hallow Park, Worcester WR2 6PG
☎01905 640663 Fax 01905 641842
✉ books@pva.co.uk
Managing Director *Paul Vaughan*

Founded 1978. Handles non-fiction only. COMMISSION 15%. Send synopsis and sample chapters together with return postage.

Real Creatives Worldwide
14 Dean Street, London W1D 3RS
☎020 7437 4188
✉ malcolm.rasala@realcreatives.com
Contacts *Mark Maco, Malcolm Rasala*

Founded 1984. Specialises in drama, science, technology, factual and entertainment. Represents Hollywood TV/film writers and directors, as well as designers, editors, producers and composers. Has a production arm making motion pictures, television, etc. 'Send letter or e-mail

requesting a writer's submission agreement covering libel, defamation, plagiarism, etc.' Reading fee: £125.

Rogers, Coleridge & White Ltd★
20 Powis Mews, London W11 1JN
☎020 7221 3717 Fax 020 7229 9084

Contacts *Deborah Rogers, Gill Coleridge, Patricia White, Peter Straus, David Miller, Zoe Waldie, Peter Straus*
Foreign Rights *Laurence Laluyaux, Stephen Edwards*

Founded 1967. Handles fiction, non-fiction and children's books. No TV or film scripts, plays or technical books. Rights representative in UK and translation for several New York agents. COMMISSION Home 10%; US & Translation 20%. OVERSEAS ASSOCIATE Melanie Jackson Agency, New York. No unsolicited mss, please and no submissions by fax or e-mail.

Uli Rushby-Smith Literary Agency
72 Plimsoll Road, London N4 2EE
☎020 7354 2718 Fax 020 7354 2718
Contact *Uli Rushby-Smith*

Founded 1993. Handles fiction and non-fiction, commercial and literary, both adult and children's. Film and TV rights handled in conjunction with a sub-agent. No plays or poetry. COMMISSION Home 15%; US & Translation 20%. Represents UK rights for Curtis Brown, New York (children's), 2.13.61 USA, Penguin (Canada), Alice Toledo Agency (NL) and Columbia University Press. Approach with an outline, two or three sample chapters and explanatory letter in the first instance (s.a.e. essential). No disks. No reading fee.

Rosemary Sandberg Ltd
6 Bayley Street, London WC1B 3HB
☎020 7304 4110 Fax 020 7304 4109
✉ rosemary@sandberg.demon.co.uk
Contact *Rosemary Sandberg*

Founded 1991. In association with Ed Victor Ltd. Specialises in children's writers and illustrators. COMMISSION 10%. No unsolicited mss as client list is currently full.

The Sayle Literary Agency★
Bickerton House, 25–27 Bickerton Road, London N19 5JT
☎020 7263 8681 Fax 020 7561 0529
Proprietor *Rachel Calder*

Handles fiction, crime and general. Non-fiction: current affairs, social issues, travel, biographies, historical. No plays, poetry, children's, text-books, technical, legal or medical books. CLIENTS Stephen Amidon, Billy Bragg, Pete Davies, Margaret Forster, Georgina Hammick, Andy Kershaw, Phillip Knightley, Denise Mina, Malcolm Pryce, Kate Pullinger, Ronald Searle, Gitta Sereny, Stanley Stewart, William Styron. COMMISSION Home 15%; US & Translation 20%. OVERSEAS ASSOCIATES Dunow & Carlson Literary Agency; Darhansoff, Verrill and Feldman; Anne Edelstein Literary Agency; Sally Wofford-Girand Agency; New England Publishing Associates, USA; translation rights handled by The Marsh Agency; film rights by Sayle Screen Ltd. No unsolicited mss. Preliminary letter essential, including a brief biographical note and a synopsis plus two or three sample chapters. Return postage essential. No reading fee.

Sayle Screen Ltd
11 Jubilee Place, London SW3 3TD
☎020 7823 3883 Fax 020 7823 3363
✉ info@saylescreen.com
www.saylescreen.com
Agents *Jane Villiers, Matthew Bates, Toby Moorcroft*

Specialises in writers and directors for film and television. Also deals with theatre and radio. Works in association with the Sayle Literary Agency and Greene & Heaton Ltd representing film and TV rights in novels and non-fiction. CLIENTS include Shelagh Delaney, Marc Evans, Margaret Forster, Rob Green, Mark Haddon, Christopher Monger, Paul Morrison, Gitta Sereny, Sue Townsend. No unsolicited material without preliminary letter.

The Sharland Organisation Ltd
The Manor House, Manor Street, Raunds NN9 6JW
☎01933 626600 Fax 01933 624860
✉ tsoshar@aol.com
www.sharlandorganisation.co.uk
Contacts *Mike Sharland, Alice Sharland*

Founded 1988. Specialises in national and international film and TV negotiations. Also negotiates multimedia, interactive TV deals and computer game contracts. Arranges and negotiates speaking engagements for major authors. Handles scripts for film, TV, radio and theatre; also non-fiction. Markets books for film and handles stage, radio, film and TV rights for authors. No scientific, technical or poetry. COMMISSION Home 15%; US & Translation

20%. OVERSEAS ASSOCIATES various. No unsolicited mss. Preliminary enquiry by letter or phone essential.

Sheil Land Associates Ltd★ ✓✓✓
(incorporating **Richard Scott Simon Ltd 1971** and **Christy Moore Ltd 1912**)
43 Doughty Street, London WC1N 2LH
☎020 7405 9351 Fax 020 7831 2127
✉ info@sheilland.co.uk
Agents, UK & US *Sonia Land, Luigi Bonomi, Vivien Green, Amanda Preston*
Film/Theatrical/TV *John Rush, Roland Baggott*
Foreign *Amelia Cummins, Vanessa Forbes*

Founded 1962. Handles full-length general, commercial and literary fiction and non-fiction, including: social politics, business, history, science, military history, gardening, thrillers, crime, romance, drama, biography, travel, cookery and humour, UK and foreign estates. Also theatre, film, radio and TV scripts. CLIENTS include Peter Ackroyd, Hugh Bicheno, Melvyn Bragg, Stephanie Calman, David Cohen, Catherine Cookson estate, Anna del Conte, Seamus Deane, Alan Drury, Erik Durschmied, Alan Garner, Bonnie Greer, Susan Hill, Richard Holmes, HRH The Prince of Wales, John Humphries, Mark Irving, Simon Kernick, James Long, Richard Mabey, Colin McDowell, Patrick O'Brian estate, Esther Rantzen, Pam Rhodes, Jean Rhys estate, Richard and Judy, Martin Riley, Colin Shindler, Tom Sharpe, Martin Stephen, Brian Sykes, Jeffrey Tayler, Alan Titchmarsh, Rose Tremain, Phil Vickery, John Wilsher, Toby Young. COMMISSION Home 15%; US & Translation 20%. OVERSEAS ASSOCIATES Georges Borchardt, Inc. (Richard Scott Simon). UK representatives for Farrar, Straus & Giroux, Inc. US film and TV representation: CAA, APA, and others. Welcomes approaches from new clients either to start or to develop their careers. Preliminary letter with s.a.e. essential. No reading fee.

Caroline Sheldon Literary Agency★
Thorley Manor Farm, Thorley, Yarmouth, Isle of Wight PO41 0SJ
☎01983 760205
Also at: 71 Hillgate Place, London W8 7SS
Contact *Caroline Sheldon*

Founded 1985. Handles adult fiction, in particular women's, both commercial and literary novels. Also full-length children's fiction. No non-fiction, TV/film scripts unless by book-writing clients. COMMISSION Home 10%; US & Translation 20%. Submissions should be sent to Isle of Wight address. Send letter with all relevant details of ambitions and first four chapters of proposed book (enclose large s.a.e.). No reading fee.

Dorie Simmonds Agency*

67 Upper Berkeley Street, London W1H 7QX
☎020 7486 9228 Fax 020 7486 8228
✉ dhsimmonds@aol.com

Contact *Dorie Simmonds*

Handles a wide range of subjects including general non-fiction and commercial fiction, children's books and associated rights. Specialities include contemporary personalities and historical biographies. COMMISSION Home & US 15%; Translation 20%. Outline required for non-fiction; a short synopsis for fiction with 2–3 sample chapters, and a c.v. with writing experience/publishing history. No reading fee. Return postage essential.

Jeffrey Simmons

15 Penn House, Mallory Street, London NW8 8SX
☎020 7224 8917 Fax 020 7224 8918
✉ jas@london-inc.com

Contact *Jeffrey Simmons*

Founded 1978. Handles biography and autobiography, cinema and theatre, fiction (both quality and commercial), history, law and crime, politics and world affairs, parapsychology and sport (but not exclusively). No science fiction/ fantasy, children's books, cookery, crafts, hobbies or gardening. Film scripts handled only if by book-writing clients. Special interest in personality books of all sorts and fiction from young writers (i.e. under 40) with a future. COMMISSION Home 10–15%; US & Foreign 15%. Writers become clients by personal introduction or by letter, enclosing a synopsis if possible, a brief biography, a note of any previously published books, plus a list of any publishers and agents who have already seen the mss.

Richard Scott Simon Ltd

See **Sheil Land Associates Ltd**

Sinclair-Stevenson

3 South Terrace, London SW7 2TB
☎020 7581 2550 Fax 020 7581 2550

Contact *Christopher Sinclair-Stevenson*

Founded 1995. Handles biography, current affairs, travel, history, fiction, the arts. No scripts, children's, academic, science fiction/fantasy.

CLIENTS include Jennifer Johnston, J.D.F. Jones, Ross King, Christopher Lee, Andrew Sinclair and the estates of Alec Guinness, John Cowper Powys and John Galsworthy. COMMISSION Home 10%; US 15%; Translation 20%. OVERSEAS ASSOCIATE T.C. Wallace Ltd, New York. Translation rights handled by David Higham Associates. Send synopsis with s.a.e. in the first instance. No reading fee.

Robert Smith Literary Agency Ltd*

12 Bridge Wharf, 156 Caledonian Road, London N1 9UU
☎020 7278 2444 Fax 020 7833 5680
✉ robertsmith.literaryagency@virgin.net

Contact *Robert Smith*

Founded 1997. Handles non-fiction; biography, health and nutrition, cookery, lifestyle, show-business and true crime. No scripts, fiction, poetry, academic or children's books. CLIENTS Martin Allen, Carol Clerk, Stewart Evans, Neil and Christine Hamilton, James Haspiel, Roberta Kray, Norman Parker, Nikola Pleasence, Mike Reid, Professor Bill Rubinstein, Keith Skinner, Douglas Thompson. COMMISSION Home 15%; US & Translation 20%. OVERSEAS ASSOCIATE Thomas Schlück Literary Agency (Germany). No unsolicited mss. Send a letter and synopsis in the first instance. No reading fee.

Standen Literary Agency

41b Endymion Road, London N4 1EQ
☎020 8245 3053 Fax 020 8245 3053
✉ yasmin@standenliteraryagency.com
www.standenliteraryagency.com

Contact *Yasmin Standen*

Founded 2004. Handles fiction, both adult and children's. No thrillers, non-fiction, academic. Interested in first time writers. COMMISSION Home 15%; Overseas 20%. See website for submissions procedure.

Elaine Steel

110 Gloucester Avenue, London NW1 8HX
☎020 8348 0918 Fax 020 8341 9807
✉ ecmsteel@aol.com

Contact *Elaine Steel*

Founded 1986. Handles scripts, screenplays and books. No technical or academic. CLIENTS include Les Blair, Anna Campion, Michael Eaton, Pearse Elliott, Gwyneth Hughes, Brian Keenan, Troy Kennedy Martin, Rob Ritchie, Albie Sachs, Ben Steiner. COMMISSION Home 10%; US & Translation 20%. Initial phone call preferred.

Abner Stein*

10 Roland Gardens, London SW7 3PH
☎020 7373 0456 Fax 020 7370 6316

Contact *Arabella Stein*

Founded 1971. Mainly represents US agents and authors but handles some full-length fiction and general non-fiction. No scientific, technical, etc. No scripts. COMMISSION Home 10%; US & Translation 20%. Send letter and outline in the first instance rather than unsolicited mss.

Micheline Steinberg Associates

Fourth Floor, 104 Great Portland Street, London W1W 6PE
☎020 7631 1310 Fax 020 7631 1146
✉ info@steinplays.com

Contacts *Micheline Steinberg, Ginny Sennett, Rachel Taylor*

Founded 1988. Specialises in plays for stage, TV, radio and film. Dramatic associate for Pollinger Limited. COMMISSION Home 10%; Elsewhere 15%. Best approach by preliminary letter (with s.a.e.).

Shirley Stewart Literary Agency

3rd Floor, 21 Denmark Street, London WC2H 8NA
☎020 7836 4440 Fax 020 7836 3482

Director *Shirley Stewart*

Founded 1993. Handles literary fiction and non-fiction. No scripts, children's, science fiction, fantasy or poetry. COMMISSION Home 10%; US & Translation 20%. OVERSEAS ASSOCIATE Curtis Brown Ltd, New York. Will consider unsolicited material; send letter with two or three sample chapters in the first instance. S.a.e. essential. Submissions by fax or on disk not accepted. No reading fee.

Sunflower Literary Agency

106 Mansfield Drive, Redhill RH1 3JN
✉ contact@sunflowerliteraryagency.com
www.sunflowerliteraryagency.com

Senior Editor *Philip Adams*
Correspondence Secretary *David Sherriff*

Founded 2003. Handles full-length fiction, especially thrillers (techno a plus); literary fiction, especially political and/or social satire (controversy a plus); erotica, in any of the above genres. No poetry, screenplays, non-fiction, short fiction, 'who-dunnits' or autobiography. COMMISSION Home 15% (first book), 10% (later books); USA & Translation additional 5% to base rate. 'We *only* consider work from unpub-

lished authors (or major changes of genre).' Electronic submissions preferred: contact via the website only. All requirements listed on the web page must be fulfilled before e-mail contact is made. No fees charged. Provides editing and pre-publication services via **Tournesol Books** (see entry under *Small Presses*) and facilitates self-publication and promotion through **The Pen Press Limited** (see entry under *Small Presses*).

The Susijn Agency Ltd

3rd Floor, 64 Great Titchfield Street, London W1W 7QH
☎020 7580 6341 Fax 020 7580 8626
✉ info@thesusijnagency.com
www.thesusijnagency.com

Contacts *Laura Susijn, Charles Buchan*

Founded April 1998. Specialises in selling rights worldwide in literary fiction and non-fiction. Also represents non-English language authors and publishers for UK, US and translation rights worldwide. COMMISSION Home 15%; US & Translation 15–20%. Preliminary letter, synopsis and first two chapters preferred. No reading fee.

The Tennyson Agency

10 Cleveland Avenue, Wimbledon Chase, London SW20 9EW
☎020 8543 5939
✉ enquiries@tenagy.co.uk
www.tenagy.co.uk

Contact *Christopher Oxford*

Founded 2001. Specialises in theatre, radio, television and film scripts. Related material considered on an ad hoc basis. No short stories, children's, poetry, travel, military/historical, academic or sport. CLIENTS Vivienne Allen, Tony Bagley, Alastair Cording, Iain Grant, Jonathan Holloway, Julian Howell, Philip Hurd-Wood, Joanna Leigh, John Ryan, Walter Saunders, Diana Ward. COMMISSION Home 12½–15%; Overseas 17½–20%. No unsolicited material; send introductory letter with résumé and proposal/outline of work. No reading fee.

Lavinia Trevor Literary Agency*

The Glasshouse, 49A Goldhawk Road, London W12 8QP
☎020 8749 8481 Fax 020 8749 7377

Contact *Lavinia Trevor*

Founded 1993. Handles general fiction (literary and commercial) and non-fiction, including popular science. No fantasy, science-fiction, poetry, academic, technical or children's books. No TV, film, radio, theatre scripts. COMMISSION rate by agreement with author. Approach with a preliminary letter, a brief autobiography and first 50–60 typewritten pages. S.a.e. essential. No reading fee.

Jane Turnbull★

Barn Cottage, Veryan, Truro TR2 5QA
☎01872 5013170
✉ jane.turnbull@btinternet.com

Contact *Jane Turnbull*

Founded 1986. Handles fiction and non-fiction. No science fiction, romantic fiction, children's literature or plays. Specialises in biography, history, current affairs, health and diet. Translation rights handled by Gillon Aitken Associates Ltd. COMMISSION Home 10%; US & Foreign 20%. No unsolicited mss. Approach with letter in the first instance. No reading fee.

Ed Victor Ltd★

6 Bayley Street, Bedford Square, London WC1B 3HE
☎020 7304 4100 Fax 020 7304 4111

Contacts *Ed Victor, Graham Greene, Maggie Phillips, Sophie Hicks, Grainne Fox*

Founded 1976. Handles a broad range of material including children's books but leans towards the more commercial ends of the fiction and non-fiction spectrums. No poetry, scripts or academic. Takes on very few new writers. After trying his hand at book publishing and literary magazines, Ed Victor, an ebullient American, found his true vocation. Strong opinions, very pushy and works hard for those whose intelligence he respects. Loves nothing more than a good title auction. CLIENTS include Eoin Colfer, Frederick Forsyth, A.A. Gill, Josephine Hart, Jack Higgins, Erica Jong, Nigella Lawson, Kathy Lette, Allan Mallinson, Anne Robinson and the estates of Douglas Adams, Raymond Chandler, Dame Iris Murdoch, Sir Stephen Spender and Irving Wallace. COMMISSION Home & US 15%; Translation 20%. No unsolicited mss.

Robin Wade Literary Agency

33 Cormorant Lodge, Thomas More Street, London E1W 1AU
☎020 7488 4171 Fax 020 7488 4172
✉ rw@rwla.com
www.rwla.com

Contact *Robin Wade*
Associate *Jo Kitching*

Founded 2001. Handles general fiction and non-fiction including children's books. No scripts, poetry, plays or short stories.

COMMISSION Home 10%; Overseas & Translation 20%. 'Fees negotiable if a contract has already been offered.' Send detailed synopsis and two specimen chapters by e-mail with a brief biography. No reading fee.

Cecily Ware Literary Agents

19C John Spencer Square, London N1 2LZ
☎020 7359 3787 Fax 020 7226 9828
✉ info@cecilyware.com

Contacts *Cecily Ware, Gilly Schuster, Warren Sherman*

Founded 1972. Primarily a film and TV script agency representing work in all areas: drama, children's, series/serials, adaptations, comedies, etc. COMMISSION Home 10%; US 10–20% by arrangement. No unsolicited mss or phone calls. Approach in writing only. No reading fee.

Watson, Little Ltd★

Capo Di Monte, Windmill Hill, London NW3 6RJ
☎020 7431 0770 Fax 020 7431 7225
✉ enquiries@watsonlittle.com

Contacts *Sheila Watson, Mandy Little, Sugra Zaman*

Handles fiction, commercial women's fiction, crime and literary fiction. Non-fiction special interests include history, science, popular psychology, self-help, business and general leisure books. Also children's fiction and non-fiction. No short stories, poetry, TV, play or film scripts. Not interested in purely academic writers. COMMISSION Home 15%; US 24%; Translation 19%. OVERSEAS ASSOCIATES worldwide. FILM & TV ASSOCIATES The Sharland Organisation Ltd; Hurley Lowe Management. No e-mails or unsolicited mss. Informative preliminary letter and synopsis with return postage essential.

A.P. Watt Ltd★

20 John Street, London WC1N 2DR
☎020 7405 6774 Fax 020 7831 2154
✉ apw@apwatt.co.uk
www.apwatt.co.uk

Directors *Caradoc King, Linda Shaughnessy, Derek Johns, Georgia Garrett, Nick Harris, Natasha Fairweather, Sheila Crowley*

Founded 1875. The oldest-established literary agency in the world. Handles full-length typescripts, including children's books, screenplays for film and TV. No poetry, academic or specialist works. CLIENTS include Trezza Azzopardi, David Baddiel, Quentin Blake, Marika Cobbold, Helen Dunmore, Nicholas Evans, Giles Foden,

Esther Freud, Janice Galloway, Martin Gilbert, Nadine Gordimer, Linda Grant, Reginald Hill, Michael Holroyd, Michael Ignatieff, Mick Jackson, Philip Kerr, Dick King-Smith, India Knight, John Lanchester, Alison Lurie, Jan Morris, Jill Murphy, Andrew O'Hagan, Susie Orbach, Tony Parsons, Caryl Phillips, Philip Pullman, Jancis Robinson, Jon Ronson, Elaine Showalter, Zadie Smith, Graham Swift, Colm Toibin, Fiona Walker and the estates of Wodehouse, Graves and Maugham. COMMISSION Home 10%; US & Translation 20%. No unsolicited mss accepted.

Josef Weinberger Plays

12–14 Mortimer Street, London W1T 3JJ
☎020 7580 2827 Fax 020 7436 9616
✉ general.info@jwmail.co.uk
www.josef-weinberger.com

Contact *Michael Callahan*

Josef Weinberger is both agent and publisher of scripts for the theatre. CLIENTS include Ray Cooney, John Godber, Peter Gordon, Debbie Isitt, Arthur Miller, Sam Shepard, John Steinbeck. OVERSEAS REPRESENTATIVES in the US, Canada, Australia, New Zealand, India, South Africa and Zimbabwe. No unsolicited mss; introductory letter essential. No reading fee.

John Welch, Literary Consultant & Agent

Mill Cottage, Calf Lane, Chipping Camden GL55 6JQ
☎01386 840237 Fax 01386 840568
✉ johnwelch@waitrose.com

Contact *John Welch*

Founded 1992. Handles military aviation and naval history, and history in general. No fiction, poetry, children's books or scripts for radio, TV, film or theatre. Already has a full hand of authors so no new authors being considered. CLIENTS include Alexander Baron, Michael Calvert, Patrick Delaforce, Timothy Jenkins, Sybil Marshall, Ewart Oakeshott, Norman Scarfe, Anthony Trew, Peter Trew, David Wragg. COMMISSION Home 10%.

Eve White Literary Agent

Irish Hill House, Hamstead Marshall, Newbury RG20 0JB
☎01488 657656
✉ evewhite@btinternet.com

Contact *Eve White*

Founded 2003. Handles full-length adult and children's fiction and non-fiction. No poetry,

short stories or textbooks. CLIENTS Deanne Ashman, Peter J. Murray. COMMISSION Home 15%; US & Translation 20%. No unsolicited mss. Send letter with s.a.e. (include e-mail address and phone number), résumé, synopsis, one-page writing sample. No initial approach by e-mail. No reading fee.

Dinah Wiener Ltd★

12 Cornwall Grove, Chiswick, London W4 2LB
☎020 8994 6011 Fax 020 8994 6044

Contact *Dinah Wiener*

Founded 1985. Handles fiction and general non-fiction: auto/biography, popular science, cookery. No scripts, children's or poetry. CLIENTS include T.J. Armstrong, Valerie-Anne Baglietto, Malcolm Billings, Alison Brodie, Hugh Brune, Guy Burt, Victoria Corby, David Deutsch, Jenny Hobbs, Sandra Howard, Mark Jeffery, Tania Kindersley, Michael Lockwood, Sarah Mason, Daniel Snowman, Peta Tayler, Mitchell Tonks, Rachel Trethewey, Marcia Willett. COMMISSION Home 15%; US & Translation 20%. Approach with preliminary letter in first instance, giving full but brief c.v. of past work and future plans. Mss submitted must include s.a.e. and be typed in double-spacing.

Rebecca Winfield Literary Agency

84 Cowper Road, London W7 1EJ
☎020 8567 6738 Fax 020 8567 6738
✉ rebecca.winfield@btopenworld.com

Contact *Rebecca Winfield*

Founded 2003. Handles quality fiction and non-fiction; biography, social politics and narrative non-fiction. No science fiction, fantasy, horror or poetry. Also provides rights consultancy service to literary agents. COMMISSION Home 15%; US & Translation 20%. Send letter, synopsis and no more than three sample chapters in the first instance together with s.a.e. for return of material. Submissions on disk or by e-mail not accepted. No reading fee.

The Wylie Agency (UK) Ltd

17 Bedford Square, London WC1B 3JA
☎020 7908 5900 Fax 020 7908 5901
✉ mail@wylieagency.co.uk

Handles fiction and non-fiction. No scripts or children's books. COMMISSION Home 10%; US 15%; Translation 20%. The Wylie Agency does not accept unsolicited submissions. Enquire by letter or e-mail before submitting. Any submission must be accompanied by return postage/ s.a.e.

Literary Scouts

Literary scouts gather information from UK agents, publishers and editors on behalf of foreign clients. They are not literary agents and work only with material that is already commissioned or being handled by an agent. They do **not** accept unsolicited material and do **not** deal directly with writers.

Louise Allen-Jones
40 Lillieshall Road, London SW4 0LP
☎020 7720 2453 Fax 020 7498 1818
✉ louise@louiseallenjones.com
Contact *Louise Allen-Jones*

Scouts for Econ Ullstein List, Germany; The English Agency, Japan; Bruna, Signet, Signature and de Boekerij 'M', The Netherlands; Distribuidora, Brazil; The Film Council, UK.

Badcock & Rozycki
Literary Scouts
1 Old Compton Street, London W1D 5JA
☎020 7734 7997 Fax 020 7734 6886

Contacts *June Badcock* (june@badcock-rozycki.co.uk), *Barbara Rozycki* (barbara@badcock-rozycki.co.uk), *Claire Holt* (claire@badcock-rozycki.co.uk)

Scouts for Wilhelm Heyne Verlag and Diana Verlag, Germany; Unieboek BV and Prometheus/Bert Bakker, The Netherlands; RCS Libri Group, Italy; Editions Jean-Claude Lattès, France; Ediciones Salamandra, Spain; Ellinika Grammata, Greece; Werner Söderström Osakeyhtiö, Finland; Forum, Sweden; NW Damm & Son A/S, Norway; Egmont Lademann A/S, Denmark; Edda Media, Iceland.

Anne Louise Fisher
and Suzy Lucas
29 D'Arblay Street, London W1F 8EP
☎020 7494 4609 Fax 020 7494 4611
✉ annelouise@alfisher.co.uk
Contacts *Anne Louise Fisher, Suzy Lucas*

Scouts for Doubleday Inc., Broadway Books and Nan A. Talese, US; Librarie Plon-Perrin, Pocket and Univers Poche, France; Karl Blessing Verlag, Germany; Arnoldo Mondadori Editore and Oscar Mondadori, Italy; Albert Bonniers Bokförlag, Sweden; Otava, Finland; Gyldendal Norsk Forlag, Norway; Mouria, The Netherlands; Plaza y Janés, Grijalbo, Editorial Debate, Editorial Lumen and Mondadori Iberica, Spain; Patakis Publications, Greece.

Koukla MacLehose
Arundel House, 3 Westbourne Road, London N7 8AR
☎020 7607 1336 Fax 020 7609 7775
✉ koukla@btopenworld.com
Contact *Koukla MacLehose*

Scouts for Tammi, Finland; Wåhlström & Widstrand, Sweden; Pax, Norway; Rosinante, Sam Perens and Forum/Fremad, Denmark; Meulenhoff and Arena, The Netherlands; Hanser, Zsolnay, Sans Souci and Nagel & Kimche, Germany; Gallimard and Denoël, France; Einaudi, Italy; Anagrama, Spain; Asa, Portugal; Psichogios, Greece; Keter, Israel.

Folly Marland
6 Elmcroft Street, London E5 0SQ
☎020 8986 0111 Fax 020 8986 0111
✉ fmarland@pobox.com
Contact *Folly Marland*

Scouts for Scherz Verlag, Krüger Verlag and Argon Verlag, Germany; Uitgeverij Het Spectrum, The Netherlands; Sony Magazines, Japan; Livani, Greece.

Rosalind Ramsay Limited
195 Lavender Hill, London SW11 5TB
☎020 7978 7444 Fax 020 7924 5455
✉ ros@rosalindramsay.com
www.rosalindramsay.com
Contacts *Rosalind Ramsay*

Scouts for Kiepenheuer & Witsch, Germany; Sperling & Kupfer, Italy; Ambo Anthos, The Netherlands; Norstedts, Sweden; Kadokawa, Japan; Dioptra, Greece.

Heather Schiller
✉ heather.schiller@virgin.net
Contact *Heather Schiller*

Scouts for BZZTÔH, The Netherlands; Cappelen, Norway; Piper, Germany; Lindhardt & Ringhof, Denmark; Prisma, Sweden.

Jane Southern

11 Russell Avenue, Bedford MK40 3TE
☎01234 400147 Fax 01234 400146
✉ jane.southern@ntlworld.com

Contact *Jane Southern*

UK Scout for Hoffmann und Campe Verlag, Germany; Bertelsmann Club, Germany; The House of Books, The Netherlands; Belfond, Presses de la Cité and France Loisirs, France.

Van Lear Limited

PO Box 21816, London SW6 5ZU
☎020 7385 1199 Fax 020 7385 6262
✉ evl@vanlear.co.uk

Contact *Liz Van Lear*

Scouts for Droemer Knaur Schneekluth, Germany; Planeta Group, Spain and Latin America; Richters, Sweden; Artist House, Japan; Oceanida, Greece; Dom Quixote, Portugal; il Saggiatore, Italy; Veen Bosch & Keuning, The Netherlands; Cicero, Denmark.

Sylvie Zannier-Betts

114 Springfield Road, Brighton BN1 6DE
☎01273 557370/07791 750864 (mobile)
Fax 01273 557370
✉ szannier@lineone.net

Contact *Sylvie Zannier-Betts*

Scouts for Uitgeverij De Geus, The Netherlands; S. Fischer Verlag, Germany; Gummerus Publishers, Finland.

National Newspapers

Departmental e-mail addresses are too numerous to include in this listing. They can be obtained from the newspaper's main switchboard or the department in question

The Business

292 Vauxhall Bridge Road, London
SW1V 1SS
☎020 7961 0000

Owner *Barclay Brothers*

Editor-in-Chief *Andrew Neil*

Circulation 282,110

Launched in February 1998. Sunday national newspaper dedicated to business, finance and politics. No unsolicited material. All ideas must be discussed with the department's editor in advance.

Political Editor *Fraser Nelson*

Daily Express

Ludgate House, 245 Blackfriars Road, London
SE1 9UX
☎020 7928 8000   Fax 020 7620 1654
www.express.co.uk

Owner *Northern & Shell Media/Richard Desmond*

Editor *Peter Hill*

Circulation 942,171

Under owner Richard Desmond, publisher of *OK!* magazine, the paper features a large amount of celebrity coverage. The general rule of thumb is to approach in writing with an idea; all departments are prepared to look at an outline without commitment. Ideas welcome but already receives many which are 'too numerous to count'.

News Editor *David Leigh*
Diary (Hickey Column) *Kathryn Spencer*
Features Editor *Heather Preen*
City Editor *Stephen Kahn*
Political Editor *Patrick O'Flynn*
Sports Editor *Bill Bradshaw*
Planning Editor (News Desk) should be circulated with copies of official reports, press releases, etc., to ensure news desk cover at all times.
Saturday magazine. Editor *Graham Bailey*
PAYMENT negotiable.

Daily Mail

Northcliffe House, 2 Derry Street, London
W8 5TT
☎020 7938 6000

Owner *Associated Newspapers/Lord Rothermere*

Editor *Paul Dacre*

Circulation 2.4 million

In-house feature writers and regular columnists provide much of the material. Photo-stories and crusading features often appear; it's essential to hit the right note to be a successful Mail writer. Close scrutiny of the paper is strongly advised. Not a good bet for the unseasoned. Accepts news on savings, building societies, insurance, unit trusts, legal rights and tax.

News Editor *Tony Gallagher*
City Editor *Alex Brummer*
'Money Mail' Editor *Tony Hazell*
Political Editor *David Hughes*
Education Correspondent *Sarah Harris*
Diary Editor *Richard Kay*
Features Editor *Leaf Kalfayan*
Literary Editor *Jane Mays*
Sports Editor *Matt Tench*
Femail *Lisa Collins*
Weekend Saturday supplement. Editor *Heather McGlone*

Daily Mirror

1 Canada Square, Canary Wharf, London
E14 5AP
☎020 7293 3000   Fax 020 7293 3409
www.mirror.co.uk

Owner *Trinity Mirror plc*

Editor *To be appointed*

Circulation 1.91 million

No freelance opportunities for the inexperienced, but strong writers who understand what the tabloid market demands are always needed.

Deputy Editor *Des Kelly*
News Editor *Conor Hanna*
Features Editor *Peter Willis*
Political Editor *James Hardy*
Business Editor *Clinton Manning*
Showbusiness Diary Editor *Jessica Callan*
Sports Editor *Dean Morse*

Daily Record

One Central Quay, Glasgow G3 8DA
☎0141 309 3000   Fax 0141 309 3340

www.record-mail.co.uk
Owner *Trinity Mirror plc*
Editor *Bruce Waddell*
Circulation 503,077

Mass-market Scottish tabloid.

Freelance material is generally welcome.
News Editor *Tom Hamilton*
Features Editor *Melanie Harvey*
Business Editor *John Penman*
Political Editor *Paul Sinclair*
Associate Sports Editor *Alan Thomson*
Magazine Editor *Angela Dewar*
Scotland Means Business Quarterly business magazine, launched March 2002. Editor *Magnus Gardham*

Daily Sport

19 Great Ancoats Street, Manchester M60 4BT
☎0161 236 4466 Fax 0161 236 4535
www.dailysport.co.uk
Owner *Sport Newspapers Ltd*
Editor *David Beevers*
Circulation 200,000

Tabloid catering for young male readership. Unsolicited material welcome; send to News Editor *Nick Appleyard*
Sports Editor *Marc Smith*
Lads Mag Monthly glossy magazine. Editor *Mark Harris*.

Daily Star

Ludgate House, 245 Blackfriars Road, London SE1 9UX
☎020 7928 8000 Fax 020 7922 7960
Owner *Northern & Shell Media/Richard Desmond*
Editor *Dawn Neesom*
Circulation 903,702

In competition with *The Sun* for off-the-wall news and features. Freelance opportunities available.
Deputy Editor *Jim Mansell*
Assistant Editor, Features *Samm Taylor*
Sports Editor *Howard Wheatcroft*

Daily Star Sunday

Ludgate House, 245 Blackfriars Road, London SE1 9UX
☎020 7928 8000
Owner *Northern & Shell Media/Richard Desmond*
Editor *Gareth Morgan*
Circulation 556,751

New Sunday, launched in September 2002 in direct competition with *News of the World* and *The People*.

Supplement: *Hot Celebs* Showbiz/glamour magazine.

The Daily Telegraph

1 Canada Square, Canary Wharf, London E14 5DT
☎020 7538 5000 Fax 020 7513 2506
www.telegraph.co.uk
Owner *Conrad Black*
Editor *Martin Newland*
Circulation 923,042

Unsolicited mss not generally welcome – 'all are carefully read and considered, but very few published'. Contenders should approach the paper in writing, making clear their authority for writing on that subject. No fiction.
Home Editor *Fiona Barton* Tip-offs or news reports from *bona fide* journalists. Must phone the news desk in first instance. Maximum 200 words. Payment minimum £40 (tip).
Arts Editor *Sarah Crompton*
City Editor *Neil Collins*
Political Editor *George Jones*
Diary Editor *Charlie Methvin* Always interested in diary pieces.
Education *John Clare*
Environment *Charles Clover*
Features Editor *Richard Preston* Most material supplied by commission from established contributors. New writers are tried out by arrangement with the features editor. Approach in writing. Maximum 1500 words.
Literary Editor *Kate Summerscale*
Sports Editor *David Welch* Occasional opportunities for specialised items.
Style Editor *Rachel Forder*
PAYMENT by arrangement.
Daily Telegraph Weekend Saturday supplement. Editor *Michele Lavery*

Financial Times

1 Southwark Bridge, London SE1 9HL
☎020 7873 3000 Fax 020 7873 3076
✉ firstname.lastname@ft.com
www.ft.com
Owner *Pearson*
Editor *Andrew Gowers*
Circulation 448,791

Founded 1888. UK and international coverage of business, finance, politics, technology, management, marketing and the arts. All feature ideas must be discussed with the department's editor in advance. Not snowed under with unsolicited contributions – they get less than any other national newspaper. Approach by e-mail with ideas in the first instance.

News Editor *Edward Carr*
Features Editor *Andrew Hill*
Arts Editor *Lorna Dolan*
Financial Editor *Jane Fuller*
Literary Editor *Jan Dalley*
Diary Editor *Sundeep Tucker*
Education *Miranda Green*
Environment *Vanessa Houlder*
Political Editor *James Blitz*
Sports Correspondent *David Owen*
Weekend FT Editor *Richard Addis*
How to Spend It Monthly magazine. Editor *Gillian de Bono*

The Guardian

119 Farringdon Road, London EC1R 3ER
☎020 7278 2332 Fax 020 7837 2114
✉ firstname.secondname@guardian.co.uk
www.guardian.co.uk
Owner *The Scott Trust*
Editor *Alan Rusbridger*
Circulation 376,287

Of all the nationals *The Guardian* probably offers the greatest opportunities for freelance writers, if only because it has the greatest number of specialised pages which use freelance work. But mss must be directed at a specific slot.

News Editor *Paul Johnson* No opportunities except in those regions where there is presently no local contact for news stories.

Home News *Ed Pilkington*
Arts Editor *Charlie English*
Literary Editor *Claire Armitstead*
Financial Editor *Paul Murphy*
City Editor *Julia Finch*
Life Editor *Simon Rogers* Thursday supplement, published in association with *Nature*. Science, technology, medicine, environment and other issues. Incorporates *Online* science and computing. Computing/communications (Internet) articles should be addressed to *Jack Schofield*; science articles to *Tim Radford*. Mss on disk or by e-mail (neil.mcintosh@guardian.co.uk).
Diary Editor *Matthew Norman*
Education Editor *Will Woodward* Expert pieces on modern education welcome.
Environment *John Vidal*
Features Editor *Ian Katz* Receives up to 50 unsolicited mss a day; these are passed on to relevant page editors.
Guardian Society Editor *Patrick Butler* Focuses on social change – the forces affecting us, from environment to government policies. Top journalists and outside commentators.
Media Editor *Charlie Burgess* Nine pages a week, plus 'New Media'. Outside contributions are considered. All aspects of modern

media, advertising and PR. Background insight important. Best approach is by e-mail (janine.gibson@guardian.co.uk).
Political Editor *Mike White*
Sports Editor *Ben Clissitt*
Women's Page *Clare Margetson* Runs three days a week. Unsolicited ideas used if they show an appreciation of the page in question. Maximum 800–1000 words. Write, e-mail (clare.margetson@guardian.co.uk) or fax on 020 7239 9935.
The Guardian Weekend Glossy Saturday issue. Editor *Katharine Viner*
The Guide Editor *Tim Lusher*

The Herald (Glasgow)

200 Renfield Street, Glasgow G2 3PR
☎0141 302 7000 Fax 0141 302 7070
www.theherald.co.uk
Owner *Gannett UK Ltd*
Editor *Mark Douglas-Home*
Circulation 83,083

One of the oldest national newspapers in the English-speaking world, *The Herald*, which dropped its 'Glasgow' prefix in February 1992, was bought by Scottish Television in 1996. Lively, quality, national Scottish daily broadsheet. Approach with ideas in writing or by phone in first instance.

News Editor *Magnus Llewelin*
Arts Editor *Keith Bruce*
Business Editor *Ian McConnell*
Diary *Ken Smith*
Education *Liz Buie*
Sports Editor *Donald Cowey*
Herald Magazine Editor *Kathleen Morgan*

The Independent

Independent House, 191 Marsh Wall, London E14 9RS
☎020 7005 2000 Fax 020 7005 2999
www.independent.co.uk
Owner *Independent Newspapers*
Editor *Simon Kelner*
Circulation 258,012

Founded 1986. Particularly strong on its arts/media coverage, with a high proportion of feature material. Theoretically, opportunities for freelancers are good. However, unsolicited mss are not welcome; most pieces originate in-house or from known and trusted outsiders. Ideas should be submitted in writing.

News Editor *Michael Ellison*
Features *Adam Leigh*
Arts Editor *Ian Irvine*

Business Editor *Jeremy Warner*
Education *Richard Garner*
Environment *Michael McCarthy*
Literary Editor *Boyd Tonkin*
Political Editor *Andrew Grice*
Sports Editor *Paul Newman*
Travel Editor *Simon Calder*
The Independent Magazine Saturday supplement. Editor *Laurence Earle*
The Independent Traveller 32-page Saturday magazine
The Information Editor *Jo Ellison*

Independent on Sunday

Independent House, 191 Marsh Wall, London E14 9RS
☎020 7005 2000 Fax 020 7005 2999
www.independent.co.uk/sindy/sindy.html

Owner *Independent Newspapers*
Editor *Tristan Davies*
Circulation 209,236

Founded 1986. Regular columnists contribute most material but feature opportunites exist. Approach with ideas in first instance.

News Editor *Robert Mendick*
 Focus Editor *Cole Moreton*
 Arts Editor *Marcus Field*
 Comment Editor *James Hanning*
 Business Editor *Jason Nissé*
 Literary Editor *Suzi Feay*
 Environment *Geoffrey Lean*
 Political Editor *Andy McSmith*
 Sports Editor *Neil Morton*
 Travel Editor *Kate Simon*
 The Sunday Review supplement. Editor *Andrew Tuck*
 ABC Arts, books and culture supplement.

International Herald Tribune

6 bis, rue des Graviers, 92521 Neuilly, Paris
☎0033 1 4143 9300
Fax 0033 1 4143 9338 (editorial)
✉ iht@iht.com
www.iht.com
Circulation 245,223

Executive Editor *Walter Wells*
Deputy Editors *Katherine Knorr, Robert Marino*

Published in France, Monday to Saturday, and circulated in Europe, the Middle East, North Africa, the Far East and the USA. General news, business and financial, arts and leisure. Uses regular freelance contributors. Contributor policy can be found on the website at: www.iht.com/contributor.htm

The Mail on Sunday

Northcliffe House, 2 Derry Street, London W8 5TS
☎020 7938 6000 Fax 020 7937 3829

Owner *Associated Newspapers/Lord Rothermere*
Editor *Peter Wright*
Circulation 2.38 million

Sunday paper with a high proportion of newsy features and articles. Experience and judgement required to break into its band of regular feature writers.

News Editor *Sebastian Hamilton*
Financial Editor *Lisa Buckingham*
Diary Editor *Adam Helliker*
Features Editor/Women's Page *Sian James*
Books *Marilyn Warnick*
Political Editor *Simon Walters*
Sports Editor *Malcolm Vallerius*
Night & Day Editor *Christena Appleyard*
Review Editor *Jim Gillespie*
You – The Mail on Sunday Magazine Colour supplement. Many feature articles, supplied entirely by freelance writers. Editor *Sue Peart*.
Features Editor *Rosalind Lowe*

Morning Star

William Rust House, 52 Beachy Road, London E3 2NS
☎020 8510 0815 Fax 020 8986 5694
✉ morsta@geo2.poptel.org.uk

Owner *Peoples Press Printing Society*
Editor *John Haylett*
Circulation 9000

Not to be confused with the *Daily Star*, the *Morning Star* is the farthest left national daily. Those with a penchant for a Marxist reading of events and ideas can try their luck, though feature space is as competitive here as in the other nationals.

News Editor *Dan Coysh*
Features & Arts Editor *Richard Bagley*
Political Editor *Adrian Roberts*
Foreign Editor *Dave Williams*
Sports Editor *Mark Barber*

News of the World

1 Virginia Street, London E98 1NW
☎020 7782 1000 Fax 020 7583 9504
www.newsoftheworld.co.uk

Owner *News International plc/Rupert Murdoch*
Editor *Andy Coulson*
Circulation 3.95 million

Highest circulation Sunday paper. Freelance

contributions welcome. News and features editors welcome tips and ideas.

Deputy Editor *Neil Wallis*
News Editor *Gary Thompson*
Features Editor *Jules Stenson*
Business/City Editor *Peter Prendergast*
Political Editor *Ian Kirby*
Sports Editor *Mike Dunn*
Sunday Magazine Colour supplement. Editor *Judy McGuire*. Showbiz interviews and strong human-interest features make up most of the content, but there are no strict rules about what is 'interesting'. Unsolicited mss and ideas welcome.

The Observer

119 Farringdon Road, London EC1R 3ER
☎020 7278 2332   Fax 020 7713 4250
✉ editor@observer.co.uk
www.observer.co.uk

Owner *Guardian Newspapers Ltd*
Editor *Roger Alton*
Circulation 452,257

Founded 1791. Acquired by Guardian Newspapers from Lonrho in May 1993. Occupies the middle ground of Sunday newspaper politics.

Unsolicited material is not generally welcome, 'except from distinguished, established writers'. Receives far too many unsolicited offerings already. No news, fiction or special page opportunities. The newspaper runs annual competitions which change from year to year. Details are advertised in the newspaper.

Executive Editor, News *Andy Malone*
Arts Editor *Jane Ferguson*
Review Editor *Louise France*
Comment Editor *Mike Holland*
Deputy Business Editor/City Editor *Richard Wachman*
Business Editor *Frank Kane*
Personal Finance Editor *Maria Scott*
Science Editor *Robin McKie*
Education Editor *Martin Bright*
Environment Correspondent *Mark Townsend*
Literary Editor *Robert McCrum*
Travel Editor *Jeannette Hyde*
Sports Editor *Brian Oliver*
The Observer Magazine Glossy arts and lifestyle supplement. Editor *Allan Jenkins*
The Observer Sport Monthly Magazine supplement launched in 2000. *Jason Cowley*
The Observer Food Monthly Launched in 2001. Editor *Nicola Jeal*
The Observer Music Monthly Launched in 2003. Editor *Caspar Llewellyn Smith*

The People

1 Canada Square, Canary Wharf, London
E14 5AP
☎020 7293 3614   Fax 020 7293 3887
www.people.co.uk

Owner *Trinity Mirror plc*
Editor *Mark Thomas*
Circulation 1.02 million

Slightly up-market version of *The News of the World*. Keen on exposés and big-name gossip. Interested in ideas for investigative articles. Phone in first instance.

News Editor *Ian Edmondson*
Features Editor *Rachael Bletchley*
Political Editor *Nigel Nelson*
Sports Editor *Lee Clayton*
Travel Associate Editor *Trisha Harbord*
Take It Easy Magazine supplement. Editor *Kerry Parnell* Approach by phone with ideas in first instance.

Scotland on Sunday

Barclay House, 108 Holyrood Road,
Edinburgh EH8 8AS
☎0131 620 8620   Fax 0131 620 8491
www.scotlandonsunday.com

Owner *Scotsman Publications Ltd*
Editor *John McLellan*
Circulation 83,952

Scotland's top-selling quality broadsheet. Welcomes ideas rather than finished articles.

News Editor *Peter Laing*
Arts Editor *Fiona Leith*
Spectrum Colour supplement. Features on personalities, etc. Editor *Eilidh MacAskill*

The Scotsman

Barclay House, 108 Holyrood Road,
Edinburgh EH8 8AS
☎0131 620 8620   Fax 0131 620 8616
(Editorial)
www.scotsman.com

Owner *Scotsman Publications Ltd*
Editor *Iain Martin*
Circulation 70,656

Scotland's national newspaper. Many unsolicited mss come in, and stand a good chance of being read, although a small army of regulars supply much of the feature material not written in-house. See website for contact details.

News Editor *Nick Drainey*
Business Editor *Nick Bevens*
Education *Seonag MacKinnon*
Features Editor *Emma Cowing*

Book Reviews *David Robinson*
Sports Editor *Donald Walker*

The Sun
1 Virginia Street, London E98 1SN
☎020 7782 4000 Fax 020 7782 4108
✉ firstname.lastname@the-sun.co.uk
www.the-sun.co.uk

Owner *News International plc/Rupert Murdoch*
Editor *Rebekah Wade*
Circulation 3.33 million

Highest circulation daily. Populist outlook; very keen on gossip, pop stars, TV soap, scandals and exposés of all kinds. No room for non-professional feature writers; 'investigative journalism' of a certain hue is always in demand, however.
Head of News *Paul Field*
Head of Features *Graham Dudman*
Head of Sport *Steve Waring*
Woman's Editor *Sharon Hendry*
Fashion Editor *Erica Davies*

Sunday Express
Ludgate House, 245 Blackfriars Road, London SE1 9UX
☎020 7928 8000 Fax 020 7620 1654

Owner *Northern & Shell Media/Richard Desmond*
Editor *Martin Townsend*
Circulation 952,171

The general rule of thumb is to approach in writing with an idea; all departments are prepared to look at an outline without commitment.
News Editor *Jim Murray*
Features Editor *Giulia Rhodes*
Business Editor *David Paisley*
Political Editor *Julia Hartley-Brewer*
Sports Editor *Scott Wilson*
S Fashion and lifestyle magazine for women. Editor *Louise Robinson.* No unsolicited mss. All contributions are commissioned. Ideas in writing only.
S2 News and lifestyle magazine for men. Editor *Phil McNeill*
PAYMENT negotiable.

Sunday Herald
200 Renfield Street, Glasgow G2 3QB
☎0141 302 7800 Fax 0141 302 7815
✉ editor@sundayherald.com
www.sundayherald.com

Owner *Newsquest*
Editor *Andrew Jaspan*

Circulation 58,303
Also at: 9/10 St Andrew Square, Edinburgh EH2 2AF ☎0131 718 6040 Fax 0131 718 6105
Launched February 1999. Scottish seven-section broadsheet.
Deputy Editor *Richard Walker*
News Editor *David Milne*
Political Editor *Douglas Fraser*
Sports Editor *David Dick*
Entertainment Editor *Andrew Burnet*
Magazine Editor *Jane Wright*

Sunday Mail
One Central Quay, Glasgow G3 8DA
☎0141 309 3000 Fax 0141 309 3587
www.sundaymail.co.uk

Owner *Trinity Mirror plc*
Editor *Allan Rennie*
Circulation 605,743

Popular Scottish Sunday tabloid.
News Editor *Jim Wilson*
Features Editor *Susie Cormack*
7Days Weekly supplement. Editor *Liz Steele*
Mailsport Monthly Monthly magazine. Editor *George Cheyne*

Sunday Mirror
1 Canada Square, Canary Wharf, London E14 5AP
☎020 7293 3000
Fax 020 7293 3939 (news desk)
www.sundaymirror.co.uk

Owner *Trinity Mirror*
Editor *Tina Weaver*
Circulation 1.58 million

In general terms contributions are welcome, though the paper patiently points out it has more time for those who have taken the trouble to study the market. Initial contact in writing preferred, except for live news situations. No fiction.
News Editor *James Scott* The news desk is very much in the market for tip-offs and inside information. Contributors would be expected to work with staff writers on news stories. Approach by telephone or fax in the first instance.
Finance *Melanie Wright*
Features Editor *Nicky Dawson* 'Anyone who has obviously studied the market will be dealt with constructively and courteously.' Cherishes its record as a breeding ground for new talent.
Sports Editor *Craig Tregurtha*
M Celebs Colour supplement. Editor *Mel Brodie*

Sunday Post

2 Albert Square, Dundee DD1 9QJ
☎01382 223131   Fax 01382 201064
✉ mail@sundaypost.com
www.sundaypost.com

Owner *D.C. Thomson & Co. Ltd*
Editor *David Pollington*
Circulation 530,168

Contributions should be addressed to the editor.

Sunday Post Magazine Monthly colour supplement. Editor *Jan Gooderham*

Sunday Sport

19 Great Ancoats Street, Manchester M60 4BT
☎0161 236 4466   Fax 0161 236 4535
www.sundaysport.com

Owner *David Sullivan*
Editor *Paul Carter*
Circulation 178,740

Founded 1986. Sunday tabloid catering for a particular sector of the male 15–35 readership. As concerned with 'glamour' (for which, read: 'page 3') as with human interest, news, features and sport. Unsolicited mss are welcome; receives about 90 a week. Approach should be made by phone in the case of news and sports items, by letter for features. All material should be addressed to the news editor.

News Editor *Nick Appleyardie* Off-beat news, human interest, preferably with photographs.

Showbiz Editor *Alice Walker* Regular items: showbiz, television, films, pop music and gossip.

Sports Editor *Marc Smith* Hard-hitting sports stories on major soccer clubs and their personalities, plus leading clubs/people in other sports. Strong quotations to back up the news angle essential.

PAYMENT negotiable and on publication.

The Sunday Telegraph

1 Canada Square, Canary Wharf, London E14 5DT
☎020 7538 5000   Fax 020 7538 6242
www.telegraph.co.uk

Owner *Conrad Black*
Editor *Dominic Lawson*
Circulation 697,771

Right-of-centre quality Sunday paper which, although traditionally formal, has pepped up its image to attract a younger readership. Unsolicited material from untried writers is rarely ever used. Contact with idea and details of track record.

News Editor *Richard Ellis*

Features Editor *Susannah Herbert*
City Editor *Robert Peston*
Political Editor *Patrick Hennessy*
Education Editor *Julie Henry*
Arts Editor *Lucy Tuck*
Environment Editor *David Harrison*
Literary Editor *Miriam Gross*
Diary Editor *Tim Walker*
Sports Editor *Jon Ryan*

Sunday Telegraph Magazine Colour supplement. Editor *Anna Murphy*

The Sunday Times

1 Pennington Street, London E98 1ST
☎020 7782 5000   Fax 020 7782 5658
www.sunday-times.co.uk

Owner *News International plc/Rupert Murdoch*
Editor *John Witherow*
Circulation 1.4 million

Founded 1820. Tendency to be anti-establishment, with a strong crusading investigative tradition. Approach the relevant editor with an idea in writing. Close scrutiny of the style of each section of the paper is strongly advised before sending mss. No fiction. All fees by negotiation.

News Editor *Charles Hymas* Opportunities are very rare.

News Review Editor *Eleanor Mills* Submissions are always welcome, but the paper commissions its own, uses staff writers or works with literary agents, by and large. The features sections where most opportunities exist are *Style* and *The Culture*.

Culture Editor *Helen Hawkins*
Business Editor *William Lewis*
City Editor *Paul Durman*
Education Editor *Geraldine Hackett*
Science/Environment *Jonathan Leake*
Literary Editor *Caroline Gascoigne*
Sports Editor *Alex Butler*
Style Editor *Tiffanie Darke*

Sunday Times Magazine Colour supplement. Editor *Robin Morgan* No unsolicited material. Write with ideas in first instance.

Sunday Times Travel Magazine Monthly supplement. Editor *Jan Knight*

The Times

1 Pennington Street, London E98 1TT
☎020 7782 5000   Fax 020 7488 3242
www.thetimes.co.uk

Owner *News International plc/Rupert Murdoch*
Editor *Robert Thomson*
Circulation 658,637

Generally right (though features can range in

tone from diehard to libertarian). *The Times* receives a great many unsolicited offerings. Writers with feature ideas should approach by letter in the first instance. No fiction.

Deputy Editor *Ben Preston*
  News Editor *John Wellman*
  Features Editor *Michael Harve*
  Associate Editor *Brian MacArthur*
  City/Financial Editor *Patience Wheatcroft*

Diary Editor *Andrew Pierce*
Arts Editor *Sarah Vine*
Literary Editor *Erica Wagner*
Political Editor *Phil Webster*
Sports Editor *David Chappell*
Weekend Review Editor *Ben MacIntyre*
The Times Magazine Saturday supplement.
Editor *Gill Morgan*
  Times 2 Editor *Sandra Parsons*

Regional Newspapers

ENGLAND

Berkshire

Reading Evening Post
8 Tessa Road, Reading RG1 8NS
☎0118 918 3000 Fax 0118 959 9363
✉ editorial@reading-epost.co.uk
Owner *Guardian Media Group*
Editor *Andy Murrill*
Circulation 20,006

Unsolicited mss welcome; one or two received every day. Fiction rarely used. Interested in local news features, human interest, well-researched investigations. Special sections include holidays & travel (Mon); food page; children's page (Tues); style page (Wed); business (Wed & Fri); motoring and motorcycling; gardening; rock music (Fri).

Cambridgeshire

Cambridge Evening News
Winship Road, Milton, Cambridge CB4 6PP
☎01223 434434 Fax 01223 434415
Owner *Cambridge Newspapers Ltd*
Editor *Colin Grant*
Circulation 34,619
  News Editor *John Deex*
  Business Editor *Jenny Chapman*
  Sports Editor *Chris Gill*

Cheshire

Chronicle Newspapers (Chester & North Wales)
Chronicle House, Commonhall Street, Chester CH1 2AA
☎01244 340151 Fax 01244 340165
✉ eric.langton@cheshirenews.co.uk
www.iccheshireonline.co.uk
Owner *Trinity Mirror Plc*
Editor-in-Chief *Eric Langton*

All unsolicited feature material considered.

Cleveland

Hartlepool Mail
New Clarence House, Wesley Square, Hartlepool TS24 8BX
☎01429 239333 Fax 01429 869024
✉ mail.news@northeast-press.co.uk
www.hartlepooltoday.co.uk
Owner *Johnston Press Plc*
Editor *Paul Napier*
Circulation 20,655
  News Editor *Pete McCusker*
  Sports Editor *Roy Kelly*

Cumbria

News & Star
Newspaper House, Dalston Road, Carlisle CA2 5UA
☎01228 612600 Fax 01228 612601
Owner *Cumbrian Newspaper Group Ltd*
Editor *Keith Sutton*
Circulation 25,029
  Deputy Editor *Nick Turner*
  Sports Editor *Mike Gardner*
  Women's Page *Jane Loughran*

North West Evening Mail
Abbey Road, Barrow in Furness LA14 5QS
☎01229 821835 Fax 01229 840164
✉ news@nwemail.co.uk
www.nwemail.co.uk
Owner *Robin Burgess*
Editor *Stephen Brauner*
Circulation 19,822

All editorial material should be addressed to the editor.
  Sports Editor *Leo Clarke*

Derbyshire

Derby Evening Telegraph
Northcliffe House, Meadow Road, Derby DE1 2DW
☎01332 291111 Fax 01332 253027
Owner *Northcliffe Newspapers Group Ltd*
Editor *Mike Norton*
Circulation 51,911
  News Editor *Cheryl Hague*
    (newsdesk@derbytelegraph.co.uk)
  News Features Editor *Sarah Newton*
    (sarahnewton@derbytelegraph.co.uk)
  Sports Editor *Peter Green*
    (sports@derbytelegraph.co.uk)
  Motoring Editor *Bob Maddox*

Devon

Evening Herald

17 Brest Road, Derriford Business Park,
Derriford, Plymouth PL6 5AA
☎01752 765500 Fax 01752 765527
✉ news@eveningherald.co.uk
www.thisisplymouth.co.uk

Owner *Northcliffe Newspapers Group Ltd*
Editor *Alan Qualtrough*
Circulation 42,983

All editorial material to be addressed to the editor or the News Editor *John Casey*.

Express & Echo

Heron Road, Sowton, Exeter EX2 7NF
☎01392 442211
Fax 01392 442294/442287 (editorial)
✉ echonews@expressandecho.co.uk
www.thisisexeter.co.uk

Owner *Westcountry Publications Limited*
Editor *Steve Hall*
Circulation 26,198

Weekly supplements: *Business Week*; *Property Echo*; *Wheels*; *Weekend Echo*.
  Head of Content *Sue Kemp*
  Features Editor/Women's Page *Lynne Turner*
  Sports Editor *Richard Davies* (Fax 01392 442416)

Herald Express

Harmsworth House, Barton Hill Road,
Torquay TQ2 8JN
☎01803 676000 Fax 01803 676228 (editorial)
✉ newsdesk@heraldexpress.co.uk
www.thisissouthdevon.co.uk

Owner *Northcliffe Newspapers Group Ltd*
Editor *B. Hanrahan*
Circulation 25,681

Drive scene, property guide, *On The Town* – leisure and entertainment guide, Monday sports, special pages, rail trail, Saturday surgery, nature and conservation column, dance scene, shop scene, *The Business*. Supplements: *Gardening* (weekly); *Visitors Guide* and *Antiques & Collectables* (fortnightly). Unsolicited mss generally not welcome. All editorial material should be addressed to the editor in writing.

Sunday Independent

Burrington Way, Plymouth PL5 3LN
☎01752 206600 Fax 01752 206164

Owner *Tindle Newspapers*
Editor *Nikki Rowlands*
Circulation 28,434

Tabloid Sunday covering the whole of the West Country from Bristol to Weymouth and Land's End. News stories/tips, news features. All editorial should be addressed to the editor.
  PAYMENT by arrangement.

Western Morning News

17 Brest Road, Derriford Business Park,
Derriford, Plymouth PL6 5AA
☎01752 765500 Fax 01752 765535
✉ wmnnewsdesk@westernmorningnews.co.uk
www.thisisplymouth.co.uk

Owner *Northcliffe Newspapers Group Ltd*
Editor *Barrie Williams*
Circulation 46,221

Unsolicited mss welcome, but must be of topical and local interest and addressed to the Assistant Editor (News) *Mark Hughes*.
  Sports Editor *Mark Stephens*

Dorset

Daily Echo

Richmond Hill, Bournemouth BH2 6HH
☎01202 554601 Fax 01202 299543

Owner *Newsquest Media Group Ltd (a Gannett company)*
Editor *Neal Butterworth*
Circulation 35,239

Founded 1900. Has a strong news and features content and invites specialist articles, particularly on unusual subjects, either contemporary or historical, but only with a local angle or flavour. Special review sections each day, including sport, property, entertainment and culture, heritage, motoring, gardening, the environment and the coastline. Also *Saturday Magazine* and monthly *Society* glossy magazine. All editorial material should be addressed to the Editor.
  PAYMENT on publication.

Dorset Echo

Fleet House, Hampshire Road, Granby
Industrial Estate, Weymouth DT4 9XD
☎01305 830930 Fax 01305 830956

Owner *Newsquest Media Group Ltd (a Gannett company)*
Editor *David Murdock*
Circulation 21,015

By-gone days, films, arts, showbiz, brides, motoring, property, weekend leisure and entertainment including computers and gardening and weekend magazine.
  News Editor *Paul Thomas*
  Sports Editor *Paul Baker*

Co. Durham

The Northern Echo
Priestgate, Darlington DL1 1NF
☎01325 381313 Fax 01325 380539
✉ echo@nne.co.uk
www.thisisthenortheast.co.uk
Owner *Newsquest (North East) Ltd (a Gannett company)*
Editor *Peter Barron*
Circulation 56,447

Founded 1870. Freelance pieces welcome but telephone first to discuss submission.

News Editor *Nigel Burton* Interested in reports involving the North East or North Yorkshire. Preferably phoned in.

Features Editor *Nick Morrison* Background pieces to topical news stories relevant to the area. Must be arranged with the features editor before submission of any material.

Business Editor *Mike Parker*
Sports Editor *Nick Loughlin*
PAYMENT and length by arrangement.

Essex

Evening Echo
Newspaper House, Chester Hall Lane, Basildon SS14 3BL
☎01268 522792 Fax 01268 469281
Owner *Newsquest Media Group (a Gannett company)*
Editor *Martin McNeill*
Circulation 38,852

Relies almost entirely on staff and regular outside contributors, but will very occasionally consider material sent on spec. Approach the editor in writing with ideas. Although the paper is Basildon-based, its largest circulation is in the Southend area.

Evening Gazette (Colchester)
Oriel House, 43–44 North Hill, Colchester CO1 1TZ
☎01206 506000 Fax 01206 508274
✉ newsdesk@thisisessex.co.uk
www.thisisessex.co.uk
Owner *Newsquest (Essex) Ltd*
Editor *Irene Kettle*
Circulation 26,449

Monday to Friday daily newspaper servicing north and mid-Essex including Colchester, Harwich, Clacton, Braintree, Witham, Maldon and Chelmsford. Unsolicited mss not generally used. Relies heavily on regular contributors.

Features Editor *Iris Clapp*

Gloucestershire

Gloucestershire Echo
1 Clarence Parade, Cheltenham GL50 3NY
☎01242 271900 Fax 01242 271848
Owner *Northcliffe Newspapers Group Ltd*
Editor *Anita Syvret*
Circulation 24,205

All material, other than news, should be addressed to the editor.

News Editor *Tanya Gledhill*

The Citizen
St John's Lane, Gloucester GL1 2AY
☎01452 424442
Fax 01452 420664 (Editorial)
Owner *Northcliffe Newspapers Group Ltd*
Editor *Ian Mean*
Circulation 30,054

All editorial material to be addressed to the Head of Content *Matt Holmes*.

Greater London

Evening Standard
Northcliffe House, 2 Derry Street, London W8 5EE
☎020 7938 6000 Fax 020 7937 2648
www.standard.co.uk/e-editions
Owner *Associated Newspapers/Lord Rothermere*
Editor *Veronica Wadley*
Circulation 393,887

Long-established evening paper, serving Londoners with both news and feature material. Genuine opportunities for London-based features. Produces a weekly colour supplement, *ES The Evening Standard Magazine*, a weekly listings magazine, *MetroLife* and regular weekly supplements: *Just the Job* (Mon) and *Homes & Property* (Wed).

Joint Deputy Editors *Andrew Bordiss, Ian MacGregor*
Executive Editors *Anne McElvoy, Philip Evans*
Assistant Editor (Features) *Guy Eaton*
News Editor *Ian Walker*
Assistant Editor (Arts) *Norman Lebrecht*
Assistant Editor (Sport) *Simon Greenberg*
ES Editor *Catherine Ostler*
MetroLife Editor *Mark Booker*

Greater Manchester

Manchester Evening News
164 Deansgate, Manchester M60 2RD
☎0161 832 7200 Fax 0161 834 3814

www.manchesteronline.co.uk
Owner *Manchester Evening News Ltd*
Editor *Paul Horrocks*
Circulation 153,125

One of the country's major regional dailies. Initial approach in writing preferred. No fiction. *Personal Finance* (Mon); *Health* (Tues); *Homes & Property* (Wed); *Small Business* (Thurs); *Lifestyle* (Fri/Sat); *Holidays* (Sat).

News Editor *Ian Wood*
Features Editor *Maggie Henfield* Regional news features, personality pieces and showbiz profiles considered. Maximum 1200 words.
Sports Editor *Peter Spencer*
Women's Page *Diane Cooke*
PAYMENT based on house agreement rates.

Hampshire

The News
The News Centre, Hilsea, Portsmouth PO2 9SX
☎023 9266 4488 Fax 023 9267 3363
✉ newsdesk@thenews.co.uk
www.portsmouth.co.uk
Owner *Portsmouth Printing & Publishing Ltd*
Editor *Mike Gilson*
Circulation 63,483

Unsolicited mss not generally accepted. Approach by letter.
News Editor *Colin McNeill*
Features Editor *John Millard* General subjects of S.E. Hants interest. Maximum 600 words. No fiction.
Sports Editor *Colin Channon* Sports background features. Maximum 600 words.

The Southern Daily Echo
Newspaper House, Test Lane, Redbridge, Southampton SO16 9JX
☎023 8042 4777 Fax 023 8042 4545
www.thisishampshire.net
Owner *Newsquest plc*
Editor *Ian Murray*
Circulation 43,291

Unsolicited mss 'tolerated'. Approach the editor in writing with strong ideas; staff supply almost all the material.

Kent

Kent Messenger
6 & 7 Middle Row, Maidstone ME14 1TG
☎01622 695666 Fax 01622 757227
✉ rgreen@thekmgroup.co.uk
www.kentonline.co.uk

Owner *Kent Messenger Group*
Editor *Ron Green*
Circulation 62,171

Very little freelance work is commissioned.

Medway Messenger
Medway House, Ginsbury Close, Sir Thomas Longley Road, Medway City Estate, Strood, Rochester ME2 4DU
☎01634 227821 Fax 01634 715256
✉ medwaytoday@thekmgroup.co.uk
Owner *Kent Messenger Group*
Editor *Bob Dimond*

Published Mondays and Fridays with the free *Medway Extra* on Wednesday.
Business Editor *Trevor Sturgess*
Community Editor *David Jones*
Sports Editor *Mike Rees*

Lancashire

Bolton Evening News
Newspaper House, Churchgate, Bolton BL1 1DE
☎01204 522345 Fax 01204 365068
✉ bennewsdesk@boltoneveningnews.co.uk
www.thisisbolton.co.uk
Owner *Newsquest Media Group Ltd (a Gannett company)*
Editor *Steve Hughes*
Circulation 35,337

Business, children's page, travel, local services, motoring, fashion and cookery.
News Editor *John Horne*
Features Editor/Women's Page *Julia Smith*

Lancashire Evening Post
Olivers Place, Eastway, Fulwood, Preston PR2 9ZA
☎01772 254841 Fax 01772 880173
www.prestontoday.net
Owner *Johnston Press plc*
Editor *Simon Reynolds*
Circulation 44,876

Unsolicited mss are not generally welcome; many are received and not used. All ideas in writing to the editor.

Lancashire Evening Telegraph
Newspaper House, High Street, Blackburn BB1 1HT
☎01254 678678 Fax 01254 680429
www.thisislancashire.co.uk
Owner *Newsquest Media Group Ltd (a Gannett company)*

Editor *Kevin Young*
Circulation 36,266

News stories and feature material with an East Lancashire flavour (a local angle, or written by local people) welcome. Approach in writing with an idea in the first instance. No fiction.
   News Editor *Andrew Turner*
   Features Editor *John Anson*

Oldham Evening Chronicle
PO Box 47, Union Street, Oldham OL1 1EQ
☎0161 633 2121   Fax 0161 652 2111
✉ editorial@oldham-chronicle.co.uk

Owner *Hirst Kidd & Rennie Ltd*
Editor *Jim Williams*
Circulation 27,668

Motoring, food and wine, lifestyle supplement, business page.
   News Editor *Mike Attenborough*

The Gazette (Blackpool)
PO Box 20, Avroe House, Avroe Crescent, Blackpool FY4 2DP
☎01253 400888   Fax 01253 361870
✉ bpl.editorial@blackpoolgazette.co.uk
www.blackpooltoday.co.uk

Owner *Johnston Press plc*
Circulation 35,986

Managing Director *Philip Welsh*
Editor *David Helliwell*

Unsolicited mss welcome in theory. Approach in writing with an idea. Supplements: *The Result* (sport, Mon); *Eve* (women, Tues); *Wheels* (motoring, Wed); *Homes* (Thurs); *The Weekend* (entertainment, Fri); *Life!* magazine (entertainment & leisure, Sat); *Jobs Plus* (jobs and careers, Sat).

Leicestershire
Leicester Mercury
St George Street, Leicester LE1 9FQ
☎0116 251 2512   Fax 0116 253 0645
www.thisisleicestershire.co.uk

Owner *Northcliffe Newspapers Group Ltd*
Editor *Nick Carter*
Circulation 93,156

   News Editor *Mark Charlton*
   Features Editor *Alex Dawson*

Lincolnshire
Grimsby Telegraph
80 Cleethorpe Road, Grimsby DN31 3EH
☎01472 360360   Fax 01472 372257

✉ newsdesk@grimsbytelegraph.co.uk
Owner *Northcliffe Newspapers Group Ltd*
Editor *Michelle Lalor*
Circulation 41,109

Sister paper of the *Scunthorpe Evening Telegraph*. Unsolicited mss generally welcome. Approach in writing. No fiction. Weekly supplements: *Business Telegraph*; *Homes and Gardens*; *Drive* (motoring); *Sports Telegraph* (Sat). All material to be addressed to the News Editor *D. Atkin*. Particularly welcomes hard news stories – approach in haste by telephone.
   Special Publications Editor *B. Farnsworth*

Lincolnshire Echo
Brayford Wharf East, Lincoln LN5 7AT
☎01522 820000   Fax 01522 804493
✉ editor@lincolnshireecho.co.uk

Owner *Northcliffe Newspapers Group Ltd*
Editor *Michael Sassi*
Circulation 27,027

Best buys, holidays, motoring, dial-a-service, restaurants, sport, leisure, home improvement, record reviews, gardening corner, stars. All editorial material to be addressed to the editor.

Scunthorpe Telegraph
4–5 Park Square, Scunthorpe DN15 6JH
☎01724 273273   Fax 01724 273101

Owner *Northcliffe Newspapers Group Ltd*
Editor *Jon Grubb*
Circulation 23,176

All correspondence should go to the Deputy Editor *Jane Manning*.

Merseyside
Daily Post (Liverpool)
PO Box 48, Old Hall Street, Liverpool L69 3EB
☎0151 227 2000   Fax 0151 236 4682
www.icliverpool.co.uk

Owner *Trinity Mirror Plc*
Editor *Jane Wolstenholme*
Circulation 20,048

Unsolicited mss welcome. Receives about six a day. Approach in writing with an idea. No fiction. Local, national/international news, current affairs, profiles – with pictures. Maximum 800–1000 words.
   Features Editor *Louise Douglas*
   News Editor *Paul Kennedy*
   Sports Editor *Richard Williamson*
   Women's Page *Penny Fray*

Liverpool Echo

PO Box 48, Old Hall Street, Liverpool
L69 3EB
☎0151 227 2000 Fax 0151 236 4682
✉ letters@liverpoolecho.co.uk
Owner *Trinity Mirror Merseyside*
Editor *Mark Dickinson*
Circulation 135,845

One of the country's major regional dailies.
Unsolicited mss welcome; initial approach
with ideas in writing preferred.
 Acting News Editor *Alison Gow*
 Features Editor *Jane Haase*
 Sports Editor *John Thompson*
 Women's Editor *Susan Lee*

Norfolk

Eastern Daily Press

Prospect House, Rouen Road, Norwich
NR1 1RE
☎01603 628311 Fax 01603 623872
www.EDP24.co.uk
Owner *Archant Regional*
Editor *Peter Franzen*
Circulation 72,323

Most pieces by commission only. Supplements:
Centro (daily); education (Tues); motoring,
business, property pages, agriculture, employ-
ment (all weekly); *Event* full-colour magazine
(Fri); Saturday full colour magazine.
 Deputy Editor *James Ruddy*
 Editor (News) *Paul Durrant*
 Features Editor *Emma Outten*
 Sports Editor *David Thorpe*
 Magazine Editor *Steve Snelling*

Evening News

Prospect House, Rouen Road, Norwich
NR1 1RE
☎01603 628311 Fax 01603 219060
✉ david.bourn@archant.co.uk
www.eveningnews24.co.uk
Owner *Archant Ltd*
Editor *David Bourn*
Circulation 29,835

Includes special pages on local property,
motoring, children's page, pop, fashion, arts,
entertainments and TV, gardening, local music
scene, home and family.
 Deputy Editor *Tim Williams*
  (tim.williams@archant.co.uk)
 Assistant Editor *Amanda Patterson*
  (amanda.patterson@archant.co.uk)

Features Editor *Derek James*
 (derek.james@archant.co.uk)

Northamptonshire

Chronicle and Echo

Upper Mounts, Northampton NN1 3HR
☎01604 467000 Fax 01604 467190
Owner *Northamptonshire Newspapers*
Editor *Mark Edwards*
Circulation 26,002

Unsolicited mss are 'not necessarily unwelcome
but opportunities to use them are rare'.
Approach in writing with an idea. No fiction.
Supplements: *Sport on Monday*; *Business Week*
(Tues); *Property Week* (Wed); *Job Search* (Thurs);
Weekend Motors and *The Guide* (Friday); *TV
Week* (Sat).
 News Editor *Richard Edmondson*
 Features Editor/Women's Page *Sarah
  Freeman*
 Sports Editor *Steve Pitts*

Evening Telegraph

Newspaper House, Ise Park, Rothwell Road,
Kettering NN16 8GA
☎01536 506100 Fax 01536 506195
✉ etnewsdesk@northantsnews.co.uk
www.northantsnews.com
Owner *Johnston Press Plc*
Managing Editor *David Penman*
Circulation 33,346

Northamptonshire Business Guide (weekly); *Entertainment Guide* and *Jobs* supplements (Thurs);
films and eating out (Fri); and *Home & Garden* –
monthly lifestyle supplement including gardening, etc.
 News Editor *Nick Tite*
 Sports Editor *Ian Davidson*

Nottinghamshire

Evening Post Nottingham

Castle Wharf House, Nottingham NG1 7EU
☎0115 948 2000 Fax 0115 964 4032
Owner *Northcliffe Newspapers Group Ltd*
Editor *Graham Glen*
Circulation 76,949

Unsolicited mss occasionally used. Good local
interest only. Maximum 800 words. No fic-
tion. Send ideas in writing.
 News Editor *Claire Catlow*
 Deputy Editor *Marc Astley*
 Sports Editor *Dave Parkinson*

Oxfordshire
Oxford Mail
Osney Mead, Oxford OX2 0EJ
☎01865 425262 Fax 01865 425554
✉ nqonews@nqo.com
www.thisisoxfordshire.co.uk

Owner *Newsquest (Oxfordshire) Ltd*
Editor *Simon O'Neill*
Circulation 27,575

Unsolicited mss are considered but a great many unsuitable offerings are received. Approach in writing with an idea, rather than by phone. No fiction.
PAYMENT All fees negotiable.

Shropshire
Shropshire Star
Ketley, Telford TF1 5HU
☎01952 242424 Fax 01952 254605

Owner *Shropshire Newspapers Ltd*
Editor *Sarah-Jane Smith*
Circulation 82,862

No unsolicited mss; approach the editor with ideas in writing in the first instance. No news or fiction.
Head of Features *Sharon Walters, Carl Jones*
Limited opportunities; uses mostly in-house or syndicated material. Maximum 1200 words.
Sports Editor *Dave Ballinger*

Somerset
Evening Post
Temple Way, Bristol BS99 7HD
☎0117 934 3000 Fax 0117 934 3575
✉ mail@epost.co.uk
www.epost.co.uk

Owner *Bristol United Press plc*
Editor *Mike Lowe*
Circulation 58,862

News Editor *Kevan Blackadder*
Features Editor *Bill Davis*
Sports Editor *Chris Bartlett*

The Bath Chronicle
Windsor House, Windsor Bridge Road, Bath
BA2 3AU
☎01225 322322 Fax 01225 322291
www.thisisbath.com

Owner *BUP Plc*
Editor *David Gledhill (editor@bathchron.co.uk)*
Circulation 15,338

Local news and features especially welcomed (news@bathchron.co.uk).
Deputy Editor *John McCready*
News Editor *Paul Wiltshire*
Features Editor *Georgette McCready*
Sports Editor *Julie Riegal*

Western Daily Press
Temple Way, Bristol BS99 7HD
☎0117 934 3000 Fax 0117 934 3574
✉ WDEditor *or* WDNews *or*
WDFeats@bepp.co.uk
www.westpress.co.uk

Owner *Bristol Evening Post & Press Ltd*
Editor *Terry Manners*
Circulation 50,756

Sports Editor *Chris Spittles*
Women's Page *Cathy Smith* (Features Production)

Staffordshire
Burton Mail
65–68 High Street, Burton upon Trent
DE14 1LE
☎01283 512345 Fax 01283 515351
✉ editorial@burtonmail.co.uk

Owner *Staffordshire Newspapers Ltd*
Editor *Paul Hazeldine*
Circulation 16,766

Fashion, health, wildlife, environment, nostalgia, financial/money (Mon); consumer (Tues); women's world, rock (Wed); property (Thurs); motoring, farming, what's on (Fri); what's on, leisure (Sat).
News *Steve Doohan*
Features *Bill Pritchard*
Sports Editor *Rex Page*
Women's Page *Emma Atkin*

The Sentinel/Sentinel Sunday
Sentinel House, Etruria, Stoke on Trent
ST1 5SS
☎01782 602525 Fax 01782 280781
(Sentinel)/201167 (Sentinel Sunday)
www.thisisstaffordshire.co.uk

Owner *Staffordshire Sentinel Newspapers Ltd*
Editor-in-Chief *Sean Dooley*
Circulation 75,366 (Sentinel)

Weekly sports final supplement. All material should be sent to the Head of Content *Martin Tideswell*.

Suffolk

East Anglian Daily Times

Press House, 30 Lower Brook Street, Ipswich
IP4 1AN
☎01473 230023 Fax 01473 324776
✉ eadt@eadt.co.uk
www.eadt.co.uk

Owner *Archant Ltd*
Editor *Terry Hunt*
Circulation 40,251

Founded 1874. Unsolicited mss generally not welcome; three or four received a week and almost none are used. Approach in writing in the first instance. No fiction. Supplements: Sport (Mon); Business (Tues); Jobs (Wed); Property (Thurs); Motoring (Fri); Magazine (Sat).

News Editor *Aynsley Davidson* Hard news stories involving East Anglia (Suffolk, Essex particularly) or individuals resident in the area are always of interest.

Features *Julian Ford* Mostly in-house, but will occasionally buy in when the subject is of strong Suffolk/East Anglian interest. Photo features preferred (extra payment). Special advertisement features are regularly run. Some opportunities here. Maximum 1000 words.

Sports Editor *Nick Garnham*
Women's Page *Victoria Hawkins*

Evening Star

30 Lower Brook Street, Ipswich IP4 1AN
☎01473 230023 Fax 01473 324850

Owner *Archant Ltd*
Editor *Nigel Pickover*
Circulation 25,924

News Editor *Martin Davey*
Sports Editor *Mike Horne*

Sussex

The Argus

Argus House, Crowhurst Road, Hollingbury,
Brighton BN1 8AR
☎01273 544544 Fax 01273 505703
✉ simonb@theargus.co.uk
www.thisisbrightonandhove.co.uk

Owner *Newsquest (Sussex) Ltd*
Editor-in-Chief *Simon Bradshaw*
Circulation 42,464

News Editor *Simon Freeman*
Sports Editor *Chris Giles*

Teesside

Evening Gazette

Borough Road, Middlesbrough TS1 3AZ
☎01642 234242 Fax 01642 232014

Owner *Trinity Mirror plc*
Editor *Steve Dyson*
Circulation 60,362

Special pages: health, education, family, business, property, entertainment, leisure, motoring, recruitment.

News Editor *Jim Horsley*
Features Editor/Women's Page *Kathryn Armstrong*
Business *Helen Logan*
Sports Editor *Allan Boughey*
Councils *Sandy McKenzie*
Consumer *David Fryer*
Health *Helen Sturdy*
Crime *Mike Underwood*

Tyne & Wear

Evening Chronicle

Groat Market, Newcastle upon Tyne
NE1 1ED
☎0191 232 7500 Fax 0191 232 2256
✉ ec.news@ncjmedia.co.uk
www.icnewcastle.co.uk

Owner *Trinity Mirror Plc*
Editor *Paul Robertson*
Circulation 90,813

Receives a lot of unsolicited material, much of which is not used. Family issues, gardening, pop, fashion, cooking, consumer, films and entertainment guide, home improvements, motoring, property, angling, sport and holidays. Approach in writing with ideas. Limited opportunities for features due to full-time feature staff.

Assistant Editor (News) *Mick Smith*
Sports Editor *Paul New*
Women's Interests *Jennifer Bradbury*

Gazette

Chapter Row, South Shields NE33 1BL
☎0191 427 4800 Fax 0191 456 8270
www.southtynesidetoday.co.uk

Owner *Northeast Press Ltd*
Editor *John Szymanski*
Circulation 21,450

News Editor *Gary Welford*
Sports Editor *Mick Worrall*
Women's Page *Caroline Sword*

The Journal

Groat Market, Newcastle upon Tyne
NE1 1ED
☎0191 232 7500
Fax 0191 232 2256/201 6044
✉ jnl.newsdesk@ncjmedia.co.uk
www.the-journal.co.uk

Owner *Trinity Mirror Plc*
Editor *Brian Aitken*
Circulation 43,333

Daily platforms include farming and business.
  Deputy Editor *Graham Pratt*
  Sports Editor *Kevin Dinsdale*
  Arts & Entertainment Editor *David Whetstone*
  Environment Editor *Tony Henderson*
  Business Editor *Iain Laing*

Sunday Sun

Newcastle Chronicle & Journal Ltd, Thomson House, Groat Market, Newcastle upon Tyne NE1 1ED
☎0191 201 6158 Fax 0191 201 6180
✉ peter.montellier@ncjmedia.co.uk

Owner *Trinity Mirror Plc*
Editor *Peter Montellier*
Circulation 86,400

All material should be addressed to the appropriate editor (phone to check), or to the editor.
  Sports Editor *Dylan Younger*

Sunderland Echo

Echo House, Pennywell, Sunderland SR4 9ER
☎0191 501 5800 Fax 0191 534 4861
✉ rob.lawson@northeast-press.co.uk

Owner *Johnston Press Plc*
Editor *Rob Lawson*
Circulation 48,551

All editorial material to be addressed to the News Editor *Patrick Lavelle* (echo.news@ northeast-press.co.uk).

Warwickshire

Coventry Evening Telegraph

Corporation Street, Coventry CV1 1FP
☎024 7663 3633 Fax 024 7655 0869
✉ news@coventry-telegraph.co.uk
www.IcCoventry.co.uk

Owner *Trinity Mirror Plc*
Editor *Alan Kirby*
Circulation 62,279

Unsolicited mss are read, but few are published. Approach in writing with an idea. No fiction. All unsolicited material should be addressed to the editor. Maximum 600 words for features.
  News Managers *Steve Chilton, Steve Williams*
  Features Manager/Women's Page *Paula Irish*
  Sports Editor *Rob Madill*
  PAYMENT negotiable.

Leamington Spa Courier

32 Hamilton Terrace, Leamington Spa
CV32 4LY
☎01926 457755 Fax 01926 451690
✉ editorial@leamingtoncourier.co.uk
www.leamingcourier.co.uk

Owner *Heart of England Newspapers (Johnston Press)*
Editor *Martin Lawson*
Circulation 13,572

One of the Leamington Spa Courier series which also includes the Warwick Courier and Kenilworth Weekly News. Unsolicited feature articles considered, particularly matter with a local angle. Telephone with idea first.
  News Editor *Calista Lewis*

West Midlands

Birmingham Evening Mail

PO Box 78, Weaman Street, Birmingham
B4 6AT
☎0121 236 3366
Fax 0121 234 5878 (editorial)

Owner *Trinity Mirror Plc*
Editor *Roger Borrell*
Circulation 107,410

Freelance contributions are welcome, particularly topics of interest to the West Midlands and Women's Page pieces offering original and lively comment.
  Deputy Editor *Colin Clark*
  Features Editor *Alison Handley*
  Women's Page *Diane Parkes*

Birmingham Post

28 Colmore Circus, Queensway, Birmingham
B4 6AX
☎0121 234 5419 Fax 0121 234 5667

Owner *Trinity Mirror Plc*
Editor *Fiona Alexander*
Circulation 16,885

One of the country's leading regional newspapers. Freelance contributions are welcome. Topics of interest to the West Midlands and pieces offering lively, original comment are particularly welcome.
  News Editor *Mo Ilyas*
  Features Editor *Sid Langley*

Express & Star
Queen Street, Wolverhampton WV1 1ES
☎01902 313131   Fax 01902 319721

Owner *Midlands News Association*
Editor *Adrian Faber*
Circulation 163,543

> Deputy Editor *Keith Harrison*
> Assistant Editor *Roy Williams*
> Head of News *Mark Drew*
> Features Editor *Dylan Evans*
> Business Editor *Jim Walsh*
> Sports Editor *Tim Walters*
> Women's Editor *Anne-Laure Domenichini*
> Lifestyle Editor *Deanna Delamotta*

Sunday Mercury (Birmingham)
Weaman Street, Birmingham B4 6AY
☎0121 234 5567   Fax 0121 234 5877
✉ sundaymercury@mrn.co.uk

Owner *Trinity Mirror Plc*
Editor *David Brookes*
Circulation 85,934

> Deputy Editor (Features) *Paul Cole*
> Head of Content *Tony Larner*
> Assistant Editor (Sport) *Lee Gibson*

Wiltshire
Evening Advertiser
100 Victoria Road, Swindon SN1 3BE
☎01793 528144   Fax 01793 542434
✉ editor@newswilts.co.uk
www.thisiswiltshire.co.uk

Owner *Newsquest (Wiltshire & Oxfordshire) Ltd*
Editor *Mark Waldron*
Circulation 24,004

Copy and ideas invited. 'All material must be strongly related or relevant to the town of Swindon or the county of Wiltshire.' Little scope for freelance work. Fees vary depending on material.

> Deputy Editor *Pauline Leighton*
> News Editor *Catherine Turnbull*
> Sports Editor *Neville Smith*

Worcestershire
Evening News
Berrow's House, Hylton Road, Worcester WR2 5JX
☎01905 748200   Fax 01905 748009

Owner *Newsquest (Midlands South) Ltd*
Editor *Stewart Gilbert*
Circulation 20,456

Local events (Tues); jobs/careers (Wed); prop-erty (Thurs); showbiz/what's on, motoring and Pulse pop page (Fri); holidays/what's on (Sat).

> Deputy Editor *Mark Higgitt*
> News Editor *Sala Lloyd*
> Features Editor *Mike Pryce*
> Consumer Page *Melanie Hill*
> Sports Editor *Paul Ricketts*

Yorkshire
Evening Press
PO Box 29, 76–86 Walmgate, York
YO1 9YN
☎01904 653051   Fax 01904 612853
✉ newsdesk@ycp.co.uk
www.thisisyork.co.uk

Owner *Newsquest Media Group (a Gannett company)*
Editor *Kevin Booth*
Circulation 36,837

Unsolicited mss not generally welcome, unless submitted by journalists of proven ability. *Business Press Pages* (Tues); *Property Press* (Thurs); *Friday Night Fever* – what's on (Fri); *8 Days* TV supplement (Sat).

> News Editor *Fran Clee*
> Picture Editor *Martin Oates*
> Sports Editor *Martin Jarred*
> PAYMENT negotiable.

Huddersfield Daily Examiner
Queen Street South, Huddersfield HD1 2TD
☎01484 430000   Fax 01484 437789

Owner *Trinity Mirror Plc*
Editor *Roy Wright*
Circulation 31,602

Home improvement, home heating, weddings, dining out, motoring, fashion, services to trade and industry.

> News Editor *Neil Atkinson*
> Features Editor *Andrew Flynn*
> Sports Editor *John Gledhill*
> Women's Page *Hilarie Stelfox*

Hull Daily Mail
Blundell's Corner, Beverley Road, Hull
HU3 1XS
☎01482 327111   Fax 01482 584353
✉ news@hulldailymail.co.uk
www.thisishull.co.uk

Owner *Northcliffe Newspapers Group Ltd*
Editor *John Meehan*
Circulation 71,337

> News Editor *Jeremy Deacon*
> Features Editor *Alex Leys*

Scarborough Evening News

17–23 Aberdeen Walk, Scarborough
YO11 1BB
☎01723 363636 Fax 01723 383825
✉ editorial@scarborougheveningnews.co.uk
www.scarboroughtoday.co.uk

Owner *Yorkshire Regional Newspapers Ltd*
Editor *Ed Asquith*
Circulation 14,936

Special pages include property (Mon); motoring (Tues/Fri).

Deputy Editor *Sue Wilkinson*
News Editor *Neil Pickford*
Sports Editor *Charles Place*
All other material should be addressed to the editor.

Telegraph & Argus (Bradford)

Hall Ings, Bradford BD1 1JR
☎01274 729511 Fax 01274 723634
www.thisisbradford.co.uk

Owner *Newsquest Media Group Ltd (a Gannett company)*
Editor *Perry Austin-Clarke*
Circulation 46,716

No unsolicited mss – approach in writing with samples of work. No fiction.

Head of News *Martin Heminway*
Features Editor *David Barnett*
Local features and general interest. Showbiz pieces. 600–1000 words (maximum 1500).

The Doncaster Star

Sunny Bar, Doncaster DN1 1NB
☎01302 344001 Fax 01302 768340
✉
rob.hollingworth@sheffieldnewspapers.co.uk
Owner *Sheffield Newspapers Ltd*
Editor/News Editor *Rob Hollingworth*
Circulation 8,312

All editorial material to be addressed to the editor.

Sports Editor *Steve Hossack*

The Star

York Street, Sheffield S1 1PU
☎0114 276 7676 Fax 0114 272 5978

Owner *Sheffield Newspapers Ltd*
Editor *Peter Charlton*
Circulation 75,881

Unsolicited mss not welcome, unless topical and local.

News Editor *Bob Westerdale* Contributions only accepted from freelance news reporters if they relate to the area.

Features Editor *John Highfield* Very rarely requires outside features, unless on specialised subject.

Sports Editor *Martin Smith*
Women's Page *Jo Davison*
PAYMENT negotiable.

Yorkshire Evening Post

Wellington Street, Leeds LS1 1RF
☎0113 243 2701 Fax 0113 238 8536
✉ eped@ypn.co.uk

Owner *Johnson Press*
Editor *Neil Hodgkinson*
Circulation 81,116

Evening sister of the *Yorkshire Post*.

News Editor *Gilian Haworth*
Features Editor *Anne Pickles*
Sports Editor *Phil Rostron*
Women's Page *Jayne Dawson*

Yorkshire Post

Wellington Street, Leeds LS1 1RF
☎0113 243 2701 Fax 0113 238 8537
✉ yp.editor@ypn.co.uk

Owner *Johnston Press*
Editor *Rachel Campey*
Circulation 64,648

A serious–minded, quality regional daily with a generally conservative outlook. Three or four unsolicited mss arrive each day; all will be considered but initial approach in writing preferred. All submissions should be addressed to the editor. No fiction, poetry or family histories.

Deputy Editor *Duncan Hamilton*
Features Editor *Catherine Scott* Open to suggestions in all fields (though ordinarily commissioned from specialist writers).

Sports Editor *Bill Bridge*
Women's Page *Jill Armstrong*

NORTHERN IRELAND

Belfast News Letter

46–56 Boucher Crescent, Belfast BT12 6QY
☎028 9068 0000 Fax 028 9066 4412

Owner *Century Newspapers Ltd*
Editor *Nigel Wareing*

Weekly supplements: *Farming Life*; *Business News Letter*; *Female Times*; *The Guide*; *Sports Ulster*.

News Editors *Ric Clark, Steven Moore, Jackie McKeown*
Features Editor *Geoff Hill*
Sports Editor *Brian Millar*
Fashion & Lifestyle/Property Editor *Sandra Chapman*

Business Editor *Adrienne McGill*
Agricultural Editor *David McCoy*
Political Editor *Ciaran McKeown*
Picture Editor *Martin Nangle*

Belfast Telegraph

Royal Avenue, Belfast BT1 1EB
☎028 9026 4000 Fax 028 9055 4506/4540
Owner *Independent News & Media (UK)*
Editor *Edmund Curran*
Circulation 108,651

Weekly business, property and recruitment supplements.

Deputy Editor *Jim Flanagan*
News Editor *Paul Connolly*
Features Editor *John Caruth*
Sports Editor *John Laverty*
Business Editor *Nigel Tilson*

The Irish News

113/117 Donegall Street, Belfast BT1 2GE
☎028 9032 2226 Fax 028 9033 7505
Owner *Irish News Ltd*
Editor *Noel Doran*
Circulation 50,223

All material to appropriate editor (phone to check), or to the news desk.

Head of Content *Fiona McGarry*
Sports Editor *Thomas Hawkins*
Arts Editor/Women's Page *Joanna Braniff*

Sunday Life

124–144 Royal Avenue, Belfast BT1 1EB
☎028 9026 4300 Fax 028 9055 4739
✉ betty.arnold@belfasttelegraph.co.uk
www.sundaylife.co.uk
Owner *Independent News & Media (UK)*
Editor/General Manager *Martin Lindsay*
Circulation 87,132

Deputy Editor *Martin Hill*
Sports Editor *Jim Gracey*
More2Life Colour supplement. Editor *Stephanie Bell*

SCOTLAND

The Courier and Advertiser

80 Kingsway East, Dundee DD4 8SL
☎01382 223131 Fax 01382 454590
✉ courier@dcthomson.co.uk
www.thecourier.co.uk
Owner *D.C. Thomson & Co. Ltd*
Editor *Bill Hutcheon*
Circulation 83,084

Circulates in East Central Scotland. Features

occasionally accepted on a wide range of subjects, particularly local/Scottish interest – including finance, insurance, agriculture, motoring, modern homes, lifestyle and fitness. Maximum length, 500 words.

News Editor *Arliss Rhind*
Features Editor/Women's Page *Catriona McInnes*
Sports Editor *Graeme Dey*

Daily Record (Glasgow)

See *National Newspapers*

Evening Express (Aberdeen)

PO Box 43, Lang Stracht, Mastrick, Aberdeen AB15 6DF
☎01224 690222 Fax 01224 699575
✉ d.martin@ajl.co.uk
Owner *Northcliffe Newspapers Group Ltd*
Editor *Donald Martin*
Circulation 59,053

Circulates in Aberdeen and the Grampian region. Local, national and international news and pictures, sport. Family platforms include *What's On, Counter* (consumer news), *Eating Out Guide, Family Days Out*. Unsolicited mss welcome 'if on a controlled basis'.

Assistant Editor *Richard Prest* Freelance news contributors welcome.

PAYMENT negotiable.

Evening News

Barclay House, 108 Holyrood Road, Edinburgh EH8 8AS
☎0131 620 8620 Fax 0131 620 8696
www.edinburghnews.com
Owner *Scotsman Publications Ltd*
Editor *Ian Stewart*
Circulation 68,803

Founded 1873. Circulates in Edinburgh, Fife, Central and Lothian. Coverage includes: entertainment, fashion, gardening, motoring, shopping, health and lifestyle, showbusiness. Occasional platform pieces, topical features and local interest. Unsolicited feature material welcome. Approach the appropriate editor in writing.

News Editor *Jim Morrison*
Sports Editor *Toby Chapman*
PAYMENT NUJ/house rates.

Evening Telegraph

80 Kingsway East, Dundee DD4 8SL
☎01382 223131 Fax 01382 454590
✉ general@eveningtelegraph.co.uk
www.eveningtelegraph.co.uk

Owner *D.C. Thomson & Co. Ltd*
Editor *Alan Proctor*
Circulation 26,766

Circulates in Tayside, Dundee and Fife. All material should be addressed to the editor.

Evening Times
200 Renfield Street, Glasgow G2 3PR
☎0141 302 7000 Fax 0141 302 6677
✉ times@eveningtimes.co.uk
Owner *Newsquest*
Editor *Charles McGhee*
Circulation 92,716

Circulates in Glasgow and the west of Scotland. Supplements: *Job Search*; *Homes etc*; *Drive times*; *Extra times*; *Times Out*; *Times Out Weekend Extra*.
  News Editor *Hugh Boag*
  Features Editor *Garry Scott*
  Sports Editor *David Stirling*

Greenock Telegraph
2 Crawfurd Street, Greenock PA15 1LH
☎01475 726511 Fax 01475 783734
Owner *Clyde & Forth Press Ltd*
Managing Editor *Steward Peterson*
Circulation 18,946

Circulates in Greenock, Port Glasgow, Gourock, Kilmacolm, Langbank, Bridge of Weir, Inverkip, Wemyss Bay, Skelmorlie, Largs. Unsolicited mss considered 'if they relate to the newspaper's general interests'. No fiction. All material to be addressed to the editor.

The Herald/Sunday Herald (Glasgow)
See *National Newspapers*

Paisley Daily Express
14 New Street, Paisley PA1 1YA
☎0141 887 7911 Fax 0141 887 6254
✉ pde@s-un.co.uk
Owner *Scottish & Universal Newspapers Ltd*
Editor *Jonathan Russell*
Circulation 11,082

Circulates in Paisley, Linwood, Renfrew, Johnstone, Elderslie, Neilston and Barrhead. Unsolicited mss welcome only if of genuine local (Paisley) interest. The paper does not commission work and will consider submitted material. Maximum 1000–1500 words. All submissions to the editor.
  News Editor *Anne Dalrymple*
  Sports Reporters *Michelle Evans, Paul Behan*

The Press and Journal
PO Box 43, Lang Stracht, Mastrick, Aberdeen AB15 6DF
☎01224 690222 Fax 01224 663575
Owner *Northcliffe Newspapers Group Ltd*
Editor *Derek Tucker*
Circulation 90,379

A well-established daily that circulates in Aberdeen, Grampians, Highlands, Tayside, Orkney, Shetland and the Western Isles. Most material is commissioned but will consider ideas.
  News Editor *Fiona McWhirr* Wide variety of hard or off-beat news and features relating especially, but not exclusively, to the north of Scotland.
  Sports Editor *Alex Martin*
  Women's Page *Victoria Banks*
  Your Life *Sonja Cox* Saturday lifestyle tabloid pullout. Features food, fashion, travel, books, arts and lifestyle.
  PAYMENT by arrangement.

The Scotsman (Edinburgh)
See *National Newspapers*

Scotland on Sunday (Edinburgh)
See *National Newspapers*

Sunday Mail (Glasgow)
See *National Newspapers*

Sunday Post (Dundee)
See *National Newspapers*

WALES
Daily Post
PO Box 202, Vale Road, Llandudno Junction, Conwy LL31 9ZD
☎01492 574455 Fax 01492 574433
✉ alistairmachray@dailypost.co.uk
Owner *Trinity Mirror Plc*
Editor in Chief *Alastair Machray*
Circulation 47,000
  Features Editor *Jill Tunstall*
  News Editor *Maria Breslyn*
  Sports Editor *Jonathan McEvoy*

Evening Leader
Mold Business Park, Wrexham Road, Mold CH7 1XY
☎01352 707707 Fax 01352 752180
✉ news@eveningleader.co.uk
Owner *North Wales Newspapers*

Editor-in-Chief *Richard Williams*
Circulation 27,163

Circulates in Wrexham, Flintshire, Deeside and Chester. Special pages/features: motoring, travel, arts, women's, children's, photography, local housing, information and news for the disabled, music and entertainment.
Assistant Editor *Barrie Jones*
Head of Content *Joanne Shone*
Sports Editor *Nick Harrison*

South Wales Argus
Cardiff Road, Maesglas, Newport
NP20 3QN
☎01633 810000 Fax 01633 777202
www.thisisgwent.co.uk

Owner *Newsquest*
Editor *Gerry Keighley*
Circulation 30,700

Circulates in Newport, Gwent and surrounding areas.
News Editor *Mark Templeton*
Sports Editor *Phil Webb*

South Wales Echo
Thomson House, Havelock Street, Cardiff
CF10 1XR
☎029 2058 3622 Fax 029 2058 3624
www.icwales.co.uk

Owner *Trinity Mirror Plc*
Editor *Alastair Milburn*
Circulation 59,590

Circulates in South and Mid Glamorgan and Gwent.
Head of News *Nick Machin*
Head of Features *Alison Stokes*
Head of Sport *Delme Parfitt*

South Wales Evening Post
Adelaide Street, Swansea SA1 1QT
☎01792 510000 Fax 01792 514697
✉ postbox@swwp.co.uk
www.thisissouthwales.co.uk

Owner *Northcliffe Newspapers Group Ltd*
Editor *Spencer Feeney*
Circulation 57,884

Circulates throughout south west Wales.
News Editor *Peter Slee*
Features Editor *Catherine Ings*
Sports Editor *David Evans*

The Western Mail
Thomson House, Havelock Street, Cardiff
CF10 1XR
☎029 2058 3583 Fax 029 2058 3652

www.icwales.com
Owner *Trinity Mirror Plc*
Editor *Alan Edmunds*
Circulation 44,559

Circulates in Cardiff, Merthyr Tydfil, Newport, Swansea and towns and villages throughout Wales. Mss welcome if of a topical nature, of Welsh interest. No short stories or travel. Approach in writing to the editor. 'Usual subjects already well covered, e.g. motoring, travel, books, gardening. We look for the unusual.' Maximum 1000 words. Opportunities also on women's page. Supplements: *Saturday Magazine*; *Education*; *WM*; *Box Office*; *Welsh Homes*; *Business*; *Sport*; *Motoring*.
Deputy Editor *Neil Bennett*
News Editor *Duncan Higgitt*
Sports Editor *Philip Blanche*
Features Editor *Ceri Gould*

Wales on Sunday
Thomson House, Havelock Street, Cardiff
CF10 1XR
☎029 2022 3333 Fax 029 2058 3725

Owner *Trinity Mirror plc*
Editor *Tim Gordon*
Circulation 50,166

Launched 1989. Tabloid with sports supplement. Does not welcome unsolicited mss.
News Editor *Laura Kemp*
Show Biz/Features Editor *Rachel Mainwaring*
Sports Editor *Nick Rippington*

CHANNEL ISLANDS
Guernsey Press & Star
Braye Road, Vale, Guernsey GY1 3BW
☎01481 240240 Fax 01481 240235
✉ newsroom@guernsey-press.com
www.guernsey-press.com

Owner *Guiton Group*
Editor *Richard Digard*
Circulation 16,411

Special pages include children's and women's interest, gardening and fashion.
News Editor *James Falla*
Sports Editor *Rob Batiste*
Features Editor *Suzanne Heneghan*

Jersey Evening Post
PO Box 582, Jersey JE4 8XQ
☎01534 611611 Fax 01534 611622
✉ editorial@jerseyeveningpost.com
www.thisisjersey.com

Owner *Jersey Evening Post Ltd*
Editor *Chris Bright*
Circulation 22,492

Special pages: gardening, motoring, property, boating, technology, young person's (16–25), women, food and drink, personal finance, rock reviews, health, business.

News Editor *Sue Le Ruez*
Features Editor *Elaine Hanning*
Sports Editor *Ron Felton*

Magazines

Abraxas
57 Eastbourne Road, St Austell PL25 4SU
☎01726 64975 Fax 01726 64975
✉ palnew7@hotmail.com
www.AbraxasMagazine.com

Owner *Paul Newman*
Editors *Paul Newman, Pamela Smith-Rawnsley*

Founded 1991. QUARTERLY incorporating the *Colin Wilson Newsletter*. Unsolicited mss welcome after a study of the magazine – initial approach by phone or letter/e-mail preferred.

FEATURES Essays, translations and reviews. Welcomes provocative, lively articles on little-known literary figures and new slants on psychology, existentialism and ideas. Max. length 2000 words.

FICTION One story per issue. Max. 2000 words. Favours compact, obsessional stories.

POETRY Double-page spread – slight penchant for the surreal but open to most styles.

PAYMENT free copy of magazine.

Acclaim
See **The New Writer**

Accountancy
145 London Road, Kingston Upon Thames KT2 6SR
☎020 8247 1387 Fax 020 8247 1424

Owner *Wolters Kluwer UK*
Editor *Chris Quick*
Circulation 53,681

Founded 1889. MONTHLY. Written ideas welcome.

FEATURES *Lesley Bolton* Accounting, tax, business-related articles of high technical content aimed at professional/managerial readers. Max. 2000 words. PAYMENT by arrangement.

Accountancy Age
32–34 Broadwick Street, London W1A 2HG
☎020 7316 9190/Features: 020 7316 9807
Fax 020 7316 9250
✉ accountancy_age@vnu.co.uk
www.accountancyage.com

Owner *VNU Business Publications*
Editor *Damian Wild*
Deputy Editor *Gavin Hinks* (020 7316 9242)
Circulation 77,806

Founded 1969. WEEKLY. Unsolicited mss welcome. Ideas may be suggested in writing provided they are clearly thought out.

FEATURES *Rachel Fielding* Topics right across the accountancy, business and financial world. Max. 2000 words. PAYMENT negotiable.

Ace Tennis Magazine
IG House, Palliser Road, London W14 9EB
☎020 7381 7100 Fax 020 7610 2794
✉ Nigel.Billen@acemag.co.uk

Owner *Tennis GB*
Editor *Nigel Billen*
Circulation 44,241

Founded 1996. MONTHLY specialist tennis magazine. News (250 words max.) and features (2000 words max.). No unsolicited mss; send feature synopses by e-mail in the first instance. No tournament reports. PAYMENT £200 per 1000 words.

Acumen
See under **Poetry Magazines**

Aeroplane
IPC Media Ltd., King's Reach Tower, Stamford Street, London SE1 9LS
☎020 7261 5849 Fax 020 7261 5269
✉ aeroplane_monthly@ipcmedia.com
www.aeroplanemonthly.com

Owner *IPC Country & Leisure Media Ltd*
Editor *Michael Oakey*
Circulation 36,656

Founded 1973. MONTHLY. Historic aviation and aircraft preservation from its beginnings to the 1960s. No post-1960 aircraft types; no poetry. Will consider news items and features written with authoritative knowledge of the subject, illustrated with good quality photographs.

NEWS *Tony Harmsworth* Max. 500 words.
FEATURES *Michael Oakey* Max. 3000 words.
Approach by letter in the first instance.

PAYMENT £60 per 1000 words; £10–40 per picture used.

African Affairs
Dept of Politics, University of Newcastle upon Tyne, 40–42 Great North Road, Newcastle upon Tyne NE1 7RL

☎0191 222 6000   Fax 0191 222 5609
✉ african.affairs@ncl.ac.uk
Owner *Royal African Society*
Editors *Tim Kelsall, Stephen Ellis*
Circulation 3185

Founded 1901. QUARTERLY learned journal publishing articles on recent political, social and economic developments in sub-Saharan countries. Also included are historical studies that illuminate current events in the continent. Unsolicited mss welcome. Max. 8000 words. No PAYMENT.

Air International
PO Box 100, Stamford PE9 1XQ
☎01780 755131   Fax 01780 757261
✉ malcolm.english@keypublishing.com
Owner *Key Publishing Ltd*
Editor *Malcolm English*

Founded 1971. MONTHLY. Civil and military aircraft magazine. Unsolicited mss welcome but initial approach by phone or in writing preferred.

AirForces Monthly
PO Box 100, Stamford PE9 1XQ
☎01780 755131   Fax 01780 757261
✉ edafm@keypublishing.com
Owner *Key Publishing Ltd*
Editor *Alan Warnes*
Circulation 25,787

Founded 1988. MONTHLY. Modern military aviation magazine. Unsolicited mss welcome but initial approach by phone or in writing preferred.

Amateur Gardening
Westover House, West Quay Road, Poole BH15 1JG
☎01202 440840   Fax 01202 440860
Owner *IPC Media*
Editor *Tim Rumball*
Circulation 56,827

Founded 1884. WEEKLY. New contributions are welcome especially if they are topical and informative. All articles/news items should be supported by colour pictures (which may or may not be supplied by the author).
FEATURES Topical and practical gardening articles. Max. 1000 words.
NEWS Compiled and edited in-house generally but all stories welcomed.
PAYMENT negotiable.

Amateur Photographer
IPC Media Ltd., King's Reach Tower, Stamford Street, London SE1 9LS
☎020 7261 5100/0870 444 5000 (switchboard)   Fax 020 7261 5404
✉ amateurphotographer@ipcmedia.com
Owner *IPC Media*
Editor *Garry Coward-Williams*
Circulation 26,253

Founded 1884. WEEKLY. For the competent amateur with a technical interest. Freelancers are used but writers should be aware that there is ordinarily no use for words without pictures.

Amateur Stage
Hampden House, 2 Weymouth Street, London W1W 5BT
☎020 7636 4343   Fax 020 7636 2323
✉ cvtheatre@aol.com
Owner *Platform Publications Ltd*
Editor *Charles Vance*

Some opportunity here for outside contributions. Topics of interest include amateur premières, technical developments within the amateur forum and items relating to landmarks or anniversaries in the history of amateur societies. Approach in writing only (include s.a.e. for return of mss). No PAYMENT.

Ancestors
See **The National Archives** under *UK Publishers*

Angler's Mail
IPC Media Ltd., King's Reach Tower, Stamford Street, London SE1 9LS
☎020 7261 5778   Fax 020 7261 6016
✉ anglersmail@ipcmedia.com
Owner *IPC Media*
Editor *Tim Knight*
Circulation 45,237

Founded 1965. WEEKLY. Angling news and matches. Interested in pictures, stories, tip-offs and features. Approach the news desk by telephone. PAYMENT £10–40 per 200 words; pictures, £20–40.

Animal Action
Wilberforce Way, Southwater, Horsham RH13 9RS
☎0870 010 1181   Fax 0870 753 0048
✉ publications@rspca.org.uk
www.rspca.org.uk
Owner *RSPCA*
Editor *Simon Corrall*

Circulation 80,000

BI-MONTHLY RSPCA youth membership magazine. Articles (pet care, etc.) are written in-house. Good-quality animal photographs welcome.

Animalprints

Worthing Animal Aid, 56 Cissbury Gardens, Worthing BN14 ODZ
☎01903 877144
✉ WorthingAnimalAid@btinternet.com

Owner *Worthing Animal Aid*
Editor *Lilian Taylor*
Circulation 500

Founded 1999. QUARTERLY magazine that aims to advance the animal movement. Welcomes contributions that are well researched, subtly thought provoking and have the potential for stimulating discussion. Approach in writing. PAYMENT Complimentary copies of relevant issue.

The Antique Dealer and Collectors' Guide

PO Box 805, Greenwich, London SE10 8TD
☎020 8691 4820 Fax 020 8691 2489
✉ antiquedealercollectorsguide@
ukbusiness.com
www.antiquecollectorsguideco.uk

Owner *Statuscourt Ltd*
Publisher *Philip Bartlam*
Circulation 12,500

Founded 1946. TEN ISSUES YEARLY. Covers all aspects of the antiques and fine art worlds. Unsolicited mss welcome.

FEATURES Practical but readable articles on the history, design, authenticity, restoration and market aspects of antiques and fine art. Max. 2000 words.

NEWS Items on events, sales, museums, exhibitions, antique fairs and markets. Max. 300 words.

PAYMENT rates for features by arrangement.

Antiques & Art Independent

PO Box 1945, Comely Bank, Edinburgh EH4 1AB
☎07000 268478
✉ antiquesnews@hotmail.com
www.antiquesnews.co.uk

Owner *Antiquesnews Ltd*
Publisher/Editor *Tony Keniston*

Founded 1997. QUARTERLY. Up-to-date information for the British antiques and art trade. News, photographs, gossip and contro-versial views on all aspects of the fine art and antiques world welcome. Articles on antiques and fine arts themselves are not featured. Approach in writing with ideas.

Apex Advertiser

PO Box 7086, Clacton-on-Sea CO15 5WN
☎0870 242 0938 Fax 0870 046 6536
✉ enquiry@apexadvertiser.co.uk
www.apexadvertiser.co.uk

Owner *Apex Publishing Ltd*
Editor *Susan Kidby*
Circulation 12,000

Founded 2002. MONTHLY advertising magazine including guides and information, features, listings and reviews. Approach by post, only.

Apollo Magazine

20 Theobald's Road, London WC1X 8PF
☎020 7430 1900 Fax 020 7404 7015
✉ editorial@apollomag.com

Owner *The Spectator (1828) Ltd*
Editor *Michael Hall*
Publisher *Kimberly Fortier*

FOUNDED 1925. MONTHLY. Specialist articles on art and antiques, exhibition and book reviews, exhibition diary, information on dealers and auction houses. Unsolicited mss welcome. Interested in specialist, usually new research in fine arts, architecture and antiques.

Architects' Journal

151 Rosebery Avenue, London EC1R 4GB
☎020 7505 6700 Fax 020 7505 6701
www.ajplus.co.uk

Owner *Emap Construct*
Editor *Isabel Allen*
Circulation 16,441

WEEKLY trade magazine dealing with all aspects of the industry. No unsolicited mss. Approach in writing with ideas.

Architectural Design

John Wiley & Sons, 4th Floor, International House, Ealing Broadway Centre, London W5 5DB
☎020 8326 3800 Fax 020 8326 3801

Owner *John Wiley & Sons Ltd*
Editor *Helen Castle*
Senior Production Editor *Mariangela Palazzi-Williams*
Circulation 5,000

Founded 1930. BI-MONTHLY. Sold as a book as well as a journal, *AD* charts theoretical and topical developments in architecture. Format consists of 128pp, the first part dedicated to a theme compiled by a specially commissioned guest-editor; the back section (AD+) carries series and more current one-off articles. Unsolicited mss not welcome generally, though journalistic contributions will be considered for the back section.

The Architectural Review
151 Rosebery Avenue, London EC1R 4GB
☎020 7505 6725 Fax 020 7505 6701
www.arplus.com

Owner *Emap Construct*
Editor *Peter Davey*
Circulation 23,925

MONTHLY professional magazine dealing with architecture and all aspects of design. No unsolicited mss. Approach in writing with ideas.

Arena
Endeavour House, 189 Shaftesbury Avenue, London WC2H 8JG
☎020 7437 9011

Owner *Emap East*
Editor *Anthony Noguera*
Circulation 40,617

MONTHLY style and general interest magazine for men. Intelligent articles and profiles.

FEATURES Fashion, lifestyle, film, television, politics, business, music, media, design, art, architecture and sport.

Art Monthly
4th Floor, 28 Charing Cross Road, London WC2H 0DB
☎020 7240 0389 Fax 020 7497 0726
info@artmonthly.co.uk
www.artmonthly.co.uk

Owner *Britannia Art Publications Ltd*
Editor *Patricia Bickers*
Circulation 6000

Founded 1976. TEN ISSUES YEARLY. News and features of relevance to those interested in modern and contemporary visual art. Unsolicited mss welcome. Contributions should be addressed to the deputy editor, accompanied by s.a.e.

FEATURES Always commissioned. Interviews and articles of up to 2000 words on art theory, individual artists, contemporary art history and issues affecting the arts (e.g. funding and arts education). Exhibition reviews of 750–1000 words; book reviews of 750–1000 words.

NEWS Brief reports (250–300 words) on art issues.

PAYMENT negotiable.

The Art Newspaper
70 South Lambeth Road, London SW8 1RL
☎020 7735 3331 Fax 020 7735 3332
contact@theartnewspaper.com
www.theartnewspaper.com

Owner *Umberto Allemandi & Co. Publishing*
Editor *Cristina Ruiz*
Circulation 22,000

Founded 1990. MONTHLY. Tabloid format with hard news on the international art market, news, museums, exhibitions, archaeology, conservation, books and current debate topics. Length 250–2000 words. No unsolicited mss. Approach with ideas in writing. Commissions only. PAYMENT £120 per 1000 words.

The Artist
Caxton House, 63–65 High Street, Tenterden TN30 6BD
☎0158076 3673 Fax 0158076 5411
www.theartistmagazine.co.uk

Owner/Editor *Sally Bulgin*
Circulation 20,500

Founded 1931. MONTHLY. Art journalists, artists, art tutors and writers with a good knowledge of art materials are invited to write to the editor with ideas for practical and informative features about art, materials, techniques and artists.

Artscene
Dean Clough Industrial Park, Halifax HX3 5AX
☎01422 322527 Fax 01422 322518
artscene@btconnect.com
www.artscene.org.uk

Owner *Arts Council England, Yorkshire*
Editor *Victor Allen*
Circulation 25,000

Founded 1973. MONTHLY. Listings magazine for Yorkshire and Humberside. No unsolicited mss. Approach by phone with ideas.

FEATURES Profiles of artists (all media) and associated venues/organisers of events of interest. Topical relevance vital. Max. length 1500 words.

NEWS Artscene strives to bring journalistic values to arts coverage – all arts 'scoops' in the region are of interest. Max. length 500 words.

PAYMENT features and news, £100 per 1000 words.

Asian Times
Unit 2, 65 Whitechapel Road, London E1 1DU
☎020 7650 2000 Fax 020 7650 2001
asiantimes@ethnicmedia.co.uk

www.ethnicmedia.co.uk
Owner *Ethnic Media Group*
Editor *Isaac Hamza*
Circulation 28,525

Founded 1983. WEEKLY community paper for the Asian community in Britain. Interested in relevant general, local and international issues. Approach in writing with ideas for submission.

Athletics Weekly

83 Park Road, Peterborough PE1 2TN
☎01733 898440 Fax 01733 898441
✉ results@athletics-weekly.co.uk
www.athleticsweekly.com
Owner *Descartes Publishing*
Editor *Jason Henderson*
Circulation 14,000

Founded 1945. WEEKLY. Covers track and field, road, fell, cross-country, race walking, athletic features and sports politics.
NEWS *Steve Landells* Max. 400 words.
FEATURES *Tony Ward* Max. 2000 words. Approach in writing.
PAYMENT negotiable.

Attitude

Northern & Shell Tower, City Harbour, 4 Selsdon Way, London E14 9GL
☎020 7308 5261 Fax 020 7308 5384
✉ attitdue@attitudemag.co.uk
Owner *Remnant Media*
Editor *Adam Mattera*
Deputy Editor *Matthew Todd*
Circulation 60,000

Founded 1994. MONTHLY. Style magazine aimed primarily, but not exclusively, at gay men. Celebrity, fashion and cultural coverage. Brief summaries of proposed features, together with details of previously published work, should be sent by post or e-mail only. 'It sounds obvious, but anyone wanting to contribute to the magazine should read it first.'

The Author

84 Drayton Gardens, London SW10 9SB
☎020 7373 6642
Owner *The Society of Authors*
Editor *Fanny Blake*
Manager *Kate Pool*
Circulation 8500

Founded 1890. QUARTERLY journal of the **Society of Authors**. Most articles are commissioned.

Auto Express

30 Cleveland Street, London W1T 4JD
☎020 7907 6200 Fax 020 7907 6234
✉ editorial@autoexpress.co.uk
www.autoexpress.co.uk
Owner *Dennis Publishing*
Editor *David Johns*
News & Features Editor *Richard Yarrow*
Circulation 96,238

Founded 1989. WEEKLY consumer motoring title with news, drives, tests, investigations, etc.
NEWS News stories and tip-offs welcome. Fillers 150 words max.; leads 300 words. Approach by e-mail.
FEATURES Welcomes ideas. No fully-written articles – features will be commissioned if appropriate and good enough. Max. 2000 words.
PAYMENT £350 per 1000 words.

Autocar

60 Waldegrave Road, Teddington TW11 8LG
☎020 8943 5630 Fax 020 8267 5759
✉ autocar@haynet.com
www.autocarmagazine.co.uk
Owner *Haymarket Magazines Ltd*
Editor *Steve Sutcliffe*
News *Tim Pollard*
Circulation 68,742

Founded 1895. WEEKLY. All news stories, features, interviews, scoops, ideas, tip-offs and photographs welcome. PAYMENT negotiable.

Aviation News

HPC, Drury Lane, St Leonards on Sea TN38 9BJ
☎01424 720477 Fax 01424 443693
✉ editor@aviation-news.co.uk
www.aviation-news.co.uk
Owner *Hastings Printing Company*
Editor *Barry C. Wheeler*
Circulation 21,000

Founded 1939. MONTHLY review of aviation for those interested in military, commercial and business aircraft and equipment – old and new. Will consider articles on military and civil aircraft, airports, air forces, current and historical subjects. No fiction.
FEATURES 'New writers always welcome and if the copy is not good enough it is returned with guidance attached.' Max. 5000 words.
NEWS Items are always considered from new sources. Max. 300 words.
PAYMENT negotiable.

B Magazine

64 North Row, London W1K 7LL
☎020 7150 7020 Fax 020 7150 7677
✉ letters@bmagazine.co.uk
www.hf-uk.com
Owner *Hachette Filipacchi (UK) Ltd*
Editor *Frances Sheen*
Circulation 165,708

MONTHLY glossy magazine aimed at women in their mid-twenties. Will consider real-life stories, emotional issues and celebrity features. Ideas for features should be sent to *Viki Wilson*. No short stories. Approach in writing or by e-mail.

Baby & You

The Publishing House, 1–3 Highbury Station Road, London N1 1SE
☎020 7226 2222
✉ amanda.burney@highburywv.com
Owner *Highbury House Communications Plc*
Editor *Amanda Burney*

MONTHLY parenting title that focuses on issues affecting the family as a whole.

Balance

Diabetes UK, 10 Parkway, London NW1 7AA
☎020 7424 1000 Fax 020 7424 1001
✉ balance@diabetes.org.uk
Owner *Diabetes UK*
Editor *Martin Cullen*
Circulation 250,000

Founded 1935. BI-MONTHLY. Unsolicited mss are not accepted. Writers may submit a brief proposal in writing. Only topics relevant to diabetes will be considered.

NEWS Short pieces about activities relating to diabetes and the lifestyle of people with diabetes. Max. 150 words.

FEATURES Medical, diet and lifestyle features written by people with diabetes or with an interest and expert knowledge in the field. General features are mostly based on experience or personal observation. Max. 1500 words.

PAYMENT NUJ rates.

The Banker

Tabernacle Court, 16–28 Tabernacle Street, London EC2A 4DD
☎020 7382 8507 Fax 020 7382 8586
✉ stephen.timewell@ft.com
www.thebanker.com
Owner *FT Business*
Editor-in-Chief *Stephen Timewell*
Circulation 25,000

Founded 1926. MONTHLY. News and features on banking, finance and capital markets worldwide and technology.

BBC Gardeners' World Magazine

Woodlands, 80 Wood Lane, London W12 0TT
☎020 8433 3959 Fax 020 8433 3986
✉ adam.pasco@bbc.co.uk
Owner *BBC Worldwide Publishing Ltd*
Editor *Adam Pasco*
Circulation 285,772

Founded 1991. MONTHLY. Gardening advice, ideas and inspiration. No unsolicited mss. Approach by phone or in writing with ideas – interested in features about exceptional small gardens. Also interested in any exciting new gardens showing good design and planting ideas as well new plants and the stories behind them. 'The magazine aims to be the first to bring news of new trends and developments, and always welcomes ideas from contributors.'

BBC Good Food

Woodlands, 80 Wood Lane, London W12 0TT
☎020 8433 2000 Fax 020 8433 3931
✉ goodfood.magazine@bbc.co.uk
Owner *BBC Worldwide Publishing Ltd*
Editorial Director *Gillian Carter*
Circulation 325,000

Founded 1989. MONTHLY food and drink magazine with television and radio links. No unsolicited mss.

BBC Good Homes Magazine

Woodlands, 80 Wood Lane, London W12 0TT
☎020 8433 2391 Fax 020 8433 2691
www.bbcgoodhomes.com
Owner *BBC Worldwide Publishing Ltd*
Editor *Lisa Allen*
Circulation 106,213

Founded 1998. MONTHLY. Decorating, interiors, homes, shopping, property and gardening. No non-homes related features, fiction or puzzles.

FEATURES *Gill Smith* Readers' homes; property features from specialists. Approach by letter with cuttings.

BBC History Magazine
(incorporating **Living History**)

14th Floor, Tower House, Fairfax Street, Bristol BS1 3BN
☎0117 927 9009
www.originpublishing.co.uk

Owner *BBC Worldwide Publishing Ltd*
Editor *Dave Musgrove*
Circulation 53,000

Founded 2000. MONTHLY. General news and features on British and international history, with books and CD reviews, listings of history events, TV and radio history programmes and regular features for those interested in history and current affairs. Winner, British Society of Magazine Editors 'Editor of the Year Award', 2002, for general interest and current affairs titles. Will consider submissions from academic or otherwise expert historians/archaeologists as well as, occasionally, from historically literate journalists who include expert analysis and historiography with a well-told narrative. Ideas for regular features are welcome. Also publishes cartoons, quizzes and crosswords. 'We cannot guarantee to acknowledge all unsolicited mss immediately.'

FEATURES should be pegged to anniversaries or forthcoming books/TV programmes, current affairs topics, etc. 750–3000 words.

NEWS 400–500 words. Send short letter or e-mail with synopsis, giving appropriate sources, pegs for publication dates, etc.

PAYMENT negotiable.

BBC Homes & Antiques

Woodlands, 80 Wood Lane, London W12 0TT
☎020 8433 3490 Fax 020 8433 3867
www.bbcworldwide.com/antiques
Owner *BBC Worldwide Publishing Ltd*
Editor *Mary Carroll*
Circulation 150,454

Founded 1993. MONTHLY traditional home interest magazine with a strong bias towards antiques and collectables. Opportunities for freelancers are limited; most features are commissioned from a regular stable of contributors. No fiction, health and beauty, fashion or general showbusiness. Approach with ideas by phone or in writing.

FEATURES *Caroline Wheater* At-home features: inspirational houses – people-led items. Pieces commissioned on recce shots and cuttings. Guidelines available on request. Send cuttings of relevant work published. Max. 1500 words. PAYMENT negotiable.

BBC Music Magazine

14th Floor, Tower House, Fairfax Street, Bristol BS1 3BN
☎0117 927 9009
www.originpublishing.co.uk
Owner *BBC Worldwide Publishing Ltd*

Editor *To be appointed*
Circulation 70,006 (worldwide)

Founded 1992. MONTHLY. All areas of classical music. Not interested in unsolicited material. Approach with ideas by e-mail or fax.

BBC Top Gear Magazine

Woodlands, 80 Wood Lane, London W12 0TT
☎020 8433 3716 Fax 020 8433 3754
www.topgear.com
Owner *BBC Worldwide Ltd*
Editor *Michael Harvey*
Circulation 136,216

Founded 1993. MONTHLY companion magazine to the popular TV series. No unsolicited material as most features are commissioned.

BBC Wildlife Magazine

14th Floor, Tower House, Fairfax Street, Bristol BS1 3BN
☎0117 927 9009
www.originpublishing.co.uk
Owner *BBC Worldwide Publishing Ltd*
Editor *Sophie Stafford*
Circulation 50,811

Founded 1963 (formerly *Wildlife*, née *Animals*). MONTHLY. Unsolicited mss generally not welcome.

FEATURES Most features commissioned from writers with expert knowledge of wildlife or conservation subjects. Max. 2500 words.

NEWS Most news stories commissioned from known freelancers. Max. 400 words. PAYMENT features, £200–450; news, £80–120

Bee World

IBRA, 18 North Road, Cardiff CF10 3DT
☎029 2037 2409 Fax 029 2066 5522
✉ mail@ibra.org.uk
www.ibra.org.uk
Owner *International Bee Research Association*
Editor *Dr P.A. Munn*
Circulation 1700

Founded 1919. QUARTERLY. High-quality factual journal, including peer-reviewed articles, with international readership. Features on apicultural science and technology. Unsolicited mss welcome but authors should write to the editor for guidelines before submitting material.

Bella

H. Bauer Publishing, Academic House, 24–28 Oval Road, London NW1 7DT
☎020 7241 8000 Fax 020 7241 8056

Owner *H. Bauer Publishing*
Editor-in-Chief *Jayne Marsden*
Circulation 429,226

Founded 1987. WEEKLY. Women's magazine specialising in real-life, human interest stories.
FEATURES *Clare Swatman* Contributions welcome for some sections of the magazine: readers' letters, 'Blush with Bella'.
FICTION *Linda O'Byrne* Max. 1000–1200 words. Send s.a.e. for guidelines.

Best
72 Broadwick Street, London W1F 9EP
☎020 7439 5000 Fax 020 7312 4175
✉ best@natmags.co.uk

Owner *National Magazine Company*
Editor *Louise Court*
Circulation 420,437

Founded 1987. WEEKLY women's magazine. Multiple features, news, short stories on all topics of interest to women. Important for would-be contributors to study the magazine's style which differs from many other women's weeklies. Approach in writing with s.a.e.
FEATURES *Helen Garston, Charlotte Seligman* Max. 1500 words. No unsolicited mss.
FICTION *Pat Richardson* Short story slot – 900–1200 words. Send s.a.e. for guidelines.
PAYMENT negotiable.

Best of British
Ian Beacham Publishing, Bank Chambers, 27a Market Place, Market Deeping PE6 8EA
☎01778 342814
✉ mail@british.fsbusiness.co.uk
www.bestofbritishmag.co.uk

Owner *Ian Beacham Publishing*
Editor-in-Chief *Ian Beacham*

Founded 1994. MONTHLY magazine celebrating all things British, both past and present. Emphasis on nostalgia – memories from the 1940s, 1950s and 1960s. Study of the magazine is advised in the first instance. All preliminary approaches should be made in writing.

Best Solutions
IBIS, 38 Broad Street, Earls Barton NN6 0ND
☎01604 466500 Fax 01604 466480
✉ info@bestsolutions.org.uk
www.bestsolutions.org.uk

Editor *Chris Cherin*

Founded 1996. QUARTERLY 32pp business to business consultancy magazine. No unsolicited mss. Interested in business solution articles (1000 words). Approach in writing.

The Big Issue
1–5 Wandsworth Road, London SW8 2LN
☎020 7526 3200 Fax 020 7526 3201
✉ editorial@bigissue.com
www.bigissue.com

Editor-in-Chief *A. John Bird*
Editor *Matt Ford*
Circulation 122,679

Founded 1991. WEEKLY. An award-winning campaigning and street-wise general interest magazine sold in London, the Midlands, the North East and South of England. Separate regional editions sold in Manchester, Scotland, Wales and the South West.
NEWS *Judy Kerr* Hard-hitting exclusive stories with emphasis on social injustice aimed at national leaders.
ARTS *Charles Howgego* Interested in interviews and analysis ideas. Reviews written in-house. Send synopses to arts editor.
FEATURES Interviews, campaigns, comment, opinion and social issues reflecting a varied and informed audience. Balance includes social issues but mixed with arts and cultural features. Freelance writers used each week – commissioned from a variety of contributors. Best approach is to e-mail or post synopses to assistant deputy editor, *Charles Howgego* with examples of work in the first instance. Max. 1500 words. PAYMENT £160 for 1000 words.

Bike
Emap Automotive Ltd, Media House, Lynch Wood, Peterborough PE2 6EA
☎01733 468181 Fax 01733 468196
✉ bike@emap.com

Owner *Emap Plc*
Editor *Tim Thompson*
Circulation 100,093

Founded 1971. MONTHLY. Broad-based motorcycle magazine. Approach by e-mail.

Bird Life Magazine
RSPB, The Lodge, Sandy SG19 2DL
☎01767 680551 Fax 01767 683262
✉ derek.niemann@rspb.org.uk

Owner *Royal Society for the Protection of Birds*
Editor *Derek Niemann*
Circulation 90,000

Founded 1965. BI-MONTHLY. Bird, wildlife and nature conservation for 8–12-year-olds (RSPB Wildlife Explorer members). No unsolicited mss. No 'captive/animal welfare' articles.
FEATURES Unsolicited material rarely used.

NEWS News releases welcome. Approach in writing in the first instance.

Bird Watching

Emap Active, Bretton Court, Peterborough PE3 8DZ
☎01733 264666 Fax 0870 046 4729
✉ david.cromack@emap.com

Owner *Emap Active*
Editor *David Cromack*
Circulation 20,447

Founded 1986. MONTHLY magazine for birdwatchers at all levels of experience. Offers practical advice of where and when to see birds, how to identify them, product reviews (particularly binoculars and telescopes), extensive bird sightings, news and general articles.

FEATURES Interested in authoratative articles on bird behaviour and bird watching/sites in the UK. Please send synopsis, not the whole piece. Max. 1000 words.

NEWS UK news pre-eminent, preferably with pictures. Max. 350 words.

FEES negotiable.

Birds

RSPB, The Lodge, Sandy SG19 2DL
☎01767 680551 Fax 01767 683262
✉ rob.hume@rspb.org.uk

Owner *Royal Society for the Protection of Birds*
Editor *R.A. Hume*
Circulation 618,174

QUARTERLY magazine which covers not only wild birds but also other wildlife and related conservation topics. No interest in features on pet birds or 'rescued' sick/injured/orphaned ones. Content refers mostly to RSPB work so opportunities for freelance work on other subjects are limited but some freelance submissions are used in most issues. Phone or e-mail to discuss.

Birdwatch

3D/F Leroy House, 436 Essex Road, London N1 3QP
☎020 7704 9495 Fax 020 7704 2767
✉ editorial@birdwatch.co.uk
www.birdwatch.co.uk

Owner *Solo Publishing*
Editor *Dominic Mitchell*
Circulation 15,000

Founded 1992. MONTHLY magazine featuring illustrated articles on all aspects of birds and birdwatching, especially in Britain. No unsolicited mss. Approach in writing with synopsis of 100 words max. Annual **Birdwatch Bird Book of the Year** award (see entry under *Prizes*).

FEATURES *Dominic Mitchell* Unusual angles/ personal accounts, if well-written. Articles of an educative or practical nature suited to the readership. Max. 2000 words.

FICTION *Dominic Mitchell* Very little opportunity although occasional short story published. Max. 1500 words.

NEWS *David Mairs* Very rarely use external material.

PAYMENT £50 per 1000 words.

Bizarre

30 Cleveland Street, London W1T 4JD
☎020 7907 6000 Fax 020 7907 6020
✉ bizarre@dennis.co.uk
www.bizarremag.com

Owner *Dennis Publishing*
Editor *Alex Godfrey*
Circulation 95,095

Founded 1997. MONTHLY magazine featuring amazing stories and images from around the world. No fiction, poetry, illustrations, short snippets.

FEATURES *James Doorne* No unsolicited mss. Send synopsis by post or e-mail.

PAYMENT negotiable.

Black Beauty & Hair

2nd Floor, Culvert House, Culvert Road, Battersea, London SW11 5HD
☎020 7720 2108 Fax 020 7498 3023
✉ info@blackbeautyandhair.com
www.blackbeautyandhair.com

Owner *Hawker Consumer Publications Ltd*
Editor *Irene Shelley*
Circulation 21,499

BI-MONTHLY with one annual special: *The Hairstyle Book* in October; and a *Bridal Supplement* in the April/May issue. Black hair and beauty magazine with emphasis on authoritative articles relating to hair, beauty, fashion, health and lifestyle. Unsolicited contributions welcome.

FEATURES Beauty and fashion pieces welcome from writers with a sound knowledge of the Afro-Caribbean beauty scene plus bridal features. Minimum 1000 words.

PAYMENT £100 per 1000 words.

Bliss Magazine

Endeavour House, 189 Shaftesbury Avenue, London WC2H 8JG
☎020 7208 3478 Fax 020 7208 3591
✉ alex.thwaites@emap.com

Owner *Emap élan*
Editor *Helen Johnston*
Circulation 241,664

Founded 1995. MONTHLY teenage lifestyle magazine for girls. No unsolicited mss; 'call the assistant editor (*Chantelle Horton*) with an idea and then send it in.'

NEWS *Charlotte Crisp* Worldwide teenage news. Max. 200 words.

FEATURES Real life teenage stories with subjects willing to be photographed. Reports on teenage issues. Max. 2000 words.

PAYMENT news, £50–100; feaures, £350.

The Book Collector

PO Box 12426, London W11 3GW
☎020 7792 3492 Fax 020 7792 3492
✉ info@thebookcollector.co.uk
www.thebookcollector.co.uk

Owner *The Collector Ltd*
Editor *Nicolas J. Barker*

Founded 1950. QUARTERLY magazine on bibliography and the history of books, bookcollecting, libraries and the book trade.

Book World Magazine

2 Caversham Street, London SW3 4AH
☎020 7351 4995 Fax 020 7351 4995

Owner *Christchurch Publishers Ltd*
Editor *James Hughes*
Circulation 5500

Founded 1980. MONTHLY news and reviews for serious book collectors, librarians, antiquarian and other booksellers. No unsolicited mss. Interested in material relevant to literature, art and book collecting. Send letter in the first instance.

Bookdealer

11 Gainsborough Court, College Road, Dulwich, London SE21 7LT
☎020 8693 5685 Fax 020 8693 5685

Editor *Barry Shaw*

WEEKLY trade paper which acts almost exclusively as a platform for people wishing to buy or sell rare/out-of-print books. Twelve-page editorial only; occasional articles and book reviews by regular freelance writers.

The Bookseller

Endeavour House, 5th Floor, 189 Shaftesbury Avenue, London WC2H 8TJ
☎020 7420 6006 Fax 020 7420 6103
www.theBookseller.com

Owner *VNU Entertainment Media*
Editor *Nicholas Clee*

Trade journal of the publishing and book trade – the essential guide to what is being done to

whom. Trade news and features, including special features, company news, publishing trends, bestseller data, etc. Unsolicited mss rarely used as most writing is either done in-house or commissioned from experts within the trade. Approach in writing first.

FEATURES *Jenny Bell*
NEWS *Joel Rickett*

Boxing Monthly

40 Morpeth Road, London E9 7LD
☎020 8986 4141 Fax 020 8986 4145
✉ mail@boxing-monthly.demon.co.uk
www.boxing-monthly.co.uk

Owner *Topwave Ltd*
Editor *Glyn Leach*
Circulation 30,000

Founded 1989. MONTHLY. International coverage of professional boxing; previews, reports and interviews. Unsolicited material welcome. Interested in small hall shows and grass-roots knowledge. No big fight reports. Approach in writing in the first instance.

Boyz

2nd Floor, Medius House, 63–69 New Oxford Street, London WC1A 1DG
☎020 7845 4300 Fax 020 7845 4309
✉ hudson@boyz.co.uk

Editor *David Hudson*
Circulation 55,000

Founded 1991. WEEKLY entertainment and features magazine aimed at a gay readership covering clubs, fashion, TV, films, music, theatre, celebrities and the UK gay scene in general. Unsolicited mss are looked at but not often used.

Brides

Vogue House, Hanover Square, London W1S 1JU
☎020 7499 9080 Fax 020 7152 3369

Owner *Condé Nast Publications Ltd*
Editor *Liz Savage*
Circulation 66,016

BI-MONTHLY. Much of the magazine is produced in-house, but a good, relevant feature on cakes, jewellery, music, flowers, etc. is always welcome. Max. 1000 words. Prospective contributors should telephone with an idea in the first instance.

British Birds

The Banks, Mountfield, Robertsbridge TN32 5JY
☎01580 882039 Fax 01580 882038

✉ editor@britishbirds.co.uk
Editor *Dr R. Riddington*
Circulation 6,000

Founded 1907. MONTHLY ornithological journal. Features main papers on topics such as behaviour, distribution, ecology, identification and taxonomy; annual *Report on Rare Birds in Great Britain* and *Rare Breeding Birds in the UK*; sponsored competition for Bird Photograph of the Year. Unsolicited mss welcome from ornithologists.

FEATURES Well-researched, original material relating to Western Palearctic birds welcome.

NEWS *Adrian Pitches* (adrian.pitches@ blueyonder.co.uk) Items ranging from conservation to humour. Max. 200 words.

PAYMENT for photographs, drawings, paintings and main papers.

British Chess Magazine

The Chess Shop, 44 Baker Street, London W1U 7RT
☎020 7486 8222 Fax 020 7486 3355
✉ bcmchess@compuserve.com
www.bcmchess.co.uk

Director/Editor *John Saunders*

Founded 1881. MONTHLY. Emphasis on tournaments, the history of chess and chess-related literature. Approach in writing with ideas. Unsolicited mss not welcome unless from qualified chess experts and players.

British Medical Journal

BMA House, Tavistock Square, London WC1H 9JR
☎020 7387 4499 Fax 020 7383 6418
✉ editor@bmj.com
www.bmj.com

Owner *British Medical Association*
Editor *Professor Richard Smith*

One of the world's leading general medical journals.

British Philatelic Bulletin

Royal Mail, 148 Old Street, London EC1V 9HQ
☎020 7250 2038 Fax 020 7250 2389

Owner *Royal Mail*
Editor *John Holman*
Circulation 22,000

Founded 1963. MONTHLY bulletin giving details of forthcoming British stamps, features on older stamps and postal history, and book reviews. Welcomes photographs of interesting, unusual or historic letter boxes.

FEATURES Articles on all aspects of British philately. Max. 1500 words.

NEWS Reports on exhibitions and philatelic events. Max. 500 words. Approach in writing in the first instance.

PAYMENT £60 per 1000 words.

British Railway Modelling

The Maltings, West Street, Bourne PE10 9PH
☎01778 391176 Fax 01778 425437
✉ johne@warnersgroup.co.uk
www.brmodelling.com

Owner *Warners Group Publications Plc*
Managing Editor *David Brown*
Editor *John Emerson*
Assistant Editor *Tony Wright*
Circulation 21,868

Founded 1993. MONTHLY. A general magazine for the practising modeller. No unsolicited mss but ideas are welcome. Interested in features on quality models, from individual items to complete layouts. Approach in writing.

FEATURES Articles on practical elements of the hobby, e.g. locomotive construction, kit conversions, etc. Layout features and articles on individual items which represent high standards of the railway modelling art. Max. 6000 words (single feature).

NEWS News and reviews containing the model railway trade, new products, etc. Max. 1000 words.

PAYMENT up to £60 per published page.

Broadcast

33–39 Bowling Green Lane, London EC1R 0DA
☎020 7505 8045 Fax 020 7505 8050

Owner *Emap Communications*
Editor *Conor Dignam*
Circulation 14,297

Founded 1960. WEEKLY. Opportunities for freelance contributions. Write to the relevant editor in the first instance.

FEATURES *Lisa Campbell* Any broadcasting issue. Max. 1500 words.

NEWS *Colin Robertson* Broadcasting news. Max. 350 words.

PAYMENT £200 per 1000 words.

Brownie

PO Box 48, Bexley DA5 1WB
☎01332 400274 Fax 01332 400274
✉ mariontbrownie@aol.com
www.girlguiding.org.uk

Owner *The Guide Association*
Editor *Marion Thompson*

Circulation 16,500

Founded 1962. MONTHLY. Aimed at Brownie members aged 7–10.

ARTICLES Crafts and simple make-it-yourself items using inexpensive or scrap materials.

FICTION Brownie content an advantage. No adventures involving unaccompanied children in dangerous situations – day or night. Max. 650 words. PAYMENT £50 per 1000 words pro rata.

Build It
1 Canada Square, Canary Wharf, London E14 5AP
☎020 7772 8440 Fax 020 7772 8584
✉ buildit@mrn.co.uk
www.buildit-online.co.uk

Owner *Inside Communications*
Editor *Catherine Monk*

Founded 1990. MONTHLY magazine covering self-build, conversion and renovation. Unsolicited material welcome on self-build case studies as well as articles on technical construction, architecture and design and dealing with builders. Max. length 2500 words. Approach by phone, post or e-mail.

The Burlington Magazine
14–16 Duke's Road, London WC1H 9SZ
☎020 7388 1228 Fax 020 7388 1230
✉ editorial@burlington.org.uk
www.burlington.org.uk

Owner *The Burlington Magazine Publications Ltd*
Managing Director *Kate Trevelyan*
Editor *Richard Shone*
Associate Editors *Bart Cornelis, Jane Martineau*

Founded 1903. MONTHLY. Unsolicited contributions welcome on the subject of art history provided they are previously unpublished. All preliminary approaches should be made in writing.

EXHIBITION REVIEWS Usually commissioned, but occasionally unsolicited reviews are published if appropriate. Max. 1000 words.

ARTICLES Max. 4500 words.

SHORTER NOTICES Max. 2000 words.

PAYMENT articles, £140 (max.); shorter notices, £80 (max.).

Business Brief
PO Box 582, Five Oaks, St Saviour JE4 8XQ
☎01534 611600 Fax 01534 611610
✉ mspeditorial@msppublishing.com

Owner *MSP Publishing*
Editor *Peter Body*

Circulation 6,500 (Jersey & Guernsey)

Founded 1989. MONTHLY magazine covering business developments in the Channel Islands and how they affect the local market. Styles itself as the magazine for business people rather than just a magazine about business. Interested in business-orientated articles only – 800 words max. Approach the editor by e-mail in the first instance with telephone follow-up. PAYMENT negotiable.

Business Traveller
Nestor House, Playhouse Yard, London EC4V 5EX
☎020 7778 0000 Fax 020 7778 0022
✉ editorial@businesstraveller.com
www.businesstraveller.com

Owner *Euromoney Institutional Investor Plc*
Editor-in-Chief *Tom Otley*
Circulation 500,000 (worldwide)

MONTHLY. Consumer publication. Opportunities exist for freelance writers but unsolicited contributions tend to be about leisure travel rather than business travel. Would-be contributors are strongly advised to study the magazine or the website first. Approach in writing with ideas.

PAYMENT varies.

Camcorder User
Highbury Entertainment London,
53–79 Highgate Road, London NW5 1TW
☎020 7331 1000 Fax 020 7331 1242
✉ rob.hull@highburywv.com
www.camuser.co.uk

Owner *Highbury WV*
Editor *Robert Hull*
Circulation 15,000

Founded 1988. MONTHLY magazine dedicated to camcorders, with features on creative technique, shooting advice, new equipment, accessory round-ups and interesting applications on location. Unsolicited mss, illustrations and pictures welcome. PAYMENT negotiable.

Campaign
22 Bute Gardens, London W6 7HN
☎020 8267 4683 Fax 020 8267 4914
✉ campaign@haynet.com
www.brandrepublic.com

Owner *Haymarket Publishing Ltd*
Editor *Caroline Marshall*
Circulation 17,700

Founded 1968. WEEKLY. Lively magazine serving the advertising and related industries.

Freelance contributors are best advised to write in the first instance.

FEATURES Ideas welcome.

NEWS Relevant news stories of up to 320 words.

PAYMENT negotiable.

Campaign Update

The Old Town Hall 367 Kennington Road, London SE1 4PT

☎020 7582 5432 Fax 020 7793 8484

Owner *Countryside Alliance*
Editor *Neville Gill*
Circulation 60,000

Founded 1996. QUARTERLY magazine on country sports and conservation issues. No unsolicited mss.

Camping and Caravanning

Greenfields House, Westwood Way, Coventry CV4 8JH

☎024 7669 4995 Fax 024 7669 4886

Owner *The Camping and Caravanning Club*
Editor *Nick Harding*
Circulation 167,025

Founded 1901. MONTHLY. Interested in journalists with camping and caravanning knowledge. Write with ideas for features in the first instance.

FEATURES Outdoor pieces in general, plus items on specific regions of Britain. Max. 1200 words. Illustrations to support text essential.

Canal and Riverboat

PO Box 618, Norwich NR7 0QT

☎01603 708930 Fax 01603 708934
✉ bluefoxfilms@themag.fsnet.co.uk
www.canalandriverboat.com

Owner *A.E. Morgan Publications Ltd*
Editor *Chris Cattrall*
Circulation 17,000

Covers all aspects of waterways, narrow boats and cruisers. Contributions welcome. Make initial approach by post or e-mail.

FEATURES Waterways, narrow boats and motor cruisers, cruising reports, practical advice, etc. Unusual ideas and personal comments are particularly welcome. Max. 2000 words. Articles should be supplied in PC Windows format disk or e-mailed with JPEG images.

NEWS Items of up to 300 words welcome on the Inland Waterways System, plus photographs if possible.

PAYMENT features, around £50 per page; news, £20.

Car Mechanics

Kelsey Publishing Group, Cudham Tithe Barn, Berry's Hill, Cudham TN16 3AG

☎01959 541444 Fax 01959 541400
✉ cm.mag@kelsey.co.uk

Owner *Kelsey Publishing Group*
Editor *Peter Simpson*
Circulation 35,000

MONTHLY. Practical guide to maintenance and repair of post–1978 cars for DIY and the motor trade. Unsolicited mss, with good-quality colour prints or transparencies, sent 'at sender's risk'. Initial approach by letter or phone strongly recommended, 'but please read a recent copy for style first.' No cartoons.

FEATURES Good, technical, entertaining and well-researched material welcome, especially anything presenting complex matters clearly and simply. PAYMENT negotiable.

Caravan Life

Warners Group Publications plc, The Maltings, West Street, Bourne PH10 9PH

☎01778 391165 Fax 01778 425437
✉ mikelec@warnersgroup.co.uk

Editor *Michael Le Caplain*
Circulation 17,000

Founded 1987. Magazine for experienced caravanners and enthusiasts providing practical and useful information and product evaluation. Opportunities for caravanning, relevant touring and travel material, also monthly reviews of the best tow cars, all with good-quality colour photographs.

Caravan Magazine

IPC Media Ltd., Leon House, 233 High Street, Croydon CR9 1HZ

☎020 8774 0600
✉ caravan@ipcmedia.com
www.caravan.com

Owner *IPC Media*
Editor *Steve Rowe*
Circulation 16,332

Founded 1933. MONTHLY. Unsolicited mss welcome. Approach in writing with ideas. All correspondence should go direct to the editor.

FEATURES Touring with strong caravan bias, technical/DIY features and how-to section. Max. 1500 words. PAYMENT by arrangement.

Caribbean Times

Unit 2, 65 Whitechapel Road, London E1 1DU

☎020 7650 2000 Fax 020 7650 2001

✉ caribbeantimes@ethnicmedia.co.uk
www.ethnicmedia.co.uk

Owner *Ethnic Media Group*
Editor *Ron Shillingford*
Circulation 25,190

Founded 1981. WEEKLY community paper for the African and Caribbean communities in Britain. Interested in general, local and international issues relevant to these communities. Approach in writing with ideas for submission.

Cat World

Avalon Court, Star Road, Partridge Green RH13 8RY
☎01403 711511 Fax 01403 711521
✉ editor@catworld.co.uk
www.catworld.co.uk

Owner *Ashdown Publishing Ltd*
Editor *Jo Rothery*
Circulation 20,000

Founded 1981. MONTHLY. Unsolicited mss welcome but initial approach in writing preferred. No poems or fiction.

FEATURES Lively, first-hand experience features on every aspect of the cat. Breeding features and veterinary articles by acknowledged experts only. Preferred length 750 or 1700 words. Accompanying pictures should be good quality and sharp.

NEWS Short, concise, factual or humorous items concerning cats. Max. 100 words. Submissions on disk (MS Word) if possible, with accompanying hard copy and s.a.e. for return or by e-mail.

The Catholic Herald

Lamb's Passage, Bunhill Row, London EC1Y 8TQ
☎020 7588 3101 Fax 020 7256 9728
✉ editorial@catholicherald.co.uk
www.catholicherald.co.uk

Acting Editor *Luke Coppen*
Features Editor *Christina Farrell*
Literary Editor *Damian Thompson*
Circulation 22,000

WEEKLY. Interested mainly in straight Catholic issues but also in general humanitarian matters, social policies, the Third World, the arts and books. PAYMENT by arrangement.

Chapman

4 Broughton Place, Edinburgh EH1 3RX
☎0131 557 2207 Fax 0131 556 9565
✉ chapman-pub@blueyonder.co.uk
www.chapman-pub.co.uk

Owner/Editor *Joy Hendry*
Circulation 2000

Founded 1970. Scotland's quality literary magazine. Features poetry, short works of fiction, criticism, reviews and articles on theatre, politics, language and the arts. Unsolicited material welcome if accompanied by s.a.e. Approach in writing unless discussion is needed. Priority is given to full-time writers.

FEATURES Topics of literary interest, especially Scottish literature, theatre, culture or politics. Max. 5000 words.

FICTION Short stories, occasionally novel extracts if self-contained. Max. 6000 words.

SPECIAL PAGES Poetry, both UK and non-UK in translation (mainly, but not necessarily, European).

PAYMENT by negotiation.

Chat

IPC Media Ltd., King's Reach Tower, Stamford Street, London SE1 9LS
☎020 7261 6565 Fax 020 7261 6534
www.ipcmedia.com/pubs/chat.htm

Owner *IPC Connect*
Editor *June Smith-Sheppard*
Circulation 604,582

Founded 1985. WEEKLY general interest women's magazine. Unsolicited mss considered; approach in writing with ideas. Not interested in contributors 'who have never bothered to read *Chat* and therefore don't know what type of magazine it is. *Chat* does not publish fiction.'

FEATURES *Anna Kingsley* Human interest and humour. Max. 1000 words. PAYMENT up to £1500 maximum.

Chemist & Druggist

Sovereign House, Sovereign Way, Tonbridge TN9 1RW
☎01732 377487 Fax 01732 367065
✉ chemdrug@cmpinformation.com
www.dotpharmacy.com

Owner *CMP Information*
Editor *Charles Gladwin*
Circulation 14,798

Founded 1859. WEEKLY news magazine for community pharmacy.

FEATURES practice, politics, professional matters, clinical articles and business advice. Contact by phone or e-mail to discuss features ideas.

NEWS Contact Assistant Editor with news articles relating to local pharmacy matters, local pharmaceutical industry events and pharmacists in the news. Max. 200 words.

PAYMENT standard rates.

Child Education

Scholastic Ltd, Villiers House, Clarendon Avenue, Leamington Spa CV32 5PR
☎01926 887799 Fax 01926 883331
www.scholastic.co.uk
Owner *Scholastic Ltd*
Acting Editor *Michael Ward*
Circulation 25,000

Founded 1923. MONTHLY magazine aimed at teachers of children aged 4–7 years. Practical articles from teachers about education for this age group are welcome. Max. 900 words. Approach in writing with synopsis.

Choice

First Floor, 2 King Street, Peterborough PE1 1LT
☎01733 555123 Fax 01733 427500
✉ editorial@choicemag.co.uk
Owner *Choice Publishing Ltd*
Editor *Norman Wright*
Circulation 90,000

Monthly full-colour, lively and informative magazine for people aged 50 plus which helps them get the most out of their lives, time and money after full-time work.

FEATURES Real-life stories, hobbies, interesting (older) people, British heritage and countryside, involving activities for active bodies and minds, health, relationships, book/entertainment reviews. Unsolicited mss read (s.a.e. for return of material); write with ideas and copies of cuttings if new contributor. No phone calls, please.

RIGHTS/MONEY All items affecting the magazine's readership are written by experts. Areas of interest include pensions, state benefits, health, finance, property, legal. PAYMENT by arrangement.

Christian Herald

Christian Media Centre, Garcia Estate, Canterbury Road, Worthing BN13 1EH
☎01903 821082 Fax 01903 821081
✉ news@christianherald.org.uk
www.christianherald.org.uk
Owner *Christian Media Centre Ltd*
Editor *Russ Bravo*
Circulation 15,000

WEEKLY. Evangelical, inter-denominational newspaper for committed Christians. News, bible-based comment and incisive features. No poetry. Contributors' guidelines available. PAYMENT Christian Media rates.

Church Music Quarterly

Cleveland Lodge, Westhumble, Dorking RH5 6BW
☎01306 872800 Fax 01306 887260
✉ cmq@rscm.com
www.rscm.com
Owner *Royal School of Church Music*
Editor *Esther Jones*
Circulation 16,500

QUARTERLY. Contributions welcome. Phone in the first instance.

FEATURES Articles on church music or related subjects considered. Max. 2000 words. PAYMENT £60 per page.

Church of England Newspaper

20–26 Brunswick Place, London N1 6DZ
☎020 7417 5800 Fax 020 7216 6410
✉ cen@parlicom.com
www.churchnewspaper.com
Owner *Parliamentary Communications Ltd*
Editor *Colin Blakely*
Circulation 9,500

Founded 1828. WEEKLY. Most material is commissioned but unsolicited mss are considered.

FEATURES *Emma Garrow* Preliminary enquiry essential. Max. 1200 words.

NEWS *Jonathan Wynne-Jones* Items must be sent promptly and should have a church/Christian relevance. Max. 200–400 words. PAYMENT negotiable.

Church Times

33 Upper Street, London N1 0PN
☎020 7359 4570 Fax 020 7226 3073
✉ news@churchtimes.co.uk *or*
features@churchtimes.co.uk
www.churchtimes.co.uk
Owner *Hymns Ancient & Modern*
Editor *Paul Handley*
Circulation 31,570

Founded 1863. WEEKLY. Unsolicited mss considered.

FEATURES *Sarah Meyrick* Articles and pictures (any format) on religious topics. Max. 2000 words.

NEWS *Helen Saxbee* Occasional reports (commissions only) and up-to-date photographs. PAYMENT features, £120 per 1000 words; news, by arrangement.

Classic Bike

EMAP Automotive, Media House, Lynchwood, Peterborough Business Park, Peterborough PE2 6EA

☎01733 468465   Fax 01733 468466
✉ classic.bike@emap.com
Owner *Emap Automotive Ltd*
Editor *Hugo Wilson*
Circulation 44,733

Founded 1978. MONTHLY. Mainly pre-1972 classic motorcycles with a heavy bias to British marques. Approach in writing.

NEWS Genuine news with good illustrations, if possible, suitable for a global audience. Max. 400 words.

FEATURES British motorcycle industry inside stories, technical features 'that can be understood by all', German, Spanish and French machine features, people. Max. 2000 words.

SPECIAL PAGES How-to features, oddball machines, stunning pictures, features with a fresh slant.

PAYMENT £100–125 per 1000 words, plus pictures.

Classic Boat

Leon House, 233 High Street, Croydon CR9 1HZ
☎020 8744 0600
✉ cb@ipcmedia.com
www.classicboat.co.uk
Owner *IPC Media*
Editor *Dan Houston*
Circulation 14,000

Founded 1987. MONTHLY. Traditional boats and classic yachts, old and new; maritime history. Unsolicited mss, particularly if supported by good photos, are welcome. Sail and power boat pieces considered. Approach in writing with ideas. Interested in well-researched stories on all nautical matters. News reports welcome. Contributor's notes available (send s.a.e.).

FEATURES Boatbuilding, boat history and design, events, yachts and working boats. Material must be well-informed and supported where possible by good-quality or historic photos. Max. 3000 words. Classic is defined by excellence of design and construction – the boat need not be old and wooden!

NEWS New boats, restorations, events, boatbuilders, etc. Max. 500 words. PAYMENT features, £75–100 per published page; news, according to merit.

Classic Cars

Media House, Peterborough Business Park, Lynchwood, Peterborough PE2 6EA
☎01733 468219   Fax 01733 468888
✉ classic.cars@emap.com
www.classiccarsmagazine.co.uk

Owner *Emap Automotive Ltd*
Editor *Martyn Moore*
Circulation 54,621

Founded 1973. TWELVE ISSUES YEARLY. International classic car magazine containing entertaining and informative articles about classic cars, events and associated personalities. Contributions welcome. PAYMENT negotiable.

Classical Guitar

1 & 2 Vance Court, Trans Britannia Enterprise Park, Blaydon on Tyne NE21 5NH
☎0191 414 9000   Fax 0191 414 9001
✉ classicalguitar@ashleymark.co.uk
www.classicalguitarmagazine.com
Owner *Ashley Mark Publishing Co.*
Editor *Macer Hall*

Founded 1982. MONTHLY.

FEATURES *Macer Hall* Usually written by staff writers. Max. 1500 words.

News *Thérèse Wassily Saba* Small paragraphs and festival concert reports welcome.

Reviews *Tim Panting* Concert reviews of up to 250 words are usually written by staff reviewers.

PAYMENT features, by arrangement; no payment for news.

Classical Music

241 Shaftesbury Avenue, London WC2H 8TF
☎020 7333 1742   Fax 020 7333 1769
✉ classical.music@rhinegold.co.uk
www.rhinegold.co.uk
Owner *Rhinegold Publishing Ltd*
Editor *Keith Clarke*

Founded 1976. FORTNIGHTLY. A specialist magazine using precisely targeted news and feature articles aimed at the music business. Most material is commissioned but professionally written unsolicited mss are occasionally published. Freelance contributors may approach in writing with an idea but should familiarise themselves beforehand with the style and market of the magazine. PAYMENT negotiable.

Classics

Berwick House, 8–10 Knoll Rise, Orpington BR6 0PS
☎01689 887200   Fax 01689 876438
✉ classics@splpublishing.co.uk
Owner *Highbury Leisure*
Editor *Tim Morgan*

Founded 1997. MONTHLY how-to magazine for classic car owners, featuring everything from repairing and restoring to buying, selling and enjoying all types of cars from the 1950s to 1980s. Includes vehicle comparison tests, price guide, practical advice and technical know-how from experts and owners, plus hundreds of readers' free ads.

FEATURES Illustrated features on classic car maintenance, repair and restoration with strong technical content and emphasis on DIY.

NEWS All classic car related news stories and topical photos.

Climber

Warners Group Publications plc, West Street, Bourne PE10 9PH
☎01778 391117
✉ bernard@warnersgroup.co.uk
www.climber.co.uk

Owner *Warners Group Publications plc*
Editor *Bernard Newman*

Founded 1962. MONTHLY. Features articles and news on climbing and mountaineering in the UK and abroad. No unsolicited mss.

Club International

2 Archer Street, London W1D 7AW
☎020 7292 8000 Fax 020 7734 5030
✉ mattb@pr-org.co.uk

Owner *Paul Raymond*
Editor *Matt Berry*
Circulation 180,000

Founded 1972. MONTHLY. Features and short humorous items aimed at young male readership aged 18–30.
FEATURES Max. 1000 words.
SHORTS 200–750 words.
PAYMENT negotiable.

Co-op Traveller

Wrap Communications Ltd, The Bake House, J108 TBBC, 100 Clements Road, London SE16 4DG
☎020 7231 0707 Fax 020 7231 1232
✉ info@wrapcom.com
www.wrapcom.com

Owner *United Co-op Travel Division/Wrap Communications*
Editor *Ciaran Jennings*
Circulation 150,000

Founded 2001. BIANNUAL. Magazine for Co-op Travel customers. Travel articles and travel-related news for the independent traveller. No unsolicited material; approach by telephone, fax, letter or e-mail in the first instance.

FEATURES Ideas for exciting travel features, including destinations, accommodation, activities etc. Max. 1000 words.

News Stories that reveal fascinating facts for holidaymakers, including interesting products, new destinations and developments in the travel market. Max. 300 words.
PAYMENT negotiable.

Coach and Bus Week

Emap Active Ltd, Bretton Court, Bretton, Peterborough PE3 8DZ
☎01733 467778 Fax 01733 467770
✉ jacqui.grobler@emap.com
www.cbwnet.co.uk

Owner *Emap Active Ltd*
Editor *Mark Williams*
Circulation 5184

WEEKLY magazine, aimed at coach and bus operators. Interested in coach and bus industry-related items only; contact by letter, e-mail or telephone.

Coin News

Token Publishing Ltd, Orchard House, Duchy Road, Heathpark, Honiton EX14 1YD
☎01404 46972 Fax 01404 44788
✉ info@tokenpublishing.com
www.tokenpublishing.com

Owners *J.W. Mussell, Carol Hartman*
Editor *J.W. Mussell*
Circulation 10,000

Founded 1964. MONTHLY. Contributions welcome. Approach by phone in the first instance.

FEATURES Opportunity exists for well-informed authors 'who know the subject and do their homework'. Max. 2500 words.
PAYMENT £25 per 1000 words.

Company

National Magazine House, 72 Broadwick Street, London W1F 9EP
☎020 7439 5000 Fax 020 7312 3797
✉ company.mail@natmags.co.uk
www.company.co.uk

Owner *National Magazine Co. Ltd*
Editor *Victoria White*
Circulation 330,751

MONTHLY. Glossy women's magazine appealing to the independent and intelligent young woman. A good market for freelancers: 'We look for great newsy features relevant to young British women'. Keen to encourage bright, new, young talent, but uncommissioned material is rarely accepted. Feature outlines are the only sensible approach in the first instance. Max. 1500–2000 words. Features to *Claire Askew*, Features Editor. PAYMENT £250 per 1000 words.

Compass Sport

Ballencrieff Cottage, Ballencrieff Toll,
Bathgate EH48 4LD
☎01506 632728 Fax 01506 632728
✉ editor@compasssport.com
www.compasssport.com

Owner *Pages Editorial & Publishing Services*
Editor *Suse Coon*

BI-MONTHLY orienteering magazine covering all
disciplines of the sport including mountain
marathons, mountain bike, ski and trail orienteering. Includes profiles and articles on relevant
topics, with subsections on fixtures, junior news,
adventure racing and mountain marathons
which are compiled by sub-editors. Letters, puzzles and competition. Phone or e-mail to discuss
content and timing. PAYMENT by arrangement.

Computer Arts

30 Monmouth Street, Bath BA1 2BW
☎01225 442244 Fax 01225 732295
✉ ca.mail@futurenet.co.uk
www.computerarts.co.uk

Owner *The Future Network*
Editor *Vicki Atkinson*

Founded 1995. MONTHLY. The world of computer arts – 3D, web design, photoshop, digital
video. No unsolicited mss. Interested in tutorials,
profiles, tips, software and hardware reviews.
Approach by post or e-mail.

Computer Weekly

Quadrant House, The Quadrant, Sutton
SM2 5AS
☎020 8652 3122 Fax 020 8652 8979
✉ computer.weekly@rbi.co.uk
www.computerweekly.com

Owner *Reed Business Information*
Editorial Director *Karl Schneider*
Editor *Hooman Bassirian*
Circulation 143,000

Founded 1966. Freelance contributions welcome.
FEATURES *To be appointed* Always looking
for good new writers with specialised industry
knowledge. Max. 1800 words.
NEWS *Mike Simons* Some openings for
regional or foreign news items. Max. 300 words.
PAYMENT negotiable.

Computing, The IT Newspaper

32–34 Broadwick Street, London W1A 2HG
☎020 7316 9000 Fax 020 7316 9160
✉ computing@vnu.co.uk
www.computing.co.uk

Owner *VNU Business Publications Ltd*
Editor *Mike Gubbins*
Circulation 110,000

Founded 1973. WEEKLY newspaper for IT professionals. Unsolicited articles welcome. Please
enclose s.a.e. for return.
NEWS *Bryan Glick*
Payment up to £350 per 1000 words.

Condé Nast Traveller

Vogue House, Hanover Square, London
W1S 1JU
☎020 7499 9080 Fax 020 7493 3758
✉ editorcntraveller@condenast.co.uk
www.cntraveller.co.uk

Owner *Condé Nast Publications*
Editor *Sarah Miller*
Circulation 82,780

Founded 1997. MONTHLY travel magazine.
Proposals rather than completed mss preferred.
Approach in writing in the first instance. No
unsolicited photographs. 'The magazine has a
no freebie policy and no writing can be
accepted on the basis of a press or paid-for trip.'

Conservative Heartland

The Spectator (1828) Ltd, 56 Doughty Street,
London WC1N 2LL
☎020 7440 9240 Fax 020 7831 6468
✉ editor@hearlandmag.co.uk

Owner *The Conservative Party*
Editor *Martin Vander Weyer*
Circulation 250,000

Founded 1999. BIANNUAL. Conservative Party
magazine. Lifestyle articles, political comment
and information. No unsolicited material;
approach by telephone or e-mail with idea in
the first instance.

Contemporary Review

PO Box 1242, Oxford OX1 4FJ
☎01865 201529 Fax 01865 201529
✉ editorial@contemporaryreview.co.uk
www.contemporaryreview.co.uk

Owner *Contemporary Review Co. Ltd*
Editor *Dr Richard Mullen*

Founded 1866. MONTHLY. Covers international affairs and politics, literature and the
arts, history and religion. No fiction. Max.
3000 words.
Literary Editor *Dr James Munson* Monthly
book section with reviews which are always
commissioned. PAYMENT £5 per page.

CosmoGIRL!

National Magazine House, 72 Broadwick Street, London W1F 9EP
☎020 7439 5000 Fax 020 7439 5400
✉ cosmogirl.mail@natmags.co.uk
www.cosmogirl.co.uk

Owner *National Magazine Co. Ltd*
Editor *Celia Duncan*
Circulation 198,324

Founded 2001. MONTHLY glossy magazine for 'fun, fearless teens'. Fashion, beauty advice and boys.

FEATURES *Miranda Eason* Interested in ideas – send synopsis by mail – no finished articles.

Cosmopolitan

National Magazine House, 72 Broadwick Street, London W1F 9EP
☎020 7439 5000 Fax 020 7439 5016
✉ cosmo.mail@natmags.co.uk
www.cosmopolitan.co.uk

Owner *National Magazine Co. Ltd*
Editor *To be appointed*
Deputy Editor *Nina Ahmad*
Circulation 460,655

MONTHLY. Designed to appeal to the mid-twenties, modern-minded female. Popular mix of articles, with emphasis on relationships and careers, and hard news. No fiction. Will rarely use unsolicited mss but always on the look-out for 'new writers with original and relevant ideas and a strong voice'. Send short synopsis of idea to features' writer *Charlotte Northedge*. All would-be writers should be familiar with the magazine.

PAYMENT about £250 per 1000 words.

Counselling at Work

Association for Counselling at Work, BACP, BACP House, 35–37 Albert Street, Rugby CV21 2SG
☎0870 443 5252
✉ acw@bacp.co.uk

Owner *British Association for Counselling and Psychotherapy*
Editor *Rick Hughes*
Circulation 1600

Founded 1993. QUARTERLY official journal of the Association for Counselling at Work, a Division of BACP. Looking for well-researched articles (500–2400 words) about *any* aspect of workplace counselling. Mss from those employed as counsellors or in welfare posts are particularly welcome. Photographs accepted. No fiction or poetry. Send A4 s.a.e.

for writer's guidelines and sample copy of the journal. No PAYMENT.

Country Homes and Interiors

IPC Media Ltd., King's Reach Tower, Stamford Street, London SE1 9LS
☎020 7261 6451 Fax 020 7261 6895

Owner *IPC Media*
Acting Editor *Arabella St John Parker*
Circulation 94,204

Founded 1986. MONTHLY. The best approach for prospective contributors is with an idea in writing as unsolicited mss are not welcome.

FEATURES *Jean Carr* Monthly personality interviews of interest to an intelligent, affluent readership (women and men), aged 25–44. Max. 1200 words.

HOUSES *Arabella St John Parker* Country-style homes with excellent design ideas. Length 1000 words.

PAYMENT negotiable.

Country Life

IPC Media Ltd., King's Reach Tower, Stamford Street, London SE1 9LS
☎020 7261 7058 Fax 020 7261 5139
www.countrylife.co.uk

Owner *IPC Media*
Editor *Clive Aslet*
Circulation 42,649

Established 1897. WEEKLY. *Country Life* features articles which relate to architecture, countryside, wildlife, rural events, sports, arts, exhibitions, current events, property and news articles of interest to town and country dwellers. Strong informed material rather than amateur enthusiasm. 'We regret we cannot be liable for the safe custody or return of any solicited or unsolicited materials.'

PAYMENT variable, depending on word length and picture size.

Country Living

National Magazine House, 72 Broadwick Street, London W1F 9EP
☎020 7439 5000 Fax 020 7439 5093
www.countryliving.co.uk

Owner *National Magazine Co. Ltd*
Editor *Susy Smith*
Circulation 174,538

Magazine aimed at both country dwellers and town dwellers who love the countryside. Covers people, conservation, wildlife, houses (gardens and interiors) and rural businesses. No unsolicited mss

Country Smallholding

Archant Publishing, Fair Oak Close, Exeter
Airport Business Park, Clysts Honiton, Nr
Exeter EX5 2UL
☎01392 888475 Fax 01392 888550
✉ editorial.csh@archant.co.uk
www.countrysmallholding.com
Owner *Archant Publishing*
Editor *Diane Cowgill*
Circulation 20,000

Founded 1975. MONTHLY magazine for small
farmers, smallholders, practical landowners and
for anyone looking for a new home in the
country. Articles welcome on organic growing,
keeping poultry, livestock and other animals,
crafts, cookery, herbs, building and energy.
Articles should be detailed and practical, based
on first-hand knowledge and experience.
Approach in writing or by e-mail.

Country Walking

Bretton Court, Bretton, Peterborough
PE3 8DZ
☎01733 282614 Fax 01733 282654
✉ country.walking@emap.com
Owner *Emap Plc*
Editor *Jonathan Manning*
Circulation 47,767

Founded 1987. MONTHLY magazine featuring
country walk ideas, highlighting flora, fauna,
country crafts, history and heritage, pubs and
landscape along walks. News, gear tests and
profiles of celebrity walkers also feature. Special
monthly pull-out section of 27 detailed walking
routes. Original high quality photography and
ideas for features considered, although very few
unsolicited mss accepted. Approach by letter or
e-mail.
   FEATURES *Jonathan Manning*
   SPECIAL PAGES 'Down your way' section of
walk routes, including outline map and step-
by-step directions. Accurately and recently
researched walk and fact file including photographs and points of interest en route. Please
contact *Trevor Rickwood* for guidelines (unsolicited submissions generally not accepted for
this section).
   PAYMENT not negotiable.

The Countryman

The School House, Compton Pauncefoot
BA22 7EJ
✉ editorial@thecountryman.co.uk
www.thecountryman.co.uk
Owner *Dalesman Publishing Co. Ltd*
Editor *Bill Taylor*

Circulation 27,683

Founded 1927. MONTHLY. Unsolicited mss
with s.a.e. welcome; about 120 received each
week. Contributors are strongly advised to
study the magazine's content in the first
instance. Articles supplied with top quality illustrations (colour transparencies, archive b&w
prints and line drawings) are far more likely to
be used. Max. article length 1200 words.

The Countryman's Weekly
(incorporating **Gamekeeper and Sporting Dog**)

Yelverton PL20 7PE
☎01822 855281 Fax 01822 855372
✉ cmansweekly@aol.com
Managing Director *Vic Gardner*
Editor *David Venner*

Founded 1895. WEEKLY. Unsolicited material
welcome.
   FEATURES On any country sports topic.
Max. 1000 words.
   PAYMENT rates available on request.

County

26C High Street, Watlington OX49 5PY
☎01491 614040 Fax 01491 614041
✉ sales@countymagazine.com
www.countymagazine.com
Owners *Mr and Mrs R. Watts*
Editor *Mrs Ashlyn Watts*
Circulation 50,000

Founded 1986. QUARTERLY lifestyle magazine
featuring homes, interiors, gardening, fashion
and beauty, motoring, leisure and dining.
Welcomes unsolicited mss. All initial approaches
should be made in writing.

The Cricketer International
See **The Wisden Cricketer**

Crimewave

5 Martins Lane, Witcham, Ely CB6 2LB
☎01353 777931
✉ ttapress@aol.com
www.ttapress.com
Owner *TTA Press*
Editor *Andy Cox*

Founded 1998. QUARTERLY B5 colour magazine of crime fiction. 'The UK's only magazine
specialising in crime short stories, publishing the
very best from across the spectrum.' Every issue
contains stories by authors who are household
names in the crime fiction world but room is
found for lesser known and unknown writers.

Taking Care of Frank by Antony Mann (Crimewave 2) and *Prussian Snowdrops* by Marion Arnott (Crimewave 4) won the **CWA/Macallan Short Story Dagger** award in 1999 and 2001 respectively. Submissions welcome (not via e-mail) with appropriate return postage. Potential contributors are advised to study the magazine. Contracts exchanged upon acceptance. PAYMENT on publication.

Cumbria and Lake District Magazine

Stable Courtyard, Broughton Hall, Skipton BD23 3AZ
☎01756 701381 Fax 01756 701326
✉ editorial@dalesman.co.uk
www.dalesman.co.uk
Owner *Dalesman Publishing Co. Ltd*
Editor *Terry Fletcher*
Circulation 14,861

Founded 1951. MONTHLY. County magazine of strong regional and countryside interest, focusing on the Lake District. Unsolicited mss welcome. Max. 1500 words. Approach in writing, by phone or e-mail with feature ideas. PAYMENT negotiable.

Cycle Sport

IPC Media Ltd., Leon House, 233 High Street, Croydon CR9 1HZ
☎020 8774 0600
✉ cycling@ipcmedia.com
www.cyclesport.co.uk
Owner *IPC Media*
Managing Editor *Robert Garbutt*
Deputy Editor *Nigel Wynn*
Circulation 20,270

Founded 1993. MONTHLY magazine dedicated to professional cycle racing. Unsolicited ideas for features welcome.

Cycling Weekly

IPC Media Ltd, Leon House, 233 High Street, Croydon CR9 1HZ
☎020 8774 0600
✉ cycling@ipcmedia.com
www.cyclingweekly.co.uk
Owner *IPC Media*
Publishing Director *Keith Foster*
Editor *Robert Garbutt*
Circulation 27,034

Founded 1891. WEEKLY. All aspects of cycle sport covered. Unsolicited mss and ideas for features welcome. Approach in writing with ideas. Fiction rarely used.

FEATURES Cycle racing, coaching, technical material and related areas. Max. 2000 words. Most work commissioned but interested in seeing new work.
NEWS Short news pieces, local news, etc. Max. 300 words.
PAYMENT features, around £60–120 per 1000 words (quality permitting); news, £15 per story.

The Dalesman

Stable Courtyard, Broughton Hall, Skipton BD23 3AZ
☎01756 701381 Fax 01756 701326
✉ editorial@dalesman.co.uk
www.dalesman.co.uk
Owner *Dalesman Publishing Co. Ltd*
Editor *Terry Fletcher*
Circulation 47,391

Founded 1939. Now the biggest-selling regional publication of its kind in the country. MONTHLY magazine with articles of specific Yorkshire interest. Unsolicited mss welcome; receives approximately ten per day. Initial approach in writing, by phone or e-mail. Max. 1500 words. PAYMENT negotiable.

Dance Theatre Journal

Laban, Creekside, London SE8 3DZ
☎020 8691 8600 Fax 020 8691 8400
✉ dtj@laban.org
www.laban.org
Owner *Laban*
Editor *Martin Hargreaves*
Circulation 2000

Founded 1982. QUARTERLY. Interested in features on every aspect of the contemporary dance scene, particularly issues such as the funding policy for dance, critical assessments of choreographers' work and the latest developments in the various schools of contemporary dance. Unsolicited mss welcome. Length 1000–3000 words

Dance Today!

The Dancing Times Ltd, Clerkenwell House, 45–47 Clerkenwell Green, London EC1R 0EB
☎020 7250 3006 Fax 020 7253 6679
✉ dancetoday!@dancing-times.co.uk
www.dancing-times.co.uk
Owner *The Dancing Times Ltd*
Editor *Sylvia Boerner*
Circulation 2500

Founded 1956 as *Ballroom Dancing Times*. Relaunched as *Dance Today!* in 2001. MONTHLY magazine for anyone interested in ballroom and social dancing. Unsolicited contributions welcome; send c.v. with sample work by post or e-mail.

The Dancing Times
45–47 Clerkenwell Green, London EC1R 0EB
☎020 7250 3006 Fax 020 7253 6679
✉ editorial@dancing-times.co.uk
www.dancing-times.co.uk
Owner *The Dancing Times Ltd*
Editor *Mary Clarke*

Founded 1910. MONTHLY. Freelance suggestions welcome from specialist dance writers and photographers only. Approach in writing.

Dare Magazine
Room A1136, Woodlands, 80 Wood Lane, London W12 0TT
Editor *Mink Kapferer*

Founded 2003. FORTNIGHTLY teen lifestyle magazine: boys, friends, fashion, beauty, celebs, quizzes, cringes, advice and posters. Welcomes real-life and spooky-psychic stories, quizzes. Approach by e-mail (Julie.Bradley@bbc.co. uk).
FEATURES Max. 900 words.
PAYMENT depends on commission.

Darts World
81 Selwood Road, Croydon CR0 7JW
☎020 8650 6580 Fax 020 8654 4343
✉ dartsworld@blueyonder.co.uk
www.dartsworld.com
Owner *World Magazines Ltd*
Editor *A.J. Wood*
Circulation 18,780

FEATURES Single articles or series on technique and instruction. Max. 1200 words.
FICTION Short stories with darts theme. Max. 1000 words.
NEWS Tournament reports and general or personality news required. Max. 800 words.
PAYMENT negotiable.

Day by Day
Woolacombe House, 141 Woolacombe Road, London SE3 8QP
☎020 8856 6249
Owner *Loverseed Press*
Editor *Patrick Richards*
Circulation 25,000

Founded 1963. MONTHLY. News commentary and digest of national and international affairs, with reviews of the arts (books, plays, art exhi-bitions, films, opera, musicals) and county cricket and Test reports among regular slots. Unsolicited mss welcome (s.a.e. essential). Approach in writing with ideas. Contributors are advised to study the magazine in the first instance. (Specimen copy £1.20) UK subscription £14.50; Europe £18.50; RoW £22.50.
NEWS *Ronald Mallone* Interested in themes connected with non-violence and social justice only. Max. 600 words.
FEATURES No scope for freelance contributions here.
POEMS *Michael Gibson* Short poems in line with editorial principles considered. Max. 20 lines.
PAYMENT negotiable.

Dazed & Confused
112 Old Street, London EC1V 1BD
☎020 7336 0766 Fax 020 7336 0966
✉ dazed@confused.co.uk
www.confused.co.uk
Owner *Waddell Ltd*
Editor *Callum McGeoch*
Circulation 80,000

Founded 1992. MONTHLY. Cutting edge fashion, music, art interviews and features. No unsolicited material. Approach in writing with ideas in the first instance.

Decanter
First Floor, Broadway House, 2–6 Fulham Broadway, London SW6 1AA
☎020 7610 3929 Fax 020 7381 5282
✉ editorial@decanter.com
www.decanter.com
Editor *Amy Wislocki*
Circulation 35,000

FOUNDED 1975. Glossy wines magazine. Feature ideas welcome – send to editor by post or fax (not e-mail). No fiction.
NEWS/FEATURES All items and articles should concern wines, food and related subjects. PAYMENT £230 per 1,000 words.

Derbyshire Life and Countryside
Heritage House, Lodge Lane, Derby DE1 3HE
☎01332 347087 Fax 01332 290688
✉ editorials@hhgroup.co.uk
Owner *B.C. Wood*
Editor *Vivienne Irish*
Circulation 11,630

Founded 1931. MONTHLY county magazine for Derbyshire. Unsolicited mss and photographs of Derbyshire welcome, but written approach with ideas preferred.

Descent
51 Timbers Square, Cardiff CF24 3SH
☎029 2048 6557 Fax 029 2048 6557
✉ descent@wildplaces.co.uk
www.caving.uk.com
Owner *Wild Places Publishing*
Editor *Chris Howes*
Assistant Editor *Judith Calford*

Founded 1969. BI-MONTHLY magazine for cavers and mine enthusiasts. Submissions welcome from freelance contributors who can write accurately and knowledgeably on any aspect of caves, mines or underground structures.

FEATURES General interest articles of under 1000 words welcome, as well as short foreign news reports, especially if supported by photographs/illustrations. Suitable topics include exploration (particularly British, both historical and modern), expeditions, equipment, techniques and regional British news. Max. 2000 words.

PAYMENT on publication according to page area filled.

Desire
1a Fentiman Road, London SW8 1LD
☎020 7820 8844 Fax 020 7820 9944
www.desire.co.uk
Owner *Moondance Media Ltd*
Editor *Ian Jackson*

Founded 1994. FIVE ISSUES YEARLY. Britain's only erotic magazine for both women and men, celebrating sex and sensuality with a mix of features, reviews, interviews, photography, reports and erotic fantasy. For a sample copy of the magazine plus contributors' guidelines and rates, please enclose four first class stamps.

Director
116 Pall Mall, London SW1Y 5ED
☎020 7766 8950 Fax 020 7766 8840
✉ director-ed@iod.com
Editor *Joanna Higgins*
Circulation 50,000

1991 Business Magazine of the Year. Published by Director Publications Ltd. for members of the Institute of Directors. Wide range of features from political and business profiles and management thinking to employment and financial issues. Also book reviews. Regular contributors used. Send letter with synopsis/published samples rather than unsolicited mss. Strictly no 'lifestyle' writing. PAYMENT negotiable.

Disability Now
6 Market Road, London N7 9PW
☎020 7619 7323 Fax 020 7619 7331
✉ editor@disabilitynow.org.uk
www.disabilitynow.org.uk
Owner *SCOPE*
Editor *Mary Wilkinson*
Circulation 19,350

Founded 1984. Leading MONTHLY newspaper with fortnightly supplement for disabled people in the UK – people with a wide range of physical disabilities, as well as their families, carers and relevant professionals. Freelance contributions welcome. No fiction. Approach in writing.

FEATURES Covering new initiatives and services, personal experiences and general issues of interest to a wide national readership. Max. 900 words. Disabled contributors welcome.

NEWS Max. 300 words.

SPECIAL PAGES Possible openings for cartoonists.

PAYMENT by arrangement.

Disabled Motorist
DDMC, Cottingham Way, Thrapston NN14 4PL
☎01832 734724 Fax 01832 733816
✉ info@ddmc.org.uk
www.ddmc.org.uk
Owner *Disabled Drivers' Motor Club*
Editor *Lesley Browne*
Circulation 18,000

MONTHLY publication of the Disabled Drivers' Motor Club, an organisation which aims to promote and protect the interests and welfare of disabled people and help and encourage them in gaining increased mobility. Various discounts available for members; membership costs £10 p.a. (single), £15 (joint). The magazine includes information for members plus members' letters. Approach in writing with ideas. Unsolicited mss welcome.

Diva, lesbian life and style
Spectrum House, 32–34 Gordon House Road, London NW5 1LP
☎020 7424 7400 Fax 020 7424 7401
✉ edit@divamag.co.uk
www.divamag.co.uk
Owner *Millivres-Prowler Ltd*
Editor *Jane Czyzselska*

Founded 1994. MONTHLY glossy magazine featuring lesbian news and culture including fashion, lifestyle and satire. Welcomes news, features, short fiction and photographs. No poetry. Contact the news editor at the e-mail address above with news items and feature ideas and photo/fashion photographs. Approach via e-mail in the first instance.

Dog World

Somerfield House, Wotton Road, Ashford
TN23 6LW
☎01233 621877   Fax 01233 645669
www.dogworld.co.uk
Owner *Dog World Ltd*
Editor *Stuart Baillie*
Circulation 26,000

Founded 1902. WEEKLY newspaper for people who are seriously interested in pedigree dogs. Unsolicited mss occasionally considered but initial approach in writing preferred.

FEATURES Well-researched historical items or items of unusual interest concerning dogs. Max. 1000 words. Photographs of unusual 'doggy' situations occasionally of interest.

NEWS Freelance reports welcome on court cases and local government issues involving dogs.

PAYMENT features, up to £50; photos £15.

Dogs Monthly

Ascot House, High Street, Ascot SL5 7HG
☎0870 730 8433   Fax 0870 730 8431
✉ dm@rtc-mail.org.uk
www.dogsmonthly.co.uk
Owner *Mr D. Cavill*
Editor *Ruth Chapman*
Circulation 17,000

Founded 1983. MONTHLY magazine suitable for serious dog owners whose dog is more than just a pet.

FEATURES Articles on breeds and topical news. Approach the editor first by e-mail. Max. length for features, news, fiction or other articles 2000 words.

PAYMENT £35 per published page for illustrated articles.

Eastern Eye

Unit 2, 65 Whitechapel Road, London
E1 1DU
☎020 7650 2000   Fax 020 7650 2001
www.ethnicmedia.co.uk
Owner *Ethnic Media Group*
Editor *Amar Singh*
Circulation 40,000

Founded 1989. WEEKLY community paper for the Asian community in Britain. Interested in relevant general, local and international issues. Approach in writing with ideas for submission.

The Ecologist

Unit 18, Chelsea Wharf, 15 Lots Road,
London SW10 0QJ
☎020 7351 3578   Fax 020 7351 3617
✉ editorial@theecologist.org
www.theecologist.org
Owner *Ecosystems Ltd*
Managing Editor *Harry Ram*
Editor *Zac Goldsmith*
Circulation 20,000

Founded 1970. MONTHLY. Unsolicited mss welcome but best approach is a brief proposal to the editor by e-mail (address above), outlining experience and background and summarising suggested article.

FEATURES Radical approach to political, economic, social and environmental issues, with an emphasis on rethinking the basic assumptions that underpin modern society. Articles of between 500 and 3000 words.

PAYMENT negotiable.

The Economist

25 St James's Street, London SW1A 1HG
☎020 7830 7000   Fax 020 7839 2968
www.economist.com
Owner *Pearson/individual shareholders*
Editor *Bill Emmott*
Circulation 146, 401 (UK)

Founded 1843. WEEKLY. Worldwide circulation. Approaches should be made in writing to the editor. No unsolicited mss.

The Edge

65 Guinness Buildings, Hammersmith,
London W6 8BD
☎020 8563 1310
✉ davec@theedge.abelgratis.co.uk
www.theedgeabelgratis.co.uk
Editor *Dave Clark*

QUARTERLY. Reviews and features: film (indie, arts), books, popular culture. Fiction: modern crime/horror/SF/erotica/slipstream. Sample issue £4 post-free (cheques payable to 'The Edge'). Writers' guidelines available on website, for s.a.e. or by e-mail.

PAYMENT up to £60 per 1000 words.

Edinburgh Review

22A Buccleuch Place, Edinburgh EH8 9LN
☎0131 651 1415
✉ edinburgh.review@ed.ac.uk
Publisher *Centre for the History of Ideas in Scotland*
Circulation 750

Founded 1969. THREE ISSUES YEARLY. Articles and fiction on Scottish and international literary, cultural and philosophical themes. Unsolicited contributions are welcome (1600 are received each year), but prospective contributors are strongly advised to study the magazine first. Allow up to six months for a reply.

FEATURES Interest will be shown in accessible articles on philosophy and its relationship to literature or visual art.

FICTION Scottish and international. Max. 6000 words.

Electrical Times

Nexus House, Swanley BR8 8HU
☎01322 611282 Fax 01322 616376
✉ b.evett@highburybiz.com

Owner *Highbury Business Communications*
Managing Editor *Bill Evett*
Circulation 14,476

Founded 1891. MONTHLY. Aimed at electrical contractors, designers and installers. Unsolicited mss welcome but initial approach preferred.

Elle

64 North Row, London W1K 7LL
☎020 7150 7000 Fax 020 7150 7670

Owner *Hachette Filipacchi*
Editor *Lorraine Candy*
Features Editor *Anna Pursglove*
Circulation 201,309

Founded 1985. MONTHLY fashion glossy. Prospective contributors should approach the relevant editor in writing in the first instance, including cuttings.

FEATURES Max. 2500 words.

HOT LIST Short articles on hot trends, events, fashion and beauty. Max. 500 words.

PAYMENT negotiable.

Embroidery

PO Box 42B, East Molesley KT8 9BB
☎01260 295735
✉ jhalld@embroiderersguild.com
www.embroiderersguild.com

Owner *Embroiderers' Guild*
Editor *Joanne Hall*
Circulation 12,000

Founded 1933. BI-MONTHLY. Features articles on historical and foreign embroidery, and contemporary artists' work with illustrations. Covers all forms of textile art, historical and contemporary. Also reviews. Unsolicited material welcome. Max. 2500 words.

PAYMENT negotiable.

Empire

4th Floor, Mappin House, 4 Winsley Street, London W1W 8HF
☎020 7436 1515 Fax 020 7343 8703
✉ empire@emap.com
www.empireonline.co.uk

Owner *Emap East*
Editor *Colin Kennedy*
Circulation 190,659

Founded 1989. Launched at the Cannes Film Festival. MONTHLY guide to the movies which aims to cover the world of films in a 'comprehensive, adult, intelligent and witty package'. Although most of *Empire* is devoted to films and the people behind them, it also looks at the developments and technology behind television and dvds plus music, multimedia and books. Wide selection of in-depth features and stories on all the main releases of the month, and reviews of over 100 films and videos. Contributions welcome but approach in writing first.

FEATURES Behind-the-scenes features on films, humorous and factual features.

PAYMENT by agreement.

The Engineer

50 Poland Street, London W1F 7AX
☎020 7970 4103 Fax 020 7970 4189
✉ george.coupe@centaur.co.uk
www.e4engineering.com

Owner *Centaur Communications*
Editor *George Coupe*
Circulation 41,000

FOUNDED 1856. FORTNIGHTLY news magazine for technology and innovation.

FEATURES Most outside contributions are commissioned but good ideas are always welcome. Max. 2000 words.

NEWS Scope for specialist regional freelancers, and for tip-offs. Max. 500 words.

TECHNOLOGY Technology news from specialists, and tip-offs. Max. 500 words.

PAYMENT by arrangement.

The English Garden

Romsey Publishing, Jubilee House, 2 Jubilee Place, London SW3 3QT
☎020 7751 4800 Fax 020 7751 4848
✉ englishgarden@romseypublishing.com
www.theenglishgarden.co.uk

Owner *Romsey Publishing Ltd*
Acting Editor *Janine Wookey*
Circulation 95,917

Founded 1996. MONTHLY. Features on beauti-

ful gardens with practical ideas on design and planting. No unsolicited mss.
FEATURES *Jackie Bennett* Max. 1000–1200 words. Approach in writing in the first instance; send synopsis of 150 words with strong design and planting ideas, feature proposals, or sets of photographs of interesting gardens.

English Nature Magazine
English Nature, Northminster House, Peterborough PE1 1UA
☎01733 455191 Fax 01733 455436
✉ gordon.leel@english-nature.org.uk
www.english-nature.org.uk
Owner *English Nature*
Editor *Amanda Giles*
Circulation 16,000
Founded 1992. BI-MONTHLY magazine which explains the work of English Nature, the government adviser on wildlife and conservation policies. No unsolicited material.

Erotic Review
30 Cleveland Street, London W1T 4JD
☎020 7907 6404 Fax 020 7437 3528
✉ info@theeroticreview.co.uk
www.theeroticreview.co.uk
Owner *The Erotic Review Limited*
Editor *Rowan Pelling*
Circulation 20,000
Founded 1997. MONTHLY erotic literary magazine containing articles, humour, fiction, poetry and art work. Unsolicited material welcome, but please read magazine first. No clichéd pornography. Approach in writing in the first instance enclosing a brief sample of work and s.a.e.
FEATURES Esoteric, humorous or real-life experiences. Max. 2000 words.
FICTION Erotic short stories. Max. 2000 words.
PAYMENT features, £40–100; fiction, £50–100.

ES (Evening Standard magazine)
See **Evening Standard** under *Regional Newspapers*

Esquire
National Magazine House, 72 Broadwick Street, London W1F 9EP
☎020 7439 5000 Fax 020 7439 5675
Owner *National Magazine Co. Ltd*
Editor *Simon Tiffin*
Circulation 70,164

Founded 1991. MONTHLY. Quality men's general interest magazine. No unsolicited mss or short stories.

Essentials
IPC Media Ltd., King's Reach Tower, Stamford Street, London SE1 9LS
☎020 7261 6970 Fax 020 7261 5262
Owner *IPC Media*
Editor *Karen Livermore*
Circulation 150,402
Founded 1988. MONTHLY women's interest magazine. Unsolicited mss (not originals) welcome if accompanied by s.a.e. Initial approach in writing preferred. Prospective contributors should study the magazine thoroughly before submitting anything. No fiction.
FEATURES Max. 2000 words (double-spaced on A4).
PAYMENT negotiable.

Essex Life & Countryside
G13 Dugard House, Peartree Road, Stanway, Colchester CO3 5JX
☎01206 571364 Fax 01206 366982
✉ enquiries@essexlife.net
www.essexlife.net
Owner *Archant Life*
Editor *Carmen Konopka*
Submissions to: PO Box 6657, Bishop's Stortford CM23 4WB
Circulation 10,000
Founded 1952. MONTHLY. Unsolicited material of Essex interest welcome. Features must include colour photos. No general interest material.
FEATURES Countryside, culture and crafts in Essex. Max.1400 words.
PAYMENT by individual agreement.

The Essex Magazine
See **The Journal Magazines**

Eve
BBC Worldwide, Room AG200, 80 Wood Lane, London W12 0TT
☎020 8433 3767 Fax 020 8433 3359
✉ eve@bbc.co.uk
Owner *BBC Worldwide Publishing Ltd*
Editor *Jane Bruton*
Deputy Editor *Lucy Dunn*
Features Director *Victoria Woodhall*
Circulation 142,382
Founded 2000. MONTHLY. Wide-ranging general interest – aimed at the intelligent 30+

woman. No unsolicited material. Send introductory letter, *recent* writings and outlines for ideas aimed at a specific section. It is essential that would-be contributors familiarise themselves with the magazine.

Eventing
See **Horse and Hound**

Evergreen
PO Box 52, Cheltenham GL50 1YQ
☎01242 537900 Fax 01242 537901
Editor *R. Faiers*
Circulation 75,000

Founded 1985. QUARTERLY magazine featuring articles and poems about Britain. Unsolicited contributions welcome.

FEATURES Britain's natural beauty, towns and villages, nostalgia, wildlife, traditions, odd customs, legends, folklore, crafts, etc. Length 250–2000 words.

PAYMENT £15 per 1000 words; poems £4.

Everything France
Medway House, Lower Road, Forest Row RH18 5HE
☎01342 828700 Fax 01342 828701
✉ efmag@brooklandsgroup.com
www.brooklandsgroup.com
Owner *Brooklands Group Limited*
Editor *Jon Stackpool*

Founded 2001. MONTHLY. 'The premier magazine for French property, travel, touring, food and drink.' Welcomes French-based features on property – buying, lifestyle and gardens; tourism, cities and regions, personalities and French culture. Approach by e-mail. Max. 3000 words.

PAYMENT negotiable.

Executive Woman
2 Chantry Place, Harrow HA3 6NY
☎020 8420 1210 Fax 020 8420 1691
✉ info@execwoman.com
www.execwoman.com
Owner *Saleworld*
Managing Editor *Angela Giveon*
Circulation 85,000

Founded 1987. BI-MONTHLY magazine for female executives in the corporate field and female entrepreneurs.

FEATURES New and interesting business issues and 'Women to Watch'. Health and conferencing, profiles, technology, beauty, fashion, training and arts items. 700 words per page.

LEGAL/FINANCIAL Opportunities for lawyers/

accountants to write on issues in their field. Max. 600 words. PAYMENT negotiable.

Fairgame Magazine
The Baltic Business Centre, Gateshead NE8 3DA
☎0191 442 4001 Fax 0191 442 4002
www.fairgamemagazine.com
Editor *Jennifer O'Neill*
Circulation 15,000

Founded 2003. BI-MONTHLY magazine for women football players. Contributions welcome.

FEATURES *Claire Foy* International reports, player and team profiles, interviews, diet, health and fitness, tactics, training advice, play improvement, fund-raising. Max. 1500 words.

NEWS *Wilf Frith* Match reports, team news, transfers, injuries, results and fixtures. Max. 600 words.

Family Circle
IPC Media Ltd., King's Reach Tower, Stamford Street, London SE1 9LS
☎0870 444 5000 Fax 020 7261 5929
Owner *IPC Media*
Editor *Julie Barton-Breck*
Circulation 162,178

Founded 1964. MONTHLY. Women's general interest. Little scope for freelancers as most material is produced in-house or by published journalists.

FEATURES *Emma Burstall*
HEALTH & CONSUMER *Sarah Touquet*
FOOD & DRINK *Emma Lewis*

Family Tree Magazine
61 Great Whyte, Ramsey, Huntingdon PE26 1HJ
☎01487 814050 Fax 01487 711361
✉ lesboon@family-tree.co.uk
www.family-tree.co.uk
Owner *ABM Publishing Ltd*
Editor *Sue Fearn*
Circulation 50,000

Founded 1984. MONTHLY. News and features on matters of genealogy. Not interested in own family histories. Approach in writing with ideas. All material should be addressed to *Sue Fearn*.

FEATURES Any genealogically related subject. Max. 2400 words. No puzzles or fictional articles.

PAYMENT news and features, £45 per 1000 words.

Fancy Fowl

The Publishing House, Station Road, Framlingham IP13 9EE
☎01728 622030 Fax 01728 622031
✉ ff@prestige.typo.co.uk

Owner *TP Publications*
Editor *Liz Fairbrother*
Circulation 3000

Founded 1979. MONTHLY. Devoted entirely to poultry, waterfowl, turkeys, geese, pea fowl, etc. – management, breeding, rearing and exhibition. Outside contributions of knowledgeable, technical poultry-related articles and news welcome. Max. 1000 words. Approach by letter.
  PAYMENT negotiable.

Farmers Weekly

Quadrant House, Sutton SM2 5AS
☎020 8652 4911 Fax 020 8652 4005
✉ farmers.weekly@rbi.co.uk
www.fwi.co.uk

Owner *Reed Business Information*
Editor *Stephen Howe*
Circulation 78,629

WEEKLY. 1996 Business Magazine of the Year. For practising farmers and those in the ancillary industries. Unsolicited mss considered.
  FEATURES A wide range of material relating to farmers' problems and interests: specific sections on arable and livestock farming, farm life, practical and general interest, machinery and business.
  NEWS General farming news.
  PAYMENT negotiable.

Fast Car

Berwick House, 8–10 Knoll Rise, Orpington BR6 0PS
☎01689 887200 Fax 01689 838844
✉ fastcar@splpublishing.co.uk
www.fastcar.co.uk

Owner *Highbury Leisure*
Editor *Gez Jones*
Circulation 127,813

Founded 1987. THIRTEEN ISSUES YEARLY. Lad's magazine about perfomance tuning and modifying cars. Covers all aspects of this youth culture including the latest street styles and music. Features cars and their owners, product tests and in-car entertainment. Also includes a free reader ads section.
  NEWS Any item in line with the above.
  FEATURES Innovative ideas in line with the above and in the *Fast Car* writing style.

Generally four pages in length. No Kit-car features, race reports or road test reports of standard cars. Copy should be as concise as possible. PAYMENT negotiable.

FHM

Mappin House, 4 Winsley Street, London W1W 8HF
☎020 7436 1515 Fax 020 7343 3000
✉ general@fhm.com
www.fhm.com

Owner *Emap Plc*
Editor *David Davies*
Circulation 601,166

Founded in 1986 as a free fashion magazine, FHM evolved to become more male oriented but without much public acclaim until Emap bought the title in 1994. Since then it has become the best-selling men's magazine in the world covering all areas of men's lifestyle. Published MONTHLY with 18 international editions worldwide. No unsolicited mss. Synopses and ideas welcome by e-mail.
  PAYMENT negotiable.

The Field

IPC Media Ltd., King's Reach Tower, Stamford Street, London SE1 9LS
☎020 7261 5198 Fax 020 7261 5358
✉ beatrice_gray@ipcmedia.com
www.thefield.co.uk

Owner *IPC Media*
Editor-in-Chief *Jonathan Young*
Circulation 32,004

Founded 1853. MONTHLY magazine for those who are serious about the British countryside and its pleasures. Unsolicited mss (and transparencies) welcome but initial approach should be made in writing or by phone on 020 7261 6225.
  FEATURES Exceptional work on any subject concerning the countryside. Most work tends to be commissioned.
  PAYMENT varies.

Film Review

Visual Imagination Ltd, 9 Blades Court, Deodar Road, London SW15 2NU
☎020 8875 1520 Fax 020 8875 1588
✉ filmreview@visimag.com
www.visimag.com

Owner *Visual Imagination Ltd*
Editor *Neil Corry*
Circulation 50,000

FOUR-WEEKLY. Reviews, profiles, interviews

and special reports on films. Unsolicited material considered. PAYMENT negotiable.

Fishing News

Telephone House, 69–77 Paul Street, London EC2A 4LQ
☎020 7017 4531 Fax 020 7017 4536
✉ tim.oliver@informa.com
www.fishingnews.co.uk
Owner *Informa Group Plc*
Editor *Tim Oliver*
Circulation 11,400

Founded 1913. WEEKLY. All aspects of the commercial fishing industry in the UK and Ireland. No unsolicited mss; telephone inquiry in the first instance. Max. 600 words for news and 1500 words for features. PAYMENT £100 per 1000 words.

The Fix

5 Martins Lane, Witcham, Ely CB6 2LB
☎01353 777931
✉ ttapress@aol.com
www.ttapress.com
Owner *TTA Press*
Editor *Andy Cox*

Founded 1994. BI-MONTHLY. Features detailed contributors' guidelines and reviews of international short story publications, plus varied articles, news, views and interviews.

FEATURES Unsolicited articles welcome on any aspect of short story publishing: market information, writing, editing, illustrating, interviews and reviews. All genres. Submissions should include adequate return postage. 'Please study the magazine: this will greatly enhance your chances of acceptance.'

Flight International

Quadrant House, The Quadrant, Sutton SM2 5AS
☎020 8652 3842 Fax 020 8652 3840
✉ flight.international@rbi.co.uk
www.flightinternational.com
Owner *Reed Business Information*
Editor *Murdo Morrison*
Circulation 52,222

Founded 1909. WEEKLY. International trade magazine for the aerospace industry, including civil, military and space. Unsolicited mss considered. Commissions preferred - phone with ideas and follow up with letter. E-mail submissions encouraged.

FEATURES *Murdo Morrison* Technically informed articles and pieces on specific geographical areas with international appeal. Analytical, in-depth coverage required, preferably supported by interviews. Max. 1800 words.

NEWS *Andrew Doyle* Opportunities exist for news pieces from particular geographical areas on specific technical developments. Max. 350 words.

PAYMENT NUJ rates.

Flora International

The Fishing Lodge Studio, 77 Bulbridge Road, Wilton, Salisbury SP2 0LE
☎01722 743207 Fax 01722 743207
✉ floramag@aol.com
Publisher/Editor *Maureen Foster*
Circulation 16,000

Founded 1974. BI-MONTHLY magazine for flower arrangers and florists. Unsolicited mss welcome. Approach in writing with ideas. Not interested in general gardening articles.

FEATURES Fully illustrated, preferably with b&w photos or illustrations/colour photographs or transparencies. Flower arranging, flower arrangers' gardens and flower crafts. Floristry items written with practical knowledge and well illustrated are particularly welcome. Max. 1000 words.

PROFILES/REVIEWS Personality profiles and book reviews.

PAYMENT £50 per 1000 words plus additional payment for suitable photographs.

FlyPast

PO Box 100, Stamford PE9 1XQ
☎01780 755131 Fax 01780 757261
✉ flypast@keypublishing.com
Owner *Key Publishing Ltd*
Editor *Ken Ellis*
Circulation 44,081

Founded 1981. MONTHLY. Historic aviation and aviation heritage, mainly military, Second World War period up to c.1970. Unsolicited mss welcome.

Focus

See **British Science Fiction Association** under *Professional Associations*

Focus

Origin Publishing, 14th Floor, Tower House, Fairfax Street, Bristol BS1 3BN
☎0117 927 9009 Fax 0117 934 9008
www.originpublishing.co.uk
Owner *Origin Publishing*
Editor *Paul Parsons*
News Editor *Graham Southorn*
Circulation 55,000

Founded 1992. MONTHLY. Popular science and discovery. Welcomes *relevant* summaries of original feature ideas by e-mail.

For Women
Fantasy Publications, 4 Selsdon Way, London E14 9EL
☎020 7308 5090

Editor *Liz Beresford*
Circulation 60,000

Founded 1992. SIX-WEEKLY magazine of erotic and sex interest for women – health and sex, erotic fiction and erotic photography. No homes and gardens articles. Approach in writing in the first instance. Send s.a.e. for submission guidelines.
FICTION *Elizabeth Coldwell* Erotic short stories. Max. 3000 words.
PAYMENT £150 total.

Fortean Times: The Journal of Strange Phenomena
PO Box 2409, London NW5 4NP
☎020 7907 6235 Fax 020 7907 6835
✉ david_sutton@dennis.co.uk
www.forteantimes.com

Editor *David Sutton*
Circulation 30,000

Founded 1973. MONTHLY. Accounts of strange phenomena and experiences, curiosities, mysteries, prodigies and portents. Unsolicited mss welcome. Approach in writing with ideas. No fiction, poetry, rehashes or politics.
FEATURES Well-researched and referenced material on current or historical mysteries, or first-hand accounts of oddities. Max. 3000 words, preferably with good relevant photos/illustrations.
NEWS Concise copy with full source references essential.
PAYMENT negotiable.

Foundation: The International Review of Science Fiction
c/o Middlesex University, White Hart Lane, London N17 8HT
✉ farah@fjm3.demon.co.uk
www.sf-foundation.org
Owner *Science Fiction Foundation (reg. Charity 1041052)*
Editor *Dr Farah Mendlesohn*

THRICE-YEARLY publication devoted to the critical study of science fiction.
PAYMENT None.

France Magazine
Archant House, Oriel Road, Cheltenham GL50 1BB
☎01242 216050 Fax 01242 216074
✉ editorial@francemag.com
www.francemag.com
Owner *Archant (Life South) Ltd*
Editor *Kate McNally*
Circulation 54,216

FOUNDED 1989. MONTHLY magazine containing all things of interest to Francophiles – in English. Approach by e-mail in the first instance.

Freelance Market News
Sevendale House, 7 Dale Street, Manchester M1 1JB
☎0161 228 2362, ext 210 Fax 0161 228 3533
✉ fmn@writersbureau.com
www.writersbureau.com/resources.htm

Editor *Angela Cox*

MONTHLY. News and information on the freelance writers' market, both inland and overseas. Includes market information, competitions, seminars, courses, overseas openings, etc. Short articles (700 words max.). Unsolicited contributions welcome.
PAYMENT by negotiation.

The Freelance
See **National Union of Journalists** under *Professional Associations*

Garden Answers
Bretton Court, Bretton, Peterborough PE3 8DZ
☎01733 264666 Fax 01733 282695
Owner *Emap Active Publications Ltd*
Editor *Nicola Dela-Croix*
Circulation 60,589

Founded 1982. MONTHLY. 'It is unlikely that unsolicited manuscripts will be used, as articles are usually commissioned and must be in the magazine style.' Prospective contributors should approach the editor in writing. Interested in hearing from gardening writers on any subject, whether flowers, fruit, vegetables, houseplants or greenhouse gardening.

Garden News
Bretton Court, Bretton, Peterborough PE3 8DZ
☎01733 264666 Fax 01733 282695
Owner *Emap Active Publications Ltd*
Editor *Sarah Page*

Circulation 53,203

Founded 1958. Britain's biggest-selling, full-colour gardening WEEKLY. News and advice on growing flowers, fruit and vegetables, plus colourful features on all aspects of gardening especially for the committed gardener. News and features welcome, especially if accompanied by top-quality photos or illustrations. Contact the editor before submitting any material.

The Garden, Journal of the Royal Horticultural Society

RHS Publications, 4th Floor, Churchgate
New Road, Peterborough PE1 1TT
✉ thegarden@rhs.org.uk
www.rhs.org.uk
Owner *The Royal Horticultural Society*
Editor *Ian Hodgson*
Circulation 306,003

Founded 1866. MONTHLY journal of the Royal Horticultural Society. Covers all aspects of the art, science and practice of horticulture and garden making. 'Articles must have depth and substance.' Approach by letter with a synopsis in the first instance. Max. 2500 words.

Gardens Illustrated

BBC Worldwide, Woodlands, 80 Wood
Lane, London W12 0TT
☎020 8433 1352 Fax 020 8433 2680
www.gardensillustrated.com
Owner *BBC Worldwide Publishing Ltd*
Editor *Clare Foster*
Circulation 32,120

Founded 1993. TEN ISSUES YEARLY. 'Britain's most distinguished garden magazine' with a world-wide readership. The focus is on garden design, with a strong international flavour. Unsolicited mss are rarely used and it is best that prospective contributors approach the editor with ideas in writing, supported by photographs.

Gay Times

Unit M, Spectrum House, 32–34 Gordon
House Road, London NW5 1LP
☎020 7424 7400 Fax 020 7424 7401
www.gaytimes.co.uk
Owner *Millivres-Prowler Group*
Editor *Vicky Powell*
Circulation 65,000

Covers all aspects of gay life, plus general interest likely to appeal to the gay community, art reviews and news. Regular freelance writers used. PAYMENT negotiable.

Gibbons Stamp Monthly

Stanley Gibbons, 7 Parkside, Christchurch
Road, Ringwood BH24 3SH
☎01425 472363 Fax 01425 470247
✉ hjefferies@stanleygibbons.co.uk
www.gibbonsstampmonthly.com
Owner *Stanley Gibbons Ltd*
Editor *Hugh Jefferies*
Circulation 22,000

Founded 1890. MONTHLY. News and features. Unsolicited mss welcome. Make initial approach in writing by telephone or e-mail to avoid disappointment.

FEATURES *Hugh Jefferies* Unsolicited material of specialised nature and general stamp features welcome. Max. 3000 words but longer pieces can be serialised.

NEWS *Michael Briggs* Any philatelic news item. Max. 500 words.

PAYMENT features £40–50 per 1000 words; news no payment.

Girl About Town

Independent House, 191 Marsh Wall, London
E14 9RS
☎020 7005 5550 Fax 020 7005 5777
www.londoncareers.net
Owner *Independent Magazines*
Editor-in-Chief *Bill Williamson*
Circulation 85,000

Founded 1972. Free WEEKLY magazine for women aged 18 to 45. Unsolicited mss may be considered. No fiction.

FEATURES Standards are 'exacting'. Commissions only. Some chance of unknown writers being commissioned. Max. 1500 words.

PAYMENT negotiable.

Glamour

6–8 Old Bond Street, London W1S 4PH
☎020 7499 9080 Fax 020 7491 2551
www.condenast.co.uk
Owner *Condé Nast*
Editor *Jo Elvin*
Circulation 582,690

Founded 2001. Handbag-size glossy women's magazine – fashion, beauty and celebrities. No unsolicited mss; send ideas for features in synopsis form to the Features Editor *Miranda Levy*.

Gliding and Motorgliding International

281 Queen Edith's Way, Cambridge
CB1 9NH
☎01223 247725

✉ bryce.smith@virgin.net
www.glidingmagazine.com
Owner *Soaring Society of America*
Editor *Gillian Bryce-Smith*

Founded November 1998 for international gliding and motorgliding enthusiasts. Few opportunities for freelance writers. Now on the Internet as the first gliding magazine to be electronic only. No PAYMENT.

The Golf+

Leon House, 233 High Street, Croydon CR9 1HZ
☎020 8774 0600
✉ thegolfmag@ipcmedia.com
www.thegolf.co.uk
Owner *IPC Media*
Editor *Steve Kirk*
Circulation 25,000

Founded 1995. MONTHLY features Volkswagen Golfs and other VAG cares. Articles on tuning, syling, performance, technical and potential feature cars. 'Not interested in anything to do with the game of golf.' Submissions should be made directly to the Editor. Articles must show excellent specialist knowledge of the subject matter. PAYMENT by negotiation.

Golf Monthly

IPC Media Ltd., King's Reach Tower, Stamford Street, London SE1 9LS
☎020 7261 7237   Fax 020 7261 7240
✉ golfmonthly@ipcmedia.com
golf-monthly.co.uk
Owner *IPC Media*
Editor *Jane Carter*
Circulation 74,587

Founded 1911. MONTHLY. Player profiles, golf instruction, general golf features and columns. Not interested in instruction material from outside contributors. Unsolicited mss welcome. Approach in writing with ideas.
    FEATURES Max. 1500–2000 words. PAYMENT by arrangement.

Golf Weekly

Bushfield House, Orton Centre, Peterborough PE2 5UW
☎01733 288035   Fax 01733 288025
✉ golf.weekly@emap.com
Owner *Emap Active Ltd*
Editor *Peter Masters*
Circulation 10,000

Founded 1890. WEEKLY. Unsolicited material welcome from full-time journalists only. 'Always looking for photographic and written news contributions.' For features, approach in writing in first instance; for news, e-mail, fax or phone.
    FEATURES Max. 1500 words.
    NEWS Max. 300 words.
    PAYMENT negotiable.

Golf World

Bushfield House, Orton, Peterborough PE2 5UW
☎01733 237111   Fax 01733 288025
www.email.golfworldmagazine.co.uk
Owner *Emap Active Publications Ltd*
Editor *Andy Calton*
Circulation 47,079

Founded 1962. MONTHLY. No unsolicited mss. Approach in writing with ideas.

Good Holiday Magazine

27A High Street, Esher KT10 9RL
☎01372 468140   Fax 01372 470765
✉ info@goodholidayideas.com
Editor *John Hill*
Circulation 100,000

Founded 1985. QUARTERLY aimed at better-off holiday-makers rather than travellers. World-wide destinations including Europe and domestic. No unsolicited material but approach in writing or by e-mail with ideas and/or synopsis. PAYMENT negotiable.

Good Housekeeping

National Magazine House, 72 Broadwick Street, London W1F 9EP
☎020 7439 5000   Fax 020 7439 5616
✉ firstname.lastname@natmags.co.uk
www.natmags.co.uk
Owner *National Magazine Co. Ltd*
Editor-in-Chief *Lindsay Nicholson*
Circulation 415,730

Founded 1922. MONTHLY glossy. No unsolicited mss. Write with ideas in the first instance to the appropriate editor.
    FEATURES *Kerry Fowler* Most work is commissioned but original ideas are always welcome. No ideas are discussed on the telephone. Send short synopsis, plus relevant cuttings, showing previous examples of work published. No unsolicited mss.
    HEALTH *Julie Powell*. Submission guidelines as for features; no unsolicited mss.

Good Motoring

Station Road, Forest Row RH18 5EN
☎01342 825676 Fax 01342 824847
✉ dh@motoringassist.com
www.roadsafety.org.uk
Owner *Gem Motoring Assist*
Editor *Derek Hainge*
Circulation 52,000

Founded 1932. QUARTERLY motoring, road
safety and travel magazine. Occasional general
features. 1500 words max. Prospective contributors should approach in writing only.

Good News

50 Loxwood Avenue, Worthing BN14 7RA
☎01903 824174 Fax 01903 824174

Owner *Good News Fellowship*
Editor *Donald Banks*
Circulation 40,000

Founded 2001. MONTHLY evangelistic newspaper which welcomes contributions. No fiction.
Send for sample copy of writers' guidelines in the
first instance. No poetry or children's stories.

NEWS Items of up to 500 words (preferably
with pictures) 'showing God at work, and
human interest photo stories. "Churchy" items
not wanted. Testimonies of how people have
come to personal faith in Jesus Christ and the
difference it has made are always welcome.
They do not need to be dramatic!'

WOMEN'S PAGE Relevant items of interest
welcome.

PAYMENT negotiable.

Good Ski Guide

PPL, 5th Floor, Mermaid House, 2 Puddle
Dock, London EC4V 3DR
☎020 7332 2000
✉ info@goodskiguide.com
www.goodskiguide.com
Owner *Profile Media Group plc*
Editor *Cate Langmuir*
Circulation 50,000

Founded 1976. FOUR ISSUES YEARLY. Unsolicited mss welcome from writers with a knowledge
of skiing and ski resorts. Prospective contributors
are best advised to make initial contact in writing
as ideas and work need to be seen before any discussion can take place. PAYMENT negotiable.

GQ

Vogue House, Hanover Square, London
W1S 1JU
☎020 7499 9080 Fax 020 7495 1679
www.gq-magazine.co.uk

Owner *Condé Nast Publications Ltd*
Editor *Dylan Jones*
Circulation 124,022

Founded 1988. MONTHLY. Men's style magazine. No unsolicited material. Write or fax
with an idea in the first instance.

Granta

2–3 Hanover Yard, Noel Road, London
N1 8BE
☎020 7704 9776 Fax 020 7704 0474
✉ editorial@granta.com
www.granta.com

Editor *Ian Jack*
Deputy Editor *Matt Weiland*

QUARTERLY magazine of new writing, including
fiction, memoirs, reportage and photography
published in paperback book form. Highbrow,
diverse and contemporary, with a thematic
approach. Unsolicited mss (including fiction)
considered. A lot of material is commissioned.
Vital to read the magazine first to appreciate its
very particular fusion of cultural and political
interests. No reviews, news articles or poetry.
Access the website for submission guidelines.

PAYMENT negotiable.

The Great Outdoors

See **TGO**

The Great War

PO Box 202, Scarborough YO11 3GE
☎01723 581329 Fax 01723 581329
✉ books@greatnorthernpublising.co.uk
www.greatnorthernpublishing.co.uk
Owner *Great Northern Publishing*
Editor *Mark Marsay*

Founded 2001. BI-MONTHLY subscription only,
non-academic magazine published in A5 format.
'The little magazine dedicated to the Great War
(1914–19) and to those who perished and those
who returned.'

FEATURES Articles, personal stories and
accounts of those who served (men and women
of all nationalities) and their families: diaries;
anecdotes; letters: postcards; poetry; unit histories; events; incidents and memorials etc.
Absolutely no fiction. Not interested in long academic works expounding historian's personal
views. New material always welcome but contact editor prior to sending. See website for submission guidelines and editorial content. 'Open
door policy: everyone and everything welcome
regardless of ability to write to high standard. No
subject or topic excluded.' Sample copy £5.

Guardian Weekend
See **The Guardian** under *National Newspapers*

Guiding magazine
17–19 Buckingham Palace Road, London
SW1W 0PT
☎020 7834 6242 Fax 020 7828 5791
✉ guiding@girlguiding.org.uk
www.girlguiding.org.uk
Owner *The Guide Association*
Editor *Wendy Kewley*
Circulation 68,000

Founded 1914. MONTHLY. Unsolicited mss welcome provided topics relate to the Movement and/or women's role in society. Ideas in writing appreciated in first instance. No nostalgic, 'when I was a Guide', pieces, please.

ACTIVITY IDEAS Interesting, contemporary ideas and instructions for activities for girls aged 5 to 18+ to do during unit meetings – crafts, games (indoor/outdoor), etc.

FEATURES Topics relevant to today's girls and young women. 650 words.

NEWS Items likely to be of interest to members. Max. 100–150 words.

PAYMENT £70 per 1000 words.

H&E Naturist
Burlington Court, Carlisle Street, Goole
DN14 5EG
☎01405 769712/764206 Fax 01405 763815
✉ editorhenaturist@btconnect.com
www.healthandefficiency.co.uk
Owner *New Freedom Publications Ltd*
Editor *Mark Nisbet*
Circulation 20,000

Founded 1898. MONTHLY naturist magazine.

FEATURES Will consider short features on social nudism, longer features on nudist holidays and nudist philosophy. 90% of every issue is by freelance contributors. 1000–1500 words.

NEWS 'We are always on the lookout for national and international nudist news stories.' 250–500 words. No soft porn, 'sexy' stories or sleazy photographs. Approach by post, e-mail or telephone.

Hair
IPC Media Ltd., King's Reach Tower, Stamford Street, London SE1 9LS
☎020 7261 6975 Fax 020 7261 7382
Owner *IPC Media*
Editor *Zoe Richards*
Circulation 157,499

Founded 1977. BI-MONTHLY hair and beauty magazine. No unsolicited mss, but always interested in good photographs. Approach with ideas in writing.

FEATURES Fashion pieces on hair trends and styling advice. Max. 1000 words.

PAYMENT negotiable.

Hairflair
Hairflair Magazines Ltd, Freebournes House, Freebournes Road, Witham CM8 3US
☎01376 534540 Fax 01376 534546
Owner *Hairflair Magazines Ltd*
Editor *Claire Muffett*
Circulation 60,000

Founded 1982. BI-MONTHLY. Original and interesting hair and beauty-related features written in a young, lively style to appeal to a readership aged 16–35 years. Unsolicited mss not welcome, although freelancers are used.

FEATURES Hair and beauty. Max. 2500 words. PAYMENT negotiable.

Harpers & Queen
National Magazine House, 72 Broadwick Street, London W1F 9EP
☎020 7439 5000 Fax 020 7439 5506
Owner *National Magazine Co. Ltd*
Editor *Lucy Yeomans*
Circulation 90,227

MONTHLY. Up-market glossy combining the stylish and the streetwise. Approach in writing (not phone) with ideas.

FEATURES *Harriet Green* Ideas only in the first instance.

NEWS Snippets welcome if very original.

PAYMENT negotiable.

Health & Fitness Magazine
Highbury – Lifestyle, The Publishing House, 1–3 Highbury Station Road, London N1 1TW
☎020 7266 2222 Fax 020 7331 1108
www.hfonline.co.uk
Owner *Highbury WV*
Editor *Mary Comber*
Circulation 65,000

Founded 1983. MONTHLY. Target reader: active, health-conscious women aged 25–40.

FEATURES news and articles on nutrition, exercise, healthy eating, holistic health and well-being. Will consider ideas; approach in writing in the first instance.

Health Education
The School of Education, University of Southampton, Southampton SO17 1BJ
☎023 8059 3707

✉ skw@soton.ac.uk
www.emeraldinsight.com
Owner *Emerald*
Editor *Professor Katherine Weare*
Circulation 2000

Founded 1992. SIX ISSUES YEARLY. Health education journal with an emphasis on schools and young people but papers on any area of health education and health promotion are welcome. Professional readership.

Heat
Endeavour House, 189 Shaftesbury Avenue, London WC2H 8JG
☎020 7437 9011 Fax 020 7859 8670
✉ heat@emap.com
Owner *Emap Entertainment*
Editor *Mark Frith*
Circulation 566,731

Founded January 1999. WEEKLY entertainment magazine dealing with TV, film and radio information, fashion and features, with an emphasis on celebrity interviews and news. Targets 18 to 40-year-old readership, male and female. Articles written both in-house and by trusted freelancers. No unsolicited mss.

Hello!
Wellington House, 69–71 Upper Ground, London SE1 9PQ
☎020 7667 8700 Fax 020 7667 8716
www.hellomagazine.com
Owner *Hola! (Spain)*
Editor *Ronnie Whelan*
Commissioning Editor *Linda Newman*
Circulation 350,374

WEEKLY. Owned by a Madrid-based publishing family, *Hello!* has grown faster than any other British magazine since its launch here in 1988. The magazine has editorial offices both in Madrid and London. Major colour features plus regular news pages. Although much of the material is provided by regulars, good proposals do stand a chance. Approach the commissioning editor with ideas in the first instance. No unsolicited mss.
    FEATURES Interested in celebrity-based features, with a newsy angle, and exclusive interviews from generally unapproachable personalities.
    PAYMENT by arrangement.

Here's Health
Greater London House, Hampstead Road, London NW1 7EJ
☎020 7347 1893 Fax 020 7347 1897

✉ hereshealth.editor@emap.com
Owner *Emap Esprit*
Editor *Sarah Wilson*
Circulation 20,015

Founded 1956. MONTHLY. Full-colour magazine dealing with alternative medicine, nutrition, natural health, wholefoods, supplements, organics and the environment. Prospective contributors should bear in mind that this is a specialist magazine with a pronounced bias towards alternative/complementary medicine, using expert contributors on the whole. No completed articles. Contact Deputy Editor *Lisa Howells* with ideas in the first instance.
    PAYMENT negotiable.

Hi-Fi News
Leon House, 233 High Street, Croydon CR9 1HZ
☎020 8774 0600
✉ hi-finews@ipcmedia.com
Owner *IPC Media*
Editor *Steve Harris*
Circulation 17,211

Founded 1956. MONTHLY. Write in the first instance with suggestions based on knowledge of the magazine's style and subject. All articles must be written from an informed technical or enthusiast viewpoint. PAYMENT negotiable, according to technical content.

High Life
37–43 Sackville Street, London W1S 3EH
☎020 7534 2400 Fax 020 7534 2555
✉ high.life@cedarcom.co.uk
www.cedarcom.co.uk
Owner *Cedar Communications*
Editor *Alex Finer*
Circulation 251,438

Founded 1973. MONTHLY glossy. British Airways in-flight magazine. Almost all the content is commissioned. No unsolicited mss. Few opportunities for freelancers.

History Today
20 Old Compton Street, London W1D 4TW
☎020 7534 8000 Fax 020 7534 8008
✉ p.furtado@historytoday.com
www.historytoday.com
Owner *History Today Trust for the Advancement of Education*
Editor *Peter Furtado*
Circulation 29,269

Founded 1951. MONTHLY. General history and archaeology worldwide, history behind the headlines. Serious submissions only; no 'jokey' material. Approach by post or e-mail.

Home

Highbury Leisure Ltd, Berwick House, 8–10 Knoll Rise, Orpington BR6 0PS
☎01689 887200 Fax 01689 896847
✉ jwooderson@splpublishing.co.uk
Owner *Highbury Leisure Ltd*
Editor *Jocelyn Garside*
Circulation 58,421

MONTHLY magazine with ideas, information and inspiration for the home. Features include style, design, home products, gardens and cookery. Synopses and ideas welcome; approach in writing. No health and lifestyle articles.

Home & Country

104 New Kings Road, London SW6 4LY
☎020 7731 5777 Fax 020 7736 4061
Owner *National Federation of Women's Institutes*
Editor *Susan Seager*
Circulation 50,000

Founded 1919. MONTHLY. Official full-colour journal of the Federation of Women's Institutes, containing articles on a wide range of subjects of interest to women. Strong environmental country slant with crafts and cookery plus gardening appearing every month. Unsolicited mss, photos and illustrations welcome.
PAYMENT by arrangement.

Home & Family

Mary Sumner House, 24 Tufton Street, London SW1P 3RB
☎020 7222 5533 Fax 020 7222 1591
Owner *MU Enterprises Ltd*
Editor *Jill Worth*
Circulation 58,000

Founded 1976. QUARTERLY. Unsolicited mss considered. No fiction or poetry. Features on family life, social problems, marriage, Christian faith, etc. Max. 1000 words.
PAYMENT 'modest'.

Homes & Gardens

IPC Media Ltd., King's Reach Tower, Stamford Street, London SE1 9LS
☎020 7261 5000 Fax 020 7261 6247
www.homesand gardens.com
Owner *IPC Media*
Editor *Deborah Barker*
Circulation 162,817

Founded 1919. MONTHLY. Almost all published articles are specially commissioned. No fiction or poetry. Best to approach in writing with an idea, enclosing snapshots if appropriate.

Horse

Room 2303, IPC Country & Leisure Media Ltd, King's Reach Tower, Stamford Street, London SE1 9LS
☎020 7261 7969 Fax 020 7261 7979
✉ amanda_gee@ipcmedia.com
www.ipcmedia.com
Owner *IPC Media*
Editor *Amanda Gee*
Circulation 30,002

Founded 1997. MONTHLY magazine which aims at people who ride regularly and is committed to learning more about current issues in the equestrian world such as riding concepts, vetinary developments and horse care as well as offering practical advice. Regular contributors provide a lot of reader interaction. Articles on leading equestrian celebrities. Send examples of published work with c.v. to the editor.

Horse and Hound

IPC Media Ltd., King's Reach Tower, Stamford Street, London SE1 9LS
☎020 7261 6315 Fax 020 7261 5429
✉ jenny_sims@ipcmedia.com
Owner *IPC Media*
Editor *Lucy Higginson*
Circulation 68,320

Founded 1884. WEEKLY. The oldest equestrian magazine on the market. Contains regular veterinary advice and instructional articles, as well as authoritative news and comment on fox hunting, national/international showjumping, horse trials, dressage, driving and endurance riding. Also weekly racing and point-to-points, breeding reports and articles. Regular book and art reviews, and humorous articles and cartoons are frequently published. Plenty of opportunities for freelancers. Unsolicited contributions welcome.
Also publishes a sister monthly publication, *Eventing*, which covers the sport of horse trials comprehensively; Acting Editor *Julie Harding*.
PAYMENT NUJ rates.

Horse and Rider

Headley House, Headley Road, Grayshott GU26 6TU
☎01428 601020 Fax 01428 601030
✉ djm@djmurphy.co.uk
www.horseandridermagazine.co.uk
Owner *D.J. Murphy (Publishers) Ltd*
Editor *Alison Bridge*
Assistant Editor *Danielle Pascoe*

Circulation 46,000

Founded 1949. MONTHLY. Adult readership, largely horse-owning. News and instructional features, which make up the bulk of the magazine, are almost all written in-house or commissioned. New contributors and unsolicited articles are occasionally used. Approach the editor in writing with ideas.

Hotline

The River Group, Victory House, Leicester Square, London WC2H 7BZ
☎020 7306 0304
✉ rstanley@riverltd.co.uk

Editor *Rod Stanley*

Founded 1997. QUARTERLY on-board magazine for Virgin trains. UK travel-based features. Ideas and outlines welcome by post or e-mail.

House & Garden

Vogue House, Hanover Square, London W1S 1JU
☎020 7499 9080 Fax 020 7629 2907
www.condenast.co.uk

Owner *Condé Nast Publications Ltd*
Editor *Susan Crewe*
Circulation 148,716

Founded 1947. MONTHLY. Most feature material is produced in-house but occasional specialist features are commissioned from qualified freelancers, mainly for the interiors, wine and food sections and travel.

FEATURES *Liz Elliot* Suggestions for features, preferably in the form of brief outlines of proposed subjects, will be considered.

House Beautiful

National Magazine House, 72 Broadwick Street, London W1F 9EP
☎020 7439 5000 Fax 020 7439 5141

Owner *National Magazine Co. Ltd*
Editor *Kerryn Harper*
Circulation 182,025

Founded 1989. MONTHLY. Lively magazine offering sound, practical information and plenty of inspiration for those who want to make the most of where they live. Over 100 pages of easy-reading editorial. Regular features about decoration, DIY, food, gardening and home finance. Approach in writing with synopses or ideas in the first instance.

i-D Magazine

124 Tabernacle Street, London EC2A 4SA
☎020 7490 9710 Fax 020 7251 2225

✉ editor@i-dmagazine.co.uk
www.i-dmagazine.com

Owner *Levelprint*
Editor *Avril Mair*
Circulation 66,000

Founded 1980. MONTHLY lifestyle magazine for both sexes with a fashion bias. International. Very hip. Does not accept unsolicited contributions but welcomes new ideas from the fields of fashion, music, clubs, art, film, technology, books, sport, etc. No fiction or poetry. 'We are always looking for freelance non-fiction writers with new or unusual ideas.' A different theme each issue – past themes have included Green politics, taste, films, sex, love and loud dance music – means it is advisable to discuss feature ideas in the first instance.

Ideal Home

IPC Media Ltd., King's Reach Tower, Stamford Street, London SE1 9LS
☎020 7261 6505 Fax 020 7261 6697

Owner *IPC Media*
Editor *Susan Rose*
Circulation 274,488

Founded 1920. MONTHLY glossy. Unsolicited feature ideas are welcome only if appropriate to the magazine. Prospective contributors wishing to submit ideas should do so in writing to the editor. No fiction.

FEATURES Furnishing and decoration of houses, kitchens or bathrooms; interior design, soft furnishings, furniture and home improvements, lifestyle and readers' homes. Length to be discussed with editor.

PAYMENT negotiable.

Ignition Motoring for Women

2 Chantry Place, Harrow HA3 6NY
☎020 8420 1210 Fax 020 8420 1691

Managing Editor *Angela Giveon*
Circulation 35,000

Founded 2003. QUARTERLY 'The only motoring magazine in the world for women.' Aimed at a readership of 17–50-year-olds, covering the 'five ages of motoring'. Features on motorsports, all with a strong feminine bias, as well as fashion and beauty.

The Illustrated London News

20 Upper Ground, London SE1 9PF
☎020 7805 5562 Fax 020 7805 5911
✉ iln@ilng.co.uk
www.ilng.co.uk

Owner *James Sherwood*

Editor *Alison Booth*
Circulation 47,547

Founded 1842. BIANNUAL: Christmas and Summer issues, plus the occasional special issue to coincide with particular events. Although the *ILN* covers issues concerning the whole of the UK, its emphasis remains on the capital and its life. Travel, wine, restaurants, events, cultural and current affairs are all covered. There are few opportunities for freelancers but all unsolicited mss are read (receives about five a week). The best approach is with an idea in writing to the editor. Particularly interested in articles relating to events and developments in contemporary London, and about people working in the capital. All features are illustrated, so ideas with picture opportunities are particularly welcome.

Image Magazine
Upper Mounts, Northampton NN1 3HR
☎01604 467000   Fax 01604 467190
✉ image@northantsnews.co.uk
www.northantsnews.com

Owner *Northamptonshire Newspapers Ltd*
Editor *Ruth Supple*
Circulation 12,000

Founded 1905. MONTHLY general interest regional magazine. No unsolicited mss.
FEATURES Local issues, personalities, businesses, etc., of Northamptonshire, Bedfordshire, Buckinghamshire interest. Max. 500 words.
NEWS No hard news as such, just monthly diary column.
OTHER Regulars on motoring, fashion, beauty, lifestyle, travel and horoscopes. Max. 500 words.
PAYMENT for features negotiable.

In Britain
Jubilee House, 2 Jubilee Place, London SW3 3TQ
☎020 7751 4800   Fax 020 7751 4848
✉ inbritain@romseypublishing.com

Editor *Andrea Spain*
Circulation 47,000

Founded in the 1930s. BI-MONTHLY. Travel magazine of 'VisitBritain'. Not much opportunity for unsolicited work – approach (by e-mail) with ideas and samples. Words and picture packages preferred (good quality transparencies only).

Independent Magazine
See **The Independent** under *National Newspapers*

Inspirations
Highbury Leisure Ltd, Berwick House, 8–10 Knoll Rise, Orpington BR6 0PS
☎01689 887200   Fax 01689 896847

Owner *Highbury Leisure Ltd*
Editor *Andrée Frieze*
Circulation 50,000

Homes and interiors covering decorating, design, house features, makeovers, cookery, property, DIY advice and gardens. Will consider unsolicited synopses on these subjects.

InStyle
IPC Media Ltd., Kings Reach Tower, Stamford Street, London SE1 9LS
☎020 7261 5000   Fax 020 7261 6664
✉ firstname_lastname@ipcmedia.com

Owner *IPC Media*
Editor *Louise Chunn*
Senior Editors (Features) *Cath Rapley, Polly Williams*
Fashion Editor *Tamasin Doe*
Circulation 187,172

Launched March 2001. MONTHLY. UK edition of US fashion, beauty, celebrity and lifestyle magazine. Unsolicited material welcome; send by e-mail to individual editors.

The International Journal of Erotica
Diverse Publications, Unit 556, 3 Courthill House, 60 Water Lane, Wilmslow SK9 5BB
✉ diversepublications@yahoo.co.uk
www.diversepublications.co.uk
Owner *Diverse Publications Ltd*
Editors *Robin Barratt, Inna Zabrodskaya*
Circulation 25,000

Founded 2003. QUARTERLY publication focusing on erotic art, poetry, photography and fiction. 'From India to Russia, from the UK to South Africa and Asia, we will be discussing and exploring the full range of erotic art and writing from a variety of countries and cultures.' Unsolicited contributions welcome, particularly from outside the UK – prose, fiction or poetry, up to 5000 words. Also monochrome or colour photographic portfolios. Absolutely *no* pornography.

Interzone: Science Fiction & Fantasy
217 Preston Drove, Brighton BN1 6FL
☎01273 504710
www.sfsite.com/interzone
Owner/Editor *David Pringle*

Circulation 10,000

Founded 1982. BI-MONTHLY magazine of science fiction and fantasy. Unsolicited mss are welcome 'from writers who have a knowledge of the magazine and its contents'. S.a.e. essential for return.

FICTION 2000–6000 words.

FEATURES Book/film reviews, interviews with writers and occasional short articles. Length by arrangement.

PAYMENT fiction, £30 per 1000 words; features, negotiable.

Investors Chronicle

Tabernacle Court, 16–28 Tabernacle Street, London EC2A 4DD

☎020 7382 8607 Fax 020 7382 8105

www.investorschronicle.co.uk

Owner *Pearson*
Editor *Matthew Vincent*
Deputy Editor *Rosie Carr*
Circulation 50,524

Founded 1860. WEEKLY. Opportunities for freelance contributors in the survey section only. All approaches should be made in writing. Over forty surveys are published each year on a wide variety of subjects, generally with a financial, business or investment emphasis. Copies of survey list and synopses of individual surveys are obtainable from the surveys editor.

PAYMENT negotiable.

Irish Pages

The Linen Hall Library, 17 Donegall Square North, Belfast BT1 5GB

☎028 90 321 707

✉ irishpages@yahoo.co.uk

www.irishpages.org

Editor *Chris Agee*
Circulation 1400

Founded 2002. BIANNUAL non-partisan, non-sectarian journal publishing writing from Ireland and abroad. 'The most important cultural journal in Ireland at the present moment' (Jonathan Allison, Director of the Yeats Summer School).

FEATURES Poetry, short fiction, essays, non-fiction, memoirs, nature-writing, translated work, literary journalism and other autobiographical, historical and scientific writing of literary distinction. Irish language and Ulster Scots writing are published in the original, with English translations. Equal editorial attention is given to established, emergent and new writers. Send submissions to the editor by post.

IRRV Valuer

The IRRV, 41 Doughty Street, London WC1N 2LF

☎01992 505529 Fax 01992 505547

✉ katemiller@globalnet.co.uk

www.irrv.org.uk

Owner *Institue of Revenues, Rating and Valuation*
Managing Editor *Kate Miller*
Circulation 1,322

Founded 2001. Six BI-MONTHLY issues yearly for property valuation professionals. Well-qualified commentary, analysis and news covering issues affecting valuers, including reforms, legislation and technology. Small amount of appropriate lifestyle coverage. No unsolicited material; approach by telephone, fax, letter or e-mail in the first instance.

FEATURES Ideas for stories must be well sourced and informed. Max. 1000 words.

NEWS Stories relevant to property professionals. Max. 300 words.

PAYMENT negotiable.

It's Hot! Magazine

Rm A1136, BBC Worldwide, Woodlands, 180 Wood Lane, London W12 0TT

☎020 8433 2447 Fax 020 8433 2763

✉ itshot@bbc.co.uk

Owner *BBC Worldwide*
Editor *Peter Hart*
Features *Kelly Wilks*
Circulation 116,515

Founded 2002. MONTHLY magazine aimed at celebrity-mad 9–13 year old girls featuring music, film & TV gossip. Interested in exclusive celebrity interviews relevant to their market, and quizzes. Approach the editor with ideas by e-mail (peter.hart@bbc.co.uk) but 'please read the magazine first for style'. PAYMENT negotiable.

Jack Magazine

30 Cleveland Street, London W1T 4JD

☎020 7907 6000 Fax 020 7907 6020

✉ jackletters@dennis.co.uk

www.jackthemag.com

Owner *Felix Dennis*
Editor *Michael Hodges*
Circulation 39,052

Founded 2002. MONTHLY upmarket men's magazine. No fiction. E-mail pitch explaining where the article would fit into the magazine; give previous writing experience.

FEATURES *Eddy Lawrence* (eddy-lawrence@dennis.co.uk)

REVIEWS Books (ben-ashby@dennis.co.uk);

Cars (brendan-fitzgerald@dennis.co.uk); Music (kim-tbennett@dennis.co.uk)

FRONT SECTION ('Most Talked About') *Dan Davies* (dan-davies@dennis.co.uk)

FASHION *William Gilchrist* (william-gilchrist@dennis.co.uk)

PAYMENT 25p per word.

Jade

PO Box 202, Scarborough YO11 3GE
☎01723 581329 Fax 01723 581329
✉ books@greatnorthernpublishing.co.uk
www.greatnorthernpublishing.co.uk

Owner *Great Northern Publishing*
Editors *Mark Marsay, Diane Crowther*

Founded 2002. BI-MONTHLY uncensored, adult subscription only magazine in A5 format. 'The erotic art and literature magazine for discerning adults.'

Features new and established international photographers, artists and writers in all erotic genres from around the world. No editorial articles, features or advice columns. Prides itself on minimal advertising stance. Contributors (photographers, artists and writers) should consult the website for submission guidelines and current requirements; contact the editors prior to sending material. Sample copy £5 – contains strong adult content.

Jane's Defence Weekly

Sentinel House, 163 Brighton Road, Coulsdon CR5 2YH
☎020 8700 3700 Fax 020 8763 1007
✉ jdw@janes.com
www.janes.com

Owner *Jane's*
Editor *Peter Felstead*
Circulation 25,500

Founded 1984. WEEKLY. No unsolicited mss. Approach in writing with ideas in the first instance.

FEATURES Current defence topics (politics, strategy, equipment, industry) of worldwide interest. No history pieces. Most features are commissioned. Max. 4000 words.

Jazz Journal International

3 & 3A Forest Road, Loughton IG10 1DR
☎020 8532 0456/0678 Fax 020 8532 0440

Owner *Jazz Journal Ltd*
Editor-in-Chief *Eddie Cook*
Circulation 8000+

Founded 1948. MONTHLY. A specialised jazz magazine, for record collectors, principally using expert contributors whose work is known to the editor. Unsolicited mss not welcome, with the exception of news material (for which no payment is made). It is not a gig guide, nor a free reference source for students.

Jersey Now

PO Box 582, Five Oaks, St Saviour JE4 8XQ
☎01534 611743 Fax 01534 611610
✉ mspeditorial@msppublishing.com

Owner *MSP Publishing*
Managing Editor *Peter Body*
Circulation 24,000

Founded 1987. QUARTERLY lifestyle magazine for Jersey covering homes, gardens, the arts, Jersey heritage, motoring, boating, fashion and technology. Upmarket glossy aimed at an informed and discerning readership. Interested in Jersey-orientated articles only – 1200 words max. Approach the editor initially. PAYMENT negotiable.

Jewish Chronicle

25 Furnival Street, London EC4A 1JT
☎020 7415 1500 Fax 020 7405 9040
✉ editorial@thejc.com
www.thejc.com

Owner *Kessler Foundation*
Editor *Edward J. Temko*
Circulation 50,000

WEEKLY. Unsolicited mss welcome if 'the specific interests of our readership are borne in mind by writers'. Approach in writing, except for urgent current news items. No fiction. Max. 1500 words for all material.

FEATURES *Gerald Jacobs*
LEISURE/LIFESTYLE *Alan Montague*
HOME NEWS *Barry Toberman*
FOREIGN NEWS *Joe Millis*
SUPPLEMENTS *Angela Kiverstein*
PAYMENT negotiable.

Jewish Quarterly

PO Box 37645, London NW7 1WB
☎020 8343 4675 Fax 020 8343 4675
✉ admin@jewishquarterly.org
www.jewishquarterly.org

Publisher *Jewish Literary Trust Ltd*
Editor *Matthew Reisz*

Founded 1953. QUARTERLY illustrated magazine featuring Jewish literature and fiction, politics, art, music, film, poetry, history, dance, community, autobiography, Hebrew, Yiddish, Israel and the Middle East, Judaism, interviews, Zionism, philosophy and holocaust studies. Features a major books and arts section. Unsolicited mss welcome but letter or phone call preferred in first instance.

Jewish Telegraph
Jewish Telegraph Group of Newspapers,
11 Park Hill, Bury Old Road, Prestwich,
Manchester M25 0HH
☎0161 740 9321 Fax 0161 740 9325
✉ editor@jewishtelegraph.com
www.jewishtelegraph.com
Editor *Paul Harris*
Circulation 16,000

Founded 1950. WEEKLY publication with local, national and international news and features. (Separate editions published for Manchester, Leeds, Liverpool and Glasgow.) Unsolicited features on Jewish humour and history welcome.

The Journal Magazines (Norfolk, Suffolk, Cambridgeshire)/ The Essex Magazine
The Old County School, Northgate Street, Bury St Edmunds IP33 1HP
☎01284 701190 Fax 01284 701680
✉ pippa@acornmagazines.co.uk
Owner *Acorn Magazines Ltd*
Editor *Pippa Bastin*
Circulation 12,000 each

Founded 1990. MONTHLY magazines covering items of local interest – history, people, conservation, business, places, food and wine, fashion, homes and sport.
FEATURES 750–1500 words max., plus pictures. Approach the editor by e-mail (see above) with ideas in the first instance.

Kerrang!
Mappin House, 4 Winsley Street, London W1N 7AR
☎020 7436 1515 Fax 020 7182 8910
www.kerrang.com
Owner *Emap Performance*
Editor *Ashley Bird*
Circulation 69,261

Founded 1980. WEEKLY rock, punk and nu-metal magazine. 'Written by fans for fans.' Will consider ideas for features but not actively seeking new contributors unless expert in specialist fields such as Black metal and nu-metal.

The Lady
39–40 Bedford Street, London WC2E 9ER
☎020 7379 4717 Fax 020 7836 4620
Editor *Arline Usden*

Circulation 40,000

Founded 1885. WEEKLY. Unsolicited mss are accepted provided they are not on the subject of politics or religion, or on topics covered by staff writers or special correspondents, i.e. fashion and beauty, health, cookery, household, gardening, finance and shopping.
FEATURES Well-researched pieces on British and foreign travel, historical subjects or events; interviews and profiles and other general interest topics. Max. 1200 words for illustrated two-page articles; 900 words for one-page features; 430 words for first-person 'Viewpoint' pieces. All material should be addressed to the editor with s.a.e. enclosed. Photographs supporting features may be supplied as colour transparencies, b&w prints or on disk. Telephone enquiries about features are not encouraged.

Land Rover World
Leon House, 233 High Street, Croydon CR9 1HZ
☎020 8774 0600
Owner *IPC Media*
Editor *Luke Evans*
Circulation 30,000

Founded 1994. MONTHLY. Incorporates *Practical Land Rover World* and *Classic Land Rover World*. Unsolicited material welcome, especially if supported by high-quality illustrations.
FEATURES All articles with a Land Rover theme of interest. Potential contributors are strongly advised to examine previous issues before starting work.
PAYMENT negotiable.

LG
Upper Mounts, Northampton NN1 3HR
☎01604 467043 Fax 01604 467190
Owner *Northamptonshire Newspapers Ltd*
Editor *Ruth Supple*
Circulation 6000

Formerly *Looking Good*, founded 1984. Relaunched in 2002 as *LG*, a MONTHLY magazine aimed at women aged 18–30. Fashion and beauty, lifestyle, true life stories. Contributions occasionally considered but majority of work is done in-house.

Life&Soul Magazine
Box 8, 94 London Road, Headington, Oxford OX3 9FN
☎01865 423435 Fax 01865 423435
✉ editor@lifeandsoul.com
www.lifeandsoul.com
Publisher *Karma Publishing Ltd*

Editor *Roy Stemman*
Circulation 3000

QUARTERLY. The only magazine in the world dealing with all aspects of reincarnation – from people who claim to recall their past lives spontaneously to those who have been regressed. It also examines other evidence for immortality, including near-death experiences, spirit communication and paranormal phenonema. Commissions only. No unsolicited mss.

Lincolnshire Life
County Life Ltd, PO Box 81, Lincoln LN1 1HD
☎01522 527127 Fax 01522 560035
✉ editorial@lincolnshirelife.co.uk
www.lincolnshirelife.co.uk

Publisher *A.L. Robinson*
Executive Editor *Judy Theobald*
Circulation 10,000

Founded 1961. MONTHLY county magazine featuring geographically relevant articles on local culture, history, personalities, etc. Max. 1500 words. Contributions supported by three or four good-quality photographs welcome. Approach in writing. PAYMENT varies.

The Lincolnshire Poacher
County Life Ltd, PO Box 81, Lincoln LN1 1HD
☎01522 527127 Fax 01522 560035
✉ editorial@lincolnshirelife.co.uk
www.lincolnshirelife.co.uk

Publisher *A.L. Robinson*
Executive Editor *Judy Theobald*
Circulation 5000

QUARTERLY county magazine featuring geographically relevant but nostalgic articles on the history, culture and personalities of Lincolnshire. Max. 1500 words. Contributions supported by three or four good-quality photography/illustrations appreciated. Approach in writing. PAYMENT varies.

The List
14 High Street, Edinburgh EH1 1TE
☎0131 558 1191 Fax 0131 557 8500
✉ editor@list.co.uk
www.list.co.uk

Owner *The List Ltd*
Publisher *Robin Hodge*
Editor *Nick Barley*
Circulation 17,500

Founded 1985. FORTNIGHTLY. Events guide covering Glasgow and Edinburgh. Interviews and profiles of people working in film, theatre, music and the arts. Max. 1200 words. No unsolicited mss. Phone with ideas. News material tends to be handled in-house. PAYMENT £100.

Literary Review
44 Lexington Street, London W1F 0LW
☎020 7437 9392 Fax 020 7734 1844
✉ litrev@dircon.co.uk

Editor *Nancy Sladek*
Circulation 15,000

Founded 1979. MONTHLY. Publishes book reviews (commissioned), features and articles on literary subjects. Contact the editor in writing. Unsolicited mss not welcome. Runs a monthly competition for 'poems which rhyme, scan and make sense'.
PAYMENT 'miniscule'.

Living France Magazine
Archant House, Oriel Road, Cheltenham GL50 1BB
☎01242 216050 Fax 01242 216074
✉ editorial@livingfrance.com
www.livingfrance.com

Owner *Archant Life*
Editor *Lucy-Jane Cypher*

Founded 1989. MONTHLY. A Francophile magazine catering for those with a passion for France, French culture and lifestyle. Editorial covers all aspects of holidaying, living and working in France. Property section for those owning or wishing to buy a property in France. No unsolicited mss; approach in writing or by e-mail with an idea.

Living History
See **BBC History Magazine**

Loaded
IPC Media Ltd., King's Reach Tower, Stamford Street, London SE1 9LS
☎020 7261 5562 Fax 020 7261 5557
✉ andrew_woods@ipcmedia.com

Owner *IPC Media*
Editor *Martin Daubney*
Features Editor *Andrew Woods*
Circulation 263,108

Founded 1994. MONTHLY men's lifestyle magazine featuring music, sport, sex, humour, travel, fashion, hard news and popular culture. Will consider material which comes into these categories; approach the features editor in writing or by e-mail in the first instance. No fiction or poetry.

Logos

5 Beechwood Drive, Marlow SL7 2DH
☎01628 433871   Fax 01628 477577
✉ logos-marlow@dial.pipex.com

Owner *Whurr Publishers Ltd*
Editor *Gordon Graham*
Associate Editor *Betty Graham*

Founded 1990. QUARTERLY. Aims to 'deal in depth with issues which unite, divide, excite and concern the world of books', with an international perspective. Each issue contains six to eight articles of between 3500 and 7000 words. 'Logos is a non-profit making professional forum, not a scholarly journal.' Suggestions and ideas for contributions are welcome, and should be addressed to the editor. 'Guidelines for Contributors' available. Contributors write from their experience as authors, publishers, booksellers, librarians, etc.

PAYMENT Contributors receive 25 offprints, a copy of the issue in which their article appears and a 50% concession on the subscription rate.

The London Magazine

32 Addison Grove, London W4 1ER
☎020 8400 5882   Fax 020 8994 1713
✉ editorial@thelondonmagazine.net
www.londonmagazine.net

Owner *Christopher Arkell*
Editor *Sebastian Barker*
Circulation 1,200

Founded originally in 1732 and relaunched in 2002. BI-MONTHLY review of literature and the arts. Publishes poems, short stories, features, memoirs, and book and performane reviews. Not interested in overtly political material or anything sent by e-mail or fax. No phone-calls. All submissions should be made by post with an s.a.e. to the editor.
FEATURES Max. 5000 words.
FICTION Max. 5000 words.
POEMS 'Any length within reason.'
PAYMENT negotiable.

London Review of Books

28 Little Russell Street, London WC1A 2HN
☎020 7209 1101   Fax 020 7209 1102
✉ edit@lrb.co.uk
www.lrb.co.uk

Owner *LRB Ltd*
Editor *Mary-Kay Wilmers*
Circulation 42,721

Founded 1979. FORTNIGHTLY. Reviews, essays and articles on political, literary, cultural and sci-entific subjects. Also poetry. Unsolicited contributions welcome (approximately 50 received each week). No pieces under 2000 words. Contact the editor in writing. Please include s.a.e.
PAYMENT £150 per 1000 words; poems, £75.

Looking Good
See **LG**

Lothian Life

Ballencrieff Cottage, Ballencrieff Toll, Bathgate EH48 4LD
☎01506 632728   Fax 01506 632728
✉ editor@lothianlife.co.uk
www.lothianlife.co.uk

Owner *Pages Editorial & Publishing Services*
Editor *Susan Coon*

QUARTERLY county magazine for people who live, work or have an interest in the Lothians. Includes three or four major features (1500 words) on successful people, businesses or initiatives. A local walk takes up the centre spread. Regular articles by experts on collectables, property, interior design, cookery, health and local gardening, plus news items, letters and a competition. Freelance writers used only for main features. Phone first to discuss content and timing.
PAYMENT by arrangement.

Machine Knitting Monthly

PO Box 1479, Maidenhead SL6 8YX
☎01628 783080   Fax 01628 633250
✉ rpa@surf3.net
www.machineknittingmonthly.co.uk

Owner *RPA Publishing Ltd*
Editor *Anne Smith*

Founded 1986. MONTHLY. Unsolicited mss considered 'as long as they are applicable to this specialist publication. We have our own regular contributors each month but we're always willing to look at new ideas from other writers.' Approach in writing in the first instance.

Management Today

174 Hammersmith Road, London W6 7JP
☎020 8267 5000
✉ management.today@haynet.com

Owner *Haymarket Business Publications Ltd*
Managing Director *Rufus Olins*
Editor *Matthew Gwyther*
Circulation 102,000

General business topics and features. Ideas welcome. Send brief synopsis to the editor.

marie claire
13th Floor, King's Reach Tower, Stamford Street, London SE1 9LS
☎020 7261 5240 Fax 020 7261 5277
✉ marieclaire@ipcmedia.com
www.ipcmedia.com
Owner *European Magazines Ltd*
Editor *Marie O'Riordan*
Circulation 360,789

Founded 1988. MONTHLY. An intelligent glossy magazine for women, with strong international features and fashion. No unsolicited mss. Approach with ideas in writing or by e-mail (marieclaireideas@ipcmedia.com). No fiction.
FEATURES *Charlotte Moore* Detailed proposals for feature ideas should be accompanied by samples of previous work.

Marketing Week
12–26 Lexington Street, London W1R 4HQ
☎020 7970 4000 Fax 020 7970 6721
✉ stuart.smith@centaur.co.uk
www.mad.co.uk/publication/mw/
Owner *Centaur Communications*
Editor *Stuart Smith*
Circulation 41,000

WEEKLY trade magazine of the marketing industry. Features on all aspects of the business, written in a newsy and up-to-the-minute style. Approach with ideas in the first instance.
FEATURES *Danny Parker*
PAYMENT negotiable.

Match
Bushfield House, Orton Centre, Peterborough PE2 5UW
☎01733 237111 Fax 01733 288150
✉ match.magazine@emap.com
www.matchmag.co.uk
Owner *Emap Active Ltd*
Editor *Simon Caney*
Deputy Editor *Ian Foster*
Circulation 72,023

Founded 1979. WEEKLY. The UK's biggest-selling football magazine aimed at 10–15-year-olds. All material is generated in-house by a strong news and features team. Work experience placements often given to trainee journalists and students; the majority of staff are recruited through this route. Approach in writing or by phone.

Match Angling Plus
Emap Active, Bushfield House, Orton Centre, Peterborough PE2 5UW
☎01733 465705 Fax 01733 465658
✉ steve.cole@emap.com
Owner *Emap Active*
Editor *Steve Cole*
Circulation 15,000

Founded 1992. MONTHLY magazine aimed at match anglers and advanced pleasure anglers. Coarse fishing only.
FEATURES only. Please send relevant articles, with or without pictures, by e-mail to the editor. Max. 2500 words.

Matrix
See **British Science Fiction Association** under *Professional Associations*

Maxim
30 Cleveland Street, London W1T 4JD
☎020 7907 6410 Fax 020 7907 6439
✉ editorial@maxim-magazine.co.uk
Owner *Dennis Publishing*
Editor *Greg Gutfield*
Circulation 243,341

Established 1995. MONTHLY glossy men's lifestyle magazine featuring sex, travel, health, motoring and fashion. No fiction or poetry. Approach in writing in the first instance, sending outlines of ideas only together with examples of published work.

Mayfair
2 Archer Street, Piccadilly Circus, London W1D 7AW
☎020 7292 8000 Fax 020 7734 5030
✉ mayfair@pr-org.co.uk
www.sexclub.co.uk
Owner *Paul Raymond Publications*
Editor *David Ryder*
Circulation 331,760

Founded 1966. THIRTEEN ISSUES YEARLY. Unsolicited material accepted if pertinent to the magazine and if accompanied by suitable illustrative material. 'We will *only* publish work if we can illustrate it.' Interested in features and humour aimed at men aged 18–80; 800–1000 words. Punchy, bite-sized humour, top ten features, etc. 'Must make the editor laugh.' Also considers erotica.

Mayfair Times
27 John Adam Street, London WC2N 6HX
☎020 7839 2455 Fax 020 7839 3789
✉ erik.brown@pubbiz.com
www.pubbiz.com
Owner *Mayfair Times Ltd*
Editor *Erik Brown*
Circulation 17,000

Founded 1985. MONTHLY. Features on Mayfair

of interest to residents, local workers, visitors and shoppers.

Medal News
Orchard House, Duchy Road, Heathpark, Honiton EX14 1YD
☎01404 46972 Fax 01404 44788
✉ info@tokenpublishing.com
www.tokenpublishing.com
Owners *J.W. Mussell, Carol Hartman*
Editor *J.W. Mussell*
Circulation 7,000

Founded 1989. MONTHLY. Unsolicited material welcome but initial approach by phone or in writing preferred.
FEATURES 'Opportunities exist for well-informed authors who know the subject and do their homework.' Max. 2500 words.
PAYMENT £25 per 1000 words.

Media Week
Quantum House, 19 Scarbrook Road, Croydon CR9 1LX
☎020 8565 4323 Fax 020 8565 4394
www.mediaweek.co.uk
Owner *Quantum Business Media*
Editor *Tim Burrowes*
Circulation 20,555

Founded 1986. WEEKLY trade magazine. UK and international coverage on all aspects of commercial media. Approach in writing with ideas. See website for e-mail addresses.

Melody Maker
See **New Musical Express**

Men's Health
7–10 Chandos Street, London W1G 9AD
☎020 7291 6000 Fax 020 7291 6053
www.menshealth.co.uk
Owner *Rodale Publishing*
Editor *Morgan Rees*
Circulation 220,446

Founded 1994. MONTHLY men's healthy lifestyle magazine covering health, fitness, nutrition, stress and sex issues. No unsolicited mss; will consider ideas and synopses tailored to men's health. No fiction or extreme sports. Approach in writing in the first instance.

MiniWorld Magazine
Leon House, 233 High Street, Croydon CR9 1HZ
☎020 8774 0600
✉ miniworld@ipcmedia.com
www.miniworld.co.uk

Owner *IPC Media*
Editor *Monty Watkins*
Circulation 37,000

Founded 1991. MONTHLY car magazine devoted to the Mini. Unsolicited material welcome but prospective contributors are advised to contact the editor.
FEATURES Maintenance, tuning, restoration, technical advice, classified, sport, readers' cars and social history of this cult car.
PAYMENT negotiable.

Mizz
IPC Media Ltd., King's Reach Tower, Stamford Street, London SE1 9LS
☎020 7261 6319 Fax 020 7261 6032
Owner *IPC Media*
Editor *Sharon Christal*
Deputy Editor *Leslie Sinoway*
Circulation 100,298

Founded 1985. FORTNIGHTLY magazine for the 10–14-year-old girl.
FEATURES 'We have a full features team and thus do not accept freelance features.'

Model Collector
IPC Focus Network, Leon House, 233 High Street, Croydon CR9 1HZ
☎020 8774 0600
✉ modelcollector@ipcmedia.com
www.modelcollector.com
Owner *AOL Time Warner/IPC Media*
Editor *Stephen Rowe*
Circulation 15,699

Founded 1987. THIRTEEN ISSUES YEARLY Britain's best selling die cast magazine. From the latest models to classic 30's Dinkys. Interested in historical articles about particular models or ranges and reviews of the latest products. Photographs welcome. Not interested in radio controlled models or model railways.
FEATURES Freelancers should contact the editor. Unsolicited material may be considered.
NEWS Trade news welcome. Call *Lindsay Armrani* (020 8774 0932) to discuss details.

Mojo
Mappin House, 4 Winsley Street, London W1W 8HF
☎020 7436 1515 Fax 020 7312 8296
✉ mojo@emap.com
www.mojo4music.com
Owner *Emap-Metro*
Editor-in-Chief *Phil Alexander*
Circulation 104,437

Founded 1993. MONTHLY magazine containing features, reviews and news stories about rock music and its influences. Receives about five mss per day. No poetry, think-pieces on dead rock stars or similar fan worship.

FEATURES Amateur writers discouraged except as providers of source material, contacts, etc.

NEWS All verifiable, relevant stories considered.

REVIEWS Write to Reviews Editor *Jenny Bulley* with relevant specimen material.

PAYMENT negotiable.

Moneywise

RD Publications Ltd, 11 Westferry Circus, Canary Wharf, London E14 4HE
☎020 7715 8465 Fax 020 7715 8733
www.moneywise.co.uk

Owner *Reader's Digest Association*
Editor *Ben Livesy*
Circulation 105,000

Founded 1990. MONTHLY. No unsolicited mss; ideas welcome. Make initial approach in writing to *Sarah Das* (c.v. preferred).

More!

Endeavour House, 189 Shaftesbury Avenue, London WC2H 8JG
☎020 7208 3165 Fax 020 7208 3595
✉ abby.woolf@emap.com
www.moremagazine.co.uk

Owner *Emap élan Publications*
Editor *Alison Hall*
Features Director *Amanda Astill*
Editorial Enquiries *Abby Woolf*
Circulation 259,550

Founded 1988. FORTNIGHTLY women's magazine aimed at the working woman aged 18–25. Features on sex and relationships plus news. Most items are commissioned; approach features director with idea. Prospective contributors are strongly advised to study the magazine's style before submitting anything.

Mother and Baby

Greater London House, Hampstead Road, London NW1 7EJ
☎020 7347 1869 Fax 020 7347 1888
✉ mother&baby@emap.com

Owner *Emap Esprit*
Editor *Elena Dalrymple*
Circulation 81,024

Founded 1956. MONTHLY. Welcomes suggestions for feature ideas about pregnancy, newborn basics, practical babycare, baby development and childcare subjects. Approaches may be made by telephone, e-mail or in writing to the Features Editor *Georgina Hersey*.

Motor Boat & Yachting

IPC Media Limited, King's Reach Tower, Stamford Street, London SE1 9LS
☎020 7261 5333 Fax 020 7261 5419
✉ mby@ipcmedia.com
www.mby.com

Owner *Time Warner*
Editor *Tom Isitt*
Circulation 18,038

Founded 1904. MONTHLY for those interested in motor boats and motor cruising.

FEATURES *Tom Isitt* Cruising features and practical features especially welcome. Illustrations/photographs (mostly colour) are just as important as text. Max. 3000 words.

NEWS *Kate Brunel-Cohen* Factual pieces. Max. 200 words.

PAYMENT features: from £100 per 1000 words or by arrangement; news: up to £50 per item.

Motor Caravan Magazine

Leon House, 233 High Street, Croydon CR9 1HZ
☎020 8774 0600
✉ simon_collis@ipcmedia.com
www.motorcaravanmagazine.co.uk

Owner *IPC Media*
Editor *Simon Collis*
Circulation 15,000

Founded 1986. MONTHLY consumer magazine delivering test reports, touring ideas and practical advice to motor caravanners. Unsolicited material welcome. Interested in holiday reports, interesting or unusual caravans, practical step-by-step motor caravanning features. Phone the editor or e-mail outlining basic ideas. Max. 2500 words. PAYMENT £60 a page.

Motor Cycle News

Media House, Lynchwood, Peterborough Business Park, Peterborough PE2 6EA
☎01733 468000 Fax 01733 468028
✉ MCN@emap.com
www.motorcylenews.com

Owner *Emap plc*
Editor *Marc Potter*
Circulation 141,914

Founded 1955. WEEKLY Interested in short news stories and features on motorcyles and motorcycle racing. Not race reports. Contact relevant desks direct.

Motorcaravan Motorhome Monthly (MMM)

PO Box 88, Tiverton EX16 7ZN
✉ mmmeditor@warnersgroup.co.uk
www.mmmonline.co.uk
Owner *Warners Group Publications Plc*
Editor *Mike Jago*
Circulation 35,000

Founded 1966. MONTHLY. 'There's no money in motorcaravan journalism but for those wishing to cut their first teeth ...' Unsolicited mss welcome if relevant, but ideas in writing preferred in first instance.

FEATURES Caravan site reports. Max. 500 words.

TRAVEL Motorcaravanning trips (home and overseas). Max. 2000 words.

NEWS Short news items for miscellaneous pages. Max. 200 words.

FICTION Must be motorcaravan-related and include artwork/photos if possible. Max. 2000 words.

SPECIAL PAGES DIY – modifications to motorcaravans. Max. 1500 words.

OWNER REPORTS Contributions welcome from motorcaravan owners. Contact the editor for requirements. Max. 2000 words.

PAYMENT varies.

Ms London

Independent House, 191 Marsh Wall, London E14 9RS
☎020 7005 5236 Fax 020 7005 5999
www.londoncareers.net
Owner *Independent Magazines*
Editor-in-Chief *Bill Williamson*
Circulation 85,000

Founded 1968. WEEKLY. Aimed at working women in London, aged 18–45. No unsolicited mss.

NEWS Handled in-house but follow-up feature ideas welcome.

FEATURES Content is varied and topical, ranging from celebrity interviews to news issues, fashion, health, careers, relationships and homebuying. Approach in writing only with ideas in the first instance, enclosing sample of published writing. Material should be London-angled, sharp or humorous and fairly sophisticated in content. Max. 1500 words.

PAYMENT about £130 per 1000 words on publication.

Mslexia (For Women Who Write)

PO Box 656, Newcastle upon Tyne NE99 2XD
☎0191 261 6656 Fax 0191 261 6636

✉ postbag@mslexia.demon.co.uk
www.mslexia.co.uk
Owner *Mslexia Publications Limited*
Editor *Debbie Taylor*
Circulation 10,000

Founded 1997. QUARTERLY. Articles, advice, reviews, interviews, events for women writers plus new poetry and prose. Will consider fiction, poetry, features and letters but contributors *must* send for guidelines first.

Music Week

Ludgate House, 245 Blackfriars Road, London SE1 9UR
☎020 7921 5000 Fax 020 7921 8326
www.musicweek.com
Owner *CMP Information*
Editor-in-Chief *Ajax Scott*
Circulation 13,900

Britain's only WEEKLY music business magazine. No unsolicited mss. Approach in writing with ideas.

FEATURES Analysis of specific music business events and trends.

NEWS Music industry news only.

Musical Opinion

2 Princes Road, St Leonards on Sea TN37 6EL
☎01424 715167 Fax 01424 712214
✉ musicalopinion2@aol.com
www.musicalopinion.com
Owner *Musical Opinion Ltd*
Editor *Denby Richards*
Circulation 5000

Founded 1877. Glossy, full-colour BI-MONTHLY magazine. Classical music content, with topical features on music, musicians, festivals, etc., and reviews (concerts, festivals, opera, ballet, jazz, CDs, DVDs, videos, books and printed music). International readership. No unsolicited mss; commissions only. Ideas always welcome though; approach by phone, fax or e-mail, giving telephone number. Visit the website for full information.

PAYMENT negotiable.

My Weekly

80 Kingsway East, Dundee DD4 8SL
☎01382 223131 Fax 01382 452491
✉ myweekly@dcthomson.co.uk
Owner *D.C. Thomson & Co. Ltd*
Editor *Harrison Watson*
Circulation 273,703

A traditional women's WEEKLY. D.C. Thomson has long had a policy of encouragement and help to new writers of promise. Ideas welcome. Approach in writing.

FEATURES Particularly interested in human interest pieces (1000–1500 words) which by their very nature appeal to all age groups.

FICTION Three stories a week, ranging in content from the emotional to the off-beat and unexpected. 1000–4000 words.

PAYMENT negotiable.

The National Trust Magazine
36 Queen Anne's Gate, London SW1H 9AS
☎020 7222 9251 Fax 020 7222 5097
✉ enquiries@thenationaltrust.org.uk

Owner *The National Trust*
Editor *Gaynor Aaltonen*
Circulation 1.47 million

Founded 1968. THREE ISSUES YEARLY. Conservation of historic houses, coast and countryside in England, Northern Ireland and Wales. No unsolicited mss. Approach in writing with ideas.

The Naturalist
c/o University of Bradford, Bradford BD7 1DP
☎01274 234212 Fax 01274 234231
✉ m.r.d.seaward@bradford.ac.uk

Owner *Yorkshire Naturalists' Union*
Editor *Prof. M.R.D. Seaward*
Circulation 5000

Founded 1875. QUARTERLY. Natural history, biological and environmental sciences for a professional and amateur readership. Unsolicited mss and b&w illustrations welcome. Particularly interested in material – scientific papers – relating to the north of England. No PAYMENT.

Nature
The Macmillan Building, 4–6 Crinan Street, London N1 9XW
☎020 7833 4000 Fax 020 7843 4596
✉ nature@nature.com
www.nature.com/nature

Owner *Nature Publishing Group*
Editor *Philip Campbell*
Circulation 65,000

Covers all fields of science, with articles and news on science and science policy only. Scope only for freelance writers with specialist knowledge in these areas.

New Beacon
105 Judd Street, London WC1H 9NE
☎020 7388 1266 Fax 020 8438 9092
www.rnib.org.uk

Owner *Royal National Institute for the Blind*

Editor *Ann Lee*
Circulation 6000

Founded 1917. MONTHLY (except August). Published in print, braille and on tape, disk and e-mail. Unsolicited mss welcome. Approach with ideas in writing. Personal experiences by writers who have sight difficulties (partial sight or blindness), and authoritative items by professionals or volunteers working in the field of sight problems welcome. Max. 1500 words.

PAYMENT negotiable.

New Humanist
1 Gower Street, London WC1E 6HD
☎020 7436 1151
✉ editor@newhumanist.org.uk

Owner *Rationalist Press Association*
Editor *Frank Jordans*
Circulation 5000

Founded 1885. QUARTERLY. Unsolicited mss welcome. No fiction.

FEATURES Articles with a humanist perspective welcome in the following fields: religion (critical), humanism, human rights, philosophy, current events, literature, history and science. 2000 words.

BOOK REVIEWS 750–1000 words, by arrangement with the editor.

PAYMENT for features is nominal, but negotiable.

New Impact
Anser House, Courtyard Offices, 140 Oxford Road, Marlow SL7 2NT
☎01628 481581 Fax 01628 475570
✉ curious@anserhouse.co.uk
www.anserhouse.co.uk

Owner *D.E. Sihera*
Editor *Elaine Sihera*
Features Editor *Sushma Mallaya*
Circulation 10,000

Founded 1993. QUARTERLY. Celebrates diversity, enterprise and achievement from a minority ethnic perspective. Unsolicited mss welcome. Interested in training, arts, features, personal achievement, small business features, profiles of personalities especially for a multicultural audience. Promotes the British Diversity Awards each November and the Windrush Awards each June, the Register of Diversity Managers among employers and managing the diversity maze for practitioners.

NEWS Local training/business features – some opportunities. Max. length 550 words.

FEATURES Original, interesting pieces with a deliberate multicultural/diversity focus. Personal/professional successes and achievements welcome. Max. length 1000 words.

FICTION Short stories, poems – especially from minority writers. Not interested in romantic/sexual narratives. Max. length 1500 words.

SPECIAL PAGES Interviews with personalities – especially Asian, African Caribbean and Chinese. Max. length 1200 words.

PAYMENT negotiable.

New Internationalist

55 Rectory Road, Oxford OX4 1BW
☎01865 728181 Fax 01865 793152
✉ ni@newint.org
www.newint.org/

Owner *New Internationalist Trust*
Co-Editors *Vanessa Baird, David Ransom, Katharine Ainger, Adam Ma'anit*
Circulation 80,000

Radical and broadly leftist in approach, but unaligned. Concerned with world poverty and global issues of peace and politics, feminism and environmentalism, with emphasis on the Third World. Difficult to use unsolicited material as they work to a theme each month and features are commissioned by the editor on that basis. The way in is to send examples of published or unpublished work; writers of interest are taken up.

New Musical Express

IPC Media Ltd., King's Reach Tower, Stamford Street, London SE1 9LS
☎020 7261 6472 Fax 020 7261 5185
www.nme.com

Owner *IPC Media*
Editor *Conor McNicholas*
Circulation 72,557

Britain's best-selling musical WEEKLY. Now incorporates *Melody Maker*. Freelancers used, but always for reviews in the first instance. Specialisation in areas of music (or film, which is also covered) is a help.

REVIEWS: LPs *Anthony Thornton* LIVE *Pat Long* Send in examples of work, either published or specially written samples.

New Nation

Unit 2, 65 Whitechapel Road, London E1 1DU
☎020 7650 2000 Fax 020 7650 2001
www.ethnicmedia.co.uk

Owner *Ethnic Media Group*
Editor *Michael Eboda*
Circulation 30,000

Founded 1996. WEEKLY community paper for the Black community in Britain. Interested in relevant general, local and international issues. Approach in writing with ideas for submission.

New Scientist

1st Floor, 151 Wardour Street, London W1F 8WE
☎020 8652 3500 Fax 020 7331 2772 (News)
www.newscientist.com

Owner *Reed Business Information Ltd*
Editor-in-Chief *Dr Alun Anderson*
Editor *Jeremy Webb*
Circulation 143,902

Founded 1956. WEEKLY. No unsolicited mss. Approach with ideas – one A4-page synopsis – by fax or e-mail.

FEATURES Commissions only, but good ideas welcome. Max. 3500 words.

NEWS *Matt Walker* Mostly commissions, but ideas for specialist news welcome. Max. 1000 words.

REVIEWS *Maggie McDonald* Reviews are commissioned.

OPINION *Michael Bond* Unsolicited material welcome if of general/humorous interest and related to science. Max. 1000 words.

PAYMENT negotiable.

The New Shetlander

11 Mounthooly Street, Lerwick ZE1 0BJ
☎01595 693816 Fax 01595 696787
✉ shetlandcss@zetnet.co.uk
www.shetlandcss.co.uk

Owner *Shetland Council of Social Service*
Editors *Brian Smith, Laureen Johnson*
Circulation 1900

Founded 1947. QUARTERLY literary magazine containing short stories, essays, poetry, historical articles, literary criticism, political comment, arts and books. The magazine has two editors and an editorial committee who all look at submitted material. Interested in considering short stories, poetry, historical articles with a northern Scottish or Scandinavian flavour, literary pieces and articles on Shetland. As a rough guide, items should be between 1000 and 2000 words although longer mss are considered. Initial approach in writing, please.

PAYMENT Complimentary copy.

New Statesman

Victoria Station House, 191 Victoria Street, London SW1E 5NE
☎020 7730 3444 Fax 020 7259 0181
www.newstatesman.co.uk

Publisher *Spencer Neal*
Editor *Peter Wilby*
Deputy Editor *Cristina Odone*
Circulation 24,860

WEEKLY magazine, the result of a merger (1988) of *New Statesman* and *New Society*. Coverage of news, book reviews, arts, current affairs, politics and social reportage. Unsolicited contributions with s.a.e. will be considered. No short stories.

ARTS & BOOKS *Lisa Allardice*

New Theatre Quarterly

Oldstairs, Kingsdown, Deal CT14 8ES
☎01304 373448
✉ simontrussler@btinternet.com
www.uk.cambridge.org

Publisher *Cambridge University Press*
Editors *Clive Barker, Simon Trussler, Maria Shevtsova*

Founded 1985 (originally launched in 1971 as *Theatre Quarterly*). Articles, interviews, documentation and reference material covering all aspects of live theatre. Recommend preliminary e-mail enquiry before sending contributions. No theatre reviews or anecdotal material.

New Welsh Review

PO Box 170, Aberystwyth SY23 1WZ
☎01970 626230 Fax 01970 626230
✉ nwr@welshnet.co.uk

Owner *New Welsh Review Ltd*
Editor *Francesca Rhydderch*
Circulation 900

Founded 1988. QUARTERLY Welsh literary magazine in the English language. Welcomes material of literary and cultural relevance to Welsh readers and those with an interest in Wales. Approach in writing in the first instance.

FEATURES Max. 3000 words.
FICTION Max. 5000 words.
REVIEWS Max. 800 words.

PAYMENT average of £150 (features); £75 (fiction); £40 (reviews); £25 per poem.

New Woman

Endeavour House, 189 Shaftesbury Avenue, London WC2H 8JG
☎020 7437 9011 Fax 020 7208 3585
✉ kate.turner@emap.com
www.newwoman.co.uk

Owner *Emap élan Ltd*
Editor *Sara Cremer*
Circulation 290,533

MONTHLY women's interest magazine. Winner of the Emap 'Magazine of the Year' award in 2002 and the BSME 'Editor of the Year' in 2001. Aimed at women aged 25–35. An 'entertaining, informative and intelligent' read. Main topics of interest include men, sex, love, health, careers, beauty and fashion. Uses mainly established freelancers but unsolicited ideas submitted in synopsis form will be considered. Welcomes ideas from male writers for humorous 'men's opinion' pieces.

FEATURES/NEWS *Katie Masters* Articles must be original and look at subjects or issues from a new or unusual perspective.

The New Writer

PO Box 60, Cranbrook TN17 2ZR
☎01580 212626 Fax 01580 212041
✉ editor@thenewwriter.com
www.thenewwriter.com

Publisher *Merric Davidson*
Editor *Suzanne Ruthven*

Founded 1996. Published BI-MONTHLY following the merger between *Acclaim* and *Quartos* magazines. TNW continues to offer practical 'nuts and bolts' advice on poetry and prose but with the emphasis on *forward-looking* articles and features on all aspects of the written word that demonstrate the writer's grasp of contemporary writing and current editorial/publishing policies. Plenty of news, views, competitions, reviews; writers' guidelines available with s.a.e. Regular e-mail Newsletter included in subscription package.

FEATURES Unsolicited mss welcome. Interested in lively, original articles on writing in its broadest sense. Approach with ideas in writing in the first instance. No material is returned unless accompanied by s.a.e.

FICTION Publishes short-listed entries from competitions and subscriber-only submissions.

POETRY Unsolicited poetry welcome. Both short and long unpublished poems, providing they are original and interesting.

PAYMENT features, £20 per 1000 words; fiction, £10 per story; poetry, £3 per poem.

New Writing Scotland

Association for Scottish Literary Studies, c/o Department of Scottish History, 9 University Gardens, University of Glasgow G12 8QH
☎0141 330 5309 Fax 0141 330 5309
✉ d.jones@scothist.arts.gla.ac.uk
www.asls.org.uk

Contact *Duncan Jones*

ANNUAL anthology of contemporary poetry and prose in English, Gaelic and Scots, produced by the **Association for Scottish Literary Studies** (see entry under *Professional Associations*). Will consider poetry, drama, short fiction or other creative prose but not full-length plays or novels, though self-contained extracts are acceptable. Contributors should be Scottish by birth or upbringing, or resident in Scotland. Max. length of 3500 words is suggested. Send no more than two short stories and six poems. Submissions should be accompanied by two s.a.e.s (one for receipt, the other for return of mss). Mss, which must be sent by 31 January, should be typed, double-spaced, on one side of the paper only with the sheets secured at top left-hand corner. Provide covering letter with full contact details but do not put name or address on individual work(s). Prose pieces should carry an approximate word count.

newBOOKSmag
15 Scots Drive, Wokingham RG41 3XF
✉ guy@newbooksmag.com
www.newbooksmag.com
Owner/Editor *Guy Pringle*
Circulation 15,000

Founded 2000. BI-MONTHLY magazine for readers and reading groups with extracts from the best new fiction and free copies to be claimed. No unsolicited contributions. Also publishes *MyBOOKSmag* for 5–7-year-olds and *tBkmag* for 8–12-year-olds.

Newcastle Life
See **North East Times**

North East Times
8 Landsdown Terrace, Gosforth, Newcastle upon Tyne NE3 1HN
☎0191 284 4494 Fax 0191 284 9995
✉ alison.conlon@accentmagazines.co.uk
Owner *North East Times Ltd*
Editor *Alison Conlon*
Circulation 10,000

MONTHLY county magazine incorporating *Newcastle Life*. No unsolicited mss. Approach with ideas in writing. Not interested in any material that is not applicable to ABC1 readers.

The North
See under *Poetry Magazines*

Now
IPC Media Ltd., King's Reach Tower, Stamford Street, London SE1 9LS
☎020 7261 6274
Owner *IPC Media*
Editor *Jane Ennis*

Circulation 592,076

Founded 1996. WEEKLY magazine of celebrity gossip, news and topical features aimed at the working woman. Unlikely to use freelance contributions due to specialist content – e.g. exclusive showbiz interviews – but ideas will be considered. Approach in writing; no faxes.

Nursing Times
Greater London House, Hampstead Road, London NW1 7EJ
☎020 7874 0500 Fax 020 7874 0505
www.nursingtimes.net
Owner *Emap Healthcare*
Editor *Rachel Downey*
Circulation 66,276

A large proportion of *Nursing Times'* feature content is from unsolicited contributions sent on spec. Pieces on all aspects of nursing and health care, both practical and theoretical, written in a lively and contemporary way, are welcome. Commissions also.

PAYMENT varies/NUJ rates apply to commissioned material from union members only.

OK! Magazine
Ludgate House, 245 Blackfriars Road, London SE1 9UX
☎020 7928 8000 Fax 020 7579 4607
✉ firstname.lastname@express.co.uk
Owner *Northern & Shell Media/Richard Desmond*
Editor *Lisa Palta*
Circulation 570,927

Founded 1996. WEEKLY celebrity-based magazine. Welcomes interviews and pictures on well known personalities, and ideas for general features. Approach the editor by phone or fax in the first instance.

Old Glory
Mortons Heritage Media, Newspaper House, Morton Way, Horncastle LN9 6JR
☎01507 529300 Fax 01507 529495
✉ info@mortons.co.uk
www.oldglory.co.uk
Owner *Mortons Media Ltd*
Editor *Colin Tyson*

Founded 1988. MONTHLY magazine covering all aspects of transport and industrial heritage both in the UK and overseas. Specialises in vintage vehicles and steam preservation. Unsolicited articles are welcome. Approach by letter addressed to the editor.

FEATURES Restoration projects from steam rollers to windmills. Max. 1000 words.

NEWS Steam and transport rally reports. News concerning industrial and heritage sites and buildings.

The Oldie

65 Newman Street, London W1T 3EG
☎020 7436 8801 Fax 020 7436 8804
✉ theoldie@theoldie.co.uk
www.theoldie.co.uk
Owner *Oldie Publications Ltd*
Editor *Richard Ingrams*
Circulation 30,000

Founded 1992. MONTHLY general interest magazine with a strong humorous slant for the older person. Submissions welcome; enclose s.a.e. No poetry.

Opera

36 Black Lion Lane, London W6 9BE
☎020 8563 8893 Fax 020 8563 8635
✉ editor@operamag.clara.co.uk
www.opera.co.uk
Owner *Opera Magazine Ltd*
Editor *John Allison*
Circulation 11,500

Founded 1950. MONTHLY review of the current opera scene. Almost all articles are commissioned and unsolicited mss are not welcome. All approaches should be made in writing.

Opera Now

241 Shaftesbury Avenue, London WC2H 8TF
☎020 7333 1740 Fax 020 7333 1769
✉ opera.now@rhinegold.co.uk
www.rhinegold.co.uk
Publisher *Rhinegold Publishing Ltd*
Editor-in-Chief *Ashutosh Khandekar*
Deputy Editor *Antonia Couling*

Founded 1989. BI-MONTHLY. News, features and reviews aimed at those involved as well as those interested in opera. No unsolicited mss. All work is commissioned. Approach with ideas in writing.

Orbis

See under *Poetry Magazines*

Organic Gardening

Sandvoe, North Roe, Shetland ZE2 9RY
☎01806 533319 Fax 01806 533319
✉ organic.gardening@virgin.net
Editor *Gaby Bartai Bevan*
Circulation 20,000

Founded 1988. MONTHLY. Articles and features on all aspects of gardening based on organic methods. Unsolicited material welcome; 800–2000 words for features and 100–300 for news items. Poetry not published. Prefers 'hands-on' accounts of projects, problems, challenges and how they are dealt with. Approach in writing.
PAYMENT by arrangement.

OS (Office Secretary) Magazine

First Floor, 63 High Street, Witney
OX28 6HS
☎01993 775545 Fax 01993 778884
Owner *Peebles Media Group Ltd*
Editor *Clare Bodel*
Circulation 35,000

Founded 1986. BI-MONTHLY. Features articles of interest to secretaries and personal assistants aged 25–60. No unsolicited mss.

FEATURES Informative pieces on technology and practices, office and employment-related topics. Length 1000 words. Approach with ideas by telephone or in writing.
PAYMENT by negotiation.

Palmtop User Magazine

Palmtop Publications, PO Box 188, Bicester
OX26 6GP
☎01869 249287 Fax 01869 246043
✉ editor@palmtop.co.uk
www.palmtop.co.uk
Owners *Mr S. Clack, Miss R.A. Rolfe*
Editor *Mr S. Clack*
Circulation 10,000

Founded 1994. BI-MONTHLY users' magazine for hand-held computers. No unsolicited mss; approach by telephone or e-mail in the first instance.

Park Home & Holiday Caravan

Leon House, 233 High Street, Croydon
CR9 1HZ
☎020 8774 0600
✉ anne_webb@ipcmedia.com
www.phhc.co.uk
Owner *IPC Country & Leisure Media*
Editor *Anne Webb*
Circulation 15,000

Founded 1960. THIRTEEN ISSUES YEARLY. News of parks, models, legislation, accessories, lifestyle for those living in residential park homes or owning holiday caravans. Welcomes material specifically related to park home and holiday caravan sites; no general touring features. Approach by letter or telephone.

The Party Magazine

Bury House Media Ltd, Bury Farm House, Bury Lane, Epping CM16 5JA
☎01992 579906 Fax 01992 579907
✉ info@thepartymagazine.co.uk
www.thepartymagazine.com

Editor *Janine Furness*

Founded 2003. MONTHLY. Food, home interest, gadgets and appliances, lifestyle, party ideas, drinks and venues.

PC Format

Future Publishing, 30 Monmouth Street, Bath BA1 2BW
☎01225 442244 Fax 01225 732295
✉ pcfmail@futurenet.co.uk
www.futurenet.co.uk

Owner *Future Publishing*
Publisher *Kelley Corten*
Editor *Geoff Harris*
Circulation 76,337

Founded 1991. FOUR-WEEKLY magazine covering everything for the consumer PC – games, hardware. Welcomes feature and interview ideas in the first instance; approach by telephone, e-mail or in writing.

People Management

Personnel Publications Limited, 1 Benjamin Street, London EC1M 5EA
☎020 7880 6200 Fax 020 7296 4215
✉ editorial@peoplemanagement.co.uk
www.peoplemanagement.co.uk

Editor *Steve Crabb*
Deputy Editor *Rima Manoche*
Circulation 116,432

FORTNIGHTLY magazine on human resources, industrial relations, employment issues, etc. Welcomes submissions but apply for 'Guidelines for Contributors' in the first instance.

FEATURES *Jane Pickard/Rebecca Johnson*
NEWS *Zoe Roberts*
LAW AT WORK *Jill Evans*.

The People's Friend

80 Kingsway East, Dundee DD4 8SL
☎01382 462276/223131 Fax 01382 452491
✉ peoplesfriend@dcthomson.co.uk

Owner *D.C. Thomson & Co. Ltd*
Editor *Margaret McCoy*
Circulation 397,080

The *Friend* is a fiction magazine, with two serials and several short stories each week. Founded in 1869, it has always prided itself on providing 'a good read for all the family'. Stories should be about ordinary, identifiable characters with the kind of problems the average reader can understand and sympathise with. 'We look for the romantic and emotional developments of characters, rather than an over-complicated or contrived plot. We regularly use period serials and, occasionally, mystery/adventure.' Guidelines on request with s.a.e.

SHORT STORIES Can vary in length from 1000 words or less to as many as 4000.
SERIALS Serials of 8–10 instalments.
ARTICLES Short fillers welcome.
PAYMENT on acceptance.

Period Living & Traditional Homes

Mappin House, 4 Winsley Street, London W1W 8HF
☎020 7343 8775 Fax 020 7343 8710
✉ period.living@emap.com

Owner *Emap East*
Editor *Sharon Parsons*
Deputy Editor *Andrew Lilwall-Smith*
Circulation 72,836

Founded 1992. Formed from the merger of *Period Living* and *Traditional Homes*. Covers interior decoration in a period style, period house profiles, traditional crafts, renovation of period properties.

PAYMENT varies according to length/type of article.

Personal Finance

Arnold House, 36–41 Holywell Lane, London EC2A 3SF
☎020 7827 5454 Fax 020 7827 0567

Owner *Charterhouse Communications plc*
Editor *Martin Fagan*
Circulation 40,000

Founded 1994. MONTHLY finance magazine.
NEWS All items written in-house.
FEATURES All issues relating to personal finance, particularly investment, insurance, banking, mortgages, savings, borrowing, health care and pensions. No corporate articles or personnel issues. Write to the editor with ideas in the first instance. No unsolicited mss.
PAYMENT £200 per 1000 words.

The Philosopher

Centre for Lifelong Learning, Newcastle University, Newcastle upon Tyne NE1 7RU
✉ thephilosophicalsociety@yahoo.co.uk
www.the-philosopher.co.uk

Owner *The Philosophical Society*
Editor *Martin Cohen*

Founded 1913. BIANNUAL journal of the Philosophical Society of Great Britain with an international readership made up of members, libraries and specialist booksellers. Wide range of interests, but leaning towards articles that present philosophical investigation which is relevant to the individual and to society in our modern era. Accessible to the non-specialist. Will consider articles and book reviews. Notes for Contributors available; send s.a.e., e-mail or see website. As well as short philosophical papers, will accept:

NEWS about lectures, conventions, philosophy groups. Ethical issues in the news. Max. 1000 words.

REVIEWS of philosophy books (max. 600 words); discussion articles of individual philosophers and their published works (max. 2000 words).

MISCELLANEOUS items, including graphics, of philosophical interest and/or merit.

PAYMENT Free copies.

Piano

241 Shaftesbury Avenue, London
WC2H 8TF
☎020 7333 1724 Fax 020 7333 1736
✉ pianomagazine@mail.com
www.rhinegold.co.uk
Owner *Rhinegold Publishing*
Editor *Jeremy Siepmann*
Deputy Editor *Sarah Smith*
Circulation 11,000

Founded 1993. BI-MONTHLY magazine containing features, profiles, technical information, news, reviews of interest to those with a serious amateur or professional concern with pianos or their playing. No unsolicited material. Approach with ideas in writing only.

Picture Postcard Monthly

15 Debdale Lane, Keyworth, Nottingham
NG12 5HT
☎0115 937 4079 Fax 0115 937 6197
✉ reflections@argonet.co.uk
www.postcardcollecting.co.uk
Owners *Brian & Mary Lund*
Editor *Brian Lund*
Circulation 4000

Founded 1978. MONTHLY. News, views, clubs, diary of fairs, sales, auctions, and well-researched postcard-related articles. Might be interested in general articles supported by postcards. Unsolicited mss welcome. Approach by phone or in writing with ideas.

Pilot

Archant Specialist, The Mill, Bearwalden Business Park, Wendens Ambo, Saffron Walden CB11 4GB
☎01799 544200 Fax 01799 544201
✉ dave.calderwood@pilotweb.co.uk
www.pilotweb.co.uk
Publisher *Archant Specialist*
Editor-in-Chief *Dave Calderwood*
Deputy Editor *Nick Bloom*
Circulation 22,308

Founded 1968. MONTHLY magazine for private plane pilots. Much of the magazine is written by outside contributors – mostly regulars. Unsolicited mss welcome but ideas in writing preferred. Perusal of any issue of the magazine will reveal the type of material bought. 700 words of 'Advice to would-be contributors' sent on receipt of s.a.e. (mark envelope 'Advice'), or see the website for details.

NEWS Contributions need to be as short as possible. See *Pilot Notes* and *Old-Timers* in the magazine.

FEATURES Many articles are unsolicited personal experiences/travel accounts from pilots of private planes; good photo coverage is very important. Max. 5000 words.

Pink Paper

2nd Floor, Medius House, 63–69 New Oxford Street, London WC1A 1DG
☎020 7845 4300 Fax 020 7845 4309
✉ editorial@pinkpaper.com
Editor *Tristan Reid-Smith*
Circulation 55,000

Founded 1987. WEEKLY. Only national newspaper for lesbians and gay men covering politics, social issues, health, the arts and all areas of concern to lesbian/gay people. Unsolicited mss welcome. Initial approach by post with an idea preferred. Interested in profiles, reviews, in-depth features and short news pieces.

PAYMENT by arrangement.

Planet: The Welsh Internationalist

See **Planet** under *Small Presses*

PN Review

See under *Poetry Magazines*

Poetry Ireland Review

See under *Poetry Magazines*

Poetry Review

See under *Poetry Magazines*

Poetry Scotland
See under *Poetry Magazines*

Poetry Wales
See under *Poetry Magazines*

PONY
D.J. Murphy (Publishers) Ltd, Headley House, Headley Road, Grayshott GU26 6TU
☎01428 601020 Fax 01428 601030
✉ pony@djmurphy.co.uk (text only)
www.ponymag.com
Owner *D.J. Murphy (Publishers) Ltd*
Editor *Janet Rising*
Assistant Editor *Zoe Cannon*
Circulation 35,857

Founded 1948. Lively MONTHLY aimed at 10–16-year-olds. News, instruction on riding, stable management, veterinary care, interviews. Approach in writing with an idea.
FEATURES welcome. Max. 900 words.
NEWS Written in-house. Photographs and illustrations (serious/cartoon) welcome.
PAYMENT £65 per 1000 words.

Popular Crafts
Highbury Leisure, Berwick House, 8–10 Knoll Rise, Orpington BR6 0PS
☎01689 899205 Fax 01689 899240
✉ dmoss@highburyleisure.co.uk
www.popularcrafts.com
Owner *Highbury Leisure*
Editor *Debbie Moss*
Circulation 32,000

Founded 1980. MONTHLY. Covers crafts of all kinds. Freelance contributions welcome – copy needs to be lively and interesting. Approach in writing or by e-mail with an outline of idea and photographs.
FEATURES Project-based under the following headings: Homecraft; Needlecraft; Popular Craft; Kidscraft; News and Columns. Any craft-related material including projects to make, with full instructions/patterns supplied in all cases; profiles of crafts people and news of craft group activities or successes by individual persons; articles on collecting crafts; personal experiences and anecdotes.
PAYMENT on publication.

PR Week
174 Hammersmith Road, London W6 7JP
☎020 8267 4429 Fax 020 8267 4509
www.prweek.com
Owner *Haymarket Business Publications Ltd*
Editor *Gidon Freeman*

Circulation 18,200
Founded 1984. WEEKLY. Contributions accepted from experienced journalists. Approach in writing with an idea.
PAYMENT negotiable.

Practical Boat Owner
Westover House, West Quay Road, Poole BH15 1JG
☎01202 440820 Fax 01202 440860
www.pbo.co.uk
Owner *IPC Media*
Editor *Sarah Norbury*
Circulation 50,107

Founded 1967. MONTHLY magazine of practical information for cruising boat owners. Receives about 1500 mss per year. Interested in hard facts about gear, equipment, pilotage and renovation, etc. from experienced yachtsmen.
FEATURES Technical articles about maintenance, restoration, modifications to cruising boats, power and sail up to 45ft, or reader reports on gear and equipment. European pilotage articles and cruising guides. Approach in writing with synopsis in the first instance.
PAYMENT negotiable.

Practical Caravan
60 Waldegrave Road, Teddington TW11 8LG
☎020 8267 5629 Fax 020 8267 5725
✉ practical.caravan@haynet.com
www.practicalcaravan.com
Owner *Haymarket Magazines Ltd*
Editor *Alex Newby*
Circulation 41,665

Founded 1967. MONTHLY. Contains caravan reviews, travel features, investigations, products, park reviews. Unsolicited mss welcome on travel relevant only to caravanning/touring vans. No motorcaravan or static van stories. Approach with ideas by phone, letter or e-mail.
FEATURES Must refer to caravanning. Written in friendly, chatty manner. Pictures essential. Max. length 2000 words.
PAYMENT negotiable.

Practical Fishkeeping
Bretton Court, Bretton, Peterborough PE3 8DZ
☎01733 264666 Fax 01733 465246
✉ karen.youngs@emap.com
www.practicalfishkeeping.co.uk
Owner *Emap Active Publications Ltd*
Editor *Karen Youngs*
Circulation 16,621

MONTHLY. Practical articles on all aspects of fish-keeping. Unsolicited mss welcome; approach in writing with ideas. Quality photographs of fish always welcome. No fiction or verse.

Practical Parenting

IPC Media Ltd., King's Reach Tower, Stamford Street, London SE1 9LS
☎020 7261 5058   Fax 020 7261 6542

Owner *IPC Media*
Editor *Mara Lee*
Deputy Editor *Kate Brophy*
Circulation 46,840

Founded 1987. MONTHLY. Practical advice on pregnancy, birth, babycare and childcare, 0–4 years. Submit ideas in writing with synopsis or send mss on spec. Interested in feature articles of up to 3000 words in length, and in readers' experiences/personal viewpoint pieces of between 750–1000 words. All material must be written for the magazine's specifically targeted audience and in-house style.
PAYMENT negotiable.

Practical Photography

Bretton Court, Bretton, Peterborough PE3 8DZ
☎01733 264666   Fax 01733 465246
✉ practical.photography@emap.com

Owner *Emap Active Publications Ltd*
Associate Editor *Andrew James*
Circulation 57,195

MONTHLY All types of photography, particularly technique-orientated pictures. No unsolicited mss. Preliminary approach may be made by e-mail. Always interested in new, especially unusual, ideas.
FEATURES Anything relevant to the world of photography, but not 'the sort of feature produced by staff writers. Features on technology, digital imaging techniques and humour are three areas worth exploring. Bear in mind that there is a three-month lead-in time.' Max. 2000 words.
PAYMENT varies.

Practical Wireless

Arrowsmith Court, Station Approach, Broadstone BH18 8PW
☎0870 224 7810   Fax 0870 224 7850
✉ name@pwpublishing.ltd.uk
www.pwpublishing.ltd.uk

Owner *PW Publishing Ltd*
Editor *Rob Mannion*
Circulation 20,000

Founded 1932. MONTHLY. News and features relating to amateur radio, radio construction and radio communications. Unsolicited mss welcome. Author's guidelines available (send s.a.e.). Approach by phone or e-mail with ideas in the first instance. Only interested in hearing from people with a thorough knowledge of radio. Copy (typed only) should be supported where possible by artwork, either illustrations, diagrams or photographs. PAYMENT £54–70 per page.

Practical Woodworking

Highbury Leisure, Berwick House, 8–10 Knoll Rise, Orpington BR6 0PS
☎01923 286421   Fax 01923 286421
✉ practical.woodworking@nexusmedia.com
www.getwoodworking.com

Owner *Highbury House Communications*
Editor *Mark Chisholm*

Founded 1965. MONTHLY. Contains articles relating to woodworking – projects, techniques, new products, tips, letters, etc. Unsolicited mss welcome. No fiction. Approach with ideas in writing, by phone or e-mail.
FEATURES Projects, techniques, etc.
PAYMENT £60–75 per published page.

Prediction

Leon House, 233 High Street, Croydon CR9 1HZ
☎020 8774 0600
✉ prediction@ipcmedia.com
www.predictionmagazine.co.uk

Owner *IPC Media*
Editor *Tania Ahsan*
Circulation 15,063

Founded 1936. MONTHLY. Covering astrology and mind, body, spirit topics. Unsolicited material in these areas welcome (about 200–300 mss received every year). Writers' guidelines available on request.
ASTROLOGY Pieces should be practical and of general interest. Charts and astro data should accompany them, especially if profiles.
FEATURES Articles on divination, shamanism, alternative healing, psychics and other supernatural phenonema considered. Please read a recent copy of the magazine before sending unsolicited material.

Pregnancy & Birth

Greater London House, Hampstead Road, London NW1 7EJ
☎020 7347 1885   Fax 020 7347 1888
✉ lucy.dimbylow@emap.com

Owner *Emap Esprit*
Editor *Kaye McIntosh*

Features Editor *Lizzie Attwood*
Circulation 53,700

MONTHLY magazine covering all aspects of pregnancy from health to fashion. Regularly commissions features from health journalists. Freelancers should approach by post in the first instance. PAYMENT varies.

Press Gazette

Quantum House, 19 Scarbrook Road, Croydon CR9 1LX
☎020 8565 4473 Fax 020 8565 4395
✉ pged@pressgazette.co.uk
www.pressgazette.co.uk

Owner *Quantum*
Editor *Ian Reeves*
Deputy Editor *Jon Slattery*
Circulation 9,500

WEEKLY magazine for all journalists – in regional and national newspapers, magazines, broadcasting, and online – containing news, features and analysis of all areas of journalism, print and broadcasting. Unsolicited mss welcome; interested in profiles of magazines, broadcasting companies and news agencies, personality profiles, technical and current affairs relating to the world of journalism. Approach with ideas by phone, e-mail, fax or in writing.

Pride

Hamilton House, 55 Battersea Bridge Road, London SW11 3AX
☎020 7228 3110 Fax 020 7228 3129
✉ info@pride.com

Owner *Carl Cushnie Junior*
Editor *Amina Taylor*
Circulation 40,000

Founded 1991. MONTHLY lifestyle magazine for Black women with features, beauty, arts and fashion. Approach in writing or by e-mail with ideas.

FEATURES Issues pertaining to the Black community. 'Ideas and solicited mss are welcomed from new freelancers.' Max. 2000 words.

FICTION Publishes the occasional short story. Max. 3000 words.

HEALTH, BEAUTY, LIFESTYLE *Sherry Dixon* Freelancers used for short features. Max. 1000 words.

Prima

National Magazine House, 72 Broadwick Street, London W1F 9EP
☎020 7439 5000
✉ prima@natmags.co.uk
www.natmags.co.uk

Owner *National Magazine Company*
Editor *Maire Fahey*
Circulation 330,128

Founded 1986. MONTHLY women's magazine. HEALTH & FEATURES Coordinator *Ruth Devine*. Mostly practical and written by specialists, or commissioned from known freelancers. Unsolicited mss not welcome.

Private Eye

6 Carlisle Street, London W1D 3BN
☎020 7437 4017 Fax 020 7437 0705
✉ strobes@private-eye.co.uk
www.private-eye.co.uk

Owner *Pressdram*
Editor *Ian Hislop*
Circulation 205,250

Founded 1961. FORTNIGHTLY satirical and investigative magazine. Prospective contributors are best advised to approach the editor in writing. News stories and feature ideas are always welcome, as are cartoons. All jokes written in-house. PAYMENT in all cases is 'not great', and length of piece varies as appropriate.

Professional Nurse

Emap Healthcare, Greather London House, Hampstead Road, London NW1 7EJ
☎020 7874 0385 Fax 020 7874 0386
✉ pn@emap.com

Owner *Emap Healthcare*
Editor *Carolyn Scott*
Deputy Editor *Amanda Clark*
Circulation 21,000

MONTHLY magazine offering clinical papers, research, opinion and reviews for nurses working in hospitals and in the community.

FEATURES Articles about the health service written by nurses preferably. Approach deputy editor by e-mail. Max. 1500 words.

CLINICAL PAPERS written by nurses. Approach editor by e-mail. Max. 3000 words. PAYMENT features, £50; clinical papers, £75.

Prospect

2 Bloomsbury Square, London WC1A 2QA
☎020 7255 1344 (editorial)/1281 (publishing)
Fax 020 7255 1279
✉ editorial@prospect-magazine.co.uk *or* publishing@prospect-magazine.co.uk
www.prospect-magazine.co.uk

Owner *Prospect Publishing Limited*
Editor *David Goodhart*
Circulation 24,400

Founded 1995. MONTHLY. Essays, reviews,

short fiction and research on current/international affairs and cultural issues. No news features. Unsolicited contributions welcome, although more useful to approach in writing with ideas in the first instance.

Psychic News
The Coach House, Stansted Hall, Stansted CM24 8UD
☎01279 817050 Fax 01279 817051
✉ pn@snu.org.uk
www.snu.org.uk
Owner *Psychic Press 1995 Ltd*
Editor *Tony Ortzen*
Circulation 40,000

Founded 1932. *Psychic News* is the world's only WEEKLY spiritualist newspaper. It covers subjects such as psychic research, hauntings, ghosts, poltergeists, spiritual healing, survival after death and paranormal gifts. Unsolicited material considered.

Publishing News
7 John Street, London WC1N 2ES
☎0870 870 2345 Fax 0870 870 0385
✉ mailbox@publishingnews.co.uk
www.publishingnews.co.uk
Editor *Liz Thomson*

WEEKLY newspaper of the book trade. Hardback and paperback reviews and extensive listings of new paperbacks and hardbacks. Interviews with leading personalities in the trade, authors, agents and features on specialist book areas.

Q
Mappin House, 4 Winsley Street, London W1W 8HF
☎020 7436 1515 Fax 020 7182 8547
www.q4music.com
Owner *Emap Performance*
Editor *Paul Rees*
Circulation 180,215

Founded 1986. MONTHLY. Glossy aimed at educated popular music enthusiasts of all ages. Few opportunities for freelance writers. Unsolicited mss are strongly discouraged. Prospective contributors should approach in writing only.

Q-News, The Muslim Magazine
55 Bryanston Street, London W1H 7AJ
☎020 7859 8217 Fax 020 7868 8600
✉ info@q-news.com
www.q-news.com
Owner *Fuad Namdi*

Editor *Shagufta Yaqub*
Circulation 15,000

Founded 1992. MONTHLY British Muslim community magazine covering news, features, current affairs. Regular health column, film/book/events reviews, Islamic religious/spiritual articles, art, culture, civilisation, history, etc. Interested in hearing from specialists on issues affecting the Muslim community, local/regional news and analysis.

FEATURES *Shagufta Yaqub* 'Writers wishing to focus on areas of interest to our readership will gain access and credibility among the relevant people.' 3000 words max.

NEWS *Fareena Alam* Analysis on news and current affairs – alternative rather than mainstream viewpoint preferred. 2000 words max.

FICTION *Shagufta Yaqub* 'An area we would like to develop. The right person could use this opportunity as a launch pad into their career.' 2000 words max. Approach by e-mail.

PAYMENT None.

Quartos Magazine
See **The New Writer**

QWF Magazine
PO Box 1768, Rugby CV21 4ZA
☎01788 334302
✉ jo@qwfmagazine.co.uk
www.qwfmagazine.co.uk
Editor *Jo Good*

BI-MONTHLY small press magazine. Founded in 1994, as a showcase for the best in women's short story writing – original and thought-provoking. Only considers stories that are previously unpublished and of less than 4000 words; articles must be less than 1000 words and of interest to the writer. Include covering letter, s.a.e. and brief biography with mss. Before submission of material send s.a.e. (50p stamp) with request for free back copy. Also runs script appraisal service and regular short story competitions. For further information and detailed guidelines for contributors please access the website or contact the editor at the address above. Submissions should be sent to Assistant Editor, *Sally Zigmond* (18 Warwick Crescent, Harrogate HG2 8JA) with s.a.e.

Racecar Engineering
Leon House, 233 High Street, Croydon CR9 1HZ
☎020 8774 0600
✉ racecar@ipcmedia.com
www.racecar-engineering.co.uk

Owner *IPC Media*
Editor *Charles Armstrong-Wilson*
Deputy Editor *Gemma Briggs*
Circulation 15,000

Founded 1990. MONTHLY. In-depth features on motorsport technology plus news and products. Interested in receiving news and features from freelancers.

FEATURES Informed insight into current motorsport technology. 3000 words max.

NEWS New cars, products or business news relevant to motorsport. No items on road cars or racing drivers. 500 words max. Call or e-mail to discuss proposal.

Racing Post (incorporating The Sporting Life)

1 Canada Square, Canary Wharf, London E14 5AP
☎020 7293 3000 Fax 020 7293 3758
✉ editor@racingpost.co.uk
www.racingpost.co.uk

Owner *Trinity Mirror Plc*
Editor *Chris Smith*

Founded 1986. DAILY horse racing paper with some general sport. In 1998, following an agreement between the owners of *The Sporting Life* and the *Racing Post*, the two papers merged.

Radio Times

80 Wood Lane, London W12 0TT
☎020 8433 3400 Fax 020 8433 3160
✉ radio.times@bbc.co.uk
www.radiotimes.com

Owner *BBC Worldwide Limited*
Editor *Gill Hudson*
Circulation 1.16 million

WEEKLY. UK's leading broadcast listings magazine. The majority of material is provided by freelance and retained writers, but the topicality of the pieces means close consultation with editors is essential. Very unlikely to use unsolicited material. Detailed BBC, ITV, Channel 4, Channel 5 and satellite television and radio listings are accompanied by feature material relevant to the week's output.

PAYMENT by arrangement.

Rail

Bretton Court, Bretton, Peterborough PE3 8DZ
☎01733 264666 Fax 01733 282720
✉ rail@emap.com

Owner *Emap Active Publications Ltd*
Managing Editor *Nigel Harris*

Circulation 27,929

Founded 1981. FORTNIGHTLY magazine dedicated to modern railway. News and features, and topical newsworthy events. Unsolicited mss welcome. Approach by phone with ideas. Not interested in personal journey reminiscences. No fiction.

FEATURES By arrangement with the editor. All modern railway British subjects considered. Max. 2000 words.

NEWS Any news item welcome. Max. 500 words.

PAYMENT features, varies/negotiable; news, up to £100 per 1000 words.

Railway Gazette International

Quadrant House, Sutton SM2 5AS
☎020 8652 8608 Fax 020 8652 3738
www.railwaygazette.com

Owner *Reed Business Information*
Editor *Murray Hughes*

Founded 1835. MONTHLY magazine written for senior railway managers and engineers worldwide. 'No material for railway enthusiast publications.' Telephone to discuss ideas in the first instance.

The Railway Magazine

IPC Media Ltd., King's Reach Tower, Stamford Street, London SE1 9LS
☎020 7261 5533/5821 Fax 020 7261 5269
✉ railway@ipcmedia.com
www.ipcmedia.com

Owner *IPC Media*
Editor *Nick Pigott*
Circulation 31,196

Founded 1897. MONTHLY. Articles, photos and short news stories of a topical nature, covering modern railways, steam preservation and railway history, welcome. Max. 2000 words, with sketch maps of routes, etc., where appropriate. Unsolicited mss welcome. No poetry.

PAYMENT negotiable.

Reader's Digest

11 Westferry Circus, Canary Wharf, London E14 4HE
☎020 7715 8000 Fax 020 7715 8716
www.readersdigest.co.uk

Owner *Reader's Digest Association Ltd*
Editor-in-Chief *Katherine Walker*
Circulation 860,000

Although in theory, a good market for general interest features of around 2500 words very few are ever accepted. However, 'a tiny proportion' comes from freelance writers, all of which are specially commissioned. Opportunities exist for short humorous contributions to regular features – 'Life's Like That', 'Laughter, the Best Medicine', 'All in a Day's Work'. Issues a helpful booklet called 'Writing for Reader's Digest', available by post at £4.50. PAYMENT up to £100.

The Reader

Reader Office, 19 Abercromby Square, Liverpool L69 7ZG
✉ readers@liv.co.uk
www.thereader.co.uk
Editor *Jane Davis*
Circulation 1200

Founded 1997. THREE ISSUES YEARLY. Poetry, short fiction, literary articles and essays, thought, reviews, recommendations. Contributions from internationally lauded and new voices. Welcomes articles/essays about reading, max. 2000 words. Recommendations for good reading, max. 1000 words. Short stories, max. 2500 words. No theoretical style literary discourses. Approach in writing.
PAYMENT negotiable.

Record Collector

43–45 St Mary's Road, Ealing, London W5 5RQ
☎0870 732 8080 Fax 0870 732 6060
✉ alan.lewis@metropolis.co.uk
www.recordcollector.com
Owner *Metropolis*
Editor *Alan Lewis*

Founded 1979. MONTHLY. Detailed, well-researched articles welcome on any aspect of record collecting or any collectable artist in the field of popular music (1950s to present day), with complete discographies where appropriate. Unsolicited mss welcome. Approach with ideas by phone or e-mail.
PAYMENT negotiable.

Red

64 North Row, London W1K 7LL
☎020 7150 7000 Fax 020 7150 7684
✉ sally.mann@hf-uk.com
www.redmagazine.co.uk
Owner *Hachette Filipacchi UK Ltd*
Acting Editor *Kerry Parnell*
Circulation 196,719

Founded 1998. MONTHLY magazine aimed at the 30-something woman. Will consider ideas sent in 'on spec' but tends to rely on regular contributors.

Report

ATL, 7 Northumberland Street, London WC2N 5RD
☎020 7930 6441 Fax 020 7782 1618
Owner *Association of Teachers and Lecturers*
Editor *Heather Pinnell*
Circulation 160,000

Founded 1978. TEN ISSUES YEARLY during academic terms. Contributions welcome. All submissions should go directly to the editor. Articles should be no more than 800 words and must be of practical interest to the classroom teacher and F.E. lecturers.

Right Now!

Box 361, 78 Marylebone High Street, London W1U 5AP
☎0845 601 3243 Fax 0845 601 3243
✉ rightnow@compuserve.com
www.right-now.org
Owner *Right Now! Press Ltd*
Editor *Derek Turner*
Circulation 3000

Founded 1993. QUARTERLY right-wing conservative commentary. Welcomes well-documented disputations, news stories and features about British heritage ('the more politically incorrect, the better!'). No fiction or poems. Initial approach in writing.
No PAYMENT.

Rugby World

IPC Media Ltd., 23rd Floor, King's Reach Tower, Stamford Street, London SE1 9LS
☎020 7261 6830 Fax 020 7261 5419
www.rugbyworld.com
Owner *IPC Media*
Editor *Paul Morgan*
Circulation 46,233

Founded 1960. MONTHLY. Features of special rugby interest only. Unsolicited contributions welcome but s.a.e. essential for return of material. Prior approach by phone or in writing preferred.

Runner's World

7–10 Chandos Street, London W1M 0AD
☎020 7291 6000 Fax 020 7291 6080
✉ rwedit@rodale.co.uk
www.runnersworld.co.uk
Owner *Rodale Press*
Editor *Steven Seaton*
Circulation 70,206

Founded 1979. MONTHLY magazine giving

practical advice on all areas of distance running including products and training, travel features, news and cross-training advice. Personal running-related articles, famous people who run or off-beat travel articles are welcome. No elite athlete or training articles. Approach with ideas in writing in the first instance.

Running Fitness
1st Floor, South Wing, Broadway Court, Broadway, Peterborough PE1 1RP
☎01733 347559 Fax 01733 352749
✉ rf.ed@kelsey.co.uk
www.running-fitness.com

Owner *Kelsey Publishing*
Editor *Paul Larkins*
Circulation 26,000

Founded 1985. MONTHLY. Instructional articles on running, fitness, and lifestyle, plus running-related activities and health.

FEATURES Specialist knowledge an advantage. Opportunities are wide, but approach with ideas in first instance.

NEWS Opportunities for people stories, especially if backed up by photographs.

Safeway The Magazine
Redwood, 7 Saint Martin's Place, London WC2N 4HA
☎020 7747 0788 Fax 020 7747 0799

Editor *Jennifer Newton*
Circulation 1.8 million

Founded 1996. MONTHLY in-store magazine covering food and recipes, beauty, health, shopping, gardens, travel and features. Regular freelancers are employed and although outside material is rarely used ideas will be considered for beauty, health, travel and features. Approach in writing in the first instance.

Saga Magazine
Saga Publishing Ltd, The Saga Building, Enbrook Park, Folkstone CT20 3SE
☎01303 771523 Fax 01303 776699
www.saga.co.uk

Owner *Saga Publishing Ltd*
Editor *Emma Soames*
Circulation 1.19 million

Founded 1984. MONTHLY magazine that sets out to celebrate the role of older people in society, reflecting their achievements, promoting their skills, protecting their interests, and campaigning on their behalf. A warm personal approach, addressing the readership in an up-beat and positive manner. It has a hard core of celebrated

commentators/writers (e.g. Keith Waterhouse, Alexander Chancellor, Angela Rippon) as regular contributors. Articles mostly commissioned or written in-house but exclusive celebrity interviews welcome if appropriate/relevant. Length 1000–1200 words (max. 1600). No short stories or poems, please.

Sailing Today
4 Chapel Row, Bath BA1 1HN
☎01225 470074 Fax 01225 313325
✉ feedback@sailingtoday.co.uk

Owner *Madforsport Ltd*
Editor *John Goode*

Founded 1997. MONTHLY practical magazine for cruising sailors. *Sailing Today* covers owning and buying a boat, equipment and products for sailing and is about improving readers' skills, boat maintenance and product tests. Most articles are commissioned but will consider practical features and cruise stories with photos. Approach by telephone or in writing in the first instance.

Sainsbury's Magazine
20 Upper Ground, London SE1 9PD
☎020 7633 0266 Fax 020 7401 9423
✉ edit@newcrane.co.uk

Owner *New Crane Publishing*
Editor *Sue Robinson*
Consultant Food Editor *Delia Smith*
Circulation 278,043

Founded 1993. MONTHLY featuring a main core of food and cookery with features, health, beauty, fashion, home, gardening and news. No unsolicited mss. Approach in writing with ideas only in the first instance.

The Salisbury Review
33 Canonbury Park South, London N1 2JW
☎020 7226 7791 Fax 020 7354 0383
✉ salisbury-review@easynet.co.uk
www.salisbury-review.co.uk

Editor *Dennis O'Keeffe*
Managing Editor *Merrie Cave*
Consulting Editors *Roger Scruton, Sir Richard Body, Myles Harris*
Circulation 1700

Founded 1982. QUARTERLY magazine of conservative thought. Editorials and features from a right-wing viewpoint. Unsolicited material welcome.

FEATURES Max. 4000 words.
REVIEWS Max. 1000 words.
No PAYMENT.

Scotland in Trust

5 Windsor Place, Edinburgh EH15 2AJ
☎0131 657 4612 Fax 0131 657 4612
✉ trust@cmyk-design.co.uk
Owner *National Trust for Scotland*
Editor *Iain Gale*
Circulation 138,878

Founded 1983. THREE ISSUES YEARLY. Magazine containing heritage/conservation features. No unsolicited mss.

Scotland on Sunday Magazine

See **Scotland on Sunday** under *National Newspapers*

The Scots Magazine

D.C. Thomson & Co., 2 Albert Square, Dundee DD1 9QJ
☎01382 223131 Fax 01382 322214
✉ mail@scotsmagazine.com
www.scotsmagazine.com
Owner *D.C. Thomson & Co. Ltd*
Editor *John Methven*
Circulation 50,000

Founded 1739. MONTHLY. Covers a wide field of Scottish interests ranging from personalities to wildlife, climbing, reminiscence, history, folklore. Outside contributions welcome; 'staff delighted to discuss in advance by letter or e-mail'.

The Scottish Farmer

SMG Magazines, 200 Renfield Street, Glasgow G2 3PR
☎0141 302 7700 Fax 0141 302 7799
✉ firstname.lastname@smg.plc.uk
Owner *SMG Magazines*
Editor *Alasdair Fletcher*
Circulation 22,000

Founded 1893. WEEKLY. Farmer's magazine covering most aspects of Scottish agriculture. Unsolicited mss welcome. Approach with ideas in writing, by fax or e-mail.

FEATURES *Alasdair Fletcher* Technical articles on agriculture or farming units. 1000–2000 words.

NEWS *John Duckworth* Factual news about farming developments, political, personal and technological. Max. 800 words.

WEEKEND FAMILY PAGES Rural and craft topics.

Scottish Field

Special Publications, Craigcrook Castle, Craigcrook Road, Edinburgh EH4 3PE
☎0131 312 4550 Fax 0131 312 4551

✉ editor@scottishfield.co.uk
Owner *Oban Times*
Editor *Archie Mackenzie*

Founded 1903. MONTHLY. Scotland's quality lifestyle magazine. Unsolicited mss welcome but writers should study the magazine first.

FEATURES Articles of general interest on Scotland and Scots abroad with good photographs or, preferably, colour slides. Approx. 1000 words.

PAYMENT negotiable.

Scottish Home & Country

42 Heriot Row, Edinburgh EH3 6ES
☎0131 225 1724 Fax 0131 225 8129
✉ magazine@swri.demon.co.uk
Owner *Scottish Women's Rural Institutes*
Editor *Liz Ferguson*
Circulation 11,000

Founded 1924. MONTHLY. Scottish or rural-related issues, health, travel, women's issues and general interest. Unsolicited mss welcome. Commissions are rare and tend to go to established contributors only.

Scottish Rugby Magazine

First Press Publishing, 1 Central Quay, Glasgow G3 8DA
☎0141 309 1400 Fax 0141 248 1099
✉ editor@scottishrugby.co.uk
Senior Editor *Alex Macleod*
Circulation 19,200

Founded 1990. MONTHLY. Features, club profiles, etc. Approach with ideas by e-mail or in writing.

Scouting Magazine

Gilwell House, Gilwell Park, Chingford E4 7QW
☎020 8433 7100 Fax 020 8433 7103
✉ scouting.magazine@scout.org.uk
www.scouts.org.uk
Owner *The Scout Association*
Editor *Anna Sorensen*
Circulation 20,000+

BI-MONTHLY magazine for adults connected to or interested in the Scout Movement. Interested in Scouting-related submissions only.

PAYMENT by negotiation.

Screen

Gilmorehill Centre for Theatre, Film and Television, University of Glasgow, Glasgow G12 8QQ
☎0141 330 5035 Fax 0141 330 3515

✉ screen@arts.gla.ac.uk
www.screen.arts.gla.ac.uk

Publisher *Oxford University Press*
Editors *Annette Kuhn, John Caughie, Simon Frith, Karen Lury, Jackie Stacey, Sarah Street*
Editorial Assistant *Caroline Beven*
Circulation 1200

QUARTERLY refereed academic journal of film and television studies for a readership ranging from undergraduates to screen studies academics and media professionals. There are no specific qualifications for acceptance of articles. Straightforward film reviews are not normally published. Check the magazine's style and market in the first instance.

Screen International
33–39 Bowling Green Lane, London
EC1R 0DA
☎020 7505 8056 Fax 020 7505 8117
✉ leo.barraclough@media.emap.com
www.screendaily.com

Owner *Emap Communications*
Managing Editor *Leo Barraclough*

International trade paper of the film, video and television industries. Expert freelance writers are occasionally used in all areas. No unsolicited mss. Approach with ideas in writing or by e-mail.

FEATURES *Louise Tutt.*
PAYMENT negotiable on NUJ basis.

Screentrade Magazine
Screentrade Media Ltd, PO Box 144,
Orpington BR6 6LZ
☎01689 833117 Fax 01689 833117
✉ philip45other@yahoo.co.uk

Owner *Screentrade Media Ltd*
Editor *Philip Turner*
Circulation 3000+

Founded 2002. QUARTERLY journal for British and European exhibitors and film distributors.

FEATURES Items on cinema management, technical, cinema building history, nostalgia, showmanship, book reviews and other managerial matters. Also film and producer/director opinions. Some film reviews but no 'film star' interviews. Most contributions are from within the industry. Items on the state of cinema exhibition, film distribution, cinema architecture, interviews with key industry personnel frequently undertaken. 1500–3000 words.

NEWS Topical items (if substantiated) welcome. Events coverage (e.g. festivals) from an exhibitor's viewpoint preferred.

ScriptWriter Magazine
2 Elliott Square, London NW3 3SU
☎020 7586 4853 Fax 020 7586 4853
✉ julian@scriptwritermagazine.com
www.scriptwritermagazine.com

Owner *Scriptease Ltd*
Editor *Julian Friedmann*
Circulation 1500

Launched November 2001. SIX ISSUES PER YEAR. Magazine for professional scriptwriters covering all aspects of the business and craft of writing for the small and large screen. Interested in serious, in-depth analysis; max. 1500–3500 words. E-mail with synopsis, sample material and c.v.

PAYMENT £20 per 1000 words.

Sea Breezes
Mannin Media Group Ltd, Media House,
Cronkbourne IM4 4SB
☎01624 696566 Fax 01624 661655
✉ seabreezes@manninmedia.co.im
www.seabreezes.co.im

Owner *Print Centres*
Editor *Captain A.C. Douglas*
Circulation 17,000

Founded 1919. MONTHLY. Covers virtually everything relating to ships and seamen. Unsolicited mss welcome; they should be thoroughly researched and accompanied by relevant photographs. No fiction, poetry, or anything which 'smacks of the romance of the sea'.

FEATURES Factual tales of ships, seamen and the sea, Royal or Merchant Navy, sail or power, nautical history, shipping company histories, epic voyages, etc. Length 1000–4000 words. 'The most readily acceptable work will be that which shows it is clearly the result of first-hand experience or the product of extensive and accurate research.' PAYMENT £14 per page (about 800 words).

She Magazine
National Magazine House, 72 Broadwick Street, London W1F 9EP
☎020 7439 5000 Fax 020 7312 3981
www.natmags.co.uk

Owner *National Magazine Co. Ltd*
Editor *Terry Tavner*
Circulation 190,033

Glossy MONTHLY for the thirty-something woman, addressing her needs as an individual, a partner and a parent. Talks to its readers in an intelligent, humorous and sympathetic way.

FEATURES should be about 1200 words long. Approach with ideas in writing or e-mail the Acting Features Editor (natasha.cook@natmags.co.uk). No unsolicited material. PAYMENT negotiable.

Ships Monthly

IPC Country & Leisure Media Ltd,
222 Branston Road, Burton-upon-Trent
DE14 3BT
☎01283 542721 Fax 01283 546436
✉ shipsmonthly@ipcmedia.com

Owner *IPC Country & Leisure Media Ltd*
Editor *Iain Wakefield*
Circulation 22,000

Founded 1966. MONTHLY A4 format magazine for ship enthusiasts and maritime professionals. News, photographs and illustrated articles on all kinds of ships – mercantile and naval, past and present. No yachting. Most articles are commissioned; prospective contributors should telephone or e-mail in the first instance.

Shoot Monthly Magazine

IPC Media Ltd., King's Reach Tower,
Stamford Street, London SE1 9LS
☎020 7261 6287 Fax 020 7261 6019
✉ shoot@ipcmedia.com

Owner *IPC Media*
Editor *Colin Mitchell*
Circulation 30,255

Founded 1969. MONTHLY football magazine. No unsolicited mss. Present ideas for news, features or colour photo-features to the editor by letter or e-mail.

FEATURES Hard-hitting, topical and off-beat.

NEWS Items welcome, especially exclusive gossip and transfer speculation.

PAYMENT negotiable.

Shooting and Conservation

BASC, Marford Mill, Rossett, Wrexham
LL12 0HL
☎01244 573000 Fax 01244 573001

Owner *The British Association for Shooting and Conservation (BASC)*
Editor *Jeffrey Olstead*
Circulation 120,000

SIX ISSUES PER YEAR. Good articles and stories on shooting, conservation and related areas may be considered although most material is produced in-house. Max. 1500 words. PAYMENT negotiable.

Shooting Times & Country Magazine

IPC Media Ltd., King's Reach Tower,
Stamford Street, London SE1 9LS
☎020 7261 6180 Fax 020 7261 7179
✉ steditorial@ipcmedia.com

Owner *IPC Media*
Editor *Robert Gray*
Circulation 27,446

Founded 1882. WEEKLY. Covers shooting, fishing and related countryside topics. Unsolicited contributions considered.

PAYMENT negotiable.

Shout Magazine

D.C. Thomson & Co., Albert Square,
Dundee DD1 9QJ
☎01382 223131 Fax 01382 200880
✉ shout@dcthomson.co.uk

Owner *D.C. Thomson Publishers*
Editor *Maria T. Welch*
Circulation 84,600

Founded 1993. FORTNIGHTLY. Pop music, emotional, beauty, fashion, soap features, quizzes.

FICTION *Maria Welch* Supernatural/spooky stories welcome. Approach by telephone in the first instance. Max. 1500 words. PAYMENT £100.

Shout!

PO Box YR46, Leeds LS9 6XG
☎0113 248 5700 Fax 0113 295 6097
✉ shout.magazine@ntlworld.com
www.shout.connectfree.co.uk

Owner/Editor *Mark Michalowski*
Circulation 7000

Founded 1995. MONTHLY lesbian/gay and bisexual news, views, arts and scene for Yorkshire; lgb health and politics. Interested in reviews of Yorkshire lgb events, happenings, news, analysis – 300 to 1000 words max. No fiction, fashion or items with no reasonable relevance to Yorkshire and the north.

PAYMENT £40 per 1000 words.

Showing World

The Publishing House, Station Road,
Framlingham IP13 9EE
☎01728 622030 Fax 01728 622031
✉ todaymagazine@btopeworld.com

Owner *T.P. Publications*
Editor *Charlotte Knight*
Circulation 3,000

Founded 1991. Features every aspect of showing horses and ponies, including natives, minia-

tures and donkeys. Knowledgeable and how-to-do-it articles welcome. Photos essential.
PAYMENT negotiable.

Shropshire Magazine
77 Wyle Cop, Shrewsbury SY1 1UT
☎01743 362175 Fax 01743 362128
Owner *Shropshire Newspapers Ltd*
Editor *Sarah-Jane Smith*

Founded 1950. MONTHLY. Unsolicited mss welcome but ideas in writing preferred.

FEATURES Personalities, topical items, historical (e.g. family) of Shropshire; also general interest: homes, weddings, antiques, etc. Max. 1000 words.
PAYMENT negotiable 'but modest'.

Sight & Sound
British Film Institute, 21 Stephen Street, London W1T 1LN
☎020 7255 1444 Fax 020 7436 2327
www.bfi.org.uk/sightandsound
Owner *British Film Institute*
Editor *Nick James*

Founded 1932. MONTHLY. Topical and critical articles on international cinema, with regular columns from the USA and Europe. Length 1000–5000 words. Relevant photographs appreciated. Also book, film and video release reviews. Approach in writing with ideas.
PAYMENT by arrangement.

The Sign
See **Hymns Ancient & Modern Ltd** under *UK Publishers*

Ski and Board
The White House, 57–63 Church Road, Wimbledon, London SW19 5SB
☎020 8410 2000 Fax 020 8410 2001
✉ s&b@skiclub.co.uk
www.skiclub.co.uk
Owner *Ski Club of Great Britain*
Editor *Arnie Wilson*

Founded 1903. FOUR ISSUES YEARLY. Features from established ski/snowboard writers only.

The Skier and Snowboarder Magazine
Mountain Marketing Ltd., PO Box 386, Sevenoaks TN13 1AQ
☎0845 310 8303 Fax 01732 779266
✉ skierandsnowboarder@hotmail.com
Publisher *Mountain Marketing Ltd*
Editor *Frank Baldwin*

Circulation 30,000

SEASONAL (from July to May). FIVE ISSUES YEARLY. Outside contributions welcome.

FEATURES Various topics covered, including race reports, resort reports, fashion, equipment update, dry slope, school news, new products, health and safety. Crisp, tight, informative copy of 800 words or less preferred.
NEWS All aspects of skiing news covered.
PAYMENT negotiable.

Slightly Foxed: The Real Reader's Quarterly
21 Alwyne Road, London N1 2HN
☎020 7359 3377 Fax 0870 199 1245
✉ all@foxedquarterly.com
www.foxedquarterly.com
Owner *Slightly Foxed Ltd*
Editors *Gail Pirkis, Hazel Wood*
Circulation 2500

Founded 2004. 'Reviews of books (fiction and non-fiction) that have stood the test of time or books that have been published recently and are of real quality but which have been overlooked by reviewers and bookshops.' Unsolicited contributions of 'lively, personal, idiosyncratic writing of real quality' are welcome but it is recommended that would-be contributors read the magazine first to gauge its approach. Send e-mail with sample work in the first instance. Not interested in anything that is not actually a review of a book or author.

Slimming
Greater London House, Hampstead Road, London NW1 7EJ
☎020 7347 1854 Fax 020 7347 1863
✉ katy.salter@emap.com
Owner *Emap Esprit*
Editor *Rashmi Madan*
Circulation 68,196

Founded 1969. TWELVE ISSUES YEARLY. Leading magazine about slimming, diet and health. Opportunities for freelance contributions on general health (diet-related); psychology related to health and fitness; celebrity interviews. It is best to approach with an idea by e-mail.
PAYMENT negotiable.

Smallholder
Hook House, Wimblington March PE15 0QL
☎01354 741182 Fax 01354 741182
✉ edit@smallholder.co.uk
www.smallholder.co.uk
Owner *Newsquest*

Editor *Liz Wright*
Circulation 20,000

Founded 1982. MONTHLY. Outside contributions welcome. Send for sample magazine and editorial schedule before submitting anything. Follow up with samples of work to the editor so that style can be assessed for suitability. No poetry or humorous, unfocused personal tales; no puzzles.

FEATURES New writers always welcome, but must have high level of technical expertise – 'not textbook stuff'. 'How to do it' articles with photos welcome. Illustrations and photos paid for. Length 750–1500 words.

NEWS All agricultural and rural news welcome. Length 200–500 words.

PAYMENT negotiable.

Smash Hits

Mappin House, 4 Winsley Street, London W1W 8HF
☎020 7436 1515 Fax 020 7636 5792
✉ letters@smashhits.net
www.smashhits.net

Owner *Emap Performance*
Editor *Lisa Smosarski*
Circulation 114,383

Founded 1978. FORTNIGHTLY. Top of the mid-teen market. Unsolicited mss are not accepted, but prospective contributors may approach in writing with ideas.

Sneak Magazine

Mappin House, 4 Winsley Street, London W1W 8HF
☎020 7436 1515 Fax 020 7312 8229
✉ michelle.garnett@emap.com
www.sneakmagazine.com

Owner *EMAP*
Editor *Michelle Garnett*
Editorial Director *Jennifer Cawthron*
Circulation 104,174

Founded 2002. WEEKLY magazine for teenagers providing gossip and entertainment. Unsolicited material welcome.

FEATURES *Leo Roberts*
NEWS *Kate Taylor*
FICTION *Louise Christie*. Approach by e-mail.

Snooker Scene

Cavalier House, 202 Hagley Road, Edgbaston, Birmingham B16 9PQ
☎0121 454 2931 Fax 0121 452 1822
✉ clive.everton@talk21.com

Owner *Everton's News Agency*

Editor *Clive Everton*
Circulation 16,000

Founded 1971. MONTHLY. No unsolicited mss. Approach in writing with an idea.

The Spectator

56 Doughty Street, London WC1N 2LL
☎020 7405 1706 Fax 020 7242 0603
✉ editor@spectator.co.uk
www.spectator.co.uk

Owner *The Spectator (1828) Ltd*
Editor *Boris Johnson*
Deputy Editor *Stuart Reid*
Circulation 63,223

Founded 1828. WEEKLY political and literary magazine. Prospective contributors should write in the first instance to the relevant editor. Unsolicited mss welcome, but no 'follow up' phone calls, please.

BOOKS *Mark Amory*.
PAYMENT nominal.

The Sporting Life
See **Racing Post**

Staffordshire Life

The Publishing Centre, Derby Street, Stafford ST16 2DT
☎01785 257700 Fax 01785 253287
✉ editor@staffordshirelife.co.uk

Owner *Staffordshire Newspapers Ltd*
Editor *Philip Thurlow-Craig*
Circulation 20,000

Founded 1982. ELEVEN ISSUES YEARLY. Full-colour county magazine devoted to Staffordshire, its surroundings and people. Contributions welcome. Approach in writing with ideas.

FEATURES Max. 1200 words.

FASHION Copy must be supported by photographs.

PAYMENT NUJ rates.

The Stage (incorporating Television Today)

Stage House, 47 Bermondsey Street, London SE1 3XT
☎020 7403 1818 Fax 020 7357 9287
✉ editor@thestage.co.uk
www.thestage.co.uk

Owner *The Stage Newspaper Ltd*
Editor *Brian Attwood*
Circulation 41,500

Founded 1880. WEEKLY. No unsolicited mss. Prospective contributors should write with ideas in the first instance.

FEATURES Preference for middle-market, tabloid-style articles. 'Puff pieces', PR plugs and extended production notes will not be considered. Max. 800 words. Profiles: 1200 words.

NEWS News stories from outside London are always welcome. Max. 300 words.

PAYMENT £100 per 1000 words.

Stamp Magazine

Leon House, 233 High Street, Croydon CR9 1HZ
☎020 8774 0600
✉ steve_fairclough@ipcmedia.com
Owner *IPC Media*
Editor *Steve Fairclough*
Circulation 12,000

Founded 1934. MONTHLY news and features on the world of stamp collecting from the past to the present day. Interested in articles by experts on particular countries or themes such as subject matter illustrated on stamps – dogs, politics, etc. Approach in writing.

NEWS *Deborah Lees* News of latest stamp issues or industry news. Max. 500 words.

FEATURES *Steve Fairclough* Any features welcome on famous stamps, rarities, postmarks, postal history, exhibitions, postcards, personal collections, auctions. Must be illustrated with colour images ('we can arrange for photography of original stamps'). Max. 2500 words, or 5000 for 2-part expert piece.

PAYMENT negotiable.

Stand Magazine

See under *Poetry Magazines*

Staple

See under *Poetry Magazines*

Steam Railway Magazine

Bretton Court, Bretton, Peterborough PE3 8DZ
☎01733 264666 Fax 01733 282720
✉ steam.railway@emap.com
Owner *Emap Active Limited*
Editor *Tony Streeter*
Circulation 32,771

Founded 1979. FOUR-WEEKLY magazine targeted at all steam enthusiasts interested in the modern preservation movement. Unsolicited material welcome. News reports, photographs, steam-age reminiscences. Approach in writing or by e-mail.

The Strad

Newsquest Magazines, 330 High Holborn, London WCV 7QTY
☎020 7203 6731 Fax 020 7203 6736
✉ thestrad@orpheuspublications.com
www.thestrad.com
Owner *Newsquest Media Group*
Editor *Naomi Sadler*
Circulation 17,500

Founded 1890. MONTHLY for classical string musicians, makers and enthusiasts. Unsolicited mss accepted occasionally 'though acknowledgement/return not guaranteed'.

FEATURES Profiles of string players, teachers, luthiers and musical instruments, also relevant research. Max. 2000 words.

REVIEWS *Ariane Todes, Zoë Rigden*
PAYMENT £150 per 1000 words.

Suffolk and Norfolk Life

The Publishing House, Framlingham IP13 9EE
☎01728 622030 Fax 01728 622031
Owner *Today Magazines Ltd*
Editor *Kevin Davis*
Circulation 17,000

Founded 1989. MONTHLY. General interest, local stories, historical, personalities, wine, travel, food. Unsolicited mss welcome. Approach by phone or in writing with ideas. Not interested in anything which does not relate specifically to East Anglia.

FEATURES *Kevin Davis* Max. 1500 words, with photos.

NEWS *Kevin Davis* Max. 1000 words, with photos.

SPECIAL PAGES *William Locks* Study the magazine for guidelines. Max. 1500 words.

PAYMENT £35–50.

Sugar Magazine

64 North Row, London W1K 7LL
☎020 7150 7050 Fax 020 7150 7678
Owner *Hachette Filipacchi (UK)*
Editor *Nick Chalmers*
Editorial Director *Lysanne Currie*
Circulation 291,794

Founded 1994. MONTHLY. Everything that might interest the teenage girl. No unsolicited mss. Will consider ideas or contacts for real-life features. No fiction. Approach in writing in the first instance.

Sunday Post Magazine

See **Sunday Post** under *National Newspapers*

Sunday Times Magazine
See **Sunday Times** under *National Newspapers*

SuperBike Magazine
IPC Media Ltd, Leon House, 233 High Street, Croydon CR9 1HZ
☎020 8774 0600
www.ipcmedia.com
Owner *IPC Media*
Publishing Director *Keith Foster*
Editor *Kenny Pryde*
Circulation 62,057

Founded 1977. MONTHLY. Dedicated to all that is best and most exciting in the world of high-performance motorcycling. Unsolicited mss, synopses and ideas welcome.

Sussex Life
Baskerville Place, 28 Teville Road, Worthing BN11 1UG
☎01903 218719 Fax 01903 820193
✉ ian@sussexlife.co.uk
www.sussexlife.com
Owner *Archant Life*
Editor *Ian Trevett*
Circulation 42,000

Founded 1965. MONTHLY. Sussex and general interest magazine. Regular supplements on education, fashion, homes and gardens. Interested in investigative, journalistic pieces relevant to the area and celebrity profiles. Unsolicited mss, synopses and ideas in writing welcome. Minimum 500 words

Swimming Magazine
Harold Fern House, Derby Square, Loughborough LE11 5AL
☎01509 618766 Fax 01509 618768
Owner *Amateur Swimming Association*
Editor *P. Hassall*
Circulation 20,000

Founded 1923. MONTHLY about competitive swimming and associated subjects. Unsolicited mss welcome.

FEATURES Technical articles on swimming, water polo, diving or synchronised swimming. Length and payment negotiable.

The Tablet
1 King Street Cloisters, Clifton Walk, London W6 0QZ
☎020 8748 8484 Fax 020 8748 1550
✉ thetablet@tablet.co.uk
www.thetablet.co.uk
Owner *The Tablet Publishing Co Ltd*

Editor *Catherine Pepinster*
Circulation 22,466

Founded 1840. WEEKLY. Quality international Roman Catholic magazine featuring articles – political, social, cultural, theological or spiritual – of interest to concerned Christian laity and clergy. Unsolicited material welcome (1500 words) if relevant to magazine's style and market. All approaches should be made in writing.
PAYMENT from about £75.

Take a Break
Academic House, 24–28 Oval Road, London NW1 7DT
☎020 7241 8000
✉ tab.features@bauer.co.uk
Owner *H. Bauer Publishing Ltd*
Editor *John Dale*
Circulation 1.25 million

Founded 1990. WEEKLY. True-life feature magazine. Approach with ideas in writing.

NEWS/FEATURES Always on the look-out for good, true-life stories. Max. 1200 words.

FICTION Sharp, succinct stories which are well told and often with a twist at the end. All categories, provided it is relevant to the magazine's style and market. Max. 1000 words.
PAYMENT negotiable.

TATE Etc
Millbank, London SW1P 4RG
☎020 7887 8030 Fax 020 7887 8729
✉ tateetc@tate.org.uk
www.tate.org.uk
Owner *Tate*
Editorial Director *Bice Curiger*
Editor *Simon Grant*
Circulation 90,000

Relaunched May 2004. THREE ISSUES YEARLY. Visual arts magazine aimed at a broad readership with articles blending the historic and the contemporary. Please send material by post.

Tatler
Vogue House, Hanover Square, London W1S 1JU
☎020 7499 9080 Fax 020 7409 0451
www.tatler.co.uk
Owner *Condé Nast Publications Ltd*
Editor *Geordie Greig*
Circulation 84,330

Up-market glossy from the Condé Nast stable. New writers should send in copies of either published work or unpublished material; writers of promise will be taken up. The magazine works largely on a commission basis: they are unlikely to publish unsolicited features, but will ask writers to work to specific projects.

FEATURES DIRECTOR *Vassi Chamberlain*

TGO (The Great Outdoors)

Newsquest Magazines, 200 Renfield Street, Glasgow G2 3QB
☎0141 302 7700 Fax 0141 302 7799
✉ cameron.mcneish@tgomagazine.co.uk

Owner *Newsquest*
Editor *Cameron McNeish*
Circulation 22,000

Founded 1978. MONTHLY. Deals with walking, backpacking and wild country topics. Unsolicited mss are welcome.

FEATURES Well-written and illustrated items on relevant topics. Max. 2500 words. Colour photographs only, please.

NEWS Short topical items (or photographs). Max. 300 words.

PAYMENT negotiable.

that's life!

Academic House, 24–28 Oval Road, London NW1 7DT
☎020 7241 8000 Fax 020 7241 8008
✉ firstname.lastname@bauer.co.uk

Owner *H. Bauer Publishing Ltd*
Editor *Jo Checkley*
Circulation 597,170

Founded 1995. WEEKLY. True-life stories, puzzles, health, homes, parenting, cookery and fun.

FEATURES *Andreina Cordani* Max. 1600 words.

FICTION *Emma Fabian* 1200 words.

PAYMENT features, varies; fiction, £300.

The Third Alternative

5 Martins Lane, Witcham, Ely CB6 2LB
☎01353 777931
✉ ttapress@aol.com
www.ttapress.com

Owner *TTA Press*
Editor *Andy Cox*

Founded 1993. QUARTERLY A4 colour magazine of horror, fantasy, science fiction and cross-genre fiction, plus interviews, profiles, comment, cinema and artwork. Publishes talented newcomers alongside famous authors. Unsolicited mss welcome if accompanied by s.a.e. or e-mail address for overseas submissions (no length restriction but no novels or serialisations). Queries and letters welcome via e-mail but submissions as hard copy only.

Potential contributors are advised to study the magazine. Contracts are exchanged upon acceptance; payment is upon acceptance. Winner of several British Fantasy Awards. The magazine is supported by Eastern Arts and the Arts Council of England.

This England

PO Box 52, Cheltenham GL50 1YQ
☎01242 537900 Fax 01242 537901

Owner *This England Ltd*
Editor *Roy Faiers*
Circulation 200,000

Founded 1968. QUARTERLY, with a strong overseas readership. Celebration of England and all things English: famous people, natural beauty, towns and villages, history, traditions, customs and legends, crafts, etc. Generally a rural basis, with the 'Forgetmenots' section publishing readers' recollections and nostalgia. Up to one hundred unsolicited pieces received each week. Unsolicited mss/ideas welcome. Length 250–2000 words.

PAYMENT £25 per 1000 words.

Time

Brettenham House, Lancaster Place, London WC2E 7TL
☎020 7499 4080
✉ edit-office@timemagazine.com
www.timeeurope.com

Owner *Time Warner*
Editor (Europe, Middle East, Africa)
  Eric Pooley
Circulation 597,038 (Europe)

Founded 1923. WEEKLY current affairs and news magazine. There are few opportunities for freelancers on *Time* as almost all the magazine's content is written by staff members from various bureaux around the world. No unsolicited mss.

Time Out

Universal House, 251 Tottenham Court Road, London W1T 7AB
☎020 7813 3000 Fax 020 7813 6001
www.timeout.com

Publisher *Lesley Gill*
Editor *Laura Lee Davies*
Circulation 86,000

Founded 1968. WEEKLY magazine of news and entertainment in London.

FEATURES *Jessica Cargill Thompson* 'Usually written by staff writers or commissioned, but it's always worth submitting an idea by post if particularly apt to the magazine.' 1000 words.

CONSUMER SECTION *Neil McLennan*
Fashion, shopping, travel, design, property.
PAYMENT negotiable.

The Times Educational Supplement
Admiral House, 66–68 East Smithfield,
London E1W 1BX
☎020 7782 3000 Fax 020 7782 3200
✉ newsdesk@tes.co.uk *or* editor@tes.co.uk
www.tes.co.uk
Owner *News International*
Editor *Bob Doe*
Circulation 118,000

Founded 1910. WEEKLY. New contributors are
welcome and should fax or e-mail ideas on one
sheet of A4 for news, features or reviews, or
e-mail the editor or newsdesk. The main
newspaper accepts contributions in the following sections:
OPINION 'Platform': a weekly slot for a well-
informed and cogently argued viewpoint. Max.
1200 words. 'Another Voice': a shorter comment on an issue of the day by non-education
professionals. Max. 700 words.
LEADERSHIP Weekly pages on practical issues
for school governors and managers. Max. 800
words.
FE FOCUS Weekly pull-out section covering
post-16 education and training in colleges, work
and the wider community. Aimed at everyone
from teachers/lecturers to leaders and opinion
formers in lifelong learning. News, features,
comment and opinion on all aspects of college
life welcome. Length from 350 words (news)
to 1000 max. (features). Contact ian.nash@tes.
co.uk
Friday A weekly magazine with *The TES*
which focuses on whole school issues, good
practice, teaching as a career and the work/life
balance (friday@tes.co.uk):
FEATURES Unsolicited features are rarely
accepted but ideas are welcome accompanied by
cuttings and/or c.v. Length from 1000–2000
words. Strong storylines are expected.
TALKBACK Short, first person pieces, max.
650 words, are welcome for consideration.
Humour from teachers is encouraged, especially for the 'Thank God it's Friday' column.
TES Teacher Weekly magazine for classroom
teachers focusing on what individual teachers
do in the classroom to teach pupils and subjects. Specific subject section each week. Max.
800 words. (teacher@tes.co.uk)
Online (Computers in Education) A magazine
devoted to information and communications
technology appearing with *The TES* six times a
year. (merlin.john@tes.co.uk)

SPECIAL ISSUES Occasional pull-out magazines
on topics including newly qualified teachers
(fiona.flynn@tes.co.uk), business links (ian.nash
@tes.co.uk), school visits – *Going Places* (yolanda.
brooks@tes.co.uk).

The Times Educational Supplement Scotland
Scott House, 10 South St Andrew Street,
Edinburgh EH2 2AZ
☎0131 557 1133 Fax 0131 558 1155
✉ scoted@tes.co.uk
www.tes.co.uk/scotland
Owner *TSL Education Ltd*
Editor *Neil Munro*
Circulation 9000

Founded 1965. WEEKLY. Unsolicited mss wel-
come.
FEATURES Articles on education in Scotland.
Max. 1000 words.
NEWS Items on education in Scotland. Max.
600 words.

The Times Higher Education Supplement
Admiral House, 66–68 East Smithfield,
London E1W 1BX
☎020 7782 3000 Fax 020 7782 3300
✉ editor@thes.co.uk
www.thes.co.uk
Owner *News International*
Editor *John O'Leary*
Circulation 26,000

Founded 1971. WEEKLY. Unsolicited mss are
welcome but most articles and almost all book
reviews are commissioned. 'In most cases it is
better to write or e-mail, but in the case of
news stories it is all right to phone.'
BOOKS *Andrew Robinson*
FEATURES *Mandy Garner* Most articles are
commissioned from academics in higher education.
NEWS *Lee Eliot-Major* Freelance opportunities very occasionally.
SCIENCE *Steve Farrar*
SCIENCE BOOKS *Andrew Robinson*
FOREIGN *David Jobbins*
PAYMENT by negotiation.

The Times Literary Supplement
Admiral House, 66–68 East Smithfield,
London E1W 1BX
☎020 7782 3000 Fax 020 7782 3100
www.the-tls.co.uk
Owner *TSL Education Ltd*

Editor *Peter Stothard*
Circulation 35,000

Founded 1902. WEEKLY review of literature. Contributors should approach in writing and be familiar with the general level of writing in the *TLS*.
LITERARY DISCOVERIES *Alan Jenkins*
POEMS *Mick Imlah*
NEWS News stories and general articles concerned with literature, publishing and new intellectual developments anywhere in the world. Length by arrangement.
PAYMENT by arrangement.

Titbits
2 Caversham Street, London SW3 4AH
☎020 7351 4995 Fax 020 7351 4995

Owner *Sport Newspapers Ltd*
Editor *James Hughes*
Circulation 150,000

Founded 1895. MONTHLY. Consumer magazine for men covering show business and general interests. Ideas in writing welcome. Max. 3000 words. News, features, particularly photo features (colour) and fiction. Always send letter or telephone first.
PAYMENT negotiable.

Today's Golfer
Bushfield House, Orton Centre, Peterborough PE2 5UW
☎01733 237111 Fax 01733 288014

Owner *Emap Active Ltd*
Editor *Paul Hamblin*
Associate Editor *John McKenzie*
Circulation 100,078

Founded 1988. MONTHLY. Golf instruction, features, player profiles and news. Most features written in-house but unsolicited mss will be considered. Approach in writing with ideas. Not interested in instruction material from outside contributors.
FEATURES/NEWS *Kevin Brown* Opinion, player profiles and general golf-related features.

Top of the Pops Magazine
Room A1136, Woodlands, 80 Wood Lane, London W12 0TT
☎020 8433 3910 Fax 020 8433 2694
www.beeb.com/totp

Owner *BBC Worldwide Publishing Ltd*
Editor *Corinna Shaffer*
Circulation 230,493

Founded 1995. MONTHLY teenage pop music magazine with a lighthearted and humorous approach. No unsolicited material apart from pop star interviews.

Total Film
99 Baker Street, London W1U 6FP
☎020 7317 2600 Fax 020 7317 0275
✉ totalfilm@futurenet.co.uk

Owner *Future Publishing*
Editor *Matt Mueller*
Circulation 90,580

Founded 1997. MONTHLY reviews-based movie magazine. Interested in ideas for features, not necessarily tied in to specific releases, and humour items. No reviews or interviews with celebrities/directors. Approach by post or e-mail.

Total Vauxhall
A&S Publishing Co Ltd, 35 St Michaels Square, Gloucester GL1 1HX
☎01452 317790 Fax 01452 415817
✉ info@totalvauxhall.co.uk
www.totalvauxhall.co.uk

Owner *A&S Publishing Co Ltd*
Editor *Jon Walsh*
Circulation 20,000

Founded 2001. MONTHLY independent newsstand magazine aimed at the Vauxhall enthusiast. Covers new, modified, historical/classic, race and rally Vauxhalls of all kinds. Substantial amount of technical content. Also covers the more interesting parts of the GM family, particularly Opel and Holden. Uses a lot of freelance contributors; 'those who hit deadlines and fulfil the brief get regular work and lots of it.' Feature ideas, news items, historical pieces and potential feature cars welcome but must have a Vauxhall/GM tilt. Call the editor directly for an informal discussion on style, approach and angle.
PAYMENT 'surprisingly generous'.

Traditional Woodworking
151 Station Street, Burton on Trent DE14 1BG
☎01283 742950 Fax 01283 742957
✉ enquiries@twonline.co.uk

Owner *Waterways World*
Editor *Alison Bell*

Founded 1988. MONTHLY. Features workshop projects, techniques, reviews of the latest woodworking tools and equipment, general articles on woodworking and furniture making. Supplement: *Power Tool Guide*.
FEATURES Technical features and furniture projects welcome. The latter must include drawings and cutting lists. A photograph of the

piece is required before commissioning. Approach in writing in the first instance.

PAYMENT negotiable.

Trail

Bretton Court, Bretton, Peterborough PE3 8DZ

☎01733 264666 Fax 01733 282653

www.trailmag.com

Owner *Emap Active Publishing Ltd*
Editor *Guy Proctor*
Circulation 37,827

Founded 1990. MONTHLY. Gear reports, where to walk and practical advice for the hill-walker and long distance walker. Inspirational reads on people and outdoor/walking issues. Health, fitness and injury prevention for high level walkers and outdoor lovers. Approach by phone or in writing in the first instance.

FEATURES *Emma Kendell* Very limited requirement for overseas articles, 'written to our style'. Ask for guidelines. Max. 2000 words. Limited requirement for guided walks articles. Specialist writers only. Ask for guidelines. 750–2000 words (depending on subject).

PAYMENT £100 per 1000 words.

Tramp Magazine

South Bank House, Black Prince Road, London SE1 7SJ

☎020 7735 8171

✉ info@trampmagazine.com

www.trampmagazine.com

Owner *Enrico Williams*
Editor *Kirsten Telfer-Beith*
Circulation 60,000

Founded 2003. MONTHLY luxury lifestyle magazine. Travel, entertainment, lifestyle and fashion items welcome; approach by e-mail.

TRAVEL *Christina Haynes*
FOOD *Malaika Aaron-Pereira*
LIFESTYLE *Paolla Steinhart-Smith*

Traveller

45–49 Brompton Road, London SW3 1DE

☎020 7589 0500 Fax 020 7581 1357

www.traveller.org.uk

Owner *Wexas International*
Editor *Jonathan Lorie*
Deputy Editor *Amy Sohanpaul*
Circulation 37,000

Founded 1970. QUARTERLY travel magazine.

FEATURES High quality, personal narratives of remarkable journeys. Articles should be off-beat, adventurous, authentic. No mainstream destinations. For guidelines, see website. Articles may be accompanied by professional quality, original slides. Freelance articles considered. Max. 1200 words. Initial contact by e-mail.

PAYMENT £150 per 1000 words.

Trout Fisherman

EMAP Active Ltd, Bushfield House, Orton Centre, Peterborough PE2 5UW

☎01733 237111 Fax 01733 465820

✉ mark.sutcliffe@emap.com

Owner *Emap Active Ltd*
Editor *Mark Sutcliffe*
Circulation 34,553

Founded 1977. MONTHLY instructive magazine on trout fishing. Most of the articles are commissioned, but unsolicited mss and quality colour transparencies welcome.

FEATURES Max. 2500 words.

PAYMENT varies.

TVTimes

IPC Media Ltd., King's Reach Tower, Stamford Street, London SE1 9LS

☎020 7261 7000 Fax 020 7261 7888

Owner *IPC Media*
Editor *Mike Hollingsworth*
Circulation 524,131

Founded 1955. WEEKLY magazine of listings and features serving the viewers of independent television, BBC, satellite and radio. Freelance contributions by commission only. No unsolicited contributions.

Ulster Tatler

39 Boucher Road, Belfast BT12 6UT

☎028 9068 1371 Fax 028 9038 1915

✉ ulstertat@aol.com

www.ulstertatler.com

Owner/Editor *Richard Sherry*
Circulation 12,689

Founded 1965. MONTHLY. Articles of local interest and social functions appealing to Northern Ireland's ABC1 population. Welcomes unsolicited material; approach by phone or in writing in the first instance.

FEATURES *Noreen Dorman* Max. 1500 words.

FICTION *Richard Sherry* Max. 3000 words

The Universe

St James's Buildings, Oxford Street, Manchester M1 6FP

☎0161 236 8856 Fax 0161 236 8892

✉ joseph.kelly@the-universe.com

www.totalcatholic.com

Owner *Gabriel Communications Ltd*

Editor *Joe Kelly*
Circulation 60,000

Occasional use of new writers, but a substantial network of regular contributors already exists. Interested in a very wide range of material: all subjects which might bear on Christian life. Fiction not normally accepted. PAYMENT negotiable.

Vector
See **British Science Fiction Association** under *Professional Associations*

The Vegan
Donald Watson House, 7 Battle Road, St Leonards on Sea TN37 7AA
☎01424 427393 Fax 01424 717064
✉ editor@vegansociety.com
www.vegansociety.com
Owner *Vegan Society*
Editor *Rick Savage*
Circulation 5000

Founded 1944. QUARTERLY. Deals with the ecological, ethical and health aspects of veganism. Unsolicited mss welcome. Max. 2000 words. PAYMENT negotiable.

Verbatim The Language Quarterly
PO Box 156, Chearsley, Aylesbury HP18 0DQ
☎01844 208474
✉ verbatim.uk@tesco.net
www.verbatimmag.com
Owner *Word, Inc.*
Editor *Erin McKean*

Founded in 1974 by Laurence Urdang. QUARTERLY journal devoted to what is amusing, interesting and engaging about the English language and languages in general. Will consider unsolicited material but write for writer's guidelines in the first instance. For a sample copy of the magazine, send 50p (stamp or IRC).
    PAYMENT ranges from £20–300, 'depending on length, wit and other merit'.

Vogue
Vogue House, Hanover Square, London W1S 1JU
☎020 7499 9080 Fax 020 7408 0559
www.vogue.co.uk
Owner *Condé Nast Publications Ltd*
Editor *Alexandra Shulman*
Circulation 202,259

Condé Nast Magazines tend to use known

writers and commission what's needed, rather than using unsolicited mss. Contacts are useful.
    FEATURES *Jo Craven* Upmarket general interest rather than 'women's'. Good proportion of highbrow art and literary articles, as well as travel, gardens, food, home interest and reviews.

The Voice Newspaper
Blue Star House, 234–244 Stockwell Road, London SW9 9UG
☎020 7737 7377 Fax 020 7274 8994
✉ newsdesk@the-voice.co.uk
www.voice-online.co.uk
Managing Director *Linda McCalla*
Group Editor *Deidre Forbes*
Circulation 40,000

Founded 1982. Leading WEEKLY newspaper for black Britons. Includes news, features, arts, sport and a comprehensive jobs section. Also includes a weekly glossy entertainment section. Illustrations: colour and b&w photos. Open to ideas for news and features on sport, business, community events and the arts.

Voyager
PSP Communications, 15 Craven Street, London WC2N 5AD
☎020 7747 9390 Fax 020 7839 5955
✉ daskadavis@pspcom.com
www.pspcom.com
Owner *PSP Communications*
Editor *Daska Davis*
Circulation 36,000

TEN ISSUES PER YEAR. In-flight magazine of bmi british midland. Lifestyle features and profiles, plus British Midland information. No unsolicited mss. Approach in writing with ideas in the first instance. No destination travel articles.

walk
2nd Floor, Camelford House, 87–90 Albert Embankment, London SE1 7TW
☎020 7339 8500 Fax 020 7339 8501
✉ ramblers@london.ramblers.org.uk
Owner *Ramblers' Association*
Editor *Christopher Sparrow*
Circulation 100,394

QUARTERLY. Official magazine of the Ramblers' Association, available to members only. Unsolicited mss welcome. S.a.e. required for return.
    FEATURES Freelance features are invited on any aspect of walking in Britain. Length 450–650 words, preferably with good photographs. No general travel articles.

The War Cry
101 Newington Causeway, London
SE1 6BN
☎020 7367 4900 Fax 020 7367 4710
✉ warcry@salvationarmy.org.uk
www.salvationarmy.org.uk/warcry
Owner *The Salvation Army*
Editor *Major Nigel Bovey*
Circulation 65,000

Founded 1879. WEEKLY magazine containing Christian comment on current issues. Unsolicited mss welcome if appropriate to contents. No fiction or poetry. Approach by phone with ideas.

NEWS relating to Christian Church or social issues. Max. length 500 words.

FEATURES Human interest articles aimed at the 'man/woman-in-the-street'. Max. length 500 words.

PAYMENT £20 per article.

Wasafiri
Dept of English & Drama, Queen Mary College, University of London, Mile End Road, London E1 4NS
☎020 7882 3120 Fax 020 7882 3120
✉ wasafiri@qmul.ac.uk
www.wasafiri.org
Editor *Susheila Nasta*
Managing Editor *Richard Dyer*
Reviews Editor *Mark Stein*

TRI-ANNUAL literary journal of African, Asian, Black British and Caribbean culture. Short stories, poetry, reviews, interviews, criticism and cross cultural debate, film and literature. Illustrations in b&w. Send double-spaced mss, in duplicate, with s.a.e. No e-mail submissions.

PAYMENT negotiable.

Water Gardener
Winchester Court, 1 Forum Place, Hatfield
AL10 0RN
☎01707 273999 Fax 01707 276555
✉ watergardener@trmg.co.uk
www.trmg.co.uk
Owner *TRMG*
Editor *Christina Guthrie*
Deputy Editor *Benidict Vanheems*

Founded 1994. MONTHLY. Everything relevant to water gardening. Will consider photonews items and features on aspects of the subject; write with idea in the first instance. Max. 2000 words.

PAYMENT by negotiation.

Waterways World
151 Station Street, Burton on Trent
DE14 1BG
☎01283 742950 Fax 01283 742957
✉ admin@wwonline.co.uk
Owner *Waterways World Ltd*
Editor *Hugh Potter*
Circulation 22,408

Founded 1972. MONTHLY magazine for inland waterway enthusiasts. Unsolicited mss welcome, provided the writer has a good knowledge of the subject. No fiction.

FEATURES *Hugh Potter* Articles (preferably illustrated) are published on all aspects of inland waterways in Britain and abroad, including recreational and commercial boating on rivers and canals.

NEWS *Chris Daniels* Max. 500 words.

PAYMENT £42 per 1000 words.

Web User
IPC Media, Room 0305, King's Reach Tower, Stamford Street, London SE1 9LS
☎020 7261 7294 Fax 020 7261 7878
✉ letters@web-user.co.uk
www.web-user.co.uk
Owner *IPC Media, a TimeWarner company*
Editor *Richard Clark*

Founded 2001. FORTNIGHTLY bestseller Internet magazine for all users of the Internet. No unsolicited material; send e-mail or letter of enquiry in the first instance.

Wedding and Home
IPC Media Ltd., King's Reach Tower, Stamford Street, London SE1 9LS
☎020 7261 7471 Fax 020 7261 7459
✉ weddingandhome@ipcmedia.com
Owner *IPC Media*
Editor *Kate Barlow*
Circulation 53,862

Founded 1985. BI-MONTHLY offering ideas and inspiration for women planning their wedding. Most features are written in-house or commissioned from known freelancers. Unsolicited mss are not welcome, but approaches may be made in writing.

Weekly News
D.C. Thomson & Co. Ltd., Albert Square, Dundee DD1 9QJ
☎01382 223131 Fax 01382 201390
✉ d.burness@dcthomson.co.uk
Owner *D.C. Thomson & Co. Ltd*
Editor *David Burness*

Circulation 120,000

Founded 1855. WEEKLY. Newsy, family-orientated magazine designed to appeal to the busy housewife. 'We receive a lot of unsolicited articles and there is great loss of life among them.' Usually commissions, but writers of promise will be taken up. Series include showbiz, royals and television. Limited general interest fiction.

PAYMENT negotiable.

What Car?

60 Waldegrave Road, Teddington TW11 8LG
☎020 8267 5683 Fax 020 8267 5750
✉ whatcar@haynet.com
www.whatcar.com

Owner *Haymarket Motoring Publications Ltd*
Editor *Rob Aherne*
Circulation 137,411

MONTHLY. The car buyer's bible, *What Car?* concentrates on road test comparisons of new cars, news and buying advice on used cars, as well as a strong consumer section. Some scope for freelancers. No unsolicited mss.

PAYMENT negotiable.

What Hi-Fi? Sound & Vision

38–42 Hampton Road, Teddington
TW11 0JE
☎020 8943 5000 Fax 020 8267 5019
www.whathifi.com

Owner *Haymarket Magazines Ltd*
Managing Director *Kevin Costello*
Editor *Clare Newsome*
Circulation 76,000

Founded 1976. THIRTEEN ISSUES YEARLY. Features on hi-fi and home cinema. No unsolicited contributions. Prior consultation with the editor essential.

FEATURES General or more specific items on hi-fi and home cinema pertinent to the consumer electronics market.

REVIEWS Specific product reviews. All material is now generated by in-house staff. Freelance writing no longer accepted.

What Investment

Arnold House, 36–41 Holywell Lane, London
EC2A 3SF
☎020 7827 5454 Fax 020 7827 0567

Owner *Charterhouse Communications*
Editor *Sally Wright*
Circulation 37,000

Founded 1982. MONTHLY. Features articles on a variety of savings and investment matters. All approaches should be made in writing.

FEATURES Length 1200–1500 words (max. 2000).

PAYMENT NUJ rates minimum.

What Mortgage

Arnold House, 36–41 Holywell Lane, London
EC2A 3SF
☎020 7827 5454 Fax 020 7827 0567
✉ hilary.osborne@
  charterhouse-communications.co.uk
www.whatmortgageonline.co.uk

Owner *Charterhouse Communications*
Editor *Hilary Osborne*

Founded 1982. MONTHLY magazine on property purchase and finance. No unsolicited material; prospective contributors may make initial contact with ideas either by telephone or in writing.

FEATURES Up to 1500 words on related topics are considered. Particularly welcome are new angles, ideas or specialities relevant to mortgages.

PAYMENT £200 per 1000 words.

What Satellite and Digital TV

Highbury – WV, 53–79 Highgate Road,
London NW5 1TW
☎020 7331 1000 Fax 020 7331 1241
✉ wotsat@wvip.co.uk
www.wotsat.com

Owner *Highbury – WV*
Editor *Alex Lane*
Circulation 65,000

Founded 1986. MONTHLY including news, technical information, equipment tests, programme background, listings. Contributions welcome – phone first.

FEATURES *Alex Lane* Unusual installations and users. In-depth guides to popular/cult shows. Technical tutorials.

NEWS *Alex Lane* Industry and programming. Max. 250 words.

What's New in Building

Ludgate House, 245 Blackfriars Road, London
SE1 9UY
☎020 7921 8228 Fax 020 7921 8247
✉ mpennington@cmpinformation.com

Owner *CMP Information*
Editor *Mark Pennington*
Circulation 29,000

MONTHLY. Specialist magazine covering new products for building. Unsolicited mss not generally welcome. The only freelance work available is rewriting press release material. This is offered on a monthly basis of 25–50

items of about 150 words each. PAYMENT
£5.25 per item.

What's On in London
180–182 Pentonville Road, London N1 9JP
☎020 7278 4393 Fax 020 7837 5838
✉ rfoss@whatsoninlondon.co.uk
www.whatsoninlondon.co.uk

Owner *S.D. Shaw*
Editor *Michael Darvell*
Circulation 40,000

Founded 1935. WEEKLY entertainment-based
guide and information magazine. Features, listings and reviews. Always interested in well-
thought-out and well-presented mss. Articles
should have London/Home Counties connection, except during the summer when they can
be of much wider tourist/historic interest, relating to unusual traditions and events. Approach
the editor by telephone in the first instance.
    FEATURES *Graham Hassell*
    ART *Fisun Güner*
    CINEMA *Jim Healy*
    POP MUSIC *John Coleman*
    CLASSICAL MUSIC *Michael Darvell*
    THEATRE *Oliver Jones*
    EVENTS *Adam Lay*
    PAYMENT by arrangement.

Wild Times
RSPB, The Lodge, Sandy SG19 2DL
☎01767 680551 Fax 01767 683262
✉ derek.niemann@rspb.org.uk

Owner *Royal Society for the Protection of Birds*
Editor *Derek Niemann*

Founded 1965. BI-MONTHLY. Bird, wildlife and
nature conservation for under 8-year-olds
(RSPB Wildlife Explorer members). No unsolicited mss. No 'captive/animal welfare' articles.
    FEATURES Unsolicited material rarely used.
    NEWS News releases welcome. Approach in
writing in the first instance.

Wine Magazine
Quest Magazines Ltd., 6–14 Underwood
Street, London N1 7JQ
☎020 7549 2572 Fax 020 7549 2550
✉ wine@wilmington.co.uk
www.wineint.com

Owner *Wilmington Publishing*
Editor *Catharine Lowe*
Circulation 35,000

Founded 1983. MONTHLY. No unsolicited mss.
    NEWS/FEATURES Wine, spirits, cigars, food
and food/wine-related travel stories. Prospective contributors should approach in writing.

Wingbeat
RSPB, The Lodge, Sandy SG19 2DL
☎01767 680551 Fax 01767 683262
✉ derek.niemann@rspb.org.uk

Owner *Royal Society for the Protection of Birds*
Editor *Derek Niemann*

Founded 1965. BI-MONTHLY. Bird, wildlife and
nature conservation for 14–18-year-olds (RSPB
Wildlife Explorer members). No unsolicited mss.
No 'captive/animal welfare' articles.
    FEATURES Unsolicited material rarely used.
    NEWS News releases welcome. Approach in
writing in the first instance.

The Wisden Cricketer
136–142 Bramley Road, London W10 6SR
☎020 7565 3000 Fax 020 7565 3090
✉ twc@wisdengroup.com

Owner *Wisden Cricketer Publishing Ltd*
Editor *John Stern*
Circulation 35,000

Founded 2003. MONTHLY. Result of a merger
between *The Cricketer International* (1921) and
Wisden Cricket Monthly (1979). Very few
uncommissioned articles are used, but would-
be contributors are not discouraged. Approach
in writing. PAYMENT varies.

Woman
IPC Media Ltd, King's Reach Tower,
Stamford Street, London SE1 9LS
☎020 7261 7023 Fax 020 7261 5997

Owner *IPC Media*
Editor *Carole Russell*
Circulation 565,393

Founded 1937. WEEKLY. Long-running, popular women's magazine which boasts a readership of over 2.5 million. No unsolicited mss.
Most work commissioned. Approach with
ideas in writing.
    FEATURES *Judy Yorke* Max. 1250 words.
    BOOKS *Sue Thomas*

Woman and Home
IPC Media Ltd., King's Reach Tower,
Stamford Street, London SE1 9LS
☎020 7261 5176 Fax 020 7261 7346

Owner *IPC Media*
Editor *Sue James*
Circulation 295,362

Founded 1926. MONTHLY. No unsolicited
mss. Prospective contributors are advised to
write with ideas, including photocopies of
other published work or details of magazines to
which they have contributed. S.a.e. essential

for return of material. Most freelance work is specially commissioned.

Woman's Own

IPC Media Ltd., King's Reach Tower, Stamford Street, London SE1 9LS
☎020 7261 5500 Fax 020 7261 5346

Owner *IPC Media*
Editor *Elsa McAlonan*
Features Editor *Jackie Hatton*
Circulation 478,687

Founded 1932. WEEKLY. Prospective contributors should contact the features editor *in writing* in the first instance before making a submission. No unsolicited fiction.

Woman's Realm

Merged with *Woman's Weekly* in 2001.

Woman's Weekly

IPC Media Ltd., King's Reach Tower, Stamford Street, London SE1 9LS
☎0870 444 5000 Fax 020 7261 6322

Owner *IPC Media*
Editor *Gilly Sinclair*
Deputy Editor *Geoffrey Palmer*
Circulation 453,153

Founded 1911. Mass-market women's WEEKLY.

FEATURES Inspiring, positive human interest stories, especially first-hand experiences, of up to 1200 words. Freelancers used regularly but only experienced magazine journalists. Synopses and ideas should be submitted in writing.

FICTION *Gaynor Davies* Short stories 1000–2500 words; serials 12,000–30,000 words. Guidelines for serials: 'a strong emotional theme with a conflict not resolved until the end'; short stories should have warmth and originality.

Women & Golf

24th Floor, IPC Media Ltd., King's Reach Tower, Stamford Street, London SE1 9LS
☎020 7261 7237 Fax 020 7261 7240
✉ women&golf@ipcmedia.com

Owner *IPC Media*
Editor *Jane Carter*
Circulation 24,000

Founded 1991. MONTHLY consumer magazine aimed at amateur lady golfers of all ability levels. Features and photography and news welcome; approach by e-mail or post.

Women's Health

Highbury – WV, 1–3 Highbury Station Road, London N1 1SE

☎020 7226 2222 Fax 020 7288 7579
✉ womenshealth@highburywv.com

Owner *Highbury House Communications*
Editor *Tracey Smith*
Circulation 100,000

FOUNDED 1998. MONTHLY lifestyle magazine with a health twist, taking an irreverant approach. Aimed at ABC1 women of 25–39. No unsolicited mss. Will consider ideas for items with interesting angles on fitness and beauty plus alternative health and food. Approach in writing or by e-mail in the first instance.

Woodworker

Highbury Leisure, Berwick House, 8–10 Knoll Rise, Orpington BR6 0EL
☎01689 899207
www.getwoodworking.com

Owner *Highbury Leisure*
Editor *Mark Ramuz*
Circulation 45,000

Founded 1901. MONTHLY. Contributions welcome; approach with ideas in writing.

FEATURES Articles on woodworking with good photo support appreciated. Max. 2000 words.

Payment £150+ per 1000 words.

World Fishing

Media House, Azalea Drive, Swanley BR8 8HU
☎01322 660070 Fax 01322 616324
✉ pilar.santamaria@nexusmedia.com

Owner *Highbury Business*
Editor *Pilar Santamaria*
Circulation 5769

Founded 1952. MONTHLY. Unsolicited mss welcome; approach by phone or in writing with an idea.

NEWS/FEATURES of a technical or commercial nature relating to the commercial fishing and fish processing industries worldwide (the magazine is read in 126 different countries). Max. 1500 words.

PAYMENT by arrangement.

The World of Interiors

Vogue House, Hanover Square, London W1S 1JU
☎020 7499 9080 Fax 020 7493 4013
✉ interiors@condenast.co.uk
www.worldofinteriors.co.uk

Owner *Condé Nast Publications Ltd*
Editor *Rupert Thomas*
Circulation 64,567

Founded 1981. MONTHLY. Best approach by

fax or letter with an idea, preferably with reference snaps or guidebooks.

FEATURES *Rupert Thomas* Most feature material is commissioned. 'Subjects tend to be found by us, but we are delighted to receive suggestions of interiors, archives, little-known museums, collections, etc. unpublished elsewhere, and are keen to find new writers.'

World Ski and Wintersports Guide
27a High Street, Esher KT10 9RL
☎01372 468140 Fax 01372 470675
✉ info@goodholidayideas.com

Editor *John Hill*
Circulation 65,000

Founded 2002. BI-ANNUAL destination guide for skiers and winter sports enthusiasts covering the top 100 ski and winter sports resorts. No unsolicited mss. Approach with ideas and/or synopsis in writing or by e-mail.

PAYMENT negotiable.

World Soccer
IPC Media Ltd., King's Reach Tower, Stamford Street, London SE1 9LS
☎020 7261 5737 Fax 020 7261 7474
✉ world_soccer@ipcmedia.com
www.worldsoccer.com

Owner *IPC Media*
Editor *Gavin Hamilton*
Circulation 55,299

Founded 1960. MONTHLY. Unsolicited material welcome but initial approach by e-mail or in writing. News and features on world soccer.

Writers' Forum incorporating
World Wide Writers
PO Box 3229, Bournemouth BH1 1ZS
☎01202 589828 Fax 01202 587757
✉ editorial@writers-forum-com
www.worldwidewriters.com

Owner *Writers International Ltd*
Editor *John Jenkins*
Deputy Editor *Mary Hogarth*

Founded 1993. ELEVEN ISSUES YEARLY. Magazine covers all aspects of the craft of writing. Well written articles welcome. Write to the editor in the first instance.

Writers Forum Short Story Competition Prizes range from £150–250 with an annual trophy and a cheque for £1000 for the best story of the year. Entrance fee: non-subscribers – £10; subscribers – £6. Winners published in every issue.

Writers' Forum Poetry Competition First prize £100, runners up £25. Entrance fee – £5 for one poem or £7 for two. Winners published in every issue. Annual subscription: £30 UK; £44 Worldwide. Send s.a.e. with 66p in stamps for free back issue.

Writers' News/Writing Magazine
First Floor, Victoria House, 143-144 The Headrow, Leeds LS1 5RL
☎0113 200 2929 Fax 0113 200 2928
www.writersnews.co.uk

Owner *Warners Group Publications plc*
Editor *Derek Hudson*

Founded 1989. MONTHLY/BI-MONTHLY magazines containing news and advice for writers. *Writers' News* is exclusive to mail-order members who also receive *Writing Magazine*, a full-colour glossy publication, which is available on newsstands. No poetry or general items on 'how to become a writer'. Receive 1000 mss each year. Approach in writing or by e-mail.

NEWS Exclusive news stories of interest to writers. Max. 350 words.

FEATURES How-to articles of interest to professional writers. Max. 1500 words.

www.50connect.co.uk
See under *Electronic Publishing and Other Services*

Yachting Monthly
IPC Media Ltd., King's Reach Tower, Stamford Street, London SE1 9LS
☎020 7261 6040 Fax 020 7261 7555
✉ paul_gelder@ipcmedia.com
www.yachtingmonthly.com

Owner *IPC Media*
Editor *Paul Gelder*
Circulation 37,001

Founded 1906. MONTHLY magazine for yachting and cruising enthusiasts – not racing. Unsolicited mss welcome, but many are received and not used. Prospective contributors should make initial contact in writing.

FEATURES A wide range of features concerned with maritime subjects and cruising under sail; well-researched and innovative material always welcome, especially if accompanied by colour transparencies. Max. 2250 words.

PAYMENT £80–110 per 1000 words.

Yachting World
IPC Media Ltd., King's Reach Tower, Stamford Street, London SE1 9LS
☎020 7261 6800 Fax 020 7261 6818

✉ yachting_world@ipcmedia.com
www.yachtingworld.com
Owner *IPC Media*
Editor *Andrew Bray*
Circulation 30,667

Founded 1894. MONTHLY with international coverage of yacht racing, cruising and yachting events. Will consider well researched and written sailing stories. Preliminary approaches should be by phone for news stories and in writing for features.
PAYMENT by arrangement.

Yorkshire Women's Life Magazine

PO Box 113, Leeds LS8 2WX
☎0113 262 1409
✉ Ywlmagenquiries@btinternet.com
Editor/Owner *Dawn Maria France*
Assistant Editor *Imogen Brown*
Fashion *Sky Taylor*
Magazine PA *Anna Jenkins*
Diary *Giles Smith*

Founded 2001. THREE ISSUES YEARLY. Features of interest to women along with regional, national, international news and lifestyle articles. Past issues have covered anorexia nervosa, mental health, stress management, children in US chain gangs, women living in pain, Windrush awards. 'It is important to study the style of the magazine before submitting material. Send A4 s.a.e. with 42p stamp for copy of submission guidelines. Unsolicited mss and new writers actively encouraged; approach in writing in the first instance with s.a.e. *No* phone calls.'

You & Your Wedding

National Magazine Company, 72 Broadwick Street, London W1F 9EP
☎020 7439 5000 (editorial)
Fax 020 7439 2985
Owner *The National Magazine Company Ltd*
Editor *To be appointed*
Circulation 62,145

Founded 1985. BI-MONTHLY. Anything relating to weddings, setting up home, and honeymoons. No unsolicited mss. Ideas may be submitted in writing only, especially travel features. No phone calls.

You – The Mail on Sunday Magazine

See **The Mail on Sunday** under *National Newspapers*

Young Voices

Voice Group Limited, Blue Star House, 234–244 Stockwell Road, London SW9 9UG
☎020 7737 7377   Fax 020 7274 8894
www.young-voices.co.uk
Managing Director *Linda McCalla*
Group Editor *Deidre Forbes*
Editor *Emelia Kenlock*

Founded 2003. MONTHLY glossy magazine aimed at 11–19-year-olds. 'Provides a new outlet for today's youth.' Latest news features, showbiz insight and reviews. Also covers current affairs topics that affect readers' lives.

Young Writer

Glebe House, Weobley, Hereford HR4 8SD
☎01544 318901   Fax 01544 318901
✉ editor@youngwriter.org
www.youngwriter.org
Editor *Kate Jones*

Describing itself as 'The Magazine for Children with Something to Say', *Young Writer* is issued three times a year, at the back-to-school times of September, January and April. A forum for young people's writing – fiction and non-fiction, prose and poetry – the magazine is an introduction to independent writing for young writers aged 5–18. PAYMENT from £20 to £100 for freelance commissioned articles (these can be from adult writers).

Your Cat Magazine

Roebuck House, 33 Broad Street, Stamford PE9 1RB
☎01780 766199   Fax 01780 766416
✉ yourcat@bournepublishinggroup.co.uk
www.yourcat.co.uk
Owner *BPG (Stamford) Ltd*
Editor *Sue Parslow*

Founded 1994. MONTHLY magazine giving practical information on the care of cats and kittens, pedigree and non-pedigree, plus a wide range of general interest items on cats. Will consider 'true life' cat stories (max. 900 words) and quality fiction. Send synopsis in the first instance. 'No articles written as though by a cat.'

Your Dog Magazine

Roebuck House, 33 Broad Street, Stamford PE9 1RB
☎01780 766199   Fax 01780 766416
Owner *BPG (Stamford) Ltd*
Editor *Sarah Wright*
Circulation 26,000

Founded 1995. MONTHLY. Practical advice for

pet dog owners. Will consider practical features and some personal experiences (no highly emotive pieces or fiction). Telephone in the first instance.

NEWS Max. 300–400 words.

FEATURES Max. 2500 words; limited opportunities.

PAYMENT negotiable.

Your Horse

Bretton Court, Bretton, Peterborough PE3 8DZ

☎01733 264666 Fax 01733 465200

Owner *Emap Active Ltd*
Editor *Natasha Simmonds*
Circulation 56,507

For people who live, breath and have fun around horses. Most writing produced in-house but well-targeted articles will always be considered.

Yours Magazine

Emap Esprit, Bretton Court, Bretton, Peterborough PE3 8DZ

☎01733 264666 Fax 01733 465266

Owner *Emap Esprit*
Editor *Valery McConnell*
Circulation 403,696

Founded 1973. MONTHLY plus four seasonal specials. Aimed at a readership aged 55 and over.

FEATURES Unsolicited mss welcome but must enclose s.a.e. Max. 1500 words.

NEWS Short, newsy items of interest to readership welcome. Length 300–500 words.

FICTION One or two short stories used in each issue. Max. 1500 words.

PAYMENT negotiable.

Zembla Magazine

61a Ledbury Road, London W11 2AL

☎020 7221 8878

✉ mail@zemblamagazine.com

www.zemblamagazine.com

Owners *Simon Finch, Dan Crowe*
Editor *Dan Crowe*
Circulation 30,000

Founded 2003. BI-MONTHLY literary magazine featuring fiction, non-fiction, reviews, interviews and 'all sorts of fun with words'. Welcomes fiction and non-fiction ideas; no review material. Approach by e-mail in the first instance.

Zest

National Magazine House, 72 Broadwick Street, London W1F 9EP

☎020 7439 5000 Fax 020 7312 3750

✉ zest.mail@natmags.co.uk

www.zest.co.uk

Owner *National Magazine Company*
Editor *Alison Pylkkanen*
Deputy Editor *Rebecca Frank*
Circulation 105,058

Founded 1994. MONTHLY. Health, beauty, fitness, nutrition and general well-being. No unsolicited mss. Prefers ideas in synopsis form; approach in writing.

News Agencies

Associated Press Limited
12 Norwich Street, London EC4A 1BP
☎020 7353 1515
Fax 020 7353 8118 (Newsdesk)

Material is either generated in-house or by regulars. Hires the occasional stringer. No unsolicited mss.

Dow Jones Newswires
10 Fleet Place, London EC4M 7QN
☎020 7842 9900 Fax 020 7842 9361

A real-time financial and business newswire operated by Dow Jones & Co., publishers of *The Wall Street Journal*. No unsolicited material.

Hayters Teamwork Sports Agency
6 Sharman Walk, Apperknowle, Sheffield S18 4BJ
☎01246 414767/07970 284848 (mobile)
Fax 01246 414767
✉ Nicksport1@aol.com

Contact *Nick Johnson*

Provides written/broadcast coverage of sport in the South Yorkshire area.

National News Press and Photo Agency
4–5 Academy Buildings, Fanshaw Street, London N1 5LQ
☎020 7684 3000 Fax 020 7684 3030
✉ news@nationalnews.co.uk

All press releases are welcome. Most work is ordered or commissioned. Coverage includes courts, tribunals, conferences, general news, etc. – words and pictures – as well as PR.

Press Association Ltd
292 Vauxhall Bridge Road, London SW1V 1AE
☎020 7963 7000/7830 (Newsdesk)

Fax 020 7963 7192 (Newsdesk)
✉ copy@pa.press.net
www.pa.press.net

No unsolicited material. Most items are produced in-house though occasional outsiders may be used. A phone call to discuss specific material may lead somewhere 'but this is rare'.

Reuters
85 Fleet Street, London EC4P 4AJ
☎020 7250 1122

No unsolicited material.

Solo Syndication Ltd
17–18 Hayward's Place, London EC1R 0EQ
☎020 7566 0360 Fax 020 7566 0388
✉ tyork@atlanticsyndication.com
www.atlanticsyndication.com

Founded 1978. Specialises in worldwide newspaper syndication of photos, features and cartoons. Professional contributors only.

Space Press News and Pictures
Bridge House, Blackden Lane, Goostrey CW4 8PZ
☎01477 533403 Fax 01477 535756
✉ Scoop2001@aol.com

Editor *John Williams*
Pictures *Emma Williams*

Founded 1972. Press and picture agency covering Cheshire and the North West, North Midlands, including Knutsford, Macclesfield, Congleton, Crewe and Nantwich, Wilmslow, Alderley Edge, serving national, regional and local press, TV, radio, and digital picture transmission. Copy and pictures produced for in-house publications and PR. Property, countryside and travel writing. A member of the National Association of Press Agencies (NAPA).

Television and Radio

For the latest information on broadcast rates for freelancers access the following websites: the National Union of Journalists' 'The Rate for the Job': www.gn.apc.org/media; the Producers Alliance for Cinema and Television: www.pact.co.uk; the Society of Authors: www.societyofauthors.org; and the Writers' Guild: www.writersguild.org.uk

BBC TV and Radio

www.bbc.co.uk
For details of TV and radio commissioning log on to www.bbc. co.uk/commissioning/

The structure of the BBC includes the following divisions: Television Division - responsible for the network television channels and for commissioning in most genres; Drama, Entertainment and Children's; Factual and Learning; Radio and Music; News; Sport; Nations and Regions; and the New Media division which develops the BBC's interactive television and online activities.

TELEVISION
BBC Television Centre, Wood Lane, London W12 7RJ
☎020 8743 8000

Director, Television *Jana Bennett*
Controller, BBC One *Lorraine Heggessey*
Controller, BBC Two *Roly Keating*
Controller, Daytime *Alison Sharman*

DIGITAL TELEVISION
Controller, BBC Three *Stuart Murphy*
Controller, BBC Four *To be appointed*

BBC Three was launched February 2003, replacing BBC Choice. Broadcasts a wide range of entertainment aimed at a 25–34-year-old audience. BBC Four, launched in March 2002, is devoted solely to the arts. Programmes include *Readers and Writers*, a weekly book programme.

RADIO
Broadcasting House, Portland Place, London W1A 1AA
☎020 7580 4468

Director of Radio & Music *Jenny Abramsky*
Controller, Radio 1 *Andy Parfitt*
Executive Producer, Radio 1 *Maria Williams*
Controller, Radio 2 *Lesley Douglas*
Commissions & Schedules Manager, Radio 2 *Julian Grundy*
Controller, Radio 3 *Roger Wright*

Commissions & Schedules Manager, Radio 3 *David Ireland*
Controller, Radio 4 *Helen Boaden*

Proposals for Radio 4 must be submitted through an in-house department or a registered independent company. For a list of these log on to www.bbc.co.uk/commissioning/structure/process_radio.shtml

Controller, Radio Five Live *Bob Shennan*
Commissioning Editor, Radio 5 Live *Moz Dee*

DIGITAL RADIO
BBC 1Xtra
BBC Five Live Sports Extra
BBC 6 Music
BBC 7 (comedy, drama and books)
BBC Asian Network

Drama, Entertainment and Children's Division

Director *Alan Yentob*

BBC *writersroom* champions writers across all BBC platforms, running targeted schemes and workshops linked directly to production. It accepts and assesses unsolicited scripts for film, single TV dramas, comedy and radio drama. The website bbc.co.uk/writersroom offers a diary of events, opportunities, competitions, interviews with established writers, submission guidelines, free formatting software and a messageboard.

BBC *writersroom* also runs *northern exposure* which focuses on new writing in the north of England, channelled through theatres in Liverpool, Manchester, Bradford, Leeds and Newcastle. Would-be contributors should send a sample, full-length drama script to: BBC *writersroom*, 1 Mortimer Street, London W1T 3JA. For guidelines on unsolicited scripts log on to the website or send a large s.a.e. to *Jessica Dromgoole*, New Writing Coordinator, BBC Drama, Entertainment and CBBC at the Mortimer Street address above.

See also www.bbc.co.uk/commissioning

DRAMA
Controller, Drama Commissioning *Jane Tranter*
Controller, Continuing Drama Series *Mal Young*
Head of Drama Commissioning *Gareth Neame*
Head of Drama Serials *Laura Mackie*
Head of Development, Drama Series *Sarah Cullen*
Controller, Daytime Drama, Factual Entertainment & Entertainment on BBC One/Two: *Alison Sharman* (daytime.proposals@bbc.co.uk)
Head of Films *David Thompson*
Head of Development, Films *Tracey Scoffield*
Creative Director, New Writing *Kate Rowland*
Head of Radio Drama *Gordon House*
Executive Producer (Birmingham)/Editor, The Archers *Vanessa Whitburn*
Executive Producer (World Service Drama) *Marion Nancarrow*

ENTERTAINMENT
Controller, Entertainment Commissioning *Jane Lush*
Head of Comedy Entertainment, Television *Jon Plowman*
Head of Comedy Commissioning *Mark Freeland*
Producer *Bill Dare*
Head of Light Entertainment, Radio 4 *John Pidgeon*

Get Writing: www.bbc.co.uk/dna/getwriting/ – BBC Learning's new service which aims 'to help people get back into or start out in creative writing'.

Programmes produced range from *The Kumars at No 42* and *The Weakest Link* on television to *Loose Ends* and *The Now Show* on Radio 4. Virtually every comic talent in Britain got their first break writing one-liners for topical comedy weeklies.

CBBC (CHILDREN'S)
Controller, CBBC *Dorothy Prior*
Head of Production *Karen Woodward*
Head of Acquisitions *Michael Carrington*
Head of CBBC Drama *Elaine Sperber*
Head of Entertainment *Anne Gilchrist*
Head of CBBC News and Factual Programmes *Roy Milani*
Head of CBBC Pre-school *Clare Elstow*
Head of CBBC Education *Sue Nott*

Factual and Learning Division
Director, Factual TV & Learning *John Willis*
Controller, Learning & Interactive *Liz Cleaver*
Controller, Documentaries and Contemporary Factual *Anne Morrison*

Commissioner, Specialist Factual *Keith Scholey*
Controller of Children's Education *Frank Flynn*
Controller of Learning with the BBC *Paul Gehardt*
Head of Independent Commissioning, Specialist Factual (including Arts) *Adam Kemp*
Head of Lifeskills TV *Seetha Kumar*
Executive Editor, Children's Education *Karen Johnson*

News Division
www.bbc.co.uk/news
news.bbc.co.uk

BBC News is the world's largest news-gathering organisation, with 2000 journalists, 250 specialist correspondents and 40 bureaux around the world. There are four specialist units: world affairs; economics and business; politics; and social affairs. BBC News serves: BBC1, BBC2, BBC Three, BBC Four, Radios 1xtra, 1, 2, 3, 4, 5 Live, Six Music, BBC News 24, BBC Parliament, BBC World, BBC World Service, News Online, Ceefax.

Director, News *Richard Sambrook*
Deputy Director, News *Mark Damazer*
Head of Current Affairs *Peter Horrocks*
Head of Newsgathering *Adrian Van Klaveran*
Head of Interactive *Richard Deverell*
Head of Political Programmes *Fran Unsworth*
Head of Radio News *Stephen Mitchell*
Head of TV News *Roger Mosey*
Deputy Head of TV News *Rachel Attwell*

TELEVISION
Editor, 1 o'clock News *Chris Rybczynski*
Editor, 6 o'clock News *Amanda Farnsworth*
Editor, 10 o'clock News *Kevin Bakhurst*
Editor, Newsnight *George Entwhistle*
Editor, Breakfast News *Richard Porter*
Editor, Breakfast With Frost *Barney Jones*
Editor, This World *Karen O'Connor*
Editor, World Service News Programmes *Alan Le Breton*

RADIO
Editor, Today *Kevin Marsh*
Editor, The World at One/World This Weekend/PM/Broadcasting House *Richard Clark*
Head of Five Live News *Ceri Thomas*
Editor, The World Tonight *David Stevenson*

CEEFAX
Room 7540, BBC Television Centre, Wood Lane, London W12 7RJ
☎020 8576 1801

Editor, Ceefax *Paul Brannan*

SUBTITLING
Room BC3A5, Broadcast Centre, Wood
Lane, London W12 7TP
☎020 8008 0596/41 339 8844 ext. 2128
✉ subtitling@bbc.co.uk

A rapidly expanding service available via Ceefax
page 888. Units based in both London and
Glasgow.

Sport Division
Director, Sport *Peter Salmon*
Head of Football & Boxing *Niall Sloane*
Head of Interactive *Andrew Thompson*

Sports news and commentaries across television
and Radios 1, 4 and 5 Live, with the majority
of output on Radio 5 Live. Regular programmes include *Grandstand*.

BBC Religion
New Broadcasting House, Oxford Road,
Manchester M60 1SJ
☎0161 200 2020   Fax 0161 244 3183

Head of Religion and Ethics *Alan Bookbinder*

Regular programmes include: TELEVISION
Heaven & Earth; *Songs of Praise*; *A Seaside Parish*.
RADIO *Good Morning Sunday*; *Sunday Half
Hour*; *Thought for the Day*; *The Daily Service*.

BBC Talent
www.bbc.co.uk/talent

The BBC's search for new talent covers a constantly changing range of outlets that has
included TV and radio producers, presenters,
filmmakers, sitcom and comedy writers. Access
the website for latest information.

BBC World Service
PO Box 76, Bush House, Strand, London
WC2B 4PH
☎020 7240 3456   Fax 020 7557 1900
www.bbc.co.uk/worldservice

Director *To be appointed*
Director, English Networks & News,
   BBCWS *Phil Harding*

The World Service broadcasts in English and 42
other languages. The English service is round-
the-clock, with news and current affairs as the
main component. With over 150 million listeners, excluding countries where research is not
possible, it reaches a bigger audience than its five
closest competitors combined. The World
Service is increasingly available throughout the
world on local FM stations, via satellite and
online as well as through short-wave frequencies.
Coverage includes world business, politics,

people/events/opinions, development issues, the
international scene, developments in science and
technology, sport, religion, music, drama, the
arts. BBC World Service broadcasting is financed
by a grant-in-aid voted by Parliament amounting
to £220 million for 2003/2004.

BBC writersroom
See **Drama, Entertainment and Children's
Division**

BBC Regions

BBC Northern Ireland
Broadcasting House, Ormeau Avenue, Belfast
BT2 8HQ
☎028 9033 8000
www.bbc.co.uk/northernireland

Controller *Anna Carragher*
Head of Broadcasting *Peter Johnston*
Head of News & Current Affairs *Andrew
   Colman*
Editor, News Gathering *Michael Cairns*
Editor, Television News *Angelina Fusco*
Editor, Radio News *Kathleen Carragher*
Head of Drama *Patrick Spence*
Head of Programme Production *Mike Edgar*
Editor, Entertainment *Alex Johnston*
Editor, Sport *Edward Smith*
Head of Creative Development *Bruce Batten*
Head of Interactive Services & Learning
   Kieran Hegarty
Managing Editor, Radio *Susan Lovell*
Editor, TV Factual *Deirdre Devlin*
Producer, Religion *Bert Tosh*
Editor, Political Programmes *Lena Ferguson*
Managing Editor, Foyle *Ana Leddy*

Regular television programmes include *BBC
Newsline 6.30* and a wide range of documentary,
popular factual and entertainment programmes.
Radio stations: BBC Radio Foyle and BBC
Radio Ulster (see entries). For further details on
television and film scripts contact: *Susan Carson*,
Development Co-ordinator Television, BBC
Northern Ireland Drama, Room 3.07, Blackstaff
House, Great Victoria Street, Belfast, BT2 7BB.
(☎028 9033 8498 ✉ tvdrama.ni@bbc.co.uk)
Radio scripts contact: *Anne Simpson*, Manager,
Radio Drama at the same address.

BBC Scotland
Broadcasting House, Queen Margaret Drive,
Glasgow G12 8DG
☎0141 338 2000
www.bbc.co.uk/scotland

Controller *Ken MacQuarrie*
Controller, Network Development, Nations and Regions *Colin Cameron*
Head of Drama, Television *Barbara McKissack*
Head of Drama, Radio *Patrick Rayner*
Head of Comedy and Entertainment *Mike Bolland*
Head of Factual Programmes *Andrea Miller*
Head of BBC Scotland Interactive *Julie Adair*
Head of CBBC and Gaelic *Donalda MacKinnon*
Editor, Education *Moira Scott*
Head of Radio *Maggie Cunningham*
Head of News and Current Affairs *Blair Jenkins*
Head of Sport *Neil Fraser*
Commissioning Editor, Television *Ewan Angus*

Headquarters of BBC Scotland with centres in Aberdeen, Dundee, Edinburgh and Inverness. Regular and recent programmes include *Reporting Scotland*, *Sportscene* and *Monarch of the Glen* on television and *Good Morning Scotland* and *Fred Macaulay* on radio.

Aberdeen
Broadcasting House, Beechgrove Terrace, Aberdeen AB9 2ZT
☎ 01224 625233

Head of North *Andrew Jones*

News, plus some features, including the regular *Beechgrove Garden*. Second TV centre, also with regular radio broadcasting.

Dundee
Nethergate Centre, 66 Nethergate, Dundee DD1 4ER
☎01382 202481

News base only; contributors' studio.

Edinburgh
The Tun, Holyrood Road, Edinburgh EH8 8JF
☎0131 557 5677

Senior Producer, Arts & Features *Jane Fowler*

News, current affairs, arts and features.

Inverness
7 Culduthel Road, Inverness 1V2 4ADT
☎01463 720720

Editor *Ishbel MacLennan*

News features for Radio Scotland.

Radio Nan Gaidheal
Rosebank, Church Street, Stornoway, Isle of Lewis PA87 2LS
☎01851 705000

Editor *Marion MacKinnon*

The Gaelic service reaching most of Scotland.

BBC Wales

Broadcasting House, Llandaff CF5 2YQ
☎029 2032 2000 Fax 029 2055 2973
www.bbc.co.uk/wales

Controller *Menna Richards*
Head of Programmes (Welsh Language) *Keith Jones*
Head of Programmes (English Language) *Clare Hudson*
Head of News & Current Affairs *Mark O'Callaghan*
Head of Drama *Julie Gardner*
Commissioning Editor, Independents and 2W *Martyn Ingram*
Producer, Pobol y Cwm *Bethan Jones*
Editor, New Media *Iain Tweedale*

Headquarters of BBC Wales, with regional centres in Bangor, Aberystwyth, Carmarthen, Wrexham and Swansea. BBC Wales television produces up to 12 hours of English language programmes a week, 12 hours in Welsh for transmission on **S4C** and an increasing number of hours on network services. BBC2W, the digital channel, was launched in 2001. Regular programmes include *Wales Today*; *Week In Week Out*, *The Exchange*; and in Welsh *Newyddion* and *Pobol y Cwm* on television and *Good Morning Wales*; *Good Evening Wales*; *Post Cyntaf* and *Post Prynhawn* on Radio Wales and Radio Cymru. Ideas for programmes should be submitted either by post to *Martyn Ingram*, Commissioning Editor, Room 3021 at the address above or by e-mail to commissioning@bbc.co.uk

Bangor
Broadcasting House, Meirion Road, Bangor LL57 2BY
☎01248 370880 Fax 01248 351443

Head of Centre *Marian Wyn Jones*

BBC Asian Network

The Mail Box, Birmingham B1 1XM
☎0121 567 6767
✉ asian.network@bbc.co.uk
www.bbc.co.uk/asiannetwork

Managing Editor *Vijay Sharma*

Commenced broadcasting in November 1996. Broadcasts to a Midlands audience during the day and nationwide coverage in the evening. Programmes in English, Bengali, Gujerati, Hindi, Punjabi and Urdu.

BBC Birmingham

The Mail Box, Birmingham B1 1RF
☎0121 567 6767 Fax 0121 567 6875
www.bbc.co.uk/birmingham

Head of Regional and Local Programmes
David Holdsworth
Output Editor *Charles Watkin*

Output for the network includes: TELEVISION
Doctors; *Countryfile*; *Top Gear*; *Dalziel and Pascoe*;
Gardener's World; *Big Strong Boys*; *Trading Up*.
RADIO *The Archers*; *Shake, Rattle and Roll*;
Farming Today; *Late Night Currie*; *Ramblings With
Clare Balding*.

BBC East Midlands (Nottingham)
East Midlands Broadcasting Centre, London
Road, Nottingham NG2 4UU
☎0115 955 0500 Fax 0115 902 1983
Website www.bbc.co.uk/nottingham
Head of Regional Programming *Alison Ford*
Output Editor *Lisa Lambden*

BBC East (Norwich)
The Forum, Millennium Plain, Norwich
NR2 1AW
☎01603 284700 Fax 01603 284399
Website www.bbc.co.uk/norfolk
Head of Regional Programming *Tim Bishop*
Output Editor *Dave Betts*

BBC Bristol
Broadcasting House, Whiteladies Road,
Bristol BS8 2LR
☎0117 973 2211
Managing Editor *Jenny Lacey*
Head of General Factual & Learning *Tom
Archer*
Head of Natural History Unit *Neil Nightingale*

BBC Bristol is the home of the BBC's Natural
History Unit, producing programmes such as
Blue Planet; *Life of Mammals*; *Wildlife on One*; *The
Natural World* and *The Really Wild Show* for
BBC1 and BBC2. It also produces natural his-
tory programmes for Radio 4 and Radio 5 Live.
The Features department produces a wide range
of television programmes, including *DIY SOS*;
Antiques Roadshow; *Bargain Hunt* and *Life of Grime*
in addition to radio programmes specialising in
history, travel, literature and human interest fea-
tures for Radio 4.

BBC London
35 Marylebone High Street, London
W1U 4QA
☎020 7224 2424
www.bbc.co.uk/london
Executive Editor *Mike MacFarlane*
(Responsible for BBC tri-media: BBC

London News, BBC London 94.9FM and
the BBC London website)
Planning Editor *Nikki O'Donnell*

BBC North/BBC North West/ BBC North East & Cumbria
The regional centres at Leeds, Manchester and
Newcastle make their own programmes on a
bi-media approach, each centre having its own
head of regional and local programmes.

BBC North (Leeds)
Broadcasting Centre, Woodhouse Lane, Leeds
LS2 9PX
☎0113 244 1188
Head of Regional and Local Programmes
Tamsin O'Brien
Editor, Newsgathering *Jake Fowler*
Output Editor, Look North Yorkshire *Jake
Fowler*
Output Editor, Look North Yorkshire and
Lincolnshire *Roger Farrant*
Assistant News Editors, Look North *Denise
Wallace, Ned Thacker*
Political Editor, North of Westminster *Len
Tingle*
Senior Broadcast Journalist, North of
Westminster *Rod Jones*
Weeklies Editor, Close Up North *Ian
Cundall*
Producers, Close Up North *Richard Taylor,
Paul Greenan*
Multimedia Planning Editor *Kate Watkins*

BBC North West (Manchester)
New Broadcasting House, Oxford Road,
Manchester M60 1SJ
☎0161 200 2020
Head of Regional and Local Programmes
Martin Brooks
Editor, Newsgathering *Michelle Mayman*
Output Editor *Tamsin O'Brien*
Producer, Northwest Tonight *Jim Clark*
Producer, Inside Out *Deborah van Bishop*
Producer, The Politics Show *Liam Fogarty*

BBC North East & Cumbria (Newcastle upon Tyne)
Broadcasting Centre, Barrack Road, Newcastle
Upon Tyne NE99 2NE
☎0191 232 1313
Head of Regional and Local Programmes
Wendy Pilmer
Editor, Newsgathering *Andrew Lambert*
Output Editor, Look North *Andy Cooper*

BBC South East (Tunbridge Wells)

The Great Hall, Mount Pleasant, Tunbridge
Wells TN1 1QQ
☎01892 670000

Head of Regional and Local Programmes *Leo
Devine* (Responsible for BBC South East
[TV], BBC Radio Kent and BBC Southern
Counties Radio)
Editor, South East Today *Quentin Smith*
Editor, Southern Counties Radio *Mike Hapgood*
Editor, Radio Kent *Robert Wallace*
Editor, Newsgathering *Talya Robertson*
Producer, Inside Out *Linda Bell*

BBC West/BBC South/ BBC South West

The three regional television stations, BBC
West, BBC South and BBC South West produce the nightly news magazine programmes,
as well as regular 30-minute local current affairs
programmes and parliamentary programmes.
Each of the regions operates a comprehensive
local radio service as well as a range of correspondents specialising in subjects like health,
education, business, local government, home
affairs and the environment.

BBC West (Bristol)

Broadcasting House, Whiteladies Road, Bristol
BS8 2LR
☎0117 973 2211

Head of Regional and Local Programmes
Andrew Wilson (Responsible for the BBC
West region, BBC Points West (evening TV
news programme), Inside Out (documentary
series), BBC Radio Bristol, BBC Somerset
Sound, BBC Radio Gloucestershire, BBC
Wiltshire, BBC Radio Swindon and the
BBC Where I Live website)
Output Editors *Jane Kinghorn, Stephanie
Marshall*
Series Producer, Inside Out *To be appointed*

BBC South (Southampton)

Broadcasting House, Havelock Road,
Southampton SO14 7PU
☎023 8022 6201

Head of Regional and Local Programmes *Eve
Turner* (Responsible for BBC South TV,
BBC Radio Berkshire, BBC Radio Oxford,
BBC Radio Solent and BBCi Southampton)
Output Editor, BBC South Today *Lee Desty*
Newsgathering Editor *Cathy Burnett*
Series Producer, Inside Out *Jane French*

BBC South West (Plymouth)

Broadcasting House, Seymour Road,
Mannamead, Plymouth PL3 5BD
☎01752 229201

Acting Head of Regional and Local
Programmes *John Lilley* (Responsible for the
BBC South West region, BBC Spotlight
(evening TV news programme), Inside Out
(documentary series), BBC Radio Devon,
BBC Radio Cornwall, BBC Radio
Guernsey, BBC Radio Jersey and the BBC
Where I Live website)
Output Editor *David Farwig*
Series Producer *Simon Willis*

BBC Local Radio

Room 2661, Broadcasting House, London
W1A 1AA
☎020 7580 4468

There are 40 local BBC radio stations in England
transmitting on FM and medium wave. These
present local news, information and entertainment to local audiences and reflect the life of the
communities they serve. Each has its own news-
room which supplies local bulletins and national
news service. Many have specialist producers. A
comprehensive list of programmes for each is
unavailable and would soon be out of date. For
general information on programming, contact
the relevant station direct.

BBC Radio Berkshire

PO Box 104.4, Reading RG4 8FH
☎0118 9464200   Fax 0118 9464555
www.bbc.co.uk/berkshire
Editor *Marianne Bell*

BBC Radio Bristol

PO Box 194, Bristol BS99 7QT
☎0117 974 1111   Fax 0117 923 8323
✉ radio.bristol@bbc.co.uk
www.bbc.co.uk/england/radiobristol
Managing Editor *Jenny Lacey*
Wide range of feature material used.

BBC Radio Cambridgeshire

104 Hills Road, Cambridge CB2 1LD
☎01223 259696   Fax 01223 589870
✉ cambs@bbc.co.uk
www.bbc.co.uk/radiocambridgeshire
Editor *David Martin*

Commenced broadcasting in May 1982. Short
stories are broadcast occasionally.

BBC Radio Cleveland

PO Box 95FM, Broadcasting House,
Newport Road, Middlesbrough TS1 5DG
☎01642 225211 Fax 01642 211356
✉ bbcradiocleveland@bbc.co.uk
www.bbc.co.uk/england/radiocleveland

Managing Editor *Andrew Glover*

Material used is mainly local to Teesside, Co.
Durham and North Yorkshire, and is almost
exclusively news and current affairs.

BBC Radio Cornwall

Phoenix Wharf, Truro TR1 1UA
☎01872 275421 Fax 01872 240679
✉ radio.cornwall@bbc.co.uk
www.bbc.co.uk/radiocornwall

Editor *Pauline Causey*

On air from 1983 serving Cornwall and the Isles
of Scilly. Broadcasts 117 hours of local programmes weekly including news, phone-ins and
specialist music. Martin Bailie's afternoon programme includes interviews with local authors
and arts-related features on Cornish themes.

BBC Radio Cumbria

Annetwell Street, Carlisle CA3 8BB
☎01228 592444 Fax 01228 511195
✉ cumbria@bbc.co.uk
www.bbc.co.uk/cumbria

Editor *Nigel Dyson*

Occasional opportunities for plays and short
stories are advertised on-air.

BBC Radio Cymru

Broadcasting House, Llandaff, Cardiff
CF5 2YQ
☎029 20 322018 Fax 029 20 322473
✉ radio.cymru@bbc.co.uk
www.bbc.co.uk/radiocymru

Editor *Aled Glynne Davies*

Welsh language station serving Welsh speaking
communities. Rich mix of news, music, sport,
features, current affairs, drama, comedy, religion and education. Writing Opportunities:
DRAMA Daily 10 minute soap *Eileen* and over
nine further hours of new radio drama each
year. COMEDY Occasional series during the
year (for details of independent commissions
see www.bbc.co.uk/wales/commissioning/).

BBC Radio Derby

PO Box 104.5, Derby DE1 3HL
☎01332 361111 Fax 01332 290794
✉ radio.derby@bbc.co.uk

www.bbc.co.uk/derby

Editor *Simon Cornes*

News, sport, information and entertainment.

BBC Radio Devon

PO Box 1034, Broadcasting House, Seymour
Road, Mannamead, Plymouth PL3 5YQ
☎01752 260323 Fax 01752 234599
✉ radio.devon@bbc.co.uk
www.bbc.co.uk/devon

Also at: Walnut Gardens, St David's Hill,
Exeter EX4 4DB
☎01392 215651 Fax 01392 425570

Managing Editor *John Lilley*
Head of Programmes *Ian Timms*
Head of News *Sarah Solftley*

On air since 1983.

BBC Essex

PO Box 765, Chelmsford CM2 9XB
☎01245 616000 Fax 01245 492983
✉ essex@bbc.co.uk
www.bbc.co.uk/essex

Managing Editor *Margaret Hyde*

Broadcasts local and regional programmes for
20 hours every day aimed at a mature audience.
Programmes are a mix of news, interviews,
expert contributors, phone-ins, sport and special interest such as gardening.

BBC Radio Foyle

8 Northland Road, Londonderry
BT48 7GD
☎028 7137 8600 Fax 028 7137 8666
www.bbc.co.uk/northernireland

Managing Editor *Ana Leddy*
News Producer *Paul McFadden*
Arts/Book Reviews *Colum Arbuckle*
Features *Michael Bradley*

Radio Foyle broadcasts about seven hours of
original material a day, seven days a week to
the north west of Northern Ireland. Other programmes are transmitted simultaneously with
Radio Ulster. The output ranges from news,
sport, and current affairs to live music recordings and arts reviews.

BBC Radio Gloucestershire

London Road, Gloucester GL1 1SW
☎01452 308585 Fax 01452 309491
✉ radio.gloucestershire@bbc.co.uk
www.bbc.co.uk/radiogloucestershire

Managing Editor *Mark Hurrell*

News and information covering the large variety

of interests and concerns in Gloucestershire. Leisure, sport and music, plus African Caribbean and Asian interests. Regular book reviews and interviews with local authors in the *Trish Campbell Show.*

BBC GLR
See **BBC London 94.9FM**

BBC GMR
PO Box 951, Oxford Road, Manchester M60 1SD
☎0161 200 2000 Fax 0161 228 6110
✉ gmr@bbc.co.uk
www.bbc.co.uk/gmr

Managing Editor *Mike Bristow*
News Editor *Mark Elliot*

On air from 1970 as Radio Manchester, becoming BBC GMR in 1988. One of the largest of the BBC local radio stations, broadcasting news, current affairs, phone-ins, help, advice and sport.

BBC Radio Guernsey
Broadcasting House, Bulwer Avenue, St Sampson's, Guernsey GY2 4LA
☎01481 200600 Fax 01481 200361
✉ radio.guernsey@bbc.co.uk
www.bbc.co.uk/radioguernsey
Managing Editor *Rod Holmes*

Opened with its sister station, BBC Radio Jersey, in March 1982. Broadcasts 80 hours of local programming a week.

BBC Hereford & Worcester
Hylton Road, Worcester WR2 5WW
☎01905 748485 Fax 01905 748006
✉ bbchw@bbc.co.uk
www.bbc.co.uk/herefordworcester
Also at: 43 Broad Street, Hereford HR4 9HH
☎01432 355252 Fax 01432 356446
Managing Editor *James Coghill*

Has an interest in writers/writing with local connections

BBC Radio Humberside
9 Chapel Street, Hull HU1 3NU
☎01482 323232 Fax 01482 621403
✉ radio.humberside@bbc.co.uk
www.bbc.co.uk/radiohumberside
Executive Editor *Helen Thomas*

On air since 1971. Occasionally broadcasts short stories by local writers and holds competitions for local amateur authors and playwrights.

BBC Radio Jersey
18 Parade Road, St Helier, Jersey JE2 3PL
☎01534 870000 Fax 01534 732569
✉ jersey@bbc.co.uk
www.bbc.co.uk/radiojersey
Managing Editor *Denzil Dudley*
Assistant Editor *Matthew Price*

Local news, current affairs and community items.

BBC Radio Kent
The Great Hall, Mount Pleasant Road, Tunbridge Wells TN1 1QQ
☎01892 670000 Fax 01892 549118
✉ radio.kent@bbc.co.uk
www.bbc.co.uk/radiokent
Managing Editor *Robert Wallace*

Occasional commissions are made for local interest documentaries and other one-off programmes.

BBC Radio Lancashire
20–26 Darwen Street, Blackburn BB2 2EA
☎01254 262411 Fax 01254 680821
✉ radio.lancashire@bbc.co.uk
www.bbc.co.uk/radiolancashire
Editor *John Clayton*

Journalism-based radio station, interested in interviews with local writers. Contact *Alison Brown*, Daily Programmes Producer, Monday to Friday (alison.brown@bbc.co.uk).

BBC Radio Leeds
Broadcasting Centre, Woodhouse Lane, Leeds LS2 9PN
☎0113 224 7300 Fax 0113 242 0652
✉ radio.leeds@bbc.co.uk
www.bbc.co.uk/radioleeds
Managing Editor *John Ryan*

One of the country's biggest local radio stations, BBC Radio Leeds was also one of the first, coming on air in the 1960s as something of an experimental venture. The station is 'all talk', with a comprehensive news, sport and information service as the backbone of its daily output. BBC Radio Leeds has been a regular finalist for the title of Sony Regional Station of the Year. Has also won two Gold Sonys for best presentation.

BBC Radio Leicester
Epic House, Charles Street, Leicester LE1 3SH
☎0116 251 6688 Fax 0116 251 1463
✉ radioleicester@bbc.co.uk
www.bbc.co.uk/radioleicester
Managing Editor *Kate Squire*

The first local station in Britain. Occasional interviews with local authors. (Moving to new premises in 2004; address not confirmed at time of writing.)

BBC Radio Lincolnshire

PO Box 219, Newport, Lincoln LN1 3XY
☎01522 511411   Fax 01522 511058
✉ radio.lincolnshire@bbc.co.uk
www.bbc.co.uk/radiolincolnshire

Managing Editor *Charlie Partridge*

Unsolicited material considered only if locally relevant. Maximum 1000 words: straight narrative preferred, ideally with a topical content.

BBC London 94.9FM

PO Box 94.9, 35 Marylebone High Street, London W1A 6FL
☎020 7224 2424   Fax 020 7208 9661
✉ yourlondon@bbc.co.uk
www.bbc.co.uk/londonlive

Editor *David Robey*

Formerly Greater London Radio (GLR), launched in 1988. Broadcasts news, information, travel bulletins, sport and music to Greater London and the Home Counties. Dotun Adebayo's *Word for Word* explores and celebrates poetry, the spoken word and song lyrics every Sunday between 5.00 pm and 7.00 pm.

BBC Radio Manchester

See **BBC GMR**

BBC Radio Merseyside

55 Paradise Street, Liverpool L1 3BP
☎0151 708 5500   Fax 0151 794 0988
✉ radio.merseyside@bbc.co.uk
www.bbc.co.uk/radiomerseyside
www.bbc.co.uk/liverpool

Editor *Mick Ord*

First Friday – a monthly poetry slot between 1.30 pm and 2.00 pm on the first Friday of every month in the Roger Phillips lunchtime programme. Merseyside writers can offer poetry by e-mailing roger.phillips@bbc.co.uk or send copies with name/address attached, to 'First Friday Poetry', c/o BBC Radio Merseyside at the address above. Only the poets used will be acknowledged and contacted.

BBC Radio Newcastle

Broadcasting Centre, Barrack Road, Newcastle upon Tyne NE99 1RN
☎0191 232 4141
✉ radio.newcastle@bbc.co.uk

www.bbc.co.uk/tyne
www.bbc.co.uk/wear

Editor *Sarah Drummond*
Senior Producer (Programmes) *Sarah Miller*

Commenced broadcasting in January 1971. One of the BBC's big city radio stations in England, it reaches an audience of 233,000.

BBC Radio Norfolk

Norfolk Tower, Surrey Street, Norwich NR1 3PA
☎01603 617411   Fax 01603 633692
✉ radionorfolk@bbc.co.uk
www.bbc.co.uk/radionorfolk

Editor *David Clayton*

Good ideas and material welcome for features/documentaries *if* directly related to Norfolk.

BBC Radio Northampton

Broadcasting House, Abington Street, Northampton NN1 2BH
☎01604 239100   Fax 01604 230709
✉ radionorthampton@bbc.co.uk
www.bbc.co.uk/radionorthampton

Managing Editor *Laura Moss*

Books of local interest are regularly featured. Authors and poets are interviewed on merit. Poems and short stories are reviewed occasionally, but not broadcast. Runs occasional competitions for local writers.

BBC Radio Nottingham

London Road, Nottingham NG2 4UU
☎0115 955 0500   Fax 0115 902 1983
✉ radio.nottingham@bbc.co.uk
www.bbc.co.uk/radionottingham

Editor *Mike Bettison*

Rarely broadcasts scripted pieces of any kind but interviews with authors form a regular part of the station's output.

BBC Radio Orkney

Castle Street, Kirkwall KW15 1DF
☎01856 873939   Fax 01856 872908

Senior Producer *John Fergusson*

Regular programmes include *Around Orkney* (weekday news programme) and *Bruck* (magazine programme).

BBC Radio Oxford

PO Box 95.2, Oxford OX2 7YL
☎08459 311444   Fax 08459 311555
✉ radio.oxford@bbc.co.uk
www.bbc.co.uk/radiooxford

Executive Editor *Steve Taschini*

Restored to its original name in 2000 having been merged with BBC Radio Berkshire in 1995 to create BBC Thames Valley. The station frequently carries interviews with local authors and offers books as prizes.

BBC Radio Scotland (Dumfries)

Elmbank, Lover's Walk, Dumfries DG1 1NZ
☎01387 268008 Fax 01387 252568
✉ dumfries@bbc.co.uk

Senior Producer *Willie Johnston*

Previously Radio Solway. The station mainly outputs news bulletins (four daily) although it has become more of a production centre with programmes being made for Radio Scotland as well as BBC Radio 2 and 5 Live. Freelancers of a high standard, familiar with Radio Scotland, should contact the producer.

BBC Radio Scotland (Selkirk)

Municipal Buildings, High Street, Selkirk
TD7 4JX
☎01750 21884 Fax 01750 22400

Senior Broadcaster *Ninian Reid*

Formerly BBC Radio Tweed. Local news bulletins.

BBC Radio Sheffield

54 Shoreham Street, Sheffield S1 4RS
☎0114 273 1177 Fax 0114 267 5454
✉ radio.sheffield@bbc.co.uk
www.bbc.co.uk/radiosheffield

Managing Editor *Gary Keown*
Programmes Editor *Angus Morat*
News Editor *Michael Woodcock*

Writer interviews, writing-related topics and readings on the Rony Robinson show at 9.00 am.

BBC Radio Shetland

Pitt Lane, Lerwick ZE1 0DW
☎01595 694747 Fax 01595 694307
✉ radio.shetland@bbc.co.uk

Senior Producer *Caroline Moyes*

Regular programmes include *Good Evening Shetland*. An occasional books programme highlights the activities of local writers and writers' groups.

BBC Radio Shropshire

2–4 Boscobel Drive, Shrewsbury SY1 3TT
☎01743 248484 Fax 01743 237018
✉ radio.shropshire@bbc.co.uk

www.bbc.co.uk/shropshire

Managing Editor *Tim Pemberton*

On air since 1985. Unsolicited literary material rarely used, and then only if locally relevant.

BBC Radio Solent

Broadcasting House, Havelock Road,
Southampton SO14 7PW
☎023 8063 2811 Fax 023 8033 9648
✉ radio.solent@bbc.co.uk
www.bbc.co.uk/radiosolent

Managing Editor *Mia Costello*

Broadcasting since 1970.

BBC Somerset Sound

Broadcasting House, Park Street, Taunton
TA1 4DA
☎01823 348920 Fax 01823 332539
✉ somerset.sound@bbc.co.uk
www.bbc.co.uk/radiobristol/somerset

Managing Editor *Jenny Lacey*
Assistant Editor *Simon Clifford*

Informal, speech-based programming with strong news and current affairs output and regular local interest features, including local writing. Poetry and short stories on the *Adam Thomas Programme*.

BBC Southern Counties Radio

Broadcasting Centre, Guildford GU2 7AP
☎01483 306306 Fax 01483 304952
✉ southern.counties.radio@bbc.co.uk
www.bbc.co.uk/southerncounties

Also at: Broadcasting House, 40–42 Queens Road, Brighton BN1 3XB

Managing Editor *Mike Hapgood*

Regular programmes include three individual breakfast shows: *Breakfast Live in Brighton with Sarah Gorrell/in Surrey with Ed Douglas/in Sussex with John Radford*.

BBC Radio Stoke

Cheapside, Hanley, Stoke on Trent
ST1 1JJ
☎01782 208080 Fax 01782 289115
✉ radio.stoke@bbc.co.uk
www.bbc.co.uk/radiostoke

Editor *Sue Owen*

On air since 1968, one of the first eight 'experimental' BBC stations. Emphasis on news, current affairs and local topics. Music represents a fifth of total output. Unsolicited material of local interest is welcome – send to *Tim Wedgwood*.

BBC Radio Suffolk
Broadcasting House, St Matthew's Street,
Ipswich IP1 3EP
☎01473 250000 Fax 01473 210887
✉ radiosuffolk@bbc.co.uk
www.bbc.co.uk/suffolk
Managing Editor *Gerald Main*

Strongly locally speech-based, dealing with
news, current affairs, community issues, the arts,
agriculture, commerce, travel, sport and leisure.
Programmes sometimes carry interviews with
writers.

BBC Radio Swindon
PO Box 1234, Swindon
☎01793 513626 Fax 01793 513650
✉ swindon@bbc.co.uk
www.bbc.co.uk/england/radioswindon
Editor *Tony Worgan*

Local news and current affairs.

BBC Thames Valley
See **BBC Radio Oxford**

BBC Three Counties Radio
1 Hastings Street, Luton LU1 5XL
☎01582 637400 Fax 01582 401467
✉ threecounties@bbc.co.uk
www.bbc.co.uk/3counties
Managing Editor *Mark Norman*

Encourages freelance contributions from the
community across a wide range of radio output, including interview and feature material.
Interested in local history topics (five minutes
maximum).

BBC Radio Ulster
Broadcasting House, Ormeau Avenue, Belfast
BT2 8HQ
☎028 9033 8000 Fax 028 9033 8805
Managing Edtor *Kathleen Carragher*

Programmes broadcast from 6.30 am to midnight weekdays and from 6.55 am to midnight
at weekends. Radio Ulster has won seven Sony
awards in recent years. Programmes include:
*Good Morning Ulster; Gerry Anderson; Talk Back;
Just Jones; Evening Extra; On Your Behalf; Your
Place and Mine* and *Across the Line.*

BBC Radio Wales
Broadcasting House, Llandaff, Cardiff CF5 2YQ
☎029 2032 2000 Fax 029 2032 2674
✉ radio.wales@bbc.co.uk
www.bbc.co.uk/radiowales
Editor *Julie Barton*

Editor, Radio Wales News *Geoff Williams*

Broadcasts news on the hour and half hour
throughout weekday daytime programmes;
hourly bulletins in the evenings and at weekends.
Programmes include *Good Morning Wales; Roy
Noble; Nicola Heywood Thomas* and *Kevin Hughes*.
Access line number: 08700 100110.

BBC Radio Wiltshire
PO Box 1234, Trowbridge & Salisbury
☎01793 513626 Fax 01793 513650
✉ radio.wiltshire@bbc.co.uk
www.bbc.co.uk/england/radiowiltshire
Editor *Tony Worgon*

Regular programmes include: Mark Seaman's
Mid-Morning Show and Graham Seaman's
Afternoon Show (reviews and author interviews).

BBC Radio WM
PO Box 206, Birmingham B5 7SD
☎08453 009956 Fax 0121 472 3174
✉ radio.wm@bbc.co.uk
www.bbc.co.uk/radiowm
Managing Editor *Keith Beech*

Commenced broadcasting in November 1970
as BBC Birmingham and has won four gold
Sony awards in recent years. Speech-based
station broadcasting to the West Midlands,
South Staffordshire, North Worcestershire and
North Warwickshire.

BBC Radio WM Coventry and Warwickshire
Holt Court, 1 Greyfriars Road, Coventry
CV1 2WR
☎024 7686 0086 Fax 024 7657 0100
✉ coventry.warwickshire@bbc.co.uk
www.bbc.co.uk/coventrywarwickshire
Managing Editor *David Clargo*

Commenced broadcasting in January 1990 as
CWR. Shares programmes with sister station,
BBC Radio WM. News, current affairs, public
service information and community involvement, relevant to its broadcast area: Coventry
and Warwickshire.

BBC Radio York
20 Bootham Row, York YO30 7BR
☎01904 641351 Fax 01904 610937
✉ northyorkshire.radio@bbc.co.uk
www.bbc.co.uk/northyorkshire
Editor *Matt Youdale*

Stories only accepted in reponse to occasional
short story competitions.

Independent Television

Anglia Television
Anglia House, Norwich NR1 3JG
☎01603 615151   Fax 01603 761245
www.angliatv.com
Managing Director *Graham Creelman*
Controller of Programmes *Neil Thompson*

Anglia Television is a major producer of programmes for the ITV network, including *Trisha* (Trisha Goddard's chat show) and major documentaries. Network drama is produced by Anglia's parent company, Granada.

Border Television plc
Television Centre, Durranhill, Carlisle
CA1 3NT
☎01228 525101   Fax 01228 541384
www.border-tv.com
Deputy Chairman *James Graham, OBE*
Controller of Programmes *Neil Robinson*

Border's programming concentrates on documentaries rather than drama. Most scripts are supplied in-house but occasionally there are commissions. Apart from notes, writers should not submit written work until their ideas have been fully discussed.

Carlton
See **ITV plc**

Central
See **ITV plc**

Channel 4
124 Horseferry Road, London SW1P 2TX
☎020 7396 4444   Fax 020 7306 8356
www.channel4.com
Director of Television *Kevin Lygo*
Head of Factual Entertainment *Julian Bellamy*
Head of Features *Sue Murphy*
Head of Specialist Factual Group *Janice Hadlow*
Head of News, Current Affairs *Dorothy Byrne*
COMMISSIONING EDITORS
Head of Drama *John Yorke*
Head of Comedy and Films *Caroline Leddy*
Head of Entertainment *Andrew Newman*
Head of Programmes, E4 & Digital
    Programming *Murray Boland*
Head of Documentaries *Peter Dale*
Head of Sport *David Kerr*
Controller of Programme Acquisition *June Dromgoole*

Channel 4 started broadcasting as a national channel in November 1982. It enjoys unique status as the world's only major public service broadcaster funded entirely by its own commercial activities. All programmes are commissioned from independent production companies and are broadcast across the whole of the UK except those parts of Wales covered by S4C. Its FilmFour channel, launched in 1998, is a premium pay-TV channel featuring modern independent cinema. A second digital channel, E4, was launched in January 2001, broadcasting a range of programmes similar to Channel 4.

Channel Television
Television Centre, La Pouquelaye, St Helier
JE1 3ZD
☎01534 816816   Fax 01534 816817
www.channeltv.co.uk
Also at: Television House, Bulwer Avenue,
St Sampsons, Guernsey GY2 4LA
☎01481 241888 Fax 01481 241878
Managing Director *Michael Lucas*
Director of Programmes *Karen Rankine*
Director of Sales *Don Miller*
Director of Resources & Transmission *Kevin Banner*

Channel Television is the independent television broadcaster to the Channel Islands, serving 143,000 residents, most of whom live on the main islands, Jersey, Guernsey, Alderney and Sark. The station has a weekly reach of more than 94% with local programmes (in the region of five and a half hours each week) at the heart of the ITV service to the islands.

Five
22 Long Acre WC2E 9LY
☎020 7550 5555   Fax 020 7550 5554
www.five.tv
CEO *Jane Lighting*
Director of Programmes *Dan Chambers*
Controller of Children's and Religious
    Programmes *Nick Wilson*
Senior Programme Controller *Chris Shaw*
Controller of Drama Programmes *Corinne Hollingworth*

Channel 5 Broadcasting Ltd won the franchise for Britain's third commercial terrestrial television station in 1995 and came on air at the end of March 1997. Regular programmes include *Family Affairs* (Monday to Friday soap opera) and *The Wright Stuff* (weekday morning chat show), plus documentaries, drama, films, children's programmes, sport and entertainment.

GMTV

The London Television Centre, Upper Ground, London SE1 9TT
☎020 7827 7000 Fax 020 7827 7249
✉ talk2us@gmtv.co.uk
www.gmtv.co.uk
Managing Director *Paul Corley*
Director of Programmes *Peter McHugh*
Managing Editor *John Scammell*
Editor *Martin Frizell*

Winner of the national breakfast television franchise. Jointly owned by Scottish Media Group, Carlton Communications, Walt Disney Company and Granada Group. GMTV took over from TV-AM on 1 January 1993, with live programming from 6.00 am to 9.25 am. Regular news headlines, current affairs, topical features, showbiz and lifestyle, sports and business, quizzes and competitions, travel and weather reports. Launched its digital service, GMTV2, in January 1999, with daily broadcasts from 6.00 am to 9.25 am. News reports, travel, health and lifestyle features, some simulcast with GMTV1. Children's programming on Saturdays.

Grampian TV

Craigshaw Business Park, West Tullos, Aberdeen AB12 3QH
☎01224 848848 Fax 01224 848800
www.grampiantv.co.uk
Managing Director *Derrick Thomson*
Head of News and Current Affairs *Henry Eagles*

Extensive regional news and reports including farming, fishing and sports, interviews and leisure features, various light entertainment, Gaelic and religious programmes, and live coverage of the Scottish political, economic and industrial scene. Serves the area stretching from Fife to Shetland. Regular programmes include *North Tonight*; *Cop College* and other varied genre shows strongly reflecting the regionality of the north of Scotland.

Granada

Quay Street, Manchester M60 9EA
☎0161 832 7211 Fax 0161 827 2180
www.granadamedia.com
Director of Programmes *John Whiston*
Director of Production *Claire Poyser*
Controller of Regional Programmes *Kieron Collins*
Controller of Drama *Carolyn Reynolds*
Controller of Current Affairs and Features *Jeff Anderson*
Controller of Documentaries, History and Science *Bill Jones*

Mss from professional writers will be considered. All mss should be addressed to the relevant departmental controller. Regular programmes include *Coronation Street* and *Tonight*.

HTV

See **ITV plc**

ITN (Independent Television News Ltd)

200 Gray's Inn Road, London WC1X 8XZ
☎020 7833 3000 Fax 020 7430 4868
✉ contact@itn.co.uk
www.itn.co.uk
Chief Executive *Mark Wood*
Editor-in-Chief, ITV News *David Mannion*
Editor, Channel 4 News *Jim Gray*
Editor, Five News *Gary Rogers*

Provider of the main national and international news for ITV, Channel 4 and Five and radio news for IRN. Programmes on ITV: *Lunchtime News*; *London Today*; *Evening News*; *London Tonight*; *News at 10.30*, plus regular news summaries and three programmes a day at weekends. Programmes on Channel 4 include the in-depth news analysis programmes *Channel 4 News at Noon* and *Channel 4 News*. Programmes on Five: *5 News at Noon* and *5 News* plus regular updates. ITN also has operating control of *Euronews*, Europe's only pan-European broadcaster. Since August 2000, ITN broadcasts in its own right on ITN News Channel, a 24-hour news service available for television, video, audio and text format.

ITV plc

The London Television Centre, Upper Ground, London SE1 9LT
www.itvplc.com
Chief Executive *Charles Allen*
Chairman *Michael Green*

ITV plc, formed following the merger of Granada and Carlton Television, holds 11 of the 15 regional ITV licences: Carlton, Central, Granada, LWT, Meridian, Yorkshire, Tyne Tees, Anglia, HTV, Westcountry and Border. See also **Granada Productions** under **Film, TV and Radio Production Companies**. (Information on how the company will be structured was not available at the time of going to press.)

ITV Broadcasting
(at London Television Centre address)
Chief Executive *Mick Desmond*
Programme Director *Nigel Pickard*

LWT (London Weekend Television)

The London Television Centre, Upper Ground, London SE1 9LT
☎020 7620 1620
www.itv.com/lwt

Managing Director *Christy Swords*
Creative Controller of Entertainment *Nigel Hall*
Controller of Drama *Michele Buck*
Controller of Arts *Melvyn Bragg*
Controller of Factual Programmes *Will Smith*

Makers of current affairs, entertainment and drama series. Provides a large proportion of ITV's drama and light entertainment, and also for BSkyB and Channel 4.

Meridian Broadcasting

Television Centre, Southampton SO14 0PZ
☎023 8022 2555   Fax 023 8033 5050
www.meridiantv.com

Managing Director *Lindsay Charlton*
Controller of Regional Programmes *Mark Southgate*

Meridian's studios in Southampton provide a base for regional productions. Regular regional programmes include the award-winning news service, *Meridian Tonight* and *Countryways*. (Meridian are moving to a new location at the end of 2004; check website for details.)

S4C

Parc Tŷ Glas, Llanishen CF14 5DU
☎029 2074 7444   Fax 029 2075 4444
✉ s4c@s4c.co.uk
www.s4c.co.uk

Chief Executive *Huw Jones*
Director of Programmes *Iona Jones*

The Welsh 4th Channel, established by the Broadcasting Act 1980, is responsible for a schedule of Welsh and English programmes on the Fourth Channel in Wales. Known as S4C, the analogue service is made up of about 34 hours per week of Welsh language programmes and more than 85 hours of English language output from Channel 4. S4C digidol broadcasts in Welsh exclusively for 80 hours per week. Ten hours a week of the Welsh programmes are provided by the BBC; the remainder are purchased from ITV1 Wales and independent producers. Drama, comedy and documentary are all part of S4C's programming. Commissioning guidelines can be viewed on the website given above.

Scottish Television Ltd

200 Renfield Street, Glasgow G2 3PR
☎0141 300 3000   Fax 0141 300 3030
www.scottishtv.co.uk

Managing Director, Scottish TV *Bobby Hain*
Head of Features & Entertainment *Agnes Wilkie*
Senior News Producer *Paul McKinney*
Head of Sport *Andrea Brownlie*

Scottish TV produces 12 hours of television a week for the central Scotland region and a number of network programmes. This is made up of news, current affairs and sport, and a wide-ranging portfolio of other programmes ranging from entertainment, documentary, religion, drama and children's such as *Taggart*; *I'm A Celebrity … Get Me Out of Here* and *Squeak!* Scottish Television together with Grampian and Scottish Screen have made a number of short films under the banner of New Found Land.

Teletext Ltd

Building 10, Chiswick Park, 566 Chiswick High Road, London W4 5TS
☎0870 731 3000   Fax 0870 731 3001
www.teletext.co.uk

Managing Director *Mike Stewart*
Editor-in-Chief *John Sage*

On 1 January 1993, Teletext Ltd took over the electronic publishing service for both ITV and Channel 4. Transmits a wide range of news pages and features, including current affairs, sport, TV listings, weather, travel, holidays, finance, games, competitions, etc. Also broadcasts on Five, digital terrestrial (Channel 9), digital cable TV and the Web and mobile services.

Tyne Tees Television

Television Centre, Newcastle upon Tyne NE1 2AL
☎0191 261 0181   Fax 0191 261 2302
www.tynetees.tv

Managing Director/Controller of Programmes *Graeme Thompson*
Head of New Media *Malcolm Wright*
Editor, Current Affairs and Features *Jane Bolesworth*
Managing Editor, News *Graham Marples*
Executive Producer & Head of Development, Yorkshire Tyne Tees Features *Mark Robinson*
Head of Regional Affairs *Norma Hope*
Head of Sport *Roger Tames*

Programming covers religion, politics, news and current affairs, regional documentaries, business, entertainment, sport and arts. Regular programmes include *North East Tonight with Mike Neville* and *Around the House* (politics). In 2004, Tyne Tees screened a series of eight dramas and documentaries – *Hot House* – showcasing North East writers and directors.

UTV (Ulster Television)

Havelock House, Ormeau Road, Belfast BT7 1EB
☎028 9032 8122 Fax 028 9024 6695
www.utvlive.com

Director of Ulster Television *Alan Bremner*
Head of News, Current Affairs and Sport *Rob Morrison*

Regular programmes on news and current affairs, politics, sport, education, music, light entertainment, arts, health and local culture.

Yorkshire Television

The Television Centre, Leeds LS3 1JS
☎0113 243 8283 Fax 0113 244 5107
www.itv.com

London office: London Television Centre, Upper Ground, London SE1 9LT
☎020 7620 1620

Chairman *Charles Allen*
Managing Director *David Croft*
Director of Programmes, Yorkshire Tyne Tees Productions *John Whiston*
Controller of Drama, Yorkshire Tyne Tees Productions *Keith Richardson*
Controller of Drama, YTV *Carolyn Reynolds*
Controller of Comedy Drama and Drama Features *David Reynolds*

Part of **ITV plc**. Drama series, situation comedies, film productions and long-running series like *Emmerdale* and *Heartbeat*. Always looking for strong writing in these areas, but prefers to find it through an agent. Documentary/current affairs material tends to be supplied by producers; opportunities in these areas are rare but adaptations of published work as a documentary subject are considered. In theory, opportunity exists within series, episode material. Best approach is through a good agent.

Cable and Satellite Television

Artsworld

Great West House, Great West Road, Brentford TW8 9DF
☎020 7805 2424
✉ tv@artsworld.com
www.artsworld.com

Chairman *John Hambley*
Programme Controller *Alison Martin*

Satellite arts channel, launched in November 2000. Broadcasts from 7.00 pm to midnight (repeated from 2.00 pm to 7.00 pm the following day) via BSkyB. Programmes include the series, *Great Books*.

British Sky Broadcasting Ltd (BSkyB)

6 Centaurs Business Park, Grant Way, Isleworth TW7 5QD
☎020 7705 3000 Fax 020 7705 3030
www.sky.com

Chief Executive *James Murdoch*
Managing Director, Sky Networks *Dawn Airey*
Chief Operating Officer *Richard Freudenstein*
Head of Sky News *Nick Pollard*
Managing Director, Sky Sports *Vic Wakeling*

Launched in 1989, British Sky Broadcasting gives over 15 million viewers (in more than 7 million households) access to movies, news, entertainment and sports channels, and interactive services on Sky digital. Launched in October 1998, Sky digital has more than 400 channels and offers a range of innovative interactive services. 2001 saw the introduction of the next-generation integrated digital satellite set-top box/personal video recorder, Sky+.

WHOLLY-OWNED SKY CHANNELS
Sky Movies 1–9/Sky Cinema 1&2
Largest TV movie service outside the US. Sky Movies 1–9 show over 90% of the top 100 grossing box-office films of the previous year. Sky Cinema 1&2 shows classic films, from Westerns to Film Noir, Chaplin to Chevy Chase, as well as a World Cinema strand that includes UK premières of new and old movies.

Sky News
Award winning 24-hours news service with hourly bulletins and expert comment.

Sky One/Sky One Mix
The most frequently watched non-terrestrial channel with the accent on entertainment for 16–34-year-olds.

Sky Sports 1/Sky Sports 2/Sky Sports 3/Sky Sports News/Sky Sports Extra
Over 30,000 hours of sport are broadcast every year across the five Sky Sports channels. Sky Sports 1, 2 and 3 are devoted to live events, support programmes and in-depth sports coverage seven days a week. Sky Sports News provides sports news and the latest results and information 24 hours a day. Sky Sports Extra carries ad-

ditional sports programming including the award-winning live interactive coverage.

Sky Travel/Sky Travel Extra
Magazine shows, documentaries and tele-shopping.

JOINT VENTURES
National Geographic; Nickelodeon; Nick Jr; The History Channel; Paramount Comedy Channel; QVC; MUTV; Music Choice Europe; Granada Men & Motors; Granada Plus; Artsworld; Adventure One; The Biography Channel; Attheraces; Chelsea Digital Media.

CNBC Europe
10 Fleet Place, London EC4M 7QS
☎020 7653 9300 Fax 020 7653 5956
www.cnbceurope.com

Managing Director *Richard Cotton*

A service of NBC and Dow Jones. 24-hour business and financial news service. Programmes include *Today's Business*; *Morning Exchange*; *Capital Ideas*; *Europe Squawk Box*.

CNN International
Turner House, 16 Great Marlborough Street, London W1F 7HS
☎020 7693 1000 Fax 020 7693 1001
www.edition.cnn.com

Managing Editor, CNN International Europe, Middle East & Africa *Nick Wrenn*

CNN, the leading global 24-hour news network, is available to one billion people worldwide via the 26 CNN branded TV, Internet, radio and mobile services produced by CNN News Group, a Time Warner company. CNN has major production centres in Atlanta, New York, Los Angeles, London, Hong Kong and Mexico City. The London bureau, the largest outside the USA, is CNN's European headquarters and produces over 50 hours of programming per week. Live business and news programmes, including *CNN Today*; *Business International*; *World News* and *World Business Today*. Weekly programmes include *International Correspondents*, a discussion programme featuring journalists and media figures and *The Daily Show*, a late night half-hour of satire and topical comedy hosted by Jon Stewart.

MTV Networks Europe
180 Oxford Street, London W1D 1DS
☎020 7284 7777 Fax 020 7284 7788
www.mtv.co.uk

President & Chief Executive *Brent Hansen*

Established 1987. Europe's 24-hour music and

youth entertainment channel, available on cable, via satellite and digitally. Transmitted from London in English across Europe.

Travel Channel
66 Newman Street, London W1T 3EQ
☎020 7636 5401
✉ enquiries@travelchannel.co.uk
www.travelchannel.co.uk

Launched in February 1994. Broadcasts programmes and information on the world of travel. Destinations reports, lifestyle programmes plus food and drink, sport and leisure pursuits. Transmits from 7.00 am to 1.00 am throughout Europe and Africa.

National Commercial Radio

Classic FM
7 Swallow Place, London W1B 2AG
☎020 7343 9000 Fax 020 7344 2700
www.classicfm.com

Managing Director/Programme Controller
   Roger Lewis
Managing Editor *Darren Henley*

Classic FM, Britain's largest national commercial radio station, started broadcasting in September 1992. Plays accessible classical music 24 hours a day and broadcasts news, weather, travel, business information, political/celebrity/general interest talks, features and interviews. Classic has gone well beyond its expectations, attracting 6.2 million listeners a week. Winner of the 'Station of the Year' Sony Award in 2000.

Digital One
7 Swallow Place, London W1B 2AG
☎020 7288 4600
✉ info@digitalone.co.uk
www.ukdigitalradio.com

The UK's only national commercial digital radio multiplex operator. Backed by radio group GWR and cable supplier ntl, Digital One began broadcasting on 15 November 1999. Channels include **Classic FM**, **Virgin Radio**, **TalkSport** and digital-only stations, **Oneword**, Planet Rock, Core, PrimeTime Radio and Life.

Oneword
Landseer House, 19 Charing Cross Road, London WC2H 0ES
☎020 7976 3030 Fax 020 7930 9460
✉ info@oneword.co.uk
www.oneword.co.uk

Managing Director *Ben Budworth*

Programme Manager *Christina Captieux*

The first commercial radio station dedicated solely to the transmission of plays, books, comedy and reviews. Broadcasts on Sky Digital (channel 877), Freeview (channel 87), ntl (channel 893) in Europe, DAB Digital Radio (Digital One – 18 hours a day) in the UK and worldwide on the Internet. Programmes include *Between the Lines*, a twice-daily conversation by Paul Blezard with different authors. Winner of the 'Station of the Year' Sony Radio Awards in 2001 and 2002.

TalkSport
PO Box 1089, London SE1 8WQ
☎020 7959 7800
www.talksport.co.uk

Programme Director *Mike Parry*

Commenced broadcasting in February 1995 as Talk Radio UK. Re-launched January 2000 as TalkSport, the UK's first sports radio station. Broadcasts 24 hours a day. News items can be e-mailed to *Mike Parry* via the website.

Virgin Radio
1 Golden Square, London W1F 9DJ
☎020 7434 1215 Fax 020 7434 1197
www.virginradio.co.uk

Chief Executive *John Pearson*
Programme Director *Paul Jackson*

Music-based station launched in 1973, bought by Chris Evans' Ginger Media Group in December 1997 and acquired by the Scottish Media Group in March 2000.

Independent Local Radio

Breeze
See **Essex FM**

95.8 Capital Radio FM
30 Leicester Square, London WC2H 7LA
☎020 7766 6000 Fax 020 7766 6100
www.capitalfm.com

Managing Director *Keith Pringle*

Commenced broadcasting in October 1973 as the country's second commercial radio station (the first being LBC, launched a week earlier). Europe's largest commercial radio station.

Central FM Ltd
201–203 High Street, Falkirk FK1 1DU
☎01324 611164 Fax 01324 611168
✉ email@centralfm.co.uk
www.centralfm.co.uk

Brand Manager and Programme Controller
  Tom Bell

Broadcasts music, sport and local news to central Scotland, 24 hours a day.

Century FM
Century House, PO Box 100, Church Street, Gateshead NE8 2YY
☎0191 477 6666 Fax 0191 477 5660

Programme Controller *Giles Squire*

Music, talk, news and interviews, 24 hours a day.

Clyde 1/Clyde 2
Clydebank Business Park, Clydebank
G81 2RX
☎0141 565 2200 Fax 0141 565 2265
www.clyde1.com
www.clyde2.com

Managing Director *Paul Cooney*

Programmes usually originate in-house or by commission. All documentary material is made in-house. Good local news items always considered. There are three book programmes presented by Alex Dickson each week on Clyde 2 at 10.00 pm – 10.30 pm: *Authors* (Monday) features author interviews while *Hardback Bookcase* (Tuesday) and *Paperback Bookcase* (Wednesday) review latest titles.

Cool FM
See **Downtown Radio**

Downtown Radio/Cool FM
Newtownards, Co. Down BT23 4ES
☎028 9181 5555 Fax 028 9181 5252
✉ programmes@downtown.co.uk
www.downtown.co.uk

Managing Director *David Sloan*

Downtown Radio first ran a highly successful short story competition in 1988, attracting over 400 stories. The competition is now an annual event and writers living within the station's transmission area are asked to submit material during the winter and early spring. The competition is promoted in association with Eason Shops. For further information, write to *Anita Downey* at the station.

Essex FM/Breeze
Radio House, Clifftown Road, Southend on Sea SS1 1SX
☎01702 333711 Fax 01702 333686
www.musicradio.com

Programme Director *Jeff O'Brien*

Music-based stations. Part of the GWR Group plc. No real opportunities for writers' work as such, but will occasionally interview local authors of published books. Contact *Lee Murphy*, News Editor.

Forth One/Forth 2
Forth House, Forth Street, Edinburgh
EH1 3LF
☎0131 556 9255 Fax 0131 475 1221
✉ scott@forth2.com
www.forthonline.co.uk
Controller, Forth One & Forth 2 *Nik Goodman*
Programme Producer, Forth 2 *Moira Millar*
News Editor *Paul Robertson*

News stories welcome from freelancers. Music-based programming.

Galaxy 102.2
See **100.7 Heart FM**

GWR FM
PO Box 2000, 1 Passage Street, Bristol
BS99 7SN
☎0117 984 3200 Fax 0117 984 3202
www.musicradio.com
Programme Controller *Paul Andrew*

Very few opportunities for writers. Almost all material originates in-house. Part of the GWR Group plc.

Hallam FM/Magic AM
Radio House, 900 Herries Road, Sheffield
S6 1RH
☎0114 209 1000
www.hallamfm.co.uk
Programme Director *To be appointed*

Launched in 1974. Music, news and features, 24 hours a day.

100.7 Heart FM/Galaxy 102.2
1 The Square, 111 Broad Street, Birmingham
B15 1AS
☎0121 695 0000 Fax 0121 695 0055
✉ mail@heartfm.co.uk *or*
mail@galaxy1022.co.uk
www.heartfm.co.uk
www.galaxy1022.co.uk
Managing Director *Paul Fairburn*
Programme Director, Heart FM *Alan Carruthers*
Programme Director, Galaxy *Neil Greenslade*

Heart FM commenced broadcasting music, regional news and information in September

1994. Galaxy broadcasts today's dance and soul, news and information.

Isle of Wight Radio
Dodnor Park, Newport PO30 5XE
☎01983 822557 Fax 01983 821690
✉ tom.stroud@iwradio.co.uk
www.iwradio.co.uk
Managing Director *Andy Shier*
Programme Manager *Tom Stroud*

Part of the Radio Investments Limited Group, Isle of Wight Radio is the island's only radio station broadcasting local news, music and general entertainment including phone-ins and interview based shows. Music, television, film, popular culture are the main areas of interest.

KM-fm
Medway House, Ginsbury Close, St Thomas Longley Road, Medway City Estate, Strood, Rochester ME2 4DU
☎01634 227808 Fax 01634 297272
www.kentonline.co.uk/kmfm
Group Programme Director *Mike Osborne*

A wide range of music programming plus news, views and local interest. Part of the Kent Messenger Group.

LBC News 1152 AM
See **LBC Radio Ltd**

LBC Radio Ltd
The Chrysalis Building, Bramley Road, London W10 6SP
☎020 7314 7300 Fax 020 7324 7373
www.lbc.co.uk
Programme Director *Steve Kyte*
Editorial Director *Jonathan Richards*

LBC 97.3 FM is a talk-based station broadcasting 24 hours a day providing entertainment, interviews, celebrity guests, music, chat shows, local interest, news and sport. LBC News 1152 AM, the sister station of LBC 87.3 FM, provides 24-hour rolling news.

105.4 FM Leicester Sound
6 Dominus Way, Meridian Business Park, Leicester LE19 1RP
☎0116 256 1300
Fax 0116 256 1303/1305 (news)
Programme Controller *Craig Boddy*

Part of GWR Group plc. Predominantly a music station. Very occasionally, unsolicited material of local interest – 'targeted at our particular audience' – may be broadcast.

Magic 1152AM (Newcastle upon Tyne)
See **Metro Radio**

Magic 1548
See **Radio City Ltd**

Magic AM
See **Hallam FM**

Marcher Radio Group
Marcher Sound Ltd., The Studios, Mold Road, Wrexham LL11 4AF
☎01978 752202 Fax 01978 722209
www.marchergold.co.uk
Programme Controller *Graham Ledger*

Occasional features and advisory programmes. Hour-long Welsh language broadcasts are aired weekdays at 6.00 pm.

Metro Radio/Magic 1152AM
Swalwell, Newcastle upon Tyne NE99 1BB
☎0191 420 0971 Fax 0191 488 8611
www.metroradio.co.uk
Programme Director *Tony McKenzie*

Very few opportunities for writers, but phone-in programmes may interview authors.

Moray Firth Radio
PO Box 271, Scorguie Place, Inverness IV3 8UJ
☎01463 224433 Fax 01463 243224
www.mfr.co.uk
Programme Controller *Danny Gallagher*
Head of Programmes *Ray Atkinson*
Book Reviews *May Marshall*

Book reviews every Sunday morning at 7.00 am until 8.00 am.

NorthSound Radio
Abbotswell Road, Aberdeen AB12 4AJ
☎01224 337000 Fax 01224 400003
www.northsound.co.uk
Managing Director *Adam Findlay*
Programme Controller *Luke McCullough*

Features and music programmes 24 hours a day including, mid-morning (9.00 am – midday), *Northsound 2* feature programme.

Premier Radio
22 Chapter Street, London SW1P 4NP
☎020 7316 1300 Fax 020 7233 6706
✉ premier@premier.org.uk
www.premier.org.uk

Managing Director *Peter Kerridge*

Broadcasts programmes that reflect the beliefs and values of the Christian faith, 24 hours a day on 1305, 1413, 1332 MW, Sky digital 873, ntl 886 and on the Web.

Radio City Ltd/Magic 1548
Radio City Tower, St John's Beacon, 1 Houghton Street, Liverpool L1 1RL
☎0151 472 6800 Fax 0151 472 6821
www.radiocity.co.uk
Managing Director *Tom Hunter*
Programme Director *Richard Maddock*

Opportunities for writers are very few and far between as this is predominantly a music station.

Radio XL 1296 AM
KMS House, Bradford Street, Birmingham B12 0JD
☎0121 753 5353 Fax 0121 753 3111
Managing Director *Arun Bajaj*

Asian broadcasting for the West Midlands, 24 hours a day. Broadcasts *Love Express* featuring love stories and poems. Writers should send material for the attention of *Hardev Nara*.

Sabras Radio
Radio House, 63 Melton Road, Leicester LE4 6PN
☎0116 261 0666 Fax 0116 266 7776
www.sabrasradio.com
Programme Controller *Don Kotak*

Programmes for the Asian community, broadcasting 24 hours a day.

Spectrum Radio
204–206 Queenstown Road, London SW8 3NR
☎020 7627 4433 Fax 020 7627 3409
✉ enquiries@spectrumradio.net
www.spectrumradio.net
Managing Director *Toby Aldrych*

Programmes for a broad spectrum of ethnic groups in London.

Spire FM
City Hall Studios, Malthouse Lane, Salisbury SP2 7QQ
☎01722 416644 Fax 01722 416688
www.spirefm.co.uk
Station Director *Ceri Herford*

Music, news current affairs, quizzes and sport. Won the Sony Award for the best local radio station in 1994 and 1996.

Sunrise Radio (Yorkshire)

Sunrise House, 30 Chapel Street, Bradford
BD1 5DN
☎01274 735043 Fax 01274 728534
www.sunriseradio.fm

Programme Controller, Chief Executive &
Chairman *Usha Parmar*

Programmes for the Asian community in
Bradford.

Sunshine 855

South Shropshire Communications Ltd., Unit
11, Burway Trading Estate, Bromfield Road,
Ludlow SY8 1EN
☎01584 873795 Fax 01584 875900
www.sunshine855.co.uk

Operations Director *Mrs G. Murfin*

Music, news and information, broadcast
24 hours a day.

Swansea Sound 1170 MW/
The Wave FM

Victoria Road, Gowerton, Swansea SA4 3AB
☎01792 511170 (MW)/ 511964 (FM)
Fax 01792 511171 (MW)/511965 (FM)

www.swanseasound.co.uk

Regional Managing Director *Esther Morton*
Programme Manager *Steve Barnes*
News Editor *Emma Thomas*

Music-based programming on FM while
Swansea Sound is interested in a wide variety
of material, though news items must be of local
relevance. An explanatory letter, in the first
instance, is advisable.

2CR-FM/Classic Gold 828

5–7 Southcote Road, Bournemouth
BH1 3LR
☎01202 259259 Fax 01202 255244
✉ newsbournemouth@creation.com
www.koko.com

Programme Controller *Graham Mack*

Wholly-owned subsidiary of the GWR Group
plc. Serves Dorset and Hampshire. All reviews/
topicality/press releases to the Programme
Controller, 2CR-FM at the address above.

The Wave FM

See **Swansea Sound 1170 MW**

Radio Drama - the Writers Medium

by Kate Rowland, BBC Creative Director, New Writing

Radio is one of the most exciting and demanding mediums for a writer. It is a place for writers to let their imaginations fly, where the audience is ready to be challenged and entertained by new ideas. And perhaps most extraordinary for a writer is that each member of your audience will be having a totally different and individual experience; no two people will be seeing your work in the same way. It is, almost without exception, one of the few places that the single authored play is the dominant form. Radio is a writer's medium and the relationship with the producer is a close and intimate one. Your original voice can be heard and your input will be valued through to the final stages of the production.

Many different dramatists are attracted to the medium. Writers cross platform more frequently now: their talents are not pigeonholed and they enjoy the different disciplines and opportunities offered by radio, theatre, TV and film. The late Peter Tinniswood created so much original radio drama alongside award winning writers Lee Hall, Mike Walker, Gill Adams, Marcy Kahan and many others who have contributed so much to the networks. Exciting new writers like Debbie Tucker Green and Avie Luthra have relished the opportunity to work in a new medium.

If we don't know your work – and a lot of people are at that starting point – the first thing we need to do is read a full script. I can't stress enough that we're interested in your original voice, in you, and not in you trying to do what you think the BBC wants, it should be what you want to write. Writer passion is the best thing we can find. It's like a fine pint of Heineken – it does refresh the parts. Once we can say this is who this writer is, and the way they write dialogue and characters and ideas, then we're interested. If people copy – and there is a lot of imitation – then we're not so interested. Keep going, and trust us. Don't hang on to one project if it's been rejected; move on to something else. It might be that the project has a life later on, but if you keep trying to flog this one thing, and are burnt up with anger as a result of failure, then it won't help your writing. Most really good writers have been rejected and understand that it doesn't mean they're not good, but that it's actually a process. And then suddenly it's as though the light goes on, it's there in the script, it communicates itself to someone else.

Obviously, writers are keen to know how long the commissioning process takes. The answer is, it really depends on the medium, but it can be anything from six months to a couple of years, less for radio, and you can be looking at three or four years for a film. So I think the most important thing is to know that if something does go into development, that's a really fantastic step forward. In radio there is very little that just stays in development. There is a 98 per cent hit rate for work that is commissioned to be produced. In television, I think ten per cent of projects being developed will be produced.

Writer passion drives so much of the creative industry but at the end of the day everybody needs a producer. In radio and in TV you can't go straight to a commissioner you need to find the right producer to represent your idea. It is a competitive industry and even where there are such opportunities for new drama as there are in radio, you must have a real advocate for your work. How a producer pitches your work really depends on your experience. If you are a first-time writer with no broadcast credit then we must see a full script to know you can do it.

For writers new to radio I suggest that you spend time listening so you get a sense of the quality and range of ideas, including the mix of genre and story-telling techniques: drama documentary, contemporary drama, comedy drama, monologue. Writers can use actuality, transcript, poetry or real events as a springboard into the drama but, whatever the approach, the form needs to match the idea. We want to see your central character/protagonist and under-stand their emotional journey. Too often I am presented with issue led pieces, not dramas where the characters' lives depend upon the action of the story.

The majority of radio drama is on Radio 4 but Radio 3 also has a reputation for producing a range of innovative drama in the Sunday Play slot and The Wire which is dedicated to new writers and new ideas. The Afternoon Play on Radio 4 has an extraordinary breadth of work with a large and dedicated audience every day. Both the writersroom and the Radio 4 website can give you detailed information about the range of slots and diversity of ideas that the commission-ers are looking for. All writers whatever their experience must pitch their idea to a producer, whether it's an in-house BBC producer or an independent one.

What we are looking for really depends on your experience. If you are a com-missioned writer in another medium with an established track record in theatre, film or TV, then we are happy to read an existing script that demonstrates your talent and ability. It is slightly different for each of the commissioners, but I like to read a writer's work so that when I read the idea I can hear your writing voice. If you are a new writer with no previous credits, then we will be looking to read a full script. It's important for writers to develop their ideas and understand the medium. One of the problems we face with first radio plays is a terrible tendency of writers to overwrite, to describe everything that people are thinking, doing, feeling. The characters don't inhabit the world, and it becomes more like a piece of prose than a drama the audience interacts with. Don't underestimate the role the audience plays in bringing your drama to life. One of the best creative thoughts was something that Georges Braque, the cubist painter said, 'It's not the objects but the spaces in-between the objects that count.'

When we read a proposal, we are looking for something that demands to be told. 'Why now?' is often a question I ask. Have I heard this story before, or are you bringing something new to the way we think about a particular theme? A long synopsis detailing plot action is not useful because it doesn't convey why you want to write this and what the emotional tone of the piece is. Be creative in your proposals, a touch of dialogue can say far more than description of the action. You should be able to tell your story in one or two pages. As a commissioner, I look at the idea from the author's perspective. Sometimes we might think a particular idea would be better served as a documentary rather than as a play, sometimes your idea duplicates something we have already seen. It's crucial you work with a producer at an early stage, because they can feed these responses back to you and help you modify your idea.

We encourage all writers to make an informed decision about the producer they choose to send their work to. It helps if you only send your work to one producer at a time. If it is a first unsolicited script, then you need to send it to the writersroom, I Mortimer Street, London W1T 3JA where your work will be considered. As well as looking at the specific idea, we are also looking at the quality of your writing. Strong work is then forwarded to the Development Team in Radio Drama. If you have any queries, then please do get in touch with the New Writing team.

I think that one of the most important things for writers to understand is that there are lots of different ways into the BBC and we are here to help and guide you to find a part of the organisation that suits your talents. It is in the BBC's interest to find new writers. The amount of production that is going on across drama, entertainment and children's television is huge and we're constantly looking for new writers – either for some of the long running returning series or original work.

Websites: writersroom: bbc.co.uk/writersroom
*   BBC Radio 4: bbc.co.uk/radio4*
*   BBC Radio 3: bbc.co.uk/radio3*

Film, TV and Radio Producers

Aardman
Gas Ferry Road, Bristol BS1 6UN
☎0117 984 8485 Fax 0117 984 8486
www.aardman.com
Head of Development (Features) *Richelle Wilder*
Script Editor (Television) *Dick Hansom*

Founded 1972. Award-winning animation studio producing films, television series, videos, commercials and new media properties. OUTPUT includes: *Rex the Runt*; *Morph Files*; *Creature Comforts*; *Wallace and Gromit*; *Angry Kid*; *Chicken Run*; *The Presentators*. No unsolicited submissions.

Above The Title
Level 2, 10/11 St Georges Mews, London NW1 8XE
☎020 7916 1984 Fax 020 7722 5706
✉ mail@abovethetitle.com
www.abovethetitle.com
Contacts *Bruce Hyman, Helen Chattwell*

Producer of radio drama and documentary programmes. OUTPUT *The National Theatre of Brent's Complete and Utter History of the Mona Lisa* (Radio 4); *40 Years of Wonder* (Radio 2); *The Joy of Sax* (Radio 3) Unsolicited mss and ideas welcome. Approach in the first instance by e-mail. 'We encourage and support new writing in every way we can.'

Absolutely Productions Ltd
Suite 226, Craven House, 121 Kingsway, London WC2B 6PA
☎020 7930 3113
✉ info@absolutely-uk.com
www.absolutely-uk.com
Executive Producer *Gordon Kennedy*

TV and film production company specialising in comedy and entertainment. OUTPUT *Absolutely* series 1–4 (Ch4); *mr don and mr george* (Ch4); *Squawkietalkie* (comedy wildlife programme for Ch4); *The Preventers* (ITV); *Scotland v England* (Ch4); *Barry Welsh is Coming* (HTV); *The Jack Docherty Show* (Ch5); *The Morwenna Banks Show* (Ch5); *Stressed Eric* (BBC2); *Armstrong & Miller* (Paramount/Ch4); *The Creatives* (BBC2); *Trigger Happy* (Ch4); *The Announcement* (Dakota Entertainment).

Abstract Images
117 Willoughby House, Barbican, London EC2Y 8BL
☎020 7638 5123
✉ productions@abstract-images.co.uk
Contact *Howard Ross*

Television documentary and drama programming. Also theatre productions. OUTPUT includes *Balm in Gilead* (drama); *Road* (drama); *Bent* (drama); *God: For & Against* (documentary); *This Is a Man* (drama/doc). New writers should send synopsis in the first instance.

Acacia Productions Ltd
80 Weston Park, London N8 9Tb
☎020 8341 9392 Fax 020 8341 4879
✉ acacia@dial.pipex.com
www.acaciaproductions.co.uk
Contact *J. Edward Milner*

Producer of award-winning television and video documentaries; also news reports, corporates and programmes for educational charities. No unsolicited mss. OUTPUT includes documentary series entitled *Last Plant Standing*; *A Farm in Uganda*; *Montserrat: Under the Volcano*; *Spirit of Trees* (8 progs.); *Vietnam: After the Fire*; *Macroeconomics – the Decision-makers*; *Greening of Thailand*; *A Future for Forests*.

Acrobat Television
107 Wellington Road North, Stockport SK4 2LP
☎0161 477 9090 Fax 0161 477 9191
✉ info@acrobat-tv.co.uk
Contacts *David Hill, Annie Broom*

Corporate video producer. OUTPUT includes instructional video for the British Association of Ski Instructors; corporate videos for Neilson Sailing, Hepworth Building Products, The Simon Group and First Choice Ski. No unsolicited mss.

All Out Productions
50 Copperas Street, Manchester M4 1HS
☎0161 834 9955 Fax 0161 834 6978

✉ mail@allout.co.uk
www.allout.co.uk

Contact *David Cook*

Producer of documentaries, features and current affairs programmes for radio. OUTPUT includes *Five Live Report* (BBC Five Live – weekly news documentary); *Lamacq Live* (BBC Radio One – music and social affairs). Ideas welcome but not mss. Approach by e-mail.

Anglo/Fortunato Films Ltd
170 Popes Lane, London W5 4NJ
☎020 8932 7676 Fax 020 8932 7491

Contact *Luciano Celentino*

Film, television and video producer/director of action comedy and psych-thriller drama. No unsolicited mss.

Ariel Productions Ltd
11 Albion Gate, Hyde Park Place, London W2 2LF
☎020 7262 7726 Fax 020 7262 7726

Producer *Otto Plaschkes*

Feature film and television producer. OUTPUT includes *Georgy Girl*; *Hopscotch*; *In Celebration*; *Butley*; *Doggin' Around*. Encourages new writers through involvement with the **National Film and Television School** and Screen Laboratory. No unsolicited mss.

Arlington Productions Limited
Cippenham Court, Cippenham Lane, Cippenham, Nr Slough SL1 5AU
☎01753 516767 Fax 01753 691785

Television producer. Specialises in popular international drama, with *occasional* forays into other areas. 'We have an enviable reputation for encouraging new writers but only accept unsolicited submissions via agents.'

The Ashford Entertainment Corporation Ltd
20 The Chase, Coulsdon CR5 2EG
✉ info@ashford-entertainment.co.uk
www.ashford-entertainment.co.uk

Managing Director *Frazer Ashford*

Founded in 1996 by award-winning film and TV producer Frazer Ashford whose credits include *Great Little Trains* (Mainline Television for Westcountry/Ch4, starring the late Willie Rushton); *Street Life* and *Make Yourself at Home* (both for WTV). Produces theatrical films and television – drama, lifestyle and documentaries. Happy to receive ideas for documentaries but submit a one-page synopsis only in the first

instance, enclosing s.a.e. 'Be patient, allow up to four weeks for a reply. Be precise with the idea; specific details rather than vague thoughts. Attach a back-up sheet with credentials and supporting evidence, i.e., can you ensure that your idea is feasible?'

Assembly Film and Television Ltd
Riverside Studios, Crisp Road, London W6 9RL
☎020 8237 1075 Fax 020 8237 1071
✉ judithmurrell@riversidestudios.co.uk

Contacts *William Burdett-Coutts, Judith Murrell*

Television documentary producer. OUTPUT includes the Prudential Awards for the Arts; the London Comedy Festival; Ch4's Black Season, *In Exile: Sitcom*; BAFTA award-winning *Black Books: Sitcom* and Jo Brand's *Hot Potatoes* for BBC1.

Beckmann International Ltd
1 The Courtyard, Court Row, Ramsey IM8 1AS
☎01624 816585 Fax 01624 816589
✉ sales@beckmanngroup.co.uk
www.beckmanngroup.co.uk

Contacts *Jo White, Stuart Semark*

Isle of Man-based company. Video and television documentary distributor. OUTPUT *Practical Guide to Europe* (travel series); *Maestro* (12-part series on classical composers); *Ivory Orphans*.

Big Heart Media
Flat 4, 6 Pear Tree Court, London EC1R 0DW
☎020 7608 0352 Fax 020 7250 1138
✉ info@bigheartmedia.com
www.bigheartmedia.com

Contacts *Colin Izod, Beth Newell*

Producers of drama and documetaries for television, radio and video. Ideas/outlines welcome by e-mail, but not unsolicted mss. 'We will respond as soon as we can. We're very keen to enourage new writing – particularly for radio drama.'

Black Coral Productions Ltd
2nd Floor, 241 High Street, London E17 7BH
☎020 8520 2830 Fax 020 8520 2358
✉ bcp@coralmedia.co.uk
www.m4media.net

Contacts *Lazell Daley*

Committed to new writing, BCP welcomes proposals and treatments and offers a script consultancy service for which a fee is payable. Please call for further information.

Blackwatch Productions Limited

3 Royal Exchange Court, 17 Royal Exchange Square, Glasgow G1 3DB
☎0141 222 2640/2641 Fax 0141 222 2646
✉ info@blackwatchtv.com
www.blackwatchtv.com

Company Director *Nicola Black*
Head of Production *Paul Gallagher*
Research & Development Officers *Heidi Proven, Anne-Claire Pilley*
Production Manager *Amanda Keown*

Film, television, video producer of drama and documentary programmes. OUTPUT includes *The Paranormal Peter Sellers*; *Snorting Coke with the BBC*; *When Freddie Mercury Met Kenny Everett*; *Designer Vaginas*; *Bonebreakers*; *Luv Bytes*; and *Can We Can We Carry On, Girls?* for Ch4. Also co-ordinates *Mesh*, animation scheme. Does not welcome unsolicited mss.

Bona Broadcasting Ltd

3rd Floor, 21 Albert Square, Dundee DD1 1DJ
☎01382 225403 Fax 01382 225408
✉ ideas@bonabroadcasting.com
www.bonabroadcasting.com

Contact *Turan Ali*

Producer of award winning-drama and documentary programmes for BBC Radio, TV and film projects. No unsolicted mss but send a one-paragraph summary by e-mail in the first instance. 'Writers new to BBC radio should expect to write a whole script on spec to win a commission.' Runs radio and TV drama training courses in the UK and internationally.

Bronco Films Ltd

The Birches, School Road, Gartocharn
G83 8RT
☎01389 710103 Fax 01389 710105
✉ broncofilm@btinternet.com
www.broncofilms.co.uk

Contact *Peter Broughan*

Film, television and video drama. OUTPUT includes *Rob Roy* (feature film) and *Young Person's Guide to Becoming a Rock Star* (TV series). No unsolicited mss.

Buccaneer Films

5 Rainbow Court, Oxhey WD19 4RP
☎01923 254000
✉ michael@gosling.com

Contact *Michael Gosling*

Corporate video production and still photography specialists in education and sport. No unsolicited mss.

Carlton Productions

See **Granada Productions (ITV plc)**

Carnival (Films & Theatre) Ltd

12 Raddington Road, Ladbroke Grove,
London W10 5TG
☎020 8968 0968 Fax 020 8968 0155
✉ info@carnival-films.co.uk
www.carnival-films.co.uk

Contact *Brian Eastman*

Film, TV and theatre producer. OUTPUT Film: *The Mill on the Floss* (BBC); *Firelight* (Hollywood Pictures/Wind Dancer Productions); *Up on the Roof* (Rank/Granada); *Shadowlands* (Savoy/Spelling); *The Infiltrator* (Home Box Office); *Under Suspicion* (Columbia/Rank/LWT). Television: *Rosemary & Thyme* (ITV/Granada); *As If* (Ch4/Columbia); *Lucy Sullivan is Getting Married* (ITV); *The Tenth Kingdom* (Sky/NBC); *Agatha Christie's Poirot* (ITV/LWT/A&E); *Every Woman Knows a Secret* and *Oktober* (both for ITV Network Centre); *The Fragile Heart* (Ch4); *Crime Traveller* (BBC); *Bugs 1–4* (BBC); *Anna Lee* (LWT); *All Or Nothing At All* (LWT); *Head Over Heels* (Carlton); *Jeeves & Wooster I–IV* (Granada); *Traffik* (Ch4); *Forever Green 1–3* (LWT); *Porterhouse Blue* (Ch4); *Blott on the Landscape* (BBC). Theatre: *What a Performance*; *Juno & the Paycock*; *Murder is Easy*; *Misery*; *Ghost Train*; *Map of the Heart*; *Shadowlands*; *Up on the Roof*.

Cartwn Cymru

32 Wordsworth Avenue, Roath, Cardiff
CF24 3FR
☎029 2046 3556/07771 640400
✉ production@cartwn-cymru.com

Contact *Naomi Jones*

Animation production company. OUTPUT *Toucan 'Tecs* (YTV/S4C); *Funnybones* and *Turandot: Operavox* (both for S4C/BBC); *Testament: The Bible in Animation* (BBC2/S4C); *The Miracle Maker* (S4C/BBC/British Screen/Icon Entertainment International); *Faeries* (HIT Entertainment plc for CITV); *Otherworld* (animated feature film for S4C Films, British Screen, Arts Council of Wales).

Celador

39 Long Acre, London WC2E 9LG
☎020 7240 8101 Fax 020 7845 6977
✉ tvhits@celador.co.uk
www.celador.co.uk

Head of Entertainment *Colman Hutchinson*
Development Executives, Comedy *Humphrey Barclay, Vanessa Haynes*
Head of Radio *Liz Anstee*

Producer of TV and radio comedy and light entertainment. OUTPUT *Who Wants to be a Millionaire*; *Winning Lines*; *Commercial Breakdown*; *Britain's Brainiest ...*; *All About Me*; *It's Been A Bad Week*. 'We are interested in original comedy and radio scripts but do not accept unsolicited entertainment formats. As a relatively small company our script-reading capacity is limited.'

Celador Films

39 Long Acre, London WC2E 9LG
☎020 7845 6998   Fax 020 7497 9541
✉ Lleibo@celador.co.uk
www.celador.co.uk

Head of Production and Development
  Christian Colson
Story Editor *Ivana MacKinnon*

Producer of feature films. OUTPUT *Dirty Pretty Things*. Currently in post-production on Julian Fellowes-helmed romantic drama, *A Way Through the Woods*. Also developing work by Neil Marshall. No unsolicited mss.

Celtic Films Ent. Ltd

22 Grafton Street, London W1S 4EX
☎020 7409 2080   Fax 020 7409 2383
✉ celticfilms@aol.com

Contact *Stuart Sutherland*

Film and television drama producer. OUTPUT includes 14 feature-length *Sharpe* TV films for Carlton and *A Life for a Life – The True Story of Stefan Kiszko* TV film for ITV. Devised *Hornblower* series for ITV. Supports new writing and welcomes unsolicited mss.

Chameleon Television Ltd

Great Minster House, Lister Hill, Horsforth, Leeds LS18 5DL
☎0113 205 0040   Fax 0113 281 9454
✉ allen@chameleontv.com

Contacts *Allen Jewhurst, Anna Hall, Simon Wells*

Film and television drama and documentary producer. OUTPUT includes *The Reckoning* (USA/Ch4); *Dunblane* (ITV); *Foul Play* (Ch5); *College Girls* and *Ken Dodd in the Dock* (both for Ch4); *Divorces From Hell*, *New Voices*; *Shipman* and *Love to Shop* (all for ITV); *Ted Hughes – Love, Loss* (BBC). Scripts not welcome unless via agents but new writing is encouraged.

Chatsworth Television Limited

97–99 Dean Street, London W1D 3TE
☎020 7734 4302   Fax 020 7437 3301
✉ television@chatsworth-tv.co.uk
www.chatsworth-tv.co.uk

Managing Director *Malcolm Heyworth*

Entertainment and factual entertainment television producer.

The Children's Film & Television Foundation Ltd

The John Maxwell Building, Elstree Film & TV Studios, Shenley Road, Borehamwood WD6 1JG
☎020 8953 0844   Fax 020 8207 0860
✉ annahome@cftf.onyxnet.co.uk

Chief Executive *Anna Home*

Involved in the development and co-production of films for children and the family, both for the theatric market and for TV.

Cinécosse

North Meadows, Oldmeldrum AB51 OGQ
☎01651 873311   Fax 01651 873300
✉ admin@cinecosse.co.uk
www.cinecosse.co.uk

Contact *Graeme Mowat*

Television and video documentary and corporate productions. OUTPUT includes *Scotland's Larder* (Scottish/Grampian TV); safety and training videos for industry; tourism promotional and sales information, interactive multimedia and DVD authoring. All scripts are commissioned; no unsolicited material.

Cinema Verity Productions Ltd

11 Addison Avenue, London W11 4QS
☎020 7460 2777   Fax 020 7371 3329

Contact *Verity Lambert*

Leading television drama producer whose credits include *She's Out* by Lynda la Plante; *Class Act* by Michael Aitkens; *May to December* (BBC series); *Running Late* by Simon Gray (Screen 1); *The Cazalets* adapt. of *The Cazalet Chronicle* by Elizabeth Jane Howard (BBC).

Clarion Film & Television

Merton Abbey Mills, Water Mill Way, London SW19 2RD
☎020 8540 0110
✉ info@clariontv.com
www.clariontv.com

Director of Programming *Kieran Matthew*
Creative Director *Andrew Linton*
Managing Director *Richard Hannah*

Film and TV production house covering news and factual entertainment commissions, corporate video production and business TV. Own facilities including house animation studio and copyright clearance bureau. Creators of news and language series *The Spoken Word*.

Cleveland Productions

5 Rainbow Court, Oxhey, Near Watford
WD19 4RP
☎01923 254000
✉ michael@gosling.com

Contact *Michael Gosling*

Communications in sound and vision A/V
production and still photography specialists in
education and sport. No unsolicited mss.

COI Communications

Hercules Road, London SE1 7DU
☎020 7261 8767 Fax 020 7261 8776

Head of Department *Jackie Huxley*

Film, video and TV: drama, documentary,
commercials, corporate and public information
films. OUTPUT includes government commercials and corporate information. No scripts.
New writing commissioned as required.

Collingwood & Convergence Productions Ltd

10–14 Crown Street, London W3 8SB
☎020 8993 3666 Fax 020 8993 9595
✉ info@crownstreet.co.uk

Producers *Christopher O'Hare, Terence Clegg,
Tony Collingwood*
Head of Development *Helen Stroud*

Film and TV. Convergence Productions produces live action, drama documentaries;
Collingwood O'Hare Entertainment specialises
in children's animation. OUTPUT **Convergence**:
Theo (film drama series); *Plastic Fantastic* (UK cos-
metic surgery techniques, Ch5); *David Starkey's
Henry VIII* (Ch4 historical documentary) and *On
the Road Again* (BBC2 documentary travel
series). **Collingwood**: *RARG* (award-winning
animated film); *Captain Zed and the Zee Zone*
(ITV); *Daisy-Head Mayzie* (Dr Seuss animated
series for Turner Network and Hanna-Barbera);
Animal Stories (animated poems, ITV network);
Eddy and the Bear (CITV) and *The King's Beard*
(CITV). Unsolicited mss not welcome 'as a general rule as we do not have the capacity to
process the sheer weight of submissions this creates. We therefore tend to review material from
individuals recommended to us through personal
contact with agents or other industry professionals. We like to encourage new writing and have
worked with new writers but our ability to do so
is limited by our capacity for development. We
can usually only consider taking on one project
each year, as development/finance takes several
years to put in place.'

The Comedy Unit

Glasgow TV & Film Studios, Glasgow Media
Park, Craigmont Street, Glasgow G20 9BT
☎0141 305 6666 Fax 0141 305 6600
✉ comedyunit@comedyunit.co.uk
www.comedyunit.co.uk

Contacts *April Chamberlain, Colin Gilbert*

Producers of comedy entertainment for chil-
dren's TV, radio, video and film. OUTPUT *Still
Game; Karen Dunbar Show; Offside; Chewin' the
Fat; Only An Excuse; Yo! Diary* and *Watson's
Wind Up*. Unsolicited mss welcome by post or
e-mail.

Convergence Productions Ltd

See **Collingwood & Convergence
Productions Ltd**

Cosgrove Hall Films

8 Albany Road, Chorlton–cum–Hardy
M21 0AW
☎0161 882 2500 Fax 0161 882 2555
✉ animation@chf.co.uk

Contact *Lee Marriott*

Children's animation producer; film video and
television. OUTPUT includes *Noddy* and *Rotten
Ralph* (both for BBC); *Lavender Castle* by Gerry
Anderson; *The Fox Busters; Animal Shelf; Rocky
& the Dodos*; Alison Uttley's *Little Grey Rabbit*
(all for children's ITV); Terry Pratchett's
Discworld (Ch4). 'We try to select writers on a
project-by-project basis.'

Creative Channel Ltd

Channel TV, Television Centre, St Helier,
Jersey JE1 3ZD
☎01534 816873 Fax 01534 816889
✉ david@channeltv.co.uk
www.channeltv.co.uk

Senior Producer *David Evans*

Producer of TV commercials and corporate
material: information, promotional, sales, training and events coverage. CD and DVD production; promotional videos for all types of
businesses throughout Europe. No unsolicited
mss; new writing/scripts commissioned as
required. Interested in hearing from local writers resident in the Channel Islands.

The Creative Partnership

13 Bateman Street, London W1D 3AF
☎020 7439 7762
✉ sallyc@thecreativepartnership.co.uk
www.thecreativepartnership.co.uk

Contacts *Christopher Fowler, Jim Sturgeon*

'Europe's largest "one-stop shop" for advertising and marketing campaigns for the film and television industries.' Clients include most major and independent film companies. No scripts. 'We train new writers in-house, and find them from submitted c.v.s. All applicants must have previous commercial writing experience.'

Cricket Ltd
Medius House, 63–69 New Oxford Street, London WC1A 1EA
☎020 7845 0300 Fax 020 7845 0303
✉ team@cricket-ltd.com
www.cricket-ltd.com

Head of Production (Film & Video) *Jonathan Freer*

Film and video, live events and conferences, print and design. 'Communications solutions for business clients wishing to influence targeted external and internal audiences.'

CSA Word
6A Archway Mews, 241A Putney Bridge Road, London SW15 2PE
☎020 8871 0220 Fax 020 8877 0712
✉ victoria@csaword.co.uk
www.csaword.co.uk

Contacts *Victoria Williams, Clive Stanhope*

Producer of drama, documentaries and readings for radio. OUTPUT *Alfie Elkins & His Little Life* (drama for BBC World Service); *Lucky Man* (reading for BBC R4); *The Scarlet Pimpernel* (reading for BBC R2); *It's a Girl*; *Chat Snaps*; *Videotape – Two* (documentaries for BBC World Service Learning); *The Glenn Miller Story* (documentary for BBC Radio 2). Unsolicited mss and ideas welcome by post or e-mail. 'We encourage new drama, short story writing and documentary/feature ideas.'

Cutting Edge Productions Ltd
27 Erpingham Road, London SW15 1BE
☎020 8780 1476 Fax 020 8780 0102
✉ juliannorridge@btconnect.com

Contact *Julian Norridge*

Corporate and documentary video and television. OUTPUT includes US series on evangelicalism, 'Dispatches' on US tobacco and government videos. No unsolicited mss: 'we commission all our writing to order, but are open to ideas.'

Dakota Films Ltd
4 Junction Mews, London W2 1PN
☎020 7706 9407 Fax 020 7402 6111

✉ info@dakota-films.demon.co.uk
Managing Director *Jonathan Olsberg*

Film and television drama. Feature films include: *Me Without You*; *Janice Beard 45wpm*; *Let Him Have It*; *Othello*. Currently developing a slate of films, including John Sayles' *Fade to Black* and John Duigan's *Head in the Clouds*, and a number of projects by new writers. Interested in working with new talent but does not consider unsolicited material.

Diverse Production Limited
Gorleston Street, London W14 8XS
☎020 7603 4567 Fax 020 7603 2148
www.diverse.tv

Contacts *Roy Ackerman, Narinder Minhas*

Broadcast television production with experience in popular prime-time formats, strong documentaries (one-offs and series), investigative journalism, science, business and history films, travel series, arts and music, talk shows, schools and education. OUTPUT includes *Secret Lives*; *Omnibus*; *Cutting Edge*; *Equinox*; *Modern Times*; *Dispatches*; *Without Walls*; *Panorama*; *The Big Idea*; *Empires and Emperors* and *The Little Picture Show*.

DMS Films Ltd
369 Burnt Oak Broadway, Edgware HA8 5XZ
☎020 8951 6060 Fax 020 8951 6050
✉ danny@argonaut.com

Producer *Daniel San*

Film drama producer. OUTPUT includes *Understanding Jane*; *Hard Edge*; *Strangers*. Unsolicited screenplays not welcome: phone, fax or e-mail synopsis or outline in first instance.

DoubleBand Films
Crescent Arts Centre, 2–4 University Road, Belfast BT7 1NH
☎028 9024 3331 Fax 028 9023 6980
✉ info@doublebandfilms.com
www.doublebandfilms.com

Contacts *Michael Hewitt, Dermot Lavery*

Specialises in documentaries and drama. Recent productions include *Seven Days that Shook the World* and *War in Mind* (both for Ch4); *Christine's Children* (BBC Northern Ireland; nominated for both the RTS and Celtic Film Festival). Currently working on documentary about Rwanda for Ch4's 'The Slot' and a Landmark D-Day documentary, *D-Day: Triumph and Tragedy* (for BBC NI).

Drake A–V Video Ltd
89 St Fagans Road, Fairwater, Cardiff
CF5 3AE
☎029 2056 0333   Fax 029 2055 4909
www.drakeav.com
Contact *Ian Lewis*

Corporate A–V film and video, mostly promotional, training or educational. Scripts in these fields welcome. Design and installation of AV systems.

The Drama House Ltd
Coach Road Cottage, Little Saxham
IP29 5LE
☎01284 810521   Fax 01284 811425
✉ jack@dramahouse.co.uk
www.dramahouse.co.uk
Contact *Jack Emery*

Film and television producer. OUTPUT *Inquisition* (Five); *Little White Lies*; *Breaking the Code* and *Witness Against Hitler* (all for BBC1); *Suffer the Little Children* (BBC2). Send two-page synopsis only. All synopses read and returned if accompanied by s.a.e. Interested especially in new writers. Consult the website before sending material.

Charles Dunstan Communications Ltd
42 Wolseley Gardens, London W4 3LS
☎020 8994 2328   Fax 020 8994 2328
Contact *Charles Dunstan*

Producer of film, video and TV for documentary and corporate material. OUTPUT *Renewable Energy* for broadcast worldwide in *Inside Britain* series; *The Far Reaches* travel series; *The Electric Environment*. No unsolicited scripts.

Ruth Evans Productions
4 Offlands Cottages, Moulsford OX10 9HP
☎01491 651331
✉ ruthgevans@msn.com
Contact *Ruth Evans*

Producer of features and documentaries for the World Service and BBC Radio 4. Unsolicited ideas and mss welcome by e-mail. New writing is 'to be encouraged'.

Fairline Productions Ltd
15 Royal Terrace, Glasgow G3 7NY
☎0141 331 0077   Fax 0141 331 0066
✉ fairprods@aol.com
Contact *Mr R. Walker*

Television and video producer of documentary and corporate programmes and commercials. OUTPUT includes *Hooked*, a 15-part angling series (Discovery Channel) plus training and instructional videos for Forbo-Nairn Ltd, Royal Bank of Scotland, and Health & Safety Executive. No unsolicited scripts.

Farnham Film Company Ltd
34 Burnt Hill Road, Lower Bourne, Farnham
GU10 3LZ
☎01252 710313   Fax 01252 725855
www.farnfilm.com
Contact *Ian Lewis*

Television and film: children's drama and documentaries. Unsolicited mss usually welcome but prefers a letter to be sent in the first instance. Check website for current requirements.

Farrant Partnership
429 Liverpool Road, London N7 8PR
☎020 7700 4647   Fax 020 7697 0224
✉ mail@farrant-partnership.com
www.farrant-partnership.com
Contact *James Farrant*

Corporate video productions, seminars, conferences.

Fast Films
Christmas House, 213 Chester Road, Castle Bromwich, Solihull B36 0ET
☎0121 749 7147/4144
Contact *Gavin Prime*

Film and television: comedy, entertainment and animation. No unsolicited mss.

Festival Film and Television Ltd
Festival House, Tranquil Passage, Blackheath, London SE3 0BJ
☎020 8297 9999   Fax 020 8297 1155
✉ info@festivalfilm.com
Contacts *Ray Marshall, Matt Marshall*

Specialises in television drama. In the last ten years has produced the Catherine Cookson drama for ITV. Now made its first feature film *Man Dancin'*. Looking primarily for commercial projects for both cinema and TV. Features: should be 'feel good'/family or projects with 'heart'. No horror or violence. TV: mainly looking for series or 2/3 parters. Not particularly interested in 'period'. Prefers submissions through an agent. Unsolicited work must be professionally presented or it will be returned unread.

Festival Productions Limited

PO Box 70, Brighton BN1 1YJ
☎01273 669595 Fax 01273 669596
✉ post@festivalradio.com
www.festivalradio.com

Managing Director *Steve Stark*

Producer of globally syndicated music shows, Sony Award winning radio campaigns, contemporary spoken word productions and a dedicated net radio service at www.totallyradio.com Unsolicited mss welcome by post or by e-mail.

Fiction Factory

14 Greenwich Church Street, London SE10 9BJ
☎020 8853 5100 Fax 020 8293 3001
✉ radio@fictionfactory.co.uk
www.fictionfactory.co.uk

Creative Director *John Taylor*

Producer of drama and documentaries for radio. OUTPUT includes Proust's *A La Recherche du Temps Perdu* (BBC R4 classic serial); *A Wild Ride to Dublin* and *After Scarborough* (new plays for R4); Susan Hill's *The Woman in Black*; *The Thin Green Line* (feature series, R4); *What About The Family* (feature series, BBC World Service). Ideas considered if sent by e-mail. Mss only from agents or writers with a professional track record in the broadcast media.

Film and General Productions Ltd

4 Bradbrook House, Studio Place, London SW1X 8EL
☎020 7235 4495 Fax 020 7245 9853
✉ cparsons@filmgen.co.uk

Contacts *Clive Parsons, Davina Belling*

Film and television drama. Feature films include *True Blue, Tea with Mussolini* and *I Am David*. Also *Seesaw* (ITV drama), *The Greatest Store in the World* (family drama, BBC) and *The Queen's Nose* (children's series, BBC). Interested in considering new writing but subject to prior telephone conversation.

Firehouse Productions

42 Glasshouse Street, London W1B 5DW
☎020 7439 2220 Fax 020 7439 2210
✉ postie@firehouse.biz
www.firehouse.biz

Contacts *Julie-anne Edwards, Gavin Knight*

Corporate films and websites, commercials and DRTV. OUTPUT includes work for De Beers; BT, Video Arts and various agencies.

The First Film Company Ltd

38 Great Windmill Street, London W1D 7LU
☎020 7439 1640 Fax 020 7437 2062
✉ info@firstfilmcompany.com

Producers *Roger Randall-Cutler, Robert Cheek*

Founded 1984. Cinema screenplays. All submissions should be made through an agent.

First Writes Theatre Company

Lime Kiln Cottage, High Starlings, Banham, Norwich NR16 2BS
☎01953 888525 Fax 01953 888974
✉ ellen@firstwrites.fsnet.co.uk
www.first-writes.co.uk

Contact *Ellen Dryden*

Producer of numerous afternoon, Friday and Saturday plays, classic serials and comedy narrative series for BBC Radio 3, 4 and World Service. Welcomes unsolictied mss or ideas by post. 'As an independent company it is difficult to obtain commissions for new writers and in-house should be your first port of call. However, we are committed to producing new work by established writers.'

Flannel

21 Berwick Street, London W1F 0PZ
☎020 7287 9277 Fax 020 7287 7785
✉ mail@flannel.net

Contact *Kate Haldane*

Producer of drama, documentaries and comedy for television and radio. OUTPUT includes *Women's Hour* (BBC R4); *The Hendersons' Christmas Party* (five-part Christmas drama – BBC R4). No unsolicited mss. 'Keen to encourage new writing, but must come via an agent. Particularly interested in 45–50 minute dramas for radio. Not in a position to produce plays for stage, but very happy to consider adaptations. Welcomes comedy with some track record.'

Flashback Television Limited

11 Bowling Green Lane, London EC1R 0BG
☎020 7490 8996 Fax 020 7490 5610
✉ mailbox@flashbacktv.co.uk
www.flashbacktv.com

Contact *Tim Ball*

Producer of documentaries and factual entertainment since 1982. Based in London and Bristol. Recent credits include *Heavy Metal/Battlestations* (A&E, Ch4); *Nigella Forever Summer* (Ch4); *No 57: The History of a House* (Ch4) and *Superhomes* (BBC).

Flicks Films Ltd
101 Wardour Street, London W1F 0UG
☎020 7734 4892 Fax 020 7287 2307
www.flicksfilms.com

Managing Director/Producer *Terry Ward*

Film and video: children's animated series and specials. OUTPUT *The Mr Men; Little Miss; Bananaman; The Pondles; Nellie the Elephant; See How They Work With Dig and Dug; Timbuctoo.* Scripts specific to their needs will be considered. 'Always willing to read relevant material.'

Focus Films Ltd
The Rotunda Studios, Rear of 116–118 Finchley Road, London NW3 5HT
☎020 7435 9004 Fax 020 7431 3562
✉ focus@focusfilms.co.uk
www.focusfilms.co.uk

Contacts *David Pupkewitz, Malcolm Kohll* (Head of Development)

Film producer. OUTPUT *The Book of Eve* (Canadian drama); *The Bone Snatcher* (Horror, UK/Can/SA); *Julia's Ghost* (German co-production); *The 51st State* (feature film); *Secret Society* (comedy drama feature film); *Crimetime* (feature thriller); *Diary of a Sane Man; Othello.* Projects in development include *Barry; Dogwatch; Indibindie.* No unsolicited scripts.

Mark Forstater Productions Ltd
27 Lonsdale Road, London NW6 6RA
☎020 7624 1123 Fax 020 7624 1124

Contact *Mark Forstater*

Active in the selection, development and production of material for film and TV. OUTPUT *Monty Python and the Holy Grail; The Odd Job; The Grass is Singing; Xtro; Forbidden; Separation; The Fantasist; Shalom Joan Collins; The Silent Touch; Grushko; The Wolves of Willoughby Chase; Between the Devil and the Deep Blue Sea; Doing Rude Things.* No unsolicited scripts.

FremantleMedia Ltd
1 Stephen Street, London W1T 1AL
☎020 7691 6000 Fax 020 7691 6100
www.fremantlemedia.com

Chief Executive *Tony Cohen*
Chief Executive, UK Production *Peter Fincham*

FremantleMedia, formerly known as Pearson Television, is the production arm of the RTL Group, Europe's largest TV and radio company. Acquired Thames Television in 1993 (producer of *The Bill*) and Grundy Worldwide (*Neighbours*) in 1995. Also Witzend Productions (*Lovejoy*) and Alomo Productions in 1996 and TalkBack Productions in 2000. FremantleMedia produces more than 260 programmes in over 39 countries and territories a year.

Full Moon Productions
rue Fenelon, Salignac Eyvigues 24590, France
☎00 33 553 29 94 06 Fax 00 33 825 17 60 28
✉ salignacfoundation@worldonline.fr
www.salignacfoundation.com

Contact *Barry C. Paton, BSc.*

Production and logistics management in France. 'We are keen to explore new and innovative drama production for broadcast and/or film. Our script advisors can assess projects. Also runs training courses in video production and screenwriting. No unsolicited scripts initially, please.' Initial contact should be by letter or e-mail.

Gabriela Productions Limited
12 Myrtle Road, London W3 6EA
✉ only4contact@yahoo.com
Contact *W. Starecki*

Film and television drama and documentary productions, including *Blooming Youth* and *Dog Eat Dog* for Ch4 and *Spider's Web* for Polish TV. Welcomes unsolicited mss.

Gaia Communications
Sanctuary House, 35 Harding Avenue, Eastbourne BN22 8PL
☎01323 734809/727183 Fax 01323 734809
✉ mail@gaiacommunications.co.uk
www.gaiacommunications.co.uk

Producer *Robert Armstrong*
Script Editor *Loni Webb*

Established 1987. Video and TV corporate and documentary. OUTPUT *Discovering* (south east regional tourist and local knowledge series); *Holistic* (therapies and general information); local interest audiobooks.

Gala Productions Ltd
25 Stamford Brook Road, London W6 0XJ
☎020 8741 4200 Fax 020 8741 2323
✉ david@galaproductions.co.uk

Producer *David Lindsay*

TV commercials, promos, film and TV documentaries.

Noel Gay Television
Shepperton Studios, Studios Road, Shepperton TW17 0QD
☎01932 592569 Fax 01932 592172

✉ charles.armitage@virgin.net

CEO *Charles Armitage*

Output: *The Fear* (BBC Choice); *Second Chance* (Ch4); *Hububb* Series 1–5 (BBC); *I-Camcorder* (Ch4); *Frank Stubbs Promotes* (Carlton/ITV); *10%ers* Series 2 (Carlton/ITV); *Call Up the Stars* (BBC1); *Smeg Outs* (BBC video); *Red Dwarf* 8xseries; *Dave Allen* (ITV); *Windrush* (BBC2). Joint ventures and companies include a partnership with Odyssey, a leading Indian commercials, film and TV producer, and the Noel Gay Motion Picture Company, whose credits include *Virtual Sexuality*; *Trainspotting* (with Ch4 and Figment Films); *Killer Tongue*; *Dog Soldiers*; *Fast Sofa*; and *Pasty Faces*. Associate NGTV companies are Grant Naylor Productions, **Rose Bay Film Productions** (see entry) and Pepper Productions. NGTV is willing to accept unsolicited material from writers but 1–2-page treatments only. No scripts, please.

Ginger Television
See **SMG & Ginger TV Productions Ltd**

Goldcrest Films International Ltd
65–66 Dean Street, London W1D 4PL
☎020 7437 8696 Fax 020 7437 4448
✉ mailbox@goldcrest-films.com

Chairman *John Quested*
Contact *Stephen Johnston*

Founded in the late 1970s. Formerly part of the Brent Walker Leisure Group but independent since 1990 following management buy-out led by John Quested. The company's core activities are film production, post-production facilities and worldwide distribution. Scripts via agents only.

The Good Film Company Ltd
The Studio, 5–6 Eton Garages, Lambolle Place, London NW3 4PE
☎020 7794 6222 Fax 020 7794 4651
✉ productions@goodfilms.co.uk
www.goodfilms.co.uk

Contact *Yanina Barry*

Commercials and pop videos. Clients include Hugo Boss, Cadbury's, Wella, National Express Coaches, Camel Cigarettes, Tunisian Tourist Board. *No* unsolicited mss.

Granada Productions (ITV plc)
The London Television Centre, Upper Ground, South Bank, London SE1 9LT
Chief Executive *Simon Shaps*
Director of Factual Entertainment *Jim Allen*

Director of Daytime & Lifestyle *Dianne Nelmes*
Director of Drama, Children's & Arts *John Whiston*

Granada Productions, **ITV plc**'s production arm, is the largest commercial TV production company in the UK. Produces original programmes, co-productions and TV movies for ITV channels and other broadcasters, both in the UK and abroad.

Granite Film & Television Productions Ltd
Vigilant House, 120 Wilton Road, London SW1V 1JZ
☎020 7808 7230 Fax 020 7808 7231

Contact *Simon Welfare*

Producer of television documentary programmes such as *Nicholas & Alexandra*; *Victoria & Albert* and *Arthur C. Clarke's Mysterious Universe*.

Green Umbrella Ltd
The Production House, 147a St Michaels Hill, Bristol BS2 8DB
☎0117 973 1729 Fax 0117 946 7432
✉ postmaster@umbrella.co.uk
www.umbrella.co.uk

Film producers specialising in science and natural history documentaries. OUTPUT includes episodes for *The Natural World*, *Wildlife on One* and original series such as *Living Europe* and *Triumph of Life*. Unsolicited treatments relating to natural history and science subjects are welcome.

Greenwich Village Productions
14 Greenwich Church Street, London SE10 9BJ
☎020 8853 5100 Fax 020 8293 3001
✉ info@greenwichvillage.tv
www.greenwichvillage.tv

Contact *John Taylor*

Producer of drama documentaries, arts features and educational programmes. OUTPUT *An Arundel Tomb* (video treatment of Philip Larkin's poem); *Pluckley – England's Haunted Village* and *The Secret Places of the Four Quartets* (drama documentaries). Welcomes ideas by e-mail. 'Mss only from agents or writers with a professional track record in the chosen medium.'

H2 Business Communications
Shepperton Studios, Shepperton TW17 0QD
☎01932 562611 (main switchboard)
✉ bob@hthc.co.uk

Contact *Bob Carson*

Conferences, videos, awards presentations and speaker training.

Hammer Film Productions Ltd

92 New Cavendish Street, London W1W 6XJ
☎020 7637 2322 Fax 020 7323 2307

Contact *Terry Ilott*

Television and feature films. Please do not send unsolicited scripts or treatments.

Hammerwood Film Productions

110 Trafalgar Road, Portslade BN41 1GS
☎01273 277333 Fax 01273 705451
✉ filmangels@freenetname.co.uk
www.filmangel.co.uk

Contacts *Ralph Harvey, Petra Ginman*

Film, video and TV drama. OUTPUT *Boadicea – Queen of Death* (film; co-production with Pan-European Film Productions and Boudicca Film Productions Ltd); *Boudicca – A Celtic Tragedy* (TV series). In pre-production: *Road to Nirvana* (Ealing-style comedy); *The Black Egg* (witchcraft in 17th century England); *The Ghosthunter; A Symphony of Spies* (true stories of WW2 espionage and resistance required); *Iceni* (documentary of the rebellion of AD61); *No Case to Answer* (legal series). 'Authors are recommended to access www.filmangel.co.uk' (see **Useful Websites**).

Hartswood Films Ltd

Twickenham Studios, The Barons, St Margarets TW1 2AW
☎020 8607 8736 Fax 020 8607 8744
✉ films.tv@hartswoodfilms.co.uk

Contact *Elaine Cameron*

Film and TV production for drama, comedy and documentary. OUTPUT *Men Behaving Badly; Border Cafe; Coupling* (all for BBC); *Me Again* (feature film).

Hat Trick Productions Ltd

10 Livonia Street, London W1F 8AF
☎020 7437 2907 Fax 020 7287 9791
www.hattrick.com

Contact *Denise O'Donoghue*

Television programmes.

Healthcare Productions Limited

Unit 1.04 Bridge House, Three Mills, Three Mill Lane, London E3 3DU
☎020 8980 9444 Fax 020 8980 1901
✉ penny@healthcareproductions.co.uk
www.healthcareproductions.co.uk

Contact *Penny Webb*

Television and video: documentary and drama. Produces training and educational material, in text, video and CD-ROM, mostly health-related, social care issues, law and marriage.

The Jim Henson Company

30 Oval Road, Camden NW1 7DE
☎020 7428 4000 Fax 020 7428 4001
www.henson.com *and*
www.muppets.com

Executive Producer *Martin Baker*

Feature films and TV: family entertainment and children's, fantasy and sci-fi. OUTPUT *Good Boy!; Buddy; Rat; The Dark Crystal; Labyrinth; The Witches* (films); *Dinosaurs* (ABC); *Muppet Tonight* (BBC/Sky); *The Muppet Show* (ITV); *The Storyteller* (Ch4/BBC); *Dr Seuss; The Secret Life of Toys* (BBC); *The Animal Show* (BBC); *Mopatop's Shop* (ITV); *Brats of the Lost Nebula* (WB); *Farscape* (Sci-Fi/USA/BBC); *Bear in the Big Blue House* (Disney Channel/Ch5); *Jim Henson's Construction Site* (ITV); *The Hoobs* (Ch4); *Jack and the Beanstalk: The Real Story* (CBS); *Telling Stories with Tomie de Paola* and *Donna's Day* (both for Odyssey); *The Fearing Mind* (Fox); *It's a Very, Merry Muppet Christmas* (NBC); *Kermit's Swamp Years* (CTHV); *Animal Jam* (Discovery); *Bambaloo* (Seven Network); *Gulliver's Travels* (CBS). Scripts via agents only.

Heritage Media Limited

Castle Eden Studios, Castle Eden TS27 4SD
☎01429 838885 Fax 01429 838775

Contact *Toby Horton*

Producer of audio publications and independent productions with a heritage/classic theme.

Heritage Theatre Ltd

8 Clanricarde Gardens, London W2 4NA
☎020 7243 2750 Fax 020 7792 8584
✉ rm@heritagetheatre.com
www.heritagetheatre.com

Contact *Robert Marshall*

Video recordings of successful stage plays, sold to the public in VHS and DVD format. 'It is possible to negotiate agreements before the production is staged.'

Hewland International Limited

Spring House, 10 Spring Place, Kentish Town NW5 3BH
☎020 7916 2266 Fax 020 7916 2244
✉ info@hewland.co.uk
www.hewland.co.uk

Contact *Jo Bierton*

Unsolicited manuscripts welcome. Scripts should be mailed to address above. 'There are never enough good new writers and we are desperate to find them ... but we specialise in commercial youth-oriented pieces.'

John Holloway
53 Daybrook Road, London SW19 3DJ
☎020 8542 7721
✉ holliesx2@aol.com

Contact *John Holloway*

Corporate video and promotional articles. Clients include the Post Office, IBM, British Gas, Freemans, Eastern Electricity, Customs & Excise.

Holmes Associates
The Studio, 37 Redington Road, London NW3 7QY
☎020 7813 4333 Fax 020 7813 4334
✉ holmesassociates@blueyonder.co.uk

Contact *Andrew Holmes*

Prolific originator, producer and packager of documentary, drama and music television and films. See also **Open Road Films**. OUTPUT has included *Prometheus* (Ch4 'Film on 4'); *The Shadow of Hiroshima* (Ch4 'Witness'); *The House of Bernarda Alba* (Ch4/WNET/Amaya); *Piece of Cake* (LWT); *The Cormorant* (BBC/Screen 2); *John Gielgud Looks Back*; *Rock Steady*; *Well Being*; *Signals*; *Ideal Home?* (all Ch4); *Timeline* (with MPT, TVE Spain & TRT Turkey); *Seven Canticles of St Francis* (BBC2).

Hourglass Productions
27 Prince's Road, London SW19 8RA
☎020 8540 8786
✉ productions@hourglass.co.uk
www.hourglass.co.uk

Directors *Martin Chilcott, Jacqueline Chilcott*

Film and video; documentary and drama. OUTPUT BAFTA nominated scientific television documentaries and educational programming. Also current affairs, health and social issues.

Icon Films
4 West End, Somerset Street, Bristol BS2 8NE
☎0117 924 8535 Fax 0117 942 0386
✉ info@iconfilms.co.uk
www.iconfilms.co.uk

Contact *Harry Marshall*

Film and TV documentaries. OUTPUT *Holy Cow!* (WNET); *A Different Ball Game* (National Geographic); *Quest for the True Cross* (Ch4/Discovery). Specialises in factual documentaries. Open-minded to new filmmakers. Proposals welcome.

Ideal Image Ltd
Cherrywood House, Crawley Down Road, Felbridge RH19 2PP
☎01342 300566

Contact *Alan Frost*

Producer of documentary and drama for film, video, TV and corporate clients. OUTPUT *24/7*; *The Pipeline*; *Beating the Market*. No unsolicited scripts.

Imari Entertainment Ltd
PO Box 158, Beaconsfield HP9 1AY
☎01494 677147 Fax 01494 677147
✉ info@imarientertainment.com

Contact *Jonathan Fowke*

TV and video producer, covering all areas of drama, documentary and corporate productions.

Impossible TV
See **Planet 24 Productions Ltd**

Isis Productions
106 Hammersmith Grove, London W6 7HB
☎020 8748 3042 Fax 020 8748 3046
✉ isis@isis-productions.com
www.isisproductions.co.uk

Directors *Nick de Grunwald, Jamie Rugge-Price*
Production Coordinator *Catriona Lawless*

Formed in 1991, Isis Productions focuses on the production of music and documentary programmes. OUTPUT *James Brown – Soul Survivor* (Ch4); *Pink Floyd* (ITV 'Classic Albums 5'); *Bernie Taupin* (ITV 'South Bank Show'); *Iron Maiden, Judas Priest* (Five 'Rock Classics'); Films on *Deep Purple, Metallica, Def Leppard, Lou Reed, Elton John, Elvis Presley, Sex Pistols* (ITV 'Classic Albums 3'); *Nosey Series 3* (Five – Children's); *The Genesis Songbook* (Five); *England's Other Elizabeth – Elizabeth Taylor* (BBC 'Omnibus').

Isolde Films
28 Twyford Avenue, London W3 9QB
☎020 8896 2860
✉ isolde@btinternet.com
www.tonypalmer.org

Contact *Michela Antonello*

Film and TV: drama and documentary. OUTPUT *Wagner*; *Menuhin*; *Maria Callas*; *Testimony*; *In From the Cold*; *Pushkin*; *England, My England* (by John Osborne); *Kipling*.

Unsolicited material is read, but please send a written outline first.

JAM Pictures and
Jane Walmsley Productions
8 Hanover Street, London W1S 1YE
☎020 7290 2676 Fax 020 7290 2677
✉ producers@jampix.com

Contacts *Jane Walmsley, Michael Braham*

JAM Pictures was founded in 1996 to produce drama for film, TV and stage. Projects include: *Hillary's Choice* (TV film, A&E Network); *Son of Pocahontas* (TV film, ABC); *Rudy: the Rudy Giuliani Story* (TV film, USA Network); *One More Kiss* (feature, directed by Vadim Jean); *Bad Blood* (UK theatre tour). Jane Walmsley Productions, formed in 1985 by TV producer, writer and broadcaster, Jane Walmsley, has completed award-winning documentaries and features such as *Hot House People* (Ch4). No unsolicited mss. 'Letters can be sent to us, asking if we wish to see mss; we are very interested in quality material, from published or produced writers only, please'

Justice Entertainment Ltd
PO Box 4377, London W1A 7SX
☎020 7467 5450 Fax 020 7467 5451
✉ info@timwestwood.com
www.timwestwood.com

Producer of shows for Radio 1. No unsolicited material.

Keo Films.com
Studio 2B, 151–157 City Road, London EC1V 1JH
☎020 7490 3580 Fax 020 7490 8419
✉ keo@keofilms.com
www.keofilms.com

Contact *Katherine Perry*

Television documentaries and factual entertainment. OUTPUT includes BBC's 'QED': *The Maggot Mogul* and *Sleeping it Off*; plus *A Cook on the Wild Side; TV Dinners; Beast of the Amazon; Big Snake* and *Jungle Trip* ('To the Ends Of The Earth' series); *River Cottage; Return to River Cottage; The Real Deal; Agia Napa Fantasy Island; Shadow People; River Cottage Forever; Brown Britain; Going To Extremes.* All for Ch4. No unsolicited mss.

Kingfisher Television Productions Ltd
Carlton Studios, Lenton Lane, Nottingham NG7 2NA

☎0115 964 5262 Fax 0115 964 5263
Contact *Tony Francis*
Broadcast television production.

Kismet Film Company
25A Old Compton Street, London W1D 5JW
☎020 7734 0099 Fax 020 7734 1222
✉ kismetfilms@dial.pipex.com

Producer *Michele Camarda*

Feature films. OUTPUT includes *Photographing Fairies; This Year's Love; Wonderland* and *Born Romantic.* Involved in workshops such as PAL Writer's Workshop, **Equinoxe Screenwriting Workshops** and North by Northwest. Kismet can no longer accept unsolicited material.

Kudos Film and Televison
65 Great Portland Street, London W1W 7LW
☎020 7580 8686 Fax 020 7580 8787
✉ reception@kudosproductions.co.uk
www.kudosfilmandtv.com

Joint Managing Directors *Jane Featherstone, Stephen Garrett*
Head of Development *Claire Parker*
General Manager *Daniel Isaacs*

Feature films such as *Among Giants* and *Pure.* Television dramas include *The Magician's House; Spooks* and *Hustle* (BBC1 series); *Psychos* (Ch4 series); *Comfortably Numb* and *Pleasureland* (Ch4). No unsolicited mss.

Ladbroke Productions (Radio) Ltd
Essel House, 29 Folet Street, London W1W 7JW
☎020 7323 2770 Fax 020 7079 2080
✉ neilgardner@ladbroke-radio.co.uk
www.ladbroke-radio.co.uk

Contacts *Neil Gardner, Richard Bannerman, Paul Kent*

Producer of radio drama, documentary, corporate, music, music documentaries and readings. OUTPUT includes *The Darling Buds of May; The True History of British Pop; The World on a String; The Colour of Music* (all for BBC Radio 2); *In the Company of Men* (BBC Radio 3 drama); *Sitting in Limbo* (BBC World Service drama); *Your Vote Counts* (Electoral Commision audio CDs). Unsolicited mss and ideas welcome; send letter in the first instance. 'We are willing to help develop for possible submission to the BBC.'

Lagan Pictures Ltd
21 Tullaghbrow, Tullaghgarley, Ballymena BT42 2LY
☎028 2563 9479/077 9852 8797

Fax 028 2563 9479
✉ laganpictures@tullaghbrow.freeserve.co.uk

Producer/Director *Stephen Butcher*

Film, video and TV: drama, documentary and corporate. OUTPUT *A Force Under Fire* (Ulster TV). In development: *Into the Bright Light of Day* (drama-doc); *The £10 Float* (feature film); *The Centre* (drama series). 'We are always interested in hearing from writers originating from or based in Northern Ireland or anyone with, preferably unstereotypical, projects relevant to Northern Ireland. We do not have the resources to deal with unsolicited mss, so please write with a brief treatment/synopsis in the first instance.'

Landseer Film and Television Productions Ltd

140 Royal College Street, London NW1 0TA
☎020 7485 7333 Fax 020 7485 7573
✉ mail@landseerfilms.com
www.landseerfilms.com

Directors *Derek Bailey, Ken Howard*

Film and video production: documentary, drama, music and arts. OUTPUT *Should Accidentally Fall* (BBC/Arts Council); *Nobody's Fool* ('South Bank Show' on Danny Kaye for LWT); *Swinger* (BBC2/Arts Council); *Auld Lang Syne* and *Retying the Knot – The Incredible String Band* (both for BBC Scotland); *Benjamin Zander* ('The Works', BBC2); *Zeffirelli, Johnnie Ray, Petula Clark* and *Bing Crosby* (all for 'South Bank Show', LWT); *Death of a Legend – Frank Sinatra* ('South Bank Show' special); *Routes of Rock* (Carlton); *See You in Court* (BBC); *Nureyev Unzipped, Gounod's Faust, The Judas Tree, Ballet Boyz, 4Dance* and *Bourne to Dance* (all for Ch4), *Proms in the Park* (Belfast).

Lilyville Screen Entertainment Ltd

7 Lilyville Road, London SW6 5DP
☎020 7371 5940 Fax 020 7736 9431
✉ tony.cash@btclick.com

Contact *Tony Cash*

Drama and documentaries for TV. OUTPUT *Poetry in Motion* (series for Ch4); 'South Bank Show': *Ben Elton* and *Vanessa Redgrave; Musique Enquête* (drama-based French language series, Ch4); *Landscape and Memory* (arts documentary series for the BBC); Jonathan Miller's production of the *St Matthew Passion* for the BBC; major documentary on the BeeGees for the 'South Bank Show'. Scripts with an obvious application to TV may be considered. Interested in new writing for documentary programmes.

London Scientific Films Ltd

Mill Studio, Crane Mead, Ware SG12 9PY
☎01920 444399
✉ lsf@londonscientificfilms.co.uk

Contact *Mike Cockburn*

Film and video documentary and corporate programming. No unsolicited mss.

Lucida Productions

49 Sunderland Road, London SE23 2PS
☎020 8699 9470

Contact *Paul Joyce*

Television and cinema: arts, adventure, current affairs, documentary, drama and music. OUTPUT has included *Motion and Emotion: The Films of Wim Wenders; Dirk Bogarde – By Myself; Sam Peckinpah – Man of Iron; Kris Kristofferson – Pilgrim; Wild One: Marlon Brando; Stanley Kubrick: 'The Invisible Man'; 2001: the Making of a Myth* (Ch4); *Mantrap – Straw Dogs, the final cut* (with Dustin Hoffman). Currently in development for documentary and drama projects.

LWT Drama

London Television Centre, Upper Ground, London SE1 9LT
☎020 7620 1620

Controller of Drama *Michele Buck*

Television drama. OUTPUT *Hornblower; Poirot; Miss Marple; Touching Evil; Where the Heart Is; The Last Detective; William and Mary.*

Malone Gill Productions Ltd

27 Campden Hill Road, London W8 7DX
☎020 7937 0557 Fax 020 7376 1727
✉ malonegill@aol.com

Contact *Georgina Denison*

Mainly documentary but also some drama. OUTPUT includes *The Face of Russia* (PBS); *Vermeer* ('South Bank Show'); *Highlanders* (ITV); *Storm Chasers; Nature Perfected* and *The Feast of Christmas* (all for Ch4); *The Buried Mirror: Reflections on Spain and the New World* by Carlos Fuentes (BBC2/Discovery Channel). Approach by letter with proposal in the first instance.

Marchmont Films

41 Marchmont Street, London WC1N 1AP
☎020 7681 0324
✉ web@marchmontfilms.com
www.marchmonfilms.com

Contact *Andrew Cussens*

Producer of short films, feature films and television drama. OUTPUT includes *Out In the*

Cold; *Platinum*; *Scooped*; *The Surveyor* and *The Boxer*. Welcomes new writers. See website for current submission criteria.

Jane Marshall Productions

The Coach-House, Westhill Road,
Blackdown, Leamington Spa CV32 6RA
☎01926 831680
✉ jane@jmproduction.freeserve.co.uk

Contact *Jane Marshall*

Producer of readings of published work both fiction and non-fiction for BBC Radio. Published work only.

Maverick Television

Progress Works, The Custard Factory, Heath Mill Lane, Birmingham B9 4AL
☎0121 771 1812 Fax 0121 771 1550
✉ maverick@mavericktv.co.uk
www.mavericktv.co.uk

Contact *Clare Welch*

Founded 1994. High quality and innovative DVC programming in both documentary and drama. Expanding into light entertainment and more popular drama. OUTPUT includes *Trade Secrets*; *Picture This: Accidental Hero* (both for BBC2); *Motherless Daughters*; *Highland Bollywood: Black Bag*; *Health Alert: My Teenage Menopause*; *Embarrassing Illnesses*; *Vee-TV* and *Home From Home* (all for Ch4); *Long Haul* (Scottish Screen/ STV); *Learning to Love the Grey* (BBC/OU).

Maya Vision International Ltd

43 New Oxford Street, London WC1A 1BH
☎020 7836 1113 Fax 020 7836 5169
www.mayavisionint.com

Contact *John Cranmer*

Film and TV: drama and documentary. OUTPUT *Saddam's Killing Fields* (for 'Viewpoint', Central TV); *3 Steps to Heaven* and *A Bit of Scarlet* (feature films for BFI/Ch4); *A Place in the Sun* and *North of Vortex* (dramas for Ch4/Arts Council); *The Real History Show* (Ch4); *In Search of Shakespeare*; *In the Footsteps of Alexander the Great*; *Conquistadors* (documentaries for BBC2); *Hitler's Search for the Holy Grail* (Ch4 documentary). Absolutely no unsolicited material; commissions only.

MBP TV

Saucelands Barn, Coolham, Horsham
RH13 8QG
☎01403 741620 Fax 01403 741647
✉ info@mbptv.com
www.mbptv.com

Contact *Phil Jennings*

Maker of film and video specialising in programmes covering equestrianism and the countryside. No unsolicited scripts, but always looking for new writers who are fully acquainted with the subject.

Melendez Films

Julia House, 44 Newman Street, London
W1T 1QD
☎020 7323 5273 Fax 020 7323 5373

Contact *Steven Melendez*

Independent producer working with TV stations. Animated films aimed mainly at a family audience, produced largely for the American market, and prime-time network broadcasting. Also develops and produces feature films (eight so far). OUTPUT has included *Peanuts*; *The Lion, the Witch and the Wardrobe*; *Babar the Elephant* (TV specials); *Dick Deadeye or Duty Done*, a rock musical based on Gilbert & Sullivan operattas. Synopses only, please. Enclose s.a.e. for return.

Mendoza Productions

75 Wigmore Street, London W1U 1QD
☎020 7935 4674 Fax 020 7935 4417
✉ debz@mendozafilms.com

Contacts *Wynn Wheldon, Debby Mendoza*

Commercials, title sequences (e.g. Alan Bleasdale's *G.B.H.*); party political broadcasts. Currently in pre-production on a feature-length comedy film. Involved with the **Screenwriters' Workshop**. Unsolicited mss welcome but 'comedies only, please'. Material will not be returned without s.a.e.

Mersey Television Company Ltd

Campus Manor, Childwall Abbey Road,
Liverpool L16 0JP
☎0151 722 9122 Fax 0151 722 1969
www.merseytv.com

Chairman *Prof. Phil Redmond*

The best known of the independents in the north of England. Makers of television drama. OUTPUT *Hollyoaks* (Ch4); *Grange Hill* (BBC)

Moonstone Films Ltd

5 Linkenholt Mansions, Stamford Brook
Avenue, London W6 0YA
☎020 8846 8511 Fax 0870 005 6839
✉ info@moonstonefilms.co.uk

Contact *Tony Stark*

TV current affairs, science and history documentaries. OUTPUT *Arafat's Authority* and *Arafat Investigated*, both for BBC 'Correspondent'. Plus various Ch4 News commissions. Unsolicited mss welcome.

MW Entertainments Ltd
48 Dean Street, London W1D 5BF
☎020 7734 7707 Fax 020 7734 7727
✉ contact@michaelwhite.co.uk

Contact *Michael White*

High-OUTPUT company whose credits include *Widow's Peak*; *White Mischief*; *Nuns on the Run*; *Enigma*; *The Comic Strip Series*. Also theatre projects, including *Notre-Dame de Paris*; *Fame*; *Me and Mamie O'Rourke*; *She Loves Me*; *Crazy for You*; *Contact*. Contributions are passed by Michael White to a script reader for consideration.

Neon
Studio One, 19 Marine Crescent, Glasgow G51 1HD
☎0141 429 6366 Fax 0141 429 6377
✉ mail@go2neon.com
www.go2neon.com

Contact *Stephanie Pordage*

Television and radio: drama and documentary producers. OUTPUT includes *The Brand New Opry*; *Man in a Briefcase*; *Peeking Past the Gates of Skibo*. Supports and encourages new writing 'at every opportunity'. Welcomes unsolicited material but telephone in the first instance.

Number 9 Films
Linton House, 24 Wells Street, London W1T 3PH
☎020 7323 4060
✉ mjensen@number9films.co.uk

Contact *Stephen Woolley*

Leading feature film producer. OUTPUT includes *Purely Belter*; *Little Voice*. Forthcoming productions: *Return to Sender*, *Mrs Harris*. No unsolicited material.

Octopus TV
See **Octopus Publishing Group** under *UK Publishers*

Odyssey Productions Ltd
72 Tay Street, Newport DD6 8AP
☎01382 542070 Fax 01382 542070
✉ billykay@sol.co.uk

Contact *Billy Kay*

Producer of radio documentaries. OUTPUT includes *Scotland's Black History*; *Gentle Shepherds* (oral history); *Street Kids* (Scottish missionaries

working with street kids in Brazil). Ideas for radio documentaries welcome; send letter with one page outlining the idea and programme content.

Omnivision
Pinewood Studios, Iver Heath SL0 0NH
☎01753 656329 Fax 01753 631146
✉ info@omnivision.co.uk
www.omnivision.co.uk

Contact *Christopher Morris*

TV and video producers of documentary, corporate, news and sport programming. Also equipment and facilities hire. Interested in ideas; approach by letter or e-mail.

ON Communication
5 East St Helen Street, Abingdon, Oxford OX14 5EG
☎01235 537400 Fax 01235 530581
✉ ON@oncomms-tv.co.uk
www.oncommunication.com

Contact *Samantha Watson*

An independent production company founded in 1985 to produce high-quality factual programming, including science, current affairs, authored documentaries for television, as well as for corporate and heritage markets.

Open Media
The Mews Studio, 8 Addison Bridge Place, London W14 8XP
✉ contact@openmedia.co.uk
www.openmedia.co.uk

Contact *Laura Cook*

Broadcast television: OUTPUT *After Dark*; *The Secret Cabaret*; *James Randi Psychic Investigator*; *Opinions*; *Is This Your Life?*; *Don't Quote Me*; *Brave New World*; *The Talking Show*; *Natural Causes*; *Equinox*; *Dispatches*.

Open Road Films
The Studio, 37 Redington Road, London NW3 7QY
☎020 7813 4333 Fax 020 7916 9172
✉ openroadfilms@blueyonder.co.uk

Development Executive *Elizabeth King*
Producer *Andrew Holmes*

Company, formed by **Holmes Associates**, to produce low to medium budget British feature films. OUTPUT *Chunky Monkey*; *Ashes & Sand*. Four projects in development. Unsolicited treatments/synopses will be considered but may take some time for response.

Orlando TV Productions

Up-the-Steps, Little Tew, Chipping Norton
OX7 4JB
☎01608 683218   Fax 01608 683364
✉ orlando.tv@btinternet.com
www.orlandodigital.co.uk

Contact *Mike Tomlinson*

Producer of TV documentaries and digital multimedia content, with science subjects as a specialisation. Approaches by established writers/journalists to discuss proposals for collaboration are welcome.

Orpheus Productions

6 Amyand Park Gardens, Twickenham
TW1 3HS
☎020 8892 3172   Fax 020 8892 4821
✉ richard-taylor@blueyonder.co.uk

Contact *Richard Taylor*

Television documentaries and corporate work. OUTPUT has included programmes for the BBC, ITV and Ch4 as well as documentaries for the United Nations, the Shell Film Unit and Video Arts. Unsolicited scripts are welcomed with caution. 'Our preference is for the more classically structured documentary that, while being hard-hitting, explores the subtleties and the paradox of an issue – and is not presented by unqualified celebrities.'

Outcast Production

92 Buckhold Road, London SW18 4AP
✉ andythewise@aol.com

Contact *Andreas Wisniewski*

Low-budget feature films. No unsolicited mss; send synopsis or treatment only. 'We are actively searching for and encouraging new writing.'

Ovation

One Prince of Wales Passage, 117 Hampstead Road, London NW1 3EF
☎020 7387 2342   Fax 020 7380 0404

Contact *John Plews*

Corporate video and conference scripts. Unsolicited mss not welcome. 'We talk to new writers from time to time.' Ovation also runs the fringe theatre, 'Upstairs at the Gatehouse' in Highgate, north London.

Oxford Scientific Films Ltd

Station Yard, Thame OX9 3UH
☎01844 262370   Fax 01844 262380
✉ enquiries@osf.uk.com
www.osf.uk.com

Chief Executive *Claire Birks*

Established media company with specialist knowledge and expertise in award-winning natural history films and science-based programmes. Film, video and TV documentaries. Scripts welcome. Operates an extensive stills and film footage library specialising in wildlife and special effects (see entry under **Picture Libraries**).

Pacificus Productions

47 Addison Avenue, London W11 4QU
☎020 7603 6991   Fax 020 7603 6593
✉ mail@pacificus.co.uk

Contacts *Clive Brill, Tom Treadwell*

Produced feature film *Before You Go* (directed by Lewis Gilbert) plus many dramas for BBC Radio 4. Clive Brill is a regular tutor at **The Arvon Foundation**. Encourages new writing with small development fund available. Approach by e-mail in the first instance with ideas and mss.

Panther Pictures Ltd

11 Southwell Gardens, London SW7 4SB
☎07976 256 610
www.pantherpictures.co.uk

Contact *Robert Sutton*

Feature films, including *Inside/Out*, a US/UK/Canada/France co-production.

Paper Moon Productions

Wychwood House, Burchetts Green Lane, Littlewick Green, Nr. Maidenhead SL6 3QW
☎01628 829819   Fax 01628 825949
✉ david@paper-moon.co.uk

Contact *David Haggas*

Broadcast documentaries and corporate communications. Recent OUTPUT includes *Bilbo & Beyond*, an affectionate glimpse into the life and work of the dedicated philologist and fantasy writer J.R.R. Tolkien.

Parallax Independent Ltd

7 Denmark Street, London WC2H 8LZ
☎020 7836 1478   Fax 020 7497 8062
www.parallaxindependent.co.uk

Contact *Sally Hibbin*

Feature films/television drama. OUTPUT *A Very British Coup*; *Riff-Raff*; *Bad Behaviour*; *Raining Stones*; *Ladybird, Ladybird*; *i.d.*; *Land and Freedom*; *The Englishman Who Went up a Hill But Came Down a Mountain*; *Bliss*; *Jump the Gun*; *Carla's Song*; *The Governess*; *My Name Is Joe*; *Stand and Deliver*; *Dockers*; *Hold Back the Night*; *Bread and*

Roses; Princesa; The Navigators; Sweet Sixteen; Innocence; The Intended; Blind Flight; Yasmin.

Passion Pictures
3rd Floor, 33–34 Rathbone Place, London W1T 1JN
☎020 7323 9933 Fax 020 7323 9030
✉ info@passion-pictures.com

Managing Director *Andrew Ruhemann*

Documentary and drama includes: *One Day in September* (Academy Award-winner for Best Feature Documentary, 2000); also commercials and music videos: Carphone Warehouse, Mini, Aero, Gorillaz, Coldplay and Robbie Williams. Unsolicited mss welcome.

Pathé Pictures
14–17 Kenthouse, Market Place, London W1W 8AR
☎020 7323 5151 Fax 020 7631 3568

Head of Creative Affairs *Celine Haddad*
Development & Acquisitions Executive *Erol Arguden*
Story Editor *Charlie Mitchell*

Produces 4–6 theatrical feature films each year. 'We are pleased to consider all material that has representation from an agent or production company.'

PBF Motion Pictures
Lilac Cottage, Portsmouth Road, Ripley GU23 6ER
☎01483 225179
✉ peter@pbf.co.uk

Contact *Peter B. Fairbrass*

Film, video and TV: drama, documentary, commercials and corporate. Also televised chess series and chess videos. No scripts. No submissions.

Pearson Television
See **FremantleMedia Ltd**

Pelicula Films
59 Holland Street, Glasgow G2 4NJ
☎0141 287 9522 Fax 0141 287 9504

Contact *Mike Alexander*

Television producer. Maker of drama documentaries and music programmes for the BBC and Ch4. OUTPUT *As an Eilean (From the Island); The Trans-Atlantic Sessions 1 & 2; Nanci Griffith, Other Voices 2; Follow the Moonstone.*

Photoplay Productions Ltd
21 Princess Road, London NW1 8JR
☎020 7722 2500 Fax 020 7722 6662

✉ photoplay@compuserve.com

Contact *Patrick Stanbury*

Documentaries for film, television and video plus restoration of silent films and their theatrical presentation. OUTPUT includes: *The Cat and the Canary; Orphans of the Storm; Cecil B. DeMille, American Epic* and the 'Channel 4 Silents' series of silent film restoration, including *The Wedding March* and *The Iron Mask.* Recently completed *The Tramp and the Dictator.* No unsolicited mss; 'we tend to create and write all our own programmes.'

Picardy Media & Communication
1 Park Circus, Glasgow G3 6AX
☎0141 333 5554 Fax 0141 332 6002
✉ jr@picardy.co.uk
www.picardy.co.uk

Head of Production *John Rocchiccioli*

Television and video: arts documentaries, training and promotional videos, education projects, multi-media productions, and TV and cinema commercials. Unsolicited mss welcome; 'keen to encourage new writing.'

Picture Palace Films Ltd
13 Egbert Street, London NW1 8LJ
☎020 7586 8763 Fax 020 7586 9048
✉ info@picturepalace.com
www.picturepalace.com

Contacts *Malcolm Craddock, Katherine Hedderly*

Leading independent producer of film and TV drama. OUTPUT *Rebel Heart* (BBC1); *Extremely Dangerous* and *A Life for A Life* (both for ITV); *Sharpe's Rifles* (14 films for Carlton TV); *Little Napoleons* (comedy drama, Ch4); *The Orchid House* (drama serial, Ch4); *Tandoori Nights; 4 Minutes; When Love Dies* (all for Ch4); *Ping Pong* (feature film); *Acid House* (Picture Palace North). Material will only be considered if submitted through an agent.

Planet 24 Productions Ltd
35–38 Portman Square, London W1H 0NU
☎020 7486 6268 Fax 020 7612 0679
✉ info@planet24.co.uk
www.planet24.com

Managing Director *Ed Forsdick*

Television producer of light and factual entertainment, comedy, music, features and computer animation. Wholly owned subsidiary of **ITV plc**. OUTPUT *The Big Breakfast; The Word; Watercolour Challenge; The Richard Blackwood Show; Little Friends; Survivor.* Also animation productions via Impossible TV. OUTPUT *Too Much TV*; *MechaNick*; *Doghouse*.

Plantagenet Films Limited

Ard-Daraich Studio B, Ardgour, Nr Fort William PH33 7AB
☎01855 841384 Fax 01855 841384
✉ plantagenetfilms@aol.com

Contact *Norrie Maclaren*

Film and television: documentary and drama programming such as *Dig* (gardening series for Ch4); various 'Dispatches' for Ch4 and 'Omnibus' for BBC. Keen to encourage and promote new writing; unsolicited mss welcome.

Portobello Pictures

PO Box 34874, London W8 7YX
☎020 7985 0132 Fax 020 7985 0131

Contacts *Eric Abraham, Will Cookson*

Film drama, including Jan Sverak's *Dark Blue World* and *Kolya*; Jez Butterworth's *Mojo* and Tim Roth's *The War Zone*, plus BBC1's *Dalziel & Pascoe* (series 1–3).

Pozzitive Television

Paramount House, 162–170 Wardour Street, London W1F 8AB
☎020 7734 3258 Fax 020 7437 3130
✉ pozzitive@pozzitive.demon.co.uk

Contact *David Tyler*

Producer of comedy and entertainment for television and radio. OUTPUT *Dinner Ladies*; *Coogan's Run*; *The 99p Challenge*. Unsolicited mss of TV comedy only welcome. 'No screenplays or stage plays, please. Send hard copy of full sample script. We read everything submitted this way.'

Promenade Enterprises Limited

6 Russell Grove, London SW9 6HS
☎020 7582 9354 Fax 020 7587 1564
✉ info@promenadeproductions.com
www.promenade productions.com

Contact *Nicholas Newton*

Producer of drama for radio and theatre predominantly. Supports new writing but only accepts unsolicited mss via agents or producers.

Redweather

Easton Business Centre, Felix Road, Easton BS5 0HE
☎0117 941 5854 Fax 0117 941 5851
✉ jayne@redweather.co.uk

Contact *Jayne Cotton*

Broadcast documentaries on arts and disability, corporate video and CD-ROM, Water Aid, British Oxygen, etc.

Renaissance Vision

256 Fakenham Road, Taverham, Norwich NR8 6QW
☎01603 260280 Fax 01603 864853
✉ bfg@renvision.co.uk

Contact *B. Gardner*

Video: full range of corporate work (training, sales, promotional, etc.). Producers of educational and special-interest video publications. Willing to consider good ideas and proposals.

Richmond Films & Television Ltd

PO Box 33154, London NW3 4AZ
☎020 7722 6464 Fax 020 7722 6232
✉ mail@richmondfilms.com

Contact *Development Executive*

Film and TV: drama and comedy. OUTPUT *Press Gang*; *The Lodge*; *The Office*; *Wavelength*; *Privates*. No unsolicited scripts.

Rose Bay Film Productions

13 Austin Friars, London EC2N 2JX
☎020 7670 1609 Fax 020 8357 0845
✉ info@rosebay.co.uk

Contacts *Matthew Steiner, Simon Usiskin*

Formats and TV production: entertainment and comedy. Unsolicited scripts (with s.a.e.) welcome.

Brenda Rowe Productions

42 Wellington Park, Clifton BS8 2UW
☎0117 973 0390 Fax 0117 973 8254
✉ br007b3169@blueyonder.co.uk

Contact *Brenda Rowe*

Produces observational, investigative, current affairs TV documentaries, and training and promotional videos for business organisations. Open to new work; unsolicited mss welcome.

RS Productions

191 Trewhitt Road, Newcastle upon Tyne NE6 5DY
☎0191 224 4301/07710 064632 (Mobile)
Fax 0191 224 4301
✉ enquiries@rsproductions.co.uk
www.rsproductions.co.uk

Contact *Mark Lavender*

Feature films and television: drama series/serials and singles. TV docs and series. Working with established and new talent.

Sands Films

119 Rotherhithe Street, London SE16 4NF
☎020 7231 2209 Fax 020 7231 2119
www.sandsfilms.co.uk

Contacts *Christine Edzard, Olivier Stockman*

Film and TV drama. OUTPUT *Little Dorrit; The Fool; As You Like It; A Dangerous Man; The Long Day Closes; A Passage to India; Topsy Turvy; Nicholas Nickleby; The Gangs of New York; The Children's Midsummer Night's Dream.* No unsolicited scripts.

Scala Productions Ltd

4th Floor, Portland House, 4 Great Portland Street, London W1W 8QJ
☎020 7612 0060 Fax 020 7612 0031
✉ scalaprods@aol.com

Contacts *Ian Prior*

Production company set up by ex-Palace Productions Nik Powell and Stephen Woolley, who have an impressive list of credits including *Company of Wolves; Absolute Beginners; Mona Lisa; Scandal; The Crying Game; Backbeat; Neon Bible; 24:7; Little Voice; Divorcing Jack; The Last September; Wild About Harry; Last Orders; A Christmas Carol – The Movie; Black and White; Leo; One Love; The Night We Called It A Day.* In development: *Brian Jones Project; The Queen & I; Meek; The Coat; Train to Glory; Du Cane's Boys; Shang-a-Lang; Level; Johnny Bollywood; English Passengers; He Kills Coppers; Eden's Team.*

Scope Productions Ltd

123 Blythswood Street, Glasgow G2 4EN
☎0141 332 7720 Fax 0141 332 1049
✉ laurakingwell@scopeproductions.co.uk
www.scopeproductions.co.uk

Corporate *Laura Kingwell*

Corporate film and video; broadcast documentaries and sport; TV commercials.

Screen First Ltd

The Studios, Funnells Farm, Down Street, Nutley TN22 3LG
☎01825 712034 Fax 01825 713511
✉ paul.madden@virgin.net

Contacts *M. Thomas, P. Madden*

Television dramas, documentaries, arts and animation programmes. Developing major drama series, feature films, animated specials and series. No unsolicited scripts.

Screen Ventures Ltd

49 Goodge Street, London W1T 1TE
☎020 7580 7448

✉ sales@screenventures.com

Contacts *Christopher Mould, Michael Evans*

Film and TV sales and production: documentary, music videos and drama. OUTPUT *Life and Limb* (documentary, Discovery Health Channel); *Pavement Aristocrats* (SABC); *Woodstock Diary; Vanessa Redgrave* and *Genet* (both for LWT 'South Bank Show'); *Mojo Working; Burma: Dying for Democracy* (Ch4); *Dani Dares* (Ch4 series on strong women); *Pagad* (Ch4 news report).

Screenhouse Productions Ltd

Chapel Allerton House, 114 Harrogate Road, Leeds LS7 4NY
☎0113 266 8881 Fax 0113 266 8882
✉ paul.bader@screenhouse.co.uk
www.screenhouse.co.uk

Contacts *Paul Bader, Barbara Govan*

Factual programmes, mainly popular science and history. Also new media. OUTPUT includes *Science Shack*, BBC2 series presented by Adam Hart-Davis; six series of *Local Heroes*, factual programmes about the greats of science; two series of *Hart-Davis on History*, a magazine series about local history and how to become involved in historical research (both for BBC2); two history series for BBC Knowledge, *History Quest* and *History Fix.* Contact with one-page outline of idea in the first instance.

Screenprojex.com – a division of Screen Production Associates Ltd

✉ enquiries@screenprojex.com
screenprojex.com
Contacts *Doug Abbott, John Jaquiss, Julia Vickers*

Feature films: *The Fourth Man; The Case; Black Badge; The Truth Game; Club Le Monde; Midnight Warriors; Strong Language; Holding On; Chunky Monkey; Sixty-three Closure.* No unsolicited mss. Send preliminary letter outlining project and c.v.

September Films Ltd

Glen House, 22 Glenthorne Road, London W6 0NG
☎020 8563 9393 Fax 020 8741 7214
✉ september@septemberfilms.com
www.septemberfilms.com

Head of Production *Elaine Day*
Head of Drama and Film Development *Nadine Mellor*

Factual entertainment and documentary specialists expanding further into television drama and film. Feature film OUTPUT includes *Breathtaking; House of America; Solomon & Gaenor.*

Serendipity Picture Company

Media Centre, Emma-Chris Way,
Abbeywood Park, Bristol BS34 7JU
☎0117 906 6541   Fax 0117 906 6542
✉ tony@serendipitypictures.com

Contacts *Tony Yeadon, Nick Dance*

Television and video; corporate and documentary programming. Encourages new writing and will consider scripts.

Shell Like

81 Whitfield Street, London W1T 4HG
☎020 7255 5204   Fax 020 7255 5255
✉ enquiries@shellike.com
www.shelllike.com

Contact *Nicola Warman-Johnston*

Produces radio commercials. Unsolicited mss and ideas welcome; send by e-mail.

Sianco Cyf

36 Y Maes, Caernarfon LL55 2NN
☎01286 676100/07831 726111 (mobile)
Fax 01286 677616
✉ post@sianco.tv

Contact *Siân Teifi*

Children's, youth and education programmes, children's drama, people-based documentaries for adults.

SilentSound Films Ltd

Cambridge Court, Cambridge Road, Frinton on Sea CO13 9HN
☎01255 676381   Fax 01255 676381
✉ thj@silentsoundfilms.co.uk
www.silentsoundfilms.co.uk
www.londonfoodfilmfiesta.co.uk

Contact *Timothy Foster*

Active in European film co-production with mainstream connections in the USA. Special interest in developing stage and film musicals and documentaries on the arts. Synopses considered via e-mail or post.

Siriol Productions

3 Mount Stuart Square, Butetown, Cardiff CF10 5EE
☎029 2048 8400   Fax 029 2048 5962
✉ enquiries@siriol.co.uk
www.siriolproductions.com

Contact *Andrew Offiler*

Animated series, mainly for children. OUTPUT includes *Meeow*; *Hilltop Hospital*; *The Hurricanes*; *Tales of the Toothfairies*; *Billy the Cat*; *The Blobs*, as well as the feature films, *Under Milkwood* and

The Princess and the Goblin. Write with ideas and sample script in the first instance.

Skyline Productions

10 Scotland Street, Edinburgh EH3 6PS
☎0131 557 4580   Fax 0131 556 4377
✉ leslie@skyline.uk.com
www.skyline.uk.com

Producer/Writer *Leslie Hills*

Produces film and television drama and documentary.

SMG & Ginger TV Productions Ltd

SMG: 200 Renfield Street, Glasgow G2 3PR
☎0141 300 3000

Also: Ginger TV Productions, 116 New Oxford Street, London WC1A 1HH
☎020 7663 2300
www.ginger.com

Managing Director (SMG) *Elizabeth Partyka*
Head of Drama *Eric Coulter*
Head of Factual Programming *Helen Alexander*

SMG (Scottish Media Group) TV Productions Ltd, which incorporates Ginger Television, makes programmes for the national television networks, including ITV, Ch4 and Sky. Specialises in drama, factual entertainment and children's programming. OUTPUT includes *Taggart*; *Rebus*; *Our Daughter Holly*; *Club Reps*.

So Television Ltd

18 Hatfields, London SE1 8GN
☎020 7960 2000   Fax 020 7960 2095

Contact *Nina Gosling*

Producer of a daily entertainment comedy show for television. Developing comedy entertainment and comedy narrative. No unsolicited mss.

Somethin Else

Units 1–4, 1A Old Nichol Street, London E2 7HR
☎020 7613 3211   Fax 020 7739 9799
✉ info@somethin-else.com
www.somethin-else.com

Contact *Jez Nelson*

Producer of television, video and radio documentaries. Ideas for TV shows welcome; send letter in the first instance.

Specific Films

25 Rathbone Street, London W1T 1NQ
☎020 7580 7476   Fax 020 7494 2676
✉ info@specificfilms.com

Contacts *Michael Hamlyn*

Founded 1991. OUTPUT includes *Mr Reliable* (feature film co-produced by PolyGram and the AFFC); *The Adventures of Priscilla, Queen of the Desert*, co-produced with Latent Image (Australia) and financed by PolyGram and AFFC; *U2 Rattle and Hum*, full-length feature – part concert film/part cinema verité documentary; *Paws* (executive producer); *The Last Seduction 2* (Polygram); and numerous pop promos for major international artists.

Spellbound Productions Ltd

90 Cowdenbeath Path, Islington, London N1 0LG

☎020 7713 8066 Fax 020 7713 8066

✉ phspellbound@hotmail.com

Contact *Paul Harris*

Specialises in feature films for cinema and drama for television. Keen to support and encourage new writing. Material will only be considered if in correct screenplay format and accompanied by s.a.e.

Spice Factory (UK) Ltd

81 The Promenade, Brighton BN10 8LS

☎01273 585275 Fax 01273 585304

✉ shirine@spicefactory.co.uk

Contacts *Lucy Shuttleworth, Shirine Best*

Founded 1995. Film producers. OUTPUT *Mr In-Between* (starring Andrew Howard); *Plots With a View* (Christopher Walken, Brenda Blethyn, Alfred Molina, Lee Evans); *Bollywood Queen* (Preeya Kallidas, James McAvoy, Ian McShane); *The Bridge of San Luis Rey* (Robert De Niro, Kathy Bates, Harvey Keitel); *A Different Loyalty* (Sharon Stone, Rupert Everett); *Head in the Clouds* (Charlize Theron, Penelope Cruz). No unsolicited material accepted.

'Spoken' Image Ltd

8 Hewitt Street M15 4GB

☎0161 236 7522 Fax 0161 236 0020

✉ multimedia@spoken-image.com

www.spoken-image.com

Contacts *Geoff Allman, Steve Foster*

Film, video and TV production for documentary and corporate material. Specialises in high-quality brochures and reports, CD-ROMs, exhibitions, conferences, film and video production for broadcast, industry and commerce.

Starz! – Film and Theatre Performing Arts

See entry under *UK Writers' Courses*

Tony Staveacre Productions

Channel View, Blagdon BS40 7TP

☎01761 462161 Fax 01761 462161

✉ staving@dircon.co.uk

Contact *Tony Staveacre*

Producer of dramas and documentaries as well as music, arts and comedy progammes. OUTPUT *The Wodehouse Notebooks* (for radio and TV); *The Liberation of Daphne, Speaking from the Belly* (Radio Four); *The Very Thought of You* (theatre). Welcomes unsolicited mss by mail or e-mail, 'especially from those who understand that it is becoming harder and harder to find a path through the commissioning maze!'

Stirling Film & TV Productions Limited

137 University Street, Belfast BT7 1HP

☎028 9033 3848 Fax 028 9043 8644

✉ anne@stirlingtelevision.co.uk

Contact *Anne Stirling*

Producer of broadcast and corporate programming – documentary, sport, entertainment and lifestyle programmes.

Storm Film Productions Ltd

32–34 Great Marlborough Street, London W1F 7JB

☎020 7439 1616 Fax 020 7439 4477

✉ sophie.storm@btclick.com

www.stormfilms.tv

Contact *Nic Auerbach*

Producer of commercials for clients such as British Airways and Shell. Unsolicited mss welcome.

Straight Forward Film & Television Productions Ltd

Building 2, Lesley Office Park, 393 Hollywood Road, Belfast BT4 2LS

☎028 9065 1010 Fax 028 9065 1012

✉ enquiries@straightforward.co.uk

Contacts *John Nicholson, Ian Kennedy*

Northern Ireland-based production company specialising in documentary, feature and lifestyle series for both regional and network transmission. OUTPUT includes *We Shall Overcome* (winner of Best Documentary at 1999 Celtic Television Festival for BBC); *Conquering the Normans* (Ch4 Learning – history of Normans in Ireland); *Gift of the Gab* (Ch4 Learning – contemporary Irish writing); *Fire School* (BBC NI – training of a team of fire-fighters); *Fish Out of Water* (BBC NI – job swaps north and south of the Irish border); *Just Jones* (BBC Radio Ulster daily show); *Sportsweek* (BBC Radio Ulster); *School Challenge* (3rd series, BBC NI); *World Indoor Bowls* (BBC NI); *Awash With Colour* (series, BBC Daytime).

Strawberry Productions Ltd
36 Priory Avenue, London W4 1TY
☎020 8994 4494 Fax 020 8742 7675

Contact *John Black*

Film, video and TV: drama and documentary; corporate and video publishing.

Sunset + Vine Productions Ltd
30 Sackville Street, London W1S 3DY
☎020 7478 7300 Fax 020 7478 7403

Sports, children's and music programmes for television. No unsolicited mss. 'We hire freelancers only upon receipt of a commission.'

Table Top Productions
1 The Orchard, Chiswick, London W4 1JZ
☎020 8742 0507 Fax 020 8742 0507
✉ alvin@tabletopproductions.com

Contact *Alvin Rakoff*

TV and film. OUTPUT *Paradise Postponed* (TV mini-series); *A Voyage Round My Father; The First Olympics 1896; Dirty Tricks; A Dance to the Music of Time; Too Marvellous for Words.* Also Dancetime Ltd. No unsolicited mss.

talkbackTHAMES Productions
20–21 Newman Street, London W1T 1PG
☎020 7861 8000 Fax 020 7861 8001
✉ reception@talkback.co.uk

Chief Executive Officer *Peter Fincham*
Chief Operating Officer *Sally Debonnaire*

talkackTHAMES Productions is a **Fremantle-Media** company. Specialises in comedy, comedy drama and drama; also feature lifestyle programmes. OUTPUT *Smith and Jones; Murder Most Horrid; The Day Today; Knowing Me Knowing You with Alan Partridge; I'm Alan Partridge; They Think It's All Over; Never Mind the Buzzcocks; Brass Eye; House Doctor; She's Gotta Have It; Grand Designs; Sword of Honour; In a Land of Plenty; Shooting the Past; 11 o'clock Show; Smack the Pony; Big Train; Los Dos Bros; Your Money or Your Life; Property Ladder; Would Like to Meet.*

Tandem TV & Film Ltd
Suite 206, Charleston House, Hemel Hempstead HP1 3AA
☎01442 261576 Fax 01442 219250
✉ info@tandemtv.com

www.tandemtv.com

Contact *Barbara Page*

Produces training videos, especially health and safety; construction and civil engineering documentaries; drama–doc life stories for satellite television; Christian church and charity documentary, training and promotional programmes. Welcomes unsolicited mss.

Taylor Made Broadcasts Ltd
PO Box 100, Woodstock OX20 1XE
☎01608 677777
✉ post@tmtv.co.uk

Contact *Trevor Taylor*

Producer of corporate videos and documentaries for television and radio. OUTPUT includes *Gardeners' Question Time* (BBC Radio 4). No unsolicited mss.

Telemagination Ltd
Royalty House, 72–74 Dean Street, London W1V 6AE
☎020 7434 1551 Fax 020 7434 3344
✉ mail@tmation.co.uk
www.telemagination.co.uk

Contact *Marion Edwards*

Producer of television animation. OUTPUT includes *The Animals of Farthing Wood; Noah's Island; The Last Polar Bears; Little Ghosts; Pongwiffy.* In production: *Heidi.* No unsolicited material.

Tern Television Productions Ltd
73 Crown Street, Aberdeen AB11 6EX
☎01224 211123 Fax 01224 211199
✉ office@terntv.com
www.terntv.com

Also at: RWF House, 5 Renfield Street, Glasgow G2 5EZ ☎0141 243 5678
Contacts *David Strachan, Gwyneth Hardy* (Aberdeen), *Harry Bell* (Glasgow)

Broadcast, television and corporate video productions. Specialises in factual entertainment. Currently developing drama.

Testbed Productions
Fifth Floor, 14–16 Great Portland Street, London W1W 8QW
☎020 7436 0555 Fax 020 7436 2800
✉ mail@testbed.co.uk
www.testbed.co.uk

Contacts *Viv Black, Nick Baker*

Producer of documentaries, light entertainment, factual and spoken word programmes for radio. OUTPUT *Straw Poll; I Should Be So Lucky.*

Welcomes unsolicited mss by post. 'We read all that comes in.'

Testimony Films
12 Great George Street, Bristol BS1 5RS
☎0117 925 8589 Fax 0117 925 7608
✉ stevehumphries@testimonyfilms.force9.co.uk

Contact *Steve Humphries*

TV documentary producer. Specialises in social history exploring Britain's past using living memory. OUTPUT includes *Hooked: History of Addictions*; *Married Love* (both Ch4 series); *A Secret World of Sex* (BBC series); *The 50s & 60s in Living Colour*; *Some Liked It Hot* (both ITV series). Welcomes ideas from those working on life stories and oral history.

Theatre of Comedy Company
See under *Theatre Producers*

Tiger Aspect Productions Ltd
5 Soho Square, London W1D 3QA
☎020 7434 0672 Fax 020 7287 1448
✉ beatriceread@tigeraspect.co.uk
www.tigeraspect.co.uk

Contact *Charles Brand*

Television producer for comedy, drama, documentary and entertainment. OUTPUT *Births, Marriages & Deaths*; *Kid in the Corner*; *Country House*; *Gimme Gimme Gimme*; *Harry Enfield & Chums*; *Howard Goodalls' Big Bangs*; *Playing the Field I, II & III*; *Streetmate I & II*; *Let Them Eat Cake*; *The Vicar of Dibley*. Only considers material submitted via an agent or from writers with a known track record.

Tintinna Ltd
Summerfield, Bristol Road, Chew Stoke BS40 8UB
☎01275 333128 Fax 01275 332316
✉ tintinna@aol.com

Contacts *W. Ian Bell, Sandy Bell*

Producer of history programmes, human interest features and documentaries for radio. OUTPUT includes *What If?*, *That's History* (BBC Radio 4); *Cuppa, Goldfish & Candy Floss* (BBC Radio 2). Most recently, *This Green Unpleasant Land* (BBC Radio 4). Welcomes unsolicited mss by e-mail but 'difficult to sell to network commissioners'.

Tonfedd Eryri
Hen Ysgol Aberpwll, Y Felinheli, Bangor LL56 4JS
☎01248 671167 Fax 01248 671172
✉ swyddfa@tonfedd-eryri.com

Contacts *Hefin Elis, Norman Williams*

Light entertainment, comedy, music and drama.

Touch Productions Ltd
The Malt House Studios, Donhead St Mary SP7 9DN
☎01747 828030 Fax 01747 828004
✉ erica@touchproductions.co.uk

Contacts *Erica Wolfe-Murray, Malcolm Brinkworth*

Over the past 17 years has produced 'investigative documentary films, history based films with a strong contemporary relevance, powerful observational series and innovative films that stretch the form.' Television documentaries such as *Life of a £10 Note*; *Afghan Warrior – the Life & Death of Abdul Haq*; *Falklands 20th Anniversary*; *OJ – The Untold Story*; *Simon Weston V*; *Siege Doctors* (all for BBC); *The Good Life*; *The Surgery*; *Coast of Dreams*; *A French Affair*, *Watching the Detectives*; *Brown Babies* (all for Ch4); *Fame School* and *Fame School – the Graduates* (both for Meridian). Also has a drama section based on real-life stories and unsolicited mss are welcome.

Transatlantic Films Production and Distribution Company
Studio One, 3 Brackenbury Road, London W6 0BE
☎020 8735 0505 Fax 020 8735 0605
✉ mail@transatlanticfilms.com
www.transatlanticfilms.com

Executive Producer *Revel Guest*

Producer of TV documentaries. OUTPUT *Belzoni* (Ch4 Schools); *Science of Sleep and Dreams*; *Science of Love* and *Extreme Body Parts* (all for Discovery Health); *Legends of the Living Dead* (Discovery Travel/S4C International); *2025* (Discovery Digital); *How Animals Tell the Time* (Discovery); *Trailblazers* (Travel Channel). No unsolicited scripts. Interested in new writers to write 'the book of the series', e.g. for *Greek Fire* and *The Horse in Sport*, but not usually drama script writers.

TV Choice Ltd
PO Box 597, Bromley BR2 OYB
☎020 8464 7402 Fax 020 8464 7845
✉ tvchoiceuk@aol.com
www.tvchoice.uk.com

Contact *Norman Thomas*

Produces a range of educational videos for schools and colleges on subjects such as history, geography, business studies and economics. No unsolicited mss; send proposals only.

Twentieth Century Fox Film Co
Twentieth Century House, 31–32 Soho Square, London W1D 3AP
☎020 7437 7766 Fax 020 7734 3187
www.fox.co.uk
London office of the American giant.

Twofour Productions Limited
Quay West Studios, Old Newnham, Plymouth PL7 5BH
☎01752 333900 Fax 01752 344224
✉ enq@twofour.co.uk
www.twofour.co.uk
Managing Director *Charles Wace*
Director of Broadcasting *Jill Lourie*

Specialises in factual and leisure programming for network and regional television; corporate communications for national/international business and public sector; special interest videos for retail/mail order; and, through its subsidiary twofourtv, webcasting and Intrantet or Intranet-based TV.

Tyburn Film Productions Limited
Cippenham Court, Cippenham Lane, Cippenham, Nr Slough SL1 5AU
☎01753 516767 Fax 01753 691785
Feature films. Subsidiary of **Arlington Productions Limited**. No unsolicited submissions.

UBA Ltd
21 Alderville Road, London SW6 2EE
☎01984 623619 Fax 01984 623733
Contacts *Peter Shaw, Joanna Shaw*

Feature films and TV for an international market. OUTPUT *Windprints; The Lonely Passion of Judith Hearne* (co-production with HandMade Films Ltd); *Taffin; Castaway; Turtle Diary; Sweeney Todd; Keep the Aspidistra Flying.* In development: *Kinder Garden; Rebel Magic; No Man's Land.* Prepared to commission new writing whether adapted from another medium or based on a short outline/treatment. Concerned with the quality of the script (*Turtle Diary* was written by Harold Pinter) and breadth of appeal. 'Exploitation material' not welcome.

UK Film and TV Production Company Plc
3 Colville Place, London W1T 2BH
☎020 7255 1650
Contact *Henrietta Fudakowski*

Film and television. Currently looking for feature film or TV drama scripts, with a prefer-

ence for stories with humour. No TV formats, please. Return postage and list of credits essential. Please phone before submitting material.

Vera Productions
66–68 Margaret Street, London W1W 8SR
☎020 7436 6116 Fax 020 7436 6117
Contact *Cree Jones*

Produces television comedy such as *Rory Bremner*.

Video Enterprises
12 Barbers Wood Road, High Wycombe HP12 4EP
☎01494 534144/07831 875216 (Mobile)
Fax 01494 534145
✉ videoenterprises@btconnect.com
www.videoenterprises-uk.co.uk
Contact *Maurice R. Fleisher*

Video and TV, mainly corporate: business and industrial training, promotional material and conferences. No unsolicited material 'but always ready to try out good new writers'.

VIP Broadcasting
8 Bunbury Way, Epsom KT17 4JP
☎01372 721196 Fax 01372 726697
✉ mail@vipbroadcasting.co.uk
Contact *Chris Vezey*

Produces radio documentaries (usually about musical people, including interviews and music) and corporate radio worldwide. Won award for 'Best Sound' at New York Festival 2000. Approach with idea by e-mail in the first instance; no unsolicited mss.

Brian Waddell Productions Ltd
Strand Studios, 5/7 Shore Road, Holywood BT18 9HX
☎028 9042 7646 Fax 028 9042 7922
✉ strand@bwpltv.co.uk
Contacts *Brian Waddell*

Producer of a wide range of television programmes in leisure activities, the arts, children's, travel/adventure and documentaries.

Wall to Wall
8–9 Spring Place, London NW5 3ER
☎020 7485 7424 Fax 020 7267 5292
www.walltowall.co.uk
Chief Executive *Alex Graham*

Factual and drama programming. OUTPUT includes *New Tricks; A Rather English Marriage; Glasgow Kiss; Sex, Chips & Rock 'n' Roll; The 1940s House; Body Story* and *Neanderthal*.

Jane Walmsley Productions
See **JAM Pictures**

Walnut Media Communications Ltd
Crown House, Armley Road, Leeds LS12 2EJ
☎08707 427070 Fax 08707 427080
✉ mail@walnutmedia.com
www.walnutmedia.com

Contact *Geoff Penn*

Walnut Media provides business communications services to large corporate clients through a range of services such as video, live events and new media. Founded as the Walnut Partnership in 1984, the company has diversified from corporate video production in order to provide a more complete visual service.

Walsh Bros. Limited
4 The Heights, London SE7 8JH
☎020 8858 6870/8854 5557/07879 816426
Fax 020 8858 6870/8854 5557
✉ john@walshbros.co.uk
www.walshbros.co.uk

Producer/Director *John Walsh*
Producer/Head of Finance *David Walsh, ACA*
Producer/Head of Development *Maura Walsh*

Producer of television, film drama and documentaries. OUTPUT *Monarch* (feature film); *Headhunting the Homeless* (BBC programme on the perception of homeless people in the work place); *Trex* (factual series on teenagers at work in China, Mexico, Vancouver and Alaska); *Trex2* (follow-up series covering Romania, India, Iceland and Louisiana); *Boyz & Girlz*, (Derbyshire dairy farm documentary series); *Cowboyz & Cowgirlz* (US sequel to hit series of Brit teens working on a ranch in Montana). Also arts documentaries: *The Comedy Store* and *Ray Harryhausen* (the work of Hollywood special effects legend). Drama: *The Sleeper*; *The Sceptic and the Psychic*; *A State of Mind.*

Paul Weiland Film Company
14 Newburgh Street, London W1F 7RT
☎020 7287 6900 Fax 020 7434 0146
✉ action@paulweiland.com

Television commercials and pop promos.

Whistledown Productions Ltd
66 Southwark Bridge Road, London SE1 0AS
☎020 7922 1120 Fax 020 7261 0939

Contact *David Prest*

Producer of Sony Award Winning Landmark Series for BBC Radio 4: *Evacuation, The Child Migrants*. Features and documentaries on wide range of social and historical subjects, contemporary series and popular culture. OUTPUT includes *Questions Questions* and *The Reunion* (Radio 4); music-based documentaries for Radio 2. 'We welcome contributions on contemporary issues for talks slots, etc., but phone or e-mail first.'

Michael White Productions Ltd
See **MW Entertainments Ltd**

Windrush Productions Ltd
7 Woodlands Road, Moseley B13 4EH
☎0121 449 6439 Fax 0121 449 6439
✉ beboyyaa@hotmail.com

Contacts *Emma Jeffares, Pogus Caesar*

Television documentaries, including a multicultural series for Carlton TV *Xpress*. Also for Carlton produced and directed *Respect; An Eye on X; The A-Force* (BBC); *I'm Black in Britain* (Central TV) and the music film *Xpress Urself Thru Muzik*. Produces films, documentaries, pop promos, corporate videos for a range of clients. 'We encourage new writing, especially from the regions and seek scripts from writers interested in developing new Black fiction/comedy.'

Working Title Films Ltd
Oxford House, 76 Oxford Street, London W1D 1BS
☎020 7307 3000 Fax 020 7307 3001/2/3

Co-Chairmen (Films) *Tim Bevan, Eric Fellner*
Head of Development (Films) *Debra Hayward*
Development Coordinator *Luke Parker Bowles*
Television *Simon Wright*

Feature films, TV drama; also family/children's entertainment and TV comedy. OUTPUT: FILMS *Love Actually; Thunderbirds; Ned Kelly; Johnny English; Bridget Jones's Diary; Captain Corelli's Mandolin; Ali G in da House; Notting Hill; Elizabeth; Plunkett & Macleane; The Borrowers; The Matchmaker; Fargo; Dead Man Walking; French Kiss; Four Weddings and a Funeral; The Hudsucker Proxy; The Tall Guy; Wish You Were Here; My Beautiful Laundrette.* TELEVISION *More Tales of the City; The Borrowers I & II; Armisted Maupin's Tales of the City; News Hounds; Randall & Hopkirk Deceased; Doomwatch.* No unsolicited mss at present.

Wortman Productions UK
48 Chiswick Staithe, London W4 3TP
☎020 8994 8886/07976 805976 (Mobile)
✉ nevillewortman@beeb.net

Producer *Neville Wortman*

Co-producers with Polestar Pictures Ltd. Feature film and TV production for drama, documentary, entertainment and corporate. OUTPUT *House in the Country* John Julius Norwich (ITV series); *Tribute to Ellington* (jazz special); *Lost Ships* (maritime historical drama series; Discovery Channel); *The Assassination of Julius Caesar* (Discovery/History Channel/Five). Open to new writing, preferably through agents; single page outline, some pages of dialogue; s.a.e. for reply.

WT2
Oxford House, 76 Oxford Street, London W1D 1BS
☎020 7307 3000 Fax 020 7307 3004

Head of WT2 *Natascha Wharton*
Head of Development *Rachael Prior*
WT2 Assistant *Hannah Farrell*

Low budget film division of **Working Title Films**. Feature films only. OUTPUT *Billy Elliot*; *Long Time Dead*; *Ali G Indahouse*; *My Little Eye*. No unsolicited screenplays at present, but keen to encourage new writing via New Writers Scheme (four-page outlines only) – contact *Hannah Farrell*.

Zenith Entertainment Ltd
43–45 Dorset Street, London W1U 7NA
☎020 7224 2440 Fax 020 7224 3194
✉ general@zenith-entertainment.co.uk

Head of Drama *Alex Jones*

Feature films and TV drama. OUTPUT: FILMS Todd Haynes' *Velvet Goldmine*; *Wisdom of Crocodiles*; Nicole Holofcener's *Walking and Talking*. TELEVISION *Hamish Macbeth*; *Rhodes*; *Bodyguards*; *Bomber*; *Two Thousand Acres of Sky*; *Hear the Silence*. No unsolicited scripts.

Theatre Producers

For latest minimum rates for writers of plays for subsidised repertory theatres (not Scotland) access the following websites: Theatrical Management Association at www.tmauk.org; and the Writers' Guild at www.writersguild.org.uk

Actors Touring Company (ATC)

Alford House, Aveline Street, London
SE11 5DQ
☎020 7735 8311
Fax 020 7735 1031 attn. ATC
✉ info@atc-online.com
www.atc-online.com

Artistic Director *Gordon Anderson*

Collaborates with writers on adaptation and/or translation work and unsolicited mss will be considered in this category as well as new writing. 'We endeavour to read mss but do not have the resources to do so quickly.' As a small-scale company, all plays must have a cast of six or less.

Almeida Theatre Company

The Almeida Theatre, Almeida Street,
London N1 1TA
☎020 7288 4900   Fax 020 7288 4901
www.almeida.co.uk

Artistic Director *Michael Attenborough*

Founded 1980. Now in its fourteenth year as a full-time producing theatre, presenting a year-round theatre and music programme in which international writers, composers, performers, directors and designers are invited to work with British artists on challenging new and classical works. Previous productions: *Ivanov; Naked; The Judas Kiss; The Iceman Cometh; The Jew of Malta; Celebration; The Room; Richard II; Coriolanus; Lulu; The Shape of Things; King Lear, The Lady from the Sea The Goat, or Who is Sylvia?; Whistling Psyche.* No unsolicited mss: 'our producing programme is very limited and linked to individual directors and actors'.

Alternative Theatre Company Ltd

Bush Theatre, Shepherds Bush Green,
London W12 8QD
☎020 7602 3703   Fax 020 7602 7614
✉ info@bushtheatre.co.uk

Literary Manager *Nicola Wilson*

Founded 1972. Trading as The Bush Theatre.

Produces nine new plays a year (principally British) including up to three visiting companies also producing new work: 'we are a writer's theatre'. Previous productions: *Kiss of the Spiderwoman* Manuel Puig; *Raping the Gold* Lucy Gannon; *The Wexford Trilogy* Billy Roche; *Love and Understanding* Joe Penhall; *This Limetree Bower* Conor McPherson; *Discopigs* Enda Walsh; *The Pitchfork Disney* Philip Ridley; *Caravan* Helen Blakeman; *Beautiful Thing* Jonathan Harvey; *Killer Joe* Tracy Letts; *Shang-a-Lang* Catherine Johnson; *Howie the Rookie* Mark O'Rowe; *The Glee Club* Richard Cameron; *Adrenalin ... Heart* Georgia Fitch. Scripts are read by a team of associates, then discussed with the management, a process which takes about four months. The theatre offers a small number of commissions, recommissions to ensure further drafts on promising plays, and a guarantee against royalties so writers are not financially penalised even though the plays are produced in a small house. Writers should send scripts (full-length plays only) with small s.a.e. for acknowledgement and large s.a.e. for return of script.

Birmingham Repertory Theatre

Centenary Square, Broad Street, Birmingham
B1 2EP
☎0121 245 2000   Fax 0121 245 2100
www.birmingham-rep.co.uk

Literary Officer *Caroline Jester*

The Birmingham Repertory Theatre aims to provide a platform for the best work from new writers from both within and beyond the West Midlands region. The Rep is committed to the production of new work which reflects the diversity of contemporary experience and approaches to writing for the stage. The commissioning of new plays takes place across the full range of the theatre's activities: in the Main House, The Door (which is a dedicated new writing space) and on tour to community venues in the region. The theatre runs a programme of writers' attachments every year in addition to its commissioning policy and maintains close links with *Script* (the regional writers' training agency) and the MA in Playwriting Studies at the University of Birmingham. For more information contact the Literary Officer.

Black Theatre Co-op
See **NITRO**

Bootleg Theatre Company
23 Burgess Green, Bishopdown, Salisbury SP1 3El
☎01722 421476
✉ colin@thebootlegtheatrecompany. fsnet.co.uk

Contact *Colin Burden*

Founded 1984. Tries to encompass as wide an audience as possible and has a tendency towards plays with socially relevant themes. A good bet for new writing since unsolicited mss are very welcome. 'Our policy is to produce new and/or rarely seen plays and anything received is given the most serious consideration.' Actively seeks to obtain grants to commission new writers for the company. Productions include: *Clubland* by Giles, Harris, Suthers and Mordell; *Hanging Hanratty*, Michael Burnham; *The Truth About Blokes*, Trevor Suthers; *Cool Blokes: Decent Suits*, Russell Mardell; *Rainy Night in Soho*, Stephen Giles; *Grass*, Russell Mardell.

Borderline Theatre
Darlington New Church, North Harbour Street, Ayr KA8 8AA
☎01292 281010 Fax 01292 263825
✉ firstname@borderlinetheatre.co.uk
www.borderlinetheatre.co.uk

Producer *Eddie Jackson*

Founded 1974. Borderline is one of Scotland's leading touring companies. Committed to new writing, it tours an innovative programme of new plays and radical adaptations/translations of classic texts in an accessible and entertaining style. Tours to main-house theatres and small venues throughout Scotland. Productions include the world premières of *The Angels' Share* by Chris Dolan; *The Prince and the Pilot* Anita Sullivan. Previous writers have included Dario Fo, Liz Lochhead and John Byrne. Borderline is also committed to commissioning and touring new plays for young people. Please contact the company before submitting synopsis or script.

Bristol Old Vic Theatre Company (Old Vic, Studio & Basement)
Theatre Royal, King Street, Bristol BS1 4ED
☎0117 949 3993 Fax 0117 949 3996
✉ admin@bristol-old-vic.co.uk
www.bristol-old-vic.co.uk

Bristol Old Vic actively seeks new writers for development and commission. 'We do not offer a formal reading service but are keen to build relationships with local writers in particular.'

Bush Theatre
See **Alternative Theatre Company Ltd**

Carnival (Films & Theatre) Ltd
See entry under *Film, TV and Radio Producers*

Guy Chapman Productions Ltd
33 Southampton Street, London WC2E 7HE
☎020 7379 7474 Fax 020 7379 8484
✉ admin@g-c-a.co.uk

Contacts *Guy Chapman*

Performs to young audiences with innovative, experimental theatre. Productions include: *Shopping and Fucking*; *Love Upon the Throne*; *Crave*; *Disco Pigs*; *Resident Alien*; *Corpus Christi*; *New Boy*.

Citizens Theatre
Gorbals, Glasgow G5 9DS
☎0141 429 5561 Fax 0141 429 7374
✉ info@citz.co.uk
www.citz.co.uk

General Manager *Anna Stapleton*

No formal new play policy. The theatre has a play reader but opportunities to do new work are limited.

Clwyd Theatr Cymru
Mold, Flintshire CH7 1YA
☎01352 756331 Fax 01352 701558
✉ drama@celtic.co.uk
www.clwyd-theatr-cymru.co.uk

Literary Manager *William James*
   (william.james@clwyd-theatr-cymru.co.uk)

Clwyd Theatr Cymru produces plays performed by a core ensemble in Mold and tours them throughout Wales (in English and Welsh). Productions are a mix of classics, revivals, contemporary drama. Recent new writing includes: *The Rabbit* Meredydd Barker; *Journey of Mary Kelly* Siân Evans; *Rape of the Fair Country*, *Hosts of Rebecca* and *Song of the Earth* all adapt. Manon Eames; *The Ballad of Megan Morgan*, *Flora's*

War/Rhyfel Flora, Word for Word/Gair am Air and *The Secret/Y Gyfrinach* all by Tim Baker; *Celf*, Yasmin Reza; *Damwain a Hap*, Dario Fo. Plays by Welsh writers or with Welsh themes will be considered.

Michael Codron Plays Ltd

Aldwych Theatre Offices, Aldwych, London WC2B 4DF

☎020 7240 8291 Fax 020 7240 8467

General Manager *Paul O'Leary* (Productions)

Michael Codron Plays Ltd manages the Aldwych Theatre in London's West End. The plays it produces don't necessarily go into the Aldwych but always tend to be big-time West End fare. Previous productions: *Bedroom Farce*; *Blue Orange*; *Copenhagen*; *The Invention of Love*; *Hapgood*; *Uncle Vanya*; *Rise and Fall of Little Voice*; *Arcadia*; *Dead Funny*; *My Brilliant Divorce*; *Dinner*. No particular rule of thumb on subject matter or treatment. The acid test is whether 'something appeals to Michael'. Straight plays rather than musicals.

Colchester Mercury Theatre Limited

Balkerne Gate, Colchester CO1 1PT

☎01206 577006 Fax 01206 769607

✉ info@mercurytheatre.co.uk

www.mercurytheatre.co.uk

Chief Executive *Dee Evans*

Associate Director *Adrian Stokes*

Producing theatre with a wide-ranging audience. Unsolicited scripts welcome. The theatre has a free playwright's group for adults with a serious commitment to writing plays.

The Coliseum, Oldham

Fairbottom Street, Oldham OL1 3SW

☎0161 624 1731 Fax 0161 624 5318

Chief Executive/Artistic Director *Kevin Shaw*

The artistic policy of the theatre is to present a high quality and diverse theatre programme with the ambition to commission a new play each year. Unsolicited scripts will be read but only returned if s.a.e. included.

Contact Theatre Company

Oxford Road, Manchester M15 6JA

☎0161 274 3434 Fax 0161 274 0640

✉ info@contact-theatre.org.uk

www.contact-theatre.org

Artistic Director *John E. McGrath*

'In partnership with the BBC, we are investing in innovative approaches to the discovery of new writers – and new kinds of writing – for stage, screen, radio and new media.' In general, Contact works primarily with the 13–30 age group and is particularly interested in materials that relate to the lives and culture of young people. 'We welcome work from writers of all ages. Hearing from a variety of voices, from different cultures and backgrounds, is also important to us. We encourage concise pitches from writers (no more than ten pages) including a summary and some sample pages.'

Crucible Theatre

55 Norfolk Street, Sheffield S1 1DA

☎0114 249 5999 Fax 0114 249 6003

Associate Directors *Michael Grandage, Anna Mackmin*

Literary Associate *Matthew Byam Shaw*

'Most of the new work we present will be the result of commissions or a prolonged exchange of ideas and script development with writers in whom we have expressed an interest. However, we are interested in all new work and offer a free script reading service for unsolicited scripts. NB We do not offer readers' reports. Please ring or send s.a.e. for full details of script reading service.'

Derby Playhouse

Eagle Centre, Derby DE1 2NF

☎01332 363271 Fax 01332 547200

www.derbyplayhouse.co.uk

Chief Executive *Karen Hebden*

Creative Producer *Stephen Edwards*

Derby Playhouse is interested in new work and has produced several world premières over the last year. 'We have a discrete commissioning budget but already have several projects under way. Due to the amount of scripts we receive, we now ask writers to send a letter accompanied by a synopsis of the play, a résumé of writing experience and any ten pages of the script they wish to submit. We will then determine whether we think it is suitable for the Playhouse, in which case we will ask for a full script.' Writers are welcome to send details of rehearsed readings and productions as an alternative means of introducing the theatre to their work.

Druid Theatre Company

Chapel Lane, Galway, Republic of Ireland

☎00 353 91 568660 Fax 00 353 91 563109

✉ info@druidtheatre.com

www.druidtheatre.com

Contact *Literary Manager*

Founded 1975. Based in Galway and playing

nationally and internationally, the company operates a major programme for the development of new writing. While focusing on Irish work, the company also accepts unsolicited material from outside Ireland.

The Dukes

Moor Lane, Lancaster LA1 1QE
☎01524 598505 Fax 01524 598519
Chief Executive *Amanda Belcham*
Artistic Director *Ian Hastings*

Founded 1971. The only producing house in Lancashire. Wide target market for cinema and theatre. Plays in a 313-seater end-on auditorium and in a 198-seater in-the-round studio. Host for **Litfest** – Lancaster's annual festival of literature. In the summer months open-air promenade performances are held in Williamson Park. Also, community based Youth Arts Centre.

Dundee Repertory Theatre

Tay Square, Dundee DD1 1PB
☎01382 227684 Fax 01382 228609
✉ hwatson@dundeereptheatre.co.uk
www.dundeereptheatre.co.uk
Artistic Directors *Dominic Hill, James Brining*

Founded 1939. Plays to a varied audience. Translations and adaptations of classics, and new local plays. Most new work is commissioned. Interested in contemporary plays in translation and in new Scottish writing. No scripts except by prior arrangement.

Eastern Angles Theatre Company

Sir John Mills Theatre, Gatacre Road, Ipswich IP1 2LQ
☎01473 218202 Fax 01473 384999
✉ admin@easternangles.co.uk
www.easternangles.co.uk
Artistic Director *Ivan Cutting*
General Manager *Jill Streatfeild*

Founded 1982. Plays to a rural audience for the most part. New work only: some commissioned, some devised by the company, some researched documentaries. Unsolicited mss welcome from regional writers. 'We are always keen to develop and produce new writing, especially that which is germane to a rural area.'

Edinburgh Royal Lyceum Theatre

See **Royal Lyceum Theatre Company**

English Touring Theatre

25 Short Street, London SE1 8LJ
☎020 7450 1990 Fax 020 7450 1991
✉ admin@englishtouringtheatre.co.uk
www.englishtouringtheatre.co.uk
Artistic Director *Stephen Unwin*

Founded 1993. National touring company visiting middle-scale receiving houses and arts centres throughout the UK. Mostly mainstream. Largely classical programme, but with increasing interest to tour one modern English play per year. Strong commitment to education work. No unsolicited mss.

Finborough Theatre

118 Finborough Road, London SW10 9ED
☎020 7244 7439 Fax 020 7835 1853
✉ admin@finboroughtheatre.co.uk
www.finboroughtheatre.co.uk
Artistic Director *Neil McPherson*

Founded 1980. 'One of London's leading new writing venues' (*Time Out*). Presents revivals of neglected 20th century plays, music theatre and UK premières of foreign work, particularly from Ireland, the United States and Canada. The theatre is available for hire and the fee is sometimes negotiable to encourage interesting work, though unsolicited mss are no longer accepted. Premièred work by Chris Lee, Anthony Neilson, Naomi Wallace, Tony Marchant, Diane Samuels and Mark Ravenhill.

Robert Fox Ltd

6 Beauchamp Place, London SW3 1NG
☎020 7584 6855 Fax 020 7225 1638
✉ info@robertfoxltd.com
Contact *Robert Fox*

Producer and co-producer of work suitable for West End production. Previous productions: *Another Country*; *Chess*; *Lettice and Lovage*; *Burn This*; *When She Danced*; *The Ride Down Mount Morgan*; *The Importance of Being Earnest*; *The Seagull*; *Goosepimples*; *Vita & Virginia*; *The Weekend*; *Three Tall Women*; *Skylight*; *Who's Afraid of Virginia Woolf*; *Masterclass*; *A Delicate Balance*; *Amy's View*; *Closer*; *The Lady in the Van*; *The Caretaker*; *The Breath of Life*. Also Broadway productions, recently *Gypsy*; *The Boy From Oz*; *Salome: The Reading*, and films including *Iris* and *The Hours*. Scripts, while usually by established playwrights, are always read.

Gate Theatre Company Ltd

11 Pembridge Road, London W11 3HQ
☎020 7229 5387 Fax 020 7221 6055
✉ gate@gatetheatre.freeserve.co.uk
www.gatetheatre.co.uk
Artistic Director *Erica Whyman*

Founded 1979. Plays to a mixed, London-wide

audience, depending on production. Aims to produce British premières of plays which originate from abroad and translations of neglected classics. Most work is with translators. Runs a biennial Translation Award. Recent productions: *The Flu Season* by Will Eno; *Ion* by Euripides, transl. by Stephen Sharkey; *Witness*, Cecilia Parkert, transl. by Kevin Halliwell. Positively encourages writers from abroad to send in scripts or translations. Most unsolicited scripts are read but it is extremely unlikely that new British plays will have any future at the theatre due to emphasis on plays translated from foreign languages. Please address submissions to 'Scripts'. Always enclose s.a.e. if play needs returning.

Graeae Theatre Company

LVS Resource Centre, 356 Holloway Road, London N7 6PA
☎020 7700 2455 Fax 020 7609 7324
✉ info@graeae.org
www.graeae.org
Minicom 020 7700 8184

Artistic Director *Jenny Sealey*
Executive Producer *Roger Nelson*

Europe's premier theatre company of disabled people, the company tours nationally and internationally with innovative theatre productions highlighting both historical and contemporary disabled experience. Graeae also runs Forum Theatre and educational programmes available to schools, youth clubs and day centres nationally, provides vocational training in theatre arts (including playwriting). Unsolicited scripts, from disabled writers, welcome. New work is commissioned.

Hampstead Theatre

Eton Avenue, Swiss Cottage, London NW3 3EU
☎020 7449 4200 Fax 020 7449 4201
✉ literary@hampsteadtheatre.com
www.hampsteadtheatre.com

Contact *Pippa Ellis*

A brand new Hampstead Theatre opened in 2003. The building is an intimate space with a flexible stage and an auditorium capable of expanding to seat 325. The artistic policy continues to be the production of British and international new plays and the development of important young writers. 'We are looking for writers who recognise the power of theatre and who have a story to tell. All plays are read and discussed. We give feedback to all writers with potential.' Writers produced at Hampstead

include Michael Frayn, Roy Williams, Shelagh Stephenson, Simon Block, Philip Ridley, Frank McGuinness, Rona Munro, Brad Fraser, Tim Firth and Abi Morgan.

Harrogate Theatre Company

Oxford Street, Harrogate HG1 1QF
☎01423 502710 Fax 01423 563205
✉ staff.name@harrogatetheatre.demon.co.uk

Artistic Director *Hannah Chissick*

Produces four to five productions a year on the main stage, one of which may be a new play but is most likely to be commissioned. Annual mainstage Youth Theatre production may also be commissioned. Over the next two years it is planned to workshop and read new plays by local writers and possibly stage them in the studio. Unsolicited scripts from outside Yorkshire are unlikely to receive a production or workshop. Please write with a brief synopsis initially.

Heritage Theatre Ltd

See entry under *Film, TV and Radio Producers*

The Hiss & Boo Company Ltd

1 Nyes Hill, Wineham Lane, Bolney RH17 5SD Fax 01444 882057
✉ hissboo@msn.com
www.hissboo.co.uk

Contact *Ian Liston*

Particularly interested in new thrillers, comedy thrillers, comedy and melodrama – must be commercial full-length plays. Also interested in plays/plays with music for children. No one-acts. Previous productions: *The Shakespeare Revue*; *Come Rain Come Shine*; *Sleighrider*; *Beauty and the Beast*; *An Ideal Husband*; *Mr Men's Magical Island*; *Mr Men and the Space Pirates*; *Nunsense*; *Corpse!*; *Groucho: A Life in Revue*; *See How They Run*; *Christmas Cat and the Pudding Pirates*; *Pinocchio* and traditional pantos written by Roy Hudd for the company. 'We are keen on revue-type shows and compilation shows but *not* tribute-type performances.' No unsolicited scripts; no telephone calls. Send synopsis and introductory letter in the first instance.

Hull Truck Theatre Company

Spring Street, Hull HU2 8RW
☎01482 224800 Fax 01482 581182

Executive Director *Joanne Gower*

John Godber, of *Teechers, Bouncers, Up 'n' Under* fame, the artistic director of this high-profile Northern company since 1984, has very much dominated the scene in the past with his own successful plays. The emphasis is still on new writing but Godber's work continues to be toured extensively. Most new plays are commissioned. Previous productions: *Studs* and *Like a Virgin* by Gordon Steel; *Oft Out* Gill Adams and *Double Top* by Ron Rose. The company receives a large number of unsolicited scripts but cannot guarantee a quick response. Bear in mind the artistic policy of Hull Truck, which is 'accessibility and popularity'. In general they are not interested in musicals, or in plays with casts of more than eight.

Stephen Joseph Theatre
Westborough, Scarborough YO11 1JW
☎01723 370540 Fax 01723 360506
www.sjt.uk.com
Artistic Director *Alan Ayckbourn*
Literary Manager *Laura Harvey*

A two-auditoria complex housing a 165-seat end stage theatre/cinema (the McCarthy) and a 400-seat theatre-in-the-round (the Round). Positive policy on new work. For obvious reasons, Alan Ayckbourn's work features quite strongly but a new writing programme ensures plays from other sources are actively encouraged. Also runs a lunchtime season of one-act plays each summer. Writers are advised however that the SJT is very unlikely to produce an unsolicited script – synopses are preferred. Recent commissions and past productions include: *Bedtime Stories* Lesley Bruce; *Making Waves* Stephen Clark; *Larkin with Women* Ben Brown; *Amaretti Angels* Sarah Phelps; *Something Blue* Gill Adams; *Clockwatching* and *A Listening Heaven* Torben Betts; *The Star Throwers* Paul Lucas; *Man for Hire* Meredith Oakes; *Safari Party* Tim Firth; *Beautiful People* Neil Monaghan; *Gameplan, Flatspin, Roleplay* and *House and Garden* Alan Ayckbourn. 'Writers are welcome to send details of rehearsed readings and productions as an alternative means of introducing the theatre to their work.' Submit to *Laura Harvey* enclosing an s.a.e. for return of mss.

Bill Kenwright Ltd
BKL House, 106 Harrow Road, London W2 1RR
☎020 7446 6200 Fax 020 7446 6222
Contact *Bill Kenwright*

Presents both revivals and new shows for West End and touring theatres. Although new work tends to be by established playwrights, this does not preclude or prejudice new plays from new writers. Scripts should be addressed to Bill Kenwright with a covering letter and s.a.e.

'We have enormous amounts of scripts sent to us although we very rarely produce unsolicited work. Scripts are read systematically. Please do not phone; the return of your script or contact with you will take place in time.'

Komedia
Gardner Street, North Lane, Brighton BN1 1UN
☎01273 647101 Fax 01273 647102
✉ info@komedia.co.uk
www.komedia.co.uk
Contact *David Lavender*

Founded in 1994, Komedia promotes, produces and presents new work. Mss of new plays welcome.

Leeds Playhouse
See **West Yorkshire Playhouse**

Leicester Haymarket Theatre
Belgrave Gate, Leicester LE1 3YQ
☎0116 253 0021 Fax 0116 251 3310
✉ enquiry@leicesterhaymarkettheatre.org
www.leicesterhaymarkettheatre.org
Artistic Directors *Paul Kerryson, Kully Thiarai*

Leicester Haymarket Theatre aims for a balanced programme of original and established works. It is a multi-cultural, racially integrated company with educational projects that support all productions and areas of work. Productions include *West Side Story; Singin' In the Rain; To Kill a Mockingbird; Master Harold and the Boys*. Works with other arts organisations in the city and county to provide external productions.

Library Theatre Company
St Peter's Square, Manchester M2 5PD
☎0161 234 1913 Fax 0161 228 6481
✉ ltc@libraries.manchester.gov.uk
www.librarytheatre.com
Artistic Director *Chris Honer*

Produces new and contemporary work, as well as occasional classics. No unsolicited mss. Send outline of the nature of the script first. Encourages new writing through the commissioning of new plays and through a programme of rehearsed readings to help writers' development.

Live Theatre Company
7/8 Trinity Chare, Newcastle upon Tyne NE1 3DF
☎0191 261 2694 Fax 0191 232 2224
✉ info@live.org.uk
www.live.org.uk

Artistic Director *Max Roberts*
Executive Director *Jim Beirne*

Founded 1973. Produces shows at its refurbished 200-seat venue, and also tours regionally and nationally. Company policy is to produce work that is rooted in the culture of the region, particularly for those who do not normally get involved in the arts. The company is particularly interested in promoting new writing. As well as full-scale productions the company organises workshops, rehearsed readings and other new writing activities. The company also enjoys a close relationship with **New Writing North** and is funded to support new writing through the BBC's *Northern Exposure Project*. Productions include: *Falling Together* Tom Hadaway; *Cooking With Elvis* Lee Hall; *Bones* Peter Straughan; *ne1*; *Tales From the Backyard* Alan Plater; *Double Lives* Julia Darling and Sean O'Brien; *Smack Family Robinson* Richard Bean; *Keepers of the Flame* and *Laughter When We're Dead* Sean O'Brien.

Llwyfan Gogledd Cymru (North Wales Stage)

c/o Theatr Gwynedd, Ffordd Deiniol, Bangor LL57 2TL
☎01248 370088 Fax 01248 370121
www.llwyfan-gogledd-cymru.com

Contact *Artistic Director*

Founded 2003, Llwyfan Gogledd Cymru is an Arts Council Wales revenue funded company dedicated to producing work about and for North Wales with a brief to tour both nationally and internationally. Though primarily a Welsh language mid-scale theatre company, it recognises the importance of placing both the Welsh language and its culture in a broader context. As a consequence, the work the company has lined up over the next three years is largely multilingual, reflecting the changing demographic of the region and the growing confidence of Welsh Wales to express itself on an international stage.

London Bubble Theatre Company

5 Elephant Lane, London SE16 4JD
☎020 7237 4434 Fax 020 7231 2366
✉ peth@londonbubble.org.uk
www.londonbubble.org.uk

Artistic Director *Jonathan Petherbridge*

Produces workshops, plays and events for a mixed audience of theatregoers and non-theatregoers, wide-ranging in terms of age, culture and class. Previous productions: *Punchkin, Enchanter, You Can't Say You Can't Play.* Unsolicited mss

are received but 'our reading service is extremely limited and there can be a considerable wait before we can give a response'. Commissions approximately one new project a year, often inspired by a promenade site, specific community of interest or workshop group.

Lyric Theatre Hammersmith

King Street, London W6 0QL
☎020 8741 0824 Fax 020 8741 5965
✉ enquiries@lyric.co.uk
www.lyric.co.uk

Artistic Director *Neil Bartlett*
Executive Director *Simon Mellor*

The main theatre stages an eclectic programme of new and revived classics. Interested in developing projects with writers, translators and adaptors. The Lyric does not accept unsolicited scripts. Its 110-seat studio focuses on work for children, young people and families.

mac

Cannon Hill Park, Birmingham B12 9QH
☎0121 440 4221 Fax 0121 446 4372
✉ enquiries@mac-birmingham.org.uk
www.macarts.co.uk
Minicom: 0121 440 4923

Director *Dorothy Wilson*

Innovative creative arts activities, including theatre, music, comedy, plays for children, literature and poetry events, family show at Christmas, films and free exhibitions.

Manchester Library Theatre

See **Library Theatre Company**

New Vic Theatre

Etruria Road, Newcastle under Lyme ST5 0JG
☎01782 717954 Fax 01782 712885
✉ admin@newvictheatre.org.uk

Artistic Director *Gwenda Hughes*

The New Vic is a purpose-built theatre-in-the-round. Produces ten in-house plays each year and is active within the education sector and community. New plays produced are the result of specific commissions. Send synopses *not* unsolicited scripts. 'We cannot guarantee that unsolicited scripts will be read; they will be returned on receipt of an s.a.e.'

Newpalm Productions

26 Cavendish Avenue, London N3 3QN
☎020 8349 0802 Fax 020 8346 8257

Contact *Lionel Chilcott*

Very rarely produces new plays (*As Is* by

William M. Hoffman, which came from Broadway to the Half Moon Theatre, was an exception). National tours and West End productions such as *Peter Pan (The Musical); Noises Off, Seven Brides for Seven Brothers* and *Rebecca*, at regional repertory theatres, are more typical examples of Newpalm's work. Both plays and musicals are, however, welcome; synopses are preferable to scripts.

NITRO

6 Brewery Road, London N7 9NH
☎020 7609 1331 Fax 020 7609 1221
www.nitro.co.uk

Artistic Director *Felix Cross*

Founded 1978. Formerly Black Theatre Co-op. Plays to a mixed audience, approximately 65% female. Usually tours nationally twice a year. 'A music theatre company, we are committed in the first instance to new writing by Black British writers and work which relates to the Black culture and experience throughout the Diaspora.' Unsolicited mss welcome.

Northcott Theatre

Stocker Road, Exeter EX4 4QB
☎01392 223999 Fax 01392 223996
www.northcott-theatre.co.uk

Artistic Director *Ben Crocker*

Founded 1967. The Northcott is the Southwest's principal subsidised producing theatre, situated on the University of Exeter campus. Describes its audience as 'geographically diverse, with a core audience of AB1s (40–60 age range)'. Continually looking to broaden the base of its audience profile, targeting younger and/or non-mainstream theatregoers. Aims to develop, promote and produce quality new writing which reflects the life of the region and addresses the audience it serves. Generally works on a commission basis but occasionally options existing new work. Unsolicited mss welcome – current turnaround on script-reading service is approximately three months and no mss can be returned unless a correct value s.a.e. is included with the original submission.

Norwich Puppet Theatre

St James, Whitefriars, Norwich NR3 1TN
☎01603 615564 Fax 01603 617578
✉ norpuppet@hotmail.com
www.puppettheatre.co.uk

Artistic Director *Luis Boy*
General Manager *Ian Woods*

Plays to a young audience (aged 3–12) but developing shows for adult audiences interested in puppetry. All year round programme plus tours to schools and arts venues. Most productions are based on traditional stories but unsolicited mss welcome if relevant.

Nottingham Playhouse

Nottingham Theatre Trust, Wellington Circus, Nottingham NG1 5AF
☎0115 947 4361 Fax 0115 947 5759

Artistic Director *Giles Croft*

Aims to make innovation popular, and present the best of world theatre, working closely with the communities of Nottingham and Nottinghamshire. Unsolicited mss will be read. It normally takes about six months, however, and 'we have never yet produced an unsolicited script. All our plays have to achieve a minimum of 60 per cent audiences in a 732-seat theatre. We have no studio.'

Nottingham Playhouse
Roundabout Theatre in Education

Wellington Circus, Nottingham NG1 5AF
☎0115 947 4361 Fax 0115 953 9055
✉ andrewb@nottinghamplayhouse.co.uk
www.nottinghamplayhouse.co.uk

Contact *Andrew Breakwell*

Founded 1973. Theatre-in-Education company of the **Nottingham Playhouse**. Plays to a young audience aged 5–18 years of age. 'Most of our current work uses existing scripts but we try and commission at least one new play every year. We are committed to the encouragement of new writing as and when resources permit. With other major producers in the East Midlands we share the resources of the *Theatre Writing Partnership* which is based at the Playhouse. See website for philosophy and play details. Please make contact before submitting scripts.'

N.T.C. Touring Theatre Company

The Playhouse, Bondgate Without, Alnwick NE66 1PQ
☎01665 602586 Fax 01665 605837
✉ admin@ntc-touringtheatre.co.uk
www.ntc-touringtheatre.co.uk

Contact *Gillian Hambleton*
General Manager *Anna Flood*

Founded 1978. Formerly Northumberland Theatre Company. An Arts Council England revenue funded organisation. Predominantly rural, small-scale touring company, playing to village halls and community centres throughout the Northern region, the Scottish Borders and countrywide. Productions range from established classics to new work and popular comedies, but must be appropriate to their audience. Unsolicited scripts welcome but are unlikely to be produced. All scripts are read and returned with constructive criticism within six months. Writers whose style is of interest may then be commissioned. The company encourages new writing and commissions when possible. Financial constraints restrict casting to a *maximum* of five.

Nuffield Theatre

University Road, Southampton SO17 1TR
☎023 8031 5500   Fax 023 8031 5511
✉ info@nuffieldtheatre.co.uk
www.nuffieldtheatre.co.uk
Artistic Director *Patrick Sandford*
Script Executive *John Burgess*

Well known as a good bet for new playwrights, the Nuffield gets an awful lot of scripts. They do a couple of new main stage plays every season. Previous productions: *Exchange* by Yuri Trifonov (transl. Michael Frayn) which transferred to the Vaudeville Theatre; *The Floating Light Bulb* Woody Allen (British première); new plays by Claire Luckham: *Dogspot; The Dramatic Attitudes of Miss Fanny Kemble;* and by Claire Tomalin: *The Winter Wife.* Open-minded about subject and style, producing musicals as well as straight plays. Also opportunities for some small-scale fringe work. Scripts preferred to synopses in the case of writers new to theatre. All will, eventually, be read 'but please be patient. We do not have a large team of paid readers. We read everything ourselves.'

Octagon Theatre Trust Ltd

Howell Croft South, Bolton BL1 1SB
☎01204 529407   Fax 01204 556502
✉ info@octagonbolton.co.uk
www.octagonbolton.co.uk
Executive Director *John Blackmore*

Founded in 1967, the award-winning Octagon Theatre stages at least eight main auditorium home-produced shows a year, and hosts UK touring companies such as the National Theatre, John Godber's Hull Truck Theatre Company, Peshkar Productions and Alan Ayckbourn's Stephen Joseph Theatre. Also hosts the work of partner companies as part of its commitment to creative partnerships. The theatre boasts a thriving and constantly developing participatory department, activ8, which operates a highly successful Youth Theatre as well as initiating and facilitating exciting edu-

cation and outreach programmes. The theatre is keen to encourage new writing but, due to the lack of a dedicated literary department, is unable to accept and process new and unsolicited scripts; the theatre uses **North West Playwrights** as a reading service instead.

Orange Tree Theatre

1 Clarence Street, Richmond TW9 2SA
☎020 8940 0141   Fax 020 8332 0369
✉ admin@orange-tree.demon.co.uk
www.orangetreetheatre.co.uk
Artistic Director *Sam Walters*

The Orange Tree, a theatre-in-the-round venue, presents a broad cross section of work. The 2003 season included plays by Rodney Ackland, John Goldsworthy and a new translation of Lorca as well as a new play by Oliver Ford Davies. The theatre no longer considers unsolicited mss; writers who may wish to approach the theatre are asked to write first.

Out of Joint

7 Thane Works, Thane Villas, London N7 7PH
☎020 7609 0207   Fax 020 7609 0203
✉ ojo@outofjoint.co.uk
www.outofjoint.co.uk
Director *Max Stafford-Clark*
Producer *Graham Cowley*
Literary Manager *Jenny Worton*

Founded 1993. Award-winning theatre company with new writing central to its policy. Produces new plays which reflect society and its concerns, placing an emphasis on education activity to attract young audiences. Welcomes unsolicited mss. Productions include: *Blue Heart* Caryl Churchill; *Our Lady of Sligo, The Steward of Christendom* and *Hinterland* Sebastian Barry; *Shopping and Fucking* and *Some Explicit Polaroids* Mark Ravenhill; *Rita, Sue and Bob Too* Andrea Dunbar; *A State Affair* Robin Soans; *Sliding with Suzanne* Judy Upton; *The Positive Hour* and *A Laughing Matter* April de Angelis; *Duck* Stella Feehily; *The Permanent Way* David Hare.

Oxford Stage Company

Chertsey Chambers, 12 Mercer Street, London WC2H 9QD
☎020 7438 9940   Fax 020 7438 9941
www.oxfordstage.co.uk
Artistic Director *Dominic Dromgoole*

A middle-scale touring company producing established and new plays. At least one new play or new adaptation a year. Due to forth-coming projects not considering unsolicited scripts at present.

Paines Plough

4th Floor, 43 Aldwych, London WC2B 4DN
☎020 7240 4533 Fax 020 7240 4534
✉ office@painesplough.com
www.painesplough.com

Artistic Director *Vicky Featherstone*
Associate Director *John Tiffany*
Literary Manager *Lucy Morrison*

Tours new plays nationally. Works with writers to develop their skills and voices through workshops, rehearsed readings and playwriting projects. Provides a supportive environment for commissioned writers to push themselves and challenge their craft. Will consider unsolicited material from UK writers (please send s.a.e. for return of script).

Perth Repertory Theatre Ltd

185 High Street, Perth PH1 5UW
☎01738 472700 Fax 01738 624576
✉ info@perththeatre.co.uk
www.perththeatre.co.uk

Artistic Director *Ken Alexander*
General Manager *Paul Hackett*

Founded 1935. Combination of one- to four-weekly repertoire of plays and musicals, incoming tours and studio productions. Unsolicited mss are read when time permits, but the timetable for return of scripts is lengthy. New plays staged by the company are usually commissioned under the SAC scheme.

Plymouth Theatre Royal

See **Theatre Royal**

Polka Theatre for Children

240 The Broadway, Wimbledon SW19 1SB
☎020 8545 8320 Fax 020 8545 8365
✉ info@polkatheatre.com
www.polkatheatre.com

Artistic Director *Annie Wood*
Executive Director *Stephen Midlane*
Director of New Writing *Richard Shannon*

Founded in 1967 and moved into its Wimbledon base in 1979. Leading children's theatre committed to commissioning and producing new plays. Programmes are planned two years ahead and at least three new plays are commissioned each year. 'Many of our scripts are commissioned from established writers. We are, however, keen to develop work from

writers new to children's and young people's theatre. We run a new writing programme which includes master classes and workshops. Potential new writers' work is read and discussed on a regular basis; thus we constantly add to our pool of interesting and interested writers. This department is now headed by a new position, Director of New Writing.'

Praxis Theatre Company Ltd

24 Wykeham Road, London NW4 2SU
☎020 8203 1916 Fax 020 8203 1916
✉ praxisco@globalnet.co.uk
www.users.globalnet.co.uk/~praxisco

Artistic Director *Sharon Kennet*

Founded 1993. Performs to a mixed European audience, 'crossing the divide between text-based theatre and visual theatre'. No unsolicited mss. Previous productions and films: *Seed*; *My Brother Whom I Love*; *The Sacred Penman*; *She's Well Out of Order*; *Dot*.

Queen's Theatre, Hornchurch

Billet Lane, Hornchurch RM11 1QT
☎01708 462362 Fax 01708 462363
✉ info@queens-theatre.co.uk
www.queens-theatre.co.uk

Artistic Director *Bob Carlton*

The Queen's Theatre is a 503-seat producing theatre in the London Borough of Havering and within the M25. Established in 1953, the theatre has been located in its present building since 1975 and produces up to nine in-house productions per year, including pantomime. The Queen's has re-established a permanent core company of actor/musicians under the artistic leadership of Bob Carlton. Aims to produce distinctive and accessible performances in an identifiable house style focused upon actor/musician shows but, in addition, embraces straight plays, classics and comedies. 'New play/musical submissions are welcome but should be submitted in treatment and not script form.' Each year there is a large-scale community play commissioned from a local writer culminating in a summer event beside the theatre. A new writers' group has been established, led currently by David Eldridge. Enquiries about joining should be directed to the education manager.

The Really Useful Group Ltd

22 Tower Street, London WC2H 9TW
☎020 7240 0880 Fax 020 7240 1204
www.reallyuseful.com

Commercial/West End, national and international theatre producer/co-producer whose output has included *Joseph and the Amazing Technicolor Dreamcoat*; *Jesus Christ Superstar*; *Cats*; *Song & Dance*; *Daisy Pulls It Off*; *Lend Me a Tenor*; *Starlight Express*; *The Phantom of the Opera*; *Aspects of Love*; *Sunset Boulevard*; *By Jeeves*; *Whistle Down the Wind*; *The Beautiful Game*; *Tell Me On a Sunday*; *Bombay Dreams*.

Red Ladder Theatre Company

3 St Peter's Buildings, York Street, Leeds
LS9 8AJ
☎0113 245 5311 Fax 0113 245 5351
✉ wendy@redladder.co.uk
www.redladder.co.uk

Artistic Director/Literary Manager *Wendy Harris*
Administrator *Janis Smyth*

Founded 1968. Commissioning company touring 2–3 shows a year with a strong commitment to new work and new writers. Aimed at an audience of young people aged between 14–25 years who have little or no access to theatre. Performances held in youth clubs and similar venues where young people choose to meet. Recent productions: *Silent Cry* Madani Younis, *Dreaming of Bones* Damian Gorman (2003); *Soulskin* Esther Wilson; *Tagged* Louise Wallwein (2004). The company is particularly keen to enter into a dialogue with writers with regard to creating new work for young people. E-mail the artistic director for more information at the address above.

Red Shift Theatre Company

TRG2 Trowbray House, 108 Weston Street, London SE1 3QB
☎020 7378 9787 Fax 020 7378 9789
✉ mail@redshifttheatreco.co.uk
www.redshifttheatreco.co.uk

Contact *Jonathan Holloway*, Artistic Director
General Manager *Emma Rees*

Founded 1982. Small-scale touring company which plays to a theatre-literate audience. Unlikely to produce an unsolicited script as most work is commissioned. Welcomes contact with writers – 'we try to see their work' – and receipt of c.v.s and treatments. Occasionally runs workshops bringing new scripts, writers and actors together. These can develop links with a reservoir of writers who may feed the company. Interested in new plays with subject matter which is accessible to a broad audience and concerns issues of importance; also new translations and adaptations. Previous productions: *The Love Child* and *The Legend of King Arthur*.

Ridiculusmus

c/o Your Imagination, BAC, Lavender Hill, London SW11 5TN
✉ ridiculusmus@yourimagination.org
www.ridiculusmus.com

Artistic Directors *Jon Hough, David Woods*

Founded 1992. Touring company which plays to a wide range of audiences. Productions have included adaptations of *Three Men In a Boat*; *The Third Policeman*; *At Swim Two Birds* and original work: *The Exhibitionists*; *Yes, Yes, Yes*; *Say Nothing* and *Ideas Men*. Unsolicited scripts not welcome.

Royal Court Theatre

Sloane Square, London SW1W 8AS
☎020 7565 5050
Fax 020 7565 5002 (Literary office)
www.royalcourttheatre.com

Literary Manager *Graham Whybrow*

The Royal Court is a leading international theatre producing up to 17 new plays each year in its 400-seat proscenium theatre and 80-seat studio. In 1956 its first director George Devine set out to find 'hard-hitting, uncompromising writers whose plays are stimulating, provocative and exciting'. This artistic policy helped transform post-war British theatre, with new plays by writers such as John Osborne, Arnold Wesker, John Arden, Samuel Beckett, Edward Bond and David Storey, through to Caryl Churchill, Jim Cartwright, Kevin Elyot and Timberlake Wertenbaker. Since 1994 it has produced a new generation of playwrights such as Joe Penhall, Rebecca Prichard, Sarah Kane, Jez Butterworth, Martin McDonagh, Mark Ravenhill, Ayub Khan-Din, Conor McPherson, Roy Williams and many other first-time writers. The Royal Court has programmes for young writers and international writers, and it is always searching for new plays and new playwrights.

Royal Exchange Theatre Company

St Ann's Square, Manchester M2 7DH
☎0161 833 9333 Fax 0161 832 0881
www.royalexchange.co.uk

Associate Artistic Director *Sarah Frankcom*
Associate Director (Literary) *Jo Combes*

Founded 1976. The Royal Exchange has developed a new writing policy which it finds is attracting a younger audience to the theatre. The company has produced new plays by Simon Stephens, Shelagh Stephenson, Brad Fraser, Simon Burke, Jim Cartwright, Peter Barnes and Owen McCafferty. Also English and foreign classics, modern classics, adaptations and new musicals. 'In 2004/05 we are concentrating on developing writers from the North West. If you are interested in submitting a script please write to us before sending it to the Royal Exchange.'

Royal Lyceum Theatre Company

Grindlay Street, Edinburgh EH3 9AX
☎0131 248 4800 Fax 0131 228 3955
www.lyceum.org.uk

Artistic Director *Mark Thomson*
Administration Manager *Ruth Butterworth*

Founded 1965. Repertory theatre which plays to a mixed urban Scottish audience. Produces classic, contemporary and new plays. Would like to stage more new plays, especially Scottish. No full-time literary staff to provide reports on submitted scripts.

Royal National Theatre

South Bank, London SE1 9PX
☎020 7452 3333 Fax 020 7452 3350
www.nationaltheatre.org.uk

Literary Manager *Jack Bradley*

The majority of the National's new plays come about as a result of direct commission or from existing contacts with playwrights. There is no quota for new work, though many of the plays presented have been the work of living playwrights especially in the Cottesloe Theatre which is dedicated to new plays. Writers new to the theatre would need to be of exceptional talent to be successful with a script here, however the Royal National Theatre Studio helps a limited number of playwrights, through readings, workshops and discussions. Scripts considered (send s.a.e).

Royal Shakespeare Company

1 Earlham Street, London WC2H 9LL
☎020 7845 0515
www.rsc.org.uk

Dramaturg *Paul Sirett*

The RSC is a classical theatre company based in Stratford upon Avon. It has recently transformed itself to create the opportunity for different ensemble companies to work on distinct projects that will open both in Stratford upon Avon and at various venues around London. The company also has an annual residency in Newcastle upon Tyne and tours both nationally and internationally. As well as Shakespeare, English classics and foreign classics in translation, new plays counterpoint the RSC's repertory, especially those which celebrate language. 'The dramaturgy department is proactive rather than reactive and seeks out the plays and playwrights it wishes to commission. It will read all translations of classic foreign works submitted, or of contemporary works where the original writer and/or translator is known. It is unable to read unsolicited work from less established writers. It can only return scripts if an s.a.e. is enclosed with submission.'

7:84 Theatre Company Scotland

333 Woodlands Road, Glasgow G3 6NG
☎0141 334 6686 Fax 0141 334 3369
✉ admin@784theatre.com
www.784theatre.com

Artistic Director *Lorenzo Mele*

Founded 1973. One of Scotland's foremost touring theatre companies committed to producing work that addresses current social, cultural and political issues. Recent productions include commissions by Scottish playwrights such as Stephen Greenhorn, Rona Munro and Isabel Wright (*Gilt*); Nicola McCartney (*Cave Dwellers*); Peter Arnott (*A Little Rain*); Stephen Greenhorn (*Dissent*); David Greig (*Caledonia Dreaming*) and the Scottish premières of Tony Kushner's *Angels in America* and Athol Fugard's *Valley Song*. 'The company is committed to a new writing policy that encourages and develops writers at every level of experience, to get new voices and strong messages on to the stage.' New writing development has always been central to 7:84's core activity and has included Summer Schools and rehearsed readings. The company continues to be committed to this work and its development. 'Happy to read unsolicited scripts.'

Shared Experience

The Soho Laundry, 9 Dufour's Place, London W1F 7SJ
☎020 7434 9248 Fax 020 7287 8763
✉ admin@sharedexperience.org.uk
www.sharedexperience.org.uk

Joint Artistic Directors *Nancy Meckler, Polly Teale*

Founded 1975. Varied audience depending on venue, since this is a touring company. Recent productions have included: *Anna Karenina, Mill on the Floss* and *War and Peace* (all adapt. by Helen Edmundson); *The Danube* Maria Irene Fornes; *Desire Under the Elms* Eugene O'Neill; *The Tempest* William Shakespeare; *Jane Eyre* (adapt. Polly Teale); *I Am Yours* Judith Thompson; *The House of Bernarda Alba* (transl. Rona Munro); *Mother Courage* (transl. Lee Hall); *A Doll's House* (transl. Michael Meyer); *The Magic Toyshop* (adapt. Bryony Lavery); *The Clearing* Helen Edmundson; *A Passage to India* (adapt. Martin Sherman). No unsolicited mss. Primarily not a new writing company but 'we are interested in innovative new scripts'.

Sherman Theatre Company
Senghennydd Road, Cardiff CF24 4YE
☎029 2064 6901 Fax 029 2064 6902
www.shermantheatre.co.uk

Artistic Director *Phil Clark*

Founded 1973. Theatre for Young People, with main house and studio. Encourages new writing; has produced 86 new plays in the last ten years. Previous productions include a David Wood adaptation of Roald Dahl's *James and the Giant Peach*, plays by Frank Vickery (*Pullin the Wool*); Helen Griffin (*Flesh and Blood*); Patrick Jones (*Everything Must Go*); Terry Deary (*Horrible Histories Crackers Christmas*); Mike Kenny (*Puff the Magic Dragon*); Brendan Murray (*Something Beginning With ...*); Roald Dahl (*The Enormous Crocodile*); Roger Williams (*Pop*); Arnold Wesker (*Break, My Heart*).

Show of Strength
74 Chessel Street, Bedminster, Bristol
BS3 3DN
☎0117 902 0235 Fax 0117 902 0196
✉ sheila@showofstrength.freeserve.co.uk
www.showofstrength.org.uk

Artistic Director *Sheila Hannon*

Founded 1986. Plays to an informal, younger than average audience. Aims to stage at least one new play each season with a preference for work from Bristol and the South West. Will read unsolicited scripts but a lack of funding means they are unable to provide written reports. Output: *The Wills Girls* by Amanda Whittington; *Lags* by Ron Hutchinson; *So Long Life* and *Nicholodeon* by Peter Nichols. Also, rehearsed readings of new work.

Snap People's Theatre Trust
29 Raynham Road, Bishop's Stortford
CM23 5PE
☎01279 461607 Fax 01279 506694
✉ info@snaptheatre.co.uk
www.snaptheatre.co.uk

Contacts *Andy Graham, Gill Bloomfield*

Founded 1979. Plays to young people (5–11; 12–19), and for the under 25s. New writing, young people and new media are the priorities. Writers should make contact in advance of sending material. New writing is encouraged and should involve, be written for or by young people. 'Projects should reflect the writer's own beliefs, be thought-provoking, challenging and accessible. The writer should be able to work with designers, directors and musicians in the early stages to develop the text and work alongside other disciplines.'

Soho Theatre Company
21 Dean Street, London W1D 3NE
☎020 7287 5060 Fax 020 7287 5061
✉ writers@sohotheatre.com
www.sohotheatre.com

Artistic Director *Abigail Morris*

Dedicated to new writing, the company has an extensive research and development programme consisting of a free script-reading service, workshops and readings. Also runs many courses for new writers. Soho Young Writers hold free 'Taster Workshops' and longer courses for promising playwrights aged 15–25. The company produces around four plays a year. Previous productions include: *Office* Shan Khan, winner of the 2000 Verity Bargate Award; *Angels and Saints* Jessica Townsend, joint winner of the 1998 Peggy Ramsay Award; *Jump Mr Malinoff Jump* Toby Whithouse, winner of the 1998 Verity Bargate Award; *Gabriel* Moira Buffini, winner of the 1996 LWT Award; *Be My Baby* Amanda Whittington; *Kindertransporte* Diane Samuels. Runs the **Verity Bargate Award**, a biennial competition (see entry under *Prizes*).

Sphinx Theatre Company
25 Short Street, London SE1 8LJ
☎020 7401 9993 Fax 020 7401 9995
✉ admin@sphinxtheatre.co.uk
www.sphinxtheatre.co.uk

Artistic Director *Sue Parrish*
General Manager *Susannah Kraft-Levene*

Founded 1973. Tours new plays by women nationally to small and mid-scale venues. Synopses and ideas are welcome.

The Steam Industry
c/o/ Finborough Theatre, 118 Finborough Road, London SW10 9ED
☎020 7244 7439 Fax 020 7835 1853
✉ admin@finboroughtheatre.co.uk
www.steamindustry.co.uk

Artistic Director *Phil Willmott*

Since June 1994, the multi-awards-winning production company The Steam Industry has become known for its diverse and prolific productions of both new writing, radical adaptations of classic texts and musicals at many venues including the Finborough Theatre, BAC, The

Bridewell, The Drill Hall and Riverside Studios. Unsolicited scripts are no longer welcome.

Talawa Theatre Company Ltd
3rd Floor, 23–25 Great Sutton Street, London EC1V 0DN
☎020 7251 6644 Fax 020 7251 5969
✉ hq@talawa.com
www.talawa.com

General Manager *Kate Sarley*

Founded 1985. 'Aims to provide high quality productions that reflect the significant creative role that Black theatre plays within the national and international arena and also to enlarge theatre audiences from the Black community.' Previous productions include all-Black performances of *The Importance of Being Earnest* and *Antony and Cleopatra*; plus Jamaican pantomime *Arawak Gold*; *The Gods Are Not to Blame*; *The Road* Wole Soyinka; *Beef, No Chicken* Derek Walcott; *Flying West* Pearl Cleage; *Othello* William Shakespeare. Seeks to provide a platform for new work from up and coming Black British writers. Send synopsis in the first instance. Runs a black script development project. Talawa is funded by the London Arts Board.

Theatre Absolute
57–61 Corporation Street, Coventry CV1 1GQ
☎024 7625 7380 Fax 024 7655 0680
✉ julia@theatreabsolute.co.uk
www.theatreabsolute.co.uk

Artistic Director/Writer *Chris O'Connell*
Producer *Julia Negus*

Founded 1992. An independent theatre company which commissions, produces and tours new plays that are based on a strong narrative text and aimed at audiences aged 15+. Productions include: *Car*, winner of an Edinburgh Fringe First Award 1999 and a *Time Out* Live Award – Best New Play on the London Fringe 1999; and most recently, *Kid*, Edinburgh Fringe 2003. The company also runs The Writing House, a script development scheme.

Theatre of Comedy Company
210 Shaftesbury Avenue, London WC2H 8DP
☎020 7379 3345 Fax 020 7836 8181
✉ mhone@toc.dltentertainment.co.uk

Theatre Manager *Mark Hone*

Founded 1983 to produce new work as well as classics and revivals. Interested in strong comedy in the widest sense – Chekhov comes

under the definition as does farce. Also entertainment, developing new scripts for television, namely situation comedy and series.

Theatre Royal, Plymouth
Royal Parade, Plymouth PL1 2TR
☎01752 230347 Fax 01752 230499
✉ d.prescott@theatreroyal.com
www.theatreroyal.com

Artistic Director *Simon Stokes*
Artistic Associate *David Prescott*

Stages small, middle and large-scale drama and music theatre. Commissions and produces new plays. Unsolicited playscripts with s.a.e. are read and responded to. Send only one script at a time – by post only. No e-mail submissions, please.

Theatre Royal Stratford East
Gerry Raffles Square, London E15 1BN
☎020 8279 1004 Fax 020 8534 8381
✉ asohoye@stratfordeast.com
www.stratfordeast.com

New Writing Manager *Ashmeed Sohoye*

In the heart of the East End, catering for a very mixed audience, both culturally and age range. Produces plays and musicals, youth theatre and local community plays/events, all of which is new work. Special interest in plays and musicals reflecting the culturally diverse communities of London and the UK. New initiatives in developing contemporary British musicals. No longer accepts unsolicited scripts but instead asks for a) synopsis of script, b) sample ten pages of writing, c) brief writer's biography. 'From this information we will decide whether or not to ask for full-length script.'

Theatre Royal Windsor
Windsor SL4 1PS
☎01753 863444 Fax 01753 831673
✉ info@theatreroyalwindsor.co.uk
www.theatreroyalwindsor.co.uk

Executive Producer *Bill Kenwright*
Executive Director *Mark Piper*

Plays to a middle-class, West End-type audience. Produces thirteen plays a year and 'would be disappointed to do fewer than two new plays in a year; always hope to do half a dozen'. Modern classics, thrillers, comedy and farce. Only interested in scripts along these lines.

Theatre Workshop Edinburgh
34 Hamilton Place, Edinburgh EH3 5AX
☎0131 225 7942 Fax 0131 220 0112

Artistic Director *Robert Rae*

First ever professional producing theatre to fully include disabled actors in all its productions. Plays to a young, broad-based audience with many pieces targeted towards particular groups or communities. Output has included *D.A.R.E.* Particularly interested in issues-based work for young people and minority groups. Frequently engages writers for collaborative work and devised projects. Commissions a significant amount of new writing for a wide range of contexts, from large-scale community plays to small-scale professional productions. Favours writers based in Scotland, producing material relevant to a contemporary Scottish audience.

Tiebreak Theatre

42–58 St George's Street, Norwich
NR3 1AB
☎01603 665899 Fax 01603 666096
✉ info@tiebreak-theatre.com
www.tiebreak-theatre.com

Artistic Director *David Farmer*

Founded 1981. Specialises in high-quality theatre for children and young people, touring schools, youth centres, small-scale theatres, museums and festivals. Productions: *Frog in Love*; *My Uncle Arly*; *Time and Tide*; *The Snow Egg*; *One Dark Night*; *Suitcase Full of Stories*; *Fast Eddy*; *Breaking the Rules*; *George Speaks*; *Frog and Toad*; *Singing in the Rainforest*; *The Invisible Boy*; *My Friend Willy*; *The Ugly Duckling*. New writing encouraged. Interested in low-budget, small-cast material only. School and educational material of special interest. 'Scripts welcome but please ring first to discuss any potential submission.'

The Torch Theatre

St Peter's Road, Milford Haven SA73 2BU
☎01646 694192 Fax 01646 698919
✉ info@torchtheatre.co.uk
www.torchtheatre.org.uk

Artistic Director *Peter Doran*

Founded 1977. Stages a mixed programme of in-house and middle-scale touring work. Unsolicited scripts will be read and guidance offered but production unlikely due to restricted funding. Please include s.a.e. for return of script and notes; mark clearly, 'FAO Peter Doran'. Torch Theatre Company productions include: *Dancing at Lughnasa*; *Neville's Island*; *The Woman in Black*; *Abigail's Party*; *Taking Steps*; *Blue Remembered Hills*; *A Prayer for Wings*; *Little Shop of Horrors*; *The Caretaker*; *One Flew Over the Cuckoo's Nest*; *One for the Road* plus annual Christmas musicals.

Traverse Theatre

Cambridge Street, Edinburgh EH1 2ED
☎0131 228 3223 Fax 0131 229 8443
✉ neil@traverse.co.uk
www.traverse.co.uk
www.virtualtraverse.co.uk (archive)

Artistic Director *Philip Howard*
International Literary Associate *Katherine Mendelsohn*
Literary Assistant *Neil Coull*

The Traverse is Scotland's only new writing theatre, with a particular commitment to producing new Scottish plays. However, it also has a strong international programme of work in translation and visiting companies. Previous productions include *The People Next Door* Henry Adam; *Dark Earth* David Harrower; *15 Seconds* François Archambarlt, version by Isabel Wright; *Iron* Rona Munro; *Outlying Islands* David Greig; *Gagarin Way* Gregory Burke; *Perfect Days* Liz Lochhead. Please address unsolicited scripts to *Neil Coull*, Literary Assistant.

Trestle Theatre Company

Trestle Arts Base, Russet Drive, St Albans
AL4 0JQ
☎01727 850950 Fax 01727 855558
✉ admin@trestle.org.uk
www.trestle.org.uk

Artistic Director *Toby Wilsher*

Founded 1981. Physical, mask touring theatre company. Usually devised work but does work with writers to create new writing for physical/visual theatre. No unsolicited scripts.

Tricycle Theatre

269 Kilburn High Road, London NW6 7JR
☎020 7372 6611 Fax 020 7328 0795
www.tricycle.co.uk

Artistic Director *Nicolas Kent*

Founded 1980. Plays to a very mixed audience, in terms of both culture and class. Previous productions: *Stones in his Pockets* Marie Jones; *The Stephen Lawrence Enquiry – The Colour of Justice* adapt. from the enquiry transcripts by Richard Norton-Taylor; *Nuremberg* adapt. from transcripts of the trials by Richard Norton-Taylor; *Joe Turner's Come and Gone*, *The Piano Lesson* and *Two Trains Runnin'* all by August Wilson; *Kat and the Kings* David Kramer. New writing welcome from women and ethnic minorities (particularly black, Asian and Irish). Looks for a strong narrative drive with popular appeal, not 'studio' plays. Fee £12 per script. Supplies written reader's report. Can only return scripts if postage coupons or s.a.e. are enclosed with original submission.

Tron Theatre Company

63 Trongate, Glasgow G1 5HB
☎0141 552 3748 Fax 0141 552 6657
✉ neil@tron.co.uk
www.tron.co.uk
Director *Neil Murray*

Founded 1981. Plays to a broad cross-section of Glasgow and beyond, including international tours. Recent productions: *San Diego* David Greig (co-production with Edinburgh International Festival); *Further Than the Furthest Thing* Zinnie Harris (co-production with the **Royal National Theatre**); *Shining Souls* Chris Hannan (co-production with V. Amp). Interested in ambitious plays by UK and international writers. No unsolicited mss.

Unicorn Theatre for Children

St Mark's Studios, Chillingworth Road,
London N7 8QJ
☎020 7700 0702 Fax 020 7700 3870
✉ admin@unicorntheatre.com
www.unicorntheatre.com
Artistic Director *Tony Graham*
Literary Manager *Carl Miller*

Founded 1947, resident at the Arts Theatre from 1967 to 1999. Produces full-length professionally performed plays for children, aged 4–12, their teachers and families. Recent work includes *Clockwork* by Philip Pullman, adapt. David Wood and Stephen McNeff; *Rumpelstiltskin* by Mike Kenny; *Merlin the Magnificent* by Stuart Paterson; *Great Expectations* by Charles Dickens, adapted by John Clifford. Currently produces at London venues including the Pleasance Theatre, Royal Opera House, the Linbury Theatre and on tour nationally and internationally. Moving to new Unicorn Children's Centre with two theatres on Bankside, London, in 2005. Does not produce unsolicited scripts but works with commissioned writers. Writers interested in working with the company should send details of relevant previous work and why they would like to write for Unicorn.

Upstairs at the Gatehouse

See **Ovation Productions** under *Film, TV and Radio Producers*

Charles Vance Productions

Hampden House, 2 Weymouth Street,
London W1W 5BT
☎020 7636 4343 Fax 020 7636 2323
✉ cvtheatre@aol.com
Contact *Charles Vance*

In the market for medium-scale touring productions and summer-season plays. Hardly any new work and no commissions but writing of promise stands a good chance of being passed on to someone who might be interested in it. Occasional try-outs for new work in the Sidmouth repertory theatre. Send s.a.e. for return of mss.

Warehouse Theatre

62 Dingwall Road, Croydon CR0 2NF
☎020 8681 1257 Fax 020 8688 6699
✉ info@warehousetheatre.co.uk
www.warehousetheatre.co.uk
Artistic Director *Ted Craig*

South London's new writing theatre (adjacent to East Croydon railway station) seats 90–100 and produces up to six new plays a year. Also co-produces with, and hosts, selected touring companies who share the theatre's commitment to new work. Continually building upon a tradition of discovering and nurturing new writers, with activities including a monthly writers' workshop and the annual **International Playwriting Festival**. Also hosts youth theatre workshops and Saturday morning children's theatre. Previous productions: *Iona Rain* by Peter Moffat and *Fat Janet is Dead* by Simon Smith (both past winners of the International Playwriting Festival); *Coming Up* James Martin Charlton and M.G. 'Monk' Lewis; *Dick Barton Special Agent*; *Dick Barton and the Curse of the Pharaoh's Tomb*; *Dick Barton: The Tango of Terror*; *Dick Barton and the Excess of Evil*; *Dick Barton and the Flight of the Phoenix* Phil Willmott. Unsolicited scripts welcome but it is more advisable to submit plays through the theatre's International Playwriting Festival.

Watford Palace Theatre

Clarendon Road, Watford WD17 1JZ
☎01923 235455 Fax 01923 819664
✉ enquiries@watfordtheatre.co.uk
www.watfordtheatre.co.uk
Artistic Director *Lawrence Till*

An important part of artistic and cultural policy is the commissioning of new plays and to discover major new playwrights and new plays of enduring stature to be produced in the region. Recent new plays: *Elton John's Glasses* David Farr (1997 Writers' Guild Best Regional Play award); *The Talented Mr Ripley* Phyllis Nagy; *The Dark*

Jonathan Holloway; *The Late Middle Classes* Simon Gray (1999 Barclays/TMA Best New Play Award); *Morning Glory* Sarah Daniels; *The True-Life Fiction of Mata Hari* Diane Samuels; *Full House* and *The Hairless Diva* (after Ionesco) John Mortimer; *Big Night Out at the Little Palace Theatre* Sandi Toksvig and Dillie Keane.

Watford Palace Theatre
See **Palace Theatre**

West Yorkshire Playhouse
Playhouse Square, Leeds LS2 7UP
☎0113 213 7800 Fax 0113 213 7250
✉ alex.chisholm@wyp.org.uk
www.wyp.org.uk
Literary Manager *Alex Chisholm*

Committed to working with new writing originating from or set in the Yorkshire and Humberside region. New writing from outside the region is programmed usually where writer or company is already known to the theatre. The Playhouse runs workshops, courses and writers' events including Thursday Night Live, an open platform held at the theatre for local writers and performers. For more information contact the Literary Manager on 0113 213 7286 or e-mail to address above. Scripts should be submitted with s.a.e. for return.

Whirligig Theatre
14 Belvedere Drive, Wimbledon, London SW19 7BY
☎020 8947 1732 Fax 020 8879 7648
✉ whirligig-theatre@virgin.net
Contact *David Wood*

Occasional productions and tours to major theatre venues, usually a musical for primary school audiences and weekend family groups. Interested in scripts which exploit the theatrical nature of children's tastes. Previous productions: *The See-Saw Tree*; *The Selfish Shellfish*; *The Gingerbread Man*; *The Old Man of Lochnagar*; *The Ideal Gnome Expedition*; *Save the Human*; *Dreams of Anne Frank*; *Babe, the Sheep-Pig*.

Michael White Productions Ltd
See **MW Entertainments Ltd** under *Film, TV and Radio Producers*

White Bear Theatre Club
138 Kennington Park Road, London SE11 4DJ
Administration: 3 Dante Road, Kennington, London SE11 4RB
☎020 7793 9193 Fax 020 7793 9193
Contact *Michael Kingsbury*
Administrator *Julia Parr*

Founded 1988. Output primarily new work for an audience aged 20–35. Unsolicited scripts welcome, particularly new work with a keen eye on contemporary issues, though not agitprop. *Absolution* by Robert Sherwood was nominated by the Writers' Guild for 'Best Fringe Play' and *Spin* by the same author was the *Time Out* Critics' Choice in 2000. The theatre received the *Time Out* award for Best Fringe Venue in 2001 and a Peter Brook award for best up-and-coming venue. The Writers' Guild, sponsored by the Mackintosh Foundation, is leading writer workshops and readings throughout the year. In 2004 *Round the Home ... Revisited* transferred to The Venue, Leicester Square.

Windsor Theatre Royal
See **Theatre Royal Windsor**

The Young Vic
66 The Cut, London SE1 8LZ
☎020 7922 8400 Fax 020 7922 8401
✉ info@youngvic.org
www.youngvic.org
Artistic Director *David Lan*
Executive Director *Kevin Fitzmaurice*

Founded 1970. The Young Vic is a theatre for everyone but, above all, for younger artists and audiences. Produces revivals of classics – old and new – as well as new plays and annual events that embrace both young people and adults. From July 2004 the theatre will be closed for two years for rebuilding but will maintain a programme of productions in other venues in the borough.

Festivals

Aberdeen Arts Carnival
Aberdeen Arts Centre, 33 King Street,
Aberdeen AB24 5AA
☎01224 635208
www.aberdeenartscentre.org.uk
Venue Manager *Arthur Deans*

Performances – mainly by local amateurs and
arts workshops in drama, music, art, dance and
creative writing – take place each summer
during the school holidays.

The Aldeburgh Literary Weekend
44 High Street, Aldebugh IP15 5AB
☎01728 453581 Fax 01728 452389
www.aldeburghbookshop.co.uk
Festival Organisers *John and Mary James*

Founded 2002. Held on the first weekend in
March. The programme includes creative writ-
ing workshops, a literary dinner and lunch, and
talks. Previous speakers have included Alan
Bennett, Craig Brown, Richard Dawkins,
Anthony Horowitz, P.D. James, Doris Lessing,
Christopher Matthew, Matt Ridley, Alexander
McCall Smith, Libby Purves, Salley Vickers,
V.S. Naipaul, A.N. Wilson and David Lodge.

Aldeburgh Poetry Festival
The Cut, 9 New Cut, Halesworth IP19 8BY
☎01986 835940
✉ info@aldeburghpoetryfestival.org
www.aldeburghpoetryfestival.org
Festival Director *Naomi Jaffa*

Now in its sixteenth year, an annual international
festival of contemporary poetry held on the first
weekend of November in Aldeburgh, attracting
large audiences. Regular features include a four-
week residency leading up to the festival, poetry
readings, children's event, workshops, public
masterclass, lecture, performance spot and the
Jerwood Aldeburgh Prize for the year's best
first collection (see entry under **Prizes**).

Aspects Literature Festival
North Down Borough Council, Town Hall,
The Castle, Bangor BT20 4BT
☎028 9127 8032 Fax 028 9127 1370
✉ gail.prentice@northdown.gov.uk

Festival Coordinator/Arts Officer *Gail Prentice*

Founded 1992. 'Ireland's Premier Literary
Festival' is held at the end of September and
celebrates the richness and diversity of living
Irish writers with occasional special features on
past generations. It draws upon all disciplines
– fiction (of all types), poetry, theatre, non-
fiction, cinema, song-writing, etc. It also
includes a day of writing for young readers and
sends writers to visit local schools during the
festival. Highlights of recent festivals include
appearances by Bernard MacLaverty, Marion
Keyes, Alice Taylor, Frank Delaney, Seamus
Heaney, Brian Keenan and Fergal Keane.

Bath Fringe Festival
The Bell, 103 Walcot Street, Bath BA1 5BW
☎01225 480079 Fax 01225 480079
✉ admin@bathfringe.co.uk
www.bathfringe.co.uk
Contact *Wendy Matthews*

Founded 1981. Complementing the international music festival, the Fringe presents
theatre, poetry, jazz, blues, comedy, cabaret,
street performance and more in venues, parks
and streets of Bath during late May and early
June.

Bath Literature Festival
Administration Office: Bath Festivals Trust,
5 Broad Street, Bath BA1 5LJ
☎01225 462231 Fax 01225 445551
✉ info@bathfestivals.org.uk
www.bathlitfest.org.uk

Box Office: Bath Festivals Box Office,
2 Church Street, Abbey Green, Bath BA1 1NL.
☎01225 463362
✉ boxoffice@bathfestivals.org.uk

Artistic Director *Sarah LeFanu*

Founded 1995. This annual festival (26 February
to 6 March in 2005) programmes over 100 different literary events from debates and lectures
to readers' groups and workshops in venues
throughout the city. In addition there are a number of events for children and young people.
Previous featured writers include A.S. Byatt,
Sebastian Faulks, Jackie Kay, Andrew Motion
and Jacqueline Wilson.

Bay Lit

Academi, Mount Stuart House, Mount Stuart Square, Cardiff CF10 5FQ
☎029 2047 2266 Fax 029 2049 2930
✉ post@academi.org
www.academi.org

Chief Executive *Peter Finch*

Biennial literature festival held in Cardiff Bay, featuring writers from Wales and beyond. Lectures, readings, performances, workshops and book launches in English and Welsh. Dates and further details available on the Academi website.

Belfast Festival at Queen's

Festival House, 25 College Gardens, Belfast BT9 6BS
☎028 9097 2600 Fax 028 9097 2630
✉ festival@qub.ac.uk
www.belfastfestival.com

Director *Stella Hall*

Founded 1964. Annual three-week festival held in October/November. Organised by Queen's University in association with the **Arts Council of Northern Ireland**, the festival covers a wide variety of events, including literature. Programme available in September.

Between the Lines – Belfast Literary Festival

Crescent Arts Centre, 2–4 University Road, Belfast BT7 1NH
☎028 9024 2338 Fax 028 9024 6748
✉ btl.cac@btconnect.com *or* mairtin.cac@btconnect.com
www.crescentarts.org

Artistic Director *Mairtin Crawford*

Founded 1998. Annual 7–10-day international event held in March/April. Features readings, workshops, open platforms, quizzes and performance. All genres covered: playwriting, prose, poetry, screenwriting, etc. and special events for children. Previous guests include David Lodge, Lemn Sissay, Sheila O'Flanagan, Medbh McGuckian, Conor O'Callaghan, Matthew Sweeney, Merlin Holland, Ciaran Carson. Telephone to join free mailing list.

Birmingham Book Festival

c/o Book Communications, Unit 116, The Custard Factory, Gibb Street, Birmingham B9 4AA
☎0121 246 2777/2770 Fax 0121 246 2771
✉ info@bookcommunications.co.uk

Contacts *Helen Thomas, Jonathan Davidson*

Founded 1999. Annual two-week-long festival held the last two weeks of October at various venues around Birmingham. Includes performances, lectures, discussion events and workshops.

Book Now!

The Arts Team, Orleans House Gallery, Riverside, Twickenham TW1 3DJ
✉ artsinfo@richmond.gov.uk
www.richmond.gov.uk

Founded 1992. Annual festival which runs throughout the month of November, administered by the Arts Section of Richmond Council. Principal focus is on poetry and serious fiction, but events also cover biography, writing for theatre, children's writing. Programme includes readings, discussions, workshops, debates, exhibitions, schools events. Writers who appeared at past festivals include Kate Adie, Sir Roy Strong, Humphrey Carpenter, David Starkey, Salley Vickers, Virginia Ironsie, Tobias Hill, Redmond O'Hanlon, Andrew Lycett, Andrew Graham Dixon, Ben Fogle, Mavis Cheek and Janet Todd.

Bradford Book Festival

Central Library, Princes Way, Bradford BD1 1NN
☎01274 433915
✉ paula.truman@bradford.gov.uk

Contact *Paula Truman*

Founded 1999. Month-long festival organised by Bradford Libraries, held during May/June.

Brighton Festival

Festival Office, 12a Pavilion Buildings, Castle Square, Brighton BN1 1EE
☎01273 700747 Fax 01273 707505
✉ info@brighton-festival.org.uk
www.brighton-festival.org.uk

Contact *General Manager*

Founded 1966. For 24 days every May, Brighton hosts England's largest mixed arts festival. Music, dance, theatre, film, opera, literature, comedy and exhibitions. Literary enquiries will be passed to the literature officer. Deadline October for following May.

Bristol Poetry Festival

The Poetry Can, Unit 11, 20–23 Hepburn Road, Bristol BS2 8UD
☎0117 942 6976 Fax 0117 944 1478
✉ festival@poetrycan.demon.co.uk
www.poetrycan.demon.co.uk

Festival Director *Colin Brown*

Founded 1996. Annual festival taking place across the city every October (7th to 17th in 2004). A celebration of the best in contemporary poetry, from readings and performances to cabaret and multimedia. Local, national and international poetry is showcased and explored in all its manifestations, with events for everyone including performances and workshops, competitions and commissions, public poetry interventions, community work and cross art form and digital projects.

Broadstairs Dickens Festival

10 Lanthorne Road, Broadstairs CT10 3NH
☎01843 861827 Fax 01843 861827
www.broadstairs.gov.uk/DickensFestival.html
Organiser *Sylvia Hawkes*

Founded 1937 to commemorate the 100th anniversary of Charles Dickens' first visit to Broadstairs in 1837, which he continued to visit until 1859. The Festival lasts for nine days in June and events include an opening gala concert, a parade, a performance of a Dickens play (*Nicholas Nickleby* in 2004), duels, melodramas, Dickens readings, a Victorian cricket match, Victorian bathing parties, talks, music hall, three-day Victorian country fair. Costumed Dickensian ladies in crinolines with top-hatted escorts promenade during the week.

Cambridge History Festival

Indicombe, West Buckland, Barnstaple
EX32 0SE
☎01598 760367
✉ wh@histfest.com
www.histfest.com
Contacts *Derek Wilson, Ruth Wilson*

Annual three-day festival held in September in the heart of the university. The major networking event for all popular history enthusiasts – academics, historical novelists, popular historians, TV producers and presenters, museum and gallery staff. Varied programme includes talks, presentations, displays, discussions, concerts of period music, publishers' receptions, etc. Programmes available from April. Among the writers who have appeared are David Starkey, Beryl Bainbridge, Louis de Bernières, Timothy West, Tracy Chevalier, Diarmaid MacCulloch, John Guy, Richard Holmes, Prunella Scales and Terry Jones.

Camelford Poetry Festival

The Indian King, Garmoe Cottage, Trefrew, Camelford PL32 9TP
☎01840 212161 Fax 01840 212161

✉ indianking@btconnect.com
Director *Helen Wood*

Founded 1997 as the Jon Silkin Memorial Poetry Festival. Jon Silkin taught annual poetry workshops and readings to raise funds for the Centre, and the festival was held to honour his life and work. Held annually the weekend before Easter in Camelford, the central town in North Cornwall, in the Indian King, North Cornwall's only community arts centre. The festival includes workshops, poetry readings and performances, writing and literary walks, a dinner in memory of Jon Silkin on the Friday evening and a weekend long poetry cafe where visitors can book reading slots. Previous guests have included Fred d'Aguilar, Sara Jane Arbury, John Branfield, Ann Gray, John Greening, Philip Gross, Derrek Hines, Christopher Logue, William Oxley, Ian Parks, Fiona Sampson, Myra Schneider and Dilys Wood. Book for individual events or buy a weekend ticket.

Canterbury Festival

Christ Church Gate, The Precincts, Canterbury CT1 2EE
☎01227 452853 Fax 01227 781830
✉ info@canterburyfestival.co.uk
Festival Director *Rosie Turner*

Founded 1984. Annual two-week festival held in October (8th to 22nd in 2005). A mixed programme of events including concerts in the cathedral by international artistes, opera, dance, drama, jazz and folk, visual arts open-house trail, community events and street theatre, talks and walks.

Centre for Creative & Performing Arts Spring Literary Festival at UEA

University of East Anglia, School of English & American Studies, Norwich NR4 8TJ
☎01603 592810
✉ v.striker@uea.ac.uk
www.uea.ac.uk/eas/events/intro.shtml
Contact *Val Striker*

Founded 1993. Annual event held in the spring.

Charleston Festival

The Charleston Trust, Charleston, Nr Firle, Lewes BN8 6LL
☎01323 811626
✉ info@charleston.org.uk
www.charleston.org.uk
Festival Programmer *Diana Reich*

Annual literary festival held in May over nine days. Novelists, biographers, travel writers, broadcasters, poets, food writers, actors and artists gather at Charleston, the country home of the Bloomsbury Group. Past speakers include Margaret Atwood, Alan Bennett, Jeanette Winterson, Patti Smith, Paula Rego, Eileen Atkins, Michael Frayn, Germaine Greer and Harold Pinter.

The Cheltenham Festival of Literature
Town Hall, Imperial Square, Cheltenham GL50 1QA
☎01242 263494 Fax 01242 256457
✉ adam.pushkin@cheltenham.gov.uk
www.cheltenhamfestivals.co.uk
Festival Director *Sarah Smyth*

Founded 1949. Annual festival held in October. The first purely literary festival of its kind, this festival has over the past decade developed from an essentially local event into the largest and most popular in Europe. A wide range of events including talks and lectures, poetry readings, novelists in conversation, exhibitions, discussions and a large bookshop.

Chester Literature Festival
8 Abbey Square, Chester CH1 2HU
☎01244 319985 Fax 01244 341200
✉ freda@chesterfestivals.co.uk
Chairman *John Scrivener*

Founded 1989. Annual festival commencing the first weekend in October every year (runs 1–23 October in 2005). Events include international and nationally known writers, as well as events by local literary groups. There is a Literary Lunch and a Festival Dinner, events for children, workshops and competitions. Free mailing list.

Children's Books Ireland – Annual Festival
See **Children's Books Ireland** under *Professional Associations*

Dartington Literary Festival
See **Ways With Words**

Derbyshire Literature Festival
c/o Arts Office, Derbyshire County Council, Cultural & Community Services Department, Alfreton Library, Severn Square, Alfreton DE55 7BQ
☎01773 832497 Fax 01773 831359
✉ ann.wright@derbyshire.gov.uk
www.derbyshire.gov.uk

Festival Organiser *Ann Wright*

Founded 2000. The festival takes place throughout June every two years and covers the whole county. The festival programming includes all types of live literature events; performance poetry, theatre, talks, readers' groups, workshops, dramatised readings, signings, song, readings, storytelling and literary trails, as well as a number of cross-art form events. The festival takes place in libraries and many other community venues including heritage centres, industrial buildings, stately homes, parks and moors, churches and schools and is specifically designed to reach as many different communities and geographical areas in the county as possible.

Dorchester Festival
Dorchester Arts Centre, School Lane, The Grove, Dorchester DT1 1XR
☎01305 266926 Fax 01305 266143
www.dorchesterarts.org.uk
Artistic Director *Sharon Hayden*

Founded 1996. A biennial four-day festival over early May Bank Holiday weekend (next to be held in 2006) which includes performing, media and visual arts, with associated educational and community projects in the run up to the Festival. Includes a wide range of events, in many venues, for all age groups, including some literature and poetry.

The Daphne du Maurier Festival of Arts & Literature
Restormel Borough Council, Penwinnick Road, St Austell PL25 5DR
☎01726 223535
www.dumaurier.org/festival.html

Annual festival, held in Fowey over ten days in May. Guests at the 2004 Festival included Benedict Allen, John Fortune, Michael Holroyd, Deborah Moggach, John Sergeant and E.V. Thompson.

Dublin Writers' Festival
Dublin City Council Arts Office, Foley Street, Dublin 1, Republic of Ireland
✉ info@dublinwritersfestival.com
www.dublinwritersfestival.com
Programme Director *Pat Boran*

Annual festival held in mid-June, including Bloomsday. Features readings, public interviews and discussions, along with a poetry slam and beginners' workshops. Major Irish and international poets and writers.

Dumfries and Galloway Arts Festival

Gracefield Arts Centre, 28 Edinburgh Road, Dumfries DG1 1JQ
☎01387 260447 Fax 01387 260447
✉ dgartsfestival@ukgateway.net

Festival Organiser *Mrs Barbara Kelly*

Founded 1980. Annual week-long festival held at the end of May with a variety of events including classical and folk music, theatre, dance, literary events, exhibitions and children's events.

Durham Literature Festival

Durham City Arts, Byland Lodge, Hawthorn Terrace, Durham City DH1 4TD
☎0191 301 8245 Fax 0191 301 8821
✉ info@durhamcityarts.demon.co.uk

Festival Coordinator *Alison Lister*

Founded 1989. Annual 2–3-week festival now held in September/October at various locations in the city. Performances and readings plus workshops, cabaret, exhibitions and other events.

Edinburgh International Book Festival

Scottish Book Centre, 137 Dundee Street, Edinburgh EH11 1BG
☎0131 228 5444 Fax 0131 228 4333
✉ admin@edbookfest.co.uk
www.edbookfest.co.uk

Director *Catherine Lockerbie*

Founded 1983. The world's largest and most dynamic annual book event takes place over 17 days in Edinburgh each August. An extensive programme showcases the work of the world's top authors and thinkers to an audience of over 185,000 adults and children. Featuring workshops, readings, lectures and a high profile debate and discussion series.

'Everybody's Reading' – Leicester's Festival of Words

Leicester City Council, Libraries, A12 New Walk Centre, Leicester LE1 6ZG
☎0116 252 7347
✉ waltd001@leicester.gov.uk

Literature Development Officer *Damien Walter*

Annual celebration of words and reading held in June. A mixture of author events, workshops, profiles of community arts and spotlights on local writing held in a range of community/library/arts venues around the city.

Fife Festival of Authors

Fife Council Libraries – Central Area, Libraries HQ, East Fergus Place, Kirkcaldy KY1 1XT
☎01592 412930
✉ david.spalding@fife.gov.uk

Contact *David Spalding*

Founded 1996. Annual festival running in March/April for adults and children. Aims to bring the best of modern writing to the public as well as stimulate and foster creative writing within the local communities. Author readings, poetry events, writing workshops, literary competitions and dramatic presentations feature in the programme.

Folkestone Literary Festival

The Metropole Galleries, The Leas, Folkestone CT20 2LS
☎01303 258594
✉ info@folkestonelitfest.com
www.folkestonelitfest.com

Festival Director *Nick Ewbank*

The Folkestone Literary Festival brings outstanding writers to this beautiful seaside town for a week packed with tours, discussions, talks and readings. Annual festival held in the last full week of September.

Frome Festival

25 Market Place, Frome BA11 iAH
☎01373 453889 Fax 01373 471574
✉ fromefestival@ukonline.co.uk
www.fromefestival.co.uk

Festival Director *Martin Bax*

An annual festival held from the first Friday in July for ten days celebrating all aspects of visual and performing arts and entertainment and with a strong literary element. Features music, film, dance, drama and visual arts plus readings, talks and workshops. Previous literary guests have included nationally renowned writers as well as local authors.

Graham Greene Festival

See **Graham Greene Birthplace Trust** under *Literary Societies*

Greenwich + Docklands Festivals

6 College Approach, London SE10 9HY
☎020 8305 1818 Fax 020 8305 1188
✉ info@festival.org
www.festival.org

Executive Director *Mathew Russell*
Artistic Director *Bradley Hemmings*

Greenwich + Docklands Festivals (GDF) is a festival and event-producing organisation working across east London in the boroughs of Greenwich, Tower Hamlets, Newham and more recently further afield. GDF's portfolio includes the International Festival, London's largest multi-artform festival; First Night, a celebration of the new year through the arts; and diversification, producing events for a wide range of contexts across London and beyond.

The Guardian Hay Festival

25 Lion Street, Hay-on-Wye HR3 5AD
☎0870 787 2848 Fax 01497 821066
www.hayfestival.com
Festival Director *Peter Florence*

Founded 1988. Annual May festival sponsored by *The Guardian*. Guests have included Paul McCartney, Bill Clinton, Salman Rushdie, Toni Morrison, Stephen Fry, Joseph Heller, Carlos Fuentes, Maya Angelou, Amos Oz, Arthur Miller.

Guildford Book Festival

c/o Tourist Information Centre, 15 Tunsgate, Guildford GU1 3QT
☎01483 444334
✉ director@guildfordbookfestival.co.uk
www.guildfordbookfestival.co.uk
Book Festival Director *Glenis Pycraft*

Founded 1990. Patrons: Sandi Toksvig, Fay Weldon, Timothy West and Jacqueline Wilson. Held annually, during October in venues throughout the ancient town of Guildford. The festival includes events with celebrated and new writers, workshops, poetry performances, children's events, competitions, First Novel Award, literary lunches and teas. Its appeal lies in its diversity and its aim is to involve, instruct and entertain all who care about literature. Guest authors in 2003 included Dannie Abse, Joan Bakewell, Patricia Duncker, Patrick Gale, Tony Hawks, Robert Lacey, Michael Rosen, Francine Stock, Lynne Truss and Penny Vincenzi.

Haringey Literature Festival

Collage Arts, The Chocolate Factory, Clarendon Road, London N22 6XJ
☎020 8829 1317 Fax 020 8365 8686
✉ dana@collage-arts.org
www.collage-arts.org
Festival Organiser *Dana Captainino*

Founded 1995. Annual literature programme is a mixture of poetry and literature in the form of readings, discussions, workshops and residencies.

A regular feature is *Poetry and Poppadums* featuring top and up-and-coming poets in the setting of La Kera, an Indian restaurant in the Chocolate Factory. Writers who have appeared at past festivals include Patience Agbabi, John Hegley, Matthew Sweeney, Fay Weldon.

Harrogate Crime Writing Festival

1 Victoria Avenue, Harrogate GH1 1EQ
☎01423 562303 Fax 10423 521264
✉ crime@harrogate-festival.org.uk
www.harrogate-festival.org.uk
Festival Director *William Culver Dodds*
Festival Coordinator *Jane Bradish-Ellames*
Festival Manager *Sharon Canavar*

Launched 2003. Weekend of events at the end of July each year featuring the best of British and American crime writers. Events also include industry 'How to ...' sessions, social events and late night shows. Part of the Harrogate International Festival.

Harrogate International Festival

1 Victoria Avenue, Harrogate HG1 1EQ
☎01423 562303 Fax 01423 521264
✉ info@harrogate-festival.org.uk
www.harrogate-festival.org.uk
Festival Director *William Culver-Dodds*
Festival Manager *Sharon Canavar*

Founded 1966. Annual two-week festival at the end of July and beginning of August. Events include international symphony orchestras, chamber concerts, ballet, celebrity recitals, contemporary dance, opera, drama, jazz and comedy.

Harwich Festival of the Arts

2A Kings Head Street, Harwich CO12 3EG
☎01255 503571
✉ anna@rendell-knights.freeserve.co.uk
Contact *Anna Rendell-Knights*

Founded 1980. Annual ten-day summer festival held in June/July. Events include concerts, drama, film, dance, art, exhibitions, historic town walks and children's competitions. The 2004 Festival celebrated the 400th Anniversary of King James I's signing of the 1604 Royal Charter granting Harwich self-governing free borough status.

Hastings International Poetry First of All

'The Snoring Cat', 16 Marianne Park, Dudley Road, Hastings TN35 5PU
Contact *Josephine Austin*

Founded 1968. Annual weekend poetry festival held in November in the Yelton Hotel, White Rock, Hastings. Runs the Hastings National Poetry Competition; entry forms available from the address above. Issues *First Time*, a biannual poetry magazine for first-time poets and others.

The Hay Festival
See **The Guardian Hay Festival**

Hebden Bridge Arts Festival
New Oxford House, Albert Street, Hebden Bridge HX7 4AH
☎01422 842684
✉ hbartsfestival@hotmail.com *or* enid.stephenson@3-c.coop
www.hebdenbridge.co.uk/festival
Contact *Enid Stephenson*

Founded 1994. Annual arts festival with increasingly strong adult and children's literature events. Previous guest writers include Roger McGough, Benjamin Zephaniah, Anne Fine, Juliet Barker, Jacqueline Wilson, Pete McCarthy, Ian McMillan, Adele Geras.

Humber Mouth – Hull Literature Festival
City Arts Unit, Central Library, Albion Street, Kingston upon Hull HU1 3TF
☎01482 616961 Fax 01482 616827
✉ humber.mouth@hullcc.gov.uk
www.humbermouth.org.uk
Contact *Maggie Hannan*, City Arts Unit

Founded 1992. Hull's largest festival, held in the summer, and one of the region's liveliest events. Features readings, talks, performances and workshops by writers and artists from around the world and from the city.

Ilkley Literature Festival
The Manor House, 2 Castle Hill, Ilkley LS29 9DT
☎01943 601210 Fax 01943 817079
✉ admin@ilkleyliteraturefestival.org.uk
www.ilkleyliteraturefestival.org.uk
Director *Rachel Feldberg*

Founded 1973. Major literature festival in the north with events running throughout the year. Large-scale annual festival each October. Recent guests include Louis de Bernières, John Simpson, A.S. Byatt, Carol Ann Duffy and Iain Banks. Telephone or e-mail to join free mailing list.

Imagine: Writers and Writing for Children
See **Royal Festival Hall Literature & Talks**

The International Festival of Mountaineering Literature
University of Leeds, Bretton Hall Campus, Wakefield WF4 4LG
☎0113 343 9063 Fax 0133 343 9148
✉ t.gifford@leeds.ac.uk
www.festivalofmountaineeringliterature.co.uk
Director *Terry Gifford*

Founded 1987. Annual one-day festival held in March 2005 celebrating recent books, commissioning new writing, overviews of national literatures, debates of issues, book signings, discussion with Chair of Judges of the adjudication of the annual **Boardman Tasker Award** for the best mountaineering book of the year. Announces the winner of the festival writing competition run in conjunction with *High* magazine. Write to join free mailing list.

International Playwriting Festival
Warehouse Theatre, Dingwall Road, Croydon CR0 2NF
☎020 8681 1257 Fax 020 8688 6699
✉ info@warehousetheatre.co.uk
www.warehousetheatre.co.uk
Festival Administrator *Rose Marie Vernon*

Founded 1985. Annual competition for full-length unperformed plays, judged by a panel of theatre professionals. Finalists given rehearsed readings during the festival week in November. Entries welcome from all parts of the world. Scripts plus two s.a.e.s (one script-sized) should reach the theatre by the end of June, accompanied by an entry form (available online or from the theatre). Previous winners produced at the theatre include: Kevin Hood *Beached*; Ellen Fox *Conversations with George Sandburgh After a Solo Flight Across the Atlantic*; Guy Jenkin *Fighting for the Dunghill*; James Martin Charlton *Fat Souls*; Peter Moffat *Iona Rain*; Dino Mahoney *YoYo*; Simon Smith *Fat Janet is Dead*; Dominic McHale *The Resurrectionists*; Philip Edwards *51 Peg*; Roumen Shomov *The Dove*; Maggie Nevill *The Shagaround*; Andrew Shakeshaft *Just Sitting*. Shares plays with its partner festival in Italy, the Premio Candoni Arta Terme.

Isle of Man Literature Festival
Isle of Man Arts Council, 10 Villa Marina Arcade, Douglas IM1 2HN
☎01624 611316 Fax 01624 615423

✉ dawn.maddrell@iomartscouncil.dtl.gov.im

Contact *Arts Development Manager*

Founded 1997. Annual festival of literature, poetry and music with events taking place over several weekends in the autumn.

King's Lynn, The Fiction Festival

19 Tuesday Market Place, King's Lynn PE30 1JW

☎01553 691661 (office hours) or 761919

Fax 01553 691779

Contact *Anthony Ellis*

Founded 1989. Annual weekend festival held in March. Over the weekend there are readings and discussions, attended by guest writers of which there are usually eight. Guests have included Beryl Bainbridge, Paul Bailey, Penelope Liveley, Christopher Bigsby, Geoff Dyer and John Fuller.

King's Lynn, The Poetry Festival

19 Tuesday Market Place, King's Lynn PE30 1JW

☎01553 691661 (office hours) or 761919

Fax 01553 691779

Contact *Anthony Ellis*

Founded 1985. Annual weekend festival held at the end of September, with guest poets (usually eight). Previous guests have included Carol Ann Duffy, Paul Durcan, Gavin Ewart, Peter Porter, Stephen Spender. Events include readings and discussion panels and the presentation of the King's Lynn Award; current Laureate is C.K. Stead.

Lancaster LitFest

26 Castle Park, Lancaster LA1 1YQ

☎01524 62166 Fax 01524 841216

✉ andy.darby@litfest.org

www.litfest.org

Founded 1978. Regional Literature Development Agency, organising workshops, readings, residencies, publications. Year-round programme of literature-based events and annual festival in November featuring a wide range of writers from the UK and overseas.

Leamington Festival

Warwick Arts Society, Pageant House, 2 Jury Street, Warwick CV34 4EW

☎01926 410747 Fax 01926 409050

✉ admin@warwickarts.org.uk

www.warwickarts.org.uk

Festival Director *Richard Phillips*

Launched 2003, the Festival has grown from an annual themed chamber music weekend to include jazz and world music events. Held in early May, it features literary events, many of which reflect the theme of the overall Festival. Extensive educational programme including workshops.

Ledbury Poetry Festival

Town Council Offices, Church Lane, Ledbury HR8 1DH

☎0845 458 1743

✉ info@poetry-festival.com

www.poetry-festival.com

Contact *Charles Bennett*

Founded 1997. Annual ten-day festival held in July. Includes readings, discussions, workshops, exhibitions, music and walks. There are also writers in residence at local schools and residential homes, a national poetry competition and the Town Party. Past guests have included Andrew Motion, Benjamin Zephaniah, Simon Armitage, Roger McGough, John Hegley and Germaine Greer. Full programme available in May.

Leicester Literature Festival

See **'Everybody's Reading'**

Lewes Live Literature

PO Box 2766, Lewes BN7 2WF

☎01273 401100 Fax 01273 401100

✉ info@leweslivelit.co.uk

www.leweslivelit.co.uk

Artistic Director *Mark Hewitt*

Founded 1995. Year-round literature organisation promoting Lewes Live Literature Festival (three-day intensive, late October/early November) and the LLL Spring Season (sometime April/May/June) as well as occasional projects outside these times. Areas of interest include poetry, fiction. non-fiction, art, art history, music, theatre, film, TV. Events include readings, performance, lectures, workshops, screenings of film and video, exhibitions.

Lichfield Festival

7 The Close, Lichfield WS13 7LD

☎01543 306270 Fax 01543 306274

✉ lichfield.fest@lichfield-arts.org.uk

www.lichfieldfestival.org

Festival Director *Meurig Bowen*

Founded 1982. Annual July festival with events taking place in the 13th century Cathedral, the new Lichfield Garrick Theatre, and various country churches and outdoor venues. Mainly music but a growing programme of literary events such as poetry, plays and talks.

City of London Festival

230 Bishopsgate, London EC2M 4HW
☎020 7377 0540 Fax 020 7377 1972
✉ admin@colf.org
www.colf.org

Director *Kathryn McDowell*

Founded 1962. Annual three-week festival held in June and July. Features over fifty classical and popular music events alongside poetry and prose readings, street theatre and open-air extravaganzas, in some of the most outstanding performance spaces in the world.

Lowdham Book Festival

4th Floor Arts, County Hall, West Bridgford NG2 7QP
✉ ross.bradshaw@nottsscc.gov.uk
www.lowdhambookfestival.co.uk

Contact *Ross Bradshaw*

Founded 1999. Annual week-long festival combining a village fête atmosphere with that of a major literature festival. Guests have included Carol Ann Duffy, Pete McCarthy, Ian McMillan, Alan Sillitoe, Jackie Kay, Sarah Harrison and Carole Blake. Talks on everything from St Kilda to the Jewish roots of rock 'n' roll. Free mailing list includes *County Lit* magazine.

Ludlow Festival

Castle Square, Ludlow SY8 1AY
☎01584 875070 (Admin)/872150 (Box Office) Fax 01584 877673
✉ info@ludlowfestival.co.uk
www.ludlowfestival.co.uk

Contact *Festival Administrator*

Now in its 45th year, the 2004 Festival ran to three weeks with two open-air Shakespeare production held at Ludlow Castle, street events and a varied programme including recitals, opera, dance, popular and classical concerts, literary and historical lectures.

Manchester Festival of Writing

Manchester Central Library, St Peter's Square, Manchester M2 5PD
☎0161 234 1981
✉ libbyt@libraries.manchester.gov.uk

Contact *Libby Tempest*

Founded 1990. An annual event organised by Manchester Libraries and Commonword community publishers. It consists of a short programme of practical writing workshops on specific themes/genres run by well-known writers. Attendance at all workshops is free to Manchester residents.

Manchester Poetry Festival

3rd Floor, 24 Lever Street, Stevenson Square, Manchester M1 1D2
☎0161 236 5725 Fax 0161 236 5719
✉ info@manchesterpoetryfestival.co.uk
www.manchesterpoetryfestival.co.uk

Contact *The Coordinator*

Held in the autumn, Manchester Poetry Festival is the largest urban poetry festival outside of London with nationally recognised poets and local poets and groups.

Mere Literary Festival

Lawrence's, Old Hollow, Mere BA12 6EG
☎01747 860475/861211 (Tourist Information)
www.merewilts.org.uk

Contact *Adrienne Howell*

Founded 1997. Annual festival held in the second week of October in aid of registered charity, The Mere & District Linkscheme. Events include readings, quiz, workshop, writer's lunch and talks. Finale is adjudication of the festival's writing competition (see entry under **Prizes**) and presentation of awards.

Arthur Miller Centre Literary Festival at UEA

University of East Anglia, School of English and American Studies, Norwich NR4 8TJ
☎01603 592810
✉ v.striker@uea.ac.uk
www.uea.ac.uk/eas/events/intro.shtml

Contact *Val Striker*

Founded 1991. Annual festival, held in the autumn

National Association of Writers' Groups (NAWG) Open Festival of Writing

The Arts Centre, Washington NE38 2AB
☎01262 609228
✉ nawg@tesco.net
www.nawg.co.uk

Festival Administrator *Mike Wilson*

Founded 1997. Annual festival held at St Aidan's College, University of Durham in September or October. Three days of creative writing tuition covering poetry, short and long fiction, playwriting, journalism, TV sitcom and many other subjects all led by professional writer-tutors. 36 workshops, 32 one-to-one tutorials and fringe events. Saturday gala dinner and awards ceremony. Full- or part-residential weekend, or single workshops only. Open to all, no qualifications or NAWG membership required.

National Eisteddfod of Wales

40 Parc Ty Glas, Llanishen, Cardiff
CF14 5WU
☎029 2076 3777   Fax 029 2076 3737
www.eisteddfod.org.uk

The National Eisteddfod, held in August, is the largest arts festival in Wales, attracting over 170,000 visitors during the week-long celebration of more than 800 years of tradition. Competitions, bardic ceremonies and concerts.

National Student Drama Festival

See **University of Hull** under *UK Writers' Courses*

New Hall School Festival of Literature

New Hall School, Chelmsford CM3 3HS
✉ library@newhallschool.co.uk
www.newhallschool.co.uk
Contact *Jenny Bignold*

Founded 1992, the week-long festival is open to parents, staff and friends. The aim is to widen students' horizons and, during the week, students from other schools in the town are invited to join in an array of events.

Northern Children's Book Festival

Schools Library Service, Sandhill Centre, Grindon Lane, Sunderland SR3 4EN
☎0191553 8866/7/8   Fax 0191 553 8869
✉ schools.library@sunderland.gov.uk
www.ncbf.org.uk
Secretary *Eleanor Dowley*

Founded 1984. Annual two-week festival during November. Events in schools and libraries for children in the North East region. One Saturday during the festival sees the staging of a large book event hosted by one of the local authorities involved.

Off the Page Literature Festival

County Library Support Services, Glaisdale Parkway, Nottingham NG8 4GP
☎0115 928 6029   Fax 0115 928 6400
✉ alison.hirst@nottscc.gov.uk
Contact *Alison Hirst*

Author visits aimed at making authors accessible to readers. In 2004 the series takes place at Nottingham Central Library in November. Programme is available from late summer/early autumn.

Off the Shelf Literature Festival

Central Library, Surrey Street, Sheffield S1 1XZ
☎0114 273 4716/4400   Fax 0114 273 5009
✉ offtheshelf@sheffield.gov.uk
www.offtheshelf.org.uk
Festival Organisers *Maria de Souza, Susan Walker, Lesley Webster*

Founded 1992. Annual two-week festival held during the last fortnight in October. Lively and diverse mix of readings, workshops, children's events, storytelling and competitions. Previous guests have included Nick Hornby, Doris Lessing, Benjamin Zephaniah, Terry Pratchett, Michael Palin, Carol Ann Duffy and Louis de Bernières.

Oxford Literary Festival

See *The Sunday Times* **Oxford Literary Festival**

Paddington International Poetry Festival

Uprise Arts, PO Box 33082, London W9 3WA
☎010 7286 1880

Contact *Seema Gill*

Founded in 1999 by the writer and painter Richard Heley, the main focus is on performance and slam poetry but the event also covers live painting, art exhibitions, plays and book launches.

Poetry Otherwise

Emerson College, Forest Row RH18 5JX
☎01342 822238   Fax 01342 826055
✉ mail@emerson.org.uk
www.emerson.org.uk
www.poetryotherwise.org
Director *Paul Matthews*

Held in August. A summer gathering of poets, writers and all lovers of language. Workshops, readings, talks, conversation, practice in the art of speaking poetry. Contributors have included Andrea Hollander Budy, John Freeman, Ashley Ramsden, Andie Lewenstein, Paul Matthews, Peter Abbs, Katherine Pierpoint, Fiona Owen, Lee Harwood. 'Wholesome food, wonderful Sussex countryside.'

ProudWords Writing Festival

PO Box 181, Newcastle upon Tyne NE6 5XG
☎07973 8949 12
✉ pwcwf@hotmail.com
www.proudwords.org.uk
Contact *Mary Lowe*

Founded 1998. The only writing festival in the

UK to celebrate the diversity of literary talent that exists within the gay community. Held annually, the festival includes workshops, bus trips, walking tours, readings, discussions and performances of both writing and music. ProudWords encourages participation, lively debate, an interest in literature-related activity and offers opportunities for gay people to express themselves in writing in a supportive, friendly atmosphere. Writers at past festivals include Jackie Kay, Julia Darling, Sarah Waters, Jake Arnott, P-P Hartness, Emma Donaghue, Paul Magrs, Stella Duffy, Julia Bell, Val McDermid, Chrissie Glazebrook and Cathal O Searcaigh. 'Lesbians, gay men and bisexuals are invited to Newcastle to discover for themselves the thriving writing culture that exists here.'

Purple Patch Poetry Convention

25 Griffiths Road, West Bromwich B71 2EH
✉ ppatch66@hotmail.com
www.poetrywednesbury.co.uk
Contact *Geoff Stevens*

Held at the Barlow Theatre near Birmingham this event celebrates the strength of small press poets. It was intended to make it a biennial event but it has been held in 1999, 2001 and 2002. A similar event was organised by Oxford Back Room poets in Oxford in July 2003. In 2004 it was held at the Barlow Theatre in June. Purple Patch Convention is a three-day event of poetry readings, talks, workshops and discussions and admission charges are kept very low, payments to participants being low to non-existent. The Convention's aims are quality and an opportunity to participate. Poets at past festivals have included Ray Avery, R.G. Bishop, Tilla Brading, Gerald England, J.F. Haines, Brendan Hawthorne, Martin Holroyd, Mike Hoy, Eamer O'Keeffe Carolyn King, Paul McDonald, Bob Mee, Les Merton, Michael Newman, Simon Pitt, Andy Robson, Sam Smith and Steve Sneyd.

Royal Court Young Writers Programme

The Site, Royal Court Theatre, Sloane Square, London SW1W 8AS
☎020 7565 5050 Fax 020 7565 5001
✉ ywp@royalcourttheatre.com
www.royalcourttheatre.com

Associate Director *Ola Animashawun*

Open to young people up to the age of 25. The YWP focuses on the process of playwriting by running a series of writers' groups throughout the year at its base in Sloane Square. Additionally the YWP welcomes unsolicited scripts from all young writers from across the country. 'We are always looking for scripts for development and possible production (not film scripts).'

Royal Festival Hall Literature & Talks

Performing Arts Department, Royal Festival Hall, London SE1 8XX
☎020 7921 0906 Fax 020 7928 2049
✉ awhitehead@rfh.org.uk
www.sbc.org.uk

Head of Literature & Talks *Ruth Borthwick*

The Royal Festival Hall presents a year-round literature programme covering all aspects of writing. Regular series range from A Life Indeed! to Fiction International and there are two biennial festivals: Poetry International and Imagine: Writers and Writing for Children. Literature events are now programmed in the Voice Box, Purcell Room and Queen Elizabeth Hall. To join the free mailing list, call ☎020 7921 0971 or ✉ Literature&Talks@rfh.org.uk

Rye Festival

PO Box 33, Rye TN31 7YB
☎01797 224442
✉ info@ryefestival.co.uk
www.ryefestival.co.uk

Festival Director *David Willison*

Founded 1972. Annual two-week September arts event, plus short winter series. Covers music, visual arts, theatre and masterclasses. Write or phone for more information.

Salisbury Festival

Festival Office, 75 New Street, Salisbury SP1 2PH
☎01722 332241 Fax 01722 410552
✉ info@salisburyfestival.co.uk
www.salisburyfestival.co.uk

Director *Trevor Davies*

Founded 1972. Annual festival held at the end of May/beginning of June, including classical music, theatre, jazz and exhibitions.

The Scottish Book Town Festival

Wigtown Book Town Company, County Buildings, Wigtown DG8 9JH
☎01988 402036 Fax 01988 402506
✉ info@wigtown-booktown.co.uk
www.wigtown-booktown.co.uk

Contact *Jennifer Bradley*

Founded 1999. A rural literary festival which takes place annually at the end of September in

Wigtown town centre, many of the town's bookshops and the nearby Bladnoch Distillery. Authors' readings, including children's authors, debates, poetry, music and film.

Southwell Poetry Festival

4th Floor Arts, County Hall, West Bridgford NG2 7QP
✉ ross.bradshaw@nottscc.gov.uk
www.southwellpoetryfestival.co.uk
Contact *Ross Bradshaw*

This festival returned in 2003 after a trial run in 2000 and is now established as an annual event.

Southwold Festival

See **Ways with Words**

StAnza: Scotland's Poetry Festival

Registered Office: 57 Lade Braes, St Andrews KY16 9DA
✉ info@stanzapoetry.org
www.stanzapoetry.org
Festival Director *Brian Johnstone*
   (admin@stanzapoetry.org)

The only regular festival dedicated to poetry in Scotland, StAnza is international in outlook. Held annually in the ancient university town of St Andrews, the festival is an opportunity to hear world class poets reading in exciting and atmospheric venues. The 2005 festival themes are 'Body & Soul' and 'Stateside Poets'. The festival, to be held 17th to 20th March, features, readings, discussions, conversations, performance poetry, poetry in exhibition, workshops and children's poetry. It will feature a strong showing of American poets and leading Scottish and UK poets as well as the festival's signature foreign language readings. Tickets can be purchased from the Byre Theatre box office on 01334 475000 early in 2005. Free programmes can be ordered from Fife Council Arts Development on 01592 414714 or by e-mail to arts.development@fife.gov.uk

Stratford-upon-Avon Poetry Festival

The Shakespeare Centre, Henley Street, Stratford-upon-Avon CV37 6QW
☎01789 204016/292176 (Box office)
Fax 01789 296083
✉ director@shakespeare.org.uk
Festival Director *Roger Pringle*

Founded 1953. Annual festival held on nine Sunday evenings during July and August. Readings by poets and professional actors by invitation.

The Sunday Times Oxford Literary Festival

301 Woodstock Road, Oxford OX2 7NY
☎01865 514149 Fax 01865 514804
✉ oxford.literary.festival@ntlworld.com
www.sundaytimes-oxfordliteraryfestival.co.uk
Directors *Sally Dunsmore, Angela Prysor-Jones*

Founded 1997. Annual six-day festival held two weekends prior to Easter. Authors speaking about their books, covering a wide variety of writing: fiction, poetry, biography, travel, food, gardening, children's art. Previous guests have included William Boyd, Andrew Motion, Candida McWilliam, Beryl Bainbridge, Sophie Grigson, Jamie McKendrick, Bernard O'Donoghue, Philip Pullman and Korky Paul.

Swansea Festivals

Dylan Thomas Centre, Somerset Place, Swansea SA1 1RR
☎01792 463980 Fax 01792 463993
✉ dylan.thomas.lit@swansea.gov.uk
www.dylanthomas.org
www.dylanthomasfestival.com
Contacts *David Woolley, Jo Furber*

Wordplay (6–11 October): tenth annual festival of literature and arts for young people. The Dylan Thomas Celebration (27 October to 9 November) is two weeks of performances, talks, lectures, films, music, poetry, exhibitions and celebrity guests. The Dylan Thomas Centre also runs a year-round programme of literary events; please e-mail for details.

Swindon Festival of Literature

Lower Shaw Farm, Shaw, Swindon SN5 5PJ
☎01793 771080 Fax 01793 771080
✉ swindonlitfest@lowershawfarm.co.uk
www.swindonfestivalofliterature.co.uk
Festival Director *Matt Holland*

Founded 1994. Annual festival held in May, starting with 'Dawn Chorus' at sunrise on May Day. Includes a wide range of authors, speakers, discussions, performances and workshops, plus the Clive Brain Memorial Lecture and the Swindon Performance Poetry Slam competition.

Tears in the Fence Festival

38 Hod View, Stourpaine, Blandford Forum DT11 8TN
☎01258 456803
✉ esp@euphony.net
www.wanderingdog.co.uk
Festival Director *David Caddy*
Festival Manager *Jonathan Ward*

Founded 1995. Annual international poetry festival based in London with readings, talks, discussions and workshops continuing the work begun by the Wessex Poetry Festivals, 1995–2001. Previous guests have included Barry MacSweeney, Jon Silkin, Doug Oliver, Alice Notley, Fred Voss, Joan Jobe Smith, Irina Ratushinskaya, Michele Roberts, Edwin Morgan and Kim Taplin.

The Dylan Thomas Celebration
See **Swansea Festivals**

Tŷ Newydd Festival
Tŷ Newydd, Llanystumdwy, Cricieth LL52 0LW
☎01766 522811 Fax 01766 523095
✉ post@tynewydd.org
www.tynewydd.org
Director *Sally Baker*

Biennial, bilingual literature festival held on alternate years with the Academi's **Bay Lit Festival**. Held in April and run by the National Writers' Centre for Wales, it is located at Tŷ Newydd Writers' Centre and other venues near Cricieth. Features writers and poets from Wales (working in both English and Welsh) and world-wide. Tŷ Newydd also holds an annual weekend festival in November devoted solely to Cynghanedd – Welsh strict meter poetry.

Warwick Festival
Warwick Arts Society, Pageant House, 2 Jury Street, Warwick CV34 4EW
☎01926 410747 Fax 01926 409050
✉ admin@warwickarts.org.uk
www.warwickarts.org.uk
Festival Director *Richard Phillips*

Founded 1980, this annual festival has had four names but since 2003 events have only taken place in Warwick town, using Warwick Castle and other historic buildings, plus new theatres The Dream Factory and Bridge House Theatre on the outskirts. Primarily a music festival but embraces drama, opera, dance, puppets, art exhibitions, poetry readings and other literary events. Extensive eduational programme including workshops.

Warwick Words
Warwick Events Group, Northgate, Warwick CV34 4JL
☎01926 497000 Fax 01926 407606
✉ admin@warwickarts.org.uk
www.WarwickLive.com

Founded 2002. Annual venture featuring both living writers and those who have had connections with Warwick – Tolkien, Larkin and Landor in particular. Also workshops and an education programme. A weekend festival of literature and spoken word for all the family. Events at The Dream Factory, Bridge House Theatre, St Mary's Church, the Lord Leycester Hospital and other historic buildings around Warwick over the first weekend in October.

Ways with Words
Droridge Farm, Dartington, Totnes TQ9 6JQ
☎01803 867373 Fax 01803 863688
✉ admin@wayswithwords.co.uk
www.wayswithwords.co.uk
Festival Director *Kay Dunbar*

Ways with Words runs a major literature festival at Dartington Hall in south Devon for ten days in July each year. Features over 200 writers giving lectures, readings, interviews, discussions, performances, masterclasses and workshops. Also, Words by the Water, a Cumbrian literature festival held in Keswick (2005: 1–6 March). There is a regular festival held in Southwold, Suffolk (2004: 11–15 November). Organises writing, reading and painting courses in Italy.

Wellington Literary Festival
Civic Offices, Larkin Way, Tan Bank, Wellington, Telford TF1 1LX
☎01952 222935 Fax 01952 222936
✉ WellTownCl@aol.com
www.wellington-shropshire.gov.uk
Contact *Derrick Drew*

Founded 1997. Annual festival held throughout October. Events include storytelling, writers' forum, 'Pints and Poetry', children's poetry competition, story competition, theatre review and guest speakers.

Wells Festival of Literature
25 Chamberlain Street, Wells BA5 2PQ
☎01749 670929
www.somersite.co.uk/wellsfest.htm

Founded 1992. Annual weekend-plus festival held at the end of October. Main venue is the historic, moated Bishop's Palace. A wide range of speakers caters for different tastes in reading. Recent guests include: Shirley Vickers, Beryl Bainbridge, Libby Purves, Margaret Drabble, Mary Warnock, William Dalrymple, Timothy West. Short story and poetry competitions and writing workshops are run in conjunction with the Festival.

Wessex Poetry Festival
See **Tears in the Fence Festival**

westwords festival
c/o London Borough of Hammersmith &
Fulham, Arts Team, Munster Centre, Filmer
Road, London SW6 6AS
☎020 7736 0864   Fax 020 7736 0103
Contact *Festival Organiser*
A month-long festival of the written and spoken
word for North West London held throughout
March. Combines the Harrow 'Words Live'
Literature Festival and the Hammersmith and
Fulham Wordwide Festival. Takes place in the
boroughs of Hammersmith and Fulham, Ealing,
Brent, Hillingdon and Harrow. Offers a range of
high-profile readings with workshops, discus-
sions and other activities for all ages with a particular emphasis on celebrating the literature of cultural communities.

Wonderful Words Book Festival
c/o Bude Library, The Wharf, Bude
EX23 8LQ
☎01288 359242
www.cornwall.gov.uk
Festival Organiser *Rebecca Rowland*
Founded 1994. Biennial two-month festival
hosted throughout Cornwall. The next and
seventh Festival will be hosted in 2006. The
festival, organised by the library service, has
grown into a prestigious two-month event for
children and adults. Offers author talks, writers'
workshops, poetry performances, theatre and
storytelling. Guest authors have included Doris
Lessing, Ruth Rendell, Margaret Drabble and
Dick King-Smith.

Wordfest: A Festival of Words in Basingstoke and Deane
Basingstoke & Deane Borough Council, Civic
Offices, London Road, Basingstoke
RG21 4AH
☎01256 845686
✉ c.gibson@basingstoke.gov.uk
www.basingstoke.gov.uk/wordfest
Contact *Ceri Gibson*
Founded 1999. Annual celebration of words
held over ten days in October. A range of events
and activities including author appearances, participatory workshops, theatre and community
projects, which take place throughout the
borough at a variety of venues.

Wordplay
See **Swansea Festivals**

Words by the Water
See **Ways with Words**

'Words Live' Literature Festival
See *westwords* festival

Wordsworth Trust
The Wordsworth Trust, Dove Cottage,
Grassmere LA22 9SH
☎015394 35544   Fax 015394 35748
✉ enquiries@wordsworth.org.uk
www.wordsworth.org.uk

Annual weekend festival at the end of January.
The programme is a mixture of lectures,
surgeries and workshops on subjects touching
on Romanticism in all its forms. Although the
speakers are experts in their fields, the aim is to
reach out to a general public. Guests have
included Charles Saumerez Smith, Patrick
Leigh Fermor, Fiona MacCarthy, Paul
Johnson, Lucasta Miller and Nicolas Barker.
Part of the programme also comprises talks by
writers in residence at The Wordsworth Trust,
including Owen Sheers, Conrad Atkinson and
Chris Bucklow.

Wordwide Festival
See *westwords* festival

European Publishers

Austria

Springer-Verlag KG
PO Box 89, A–1200 Vienna
☎00 43 1 3302415 Fax 00 43 1 3302426
www.springer.at
Founded 1924. Publishes academic, anthropology, architecture, art, business, chemistry, computer science, communications, electronics, economics, education, environmental studies, engineering, law, mathematics, dentistry, medicine, nursing, philosophy, physics, psychology, technology and general science.

Verlag Carl Ueberreuter GmbH
Postfach 306, A–1091 Vienna
☎00 43 1 404440 Fax 00 43 1 404445
www.ueberreuter.de
Founded 1548. Publishes fiction and general non-fiction; art, biography, government, history, economics, political science, general science, health and nutrition, science fiction, fantasy, music and dance.

Paul Zsolnay Verlag GmbH
Prinz-Eugen-Strasse 30, A–1040 Vienna
☎00 43 1 50576610 Fax 00 43 1 505766110
www.zsolnay.at
Founded 1923. Publishes biography, fiction, general non-fiction, history, poetry.

Belgium

Brepols Publishers NV
Begijnhof 67, 2300 Turnhout
☎00 32 14 448020 Fax 00 32 14 428919
www.brepols.net
Founded 1796. Publishes academic – architecture, archaeology, art, interior design, Asian studies, history, language studies, linguistics, literature, literary criticism, essays, philosophy, religion.

Facet NV
Willem Linnigstr 13, 2060 Antwerp
☎00 32 3 2274028 Fax 00 32 3 2273792
Founded 1986. Publishes children's books.

Uitgeverij Lannoo NV
Kasteelstr 97, B–8700 Tielt
☎00 32 51 424211 Fax 00 32 51 401152
www.lannoo.be
Founded 1909. Publishes general non-fiction, art, architecture and interior design, cookery, biography, economics, gardening, health and nutrition, history, management, photography, self-help, poetry, government, political science, religion, travel.

Standaard Uitgeverij
Belgiëlei 147a, 2018 Antwerp
☎00 32 3 2857200 Fax 00 32 3 2857299
www.standard.com
Founded 1919. Publishes education, fiction, poetry, humour, children's and young adult.

Denmark

Forlaget Apostrof ApS
Postboks 2580, DK–2100 Copenhagen O
☎00 45 39 208420 Fax 00 45 39 208453
www.apostrof.dk
Founded 1980. Publishes psychology and psychiatry.

Aschehoug Dansk Forlag A/S
Landemærket 8, 1119 Kbh. K. Postbox 2179,
DK–1017 Copenhagen K
☎00 45 33 305522 Fax 00 45 33 305822
www.aschehoug.dk
Founded 1977. Merged with Egmont Lademann A/S in 2003. Publishes fiction, biography, cookery, children's, art, adventure and reference.

Blackwell Munksgaard
PO Box 227, DK–1502 Copenhagen V
☎00 45 77 333333 Fax 00 45 77 333377
www.blackwellmunksgaard.com
Founded 1917. Publishes academic books and journals for higher education, research and professional markets.

Borgens Forlag A/S
Valbygardsvej 33, DK–2500 Valby
☎00 45 36 153615 Fax 00 45 36 153616
www.borgens.dk

Founded 1948. Publishes fiction, literature, literary criticism, general non-fiction, art, astrology, child care, crafts, education, environmental studies, essays, games, hobbies, health and nutrition, how-to, humour, music, dance, occult, philosophy, poetry, psychology, psychiatry, self-help, religion.

Egmont Lademann A/S
See **Aschehoug Dansk Forlag A/S**.

Forum Publishers
PO Box 2252, DK–1019 Copenhagen K
☎00 45 33 411830 Fax 00 45 33 411831
www.gyldendal.dk
Founded 1940. Part of **Gyldendalske Boghandel–Nordisk Forlag A/S**. Publishes fiction, history, humour, mysteries, children's and young adults.

Gyldendalske Boghandel–Nordisk Forlag A/S
PO Box 11, DK–1001 Copenhagen K
☎00 45 33 755555 Fax 00 45 33 755556
www.gyldendal.dk
Founded 1770. Publishes fiction, art, biography, dance, dentistry, education, history, how-to, medicine, music, poetry, nursing, philosophy, psychology, psychiatry, reference, general and social sciences, sociology, textbooks.

Hekla Forlag
Valbygaardsvej 33, DK–2500 Valby
☎00 45 36 153615 Fax 00 45 36 153616
www.borgens.dk
Founded 1979. Part of **Borgens Verlag A/S**. Publishes general fiction and non-fiction.

Høst & Søn Publishers Ltd
PO Box 2212, DK–1018 Copenhagen K
☎00 45 33 382888 Fax 00 45 33 382898
Founded 1836. Publishes fiction, crafts, environmental studies, games, hobbies, history, children's.

Lindhardt og Ringhof
Frederiksborggade 1, DK–1360 Copenhagen K
☎00 45 33 695000 Fax 00 45 33 695001
www.lrforlag.dk
Founded 1971. Publishes fiction and general non-fiction.

Nyt Nordisk Forlag Arnold Busck A/S
Købmagergade 49, DK–1150 Copenhagen K

☎00 45 33 733575 Fax 00 45 33 733576
www.nytnordiskforlag.dk
Founded 1896. Publishes fiction, art, biography, dance, dentistry, dictionaries, history, how-to, music, philosophy, religion, medicine, nursing, psychology, psychiatry, reference, general and social sciences, sociology, textbooks.

Samlerens Forlag A/S
Postboks 22, DK–1019 Copenhagen K
☎00 45 33 411800 Fax 00 45 33 411801
www.samleren.dk
Founded 1943. Publishes essays, fiction, government, history, literature, literary criticism, political science.

Det Schønbergske Forlag
Landemaerket 5, DK–1119 Copenhagen K
☎00 45 33 733585 Fax 00 45 33 733586
www.nytnordiskforlag.dk
Founded 1857. Part of **Nyt Nordisk Forlag Arnold Busck A/S**. Publishes art, biography, careers, directories, fiction, history, humour, philosophy, poetry, psychology, psychiatry, reference, textbooks, travel

Spektrum Forlagsaktieselskab
PO Box 2252, DK–1019 Copenhagen K
☎00 45 33 147714 Fax 00 45 33 147791
Founded 1990. Publishes general non-fiction.

Tiderne Skifter Forlag A/S
Købmagergade 62, DK–1019 Copenhagen K
☎00 45 33 411820 Fax 00 45 33 411821
www.tiderneskifter.dk
Founded 1973. Publishes fiction, literature and literary criticism, essays, ethnicity, photography, behavioural sciences.

Finland
Gummerus Publishers
PO Box 749, SF–00101 Helsinki
☎00 358 9 584301 Fax 00 358 9 58430200
www.gummerus.fi
Founded 1872. Publishes fiction and general non-fiction, dictionaries and reference.

Karisto Oy
Paroistentie 2, SF–13600 Hämeenlinna
☎00 358 3 6161551 Fax 00 358 3 6161555
www.karisto.fi
Founded 1900. Publishes fiction and general non-fiction.

Kirjayhtymä Oy
Urho Kekkosen Katu 4–6E,
SF–00100 Helsinki
☎00 358 9 6937641   Fax 00 358 9 69376366
Founded 1958. Publishes fiction and general non-fiction, textbooks.

Kustannusosakeyhtiö Tammi
PO Box 410, SF–00101 Helsinki
☎00 358 9 6937621   Fax 00 358 9 69376266
www.tammi.net
Founded 1943. Publishes fiction, general non-fiction. Part of the Bonnier Group.

Otava Publishing Co. Ltd
PO Box 134, SF–00121 Helsinki
☎00 358 9 19961   Fax 00 358 9 643136
www.otava.fi
Founded 1890. Publishes fiction, general non-fiction, art, architecture and interior design, history, how-to.

Werner Söderström Osakeyhtiö (WSOY)
PO Box 222, SF–00121 Helsinki
☎00 358 9 61681   Fax 00 358 9 6168467
Founded 1878. Publishes fiction, general non-fiction, education, dictionaries, encyclopedias, textbooks.

France

Editions Arthaud SA
26 rue Racine, F–75006 Paris
☎00 33 1 4051 3008   Fax 00 33 1 4325 0118
Founded 1890. Imprint of **Flammarion SA**.

Editions Belfond
12 avenue d'Italie, F–75013 Paris
☎00 33 1 4544 3823   Fax 00 33 1 4544 9804
www.belfond.fr
Founded 1963. Publishes fiction, literature, literary criticism, essays, mysteries, romance, poetry, general non-fiction, art, biography, dance, health, history, how-to, music, nutrition.

Editions Bordas
89 blvd Auguste Blanqui, F–75013 Paris
☎00 33 1 4439 5445   Fax 00 33 1 4439 4350
www.editions-bordas.com
Founded 1946. Publishes education and general non-fiction: dictionaries, directories, encyclopedias, reference.

Editions Calmann-Lévy-Stock SA
3 rue Auber, F–75009 Paris
☎00 33 1 4742 3833   Fax 00 33 1 4742 7781
Founded 1836. Publishes fiction, science fiction, fantasy, biography, history, humour, economics, philosophy, psychology, psychiatry, social sciences, sociology, sport.

Editions Denoël Sàrl
9 rue du Cherche-Midi, F–75006 Paris
☎00 33 1 4439 7373   Fax 00 33 1 4439 7390
Founded 1932. Part of **Editions Gallimard**. Publishes fiction, science fiction, fantasy, art, directories, economics, government, history, philosophy, political science, psychology, psychiatry, reference.

Editions Larousse
21 rue de Montparnasse, F–75283 Paris Cedex 06
☎00 33 1 4439 4400   Fax 00 33 1 4439 4343
Founded 1852. Publishes animals, children's, childcare, cookery, dictionaries, directories, encyclopedias, gardening, history, medicine, nursing, dentistry, music, dance, self-help, psychology, psychiatry, reference, general science, social sciences, sociology, language arts, linguistics, technology.

Librairie Arthème Fayard
75 rue des Saints-Pères, F–75006 Paris Cedex 06
☎00 33 1 4549 8200   Fax 00 33 1 4222 4017
Founded 1854. Publishes fiction, biography, directories, history, dance, music, philosophy, religion, reference, social sciences, sociology, general science, technology.

Flammarion SA
26 rue Racine, F–75006 Paris
☎00 33 1 4051 3008   Fax 00 33 1 4325 0118
www.flammarion.com
Founded 1875. Publishes general fiction and non-fiction, art, architecture, children's, gardening, plants, interior design, literature, literary criticism, essays, medicine, nursing, dentistry, wine and spirits.

Editions Gallimard
5 rue Sébastien-Bottin, F–75341 Paris Cedex 07
☎00 33 1 4954 4200   Fax 00 33 1 4544 9403
www.gallimard.fr
Founded 1911. Publishes fiction, poetry, art, biography, dance, history, music, philosophy.

Editions Grasset & Fasquelle
61 rue des Saints-Pères, F–75006 Paris

☎00 33 1 4439 2200   Fax 00 33 1 4222 6418
www.edition-grasset.fr

Founded 1907. Publishes fiction and general non-fiction, essays, literature, literary criticism, philosophy.

Hachette-Livre

43 quai de Grenelle, F–75905 Paris Cedex 15
☎00 33 1 4392 3000   Fax 00 33 1 4392 3030

Founded 1826. Publishes fiction and general non-fiction, architecture and interior design, art, directories, economics, education, general engineering, government, history, language and linguistics, political science, philosophy, reference, general science, self-help, social sciences, sociology, sport, textbooks, travel.

Editions Robert Laffont, Nil, Fixot, Seghers, Julliard

24 ave Marceau, F–75381 Paris Cedex 08
☎00 33 1 5367 1400   Fax 00 33 1 5367 1414
www.laffont.fr

Founded 1941. Publishes fiction and non-fiction; literature, literary criticism, essays, science fiction and fantasy, poetry, dictionaries, encyclopedias, philosophy, self-help, psychology, psychiatry, general science, social sciences, sociology.

Editions Jean-Claude Lattès

17 rue Jacob, F–75006 Paris
☎00 33 1 4441 7400   Fax 00 33 1 4325 3047

Founded 1968. Part of **Hachette-Livre**. Publishes fiction, criminology, general non-fiction.

Magnard SA

20 rue Berbier-du-Mets, F–75647 Paris Cedex 13
☎00 33 1 4408 8585   Fax 00 33 1 4408 4979

Founded 1933. Publishes education.

Michelin et Cie (Services de Tourisme)

46 ave de Breteuil, F–75324 Paris
☎00 33 1 4566 1234   Fax 00 33 1 4566 1163

Founded 1900. Publishes travel.

Les Editions de Minuit SA

7 rue Bernard-Palissy, F–75006 Paris
☎00 33 1 4439 3920   Fax 00 33 1 4539 3923
www.leseditionsdeminuit.fr

Founded 1942. Publishes fiction, essays, literature, literary criticism, philosophy, social sciences, sociology.

Editions Fernand Nathan

9 rue Méchain, F–75014 Paris
☎00 33 1 4587 5000   Fax 00 33 1 4537 5300
www.nathan.fr

Founded 1881. Publishes dictionaries, directories, education, encyclopedias, history, philosophy, psychology, psychiatry, reference, general and social sciences, sociology.

Presses de la Cité

12 ave d'Italie, F–75627 Paris Cedex 13
☎00 33 1 4416 0500   Fax 00 33 1 4416 0505
www.pressesdelacite.com

Founded 1947. Imprint of **Editions Belfond**. Publishes fiction and general non-fiction, science fiction, fantasy, history, mysteries, humour, romance, biography.

Presses Universitaires de France (PUF)

6 ave Reille, F–75685 Paris Cedex 14
☎00 33 1 5810 3100   Fax 00 33 1 5810 3182
www.puf.com

Founded 1921. Publishes art, biography, dance, dentistry, dictionaries, directories, encyclopedias, government, general engineering, geography, geology, history, law, medicine, music, nursing, philosophy, psychology, psychiatry, religion, political science, reference, social science, sociology, textbooks.

Editions du Seuil

27 rue Jacob, F–75006 Paris
☎00 33 1 4046 5050   Fax 00 33 1 4046 4300
www.seuil.com

Founded 1935. Publishes fiction, literature, literary criticism, essays, poetry, art, biography, dance, government, political science, history, how-to, music, photography, philosophy, psychology, psychiatry, religion, general and social sciences, sociology.

Les Editions de la Table Ronde

7 rue Corneille, F–75006 Paris
☎00 33 1 4046 7070   Fax 00 33 1 4046 7101

Founded 1944. Publishes fiction and general non-fiction, biography, history, psychology, psychiatry, religion.

Librairie Vuibert

20 rue Babier-du-Mets, F–75647 Paris Cedex 13
☎00 33 1 4408 4900   Fax 00 33 1 4408 4939
www.vuibert.com

Founded 1877. Publishes biological and earth

sciences, chemistry, chemical engineering, children's, economics, law, mathematics, physics, textbooks.

Germany

Verlag C.H. Beck (OHG)
Postfach 400340, 80703 Munich
☎00 49 89 381890 Fax 00 49 89 38189402
www.beck.de
Founded 1763. Publishes general non-fiction, anthropology, archaeology, art, dance, dictionaries, directories, economics, essays, encyclopedias, history, language arts, law, linguistics, literature, literary criticism, music, philosophy, reference, social sciences, sociology, theology.

Bertelsmann
Verlagsgruppe Random House, Neumarkter Strasse 28, 81673 Munich
☎00 49 89 4372-0 Fax 00 49 89 4372-2812
www.randomhouse.de
Founded 1835. Part of the **Random House Group**. Publishes fiction and general non-fiction, art, biography, government and political science.

Carlsen Verlag GmbH
Postfach 500380, 22703 Hamburg
☎00 49 40 398040 Fax 00 49 40 39804390
www.carlsen.de
Founded 1953. Publishes fiction, humour, children's and picture books.

Deutscher Taschenbuch Verlag GmbH & Co. KG (dtv)
Postfach 400422, 80704 Munich
☎00 49 89 38167-0 Fax 00 49 89 346428
www.dtv.de
Founded 1961. Publishes fiction and general non-fiction; art, astronomy, biography, child care and development, children's, cookery, computer science, dance, dictionaries, directories, education, government, history, how-to, music, poetry, psychiatry, psychology, philosophy, political science, reference, religion, medicine, dentistry, nursing, social sciences, literature, literary criticism, essays, humour, textbook, travel.

Econ-Verlag GmbH
Paul-Heyse-Strasse 28, 80336 Munich
☎00 49 89 5148-0 Fax 00 49 89 5148-2229
www.econ-verlag.de

Founded 1950. Publishes general non-fiction and fiction, directories, economics, reference and general science.

S Fischer Verlag GmbH
Postfach 700355, 60553 Frankfurt am Main
☎00 49 69 60620 Fax 00 49 69 6062352
www.s-fischer.de
Founded 1886. Part of the **Holtzbrinck Group**. Publishes fiction, general non-fiction, directories, essays, literature, literary criticism, reference.

Carl Hanser Verlag
Kolbergerstrasse 22, 81679 Munich
☎00 49 89 998300 Fax 00 49 89 984809
✉ info@hanser.de
www.hanser.de
Founded in 1928 in Munich. Publishes international and German contemporary literature; classics, anthropology, non-fiction on social sciences and the arts; children's and juveniles; specialist books on engineering, natural science, plastics, computers and computer science, economics and management, dentistry.

Wilhelm Heyne Verlag
Paul-Heyse-Strasse 28, 80336 Munich
☎00 49 89 5148-0 Fax 00 49 89 5148-2229
www.heyne.de
Founded 1934. Publishes fiction, mystery, romance, humour, science fiction, fantasy, astrology, biography, cookery, film, history, how-to, occult, psychology, psychiatry, video.

Hoffmann und Campe Verlag GmbH
Postfach 130444, 20139 Hamburg
☎00 49 40 441880 Fax 00 49 40 44188-202
www.hoffmann-und-campe.de
Founded 1781. Publishes fiction and general non-fiction; art, biography, dance, history, music, poetry, philosophy, psychology, psychiatry, general science, social sciences, sociology.

Verlagsgruppe Georg von Holtzbrinck GmbH
Gänsheidestrasse 26, 70184 Stuttgart
☎00 49 711 21500 Fax 00 49 711 215269
✉ info@holtzbrinck.com
www.holtzbrinck.com
Founded 1948. One of the world's largest publishing groups with 12 book publishing houses and 40 imprints. Also publishes the newspapers, *Handelsblatt* and *Die Zeit*.

Hüthig GmbH & Co. KG
Postfach 102869, 69121 Heidelberg
☎00 49 6221 489-0 Fax 00 49 6221 489-279
www.huethig.de
Founded 1925. Germany's fourth largest professional publisher.

Ernst Klett Verlag GmbH
Postfach 106016, 70049 Stuttgart
☎00 49 711 6672-0
 Fax 00 49 711 6672-2000
www.klett.de
Founded 1897. Publishes education, geography, geology; textbooks.

Langenscheidt KG
Postfach 401120, 80711 Munich 40
☎00 49 89 36096-0 Fax 00 49 89 36096-222
www.langenscheidt.de
Founded 1856. Publishes dictionaries, encyclopedias, reference, maps, travel guides, how-to, language.

Gustav Lübbe Verlag GmbH
Postfach 200180, 51431 Bergisch Gladbach
☎00 49 2202 121330
Fax 00 49 2202 121920
www.lubbe.de
Founded 1963. Publishes fiction and general non-fiction, archaeology, biography, history, how-to.

Propylän Verlag, Zweigniederlassung Berlin der Ullstein Buchverlage GmbH
Charlottenstrasse 13, 10969 Berlin
☎00 49 30 25913500
Fax 00 49 30 25913533
Founded 1903. Publishes fiction and general non-fiction, romance, mysteries, architecture and interior design, art, biography, dance, dictionaries, encyclopedias, film, video, education, essays, ethnology, geography, geology, government, health, history, how-to, humour, literature, literary criticism, maritime, military science, music, nutrition, poetry, political science, general science, social sciences, sociology, travel.

Rowohlt Verlag GmbH
Hamburgerstr 17, 21465 Reinbeck
☎00 49 30 72720 Fax 00 49 40 7272319
www.rowohlt.de
Founded 1908. Publishes general non-fiction.

Springer-Verlag GmbH & Co KG
Postfach 105280, 69042 Heidelberg
☎00 49 6221 4870 Fax 00 49 6221 487-8366
www.springer.de
Founded 1842. Publishes agriculture, architecture and interior design, art, astronomy, behavioural sciences, business, biological sciences, chemical engineering, civil engineering, computer science, criminology, dentistry, dictionaries, directories, economics, encyclopedias, finance, geography, geology, government, health, nutrition, history, library and information sciences, management, marketing, mechanical engineering, electronics, electrical engineering, general engineering, earth sciences, environmental studies, law, mathematics, medicine, nursing, political science, philosophy, psychology, psychiatry, physics, reference, general science, social sciences, sociology, technology, textbooks.

Suhrkamp Verlag
Postfach 101945, 60019 Frankfurt am Main
☎00 49 69 756010 Fax 00 49 69 75601314
www.suhrkamp.de
Founded 1950. Publishes fiction, poetry, biography, philosophy, psychology, psychiatry, general science.

Taschen GmbH
Hohenzollernring 53, 50672 Cologne
☎00 49 221 201800 Fax 00 49 221 254919
✉ contact@taschen.com
www.taschen.com
Founded 1980. Publishes photography, art, erotica, architecture and interior design.

K. Thienemanns Verlag
Blumenstr 36, 70182 Stuttgart
☎00 49 711 210550 Fax 00 49 711 2105539
www.thienemanns.de
Founded 1849. Publishes fiction and general non-fiction.

WEKA Firmengruppe GmbH & Co KG
Postfach 1209, 86425 Kissing
☎00 49 8233 230 Fax 00 49 8233 237500
Founded 1973. Germany's largest professional publisher.

Italy

Adelphi Edizioni SpA
Via S. Giovanni sul Muro 14, 20121 Milan
☎00 39 2 725731 Fax 00 39 2 89010337

www.adelphi.it
Founded 1962. Publishes fiction, literature, literary criticism, essays, mysteries, poetry, anthropology, biography, history, mathematics, philosophy, physics, psychology, religion, general science.

Bompiani–RCS Libri

Via Mecenate 91, 20138 Milan
☎00 39 2 50951 Fax 00 39 2 5065361
www.rcslibri.it
Founded 1929. Publishes fiction, general nonfiction, art, drama, theatre and general science.

Bulzoni Editore SRL (Le Edizioni Universitarie d'Italia)

Via Dei Liburni 14, 00185 Rome
☎00 39 6 4455207 Fax 00 39 6 4450355
www.bulzoni.it
Founded 1969. Publishes fiction, literature, literary criticism, essays, art, drama, general engineering, film, law, language, linguistics, philosophy, general science, social sciences, sociology, theatre, video.

Cappelli Editore

Via Farini 14, 40124 Bologna
☎00 39 51 239060 Fax 00 39 51 239286
www.cappellieditore.com
Founded 1851. Publishes fiction, art, biography, drama, film, government, history, music, dance, poetry, medicine, nursing, dentistry, philosophy, political science, psychology, psychiatry, religion, general science, social sciences, sociology, theatre, video.

Garzanti Editore

Via Gasparotto 1, 20124 Milan
☎00 39 2 674171 Fax 00 39 2 67417229
Founded 1861. Publishes fiction, literature, literary criticism, essays, art, biography, dictionaries, directories, encyclopedias, history, poetry, government, political science, reference, textbooks.

Giunti Gruppo Editoriale

Via Bolognese 165, 50139 Florence
☎00 39 55 5062376 Fax 00 39 55 5062397
www.giunti.it
Founded 1840. Publishes fiction, literature, literary criticism, essays, art, chemistry, chemical engineering, dictionaries, directories, education, encyclopedias, history, how-to, language arts, linguistics, mathematics, psychology, psychiatry, reference, general science. Italian publishers of National Geographical Society books.

Ernesto Gremese Editore SRL

Via Virginia Agnelli 88, 00151 Rome
☎00 39 6 657 40507 Fax 00 39 6 657 40509
www.gremese.com
Founded 1954. Publishes fiction, art, erotica, astrology, cookery, crafts, dance, drama, film, video, fashion, games, hobbies, essays, literature, literary criticism, dictionaries, directories, encyclopedias, health and nutrition, house and home, how-to, music, occult, reference, sport, travel, theatre, television, radio, wine and spirits.

Longanesi & C

Corso Italia 13, 20122 Milan
☎00 39 2 80206310 Fax 00 39 2 72000306
www.longanesi.it
Founded 1946. Publishes fiction, art, biography, dance, history, how-to, medicine, nursing, dentistry, music, philosophy, psychology, psychiatry, religion, general and social sciences, sociology.

Arnoldo Mondadori Editore SpA

Via Mondadori, 20090 Segrate (Milan)
☎00 39 2 75421 Fax 00 39 2 75422302
www.mondadori.com
Founded 1907. Publishes fiction, mystery, romance, art, biography, dance, dentistry, directories, history, how-to, medicine, music, poetry, philosophy, psychology, psychiatry, reference, religion, nursing, general science, education, textbooks.

Società Editrice Il Mulino

Str Maggiore 37, 40125 Bologna
☎00 39 51 256011 Fax 00 39 51 256034
www.mulino.it
Founded 1954. Publishes economics, government, history, law, language arts, linguistics, philosophy, political science, psychology, psychiatry, social sciences, sociology, textbooks.

Gruppo Ugo Mursia Editore SpA

Via Melchiorre Gioia 45, 20124 Milan
☎00 39 2 6737 8500 Fax 00 39 2 6737 8605
www.mursia.com
Founded 1922. Publishes fiction, poetry, art, biography, directories, education, history, maritime, philosophy, reference, religion, sport, general science, social sciences, sociology, textbooks.

RCS Rizzoli Libri SpA

Via Mecenate 91, 20138 Milan
☎00 39 2 50951 Fax 00 39 2 5065361
Founded 1945. Publishes art, crafts, dance,

business, dictionaries, directories, encyclopedias, games, hobbies, history, music, medicine, nursing, dentistry, general science, textbooks.

Società Editrice Internazionale – SEI

Corso Regina Margherita 176, 10152 Turin
☎00 39 11 52271 Fax 00 39 11 5211320
Founded 1908. Publishes literature, literary criticism, essays, children's, dictionaries, encyclopedias, education, geography, geology, history, mathematics, philosophy, physics, religion, psychology, psychiatry, textbooks.

Sonzogno

Via Mecenate 91, 20138 Milan
☎00 39 2 50951 Fax 00 39 2 5065361
www.rcslibri.it
Founded 1818. Publishes fiction, mysteries, and general non-fiction.

Sperling e Kupfer Editori SpA

Via Durazzo 4, 20134 Milan
☎00 39 2 217211 Fax 00 39 2 21721277
www.sperling.it
Founded 1899. Publishes fiction and general non-fiction, biography, economics, health, how-to, management, nutrition, general science, sport, travel.

Sugarco Edizioni SRL

Via Gnocchi 4, 21048 Milan
☎00 39 2 407 8370 Fax 00 39 2 407 8493
Founded 1956. Publishes fiction, biography, history, how-to, philosophy.

Todariana Editrice

Via Gardone 29, 20139 Milan
☎00 39 2 56812953 Fax 00 39 2 55213405
Founded 1967. Publishes fiction, poetry, science fiction, fantasy, literature, literary criticism, essays, language arts, linguistics, psychology, psychiatry, social sciences, sociology, travel.

The Netherlands

A.W. Bruna Uitgevers BV

Postbus 40203, 3504 AA Utrecht
☎00 31 30 247 0411 Fax 00 31 30 241 0018
www.awbruna.nl
Founded 1868. Publishes fiction and general non-fiction; mysteries, computer science, history, philosophy, psychology, psychiatry, general science, social sciences, sociology.

BZZTÔH Publishers

Laan van Meerdervoort 10, 2517 AJ The Hague
☎00 31 70 363 2934 Fax 00 31 70 363 1932
www.bzztoh.nl
Founded 1970. Publishes fiction, mysteries, romance, literature, literary criticism, essays, general non-fiction, animals, astrology, biography, cookery, dance, humour, music, philosophy, self-help, health and nutrition, occult, pets, religion (Buddhist, Hindhu, Jewish), sport, travel, women's studies.

Elsevier Science BV

Sara Burgehartst. 25, 1055 KV Amsterdam
☎00 31 20 586 2911 Fax 00 31 20 485 2457
www.elsevier.nl
Founded 1946. Parent company Reed Elsevier. Publishes sciences (all fields), medicine, nursing, dentistry, economics, engineering (chemical and general), mathematics, physics, technology.

Kluwer Academic Publishers

Postbus 17, 3300 AA Dordrecht
☎00 31 78 657 6000 Fax 00 31 78 657 6254
Founded 1889. Publishes education, CD-ROMs and journals, law, behavioural science, medicine, nursing, dentistry, social sciences, sociology, technology.

Uitgeversmaatschappij J. H. Kok BV

PO Box 5019, 8260 GA Kampen
☎00 31 38 339 2555 Fax 00 31 38 331 1776
Founded 1894. Publishes fiction, poetry, history, religion, directories, reference, general science, social sciences, sociology, textbooks.

J.M. Meulenhoff & Co BV

Postbus 100, 1000 AC Amsterdam
☎00 31 20 553 3500 Fax 00 31 20 625 8511
www.meulenhoff.nl
Founded 1895. Publishes international co-productions, fiction and general non-fiction. Specialises in Dutch and translated literature.

Pearson Education Netherlands

Concertgebouwplein 25, 1071 LM Amsterdam
☎00 31 20 575 5800 Fax 00 31 20 664 5334
www.pearsoneducation.nl
Founded 1942. Publishes education, business, computer science, directories, economics, management, reference, textbooks, technology.

Uitgeverij Het Spectrum BV

Postbus 2073, 3500 GB Utrecht
☎00 31 30 265 0650 Fax 00 31 30 262 0850
www.spectrum.nl

Founded 1935. Publishes science fiction, fantasy, literature, literary criticism, essays, mysteries, criminology, general non-fiction, computer science, dictionaries, encyclopedias, history, astrology, occult, management, environmental studies, travel.

Unieboek BV

Postbus 97, 3990 DB Houten
☎00 31 30 637 7660 Fax 00 31 30 637 7600
www.unieboek.nl

Founded 1891. Publishes fiction, mysteries, romance, general non-fiction, children's, directories, reference, animals, architecture and interior design, childcare, crafts, hobbies, games, how-to, literature, literary criticism, essays, cookery, history, self-help, photography, travel.

Uniepers BV

Postbus 69, 1390 AB Abcoude
☎00 31 29 428 5111 Fax 00 31 29 428 3013
www.uniepers.nl

Founded 1961. Publishes (mostly in co-editions) antiques, anthropology, archaeology, architecture and interior design, art, dance, history, music, natural history, photography.

Norway

H. Aschehoug & Co (W. Nygaard) A/S

Postboks 363, Sentrum, 0102 Oslo
☎00 47 22 400400 Fax 00 47 22 206395
www.aschehoug.no

Founded 1872. Publishes fiction and general non-fiction, antiques, architecture and interior design, art, business, directories, economics, education, gardening, health and nutrition, how-to, language arts, linguistics, law, mathematics, philosophy, poetry, reference, general science, science fiction and fantasy, self-help, social sciences, sociology, textbooks, travel.

J.W. Cappelens Forlag A/S

Postboks 350, Sentrum, 0101 Oslo
☎00 47 22 365000 Fax 00 47 22 365040
www.cappelen.no

Founded 1829. Publishes fiction, general non-fiction, dictionaries, directories, encyclopedias, reference, religion, textbooks.

N.W. Damm & Søn A/S

Fridtjof Nansenvei 14, 0055 Oslo
☎00 47 24 051000 Fax 00 47 24 051290
www.damm.no

Founded 1843. Owned by the Egmont Group. Publishes general non-fiction, reference, dictionaries, encyclopedias and translated fiction.

Ex Libris Forlag A/S

Tordenskioldsgt 6B, 0055 Oslo
☎00 47 22 471100 Fax 00 47 22 471149

Founded 1982. Publishes cookery, health, nutrition, humour, human relations, publishing and book trade reference.

Gyldendal Norsk Forlag A/S

Postboks 6860, St Olavs Plass, 0130 Oslo
☎00 47 22 034100 Fax 00 47 22 034105
www.gyldendal.no

Founded 1925. Publishes fiction, science fiction, fantasy, art, dance, biography, children's, dictionaries, directories, encyclopedias, government, political science, history, how-to, music, social sciences, sociology, poetry, philosophy, psychology, psychiatry, reference, religion, textbooks.

Tiden Norsk Forlag

Postboks 6704, St Olavs Plass, 0130 Oslo
☎00 47 22 2332 7660 Fax 00 46 22 2332 7697
www.tiden.no

Founded 1933. Publishes fiction, general non-fiction; essays, literature, literary criticism, science fiction, fantasy, directories, management, reference.

Portugal

Bertrand Editora Lda

Rua Anchieta 29–1, 1200 Lisbon
☎00 351 21 3468286
Fax 00 351 21 3479728

Founded 1727. Publishes art, essays, literature, literary criticism, dictionaries, encyclopedias, social sciences, sociology.

Editorial Caminho SARL

Al Santo Antonio dos Capuchos 6B,
1100 Lisbon
☎00 351 1 3152683 Fax 00 351 1 534346

Founded 1977. Publishes fiction, government, political science.

Livraria Civilização (Américo Fraga Lamares & Ca Lda)
Rua Dr Alberto Aires de Gouveia 27,
4000 Porto
☎00 351 2 20002286
Founded 1921. Publishes fiction, art, economics, history, social sciences, political science, government, sociology.

Publicações Dom Quixote Lda
Rua Cintura Porto Lote-A, 2-C Urbaniz
Matinha, 1900–649 Lisbon
☎00 351 21 8610440
Fax 00 351 21 8610456
Founded 1965. Publishes fiction, poetry, children's, directories, education, history, philosophy, reference, general science, social sciences, sociology.

Publicações Europa-América Lda
Estrada Lisboa-Sintra, Km 14,
2725 Mem Martins
☎00 351 21 921 1461
Fax 00 351 21 921 7846
Founded 1945. Publishes fiction, poetry, art, biography, children's, dance, directories, education, general engineering, history, how-to, music, philosophy, medicine, nursing, dentistry, psychology, psychiatry, reference, general science, social sciences, sociology, technology, textbooks.

Gradiva–Publicações Lda
Rua Almeida e Sousa 21–r/c Esq,
1399 041 Lisbon
☎00 351 1 3974067 Fax 00 351 1 3953471
www.gravida.pt
Founded 1981. Publishes fiction, literature, literary criticism, essays, science fiction, fantasy, romance, anthropology, Asian studies, astronomy, behavioural sciences, biological science, children's, communications, computer science, crafts, directories, earth sciences, education, games, hobbies, economics, general engineering, geography, geology, government, political studies, journalism, natural history, history, humour, environmental studies, human relations, management, mathematics, philosophy, general science, physics, psychology, psychiatry, reference, social sciences, sociology.

Livros Horizonte Lda
Rua Chagas 17 - 1 Dto, 1200 Lisbon
☎00 351 1 3466917 Fax 00 351 1 3326921
Founded 1953. Publishes art, children's, education, history, psychology, psychiatry, social sciences, sociology, textbooks.

Editorial Verbo SA
Av Antonio Augusto de Aguiar 148–6,
1069–019 Lisbon
☎00 351 21 380 2131
Fax 00 351 21 386 1122
Founded 1959. Publishes dictionaries, education, encyclopedias, history, general science.

Spain

Alianza Editorial SA
Juan Ignacio Luca de Tena 15,
28027 Madrid
☎00 349 1 393 8888 Fax 00 349 1 320 7480
alianzaeditorial.es
Founded 1965. Publishes fiction, poetry, art, history, mathematics, dance, music, philosophy, government, political science, social sciences, sociology, general science.

Ediciones Anaya SA
Juan Ignacio Luca de Tena 15,
28027 Madrid
☎00 349 1 393 8600 Fax 00 349 1 742 6631
Founded 1959. Publishes education.

CEAC Grupo Editorial SA
Peru 164, 08020 Barcelona
☎00 349 3 307 3004 Fax 00 349 3 266 0667
www.ceacedit.com
Founded 1957. Publishes CD-ROMs, children's, education, architecture and interior design, electronics, electrical engineering, general engineering, health and nutrition, photography, professional, textbooks, fiction, science fiction, fantasy.

Editorial Don Quijote
Compás del Porvenir 6, 41013 Seville
☎00 349 5 423 5080
Founded 1981. Publishes fiction, literature, literary criticism, poetry, essays, drama, theatre, history.

EDHASA (Editora y Distribuidora Hispano – Americana SA)
Av Diagonal 519–521, 2 piso, 08029 Barcelona
☎00 349 3 494 9720 Fax 00 349 3 419 4584
www.edhasa.es
Founded 1946. Publishes fiction, literature, literary criticism, essays, history.

Editorial Espasa-Calpe SA
Apdo de correos 547, Carreterade Irún Km 12,
200, 28049 Madrid
☎00 349 1 358 9689   Fax 00 349 1 358 9364
www.espasa.com
Founded 1925. Publishes fiction, science fiction, fantasy, English as a second language, general non-fiction, academic, art, children's, child care and development, cookery, biography, essays, history, literature, literary criticism, self-help, social sciences, sociology, CD-ROMs.

Grijalbo Mondadori SA
Arago 385, 08013 Barcelona
☎00 349 3 476 7110   Fax 00 349 3 476 7121
www.grijalbo.com
Founded 1962. Publishes fiction, general non-fiction, architecture and interior design, children's, dictionaries, directories, encyclopedias, gardening, plants, humour, literature, literary criticism, essays, poetry, human relations, reference.

Ediciónes Hiperión SL
Calle Salustiano Olózaga 14, 28001 Madrid
☎00 349 1 557 6015   Fax 00 349 1 435 8690
www.hiperion.com
Founded 1976. Publishes literature, literary criticism, essays, poetry, language arts, children's, religion (Islamic and Jewish), translations.

Editorial Luis Vives (Edelvives)
Calle Xaudaró 25, 28034 Madrid
☎00 349 1 334 4883   Fax 00 349 1 334 4893
Founded 1890. Publishes education.

Editorial Molino
Calabria 166, 08015 Barcelona
☎00 349 3 226 0625   Fax 00 349 3 226 6998
www.editorialmolino.com
Founded 1933. Publishes children's, education, sport, fiction.

Pearson Educacion SA
Nunez de Balboa 120, 28006 Madrid
☎00 349 1 590 3432   Fax 00 349 1 590 3448
Founded 1942. Publishes art, children's, education, history, language arts, linguistics, medicine, nursing, dentistry, general science, psychology, psychiatry, philosophy, textbooks.

Editorial Planeta SA
Edifici Planeta Diagonal 662–664,
08034 Barcelona
☎00 349 3 228 3700   Fax 00 349 3 217 7140
www.planeta.es
Founded 1952. Publishes fiction and general non-fiction.

Editorial Seix Barral SA
Edifici Planeta Diagonal 662–664,
08034 Barcelona
☎00 349 3 496 7003   Fax 00 349 3 496 7004
www.seix-barral.es
Founded 1945. Part of Grupo Planeta. Foreign language publisher of literature.

Tusquets Editores
Cesare Cantù 8, 08023 Barcelona
☎00 349 3 253 0400   Fax 00 349 3 417 6703
www.tusquets-editores.com
Founded 1969. Publishes fiction, biography, essays, literature, literary criticism, general science.

Sweden

Albert Bonniers Förlag
PO Box 3159, S-103 63 Stockholm
☎00 46 8 696 8620   Fax 00 46 8 696 8369
www.albertbonniersforlag.com
Founded 1837. Publishes fiction and general non-fiction.

Bokförlaget Bra Böcker AB
PO Box 890, S-20180 Malmo
☎00 46 40 665 4600   Fax 00 46 40 665 4622
www.bbb.se
Founded 1965. Publishes fiction, dictionaries, encyclopedias, geography, geology, history.

Brombergs Bokförlag AB
PO Box 12886, S-112 98 Stockholm
☎00 46 8 5626 2080   Fax 00 46 8 5626 2085
www.brombergs.se
Founded 1973. Publishes fiction and general non-fiction.

Bokförlaget Forum AB
PO Box 70321, S-107 23 Stockholm
☎00 46 8 696 8440   Fax 00 46 8 696 8367
Founded 1944. Publishes fiction and general non-fiction.

Bokförlaget Natur och Kultur
PO Box 27323, S-102 54 Stockholm
☎00 46 8 453 8600   Fax 00 46 8 453 8790
✉ info@nok.se
www.nok.se
Founded 1922. Publishes fiction and general non-fiction; biography, children's, history,

psychology, psychiatry and general science, textbooks.

Norstedts Förlag
Box 2052, S-103 12 Stockholm
☎00 46 8 769 8850 Fax 00 46 8 769 8864
www.norstedt.se
Founded 1823. Publishes fiction and general non-fiction.

Rabén och Sjögren Bokförlag
PO Box 2052, S-103 12 Stockholm
☎00 46 8 769 8800 Fax 00 46 8 769 8813
www.raben.se
Founded 1942. Publishes general non-fiction and children's books.

Richters Egmont
Sallerupsvaegen 9, 205 75 Malmö
☎00 46 40 380600 Fax 00 46 40 933708
www.egmont.com
Founded 1942. Publishes fiction and non-fiction; children's, dictionaries, directories, reference.

B. Wählströms Bokförlag AB
Box 30022, S-104 25 Stockholm
☎00 46 8 6198600 Fax 00 46 8 6189761
www.wahlstroms.se
Founded 1911. Publishes fiction and general non-fiction.

Switzerland

Arche Verlag AG, Raabe und Vitali
Niederdorfstr 90, CH-8001 Zurich
☎00 41 1 2522410 Fax 00 41 1 2611115
www.arche-verlag.com
Founded 1944. Publishes literature and literary criticism, essays, biography, fiction, poetry, music, dance, travel.

Diogenes Verlag AG
Sprecherstr 8, CH-8032 Zurich
☎00 41 1 2548511 Fax 00 41 1 2528407
✉ info@diogenes.ch
www.diogenes.ch
Founded 1952. Publishes fiction, essays, literature, literary criticism, mysteries, art, children's, drama, theatre, philosophy.

Langenscheidt AG Zürich-Zug
Postfach 326, CH-8021 Zurich
☎00 41 1 2115000 Fax 00 41 1 2122149
Part of **Langenscheidt Group**, Germany. Publishes language arts and linguistics.

Larousse (Suisse) SA
c/o Acces-Direct, 3 Route du Grand-Mont, CH-1052 Le Mont-sur-Lausanne
☎00 41 21 335336
Publishes dictionaries, directories, encyclopedias, reference and textbooks. Part of **Librairie Larousse**, France.

Neptun-Verlag
Postfach 307, CH-8280 Kreuzlingen
☎00 41 72 727262 Fax 00 41 72 642023
www.neptunart.ch
Founded 1946. Publishes children's, history and travel.

Orell Füssli Verlag
Dietzingerstr 3, CH-8036 Zurich
☎00 41 1 466 7711 Fax 00 41 1 466 7412
www.ofv.ch
Founded 1519. Publishes accountancy, art, biography, business, children's, economics, education, geography, geology, history, how-to, law.

Editions Payot Lausanne
CP 529, CH-1001 Lausanne
☎00 41 21 329 0264 Fax 00 41 21 329 0266
Founded 1875. Publishes general non-fiction, anthropology, archaeology, architecture and interior design, dance, education, history, law, medicine, nursing, dentistry, music, philosophy, literature, literary criticism, essays, general science, social sciences and sociology, textbooks.

Sauerländer AG
Laurenzenvorstadt 89, CH-5001 Aarau
☎00 41 64 2836 8626
Fax 00 41 64 2836 8620
www.sauerlaender.ch
Founded 1807. Publishes education and general non-fiction.

Scherz Verlag AG
Postfach 66, CH-3000 Berne 7
☎00 41 31 227337 Fax 00 41 31 3277171
Founded 1938. Publishes general non-fiction; biography, history, psychology, psychiatry, philosophy, parapsychology.

European Television Companies

Austria

ORF (Österreichisher Rundfunk)
Würzburggasse 30, A–1136 Vienna
☎00 43 1 87 8780 Fax 00 43 1 87 8782550
www.orf.at

Belgium

Radio-Télévision Belge de la Communauté Française (RTBF)
Boulevard Auguste Reyers 52,
B–1044 Brussels
☎00 32 2 737 2111 Fax 00 32 2 737 2936
www.rtbf.be

Vlaamse Radio en Televisieomroep (VRT)
Omroepcentrum, Reyerslaan 52,
B–1043 Brussels
☎00 32 2 741 3111 Fax 00 32 2 739 9351
www.vrt.be

Vlaamse Televisie Maatschappij (VTM) (cable)
Medialaan 1, B–1800 Vilvoorde
☎00 32 2 255 3211 Fax 00 32 2 252 5141
✉ info@vtm.be
www.vtm.be

Denmark

Danmarks Radio–TV
TV-Byen, DK–2860 Søborg
☎00 45 35 20 3040 Fax 00 45 35 20 2644
✉ dr@dr.dk
www.dr.dk

TV Danmark
Langebrogade 6A, DK–1411 Copenhagen K
☎00 45 70 10 1010 Fax 00 45 32 69 9699
✉ info@tvdanmark.dk
www.tvdanmark.dk

TV–2 Danmark
Rugaardsvej 25, DK–5100 Odense C
☎00 45 65 91 1244 Fax 00 45 65 91 3322
✉ tv2@tv2.dk
www.tv2.dk

Finland

MTV3 Finland
Ilmalantori 2, FIN–00240 Helsinki
☎00 358 9 15001 Fax 00 358 9 1500707
www.mtv3.fi

Yleisradio Oy (YLE)
PO Box 90, FIN–00024 Yleisradio
☎00 358 9 14801 Fax 00 358 9 14803215
www.yle.fi

France

Arte France (cable & satellite)
8 rue Marceau, 92785 Issy les Moulineaux
Cedex 9
☎00 33 1 55 00 77 77
Fax 00 33 1 55 00 77 00
www.artefrance.fr

Canal + (pay TV)
85–89 quai André Citroën, 75711 Paris
Cedex 15
☎00 33 1 44 25 10 00
www.cplus.fr

France 5
10–12 rue Horace-Vernet, 92785 Issy-les-
Moulineaux Cedex 9
☎00 33 1 56 22 91 91
Fax 00 33 1 56 22 95 95
www.france5.fr

France Télévision (France 2/ France 3)
7 Esplanade Henri de France, 75907 Paris
Cedex 15
☎00 33 1 56 22 42 42(France 2)/30 30
(France 3)
www.france2.fr
www.france3.fr

M6 (Métropole Télévision)
89 ave Charles de Gaulle, 92575 Neuilly-sur-
Seine Cedex
☎00 33 1 41 92 66 66
Fax 00 33 1 41 92 66 10
www.m6.fr

RFO (Radio Télévision Française d'Outre-mer)
5 ave du Recteur Poincaré, 75016 Paris
☎00 33 1 42 15 71 00
www.rfo.fr

TF1 (Télévision Française 1)
1 quai du Pont du Jour, 92656 Boulogne
☎00 33 1 41 41 12 34
Fax 00 33 1 41 41 28 40
www.tf1.fr

Germany
ARD – Das Erste
ARD Büro, Bertramstr 8, 60320 Frankfurt am Main
☎00 49 69 59 0607 Fax 00 49 69 15 52075
www.daserste.de

Arte Germany (cable & satellite)
Schützenstrasse 1, 76530 Baden–Baden
☎00 49 7221 9369–0
www.arte.de

ZDF (Zweites Deutsches Fernsehen)
Postfach 40 40, 55100 Mainz
☎00 49 61 31/701 Fax 00 49 61 31 702157
www.zdf.de

Republic of Ireland
Radio Telefís Éireann (RTE – RTE 1)
Donnybrook, Dublin 4
☎00 353 1 208 3111 Fax 00 353 1 208 3080
www.rte.ie

Teilefís na Gaelige
Baile na hAbhann, Co. na Gaillimhe
☎00 353 91 505050 Fax 00 353 91 505021
www.tg4.ie

Italy
RAI (RadioTelevisione Italiana)
Viale Mazzini 14, 00195 Rome
☎00 39 06 3878–1 Fax 00 39 06 372 5680
www.rai.it

The Netherlands
AVRO (Algemene Omroep Vereniging)
Postbus 2, 1200 JA Hilversum
☎00 31 35 671 79 11 Fax 00 31 35 671 74 39
www.central.avro.nl/index.asp

IKON
Postbus 10009, 1201 DA Hilversum
☎00 31 35 672 72 72 Fax 00 31 35 621 51 00
✉ ikon@ikon.nl
www.omroep.nl/ikon

NCRV (Nederlandse Christelijke Radio Vereniging)
Postbus 25000, 1202 HB Hilversum
☎00 31 35 671 99 11 Fax 00 31 35 671 92 85
info.omroep.nl/ncrv

NOS (Nederlandse Omroep Stichting)
Sumatralaan 45, 1217 GP Hilversum
☎00 31 35 677 92 22 Fax 00 31 35 677 4863
www.nos.nl

NPS (Nederlandse Programma Stichting)
Postbus 29000, 1202 MA Hilversum
☎00 31 35 677 9333
www.omroep.nl/nps

TROS (Televisie en Radio Omroep Stichting)
Postbus 28450, 1202 LH Hilversum
☎00 31 35 671 57 15 Fax 00 31 35 671 53 16
www.omroep.nl/tros

VARA
Postbus 175, 1200 AD Hilversum
☎00 31 35 671 19 11 Fax 00 31 35 671 13 40
www.omroep.nl/vara

VPRO
Postbus 11, 1200 JC Hilversum
☎00 31 35 671 29 11 Fax 00 31 35 671 21 00
✉ info@vpro.nl
www.vpro.nl

Norway
NRK (Norsk Rikskringkasting)
N–0340 Oslo
☎00 47 23 04 7000 Fax 00 47 23 04 7575

✉ info@nrk.no
www.nrk.no

TVNorge
Postboks 11, Sentrum, N–0101 Oslo
☎00 47 21 02 2000 Fax 00 47 22 05 1000
✉ tvnorge@tvnorge.no
www.tvnorge.no

TV2
Postboks 7222, N–5020 Bergen
☎00 47 55 90 8070
✉ info@tv2.no
www.tv2.no

Portugal
Radiotelevisão Portuguesa (RTP)
Avenida Marechal, Gomes da Costa 37,
1800–255 Lisbon
☎00 351 21 794 7000
www.rtp.pt

TVI (Televisão Independente)
Rua Mário Castelhano 40, Queluz de Baixo,
2745 Concelho de Oeiras
☎00 351 21 434 7500
www.tvi.pt

Spain
RTVE (RadioTelevision Española)
Edificio Prado del Rey, E–28223 Madrid
☎00 349 1 581 7238 Fax 00 349 1 581 7239
www.rtve.es

Sweden
Sveriges Television AB–SVT
Oxenstierngatan 26–34, S–105 10 Stockholm
☎00 46 8 784 0000 Fax 00 46 8 784 1500
www.svt.se

TV4
Tegeluddsvägen 3, S–115 79 Stockholm
☎00 46 8 459 4000 Fax 00 46 8 459 4444
www.tv4.se

Switzerland
RTR (Radio e Televisiun Rumantscha) (Romansch language TV)
Via dal Teater 1, CH–7002 Cuira
☎00 41 81 255 7575 Fax 00 41 81 255 7500
✉ contact@rtr.ch
www.rtr.ch

RTSI (Radiotelevisione svizzera di lingua Italiana) (Italian language TV)
Casella postale, CH–6903 Lugano
☎00 41 91 803 51 11
✉ info@rtsi.ch
www.rtsi.ch

SF DRS (Schweizer Fernsehen) (German language TV)
Fernsehenstrasse 1–4, CH–8052 Zurich
☎00 41 1 305 66 11 Fax 00 41 1 305 56 60
✉ sfdrs@sfdrs
www.sfdrs.ch

SRG SSR idée suisse (Swiss Broadcasting Corp.)
Postfach 26, CH–3000 Berne15
☎00 41 31 350 91 11
Fax 00 41 31 350 92 56
www.srg-ssr.ch

TSR (Télévision Suisse Romande)
Quai Ernest Ansermet 20, CH–1211 Geneva 8
☎00 41 22 708 20 20 Fax 00 41 22 708 98 00
www.tsr.ch

US Publishers

Anyone corresponding with the big American publishers should know that following the terrorist attacks of 2001 they are wary of any package or letter that looks in any way suspicious. This, of course, begs the question what is or what is not suspicious which is as difficult to answer as what makes or does not make a good novel. The best policy is to make an initial enquiry by e-mail.

International Reply Coupons (IRCs)
For return postage, send IRCs, available from post offices. Letters, 60 pence; mss according to weight. For current postal rates to the UK go to the United States Postal Service website at www.usps.com and click on 'Calculate Postage'.

ABC–CLIO
PO Box 1911, Santa Barbara, CA 93116–1911
☎001 805 968 1911 Fax 001 805 685 9685
✉ sales@abc-clio.com
www.abc-clio.com
CEO *Ronald J. Boehm*
Founded 1953. Publishes academic and reference, focusing on history and social studies; books and multimedia. UK SUBSIDIARY **ABC-Clio Ltd**, Oxford. No unsolicited mss; synopses and ideas welcome.
   ROYALTIES annually.

Abingdon Press
PO Box 801, Nashville, TN 37202–0801
☎001 615 749 6290 Fax 001 615 749 6056
www.abingdonpress.com
Snr. VP/Editorial Director *Harriett Jane Olson*
Founded 1789. Publishes non–fiction: religious (lay and professional), reference, professional and academic texts. Over 100 titles a year.

Harry N. Abrams, Inc.
100 Fifth Avenue, New York, NY 10011
☎001 212 206 7715 Fax 001 212 645 8437
www.abramsbooks.com
VP/Editor-in-Chief *Eric Himmel*
Founded 1950. Publishes illustrated books: art, natural history, photography. No fiction. About 200 titles a year.

Academy Chicago Publishers
363 W. Erie Street, Chicago, IL 60610
☎001 312 751 7300 Fax 001 312 751 7306
✉ info@academychicago.com
www.academychicago.com

President/Senior Editor *Anita Miller*
Founded 1975. Publishes mainstream fiction; non-fiction: art, history, mysteries. No romance, children's, young adult, religious, sexist or avant-garde. *Distributed* in the UK and Europe by Gazelle, Lancaster.
   ROYALTIES twice-yearly.

Access Press
See **HarperCollins Publishers, Inc.**

Ace
See **Penguin Group (USA) Inc.**

Addison Wesley
75 Arlington Street, Boston, MA 02116
☎001 617 848 7500 Fax 001 617 848 6016
✉ firstname.lastname@pearsoned.com
www.awl.com
Part of Pearson Education. Publishes academic textbooks, multimedia and learning programs in computer science, economics, finance, mathematics and statistics. See the website for submission guidelines.

University of Alabama Press
Box 870380, Tuscaloosa, AL 35487–0380
☎001 205 348 5180 Fax 001 205 348 9201
Director *Daniel J.J. Ross*
Founded 1945. Publishes American history, Latin American history, American religious history; African-American and Native American studies, Judaic studies, archaeology, anthropology, enthnohistory and American letters. About 60 titles a year. Submissions are not invited in poetry, fiction or drama.

Aladdin Books
See **Simon & Schuster Children's Publishing**

University of Alaska Press
PO Box 756240, University of Alaska, Fairbanks, AK 99775–6240
☎001 907 474 5831   Fax 001 907 474 5502
✉ fypress@uaf.edu
www.uaf.edu/uapress

Director *Claus M. Naske*
Senior Editor *Jennifer Collier*
Acquisitions *Erica Hill*

Traces its origins back to 1927 but was relatively dormant until the early 1980s. Publishes scholarly works about Alaska and the North Pacific rim, with a special emphasis on circumpolar regions. No fiction or poetry.

DIVISIONS **Rasmuson Library Historical Translation Series**; **Oral Biography Series**; **Classic Reprint Series** Informal non-fiction covering Northern interest. 5–10 titles a year. Unsolicited mss, synopses and ideas welcome.

Alpha
See **Penguin Group (USA) Inc.**

Alyson Publications
PO Box 4371, Los Angeles, CA 90078
☎001 323 860 6065   Fax 001 323 467 0152
✉ mail@alyson.com
www.alyson.com

Publisher *Greg Constante*
Senior Editor *Angela Brown*

Founded 1980. Publishes fiction and non-fiction books of general interest to the gay and lesbian community. No unsolicited mss. Synopses and ideas for books welcome; initial contact by mail or e-mail.
ROYALTIES twice-yearly.

AMACOM Books
1601 Broadway, New York, NY 10019–7406
☎001 212 586 8100   Fax 001 212 903 8168

President & Publisher *Harold V. Kennedy*

Founded 1972. Owned by American Management Association. Publishes business books only, including general management, business communications, sales and marketing, finance, computers and information systems, human resource management and training, career/personal growth skills. About 80 titles a year.
ROYALTIES twice-yearly.

Amistad
See **HarperCollins Publishers, Inc.**

Anchor Books
See **Doubleday Broadway Publishing Group**

Anvil
See **Krieger Publishing Co.**

Shaye Areheart Books
See **The Crown Publishing Group**

University of Arizona Press
355 S. Euclid Avenue, Ste. 103, Tucson, AZ 85719–6654
☎001 520 621 1441   Fax 001 520 621 8899
www.uapress.arizona.edu

Director/Editor-in-Chief *Christine Szuter*

Founded 1959. Publishes academic non-fiction, particularly with a regional/cultural link, plus Native-American and Hispanic literature. About 50 titles a year.

University of Arkansas Press
McIlroy House, 201 Ozark Avenue, Fayetteville, AR 72701
☎001 479 575 3246   Fax 001 479 575 6044
www.uapress.com

Director *Lawrence J. Malley*

Founded 1980. Publishes scholarly monographs, poetry and general trade books. Particularly interested in scholarly works in history, politics and literary criticism. About 30 titles a year.
ROYALTIES annually.

ASM Press
1752 N. Street NW, Washington, DC 20036–2904
☎001 202 737 3600   Fax 001 202 942 9342
✉ books@asmusa.org
www.asmpress.org

Director *Jeffrey Holtmeier*

Founded 1899. The book publishing division of the American Society for Microbiology. Publishes monographs, texts, reference books and manuals in microbiological sciences.
ROYALTIES annually.

Aspect
See **Warner Books Inc.**

Atheneum Books for Young Readers
See **Simon & Schuster Children's Publishing**

Atlantic Monthly Press
See **Grove/Atlantic Inc.**

Atria Books
See **Simon & Schuster Adult Publishing Group**

Avalon Publishing Group
1400 65th Street, Suite 250, Emeryville, CA 94608
www.avalonpub.com
Also at: 245 West 17th Street, 11th floor New York, NY 10011–5300
Chairman *Charlie Winton*

Founded 1984. Independent publisher of fiction and non-fiction; current affairs, self-help, health, women's studies, gay and lesbian, travel, music, photography and poetry.

DIVISIONS **Avalon Publishing Group California** IMPRINTS **Avalon Travel Publishing**; **Seal Press** (books by and about women); **Avalon Publishing Group New York** IMPRINTS **Carroll & Graf Publishers** (history, current affairs); **Thunder's Mouth Press** (current affairs, popular culture, film, music, photography); **Marlowe & Company** (psychology, self-help, health); **Blue Moon Books** (classic and new erotica); **Shoemaker & Hoard Publishers** (literary division). 438 titles in 2003. No unsolicited material.

Avery
375 Hudson Street, New York, NY 10014
☎001 212 366 2000 Fax 001 212 366 2643
www.penguingroup.com
Publisher *John Duff*
Senior Editor *Amy Tecklenburg*

Founded 1976. Imprint of **Penguin Group (USA) Inc.** Publishes alternative and complementary health care, nutrition, disease prevention, diet, supplements, functional foods, mind/body therapies, holistic healing. About 30 titles a year. No unsolicited mss; synopses and ideas welcome if accompanied by s.a.e./IRCs.
ROYALTIES twice-yearly.

Avon
See **HarperCollins Publishers, Inc.**

Baker Book House
PO Box 6287, Grand Rapids, MI 49516–6287
☎001 616 676 9185 Fax 001 616 676 9573
www.bakerbooks.com
President *Dwight Baker*
Director of Publications *Don Stephenson*

Founded 1939. Began life as a used-book store and began publishing in earnest in the 1950s, primarily serving the evangelical Christian market. Additional information for authors on website.

DIVISIONS/IMPRINTS
Baker Books Publishes religious non-fiction and fiction, Bible reference, professional (pastors and church leaders) books, children's books. About 80 titles a year. No unsolicited proposals.
Baker Academic *Jim Kinney* Publishes college/seminary textbooks, religious reference books, biblical studies monographs. About 45 titles a year. No unsolicited proposals.
Fleming H. Revell *Lonnie Hull Du Pont* Founded 1870. A family-owned business until 1978, Revell was one of the first Christian publishers to take the step into secular publishing. Joined Baker Book House in 1992. Publishes adult fiction and non-fiction for evangelical Christians. About 75 titles a year. No unsolicited proposals.
Brazos Press *Rodney Clapp* Publishes academic and trade books in theology, biblical studies, ethics, cultural criticism and spirituality (trade editions only). About 20 titles a year. No unsolicited mss.
Chosen Books *Jane Campbell* Founded 1971; joined Baker Book House in 1992. Publishes charismatic adult non-fiction for evangelical Christians. About 30 titles a year. No unsolicited proposals.

Ballantine Books/
Ballantine Reader's Circle
See **Random House Publishing Group**

Banner Books
See **University Press of Mississippi**

Bantam Dell Publishing Group
1745 Broadway, New York, NY 10019
☎001 212 782 9000 Fax 001 212 302 7985
www.randomhouse.com/bantamdell
President/Publisher *Irwyn Applebaum*

Founded 1945. The largest mass market paperback publisher in the USA. A division of the **Random House Publishing Group**. Publishes general commercial fiction and non-fiction, young readers and children's: mysteries, science fiction and fantasy, romance, health and nutrition, self-help.

DIVISIONS/IMPRINTS **Bantam Classics**; **Delacorte Press**; **Dell**; **Delta Books**; **Dial Press**.

Barron's Educational Series, Inc.
250 Wireless Boulevard, Hauppauge,
NY 11788–3917
☎001 516 434 3311 Fax 001 516 434 3723
✉ waynebarr@barronseduc.com
www.barronseduc.com

President *Manuel H. Barron*
Acquisitions Editor *Wayne Barr*

Founded 1942. *Publishes* adult non-fiction, children's fiction and non-fiction, test preparation materials and language materials, cookbooks, pets, hobbies, sport, photography, health, business, law, computers, travel, business, art and painting. No adult fiction. 400 titles a year. Unsolicited mss, synopses and ideas for books welcome.

ROYALTIES twice-yearly.

Basic Books
See **Perseus Books Group**

Beacon Press
25 Beacon Street, Boston, MA 02108
☎001 617 742 2110 Fax 001 617 723 3097
www.beacon.org

Director *Helene Atwan*

Founded 1854. Publishes general non-fiction. About 80 titles a year. Does not accept unsolicited mss. For further information, refer to website page.

Belknap Press
See **Harvard University Press**

Berkley
See **Penguin Group (USA) Inc.**

Bison Books
See **University of Nebraska Press**

Blackbird Press
See **Gale**

Blackwell Publishing
2121 State Avenue, Ames, IA 50014
☎001 515 292 0140 Fax 001 515 292 3348
✉ acquisitions@blackwellprofessional.com
www.blackwellprofessional.com

Publishing Director *Antonia Seymour*

Formerly Iowa State Press. Founded 1934 as an offshoot of the Iowa State University's journalism department. Publishes reference books and textbooks on aviation, food science, human dentistry, dietetics, journalism, and veterinary medicine. No fiction, trade books or poetry.

ROYALTIES annually.

H.&R. Block
See **Simon & Schuster Adult Publishing Group**

Blue Moon Books
See **Avalon Publishing Group**

Boyds Mills Press
815 Church Street, Honesdale, PA 18431
☎001 570 253 1164 Fax 001 570 253 0179
www.boydsmillspress.com

Publisher *Kent Brown*

A subsidiary of Highlights for Children, Inc. Founded 1990 as a publisher of children's trade books. Publishes children's and young adult's fiction, non-fiction and poetry. About 50 titles a year.

ROYALTIES twice-yearly.

Brassey's, Inc.
22841 Quicksilver Drive, Dulles, VA 20166
☎001 703 661 1548 Fax 001 703 661 1547
✉ djacobs@booksintl.com
www.brasseysinc.com

Publisher *Don McKeon*

Founded 1984 (acquired in 1999 by Books International of Dulles, Virginia). Publishes non-fiction titles on topics of history (especially military history), world and US affairs, US foreign policy, defence, intelligence, biography and sports. About 80 titles a year. No unsolicited mss; synopses and ideas welcome.

ROYALTIES annually.

Brazos Press
See **Baker Book House**

Broadway Books
See **Doubleday Broadway Publishing Group**

University of California Press
2120 Berkeley Way, Berkeley, CA 94720
☎001 510 642 4247 Fax 001 510 643 7127
www.ucpress.edu

Director *Lynne Withey*

Founded 1893. Publishes scholarly and scientific non-fiction; some fiction and poetry in translation. Preliminary letter with outline preferred.

Carolrhoda Books, Inc.
241 First Avenue N, Minneapolis, MN 55401
☎001 612 332 3344 Fax 001 612 332 7615
www.lernerbooks.com

VP & Editor-in-Chief *Mary M. Rodgers*

Founded 1969. A division of the **Lerner Publishing Group**. Publishes: animals, biography, earth sciences, ethnology, history, geography, geology, general science, historical fiction and picture books. Please send s.a.e. for author guidelines, making sure guideline requests are clearly marked on the envelope or they will be returned. 'We are *only* accepting submissions twice a year: from 1–31 March and 1–31 October. Submissions postmarked with other dates will be returned unopened. Also, only submissions with s.a.e./IRCs will receive a response.'

Carroll & Graf Publishers
See **Avalon Publishing Group**

Charlesbridge Publishing
85 Main Street, Watertown, MA 02472
☎001 617 926 0329 Fax 001 617 926 5720
✉ books@charlesbridge.com
www.charlesbridge.com

President/Publisher *Brent Farmer*
Managing Editor, School Division *Elena Dworkin Wright*

Founded 1980 as an educational publisher focused on a strategic approach to reading, writing, maths and science. Publishes children's educational programmes, non-fiction picture books and fiction for 3- to 12-year-olds. School division publishes mathematical fiction, *Maths Adventures*, in picture-book format and astronomy-related picture books.

University of Chicago Press
1427 East 60th Street, Chicago, IL 60637
☎001 773 702 7700 Fax 001 773 702 9756
✉ general@press.uchicago.edu
www.press.uchicago.edu

Founded 1891. Publishes academic non-fiction only.

Children's Press
See **Scholastic Library Publishing**

Chosen Books
See **Baker Book House**

Chronicle Books LLC
85 Second Street, Sixth Floor, San Francisco, CA 94105
☎001 415 537 4200 Fax 001 415 437 4460
✉ frontdesk@chroniclebooks.com
www.chroniclebooks.com

President/Publisher *Jack Jensen*

Founded 1966. Publishes illustrated and non-illustrated adult trade and children's books as well as stationery and gift items. About 200 titles a year. Query or submit outline/synopsis and sample chapters and artwork. Guidelines for ms submissions on the website.
ROYALTIES twice-yearly.

Clarkson Potter
See **The Crown Publishing Group**

Columbia University Press
61 West 62nd Street, New York, NY 10023
☎001 212 459 0600 Fax 001 212 459 3679
www.columbia.edu/cu/cup

Managing Director *James D. Jordan*
Editorial Director *Jennifer Crewe*
Approx. Annual Turnover $10 million

Founded 1893. Publishes scholarly and general interest non-fiction, reference, translations of Asian literature. No fiction or poetry. 160 titles in 2003. Welcomes unsolicited material if the subject fits their programme (see website). Approach by regular mail only.
ROYALTIES annually.

Contemporary Books
1 Prudential Plaza, Suite 900, Chicago, IL 60601
☎001 312 233 7500 Fax 001 312 233 7570

Founded 1947. Publishes general adult non-fiction. About 400 titles a year. Submissions require s.a.e./IRCs for response.

Copper Beech Books
See **The Millbrook Press, Inc.**

Joanna Cotler Books
See **HarperCollins Publishers, Inc.**

Counterpoint Press
See **Perseus Books Group**

Crocodile Books, USA
See **Interlink Publishing Group, Inc.**

The Crown Publishing Group
1745 Broadway, New York, NY 10019
☎001 212 782 9000 Fax 001 212 940 7408
www.randomhouse.com

Founded 1933. Division of the **Random House Publishing Group**. Publishes popular trade fiction and non-fiction.
IMPRINTS **Clarkson Potter** Illustrated books – cookery, gardening, style, decorating and design; **Crown Business** Editorial Director *Steve Ross* Business books; **Crown** Editorial Director *Steve Ross* General fiction and non-

fiction; **Harmony Books** Editorial Director *Shaye Areheart* New Age, spirituality, religion, some fiction; **Shaye Areheart Books** Editorial Director *Shaye Areheart* Fiction; **House of Collectibles** Antiques and collectables; **Three Rivers Press** *Becky Cabaza* Non-fiction paperbacks.

Cumberland House Publishing

431 Harding Industrial Drive, Nashville, TN 37211
☎001 615 832 1171 Fax 001 615 832 0633
✉ info@cumberlandhouse.com
www.cumberlandhouse.com

Founded 1996. Publishes fiction, non-fiction, humour, mysteries, travel cookery and sports.
ROYALTIES annually.

Benjamin Cummings

1301 Sansome Street, San Francisco, CA 94111
☎001 415 402 2500 Fax 001 415 402 2591
✉ question@aw.com
www.awl.com

Publishes academic textbooks, multimedia and learning programs in chemistry, health and life science. See the website for submission guidelines.

Currency

See **Doubleday Broadway Publishing Group**

Da Capo Press

See **Perseus Books Group**

DAW Books, Inc.

375 Hudson Street, 3rd Floor, New York, NY 10014–3658
☎001 212 366 2096/Submissions: 366 2095
Fax 001 212 366 2090
✉ daw@penguingroup.com
www.dawbooks.com

Publishers *Elizabeth R. Wollheim, Sheila E. Gilbert*
Submissions Editor *Peter Stampfel*

Founded 1971 by Donald and Elsie Wollheim as the first mass-market publisher devoted to science fiction and fantasy. An imprint of **Penguin Group (USA) Inc.** Publishes science fiction/fantasy, and some horror. No short stories, anthology ideas or non-fiction. Unsolicited mss, synopses and ideas for books welcome. About 36 titles a year.
ROYALTIES twice-yearly.

DD Equestrian Library

See **Doubleday Broadway Publishing Group**

Dearborn Financial Publishing, Inc.

155 S. Wacker Drive, Chicago IL 60606–1719
☎001 312 836 4400 Fax 001 312 836 1021
www.dearborn.com

President *Eric Cantor*

Founded 1967. A niche publisher serving the financial services industries. Publishes real estate, insurance, financial planning, securities, commodities, investments, banking, professional education, motivation and reference titles, investment reference for the consumer (personal finance, real estate) and small business owner. About 200 titles a year.
ROYALTIES twice-yearly.

Del Rey

See **Random House Publishing Group**

Delacorte Press

See **Bantam Dell Publishing Group**

Dell

See **Bantam Dell Publishing Group**

Delta Books

See **Bantam Dell Publishing Group**

Dial Books for Young Readers

345 Hudson Street, New York, NY 10014–3657
☎001 212 366 2800

Queries *Submissions Coordinator*

Founded 1961. A division of Penguin Books for Young Readers. Publishes children's books, including picture books, beginning readers, fiction and non-fiction for middle grade and young adults.
IMPRINTS Hardcover only: **Dial Books for Young Readers**; **Dial Easy-to-Read**. 50 titles a year. Accepts unsolicited picture book mss and up to ten pages for longer works with query letter.
ROYALTIES twice-yearly.

Dial Press

See **Bantam Dell Publishing Group**

Doubleday Broadway Publishing Group

1745 Broadway, New York NY 10019
☎001 212 782 9000 Fax 001 212 302 7985
www.randomhouse.com

President & Publisher *Stephen Rubin*

The Doubleday Broadway Publishing Group, a division of the **Random House Publishing Group**, was formed by a merger of Doubleday and Broadway Books in 1999. Publishes fiction and non-fiction.

DIVISION/IMPRINTS **The Anchor Bible**; **Anchor Books**; **Currency**; **DD Equestrian Library**; **Galilee Books**; **Image Books**; **Made Simple Books**; **Main Street/Back List**; **New Jerusalem Bible**; **Nan A. Talese Books**; **Outdoor Bible Series**. No unsolicited material.

Downtown Press
See **Pocket Books**

Lisa Drew Books
See **Simon & Schuster Adult Publishing Group**

Thomas Dunne Books
See **St Martin's Press LLC**

Sanford J. Durst Publications
11 Clinton Avenue, Rockville Centre, New York, NY 11570
☎001 516 766 4444   Fax 001 516 766 4520
Owner *Sanford J. Durst*

Founded 1975. Publishes non-fiction: numismatic and related, philatelic, legal, classical history and art. Also children's books. About 12 titles a year.
ROYALTIES twice-yearly.

Dutton/Dutton's Children's Books
See **Penguin Group (USA) Inc.**

ecco
See **HarperCollins Publishers, Inc.**

William B. Eerdmans Publishing Co.
255 Jefferson Avenue SE, Grand Rapids, MI 49503
☎001 616 459 4591   Fax 001 616 459 6540
www.eerdmans.com
President *William B. Eerdmans Jr*
Vice President/Editor-in-Chief *Jon Pott*

Founded 1911 as a theological and reference publisher. Gradually began publishing in other genres with authors like C.S. Lewis, Dorothy Sayers and Malcolm Muggeridge on its lists. Publishes religious: theology, biblical studies, ethical and social concern, social criticism and

children's, religious history, religion and literature.
DIVISIONS **Children's** *Judy Zylstra*; **Other** *Jon Pott*. About 120 titles a year. Unsolicited mss, synopses and ideas welcome.
ROYALTIES twice-yearly.

Eos
See **HarperCollins Publishers, Inc.**

M. Evans & Co., Inc.
216 East 49th Street, New York, NY 10017
☎001 212 688 2810   Fax 001 212 486 4544
✉ editorial@mevans.com
www.mevans.com
Associate Publisher *Harry McCullough*

Founded 1954 as a packager. Began publishing in 1962. Best known for its popular psychology and health books, with titles like *Dr Atkins' New Diet Revolution*, *This is How Love Works*, *Bragging Rights* and *Robert Crayhon's Nutrition Made Simple*. Publishes general non-fiction and fiction. About 30 titles a year. No unsolicited mss; query first. Synopses and ideas welcome.
ROYALTIES twice-yearly.

Faber & Faber, Inc.
19 Union Square West, New York, NY 10003
☎001 212 741 6900   Fax 001 212 633 9385
Editor *Denise Oswald*

Founded 1976. An affiliate of **Farrar, Straus & Giroux, Inc.** Publishes primarily non-fiction books for adults with a focus on film, theatre, music, popular culture and literary and cultural criticism. Unsolicited mss accepted; please query first and include IRCs with letter.
ROYALTIES twice-yearly.

Facts On File, Inc.
132 West 31st Street, New York, NY 10001
☎001 212 967 8800   Fax 001 212 967 9196
President *Mark McDonnell*
Publisher *Laurie E. Likoff*

Started life in the early 1940s with News Digest subscription series to libraries. Began publishing on specific subjects with the Facts On File imprint and developed its current reference and trade book programme in the 1970s. Publishes general trade, young adult trade and academic reference for the school and library markets. Specialises in single subject encyclopedias, atlases and biographical dictionaries. No fiction, cookery or popular non-fiction.
DIVISIONS **General Reference** *Laurie Likoff*;

Academic Reference *Owen Lancer*; **Adult Trade** *James Chambers*; **Young Adult & US History** *Nicole Bowen*; **Electronic Publishing** *James Housley*; **Literary Studies** *Jeff Soloway*. About 150 titles a year. Unsolicited synopses and ideas welcome; no mss. Send query letter in the first instance.

ROYALTIES twice-yearly.

Farrar, Straus & Giroux, Inc.

19 Union Square West, New York, NY 10003
☎001 212 741 6900 Fax 001 212 741 6973
www.fsgbooks.com

Founded 1946. Publishes general fiction, non-fiction, juveniles. No unsolicited material.

Fawcett

See **Random House Publishing Group**

Firebird

See **Penguin Group (USA) Inc.**

Fireside

See **Simon & Schuster Adult Publishing Group**

First Avenue Editions

See **Lerner Publishing Group**

Fisher Books

See **Perseus Books Group**

Five Star

See **Gale**

The Free Press

See **Simon & Schuster Adult Publishing Group**

Samuel French, Inc.

45 West 25th Street, New York, NY 10010–2751
☎001 212 206 8990 Fax 001 212 206 1429
✉ samuelfrench@earthlink.net
www.samuelfrench.com

Senior Editor *Lawrence Harbison*

Founded 1830. Publishes plays in paperback: London, Broadway and off-Broadway hits, light comedies, mysteries, one-act plays and plays for young audiences. OVERSEAS ASSOCIATES in London, Toronto, Sydney and Johannesburg. Unsolicited mss welcome. No synopses.

ROYALTIES annually (books); twice-yearly (amateur productions); monthly (professional productions).

Gale (formerly Gale Group)

27500 Drake Road, Farmington Hills, MI 48331
☎001 248 699 4253 Fax 001 248 699 8070
✉ galeord@gale.com
www.gale.com

CEO *Charles Siegel*
Executive VP, Editorial *Dennis Poupard*

Founded 1954. A subsidiary of The Thomson Corporation, Gale is a world leader in e-information publishing. Publishes electronic, print and microfiche reference material for libraries, schools and businesses. IMPRINTS **Blackbird Press; Charles Scribner & Sons; Five Star; Graham & Whiteside Ltd; Greenhaven Press; G.K. Hall & Co; KG Saur Verlag GmbH & Co KG; Kidhaven Press; Lucent Books; Macmillan Reference USA; Primary Source Media; St James Press; Schirmer Reference; The Taft Group; Thorndike Press; Twayne Publishers; UXL; Wheeler Publishing**. Initial contact should be made to *Dennis Poupard*, Executive VP, Editorial.

Galilee Books

See **Doubleday Broadway Publishing Group**

Laura Geringer Books

See **HarperCollins Publishers, Inc.**

The Globe Pequot Press

PO Box 480, Guilford, CT 06437–0480
☎001 203 458 4500 Fax 001 203 458 4601
✉ info@GobePequot.com
www.GlobePequot.com

President *Linda Kennedy*

Founded 1947. Publishes regional and international travel, how-to, regional and outdoor recreation. Also publishes the *Insiders'* guides. About 500 titles a year. Unsolicited mss, synopses and ideas welcome, particularly for travel and outdoor recreation books.

ROYALTIES 'occasionally'.

The Globe Pequot Press

See **The Lyons Press Inc.**

Gotham Books

See **Penguin Group (USA) Inc.**

Great Source Education Group

See **Houghton Mifflin Co.**

Greenhaven Press

See **Gale**

Greenwillow Books
See **HarperCollins Publishers, Inc.**

Griffin
See **St Martin's Press LLC**

Grolier Educational/ Grolier Online
See **Scholastic Library Publishing**

Grosset & Dunlap
See **Penguin Group (USA) Inc.**

Grove/Atlantic Inc.
841 Broadway, 4th Floor, New York,
NY 10003–4793
☎001 212 614 7850 Fax 001 212 614 7886
www.groveatlantic.com
President/Publisher *Morgan Entrekin*
Managing Editor *Michael Hornburg*
Founded 1952. Publishes general fiction and non-fiction. IMPRINTS **Atlantic Monthly Press; Grove Press**.

Gulliver Green Books
See **Harcourt Trade Publishers**

G.K. Hall & Co
See **Gale**

Harcourt School Publishers
6277 Sea Harbor Drive, Orlando, FL 32887
☎001 407 345 2000 Fax 001 407 352 3445
www.harcourtschool.com
President/CEO *Jan Spalding*
A division of Harcourt Inc., founded 1919. Publishes education materials – books, CD-ROMs, Internet and audio.

Harcourt Trade Publishers
(formerly **Harcourt Trade Division**)
525 'B' Street, Suite 1900, San Diego,
CA 92101–4495
☎001 619 231 6616 Fax 001 619 699 6777
www.harcourtbooks.com
Managing Editor, Adult *David Hough*
Managing Editor, Children's *Robin Cruise*
A division of Harcourt Inc. Publishes fiction, poetry and non-fiction covering a wide range of subjects: biography, environment and ecology, history, travel, science and current affairs for children and adults.
IMPRINTS **Greenlight Readers; Gulliver Green Books; Harcourt Young Classics; Harcourt Brace Young Classics; Harvest**

Books; **Libros Viajeros; Magic Carpet Books; Odyssey Classics; Red Wagon Books; Silver Whistle Books; Voyager Books; Helen & Kurt Wolff Books**. About 300 titles a year. No unsolicited mss.

Harlequin Historicals
See **Silhouette Books**

Harmony Books
See **The Crown Publishing Group**

HarperCollins Publishers, Inc.
10 East 53rd Street, New York, NY 10022
☎001 212 207 7000 Fax 001 212 207 6968
www.harpercollins.com
President/Chief Executive Officer *Jane Friedman*
Founded 1817. Subsidiary of News Corporation. Publishes general and literary fiction, general non-fiction, business, children's, reference and religious books.
DIVISIONS/IMPRINTS **Adult Trade; HarperCollins/HarperCollins Children's Books; HarperAudio; HarperBusiness; Harper Design International; HarperFestival; HarperTorch; HarperTrophy; Access Press; Amistad; Avon; Joanna Cotler Books; Laura Geringer Books; Greenwillow Books; Perennial; Quill; Rayo; ReganBooks; ecco; Eos; Tempest; William Morrow**.
SUBSIDIARY **Zondervan Publishing House** (see entry). About 1700 titles a year. No unsolicited material.

Harvard University Press
79 Garden Street, Cambridge, MA 02138–1499
☎001 617 495 2600 Fax 001 617 495 5898
✉ firstname_lastname@harvard.edu
www.hup.harvard.edu
Director *William P. Sisler*
Founded 1913. Publishes scholarly non-fiction only; humanities, social sciences, sciences.
IMPRINT **Belknap Press**.

Harvest Books
See **Harcourt Trade Publishers**

University of Hawai'i Press
2840 Kolowalu Street, Honolulu, HI 96822
☎001 808 956 8255 Fax 001 808 988 6052
✉ uhpbooks@hawaii.edu
www.uhpress.hawaii.edu
Director *William Hamilton*
Executive Editor *Patricia Crosby*
Founded 1947. Publishes scholarly books pertaining to East Asia, Southeast Asia, Hawaii and

the Pacific. IMPRINT **Kolowalu Books**; **Latitude 20**. Unsolicited mss; synopses and ideas welcome; approach by mail. No poetry, children's books or any topics other than Asia and the Pacific.

ROYALTIES twice-yearly.

HiddenSpring

See **Paulist Press**

Hill Street Press

191 E. Broad Street, Suite 209, Athens, GA 30601–2848

☎001 706 613 7200 Fax 001 706 613 7204

www.hillstreetpress.com

Senior Editor *Patrick Allen*

Founded 1998. Publishes books on the American South – fiction and non-fiction. No poetry, erotica, romance, children's or young adults. Unsolicited material welcome; approach in writing in the first instance.

ROYALTIES twice-yearly.

Hippocrene Books, Inc.

171 Madison Avenue, New York, NY 10016

☎001 212 685 4371 Fax 001 212 779 9338

✉ hippocrene.books@verizon.net

www.hippocrenebooks.com

President/Editorial Director *George Blagowidow*
Foreign Language Editor *Nicholas Williams*
Cookbook Editor *Anne McBride*
History Editor *Anne Kemper*

Founded 1971. Publishes general non-fiction and reference books. Particularly strong on foreign language dictionaries, language studies and international cookbooks. No fiction. Send brief summary, table of contents and one chapter for appraisal. S.a.e. essential for response. For manuscript return include sufficient postage cover (IRCs).

Holiday House, Inc.

425 Madison Avenue, New York, NY 10017

☎001 212 688 0085 Fax 001 212 421 6134

Vice President/Editor-in-Chief *Regina Griffin*

Publishes children's general fiction and non-fiction (pre-school to secondary). About 50 titles a year. Send query letters only. IRCs for reply must be included.

Henry Holt & Company Inc.

115 West 18th Street, New York, NY 10011

☎001 212 886 9200 Fax 001 212 633 0748

www.henryholt.com

President/Publisher *John Sterling*
Editor-in-Chief *Jennifer Barth*

Associate Publisher, Books for Young Readers *Laura Godwin*

Founded in 1866, Henry Holt is one of the oldest publishers in the United States. Part of Holtzbrinck Publishing Holdings. Publishes fiction, by both American and international authors, biographies, and books on history and politics, ecology and psychology.

DIVISIONS/IMPRINTS **Adult Trade**; **Books for Young Readers**; **John Macrae Books** *John Macrae*; **Metropolitan Books** *Sara Bershtel*; **Owl Books**; **Red Feather Books**; **Times Books**. About 250 titles a year.

Houghton Mifflin Co.

222 Berkeley Street, Boston, MA 02116–3764

☎001 617 351 5000 Fax 001 617 351 1125

www.hmco.com

Contact *Submissions Editor*

Founded 1832. Acquired by Vivendi in June 2001. Publishes literary fiction and general non-fiction, including autobiography, biography and history. Also school and college textbooks; children's fiction and non-fiction.

DIVISIONS/SUBSIDIARY COMPANIES **Houghton Mifflin College Division**; **Houghton Mifflin School Division**; **Houghton Mifflin Trade & Reference Division**; **Great Source Education Group**; **McDougal Littell Inc.**; **The Riverside Publishing Co.**; **Promissor Inc**. About 100 titles a year. Unsolicited adult mss no longer accepted. Send synopses, outline and sample chapters for children's non-fiction; complete mss for children's fiction. IRCs required with all submissions/queries.

House of Collectibles

See **The Crown Publishing Group**

HP Books

See **Penguin Group (USA) Inc.**

Hudson Street Press

See **Penguin Group (USA) Inc.**

Humanity Books

See **Prometheus Books**

Hydra

See **Northwestern University Press**

University of Illinois Press

1325 South Oak Street, Champaign, IL 61820–6903

☎001 217 333 0950 Fax 001 217 244 8082

✉ uipress@uillinois.edu
www.press.uillinois.edu

Director *Willis Regier*

Publishes non-fiction, scholarly and general, with special interest in Americana, women's studies, African–American studies, film, religion, American music and regional books. About 140–150 titles a year.

Image Books
See **Doubleday Broadway Publishing Group**

Indiana University Press
601 North Morton Street, Bloomington, IN 47404–3797
☎001 812 855 8817 Fax 001 812 855 8507
✉ iupress@indiana.edu
www.indiana.edu/~iupress

Director *Janet Rabinowitch*

Publishes scholarly non-fiction in the following subject areas: African studies, anthropology, Asian studies, Afro-American studies, environment and ecology, film, folklore, history, Jewish studies, literary criticism, medical ethics, Middle East studies, military, music, paleontology, philanthropy, philosophy, politics, religion, semiotics, Russian and East European studies, Victorian studies, women's studies. Query in writing in first instance.

Interlink Publishing Group, Inc.
46 Crosby Street, Northampton, MA 01060
☎001 413 582 7054 Fax 001 413 582 7057
✉ info@interlinkbooks.com
www.interlinkbooks.com

Publisher *Michel Moushabeck*

Founded 1987. Publishes fiction, travel, politics, cookbooks. Specialises in Middle East titles and ethnicity. IMPRINTS **Crocodile Books, USA** Editorial Head *Ruth Lane Moushabeck*; **Olive Branch Press** Editorial Head *Phyllis Bennis*. See submission guidelines on the website before making an approach.
ROYALTIES annually.

University of Iowa Press
100 Kuhl House, 119 West Park Road, Iowa City, IA 52242–1000
☎001 319 335 2000 Fax 001 319 335 2055
✉ uipress@uiowa.edu
www.uiowapress.org

Director *Holly Carver*

Founded 1969 as a small scholarly press pub-

lishing about five books a year. Now publishing about 35 a year in a variety of scholarly fields, plus local interest, short stories, creative non-fiction and poetry anthologies. No unsolicited mss; query first. Unsolicited ideas and synopses welcome.
ROYALTIES annually.

Iowa State University Press
See **Blackwell Publishing**

Ivy
See **Random House Publishing Group**

Jove
See **Penguin Group (USA) Inc.**

University Press of Kansas
2501 West 15th Street, Lawrence, KS 66049–3905
☎001 785 864 4154 Fax 001 785 864 4586
✉ upress@ku.edu
www.kansaspress.ku.edu

Director *Fred M. Woodward*

Founded 1946. Became the publishing arm for all six state universities in Kansas in 1976. Publishes scholarly books in American history studies, legal studies, presidential studies, American studies, political philosophy, political science, military history and environmental. About 55 titles a year. Proposals welcome.
ROYALTIES annually.

Kar-Ben Publishing
See **Lerner Publishing Group**

Jean Karl Books
See **Simon & Schuster Children's Publishing**

Kent State University Press
307 Lowry Hall, Terrace Drive, Kent, OH 44242
☎001 330 672 7913 Fax 001 330 672 3104
www.kentstateuniversitypress.com

Director *Will Underwood*
Editor-in-Chief *Joanna Hildebrand Craig*

Founded 1965. Publishes scholarly works in history, literary studies and general non-fiction with an emphasis on American studies. 25–30 titles a year. Queries welcome; no mss.
ROYALTIES annually.

Kidhaven Press
See **Gale**

Kluwer Academic Publishers

101 Philip Drive, Assinippi Park, Norwell, MA 02061
☎001 781 871 6600 Fax 001 781 871 6528
✉ kluwer@wkap.com
www.wkap.nl

CEO *Peter Hendriks*
Managing Editor *Claire Stanton*

Founded 1972. Publishes scholarly scientific, technical, medical, business and professional books and journals. IMPRINTS **Kluwer Academic Publishers/Plenum Publishers**. Over 300 titles a year.

Kolowalu Books
See **University of Hawai'i Press**

Krieger Publishing Co.

PO Box 9542, Melbourne, FL 32902–9542
☎001 321 724 9542 Fax 001 321 951 3671
✉ info@krieger-publishing.com
www.krieger-publishing.com

Chairman *Robert E. Krieger*
President *Donald E. Krieger*
Vice-President *Maxine D. Krieger*

Founded 1970. Publishes science, education, ecology, humanities, history, mathematics, chemistry, space science, technology and engineering.
IMPRINTS/SERIES **Anvil**; **Open Forum**; **Orbit**; **Professional Practices**; **Exploring Community History**; **Public History**. Unsolicited mss welcome. Not interested in synopses/ideas or trade type titles.
ROYALTIES annually.

Latino Voices
See **Northwestern University Press**

Latitude 20
See **University of Hawai'i Press**

Lerner Publishing Group

241 First Avenue North, Minneapolis, MN 55401
☎001 612 332 3344 Fax 001 612 332 7615
✉ info@lernerbooks.com
www.lernerbooks.com

Chairman *Harry J. Lerner*
President & Publisher *Adam M. Lerner*

Founded 1959. Publishes primarily children's non-fiction, fiction and curriculum material for readers of all grade levels.
DIVISIONS/IMPRINTS Editorial Head *Mary Rodgers* **Lerner Publications**; **Carolrhoda**

Books (see entry); **LernerSports**; **LernerClassroom**; **First Avenue Editions**; **Kar-Ben Publishing** Editorial Heads *Judye Groner*, *Madeline Wikler*. No puzzle, work, song or text books, or plays. Submissions are accepted in the months of March and October *only*. Work received in any other month will be returned unopened. S.a.e./IRCs required for authors who wish to have their material returned. Please allow two to six months for response. No phone calls.
ROYALTIES twice-yearly.

Libros Viajeros
See **Harcourt Trade Publishers**

Little Simon
See **Simon & Schuster Children's Publishing**

Little, Brown and Company

1271 Avenue of the Americas, New York, NY 10020
☎001 212 522 8700 Fax 001 212 522 2067
www.twbookmark.com

Imprint of Time Warner Book Group. Founded 1837. Publishes fiction, non-fiction and children's. DIVISIONS **Adult Trade** VP/Publisher *Michael Pietsch*; **Children's Books** VP/Editor-in-Chief *Maria Modugno*. No unsolicited mss.

Llewellyn Publications

PO Box 64383, St Paul, MN 55164–0383
☎001 612 291 1970 Fax 001 612 291 1908
✉ nancym@llewellyn.com
www.llewellyn.com

President/Publisher *Carl L. Weschcke*
Acquisitions Manager *Nancy J. Mostad*

Division of Llewellyn Worldwide Ltd. Founded 1901. Publishes self-help and how-to: astrology, alternative health, tantra, Fortean studies, tarot, yoga, Santeria, dream studies, metaphysics, magic, witchcraft, herbalism, shamanism, organic gardening, women's spirituality, graphology, palmistry, parapsychology. Also fiction with an authentic magical or metaphysical theme. About 100 titles a year. Unsolicited mss welcome; proposals preferred. IRCs essential in all cases.

Louisiana State University Press

PO Box 25053, Baton Rouge, LA 70894–5053
☎001 225 578 6295 Fax 001 225 578 6461
✉ lsupress@lsu.edu
www.lsu.edu/lsupress

Director *Mary Katherine Calloway*

Publishes non-fiction: Southern history, American history, Southern literary criticism, American literary criticism, biography, political science, music (jazz) and Latin American studies. About 80 titles a year. Send IRCs for mss guidelines.

Love Inspired
See **Silhouette Books**

Lucas Books
See **Random House Publishing Group**

Lucent Books
See **Gale**

Luna Books
See **Silhouette Books**

The Lyons Press Inc.
246 Goose Lane, Guilford, CT 06347
☎001 203 458 4500
www.lyonspress.com
Publisher *Tony Lyons*
Managing Editor *Alicia Solis*

Founded 1978. Imprint of The Globe Pequot Press. Publishes general fiction and non-fiction; outdoor, natural history, sports, gardening, history and art. About 200 titles a year. No unsolicited mss; synopses and ideas welcome.
ROYALTIES twice-yearly.

McDougal Littell Inc.
See **Houghton Mifflin Co.**

Margaret K. McElderry Books
See **Simon & Schuster Children's Publishing**

McFarland & Company, Inc., Publishers
PO Box 611, Jefferson, NC 28640
☎001 336 246 4460   Fax 001 336 246 5018
✉ info@mcfarlandpub.com
www.mcfarlandpub.com
President/Editor-in-Chief *Robert Franklin*
Executive Vice President *Rhonda Herman*
Executive Editor *Steve Wilson*
Editorial Development Chief *Virginia Tobiassen*

Founded 1979. A library reference and upper-end speciality market press publishing scholarly books in many fields: international studies, performing arts, popular culture, sports, automotive history, women's studies, music and fine arts, chess, history and librarianship. Specialises in general reference. Especially strong in cinema studies. No fiction, poetry, children's, New Age or inspirational/devotional works. About 275

titles a year. No unsolicited mss; send query letter first. Synopses and ideas welcome; submissions by mail preferred.
ROYALTIES annually.

The McGraw-Hill Companies, Inc.
1221 Avenue of the Americas, 50th Floor, New York, NY 10020
☎001 212 512 2000
www.mcgraw-hill.com
Chairman/President/CEO *Harold W. McGraw*

Founded 1888. Parent of **McGraw-Hill Education** which has offices in the UK (see entry under *UK Publishers*). Publishes a wide range of educational, professional, business, science, engineering and computing books.

Macmillan Reference USA
See **Gale**

John Macrae Books
See **Henry Holt & Company Inc.**

Made Simple Books
See **Doubleday Broadway Publishing Group**

Magic Carpet Books
See **Harcourt Trade Publishers**

Main Street
See **Doubleday Broadway Publishing Group**

Marlow & Company
See **Avalon Publishing Group**

University of Massachusetts Press
PO Box 429, Amherst, MA 01004–0429
☎001 413 545 2217   Fax 001 413 545 1226
✉ info@umpress.umass.edu
www.umass.edu/umpress
Director *Bruce Wilcox*
Senior Editor *Clark Dougan*

Founded 1964. Publishes scholarly, general interest, African-American, ethnic, women's and gender studies, cultural criticism, economics, fiction, literary criticism, poetry, philosophy, biography, history. About 40 titles a year. Unsolicited mss considered but query letter preferred in the first instance. Synopses and ideas welcome.
ROYALTIES annually.

Metropolitan Books
See **Henry Holt & Company Inc.**

The University of Michigan Press
839 Greene Street, Ann Arbor, MI 48104
☎001 734 764 4388 Fax 001 734 615 1540
✉ um.press@umich.edu
www.press.umich.edu

Founded 1930. Publishes non-fiction, text-books, literary criticism, theatre, economics, political science, history, classics, anthropology, law studies, gender studies, English as a second language.
ROYALTIES twice-yearly.

The Millbrook Press, Inc.
2 Old New Milford Road, Brookfield,
CT 06804
☎001 203 740 2220 Fax 001 203 740 2526
www.millbrookpress.com

Executive VP/Publisher *Jean E. Reynolds*
Managing Editor *Colleen Seibert*

Founded 1989. Publishes mainly non-fiction, children's and young adult, for trade, school and public library. IMPRINTS **Copper Beech Books**; **Twenty-First Century Books**; **Roaring Brook Press** Fiction. About 150 titles a year.
ROYALTIES twice-yearly.

University of Minnesota Press
111 Third Avenue South, Suite 290,
Minneapolis, MN 55401–2520
☎001 612 627 1970
www.upress.umn.edu

Director *Douglas Armato*
Associate Editor, Cinema & Media Studies, Visual Cultures *Andrea Kleinhuber*
Associate Editor, Architecture & Public Art *Pieter Martin*
Acquisitions Editor, American Studies, Cultural Theory, Gay & Lesbian Studies, Humanities *Richard Morrison*
Executive Editor, Anthropology, Geography, Political & Social Theory, Race & Ethnic Studies, Sociology, Urban Studies, Native American Studies *Carrie Mullen*

Founded 1927. Publishes academic books for scholars and selected general interest titles: American studies, anthropology, art and aesthetics, cultural theory, film and media studies, gay and lesbian studies, geography, literary theory, political and social theory, race and ethnic studies, sociology and urban studies. No original fiction or poetry. About 110 titles a year. No unsolicited mss. Welcomes synopses and proposals sent by mail (no e-mails). See website for submission details.

Minotaur
See **St Martin's Press LLC**

University Press of Mississippi
3825 Ridgewood Road, Jackson,
MS 39211–6492
☎001 601 432 6205 Fax 001 601 432 6217
✉ press@ihl.state.ms.us
www.upress.state.ms.us

Director *Seetha Srinivasan*
Editor-in-Chief *Craig Gill*

Founded 1970. Non-profit book publisher partially supported by the eight State universities. Publishes scholarly and trade titles in literature, history, American culture, Southern culture, African-American, women's studies, popular culture, folklife, ethnic, performance, art, architecture and photography and other liberal arts.
IMPRINTS **Muscadine Books** *Craig Gill* Regional trade titles. **Banner Books** Paperback reprints of significant fiction and non-fiction. REPRESENTED worldwide. UK representatives: **Roundhouse Publishing Group**. About 60 titles a year. Send letter of enquiry, prospectus, table of contents and sample chapter prior to submission of full mss.
ROYALTIES annually.

University of Missouri Press
2910 LeMone Boulevard, Columbia,
MO 65201
☎001 573 882 7641 Fax 001 573 884 4498
www.system.missouri.edu/upress

Director *Beverly Jarrett*

Founded 1958. Publishes academic: history, literary criticism, intellectual history and related humanities disciplines and occasional volumes of short stories. About 60 titles a year. Best approach is by letter. Send one short story for consideration, and synopses for academic work.

Modern Library
See **Random House Publishing Group**

William Morrow
See **HarperCollins Publishers, Inc.**

MTV Books
See **Pocket Books**

Muscadine Books
See **University Press of Mississippi**

Mysterious Press
See **Warner Books Inc.**

NAL
See **Penguin Group (USA) Inc.**

University of Nebraska Press
233 North 8th Street, Lincoln,
NE 68588–0255
☎001 402 472 3581 Fax 001 402 472 6214
✉ pressmail@unl.edu
www.nebraskapress.unl.edu

Chairman *Paul Royster*

Founded 1941. Publishes scholarly, Native American studies, history of the American West, literary and cultural studies, music, Jewish studies, military history, sports history, environmental history. IMPRINT **Bison Books**. 152 titles in 2003. No unsolicited mss; welcomes synopses and ideas for books. Send enquiry letter in the first instance with description of project and sample material. No original fiction, children's books or poetry.
ROYALTIES annually.

University of Nevada Press
MS 166, Reno, NV 89557–0076
☎001 775 784 6573 Fax 001 775 784 6200
www.nvbooks.nevada.edu

Director *Joanne O'Hare*

Founded 1961. Publishes scholarly and popular books; serious fiction, Native American studies, natural history, Western Americana, Basque studies and regional studies. About 25 titles a year. Unsolicited material welcome if it fits in with areas published, or offers a 'new and exciting' direction.
ROYALTIES twice-yearly.

New American Library
See **Penguin Group (USA) Inc.**

University Press of New England
One Court Street, Suite 250, Lebanon,
NH 03766
☎001 603 448 1533 Fax 001 603 448 7006
www.upne.com

Director & Editor-in-Chief *Richard Abel*
Executive Editor *Phyllis Deutsch*

Founded 1970. A scholarly books publisher sponsored by five institutions of higher education in the region: Brandeis, Dartmouth, University of Vermont, Tufts and the University of New Hampshire. Publishes general and scholarly non-fiction and Hardscrabble Books fiction of New England. OVERSEAS ASSOCIATES Canada – University of British Columbia; UK, Europe, Middle East – European University Press Group;

Australia, New Zealand, Asia & the Pacific – East-West Export Books. About 80 titles a year. Unsolicited material welcome.
ROYALTIES annually.

University of New Mexico Press
1720 Lomas Boulevard NE, Albuquerque,
NM 87131–0001
☎001 505 277 2346 Fax 001 505 277 9270
www.unmpress.com

Director *Luther Wilson*
Editor-in-Chief *David V. Holtby*

Founded 1929. Publishes scholarly and regional books. No fiction, how-to, humour, self-help or technical.

University of North Texas Press
PO Box 311336, Denton, TX 76203–1336
☎001 940 565 2142 Fax 001 940 565 4590
✉ rchrisman@unt.edu
www.unt.edu/untpress

Director *Ronald Chrisman*

Founded 1987. Publishes folklore, regional interest, contemporary, social issues, Texas history, military history, women's issues, multicultural. Publishes annually the winners of the Vassar Miller Poetry Prize and the Katherine Anne Porter Prize in Short Fiction. About 15 titles a year. No unsolicited mss; synopses and ideas welcome.
ROYALTIES annually.

Northwestern University Press
629 Noyes Street, Evanston, IL 60208
☎001 847 491 2046 Fax 001 847 491 8150
✉ nupress@northwestern.edu
www.nupress.northwestern.edu

Chairman *Peter Hayes*
Managing Director *Donna Shear*

Publishes general and academic books: philosophy, theatre and performance studies, Slavic studies, Latino fiction and biography, contemporary fiction, poetry. No children's, art books. IMPRINTS **Hydra**; **Latino Voices** Editorial Head *Susan Betz*. 60 titles in 2003. Unsolicited mss, synopses and ideas welcome; approach by mail.
ROYALTIES annually.

W.W. Norton & Company, Inc.
500 Fifth Avenue, New York,
NY 10110–0017
☎001 212 354 5500 Fax 001 212 869 0856
www.wwnorton.com

Vice-President/Managing Editor *Nancy K. Palmquist*

Founded 1923. Publishes fiction and non-fiction, college textbooks and professional books. About 300 titles a year.

Odyssey Classics
See **Harcourt Trade Division**

University of Oklahoma Press
1005 Asp Avenue, Norman,
OK 73019–6051
☎001 405 325 2000 Fax 001 405 325 4000
www.oupress.com

Director *John N. Drayton*

Founded 1928. Publishes general scholarly non-fiction only: American Indian studies, American West, classical studies, anthropology, natural history and political science. About 100 titles a year.

Olive Branch Press
See **Interlink Publishing Group, Inc.**

One World
See **Random House Publishing Group**

Onyx
See **Penguin Group (USA) Inc.**

Open Forum
See **Krieger Publishing Co.**

Orbit
See **Krieger Publishing Co.**

Outdoor Bible Series
See **Doubleday Broadway Publishing Group**

Owl Books
See **Henry Holt & Company Inc.**

Palgrave
See **St Martin's Press LLC**

Paragon House
2285 University Avenue, Suite 200, St Paul, MN 55114–1635
☎001 651 644 3087 Fax 001 651 644 0997
✉ paragon@paragonhouse.com
www.paragonhouse.com

Executive Director *Dr Gordon L. Anderson*

Founded 1982. Publishes non-fiction: reference and academic. Subjects include history, religion, philosophy, spirituality, Jewish interest, political science, international relations, psychology.

ROYALTIES twice-yearly.

Paulist Press
997 Macarthur Boulevard, Mahwah, NJ 07430
☎001 201 825 7300 Fax 001 201 825 8345
✉ sales@paulistpress.com
www.paulistpress.com

Owner *Missionary Society of St Paul the Apostle, New York*
Publisher *Fr. Lawrence Boadt*
Managing Editor *Paul McMahon*

Founded in 1866 by the Paulist Fathers as the Catholic Publication Society, it is now one of the largest Catholic publishing houses in the world. Publishes religious, spiritual, theology and children's religious books. IMPRINTS **Paulist Press** *Paul McMahon* Spirituality, ministry resources, ethics and social issues, ecumenical and inter-religious; *Chris Bellitto* Theology and philosophy, children's religious. **HiddenSpring** *Paul McMahon* General religious trade books. 90 titles a year. Unsolicited mss, synopses and ideas welcome; approach through direct mail with IRCs for return postage of material and/or letter. No New Age, Evangelical Christian books.

Pearson Scott Foresman
1900 E Lake Avenue, Glenview, IL 60025
☎001 847 729 3000 Fax 001 847 729 8910
✉ firstname.lastname@scottforesman.com
www.scottforesman.com

President *Paul McFall*

Founded 1896. Publishes elementary education materials. No unsolicited material.

Pelican Publishing Company
Box 3110, Gretna LA 70054–3110
☎001 504 368 1175
www.pelicanpub.com

Editor-in-Chief *Nina Kooij*

Publishes general non-fiction: popular history, cookbooks, travel, art, business, children's, editorial cartoon, architecture, golf, Scottish interest, collectibles guides and motivational. About 100 titles a year. Initial enquiries required for all submissions.

Pelion Press
See **The Rosen Publishing Group, Inc.**

Penguin Group (USA) Inc.
375 Hudson Street, New York, NY 10014
☎001 212 366 2000 Fax 001 212 366 2666
✉ online@penguingroup.com

www.penguin.com
CEO *David Shanks*
President *Susan Petersen Kennedy*

The second-largest trade book publisher in the world. Publishes fiction and non-fiction in hardback and paperback; adult and children's.
ADULT DIVISION IMPRINTS Hardcover: **Avery** (see entry); **Dutton**; **G.P. Putnam's Sons**; **Gotham Books**; **Hudson Street Press**; **Jeremy P. Tarcher/Putnam**; **The Penguin Press**; **Portfolio**; **Riverhead Books**; **Sentinel**; **Viking**; Trade Paperback: **Ace**; **Alpha**; **Berkley**; **HP Books**; **New American Library**; **Perigee**; **Penguin Books**; **Plume**; **Riverhead**; **Roc**. Mass Market Paperback: **Ace**; **Berkley**; **DAW**; **Jove**; **Onyx**; **Roc**; **Signet**.
CHILDREN'S DIVISION: Hardcover: **Dial Books for Young Readers** (see entry); **Dutton Children's Books**; **Frederick Warne**; **G.P. Putnam's Sons** (see entry); **Philomel Books**; **Viking Children's Books**. Paperback: **Firebird**; **Puffin Books**; **Speak**; **Razorbill**. Mass Merchandise: **Grosset & Dunlap**; **Price Stern Sloan**. No unsolicited mss.
ROYALTIES twice-yearly.

University of Pennsylvania Press
4200 Pine Street, Philadelphia,
PA 19104–4011
☎001 215 898 6261 Fax 001 215 898 0404
www.upenn.edu/pennpress
Director *Eric Halpern*

Founded 1890. Publishes serious non-fiction: scholarly, reference, professional, textbooks and semi-popular trade. No original fiction or poetry. About 75 titles a year. No unsolicited mss but synopses and ideas for books welcome.
ROYALTIES annually.

Perennial
See **HarperCollins Publisers, Inc.**

Perigee
See **Penguin Group (USA) Inc.**

Perseus Books Group
387 Park Avenue S, 12th Floor, New York,
NY 10016
☎001 212 340 8100 Fax 001 212 340 8115
www.perseusbooksgroup.com
President/CEO *Jack McKeown*

Founded 1997. Subsidiary of Perseus Capital LLC. Publishes general, academic and professional. IMPRINTS **Basic Books**; **Perseus Publishing**; **Counterpoint Press**; **Da Capo Press**; **Fisher Books**; **PublicAffairs**. No unsolicited mss.

Philomel Books
See **Penguin Group (USA) Inc.**

Picador USA
See **St Martin's Press LLC**

Players Press
PO Box 1132, Studio City CA 91614-0132
☎001 818 789 4980
CEO *William-Alan Landes*

Founded 1965 as a publisher of plays; now publishes across the entire range of performing arts: plays, musicals, theatre, film, cinema, television, costume, puppetry, plus technical theatre and cinema material. OVERSEAS SUBSIDIARIES in Canada, Australia, Germany and the UK. No unsolicited mss; synopses/ideas welcome. Send query letter s.a.e. for response.
ROYALTIES twice-yearly.

Plenum Publishers
See **Kluwer Academic Publishers**

Plume
See **Penguin Group (USA) Inc.**

Pocket Books
1230 Avenue of the Americas, New York,
NY 10020
☎001 212 698 1260 Fax 001 212 698 7284
www.simonsays.com
Executive VP/Publisher *Louise Burke*

Founded 1939. A division of **Simon & Schuster Adult Publishing Group**. Publishes trade paperbacks and hardcovers; mass-market, reprints and originals. IMPRINTS **Downtown Press**; **Pocket Star**; **MTV Books**.

Portfolio
See **Penguin Group (USA) Inc.**

Presidio Press
See **Random House Publishing Group**

Price Stern Sloan
See **Penguin Group (USA) Inc.**

Primary Source Media
See **Gale**

Professional Practices
See **Krieger Publishing Co.**

Prometheus Books

59 John Glenn Drive, Amherst,
NY 14228–2197
☎001 800 421 0351 Fax 001 716 691 0137
✉ editorial@prometheusbooks.com
www.prometheusbooks.com

Chairman *Paul Kurtz*
Editor-in-Chief *Steven L. Mitchell*

Founded 1969. Publishes books and journals
for the educational, scientific professional,
library, popular and consumer markets; adult
non-fiction, literary classics, popular science,
philosophy and young readers. IMPRINT
Humanity Books Acquisitions Editor *Ann
O'Hear*. About 100 titles a year. Unsolicited
mss, synopses and ideas for books welcome.
    ROYALTIES twice-yearly.

Promissor Inc
See **Houghton Mifflin Co.**

Public History
See **Krieger Publishing Co.**

PublicAffairs
See **Perseus Books Group**

Puffin Books
See **Penguin Group (USA) Inc.**

G.P. Putnam's Sons (Children's)

345 Hudson Street, New York, NY 10014
☎001 212 366 2000
www.penguingroup.com
President/Publisher *Nancy Paulsen*
Executive Editor *Kathryn Dawson*

A children's book imprint of Penguin Young
Readers Group, a member of **Penguin Group
(USA) Inc.** Publishes picture books, middle-
grade fiction and young adult fiction.

Quill
See **HarperCollins Publishers, Inc.**

Rand McNally

PO Box 7600, Chicago, IL 60680
☎001 847 329 8100 Fax 001 847 673 0539
www.randmcnally.com
President/CEO *Rob Apatoff*

Founded 1856. Publishes world atlases and maps,
road atlases of North America and Europe, city
and state maps of the United States and Canada,
educational wall maps, atlases and globes, plus

children's products. Includes electronic multimedia products. IMPRINT **Rand McNally for
Kids**.

Random House Publishing Group

1745 Broadway, New York, NY 10019
☎001 212 782 9000
www.randomhouse.com
President/Publisher *Gina Centrello*

Publishes fiction, non-fiction, science fiction in
hardcover, trade paperback and mass market.
    IMPRINTS **Ballantine Books**; **Ballantine
Reader's Circle**; **Del Rey**; **Del Rey/Lucas
Books**; **Fawcett**; **Ivy**; **Modern Library**; **One
World**; **Presidio Press**; **Random House**;
Random Trade Paperbacks; **Villard**. No
unsolicited mss.

Rawson Associates
See **Simon & Schuster Adult Publishing
Group**

Rayo
See **HarperCollins Publishers, Inc.**

Razorbill
See **Penguin Group (USA) Inc.**

Reader's Digest Association Inc

Reader's Digest Road, Pleasantville,
NY 10570–7000
☎001 914 238 1000 Fax 001 914 238 4559
www.rd.com
Chairman/CEO *Thomas Ryder*

Publishes home maintenance reference, cookery, DIY, health, gardening, children's books;
videos and magazines.

Red Feather Books
See **Henry Holt & Company Inc.**

Red Wagon Books
See **Harcourt Trade Division**

ReganBooks
See **HarperCollins Publishers, Inc.**

Fleming H. Revell
See **Baker Book House**

Riverhead Books
See **Penguin Group (USA) Inc.**

The Riverside Publishing Co.
See **Houghton Mifflin Co.**

Roaring Brook Press
See **The Millbrook Press, Inc.**

Roc
See **Penguin Group (USA) Inc.**

The Rosen Publishing Group, Inc.
29 East 21st Street, New York, NY 10010
☎001 212 777 3017 Fax 001 212 777 0277
www.rosenpublishing.com

President *Roger Rosen*
Vice-President *Gina Strazzabosco-Hayn*

Founded 1950. Publishes non-fiction books (supplementary to the curriculum, reference and self-help) for a young adult audience. Reading levels are years 7–12, 4–6 (books for teens with literacy problems), and 5–9. Subjects include conflict resolution, character building, health, safety, drug abuse prevention, self-help and multicultural titles. IMPRINT **Pelion Press**. 140 titles a year. For all imprints, write with outline and sample chapters.

Rutgers University Press
100 Joyce Kilmer Avenue, Piscataway,
NJ 08854–8099
☎001 732 445 7762 Fax 001 732 445 7039
rutgerspress.rutgers.edu

Director *Marlie Wasserman*
Associate Director/Editor-in-Chief *Leslie Mitchner*

Founded 1936. Publishes scholarly books, regional, social sciences and humanities. About 80 titles a year. Unsolicited mss, synopses and ideas for books welcome. No original fiction or poetry.
ROYALTIES annually.

St James Press
See **Gale**

St Martin's Press LLC
175 Fifth Avenue, New York, NY 10010
☎001 212 674 5151 Fax 001 212 420 9314
✉ inquiries@stmartins.com
www.stmartins.com

CEO (Holtzbrinck) *John Sargent*
President/Publisher (Trade Division) *Sally Richardson*

Founded 1952. A subsidiary of **Macmillan Publishers** (UK), St Martin's Press made its name and fortune by importing raw talent from the UK to the States and has continued to buy heavily in the UK. Publishes general fiction, especially mysteries and crime; and adult non-fiction: history, self-help, political science, travel, biography, scholarly, popular reference, college textbooks.
IMPRINTS **Picador USA**; **Griffin** (Trade paperbacks); **St Martin's Paperbacks** (Mass market); **Thomas Dunne Books**; **Minotaur**; **Palgrave**; **Truman Talley Books**. All submissions via legitimate literary agents only.

Scarecrow Press Inc.
4501 Forbes Boulevard, Suite 200, Lanham,
MD 20706
☎001 301 459 3366 Fax 001 301 429 5747
www.scarecrowpress.com

President *Jed Lyons*
Publisher/Editorial Director *Edward Kurdyla*

Founded 1950 as a short-run publisher of library reference books. Acquired by **University Press of America, Inc.** in 1995 which is now part of Rowman and Littlefield Publishing Group. Publishes reference, scholarly and monographs (all levels) for libraries. Reference books in all areas except sciences, specialising in the performing arts, music, cinema and library science. About 160 titles a year. Unsolicited mss welcome but material will not be returned unless requested and accompanied by return postage. Unsolicited synopses and ideas for books welcome.
ROYALTIES annually.

Schirmer Reference
See **Gale**

Anne Schwartz Books
See **Simon & Schuster Children's Publishing**

Scholastic Library Publishing
90 Old Sherman Turnpike, Danbury,
CT 06816
☎001 203 797 3500 Fax 001 203 797 3657
www.scholasticlibrary.com

President *Greg Worrell*

Publishes juvenile non-fiction, encyclopedias, speciality reference sets and picture books.
DIVISIONS/IMPRINTS **Children's Press**; **Grolier Educational**; **Grolier Online**; **Franklin Watts**. About 500 titles a year.

Scott Foresman
See **Pearson Scott Foresman**

Scribner
See **Simon & Schuster Adult Publishing Group**

Charles Scribner & Sons
See **Gale**

Seal Press
See **Avalon Publishing Group**

Sentinel
See **Penguin Group (USA) Inc.**

Seven Stories Press
140 Watts Street, New York, NY 10013
☎001 212 226 8760 Fax 001 212 226 1411
✉ info@sevenstories.com
www.sevenstories.com
CEO *Daniel Simon*
Founded 1995. Named by *Publishers Weekly* in 2001 as the fastest growing independent publisher in America. Publishes fiction, literature, literary translations, memoirs, political non-fiction, health, history, current affairs. DIVISION **Siete Cuentos Editorial** *Sara Villa*. *Overseas subsidiaries:* Turnaround Publishing Services, UK; Tower Books, Australia; Hushion House, Canada. No unsolicited mss; synopses and ideas from agents welcome or send query letter. No children's or business books.
ROYALTIES twice-yearly.

Shoemaker & Hoard Publishers
See **Avalon Publishing Group**

Siete Cuentos Editorial
See **Seven Stories Press**

Signet
See **Penguin Group (USA) Inc.**

Silhouette Books
233 Broadway, Suite 1001, New York, NY 10279
☎001 212 553 4200 Fax 001 212 227 8969
Editorial Director *Tara Gavin*
Founded 1979 as an imprint of Simon & Schuster and was acquired by a wholly owned subsidiary of Toronto-based Harlequin Enterprises Ltd in 1984. Publishes category, contemporary romance fiction and historical romance fiction only.
IMPRINTS **Silhouette Romance** *Mavis Allen*; **Silhouette Bombshell** *Lynda Curnyn*; **Silhouette Desire** *Melissa Jeglinski*; **Silhouette Special Edition** *Gail Chasan*; **Silhouette Intimate Moments** *Leslie Wainger*; **Harlequin Historicals** *Tracy Farrell*; **Luna Books** *Theresa Hussey*; **Steeple Hill** *Joan Marlow Golan*; **Love Inspired** publishes a line of inspirational con-temporary romances with stories designed to 'lift readers' spirits and gladden their hearts'.
See also **Harlequin Mills & Boon Ltd** under *UK Publishers*. OVERSEAS ASSOCIATES worldwide. Over 360 titles a year across a number of lines. No unsolicited mss. Submit query letter in the first instance or write for detailed submission guidelines/tip sheets.
ROYALTIES twice-yearly.

Silver Whistle Books
See **Harcourt Trade Division**

Simon & Schuster Adult Publishing Group (Division of Simon & Schuster, Inc)
1230 Avenue of the Americas, New York, NY 10020
☎001 212 698 7000 Fax 001 212 698 7007
www.simonsays.com
President *Carolyn K. Reidy*
Publishes fiction and non-fiction. DIVISIONS **The Free Press** VP & Editorial Director *Dominick Anfuso*; **Fireside/Touchstone** VP & Editor-in-Chief Trish Todd; **Scribner** VP & Editor-in-Chief *Nan Graham*; **Simon and Schuster** Senior VP & Editor-in-Chief *Michael V. Korda*; **Pocket Books** (see entry).
IMPRINTS **Atria Books; H.&R. Block; Lisa Drew Books; Fireside; The Free Press; Rawson Associates; Scribner; Scribner Classics; Scribner Paperback Fiction; S&S Libros eñ Espanol; Simon & Schuster; Touchstone**. No unsolicited mss.
ROYALTIES twice-yearly.

Simon & Schuster Children's Publishing
1230 Avenue of the Americas, New York, NY 10020
☎001 212 698 7200
President/Publisher *Rick Richter*
VP/Publisher, Hardcover & Paperback Imprints *Brenda Bowen*
A division of the Simon & Schuster Consumer Group. Publishes pre-school to young adult, picture books, hardcover and paperback fiction, non-fiction, trade, library and mass-market titles.
IMPRINTS **Aladdin Books** *Ellen Krieger* Picture books, paperback fiction and non-fiction reprints and originals, and limited series for ages pre-school to young adult; **Atheneum Books for Young Readers** *Ginee Seo* Picture books, hardcover fiction and non-fiction books across

all genres for ages three to young adult. Two lines within this imprint are **Jean Karl Books** quality fantasy-fiction and **Anne Schwartz Books** distinct picture books and high-quality fiction; **Little Simon** *Robin Corey* Mass-market novelty books (pop-ups, board books, colouring & activity) and merchandise (book and audio-cassette) for ages birth through eight; **Margaret K. McElderry Books** *Margaret K. McElderry, Emma Dryden* Picture books, hardcover fiction and non-fiction trade books for children ages three to young adult; **Simon & Schuster Books for Young Readers** *Elizabeth Law* Picture books, hardcover fiction and non-fiction for children ages three to young adult. **Simon Spotlight** *Jennifer Bergstrom* New imprint devoted exclusively to children's media tie-ins and licensed properties. About 480 titles a year. For submissions to all imprints: send envelope (US size 10) for guidelines, attention: *Manuscript Submissions Guidelines.*

Simon Spotlight
See **Simon & Schuster Children's Publishing**

Southern Illinois University Press
PO Box 3697, Carbondale, IL 62902–3697
☎001 618 453 2281 Fax 001 618 453 1221
www.siu.edu/~siupress

Director *John F. Stetter*

Founded 1956. Publishes scholarly and general interest non-fiction books and educational materials. 50 titles a year.

ROYALTIES annually.

Speak
See **Penguin Group (USA) Inc.**

Stackpole Books
5067 Ritter Road, Mechanicsburg, PA 17055
☎001 717 796 0411 Fax 001 717 796 0412
www.stackpolebooks.com

President *David Ritter*
Vice President/Editorial Director *Judith Schnell*

Founded 1933. Publishes outdoor sports, fishing, nature, Pennsylvania and regional, military reference, history. About 100 titles a year.

ROYALTIES twice-yearly.

Stanford University Press
1450 Page Mill Road, Palo Alto, CA 94304–1124
☎001 650 723 9434 Fax 001 650 725 3457
www.sup.org

Managing Director *Geoffrey R.H. Burn*

Founded 1925. Publishes non-fiction: scholarly works in all areas of the humanities, social sciences, history and literature, also professional lists in business, economics and law. About 120 titles a year. No unsolicited mss; query in writing first.

Steeple Hill
See **Silhouette Books**

Sterling Publishing Co. Inc.
387 Park Avenue South, 5th Floor, New York, NY 10016–8810
☎001 212 532 7160 Fax 001 212 213 2495
www.sterlingpub.com

VP/Publisher *Andrew Martin*
President/CEO *Charles Nurnberg*
VP, Editorial *Steve Magnuson*

Founded 1949. Publishes illustrated non-fiction: reference and information books, science, business, nature, arts and crafts, home improvement, history, photography, children's humour, complementary health, wine and food, sports, music, psychology, New Age, woodworking, pets, hobbies, gardening, puzzles. Submission guidelines available.

Syracuse University Press
621 Skytop Road, Suite 110, Syracuse, NY 13244–5290
☎001 315 443 5534 Fax 001 315 443 5545
www.SyracuseUniversityPress.syr.edu

Acting Director *Peter B. Webber*

Founded 1943. Publishes scholarly books in the following areas: Middle East studies, Middle East literature in translation, international affairs, Irish studies, Iroquois studies, women and religion, Jewish studies, medieval studies, religion and politics, television, geography and regional books. Also co-publishes with a number of organisations such as the American University of Beirut and the Adirondack Museum. About 50 titles a year. No unsolicited mss. Send query letter with IRCs.

ROYALTIES annually.

The Taft Group
See **Gale**

Nan A. Talese
See **Doubleday Broadway Publishing Group**

Jeremy P. Tarcher/Putnam
See **Penguin Group (USA) Inc.**

Tempest
See **HarperCollins Publishers, Inc.**

Temple University Press
1601 N. Broad Street, 083–42, Philadelphia, PA 19122–6099
☎001 215 204 8787 Fax 001 215 204 4719
www.temple.edu/tempress
Editor-in-Chief *Janet M. Francendese*

Founded 1969. Publishes scholarly books. Authors generally academics. Letter of inquiry with brief outline. Include fax/e-mail address. About 60 titles a year.

University of Tennessee Press
110 Conference Center Bldg., Knoxville, TN 37996
☎001 865 974 3321 Fax 001 865 974 3724
✉ custserv@utpress.org
www.utpress.org
Managing Editor *Stan Ivester*
Acquisitions Editor *Scot Danforth*

Founded in 1940. Publishes scholarly and regional non-fiction. Submission guidelines are posted on the website.
ROYALTIES annually.

University of Texas Press
PO Box 7819, Austin, TX 78713-7819
☎001 512 471 7233/Editorial: 471 4278
Fax 001 512 232 7178
www.utexas.edu/utpress/
Director *Joanna Hitchcock*
Assistant Director/Editor-in-Chief *Theresa J. May*

Publishes scholarly and regional non-fiction: anthropology, architecture, classics, environmental studies, humanities, social sciences, geography, language studies, literary modernism; Latin American/Latino/Mexican American/Middle Eastern/Native American studies, natural history and ornithology, regional books (Texas and the southwest). Unsolicited material welcome in above subject areas only. About 90 titles a year and 11 journals.
ROYALTIES annually.

Thorndike Press
See **Gale**

Three Rivers Press
See **The Crown Publishing Group**

Thunder's Mouth Press
See **Avalon Publishing Group**

Times Books
See **Henry Holt & Company Inc.**

Touchstone
See **Simon & Schuster Adult Publishing Group**

Transaction Publishers Ltd
c/o Rutgers – The State University of New Jersey, 35 Berrue Circle, Piscataway, NJ 08854–8042
☎001 732 445 2280 Fax 001 732 445 3138
✉ ihorowitz@transactionpub.com
www.transactionpub.com
Chairman *I.L. Horowitz*
President *Mary E. Curtis*

Founded 1962. Independent publisher of academic social scientific books, periodicals and serials.

Truman Talley Books
See **St Martin's Press LLC**

Twayne Publishers
See **Gale**

Twenty-First Century Books
See **The Millbrook Press, Inc.**

Tyndale House Publishers, Inc.
PO Box 80, Wheaton, IL 60189
☎001 630 668 8310 Fax 001 630 784 5011
www.tyndale.com
President *Mark D. Taylor*

Founded 1962. Books cover a wide range of categories from non-fiction to gift books, theology, doctrine, Bibles, fiction, children's and youth. Also produces video material, calendars and audio books for the same market. No poetry. Non-denominational religious publisher of around 300 titles a year for the evangelical Christian market. No unsolicited mss. Synopses and ideas considered. Send query letter summarising contents of book and length. Include a brief biography, detailed outline and three sample chapters. IRCs essential for response or return of material. No audio cassettes, disks or video tapes in lieu of mss. Response time around 12–16 weeks. No phone calls or e-mail submissions. Send s.a.e. for submission guidelines.
ROYALTIES annually.

University Press of America, Inc.
4501 Forbes Boulevard, Suite 200, Lanham, MD 20706
☎001 301 459 3366 Fax 001 301 429 5748

www.univpress.com
President/Publisher *James E. Lyons*
VP/Editorial Director *Judith L. Rothman*

Founded 1974. Publishes scholarly monographs, college and graduate level textbooks. No children's, elementary or high school. About 450 titles a year. Submit outline or request proposal questionnaire.

ROYALTIES annually.

UXL
See **Gale**

Viking/Viking Children's Books
See **Penguin Group (USA) Inc.**

Villard
See **Random House Publishing Group**

University of Virginia Press
PO Box 400318, Charlottesville,
VA 22904–4318
☎001 434 924 3468 Fax 001 434 982 2655
✉ upressvirginia@virginia.edu
www.upress.virginia.edu

Director *Penelope J. Kaiserlian*

Founded 1963. Publishes academic books in humanities and social science with concentrations in American history, African-American studies, architecture, Victorian literature, Caribbean literature and ecocriticism. No unsolicited mss; will consider synopses and ideas for books if in their specific areas of concentration. Approach by mail for full proposal; e-mail for short inquiry. No fiction, children's, poetry or academic books outside interests specified above.

ROYALTIES annually.

Voyager Books
See **Harcourt Trade Division**

J. Weston Walch, Publisher
PO Box 658, Portland, ME 04104
☎001 207 772 2846 Fax 001 207 772 3105
www.walch.com

President *John Thoreson*
Editor-in-Chief *Susan Blair*

Founded 1927. Publishes supplementary educational materials for middle and secondary schools across a wide range of subjects, including English/language arts, literacy, special needs, mathematics, social studies, science and school-to-career. Always interested in ideas from secondary school teachers who develop materials in the classroom. Proposal letters, synopses and ideas welcome.

Walk Worthy Press
See **Warner Books Inc.**

Walker & Co.
104 Fifth Avenue, New York, NY 10011
☎001 212 727 8300 Fax 001 212 727 0984
www.walkerbooks.com (trade non-fiction)
www.walkeryoungreaders.com (BFYR)

Contact *Submissions Editor*

Founded 1959. Publishes children's fiction and non-fiction and adult non-fiction. Please contact the following editors in advance before sending any material to be sure of their interest, then follow up as instructed: **Trade Non-fiction** *George Gibson* Permission and documentation must be available with mss. Submit prospectus first, with sample chapters and marketing analysis. **Books for Young Readers** *Emily Easton* Fiction and non-fiction for all ages. Query before sending non-fiction proposals. Especially interested in picture books – fiction and non-fiction, historical and contemporary fiction for middle grades and young adults. BFYR will consider unsolicited submissions.

Frederick Warne
See **Penguin Group (USA) Inc.**

Warner Books Inc.
1271 Avenue of the Americas, New York,
NY 10020
☎001 212 522 7200 Fax 001 212 522 7991
www.twbookmark.com

Senior Vice-President/Publisher *Jamie Raab*
Associate Publishers *Les Pockell, Ivan Held*

Founded 1961. A subsidiary of Time Warner Book Group. Publishes fiction and non-fiction, audio books.

IMPRINTS **Aspect** *Jaime Levine;* **Mysterious Press** *Kristen Weber;* **Time Warner Audio Books; Warner Vision; Walk Worthy Press; Warner Faith; Warner Forever.** About 250 titles a year. No unsolicited mss.

Washington State University Press
PO Box 645910, Pullman, WA 99164–5910
☎001 509 335 3518 Fax 001 509 335 8568
✉ wsupress@wsu.edu
www.wsu.edu/wsupress

Editor *Glen Lindeman*

Founded 1928. Publishes hardcover originals, trade paperbacks and reprints. Publishes mainly on the history, prehistory, culture, politics and natural history of the Northwest United States (Washington, Idaho, Oregon, Montana, Alaska) and British Columbia, but works that focus on national topics or other regions may also be considered if they have a Northwest connection. Subjects include history, biography, cooking/food history, nature/environment, politics. 8–10 titles a year. Queries welcome.

ROYALTIES annually.

Franklin Watts
See **Scholastic Library Publishing**

Wheeler Publishing
See **Gale**

John Wiley & Sons, Inc.
111 River Street, Hoboken, NJ 07030
☎001 201 748 6000   Fax 001 201 748 6088
✉ info@wiley.com
www.wiley.com

President/CEO *William J. Pesce*

Founded 1807. Acquired a major stake in Oxford-based business publisher Capstone Publishing Ltd in 2000. Publishes professional and trade print and electronic products in the following fields: culinary arts and hospitality, architecture/design, business, accounting, psychology, non-profit institution management, computers, engineering and general interest. Educational products: the sciences, mathematics, engineering, accounting, business, teacher education, modern languages, religion. Scientific, technical and medical publishers of journals, encyclopedias, available in print and electronic media. About 1500 titles a year. Unsolicited mss not accepted.

The University of Wisconsin Press
1930 Monroe Street, 3rd Floor, Madison, WI 53711–2059
☎001 608 263 1110   Fax 001 608 263 1120
✉ uwiscpress@uwpress.wisc.edu
www.wisc.edu/wisconsinpress

Director *Robert A. Mandel*

Founded 1936. Publishes scholarly, general interest non-fiction and regional books about Wisconsin and the mid-west. About 50 titles a year. No unsolicited mss; proposals (sent by mail) welcome. 'No unrevised dissertations, no Festschrifts, no genre, no how-to.'

Helen & Kurt Wolff Books
See **Harcourt Trade Publishers**

Zondervan Publishing House
5300 Patterson Avenue SE, Grand Rapids, MI 49530
☎001 616 698 6900   Fax 001 616 698 3439
www.zondervan.com

President/Chief Executive *Bruce E. Ryskamp*

Founded 1931. Subsidiary of **HarperCollins Publishers, Inc.** Publishes Protestant religion, Bibles, books, audio & video, computer software, calendars and speciality items.

US Literary Agents

★ = Members of the **Association of Authors' Representatives, Inc.**

Dominick Abel
Literary Agency, Inc★
146 West 82nd Street, Suite 1B, New York, NY 10024
☎001 212 877 0710 Fax 001 212 595 3133
✉ agency@dalainc.com
Contact *Dominick Abel*
Established 1975. No scripts, children's books or poetry. COMMISSION Home 15%; Translation 20%. No unsolicited material. Send query letter with s.a.e. in the first instance. No reading fee.

Altair Literary Agency LLC★
PO Box 11656, Washington, DC 20008
☎001 202 237 8282
✉ APedolsky *or*
NSmith@AltairLiteraryAgency.com
www.AltairLiteraryAgency.com
Contacts *Andrea Pedolsky, Nicholas T. Smith*
Founded 1996. Handles historical, pre-20th century, literary and women's related fiction; activity/novelty science books for children; and non-fiction covering history, biography, women's issues, contemporary issues, illustrated/photography, history of science and invention. COMMISSION Home 15%; Foreign 20%. Send query letter and proposal for non-fiction; query letter and synopsis for fiction. Return postage essential. No reading fee. 'Authors who wish to query via e-mail, and who do so via our website, will be given priority.'

Miriam Altshuler Literary Agency★
53 Old Post Road North, Red Hook, NY 12571
☎001 845 758 9408
Contact *Sara McGhee*
Founded 1994. Handles literary and commercial fiction; general non-fiction, psychology, biography. No romance, science fiction, mysteries, thrillers or self-help. COMMISSION Home 15%; Foreign/Translation 20%. Send query letter and synopsis in the first instance with return postage (no e-mail or fax queries). No reading fee.

Bart Andrews & Associates Inc
7510 Sunset Boulevard, Suite 100, Los Angeles, CA 90046–3418

☎001 310 271 9916
Contact *Bart Andrews*
Founded 1982. General non-fiction: show business, biography and autobiography, film books, trivia, TV and nostalgia. No scripts. No fiction, poetry, children's or science. No books of less than major commercial potential. Specialises in working with celebrities on autobiographies. COMMISSION Home & Translation 15%. OVERSEAS ASSOCIATE Abner Stein, UK. No unsolicited mss. 'Send a brilliant letter (with IRCs for response) extolling your manuscript's virtues. Sell me!' No reading fee.

Malaga Baldi Literary Agency
233 West 99th Street, Suite 19C, New York, NY 10025
☎001 212 222 3213
✉ MBALDI@aol.com
Contact *Malaga Baldi*
Founded 1986. Handles quality fiction and non-fiction. No scripts. No westerns, men's adventure, science fiction/fantasy, romance, how-to, young adult or children's. COMMISSION 15%. OVERSEAS ASSOCIATES **Abner Stein**, UK; Japan Uni; Eliane Benisti, France; **Marsh Agency**. Writers of fiction should send query letter describing the novel plus IRCs. Allow ten weeks *minimum* for response. For non-fiction, approach in writing with a proposal, table of contents and two sample chapters. No reading fee.

The Balkin Agency, Inc.★
PO Box 222, Amherst, MA 01004
☎001 413 548 9835 Fax 001 413 548 9836
✉ balkin@crocker.com
Contact *Richard Balkin*
Founded 1973. Handles adult non-fiction only. COMMISSION Home 15%; Foreign 20%. No reading fee for outlines and synopses.

Loretta Barrett Books, Inc.★
101 Fifth Avenue, New York, NY 10003
☎001 212 242 3420 Fax 001 212 807 9579
Contacts *Loretta Barrett, Nick Mullendore*
Founded 1990. Handles all non-fiction and fiction genres except children's, poetry, science

fiction/fantasy. Specialises in women's fiction, history, spirituality. No scripts. COMMISSION Home 15%; Foreign 20%. No e-mail submissions. Send query letter with biography and return postage only in the first instance.

Meredith Bernstein Literary Agency, Inc.★

2112 Broadway, Suite 503A, New York, NY 10023
☎001 212 799 1007 Fax 001 212 799 1145
Contacts *Meredith Bernstein, Elizabeth Cavanaugh*

Founded 1981. Handles commercial and literary fiction, mysteries and non-fiction (women's issues, business, memoirs, health, current affairs, crafts). COMMISSION Home & Dramatic 15%; Translation 20%. OVERSEAS ASSOCIATES **Abner Stein**, UK; Lennart Sane, Holland, Scandinavia and Spanish language; Thomas Schluck, Germany; Bardon Chinese Media Agency; William Miller, Japan; Frederique Porretta, France; Agenzia Letteraria, Italy.

Bleecker Street Associates, Inc.★

532 LaGuardia Place, #617, New York, NY 10012
☎001 212 677 4492 Fax 001 212 388 0001

Founded 1984. Handles fiction – women's, mystery, suspense, literary; non-fiction – history, women's interests, parenting, health, relationships, psychology, sports, sociology, current events, biography, spirituality, New Age, business. No poetry, children's, westerns, science fiction, professional, academic. COMMISSION Home 15%; Foreign 25%. Send query letter in the first instance. Will only respond if envelope and return postage enclosed. No phone calls, faxes or e-mails. No reading fee.

The Blumer Literary Agency★

PO Box 20754, Park West Station, New York, NY 10025–1516
☎001 212 749 8853 Fax 001 212 749 1603
Contact *Olivia Blumer*

Founded 2002. Handles a broad range of commercial and literary fiction and non-fiction. Strong background in memoir, inspiration, commercial, literary fiction, illustrated and nonfiction. Specialist subject: cookery. No TV, film, radio or theatre scripts. No children's, science fiction and fantasy or romances. COMMISSION Home 15%; Foreign 20%; Translation 20%. Send initial introductory letter. No reading fee.

Book Deals, Inc.★

244 Fifth Avenue, Suite 2164, New York, NY 1001-7604
☎001 212 252 2701 Fax 001 212 591 6211
✉ bookdeals@aol.com
www.bookdealsInc.com
President *Caroline Carney*

Founded 1997. Handles health, finance, business, self-help, parenting, narrative non-fiction and literary fiction. No scripts, genre fiction, cookbooks, illustrated children's, coffee table books, travel guides, military history, paranormal experience. COMMISSION Home 15%; Foreign/Translation 20%. No unsolicited material; query letter welcome. No reading fee.

Georges Borchardt, Inc.★

136 East 57th Street, New York, NY 10022
☎001 212 753 5785 Fax 001 212 838 6518

Founded 1967. Works mostly with established/published authors. Specialises in fiction, biography, and general non-fiction of unusual interest. COMMISSION Home, UK & Dramatic 15%; Translation 20%. UK ASSOCIATE **Sheil Land Associates Ltd** (Richard Scott Simon), London. Unsolicited mss not read.

Brandt & Hochman Literary Agents, Inc.★

1501 Broadway, New York, NY 10036
☎001 212 840 5760
Contacts *Carl D. Brandt, Gail Hochman, Marianne Merola, Charles Schlessiger, Bill Contardi*

Founded 1914. Handles non-fiction and fiction. No poetry. COMMISSION Home & Dramatic 15%; Foreign 20%. UK ASSOCIATE **A.M. Heath & Co. Ltd**. No unsolicited mss. Approach by letter describing background and ambitions; include return postage. No reading fee.

Barbara Braun Associates, Inc★

104 Fifth Avenue, 7th Floor, New York, NY 10011
☎001 212 604 9023 Fax 001 212 604 9041
✉ bba.230@earthlink.net
www/barbarabraunagency.com
Contacts *Barbara Braun, John Baker*

Founded 1995. Handles literary and mainstream, women's and historical fiction, also serious non-fiction, including psychology and biography. Also young adult and mystery books. Specialises in art history, archaeology, architecture and cultural history. No scripts, self-help, science fiction. COMMISSION Home

15%; Foreign 20%. OVERSEAS ASSOCIATE Chandler Crawford Literary Agency. No unsolicited mss; send query letter in the first instance. No reading fee.

Browne & Miller Literary Associates

410 S. Michigan Avenue, Suite 460, Chicago, IL 60605
☎001 312 922 3063 Fax 001 312 922 1905
✉ mail@browneandmiller.com

President *Danielle Egan-Miller*

Founded 1971. Handles commercial and literary fiction, and practical non-fiction with wide appeal. No scripts, juvenile, science fiction or poetry. COMMISSION Home 15%; Foreign/Translation 20%. OVERSEAS ASSOCIATES in Europe, Latin America, Japan and Asia. In the first instance, send query letter with return postage. No unsolicited material. No reading fee.

Pema Browne Ltd, Illustration and Literary Agents

11 Tena Place, Valley Cottage, NY 10989
☎001 845 268 0029
✉ ppbltd@earthlink.net
www.pemabrowneltd.com

Contacts *Pema Browne, Perry Browne*

Founded 1966. ('Pema rhymes with Emma.') Handles mass-market mainstream and hardcover fiction: romance, business, children's picture books and young adult; non-fiction: how-to and reference. COMMISSION Home 15%; Translation 20%; Overseas authors 20%. No unsolicited mss; send query letter with IRCs. No fax or e-mail queries. Also handles illustrators' work. No longer accepting screenplays. 'We are accepting very few new clients at this time.'

Sheree Bykofsky Associates, Inc.★

577 Second Avenue, PMB 109, New York, NY 10016
☎001 212 244 4144
✉ shereebee@aol.com

Contact *Sheree Bykofsky*

Founded 1991. Handles adult fiction and non-fiction. No scripts. No children's, young adult, horror, science fiction, romance, westerns, occult or supernatural. COMMISSION Home 15%; UK (including sub-agent's fee) 20%. No unsolicited mss. Send query letter first with brief synopsis or outline and writing sample (1–3 pp) for fiction. IRCs essential for reply or

return of material. 'Please do not send material via methods that require signature, such as FedEx, etc.' No phone calls. No reading fee.

Carlisle & Company LLC★

6 West 18th Street, New York, NY 10011
☎001 212 813 1881 Fax 001 212 813 9567
✉ mvc@carlisleco.com
www.carlisleco.com

Contacts *Michael V. Carlisle, Christy Fletcher, Emma Parry, Michelle Tessler*

Founded 1998. Handles history, science, travel, narrative non-fiction, literary and category fiction. No scripts, children's, juvenile, romance, science fiction/fantasy, mysteries. COMMISSION Home 15%; Foreign/Translation 20%. ASSOCIATES Co-agents in every major territory. No unsolicited mss. Query letter for fiction by mail or through website; proposal with query for non-fiction. No reading fee.

Maria Carvainis Agency, Inc.★

1350 Avenue of the Americas, Suite 2905, New York, NY 10019
☎001 212 245 6365 Fax 001 212 245 7196
✉ mca@mariacarvainisagency.com

President *Maria Carvainis*

Founded 1977. Handles fiction: literary and mainstream, contemporary women's, mystery, suspense, historical, young adult novels; non-fiction: business, finance, women's issues, politics, film, memoirs, reportage, biography, medicine, psychology and popular science. No film scripts unless from writers with established credits. No science fiction. COMMISSION Domestic & Dramatic 15%; Translation 20%. No faxed or e-mailed queries. No unsolicited mss; they will be returned unread. Queries only, with IRCs for response. No reading fee.

Castiglia Literary Agency★

1155 Camino del mar, #510, Del Mar, CA 92014
☎001 858 755 8761 Fax 001 858 755 7063
✉ jaclagency@aol.com

Contacts *Julie Castiglia, Winifred Golden*

Founded 1993. Handles fiction: literary, mainstream, ethnic; non-fiction: narrative, biography, science, health, parenting, memoirs, psychology, women's and contemporary issues. Specialises in science, biography and literary fiction. No scripts, horror or true crime. COMMISSION Home 15%; Foreign/Translation 25%. No unsolicited material; send query letter only in the first instance. No reading fee.

The Catalog Literary Agency
PO Box 2964, Vancouver, WA 98668
☎001 360 694 8531

Contact *Douglas Storey*

Founded 1986. Handles popular, professional and textbook material in all subjects, especially business, health, money, science, technology, computers, electronics and women's interests; also how-to, self-help, mainstream fiction and children's non-fiction. No genre fiction. No scripts, articles, screenplays, plays, poetry or short stories. COMMISSION 15%. No unsolicited mss. Query with an outline and sample chapters, and include IRCs. No reading fee.

Linda Chester & Associates★
Rockefeller Center, 630 Fifth Avenue, New York, NY 10111
☎001 212 218 3350 Fax 001 212 218 3343
✉ lcassoc@mindspring.com
www.lindachester.com

Contact *Linda Chester*

Founded 1978. Handles literary and commercial fiction and non-fiction in all subjects. No scripts, children's or textbooks. COMMISSION Home & Dramatic 15%; Translation 25%. No unsolicited mss or queries. No reading fee for solicited material.

Clausen, Mays & Tahan Literary Agency
PO Box 1015, New York, NY 10276
☎001 212 714 8181
✉ cmtassist@aol.com

Contacts *Stedman Mays, Mary M. Tahan*

Handles fiction and non-fiction work such as memoirs, biography, true crime, true stories, how-to, psychology, spirituality, relationships, style, health/nutrition, fashion/beauty, women's issues, humour and cookbooks. Some fiction. UK ASSOCIATE **David Grossman Literary Agency Ltd**. For fiction send synopsis and first ten pages. For non fiction send query letter only. Include IRCs.

Ruth Cohen, Inc.★
PO Box 2244, La Jolla, CA 92038–2244

Contact *Ruth Cohen*

Handles mystery, women's literature, romance, fiction, young adult and children's books. No scripts. No unsolicited mss; send synopsis and one sample chapter only. Include a brief, well thought-out synopsis, the opening ten pages (carefully edited) and return postage. No reading fee.

Frances Collin Literary Agent★
PO Box 33, Wayne, PA 19087–0033
☎001 610 254 0555 Fax 001 610 254 5029

Contact *Frances Collin*

Founded 1948. Successor to Marie Rodell. Handles general fiction and non-fiction. No scripts. OVERSEAS ASSOCIATES worldwide. No unsolicited mss. Send query letter only, with IRCs for reply, for the attention of *Marsha Kear*. No fax or telephone queries, please. No reading fee. Rarely accepts non-professional writers or writers not represented in the UK.

Don Congdon Associates, Inc.★
156 Fifth Avenue, Suite 625, New York, NY 10010–7002
☎001 212 645 1229 Fax 001 212 727 2688

Contacts *Don Congdon, Michael Congdon, Susan Ramer, Cristina Concepcion*

Founded 1983. Handles fiction and non-fiction. No academic, technical, romantic fiction or scripts. COMMISSION Home 15%; UK & Translation 19%. OVERSEAS ASSOCIATES worldwide. No unsolicited mss. Query letter with return postage in the first instance. No reading fee.

Cornerstone Literary Agency★
4500 Wilshire Boulevard, Los Angeles, CA 90010
☎001 323 930 6039 Fax 001 323 930 0407
✉ info@cornerstoneliterary.com
www.cornerstoneliterary.com

Contact *Helen Breitwieser*

Founded 1998. Handles literary and commercial fiction. Specialises in thrillers and commercial women's fiction. No scripts, children's, self-help, science fiction or fantasy. COMMISSION Home 15%; Foreign/Translation 20%. No unsolicited mss via mail, e-mail or fax; send query letter and one-page synopsis via fax or mail (enclosing return postage with latter). No reading fee.

Curtis Brown Ltd★
10 Astor Place, New York, NY 10003
☎001 212 473 5400

Book Rights *Laura Blake Peterson, Ellen Geiger, Peter L. Ginsberg, Emilie Jacobson, Ginger Knowlton, Maureen Walters, Mitchell Waters, Elizabeth Harding, Kirsten Manges*
Film & TV Rights *Timothy Knowlton, Edwin Wintle*
Translation *Dave Barbor*

Founded 1914. Handles general fiction and non-fiction. Also some scripts for film, TV and theatre. OVERSEAS ASSOCIATES Representatives in all major foreign countries. No unsolicited mss; queries only, with IRCs for reply. No reading fee.

Joan Daves Agency

21 West 26th Street, New York, NY 10010-1003
☎001 212 685 2663   Fax 001 212 685 1781
Director *Jennifer Lyons*

Founded 1952. See also **Writers House LLC**. Literary fiction and non-fiction. No romance or textbooks. No scripts. Send query letter in the first instance. COMMISSION Home 15%; Dramatic/Film 15%; Foreign 20%. 'A detailed synopsis seems valuable only for non-fiction work. Material submitted should specify the author's background, publishing credits and similar pertinent information.' No reading fee.

Sandra Dijkstra Literary Agency★

PMB 515, 1155 Camino Del Mar, Del Mar, CA 92014
☎001 858 755 3115   Fax 001 858 794 2822
Contact *Babette Sparr*

Founded 1981. Handles quality and commercial non-fiction and fiction, including some genre fiction. No scripts. No westerns, contemporary romance or poetry. Willing to look at children's projects. Specialises in quality fiction, mystery/ thrillers, narrative non-fiction, psychology, self-help, science, health, business, memoirs, biography. 'Dedicated to promoting new and original voices and ideas.' COMMISSION Home 15%; Translation 20%. OVERSEAS ASSOCIATES **Abner Stein**, UK; Ursula Bender, Agence Hoffman, Germany; Licht & Burr, Scandinavia; Luigi Bernabo, Italy; Sandra Bruna, Spain; Caroline Van Gelderen, Netherlands; M. Kling (La Nouvelle Agence), France; William Miller, The English Agency, Japan. For fiction: send brief synopsis (one page) and first 50 pages; for non-fiction: send proposal with overview, chapter outline, author biog, two sample chapters and profile of competition. All submissions should be accompanied by IRCs. No reading fee.

Dunham Literary Inc★

156 Fifth Avenue, Suite 625, New York, NY 10010
☎001 212 929 0994   Fax 001 212 929 0904
www.dunhamlit.com
Contacts *Jennie Dunham, Irina Kendall*

Founded 2000. Handles literary fiction and non-fiction, New Age spirituality, mysteries

and children's (from picture books through young adult). No scripts, romance, westerns, horror, science-fiction/fantasy or poetry. COMMISSION Home 15%; Foreign/Translation 20%. OVERSEAS ASSOCIATE UK & Europe: **A.M. Heath & Co. Ltd**. The Rhoda Weyr Agency is now a division of Dunham Literary Inc. No unsolicited material. Send query letter (with return postage) giving information on the author and ms. No e-mail or faxed queries; see the website for further contact information. No reading fee.

Dystel & Goderich Literary Management★

One Union Square West, Suite 904, New York, NY 10003
☎001 212 627 9100   Fax 001 212 627 9313
www.dystel.com

Contacts *Jane Dystel, Miriam Goderich, Stacey Glick, Michael Bourret, Jim McCarthy, Jessica Papin*

Founded 1991. Handles non-fiction and fiction. Specialises in politics, history, biography, cookbooks, current affairs, celebrities, commercial and literary fiction. No reading fee.

Anne Edelstein Literary Agency LLC★

20 West 22nd Street, #1603, New York, NY 10010
☎001 212 414 4923   Fax 001 212 414 2930
✉ rights@aeliterary.com
www.aeliterary.com
Contact *Emilie Stewart*

Founded 1990. No film, TV, theatre or radio scripts. COMMISSION Home 15%; Translation 20%. OVERSEAS ASSOCIATES Ulf Toregard; Eliane Benisti; Caroline van Gelderen; Luigi Bernabo; Rachel Calder, **The Sayle Literary Agency**; Raquel de la Concha; Petra Eggers. Unsolicited material welcome; send query letter in the first instance.

Educational Design Services, Inc.

PO Box 253, Wantagh, NY 11793
☎001 718 539 4107/516 221 0995
✉ linder.eds@juno.com *or* eselzer@nyc.rr.com
President *Bertram Linder*
Vice-President *Edwin Selzer*

Founded 1979. Specialises in educational material and textbooks for sale to school markets. COMMISSION Home 15%; Foreign 25%. IRCs must accompany submissions.

Ethan Ellenberg Literary Agency★

548 Broadway, #5E, New York, NY 10012
☎001 212 431 4554 Fax 001 212 941 4652
✉ agent@ethanellenberg.com
www.ethanellenberg.com

Contacts *Ethan Ellenberg, Michael Psaltis*

Founded 1984. Handles fiction: commercial, genre, literary and children's; non-fiction: history, biography, business, science, health, cooking, current affairs. Specialises in commercial fiction, thrillers, suspense and romance. No scripts, poetry or short stories. COMMISSION Home 15%; Translation 20%. Prefers submissions by mail with return postage. For fiction send synopsis and three chapters; for non-fiction send proposal and sample chapters, if available. No reading fee. For e-mail submissions send query letter only; no attachments.

Ann Elmo Agency, Inc.★

60 East 42nd Street, New York, NY 10165
☎001 212 661 2880/1 Fax 001 212 661 2883

Contacts *Lettie Lee, Mari Cronin, Andree Abecassis*

Founded in the 1940s. Handles literary and romantic fiction, mysteries and mainstream; also non-fiction in all subjects, including biography and self-help. Some children's (8–12-year-olds). COMMISSION Home 15–20%. Query letter with outline of project in the first instance. No reading fee.

The Fogelman Literary Agency★

7515 Greenville Avenue, Suite 712, Dallas, TX 75231
☎001 214 361 9956 Fax 001 214 361 9553
✉ FogLit@aol.com
www.fogelman.com

Also at: 445 Park Avenue, 9th Floor, New York, NY 10022

Contacts *Evan Fogelman, Linda Kruger, Helen Brown*

Founded 1989. Handles non-fiction and fiction: romance (including historical and contemporary) and some mystery/suspense. No scripts, poetry, westerns, science fiction/fantasy or children's books. COMMISSION Home 15%; Foreign/ Translation 10%. OVERSEAS ASSOCIATES Thomas Schluck Agency; Shin Won Literary Agency; Bastei Lubbe Taschenbucher; Big Apple Tuttle-Mori Agency. No unsolicited material. Published authors are welcome to call but unpublished authors should send query by e-mail or letter with return postage. No reading fee.

ForthWrite Literary Agency & Speakers Bureau

A subsidiary of Keller Media, Inc,
100 Wilshire Boulevard, Suite 625,
Santa Monica, CA 90401
☎001 310 456 5698 Fax 001 310 456 6589
✉ agent@KellerMedia.com
www.KellerMedia.com

Contact *Wendy L. Keller*

Founded 1988. Specialises in promoting the careers of speakers and authors in the categories of biography, business (marketing, finance, management and sales), alternative health, cookery, gardening, nature, popular psychology, history, self-help, home and health, crafts, computer, how-to. Handles electronic, foreign (translation and distribution) and resale rights for previously published books. COMMISSION Foreign 20%. Send query letter with IRCs. No reading fee.

Jeanne Fredericks Literary Agency, Inc.★

221 Benedict Hill Road, New Canaan, CT 06840
☎001 203 972 3011 Fax 001 203 972 3011
✉ jfredrks@optonline.net

Contact *Jeanne Fredericks*

Founded 1997. Handles quality adult non-fiction, usually of a practical and popular nature by authorities in their fields. Specialises in health, gardening, business, self-help, reference. No fiction, juvenile, poetry, essays, politics, academic or textbooks. COMMISSION Home 15%; Foreign 25% (with co-agent) or 20% (direct). No unsolicited material; send query by e-mail (no attachments) or letter with return postage in the first instance. No reading fee.

Robert A. Freedman Dramatic Agency, Inc.★

Suite 2310, 1501 Broadway, New York, NY 10036
☎001 212 840 5760

President *Robert A. Freedman*
Senior Vice-President *Selma Luttinger*
Vice-President *Robin Kaver*
Associate *Marta Praeger*

Founded 1928 as Brandt & Brandt Dramatic Department, Inc. Took its present name in 1984. Works mostly with established authors. Specialises in plays, film and TV scripts. COMMISSION Dramatic 10%. Unsolicited mss not read.

Gelfman Schneider Literary Agents, Inc.★

250 West 57th Street, Suite 2515, New York, NY 10107

☎001 212 245 1993 Fax 001 212 245 8678

Contacts *Deborah Schneider, Jane Gelfman*

Founded 1919 (London), 1980 (New York). Formerly John Farquharson Ltd. Works mostly with established/published authors. Specialises in general trade fiction and non-fiction. No poetry, short stories or screenplays. COMMISSION Home 15%; Dramatic 15%; Foreign 20%. OVERSEAS ASSOCIATE **Curtis Brown Group Ltd**, UK. No reading fee for outlines. Submissions must be accompanied by IRCs. No e-mail queries please.

Sanford J. Greenburger Associates, Inc.★

55 Fifth Avenue, 15th Floor, New York, NY 10003

☎001 212 206 5600 Fax 001 212 463 8718

www.greenburger.com

Contacts *Heide Lange, Faith Hamlin, Theresa Park, Elyse Cheney, Daniel Mandel*

Handles fiction and non-fiction. No unsolicited mss. First approach with query letter, sample chapter and synopsis. No reading fee.

The Charlotte Gusay Literary Agency

10532 Blythe Avenue, Los Angeles, CA 90064

☎001 310 559 0831 Fax 001 310 559 2639

✉ gusay1@aol.com (queries only)

www.mediastudio.com/gusay

Contact *Charlotte Gusay*

Founded 1988. Handles fiction, both literary and commercial, books to film and screenplays, plus non-fiction: children's and adult humour, parenting, gardening, women's and men's issues, feminism, psychology, memoirs, biography, travel. No science fiction, horror, short pieces or collections of stories. COMMISSION Home 15%; Dramatic 10%; Translation & Foreign 25%. No unsolicited mss; send query letter by snailmail first, then if your material is requested, send succinct outline and first three sample chapters for fiction, or proposal for non-fiction. No response without IRCs or self-addressed stamped envelope. No reading fee but may require a processing fee to cover handling of material.

Joy Harris Literary Agency, Inc.★

156 Fifth Avenue, Suite 617, New York, NY 10010

☎001 212 924 6269 Fax 001 212 924 6609

✉ gen.office@jhlitagent.com

Contacts *Joy Harris, Stephanie Abou, Leslie Daniels, Alexia Paul*

Handles adult non-fiction and fiction. COMMISSION Home & Dramatic 15%; Foreign 20%. No unsolicited mss. Query letter in the first instance. No reading fee.

John Hawkins & Associates, Inc.★

71 West 23rd Street, Suite 1600, New York, NY 10010

☎001 212 807 7040 Fax 001 212 807 9555

✉ jha@jhaliterary.com

Contacts *John Hawkins, William Reiss*

Founded 1893. Handles film and TV rights. COMMISSION Apply for rates. No unsolicited mss; send queries with 1–3-page outline and one-page c.v. IRCs necessary for response. No reading fee.

The Jeff Herman Agency, LLC

PO Box 1522, Stockbridge, MA 01262

☎001 413 298 0077 Fax 001 413 298 8188

✉ jeff@jeffherman.com

www.jeffherman.com

Contact *Jeffrey H. Herman*

Handles all areas of non-fiction, textbooks and reference. No scripts. COMMISSION Home 15%; Translation 10%. No unsolicited mss. Query letter with IRCs in the first instance. No reading fee. Jeff Herman publishes a useful reference guide to the book trade called *Herman's Guide to Book Editors, Publishers & Literary Agents* (Kalmbach).

Frederick Hill Bonnie Nadell Inc.

1842 Union Street, San Francisco, CA 94123

☎001 415 921 2910 Fax 001 415 921 2802

Contacts *Fred Hill, Bonnie Nadell, Irene Moore*

Founded 1979. General fiction and non-fiction. No scripts. COMMISSION Home & Dramatic 15%; Foreign 20%. *Overseas associate* **Mary Clemmey Literary Agency**, UK. Send query letter detailing past publishing history if any. IRCs required.

IMG Literary US

See entry under *UK Literary Agents*

Janklow & Nesbit Associates
445 Park Avenue, New York, NY 10022
☎001 212 421 1700 Fax 001 212 980 3671

Partners *Morton L. Janklow, Lynn Nesbit*
Senior Vice-President *Anne Sibbald*
Agents *Tina Bennett, Luke Janklow, Richard Morris, Eric Simonoff*

Founded 1989. Handles fiction and non-fiction; commercial and literary. See also **Janklow & Nesbit (UK) Ltd** under **UK Literary Agents**. No unsolicited mss.

JCA Literary Agency, Inc★
27 West 20th Street, Suite 1103, New York, NY 10011
☎001 212 807 0888 Fax 001 212 807 0461

Contacts *Jeff Gerecke, Tony Outhwaite, Peter Steinberg*

Founded 1978. Handles general fiction and non-fiction. No scripts, poetry, science fiction/fantasy or children's books. COMMISSION Home 15%; Foreign 20%. OVERSEAS ASSOCIATE **Vanessa Holt Ltd**, UK. No unsolicited mss; send query letter with return postage. No reading fee.

Kirchoff/Wohlberg, Inc.★
866 United Nations Plaza, Suite 525, New York, NY 10017
☎001 212 644 2020 Fax 001 212 223 4387
www.kirchoffwohlberg.com

Authors' Representative *Elizabeth Pulitzer-Voges*

Founded 1930. Handles books for children and young adults, specialising in children's picture books. No adult material. No scripts for TV, radio, film or theatre. Send letter of enquiry with synopsis or outline and writing sample plus IRCs for reply or return. No reading fee.

Harvey Klinger, Inc.★
301 West 53rd Street, New York, NY 10019
☎001 212 581 7068 Fax 001 212 315 3823
harveyklinger.com

Contact *Harvey Klinger*

Founded 1977. Handles mainstream fiction and non-fiction. Specialises in commercial and literary fiction, psychology, health and science. No scripts, poetry, computer or children's books. COMMISSION Home 15%; Foreign 25%. OVERSEAS ASSOCIATES in all principal countries. Welcomes unsolicited material; send by e-mail or post (no faxes). No reading fee.

Linda Konner Literary Agency★
10 West 15 Street, Suite 1918, New York, NY 10011
☎001 212 691 3419
✉ ldkonner@cs.com

Contact *Linda Konner*

Founded 1996. Handles non-fiction only, specialising in health, self-help, diet/fitness, pop psychology, relationships, parenting, personal finance. Also some pop culture/celebrities. COMMISSION Home 15%; Foreign 25%. Books must be written by or with established experts in their field. No scripts, fiction, poetry or children's books. No unsolicited material; send one-page query with return postage. No reading fee.

Peter Lampack Agency, Inc.
551 Fifth Avenue, Suite 1613, New York, NY 10176
☎001 212 687 9106
✉ ALampack@verizon.net

Contact *Andrew Lampack*

Founded in 1977. Handles commercial fiction: male action and adventure, contemporary relationships, historical, mysteries and suspense, literary fiction; also non-fiction from recognised experts in a given field, plus biographies, autobiographies. Also handles theatrical, motion picture, and TV rights from book properties. No original scripts or screenplays, series or episodic material. COMMISSION Home & Dramatic 15%; Translation & UK 20%. Best approach by letter in first instance. No reply without s.a.e. 'We will respond within three weeks and invite the submission of manuscripts which we would like to examine.' No reading fee. No unsolicited mss.

Michael Larsen/Elizabeth Pomada Literary Agency★
1029 Jones Street, San Francisco, CA 94107
☎001 415 673 0939
✉ larsenpoma@aol.com
www.larsenpomada.com

Contact (non-fiction) *Michael Larsen*
Contact (fiction) *Elizabeth Pomada*

Founded 1972. Handles adult fiction and non-fiction – literary and commercial. No scripts, poetry, children's, science fiction. COMMISSION Home 15%; Foreign 20–30%. OVERSEAS ASSOCIATES **David Grossman Literary Agency Ltd**, British rights; Chandler Crawford (foreign rights). Fiction: send first ten pages with

2-page synopsis and s.a.e.; non-fiction: e-mail title and promotion plan. Consult website for guidelines.

Sarah Lazin Books★

126 Fifth Avenue, Suite 300, New York, NY 10011
☎001 212 989 5757 Fax 001 212 989 1393

Contacts *Sarah Lazin, Paula Balzer*

Handles adult narrative non-fiction in pop culture, biography, social issues, music reference, photography, fiction. Specialises in music and biography. COMMISSION Home 15%; Foreign 10%. Send query letter with references and writing sample.

The Ned Leavitt Agency★

70 Wooster Street, Suite 4F, New York, NY 10012
www.nedleavittagency.com
President *Ned Leavitt*
Agent *Britta Steiner*

Specialises in creativity, spirituality, health and literary fiction. No scripts or genre fiction. COMMISSION Home 15%. Send 2–3 sample chapters with synopsis, by post, with s.a.e. No reading fee.

Lescher & Lescher Ltd★

47 East 19th Street, New York, NY 10003
☎001 212 529 1790 Fax 001 212 529 2716

Contacts *Robert Lescher, Mickey Choate*

Founded 1964. Handles a broad range of serious non-fiction including current affairs, history, biography, memoir, government, politics, law, contemporary issues, sociology, psychology, popular culture, food and wine, literary and commercial fiction including mysteries and thrillers; some children's books. Specialises in wine books and cookbooks. No poetry, science fiction, New Age, spiritual, romance. COMMISSION Home 10%; Foreign 20%. No unsolicited manuscripts – please query first. No reading fee.

Sterling Lord Literistic, Inc.

65 Bleecker Street, New York, NY 10012
☎001 212 780 6050 Fax 001 212 780 6095

Contacts *Philippa Brophy, Chris Calhoun*

Founded 1979. Handles all genres, fiction and non-fiction, plus scripts for TV and film. COMMISSION Home 15%; UK & Translation 20%. No unsolicited mss. Prefers letter outlining all non-fiction. No reading fee.

Lowenstein–Yost Associates Inc★

121 West 27th Street, Suite 601, New York NY 10001
☎001 212 206 1630 Fax 001 212 727 0280
www.lowensteinyost.com

Agents *Barbara Lowenstein, Nancy Yost, Eileen Cope, Dorian Karchmar*

Founded 1976. Handles fiction: literary and commercial, women's, mainstream, romance, mystery, thrillers. Non-fiction: narrative, health, business, women's issues, adventure travel, science, spirituality, psychology, social issues, ethnic and cultural issues, history, biography and the arts. No textbooks, westerns, science fiction, cookery or children's books. COMMISSION Home 15%; Foreign/Translation 20%. OVERSEAS ASSOCIATES in all major countries. Fiction: send query letter, synopsis and first chapter; nonfiction: send query with proposal, if available, or overview. Include return postage. No reading fee.

Carol Mann Agency★

55 Fifth Avenue, New York NY 10003
☎001 212 206 5635 Fax 001 212 675 4809
✉ carol.mann@carolmannagency.com *or* kristy@carolmannagency.com *or* emily@carolmannagen

Contacts *Carol Mann, Emily Nurkin, Kristy Mayer*

Founded 1977. Handles literary fiction and narrative non-fiction, including psychology, biography, memoirs, history, pop culture, spirituality. No scripts or genre fiction. COMMISSION Home 15%; Foreign 20%. No unsolicited material; send query letter with return postage. No reading fee.

Manus & Associates Literary Agency, Inc.★

425 Sherman Avenue, Suite 200, Palo Alto CA 94306
✉ ManusLit@ManusLit.com
www.ManusLit.com

Also at: 445 Park Avenue, New York, NY 10022

Contacts *Janet Manus, Jillian Manus, Jandy Nelson, Stephanie Lee, Donna Levin, Penny Nelson*

Handles commercial and literary fiction; non-fiction, including true crime, self-help, memoirs, history, pop culture and popular science. No scripts, science fiction/fantasy, westerns, romance, horror, poetry or children's books.

COMMISSION Home 15%; Foreign 25%. No unsolicited mss. Fiction: send query letter and first 30 pages; non-fiction: query letter and proposal. Include return postage. No reading fee.

The Evan Marshall Agency★

Six Tristam Place, Pine Brook,
NJ 07058–9445
☎001 973 882 1122 Fax 001 973 882 3099
✉ evanmarshall@TheNovelist.com
www.TheNovelist.com

Contact *Evan Marshall*

Founded 1987. Handles general adult fiction. COMMISSION Home 15%; UK & Translation 20%. No unsolicited mss; send query letter first. No reading fee.

Helen Merrill Ltd★

295 Lafayette Street, Suite 915, New York,
NY 10012–2700
☎001 212 226 5015 Fax 001 212 226 5079
✉ litasst@hmlartists.com

Contacts *Patrick Herold, Morgan Jenness,*
Beth Blickers

Founded 1974. Handles film and television scripts and plays only. No unsolicited material. New clients through professional reference only.

Mews Books Ltd

c/o Sidney B. Kramer, 20 Bluewater Hill,
Westport, CT 06880
☎001 203 227 1836 Fax 001 203 227 1144
✉ mewsbooks@aol.com (initial contact only; submission by regular mail)

Contacts *Sidney B. Kramer, Fran Pollak*

Founded 1970. Handles adult fiction and non-fiction, children's, pre-school and young adult. No scripts, short stories or novellas (unless by established authors). Specialises in cookery, medical, health and nutrition, scientific non-fiction, children's and young adult. COMMISSION Home 15%; Film & Translation 20%. OVERSEAS ASSOCIATE **Abner Stein**, UK. Unsolicited material welcome. Presentation must be professional and should include summary of plot/characters, one or two sample chapters, personal credentials and brief on target market, all suitable for forwarding to a publisher. No reading fee. Charges for photocopying, postage expenses, telephone calls and other direct costs. Principal agent is an attorney and former publisher (a founder of Bantam Books). Offers consultation

service through which writers can get advice on a contract or on publishing problems.

Doris S. Michaels
Literary Agency Inc.★

1841 Broadway, Suite 903, New York,
NY 10023
☎001 212 265 9474 Fax 001 212 265 9480
✉ query@dsmagency.com
www.dsmagency.com

Contact *Doris Michaels*

Handles literary fiction that has a commercial appeal and strong screen potential and women's fiction; non-fiction: current affairs, biography and memoirs, self-help, business, history, health, classical music, sports, women's issues, computers and pop culture. No action/adventure, suspense, science fiction, romance, New Age, religion/spirituality, gift books, art books, fantasy, thrillers, mysteries, westerns, occult and supernatural, horror, historical fiction, poetry, children's literature, humour or travel books. COMMISSION Home 15% Send query letter via e-mail with a one-page synopsis and include a short paragraph detailing credentials. No reading fee. .

Howard Morhaim
Literary Agency★

11 John Street, Suite 407, New York,
NY 10038
☎001 212 529 4433 Fax 001 212 995 1112

Contact *Howard Morhaim*

Founded 1979. Handles general adult fiction and non-fiction. No scripts. No children's or young adult material, poetry or religious. COMMISSION Home 15%; UK & Translation 20%. OVERSEAS ASSOCIATES worldwide. No unsolicited mss. Send query letter with synopsis and sample chapters for fiction; query letter with outline or proposal for non-fiction. Include return postage. No reading fee.

Henry Morrison, Inc.

PO Box 235, Bedford Hills, NY 10507
☎001 914 666 3500 Fax 001 914 241 7846

Contact *Henry Morrison*

Founded 1965. Handles general fiction, crime and science fiction, and non-fiction. No scripts unless by established writers. COMMISSION Home 15%; UK & Translation 25%. Unsolicited material welcome but send query letter with outline (1–5 pp) in the first instance. No reading fee.

The Jean V. Naggar Literary Agency*

216 East 75th Street, Suite 1-E, New York,
City NY 10021

Contacts *Jean Naggar, Alice Tasman, Jennifer Weltz*

Founded 1978. Handles strong mainstream fiction, literary fiction, memoir, biography, sophisticated self-help, popular science and psychology. No scripts. COMMISSION Home 15%; Foreign 20%. No unsolicited material; send query letter *only* with return postage initially. No reading fee.

B.K. Nelson Literary Agency

84 Woodland Road, Pleasantville,
NY 10570

☎001 914 741 1322 Fax 001 914 741 1324

✉ bknelson4@cs.com

www.bknelson.com

Also at: 1565 Paseo Vida, Palm Springs,
CA 92264

☎001 760 880 7800 Fax 001 760 778 0034

President *Bonita K. Nelson*

Vice President *Leonard 'Chip' Ashbach*

Editorial Director *John W. Benson*

Founded 1979. Specialises in novels, business, self-help, how-to, political, autobiography, celebrity biography. Major motion picture and TV documentary success. COMMISSION 20%. Lecture Bureau for Authors founded 1994; Foreign Rights Catalogue established 1995; BK Nelson Infomercial Marketing Co. 1996, primarily for authors and endorsements, and BKNelson, Inc. for motion picture production in 1998. Signatory to Writers Guild of America, West (WGAW). No unsolicited mss. Letter of inquiry. Reading fee charged.

New England Publishing Associates, Inc.*

Box 5, Chester, CT 06412

☎001 860 345 7323 Fax 001 860 345 3660

✉ nepa@nepa.com

www.nepa.com

Contacts *Elizabeth Frost-Knappman, Edward W. Knappman, Kris Schiavi, Ron Formica, Victoria S. Harlow* (photo/research editor)

Founded 1983. Handles non-fiction. Specialises in current affairs, business, history, science, women's studies, reference, psychology, politics, biography, true crime and literature. No textbooks or anthologies. No scripts, poetry or fiction. COM-MISSION Home 15%. OVERSEAS ASSOCIATES throughout Europe and Japan; Rachel Calder, UK. Dramatic rights: Joel Gotler, Intellectual Property Group, Los Angeles. Unsolicited mss considered but query letter or phone call preferred first. No reading fee.

Richard Parks Agency*

PO Box 693, Salem, NY 12865

☎001 212 254 9067 Fax 001 212 228 1786

✉ rp@richardparksagency.com

Contact *Richard Parks*

Founded 1989. Handles general trade fiction and non-fiction: literary novels, mysteries and thrillers, commercial fiction, science fiction, biography, pop culture, psychology, self-help, parenting, medical, cooking, gardening, history, etc. No scripts. No technical or academic. COMMISSION Home 15%; UK & Translation 20%. OVERSEAS ASSOCIATES **The Marsh Agency; Barbara Levy Literary Agency**. No unsolicited mss. Fiction read by referral only. No reading fee.

James Peter Associates, Inc.*

PO Box 358, New Canaan, CT 06840

☎001 203 972 1070 Fax 001 203 972 1759

✉ gene_brissie@msn.com

President *Eugene Brissie*

Founded 1971. Non-fiction only. 'Many of our authors are historians, psychologists, physicians – all are writing trade books for general readers.' No scripts. No fiction or children's books. Specialises in history, popular culture, business, health, biography and politics. COMMISSION 15%. No unsolicited mss. Send query letter first with brief project outline, samples and biographical information. No reading fee.

Alison J. Picard Literary Agent

PO Box 2000, Cotuit, MA 02635

☎001 508 477 7192 Fax 001 508 477 7192
(notify before faxing)

✉ ajpicard@aol.com

Contact *Alison Picard*

Founded 1985. Handles mainstream and literary fiction, contemporary and historical romance, children's and young adult, mysteries and thrillers; plus non-fiction. No short stories or poetry. Rarely any science fiction and fantasy. Particularly interested in expanding non-fiction titles. COMMISSION 15%. *Overseas associate* **John Pawsey**, UK. Approach with written query. No reading fee.

Pinder Lane & Garon-Brooke Associates Ltd★

159 West 53rd Street, Suite 14–E, New York NY 10019
☎001 212 489 0880 Fax 001 212 489 7104
✉ pinderl@interport.net

Owner Agents *Dick Duane, Robert Thixton*

Founded 1951. Fiction and non-fiction. No category romance, westerns or mysteries. COMMISSION Home 15%; Dramatic 10–15%; Foreign 30%. OVERSEAS ASSOCIATES **Abner Stein**, UK; Translation: Rights Unlimited. No unsolicited mss. First approach by query letter. No reading fee.

PMA Literary & Film Management, Inc.

PO Box 1817, Old Chelsea Sta., New York, NY 10011
☎001 212 929 1222 Fax 001 212 206 0238
✉ pmalitfilm@aol.com
www.pmalitfilm.com

President *Peter Miller*
Associates *Scott Hoffman, Lisa Silverman*

Founded 1976. Commercial fiction and non-fiction. Specialises in books with motion picture and television potential, and in true crime. No poetry, pornography, non-commercial or academic. COMMISSION Home 15%; Dramatic 10–15%; Foreign 20–25%. No unsolicited mss. Approach by letter with one-page synopsis.

The Aaron M. Priest Literary Agency★

708 Third Avenue, 23rd Floor, New York, NY 10017
☎001 212 818 0344 Fax 001 212 373 9417

Founded 1974. Handles literary and commercial fiction. No scripts, children's fantasy or sci-fi. Submissions by mail only. No reading fee.

Susan Ann Protter Literary Agent★

110 West 40th Street, Suite 1408, New York, NY 10018
☎001 212 840 0480

Contact *Susan Ann Protter*

Founded 1971. Handles general fiction, mysteries, thrillers, science fiction and fantasy; non-fiction: history, general reference, biography, science, health and parenting. No romance, poetry, westerns, religious, children's or sport manuals. No scripts. COMMISSION Home & Dramatic 15%. OVERSEAS ASSOCIATES **Abner**

Stein, UK; agents in all major markets. First approach with letter, including IRCs. No reading fee.

Quicksilver Books, Literary Agents

508 Central Park Avenue, #5101, Scarsdale, NY 10583
☎001 914 722 4664 Fax 001 914 722 4664

President *Bob Silverstein*

Founded 1973. Handles literary fiction and mainstream commercial fiction: blockbuster, suspense, thriller, contemporary, mystery and historical; and general non-fiction, including self-help, psychology, holistic healing, ecology, environmental, biography, fact crime, New Age, health, nutrition, cookery, enlightened wisdom and spirituality. No scripts, science fiction and fantasy, pornographic, children's or romance. COMMISSION Home & Dramatic 15%; Translation 20%. UK material being submitted must have universal appeal for the US market. Unsolicited material welcome but must be accompanied by IRCs for response, together with biographical details, covering letter, etc. No reading fee.

Raines & Raines★

103 Kenyon Road, Medusa NY 12120
☎001 518 239 8311 Fax 001 518 239 6029

Contacts *Theron Raines, Joan Raines, Keith Korman*

Founded 1961. *Handles* general non-fiction. No scripts. COMMISSION Home 15%; Foreign & Translation 20%. No unsolicited material; send one-page letter in the first instance. No reading fee.

Reece Halsey North★

98 Main Street, #704, Tiburon, CA 94920
☎001 415 789 9191 Fax 001 415 789 9177
✉ info@reecehalseynorth.com
www.kimberleycameron.com

Also: Reece Halsey Agency, 8733 Sunset Blvd. #101, Los Angeles, CA 90069
☎001 310 652 2409 Fax 001 310 652 7595

Contact (Tiburon) *Kimberley Cameron*
Contact (Los Angeles) *Dorris Halsey*

Founded 1957. *Represents* literary and mainstream fiction, non-fiction. No scripts, poetry or children's books. COMMISSION Home 15%; Foreign 20%. Send query letter with first ten pages together with return postage. No e-mail submissions. No reading fee.

Helen Rees Literary Agency*

376 North Street, Boston, MA 02113–2103
☎001 617 227 9014 Fax 001 617 227 8762
✉ wwhelen@aol.com *or* joanmaz@aol.com *or*
agent10702@aol.com

Contact *Joan Mazmanian*
Associates *Ann Collette, Lorin Rees*

Founded 1982. Specialises in books on health
and business; also handles biography, autobiography and history; quality fiction. No scholarly
or technical books. No scripts, science fiction,
children's, poetry, photography, short stories,
cooking. COMMISSION Home 15%; Foreign
20%. No unsolicited mss; no email queries or
attachments. Send query letter with IRCs. No
reading fee.

Rights Unlimited, Inc.*

101 West 55th Street, Suite 2D, New York,
NY 10019
☎001 212 246 0900 Fax 001 212 246 2114
✉ bkurman@rightsunlimited.com

Contact *Bernard Kurman*

Founded 1985. Handles adult fiction, non-
fiction. No scripts, poetry, short stories, educational or literary works. COMMISSION Home
15%; Translation 20%. Query letter with synopsis preferred in the first instance. No reading
fee.

The Angela Rinaldi
Literary Agency*

PO Box 7877, Beverly Hills, CA 90212–7877
☎001 310 842 7665 Fax 001 310 837 8143
✉ amr@rinaldiliterary@com

Contact *Angela Rinaldi*

Founded 1995. Handles commercial and literary fiction; narrative non-fiction, practical and
pro-active self-help. No scripts, cookery, science fiction, westerns, romance, poetry,
children's/young adult. COMMISSION Home
15%; Foreign 20%. Send brief e-mail or query
letter with return postage in the first instance.
No reading fee.

B.J. Robbins Literary Agency*

5130 Bellaire Avenue, North Hollywood,
CA 91607
☎001 818 760 6602 Fax 001 818 760 6616
✉ robbinsliterary@aol.com

Contacts *B.J. Robbins, Regina Su Mangum*

Founded 1992. Handles literary fiction, narrative and general non-fiction. No scripts, genre
fiction, romance, horror, science fiction or
children's books. COMMISSION Home 15%;

Foreign/Translation 20%. OVERSEAS ASSOCI-
ATES **Abner Stein** and **The Marsh Agency**,
UK. Send covering letter with first three chapters or e-mail query in the first instance. No
reading fee.

Linda Roghaar
Literary Agency, Inc.*

133 High Point Drive, Amherst, MA 01002
☎001 413 256 1921 Fax 001 413 256 2636
✉ contact@LindaRoghaar.com
www.LindaRoghaar.com

Contact *Linda L. Roghaar*

Founded 1997. Handles fiction and non-fiction, specialising in religious titles. No science
fiction or horror. COMMISSION Home 15%;
Foreign/Translation rate varies. Send query by
e-mail or letter with return postage (for fiction,
include the first five pages). No reading fee.

The Rosenberg Group*

23 Lincoln Avenue, Marblehead, MA 01945
www.rosenberggroup.com
Contact *Barbara Collins Rosenberg*

Founded 1998. Handles non-fiction (please see
website for areas of interest), fiction, specialising
in romance (single title and category) and
women's; non-fiction, specialising in college
textbooks. No scripts, science fiction, true crime,
inspirational fiction, children's and young adult.
COMMISSION Home 15%; Foreign 25%. No unsolicited material; send query letter by post only.
No reading fee.

Rosenstone/Wender*

38 East 29th Street, 10th Floor, New York,
NY 10016
☎001 212 725 9445 Fax 001 212 725 9447

Contacts *Phyllis Wender, Susan Perlman Cohen,
Sonia E. Pabley*

Founded 1981. Handles fiction, non-fiction,
children's, and scripts for film, TV and theatre.
No material for radio. COMMISSION Home 15%;
Dramatic 10%; Foreign 20%. OVERSEAS ASSOCI-
ATES La Nouvelle Agence, France; Andrew
Nurnberg, Netherlands; The English Agency,
Japan; Mohrbooks, Germany; Ole Licht,
Scandinavia. No unsolicited mss. Send letter out-
lining the project, credits, etc. No reading fee.

The Sagalyn Literary Agency*

7201 Wisconsin Avenue, Suite 675, Bethesda,
MA 20814
☎001 301 718 6440 Fax 001 301 718 6444
✉ agency@sagalyn.com
www.sagalyn.com

Founded 1980. Handles mostly upmarket non-fiction with some fiction. No screenplays, romance, science fiction/fantasy, children's literature. No unsolicited material. See website for submissions procedure. No reading fee.

Victoria Sanders & Associates LLC★

241 Avenue of the Americas, Suite 11H, New York, NY 10014
☎001 212 633 8811 Fax 001 212 633 0525
✉ queriesvsa@hotmail.com
www.victoriasanders.com

Contacts *Victoria Sanders, Diane Dickensheid*

Founded 1993. Handles general trade fiction and non-fiction, plus ancillary film and television rights. COMMISSION Home & Dramatic 15%; Translation 20%. Please send all queries via e-mail.

Sandum & Associates

144 East 84th Street, New York, NY 10028
☎001 212 737 2011

Contact *Howard E. Sandum*

Founded 1987. Handles all categories of general adult non-fiction, plus occasional fiction. No scripts. No children's, poetry or short stories. COMMISSION Home & Dramatic 15%; Translation & Foreign 20%. *Overseas associate* Scott Ferris Associates. No unsolicited mss. Third-party referral preferred but direct approach by letter, with synopsis, brief biography and IRCs, is accepted. No reading fee.

Jack Scagnetti
Talent & Literary Agency

5118 Vineland Avenue, Suite 102, North Hollywood CA 91601
☎001 818 762 3871

Contact *Jack Scagnetti*

Founded 1974. Works mostly with established/published authors. Handles non-fiction, fiction, film and TV scripts. No reading fees. COMMISSION Home & Dramatic 10% (scripts), 15% (books); Foreign 15%.

Schiavone Literary Agency, Inc.

236 Trails End, West Palm Beach, FL 33413–2135
☎001 561 966 9294 Fax 001 561 966 9294
✉ profschia@aol.com
www.freeyellow.com/members8/schiavone/index.html

Branch office (June/July/Aug. only): 3671 Hudson Manor Terrace, Suite 11H, Bronx, NY 10463

☎/Fax 001 718 548 5332
President *James Schiavone*
Vice-President *Jennifer Duvall*

Founded 1996. Handles fiction and non-fiction (all genres). Specialises in biography, autobiography, celebrity memoirs. No poetry. COMMISSION Home 15%; Foreign & Translation 20%. OVERSEAS ASSOCIATES in Europe. No unsolicited mss; send query letter only with s.a.e. and IRCs. No response without s.a.e. For fastest response, e-mail queries of one page (no attachments) are acceptable and encouraged. No reading fee.

Susan Schulman,
A Literary Agency★

454 West 44th Street, New York, NY 10036
☎001 212 713 1633/4/5
Fax 001 212 581 8830
✉ schulman@aol.com
www.susanschulmanagency.com

Submissions Editor (books) *Christine Morin*
Submissions Editor (plays) *Brian Leifert*

Founded 1979. Specialises in non-fiction of all types but particularly in health and psychology-based self-help for men, women and families. Other interests include business, memoirs, the social sciences, biography, language and international law. Fiction interests include contemporary fiction, including women's, mysteries, historical and thrillers 'with a cutting edge'. Always looking for 'something original and fresh'. Represents properties for film and television, and works with agents in appropriate territories for translation rights. COMMISSION Home & Dramatic 15%; Translation 20%. OVERSEAS ASSOCIATES Plays: **Rosica Colin Ltd** and **The Agency Ltd**, UK; Commercial fiction: Laura Morris, UK. No unsolicited mss. Query first, including outline and three sample chapters with IRCs. No reading fee.

Scovil Chichak Galen
Literary Agency, Inc.★

381 Park Avenue South, Suite 1020, New York, NY 10016
☎001 212 679 8686 Fax 001 212 679 6710
✉ mailroom@scglit.com
www.scglit.com

Contacts *Russell Galen, Anna M. Ghosh, Jack Scovil*

Founded 1993. Handles all categories of books. No scripts. COMMISSION Home 15%; Foreign 20%. No unsolicited material; send query by e-mail or letter. No reading fee.

Shapiro-Lichtman – Talent Agency

8827 Beverly Boulevard, Los Angeles, CA 90048
☎001 310 859 8877 Fax 001 310 859 7153

Founded 1969. Works mostly with established/published authors. Handles film and TV scripts. COMMISSION Home & Dramatic 10%; Foreign 20%. Unsolicited mss will not be read.

Rosalie Siegel, International Literary Agency, Inc.★

1 Abey Drive, Pennington, NJ 08534
☎001 609 737 1007 Fax 001 609 737 3708
Contact *Rosalie Siegel*

Founded 1978. A one-woman, highly selective agency that takes on only a limited number of new projects. Handles fiction and non-fiction (especially narrative). Specialises in French history and literature; Europe in general; American history, social history. No science fiction, photography, illustrated art books or children's. COMMISSION Home 15%; Foreign 20%. OVERSEAS ASSOCIATE **Louise Greenberg**, UK; plus associates worldwide. No unsolicited material; send query letter citing background, previously published books and brief description of current book. Include return postage. No reading fee.

Michael Snell Literary Agency

PO Box 1206, Truro, MA 02666–1206
☎001 508 349 3718
President *Michael Snell*
Vice President *Patricia Smith*

Founded 1980. Adult non-fiction, especially psychology, science, business and women's issues. Specialises in business and pet and animal books (professional and reference to popular trade how-to); general how-to and self-help on all topics, from diet and exercise to parenting, relationships, health, sex, psychology, personal finance and dogs, cats and horses, plus literary and suspense fiction. COMMISSION Home 15%. No unsolicited mss. Send outline and sample chapter with return postage for reply. No reading fee for outlines. Brochure available on how to write a book proposal. Author of *From Book Idea to Bestseller*, published by Prima. Rewriting, developmental editing, collaborating and ghostwriting services available on a fee basis. Send IRCs.

Spectrum Literary Agency★

320 Central Park West, Ste. 1-D, New York, NY 10025

☎001 212 362 4323 Fax 001 212 362 4562
www.spectrumliteraryagency.com
President and Agent *Eleanor Wood*
Agent *Lucienne Diver*

Founded 1976. Handles science fiction, fantasy, mystery, suspense and romance. No scripts. Not interested in self-help, New Age, religious fiction/non-fiction, children's books, poetry, short stories, gift books or memoirs. COMMISSION Home 15%; Translation 20%. Send query letter in first instance with s.a.e. Faxed or electronic submissions are not accepted. No reading fees.

The Spieler Agency

154 West 57th Street, Room 135, New York, NY 10019
☎001 212 757 4439 Fax 001 212 333 2019
✉ spieleragency@spieleragency.com
The Spieler Agency/West, 4096 Piedmont Avenue, Oakland, CA 94611
☎001 510 985 1422 Fax 001 510 985 1323

Contacts *Joseph Spieler, John Thornton, Lisa M. Ross, Dierdre Mullane, Katya Balter* (NY); *Victoria Shoemaker* (Oakland)

Founded 1980. Handles literary fiction and non-fiction. No how-to, genre romance, humour or science fiction. Specialises in history, science, ecology, social and political issues and business. No scripts. COMMISSION Home 15%; Translation 20%. OVERSEAS ASSOCIATES **Abner Stein**; **The Marsh Agency**, UK. Approach in writing with IRCs. No reading fee.

Philip G. Spitzer Literary Agency★

50 Talmage Farm Lane, East Hampton, NY 11937
☎001 631 329 3650 Fax 001 631 329 3651
✉ spitzer516@aol.com
Contact *Philip Spitzer*

Founded 1969. Works mostly with established/published authors. Specialises in general non-fiction and fiction – thrillers. COMMISSION Home & Dramatic 15%; Foreign 20%. No reading fee for outlines.

Steele–Perkins Literary Agency★

26 Island Lane, Canandaigua, NY 14424
☎001 585 396 9290 Fax 001 585 396 3579
✉ pattiesp@aol.com
Contact *Pattie Steele-Perkins*

Handles mainstream women's fiction, romance. No scripts. COMMISSION Home 15%. Send query letter, synopsis, three chapters and return postage. No reading fee.

Gloria Stern Agency (Hollywood)

12535 Chandler Boulevard, Suite 3, North Hollywood, CA 91607
☎001 818 508 6296 Fax 001 818 508 6296
✉ wryter21@excite.com

Contact *Gloria Stern*

Founded 1984. Handles film scripts, genre (romance, detective, thriller and sci-fi) and mainstream fiction; electronic media. Accepts interactive material, games and electronic data. COMMISSION Home 15%; Offshore 20%. Currently not accepting unsolicited material.

Stimola Literary Studio★

308 Chase Court, Edgewater, NJ 07020
☎001 201 945 9353 Fax 001 201 945 9353
✉ LtryStudio@aol.com

Contact *Rosemary B. Stimola*

Founded 1997. Handles children's books – pre-school through young adult – fiction and non fiction. Specialises in picture books, middle/young adult novels. No adult fiction. COMMISSION Home 15%; Foreign 20%. No unsolicited material; send query e-mail. No reading fee.

Barbara W. Stuhlmann Author's Representative

PO Box 276, Becket, MA 01223
☎001 413 623 5170

Contact *Barbara Ward Stuhlmann*

Founded 1954. Handles literary fiction, biography and serious non-fiction. 'At the present time we are not taking on any new clients.' No short stories, detective, romance, adventure, poetry, technical or computers. COMMISSION Home 10%; Foreign 15%; Translation 20%. Query first with IRCs, including sample chapters and synopsis of project. No reading fee.

Roslyn Targ★

105 West 13th Street, 15 E, New York, NY 10011
☎001 212 206 9390 Fax 001 212 989 6233
✉ roslyntarg@aol.com

Contact *Roslyn Targ*

Founded 1970. Handles non-fiction, particularly biography, self-help, and literary fiction. No screenplays or cookbooks. COMMISSION Home 15%; Foreign 20%. No unsolicited material; send query e-mail or letter describing the work. No reading fee.

Patricia Teal Literary Agency★

2036 Vista del Rosa, Fullerton, CA 92831
☎001 714 738 8333 Fax 001 714 738 8333

Contact *Patricial Teal*

Founded 1978. Handles women's fiction: series and single-title works; commercial and popular non-fiction. Specialises in romantic fiction. No scripts, science fiction, fantasy, horror, academic texts. COMMISSION Home 15%; Foreign 20%. No unsolicited material. Send query letter in the first instance. No reading fee.

S©ott Treimel NY★

434 Lafayette Street, New York NY 10003
☎001 212 505 8353 Fax 001 212 505 0664
✉ st.ny@verizon.net

Founded 1995. Handles children's books only, from concept/board books to teen fiction. No scripts. COMMISSION Home 15%; Foreign 20%. No unsolicited material. 'Not accepting anyone unless recommended by professional authors or editors.' No reading fee.

2M Communications Ltd

121 West 27th Street, Suite 601, New York, NY 10001
☎001 212 741 1509 Fax 001 212 691 4460
✉ morel@bookhaven.com
www.2mcommunications.com

Contact *Madeleine Morel*

Founded 1982. Handles non-fiction only: everything from pop psychology and health to cookery books, biographies and pop culture. No scripts. No fiction, children's, computers or science. COMMISSION Home & Dramatic 15%; Translation 20%. OVERSEAS ASSOCIATES Thomas Schluck Agency, Germany; Asano Agency, Japan; EAIS, France; Living Literary Agency, Italy; Nueva Agencia Literaria Internacional, Spain. No unsolicited mss; send letter with sample pages and IRCs. No reading fee.

The Vines Agency, Inc.★

648 Broadway, Suite 901, New York, NY 10012
☎001 212 777 5522 Fax 001 212 777 5978
✉ JV@vinesagency.com
www.vinesagency.com

Contacts *James C. Vines, Kate Payne*

Founded 1995. Handles fiction – literary, women's, thrillers, love stories; narrative non-fiction, historical, biography, advice, how-to. Specialises in women's fiction and thrillers. No children's picture books or poetry. COMMISSION Home 15%; Foreign/Translation 25%. *Overseas associate* Baror International (foreign rights). Unsolicited mss, synopses and sample chapters welcome. Send query with one-page letter and return postage. No reading fee.

Wales Literary Agency, Inc.*

PO Box 9428, Seattle, WA 98109–0428
☎001 206 284 7114
✉ waleslit@waleslit.com

Contacts *Elizabeth Wales, Adrienne Reed, Josie Di Bernardo*

Founded 1988. Handles quality fiction and non-fiction. No genre fiction, westerns, romance, science fiction or horror. Special interest in 'Pacific Rim', West Coast and Pacific Northwest stories. COMMISSION Home 15%; Dramatic & Translation 20%. No unsolicited mss; send query letter with publication list and writing sample. No e-mail queries longer than one page and no attachments. No reading fee.

John A. Ware Literary Agency

392 Central Park West, New York, NY 10025
☎001 212 866 4733 Fax 001 212 866 4734

Contact *John Ware*

Founded 1978. Specialises in non-fiction: biography, history, current affairs, investigative journalism, science, nature, inside looks at phenomena, medicine and psychology (academic credentials required). Also handles literary fiction, mysteries/thrillers, sport, oral history, Americana and folklore. COMMISSION Home & Dramatic 15%; Foreign 20%. Unsolicited mss not read. Send query letter first with IRCs to cover return postage. No reading fee.

Watkins Loomis Agency, Inc.

133 East 35th Street, Suite 1, New York, NY 10016
☎001 212 532 0080 Fax 001 212 889 0506

Contact *Katherine Fausset*

Founded 1904. Handles fiction and non-fiction. No scripts for film, radio, TV or theatre. No science fiction, fantasy or horror. COMMISSION Home 15%; UK & Translation 20%. OVERSEAS ASSOCIATES **Abner Stein**; **The Marsh Agency**, UK. No unsolicited mss. Approach in writing with enquiry or proposal and s.a.e. No reading fee.

Wecksler-Incomco

170 West End Avenue, New York, NY 10023
☎001 212 787 2239 Fax 001 212 496 7035
✉ jacinny@aol.com

Contacts *Sally Wecksler, Joann Amparan-Close*

Founded 1971. Handles literary fiction and non-fiction: business, reference, biography, performing arts, history and heavily illustrated books; also children's books (picture to young adult). Foreign rights. COMMISSION Home 15%; Translation & UK 20%. Send queries only. No unsolicited mss. No submissions by fax or e-mail; hard copy only. No reading fee.

Cherry Weiner Literary Agency

28 Kipling Way, Manalapan, NJ 07726
☎001 732 446 2096 Fax 001 732 792 0506
✉ Cherry8486@aol.com

Contact *Cherry Weiner*

Founded 1977. Handles all types of fiction: science fiction and fantasy, mainstream, romance, mystery, westerns. COMMISSION 15%. OVERSEAS ASSOCIATES **Abner Stein**, UK; Thomas Schluck, Germany; International Editors Inc., Spain; Prava Prevodi Agency (Eastern Europe), Serbia; Elaine Benisti Agency, France; Borderline Literary Agency, Italy; Nucihan Kesim Literary Agency, Turkey; English Agency (Japan) Ltd; Alex Korzhenevski Agency, Russia; Renaissance Media – movie agent. Also dealing with various e-book publishers. No submissions except through referral. No reading fee.

Wieser & Elwell, Inc.

80 Fifth Avenue, #1101, New York, NY 10011
☎001 212 260 0860

President *Jake Elwell*

Founded 1976. Works mostly with established/published authors. Specialises in literary and mainstream fiction, serious and popular historical fiction, and general non-fiction: business, finance, aviation, sports, travel and popular medicine. No poetry, children's, science fiction or religious. COMMISSION Home & Dramatic 15%; Foreign 20%. No unsolicited mss. First approach by letter with IRCs. No reading fee for outlines.

Ann Wright Representatives

165 West 46th Street, Suite 1105, New York, NY 10036–2501
☎001 212 764 6770 Fax 001 212 764 5125

Contact *Dan Wright*

Founded 1961. Specialises in material with strong film potential. Handles screenplays and novels, drama and fiction. No academic, scientific or scholarly. COMMISSION Literary 10–20%; Screenplays 10% of gross. Approach by letter; no reply without IRCs. Include outline and credits only. 'Has reputation for encouraging new writers.' No reading fee. Signatory to the Writers Guild of America Agreement.

Writers House, LLC.★

21 West 26th Street, New York, NY 10010
☎001 212 685 2400 Fax 001 212 685 1781
Contacts *Albert Zuckerman, Amy Berkower,
Merrilee Heifetz, Susan Cohen, Susan
Ginsburg, Robin Rue, Simon Lipskar, Steven
Malk, Jennifer Lyons, Jodi Reamer*

Founded 1974. See also **Joan Daves Agency**.
Handles all types of fiction, including children's
and young adult, plus narrative non-fiction: history, biography, popular science, pop and rock
culture as well as how-to, business and finance,
and New Age. Specialises in popular and literary
fiction, women's novels, thrillers and children's.
No scripts. No professional or scholarly.
COMMISSION Home & Dramatic 15%; Foreign
20%. Albert Zuckerman is author of *Writing the
Blockbuster Novel*, published by Little, Brown &
Co. and Warner Paperbacks. For consideration
of unsolicited mss, send one-page letter of
enquiry, 'explaining why your book is wonderful, briefly what it's about and outlining your
writing background'. No reading fee.

The Zack Company, Inc.★

243 West 70th Street, Suite 8D, New York,
NY 10023–4366
www.zackcompany.com

Contact *Andrew Zack*

Founded 1996. Handles serious narrative nonfiction by qualified experts: history, particularly
military, politics, current affairs, science and
technology, biography, autobiography, memoirs, personal finance, parenting, health and
medicine, business, relationships. Commercial
fiction – thrillers, mysteries, crime, science fiction/fantasy. No women's fiction, westerns, gay
or lesbian, scripts. COMMISSION Home 15%
(published authors)/20% (new, unpublished);
Foreign/Translation 25%. *See website for full listing of areas of representation and submission guidelines.* No unsolicited material. No reading fee.

Susan Zeckendorf Associates, Inc★

171 West 57th Street, Suite 11B, New York,
NY 10019
☎001 212 245 2928
Contact *Susan Zeckendorf*

Founded 1979. Handles non-fiction of all kinds:
self help, social history, biography; fiction. No
scripts, romance, science fiction or children's
books. COMMISSION Home 15%; Foreign &
Translation 20%. ASSOCIATES Rosemarie
Buckman (translation); **Abner Stein**, UK. No
unsolicited material; send query letter with s.a.e.
in the first instance. No reading fee.

US Media Contacts in the UK

ABC News Intercontinental Inc.
3 Queen Caroline Street, Mail Code 2303,
London W6 9PE
☎020 8222 5000 Fax 020 8222 5020

Bureau Chief & Director of News Coverage,
Europe, Middle East & Africa *Marcus
Wilford*

The Associated Press
12 Norwich Street, London EC4A 1BP
☎020 7353 1515 Fax 020 7353 8118 (news)

Chief of Bureau/Managing Director, AP Ltd
To be appointed

The Baltimore Sun
11 Kensington Court Place, London W8 5BJ
☎020 7460 2200

Bureau Chief *Ted Richissin*

Bloomberg Business News
City Gate House, 39–45 Finsbury Square,
London EC2A 1PQ
☎020 7330 7500 Fax 020 7392 6666

Print – London Bureau Chief *Chris Collins*

Boston Globe
6 Holly Mount, London NW3 6SG
☎020 7431 5797 Fax 020 7431 5807
✉ sennott@globe.com

Bureau Chief *Charles Sennott*

Business Week
20 Canada Square, Canary Wharf, London
E14 5LH
☎020 7176 6060 Fax 020 7176 6070

Bureau Chief *Stanley Reed*

Cable News Network Inc. (CNN)
Turner House, 16 Great Marlborough Street,
London W1P 1DF
☎020 7693 1000 Fax 020 7693 1552

Office Manager *Rosalind Jackman*

CBC Television and Radio
43/51 Great Titchfield Street, London
W1P 8DD
☎020 7412 9200 Fax 020 7412 9226

London Bureau Manager *Ann Macmillan*

CBS News
68 Knightsbridge, London SW1X 7LL
☎020 7581 4801 Fax 020 7581 4431

Vice President/Bureau Chief *John Paxson*

Chicago Tribune Press Service
116 Brompton Road, London SW3 1JJ
☎020 7225 0345 Fax 020 7225 0345

Chief European Correspondent *Tom Hundley*

CNBC
10 Fleet Place, Limeburner Lane, London
EC4M 7QS
☎020 7653 9451 Fax 020 7653 9393

Assignments Manager *Harry Fuller*

Dallas Morning News
☎020 8995 0513 Fax 020 8995 5072
✉ trobberson@dallasnews.com

European Bureau Chief *Tod Robberson*

Dow Jones Newswires
10 Fleet Place, Limeburner Lane, London
EC4M 7QN
☎020 7842 9900

Editor (Europe, Middle East, Africa) *Jan Boucek*

Fairchild Publications
of New York
20 Shorts Gardens, London WC2H 9AU
☎020 7240 0420 Fax 020 7240 0290

Bureau Chief *Samantha Conti*

Forbes Magazine
36/38 Picadilly, London W1J 0DP
☎020 7286 6251 Fax 020 7266 9873
✉ mfreedman@forbes.com

European Bureau Chief *Michael Freedman*

Fox News Channel
6 Centaurs Business Park, Grant Way,
Isleworth TW7 5QD
☎020 7805 7143 Fax 020 7805 1111

Bureau Chief *Scott Norvell*

The Globe and Mail
43–51 Great Titchfield Street, London
W1W 7DA

☎020 7323 0449 Fax 020 7323 0428
European Correspondent *Alan Freeman*

International Herald Tribune
40 Marsh Wall, London E14 9TP
☎020 7510 5718 Fax 020 7987 3470
London Correspondent *Eric Pfanner*
See entry under *National Newspapers*

Los Angeles Times
Moreau House, 116–118 Brompton Road,
London SW3 1HX
☎020 7823 7315 Fax 020 7823 7308
Bureau Chief *John Daniszewski*
company:Market News International
Ocean House, 10–12 Little Trinity Lane,
London EC4A 2AR
☎020 7634 1655 Fax 020 7236 7122
✉ ukeditorial@marketnews.com
Deputy Bureau Chief *Ralph Johnston*

National Public Radio
Room G-10 East Wing, Bush House, Strand,
London WC2B 4PH
☎020 7557 1087 Fax 020 7379 6486
Correspondent *Guy Raz*

NBC News Worldwide Inc.
4th Floor, 3 Shortlands, Hammersmith,
London W6 8HX
☎020 8600 6600 Fax 020 8600 6601
Bureau Chief *Chris Hampson*

The New York Times
66 Buckingham Gate, London SW1E 6AU
☎020 7799 5050 Fax 020 7799 2962
Bureau Chief *Patrick E. Tyler*

Newsweek
Academy House, 36 Poland Street, London
W1F 7LU
☎020 7851 9750 Fax 020 7851 9762
Bureau Chief *Stryker McGuire*

People Magazine
Brettenham House, Lancaster Place, London
WC2E 7TL
☎020 7499 4080 Fax 020 7322 1125
Bureau Chief *Bryan Alexander*

Reader's Digest Association Ltd
11 Westferry Circus, Canary Wharf, London
E14 4HE
See entries under *UK Publishers* and
   Magazines

Time Magazine
Brettenham House, Lancaster Place, London
WC2E 7TL
☎020 7499 4080 Fax 020 7322 1230
Bureau Chief *Jef McAllister*
See entry under *Magazines*

USA Today
69 New Oxford Street, London
WC1A 1DG
☎020 7559 5859 Fax 020 7559 5895
Correspondent *Ellen Hale*

Voice of America
☎020 7410 0960 Fax 020 7410 0966
Bureau Chief/Senior Editor *Al Pessin*

Wall Street Journal
10 Fleet Place, Limeburner Lane, London
EC4M 7QN
☎020 7842 9200 Fax 020 7842 9201
London Bureau Chief *Paul Beckett*

Washington Post
17 Dartmouth Street, London SW1H 9BL
☎020 7222 8512 Fax 020 7233 4597
✉ frankelg@washpost.com
Bureau Chief *Glenn Frankel*

US Writers' Courses

In general, courses are open to students from overseas though, of course, in some cases the financial aid information varies for international students.

Arkansas
University of Arkansas
Programs in Creative Writing, 333 Kimpel Hall, Fayetteville, AR 72701
☎001 479 575 4301
www.uark.edu/depts/english/PCWT.html

Contact *Donald Hays, Director*

MFA in *Creative Writing*, offering small, intensive workshops and innovative classes in fiction, non-fiction, translation and poetry.

California
American Film Institute
2021 N. Western Avenue, Los Angeles, CA 90027
☎001 323 856 7600
✉ screened@afi.com

Contact *Admissions Manager*

Screenwriting at AFI focuses on narrative storytelling in an environment designed to stimulate the world of the professional screenwriter. Screenwriting Fellows in the First Year are immersed in the production process in order to learn how screenplays are visualised. Initially writing short screenplays – one of which will be the basis for a first year production – writers collaborate with Producing and Directing Fellows to see their work move from page to screen. The remainder of the first year is devoted to the completion of a feature-length screenplay. Second Year Fellows may write a second feature-length screenplay, or develop materials for television, including biopics, television movies and spec scripts for sitcoms and one-hour dramas. They also have the opportunity to work closely with other disciplines by writing a Second Year thesis script.

California Institute for the Arts
MFA Writing Program, School of Critical Studies, 24700 McBean Parkway, Valencia, CA 91355-2397
☎001 661 253 7701
✉ writing@calarts.edu

Contact *Program Coordinator*

The two-year MFA Writing Programme is rooted in principles of critical thought, experimentation and innovation. It is intended as an alternative to traditional programmes, with a founding premise that distinctions between creative and critical writing should be suspended. Students are encouraged to work across genres and often work in various multi-media forms in addition to their literary production.

Chapman University
Master of Fine Arts Degree, Office of Admissions, One University Drive, Orange, CA 92866
☎001 714 997 6711
www.chapman.edu

Contact *Admissions*

Three-year Master of Fine Arts (MFA) degree in *Creativing Writing* includes courses in fiction writing, poetry and screenwriting as well as courses in world and comparative literature. Programme connected with the John Fowles Center for Creative Writing.

Saint Mary's College of California
MFA Program in Creative Writing, PO Box 4686, Moraga, CA 94575–4686
☎001 925 631 4762 Fax 001 925 631 4471
✉ writers@stmarys-ca.edu

Programme Coordinator *Thomas Cooney*

Two-year MFA course in *Fiction, Non-fiction* or *Poetry*. Students have the opportunity to gain knowledge of the world of publishing through internships in the College's in-house press, Momotombo Press and literary journal, *26*.

Strawberry Mansion Films
13586 Mahogany Place, Tustin, CA 92780
☎001 714 997 6586
✉ axelrod@chapman.edu

Contact *Mark Axelrod*

One-day, three-day and five-day seminar/workshops in *Screenwriting*. A practising screenwriter, Mark Axelrod has conducted such programmes at the Escuela Internacional de Cine y

TV in San Antonio de los Baños, Cuba (founded by García Márquez); the Goethe Institute, Santiago, Chile (with Antonio Skármeta – *Il Postino*); the National Film School of Denmark, as well as the University of East Anglia in Norwich, Columbia College, Chicago, and the Film Stadium der Universität, Hamburg, Germany. Latest film books include: *Aspects of the Screenplay* and *Character and Conflict*.

Colorado

Colorado State University

Department of English, Creative Writing Program, Fort Collins, CO 80523
☎001 970 491 6428 Fax 001 970 491 5601
✉ english@lamar.colostate.edu
www.colostate.edu/Depts/English/
    programs/mfa.htm

Contact *Assistant to the Director of Creative Writing or Director of Creative Writing*

Three-year Master of Fine Arts (MFA) programme in creative writing with concentrations in fiction or poetry. The programme offers a balance of intimate and intensive writing and translation. Course work culminates in a thesis – a collection of poetry or short stories or a novel. Students have the opportunity to teach introductory creative-writing courses, intern with literary journals including the *Colorado Review* and be a part of a thriving community.

Columbia

University of Missouri–Columbia

Creative Writing Program, Department of English, 107 Tate Hall, Columbia, MO 65211-1500
☎011 573 884 7773
✉ creativewriting@missouri.edu/~cwp
www.missouri.edu/~cwp

Contact *Sharon Fisher*

Creative Writing MA and PhD in English programmes in fiction, poetry and non-fiction. Access the website for further information.

Florida

University of West Florida

Department of English and Foreign Languages, College of Arts and Sciences, 11000 University Parkway, Pensacola, FL 32514
☎001 850 474 2923 Fax 001 850 474 2935
✉ English@uwf.edu
uwf.edu/english

BA in *English (Writing Specialization)*: students who choose to develop their creative writing skills or editing can take courses in poetry, fiction, creative non-fiction, magazine writing and editing, and feature writing. *MA in English (Creative Writing Specialization)*: workshop courses in the specialisation include fiction, creative non-fiction, poetry, editing, teaching creative writing and special topics in creative writing. Students also have the opportunity to work on the literary magazine *Bayou*.

Georgia

Georgia State University

Department of English, MSC 8R0322, 33 Gilmer Street SE, Unit 8, Atlanta, GA 30303–3088
☎001 404 651 2900 Fax 001 404 651 1710
✉ jholman@gsu.edu
www.gsu.edu/~wwweng/

Contact *Director of Creative Writing*

BA, MA, MFA and PhD programmes in *Creative Writing* – fiction or poetry. The writing faculty includes poet and novelist David Bottoms; poet Beth Gylys, fiction writers Sheri Joseph, John Holman and Josh Russell; poet Leon Stokesbury.

Illinois

Southern Illinois University

Department of English, Carbondale, IL 62901–4503
☎001 618 453 6849 Fax 001 618 453 3253
✉ crwr@siu.edu

Contact *Professor Beth Lordan*

Three-year MFA in *Creative Writing*. The programme accepts a maximum of eight students each year, so workshops are small and faculty members work closely with students.

Indiana

Taylor University

Department of English, 1025 West Rudisill Boulevard, Fort Wayne, IN 46807–2170
☎001 260 744 8647
✉ DNHensley@TaylorU.edu

Contact *Dr Dennis E. Hensley*

One-day seminars on *Freelance Writing* and *Fiction Writing* held on Saturdays each spring and autumn. Taught by Dr Hensley, Director of the Professional Writing major at the University.

Louisiana

Louisiana State University

English Department, 260 Allen Hall, Baton Rouge, LA 70803
www.english.lsu.edu
Contacts *James Wilcox, Judy Kahn*

Master of Fine Arts (MFA) course with a focus in *Poetry, Fiction, Playwriting, Screenwriting* or *Creative Non-fiction*. Includes opportunity to edit literary journals.

Maryland

Goucher College

Welch Center for Graduate Studies, 1021 Dulaney Valley Road, Baltimore, MD 21204–2794
☎001 800 697 4646 Fax 001 410 337 6085
✉ center@goucher.edu
Programme Director *Patsy Sims* (☎001 800 697 4646)

The two-year MFA Program in *Creative Nonfiction* is a limited-residency programme that allows students to complete most of the requirements off campus while developing their skill as non-fiction writers under the close supervision of a faculty mentor. Provides instruction in the following areas: the personal essay, memoir, literary journalism, travel/nature/science writing, biography/profiles, and narrative non-fiction.

Johns Hopkins University

The Writing Seminars, 3400 N. Charles Street, Baltimore, MD 21218
☎001 410 516 7563
✉ regina@jhu.edu

Two-year Master of Arts in *Creative Writing* – concentrates on fiction or poetry. One-year Master of Arts in *Creative Writing* – concentrates on science writing.

Minnesota

Minnesota State University Moorhead

Graduate Studies Office, MSUM, Moorhead, MN 56563
☎001 218 477 4681
✉ davisa@mnstate.edu
www.mnstate.edu/finearts
Programme Coordinator *Alan Davis*

MFA in *Creative Writing* (*Fiction, Non-fiction, Playwriting, Poetry, Screenwriting*). The programme offers the opportunity to take work-shops, seminars and tutorials in chosen areas and to work with New Rivers Press (www.newriverspress.com). A limited number of teaching assistantships are available. Credits are also available each May through participation in the University's 'British Isles Tour'.

New York

New York University

19 University Place, 2nd Floor, New York, NY 10003
✉ creative.writing@nyu.edu
www.nyu.edu/gsas/program/cwp
Contact *Russell Carmony*
Director *Melissa Hammerle*

Offers MFA in *Creative Writing* and MA in *English* with focus in *Creative Writing* in poetry and fiction. Includes writing workshops and craft courses, literary outreach programmes, a public reading series, student readings, special literary seminars and student teaching opportunities. Publishes a literary journal, *Washington Square*. Contact the department via e-mail.

North Carolina

University of North Carolina at Greensboro

MFA Writing Program, Department of English, 134 Melver Building, UNCG, PO Box 26170, Greensboro, NC 27402-6170
☎001 336 334 5459 Fax 001 336 256 1470
✉ jlclark@uncg.edu
www.uncg.edu/eng/mfa
Contact *Jim Clark, Director*

BA and MFA programes in *Creative Writing: fiction and poetry*.

The university offers writing courses for undergraduate English majors. Courses in journalism, expository, technical and creative writing as well as publishing are available. The student may plan a course of study suited to individual needs. A limited number of scholarships are available to undergraduates in creative writing.

MFA in Creative Writing (poetry, fiction) One of the oldest of its kind in the country, the MFA Writing Program at Greensboro is a two-year residency with an emphasis on providing students with studio time in which to study the writing of poetry or fiction with a flexibility that permits students to develop their particular talents through small classes in writing, literature and the arts.

University of North Carolina at Wilmington

Department of Creative Writing, 601 S. College Road, Wilmington, NC 28403–5938
☎001 910 962 7711
✉ mfa@uncw.edu
www.uncw.edu/mfa

Chair *Dr Philip Furia*

An intensive studio-academic programme in the writing of fiction, poetry and creative nonfiction leading to either the Master of Fine Arts or Bachelor of Fine Arts degree in *Creative Writing*. Courses include workshops in the three genres, special topics and forms courses as well as a range of courses in literature. Course work in publishing and editing is also offered in the Publishing Laboratory, a university press imprint which supports local, regional and national publishing projects.

Ohio

Bowling Green State University,

Bowling Green, OH 43403
☎001 419 372 8370 Fax 001 419 372 6805
www.bgsu.ed/departments/creative-writing/

Director of Creative Writing *Dr Lawrence Coates*

Undergraduate BFA programme – a four-year programme which offers comprehensive and rigorous training in the art of writing and develops students' skills in preparation for numerous post-graduate careers.

Graduate MFA programme – a two-year studio/academic composite, mostly work in writing itself in either poetry or fiction. Also offers ten new teaching assistantships each autumn. See the website for details on both programms.

Philadelphia

Seton Hill University

1 Seton Hill Drive, Greensburg, PA 15601
☎001 724 838 4221
✉ gadmit@setonhill.edu
www.setonhill.edu

Contact *Jenell Krymowski*

The MA in *Writing Popular Fiction* programme at Seton Hill University allows students to earn a graduate degree by writing fiction that people *actually* read. Students attend week-long residencies in January and June and complete writing projects off-campus, working with a faculty mentor who is a published author in the chosen genre. Students can choose to specialise in science fiction, fantasy, horror, children's literature, romance or mystery. Programmes can be completed in 24 months.

Temple University

1024 Anderson Hall, Philadelphia, PA 19122–6090
✉ creatwrt@blue.temple.edu
www.temple.edu/english

Director of Creative Writing *Rachel Blau DuPlessis*

MA in *English/Creative Writing*. Two-year programme with workshops in poetry and fiction; one-on-one tutorials in poetry, fiction and translation; also graduate literature courses in genre.

Rhode Island

Rhode Island Brown University

Literary Arts, Box 1852, Providence, RI 02912
☎001 401 863 3260
✉ Writing@brown.edu

Contact *Director of Literary Arts*

Two-year MFA in *Fiction, Poetry, Playwriting and Electronic Writing*. Students take three workshops, four electives and one independent study (through which they complete a thesis project).

Texas

University of Texas at Austin

Department of Radio-Television-Film, Austin, TX 78712
☎001 512 475 7399 (Admissions)
www.utexas.edu/coc/rtf

Four-year BSc course in *Radio-Television-Film* during which writing for film and television may be studied in the third and fourth years. At graduate level, an MA in *Screenwriting* is offered.

Virginia

Virginia Commonwealth University

Department of English, PO Box 842005, Richmond, VA 23284–2005
☎001 804 828 1329
✉ eng-grad@vcu.edu
www.has.vcu.edu/eng

Graduate Programmes Coordinator *Jeff Lodge*

Three-year MFA in *Creative Writing* with tracks in fiction and poetry and workshops in short fiction, the novel, poetry, drama, screenwriting and creative non-fiction. Opportunities to work with *Blackbird*: an online journal of literature and the arts (www.blackbird.vcu.edu), *Stand Magazine*, the Levis Reading Prize and the First Novelist Award.

Washington

Eastern Washington University

Inland Northwest Center for Writers, Creative Writing, 705 W. 1st Avenue, Spokane, WA 99201
☎001 509 623 4221
✉ writing@mail.ewu.edu

www.creativewriting.ewu.edu

Director *Gregory Spatz*

The MFA Program is an intensive two-year, pre-professional course of study with an emphasis on the practise of literature as a fine art. Includes course work in the study of literature from the vantage point of its composition and history, but the student's principal work is done in advanced workshops and in the writing of a book-length thesis of publishable quality in fiction, literary non-fiction or poetry. Students have the opportunity to work as interns on several projects: the literary magazine, *Willow Springs*; the community outreach programme, Writers in the Community; and Eastern Washington University Press. The MFA is a terminal degree programme.

Commonwealth Publishers

Australia

ACER Press
Private Bag 55, Camberwell, Victoria 3124
☎00 61 3 9277 5555 Fax 00 61 3 9277 5500
www.acer.edu.au
Founded 1930. Publishes education, human relations, psychology, psychiatry.

Allen & Unwin Pty Ltd
PO Box 8500, St Leonards, Sydney,
NSW 1590
☎00 61 2 8425 0100 Fax 00 61 2 9906 2218
www.allenandunwin.com
Founded 1976. Publishes fiction, literature, literary criticism, essays; general non-fiction, art, Asian studies, behavioural sciences, business, children's, cookery, earth sciences, economics, education, gay and lesbian, government, labour, political science, health and nutrition, history, industrial relations, general science.

Edward Arnold (Australia) Pty Ltd
PO Box 885, Kew, Victoria 3101
☎00 61 3 985 9011 Fax 00 61 3 985 9141
Founded 1966. Part of Hodder & Stoughton (Australia) Pty Ltd. Publishes general non-fiction: accountancy, Asian studies, behavioural sciences, career development, computer science, cookery, geography, geology, government, political science, health and nutrition, law, mathematics, psychology and psychiatry, technology, textbooks.

Blackwell Science Pty Ltd
PO Box 378, South Carlton, Victoria 3053
☎00 61 3 9347 0300 Fax 00 61 3 9347 5001
www.blacksci.co.uk
Founded 1971. Part of Blackwell Science Ltd, UK. Publishes general science, medicine, nursing, dentistry, earth sciences, general engineering, computer science, mathematics, physical sciences, physics, psychology, psychiatry, textbooks.

Currency Press Pty Ltd
PO Box 2287, Strawberry Hills, NSW 2012
☎00 61 2 9319 5877 Fax 00 61 2 9319 3649
www.currency.com.au
Founded 1971. Performing arts publisher – directories and reference – drama, theatre, music, dance, film and video.

Dangaroo Press
PO Box 93, New Lambton, NSW 2305
☎00 61 2 4954 5938 Fax 00 61 2 4954 6531
Founded 1978. Publishes general non-fiction, art, literature, literary criticism, essays, poetry, social sciences, sociology, women's studies.

E.J. Dwyer (Australia) Pty Ltd
Locked Bag 71, Alexandria, NSW 2015
☎00 61 2 9550 2355 Fax 00 61 2 9519 3218
Founded 1904. Publishes general non-fiction, self-help, marketing, social sciences, sociology, religion, theology.

HarperCollins Publishers (Australia) Pty Ltd
PO Box 321, Pymble, NSW 2073
☎00 61 2 9952 5000 Fax 00 61 2 9952 5555
www.harpercollins.com.au
Founded 1872. Part of the HarperCollins Publishers Group. Publishes fiction and general non-fiction, biography, children's, gardening, humour, government, political science, regional interests, literature, literary criticism, essays, women's studies.

Hodder Headline Australia
Level 22, 201 Kent Street, Sydney,
NSW 2000
☎00 61 2 8248 0800 Fax 00 61 2 8248 0810
www.hha.com.au
Founded 1958. Owned by Hodder Headline, UK. Publishes general non-fiction and fiction (adult and children's), education.

Hyland House Publishing Pty Ltd
PO Box 122, Flemington, Victoria 3031
☎00 61 3 9696 9065 Fax 00 61 3 9696 9064
Founded 1976. Publishes general non-fiction, Asian studies, biography, cookery, animals, pets, history, essays, fiction, gardening, literature, literary criticism.

LexisNexis Australia Ltd
Tower 2, 475–495 Victoria Avenue,
Chatswood, NSW 2067

☎00 61 2 9422 2222 Fax 00 61 2 9422 2405
www.butterworths.com.au
Founded 1910. A division of Reed Elsevier.
Publishes accountancy, business and law.

Thomas C. Lothian Pty Ltd
Level 5, 132–136 Albert Road, South
Melbourne, Victoria 3205
☎00 61 3 9694 4900 Fax 00 61 3 9645 0705
www.lothian.com.au
Founded 1888. Publishes general non-fiction:
business, health and nutrition, children's,
astrology, occult, self-help.

Macmillan Education Australia Pty Ltd
Locked Bag 1400, South Yarra, Victoria 3141
☎00 61 3 9825 1025 Fax 00 61 3 9825 1010
www.macmillan.com.au
Founded 1896. Part of **Macmillan Publishers**,
UK. Publishes accountancy, behavioural sciences, children's, economics, education, geography, geology, government, political science,
history, management, mathematics, physics, professional, general science, social sciences, sociology, textbooks.

McGraw-Hill Australia Pty Ltd
Locked Bag 2233, Business Centre, North
Ryde, NSW 1670
☎00 61 2 9900 1800 Fax 00 61 2 9878 8200
www.mcgraw-hill.com.au
Founded 1964. Owned by **McGraw-Hill
Inc.**, USA. Publishes accountancy, education,
health and nutrition, advertising, aeronautics,
aviation, anthropology, architecture and interior design, art, behavioural sciences, chemistry, chemical engineering, child care and
development, computer science, criminology,
disability, earth sciences, economics, electronics, electrical engineering, general engineering,
English as a second language, environmental
studies, film and video, geography, geology,
journalism, industrial relations, labour, language arts, linguistics, management, marketing,
maritime, mathematics, mechanical engineering, medicine, nursing, dentistry, philosophy,
photography, physics, professional, psychology, psychiatry, sport, social sciences and sociology, textbooks.

Melbourne University Press
PO Box 1167, Carlton South, Victoria 3053
☎00 61 3 9342 0300 Fax 00 61 3 9342 0399
www.mup.unimelb.edu.au
Founded 1922. Academic publishers; general

non-fiction, biography, essays, history, literature, literary criticism, natural history, psychology, psychiatry, travel.

Openbook Publishers
GPO Box 1368, Adelaide, SA 5001
☎00 61 8 8223 5468 Fax 00 61 8 8223 4552
www.openbook.com.au
Founded 1913. Publishes religious and educational books.

Oxford University Press Australia and New Zealand
GPO Box 2784Y, Melbourne, Victoria 3001
☎00 61 3 9934 9123 Fax 00 61 3 9934 9100
www.oup.com.au
Founded 1908. Owned by **Oxford University
Press**, UK. Publishes for the college, school and
trade markets.

Pan Macmillan Australia Pty Ltd
Level 18, St Martin's Tower, 31 Market
Street, Sydney, NSW 2000
☎00 61 2 9285 9100 Fax 00 61 2 9285 9190
www.panmacmillan.com.au
Founded 1983. Part of **Macmillan Publishers**,
UK. Publishes fiction, essays, literature, literary
criticism; general non-fiction, biography, children's, health and nutrition, humour, self-help,
travel.

Pearson Education Australia
LMB 507, Frenchs Forest, NSW 1640
☎00 61 3 9454 2200 Fax 00 61 3 9453 0089
www.awl.com.au
Australia's largest educational publisher.

Penguin Books Australia Ltd
PO Box 701, Hawthorn, Victoria 3122
☎00 61 3 9811 2400 Fax 00 61 3 9811 2620
www.penguin.com.au
Founded 1946. Publishes general non-fiction
and fiction; biography, children's, cookery,
humour, literature, literary criticism, essays,
science fiction, fantasy, self-help, travel.

University of Queensland Press
PO Box 6042, St Lucia, Queensland 4067
☎00 61 7 3365 2127 Fax 00 61 7 3365 7579
www.uqp.uq.edu.au
Founded 1948. Publishes academic, textbooks,
children's, general non-fiction and fiction,
literature, literary criticism, essays, poetry,
biography, history, sport, travel.

Random House Australia
20 Alfred Street, Milsons Point, NSW 2061
☎00 61 2 9954 9966 Fax 00 61 2 9954 4562
✉ random@randomhouse.com.au
www.randomhouse.com.au
Subsidiary of **Bertelsmann AG**. Publishes fiction and non-fiction.

Reader's Digest (Australia) Pty Ltd
PO Box 4353, Sydney, NSW 2001
☎00 61 2 9690 6935 Fax 00 61 2 9690 6390
Founded 1946. Associate company of **Reader's Digest Association, Inc.** (USA). Educational publisher.

Reed Educational Publishing Australia
PO Box 460, Port Melbourne, Victoria 3207
☎00 61 3 9245 7188 Fax 00 61 3 9245 7265
www.reededucation.com.au
Founded 1982. Publishes art, CD-ROMs, chemistry, chemical engineering, children's, dictionaries, encyclopedias, environmental studies, geography, geology, health and nutrition, history, mathematics, physics, textbooks.

Scholastic Australia Pty Limited
PO Box 579, Gosford, NSW 2250
☎00 61 2 4328 3555 Fax 00 61 2 4323 3827
www.scholastic.com.au
Founded 1968. Educational publisher.

Science Press
54a Fitzroy Street, Marrickville, NSW 2204
☎00 61 2 9516 1122 Fax 00 61 2 9550 1915
Founded 1945. Educational publisher.

Simon & Schuster Australia Pty Ltd
PO Box 507, East Roseville, NSW 2069
☎00 61 2 9415 9900 Fax 00 61 2 9417 3188
Founded 1987. Part of **Simon & Schuster Inc.**, USA. Publishes general non-fiction; animals and pets, anthropology, childcare, children's, cookery, crafts, games and hobbies, history, how-to, management, natural history, self-help.

University of Western Australia Press
35 Stirling Highway, Crawley, WA 6009
☎00 61 8 9380 3670 Fax 00 61 8 9380 1027
www.uwapress.uwa.edu.au
Founded 1954. Publishes general non-fiction, essays, literature, literary criticism, science fic-

tion, fantasy, history, social sciences, sociology, natural history, chilren's, directories, biography, reference, textbooks, women's studies.

John Wiley & Sons Australia Ltd
PO Box 1226, Milton, Queensland 4064
☎00 61 7 3859 9755 Fax 00 61 7 3859 9715
✉ brisbane@johnwiley.com.au
www.johnwiley.com.au
Founded 1954. Owned by **John Wiley & Sons Inc.**, USA. Publishes general non-fiction and education books.

Canada

Canadian Scholars' Press, Inc
180 Bloor Street W, Suite 1202, Toronto, Ontario M5S 2V6
☎001 416 929 2774 Fax 001 416 929 1926
✉ info@cspi.org
www.cspi.org
Founded 1987. Publishes academic books in English and French.

Fenn Publishing Co Ltd
34 Nixon Road, Bolton, Ontario L7E 1W2
☎001 905 951 6600 Fax 001 905 951 6601
www.hbfenn.com
Founded 1977. Publishes fiction and non-fiction, children's.

Fitzhenry & Whiteside Limited
195 Allstate Parkway, Markham, Ontario L3R 4T8
☎001 905 477 9700 Fax 001 905 477 9179
✉ godwit@fitzhenry.ca
www.fitzhenry.ca
Founded 1966. Publishes trade, reference and children's books; educational material.

Harcourt Canada Ltd
55 Horner Avenue, Toronto Ontario M8Z 4X6
☎001 416 255 4491 Fax 001 416 255 6708
www.harcourtcanada.com
Founded 1922. Publishes educational material.

HarperCollins Publishers Limited
2 Bloor Street E, 20th Floor, Toronto, Ontario M4W 1A8
☎001 416 975 9334 Fax 001 416 975 9884
www.harpercanada.com
Founded 1989. Publishes fiction and non-fiction, children's and religious.

Lexis Nexis Canada Ltd
75 Clegg Road, Markham, Ontario L6G 1A1
☎001 905 479 2665 Fax 001 905 479 2826
www.lexisnexis.ca
Founded 1912. Publishes law books, CD-ROMs, journals, newsletters, law reports.

McClelland & Stewart Ltd
481 University Avenue, Suite 900, Toronto,
Ontario M5G 2E9
☎001 416 598 1114 Fax 001 416 598 7764
www.mcclelland.com
Founded 1906. Publishes fiction and general
non-fiction, poetry.

McGraw-Hill Ryerson Ltd
300 Water Street, Whitby, Ontario L1N 9B6
☎001 905 430 5000 Fax 001 905 430 5020
www.mcgrawhill.ca
Founded 1944. Subsidiary of **McGraw-Hill
Education**. Publishes education and professional.

Nelson
1120 Birchmount Road, Scarborough,
Ontario M1K 5G4
☎001 416 752 9448 Fax 001 416 752 8101
www.nelson.com
Founded 1914. Division of Thomson Canada
Ltd. Leading educational publisher. Also publishes professional and reference.

New Star Books Ltd
107–3477 Commercial Street, Vancouver,
BC V5N 4E8
☎001 604 738 9429 Fax 001 604 738 9332
✉ info@newstarbooks.com
www.NewStarBooks.com
Founded 1974. Publishes literature, literary
criticism, essays, environmental studies,
geography, geology, government and political
science, history, industrial relations, journalism,
politics, labour, women's studies, gay and
lesbian studies, sociology, social sciences.

Oxford University Press, Canada
70 Wynford Drive, Don Mills, Onatario
M3C 1J9
☎001 416 441 2941 Fax 001 416 444 0427
www.oup.com/ca
Founded 1904. Owned by **Oxford University
Press**, UK. Publishes for college, school and
trade markets.

Pearson Education Canada Inc.
PO Box 580, Don Mills, Ontario M3C 2T8

☎001 416 447 5101 Fax 001 416 443 0948
www.pearsoned.com
Founded 1966. Fourth-largest educational
publisher in Canada. Publishes in English and
French.

Penguin Books Canada Limited
10 Alcorn Avenue Street, Suite 300, Toronto,
Ontario M4V 3B2
☎001 416 925 2249 Fax 001 416 925 0068
www.penguin.ca
Founded 1974. Publishes fiction and non-fiction books and audio cassettes.

Random House of Canada Ltd
One Toronto Street, Unit 300, Toronto,
Ontario M5C 2V6
☎001 416 364 4449 Fax 001 416 364 6863
www.randomhouse.ca
Founded 1944. Publishes fiction and non-fiction and children's.

Scholastic Canada Ltd
175 Hillmount Road, Markham, Ontario
L6C 1Z7
☎001 905 887 7323 Fax 001 905 887 1131
www.scholastic.ca
Founded 1957. Publishes (in English and
French) children's books and educational
material.

Tundra Books
481 University Avenue, Suite 900, Toronto,
Ontario M5G 2E9
☎001 416 598 4786 Fax 001 416 598 0247
Founded 1967. Division of **McClelland &
Stewart Ltd**. Publishes (in English and
French) children's and young adult books.

John Wiley & Sons Canada Ltd
22 Worcester Road, Etobicoke, Ontario
M9W 1L1
☎001 416 236 4433 Fax 001 416 236 4447
www.wiley.ca
Founded 1968. Subsidiary of **John Wiley &
Sons Inc.**, USA. Publishes professional, reference and textbooks.

India

Affiliated East West Press Pvt Ltd
104 Nirmal Tower, 26 Barakhamba Road,
New Delhi 110 001
☎00 91 11 331 5398 Fax 00 91 11 326 0538
Founded 1962. Publishes aeronautics, aviation,

agriculture, anthropology, biological sciences, chemistry, engineering (chemical, civil, electrical, mechanical), computer science, economics, electronics, mathematics, management, microcomputers, physical sciences, physics, general science, textbooks, veterinary science, women's studies.

Arnold Heinman Publishers (India) Pvt Ltd

AB-9, 1st Floor, Safdaoung Enclave, New Delhi 110 029
☎00 91 11 638 3422 Fax 00 91 11 687 7571

Founded 1969. Associate company of Edward Arnold (Publishers) Ltd, UK. Publishes fiction, poetry, essays, literature, literary criticism, directories, reference, textbooks, art, general engineering, government, political science, philosophy, religion, medicine, nursing, dentistry, social sciences and sociology.

S. Chand & Co Ltd

7361 Ram Nagar, Qutab Road, Hotel Tourist Complex, New Delhi 110 055
☎00 91 11 367 2080 Fax 00 91 11 367 7446

Founded 1917. Publishes art, business, economics, government, political science, medicine, nursing, dentistry, philosophy, social sciences, sociology, general science, technology.

Current Books

DC Bookshop, Pooma Complex, Trichur 680 001
☎00 91 487 244 4322

Founded 1952. Publishes fiction and general non-fiction.

General Book Depot

86 University Block, Jawahar Nagar, Delhi 110 007
☎00 91 11 326 3695 Fax 00 91 11 294 0861

Founded 1936. Publishes general nonfiction, reference, textbooks; business, career development, dictionaries, directories, encyclopedias, how-to, English as a second language, language arts, linguistics, self-help, travel.

Hind Pocket Books Private Ltd

18–19 Dilshad Garden G T Road, Shadar, Delhi 110 095 Fax 00 91 11 228 2332
Founded 1957. Publishes fiction and general non-fiction; biography, how-to and self-help.

Jaico Publishing House

121–125 Mahatma Gandhi Road, Mumbai 400 023

☎00 91 22 267 6702 Fax 00 91 22 204 1673
www.jaicobooks.com

Founded 1946. Publishes biography, behavioural sciences, language arts, linguistics, health and nutrition, cookery, law, criminology, astrology, directories, reference, self-help, occult, philosophy, religion, general engineering, economics, humour, history, government, political science, psychology, psychiatry.

Macmillan India Ltd

315/316 Raheja Chambers, 12 Museum Road, Bangalore 560 052
☎00 91 80 558 6563 Fax 00 91 80 558 8713
www.macmillan-india.com

Founded 1903. Part of **Macmillan Publishers**, UK. Educational publisher.

Munshiram Manoharlal Publishers Pvt Ltd

PO Box 5715, New Delhi 110 055
☎00 91 11 367 1668 Fax 00 91 11 361 2745
www.mrmlbooks.com

Founded 1952. Publishes academic, dictionaries, encyclopedias, professional, art, architecture and interior design, anthropology, archaeology, astrology, occult, religion (Buddhist, Hindu, Islamic), philosophy, history, language arts and linguistics, music, dance, drama, theatre, Asian studies.

National Book Trust India

A5 Green Park, New Delhi 110 016
☎00 91 11 651 8378 Fax 00 91 11 685 1795

Founded 1957. Publishes human relations and foreign countries.

National Publishing House

23 Daryaganj, New Delhi 110 002
☎00 91 11 327 4161

Founded 1950. Publishes human relations, ethnicity, social sciences, sociology.

Orient Paperbacks

1590 Madarsa Road, Kashmere Gate, Delhi 110 006
☎00 91 11 386 2267 Fax 00 91 11 386 2935
www.orientpaperbacks.com

Founded 1977. Publishes fiction and general non-fiction; business, career development, directories, cookery, crafts, games, hobbies, humour, drama, theatre, health and nutrition, how-to, poetry, astrology, occult, reference, self-help, sport.

Oxford University Press India
2/11 Ansari Road, Daryaganj,
New Delhi 110 002
☎00 91 11 202 1029 Fax 00 91 11 373 2312
Founded 1912. Owned by **Oxford University Press**, UK. Academic publishers.

Rajpal & Sons
1590 Madarasa Road, Kashmere Gate,
Delhi 110 006
☎00 91 11 296 3904 Fax 00 91 11 296 7791
Founded 1891. Publishes fiction, literature, literary criticism, essays, human relations, general science, children's, dictionaries, encyclopedias, textbooks.

Tata McGraw-Hill Publishing Company
7 West Patel Nagar, New Delhi 110 008
☎00 91 11 2588 2743 Fax 00 91 11 2588 3902
www.tatamcgrawhill.com
Founded 1970. Publishes general engineering and science, business, social sciences, sociology and management.

Vidyarthi Mithram Press
Market Road, Kochi 11
☎00 91 481 354 003 Fax 00 91 481 562 616
Founded 1928. Publishes children's, CD-ROMs, dictionaries, directories, encyclopedias, cookery, drama and theatre, economics, biography, biological sciences, chemistry and chemical engineering, computer science, reference.

A.H. Wheeler & Co Ltd
23 Lal Bahadur Shasti Marg,
Allahabad 211 001
☎00 91 11 331 2629 Fax 00 91 11 335 7798
www.ahwheeler.com
Founded 1879. Publishes CD-ROMs, professional, textbooks; computer science, behavioural sciences, accountancy, advertising, business, career development, civil engineering, communications.

New Zealand

Auckland University Press
University of Auckland, Private Bag 92019,
Auckland
☎00 64 9 373 7528 Fax 00 64 9 373 7465
www.auckland.ac.nz/aup
Founded 1966. Publishes academic, art, archaeology, biography, dictionaries, encyclopedias, government, political science, history, social sciences, sociology, women's studies, essays, poetry, literature, literary criticism.

Butterworths New Zealand Ltd
PO Box 472, Wellington 1
☎00 64 4 385 1479 Fax 00 64 4 385 1598
www.butterworths.co.nz
Founded 1914. Publishes law.

Canterbury University Press
University of Canterbury, Private Bag 4800,
Christchurch
☎00 64 3 364 2914 Fax 00 64 3 364 2044
✉ mail@cup.canterbury.ac.nz
Founded 1960. Academic publishers; general non-fiction; biography, biological sciences, history, natural history.

The Caxton Press
113 Victoria Street, Christchurch
☎00 64 3 366 8516 Fax 00 64 3 365 7840
Founded 1935. Publishes general non-fiction; biography, gardening and plants, textbooks.

HarperCollins Publishers (New Zealand) Ltd
31 View Road, Auckland
☎00 64 9 443 9400 Fax 00 64 9 443 9403
www.harpercollins.co.nz
Founded 1888. Publishes fiction, children's, art, dictionaries, directories, encyclopedias, history, humour, natural history, biography, cookery, plants, gardening, reference, sport, travel, self-help.

Hodder Moa Beckett Publishers Ltd
PO Box 100749, Auckland 1330
☎00 64 9 478 1000 Fax 00 64 9 478 1010
Founded 1971. Owned by **Hodder Headline**, UK. Publishes fiction and general non-fiction; biography, business, cookery, humour, sport.

Huia Publishers
PO Box 17335, Aotearoa, Wellington
☎00 64 4 473 9262 Fax 00 64 4 473 9265
www.huia.co.nz
Founded 1991. Publishes Maori cultural history and language, children's books in Maori and English, histories of colonisation in New Zealand, textbooks, drama and theatre, fiction.

University of Otago Press
PO Box 56, Dunedin
☎00 64 3 479 8807 Fax 00 64 3 479 8385

✉ university.press@otago.ac.nz
www.otago.ac.nz
Founded 1958. Publishes fiction, textbooks, essays, literature, literary criticism, poetry, art, history, education, biography, anthropology, natural history, environmental studies, photography, psychology, psychiatry, government and political science.

Pearson Education New Zealand Ltd
Private Bag 102908, North Shore Mail Centre, Auckland 10
☎00 64 9 444 4968 Fax 00 64 9 444 4957
www.pearson.co.nz
Founded 1968. Educational publishers.

Penguin Books (NZ) Ltd
Private Bag 102–902, North Shore Mail Centre, Auckland 1310
☎00 64 9 415 4700 Fax 00 64 9 415 4703
www.penguin.co.nz
Founded 1976. Owned by **Penguin UK**.

Reed Publishing (NZ) Ltd
Private Bag 34901, Birkenhead, Auckland 10
☎00 64 9 480 4950 Fax 00 64 9 419 4999
www.reed.co.nz
Founded 1988. Publishes fiction and general non-fiction, biography, cookery, history, natural history, regional interests, travel.

Southern Press Ltd
R D 1, Porirua 6221
☎00 64 4 239 9063 Fax 00 64 4 239 9835
Founded 1971. Publishes aviation, aeronautics, maritime, transport, technology, mechanical and civil engineering, archaeology.

Tandem Press
PO Box 34–272, Birkenhead, Auckland 10
☎00 64 9 480 1452 Fax 00 64 9 480 1455
www.tandempress.co.nz
Founded 1990. Publishes fiction and general non-fiction; cookery, business, alternative, health and nutrition, photography, psychology, psychiatry, self-help, travel, women's studies.

Victoria University Press
PO Box 600, Wellington
☎00 64 4 463 6580 Fax 00 64 4 463 6581
www.vup.vuw.ac.nz
Founded 1979. Publishes government, political science, essays, poetry, literature, literary criti-

cism, drama, theatre, history, social sciences and sociology, anthropology, language and linguistics, law, architecture and interior design.

Viking Sevenseas NZ Ltd
PO Box 152, Paraparaumu 6150, Wellington
☎00 64 4 297 1990 Fax 00 64 4 297 2040
Founded 1957. Publishes natural history and ethnicity.

Bridget Williams Books Ltd
PO Box 5482, Wellington
☎00 64 4 473 8317 Fax 00 64 4 473 8417
Founded 1990. Publishes academic, general non-fiction, biography, government, political science, history, women's studies.

South Africa

Butterworths South Africa
PO Box 4, Mayville, Durban 4058
☎00 27 31 268 3111 Fax 00 27 31 268 3100
www.butterworths..co.za

Owned by **Butterworth & Co**. UK. Publishes professional and text books; general science, medicine, nursing and dentistry, economics, education, law.

Flesch Financial Publications (Pty) Ltd
4 Gordon Street Gardens, Cape Town 8001
☎00 27 21 461 7472 Fax 00 27 21 461 3758
Founded 1966. Publishes reference, aviation, aeronautics, directories, maritime, animals, pets, business.

Heinemann Educational Publishers Southern Africa
PO Box 781940, Sandton,
Johannesburg 21461
☎00 27 11 322 8600 Fax 00 27 11 322 8717
www.heinemann.co.za
Founded 1986. Parent company: Reed Educational & Professional Publishing, UK. Publishes economics, education, English as a second language, mathematics, mechanical engineering.

Maskew Miller Longman
PO Box 396, Cape Town 8000
☎00 27 21 531 7750 Fax 00 27 21 531 4877
Founded 1893. Publishes education, children's, language arts and linguistics, essays, literature, literary criticism, textbooks.

University of Natal Press

PB X01, Scottsville, Pietermaritzburg 3209
☎00 27 331 260 5226
Fax 00 27 331 260 5801
✉ books@press.unp.ac.za

Founded 1947. Academic publishers; biography, biological sciences, education, essays, genealogy, government, political science, literature and literary criticism, poetry, health and nutrition, psychology, psychiatry, natural history, history, women's studies, sociology, social sciences.

Oxford University Press Southern Africa

PO Box 12119, N1 City 7463
☎00 27 21 595 4400   Fax 00 27 21 595 4430
✉ oxford.za@oup.com
www.oup.com/za

Founded 1915. Parent company: **Oxford University Press**, UK. Publishes academic, educational and general books.

Ravan Press (Pty) Ltd

PO Box 32484, Braamfontein,
Johannesburg 2125
☎00 27 11 484 0916
Fax 00 27 11 484 42631

Founded 1972. Part of Hodder & Stoughton Educational South Africa. Publishes fiction and general non-fiction; children's, anthropology, biography, business, economics, environmental studies, government, political science, history, labour, industrial relations, music, dance, sociology, social sciences, women's studies.

Shuter & Shooter (Pty) Ltd

PO Box 109, Pietermaritzburg 3200
☎00 27 33 394 8881   Fax 00 27 33 342 7419

Founded 1925. Publishes general non-fiction; biography, history, ethnicity, general science, technology, social sciences, sociology, textbooks.

Struik Publishers (Pty) Ltd

Cornelis Struik House, 80 McKenzie Street,
Cape Town 8001
☎00 27 21 462 4360   Fax 00 27 21 462 4379

Founded 1962. Publishes child care and development, general non-fiction, children's, cookery, directories, gardening, plants, environmental studies, natural history, reference.

Witwatersrand University Press

PO Wits, Johannesburg 2050
☎00 27 11 484 5907   Fax 00 27 11 484 5971
www.wirs.ac.za/wup.html

Founded 1922. Publishes academic, dictionaries, textbooks, encyclopedias, education, economics, essays, literature and literary criticism, drama, theatre, history, business, anthropology, archaeology, crafts, games and hobbies, government, political science, language arts, linguistics, law, general science, natural history, religion (Jewish), medicine, nursing and dentistry.

Professional Associations

ABSW

Wellcome Wolfson Building, 165 Queen's Gate, London SW7 5HE
☎0870 770 3361
✉ absw@absw.org.uk
www.absw.org.uk
Chairman *Pallab Ghosh*
Administrator *Barbara Drillsma*
MEMBERSHIP £40 (Full) p.a.; £36 (Associate); £5 (Student)

ABSW has played a central role in improving the standards of science journalism in the UK over the last 40 years. The Association seeks to improve standards by means of networking, lectures and organised visits to institutional laboratories and industrial research centres. Puts members in touch with major projects in the field and with experts worldwide. A member of the European Union of Science Journalists' Associations, ABSW is able to offer heavily subsidised places on visits to research centres in most other European countries, and hosts reciprocal visits to Britain by European journalists. Membership open to those who are considered to be *bona fide* science writers/editors, or their film/TV/radio equivalents, who earn a substantial part of their income by promoting public interest in and understanding of science. Runs the administration and judging of the **Glaxo Science Writers' Awards**, for outstanding science journalism in newspapers, journals and broadcasting and, with The Wellcome Trust, awards bursaries for science undergraduates taking a science communication course.

Academi (Yr Academi Gymreig)

3rd Floor, Mount Stuart House, Mount Stuart Square, Cardiff CF10 5FQ
☎029 2047 2266   Fax 029 2049 2930
✉ post@academi.org
www.academi.org

North West Wales office: TŷNewydd, Llanystumdwy, Cricieth, Gwynedd LL52 0LW
☎01766 522817 Fax 01766 523095
✉ olwen@academi.org

West Wales office: Dylan Thomas Centre, Somerset Place, Swansea SA1 1RR
☎01792 463980 Fax 01792 463993

✉ academi.dylan.thomas@business.ntl.com
Chief Executive *Peter Finch*

Academi is the trading name of Yr Academi Gymreig, the Welsh National Literature Promotion Agency and Society for Writers. Yr Academi Gymreig was founded in 1959 as an association of Welsh language writers. An English language section was established in 1968. Membership, for those who have made a significant contribution to the literature of Wales, is by invitation. Membership currently stands at 500. The Academi runs courses, competitions (including the **Cardiff International Poetry Competition**), conferences, tours by authors, festivals and represents the interests of Welsh writers and Welsh writing both inside Wales and beyond. Its publications include *Taliesin*, a quarterly literary journal in the Welsh language, *The Oxford Companion to the Literature of Wales*, *The Welsh Academy English-Welsh Dictionary* and a variety of translated works.

The Academi won the franchise from the Arts Council of Wales to run the Welsh National Literature Promotion Agency. The new, much enlarged organisation now administers a variety of schemes including bursaries, the annual **Book of the Year Award**, critical services, writers' mentoring, Writers on Tour, Writers Residencies and a number of literature development projects. It promotes an annual literary festival alternating between North and South Wales, runs its own programme of literary activity and publishes *A470*, a bi-monthly literature information magazine. The Academi is also in receipt of a lottery grant to publish the first Welsh National Encyclopedia. This is expected to be ready in 2006.

Those with an interest in literature in Wales can become an associate of the Academi (which carries a range of benefits). Rates are £15 p.a. (waged); £7.50 (unwaged).

ALCS

See **Authors' Licensing & Collecting Society**

Alliance of Literary Societies

22 Belmont Grove, Havant PO9 3PU
☎023 9247 5855   Fax 08700 560330
✉ rosemary@sndc.demon.co.uk

www.allianceofliterarysocieties.org
Honorary Secretary *Mrs Rosemary Culley*
Founded 1974. Aims to help and support its 100+ member societies and, when necessary, to act as a pressure group. Produces a handbook which holds useful information that is deemed important for the successful running of a literary society. It also contains details of the member societies to publicise them to the ALS members and the wider public. In addition, the Alliance produces two newsletters and *The Open Book*, an annual publication.

Arts & Business (A&B)

Nutmeg House, 60 Gainsford Street, Butlers Wharf, London SE1 2NY
☎020 7378 8143 Fax 020 7407 7527
✉ head.office@AandB.org.uk
www.AandB.org.uk

P.R. Manager *Jonathan Tuchner*

The purpose of Arts & Business (formerly the Association for Business Sponsorship of the Arts) is to help strengthen communities by developing creative and effective partnership between Business and the Arts. It provides a wide range of services to over 350 business members as well as to 700 arts organisations and museums through the Development Forum. The Arts & Business Skills Bank, Board Bank and mentoring schemes enable individual business people to share their skills with arts managers. On behalf of the Department for Culture, Media and Sport, it manages the Arts & Business New Partners Programme, an incentive programme for new and established sponsors of the arts. Arts & Business is working with forward-looking businesses to determine the future of business/arts partnerships. With the support of its President, HRH The Prince of Wales, it is exploring and developing new ways for business, the arts and society to interact. Arts & Business has 15 offices offering a range of services throughout the UK.

Arvon Foundation

See entry under *UK Writers' Courses*

ASLS

See **Association for Scottish Literary Studies**

Association for Business Sponsorship of the Arts (ABSA)

See **Arts & Business**

Association for Scottish Literary Studies

c/o Department of Scottish History,
9 University Gardens, University of Glasgow,
Glasgow G12 8QH
☎0141 330 5309 Fax 0141 330 5309
✉ d.jones@scothist.arts.gla.ac.uk
www.asls.org.uk

Contact *Duncan Jones*
SUBSCRIPTION £38 (Individual);
£67 (Institutional)

Founded 1970. ASLS is an educational charity promoting the languages and literature of Scotland. Publishes works of Scottish literature; essays, monographs and journals; and *Scotnotes*, a series of comprehensive study guides to major Scottish writers. Also produces *New Writing Scotland*, an annual anthology of contemporary poetry and prose in English, Gaelic and Scots (see entry under *Magazines*).

Association of American Correspondents in London

c/o Time Magazine, Brettenham House,
Lancaster Place, London WC2E 7TL
☎020 7322 1084 Fax 020 7322 1230

Secretary/Treasurer *Elizabeth Lea*
SUBSCRIPTION £100 (Organisations)

Founded 1919 to serve the professional interests of its member organisations, promote social cooperation among them, and maintain the ethical standards of the profession. (An extra £40 is charged for each department of an organisation which requires separate listing in the Association's handbook and a charge of £10 for each full-time editorial staff listed, up to a maximum of £120 regardless of the number listed.)

Association of American Publishers, Inc

71 Fifth Avenue, 2nd Floor, New York,
NY 10003–3004, USA
☎001 212 255 0200 Fax 001 212 255 7007
www.publishers.org

Also at: 50 f Street, NW, Washington,
DC 20001–1564
☎001 202 347 3375 Fax 001 202 347 3690

Contact *Judith Platt*

Founded 1970. For information, visit the Association's website.

Association of Authors' Agents

A.P. Watt Ltd, 20 John Street, London
WC1N 2DR
☎020 7405 6774 Fax 020 7831 2154

✉ aaa@apwatt.co.uk
www.agentsassoc.co.uk
President *Derek Johns*
MEMBERSHIP £50 p.a.

Founded 1974. Membership voluntary. The AAA maintains a code of practice, provides a forum for discussion and represents its members in issues affecting the profession. For a full list of members and a list of frequently asked questions visit the AAA website. The AAA is a voluntary body and unable to operate as an information service to the public.

Association of Authors' Representatives

PO Box 237201, Ansonia Station, New York, NY 10003, USA
☎001 212 252 3695
✉ info@aar-online.org
www.aar-online.org

Administrative Secretary *Leslie Carroll*

Founded in 1991 through the merger of the Society of Authors' Representatives and the Independent Literary Agents Association. Membership of this US organisation is restricted to agents of at least two years' operation. Provides information, education and support for its members and works to protect their best interests.

Association of British Editors
See **Society of Editors**

Association of British Science Writers
See **ABSW**

Association of Canadian Publishers

161 Eglinton Avenue East, Suite 702, Toronto, Ontario M4P 1J5, Canada
☎001 416 487 6116 Fax 001 416 487 8815
✉ admin@canbook.org
www.publishers.ca

Executive Director *John Pelletier*

Founded 1971. ACP represents over 140 Canadian-owned book publishers country-wide from the literary, general trade, scholarly and education sectors. Aims to encourage the writing, publishing, distribution and promotion of Canadian books and to support the development of a 'strong, independent and vibrant Canadian-owned publishing industry'. The organisation's website has information on getting published and links to many of their member publishers' websites.

Association of Christian Writers

All Saints Vicarage, 43 All Saints Close, London N9 9AT
☎020 8884 4348 Fax 020 8884 4348
✉ admin@christianwriters.org.uk
www.christianwriters.org.uk

Administrator *Mrs Jenny Kyriacou*
SUBSCRIPTION Single: £20 (£17 Direct Debit); Joint Husband/Wife: £23 (£20 DD); Overseas: £27 (£24 DD on UK a/c)

Founded in 1971 'to inspire and equip men and women to use their talents and skills with integrity to devise, write and market excellent material which comes from a Christian world-view. In this way we seek to be an influence for good and for God in this generation.' Publishes a quarterly magazine. Runs three training events each year, biennial conference, competitions, postal workshops, area groups, prayer support and manuscript criticism. Charity No. 1069839.

Association of Freelance Editors, Proofreaders & Indexers (Ireland)

3 The Lawn, Oldtown Mill, Celbridge, Co. Kildare, Republic of Ireland
☎00 353 1 601 2846

Contact *Priscilla O'Connor*
SUBSCRIPTION €40 p.a.

The organisation was established in Ireland to protect the interests of its members and to provide information to publishers on freelancers working in the relevant fields. Membership is restricted to freelancers with experience and/or references (but does not test or evaluate the skills of members). New category of membership – Associate Member – available for trainees in proofreading/editing who are taking the Book House Training Centre correspondence courses in Proofreading and Copy-editing.

Association of Freelance Journalists

2 Glen Cottage, Brick Hill Lane, Ketley, Telford TF2 6SB Fax 0870 133 7210
✉ afj_info@yahoo.com
www.afj.home-page.org
Official Patron *Dr Carl Chinn, PhD, MBE*
Founding President *Martin Scholes*
SUBSCRIPTION £30 p.a.

Offers membership to all who work in the field of journalism but especially local correspondents, stringers, freelance journalists, news photographers, those at the beginning of their careers or long established. Also welcomes those who make a modest income writing for the specialist press or who self-publish; who have written for a hobby but now wish to make a career of their writing. Members receive a regular e-mail newsletter, a laminated press card, a free postal/e-mail advice service, the opportunity to network with other members (through the newsletter and a special Internet service) and editors who contact the AFJ. There are discounts on products and services, including the AFJ writing course.

Association of Freelance Writers

Sevendale House, 7 Dale Street, Manchester M1 1JB
☎0161 228 2362, ext 210
Fax 0161 228 3533
✉ fmn@writersbureau.com
www.writersbureau.com/resources.htm

Contact *Angela Cox*
SUBSCRIPTION £29 p.a.

Founded in 1995 to help and advise new and established freelance writers. Members receive a copy of *Freelance Market News* each month which gives news, views and the latest advice and guidelines about publications at home and abroad. Other benefits include one free appraisal of prose or poetry each year, reduced entry to **The Writers Bureau** writing competition, reduced fees for writing seminars and discounts on books for writers.

Association of Golf Writers

1 Pilgrims Bungalow, Mulberry Hill, Chilham CT4 8AH
☎01227 732496 Fax 01227 732496
✉ andyfarrell@compuserve.com
Honorary Secretary *Andy Farrell*

Founded 1938. Aims to cooperate with golfing bodies to ensure best possible working conditions.

Association of Illustrators

81 Leonard Street, London EC2A 4QS
☎020 7613 4328 Fax 020 7613 4417
✉ info@a-o-illustrators.demon.co.uk
www.theaoi.com

Contact *Membership & Publications Secretary*

Founded 1973 to promote illustration, protect illustrators' rights, and encourage professional standards. The AOI is a non-profit-making trade association dedicated to its members, to protecting their interests and promoting their work. Talks, seminars, a journal, regional groups, legal and portfolio advice as well as a number of related publications such as *Rights, The Illustrator's Guide to Professional Practice, Survive, The*

Illustrator's Guide to a Professional Career and *Images*, the only jury-selected annual of British illustration.

Association of Independent Libraries

Leeds Library, 18 Commercial Street, Leeds LS1 6AL
☎0113 245 3071

Chairman *Geoffrey Forster*
Secretary *Krystyna Smithers*

Established to 'further the advancement, conservation and restoration of a little-known but important living portion of our cultural heritage'. Members include the **London Library, Devon & Exeter Institution, Linen Hall Library** and **Plymouth Proprietary Library**.

Association of Learned and Professional Society Publishers

South House, The Street, Clapham, Worthing BN13 3UU
☎01903 871686 Fax 01903 871457
✉ chief.exec@alpsp.org
www.alpsp.org

Chief Executive *Sally Morris*
Business Manager *Jill Tolson*
Editors, Learned Publishing *Robert Welham* (UK), *Alma Wills* (USA)

The international trade association for not-for-profit publishers and those who work with them. It currently has 280 members in 28 countries. ALPSP provides representation of its sector, cooperative services such as the ALPSP Learned Journals Collection, professional development activities and a wealth of information and advice.

Association of Scottish Motoring Writers

c/o Scottish and Universal Newspapers, 5/15 Bank Street, Airdrie ML6 6AF
☎01236 748048 Fax 01236 748098
✉ jmurdoch@s-un.co.uk

Secretary *John Murdoch*
SUBSCRIPTION £45 (Full); £25 (Associate)

Founded 1961. Aims to co-ordinate the activities of, and provide shared facilities for, motoring writers resident in Scotland. Membership is by invitation only.

Australian Copyright Council

PO Box 1986, Strawberry Hills, NSW 2016, Australia
☎00 61 29318 1788 Fax 00 61 29698 3536

info@copyright.org.au
www.copyright.org.au

Contact *Customer Service*

Founded 1968. The Council's activities and services include a range of publications, organising and speaking about copyright at seminars, research, consultancies and free legal advice. Aims include assistance for copyright owners to exercise their rights effectively, raising awareness about the importance of copyright and seeking changes to the law of copyright.

Australian Publishers Association

60/89 Jones Street, Ultimo, NSW 2007, Australia
☎00 61 2 9281 9788
apa@publishers.asn.au
www.publishers.asn.au

Chief Executive *Susan Bridge*

Annual membership subscription open to Australian publishers

Founded 1948. The APA initiates programmes that contribute to the development of publishing in Australia, virgorously protects and furthers the interests of copyright owners, agents and licensees and actively represents members' interests to government and other organisations as appropriate. The Association encourages excellence in writing, editing, design, production, marketing and distribution of published works in Australia, protects freedom of expression and manages members' funds to further the interests of the industry.

Australian Society of Authors

PO Box 1566, Strawberry Hills, NSW 2012, Australia
☎00 61 2 9318 0877   Fax 00 61 2 9318 0530
asa@asauthors.org
www.asauthors.org

Executive Director *José Borghino*

Founded 1963. The ASA aims to promote and protect the professional interests of Australian authors. Provides contract advice and assists authors on industry standards and practices. Publishes *Australian Author* magazine.

Authors' Club

40 Dover Street, London W1S 4NP
☎020 7499 8581   Fax 020 7409 0913
www.authorsclub.co.uk

Secretary *Lucy Jane Tetlow*

Founded in 1891 by Sir Walter Besant, the Authors' Club welcomes as members writers, agents, publishers, critics, journalists, academics and anyone involved with literature and the written word. Administers the **Authors' Club Best First Novel Award** and **Sir Banister Fletcher Award**, and organises regular talks and dinners with well-known guest speakers. Membership fee: apply to secretary.

Authors' Licensing & Collecting Society Limited (ALCS)

Marlborough Court, 14–18 Holborn, London EC1N 2LE
☎020 7395 0600   Fax 020 7395 0660
alcs@alcs.co.uk
www.alcs.co.uk

Chief Executive *Jane Carr*

SUBSCRIPTION £10.00 incl. VAT (UK; free to members of Society of Authors, Writers' Guild, NUJ, BAJ and CIOJ)

Founded 1977. The UK collective rights management society for writers and their successors, ALCS is a non-profit organisation whose principal purpose is to ensure that hard-to-collect revenues due to writers are efficiently collected and speedily distributed. Established to give assistance to writers through the protection and exploitation of collective rights, ALCS has distributed over £100 million in secondary royalties to writers since its creation.

ALCS represents all types of writer, fiction and non-fiction, including educational, research and academic authors, scriptwriters, playwrights, poets, editors and freelance journalists across the print and broadcast media. On joining, members give ALCS a mandate to administer on their behalf those rights which the law determines must be received or which are best handled collectively. Chief among these are: photocopying, cable retransmission (including the fees for BBC Prime and BBC World Service programming), rental and lending rights (but not British Public Lending Right), off-air recording, electronic rights, the performing right and public reception of broadcasts. The society is a prime resource and a leading authority on copyright matters and writers' collective interests. It maintains a watching brief on all matters affecting copyright both in Britain and abroad, making representations to UK government authorities and the EU. Visit the ALCS website or contact the office for registration forms and further information.

BAPLA (British Association of Picture Libraries and Agencies)

18 Vine Hill, London EC1R 5DZ
☎020 7713 1780   Fax 020 7713 1211
enquiries@bapla.org.uk

www.bapla.org
Everything you need to know about finding, buying and selling pictures. Established 1975.

BFC
See **British Film Commission**

The Bibliographical Society
c/o Institute of English Studies, Room 304, Senate House, Malet Street, London WC1E 7HU
☎020 7862 8679   Fax 020 7862 8720
✉ secretary@bibsoc.org.uk
President *D. Shaw*
Honorary Secretary *M. L. Ford*
SUBSCRIPTION £33 p.a.

Aims to promote and encourage the study and research of historical, analytical, descriptive and textual bibliography, and the history of printing, publishing, bookselling, bookbinding and collecting; to hold meetings at which papers are read and discussed; to print and publish works concerned with bibliography; to form a bibliographical library. Awards grants and bursaries for bibliographical research. Publishes a quarterly magazine called *The Library*.

Booksellers Association of the UK & Ireland Ltd
Minster House, 272 Vauxhall Bridge Road, London SW1V 1BA
☎020 7802 0802   Fax 020 7802 0803
✉ mail@booksellers.org.uk
www.booksellers.org.uk
Chief Executive *Tim Godfray*

Founded 1895. The BA helps 3200 independent, chain and multiple members to sell more books, reduce costs and improve efficiency. It represents members' interests to the UK Government, European Commission, publishers, authors and others in the trade as well as offering marketing assistance, running training courses, conferences, seminars and exhibitions. Together with **The Publishers Association**, coordinates World Book Day. Publishes directories, catalogues, surveys and various other publications connected with the book trade and administers the **Whitbread Book Awards**.

Booktrust
Book House, 45 East Hill, London SW18 2QZ
☎020 8516 2977   Fax 020 8516 2978
✉ info@booktrust.org.uk
www.booktrust.org.uk
www.booktrusted.com

Director *Chris Meade*
Press & Publicity *Helen Hayes*

Founded 1925. Booktrust, the independent educational charity promoting books and reading, runs the Book Information Line giving accurate facts about topical books and the book world (☎0906 516 1193, weekdays 10 am to 1.00 pm; calls charged at £1.50 per minute). Runs Booktrusted.com, their website for all those who care what young people read which includes details of Children's Book Week and Booktrusted publications. Administers many literary prizes such as the **Orange** and **Booktrust Teenage Prize** for fiction only, creative reading projects like Bookscapes, and runs Bookstart, the acclaimed national scheme which aims to supply a free introductory bag of baby books to all babies at their eight-month health check.

British Academy of Composers and Songwriters
2nd Floor, British Music House, 25–27 Berners Street, London W1T 3LR
☎020 7636 2929   Fax 020 7636 2212
✉ info@britishacademy.com
www.britishacademy.com
Head of Membership *Kizzy Donaldson*

The Academy represents the interests of music writers of all genres, providing advice on professional and artistic matters. Publishes bimonthly magazines and administers the annual Ivor Novello Awards and British Composer Awards.

British Association of Communicators in Business (CiB)
Suite A, First Floor, The Auriga Building, Davy Avenue, Knowhill, Milton Keynes MK5 8HG
☎0870 121 7606   Fax 0870 121 7601
✉ enquiries@cib.uk.com
www.cib.uk
Secretary General *Kathie Jones*

Founded 1949. The Association aims to be the 'market leader for those involved in corporate media management and practice by providing professional, authoritative, dynamic, supportive and innovative services'.

British Association of Journalists
89 Fleet Street, London EC4Y 1DH
☎020 7353 3003   Fax 020 7353 2310
General Secretary *Steve Turner*
SUBSCRIPTION National newspaper staff, national broadcasting staff, national news

agency staff: £17.50 a month. Other seniors, including magazine journalists, PRs and freelances who earn the majority of their income from journalism: £10 a month. Journalists under 24: £7.50 a month.

Founded 1992. Aims to protect and promote the industrial and professional interests of journalists.

British Association of Picture Libraries and Agencies
See **BAPLA**

British Centre for Literary Translation
University of East Anglia, Norwich NR4 7TJ
☎01603 592785 Fax 01603 592737
www.uea.ac.uk/eas/centres/bclt/bclt.intro.shtm
Contact *Catherine Fuller*

Founded 1989, BCLT is funded jointly by Arts Council England and the University of East Anglia. It aims to raise the profile of literary translation in the UK through events, publications, activities and research aimed at professional translators, students and the general reader. Member of the international RECIT literary translation network. Activities include the annual NESTA Sebald Lecture in London, Summer School, translator in residence scheme funded by the EC Culture 2000 programme and a joint website with the British Council (www.literary-translation.com). BCLT has a PhD programme in literary translation and is developing undergraduate and postgraduate provision. Joint sponsor with BCLA of the John Dryden Translation Prize. Publishes a journal *In Other Words* and *New Books in German*. Free mailing list.

British Copyright Council
Copyright House, 29–33 Berners Street, London W1T 3AB
☎01986 788122 Fax 01986 788847
✉ copyright@bcc2.demon.co.uk
Contact *Janet Ibbotson*

Works for the national and international acceptance of copyright and acts as a lobby/watchdog organisation on behalf of creators, publishers and performers on copyright and associated matters. Publications include *Guide to the Law of Copyright and Rights in Performances in the UK*.

The British Council
10 Spring Gardens, London SW1A 2BN
☎020 7930 8466/7389 4268 (Press Office)
Fax 020 7839 6347

www.britishcouncil.org
Head of Literature *Margaret Meyer*

The British Council promotes Britain abroad. It provides access to British ideas, expertise and experience in education, the English language, literature and the arts, science and technology and governance. Works in 110 countries running a mix of offices, libraries, resource centres and English teaching operations.

British Equestrian Writers' Association
Priory House, Station Road, Swavesey, Cambridge CB4 5QJ
☎01954 232084 Fax 01954 231362
✉ gnewsumn@aol.com
Contact *Gillian Newsum*
SUBSCRIPTION £15

Founded 1973. Aims to further the interests of equestrian sport and improve, wherever possible, the working conditions of the equestrian press. Membership is by invitation of the committee. Candidates for membership must be nominated and seconded by full members and receive a majority vote of the committee.

British Film Commission (BFC)
10 Little Portland Street, London W1W 7JG
☎020 7861 7860 Fax 020 7861 7864
www.bfc.co.uk

Founded in 1991, the British Film Council is now a division of the Film Council. Its remit is to promote the UK as an international production centre by encouraging the use of British artists and technicians, technical services, facilities and locations, and to provide wide-ranging support to those filming and contemplating filming in the UK.

British Film Institute
21 Stephen Street, London W1T 1LN
☎020 7255 1444 Fax 020 7436 0439
www.bfi.org.uk
Chair *Anthony Minghella CBE*
Director *Amanda Nevill*
24-hour *bfi* events line: 0870 240 4050

The **British Film Institute** was established in 1933 to promote greater understanding, appreciation and access to film and television culture. Its activities and services include preserving the world's largest collection of film and television material and running the National Film Theatre, the *bfi* London IMAX cinema, the Times *bfi* London Film Festival and the *bfi* National Library. It also releases films in cinemas and on video and DVD, and publishes books and educational resources. Visit the website to find out more.

British Guild of Beer Writers

68b Elmwood Road, London SE24 9NR
✉ peterhaydon@onetel.net.uk
www.beerwriters.co.uk
Secretary *Peter Haydon*
SUBSCRIPTION £40 p.a.

Founded 1988. Aims to improve standards in beer writing and at the same time extend public knowledge of beers and brewing. Publishes a directory of members with details of their publications and their particular areas of interest; this is then circulated to newspapers, magazines, trade press and broadcasting organisations. Also publishes a monthly newsletter, the *BGBW Newsletter*. As part of the plan to improve writing standards and to achieve a higher profile for beer, the Guild offers annual awards, The Gold and Silver Tankard Awards, to writers and broadcasters judged to have made the most valuable contribution towards this end in their work. Meetings are held regularly.

British Guild of Travel Writers

12 Askew Crescent, London W12 9DW
☎020 8749 1128 Fax 020 8749 1128
✉ charlotte.c@virtualnecessities.com
www.bgtw.org
Chairman *Melissa Shales*
Secretariat *Charlotte Copeman*
SUBSCRIPTION £100 p.a.

The professional association of travel writers, broadcasters, photographers and editors which aims to serve its members' professional interests by acting as a forum for debate, discussion and 'networking'. The Guild publishes an annual Year Book and has a website giving full details of all its members and useful trade contacts, holds monthly meetings and has a monthly newsletter. Members are required to spend a significant proportion of their working time on travel.

British Science Fiction Association

1 Long Row Close, Everdon, Daventry
NN11 3BE
☎01327 361661
✉ bsfa@enterprise.net
Chair *Paul and Elizabeth Billinger*
SUBSCRIPTION £21 p.a. (reduction for unwaged)

Founded originally in 1958 by a group of authors, readers, publishers and booksellers interested in science fiction. With a worldwide membership, the Association aims to promote the reading, writing and publishing of science fiction and to encourage SF fans to maintain contact with each other. Publishes *Matrix* bimonthly newsletter with comment and opinions, news of conventions, etc. Contributions from members welcomed; *Vector* bi-monthly critical journal – reviews of books and magazines; *Focus* biannual magazine with articles, original fiction and letters column. Also offers postal writer's workshop. For further information, contact the Membership Secretary Estelle Roberts at 97 Sharp Street, Newland Avenue, Hull HU5 2AE or via e-mail.

British Society of Comedy Writers

61 Parry Road, Ashmore Park,
Wolverhampton WV11 2PS
☎01902 722729 Fax 01902 722729
✉ comedy@bscw.co.uk
www.bscw.co.uk
Contact *Ken Rock*

Founded 1999. The Society aims to develop good practice and professionalism among comedy writers while bringing together the best creative professionals, and working to standards of excellence agreed with the light entertainment industry. Offers a network of industry contacts and a range of products, services and training initiatives including specialised workshops, an annual international conference, script assessment service and opportunities to visit international festivals.

British Society of Magazine Editors (BSME)

137 Hale Lane, Edgware HA8 9QP
☎020 8906 4664 Fax 020 8959 2137
✉ admin@bsme.com
www.bsme.com
Contact *Gill Branston*

Holds regular industry forums and events as well as an annual awards dinner.

British Universities Film & Video Council

See **Learning on Screen**

Broadcasting Press Guild

Tiverton, The Ridge, Woking GU22 7EQ
☎01483 764895 Fax 01483 765882
✉ torin.douglas@bbc.co.uk
Membership Secretary *Richard Last*
Lunch Secretary *Torin Douglas*
SUBSCRIPTION £15 p.a.

Founded 1974 to promote the professional interests of journalists specialising in writing or broadcasting about the media. Organises monthly lunches addressed by leading industry figures, and annual TV and radio awards. Membership by invitation.

BSME
See **British Society of Magazine Editors**

Bureau of Freelance Photographers
Focus House, 497 Green Lanes, London
N13 4BP
☎020 8882 3315 Fax 020 8886 5174
✉ info@thebfp.com
Membership Secretary *Emma Farrell*
SUBSCRIPTION £45 p.a. (UK);
    £60 p.a. (Overseas)

Founded 1965. Assists members in selling their pictures through monthly *Market Newsletter*, and offers advisory, legal assistance and other services.

Campaign for Press and Broadcasting Freedom
Second Floor, 23 Orford Road, London
E17 9NL
☎020 8521 5932
✉ freepress@cpbf.org.uk
www.cpbf.org.uk
Subscription £15 p.a. (concessions available);
    £25 p.a. (Institutions/Organisations)

Broadly based pressure group working for more accountable and accessible media in Britain. Advises on right of reply and takes up the issue of the portrayal of minorities. Members receive *Free Press* (bi-monthly), discounts on publications and news of campaign progress.

Canadian Authors Association
National Office: Box 419, 320 South Shores Road, Campbellford, Ontario K0L 1L0, Canada
☎001 705 653 0323 Fax 001 705 653 0593
✉ admin@canauthors.org
www.canauthors.org
Contact *The Administrator*

Founded 1921. The CAA 'has expanded from a group of published authors concerned with protection of their own property to one that now includes those not yet published who want protection of what they might eventually produce and who need help producing it.' The Association has branches across the country providing support to local members in the form of advice, local contests, publications and writers' circles. Publishes *National Newsline* (quarterly) and *The Canadian Writer's Guide*.

Canadian Publishers' Council
250 Merton Street, Suite 203, Toronto
M4S 1B1, Canada
☎001 416 322 7011 Fax 001 416 322 6999
✉ pubadmin@pubcouncil.ca
www.pubcouncil.ca
Executive Director, External Relations
    Jacqueline Hushion

Founded 1910. Trade association of English-language publishers which represents the domestic and international interests of member companies.

Careers Writers' Association
www.careerswriters.co.uk

Founded 1979. An association of professional careers writers whose work meets its high standards of accuracy and impartiality. It provides a network for members to exchange information and experience and holds meetings on topics of interest to its members. Forges links with organisations that share related interests and maintains regular contact with national education and training bodies, government agencies and publishers. 'The Association can provide a list of its members to organisations that require high standards of careers writing.' See website for details.

Chartered Institute of Journalists
2 Dock Offices, Surrey Quays Road, London
SE16 2XU
☎020 7252 1187 Fax 020 7232 2302
✉ memberservices@ioj.co.uk
www.ioj.co.uk
General Secretary *Dominic Cooper*
SUBSCRIPTION £190 p.a.; £16 (monthly)

Founded 1884. The Institute is concerned with professional journalistic standards and with safeguarding the freedom of the media. It is open to writers, broadcasters and journalists (including self-employed) in all media. Affiliate membership (£120) is available to part-time or occasional practitioners and to overseas journalists who can join the Institute's International Division. Members also belong to the IOJ (TU), an independent trade union which protects, advises and represents them in their employment or freelance work; negotiates on their behalf and provides legal assistance and support. The IOJ (TU) is a certificated independent trade union which represents members' interests in the workplace, and the CIOJ is also a constituent member of the National Council for the Training of Journalists, the **British Copyright Council** and the Journalists Copyright Fund. Editor of the Institute's quarterly magazine is *Andrew Smith*.

Children's Book Circle
c/o Egmont Books Ltd, 239 Kensington High Street, London W8 6SA
✉ nwilkinson@euk.egmont.com
www.childrensbookcircle.org.uk
Membership Secretary *Nicola Wilkinson*

The Children's Book Circle provides a discussion forum for anybody involved with children's books. Regular meetings are addressed by a panel of invited speakers and topics focus on current and controversial issues. Administers the **Eleanor Farjeon Award**.

Children's Books Ireland
17 Lower Camden Street, Dublin 2, Republic of Ireland
☎00 353 1 872 5854 Fax 00 353 1 872 5854
✉ info@childrensbooksireland.com
www.childrensbooksireland.com

Contact *Claire Ranson*
SUBSCRIPTION €25 p.a. (Individual);
€35 (Institutions); €15 (Students);
€45/US$40 (Overseas)

Aims to promote quality children's books and reading. Holds annual spring seminar, summer school and autumn conference for adults. Quarterly magazine, *Inis* and bi-monthly newsletter, *Children's Book News*. Annual children's book festival in October; **Bisto/CBI Book of the Year Award** (see entry under *Prizes*). Publishes *Book Choice for Primary Schools*; *Book Choice for Post Primary Schools*; *The Big Guide 2: Irish Children's Books, What's The Story? The Reading Choices of Young People in Ireland*.

CiB
See **British Association of Communicators in Business**

CILIP in Scotland
1st Floor, Building C, Brandon Gate, Leechlee Road, Hamilton M13 6AU
☎01698 458888 Fax 01698 283170
✉ cilips@slainte.org.uk
www.slainte.org.uk

Director *Elaine Fulton*

CILIP in Scotland (Chartered Institute of Library and Information Professionals in Scotland) – formerly the Scottish Library Association – aims to bring together everyone engaged in or interested in library work in Scotland. The Association has over 2300 members, covering all aspects of library and information work. Its main aims are the promotion of library services and the qualifications and status of librarians.

CILIP: The Chartered Institute of Library and Information Professionals
7 Ridgmount Street, London WC1E 7AE
☎020 7255 0500 Fax 020 7255 0501
✉ info@cilip.org.uk
www.cilip.org.uk

Chief Executive *Bob McKee*

The leading membership body for library and information professionals, formed in 2002 following the unification of the Library Association and the Institute of Information Scientists. **Facet Publishing** (successor to LA Publishing) produces 25–30 new titles each year and has over 200 in print from the LA's back catalogue. Further information from Marketing & External Relations, CILIP.

Circle of Wine Writers
166 Meadvale Road, London W5 1LS
☎020 8930 0181
✉ administration@winewriters.org
www.winewriters.org

Administrator *Andrea Warren*
MEMBERSHIP £35 p.a.

Founded 1960. Membership is open to all those professionally engaged in communicating about wines and spirits, with the exception of people primarily doing so for promotional purposes. Aims to improve the standard of writing, broadcasting and lecturing about wines, spirits and beers; to contribute to the growing knowledge and interest in wine; to promote wines and spirits of quality and to comment adversely on faulty products or dubious practices; to establish and maintain good relations with the news media and the wine trade; to provide members with a strong voice with which to promote their views; to provide a programme of workshops, meetings, talks and tastings.

Cleveland Arts
See **Tees Valley Arts**

Clé, The Irish Book Publishers' Association
19 Parnell Square, Dublin 1, Republic of Ireland
☎00 353 1 670 7393 Fax 00 353 1 670 7642

✉ info@publishingireland.com
www.publishingireland.com

President *Fergal Tobin*
Administrator *Jolly Ronan*

Founded 1970 to promote Irish publishing, protect members' interests and train the industry.

Comedy Writers' Association UK

118 Forest Edge, Buckhurst Hill IG9 5AB
☎020 8505 2476
www.cwauk.co.uk

Honorary President *Ken Dodd*
Chairman *Bob Orr*
MEMBERSHIP Secretary *Doreen Friend*

Founded 1981 to assist and promote the work of comedy writers, the Association has grown to become the largest group of independent comedy writers in the UK. Holds annual and one-day seminars. Members receive a monthly newsletter and regular market opportunities.

Comhairle nan Leabhraichean/ The Gaelic Books Council

22 Mansfield Street, Glasgow G11 5QP
☎0141 337 6211 Fax 0141 341 0515
✉ brath@gaelicbooks.net
www.gaelicbooks.net

Chairman *Professor Donald E. Meek*
Director *Ian MacDonald*

Founded 1968 and now a charitable company with its own bookshop. Encourages and promotes Gaelic publishing by giving grants to publishers and writers; providing editorial and word-processing services; retailing Gaelic books; producing a catalogue of all Gaelic books in print and answering enquiries about them; mounting occasional literary evenings and training courses.

Commercial Radio Companies Association

77 Shaftesbury Avenue, London W1D 5DU
☎020 7306 2603 Fax 020 7470 0062
✉ info@crca.co.uk
www.crca.co.uk

Chairman *Lord Eatwell*
Chief Executive *Paul Brown, CBE*
Research and Communications Manager
  Alison Winter
Public Affairs Manager *Lisa Kerr*

The CRCA is the trade body for the independent radio stations. It represents members' interests to Government, Ofcom, trade unions, copyright organisations and other bodies.

The Copyright Licensing Agency Ltd

90 Tottenham Court Road, London
W1T 4LP
☎020 7631 5555 Fax 020 7631 5500
✉ cla@cla.co.uk
www.cla.co.uk

Chief Executive *Peter Shepherd*

CLA is the UK's reproduction rights organisation which looks after the interests of authors, publishers and artists in the photocopying and scanning of extracts from books, journals and periodicals. Founded in 1982 by the **Authors' Licensing and Collecting Society (ALCS)** and the **Publishers Licensing Society Ltd (PLS)** to promote and enforce intellectual property rights of UK rightsholders both at home and abroad. CLA works closely with Reproductive Rights Organizations (RROs) from other countries and has close ties with the Design and Artists Copyright Society (DACS) which represents artists and illustrators. A not-for-profit organisation, CLA licenses the use of copyright text by business, education and government and distributes fees collected via authors, publishers and artists collective societies. CLA has also developed licences which enable digitisation of existing print material The licence enables users to scan and electronically send extracts from copyright works. Scanning and e-mail distribution is only available for UK works at present. Since its inception in 1982, CLA has distributed over £100 million.

Council for British Archaeology

Bowes Morrell House, 111 Walmgate, York
YO1 9WA
☎01904 671417 Fax 01904 671384
✉ info@britarch.ac.uk
www.britarch.ac.uk

Information Officer *Jonathan Bateman*

Founded 1944 to represent and promote archaeology at all levels. Its aims are to improve the public's awareness in and understanding of Britain's past; to carry out research; to survey, guide and promote the teaching of archaeology at all levels of education; to publish a wide range of academic, educational, general and bibliographical works (see **CBA Publishing** under *UK Publishers*).

Council of Academic and Professional Publishers

See **The Publishers Association**

Crime Writers' Association (CWA)

PO Box 273, Boreham Wood WD6 2XA
✉ secretary@thecwa.co.uk
www.thecwa.co.uk
Hon. Secretary *Liz Evans*
MEMBERSHIP Secretary *Rebecca Tope* at
 Crossways Cottage, Walterstone HR2 0DX
MEMBERSHIP £45, £60 (Associate)

Full membership is limited to professional crime writers, but publishers, literary agents, booksellers, etc. who specialise in crime, are eligible for Associate membership. The Association has regional chapters throughout the country, including Scotland. Meetings are held regularly with informative talks frequently given by police, scenes of crime officers, lawyers, etc., and a weekend conference is held annually in different parts of the country. Produces a monthly newsletter for members called *Red Herrings* and presents various annual awards (see entries under *Prizes*).

The Critics' Circle

c/o Catherine Cooper, 69 Marylebone Lane, London W1U 2PH
☎020 7224 1410
www.criticscircle.org.uk
President *Charles Osborne*
Honorary General Secretary *Charles Hedges*
SUBSCRIPTION £25 p.a.

Membership by invitation only. Aims to uphold and promote the art of criticism (and the commercial rates of pay thereof) and preserve the interests of its members: professionals involved in criticism of film, drama, music and dance.

Cyngor Llyfrau Cymru

See **Welsh Books Council**

Department for Culture, Media and Sport

2–4 Cockspur Street, London SW1Y 5DH
☎020 7211 6000 Fax 020 7211 6270
✉ lauren.mcgovern@culture.gsi.gov.uk
Head of News *Paddy Feeny*

The Department for Culture, Media and Sport has responsibilities for Government policies relating to the arts, museums and galleries, public libraries, sport, gambling, broadcasting, Press standards, the built heritage, the film and music industries, tourism and the National Lottery. It funds the **Arts Council**, national museums and galleries, the **British Library**, the **Public Lending Right** and the Royal Commission on Historical Manuscripts. It is responsible within Government for the public library service in England, and for library and information matters generally, where they are not the responsibility of other departments.

Directory & Database Publishers Association

PO Box 23034, London W6 0RJ
☎020 8846 9707
✉ rosemarypettit@onetel.net.uk
www.directory-publisher.co.uk
Contact *Rosemary Pettit*
SUBSCRIPTION £120 – £1200 p.a.

Founded 1970 to promote the interests of *bona fide* directory and database publishers and protect the public from disreputable and fraudulent practices. The objectives of the Association are to maintain a code of professional practice to safeguard public interest; to raise the standard and status of directory publishing throughout the UK; to promote business directories as a medium for advertising; to protect the legal and statutory interests of directory publishers; to foster bonds of common interest among responsible directory publishers and to provide for the exchange of technical, commercial and management information between members. Meetings, seminars, conference, newsletter, awards, statistics, business support helpline.

Drama Association of Wales

The Old Library Building, Singleton Road, Splott, Cardiff CF24 2ET
☎029 2045 2200 Fax 029 2045 2277
✉ aled.daw@virgin.net
Contact *Teresa Hennessy*

Runs a large playscript lending library; holds an annual playwriting competition (see entry under *Prizes*); offers a script-reading service (£15 per script) which usually takes three months from receipt of play to issue of reports. From plays submitted to the reading service, selected scripts are considered for publication of a short run (70–200 copies). Writers receive a percentage of the cover price on sales and a percentage of the performance fee.

Edinburgh Bibliographical Society

National Library of Scotland, George IV Bridge, Edinburgh EH1 1EW
✉ warrenmcdougall@aol.com
www.edbibsoc.lib.ed.ac.uk
Honorary Secretary *Warren McDougall*
SUBSCRIPTION £10; £15 (Institution);
 £7 (Students)

Founded 1890. Organises lectures on bibliographical topics and visits to libraries. Publishes an occasional journal called *Transactions*, which is free to members, and other occasional publications.

Educational Publishers Council
See **The Publishers Association**

Electronic Publishers' Forum
See **The Publishers Association**

The English Association
University of Leicester, University Road
LE1 7RH
☎0116 252 3982 Fax 0116 252 2301
✉ engassoc@le.ac.uk
www.le.ac.uk/engassoc/

Chief Executive *Helen Lucas*

Founded 1906 to promote understanding and appreciation of the English language and its literatures. Activities include sponsoring a number of publications and organising lectures and conferences for teachers, plus annual sixthform conferences. Publications include *Year's Work in Critical and Cultural Theory, English, Use of English, English 4–11, Essays and Studies* and *Year's Work in English Studies*.

English PEN
Lancaster House, 33 Islington High Street,
London N1 9LH
☎020 7713 0023 Fax 020 7713 0005
✉ enquiries@englishpen.org
www.englishpen.org

Executive Director *Susanna Nicklin*
MEMBERSHIP Cheque/standing order:
£45/£40 (London/Overseas);
£40/£35 (Country)

English PEN is part of International PEN, a worldwide association of writers and other literary professionals which promotes literature, fights for freedom of expression and speaks out for writers who are imprisoned or harassed for having criticised their governments, or for publishing other unpopular views.

Founded in London in 1921, International PEN now consists of over 130 centres in almost 100 countries. PEN originally stood for poets, essayists and novelists, but membership is now open to all literary professionals. It is also possible to become a 'Friend of English PEN'. A programme of talks and discussions, and other activities such as social gatherings, is supplemented by mailings, website and annual congress at one of the centre countries.

Federation of Entertainment Unions
1 Highfield, Twyford, Nr Winchester
SO21 1QR
☎01962 713134 Fax 01962 713134
✉ harris.s@btconnect.com

Secretary *Steve Harris*

Plenary meetings six times annually and meetings of the Film and Electronic Media Committee six times annually on alternate months. Additionally, there are Training & European Committees. Represents the following unions: British Actors' Equity Association; Broadcasting Entertainment Cinematograph and Theatre Union; Musicians' Union; AEEU; **National Union of Journalists**; **The Writers' Guild of Great Britain**.

The Federation of Worker Writers and Community Publishers (FWWCP)
Burslem School of Art, Queen Street, Stoke on Trent ST6 3EJ
☎01782 822327
✉ thefwwcp@tiscali.co.uk
www.thefwwcp.org.uk

Administrator/Coordinator *Tim Diggles*

The FWWCP is a federation of writing groups committed to writing and publishing based on working-class experience and creativity. The FWWCP is the membership's collective national voice and has for some time been given funding by the **Arts Council**. Founded in 1976, it comprises around 80 member groups, each one with its own identity, reflecting its community and membership. These groups represent over 5000 people who regularly (often weekly) meet to offer constructive criticism, produce books and tapes, perform and share skills, offering creative and critical support. There are writers' workshops of long standing; adult literacy organisations; groups working mainly in oral and local history; groups and local networks of writers who come together to publish, train or perform; groups with a specific remit to further the aims of a section of the community such as the homeless or disabled.

Although diverse in nature, member organisations share the aim of making writing and publishing accessible to people and encourage them to take an active, cooperative and democratic role in writing, performing and publishing. The main activities include training days and weekends to learn and share skills, a quarterly magazine, a quarterly broadsheet of members' writing, a major annual festival of writing and networking between member organisations.

The FWWCP has published a number of anthologies and is willing to work with other organisations on publishing projects. Membership is open only to groups but individuals will be put in touch with groups which can help them, and become friends of the Federation. Contact the address above for an information leaflet.

Fellowship of Authors and Artists

PO Box 158, Hertford SG13 8FA
☎0870 747 2514   Fax 0870 747 2557
✉ fellowship@compassion-in-business.co.uk
www.author-fellowship.co.uk

Contact *Graham Irwin*

Founded in 2000 to promote and encourage the use of writing and all art forms as a means of therapy and self healing; to provide a valuable resource and meeting point for all interested parties including, but not limited to, writers, artists, counsellors and healers; to publish as web pages or e-books any suitable works that may help to support or promote the aims of the fellowship.

Film Council

See **UK Film Council**

Foreign Press Association in London

11 Carlton House Terrace, London
SW1Y 5AJ
☎020 7930 0445   Fax 020 7925 0469
✉ secretariat@foreign-press.org.uk
www.foreign-press.org.uk

General Manager *Bob Jenner*
MEMBERSHIP (incl. VAT) £153 p.a. (Full);
   £142 (Associate Journalists); £215
   (Associate Non-Journalists)

Founded 1888. Non-profit-making service association for foreign correspondents based in London, providing a variety of press-related services.

The Gaelic Books Council

See **Comhairle nan Leabhraichean**

The Garden Writers' Guild

c/o Institute of Horticulture, 14/15 Belgrave Square SW1X 8PS
☎020 7245 6943
✉ gwg@horticulture.org.uk

www.gardenwriters.co.uk
Contact *Angela Clarke*
SUBSCRIPTION £45; (£40 to Institute of
   Horticulture members); £55 (Associate
   members)

Founded 1990. Aims to raise the quality of gardening communication, to help members operate efficiently and profitably, to improve liaison between garden communicators and the horticultural industry. Administers an annual awards scheme. Operates a mailing service and organises press briefing days.

Guild of Agricultural Journalists

Isfield Cottage, Church Road, Crowborough TN6 1BN
☎01892 611618   Fax 01892 613394
✉ don.gomery@farmingline.com
www.gaj.org.uk

Honorary General Secretary *Don Gomery*
SUBSCRIPTION £40 p.a.

Founded 1944 to promote a high professional standard among journalists who specialise in agriculture, horticulture and allied subjects. Represents members' interests with representative bodies in the industry; provides a forum through meetings and social activities for members to meet eminent people in the industry; maintains contact with associations of agricultural journalists overseas; promotes schemes for the education of members and for the provision of suitable entrants into agricultural journalism.

Guild of Editors

See **Society of Editors**

The Guild of Food Writers

48 Crabtree Lane, London SW6 6LW
☎020 7610 1180   Fax 020 7610 0299
✉ gfw@gfw.co.uk
www.gfw.co.uk

Administrator *Christina Thomas*
SUBSCRIPTION £70

Founded 1985. The objects of the Guild are to bring together professional food writers including journalists, broadcasters and authors, to extend the range of members' knowledge and experience by arranging discussions, tastings and visits, and to encourage new writers through competitions and awards. The Guild aims to contribute to the growth of public interest in, and knowledge of, the subject of food and to campaign for improvements in the quality of food.

Guild of Motoring Writers

39 Beswick Avenue, Ensbury Park,
Bournemouth BH10 4EY
☎01202 518808   Fax 01202 518808
✉ gensec@gomw.co.uk
www.guildofmotoringwriters.co.uk
General Secretary *Patricia Lodge*

Founded 1944. Represents members' interests
and provides a forum for members to exchange
information.

Horror Writers Association

UK Contact: 24 Pearl Road, London E17 4QZ
✉ hwa@horror.org
www.horror.org
US Contact: HWA Membership, PO Box
50577, Palo Alto, CA 94303, USA
☎001 650 561 9511

Contact (UK) *Jo Fletcher*

Founded 1987. World-wide organisation of
writers and publishers dedicated to promoting
the interests of writers of horror and dark fantasy. Publishes a bi-monthly newsletter, issues
e-mail bulletins, gives access to lists of horror
agents, reviewers and bookstores; and keys to
the 'Members Only' area of the HWA website.
Presents the annual **Bram Stoker Awards**
(see entry under *Prizes*).

HWA

See **Horror Writers Association**

Independent Publishers Guild

PO Box 93, Royston SG8 5GH
☎01763 247014   Fax 01763 246293
✉ info@ipg.uk.com
www.ipg.uk.com
Executive Director *Sheila Bounford*
Subscription £150 + VAT p.a.

Founded 1962. Membership open to independent publishers, packagers and suppliers, i.e.
professionals in allied fields. Regular meetings,
annual conference, seminars, mailings and
e-mail bulletin.

Independent Television Association

See **ITV Network Ltd**

Independent Theatre Council

12 The Leathermarket, Weston Street,
London SE1 3ER
☎020 7403 1727   Fax 020 7403 1745
✉ admin@itc-arts.org
www.itc-arts.org
Director *Charlotte Jones*

The management association and representative
body for small/middle-scale performing arts
organisations and individuals. Publications available from ITC includes *A Guide for Writers and
Companies*. Negotiates contracts and has established standard agreements for theatre professionals with Equity. The rights and fee structure
agreement, reached with **The Writers' Guild**
in 1991, was updated in December 2002.
Contact The Writers' Guild for details.

Institute of Copywriting

Honeycombe House, Bagley, Wedmore
BS28 4TD
☎01934 713563   Fax 01934 713492
✉ copy@inst.org
www.inst.org/copy
Secretary *Lynn Hall*

Founded 1991 to promote copywriters and
copywriting (writing publicity material). Maintains a code of practice. Membership is open to
students as well as experienced practitioners.
Runs training courses (see entry under *UK
Writers' Courses*). Has a list of approved copywriters. Answers queries relating to copywriting.
Contact the Institute for a free booklet.

Institute of Linguists

Saxon House, 48 Southwark Street, London
SE1 1UN
☎020 7940 3100   Fax 020 7940 3101
✉ info@iol.org.uk
www.iol.org.uk
Chief Executive Officer *Henry Pavlovich*
Membership Services Manager *Stephen Eden*

Founded 1910. Professional association for
translators, interpreters and trainers; examining
body for languages at degree level and above for
vocational purposes; the National Register of
Public Service Interpreters is managed by
NRPSI Limited, an IoL subsidiary. Subscription
rates on application. The Institute's limited
company, Language Services Ltd, provides
customised assessments of language-oriented
requirements, skills, etc.

Institute of Translation and Interpreting (ITI)

Fortuna House, South Fifth Street, Milton
Keynes MK9 2EU
☎01908 325250   Fax 01908 325259
✉ info@iti.org.uk
www.iti.org.uk

Founded 1986. The ITI is an association of
translators and interpreters to promote the high-

est standards in their field. It has strong corporate membership and runs professional development courses and conferences. Membership is open to those with a genuine and proven involvement in translation and interpreting (including students). ITI's *Directory of Members*, its bi-monthly *Bulletin* and other publications are available from the Secretariat, which also offers a free referral service for those in need of a professional translator/interpreter. ITI is a full and active member of FIT (International Federation of Translators).

Irish Book Publishers' Association
See **Clé**

Irish Copyright Licensing Agency Ltd
Irish Writers' Centre, 19 Parnell Square, Dublin 1, Republic of Ireland
☎00 353 1 872 9202 Fax 00 353 1 872 2035
✉ info@icla.ie
www.icla.ie
Executive Director *Samantha Holman*

Founded 1992 by writers and publishers in Ireland to provide a scheme through which rights holders can give permission, and users of copyright material can obtain permission, to copy.

Irish Playwrights and Screenwriters Guild
Irish Writers' Centre, 19 Parnell Square, Dublin 1, Republic of Ireland
☎00 353 1 492 3808 Fax 00 353 1 872 6282
✉ david.cavanagh@script.ie
www.script.ie
Contact *David Cavanagh*
SUBSCRIPTION details available on request

Founded in 1969 to safeguard the rights of scriptwriters for radio, stage and screen.

Irish Translators' & Interpreters' Association
Irish Writers' Centre, 19 Parnell Square, Dublin 1, Republic of Ireland
☎00 353 1 872 1302 Fax 00 353 1 872 6282
✉ secretary-itia@ntlworld.com
www.translatorsassociation.ie
Honorary Secretary *Anette Schiller*
Annual Membership €80 (Corporate); €55 (Professional); €30 (Ordinary); €15 (Student)

Founded 1986. The Association is open to all translators: technical, commercial, literary and cultural, and to all classes of interpreters. It is also for those with an interest in translation such as teachers and third-level students. Issues a yearly *Register of Members*, a quarterly magazine, *Translation Ireland* and a montly eZine, the *ITIA Bulletin*, as well as a series of leaflets and brochures referring to the joint professions.

Irish Writers' Union
Irish Writers' Centre, 19 Parnell Square, Dublin 1, Republic of Ireland
☎00 353 1 872 1302 Fax 00 353 1 872 6282
✉ info@writerscentre.ie
www.ireland-writers.com
Chairman *Conor Kostick*
Secretary *Anthony P. Quinn*
SUBSCRIPTION €45 p.a.; €25 (Associate)

Founded 1986 to promote the interests and protect the rights of writers in Ireland.

ISBN Agency
3rd Floor, Midas House, 62 Goldsworth Road, Woking GU21 6LQ
☎0870 777 8712 Fax 0870 777 8714
✉ isbn@nielsenbookdata.co.uk
www.nielsenbookdata.com

ISBNs are product numbers used by all sections of the book trade for ordering and listing purposes. While ISBNs have no links to copyright and carry no form of legal protection for the book, they will enable your books to be listed on bibliographic databases and may therefore help sales. The UK Standard Book Numbering Agency is the national ISBN agency, responsible for assigning ISBN prefixes to publishers based in the UK or Republic of Ireland. Its services include advising publishers on the correct implementation of the ISBN system and maintaining a database of publishers and their prefixes, as well as providing technical advice and assistance to publishers and the booktrade on all aspects of ISBN usage. Applications for ISBNs for new publishers, help with calculating ISBNs and additional prefixes are all available from the Agency.

Isle of Man Authors
11 Christian Avenue, Ballastowell Gardens, Ramsey IM8 2AU
☎01624 815634
Secretary *Mrs Beryl Sandwell*
SUBSCRIPTION £5 p.a.

An association of writers living on the Isle of Man, which has links with the **Society of Authors**.

ITC
See **Independent Theatre Council**

ITI
See **Institute of Translation and Interpreting**

ITV Network Ltd.
200 Gray's Inn Road, London WC1X 8HF
☎020 7843 8000 Fax 020 7843 8158
www.itv.com
Director of Programmes *Nigel Pickard*

The ITV Network Ltd., wholly owned by the ITV companies, independently commissions and schedules the television programmes which are shown across the ITV network. As a successor to the Independent Television Association, it also provides a range of services to the ITV companies where a common approach is required.

IVCA (International Visual Communication Association)
19 Pepper Street, Glengall Bridge, London E14 9RP
☎020 7512 0571 Fax 020 7512 0591
✉ info@ivca.org
www.ivca.org
Chief Executive *Wayne Drew*
Publications and Information Officer *Louise Miller*

The IVCA is a professional association representing the interests of the users and suppliers of visual communications. In particular it pursues the interests of producers, commissioners and manufacturers involved in the non-broadcast and independent facilities industries and also business event companies. It represents all sizes of company and freelance individuals, offering information and advice services, publications, a professional network, special interest groups, a magazine and a variety of events including the UK's Film and Video Communications Festival.

Learning on Screen (British Universities Film & Video Council)
77 Wells Street, London W1T 3QJ
☎020 7393 1500 Fax 020 7393 1555
www.bufvc.ac.uk/learningonscreen.org.uk

Learning on Screen is the title which was used by the Society for Screen-Based Learning (SSBL) for its courses and conferences. In January 2004 the SSBL merged with the British Universities Film & Video Council (BUFVC). The title

Learning on Screen, now adopted by the BUFVC, will continue for a range of practical, 'hands-on' on-day courses and events around the country as well as the annual Learning on Screen conference and Awards. The BUFCV promotes the production, study and use of moving images and related media for learning, teaching and research. It offers a specialist information service, publications, online services and the unique Off-Air Recording Back-Up Service, recording 44,000 hours per year of UK television.

Lewes Live Literature
See entry under *Festivals*

The Library Association
See **CILIP: The Chartered Institute of Library and Information Professionals**

literaturetraining
PO Box 23595, Leith, Edinburgh EH6 7YXU
☎0131 553 2210
✉ info@literaturetraining.com
www.literaturetraining.com
Coordinator *Philippa Johnston*

A group of seven literature organisations working in partnership to provide information, advice and guidance on professional development for writers and others involved with new writing and literature. Their easy to use, fully searchable website provides a central source of information on literature training and professional development opportunities in the UK and is supported by a range of advisory services. The literaturetraining partners are **The National Association of Writers in Education**, **The National Association for Literature Development**, **writernet**, **The Federation of Worker Wriiters and Community Publishers**, Lapidus, **Survivors' Poetry**, **Apples & Snakes** and **Scottish Book Trust**. literaturetraining is a partner in the CreativePeople Network.

Medical Journalists' Association
Fairfield, Cross in Hand, Heathfield TN21 0SH
☎01435 868786 Fax 01435 865714
✉ pigache@globalnet.co.uk
www.mja-uk.org
Chairman *Pete Moore*
Honorary Secretary *Philippa Pigache*
SUBSCRIPTION £30 p.a.

Founded 1967. Aims to improve the quality and practice of medical and health journalism and to improve relationships and understanding between medical and health journalists and the health and medical professions. Regular meetings with senior figures in medicine and medico politics; educational workshops on important subject areas or issues of the day; debates; awards for medical journalists from commercial sponsors, plus the MJA's own awards financed by members. Publishes a newsletter five times a year.

Medical Writers' Group
The Society of Authors, 84 Drayton Gardens, London SW10 9SB
☎020 7373 6642 Fax 020 7373 5768
✉ info@societyofauthors.org
www.societyofauthors.org/medical

Contact *Dorothy Sym*

Founded 1980. A specialist group within the **Society of Authors** offering advice and help to authors of medical books.

Mystery Writers of America, Inc.
17 East 47th Street, 6th Floor, New York, NY 10017, USA
☎001 212 888 8171 Fax 001 212 888 8107
✉ mwa@mysterywriters.org
www.mysterywriters.org

Office Manager *Margery Flax*
SUBSCRIPTION $95(US)

Founded 1945. Aims to promote and protect the interests of writers of the mystery genre in all media; to educate and inform its membership on matters relating to their profession; to uphold a standard of excellence and raise the profile of this literary form to the world at large. Holds an annual banquet at which the 'Edgars' are awarded (named after Edgar Allan Poe).

National Association for Literature Development
PO Box 140, Ilkley LS29 7ET
☎01943 862107
✉ steve@nald.org
www.nald.org

Coordinator *Steve Dearden*

NALD exists to enable literature professionals to talk to each other, develop their professional skills and make the case for increased investment in their work. Offers individual, organisational or corporate membership.

National Association of Writers Groups
The Arts Centre, Biddick Lane, Washington NE38 2AB
☎01262 609228
✉ nawg@tesco.net
www.nawg.co.uk

Secretary *Diane Wilson*
SUBSCRIPTION £25 p.a. + £5 registration (Group); £12 p.a. (Individual)

Founded 1995 with the object of furthering the interests of writers' groups throughout the UK. A registered charity, No: 1059047, NAWG is strictly non-sectarian and non-political. *Publishes* a bi-monthly newsletter, distributed to member groups; gives free entry to competitions for group anthologies, poetry, short stories, articles, novels and sketches; holds an annual open festival of writing with 36 workshops, seminars, individual surgeries led by professional, high-profile writers. Membership is open to all writers' groups and individual writers – there are no restrictions or qualifications required for joining; 160 groups are affiliated to-date.

National Association of Writers in Education
PO Box 1, Sheriff Hutton, York YO60 7YU
☎01653 618429
✉ paul@nawe.co.uk
www.nawe.co.uk

Contact *Paul Munden*
Subscription £20 p.a. (Individual); £10 (Student); £60 (Institution); £30 (Overseas)

Founded 1991. Aims to promote the contribution of living writers to education and to encourage both the practice and the critical appreciation of creative writing. Has over 600 members. Organises national conferences and training courses. A directory of writers who work in schools, colleges and the community is available online. Publishes a magazine, *Writing in Education*, issued free to members three times per year.

National Campaign for the Arts
Pegasus House, 37–43 Sackville Street, London W1S 3EH
☎020 7333 0375 Fax 020 7333 0660
✉ nca@artscampaign.org.uk
www.artscampaign.org.uk

Director *Victoria Todd*
Deputy Director *Anna Leatherdale*

Founded 1984 to represent the cultural sector in Britain and to make sure that the problems facing the arts are properly put to Government, at local and national level. The NCA is an independent body relying on finance from its members. Involved in all issues which affect the arts: public finance, education, lottery funding for the arts, public entertainment licensing, the rights of artists, the place of the arts on the public agenda and structures for supporting culture. Membership open to all arts organisations and to individuals. Literature subscriptions available.

National Literacy Trust

Swire House, 59 Buckingham Gate, London SW1E 6AJ
☎020 7828 2435   Fax 020 7931 9986
✉ contact@literacytrust.org.uk
www.literacytrust.org.uk
www.rif.org.uk
Director *Neil McClelland*

Founded 1993. Independent registered charity (No: 1015539) 'dedicated to building a literate nation in which everyone enjoys the skills, self-esteem and pleasures that literacy can bring.' The only organisation concerned with raising literacy standads for all age groups throughout the UK. Maintains an extensive website with literacy news, summaries of key issues, research and examples of practice nationwide; organises an annual conference, courses and training events; publishes a quarterly magazine, *Literacy Today* and runs a range of initiatives to turn promising ideas into effective action. These include the National Reading Campaign, funded by the government; Reading Is Fundamental, UK, which provides free books to children; Reading The Game, involving the professional football community; the Talk To Your Baby campaign; the Literacy and Social Inclusion Project, a partnership wth the Basic Skills Agency.

National Union of Journalists

Headland House, 308 Gray's Inn Road, London WC1X 8DP
☎020 7278 7916   Fax 020 7837 8143
✉ acorn.house@nuj.org.uk
www.nuj.org.uk
General Secretary *Jeremy Dear*
SUBSCRIPTION £177 p.a. (freelance) or 1% of annual income if lower; or 0.5% if income less than £13,600 p.a.

Represents journalists in all sectors of publishing, print and broadcast. Responsible for wages and conditions agreements which apply across the industry. Provides advice and representation for its members, as well as administering unemployment and other benefits. Publishes various guides and magazines: *On-Line Freelance Directory, Fees Guide, The Journalist* and *The Freelance*.

New Playwrights Trust

See **Writernet**

New Producers Alliance (NPA)

9 Bourlet Close, London W1W 7BP
☎020 7580 2480   Fax 020 7580 2484
✉ queries@npa.org.uk
www.newproducer.co.uk

National membership and training organisation for independent new filmmakers, the NPA provides a forum and focus for over 800 members, ranging from students and first timers to highly experienced feature filmmakers and industry affiliates. Services include: producer training from 'entrance' to 'advanced' levels; seminars, masterclasses, business breakfasts, themed networking evenings and preview screenings; in addition the NPA supports its members at film festivals including Cannes and Edinburgh with events and industry receptions. Provides free advice services including Legal and Tax & Accounting; the NPA also publishes a monthly newsletter and online members directory included in the website. In 2003 the Alliance celebrated its tenth anniversary.

The New SF Alliance (NSFA)

c/o BBR, PO Box 625, Sheffield S1 3GY
www.bbr-online.com/catalogue
Contact *Chris Reed*

Founded 1989. Committed to supporting the work of new writers and artists by promoting independent and small press publications worldwide. 'Helps with finding the right market for your material by providing a mail-order service which allows you to sample magazines, quickly and conveniently from a single address, to help you to find the ones best suited to your needs. What's more, you'll find useful information about many more outlets in the review pages of these magazines, whilst *Light's List* provides contact addresses for a whole host of small press publications, and the *BBR Directory* features books, magazines and other independently-published items as they appear.'

New Writing North

2 School Lane, Whickham, Newcastle upon Tyne NE16 4SL
☎0191 488 8580   Fax 0191 488 8576
✉ mail@newwritingnorth.com
www.newwritingnorth.com
Director *Claire Malcolm*
Administrator *Silvana Michelini*

New Writing North is the literature development agency for the Arts Council North East region and offers many useful services to writers, organising events, readings and courses. NWN produces writing guides and has a website with literary news, events and opportunities. Administers the **Northern Rock Foundation Writer's Award** (see entry under *Bursaries, Fellowships and Grants*) and the Northern Writers' Awards, which include tailored development packages (mentoring and financial help). NWN has strong links with the post of Northern Literary Fellow. NWN also works to develop theatre writing and creative radio writing projects within the region.

The Newspaper Society

Bloomsbury House, 74–77 Great Russell Street, London WC1B 3DA
☎020 7636 7014 Fax 020 7631 5119
✉ ns@newspapersoc.org.uk
www.newspapersoc.org.uk

Director *David Newell*

Founded in 1836, the Newspaper Society is the voice of Britain's regional and local newspapers. It represents and promotes the interests of around 1300 regional daily and weekly, paid for and free, titles. The range of activities and services provided by the Society can be split into two broad areas: marketing and lobbying. Holds a series of conferences and seminars each year and runs the annual Local Newspaper Week.

NPA
See **New Producers Alliance**

NSFA
See **The New SF Alliance**

Outdoor Writers' Guild

PO Box 118, Twickenham TW1 2XB
☎020 8538 9468 Fax 020 8538 9468
www.owg.org.uk

Secretary *Hazelle Jackson*
SUBSCRIPTION £60 p.a.

Founded 1980 to promote, encourage and assist the development and maintenance of professional standards among those involved in all aspects of outdoor journalism. Membership includes all those engaged in outdoor related journalism including writers, photographers, broadcasters, filmmakers, editors, publishers and illustrators. Publishes a quarterly journal, *Bootprint*, and an annual *Directory* (£35; free to members). Presents five Awards for Excellence plus other awards in recognition of achievement. Maintains a website of members' details; informal members' e-mail 'chatline' to exchange news and information; sends out regular media press releases; organises press trips.

PACT (Producers Alliance for Cinema and Television)

45 Mortimer Street, London W1W 8HJ
☎020 7331 6000 Fax 020 7331 6700
✉ enquiries@pact.co.uk
www.pact.co.uk

Chief Executive *John McVay*
Information Manager *David Alan Mills*

Founded 1991. PACT is the trade association of the UK independent feature film, television, animation and interactive media production sector and is a key contact point for foreign producers seeking British co-production, co-finance partners and distributors. Works for producers in the industry at every level and operates a members' regional network throughout the UK with a divisional office in Scotland. Membership services include: a dedicated industrial relations unit; discounted legal advice; a varied calendar of events; business advice; representation at international film and television markets; a comprehensive research programme; various publications: a monthly magazine, an annual members' directory; affiliation with European and international producers' organisations; extensive information and production advice. Lobbies actively with broadcasters, financiers and governments to ensure that the producer's voice is heard and understood in Britain and Europe on all matters affecting the feature film, television, animation and interactive production industry.

PEN
See **English PEN**

Performing Right Society

29–33 Berners Street, London W1T 3AB
☎020 7580 5544 Fax 020 7306 4455
✉ info@prs.co.uk
www.prs.co.uk

PRS collects licence fees for the public performance and broadcast of musical works and distributes this money to its members –writers and publishers of music.

Periodical Publishers Association (PPA)

Queens House, 28 Kingsway, London WC2B 6JR
☎020 7404 4166 Fax 020 7404 4167
✉ info1@ppa.co.uk
www.ppa.co.uk

Founded 1913 to promote and protect the interests of its members in particular and the magazine industry as a whole.

The Personal Managers' Association Ltd

1 Summer Road, East Molesey KT8 9LX
☎020 8398 9796 Fax 020 8398 9796
✉ info@thepma.com
Co-chairs *Michelle Kass, Alan Brodie, Nicholas Young*
Secretary *Angela Adler*
SUBSCRIPTION £250 p.a.

An association of artists' and dramatists' agents (membership not open to individuals). Monthly meetings for exchange of information and discussion. Maintains a code of conduct and acts as a lobby when necessary. Applicants screened. A high proportion of play agents are members of the PMA.

The Picture Research Association

c/o Scala Art Resource, 1 Willow Court, off Willow Street, London EC2A 4QB
☎020 7739 8544 Fax 020 7782 0011
✉ chair@picture-research.org.uk
www.picture-research.org.uk

Chair *To be appointed*
MEMBERSHIP Secretary *Wendy Wilders*
SUBSCRIPTION Members: £45 (Introductory); £55 (Full); £50 (Associate). Magazine only: £25

Founded 1977 as the Society of Picture Researchers & Editors, the Association is a professional body for picture researchers, managers, picture editors and all those involved in the research, management and supply of visual material to all forms of the media. The Association's main aims are to promote the interests and specific skills of its members internationally; to promote and maintain professional standards; to bring together those involved in the research and publication of visual material; to provide a forum for the exchange of information and to provide guidance to its members. Free advisory service for members, regular meetings, quarterly magazine, monthly newsletter and Freelance Register.

Player–Playwrights

9 Hillfield Park, London N10 3QT
☎020 8883 0371
✉ P-P@dial.pipex.com

President *Olwen Wymark*
Contact *Peter Thompson* (at the address above)
SUBSCRIPTION £10 (Joining fee); £6 p.a. thereafter, plus £2 per attendance

Founded 1948. A society giving opportunity for writers new to stage, radio and television, as well as others finding difficulty in achieving results, to work with writers established in those media. At weekly meetings (7.45 pm–10.00 pm, Mondays, upstairs at the Horse and Groom, 128 Great Portland Street, London W1), members' scripts are read or performed by actor members and afterwards assessed and dissected in general discussion. Newcomers and new acting members are always welcome.

PLR

See **Public Lending Right**

PLS

See **Publishers Licensing Society Ltd**

PMA

See **The Personal Managers' Association Ltd**

Poetry Book Society

See under *Organisations of Interest to Poets*

Poetry Ireland

See under *Organisations of Interest to Poets*

The Poetry Society

See under *Organisations of Interest to Poets*

Press Complaints Commission

1 Salisbury Square, London EC4Y 8JB
☎020 7353 1248 Fax 020 7353 8355
✉ pcc@pcc.org.uk
www.pcc.org.uk

Acting Director *Tim Toulmin*
Information Officer *Tonia Milton*

Founded in 1991 to deal with complaints from members of the public about the editorial content of newspapers and magazines. Administers the editors' Code of Practice covering such areas as accuracy, privacy, harrassment and intrusion into grief. Publications available: *Code of Practice, How to Complain* and *Annual Review*.

Private Libraries Association

55 Hamilton Park West, London N5 1AE
☎020 7503 9827 Fax 020 7503 9826
✉ pla@illuminata.co.uk

Honorary Secretary *James Brown*
MEMBERSHIP £25 p.a.

Founded 1956. An international society of book collectors. The Association's objectives are to promote and encourage the awareness of the benefits of book ownership, and the study of books, their production and ownership; to publish works concerned with this, particularly those which are not commercially profitable, to hold meetings at which papers on cognate subjects can be read and discussed. Lectures and exhibitions are open to non-members.

Producers Alliance for Cinema and Television
See **PACT**

Public Lending Right
Richard House, Sorbonne Close, Stockton-on-Tees TS17 6DA
☎01642 604699 Fax 01642 615641
✉ authorservices@plr.com
www.plr.uk.com

Registrar *Jim Parker*

Founded 1979. Public Lending Right is funded by the Department for Culture, Media and Sport to recompense authors for books borrowed from public libraries. Authors and books can be registered for PLR only when application is made during the author's lifetime. To qualify, an author must be resident in the UK or Germany (the latter as part of a reciprocal deal) and the book must be printed, bound and put on sale with an ISBN. In 2004, £6.4 million was distributed to over 18,700 authors (£6.2 million in the previous year) with 280 authors reaching the maximum payment threshold of £6000. The rate per loan was raised in 2004 to 4.85 pence, its highest level to date. Consult the website for further information.

The Publishers Association
29B Montague Street, London WC1B 5BW
☎020 7691 9191 Fax 020 7691 9199
✉ mail@publishers.org.uk
www.publishers.org.uk

Chief Executive *Ronnie Williams, OBE*

The national UK trade association for books, learned journals, and electronic publications, with around 200 member companies in the industry. Very much a trade body representing the industry to Government and the European Commission, and providing services to publishers. Publishes the *Directory of Publishing* in association with **Continuum**. Also home of the Educational Publishers Council (school books), PA's International Division (BDCI), the Council of Academic and Professional Publishers, the Trade Publishers Council and the Electronic Publishers' Forum.

Publishers' Association of South Africa
PO Box 15277, Vlaberg 8018, Cape Town, South Africa

☎00 27 21 426 1726 Fax 00 27 21 426 2728
✉ pasa@publishsa.co.za
www.publishsa.co.za

Founded in 1992 to represent publishing in South Africa, a small but key industry sector. With a membership of approximately 120 companies, the Association includes commercial organisations, university presses, one-person privately-owned publishers as well as importers and distributors.

Publishers Licensing Society Ltd
37–41 Gower Street, London WC1E 6HH
☎020 7299 7730 Fax 020 7299 7780
✉ pls@pls.org.uk
www.pls.org.uk

Chief Executive *Alicia Wise*
Manager *Caroline Elmslie*

Founded in 1981, the PLS obtains mandates from publishers which grant PLS the authority to license photocopying of pages from published works. Some licences for digitisation of printed works are available. PLS aims to maximise revenue from licences for mandating publishers and to expand the range and repertoire of mandated publishers available to licence holders. It supports the **Copyright Licensing Agency (CLA)** in its efforts to increase the number of legitimate users through the issuing of licences and vigorously pursues any infringements of copyright works belonging to rights' holders.

Publishers Publicity Circle
65 Airedale Avenue, London W4 2NN
☎020 8994 1881
✉ ppc-@lineone.net
www.publisherspublicitycircle.co.uk

Contact *Heather White*

Enables book publicists from both publishing houses and freelance PR agencies to meet and share information regularly. Meetings, held monthly in central London, provide a forum for press journalists, television and radio researchers and producers to meet publicists collectively. A directory of the membership is published each year and distributed to over 2500 media contacts.

The Radio Academy
5 Market Place, London W1W 8AE
☎020 7255 2010 Fax 020 7255 2029
✉ info@radioacademy.org
www.radioacademy.org

Director *John Bradford*

SUBSCRIPTIONS £49 (Full); £24.50 (Joint Fund Full); £36 (Associate); £18 (Post-Graduate/Concessionary/E-membership)

Founded 1983. The professional body for people working in the radio industry, the Academy is dedicated to the encouragement, recognition and promotion of excellence throughout the UK radio industry. Membership ranges from students to Governors of the BBC. Hosts the annual Radio Festival which features speakers from all aspects of the industry; holds events in London and the regions; runs masterclasses for those who aspire to enter the radio industry and seminars for the further development of professionals within the industry at various levels. Services include a directory covering all aspects of the industry, a quarterly newsletter and the Academy website.

Romance Writers of America

1600 Stuebner Airline Road, Suite 140, Spring, TX 77379, USA
☎001 832 717 5200 Fax 001 832 717 5201
✉ info@rwanational.org
www.rwanational.org

PR Coordinator *Nicole Kennedy*
MEMBERSHIP $75 p.a. plus $25 joining fee

Founded 1980. RWA, a non-profit association with more than 8400 members worldwide, provides a service to authors at all stages of their careers as well as to the romance publishing industry and its readers. Anyone pursuing a career in romantic fiction may join RWA. Holds an annual conference, and provides contests for both published and unpublished writers through the RITA Awards and Golden Hearts Awards.

The Romantic Novelists' Association

38 Maes y Llan, Dwygyfylchi, Penmaenmawr LL34 6RY
✉ trisha.ashley@tesco.net
www.rna-uk.org
Contact *Trisha Ashley*
SUBSCRIPTION Full & Associate: £28 p.a.;
£33 (Overseas, non-EU); New Writers:
£78; £83 (Overseas, non-EU)

Membership is open to published writers of romantic fiction (modern or historical), or those who have had one or more full-length serials published. Associate membership is open to publishers, editors, literary agents, booksellers, librarians and others having a close connection with novel writing and publishing. Membership in the New Writers' Scheme is available to writers who have not yet had a full-length novel published. New Writers must submit a manuscript each year. The mss receive a report from experienced published members and the reading fee is included in the subscrip-

tion of £78. Meetings are held in London and the regions with guest speakers. The *RNA News* is published bi-monthly and issued free to members. The Association makes three annual awards: The Major Award for the **Romantic Novel of the Year**, and The New Writers Award for the best published novel by a new writer and the category Romance of the Year.

Royal Festival Hall Literature & Talks

See entry under *Festivals*

Royal Society of Literature

Somerset House, Strand, London WC2R 1LA
☎020 7845 4676 Fax 020 7845 4679
✉ info@rslit.org
www.rslit.org
Chairman *Maggie Gee, FRSL*
SUBSCRIPTION £30 p.a.

Founded 1820. Membership by application to the Secretary. Fellowships are conferred by the Society on the proposal of two Fellows. Membership benefits include lectures, discussion meetings, poetry readings and two annual joint meetings with the Royal Society. Lecturers have included John Carey, Michael Holroyd, P.D. James, Jan Morris and Philip Pullman. Presents the **W.H. Heinemann Award**, the **Royal Society of Literature Ondaatje Prize**, the **Royal Society of Literature/Jerwood Awards** and the **V.S. Pritchett Memorial Prize**.

Royal Television Society

Holborn Hall, 100 Gray's Inn Road, London WC1X 8AL
☎020 7430 1000 Fax 020 7430 0924
✉ info@rts.org.uk
www.rts.org.uk
MEMBERSHIP £80 p.a.

Founded 1927. Covers all disciplines involved in the television industry. Provides a forum for debate and conferences on technical, social and cultural aspects of the medium. Presents various awards including journalism, programmes, technology, design and commercials. Publishes *Television Magazine* nine times a year for members and subscribers.

Science Fiction Foundation

Department of Media and Arts, Canterbury Christ Church University College, North Holmes Road, Canterbury CT1 1QU
www.sf-foundation.org
Membership Secretary *Andrew M. Butler*

The SFF is an international academic body for the furtherance of science fiction studies. Publishes a thrice-yearly magazine, *Foundation* (see entry under *Magazines*), which features academic articles and reviews of new fiction. It also has a reference library (see entry under *Library Services*), housed at Liverpool University.

Scottish Book Trust

Sandeman House, Trunk's Close, 55 High Street, Edinburgh EH1 1SR
☎0131 524 0161 Fax 0131 524 0160
✉ info@scottishbooktrust.com
www.scottishbooktrust.com

Contact *Mark Lambert*

Founded 1956. Scottish Book Trust exists to serve readers and writers in Scotland. 'We work to ensure that everyone has access to good books and to related resources and opportunities. We do this by operating the 'Live Literature Scotland' which funds over 1400 visits a year by Scottish writers to a variety of institutions and groups; by supporting Scottish writing through a programme of professional training opportunities for writers; by publishing a wide variety of resources and leaflets to support readership; by promoting initiatives such as National Poetry Day and World Book Day; through our Book Information Service providing free advice and support to readers and writers and the general public.'

Scottish Daily Newspaper Society

48 Palmerston Place, Edinburgh EH12 5DE
☎0131 220 4353 Fax 0131 220 4344
✉ info@sdns.org.uk

Director *Mr J.B. Raeburn*

Founded 1915. Trade association representing publishers of Scottish daily and Sunday newspapers including the major Scottish editions of UK national newspapers.

Scottish Library Association
See **CILIP in Scotland**

Scottish Newspaper Publishers Association

48 Palmerston Place, Edinburgh EH12 5DE
☎0131 220 4353 Fax 0131 220 4344
✉ info@snpa.org.uk
www.snpa.org.uk

Director *Mr J.B. Raeburn*

The representative body for the publishers of paid-for weekly and associated free newspapers in Scotland. Represents the interests of the industry to Government, public and other bodies and provides a range of services including marketing of *The Scottish Weekly Press*, industrial relations, and education and training. It is an active supporter of the Press Complaints Commission.

Scottish Print Employers Federation

48 Palmerston Place, Edinburgh EH12 5DE
☎0131 220 4353 Fax 0131 220 4344
✉ info@spef.org.uk
www.spef.org.uk

Director *Mr J.B. Raeburn*

Founded 1910. Employers' organisation and trade association for the Scottish printing industry. Represents the interests of the industry to Government, public and other bodies and provides a range of services including industrial relations, education, training and commercial activities. Negotiates a national wages and conditions agreement with the Graphical, Paper and Media Union. The Federation is a member of Intergraf, the international confederation for employers' associations in the printing industry. In this capacity its views are channelled on the increasing number of matters affecting print businesses emanating from the European Union.

Scottish Publishers Association

Scottish Book Centre, 137 Dundee Street, Edinburgh EH11 1BG
☎0131 228 6866 Fax 0131 228 3220
✉ carol.lothian@scottishbooks.org
www.scottishbooks.org

Director *Lorraine Fannin*
Member Services Manager *Liz Small*
Financial and Office Administrator *Carol Lothian*
Information and Professional Development Administrator *Katherine A. Naish*

The Association represents over 80 Scottish publishers, from multinationals to small presses, in a number of capacities, but primarily in the co-operative promotion and marketing of their books. The SPA also acts as an information and advice centre for both the trade and general public. Publishes membership lists and the annual *Directory of Publishing in Scotland*. Represents members at international book fairs; runs an extensive training programme in publishing skills; carries out market research; and encourages export initiatives.

Scottish Screen

2nd Floor, 249 West George Street, Glasgow
G2 4QE
☎0141 302 1700   Fax 0141 302 1778
✉ info@scottishscreen.com
www.scottishscreen.com
Infomation Manager *Isabella Edgar*

Founded 1997. Scottish Screen develops, encourages and promotes every aspect of film, television and new media in Scotland through script and company development, short film production, distribution of national lottery film production finance, training, education, exhibition funding, film commission locations support and the Scottish Screen Archive.

Society for Children's Book Writers & Illustrators

Flat 3, 124 Norwood Road, London SE24 9AY
✉ scbwi_bi@hotmail.com
www.wordpool.co.uk/scbwi
British Isles Regional Advisor *Natascha Biebow*

Founded in 1968 by a group of Los Angeles-based writers, the SCBWI is the only international professional organisation for the exchange of information between writers, illustrators, editors, publishers, agents and others involved with literature for young people. With a membership of 18,000 worldwide, it holds three annual international conferences plus a number of regional events, publishes a bi-monthly newsletter and awards grants for works in progress. The British Isles region meets quarterly for speaker events and holds an Illustrator's Day in the spring and a Writer's Day in the autumn. It facilitates critique groups and publishes a quarterly regional newsletter. For membership enquiries, contact the address above.

Society for Editors and Proofreaders (SfEP)

1 Riverbank House, 1 Putney Bridge
Approach, London SW6 3JD
☎020 7736 3278/7736 0901 (Training Dept)
Fax 020 7736 3318
✉ administration@sfep.org.uk
www.sfep.org.uk
Chair *Naomi Laredo*
Vice-Chair *Penny Williams*
Secretary *Val Rice*
SUBSCRIPTION £67.50 p.a. (Individuals) plus
£25 joining fee; Corporate membership
available.

Founded 1988 in response to the growing number of freelance editors and their increasing importance to the publishing industry. Aims to promote high editorial standards by disseminating information through advice and training, and to achieve recognition of the professional status of its members. The Society also supports moves towards recognised standards of training and accreditation for editors and proofreaders. It launched its own Accreditation in Proofreading test in 2002.

Society for Technical Communications (STC)

901 N. Stuart Street, Suite 904, Arlington,
Virginia 22203, USA
☎001 703 522 4114   Fax 001 703 522 2075
www.stc.org
www.stc-europe.org/uk
UK Chapter Contact *Liz Hale*
   (liz35.hale@virgin.net)

Dedicated to advancing the arts and sciences of technical communication, the STC has 25,000 members world-wide, including technical writers, editors, graphic designers, videographers, multimedia artists, Web and intranet page information designers, translators and others whose work involves making technical information available to those who need it. Publishes a quarterly scholarly journal, *Technical Communications* and the magazine, *Intercom*, ten times a year (both available to members only). The UK Chapter, which has about 140 members, hosts meetings and seminars, runs an annual technical publications competition, and publishes its own newsletter six times a year.

The Society of Authors

84 Drayton Gardens, London SW10 9SB
☎020 7373 6642   Fax 020 7373 5768
✉ info@societyofauthors.org
www.societyofauthors.org
General Secretary *Mark Le Fanu*
SUBSCRIPTION £80/75 p.a.

The Society of Authors is an independent trade union, chaired by Antony Beevor, with some 7500 members. As well as campaigning for the profession, it advises members on negotiations with publishers, broadcasting organisations, theatre managers and film companies and on queries or concerns members may have about the business aspects of their writing. The Society assists with complaints and takes action for breach of contract, copyright infringement, etc. Together with the **Writers' Guild**, the Society has played a major role in advancing the Minimum Terms Agreement for authors. Among the Society's publications are *The Author* (quarterly) and the *Quick Guides* series to various aspects of writing (all free of charge to members). Other services include vetting of contracts, emergency funds for writers, and various special discounts. There are groups within the Society for scriptwriters, children's writers and illustrators, educational writers, academic writers, medical writers and translators. Authors under 35 or over 65, not earning a significant income from their writing, may apply for lower subscription rates (after their first year in the case of over-65s). Contact the Society for a free booklet and a copy of *The Author*.

The Society of Authors in Scotland

8 Briar Road, Kirkintilloch, Glasgow G66 3SA
☎0141 776 4280 Fax 0141 776 4280
✉ brian@bdosborne.fsnet.co.uk
www.writersorg.co.uk
Secretary *Brian D. Osborne*

The Scottish branch of the **Society of Authors**, which organises business meetings, social and bookshop events throughout Scotland.

Society of Civil and Public Service Writers

17 The Green, Corby Glen, Grantham
NG33 4NP
✉ joan@lewis.fsnet.co.uk
www.scpsw.co.uk
Membership Secretary *Mrs Joan Lewis*
SUBSCRIPTION £15 p.a.

Founded 1935. Welcomes serving and retired members of the Civil Service, armed forces, Post Office, BT, nursing profession and other public servants who are aspiring or published writers. Offers competitions for short story, article and poetry; e-mail and postal folios for short story and article; AGM, occasional meetings and luncheon held in London; quarterly magazine, *Civil Service Author*, to which members may submit material; Poetry Workshop (extra £3) offers annual weekend outside London, anthology, newsletter, postal folio, competitions. S.a.e. to Secretary for details.

Society of Editors

University Centre, Granta Place, Mill Lane,
Cambridge CB2 1RU
☎01223 304080 Fax 01223 304090
✉ info@societyofeditors.org
www.societyofeditors.org
Executive Director *Bob Satchwell*

Formed by a merger of the Association of British Editors and the Guild of Editors, the Society of Editors has nearly 500 members in national, regional and local newspapers, magazines, broadcasting, new media, journalism education and media law. Campaigns for media freedom and self-regulation. For further information contact *Bob Satchwell* at the address above.

Society of Indexers

Blades Enterprise Centre, John Street,
Sheffield S2 4SU
☎0114 292 2350 Fax 0114 292 2351
✉ admin@indexers.org.uk
www.indexers.org.uk
Secretary *Ann Kingdom*
Administrator *Wendy Burrow*
SUBSCRIPTION £60 p.a.; Institutions from £120

Founded 1957. Publishes *The Indexer* (bi-annual, April and October) and a quarterly newsletter. Issues an annual list of members and *Indexers Available (IA)*, which lists members and their subject expertise. In addition, the Society runs an open-learning course entitled *Training in Indexing* and recommends rates of pay (currently £16–30 per hour or £1.20-£5 per page).

Society of Medical Writers

The Barn, Tonacliffe Road, Whitworth
OL12 8SJ
Contact *Dr David Brooks*
SUBSCRIPTION £30 p.a.; £40 (Joint)

Founded in 1986 and expanding rapidly in membership and influence. Exists to promote and improve professional and lay writing activities within and for general practice. Open to doctors and other health professionals especially those working in the field of general practice; also to professional journalists writing on anything pertaining to general practice. Keen to develop input from interested parties who work mainly outside the profession. Regular workshops held around Britain. Publishes a twice-yearly journal (*The GP Writer*), anthologies and books from members, and a register of members and their writing interests.

Society of Picture Researchers & Editors

See **The Picture Research Association**

Society of Women Writers & Journalists

Calvers Farm, Thelverton, Diss IP21 4NG
☎01379 740550 Fax 01379 741716

✉ zoe@zoeking.com
www.swwj.co.uk
Honorary Secretary *Zoe King*
Subscription £35 (Town); £30 (Country);
£25 (Overseas). £15 Joining fee
Founded 1894. The first of its kind to be run as an association of women engaged in journalism. Aims to encourage literary achievement, uphold professional standards, and establish social contacts with other writers. Offers advice to members and has regular seminars, etc. Publishes a society journal, *The Woman Writer*.

Society of Young Publishers
c/o The Bookseller, Endeavour House, 189 Shaftesbury Avenue, London WC2H 8JT
✉ info@thesyp.org.uk
www.thesyp.org.uk
Subscription £25 p.a.; £15 (Student/ Unwaged); £30 (Associate)

Provides facilities whereby members can increase their knowledge and widen their experience of all aspects of publishing, and holds regular social events. Open to those in related occupations, students, and associate membership is available for over-35s. Publishes a monthly newsletter called *Inprint* and holds meetings on the last Wednesday of each month featuring trade professionals. Please enclose an s.a.e. when writing to the Society.

The South and Mid-Wales Association of Writers (SAMWAW)
c/o I.M.C. Consulting Group, Denham House, Lambourne Crescent, Cardiff CF14 5ZW
☎029 2076 1170 Fax 029 2076 1304
✉ info@imcconsultinggroup.co.uk
Subscription £10 (Single); £15 (Joint)

Founded 1971 to foster the art and craft of writing in all its forms. Provides a common meeting ground for writers, critics, editors, adjudicators from all over the UK and abroad. Organises residential weekend conferences and day seminars throughout the year. Holds competitions, two for members only and two which are open to the public, in addition to **The Mathew Prichard Award for Short Story Writing** (see entry under *Prizes*).

Spoken Word Publishing Association (SWPA)
c/o HarperCollins Publishers Ltd, 77–85 Fulham Palace Road, London W6 8JB
☎020 Fax 020

www.swpa.co.uk
Chairman *Barry Clark*
Secretary *Zoe Howes*
Founded 1994. SWPA is the UK trade association for the spoken word industry with membership open to all those involved in the publishing of spoken word audio. Publishes *SWPA Resources Directory*, available from the address above.

Sports Journalists' Association of Great Britain
c/o Sport England Events, 3rd Floor, Victoria House, Bloomsbury Square, London WC1B 4SE
☎020 7273 1789 Fax 020 7383 0273
✉ trevjanbond1@aol.com
www.sportsjournalists.org.uk

Secretary *Trevor Bond* (244 Perry Street, Billericay CM12 0QP ☎01277 651708 Fax 01277 622890)
Subscription £23.50 p.a. incl. VAT (London); £11.75 (Regional)

Founded 1948 to promote and maintain a high professional standard among journalists who specialise in sport in all its branches and to serve members' interests. Publishes a biannual bulletin, a quarterly *Newsletter* and an annual *Handbook* for members, and promotes jointly with Sport England the annual British Sports Personalities of the Year Awards, the British Sports Journalism Awards and the Sports Photographer of the Year award.

SWPA
See **Spoken Word Publishing Association**

Tees Valley Arts
Third Floor, Melrose House, Melrose Street, Middlesbrough TS1 2HZ
☎01642 264651 Fax 01642 264955
Contact *Programme Manager (Literature)*

Tees Valley Arts is a cultural education agency working throughout the Tees Valley. The company works in partnership with local authorities, public agencies, the business sector, schools, colleges, individuals and organisations to coordinate, promote and develop the arts – crafts, film, video, photography, music, drama, dance, literature, public arts, disability, diverse arts, community arts.

Theatre Writers' Union
See **The Writers' Guild of Great Britain**

Trade Publishers Council
See **The Publishers Association**

The Translators Association
84 Drayton Gardens, London SW10 9SB
☎020 7373 6642 Fax 020 7373 5768
✉ info@societyofauthors.org
www.societyofauthors.org/translators
Secretary *Dorothy Sym*

Founded 1958 as a subsidiary group within the
Society of Authors to deal exclusively with
the special problems of literary translators into
the English language. Benefits to members
include free legal and general advice and assistance on all business matters relating to translators' work, including the vetting of contracts
and advice on rates of remuneration. Membership is normally confined to translators who
have had their work published in volume or
serial form or produced in this country for
stage, television or radio. The Association
administers several prizes for translators of published work (see *Prizes*) and maintains a database to enable members' details to be supplied
to publishers who are seeking a translator for a
particular work.

UK Film Council
10 Little Portland Street, London W1W 7JG
☎020 7861 7861 Fax 020 7861 7862
✉ info@ukfilmcouncil.org.uk
www.ukfilmcouncil.org.uk

The UK's leading film body. Uses lottery money
and Government Grant-in-Aid to encourage the
development of new talent, skills and creative
and technological innovation in UK film; help
new and established filmmakers make distinctive
British films; support the creation and growth of
stable businesses in the film sector; provide access
to finance and help the UK film industry to
compete in the global marketplace. Also promotes enjoyment and understanding of the
cinema and ensures that film's economic and
creative and cultural interests are properly represented in public policy making.

Voice of the Listener and Viewer (VLV)
101 Kings Drive, Gravesend DA12 5BQ
☎01474 352835 Fax 01474 351112
✉ vlv@btinternet.com

VLV represents the citizen and consumer interests in broadcasting. It is an independent, non-
profit-making society working to ensure inde-
pendence, quality and diversity in broadcasting.
VLV is the only consumer body speaking for
listeners and viewers on the full range of broadcasting issues. VLV is funded by its members
and is free from sectarian, commercial and
political affiliations. Holds public lectures, seminars and conferences, and has frequent contact
with MPs, civil servants, the BBC and independent broadcasters, regulators, academics
and other consumer groups. Provides an independent forum where all with an interest in
brodcasting can speak on equal terms. Produces
a quarterly news bulletin and regular briefings
on broadcasting issues. Holds its own archive
and those of the former Broadcasting Research
Unit (1980–90) and BACTV (British Action
for Children's Television). Maintains a panel of
speakers, the VLV Forum for Children's
Broadcasting, the VLV Forum for Educational
Broadcasting, and acts as secretariat for the
European Alliance of Listeners' and Viewers'
Associations (EURALVA). VLV has responded
to all major public enquiries on broadcasting
since 1984 and to all consultation documents
issued by the ITC and Radio Authority since
1990. The VLV does not handle complaints.

W.A.T.C.H.
See **Writers, Artists and their Copyright Holders**

Welsh Academy
See **Academi**

Welsh Books Council (Cyngor Llyfrau Cymru)
Castell Brychan, Aberystwyth SY23 2JB
☎01970 624151 Fax 01970 625385
✉ castellbrychan@cllc.org.uk
www.cllc.org.uk
www.gwales.com
Director *Gwerfyl Pierce Jones*
Head of Editorial Department *Dewi Morris Jones*

Founded 1961 to stimulate interest in Welsh literature and to support publishing in Wales. The
Council distributes publishing grants and promotes and fosters all aspects of both Welsh and
Welsh-interest book production. Its Editorial,
Design, Marketing and Children's Books departments and wholesale distribution centre offer
central services to publishers in Wales. Writers in
Welsh and English are welcome to approach the
Editorial Department for advice on how to get
their manuscripts published.

Welsh National Literature Promotion Agency
See **Academi**

West Country Writers' Association
High Wotton, Wotton Lane, Lympstone,
Exmouth EX8 5AY
☎01395 222749
✉ judy@josser.freeserve.co.uk
www.westcountrywriters.co.uk
President *Christopher Fry*
Honorary Secretary *Judy Joss*

Founded 1951 in the interest of published
authors with an interest in the West Country.
Meets to discuss news and views and to listen
to talks. Conference and newsletters.

Women in Publishing
Membership Secretary: PO Box 402, West
Byfleet KT14 7ZF
✉ membership@wipub.org.uk *and*
info@wipub.org.uk
www.wipub.org.uk
Membership Secretary *Alexandra McDonald*

Aims to promote the status of women working
in publishing and related trades by helping them
to develop their careers. Through WiP there are
opportunities for members to learn more about
their area of work, share information and expertise, give and receive support and partake in a
practical forum for the exchange of information
about different industry sectors. Monthly meetings provide a forum for discussion on various
topics of interest within the industry. Meetings
are held on the second Wednesday of each
month. See website for further information.
Publishes monthly newsletter, *WiPlash* and
Women in Publishing Directory.

Women Writers Network (WWN)
23 Prospect Road, London NW2 2JU
☎020 7794 5861
Membership Secretary *Cathy Smith*
Subscription £45 p.a. (incl. meeting admissions
& 6 newsletters p.a., WWN website and
online directory access); £35 p.a. (Overseas);
£30 p.a. ('Newsletter only' UK
membership')

Founded 1985. Provides a forum for the exchange of information, support, career and networking opportunities for working women
writers. Meetings, seminars, excursions, newsletter and directory. Full membership includes
free admission to monthly meetings and a
monthly newsletter. Details from the Membership Secretary at the address above.

Writernet
Cabin V, Clarendon Buildings, 25 Horsell
Road, London N5 1XL
☎020 7609 7474 Fax 020 7609 7557
✉ info@writernet.org.uk
www.writernet.org.uk
Executive Director *Jonathan Meth*
SUBSCRIPTION (information on rates available
by post or on website)

Writernet (formerly the New Playwrights Trust)
is the national research and development organisation for writing for all forms of live and
recorded performance. Publishes a range of information pertinent to writers on all aspects of
development and production in the form of
pamphlets, and a six-weekly journal which also
includes articles and interviews on aesthetic and
practical issues. Writernet also runs a script-reading service and a link service between writers and
producers, organises seminars and conducts
research projects.

The Writers' Guild of Great Britain
15 Britannia Street, London WC1X 9JN
☎020 7833 0777 Fax 020 7833 4777
✉ admin@writersguild.org.uk
www.writersguild.org.uk
President *J.C. Wilsher*
Chair *Graham Lester George*
General Secretary *Bernie Corbett*
Assistant General Secretaries *Anne Hogben,
Christine Paris*
ANNUAL SUBSCRIPTION Full Member: 1% of
earnings from professional writing (min.
£150, max. £1,500); Candidate Member:
£75; Student Member: £20; Affiliate
Member (agent or writers' group): £275; Life
Member: voluntary contribution

Founded in 1959 as the Screenwriters' Guild, the
Writers' Guild is a trade union, affiliated to the
TUC, representing professional writers in television, radio, theatre, film, books and new
media. It negotiates Minimum Terms Agreements governing writers' contracts and covering
minimum fees; advances; repeat fees; royalties
and residuals; rights; credits; number of drafts;
script alterations and the resolution of disputes.
The most important MTAs cover BBC TV
Drama; BBC Radio Drama; ITV Companies;
PACT (independent TV and film producers);
TAC (Welsh language independent TV producers); Theatrical Management Association;
Independent Theatre Council; and an agreement covering the **Royal National Theatre**,
Royal Shakespeare Company, and **Royal
Court Theatre**. These agreements are regularly
renegotiated and in most cases the minimum fees
are reviewed annually.

The Guild advises members on all aspects of their working lives, including contract vetting, legal advice, help with copyright problems and representation in disputes with producers, publishers or other writers.

Recent events organised by the Guild include a seminar on writing sitcoms, a networking evening for TV soap writers, a panel discussion on marketing theatre plays and lectures on forensic science aimed at TV series writers. *The Writers' Bulletin*, the Guild's bimonthly magazine, is free to members and contains features about professional writing, Guild news and details of work opportunities, training courses, literary competitions, etc.

Full Membership is open to anyone who has received payment for a piece of written work under a contract with terms not less than those negotiated by the Guild. Writers who do not qualify can join as Candidate Members and those on accredited writing courses or theatre attachments can become Student Members. Aged writers and those with long service in the Guild are entitled to free Life Membership.

Writers, Artists and their Copyright Holders (W.A.T.C.H.)

The Library, The University of Reading, PO Box 223, Whiteknights, Reading RG6 6AE
☎0118 378 8783 Fax 0118 378 6636
www.watch-file.com

Contact *Dr David Sutton*

Founded 1994. Provides an online database of information about the copyright holders of literary authors and artists. The database is available free of charge on the Internet and the Web. W.A.T.C.H. is the successor project to the Location Register of English Literary Manuscripts and Letters, and continues to deal with location register enquiries.

Yachting Journalists' Association

Sutton's, Church Lane, Eastergate PO20 3UZ
☎01243 542196 Fax 01243 555562
✉ ysa@mistral.co.uk
Honorary Secretary *Maggie Milne*
SUBSCRIPTION £40 p.a.

To further the interest of yachting, sail and power, and to provide support and assistance to journalists in the field; current membership is just over 260 with 31 from overseas. A handbook, listing details of members and subscribing PR organisations, press facility recommendations, forthcoming events and other useful information, is published annually at a cost to non-members and non-advertisers of £10. Information for inclusion should be submitted by the end of August. The YJA organises the Yachtsman of the Year and Young Sailor of the Year Awards, presented annually at the beginning of January.

Yr Academi Gymreig

See **Academi**

What Is Mine Is Yours
– at a Price

Kate Pool, Deputy General Secretary of the Society of Authors, gives an update on the law of copyright

Copyright is the legal right of authors, dramatists, artists and composers to prevent others from exploiting their work without their permission. All original material qualifies for protection, regardless of its artistic merit, immediately it is recorded in writing or in another form. There are no formalities in any country which is a member of the Berne Copyright Union – which now includes virtually all the principal countries of the world. Contrary to some popular misunderstandings, and while it may sometimes be harder to police infringements, copyright applies as much to work appearing on the internet as it does to work appearing anywhere else.

Generally, the owner of the copyright in a work is the author who created it. The main exceptions are when you produce work in the course of your employment, in which case your employer will own the copyright; or when you assign your copyright to someone else. A translator owns copyright in the translation, in addition to any copyright which exists in the original work. Likewise, a screenwriter owns copyright in a screenplay, in addition to any copyright in the work from which the script was adapted.

Length of copyright

Throughout the European Economic Area, and also the USA, copyright lasts until seventy years from the end of the year of the author's death. In most other countries of the world (including Canada and Australia) copyright lasts until fifty years from the end of the year of the author's death. However, there are many exceptions to this general rule. In particular:

Literary, dramatic and musical works unpublished during the author's lifetime (including letters and private papers)
If the author died before 1 August 1989, copyright lasts for fifty years from the end of the year of first posthumous publication or until 31 December 2039, whichever is the sooner. If the length of the author's life plus seventy years is longer than that period, then the life plus seventy rule will prevail, but not otherwise. Where the author died after 1 August 1989, the copyright period is seventy years from death; and artistic works, whenever the artist died and whether published or not, are protected for life plus seventy.

The works of non-European authors
These are protected in Europe only for as long as they are protected in their country of origin.

The copyright status of old works in the USA
This is a complex affair. The Society of Authors' *Quick Guide to Copyright and Moral Rights* has a section covering American copyright law as it relates to British authors.

The works of European authors who died between 1 January 1925 and 31 December 1944 which went out of copyright fifty years after their death
On 1 January 1996 these works went back into copyright for what remains of seventy years from the author's death. The new period of protection is known as 'revived copyright' You may use revived copyright material without permission from the rights holder but you have to give notice of your intentions and may have to pay a reasonable royalty.

The typographical arrangement of a published work is owned by the publisher
This means the work cannot, for example, be photocopied without the publisher's consent. The protection lasts for twenty-five years from the end of the year in which the first edition of the work appeared.

Copyright in ideas or information

There is no copyright in ideas or information. In general, anyone may use published ideas and facts provided they do not copy the precise wording in which they are expressed. But be careful, it is an infringement of copyright to rely on someone else's 'skill and labour' in creating a work. The second writer is expected to check all the facts at their original source.

Protecting your material when you are submitting it to publishers
Copyright is yours, and applies as soon as something is recorded. When sending out a typescript, you should include a copyright line: (c) [your name] 2004 (although copyright is not forfeited if you forget to do so). Always send your proposal to a specific person by name (not just 'The Commissioning Editor'), with a covering letter making clear that all rights in the work are yours, you are showing it to them in confidence, and you would be pleased to discuss terms if they are interested in publishing it. Always send a copy, not the original.

You can establish proof of the date your work was created by putting a copy in a sealed, dated envelope, and depositing it with a bank or a solicitor - or even by posting it to yourself and storing it in a safe place.

Submitting an article to a journal

Find out what terms the journal will want before, not after, committing yourself. Ideally you should be granting 'first serial rights' only - which means the publisher has the right to be the first to publish the article (generally in paper and electronic form), but having done so, all further rights belong to you. Be aware that many journals seek a wider grant of rights. Indeed, academic and learned journals frequently seek an outright assignment of copyright from their contributors (something that the writers' unions deplore).

A book publishing contract

You should be keeping your copyright and giving the publisher the 'exclusive licence' to publish the work.

Assigning copyright

If you do have to assign copyright, make sure there is a termination clause under which you can get your rights back if things go wrong - if, for example, you are not paid. Also make sure that no major changes will be made to your text without your agreement; that you will be credited as the author and your moral right of paternity is asserted (see moral rights below); and that if the work is exploited in some further way, you will be paid for and credited on the adaptation. It should also be clear that the assignment is not valid until you have received full payment of any monies due to you.

Small complete items like short stories, poems and illustrations

In most cases it will be appropriate to grant only a non-exclusive licence to reproduce the material in a particular anthology or journal, leaving you free to use the work elsewhere.

Moral rights

The main moral rights conferred by the Copyright, Designs and Patents Act 1988 are the right of paternity (the right of an author to be identified whenever a work is published, performed or broadcast: in other words, book writers, scriptwriters, illustrators and translators must be properly credited); and the right of integrity (the right of an author to object to 'derogatory' treatment of a work. Treatment is 'derogatory' if it amounts to 'distortion or mutilation . . . or is otherwise prejudicial to the honour or reputation of the author . . .')

While the right of integrity is automatic, the right of paternity must be 'asserted' in writing. The easiest way to do this is to include a suitable clause in your publishing contract - the assertion should also appear in the book, generally under the copyright line.

The rights of paternity and integrity do not apply to work published in a newspaper, magazine or similar periodical. Nor do the rights benefit authors contributing to an encyclopaedia, dictionary, yearbook or similar collective work of reference.

When do you need permission to make use of someone else's copyright work?

The simple answer is 'on most occasions', but there are exceptions worth noting.

If the quotation has been previously published and your intended use can be regarded as 'fair dealing . . . for purposes of criticism or review', whether of the work quoted or of another work, for a 'non-commercial purpose', you need not ask permission but must ensure that either in the text itself or in an acknowledgements page you give the title and author of the work quoted. It is not possible to give specific guidance on what constitutes 'fair dealing'; it is a matter of impression and common sense according to the circumstances. However, it may be relevant to take into account:

- the length and importance of the quotation;
- the amount quoted in relation to your commentary;
- the extent to which your work competes with or rivals the work quoted;
- the extent to which works quoted are saving you work.

Some years ago the Society of Authors and the Publishers' Association stated that they would usually regard as 'fair dealing' the use of a single extract of up to 400 words or a series of extracts (of which none exceeds 300 words) to a total of 800 words from a prose work, or of extracts to a total of 40 lines from a poem, provided that this did not exceed a quarter of the poem. The words must be quoted in the context of 'criticism or review'. While this statement does not have the force of law, it has carried weight with a judge experienced in copyright in a leading infringement case. It does not mean, however, that a quotation 'for purposes of criticism or review' in excess of these limits cannot rank as 'fair dealing' in some circumstances.

There are special provisions covering educational use - the Society of Authors can give further information on this.

For quotations other than those in the above categories you should ask permission to use any 'substantial' extract from a copyright work. The difficulty, once again, is that the meaning of 'substantial' is not defined, but is a matter of fact and degree. A short extract may be a vital part of a work. It has often been said that the test is much more about the quality than the quantity of what has been used. A few sentences taken from a long novel or biography are unlikely to a 'substantial part' of the original work, but a few lines of poetry may be. The only safe course, if in doubt, is to ask permission.

Permission should be obtained for the use of any quotation of copyright material, however short, to be included in an anthology. Also any quotation of previously unpublished material. And if you want to quote from song lyrics that are in copyright, be aware that permission fees can be much higher than those charged by book publishers.

When reproducing extracts from letters or private papers, remember that they may still be in copyright long after the author's death. The letter itself belongs to the recipient, but the copyright in it belongs to the writer of the letter and, after death, to the writer's estate.

Who grants permission?

With published material, it is best to write first to the publishers of the original edition of the book. Address your letter to the Permissions Department. It is very much in your interest to clear permissions as early as possible. If the publisher cannot help, or if the work is unpublished, the Society of Authors' *Quick Guide to Permissions* (also on its website at www.societyofauthors.org) gives suggestions as to how to track down rights holders.

Further information on copyright

The *Quick Guide to Permissions*, the *Quick Guide to Copyright and Moral Right,* the *Quick Guide to Copyright in Artistic Works* and the *Quick Guide to Dealing with Newspapers and Magazines* are available from the Society of Authors, 84 Drayton Gardens, London SW10 9SB, ☎020 7373 6642, ✉ info@societyofauthors.org (free to members, £2 post free in the UK to non-members).

For details about copyright in the USA refer to the Library of Congress Copyright Office at www.loc.gov/copyright/ or call the Public Information Office on 001 202 707 3000.

Some useful websites when tracing rights holders

Authors' Licensing and Collecting Society: www.alcs.co.uk
Association of Authors' Agents: www.agentsassoc.co.uk
British Library http://blpc.bl.uk/
Location Register of 20th-Century Literary Manuscripts and Letters: www.
  library.rdg.ac.uk/colls/projects/locreg.html
National Library of Scotland: www.nls.uk/
US Library of Congress Copyright Office: www.loc.gov/copyright/
WATCH (Writers Artists and their Copyright Holders): www.watch-file.com

Literary Societies

Margery Allingham Society

2B Higham Green, Winchelsea TN36 4HB
☎01797 222363 Fax 01797 222363
www.margeryallingham.org.uk
Contact *Mrs Pamela Bruxner*
SUBSCRIPTION £14 p.a.

Founded 1988 to promote interest in and study of the works of Margery Allingham. The Society publishes two issues of the newsletter, *The Bottle Street Gazette*, per year. Contributions welcome. Two social events a year. Open membership.

Jane Austen Society

22 Belmont Grove, Bedhampton, Havant
PO9 3PU
☎023 9247 5855
✉ rosemary@sndc.demon.co.uk
www.sndc.demon.co.uk/jas.htm
Membership Secretary *Mrs Rosemary Culley*
SUBSCRIPTION UK: £7.50 (Student); £15 (Annual); £20 (Joint); £45 (Corporate); £250 (Life); Overseas: £18 (Annual by credit card or UK banker's order only); £50 (Corporate); Overseas Membership £50/€75 (for 3 years); £300/€450 (Life)

Founded 1940 to promote interest in and enjoyment of Jane Austen's novels and letters. The society has branches in Bath and Bristol, Midlands, London, Oxford, Kent and Hampshire. There are independent Societies in North America and Australia.

The Baskerville Hounds

6 Bramham Moor, Hill Head, Fareham
PO14 3RU
☎01329 667325
Chairman *Philip Weller*
SUBSCRIPTION £6 p.a.

Founded 1989. An international Sherlock Holmes society specialising solely in studies of The Hound of the Baskervilles and its Dartmoor associations. Publishes an annual journal and specialist monographs. It also organises many social functions, usually on Dartmoor. Open membership.

The BB Society

8 Park Road, Solihull B91 3SU
☎01564 741847
✉ bryan@barbryn.co.uk

Chairman *Bill Humphreys*
Secretary *Bryan Holden*
SUBSCRIPTION £10 (Individual); £17.50 (Family); £50 (Corporate); £5 (Student); £17.50 (Overseas)

Founded in 2000 to bring together devotees of the writer/illustrator BB (Denys Watkins-Pitchford). BB's oeuvre included books on wildfowling, angling, children's fantasy and the countryside. The Society holds two meetings a year and publishes newsletters and an annual journal, *Sky Gypsy*. BB's centenary year will be celebrated in 2005 with a series of special events and Society publications.

The Beckford Society

The Timber Cottage, Crockerton,
Warminster BA12 8AX
☎01985 213195
✉ Sidney.Blackmore@btinternet.com
Secretary *Sidney Blackmore*
SUBSCRIPTION £10 (min.) p.a.

Founded 1995 to promote an interest in the life and works of William Beckford (1760–1844) and his circle. Encourages Beckford studies and scholarship through exhibitions, lectures and publications, including an annual journal, *The Beckford Journal* and occasional newsletters.

Thomas Lovell Beddoes Society

11 Laund Nook, Belper DE56 1GY
☎01773 828066 Fax 01773 828066
✉ john@beddoes.demon.co.uk
www.beddoes.demon.co.uk
Chairman *John Lovell Beddoes*
Secretary *Christine Hunkinson*

Formed to research the life, times and work of poet Thomas Lovell Beddoes (1803–1849), encourage relevant publications, further the reading and appreciation of his works by a wider public and liaise with other groups and organisations. Publishes an annual newsletter.

The Adrian Bell Society

3 The Maltings, Church Close, Coltishall
NR12 7DZ
☎01603 737168
Secretary *Moya Leighton*

SUBSCRIPTION £5 p.a.

Founded 1995, the Society aims to promote the study and enjoyment of the writing of Adrian Bell (1901–80); to publish journals twice a year and hold meetings to help members obtain copies of out of print titles; to assemble a collection of photocopies of his 1500 *Countryman's Notebooks* that appeared in the *Eastern Daily Press* and to index them; to commemorate his career as *The Times* first crossword compiler; to share knowledge of the places and factual background mentioned in his books. The society has 250 members worldwide who keep in touch through the journal *A Centenary Countryman's Notebook*, published 2001 (£7.00 + p&p).

Hilaire Belloc Society

1 Hillview, Elsted, Midhurst GU29 0JX
☎01730 825575
✉ HilaireBelloc1@aol.com
Contact *Dr Grahame Clough*

Founded in 1996 to promote the life and work of Hilaire Belloc through the publication of newsletters containing rare and previously unpublished material. Organises walks, social events, a Belloc weekend and a three-day conference. Currently 70 members, of which 30% are from overseas.

Arnold Bennett Society

34 Field End Close, Trentham, Stoke on Trent ST4 8DA
www.arnoldbennett.co.uk
Secretary *Mrs Carol Gorton*
SUBSCRIPTION £9 p.a. (Single); £11 (Family) plus £2 for membership outside the UK; £5 (Student)

Aims to promote interest in the life and works of 'Five Towns' author Arnold Bennett and other North Staffordshire writers. Annual dinner. Regular functions in and around Burslem plus annual seminar in London. Three newsletters a year. Open membership.

E.F. Benson Society

The Old Coach House, High Street, Rye TN31 7JF
☎01797 223114
www.efbensonsociety.org
Secretary *Allan Downend*
SUBSCRIPTION £7.50 (UK/Europe); £12.50 (Overseas)

Founded 1985 to promote the life and work of E.F. Benson and the Benson family. Organises social and literary events, exhibitions, talks and Benson interest walks in Rye. Publishes a quarterly newsletter and annual journal, *The Dodo*, postcards and reprints of E.F. Benson articles and short stories in a series called 'Bensoniana' plus other books of Benson interest. Holds an archive which includes the Seckersen Collection (transcriptions of the Benson collection at the Bodleian Library in Oxford).

E.F. Benson/The Tilling Society

5 Friars Bank, Guestling, Hastings TN35 4EJ
Fax 01424 813237
www.tilling.org.uk/society
Contact *Cynthia Reavell*
SUBSCRIPTION Full starting membership (members receive all back newsletters) £34 (UK); £38 (Overseas); or Annual Membership (members receive only current year's newsletters) £8 (UK); £10 (Overseas).

Founded 1982 for the exchange of news, information and speculation about E.F. Benson, his works and, in particular, his *Mapp & Lucia* novels. Readings, talks and journal–length biannual newsletter. Annual get-together in Rye/ 'Tilling'. Acts as a clearing house for every sort of news and activity concerning E.F. Benson.

The Betjeman Society

7 Copthorn Close, Maidenhead SL6 3PN
☎01628 823704
Honorary Secretary *Andrew Curtis*
SUBSCRIPTION £10 (Individual); £12 (Family); £3 (Student); £3 additional for Overseas members

Aims to promote the study and appreciation of the work and life of Sir John Betjeman. Annual programme includes poetry readings, lectures, discussions, visits to places associated with Betjeman, and various social events. Meetings are held in London and other centres. Regular newsletter and annual journal, *The Betjemanian*.

The Bewick Society

c/o The Hancock Museum, Newcastle upon Tyne NE2 4PT
☎01207 562196
✉ juneholmes@lineone.net
www.bewicksociety.org
Membership Secretary *June Holmes*
SUBSCRIPTION £7 p.a. (Individual); £10 (Family)

Founded 1988 to promote an interest in the life and work of Thomas Bewick, wood-engraver and naturalist (1753–1828). Organises related events and meetings, and is associated with the Bewick birthplace museum at Cherryburn, Northumberland.

Birmingham Central Literary Association

23 Arden Grove, Ladywood, Birmingham
B16 8HG
☎0121 454 9352
✉ bakerbrum@aol.com

Contact *The Secretary*

Holds fortnightly meetings in central Birmingham to discuss the lives and work of authors and poets. Holds an annual dinner to celebrate Shakespeare's birthday.

The George Borrow Society

60 Upper Marsh Road, Warminster BA12 9PN
www.clough5.fsnet.co.uk/gb.html
Chairman/Bulletin Editor *Dr Ann M. Ridler*
Membership Secretary *Michael Skillman*
Honorary Treasurer *David Pattinson*
Bulletin Editor: St Mary's Cottage, 61 Thame
  Road, Warborough, Wallingford, Oxford
  OX10 7EA ☎01865 858379
  Fax 01865 858575
SUBSCRIPTION £15 p.a.

Founded 1991 to promote knowledge of the life and works of George Borrow (1803–81), traveller, linguist and writer. The Society holds biennial conferences (with published proceedings) and informal intermediate gatherings, all at places associated with Borrow. Publishes the *George Borrow Bulletin* twice yearly, containing scholarly articles, reviews of publications relating to Borrow, reports of past events and news of forthcoming events. Member of the **Alliance of Literary Societies** and corporate associate member of the Centre of East Anglian Studies (CEAS) at the University of East Anglia, Norwich (Borrow's home city for many years).

Elinor Brent-Dyer

See **Friends of the Chalet School** and **The New Chalet Club**

British Fantasy Society

201 Reddish Road, South Reddish, Stockport
SK5 7HR
☎0161 476 5368 (after 6pm)
✉ faliol@yahoo.com
www.britishfantasysociety.org.uk
President *Ramsey Campbell*
Chairman *Nicki Robson*
Secretary *Robert Parkinson*
SUBSCRIPTION from £25 p.a.

Founded 1971 for devotees of fantasy, horror and related fields in literature, art and the cinema. Publishes a regular newsletter with information and reviews of new books and films, plus related fiction and non-fiction magazines. Annual conference at which the **British Fantasy Awards** are presented. These awards are voted on by the membership and are not an open competition.

The Brontë Society

Brontë Parsonage Museum, Haworth,
Keighley BD22 8DR
☎01535 642323 Fax 01535 647131
✉ bronte@bronte.org.uk
www.bronte.info

Contact *Membership Officer*
SUBSCRIPTION £18.50 p.a. (UK/Europe);
£10.50 (Student); £5 (Junior – up to age
14); £27.50 (Overseas); Joint subscriptions
available

Founded 1893. Aims and activities include the preservation of manuscripts and other objects related to or connected with the Brontë family, and the maintenance and development of the museum and library at Haworth. The society holds regular meetings, lectures and exhibitions; and publishes information relating to the family and a triannual *Gazette*. Freelance contributions for either publication should be sent to the Publications Secretary at the address above. Members can receive the journal, *Brontë Studies*, at a reduced subscription of £13.50 p.a.

The Rupert Brooke Society

The Orchard, 45/47 Mill Way, Grantchester
CB3 9ND
☎01223 551118 Fax 01223 551119
✉ rbs@callan.co.uk
www.rupertbrooke.com

Contacts *Claire Pidoux, Karen Smith*
SUBSCRIPTION £7.50 (UK); £10.50
  (Overseas)

Founded in 1999 to foster an interest in the work of Rupert Brooke, help preserve places associated with him and to increase the knowledge and appreciation of the village of Grantchester. Members receive a newsletter with information about events, new books and activities.

The Browning Society

9 Duncan Terrace, London N1 8BZ
☎020 7833 4228 Fax 020 7833 5834
✉ anneke.berrill@btconnect.com
Honorary Secretary *Anneke Berrill*
SUBSCRIPTION £15 p.a.

Founded 1969 to promote an interest in the

lives and poetry of Robert and Elizabeth Barrett Browning. Meetings are arranged in the London area, one of which occurs in December at Westminster Abbey to commemorate Robert Browning's death.

The John Buchan Society

Greenmantle, Main Street, Kings Newton, Melbourne DE73 1BX
☎01332 865315
✉ kah@greenmantle63.freeserve.co.uk
Secretary *Kenneth Hillier*
SUBSCRIPTION £12 (Full/Overseas);
   £5 (Associate); £6 (Junior);
   £20 (Corporate); £100 (10 years)

To perpetuate the memory of John Buchan and to promote a wider understanding of his life and works. Holds regular meetings and social gatherings, publishes a journal, and liaises with the John Buchan Centre at Broughton in the Scottish borders.

The Robert Burns World Federation Ltd

Dean Castle Country Park Dower House, Kilmarnock KA3 1XB
☎01563 572469 Fax 01563 572469
✉ robertburnsfederation@
   kilmarnock26.freeserve.co.uk
www.robertburnsfederation.co.uk
Chief Executive *Shirley Bell*
SUBSCRIPTION £23 p.a.(Individual);
   £25 (Family); £46 (Club subscription)

Founded 1885 to encourage interest in the life and work of Robert Burns and keep alive the old Scottish Tongue. The Society's interests go beyond Burns himself in its commitment to the development of Scottish literature, music and arts in general. Publishes the triannual *Burns Chronicle/Burnsian*.

The Byron Society

Byron House, 6 Gertrude Street, London SW10 0JN
☎020 7352 5112

Honorary Director, Byron Society *Mrs Elma Dangerfield CBE*
SUBSCRIPTION £20 p.a.

Founded 1876; revived in 1971. Aims to promote knowledge and discussion of Lord Byron's life and works, and those of his contemporaries, through lectures, readings, concerts, performances and international conferences. Publishes annually in June *The Byron Journal*, a scholarly journal (£5.50 plus £2 postage).

Randolph Caldecott Society

Clatterwick House, Little Leigh, Northwich CW8 4RJ
☎01606 891303 (day)/781731 (evening)
Honorary Secretary *Kenneth N. Oultram*
SUBSCRIPTION £8–£12 p.a.

Founded 1983 to promote the life and work of artist/book illustrator Randolph Caldecott. Meetings held in the spring and autumn in Caldecott's birthplace, Chester. Guest speakers, outings, newsletter, exchanges with the Society's American counterpart. (Caldecott died and was buried in St Augustine, Florida.) A medal in his memory is awarded annually in the US for children's book illustration.

The Carlyle Society, Edinburgh

Dept of English Literature, The University of Edinburgh, David Hume Tower, George Square, Edinburgh EH8 9JX
Fax 0131 650 6898
✉ ian.campbell@ed.ac.uk
President *Ian Campbell*
SUBSCRIPTION £2 p.a.; £10 (Life); $20 (US)

Founded 1929 to examine the lives of Thomas Carlyle and his wife Jane, their writings, contemporaries, and influences. Meetings are held about six times a year and occasional papers are published annually. Enquiries should be addressed to the President of the Society at the address above.

Lewis Carroll Society

69 Cromwell Road, Hertford SG13 7DP
☎01992 584530
✉ alanwhite@tesco.net
www.lewiscarrollsociety.org.uk
Secretary *Alan White*
SUBSCRIPTION from £15 p.a. (Individual);
   apply to Secretary

Founded 1969 to bring together people with an interest in Charles Dodgson and promote research into his life and works. Publishes bi-annual journal *The Carrollian*, featuring scholarly articles and reviews; a newsletter (*Bandersnatch*) which reports on Carrollian events and the Society's activities; and *The Lewis Carroll Review*, a book-reviewing journal. Regular meetings held in London with lectures, talks, outings, etc.

Lewis Carroll Society (Daresbury)

Clatterwick House, Little Leigh, Northwich CW8 4RJ
☎01606 891303 (day)/781731 (evening)
Honorary Secretary *Kenneth N. Oultram*
SUBSCRIPTION £5 p.a.

Founded 1970. To promote the life and work of Charles Dodgson, author of the world-famous *Alice's Adventures*. Holds meetings in the spring and autumn in Carroll's birthplace, Daresbury, Cheshire. Guest speakers and theatre visits. Appoints annually a 10-year-old 'Alice' who is available for public invitations.

The New Chalet Club

94 Bangor Street, Y Felinheli LL56 4PJ
www.newchaletclub.co.uk

Membership Secretary *Sera Roberts*
SUBSCRIPTION £6 p.a. (UK under 18);
£10 (UK Adults & Europe); £12 (RoW)

Founded 1995 for all those with an interest in the books of Elinor Brent-Dyer. Publishes a quarterly journal and occasional supplements, including *The A-Z of Chalet Characters*, and regularly holds local and national meetings.

Friends of the Chalet School

4 Rock Terrace, Coleford, Bath BA3 5NF
☎01373 812705
✉ focs@rockterrace.demon.co.uk
www.rockterrace.demon.co.uk/FOCS

Contacts *Ann Mackie-Hunter, Clarissa Cridland*
SUBSCRIPTION £7.50 p.a.; £6 (Under-18);
Outside UK: details on application

Founded 1989 to promote the works of Elinor Brent-Dyer. The society has members worldwide; publishes four magazines a year and runs a lending library.

The Chesterton Society UK

11 Lawrence Leys, Bloxham, Near Banbury OX15 4NU
☎01295 720869/07747 786428 (mobile)
Honorary Secretary *Robert Hughes, KHS*
SUBSCRIPTION £12.50 p.a.

Founded 1964 to promote the ideas and writings of G.K. Chesterton.

The Children's Books History Society

25 Field Way, Hoddesdon EN11 0QN
☎01992 464885
✉ cbhs@abcgarrett.demon.co.uk

Chair/Membership Secretary *Mrs Pat Garrett*
SUBSCRIPTION £10 p.a. (UK/Europe); write for Overseas subscription details

Established 1969. Aims to promote an appreciation of children's books and to study their history, bibliography and literary content. The Society holds approximately six meetings per year in London and a summer meeting to a collection, or to a location with a children's book connection. Three substantial newsletters issued annually, with an occasional paper. Review copies should be sent to Newsletter co-editor Mrs Pat Garrett (address above). The Society constitutes the British branch of the Friends of the Osborne and Lillian H. Smith Collections in Toronto, Canada, and also liaises with **CILIP** (formerly The Library Association). In 1990, the Society established its biennial Harvey Darton Award for a book, published in English, which extends our knowledge of some aspect of British children's literature of the past. 2004 winner: Jane Cooper for her book on Mrs Molesworth.

The John Clare Society

9 The Chase, Ely CB6 3DR
☎01353 668438
vzone.virgin.net/linda.curry/jclaresociety.htm
human.ntu.ac.uk/clare/clare.html

Honorary Secretary *Miss Sue Holgate*
SUBSCRIPTION £10 (Individual); £13 (Joint);
£8 (Fully Retired); £10 (Joint Retired);
£13 (Group); £15 (Library); £5 (Student, Full-time); £15 sterling draft/$30/€25 (eurocheque) (Overseas)

Founded 1981 to promote a wider appreciation of the life and works of the poet John Clare (1793–1864). Organises an annual festival in Helpston in July; arranges exhibitions, poetry readings and conferences; and publishes an annual society journal and quarterly newsletter.

William Cobbett Society

10 Grenehurst Way, Petersfield GU31 4AZ
☎01730 262060

Chairman *Molly Townsend*
Also: Boynell House, Outlands Lane,
Curdridge, Southampton SO30 2HR
☎01489 782453
Contact *David Chun*
SUBSCRIPTION £8 p.a.

Founded in 1976 to bring together those with an interest in the life and works of William Cobbett (1763–1835) and to extend the interest to a wider public. Society activities include an annual Memorial Lecture; publication of an annual journal (*Cobbett's New Register*) containing articles on various aspects of his life and times; an annual expedition retracing routes taken by Cobbett on his Rural Rides in the 1820s; visits to his birthplace and his tomb in Farnham, Surrey. In association with the Society, the Museum of Farnham holds bound volumes of *Cobbett's Political Register*, a large collection of

Cobbett's works, books about Cobbett, and has various Cobbett artefacts on display.

The Friends of Coleridge

87 Richmond Road, Montpelier, Bristol
BS6 5EP
☎0117 942 6366
✉ gcddavidson@compuserve.com
www.friendsofcoleridge.com

Membership Secretary *Shirley Watters* (11 Castle Street, Nether Stowey TA5 1LN)
Editor (Coleridge Bulletin) *Graham Davidson*
SUBSCRIPTION £10 (UK); £15 or £20 (Overseas)

Founded in 1987 to advance knowledge about the life, work and times of Samuel Taylor Coleridge and his circle, and to support his Nether Stowey Cottage, with the National Trust, as a centre of Coleridge interest. Holds literary evenings, study weekends and a biennial international academic conference. Publishes *The Coleridge Bulletin* biannually. Short articles on Coleridge-related topics may be sent to the editor at the (Bristol) address above.

Wilkie Collins Society

4 Ernest Gardens, London W4 3QU
✉ paul@wilkiecollins.org
www.wilkiecollins.org

Chairman *Andrew Gasson*
Membership Secretary *Paul Lewis* (at address above)
SUBSCRIPTION £10 (UK/Europe); £18 (RoW – remittance must be made in UK sterling)

Founded 1980 to provide information on and promote interest in the life and works of Wilkie Collins, one of the first English novelists to deal with the detection of crime. *The Woman in White* appeared in 1860 and *The Moonstone* in 1868. Publishes newsletters, reprints of Collins' work and an annual academic journal.

The Arthur Conan Doyle Society

PO Box 1360, Ashcroft, British Columbia, Canada V0K 1A0
☎001 250 453 2045 Fax 001 250 453 2075
✉ ashtree@ash-tree.bc.ca
www.ash-tree.bc.ca/acdsocy.html

Joint Organisers *Christopher Roden, Barbara Roden*

Founded 1989 to promote the study and discussion of the life and works of Sir Arthur Conan Doyle. Occasional meetings, functions and visits. Publishes an occasional journal together with reprints of Conan Doyle's writings.

Joseph Conrad Society (UK)

c/o P.O.S.K., 238–246 King Street, Hammersmith, London W6 0RF
Fax 020 8240 4365
✉ AllanSimmons@compuserve.com
www.bathspa.ac.uk/conrad/

Secretary *Hugh Epstein*
Treasurer/Editor (The Conradian) *Allan Simmons*
SUBSCRIPTION £20 p.a. (Individual); £20 (Institutions)

Founded in 1973 to promote the study of the works and life of Joseph Conrad (1857–1924). A scholarly society, supported by the Polish Library at the Polish Cultural Association where a substantial library of Conrad texts and criticism is held in the Study Centre. Publishes a journal of Conrad studies (*The Conradian*) biannually and holds an annual International Conference in the first week of July. Awards an essay prize and travel and study grants to scholars on application.

The Rhys Davies Trust

10 Heol Don, Whitchurch, Cardiff
CF14 2AU
☎029 2062 3359

Contact *Professor Meic Stephens*

Founded 1990 to perpetuate the literary reputation of the Welsh prose writer, Rhys Davies (1901–78), and to foster Welsh writing in English. Organises competitions in association with other bodies such as the **Welsh Academy**, puts up plaques on buildings associated with Welsh writers, offers grant-aid for book production, etc.

The Walter de la Mare Society

Flat 15, Trinity Court, Vicarage Road, Twickenham TW2 5TY
www.bluetree.co.uk/wdlmsociety

Honorary President *John Bayley, CBE*
Honorary Secretary & Treasurer *Julie de la Mare*
SUBSCRIPTION £15 p.a.

Founded in 1997 to honour the memory of Walter de la Mare; to promote the study and deepen the appreciation of his works; to widen the readership of his works; to facilitate research by making available the widest range of contacts and information about de la Mare; and to encourage and facilitate new Walter de la Mare publications. Produces a regular newsletter and organises events. Membership information from the address above.

Warwick Deeping Appreciation Society

23 Merton Road, Enfield EN2 0LS
☎020 8367 0263
✉ geoffrey@gillam.fsworld.co.uk
Secretary *Geoffrey Gillam*
SUBSCRIPTION £3.50 p.a.

Open to all with an interest in the life and work of Warwick Deeping who produced 70 novels and many short stories. A quarterly newsletter includes reviews of his books and results of research into his life.

The Dickens Fellowship

48 Doughty Street, London WC1N 2LX
☎020 7405 2127 Fax 020 7831 5175
✉ arwilliams33@compuserve.com
www.dickens.fellowship.btinternet.co.uk
Joint Honorary General Secretaries *Mrs Thelma Grove, Dr Tony Williams*
SUBSCRIPTION £6 (First year); £12 (Renewal)

Founded 1902. The Society's particular aims and objectives are: to bring together lovers of Charles Dickens; to spread the message of Dickens, his love of humanity ('the keynote of all his work'); to remedy social injustice for the poor and oppressed; to assist in the preservation of material and buildings associated with Dickens. Annual conference. Publishes journal called *The Dickensian* (available at special rate to members) and organises a full programme of lectures, discussions, visits and conducted walks throughout the year. Branches worldwide.

Dymock Poets

See **The Friends of the Dymock Poets**

Early English Text Society

Christ Church, Oxford OX1 1DP
Fax 01865 286581
www.oets.org.uk
Executive Secretary *R.F.S. Hamer* (at address above)
Editorial Secretary *Dr H.L. Spencer* (at Exeter College, Oxford OX1 3DP)
Membership Secretary *Mrs J.M. Watkinson* (at 12 North End, Durham DH1 4NJ)
SUBSCRIPTION £15 p.a. (UK); $30 (US); $35 (Canada)

Founded 1864. Concerned with the publication of early English texts. Members receive annual publications (one or two a year) or may select titles from the backlist in lieu.

The George Eliot Fellowship

71 Stepping Stones Road, Coventry CV5 8JT
☎024 7659 2231
www.george-eliot-fellowship.com
Contact *Mrs Kathleen Adams*
SUBSCRIPTION £10 p.a.; £100 (Life); Concessions for pensioners

Founded 1930. Exists to honour George Eliot and promote interest in her life and works. Readings, memorial lecture, birthday luncheon and functions. Issues a quarterly newsletter and an annual journal. Awards an annual prize for a George Eliot essay.

Rev. G. Bramwell Evens

See **The Romany Society**

The John Meade Falkner Society

Greenmantle, Main Street, Kings Newton, Melbourne DE73 1BX
☎01332 865315
✉ kah@greenmantle63.freeserve.co.uk
Secretary *Kenneth Hillier*
SUBSCRIPTION £5 (UK); $10 (Overseas)

Founded in 1999 to promote the appreciation and study of John Meade Falkner's life, times and works. Produces three newsletters a year and an annual journal.

Folly (Fans of Light Literature for the Young)

21 Warwick Road, Pokesdown, Bournemouth BH7 6JW
☎01202 432562 Fax 01202 460059
✉ folly@sims.abel.co.uk
Contact *Mrs Sue Sims*
SUBSCRIPTION £9 p.a. (UK); £11 (Europe); £14 (Worldwide)

Founded 1990 to promote interest in a wide variety of children's authors – with a bias towards writers of girls' books and school stories. Publishes three magazines a year.

The Ford Madox Ford Society

c/o Dr Sara Haslam, Dept of Literature, The Open University, Milton Keynes MK7 6AA
☎01908 653453 Fax 01908 653750
✉ s.haslam@open.ac.uk
www.rialto.com/fordmadoxford_society
Chairman *Professor Max Saunders*
Treasurer *Dr Sara Haslam*
SUBSCRIPTION £12 or £6 Concession

Founded 1996 to promote the works of Ford Madox Ford and to increase knowledge of his writing and impact on writing in the 20th century. Meets for academic conferences and more popular events annually. Distributes *International Ford Madox Ford Studies* free to members. Welcomes all with an interest in Ford and his works. Has members in the UK, USA, Italy, France and Germany and holds events in as many different places as possible.

C.S. Forester Society

11 Park Town, Oxford OX2 6SN
☎01865 512111 Fax 01865 515292
✉ csforester@hotmail.com
www.csforester.com

Contact *Colin Blogg*
SUBSCRIPTION £10 or $15 p.a.

Founded in 1999 to provide an informal forum to promote knowledge and enjoyment of the works and life of C.S. Forester; to write a definitive bibliography and, ultimately, a biography. Publishes a newsletter 3–4 times a year containing contributions from members, and holds meetings for film shows, readings and lectures and a literary supplement.

The Franco-Midland Hardware Company

6 Bramham Moor, Hill Head, Fareham PO14 3RU
☎01329 667325
✉ fmhc@acd-221b.info
www.btinternet.com/~sherlock.fmhc

Chairman *Philip Weller*
SUBSCRIPTION £5 p.a. (UK); £10 (Europe); £15 (RoW)

Founded 1989. 'The world's leading Sherlock Holmes correspondence study group and the most active Holmesian society in Britain.' Publishes annual journal, a biannual news magazine and an individual case study as a subscription package. Also publishes at least two specialist monographs a year. It provides certificated self-study courses and organises monthly functions at Holmes-associated locations. Open membership.

The Friends of Shandy Hall (The Laurence Sterne Trust)

Shandy Hall, Coxwold, York YO61 4AD
☎01347 868465 Fax 01347 868465
www.shandy-hall.org.uk

Curator *Patrick Wildgust*
SUBSCRIPTION £7 (Annual); £70 (Life)

Promotes interest in the works of Laurence Sterne and aims to preserve the house in which they were created (open to the public). Publishes annual journal, *The Shandean*. An

Annual Memorial Lecture is delivered each summer.

The Friends of the Dymock Poets

19 The Southend, Ledbury HR8 2EY
☎01531 6834796
✉ cateluck2003@yahoo.com
www.dymockpoets.co.uk

Chairman *Roy Palmer*
Hon. Secretary *Catharine Luck*
Membership Secretary *Jeff Cooper*
SUBSCRIPTION £7 (Individuals); £12 (Couples); £3 (Students); £12 (Societies/ Families)

Founded 1993. Established to foster an interest in the work of the Dymock Poets – Edward Thomas, Robert Frost, Wilfrid Gibson, Rupert Brooke, John Drinkwater, Lascelles Abercrombie; help preserve places and things associated with them; keep members informed of literary and other matters relating to the poets; increase knowledge and appreciation of the landscape between May Hill (Gloucestershire) and the Malvern Hills. Members are offered lectures, poetry readings, social meetings, newsletters and annual journal, guided walks in the countryside around Dymock; links with other literary societies; and annual event to commemorate the first meeting between Edward Thomas and Robert Frost on 6 October 1913.

The Gaskell Society

Far Yew Tree House, Over Tabley, Knutsford WA16 0HN
☎01565 634668
✉ JoanLeach@aol.com
gaskellsociety.users.btopenworld.com
lang.nagoya-u.ac.jp/~matsuoka/
    EG-Society.html

Honorary Secretary *Joan Leach*
SUBSCRIPTION £12 p.a.; £16 (Corporate & Overseas)

Founded 1985 to promote and encourage the study and appreciation of the life and works of Elizabeth Cleghorn Gaskell. Meetings held in Knutsford, Manchester, Bath and London; residential study weekends and visits; annual journal and biannual newsletter. On alternate years holds either a residential weekend conference or overseas visit.

The Ghost Story Society

PO Box 1360, Ashcroft, British Columbia, Canada V0K 1A0
☎001 250 453 2045 Fax 001 250 453 2075
✉ ashtree@ash-tree.bc.ca

www.ash-tree.bc.ca/GSS.html

Joint Organisers *Barbara Roden, Christopher Roden*

SUBSCRIPTION UK: £20 (Airmail); $29 (US$); $36 (Canadian$)

Founded 1988. Devoted mainly to supernatural fiction in the literary tradition of M.R. James, Walter de la Mare, Algernon Blackwood, E.F. Benson, A.N.L. Munby, R.H. Malden, etc. Publishes a thrice-yearly journal, *All Hallows*, which includes new fiction in the genre and non-fiction of relevance to the genre.

Graham Greene Birthplace Trust
Rhenigidale, Ivy House Lane, Berkhamsted HP4 2PP
☎01442 865158
✉ secretary@grahamgreenebt.org
www.grahamgreenebt.org

Secretary *Ken Sherwood*

SUBSCRIPTION £8 (UK, £20 for 3 years); £11 (Europe, £27); £15 (RoW, £40)

Founded on 2 October 1997, the 93rd anniversary of Graham Greene's birth, to promote the appreciation and study of his works. Publishes a quarterly newsletter, occasional papers, videos and compact discs. Organises the annual four-day Graham Greene Festival during the weekend nearest to the writer's birthday (2nd October) and administrates the Graham Greene Memorial Awards.

The Ivor Gurney Society
4 Myton Road, London SE21 8EB
☎0208 761 3180
✉ william.marshall@kcl.ac.uk
www.ivor.gurney.net

SUBSCRIPTION £10 (Individual); £4 (Student); £10 (Group/Library)

To promote interest in Ivor Gurney and his context and to make his music and poetry available to a wider audience by way of performances, readings, conferences, recordings and publications. To enhance and promote informed scholarship on all aspects of his life and work through the publication of a regular newsletter and an annual journal, available to society members. To maintain and expand the Gurney archive at Gloucester Central Library.

Rider Haggard Society
27 Deneholm, Whitley Bay NE25 9AU
☎0191 252 4516 Fax 0191 252 4516
✉ RB27Allen@aol.com
www.riderhaggardsociety.org.uk

Contact *Roger Allen*

SUBSCRIPTION £9 p.a. (UK); £10 (Overseas)

Founded 1985 to promote appreciation of the life and works of Sir Henry Rider Haggard, English novelist, 1856–1925. News/books exchange and meetings every 18 months.

James Hanley Network
Old School House, George Green Road, George Green, Wexham SL3 6BJ
☎01753 578632
✉ gostick@london.com
www.jameshanley.mcmail.com/index.htm

Network Coordinator *Chris Gostick*

An informal international association founded in 1997 for all those interested in exploring and publicising the works and contribution to literature of the novelist and dramatist James Hanley (1901–1985). Publishes an annual newsletter. Occasional conferences are planned for the future. All enquiries welcome.

The Thomas Hardy Society
PO Box 1438, Dorchester DT1 1YH
☎01305 251501 Fax 01305 251501
✉ info@hardysociety.org
www.hardysociety.org

Honorary Secretary *Mrs Helen Gibson*

SUBSCRIPTION £18 (Individual); £25 (Corporate); £22.50 (Individual Overseas); £30 (Corporate Overseas)

Founded 1967 to promote the reading and study of the works and life of Thomas Hardy. Thrice-yearly journal, events and a biennial conference. An international organisation.

The Henty Society
Hayfield, Bourne Fields, Twyford, Winchester SO21 1NY
☎01962 713164

Honorary Secretary *Bruce Lees*

SUBSCRIPTION £13 p.a. (UK); £16 (Overseas)

Founded 1977 to study the life and work of George Alfred Henty, and to publish research, bibliographical data and lesser-known works, namely short stories. Organises conferences and social gatherings in the UK and North America, and publishes bulletins to members. Published in 1996: *G.A. Henty (1832–1902) a Bibliographical Study* by Peter Newbolt.

James Hilton Society
49 Beckingthorpe Drive, Bottesford, Nottingham NG13 0DN
www.jameshiltonsociety.co.uk

Honorary Secretary *J.R. Hammond*
SUBSCRIPTION £10 (UK/EU); £7
  Concessions

Founded 2000 to promote interest in the life
and work of novelist and scriptwriter James
Hilton (1900–1954). Publishes *The James Hilton
Newsletter* (quarterly) and organises meetings
and conferences.

Sherlock Holmes Society (Northern Musgraves)

Hallas Lodge, Greenside Lane, Cullingworth,
Bradford BD13 5AP
☎01535 273468
✉ hallaslodge@btinternet.com

Contacts *John Hall, Anne Jordan*
SUBSCRIPTION £17 p.a. (UK)

Founded 1987 to promote enjoyment and study
of Sir Arthur Conan Doyle's Sherlock Holmes
through publications and meetings. One of the
largest Sherlock Holmes societies in Great
Britain. Honorary members include Bert Coules,
Richard Lancelyn Green, Edward Hardwicke,
Clive Merrison and Douglas Wilmer. Past hon-
orary members: Dame Jean Conan Doyle, Peter
Cushing, Jeremy Brett and Michael Williams.
Open membership. Lectures, presentations and
consultation on matters relating to Holmes and
Conan Doyle available.

Sherlock Holmes

See **The Franco-Midland Hardware Company**

Hopkins Society

41 North Drive, Rhyl LL18 4SW
☎01745 354151
✉ bill&meljones@aol.com
www.hopkinsoc.freeserve.co.uk

Contact *Imelda Jones*
SUBSCRIPTION £7 p.a. (UK); £10 (Overseas)

Founded 1990 to celebrate the life and work of
Gerard Manley Hopkins; to inform members
of any publications, courses or events about the
poet. Holds an annual lecture on Hopkins in
the spring; produces two newsletters a year;
sponsors and organises educational projects
based on Hopkins' life and works.

Housman Society

80 New Road, Bromsgrove B60 2LA
☎01527 874136
✉ info@housman-society.co.uk
www.housman-society.co.uk

Contact *Jim Page*

SUBSCRIPTION £10 (UK); £12.50 (Overseas)

Founded 1973 to promote knowledge and
appreciation of the lives and work of A.E.
Housman and other members of his family, and
to promote the cause of literature and poetry.
Sponsors a lecture at the **Hay Festival** each year
under the title of 'The Name and Nature of
Poetry'. Publishes an annual journal and biannual
newsletter.

W.W. Jacobs Appreciation Society

3 Roman Road, Southwick BN42 4TP
☎01273 871017   Fax 01273 871017

Contact *A.R. James*

Founded 1988 to encourage and promote the
enjoyment of the works of W.W. Jacobs, and
stimulate research into his life and works. No
subscription charge. Material available for purchase includes *W.W. Jacobs*, a biography published in 1999, price £12, post paid, and *WWJ
Book Hunter's Field Guide*, a narrative bibliography published in 2001, price £6, post paid.

Richard Jefferies Society

Eidsvoll, Bedwells Heath, Boars Hill, Oxford
OX1 5JE
☎01865 735678
www.bath.ac.uk/~lissmc/rjeffs.htm

Honorary Secretary *Lady Phyllis Treitel*
Membership Secretary *Mrs Margaret Evans*
SUBSCRIPTION £7 p.a. (Individual); £8
  (Joint); Life membership for those over 50

Founded 1950 to promote understanding of the
work of Richard Jefferies, nature/country writer,
novelist and mystic (1848–87). Produces newsletters, reports and an annual journal; organises
talks, discussions and readings. Library and
archives. Assists in maintaining the museum in
Jefferies' birthplace at Coate near Swindon.
Membership applications should be sent to
Margaret Evans, 23 Hardwell Close, Grove, Nr
Wantage OX12 0BN.

Jerome K. Jerome Society

c/o Fraser Wood, Mayo and Pinson, 15/16
Lichfield Street, Walsall WS1 1TS
☎01922 629000   Fax 01922 721065
✉ tonygray@jkj.demon.co.uk
www.jeromekjerome.com

Honorary Secretary *Tony Gray*
SUBSCRIPTION £7.50 p.a. (Ordinary); £25
  (Corporate); £3.75 (Under 21/Over 65)

Founded 1984 to stimulate interest in Jerome
K. Jerome's life and works (1859–1927). One
of the Society's principal activities is the

support of a small museum in the author's birthplace, Walsall. Meetings, lectures, events and a newsletter, *Idle Thoughts*. Annual dinner in Walsall near Jerome's birth date (2nd May).

The Captain W.E. Johns Appreciation Society

Nottingham meeting: Wendover, Windy Harbour Lane, Bromley Cross, Bolton BL7 9AP
☎01204 306051
✉ Biggles.uk@LineOne.net
website.lineone.net/~biggles.uk

Hertford meeting: 8 Holmes Close, Castlefields, Stafford ST16 1AR

Contacts *Mrs A. Thompson* (Nottingham), *Joy Tilley* (Hertford, ☎01785 240299)

Society for the appreciation of W.E. Johns, creator of Biggles. Meets twice a year in Nottingham and Hertford. See contacts above.

Johnson Society

Johnson Birthplace Museum, Breadmarket Street, Lichfield WS13 6LG
☎01543 264972
www.lichfieldrambler.co.uk

Hon. General Secretary *Mrs Norma Hooper*
Hon. Literary Secretary *John Dudley* (honlitsec@lichfieldrambler.co.uk)
SUBSCRIPTION £7.50 p.a.; £10 (Joint)

Founded 1910 to encourage the study of the life, works and times of Samuel Johnson (1709–1784) and his contemporaries. The Society is committed to the preservation of the Johnson Birthplace Museum and Johnson memorials.

Johnson Society of London

255 Baring Road, Grove Park, London SE12 0BQ
☎020 8851 0173
✉ JSL@nbbl.demon.co.uk
www.nbbl.demon.co.uk/index.html

President *Lord Harmsworth*
Honorary Secretary *Mrs Z.E. O'Donnell*
SUBSCRIPTION £12 p.a.; £15 (Joint)

Founded 1928 to promote the knowledge and appreciation of Dr Samuel Johnson and his works. Publishes an annual journal, *New Rambler* and occasional newsletter. Regular meetings from October to April in the meeting room of Wesley's Chapel, City Road, London on the second Saturday of each month, and a commemoration ceremony around the anniversary of Johnson's death (December) held in Westminster Abbey.

The David Jones Society

48 Sylvan Way, Sketty, Swansea SA2 9JB
☎01792 206144   Fax 01792 205305
✉ anne.price-owen@sihe.ac.uk
www.sihe/ac/uk/davidjones

Contact *Anne Price-Owen*
SUBSCRIPTION £18 (Individual); £30 (Corporate)

Founded 1996, the Society aims to promote and encourage knowledge of the painter-poet David Jones. The Society hosts annual scholarly meetings. The annual subscription includes a copy of the *David Jones Journal*. Unsolicited material relating to David Jones, art, literarure or any of his philosophies may be sent for consideration for publication in the journal.

The Just William Society

Easter Badbea, Dundonnell IV23 2QX
✉ philandpaula@easter-badbea.co.uk
Secretary/Treasurer *Paula Cross*
SUBSCRIPTION £7 p.a. (UK); £10 (Overseas); £5 (Juvenile/Student); £15 (Family)

Founded 1994 to further knowledge of Richmal Crompton's *William* and *Jimmy* books. An annual 'William' meeting is held in April. The Honorary President of the Society is Richmal Crompton's niece, Richmal Ashbee.

The Keats–Shelley Memorial Association (Inc)

Registered office: 1 Satchwell Walk, Royal Priors, Leamington Spa CV32 4QE
☎01926 427400   Fax 01926 335133

Contact *Honorary Secretary*
SUBSCRIPTION £10 p.a.

Founded 1903 to promote appreciation of the works of Keats and Shelley, and their circle. One of the Society's main tasks is the preservation of 26 Piazza di Spagna in Rome as a memorial to the British Romantic poets in Italy, particularly Keats and Shelley. Publishes an annual review of Romantic Studies called the *Keats-Shelley Review*, arranges events and lectures for Friends and promotes bursaries and competitive writing on Romantic Studies (see **Keats–Shelley Prize** under *Prizes*). The *Review* is edited by *Angus Graham-Campbell*, c/o Eton College, Windsor SL4 6EA.

The Kenny/Naughton Society

Aghamore, Ballyhaunis, Co. Mayo, Republic of Ireland
✉ paulwdrogers@hotmail.com

www.aghamorgegaa.com/society/knsociety.htm
Chairman *Paul W.D. Rogers*
Patron *Mrs Erna Naughton*
SUBSCRIPTION

Founded in 1993 to commemorate two writers who had links with Aghamore: P.D. Kenny (1862–1944), who wrote under the pseudonym 'Pat' and Bill Naughton (1910–1992), best known as the author of *Alfie*. Holds an annual school over the October bank holiday weekend which includes lectures, drama, debate and competition (the **Bill Naughton Short Story Competition** – see entry under *Prizes*).

Kent & Sussex Poetry Society
39 Rockington Way, Crowborough TN6 2NJ
☎01892 662781
✉ joyce@kentandsussexpoetrysociety.org
www.kentandsussexpoetrysociety.org
Publicity Secretary *John Arnold*
SUBSCRIPTION £10 p.a. (Full); £6 (Concessionary – country members living farther afield, senior citizens, under-16s, unemployed)

Founded 1946 to promote the enjoyment of poetry. Monthly meetings are held in Tunbridge Wells, including readings by major poets, a monthly workshop and an annual writing retreat week. Publishes an annual folio of members' work based on Members' Competition, adjudicated and commented upon by a major poet. Runs an annual **Open Poetry Competition** (see entry under *Prizes* and details on website) and Saturday workshops twice a year with leading poets.

The Kilvert Society
Sandalwood, North End Road, Steeple Claydon, Buckingham MK18 2PG
☎01296 730498
Secretary *Mr D. Elvins*
SUBSCRIPTION £6 p.a.; £9 (2 persons at same address)

Founded 1948 to foster an interest in the Diary, the diarist and the countryside he loved. Publishes three journals each year; during the summer holds three weekends of walks, commemoration services and talks.

The Kipling Society
6 Clifton Road, London W9 1SS
☎020 7286 0194 Fax 020 7286 0194
✉ jane@keskar.fsworld.co.uk
www.kipling.org.uk

Honorary Secretary *Jane Keskar*
SUBSCRIPTION £20 p.a.

Founded 1927. The Society's main activities are: maintaining a specialised library in London; answering enquiries from the public (schools, publishers, writers and the media); arranging a regular programme of lectures, especially in London and in Sussex, and an annual luncheon with guest speaker; maintaining a small museum and reference at The Grange, in Rottingdean near Brighton; issuing a quarterly journal. (For the Kipling mailbox discussion list, e-mail to: Rudyard-Kipling@jiscmail.ac.uk) This is a literary society for all who enjoy the prose and verse of Rudyard Kipling (1865–1936) and are interested in his life and times. Please contact the Secretary by letter, telephone, fax or e-mail for further information.

The Kitley Trust
Woodstock, Litton Dale, Litton SK17 8QL
☎01298 871564
✉ stottie2@waitrose.com
Contact *Rosie Ford*

Founded 1990 by a teacher in Sheffield to promote the art of creative writing, in memory of her mother, Jessie Kitley. Activities include: biannual poetry competitions; a 'Get Poetry' day (distribution of children's poems in shopping malls); annual sponsorship of a writer for a school; campaigns; organising conferences for writers and teachers of writing. Funds are provided by donations and profits (if any) from competitions.

Charles Lamb Society
BM Elia, London WC1N 3XX
SUBSCRIPTION £12 p.a. (Single); £18 (Joint & Corporate); US$28 (Overseas Personal); US$42 (Overseas Corporate)

Founded 1935 to promote the study of the life, works and times of English essayist Charles Lamb (1775–1834). Holds regular bi-monthly meetings and lectures in London and organises society events over the summer. Annual luncheon in February. Publishes a quarterly bulletin, *The Charles Lamb Bulletin*. Contributions of Elian interest are welcomed by the editor *Rick Tomlinson* at 669 South Monroe Street, Decatur, Illinois 62522–3225, USA (✉ romanticism@ameritech.net). Membership applications should be sent to the box number address above. The Society's library is housed in the **Guildhall Library**, Aldermanbury, London EC2P 2EJ. Requests to consult printed sources must be made 48 hours in advance by letter to the

Principal Reference Librarian, in person at the Printed Books Enquiry Desk or by telephone (020 7332 1868/1870). Member of the **Alliance of Literary Societies**. Registered Charity No: 803222.

Lancashire Authors' Association

Heatherslade, 5 Quakerfields, Westhoughton, Bolton BL5 2BJ
☎01942 791390
✉ eholt@cwctv.net

General Secretary *Eric Holt*
SUBSCRIPTION £10 p.a.; £13 (Joint); £1 (Junior)

Founded 1909 for writers and lovers of Lancashire literature and history. Aims to foster and stimulate interest in Lancashire history and literature as well as in the preservation of the Lancashire dialect. Meets three times a year on Saturday at various locations. Publishes a quarterly journal called *The Record*, which is issued free to members, and holds eight annual competitions (open to members only) for both verse and prose. Comprehensive library with access for research to members.

The Landor Society of Warwick

11 Watersfield Gardens, Sydenham, Leamington Spa CV31 1NT
☎01926 337874
✉ portlandbooks@quicknetuk.com

Honorary Secretary *Mrs Jean Field*
SUBSCRIPTION £7 p.a. (UK/EU); £10 (Joint); £12 (Overseas)

Founded 2000 to promote interest in the life and works of the Warwick-born writer Walter Savage Landor (1775–1864). Holds a Landor Birthday Dinner each year, and reading and discussion meetings most months. Publishes newsletter twice a year.

The Philip Larkin Society

c/o Department of Humanities, The University of Hull, Hull HU6 7RX
☎01482 465640 Fax 01482 465303
✉ j.a.osborne@hull.ac.uk
www.philiplarkin.com

Contact *Dr John Osborne*
SUBSCRIPTION £18 (Full rate); £12 (Unwaged/ Senior Citizen); £8 (Student)

Founded in 1995 to promote awareness of the life and work of Philip Larkin (1922–1985) and his literary contemporaries; to bring together all those who admire Larkin's work as a poet, writer and librarian; to bring about publications on all things Larkinesque. Organises a pro-

gramme of events ranging from lectures to rambles exploring the countryside of Larkin's schooldays and publishes a biannual newsletter, *About Larkin*.

The D.H. Lawrence Society

24 Briarwood Avenue, Nottingham NG3 6JQ
☎0115 950 3008

Secretary *Ron Faulks*
SUBSCRIPTION £14; £12 (Concession); £16 (European); £19 (RoW)

Founded 1974 to increase knowledge and the appreciation of the life and works of D.H. Lawrence. Monthly meetings, addressed by guest speakers, are held in the library at Eastwood (birthplace of DHL). Organises visits to places of interest in the surrounding countryside, supports the activities of the D.H. Lawrence Centre at Nottingham University, and has close links with DHL Societies worldwide. Publishes two newsletters and one journal each year, free to members.

The T.E. Lawrence Society

PO Box 728, Oxford OX2 6YP
www.telsociety.org

Honorary Secretary *Suzanne Fox*
SUBSCRIPTION £18 (UK); £23 (Overseas)

Founded 1985 as a non-profit making, educational, registered charity to advance awareness of the life and work of Thomas Edward Lawrence and to promote research into his life and work. Publishes four newsletters and two journals per year. A biennial symposium is held, usually in Oxford, to bring members together to share both academic and social interests. The Society encourages the formation of regional groups of which, currently, there are seven: three in England (Northwest, London, Dorset), one in Europe (Netherlands), two in the USA (Eastern and Western States) and one in Japan.

The Leamington Literary Society

52 Newbold Terrace East, Leamington Spa CV32 4EZ
☎01926 425733

Honorary Secretary *Mrs Margaret Watkins*
SUBSCRIPTION £10 p.a.

Founded 1912 to promote the study and appreciation of literature and the arts. Holds regular meetings every second Tuesday of the month (except August) at the Royal Pump Rooms, Leamington Spa. Also smaller groups which meet regularly to study poetry and the modern novel. The Society has published various books of local interest.

Lewes Monday Literary Club

c/o 1c Prince Edward's Road, Lewes BN7 1BJ
☎01273 478512
✉ chris.lutrario@btinternet.com

Contact *Christopher Lutrario*
SUBSCRIPTION £20 p.a.; £5 (Guest, per
meeting)

Founded in 1948 for the promotion and enjoyment of literature. Seven meetings are held
during the winter on the last Monday of each
month (from October to April) at the White
Hart Hotel in Lewes. The Club attracts speakers of the highest quality and a balance between
all forms of literature is aimed for. Guests are
welcome to attend meetings.

The George MacDonald Society

The Library, Kings College, Strand, London
WC2R 2LS
☎01342 823859
✉ macdonald-society@britishlibrary.net
www.gmsociety.org.uk linked with
www.george-macdonald.com

Contact *John Docherty*
SUBSCRIPTION £10 p.a. (Individual);
£13 (Joint); £7 (Unwaged); £11 (Overseas)

Founded 1981 to increase awareness of 'the
uniqueness and importance of MacDonald's
writings'. Notable among Victorian writers for
his radical mixture of genres: MacDonald's fantasy works influenced H.G. Wells, C.S. Lewis
and J.R.R. Tolkien, among many others, and his
'realistic' novels offered a fascinating glimpse into
Victorian Scottish life. The Society organises
conferences and workshops in Britain and
abroad, often in association with other societies
with related interests. Publishes an annual journal, *North Wind*, with contributions from most of
the leading MacDonald scholars worldwide and
a newsletter, *Orts*.

The Friends of Arthur Machen

78 Greenwich South Street, Greenwich,
London SE10 8UN
☎020 8691 7836
✉ jrc@amarantus.ndo.co.uk
www.machensoc.demon.co.uk

Contact *Jeremy Cantwell*
SUBSCRIPTION £15 p.a. (UK); £18 (EU/
Overseas); $32 (US)

Founded 1998. (Formerly the Arthur Machen
Society.) Promotes a wider readership of
Arthur Machen and a greater understanding of
his life and work. Members receive hardback
journals (*Faunus*) and newsletters (*Machenalia*).

The Marlowe Society

9 Middlefield Gardens, Hurst Green Road,
Halesowen B62 9QH
☎0121 421 1482 Fax 0121 421 1482
✉ marsoct@ntlworld.com
www.marlowe-society.org

Membership Secretary *Frieda Barker*
Treasurer *Bruce Young*
SUBSCRIPTION £12 p.a. (Individual);
£7 p.a. (Pensioners/Student/Unwaged);
£15 p.a. (Overseas); £200 (Group);
£100 (Individual Life Membership)

Founded 1955. Holds meetings, lectures and
discussions, stimulates research into Marlowe's
life and works, encourages production of his
plays and publishes a biannual newsletter. At a
ceremony on 11th July 2002 the Society celebrated their success in establishing a memorial
to the playwright and poet in Poets' Corner in
Westminster Abbey.

The John Masefield Society

The Frith, Ledbury HR8 1LW
☎01531 631647 Fax 01531 631647
✉ petercarter@btinternet.com
www.sas.ac.uk/ies/Full%20Text%20Archive/
Masefield/Society/jmsws.htm

Chairman *Peter Carter*
SUBSCRIPTION £5 p.a. (Individual);
£8 (Family, Institutions, Libraries);
£10 (Overseas); £2.50 (Junior, Student)

Founded in 1992 to stimulate the appreciation
of and interest in the life and works of John
Masefield (Poet Laureate 1930–1967). The
Society is based in Ledbury, the Herefordshire
market town of his birth and holds various public events in addition to publishing a journal and
occasional papers.

William Morris Society

Kelmscott House, 26 Upper Mall,
Hammersmith, London W6 9TA
☎020 8741 3735 Fax 020 8748 5207
✉ william.morris@care4free.net
www.morrissociety.org

Contact *Helen Elletson*
SUBSCRIPTION £15 p.a.

Founded 1955 to promote interest in the life,
work and ideas of William Morris (1834–
1896), English poet and craftsman.

The Neil Munro Society

8 Briar Road, Kirkintilloch, Glasgow G66 3SA
☎0141 776 4280
✉ brian@bdosborne.fsnet.co.uk

www.neilmunro.co.uk
Secretary *Brian D. Osborne*
SUBSCRIPTION £10 (Annual); £11 (Family);
£5 (Unwaged); £15 (Institutional)

Founded in 1996 to encourage interest in the works of Neil Munro (1863–1930), the Scottish novelist, short story writer, poet and journalist. An annual programme of meetings is held in Glasgow and Munro's home-town of Inveraray. Publishes *ParaGraphs*, a twice-yearly magazine, sponsors reprints of Munro's work and is developing a Munro archive.

Bill Naughton
See **The Kenny/Naughton Society**

Violet Needham Society
c/o 19 Ashburnham Place, London SE10 8TZ
☎020 8692 4562
✉ richardcheffins@aol.com
Honorary Secretary *R.H.A. Cheffins*
SUBSCRIPTION £7.50 p.a. (UK & Europe);
£11 (RoW)

Founded 1985 to celebrate the work of children's author Violet Needham and stimulate critical awareness of her work. Publishes thrice-yearly *Souvenir*, the Society journal with an accompanying newsletter; organises meetings and excursions to places associated with the author and her books. The journal includes articles about other children's writers of the 1940s and '50s and on ruritanian fiction. Contributions welcome.

The Edith Nesbit Society
21 Churchfields, West Malling ME19 6RJ
www.imagix.dial.pipex.com
Chairman *Margaret McCarthy*
SUBSCRIPTION £6 p.a.; £8 (Joint); £75 (Life)

Founded in 1996 to celebrate the life and work of Edith Nesbit (1858–1924), best known as the author of *The Railway Children*. The Society's activities include a regular newsletter, booklets, talks and visits to relevant places.

The Wilfred Owen Association
c/o 17 Belmont, Shrewsbury SY1 1TE
☎01743 460089
www.1914-19.co.uk/owen
Chairman *Michael Grayer*
SUBSCRIPTION Adults £6 (£10 Overseas);
£4 (Senior Citizens/Students/Unemployed);
£15 (UK Groups/Institutions);
£25 (Overseas Groups/Institutions)

Founded 1989 to commemorate the life and works of Wilfred Owen by promoting readings, visits, talks and performances relating to Owen and his work. The Association offers practical support for students of literature and future poets through links with education, support for literary foundations and information on historical and literary background material. Membership is international with 700 members. Publishes a regular newsletter and annual journal. Speakers are available.

The Elsie Jeanette Oxenham Appreciation Society
32 Tadfield Road, Romsey SO51 5AJ
☎01794 517149 Fax 01794 517149
✉ abbey@bufobooks.demon.co.uk
www.bufobooks.demon.co.uk/abbeylnk.htm
Membership Secretary/Treasurer *Ms Ruth Allen*
SUBSCRIPTION £7.50 p.a.; enquire for
Overseas rates

Founded 1989 to promote the works of Elsie J. Oxenham. Publishes a newsletter for members, *The Abbey Chronicle*, three times a year; Editor *Fiona Dyer* (fionadyer@btopenworld.com). 500+ members.

Thomas Paine Society
43 Eugene Gardens, Nottingham NG2 3LF
☎0115 986 0010
President *The Rt. Hon. Michael Foot*
Honorary Secretary *R.W. Morrell, MBE*
Treasurer *Stuart Wright*
SUBSCRIPTION (Minimum) £15 p.a. (UK);
$35 (Overseas); £5 (Unwaged/Pensioners/
Students)

Founded 1963 to promote the life and work of Thomas Paine, and continues to expound his ideals. Meetings, newsletters, lectures and research assistance. The Society has members worldwide and keeps in touch with American and French Thomas Paine associations. Publishes magazine, *The Journal of Radical History*, twice yearly (Editor, *R.W. Morrell*) and a newsletter. Holds occasional exhibitions and lectures, including the biannual Thomas Paine Memorial Lecture and the annual Eric Paine Memorial Lecture.

The John Polidori Literary Society
PO Box 6078, Nottingham NG16 4HX
Founder & President *Franklin Bishop*
SUBSCRIPTION on application

Founded 1990 to promote and encourage appreciation of the life and works of John William Polidori MD (1795–1821) – novelist, poet, tragedian, philosopher, diarist, essayist, reviewer, traveller and one of the youngest students to obtain a medical degree (at the age of 19). He was one-time intimate of the leading figures in the Romantic movement and travelling companion and private physician to Lord Byron. He was a pivotal figure in the infamous Villa Diodati ghost story sessions in which he assisted Mary Shelley in the creation of her *Frankenstein* tale. Polidori introduced into literature the enduring icon of the vampire portrayed as an aristocratic, handsome seducer with his seminal work *The Vampyre – A Tale*, published in 1819. Polidori was honoured in 1998 by the erection of a City of Westminster Plaque at his birthplace – 38 Great Pulteney Street, Westminster, London – officially unveiled by the Italian ambassador. The Society issues unique publications of the rare works of Polidori. International membership in Italy, USA, Canada and Spain.

The Beatrix Potter Society

9 Broadfields, Harpenden AL5 2HJ
☎01582 769755
✉ beatrixpottersociety@tiscali.co.uk
www.beatrixpottersociety.org.uk
SUBSCRIPTION UK: £15 p.a. (Individual);
£20 (Institution); Overseas: £20
(Individual); £25 (Institution)

Founded 1980 to promote the study and appreciation of the life and works of Beatrix Potter (1866–1943). Potter was not only the author of *The Tale of Peter Rabbit* and other classics of children's literature; she was also a landscape and natural history artist, diarist, farmer and conservationist, and was responsible for the preservation of large areas of the Lake District through her gifts to the National Trust. The Society upholds and protects the integrity of the unique work of Potter, her aims and bequests; holds regular talks and meetings in London and elsewhere with visits to places connected with Beatrix Potter. International Study Conferences are held in the UK and the USA. The Society has an active publishing programme. (UK Registered Charity No. 281198.)

The Anthony Powell Society

76 Ennismore Avenue, Greenford UB6 0JW
☎020 8864 4095 Fax 020 8864 6109
✉ secretary@anthonypowell.org.uk
www.anthonypowell.org.uk
Patron *John M. A. Powell*
President *Hugh Massingberd*
Honorary Secretary *Dr Keith C. Marshall*
SUBSCRIPTION £20 p.a. (Individual);

£30 (Joint/Gold); £12 (Students);
£100 (Organisation)

Founded in June 2000 by a group of scholars and enthusiasts following Powell's death earlier that year at the age of 94. The Society's first project was the First Biennial Anthony Powell Conference, held at Eton College (Powell's old school); the second conference was in April 2003 at Balliol College, Oxford (Powell's *alma mater*). Also organises events for members, ranging from 'pub meets' to talks and visits to places of Powell interest. Publishes a quarterly newsletter. The Society is a member of the **Alliance of Literary Societies**.

The Powys Society

82 Linden Road, Gloucester GL1 5HD
☎01452 304539
✉ pjf@retepssof.freeserve.co.uk
www.powys-society.org
Honorary Secretary *Peter J. Foss*
SUBSCRIPTION £13.50 (UK); £16 (Overseas);
£6 (Students)

The Society (with a membership of 350) aims to promote public education and recognition of the writings, thought and contribution to the arts of the Powys family; particularly of John Cowper, Theodore and Llewelyn, but also of the other members of the family and their close associates. The Society holds two major collections of Powys published works, letters, manuscripts and memorabilia. Publishes the *Powys Society Newsletter* in April, June and November and *The Powys Journal* in August. Organises an annual conference as well as lectures and meetings in Powys places.

The J.B. Priestley Society

Eldwick Crag Farm, High Eldwick, Bingley
BD16 3BB
☎01274 563078
✉ reavill@globalnet.co.uk
www.jbpriestley-society.com
President *Roy Hattersley*
Chairman *Dr Ken Smith*
Honorary Secretary *R.E.Y. Slater*
Membership Secretary *Tony Reavill*
SUBSCRIPTION £10 (Individual); £5
(Concession); £15 (Group/Family)

Founded 1997 to widen the knowledge and understanding of Priestley's works; promote the study of his life and his social, cultural and political influences; provide members of the Society with lectures, seminars, films, journals and stimulate education projects; promote public performances of his works and the distribution of material associated with him. For further information, contact the Membership Secretary at the address above.

The Barbara Pym Society

St Hilda's College, Oxford OX4 1DU
☎01865 276867 Fax 01865 276820
✉ eileen.roberts@st-hildas.oxford.ac.uk
www.pym.org
Chairman *Kate Charles*
SUBSCRIPTION £15 p.a. (Individual); £22 p.a.
(Household); £8 p.a. (Concession)

Aims to promote interest in and scholarly research into the works of Barbara Pym; to bring together like-minded people to enjoy the exploration of all aspects of her novels and to continue to encourage publishers to keep her novels in print. Annual weekend conference at St. Hilda's College in September, focusing on a theme or a particular novel. Annual North American Conference at Harvard Law School. Annual one-day spring meeting in London, with speaker. Publishes a newsletter, *Green Leaves*, biannually. In addition to reports on conferences and society activities, the newsletter includes scholarly papers and various unpublished items from the Pym archives at the Bodleian Library (i.e. short stories).

The Queen's English Society

Membership Secretary: Fernwood,
Nightingales, West Chiltington, Pulborough
RH20 2QT
☎01798 813001
✉ enquiries@queens-english-society.com
www.queens-english-society.com
Hon. Membership Secretary *David Ellis*
SUBSCRIPTION £10 p.a. (Ordinary);
£12 (Family/Corporate); £100 (Life
member); reduced rates available for
students and long-term unemployed

Founded in 1972 to promote and uphold the use of good English and to encourage the enjoyment of the language. Holds regular meetings to which speakers are invited, an annual luncheon and publishes a quarterly journal, *Quest*, for which original articles are welcome.

Rainbow Poetry Recitals

14 Lewes Crescent, Brighton BN2 1FH
☎01424 444072
Administrators *Hugh Hellicar, Dorothy Steers*
SUBSCRIPTION £6 (Individual); £10
(Joint/Family); £15 (Schools)

Founded 1994. Regular recitals of poetry and

other literature are held in Sussex and London, mostly in churches and civic buildings. Seminars and creative writing groups in some branches. Members' library in Sussex. Quarterly magazine.

The Arthur Ransome Society Ltd

Abbot Hall Art Gallery & Museum, Kendal
LA6 5AL
☎01539 722464 Fax 01539 722494
✉ tarsinfo@arthur-ransome.org
www.arthur-ransome.org/ar
Trustee Chairman *Geraint Lewis*
Company Secretary *Mike Glover*
SUBSCRIPTION UK: £5 (Junior); £10 (Student);
£15 (Adult); £20 (Family); £40 (Corporate);
Overseas: £5 (Junior); £10 (Student);
£20 (Adult); £25 (Family) Payable in local
currency in US, Canada, Australia, Japan and
New Zealand

Founded in 1990 to celebrate the life and to promote the works and ideas of Arthur Ransome, author of *Swallows and Amazons* titles for children, biographer of Oscar Wilde, works on the Russian Revolution and extensive articles on fishing. TARS seeks to encourage children and adults to engage in adventurous pursuits, to educate the public about Ransome and his works, and to sponsor research into his literary works and life.

The Romany Society

10 Haslam Street, Bury BL9 6EQ
☎0161 764 7078
✉ philshelley@btopenworld.com
www.romanysociety.org.uk
Honorary Secretary *John Thorpe*
Publications Officer *Phil Shelley*
SUBSCRIPTION £5 (Individual); £9 (Family);
£10 (Institutions); £3.50 (Student/
Unwaged)

Promotes the life, work and conservation message of the Rev. G. Bramwell Evens – 'Romany' – the first broadcasting naturalist who influenced generations of listeners to his *Out With Romany* radio programmes on the BBC during the 1930s and 1940s and with his series of natural history books. The Romany Society was established orignally following Evens' death at the age of 59 in 1943 and ran until 1965. Revived in 1996, the Society holds an annual members' weekend to areas of significance in the Romany story, erects memorial plaques where appropriate, encourages media coverage of Romany and supports young naturalists with the Romany Memorial Grant.

The Followers of Rupert
31 Whiteley, Windsor SL4 5PJ
☎01753 865562
✉ followersofrupert@hotmail.com
www.rupertthebear.org.uk

Membership Secretary *Mrs Shirley Reeves*
SUBSCRIPTION UK: £15; £17 (Joint); Europe,
   airmail: £18 (Individual); £20 (Joint); RoW,
   airmail: £20 (Individual); £22 (Joint)

Founded in 1983. The Society caters for the growing interest in the Rupert Bear stories, past, present and future. Publishes the *Nutwood Newsletter* quarterly which gives up-to-date news of Rupert and information on Society activities. A national get-together of members – the Followers Annual – is held during the autumn.

The Ruskin Society
49 Hallam Street, London W1W 6JP
☎020 7580 1894

Honorary Secretary *Dr Cynthia. J. Gamble*
Honorary Treasurer *The Hon. Mrs Catherine Edwards*
SUBSCRIPTION £10 p.a. (payable on 1 January)

Founded in 1997 to encourage a wider understanding of John Ruskin and his contemporaries. Organises lectures and events which seek not only to explain to the public at large the nature of Ruskin's theories but also to place these in a modern context.

The Ruskin Society of London
351 Woodstock Road, Oxford OX2 7NX
☎01865 310987/515962 Fax 01865 240448

Honorary Secretary *Miss O.E. Forbes-Madden*
SUBSCRIPTION £10 p.a.

Founded 1986 to promote interest in John Ruskin (1819–1900) and his contemporaries. All aspects of Ruskinia are introduced. Functions are held in London. Publishes the annual *Ruskin Gazette*, a journal concerned with Ruskin's influence. Affiliated to other literary societies.

The Malcolm Saville Society
78a Windmill Road, Mortimer RG7 3RL
✉ mystery@witchend.com
www.witchend.com
Membership Secretary *Richard Griffiths*
SUBSCRIPTION £7.50 p.a. (UK);
   £12 (Overseas)

Founded in 1994 to remember and promote interest in the work of the popular children's author. Regular social activities, booksearch, library, contact directory and four magazines per year.

The Dorothy L. Sayers Society
Rose Cottage, Malthouse Lane,
Hurstpierpoint BN6 9JY
☎01273 833444 Fax 01273 835988
www.sayers.org.uk

Contact *Christopher Dean*
SUBSCRIPTION £14 p.a. (UK);
   £16.50 (Europe); $28 (US)

Founded 1976 to promote the study of the life, works and thoughts of Dorothy Sayers; to encourage the performance of her plays and publication of her books and books about her; to preserve original material and provide assistance to researchers. Acts as a forum and information centre, providing material for study purposes which would otherwise be unavailable. Annual seminars and other meetings. Co-founder of the Dorothy L. Sayers Centre in Witham. Publishes bi-monthly bulletin, annual proceedings and other papers.

The Bernard Shaw
Information & Research Service
27 Cavendish Avenue, South Ruislip
HA4 6QJ
✉ dianeuttley@georgebernardshaw.com
www.georgebernardshaw.com

President *Diane S. Uttley*

Established in 1997 by writer and Shaw specialist Diane S. Uttley who was custodian of and lived in the writer's home, Shaw's Corner, from 1989 to 1997. The service is used by enthusiasts and academics; literary, theatrical and biographical.

The Shaw Society
51 Farmfield Road, Downham, Bromley
BR1 4NF
☎020 8697 3619 Fax 020 8697 3619
✉ anthnyellis@aol.com

Honorary Secretary *Ms Barbara Smoker*
SUBSCRIPTION £15 p.a. (Individual);
   £22 (Joint)

Founded 1941 to promote interest in the life and works of G. Bernard Shaw. Meetings are held on the last Friday of every month (except July, August and December) at Conway Hall, Red Lion Square, London WC1 (6.30 pm for 7.00 pm) at which speakers are invited to talk on some aspect of Shaw's life or works. Monthly playreadings are held on the first Friday of each month (except August). A 'Birthday Tribute' is held at Shaw's Corner, Ayot St Lawrence in Hertfordshire, on the weekend nearest to Shaw's birthday (26th July). Publishes a quarterly newsletter and a magazine, *The Shavian*, which appears approximately every nine months. (No payment for contributors.)

The Robert Southey Society
1 Lewis Terrace, Abergarwed, Neath
SA11 4DL
☎01639 711480
Contact *Robert King*
SUBSCRIPTION £10 p.a.

Founded 1990 to promote the work of Robert Southey. Publishes an annual newsletter and arranges talks on his life and work. Open membership.

The Laurence Sterne Trust
See **The Friends of Shandy Hall**

Robert Louis Stevenson Club
12 Dean Park, Longniddry EH32 0QR
☎01875 852976 Fax 01875 853328
✉ alan@marchbank.freeserve.co.uk
Secretary *Alan Marchbank*
SUBSCRIPTION £15 p.a. (Individual); £20 p.a. (Overseas); £100 (Ten-year); £180 (Life)

Founded in 1920 to foster interest in Robert Louis Stevenson's life and works. The Club organises an annual lunch and other events. Publishes *RLS Club News* twice a year.

The Bram Stoker Society
Regent House, Trinity College, Dublin 2, Republic of Ireland
Fax 00 353 1 671 9003 (attn: David Lass)
✉ dlass@tcd.ie
benecke.com/stoker.html
benecke.com/vampire.hrml
Honorary Secretary *David Lass*
Honorary Treasurer *Dr Albert Power* (43 Castle Court, Killiney Hill Road, Killiney, Co. Dublin, Republic of Ireland)
SUBSCRIPTION £10 p.a. (UK); €10 (Europe); $20 (US/RoW)

Founded 1980. Aims to promote the study and appreciation of Bram Stoker's works, including his place in the Gothic horror tradition, and his influence on later writers in the areas of cinema, music and theatre. Publishes an occasional newsletter, an annual journal of scholarly articles and organises a regular programme of activities with its affiliated body, The Bram Stoker Club of Trinity College Dublin. These include screenings, annual memorial lectures and the annual summer school held in July. Subscription payments by cheque or postal order (made out to The Bram Stoker Society) should be sent to the Hon. Treasurer at his address above.

The R.S. Surtees Society
Manor Farm House, Nunney, Near Frome BA11 4NJ
☎01373 836937 Fax 01373 836574
✉ rssurtees@fsmail.net
www.r.s.surteessociety.org
Contact *Orders and Membership Secretary*
SUBSCRIPTION £10

Founded 1979 to republish the works of R.S. Surtees and others.

The Tennyson Society
Central Library, Free School Lane, Lincoln LN2 1EZ
☎01522 552862 Fax 01522 552858
✉ kathleenjefferson@lincolnshire.gov.uk
www.tennysonsociety.org.uk
Honorary Secretary *Miss K. Jefferson*
SUBSCRIPTION £8 p.a. (Individual); £10 (Family); £15 (Corporate); £125 (Life)

Founded 1960. An international society with membership worldwide. Exists to promote the study and understanding of the life and work of Alfred, Lord Tennyson. The Society is concerned with the work of the Tennyson Research Centre, 'probably the most significant collection of mss, family papers and books in the world'. Publishes annually the *Tennyson Research Bulletin*, which contains articles and critical reviews; and organises lectures, visits and seminars. Annual memorial service at Somersby in Lincolnshire.

The Angela Thirkell Society
54 Belmont Park, London SE13 5BN
☎020 8244 9339
✉ penny.aldred@ntlworld.com
www.angelathirkellsociety.com
www.angelathirkell.org (N. American branch)
Honorary Secretary *Mrs. P. Aldred*
SUBSCRIPTION £7 p.a.

Founded in 1980 to honour the memory of Angela Thirkell as a writer and to make her works available to new generations. Publishes an annual journal, holds an AGM in early October and a spring meeting which usually takes the form of a visit to a location associated with Thirkell. Has a flourishing North American branch which has frequent contact with the UK parent society.

The Dylan Thomas Society of Great Britain
5 Church Park, Mumbles, Swansea SA3 4DE
☎01792 520080

Contact *Mrs Eryl Jenkins*
SUBSCRIPTION £5 (Individual); £8 (2 adults from same household)

Founded 1977 to foster an understanding of the work of Dylan Thomas and to extend members' awareness of other 20th century writers, especially Welsh writers in English. Meetings take place monthly, mainly in Swansea.

The Edward Thomas Fellowship
1 Carfax, Undercliff Drive, St Lawrence, Isle of Wight PO38 1XG
☎01983 853366 Fax
colin.g.thornton@btopenworld.com
Hon. Secretary *Colin G. Thornton*
SUBSCRIPTION £7 p.a. (Single); £10 p.a. (Joint)

Founded 1980 to perpetuate and promote the memory of Edward Thomas and to encourage an appreciation of his life and work. The Fellowship holds a commemorative birthday walk on the Sunday nearest the poet's birthday, 3rd March; issues newsletters and holds various events.

The Tolkien Society
65 Wentworth Crescent, Ash Vale GU12 5LF
Fax 0870 0525569
✉ membership@tolkiensociety.org
www.tolkiensociety.org
Membership Secretary *Trevor Reynolds*
SUBSCRIPTION £20 p.a. (UK); £22 (Overseas)

An international organisation which aims to encourage and further interest in the life and works of the late Professor J.R.R. Tolkien, CBE, author of *The Hobbit* and *Lord of the Rings*. Current membership stands at 1200. Publishes *Mallorn* annually and *Amon Hen* bi-monthly.

The Trollope Society
9A North Street, Clapham, London SW4 0HN
☎020 7720 6789 Fax 020 7978 1815
✉ trollsoc@barset.fsnet.co.uk
www.trollopesociety.org
Contacts *John Letts, Phyllis Eden*

Founded 1987 to study and promote Anthony Trollope's works. Publishes the complete works of Trollope's novels and travel books.

Wainwright Society
Kendal Museum, Station Road, Kendal LA9 6BT
☎01539 721374
✉ membership@wainwright.org.uk

www.wainwright.org.uk
Membership Secretary *Morag Clement*
SUBSCRIPTION £10 p.a. (per household – from 1 Jan.)

Founded in 2002 'to keep alive the things that Alfred Wainwright (1907–1991) promoted through his guidebooks (*Pictorial Guides to the Lakeland Fells*), started 50 years ago, and the many other publications which were the "labour of love" of a large portion of his life'. Produces a newsletter three times per year, organises walks, events, annual dinner and lecture.

Edgar Wallace Society
84 Ridgefield Road, Oxford OX4 3DA
www.edgarwallace.org
Organiser *Miss Penny Wyrd*
SUBSCRIPTION £15 p.a.; £10 (Senior Citizen/ Student); Overseas: £20; £15 (Senior Citizen/Student)

Founded in 1969 by Wallace's daughter, Penelope, to bring together all who have an interest in Edgar Wallace. Members receive a brief biography of Edgar by Penelope Wallace, with a list of published book titles. A newsletter, *Crimson Circle*, is published three times a year.

The Walmsley Society
April Cottage, No 1 Brand Road, Hampden Park, Eastbourne BN22 9PX
☎01323 506447
✉ walmsley@haughshw.demon.co.uk
Honorary Secretary *Fred Lane*
SUBSCRIPTION £10 p.a.; £12 (Family); £9 (Students/Senior Citizens); £15 (Overseas, £25 for 2 years)

Founded 1985 to promote interest in the writings of Leo Walmsley and to foster an appreciation of the work of his father, the artist Ulric Walmsley. Two annual meetings – one held in Robin Hood's Bay on the East Yorkshire coast, spiritual home of the author Leo Walmsley. Publishes a journal twice-yearly and newsletters, and is involved in other publications which benefit the aims of the Society. A biography of Leo Walmsley is now available.

Sylvia Townsend Warner Society
2 Vicarage Lane, Dorchester DT1 1LH
☎01305 266028
✉ judith@bond.vispa.com
www.townsendwarner.com
Contact *Eileen Johnson*
SUBSCRIPTION £10 p.a.; $20 (Overseas)

Founded in 2000 to promote a wider readership and better understanding of the writings of Sylvia Townsend Warner.

Mary Webb Society

8 The Knowe, Willaston, Neston
CH64 1TA
☎0151 327 5843
✉ suehigginbotham@yahoo.co.uk
www.marywebb.2ya.com

Secretary *Sue Higginbotham*
SUBSCRIPTION £10 p.a. (Individual);
£13 p.a. (Joint/Overseas)

Founded 1972. Attracts members from the UK and overseas who are devotees of the literature of Mary Webb and of the beautiful Shropshire countryside of her novels. Publishes biannual journal, organises summer schools in various locations related to the authoress's life and works. Archives; lectures; tours arranged for individuals and groups.

H.G. Wells Society

Dept. of English Literature, University of Sheffield, Shearwood Mount, Shearwood Road, Sheffield S10 2TD
hgwellsusa.50megs.com

Honorary Secretary *Steve McClean*
SUBSCRIPTION £16 (UK/EU); £19 (Overseas);
£20 (Corporate); £10 (Concessions)

Founded 1960 to promote an interest in and appreciation of the life, work and thought of Herbert George Wells. Publishes *The Wellsian* (annual) and *The H.G. Wells Newsletter* (three issues yearly). Organises meetings and conferences.

The Oscar Wilde Society

100 Peacock Street, Gravesend DA12 1EQ
☎01474 535978
✉ vanessaharris@members.vzi.co.uk

Honorary Secretary *Vanessa Harris*

Founded 1990 to promote knowledge, appreciation and study of the life, personality and works of the writer and wit Oscar Wilde. Activities include meetings, lectures, readings and exhibitions, and visits to locations associated with Wilde. Members receive a journal, *The Wildean*, twice-yearly and a newsletter, *Intentions* (six per year).

The Charles Williams Society

35 Broomfield, Stacey Bushes, Milton Keynes
MK12 6HA
✉ charles_wms_soc@yahoo.co.uk
www.geocities.com/charles_wms_soc

Contact *Honorary Secretary*

Founded 1975 to promote interest in, and provide a means for the exchange of views and information on the life and work of Charles Walter Stansby Williams (1886–1945).

The Henry Williamson Society

7 Monmouth Road, Dorchester DT1 2DE
☎01305 264092
✉ zseagull@aol.com
www.henrywilliamson.org

General Secretary *Mrs Sue Cumming*
Membership Secretary *Mrs Margaret Murphy*
(16 Doran Drive, Redhill RH1 6AX
☎01737 763228; ✉ mm@misterman.
freeserve.co.uk)
SUBSCRIPTION £12 p.a.; £15 (Family);
£5 (Students)

Founded 1980 to encourage, by all appropriate means, a wider readership and deeper understanding of the literary heritage left by the 20th-century English writer Henry Williamson (1895–1977). Publishes annual journal.

The P.G. Wodehouse Society (UK)

26 Radcliffe Road, Croydon CR0 5QE
www.eclipse.co.uk/wodehouse

Membership Secretary *Christine Hewitt*
SUBSCRIPTION £15 p.a.

Relaunched in May 1997 to advance the genius of P.G. Wodehouse. Publications include the *Wooster Source* quarterly journal and the *By The Way* newsletter. Regular national and international group meetings. Members in most countries throughout the world. Society patrons include Rt. Hon. Tony Blair MP and Stephen Fry. Wodehouse's grandson, Sir Edward Cazalet, is on the committee.

The Parson Woodforde Society

22 Gaynor Close, Wymondham NR18 0EA
☎01953 604124
✉ mabrayne@supanet.com
www.parsonwoodforde.org.uk

Membership Secretary *Mrs Ann Elliott*
SUBSCRIPTION £12.50 (UK); £25 (Overseas)

Founded 1968. Aims to extend and develop knowledge of James Woodforde's life and the society in which he lived and to provide the opportunity for fellow enthusiasts to meet together in places associated with the diarist. Publishes a quarterly journal and newsletter. The Society is producing a complete edition of the diary of James Woodforde. To date, thirteen volumes of diary material have been published covering the period 1759–1793.

The Virginia Woolf Society of Great Britain

Fairhaven, Charnleys Lane, Banks, Southport PR9 8HJ

✉ stuart.n.clarke@btinternet.com
www.virginiawoolfsociety.co.uk

Contact *Stuart N. Clarke*
SUBSCRIPTION £15 p.a.; £20 (Overseas)

Founded 1998 to promote interest in the life and work of Virginia Woolf, author, essayist and diarist. The Society's activities include trips away, walks, reading groups and talks. Publishes a literary journal, *Virginia Woolf Bulletin*, three times a year.

The Wordsworth Trust

Dove Cottage, Grasmere LA22 9SH
☎01539 435544 Fax 01539 435748
✉ enquiries@wordsworth.org.uk
www.wordsworth.org.uk

Contacts *Natalie Thompson, Allan King*
SUBSCRIPTION

Founded in 1890, the Trust is a living memorial to the life and poetry of William Wordsworth and his contemporaries. As the centre for British Romanticism, the Trust, with its wealth of manuscripts, books, drawings and pictures, provides the full context for understanding and celebrating a major cultural moment in history in which Britain played a profound role. (Registered Charity No. 1066184.)

WW2 HMSO PPBKS Society

3 Roman Road, Southwick BN42 4TP
☎01273 871017 Fax 01273 871017

Contact *A.R. James*

Founded 1994 to encourage collectors and to promote research into HMSO's World War II series of paperbacks. Most of them were written by well-known authors, though in many cases anonymously. No subscription charge. Available for purchase: Collectors' Guide (£5); Bibliography (£3); Handbook, *Informing the People* (£10).

The Yeats Society Sligo

Yeats Memorial Building, Douglas Hyde Bridge, Sligo, Republic of Ireland
☎00 353 71 42693 Fax 00 353 71 42780
✉ info@yeats-sligo.com
www.yeats-sligo.com

President *Michael Keohane*
SUBSCRIPTION €25 (Single); €38 (Couple); €127 (Corporate)

Founded in 1958 to promote the heritage of W.B. Yeats and the Yeats family. Attractions include continuous updated Yeats exhibitions for public viewing, annual Yeats International Summer School in August and Yeats Winter School in January. The Yeats Summer Festival is held each August and lectures are held in the winter and spring, sponsored by the Institute of Technology, Sligo. Publishes a newsletter and organises year-round events/programmes in arts, culture, education for writers' groups, poetry/drama groups, etc.

Yorkshire Dialect Society

51 Stepney Avenue, Scarborough YO12 5BW

Secretary *Michael Park*
SUBSCRIPTION £10 p.a.

Founded 1897 to promote interest in and preserve a record of the Yorkshire dialect. Publishes dialect verse and prose writing. Two journals to members annually. Details of publications are available from YDS, 61 Moor Lane, Carnaby, Bridlington YO16 4UT.

Francis Brett Young Society

92 Gower Road, Halesowen B62 9BT
☎0121 422 8969
www.fbysociety.co.uk

Honorary Secretary *Mrs Jean Hadley*
SUBSCRIPTION Subscription £7 p.a.
(Individuals); £10 (Couples sharing a journal); £5 (Students); £7 (Organisations/Overseas); £70 (Life); £100 (Joint, Life)

Founded 1979. Aims to provide a forum for those interested in the life and works of English novelist Francis Brett Young and to collate research on him. Promotes lectures, exhibitions and readings; publishes a regular newsletter.

Arts Councils and Regional Offices

The Arts Council England
14 Great Peter Street, London SW1P 3NQ
☎020 7333 0100 Textphone 020 7973 6564
Fax 020 7973 6590
✉ enquiries@artscouncil.org.uk
www.artscouncil.org.uk
Chairman *Professor Sir Christopher Frayling*
Chief Executive *Peter Hewitt*
Director of Literature *Gary McKeone*

Founded 1946. Arts Council England is the national development agency for the arts in England, distributing public money from government and the National Lottery to artists and arts organisations. Arts Council England works independently and at arm's length from government. Information about Arts Council England funding is available on the website, by e-mail or by contacting the enquiry line on 0845 300 6200.

Arts Council England has 9 regional offices:

Arts Council England, East
Eden House, 48–49 Bateman Street, Cambridge CB2 1LR
☎0845 300 6200 Fax 0870 242 1271
Textphone 01223 306893

Arts Council England, East Midlands
St Nicholas Court, 25–27 Castle Gate, Nottingham NG1 7AR
☎0845 300 6200 Fax 0115 950 2467

Arts Council England, London
2 Pear Tree Court, London EC1R 0DS
☎0845 300 6200 Fax 020 7608 4100
Textphone 020 7608 4101

Arts Council England, North East
Central Square, Forth Street, Newcastle upon Tyne NE1 3PJ
☎0845 300 6200 Fax 0191 230 1020
Textphone 0191 255 8500

Arts Council England, North West
Manchester House, 22 Bridge Street, Manchester M3 3AB
☎0845 300 6200 Fax 0161 834 6969
Textphone 0161 834 9131

Arts Council England, South East
Sovereign House, Church Street, Brighton BN1 1RA
☎0845 300 6200 Fax 0870 242 1257
Textphone 01273 710659

Arts Council England, South West
Bradninch Place, Gandy Street, Exeter EX4 3LS
☎0845 300 6200 Fax 01392 229229
Textphone 01392 433503

Arts Council England, West Midlands
82 Granville Street, Birmingham B1 2LH
☎0845 300 6200 Fax 0121 643 7239
Textphone 0121 643 2815

Arts Council England, Yorkshire
21 Bond Street, Dewsbury WF13 1AX
☎0845 300 6200 Fax 01924 466522
Textphone 01924 438585

The Arts Council/ An Chomhairle Ealaíon
70 Merrion Square, Dublin 2, Republic of Ireland
☎00 353 1 618 0200 Fax 00 353 1 676 1302
✉ artistsservices@artscouncil.ie
www.artscouncil.ie

Director *Patricia Quinn*
Literature Specialist (English language)
  Bronwen Williams
Literature Specialist (Irish language) *Róisín Ní Mhianáin*
Artists' Services Manager *Paul Johnson*

The development agency for the arts in Ireland. An autonomous statutory body, appointed by the Irish government to promote and assist the arts. Established by the Arts Act of 1951. In fulfilling its remit, the Council provides advice to the Irish government on artistic matters; advice, assistance and support to individuals, arts organisations and a wide range of governmental and non-governmental bodies; and financial assistance to individuals and organisations for artistic purposes. The Council also part funds county and city arts officers throughout the country. It consists of 12 members and a chair appointed by the Minister for Arts, Sport and Tourism for a period of not more than five years. Its state grant in 2004 was €52.5 million.

Of particular interest to individual writes is the Council's free booklet, *Support for Artists*, which describes bursaries, awards and schemes on offer and how to apply for them. Applicants to these awards must be of Irish birth or resident in Ireland.

The Arts Council of Northern Ireland

MacNeice House, 77 Malone Road, Belfast BT9 6AQ
☎028 9038 5200 Fax 028 9066 1715
✉ rmeredith@artscouncil-ni.org
www.artscouncil-ni.org
Literature and Language Arts Officer *Robbie Meredith*

Funds book production by established publishers, programmes of readings, literary festivals, writers-in-residence schemes and literary magazines and periodicals. Occasional schools programmes and anthologies of children's writing are produced. Annual awards and bursaries for writers are available. Holds information also on various groups associated with local arts, workshops and courses.

Scottish Arts Council

12 Manor Place, Edinburgh EH3 7DD
☎0131 226 6051 Fax 0131 225 9833
✉ administrator@scottisharts.org.uk
www.scottisharts.org.uk
Chairman *James Boyle*
Director *Graham Berry*
Head of Literature *Gavin Wallace*

Literature Officers *Jenny Attala, Sophy Dale*
Literature Secretary *Catherine Allen*

Principal channel for government funding of the arts in Scotland. The Scottish Arts Council (SAC) is funded by the Scottish Executive. It aims to develop and improve the knowledge, understanding and practice of the arts, and to increase their accessibility throughout Scotland. It offers around 1300 grants a year to artists and arts organisations concerned with the visual arts, crafts, dance and mime, drama, literature, music, festivals and traditional, ethnic and community arts. It is also a distributor of National Lottery funds to the arts in Scotland. SAC's support for Scottish-based writers with a track record of publication includes bursaries, writing fellowships and book awards (see entries under **Bursaries, Fellowships and Grants** and **Prizes**). Information offered includes lists of literature awards, literary magazines, agents and publishers.

The Arts Council of Wales

Museum Place, Cardiff CF10 3NX
☎029 2037 6500 Fax 029 2022 1447
www.artswales.org.uk/language
Senior Officer: Drama *Sandra Wynne*

In April 2003 the responsibility for funding literary magazines and book production transferred to the **Welsh Books Council**. Services for individual writers, including bursaries, mentoring, the critical writers service and writers in residency/writers on tour are provided by the **Welsh Academy, Hay-on-Wye Literature Festival** and **Tŷ Newydd Writers' Centre** at Cricieth. The Council aims to develop theatrical experience among Wales-based writers through a variety of schemes – in particular, by funding writers on year-long attachments.

UK Writers' Courses

ENGLAND

Berkshire

University of Reading
The School of Continuing Education,
London Road, Reading RG1 5AQ
☎0118 378 8347
✉ Cont-Ed@reading.ac.uk
www.reading.ac.uk/ContEd

An expanding programme of creative writing courses, including *Life into Fiction*; *Poetry Workshop*; *Getting Started*; *Writing Fiction*; *Publishing Poetry*; *Scriptwriting*; *Travel Writing*; *Comedy Writing* and *Writing for Radio*. There is also a public lecture by a writer and a reading by students of their work, and various Saturday workshops. Tutors include novelist Leslie Wilson and poets Jane Draycott, Elizabeth James and Susan Utting, David Grubb and Paul Bavister. Fees vary depending on the length of course. Concessions available.

The Write Coach
2 Rowan Close, Wokingham RG41 4BH
☎0118 978 4904
✉ enquiries@thewritecoach.co.uk
www.thewritecoach.co.uk

Contact *Rebecca Hill*

Workshops and one-to-one coaching (both in person and by telephone) 'to assist both professional and aspiring writers to become more successful, break through their blocks, build confidence, increase motivation and expand creativity'. Free e-zine and free trial session available. See website for details.

Buckinghamshire

Missenden Abbey Adult Learning
Great Missenden HP16 0BD
☎0845 045 4040 Fax 01753 783756
✉ adultlearningchil@buckscc.gov.uk
www.aredu.org.uk/missendenabbey

Residential and non-residential weekend workshops, Easter and summer school. Programmes have included *Writing Stories for Children*; *Short Story Writing*; *Poetry Workshop*; *Writing for TV and Film*; *Writing Comedy for Television*; *Life Writing*; *Travel Tales*.

National Film & Television School
Beaconsfield Studios, Station Road,
Beaconsfield HP9 1LG
☎01494 731425 Fax 01494 674042
✉ admin@nftsfilm-tv.ac.uk
www.nftsfilm-tv.ac.uk
www.nftsscreenwritingorg

Two-year programme covering all aspects of screenwriting from the development of ideas through to final production. Studying alongside other filmmaking students allows writers to have their work tested in workshops and productions. The emphasis on practical exploration and filmmaking and degree of contact with industry personnel through seminars and pitching sessions makes the course unique among screenwriting programmes. Year One deals with the basic principles of storytelling, the craft of screenwriting for film and television and the collaborative nature of production, while in Year Two students attend classes part-time while developing a portfolio of screenplays and writing the dissertation. A five-week *Feature Development* course is also offered at intervals during the year – details available from the Screenwriting Department's website or the main School website.

Cambridgeshire

National Extension College
Michael Young Centre, Purbeck Road,
Cambridge CB2 2HN
☎01223 400350 Fax 01223 400325
✉ info@nec.ac.uk
www.nec.ac.uk/courses/arts

Runs a number of home-study courses on writing which include: *Essential Editing*; *Creative Writing* (which leads to an OCN Level 2 Cert.); *Writing for Money*; *Essential Design*. Contact the NEC for a free copy of the *Guide to Courses* which includes details of fees and course enrolment. 'You can enrol at any time, study at home, work at your own pace and fit learning into your lives.'

University of Cambridge Institute of Continuing Education
Madingley Hall, Madingley, Cambridge
CB3 8AQ

☎01954 280399   Fax 01954 280200
www.cont-ed.cam.ac.uk
A wide range of weekend, five-day and week-long creative writing courses for adults is offered by the University at the Institute of Continuing Education's residential head-quarters at Madingley Hall. Evening courses are also available in Cambridgeshire and sur-rounding areas. Details of all courses can be found on the website or phone for a brochure.

Cheshire

Burton Manor
Burton Village, Neston CH64 5SJ
☎0151 336 5172   Fax 0151 336 6586
✉ enquiry@burtonmanor.com
www.burtonmanor.com

Wide variety of short courses, residential and non-residential on writing and literature, including *Creative Writing Workshop* and *Press Workshop*. Full details in brochure.

The College of Technical Authorship –
Distance Learning Course
The College of Technical Authorship, PO Box 7, Cheadle SK8 3BY
☎0161 437 4235   Fax 0161 437 4235
✉ crossley@coltecha.u-net.com
www.coltecha.com

Contact *John Crossley, DipDistEd, DipM, MCIM, FISTC, LCGI*

Distance learning courses for City & Guilds Tech 5360, Part 1, Technical Communication Techniques, and Part 2, Technical Authorship. Individual tuition by letter or e-mail; includes some practical work done at home. A member of the British Learning Association.

Cornwall

Falmouth College of Arts
Woodlane, Falmouth TR11 4RH
☎01326 211077
www.falmouth.ac.uk
(magazine) www.bloc-online.com

Contact *Admissions*

Postgraduate/MA professional writing pro-gramme. An intensive vocational writing pro-gramme developing skills in fiction, magazine journalism/features, screenwriting. Students work on an extended writing project and form

links with other PgDips such as television pro-duction and broadcast journalism. The course website won a Guardian Media Award 1999.

Cumbria

Higham Hall College
Bassenthwaite Lake, Cockermouth CA13 9SH
☎01768 776276   Fax 01768 776013
✉ admin@highamhall.com
www.highamhall.com

Winter and summer residential courses. Programme has included *Creative Writing*. Brochure available.

Derbyshire

Real Writers
PO Box 170, Chesterfield S40 1FE
☎01246 238492   Fax 01246 238492
✉ info@real-writers.com
www.real-writers.com

Correspondence service with personal tuition from working writers. Also runs an annual short story competition. Send s.a.e. for details.

Swanwick – The Writers' Summer School
The Hayes Conference Centre, Swanwick
✉ jean.sutton@lineone.net

Secretary *Jean Sutton*

A six-day Summer School of informal talks, dis-cussion groups, panels and competitions. Competitions for all and 'a lot of fun'. All levels welcome. Held mid-August from Saturday to Friday morning. Cost (2004) £265–395 all inclusive. S.a.e. to the Secretary at 10 Stag Road, Lake, Sandown, Isle of Wight PO36 8PE (☎01983 406759).

University of Derby
Student Information Centre, Kedleston Road, Derby DE22 1GB
☎01332 622236   Fax 01332 622754
✉ J.Bains@derby.ac.uk (prospectus requests only)
www.derby.ac.uk

Contact *Graham Parker*

With upwards of 300 students, *Creative Writing* runs 21 modules as part of the undergraduate degree programme, including *Storytelling*; *Poetry*; *Playwriting*; *Writing for TV and Radio*; *The Short Story*; *Journalism*; *Writing for Children*. The courses are all led by practising writers.

Devon

Arvon Foundation (Devon)
See entry under **Greater London**

Dartington College of Arts
Totnes TQ9 6EJ
☎01803 862224 Fax 01803 861666
✉ registry@dartington.ac.uk
www.dartington.ac.uk

BA(Hons) *Writing* or *Writing (Contemporary Practices)* or *Writing (Scripted Media)*: exploratory approaches to writing as it relates to performance, visual arts, sound arts and contemporary culture. Encourages the interdisciplinary, with minor awards and electives in arts and cultural management, choreography, music, theatre, visual performance. Contact Director of Writing: see dartington.ac.uk/pw/

Exeter Phoenix
Bradninch Place, Gandy Street, Exeter
EX4 3LS
☎01392 667080 Fax 01392 667599
www.exeterphoenix.org.uk

Regular literature events, focusing on readings by living poets and other writers, often linked to wider performance programmes including the annual tEXt festival in May. Tutors in a wide range of writing skills run classes and workshops, listed in the brochure of Phoenix activities. 'Uncut Poets' group holds monthly meetings.

Fire in the Head
Creative Writing Programme
PO Box 17, Yelverton PL20 6YF
☎01822 841081
✉ roselle.angwin@internet-today.co.uk
www.fire-in-the-head.co.uk

Contact *Roselle Angwin*

Imaginative and comprehensive year-round writing programme in poetry, fiction (short and novel-writing), reflective writing and creative development. Roselle Angwin, director and tutor, is a poet and author whose courses have been featured in *The Guardian* and *The Sunday Times*. Also available is an editorial consultancy.

University of Exeter
Exeter EX4 4QW
☎01392 264580 Fax 01392 264594
✉ drama@ex.ac.uk
www.ex.ac.uk/drama

Contact *The Secretary* (Drama Department, Thornlea, New North Road, Exeter EX4 4LA)

BA(Hons) in *Drama* with a third-year option in *Playwriting*. MA in *Theatre Practice* with playwriting pathway. MPhil and PhD in *Performance Practice* (including *Playwriting*).

Dorset

Bournemouth University
Bournemouth Media School, Weymouth House, Talbot Campus, Fern Barrow, Poole BH12 5BB
☎01202 595553 Fax 01202 595530

Programme Administrator *Katrina King*

Three-year, full-time BA(Hons) course in *Scriptwriting for Film and Television*.

Essex

National Council for the Training of Journalists
Latton Bush Centre, Southern Way, Harlow CM18 7BL
☎01279 430009 Fax 01279 438008
✉ info@nctj.com
www.nctj.com

For details of journalism courses, both full-time and via distance learning, please write to the NCTJ enclosing a large s.a.e. or visit the website.

Writing Life
PO Box 4065, Braintree CM7 9RJ
☎01376 343759
✉ info@creativewritinglife.co.uk
www.creativewritinglife.co.uk

Contact *Mrs Bernie Ross*

Home study course. Postal and e-mail tuition in *Creative Writing*, from anywhere in the world. Fiction speciality: one-off critiques and on-going mentoring.

Gloucestershire

Chrysalis – The Poet In You with Jay Ramsay, BA Hons (Oxon), PGDip
5 Oxford Terrace, Uplands, Stroud GL5 1TW
☎01453 759436/020 7794 8880
✉ jay@ramsay3892.fsnet.co.uk
www.lotusfoundation.org.uk

Offers postal courses, day and weekend workshops (including 'The Sacred Space of the

Word'), an on-going poetry group based in London and individual therapy related to the participant's creative process. The Chrysalis course itself consists of Part 1, 'for those who feel drawn to reading more poetry as well as wanting to start to write their own', and Part 2, 'a more in-depth course designed for those who are already writing and who want to go more deeply into its process and technique, its background and cultural history'. Editing and information about publication also provided. Brochure and workshop dates available from the address above.

Wye Valley Arts Centre

The Coach House, Mork, St Briavel's, Lydney GL15 6QH
☎01594 530214/01291 689463
Fax 01594 530321
✉ wyeart@cwcom.net
www.wyeart.cwc.net

Residential courses (Monday to Friday) – held at The Coach House, a country house near Tintern Abbey – include *Creative Writing* and *Fiction Workshop*. 'All styles and abilities. Companions and other guests not taking the courses are welcome to stay.'

Hampshire

Annual Writers' Conference, Bookfair & Workshops, Winchester

'Chinook', Southdown Road, Winchester SO21 2BY
☎01962 712307
✉ WriterConf@aol.com
www.gmp.co.uk/writers/conference
www.awc-workshops.ndo.co.uk

Conference Director *Barbara Large, MBE, FRSA*

Honorary Patron *Beryl Bainbridge*

24 June–1 July 2005. This Festival of Writing, now in its 25th year, attracts international authors, playwrights, poets, agents and editors who give workshops, mini courses, editor appointments, lectures and seminars to help writers harness their creativity and develop their writing, editing and marketing skills. Fifteen writing competitions are attached to the conference. All first-place winners are published in *The Best of* series annually. The Bookfair offers delegates a wide choice of exhibits including Internet author services, publishers, booksellers, printers and trade associations. See also **Pitstop**

Refuelling Writers' Weekend Workshops under *Writers' Circles and Workshops.*

Highbury College, Portsmouth

Dovercourt Road, Cosham, Portsmouth PO6 2SA
☎023 9238 3131   Fax 023 9237 8382
✉ media.journalism@highbury.ack.uk
www.highbury.ac.uk

Contact *Course Administrator* (☎023 9231 3287)

The 20-week fast-track courses include: *Pre-entry Magazine Journalism*; *Pre-entry Newspaper Journalism*; and Postgraduate Diploma in *Broadcasting Journalism*, run under the auspices of the Periodicals Training Council, the National Council for Training of Journalists and the Broadcast Journalism Training Council respectively.

King Alfred's College

Winchester SO22 4NR
☎01962 841515   Fax 01962 842280
www.kingalfreds.ac.uk

Three-year degree course in *Drama, Community Theatre and Media Creative Writing* (as part of joint honours), including *Writing for Devised Community Theatre* and *Writing for Television Documentary*. Contact the Admissions Office (☎01962 827262).

MA course in *Theatre for Development* – one year, full-time course with major project overseas or in the UK. MA course in *Writing for Children* available on either a one- or two-year basis. Enquiries: Admissions Officer (☎01962 827235). Also MA in *Creative and Critical Writing*.

Southampton Institute

East Park Terrace, Southampton SO14 0YN
☎023 4031 9000
✉ Richard.Hudson@Solent.ac.uk
www.solent.ac.uk

Contact *Rick Hudson* (☎023 8031 9097)

Courses offered: BA(Hons) *Media Writing*; BA (Hons) *Writing Fashion & Culture*; BA (Hons) *Journalism*. Writing may be taken as a specialism in MA *Media*.

University of Portsmouth

School of Creative Arts, Film and Media, Portsmouth PO1 2DZ
☎023 9284 8484   Fax 023 9284 3082
✉ info.centre@port.ac.uk

Contact *School of Creative Arts, Film and Media*

Offers creative writing degrees from undergraduate to PhD (*Creative and Critical Writing*) level. The School offers writers additional opportunities to combine creative writing with a number of other creative and critical course choices, including film and media options, and is a proactive centre or creative writing research through practice.

Hertfordshire

Liberato Breakaway Writing Courses

9 Bishop's Avenue, Bishop's Stortford CM23 3EJ
☎01279 833690
✉ Liberato@tesco.net
www.liberato.co.uk

Contact *Maureen Blundell*

Specialises in beginner fiction writers with day, weekend and week-long courses. Emphasis on individual writing with written ms critiques and one-to-one sessions. Weekend held at Polstead in Suffolk throughout the year. Greek weeks in June on the Saroni island of Agistri – fiction and songwriting courses. Four-day fiction/poetry course at Leiston, near Aldeburgh in Suffolk in September. Fiction and poetry days in the Gibberd Garden, Old Harlow, Essex, March to November. Also offers postal and e-mail ms critiques on all fiction/autobiography.

Isle of Wight

Annual Writers' Weekend Conference

F ★ F Productions, 39 Ranelagh Road, Sandown PO36 8NT
☎01983 407772 Fax 01983 407772
✉ felicity@writeplot.co.uk
www.writeplot.co.uk

Contact *Felicity Fair Thompson*

Kent

North West Kent College

Oakfield Lane, Dartford DA1 2JT
☎01322 629436 Fax 01322 629468
www.nwkent.ac.uk

Contact *Neil Nixon*, Head of School, Media & Communications

Two-year, full-time course that explores writing from a number of angles, teaching essential skills, market and academic aspects of the subject. Successful students progress to work or the University of Greenwich, the latter option allowing them to gain a BA(Hons) in Humanities from a further year of study. Staff include scriptwriters, novelists and a book publisher. Students compile a portfolio in the final year.

University of Kent at Canterbury

Information, Advice & Guidance Unit, APS, The Registry, Canterbury CT2 7NZ
✉ information@kent.ac.uk
www.kent.ac.uk

Undergraduate certificate courses in *Practical Writing* and *Imaginative Writing*. Also combined studies – *English and Creative Writing*.

Lancashire

Alston Hall College

Alston Lane, Longridge, Preston PR3 3BP
☎01772 784661 Fax 01772 785835
✉ alston.hall@ed.lancscc.gov.uk
www.alstonhall.u-net.com

Holds regular day and residential *Creative Writing* workshops. Full colour brochure available.

Edge Hill College of Higher Education

St Helen's Road, Ormskirk L39 4QP
☎01695 575171
✉ sheppard@edgehill.ac.uk

Contact *Dr R. Sheppard*

Offers a two-year, part-time MA in *Writing Studies*. Combines advanced-level writers' workshops with closely related courses in the poetics of writing and contemporary writing in English. There is also provision for MPhil and PhD-level research in writing and poetics. A full range of creative writing courses is available at undergraduate level, in poetry and fiction writing which may be taken as part of a modular BA.

Lancaster University

Department of Creative Writing, Lonsdale College, Bailrigg, Lancaster LA1 4YN
☎01524 594169 Fax 01524 843934
✉ l.kellett@lancaster.ac.uk

Contact *Lyn Kellett*

Offers practical graduate and undergraduate courses in writing fiction, poetry and scripts. All based on group workshops – students' work-in-progress is circulated and discussed. Distance learning MA now available. Graduates include Andrew Miller, Justin Hill, Monique Roffey, Alison MacLeod, Jacob Polley.

Leicestershire

Leicester Adult Education College, Writing School

2 Wellington Street, Leicester LE1 6HL
☎0116 233 4343 Fax 0116 233 4344
✉ vm1@leicester-adult-ed.ac.uk
www.leicester-adult-ed.ac.uk

Contact *Valerie Moore*

Offers a wide range of part time creative writing and journalism courses throughout the year. The programme offers a mix of critical workshops, one-day and term-length courses, and short craft modules. Supports writers through to publication and has strong links with local media.

London

Arvon Foundation

National Administration: 2nd Floor,
42A Buckingham Palace Road, London
SW1W 0RE
☎020 7931 7611 Fax 020 7963 0961
www.arvonfoundation.org

Devon: Totleigh Barton, Sheepwash,
Beaworthy EX21 5NS
☎01409 231338 Fax 01409 231144
✉ t-barton@arvonfoundation.org

Yorkshire: Lumb Bank, Heptonstall, Hebden
Bridge HX7 6DF
☎01422 843714 Fax 01422 843714
✉ l-bank@arvonfoundation.org

Inverness-shire: Moniack Mhor, Teavarran,
Kiltarlity, Beauly IV4 7HT
☎01463 741675
✉ m-mhor@arvonfoundation.org

Shropshire: The Hurst, Clunton, Craven
Arms SY7 0JA
☎01588 640658 Fax 01588 640509
✉ hurst@arvonfoundation.org

Joint Presidents *Terry Hands, Sir Robin Chichester-Clark*
Chairman *Prue Skene, CBE*
National Director *Helen Chaloner*

Founded 1968. Offers people of any age (over 16) and any background the opportunity to live and work with professional writers. Four-and-a-half-day residential courses are held throughout the year at Arvon's four centres, covering poetry, fiction, drama, writing for children, songwriting and the performing arts. Bursaries towards the cost of course fees are available for those on low incomes, the unemployed, students and pensioners. Runs a biennial poetry competition (see entry under *Prizes*).

Birkbeck College University of London

School of English and Humanities, Malet
Street, London WC1E 7HX
☎0845 601 0174
✉ A.Whiting@bbk.ac.uk
www.bbk.ac.uk/eh/eng

Contact *Anne Marie Whiting*

Taught by published writers, Birkbeck offers MA courses in *Fiction Writing* and *Writing for Performance*. Both courses will extend and cultivate existing writing skills, help develop writing to a professional level and are supported by masterclasses and readings from visiting professionals. All classes are held in the evening. Study part-time over two years or full-time over one year. Applications must be supported by a portfolio of creative writing. Download an application form from the website.

Blaze the Trail

2nd Floor, 241 High Street, London E17 7BH
☎020 8520 4569 Fax 020 8520 2358
✉ training@coralmedia.co.uk
www.blaze-the-trail.com

Contact *Course Administrator*

Offers vocational training including *Script Development*; *Production Management* and *Research 4 Media* for all levels. Writers, readers, script editors, researchers and production managers acquire broadcast training to develop their knowledge and understanding in the field of television and film screenwriting and production. Works with a number of broadcasters such as BBC, LWT and Channel Four and with support from Skillset, the company is continually evolving to match the changing needs of the film and television industry. *Blaze the Trail* offers individually tailored internship programmes. These placements are based in the UK, Ireland, Germany, France and Sweden. Please call Course Administrator or see the website for full details.

The Central School of Speech and Drama

Embassy Theatre, Eton Avenue, London
NW3 3HY
☎020 7722 8183 Fax 020 7722 4132
✉ n.wood@cssd.ac.uk

Contact *Nick Wood*, Writing and
Dramaturgy Tutor

MA in *Advanced Theatre Practice*. One-year, full-time course aimed at providing a grounding in principal areas of professional theatre practice – *Writing*, *Dramaturgy*, *Directing*, *Performance*, *Puppetry* and *Design*, with an emphasis on collaboration between the various strands. Prospectus available. Nick Wood is also editor of the Dramaturgy Forum website www.dramforum. net

The City Literary Institute
Humanities Dept, Stukeley Street, London WC2B 5LJ
☎020 7430 0542 Fax 020 7405 3347
✉ humanities@citylit.ac.uk

The Writing School offers a wide range of courses from *Ways Into Creative Writing* and *Writing for Children* to *Playwriting* and *Writing Short Stories*. Various lengths of course available. The Department offers information and advice during term time.

City University
Department of Continuing Education, Northampton Square, London EC1V 0HB
☎020 7040 8268
✉ conted@city.ac.uk
www.city.ac.uk/conted/cfa/write

The Courses for Adults evening programme includes: *Certificate in Novel Writing* (three term course); *Novel Writing and Longer Works*; *Towards Publication*; *Writing Crime Fiction*; *Writing for Children*; *Writing Television Drama*.

The Complete Creative Writing Course at the Groucho Club
☎020 7249 3711 Fax 020 7683 8141
✉ maggie.h@blueyonder.co.uk
www.creative-writing.pwp.blueyonder.co.uk
Contact *Maggie Hamand*

Courses of ten two-hour sessions held at the Groucho Club in London's Soho, starting in January, April and September, Monday or Saturday afternoons, 2.30pm–4.30pm. Beginners and advanced courses offered. Courses include stimulating exercises, discussion and weekly homework. The tutors are novelists Maggie Hamand and Henrietta Seredy. £195 for whole course.

The Drill Hall
16 Chenies Street, London WC1E 7EX
☎020 7307 5061 Fax 020 7307 5062
✉ admin@drillhall.co.uk

Holds a number of writing classes and work-shops. Regular tutors include Carol Burns and Peter Carty.

London College of Communication
Elephant & Castle, London SE1 6SB
☎020 7514 6562
www.lcptraining.co.uk

Intensive courses in journalism. Short courses, run by DALI (Developments at the London Institute) at the Elephant & Castle address above, include: *News Writing*; *Feature Writing*; *Sub-editing*; *Scriptwriting for TV & Film*. Also offers five-day specialist journalism courses in newswriting, subediting, print journalism, radio journalism and online journalism plus a three-week course in broadcast TV journalism. In addition, *Effective Copywriting*, *Effective Writing Techniques for Public Relations* and *Handling the Media Successfully*. For individuals and companies 'tailor-made training' services can be provided. Prospectus and information leaflets available; ☎020 7514 8193 or access the website.

London School of Journalism
126 Shirland Road, London W9 2BT
☎020 7289 7777 Fax 020 7432 8141
✉ info@lsjournalism.com
www.home-study.com

Contact *Student Administration Office*

Distance learning courses with an individual and personal approach. Students remain with the same tutor throughout the course. Options include: *Short Story Writing*; *Writing for Children*; *Poetry*; *Freelance Journalism*; *Media Law*; *Improve Your English*; *Cartooning*; *Thriller Writing*. Fees vary but range from £295 for *Enjoying English Literature* to £395 for *Journalism and Newswriting*. NUJ-recognised Postgraduate Diploma Courses taught in London (three month full-time, six month part-time, nine month evening classes). Online postgraduate diploma course also available.

Middlesex University
School of Humanities, White Hart Lane, London N17 8HR
☎020 8411 5000 Fax 020 8411 6652
✉ tmadmissions@mdx.ac.uk
www.mdx.ac.uk

The UK's longest established writing degree offers a Single or Joint Honours programme in *Creative and Media Writing* (full- or part-time). This modular programme gives an opportunity to explore journalism, poetry, prose fiction and dramatic writing for a wide range of genres and audiences. Option for work experience in the media and publishing. Contact Admissions or *Maggie Butt*, Programme Leader (m.butt@mdx. ac.uk)

MA in *Writing* (full-time, part-time; day and evening classes) includes writing workshops; critical seminars; lectures and workshops from established writers; introduction to agents and publishers. Options available: Fiction, Poetry or Scriptwriting. Contact *Sue Gee* ☎020 8411 5941 (s.gee@mdx.ac.uk)

Also offer research degrees M.Phil/PhD in *Creative Writing*. The University has a thriving Writing Centre running an annual literary festival, weekly talks, community projects and writers in residence.

PMA Training
The PMA Centre for Media Excellence, 10 Cynthia Street, London N1 9JF
☎020 7278 0606
✉ training@pma-group.com
www.pma-group.com

One-/two-/three-day editorial, PR, design and publishing courses held in central London. High-powered, intensive courses run by Fleet Street journalists and magazine editors. Courses include: *News-Writing*; *Feature Writing*; *Investigative Reporting*. Fees range from £360 to £780 plus VAT. Special rates for freelances.

Soho Theatre Company
See entry under *Theatre Producers*

University of Surrey Roehampton
School of Arts, Roehampton Lane, London SW15 5PH
☎020 8392 3000 Fax 020 8392 3289
www.roehampton.ac.uk

Three-year BA(Hons) programmes in *Drama, Theatre and Performance Studies* and *Film and Television Studies* include courses on writing for stage and screen.

University of Westminster
School of Media, Arts and Design, Harrow Campus, Watford Road, Harrow HA1 3TP
☎020 7911 5903 Fax 020 7911 5955
✉ harrow-admissions@wmin.ac.uk
www.wmin.ac.uk

Courses include part-time MAs available in *Journalism Studies; Film and Television Studies; Screenwriting and Producing; Public Communication and Public Relations; Communication and Communication Policy*.

Greater Manchester

Manchester Metropolitan University – The Writing School
Department of English, Geoffrey Manton Building, Rosamond Street West, off Oxford Road, Manchester M15 6LL
☎0161 247 1732/1 Fax 0161 247 6345
✉ m.schmidt@mmu.ac.uk

Course Convenor *Michael Schmidt*

Closely associated with **Carcanet Press Ltd** and *PN Review*, The Writing School offers four 'routes' for students to follow: *Poetry, The Novel, Life Writing* and *Writing for Children*. A key feature of the programme is regular readings, lectures, workshops and masterclasses by writers, publishers, producers, booksellers, librarians and agents. Tutors include Simon Armitage, Carol Ann Duffy, Sophie Hannah, Jeffrey Wainwright.

University of Manchester
Department of English & American Studies, Arts Building, Oxford Road, Manchester M13 9PL
☎0161 275 3144 Fax 0161 275 3256
✉ englishpg@man.ac.uk
www.art.man.ac.uk/english/pgdegree/ ma.htm#novel

Course Director *Suzannah Dunn*

Offers a one-year MA in *Novel Writing*.

University of Salford
Postgraduate Admissions, School of Media, Music & Performance, Adelphi Building, Peru Street, Salford M3 6EQ
☎0161 295 6027
✉ r.humphrey@salford.ac.uk
www.smmp.salford.ac.uk

MA in *Television and Radio Scriptwriting*. Two-year, part-time course taught by professional writers and producers. Also offers masterclasses with leading figures in the radio and television industry.

The Writers Bureau
Sevendale House, 7 Dale Street, Manchester M1 1JB
☎0161 228 2362 Fax 0161 236 9440
✉ studentservices@writersbureau.com
www.writersbureau.com

Comprehensive home-study writing course with personal tuition service from professional writers. Fiction, non-fiction, articles, short stories, novels, TV, radio and drama all covered in detail. Trial period, guarantee and no time limits. Writing for children and biographies, memoirs and family history courses also available. ODLQC accredited. Quote Ref. EH04. Free enquiry line: 0800 856 2008.

The Writers Bureau College of Journalism

Address etc. as The Writers Bureau above

Home-study course covering all aspects of journalism. Real-life assignments assessed by qualified tutors with the emphasis on getting into print. Comprises 28 modules and three handbooks. Ref: EHJ04. Free enquiry line: 0800 298 7008.

The Writers College

Address etc. as The Writers Bureau above

The Art of Writing Poetry Course from The Writers Bureau sister college. A home-study course with a more 'recreational' emphasis. The 60,000-word course has 17 modules and lets you complete six written assignments for tutorial evaluation. Quote Ref. EHP04. Free enquiry line: 0800 856 2008.

The Writer's Muse

5 Churchdale Road, Higher Blackley, Manchester M9 8NE
☎0161 720 9307/07930 322451 (mobile)
Course Director *Rosetta Jallow*
Secretary *Wendy Adeforoye*

Offers courses designed to meet aspiring writers' individual needs. Twelve monthly assignments marked by qualified teachers/freelance writers (no poetry). £70 p.a. Certificate of course participation upon completion. Also offers evaluation service £50 per manuscript. Workshops held in Greater Manchester area. Fees upon request. Send A4 s.a.e. for full details.

Merseyside

University of Liverpool

Continuing Education, 126 Mount Pleasant, Liverpool L69 3GR
☎0151 794 6900/6952 (24 hours)
Fax 0151 794 2544
✉ conted@liverpool.ac.uk
www.liv.ac.uk/conted

Course Organiser *Dr John Redmond*

Courses include: *An Introduction to Creative Writing*; *The Short Story and the Novel*; *Introduction to Writing Poetry*; *The Craft of Creative Writing*; *Writing Your Life Story*; *Science Fiction Writing*; *An Introduction to Journalism*; *Scriptwriting: Theatre*

Playwrights' Workshop and Situation Comedy. Most courses take place on one evening or daytime meeting weekly, with some Saturdays and linked days. Courses offer university credits towards a Certificate in Higher Education in Creative Writing or for personal development purposes. For most courses no previous knowledge is required. There are fee concessions for those who are receiving certain benefits or retired. Free prospectus on request or see the website.

Norfolk

University of East Anglia

School of English & American Studies, Norwich NR4 7TJ
☎01603 593820 Fax 01603 593799
✉ pgeas@uea.ac.uk
www.uea.ac.uk/eas

Contact *Kerry Duinford*, Postgraduate Admissions

UEA has a history of concern with contemporary literary culture. Among its programmes is the MA in *Creative Writing* (founded by Angus Wilson and Malcolm Bradbury in 1970/71). The course has three parallel entry points: prose fiction, poetry, and scriptwriting. A series of weekly workshops provide intensive examination of students' own work, and also draw on aspects of teaching in nineteenth and twentieth century literature, literary theory and film and cultural studies.

Northamptonshire

Knuston Hall Residential College for Adult Education

Irchester, Wellingborough NN29 7EU
☎01933 312104 Fax 01933 357596
✉ enquiries@knustonhall.org.uk
www.knustonhall.org.uk

Writing courses being held in 2004 included: *Write – and Illustrate a Picture Book for Children*; *Reminiscence Writing*; *Telling a Tale*; *Creative Writing – First Steps*; *Writing for Children* and *Writing Your Own Murder Mystery*.

Nottinghamshire

The Nottingham Trent University

Humanities Faculty Office (Post Graduate Studies), Clifton Lane, Nottingham NG11 8NS
☎0115 848 6677 Fax 0115 848 6632
✉ hum.postgrad@ntu.ac.uk

www.human.ntu.ac.uk/writing

MA in *Creative Writing*. Hands-on and work-shop-based, the course concentrates primarily on the practice and production of writing. A choice of options from *Fiction, Poetry, Creative Non-Fiction, New Media Writing, Children's Writing* and *Scriptwriting*. Assignments and a dissertation, but no formal exams. Staff are all established writers. Current visiting professors: Peter Porter and Jenny Diski. Also a full programme of visiting speakers. Study either full-time or part-time – all classes held in the evenings. Further details and application forms from the Faculty Office.

Oxfordshire

University of Oxford Department for Continuing Education

Rewley House, 1 Wellington Square, Oxford OX1 2JA

☎01865 280356 Fax 01865 270309

✉ pp@conted.ox.ac.uk

www.conted.ox.ac.uk

Creative writing classes held during the autumn and spring terms. There are also one-week summer school courses in *Creative Writing* and a two-year part-time Diploma. Early booking advised.

Shropshire

Arvon Foundation (Shropshire)

See entry under **Greater London**

Somerset

Ammerdown Centre

The Ammerdown Conference and Retreat Centre, Radstock, Bath BA3 5SW

☎01761 433709 Fax 01761 433094

✉ centre@ammerdown.org

www.ammerdown.org

Courses include a five-day creative writing course. Residential facilities. Brochure available or full details on the website.

Bath Spa University College

Newton Park, Bath BA2 9BN

☎01225 875875 Fax 01225 875444

✉ enquiries@bathspa.ac.uk

www.bathspa.ac.uk

Contact *Admissions Officer* (☎01225 875821)

MA in *Creative Writing*. A course for creative writers wanting to develop their work. Teaching is by published writers in the novel, poetry, short stories and scriptwriting. In

recent years, several students from this course have received contracts from publishers for novels, awards for poetry and short stories and have had work produced on BBC Radio.

Dillington House

Ilminster TA19 9DT

☎01460 52427/Minicom: 01460 258640

Fax 01460 52433

✉ dillington@somerset.gov.uk

www.dillington.co.uk

Dillington House is one of the finest historic houses in Somerset. Provides short residential courses across a wide range of subjects, including writing and literary appreciation. Full details of the programme are available in the free brochure and on the website.

Institute of Copywriting

Honeycombe House, Bagley, Wedmore BS28 4TD

☎01934 713563 Fax 01934 713492

✉ copy@inst.org

www.institute.org/copy

Comprehensive copywriting home-study course, including advice on becoming a self-employed copywriter. Each student has a personal tutor who is an experienced copywriter and who provides detailed feedback on the student's assignments.

University of Bristol

Department of English, 3/5 Woodland Road, Bristol BS8 1TB

☎0117 954 6969 Fax 0117 928 8860

www.bris.ac.uk/Depts/English/ce_creat.html

Contact *Continuing Education Course Organiser*

A variety of courses open to the general public, including *Women and Writing*, for women who write or would like to begin to write (poetry, fiction, non-fiction, journals). Also offers *Diploma in Creative Writing*. Detailed brochure available.

Staffordshire

Keele University

The Centre for Continuing and Professional Education, Keele University, (Freepost ST1666), Newcastle under Lyme ST5 5BR

☎01782 583436

Evening and weekend courses on literature and creative writing. The 2004/5 programme includes courses on novel writing, writers workshops and sessions on poetry writing.

Surrey

Guildford Institute

Guildford Institute of the University of Surrey, Ward Street, Guildford GU1 4LH
☎01483 562142 Fax 01483 451034
✉ gi-reception@surrey.ac.uk
www.surrey.ac.uk/education

Several of the **University of Surrey**'s *Creative Writing* courses take place at the Guildford Institute. The courses carry credits at Higher Education Level 1 (first-year undergraduate level). For details contact the Institute (details above), or *Dr Christopher Joyce*, Subject Leader for Creative Writing and Literature, at the University (☎01483 683122; c.joyce@surrey. ac.uk).

Royal Holloway

University of London, Department of Drama and Theatre, Egham Hill, Egham TW20 0EX
☎01784 443922 Fax 01784 431018
✉ drama@rhul.ac.uk

Contacts *Dan Rebellato, David Wiles*

Three-year BA courses in *Drama and Creative Writing* or *English and Creative Writing*, during which students progressively specialise in playwriting, poetry or fiction. Playwriting can be studied as part of the BA *Drama and Creative Writing* degree and poetic practice is an option in the *English* programme. Playwriting can be studied at postgraduate level in the MA in *Theatre* and there is an MA in *Poetic Practice*.

University of Surrey

Adult and Continuing Education, University of Surrey, Guildford GU2 7XH
☎01483 683151 Fax 01483 686191
✉ ace@surrey.ac.uk
www.surrey.ac.uk

The Open Studies programme includes several *Creative Writing* courses. For autumn 2003 these will be held at the **Guildford Institute**, Caterham and Reigate. The courses carry credits and can build to a university award. For details, contact *Jane Bradford*, Courses Secretary or *Dr Christopher Joyce*, Subject Leader in Creative Writing.

Sussex

The Earnley Concourse

Earnley, Chichester PO20 7JL
☎01243 670392 Fax 01243 670832
✉ info@earnley.co.uk
www.earnley.co.uk

Offers a range of residential and non-residential courses throughout the year. Previous programme has included *Writing for Publication*; *You Can Sell What You Write*. Brochure available.

University College Chichester

Bishop Otter Campus, College Lane, Chichester PO19 6PE
☎01243 816000 Fax 01243 816080
✉ s.norgate@ucc.ac.uk

Contact *Stephanie Norgate*, Route Leader, MA in Creative Writing (☎01243 816296)

Postgraduate Certificate/Diploma/MA in *Creative Writing*, both full- and part-time.

University of Sussex

Centre for Continuing Education, Education Development Building, Falmer, Brighton BN1 9RG
☎01273 678537/877888 Fax 01273 678848
✉ y.d.barnes@sussex.ac.uk/cce
www.sussex.ac.uk

Contact (for all courses) *Yvonne Barnes*

MA in *Dramatic Writing*: the student is treated as a commissioned writer working in theatre, TV, radio or film with professional directors and actors. Includes workshops, masterclasses, a residential weekend and a showcase of new work. Two years, part-time. Convenor: *Richard Crane*. Certificate in *Creative Writing*: short fiction, novel and poetry for imaginative writers. Two-year, part-time. Convenors: *Richard Crane, Mark Slater*.

Tyne & Wear

University of Sunderland

Centre for Lifelong Learning, Joseph Cowen House, Newcastle upon Tyne NE1 7RU
☎0191 515 2800 Fax 0191 515 2890
www.sunderland.ac.uk/cll

Courses held in 2004 included: *Creative Writing: Feature Writing* and *Writing From the Inside Out*, a workshop for women. Contact the Secretary, Adult Education Programme.

West Midlands

National Academy of Writing

Calthorpe House, 30 Hagley Road, Edgbaston, Birmingham B16 8QY
☎0121 455 7888 Fax 0121 456 5999
✉ info@writingacademy.org
www.writingacademy.org

The National Academy of Writing is a new

teaching institution designed to nurture and promote writing talent for the creative industries: publishing, journalism, theatre, film, radio and television. Summer 2003 courses were in prose narrative, adaptation and advanced screenwriting. Admission is based on a demonstrable talent, and the student's commitment to a writing career is axiomatic. Tuition is augmented by regular public events and masterclasses given by patrons of the Academy. The 'Adventures in the Writing Trade' series introduces top writers to young audiences and new writers, and encourages them to consider a writing career. The Academy also develops interactive schools events with high-profile writers. Access the website for full details of future courses.

Starz! – Film and Theatre Performing Arts

Christmas House, Chester Road, Castle Bromwich, Solihull B36 0ET
☎0121 749 7147

Creative Director *Gavin Prime*

Teaching disabled, disadvantaged and mainstream children. The only totally free theatre and film school of this type in England. Students range in age from eight to 19 and work in all ways connected to performing arts. This includes writing and showing them the structure of the business and how to try and get work accepted.

University of Birmingham

Centre for Lifelong Learning (CLL), Selly Oak, Birmingham B29 6LL
☎0121 414 3413 Fax 0121 414 5619
✉ e.m.braekkanpayne@bham.ac.uk

Certificate of Higher Education in *Creative Writing* – two years, part-time in Birmingham and Worcester. Classes in theory and practice of writing in a wide range of literary genres. Course brochures are available from the address above. The course includes progression routes to Diploma and BA(Hons) Degree. Students who can demonstrate qualifications or writing skills equivalent to Certificate level may apply to join the Diploma of Creative Writing.

The University also offers an MPhil. in *Playwriting Studies*. Contact *Sarah Woods*, Senior Tutor, at the Department of Drama and Theatre Arts (☎0121 414 5998).

University of Warwick

Open Studies, Centre for Lifelong Learning, Coventry CV4 7AL
☎024 7652 8286
✉ k.rainsley@warwick.ac.uk *or*

l.downs@warwick.ac.uk

Creative writing courses held at the university or in regional centres. Subjects include: *Creative Writing*; *Lifestory Writing*; *Creative Writing for All*; *Writing Creatively*; *Writing for Pleasure*. One-year certificates in *Creative Writing* and *Journalism* available.

Wiltshire

Marlborough College Summer School

Marlborough SN8 1PA
☎01672 892388/9 Fax 01672 892476
✉ admin@mcsummerschool.org.uk
www.mcsummerschool.org.uk

Summer School with literature and creative writing included in its programme. Caters for residential and day students. Brochure available giving full details and prices.

Urchfont Manor College

Urchfont, Devizes SN10 4RG
☎01380 840495 Fax 01380 840005

Short courses – days, residential weeks and weekends – offered in a varied programme which includes literature and creative writing. 'Beautiful location; historic environment; delicious home cooking.' Send for a brochure.

Yorkshire

Arvon Foundation (Yorkshire)

See entry under **Greater London**

Hull College

Queen's Gardens, Hull HU1 3DG
☎01482 329943 Fax 598733219079
✉ cjackson@hull-college.ac.uk

Contact *Daphne Glazer*

Offers part-time evening writing courses in *Novel Writing*. Courses begin each academic term.

Leeds Metropolitan University

H505, City Site, Calverley Street, Leeds LS1 3HE
☎0113 283 2600 ext 3330
✉ r.hibbert@leedsmet.ac.uk
www.lmu.ac.uk

Administrator *Richard Hibbert*

Offers a Postgraduate Certificate/Diploma/ MA in *Screenwriting (Fiction)*.

Open College of the Arts

Unit 1B, Redbrook Business Park, Wilthorpe Road, Barnsley S75 1JN
☎01226 730495   Fax 01226 730838
✉ open.arts@ukonline.co.uk
www.oca-uk.com

The OCA correspondence course, *Starting to Write*, offers help and stimulus from experienced writers/tutors. Emphasis is on personal development rather than commercial genre. Subsequent levels available include specialist poetry, fiction and autobiographical writing courses. OCA writing courses are accredited by the University of Glamorgan. Prospectus and Guide to Courses available on request.

Sheffield Hallam University

School of Cultural Studies, Sheffield Hallam University, Collegiate Crescent, Sheffield S10 2BP
☎0114 225 2607   Fax 0114 225 2603
✉ cspgenquiry@shu.ac.uk
www.shu.ac.uk/schools/cs/english/english.htm

Offers MA in *Creative Writing* (one-year, full-time; also part-time).

University of Hull

Scarborough Campus, Filey Road, Scarborough YO11 3AZ
☎01723 362392   Fax 01723 370815
www.hull.ac.uk

Director of Studies *David Hughes*

BA Single Honours in *Theatre and Performance Studies* incorporates modules in writing and other media across each level of the programme. Works closely with the Stephen Joseph Theatre and its artistic director Alan Ayckbourn. The theatre sustains a policy for staging new writers (see entry under *Theatre Producers*). The campus hosts the annual National Student Drama Festival which includes the International Student Playscript Competition (details from The National Information Centre for Student Drama; nsdf@hull.ac.uk).

University of Leeds

School of Continuing Education, Springfield Mount, Leeds LS2 9JT
✉ sce@leeds.ac.uk
www.leeds.ac.uk/sce
Contact *Rebecca O'Rourke*

A well-established provider of weekly part-time creative writing courses for adults held on campus and at several venues throughout Cleveland, North Yorkshire and West Yorkshire during the day and in the evening. Course tutors are published writers and include Bob Beagrie, Pat Borthwick, Craig Bradley, Bernie Crosthwaite, Cynthia Fuller, Kath McKay and Rommi Smith. Students can choose a general writing module or specialise in drama, fiction, lifestory, poetry or short story. Modules are pitched at introductory, intermediate and advanced levels to encourage progressive development. Students can register for certificate, diploma or degree awards or take modules on a stand alone basis. All courses carry university credit.

University of Leeds, Bretton Hall Campus

School of Performance and Cultural Industries, Bretton Hall Campus, West Bretton, Wakefield WF4 4LG
☎0113 343 9022/9241
✉ g.s.lyons@leeds.ac.uk

Contact *Garry Lyons* or *Linda Smith*, Secretary (pculs@leeds.ac.uk)

Offers one-year full-time/two-year part-time MA course in *Creative Writing* designed for competent though not necessarily published writers. Also offers a three-year *Creative Writing* BA. Details from *Simon Ross* (s.j.ross@leeds.ac.uk).

University of Sheffield

Institute for Lifelong Learning, 196–198 West Street, Sheffield S1 4ET
☎0114 222 7000   Fax 0114 222 7001
www.shef.ac.uk/till

Certificate in *Creative Writing* (Degree Level 1) and a wide range of courses, from foundation level to specialist writing areas, open to all. Courses in poetry, prose, journalism, scriptwriting, comedy, travel writing, writing using ICT/Web, writing for children. Brochures and information available from the address above.

Yorkshire Art Circus

School Lane, Glasshoughton, Castleford WF10 4QH
☎01977 550401
✉ admin@artcircus.org.uk
www.artcircus.org.uk

Administrator *Angela Sibbit*

Offers an annual programme of courses in creative writing, poetry, self-publishing and book production. Mostly daytime courses. Brochure available. Yorkshire Arts Circus is now offering a Writer Development Programme which will provide advanced support for writers wishing to extend their careers, and include a mentoring scheme, skills development in areas such as editing, proofreading and publicity, and the presentation and sale of mss. The scheme is aimed at serious writers who have already reached a certain level of ability. Participants will be expected to contribute their expertise to assist other writers.

IRELAND

Dingle Writing Courses Ltd
Ballintlea, Ventry Co. Kerry
☎00 353 66 915 9815
Fax 00 353 66 915 9815
✉ info@dinglewritingcourses.ie
www.dinglewritingcourses.ie

Directors *Abigail Joffe, Nicholas McLachlan*

An autumn programme of weekend residential courses for beginners and experienced writers alike. Tutored by professional writers the courses include poetry, fiction, starting to write and writing for theatre as well as special themed courses. Past tutors have included Michael Donaghy, Paul Durcan, Anne Enright, Nuala Ni Dhomhnaill, Carlo Gébler, Jennifer Johnston, Paula Meeham. Also organises tailor-made courses for schools, writers' groups or students on a *Creative Writing* programme.

Queen's University of Belfast
Institute of Lifelong Learning, Belfast BT7 1NN
☎028 9097 3323 Fax 028 9097 1084
✉ ill@qub.ac.uk
www.qub.ac.uk/ill

Courses have included *Creative Writing*; *Writing for Profit and Pleasure*; *Scriptwriting* and *Creative Writing for Beginners*.

University of Dublin (Trinity College)
Graduate Studies Office, Arts Building, Trinity College, Dublin 2
☎00 353 1 608 1166 Fax 00 353 1 671 2821
✉ gradinfo@tcd.ie
www.tcd.ie/owc

Contact *Admissions*

Offers an MPhil *Creative Writing* course. A one-year, full-time course intended for students who are seriously committed to writing or prospective authors.

University of Ulster
Conference & Professional Development Unit, Room 17C21, University of Ulster, Belfast BT37 0QB

☎028 9036 6680 Fax 028 9036 6060

Creative writing course/workshop, usually held in the autumn and spring terms. Concessions available.

SCOTLAND

Arvon Foundation (Inverness-shire)
See entry under **Greater London**

Edinburgh University
Office of Lifelong Learning, 11 Buccleuch Place, Edinburgh EH8 9LW
☎0131 650 4400 Fax 0131 667 6097
✉ cce@ed.ac.uk
www.cce.ed.ac.uk
www.lifelong.ed.ac.uk

Several writing-orientated courses and summer schools. Course brochure available.

7:84 Summer School
See **7:84 Theatre Company Scotland** under *Theatre Producers*

University of Dundee
Continuing Education, Nethergate, Dundee DD1 4HN
☎01382 344809 Fax 01382 221057
✉ s.z.norrie@dundee.ac.uk
www.dundee.ac.uk/education

Various creative writing courses held at the University and elsewhere in Dundee, Perth, Angus and Perthshire. Detailed course brochure available.

University of Glasgow
Department of Adult and Continuing Education, 11 Eldon Street, Glasgow G3 6NH
☎0141 330 1835/1829 (Enquiries/Brochure)
Fax 0141 330 1821
✉ enquiry@ace.gla.ac.uk
www.gla.ac.uk/adulteducation

Runs writers' workshops and courses at all levels; all friendly and informal. Daytime and evening meetings. Tutors are all experienced published writers.

University of St Andrews
School of English, The University, St Andrews KY16 9AL
☎01334 462666 Fax 01334 462655
✉ english@st-andrews.ac.uk
www.st-andrews.ac.uk

Offers postgraduate study in *Creative Writing*.

Modules in Writing Fiction and Writing Poetry. Students submit a dissertation of original writing – prose fiction of 15,000 words or a collection of around 30 short poems. Taught by Professor Douglas Dunn, John Burnside, Kathleen Jamie, A.L. Kennedy and Don Paterson.

Also offers PhD in *Creative Writing*.

WALES

Tŷ Newydd Writers' Centre

Llanystumdwy, Cricieth LL52 0LW
☎01766 522811   Fax 01766 523095
✉ post@tynewydd.org
www.tynewydd.org

Residential writers' centre set up by the Taliesin Trust with the support of the **Arts Council of Wales** to encourage and promote writing in both English and Welsh. Most courses run from Monday evening to Saturday morning. Each course has two tutors and a maximum of 16 participants. A wide range of courses for all levels of experience. Early booking essential. Fee: £370 (single)/£345 (shared) inclusive. People on low incomes may be eligible for a grant or bursary. Course leaflet available. (See also *Organisations of Interest to Poets*.)

University of Glamorgan

Treforest, Pontypridd CF37 1DL
☎01443 483598
www.glam.ac.uk

Director, The National Centre for Writing *Professor Tony Curtis, FRSL*

MPhil in *Writing*: a two-year part-time Masters degree for writers of fiction and poets. Established 1993. Contact *Professor Tony Curtis* at the School of Humanities, Law and Social Sciences.

MA in *Scriptwriting (Theatre, TV or Radio)*: a two-year part-time Masters degree for scriptwriters. Contact *Dr Richard J. Hand*.

BA in *Creative and Professional Writing*: a three-year course for undergraduates. Contact *Rob Middlehurst*.

University of Wales, Aberystwyth

Department of English, Hugh Owen Building, Aberystwyth SY23 3DY
☎01970 622534   Fax 01970 622530
www.aber.ac.uk/english

BA in *English and Creative Writing*, a three-year course taught in part by practising writers: Director of Creative Writing, novelist and poet, Jem Poster and poets Tiffany Atkinson and Matthew Francis. Also offers PhD and taught MA in *Writing* with modules in narratology and poetry, writing and publication.

University of Wales, Bangor

Department of English, College Road, Bangor LL57 2DG
☎01248 382102   Fax 01248 382102
✉ els029@bangor.ac.uk
www.bangor.ac.uk/ccpa

PhD *Creative and Critical Writing*; MA *Creative Studies (Creative Writing)*; BA *English Literature with Creative Writing*; BA *English Language with Creative Writing* and new BA *Creative Studies* (pending). Also MA *Creative Studies (Film Practice)*; MA *Creative Studies (Drama Practice)*; MA *Creative Studies (Media Practice)*. The Centre for the Creative and Performing Arts launched the UK national database on creative writing education in universities and colleges and is the location of the research programme, Creative Writing in Universities.

Writers' Holiday at Caerlon

School Bungalow, Church Road, Pontnewydd, Cwmbran NP44 1AT
☎01633 489438
✉ writersholiday@lineone.net
www.writersholiday.net

Contact *Anne Hobbs*

Annual six-day conference for writers of all standards held in the summer at the University of Wales' Caerlon Campus. Courses, lectures, concert and excursion all included in the fee. Private, single and en-suite, full board accommodation. Courses have included *Writing for Publication*; *Writing Poetry*; *Writing Romantic Fiction* and *Writing for the Radio*.

Writers' Circles and Workshops

Directory of Writers' Circles
39 Lincoln Way, Harlington LU5 6NG
☎01525 873197
✉ diana@writers-circles.com
www.writers-circles.com

Directory of Writers' Circles, edited by Diana Hayden. Contains contact details and information about meetings in the UK and Republic of Ireland. Updated twice annually.

Writers' Circles Handbook
Oldacre, Horderns Park Road, Chapel-en-le-Frith SK23 9SY
☎01298 812305
✉ oldacre@btinternet.com
www.btinternet.com/~oldacre

Contact *Jill Dick*

Handbook for writers' circles, with invaluable information, articles and a comprehensive list of all known UK circles and groups meeting in the UK. Some overseas entries too. Free regular updates available after initial purchase (£5, post free).

Biscuit, Writers Conference 2005
Biscuit Publishing, PO Box 123, Washington, Newcastle upon Tyne NE37 2YW
☎0191 431 1263 Fax 0191 431 1263
✉ info@biscuitpublishing.com
www.biscuitpublishing.com

Contact *Brian Lister*

Second annual conference, to be held at the Lindisfarne Centre, University of Durham in April 2005. Residential weekend of masterclasses, exhibitions, seminars, debates and other fringe events. Open to all poets and prose writers.

Carmarthen Writers' Circle
Lower Carfan, Tavernspite, Whitland SA34 0NP
☎01994 240441

Contact *Jenny White*

Founded 1989. The Circle meets monthly on the second Monday of the month at the Indoor Bowls Centre, Carmarthen. All levels and genres welcome.

Chiltern Writers' Group
151 Chartridge Lane, Chesham HP5 2SE
☎01494 772308
✉ chilwriters@netscape.net
chilternwriters.netfirms.com

ANNUAL SUBSCRIPTION £15; concessions: £10.
NON-MEMBERS MEETING £3.

Guest speakers, workshops, manuscript critiques and monthly meetings. Regular newsletter and competitions.

The Cotswold Writers' Circle
Bliss's Cottage, Lower Chedworth, Cheltenham GL54 4AN
☎01285 720668
✉ elaine@pandelunt.co.uk

Patron *Elizabeth Webster*
Membership Secretary *Elaine Lunt*
Competition Secretary *Mrs Anne Brookes*

The Circle meets every Tuesday morning (except 2nd Tuesday of the month) in Cirencester. Activities include workshops with well-known authors and an International Open Writing Competition; closing date 31 January annually (send s.a.e. for details). Winners published in the Circle's anthology, *Pen Ultimate*.

Cumbrian Literary Group
'Calgarth', The Brow, Flimby, Maryport CA15 8TD
☎01900 813444

President *Glyn Matthews*
Secretary *Joyce E. Fisher*
SUBSCRIPTION £8 p.a.

Founded 1946 to provide a meeting place for readers and writers in Cumbria. The Group meets once a month (April to November) in Windermere. Invites speakers to meetings and holds annual competitions for poetry and prose. Publishes *Bookshelf* magazine. Further details from the Secretary.

'Sean Dorman' Manuscript Society
Cherry Trees, Crosemere Road, Cockshutt, Ellesmere SY12 0JP
☎01939 270293

Director *Mary Driver*
SUBSCRIPTION: £6.50 p.a.

Founded 1957. Provides mutual help among

writers and aspiring writers in England, Wales and Scotland. By means of circulating manuscript parcels, members receive constructive criticism of their own work and read and comment on the work of others. Full details and application forms available on receipt of s.a.e.

East Anglian Writers
77 Marlborough Road, Norwich NR3 4PL
✉ benjamin.scott@ntlworld.com
Chair *Benjamin Scott*

A group of over 80 professional writers living in Norfolk, Cambridgeshire and Suffolk. Affiliated to the **Society of Authors**. Informal pub meetings, occasional speakers' evenings and contact point for professional writers new to the area.

Eastbourne's Anderida Writers
20 Vian Avenue, Eastbourne BN23 6EY
☎01323 737677
Secretary *Stella Freshney*
SUBSCRIPTION £15 p.a.

Creative workshops for Sussex authors. Talks and competitions.

Euroscript
Suffolk House, 1–8 Whitfield Place, London W1T 5JU
☎020 7387 5880 Fax 020 7387 5880
✉ info@euroscript.co.uk
www.euroscript.co.uk

Script development organisation offering creative and editorial input to professional writers and producers. Develops screenplays through an intensive modular programme, including residential script workshops; provides script reports and runs two film story competitions per year. Open to writers of any nationality. Write or access the website for further information.

Gay Authors Workshop
BM Box 5700, London WC1N 3XX
Contact *Kathryn Byrd*

Established 1978 to encourage and support lesbian/gay writers. Regular meetings and a newsletter. GAW gave rise to **Paradise Press** (see entry under *Small Presses*).

Historical Novel Folio
17 Purbeck Heights, Mount Road, Parkstone, Poole BH14 0QP
☎01202 741897
Contact *Doris Myall-Harris*

An independent postal workshop – single folio dealing with any period before World War II. Send s.a.e. for details.

'How to Self-Publish Your Book' Workshops
'Chinook', Southdown Road, Winchester SO21 2BY
☎01962 712307
✉ WriterCon@aol.com
www.gmp.co.uk/writers/conference
www.awc-workshops.ndo.co.uk 558
Contact *Barbara Large*

One-day workshops to inform writers who wish to self-publish their books abot the digital and lithographic processes. Participants will learn the skills of researching, writing and revising their mss; the use of photographs, maps, diagrams, illustrations, desgn and formatting; types of paper, fonts, sizes, ISBN numbers and costs.

Kops and Ryan Advanced Playwriting Workshops
41B Canfield Gardens, London NW6 3JL
☎020 7624 2940/7263 8740
Tutors *Bernard Kops, Tom Ryan*

Three ten-week terms per year from September. Small group writing and improvisation workshops. Instruction in film technique and private tutorials. Call for details.

London Writers' Circle
27 Braycourt Avenue, Walton-on-Thames KT12 2AZ
☎01932 702874
✉ wendy@stickler.org.uk
Membership Secretary *Wendy Hughes*
SUBSCRIPTION £20 (London); £10 (Country); £6 (Overseas)

Founded 1924. Encourages writers of all grades in poetry, short story and feature writing. Monthly meetings, social events and quarterly magazine.

North West Playwrights (NWP)
18 St Margaret's Chambers, 5 Newton Street, Manchester M1 1HL
☎0161 237 1978 Fax 0161 237 1978
www.newplaysnw.com

Founded 1982. Operates a script-reading service, classes and script development scheme and *The Lowdown* newsletter. Services available to writers in the region only.

Pier Playwrights

PO Box 141, Brighton BN2 1LZ
☎01273 625132
✉ admin@pierplaywrights.co.uk
www.pierplaywrights.co.uk

Contact *Chris Taylor*
SUBSCRIPTION £15 (Individual); £5 (Unwaged);
£30 (Company)

Run by playwrights for playwrights throughout
the south east region. Workshops by visiting
professionals, script reading, courses, residencies,
etc and a monthly newsletter.

Pitstop Refuelling Writers' Weekend Workshops

'Chinook', Southdown Road, Winchester
SO21 2BY
☎01962 712307
✉ WriterCon@aol.com
www.gmp.co.uk/writers/conference
www.awc-workshops.ndo.co.uk

Director *Barbara Large, MBE, FRSA*

Following on from the **Annual Writers'
Conference** in Winchester, these are small-
group writing workshops under the guidance
of professional writers. 2005 workshop dates
are 18–20 March and 21–23 October.

Screenwriters' Workshop

Suffolk House, 1–8 Whitfield Place, London
W1T 5JU
☎020 7387 5511
✉ screenoffice@tiscali.co.uk
www.lsw.org.uk

MEMBERSHIP £40 p.a

Established 1983, this educational charity helps
writers into the film and TV industries. Runs
Feedback – a script-reading service. Full details on
the website.

Scribo

1/31 Hamilton Road, Bournemouth
BH1 4EQ
☎01202 302533

Contacts *K. & P. Sylvester*

Scribo (established over 20 years ago) is a postal
workshop for novelists dealing with both manuscript folios (e.g. fantasy/sci-fi, mainstream,
women's fiction, crime, literary) and forum
folios (discussion, information exchange). No
annual subscription. Send s.a.e. for further
details.

Short Story Writers' Folio/ Children's Novel Writers' Folio

5 Park Road, Brading, Sandown, Isle of
Wight PO36 0HU
☎01983 407697
✉ dawn.wortley-nott@lineone.net

Contact *Mrs Dawn Wortley-Nott*

Postal workshops – members receive constructive criticism of their work and read and offer
advice on fellow members' contributions. Send
an s.a.e. for further details.

Society of Sussex Authors

Bookends, Lewes Road, Horsted Keynes,
Haywards Heath RH17 7DP
☎01825 790755 Fax 01825 790755
✉ michael@bookends.claranet.com

Contact *Michael Legat*
SUBSCRIPTION £10

Founded 1968. Six meetings per year, held in
Lewes, plus social events. Membership restricted
to Sussex-based writers only.

South Manchester Writer's Workshop

c/o Didsbury Methodist Church Hall,
Sandhurst Road, Didsbury
✉ mail@manchester-writers.freeserve.co.uk
www.manchester-writers.freeserve.co.uk
Contact *Philip Caveney*

Weekly meetings, open to all, held every Tuesday. Phone or access the website for details.

Southwest Scriptwriters

☎0117 909 5522
✉ info@southwest-scriptwriters.co.uk
www.southwest-scriptwriters.co.uk

Secretary *John Colborn*
SUBSCRIPTION £5 p.a.

Founded 1994 to offer support to regional
writers for all media. The group meets at the
Theatre Royal, Bristol.

Speakeasy – Milton Keynes Writers' Group

46 Wealdstone Place, Springfield, Milton
Keynes MK6 3JG
☎01908 663860
✉ speakeasy@writerbrock.co.uk
www.mkweb.co.uk/speakeasy

Contact *Martin Brocklebank*

Monthly meetings on the first Tuesday of each
month at 8.00 p.m. Full and varied programme
includes Local Writer Nights where work can be

read and peformed and Guest Nights where writers, poets and journalists are invited to speak. Mini-workshops and information nights are also in the programme. Invites entries to Open Creative Writing Competitions. Phone, e-mail or send s.a.e. for details to address above.

Spread the Word
77 Lambeth Walk, London SE11 6DX
☎020 7735 3111 Fax 020 7735 2666
✉ info@spreadtheword.org.uk
www.spreadtheword.org.uk

Contact *Development Officer*

Supports new writing and live literature in London, with a focus in the South and West. Live events, creative writing workshops, talks, reading groups, cross arts projects and one-to-one surgeries.

Sussex Playwrights' Club
2 Brunswick Mews, Hove BN3 1HD
☎01273 730106
www.newventure.org.uk

Secretary *Dennis Evans*
ANNUAL SUBSCRIPTION £7; Guests £1 per meeting

Founded 1935. Monthly readings of members' work by experienced actors. Membership open to all. Meetings held at New Venture Theatre, Bedford Place, Brighton.

Tooting and Balham Writers' Circle
See **Wandsworth Writers' Circle**

Ver Poets
Haycroft, 61–63 Chiswell Green Lane, St Albans AL2 3AL
☎01727 867005
✉ may.badman@virgin.net

Chairman *Ray Badman*

Editor/Organiser *May Badman*
MEMBERSHIP £15 p.a. (UK);
  £20/US$30 (Overseas)

Founded 1966 to promote poetry and help poets. Postal and local members. Meet in St Albans, publishes members' work and organises competitions, including the annual **Ver Poets Open** competition and an open competition for younger poets (15–19 years) called 'High Lights'. Gives help and advice and makes information available about other poetry groups, events and opportunities for publication.

Verulam Writers' Circle
46 Gadebridge Lane, Hemel Hempstead HP1 3HF
☎020 8424 5134
✉ ncook@kodak.com
www.verulamwriterscircle.org.uk

Contact *Nick Cook*

Founded 1956. Offers constructive criticism, talks and workshops. Meetings are held fortnightly at St Michael's Church Hall, St Michael's Road, St Albans.

Walton Wordsmiths
27 Braycourt Avenue, Walton on Thames KT12 2AZ
☎01932 702874
✉ words@stickler.org.uk

Contact *Wendy Hughes*

Founded in 1999 by Wendy Hughes. Supports writers of all grades and capabilities by offering constructive criticism and advice.

Wandsworth Writers' Circle
1a Gambole Road, Tooting Broadway, London SW17 0QJ
☎07970 715080
✉ jasonyoung72@yahoo.com
www.writers-circles.com/wandsworth.html

Contact *Jason Young*

Founded 2003 as Tooting and Balham Writers' Circle. A local version of the London Writers' Circle providing a weekly newsletter *The Literary Voice*. Encourages writers to attend courses supported by the **Arvon Foundation** and informs them of conferences held throughout the year.

Workers' Educational Association
National Office: Temple House, 17 Victoria Park Square, London E2 9PB
☎020 8983 1515 Fax 020 8983 4840
✉ national@wea.org.uk
www.wea.org.uk

Founded in 1903, the WEA is a voluntary body with members drawn from all walks of life. Runs writing courses and workshops throughout the country which are open to everyone. Contact the District Secretary at your district WEA office for courses in your region.

Cheshire, Merseyside & West Lancashire
7/8 Bluecoat Chambers, School Lane, Liverpool L1 3BX
☎0151 709 8023

Eastern
Botolph House, 17 Botolph Lane, Cambridge
CB2 3RE
☎01223 350978

East Midlands
39 Mapperley Road, Mapperley Park,
Nottingham NG3 5AQ
☎0115 962 8400

London
4 Luke Street, London EC2A 4XW
☎020 7613 7550

Northern
1st Floor, Unit 6, Metro Riverside Business
Park, Delta Bank Road, Gateshead
NE11 9DJ
☎0191 461 8100

North Western
4th Floor, Crawford House, University
Precinct Centre, Oxford Road, Manchester
M13 9GH
☎0161 273 7652

South Eastern
57 Riverside 2, Sir Thomas Longley Road,
Rochester ME2 4DP
☎01634 730101

South Western
Sandon Court, The Millfields, 1 Craigie
Drive, Stonehouse, Plymouth PL1 3JB
☎01752 664989

Thames & Solent
6 Brewer Street, Oxford OX1 1QN
☎01865 246270

Western
7 York Court, Wilder Street, Bristol
BS2 8QH
☎0117 916 6500

West Mercia
78–80 Sherlock Street, Birmingham B5 6LT
☎0121 603 9089

Yorkshire North
6 Woodhouse Square, Leeds LS3 1AD
☎0113 245 3304

Yorkshire South
Chantry Buildings, 6–20 Corporation Street,
Rotherham S60 1NG
☎01709 837001)

Scottish Association
Riddle's Court,
322 Lawnmarket, Edinburgh EH1 2PG
☎0131 226 3456

Writers in Oxford
✉ hampton.oxford@dial.pipex.com
www.writersinoxford.org
Membership Secretary *Rob Walters*
Chairman *Janie Hampton*
SUBSCRIPTION £20 p.a.

Founded 1992. Open to published authors, play-wrights, poets and journalists. Literary seminars and social functions. Publishes *The Oxford Writer* newsletter.

The Writers' Workshop
Cowfields Farm, Rotherfield Greys, Henley-on-Thames RG9 4PX
☎01491 628819 Fax 01491 628581

Runs regular daytime writing sessions on aspects of creative writing together with talks from guest speakers.

Yorkshire Playwrights
Membership: 9 Barker's Road, Sheffield
S7 1SD
✉ info@yorkshireplaywrights.com
www.yorkshireplaywrights.com
Membership *Caroline Small*

Founded 1989. A group of professional writers of plays for stage, TV and radio whose aims are to encourage the writing and performance of new plays in Yorkshire. Open to any writers living in Yorkshire who are members, prefer-ably, of the **Writers' Guild**, or the **Society of Authors**. Contact the Administrator for an information sheet.

The Words Complained Of ...

*David Hooper gives advice on how to avoid
an expensive court appearance*

The main area of risk in libel is in non-fiction. The best working test is whether the tendency of the words used is to diminish the reputation of the claimant. If you were in the claimant's position, could you validly object to what was written about you? It is sensible to ask yourself who might complain about what you have written and how you would respond to that complaint bearing in mind that the burden of proving by legally admissible evidence will be upon you. There is unfortunately no substitute for careful research and checking. Some errors pass into mythology. A British police officer called Morton collected damages on no less than three occasions from W. H. Allen, Secker & Warburg and Weidenfeld & Nicolson for the repetition of the canard that he was responsible for the shooting in cold blood of Abram Stern, head of the Stern gang in Palestine. The Court of Appeal has recently rejected attempts to use the freedom of expression principles under the European Convention of Human Rights Article 10, to reduce the strict application of the repetition rule in libel. If you repeat someone else's libel you are liable to have to prove that it is true even if you believed your source of information was reliable.

The issue is what readers would reasonably conclude that the words meant. The fact that the author did not intend to libel the claimant is not a defence. The reader is in any event unlikely to know what the author's intention was and would form his own view on the interpretation of the words on the page. The fact that a libel was the result of an honest mistake rather than deliberate would be relevant to the amount of damages awarded. Unhappily experience shows that libel is, particularly in the area of publishing, usually the product of mistake rather than the product of a failed exposé Publishers are in any event increasingly reluctant to run the risk of publishing investigative books. Recently Random House decided not to publish in this country a book about possible links between a Saudi businessman and Al Qaeda, which had been successfully published in the USA. Cases involving the exposure of the wrongdoing of footballers, policemen or doctors normally involve newspapers or television companies. Writers need therefore to check the accuracy of what they write. They do well, for example, not to confuse the Chancellor of Glasgow University, Sir Alec Cairncross with his brother, a suspected member of the Cambridge spy ring. Nor is it wise to suggest that a Nigerian-born singer had said that 'it was time to support apartheid' when in reality she had said nothing more sinister than 'it was time to support a party'.

The writer should focus on all people who might bring a claim. Often controversial books successfully avoid an action from the principal target only to invite a claim from some minor character over a relatively trivial indiscretion. Claims can come from unlikely sources. *The Sunday Telegraph* can scarcely have expected to be sued by the son of Qaddafi but when he turned up at court he obtained an apology although no damages. Recently a Russian businessman, Grigori Loutchansky, successfully sued The Times over a report linking him with money laundering. The paper may have felt such a claim was unlikely as Loutchansky was banned from this country because his presence was deemed undesirable by the Home Secretary and he had served a lengthy prison sentence for dishonesty in the USSR.

The Loutchansky case was a salutary reminder of the severity of English libel law. Although it is the case that the limitation period for bringing libel actions is one year, the courts upheld - which is bad news for writers of books - what is known as the single publication rule, namely that each book sale or downloading from the Internet is a fresh act of publication with its own one-year limitation period. Journalists whose material might be published electronically in an archive or otherwise accessible on a website should take care to ensure that if there is a valid libel complaint steps are taken to stop any further publication of the material electronically. Otherwise they may face another claim. Unfortunately, the libel laws in this country have attracted a number of libel tourists wishing to impress on the world their spotless reputation. Writers should bear in mind that the libel laws in the United States are unfavourable to plaintiffs with the result that a monster like Dr Armand Hammer sued the English edition of a hostile biography in this country but decided not to bring a claim in the USA.

If a claim for libel is notified, advice should be sought from a specialist lawyer, preferably one recommended by the publisher. An outraged response can raise the level of damages. If a claim is made, immediate consideration must be given as to whether any amendment or footnote is required in respect of any electronic version of the article which can be accessed by third parties. Section 2 of the Defamation Act 1996 has significantly amended the defence of offer of amends which enables a swift and less expensive resolution of a claim where a mistake has been made. It involves an admission of liability and, if the parties cannot agree, an assessment of damages by the judge but it can stop the greed of the claimant in its tracks. Writers need to discover whether they are covered by the publisher's insurance and, if so, what excess attaches to any claim. If the writer believes that the claim may be covered by insurance, he or she must ensure that the insurers are promptly notified and that any letter of complaint is forwarded to them and that no admission of liability is made without the authority of the insurers. Increasingly, libel insurance only cuts in after the claim has cost five figures - scant consolation for the author who is likely to have warranted in the publishing contract that the book is free from libel. Very often publishers will not enforce that indemnity in the absence of serious blameworthy conduct on the part of the writer but again that is little consolation, as publishers will not commit themselves in advance to their probable reaction to a libel claim. It is important therefore to consider whether the book should be read for libel and, if so, whether it is necessary to have it all read or simply parts of it.

Many publishing contracts are silent on the question of who pays for the libel reading. Writers who try to modify the standard form indemnity given to publishers normally face a thankless task, but it is worth considering whether there is scope for agreeing that the writer's liability should be modified in respect of potential defamations of which the publisher is aware where the writer has complied with all the requirements of the lawyer reading the book for libel. Practical steps which can be taken include considering whether a particular passage should be sent to the person written about. If it can be shown that the person consented to what was written, that is a defence to a claim for libel. The problem, however, is that normally such persons will not give consent.

Libel actions cannot be brought on behalf of those who are dead. The death of a plaintiff in the course of a libel action, as happened with Robert Maxwell's claim against Faber, brings the claim to an immediate halt, but each side is left bearing their own legal costs. Writers are sometimes well advised to consult a helpful volume called *Who Was Who*.

Another defence is justification, which involves the author proving that what was written was true. If what was written was fair comment on a matter of public interest based on facts which were substantially true the writer will have a defence. By virtue of the Human Rights Act 1998 the English courts will increasingly take note of the decisions made under Article 10 of the European Convention of Human Rights which upholds the freedom of speech and which has a greater tendency to rule that criticisms made of a claimant were matters of comment rather than allegations of fact which have to be justified If a court is told that the disputed passage in a libel claim will be defended, the court will not grant an interim injunction pending trial. The downside is that if the defence fails the damages are likely to be that much greater. Consideration often has to be given to whether it would be appropriate and less expensive to deal with the claim at an early stage, possibly by altering the disputed passage if that can still be done or by revising it in a later edition.

One of the most promising developments has been the expansion of the defence of qualified privilege by the libel action brought by the former Irish Prime Minister Albert Reynolds against the *Sunday Times*. If the writer can prove that on a matter of public interest there was a duty to inform the public who had a corresponding interest in receiving that information, there will be a defence which does not require proving that the particular allegation was true. The Court will, however, look very carefully at the research carried out, the language used and the attempt to put both sides of the matter.

Qualified privilege was the issue in the Loutchansky case, where the newspaper argued that it required the protection of qualified privilege to write about the alleged activities of Loutchansky which were by their nature very difficult to prove. The judge concluded, however, that the paper had made insufficient attempts to contact Loutchansky and should not have published until it had done so. The most helpful development for writers is the recognition by the courts of the importance of freedom of speech. The press has to discharge vital functions as a bloodhound as well as a watchdog and any lingering doubts should be resolved in favour of publication. The courts have recognised that freedom of speech is essential to informed political debate and that restrictions imposed upon that freedom must be proportionate and no more than is necessary to promote the legitimate object of the restriction. The courts also recognise that news is a perishable commodity and that the decision to publish must be assessed in the light of the facts then known.

To date, however, despite all the ringing endorsements of the freedom of the press, the courts have often been unwilling to uphold defences of qualified privilege. Too often they have found that there was some step which ought to have been taken before going into print. Journalists with publication deadlines may have a better prospect of establishing qualified privilege than authors who may be expected to undertake more research to get to the truth of the matter. The recent case of Jameel *v Wall Street Journal*, which is under appeal, suggests that only rarely will the courts uphold the publishing of serious allegations against named individuals which cannot be proved. The existence of the defence and the unpredictability of the view the judge may take of the research carried out is likely to deter many claimants, particularly those in public life. The Court of Appeal has recently held that a balanced account of the allegations, which it termed neutral reportage, made by a Saudi dissident was protected by qualified privilege. However, this defence is more likely to be applicable to the reporting of political matters. Previously, a writer repeating the allegations was likely to have had to prove that they were true. If there is not the pressure of a newspaper deadline the courts are going to expect an even higher standard of research and balance on the part of an author.

Writers of fiction face fewer libel problems. However, their use of autobiographical material can lead to some of their characters being identifiable. The inadvertent use of the name of a real peer has led to a novel being pulped. Directories should, where possible, be consulted to ensure there are no similarly named people in a comparable occupation. Care should be taken to see on whom characters are based and whether any of the surrounding events actually happened. Often there is much to be said for a carefully worded disclaimer of reference to living individuals. Compton Mackenzie used to pick names from old telephone directories. Unfortunately, even when this expedient was used by the novelist Paul Watkins in his book Stand up before your God, a randomly chosen name of a villainous character was by ill-fortune the name of one of his contemporaries at Eton College. Damages had to be paid as checks in the school directories could have avoided this error. Choosing the names of friends or acquaintances and involving them in defamatory escapades may be very difficult to defend and could result in the payment of damages and costs.

Writers of fiction will benefit from the defence of accidental defamation under Section 2 of the Defamation Act which will limit damages and costs but, even so, failure to make these checks can be expensive. Derek Jameson's experiences of accidentally changing the name of a sergeant who had been convicted of treason to spare that man's family's feelings to a randomly chosen name which turned out to be that of a journalist showed that the road to libel can be paved with good intentions.

The growth of faction and the introduction of living people into works of fiction do increase the risk of libel claims by blurring the distinction between fact and imagination. A *roman-à-clef* can present significant libel problems and it was perhaps not surprising that recently a publisher could not be found for a novel featuring unattractive characteristics of a person described as the wife of a Labour Prime Minister who as 'a young chap with a phoney smile' was felt not to be sufficiently unrecognisable.

Changes introduced by the Defamation Act 1996 and procedural changes regarding the conduct of libel actions to make them less tortuous and expensive and to require each side to disclose the strengths and weaknesses of their cases at an earlier stage certainly are an improvement. Libel nevertheless remains a very costly pitfall even if the damages awarded are much reduced. Damages are now capped but are slowly moving upwards for the most serious libels. In the last year two nursery workers accused of child abuse were awarded £200,000 each and a company that was falsely linked to al-Qaeda was reputed to have recovered £500,000 from the BBC, although part of those damages may have related to loss of business contracts. On top of that there are the legal costs. Most cases settle for a fraction of that. There are fast-track procedures where libel damages will be capped at £10,000. This is little consolation to writers, as these changes together with the willingness of lawyers to bring libel claims on a conditional fee basis - that is to say the lawyer does not get paid unless he wins the case, but he can recover from the defendant a success fee on top of his not inconsiderable normal legal fees - serve only to encourage the bringing of smaller, but nevertheless expensive, claims. Things are improving but at present the only certainty about libel is its expense. The Court of Appeal has considered in the case of Musa *v* The Telegraph Ltd whether solicitors should be entitled to charge as much as £800 per hour and whether there is any substance in the media's complaint that the size of conditional fees are compelling them to pay up on worthless claims.

Article 8 of the European Convention of Human Rights protects the right to respect for private and family life. To date, claims have related either to intrusive tabloid exposés or to celebrities exploiting publicity rights, such as Michael Douglas in his spat with *Hello! Magazine* who published unauthorised paparazzi photographs. That case was really about the right to control publicity and to prevent unauthorised breach of confidence in such circumstances where the parties from their commercial dealings were aware of the confidentiality that attached to the private, albeit much hyped, wedding party. The court felt that there was no public interest in such intrusive behaviour on the part of *Hello!*

Magazine and the Douglases were entitled to damages for distress and with *OK! Magazine* for any reduced syndication revenues. The court did not uphold a general right of privacy and to that extent there has been some back-peddling by the courts, which had looked as if they were going to establish a general right of privacy. If there is a remedy it is likely to be under the law of confidence and much will depend on the facts in each case. Where a person has a reasonable expectation of privacy, intrusion into that privacy will need to be justified and the threshold may be that much lower for public figures. The unauthorised use of photographs is more likely to be restrained than the written word. At present the law of privacy and of confidence is likely to present few problems, if any, for the tabloids and for those who seek to interfere with the legitimate commercial exploitation of what would otherwise be considered private matters. It is a developing area of law but at present it need not cause concern to serious writers. The approach of the court seems to have been that just as the court would have protected a written account by the Douglases of their wedding so they should be able to control the commercial exploitation of the events.

Naomi Campbell recovered £3,500 in respect of photographs of her leaving a drugs rehabilitation clinic and Amanda Holden and her husband received £40,000 from the *Daily Star*, which had published intrusive pictures of them on holiday. The TV presenter Sarah Cox received £50,000 from a Sunday tabloid for even more intrusive photos taken of her whilst on honeymoon. Although the Court of Appeal has restricted the scope of privacy claims in the case brought by the footballer Gary Flitcroft, claims based in privacy or breach-of-confidence claims can be brought where the writer knew or ought to have known that the other person could reasonably expect his privacy to be protected. Certain kinds of information about a person, for example relating to health, private relationships or finances, might well be viewed by the court as private, as could certain kinds of activity which a reasonable person applying contemporary standards of morals and behaviour would understand to be meant to be unobserved. A useful practical test of what is private is whether the disclosure of that information or conduct would be highly offensive to a reasonable person of ordinary sensibilities. Writers who are publishing details of people's private lives or their personal finances need to be able to justify the publication of such material and they may need to limit the amount of detail they do in fact publish.

Libel Health Check

Non-fiction

1. Do the persons written about belong to a group likely to sue? Celebrities rely on their reputation and tend to have aggressive lawyers. The police are backed by the Police Federation. Companies can sue for damage to their trading reputation, particularly if accused of selling dangerous products or

being insolvent. England is a claimant-friendly jurisdiction and foreigners may sue here, when they cannot sue in the USA.

2. Libel is no longer the preserve of the very rich. Conditional fee agreements for litigants who cannot pay are increasingly common.
3. Should all or any part of the book be read for libel?
4. Do the words mean what you intend? Is there any ambiguity?
5. Do you have evidence (i.e. witnesses) to prove the truth of what you have written, if there is a complaint?
6. If you repeat allegations or rumours, you may have to prove the truth of the underlying facts, not just that there is such a rumour.
7. Try and reduce what you might have to prove. Can you say that something is incorrect rather than accusing a person of deliberately lying?
8. What steps have been taken to verify the facts? Have you sought the other side's comments and is it worth sending them the relevant pages for comment?
9. Check the captions to photos, press releases and the index (particularly after any change has been made to reduced the libel risk).
10. Keep your notes or taped interviews.
11. Is the comment truly a matter of comment or is it a hidden allegation of fact (e.g. that X is dishonest) which would have to be proved to be true.

Fiction
1. What are the facts and events based on? How autobiographical are they?
2. How are the names chosen?
3. Could a disreputable character be identified from the events even if not named?
4. If writing about professions or limited groups, is there a directory which should be checked to see that there is no person with a similar name?
5. Do not assume your acquaintances will welcome their names being used and in any event do not use your characters to settle old scores.

David Hooper is a media partner at Reynolds Porter Chamberlain and author of Reputations under Fire, *published by Little Brown (2001).*

Miscellany

AR&E
25 Barrow Street, New York, NY 10014, USA
☎001 212 924 9942 Fax 001 212 924 1864
✉ info@agentresearch.com
www.agentresearch.com
Contact *Bill Martin*

US service for writers seeking representation. 'Helps you locate the agent who is right for you at this stage of your career.' Offers subscription newsletter, new agent listings as well as a free agent verification service.

Arjay Research
20 Rookery View, Little Thurrock, Grays RM17 6AS
☎01375 372199 Fax 01375 372199
✉ RogWJ@aol.com
www.copy-editing.net
Contact *Roger W. Jordan*

All aspects of international merchant shipping and naval research undertaken by former shipping archivist and editor. Extensive maritime library and comprehensive databases on *inter alia* ships wrecked/lost and passenger and cruise ships. Terms by arrangement.

Combrógos
10 Heol Don, Whitchurch, Cardiff CF14 2AU
☎029 2062 3359
Contact *Professor Meic Stephens*

Founded 1990. Arts and media research, editorial services, specialising in books about Wales or by Welsh authors. 'Encyclopaedic knowledge of Welsh history, language, literature and culture.'

Jacqueline Edwards
104 Earlsdon Avenue South, Coventry CV5 6DQ
✉ twigsbranches@yahoo.co.uk
Contact *Jacqueline Edwards, MA, LLB(Hons)*

Historical research – family, local and 19th and 20th century legal history. Covers Warwickshire, Gloucestershire, Wiltshire, Worcestershire, Cambridgeshire and the National Archive, Kew, London.

Impressions of Monmouth
Unit 3, The New Building, Ellwood Road, Milkwall, Coleford GL16 7LE
☎01594 839407 Fax 01594 839287
✉ books@impressionsmon.demon.co.uk
Contact *David James*

Advice and technical assistance for those wishing to self-publish with full design, printing and binding services. Yearbooks, commemorative books, personal, family, local histories, etc. Print runs as low as 25 copies. Fixed prices.

International Booksearch Service
☎020 7639 8900
✉ scfordham@talk21.com
www.scfordham.com
Contact *S.C. Fordham*

Founded 1992. International book search service for out-of-print books. A free service with no obligation to buy the book when found. Experienced in finding books for authors, researchers, TV and film companies, newspapers, magazines, etc.

Caroline Landeau
8 Elystan Place, London SW3 3LF
☎07050 600420 Fax 07050 605641
✉ winmacweb@hotmail.com
Contact *Caroline Landeau*

Experienced research and production – films, multimedia, books, magazines, exhibitions, animation, general interest, art, music, crime, travel, food, film, theatre.

M-Y Books Ltd
The Seed Warehouse, Maidenhead Yard, Hertford SG14 3AW
☎01992 586279
www.m-ybooks.co.uk
Contact *Jonathan Miller*

Offers promotional and marketing services to the self-published author or small publisher.

Murder Files
Dommett Hill Farm, Hare Lane, Buckland St. Mary, Chard TA20 3JS
☎01460 234065
✉ enquiry@murderfiles.com

www.murderfiles.com

Contact *Paul Williams*

Founded 1994. Crime writer and researcher specialising in GB murders. Holds information on thousands of well-known and less well-known murders dating from 1400 to the present day. Copies of press cuttings available from 1920 onwards. Details of executions, particularly at the Tyburn and Newgate. Information on British hangmen. Specialist in British police murders since 1700. CD-Rom *The Ultimate Price – The Unlawful Killing of British Police Officers*, Part 1 (1700–1899) & Part 2 (1900–2000) available. Service available to general enquirers, writers, researchers, TV, radio, video, etc.

Ormrod Research Services

Weeping Birch, Burwash TN19 7HG

☎01435 882541

✉ richardormrod@aol.com

Contact *Richard Ormrod*

Established 1982. Comprehensive research service: literary, historical, academic, biographical, commercial. Verbal quotations available. Also editing, indexing, ghost-writing and critical reading.

Patent Research

Dachsteinstr. 12a, D–81825 Munich, Germany

☎00 49 89 430 7833

Contact *Gerhard Everwyn*

All world, historical patents for researchers, authors, archives, museums and publishers. Rates on application.

Teral Research Services

45 Forest View Road, Moordown, Bournemouth BH9 3BH

☎01202 516834   Fax 01202 516834

✉ terry@judgetread/fsnet.co.uk

Contact *Terry C. Treadwell*

All aspects of research undertaken but specialises in all military, aviation, naval and defence subjects, both past and present. Extensive book and photographic library, including a leading collection of World War One aviation photographs. Terms by arrangement.

The United Kingdom Copyright Bureau

110 Trafalgar Road, Portslade BN41 1GS

☎01273 277333   Fax 01273 705451

✉ info@copyrightbureau.co.uk

www.copyrightbureau.co.uk

Contacts *Ralph de Straet von Kollman, Petra Ginman*

The UKCB provides a secure copyright service at reasonable cost, enabling multiple copyrights to be registered nominally when required. Prices are advertised on the website including the UKCB's solicitors, etc. Copyrights preferred on floppy disk or CD-Rom; mss are not accepted due to storage space.

Melanie Wilson

72 High Street, Syston LE7 1GQ

☎0116 260 4442   Fax 0116 260 1396

✉ MelanieWilson@dragonflight.co.uk

Contact *Melanie Wilson*

Comprehensive research service for books, magazines, newspapers, documentaries, films, radio, education, TV drama. Includes free worldwide booksearch service and groundwork for factual basis for all media presentations, particularly in historical research, costume and textiles, crafts, food and cooking, weapons and uniforms, traditional storytelling, past technology, living history displays and exhibitions.

Press Cuttings Agencies

Durrants

Discovery House, 28–42 Banner Street,
London EC1Y 8QE
☎020 7674 0200 Fax 020 7674 0222
✉ contact@durrants.co.uk
www.durrants.co.uk

Wide coverage of all print media sectors plus Internet, newswire and broadcast monitoring; foreign press in association with agencies abroad. High speed, early morning press cuttings from the national press e-mailed to your desktop. Overnight delivery via courier to most areas or first-class mail. Well presented, laser printed, A4 cuttings. Rates on application.

International Press-Cutting Bureau

224–236 Walworth Road, London SE17 1JE
☎020 7708 2113 Fax 020 7701 4489
✉ ipcb2000@aol.com

Contact *Robert Podro*

Covers national, provincial, trade, technical and magazine press. Cuttings are normally sent twice weekly by first-class post. Basic charges are £60 per month + 60p per cutting.

Romeike Media Intelligence

Romeike House, 290—296 Green Lanes,
London N13 5TP
☎0800 289543 Fax 020 8882 6716
✉ info@romeike.com
www.romeike.com

Contact *Alistair Hails*

Monitors national and international dailies and Sundays, provincial papers, consumer magazines, trade and technical journals, teletext services as well as national radio and TV networks. Back research, advertising checking and Internet monitoring, plus analysis and editorial summary service available.

We Find It (Press Clippings)

40 Galwally Avenue, Belfast BT8 7AJ
☎028 9064 6008 Fax 028 9064 6008

Contact *Avril Forsythe*

Specialises in Northern Ireland press and magazines, both national and provincial. Rates on application.

Xtreme Information

89½ Worship Street, London EC2A 2BF
☎020 7377 1742 Fax 020 7377 6103
✉ info@news.xtremeinformation.com
www.news.xtremeinformation.com

Newcastle office: Earl Grey House, 75–85 Grey Street, Newcastle upon Tyne NE1 6EF
☎0191 203 1020 Fax 0191 203 1010

National and European press monitoring agency. Cuttings from national and all major European press available seven days a week, with early morning delivery. Also monitoring of internet and newswire channels. Delivery available online; account management available 24 hours a day.

Bursaries, Fellowships and Grants

Arts Council Bursaries, Ireland
See **The Arts Council/An Chomhairle Ealaíon** under *Arts Councils and Regional Offices*

The Authors' Contingency Fund
The Society of Authors, 84 Drayton Gardens, London SW10 9SB
☎020 7373 6642 Fax 020 7373 5768
✉ info@societyofauthors.org
www.societyofauthors.org

This fund makes modest grants to published authors who find themselves in sudden financial difficulties. Contact the **Society of Authors** for an information sheet and application form.

The Authors' Foundation
The Society of Authors, 84 Drayton Gardens, London SW10 9SB
☎020 7373 6642 Fax 020 7373 5768
✉ info@societyofauthors.org
www.societyofauthors.org

Grants to writers whose publisher's advance is insufficient to cover the costs of research involved. Application by letter to The Authors' Foundation giving details, in confidence, of the advance and royalties, together with the reasons for needing additional funding. Grants are sometimes given even if there is no commitment by a publisher, so long as the applicant has had a book published and the new work will almost certainly be published. About £80,000 is distributed each year. Contact the **Society of Authors** for full entry details. Final entry dates: 30 April and 30 September.

The K. Blundell Trust
The Society of Authors, 84 Drayton Gardens, London SW10 9SB
☎020 7373 6642 Fax 020 7373 5768
✉ info@societyofauthors.org
www.societyofauthors.org

Grants to writers whose publisher's advance is insufficient to cover the costs of research. Author must be under 40, has to submit a copy of his/her previous book and the work must 'contribute to the greater understanding of existing social and economic organisation'. Application by letter. Contact the **Society of Authors** for full entry details. Final entry dates: 30 April and 30 September.

Alfred Bradley Bursary Award
c/o BBC Radio Drama, Room 2130, New Broadcasting House, Oxford Road, Manchester M60 1SJ
☎0161 244 4052 Fax 0161 244 4248
Contact *Coordinator*

Established 1992. Biennial award in commemoration of the life and work of the distinguished radio producer Alfred Bradley. Aims to encourage and develop new radio writing talent in the BBC North region. There is a change of focus for each award, e.g. previous years have targeted comedy drama, verse drama, etc. Entrants must live in the north of England. The award is given to help writers to pursue a career in writing for radio. The next award was launched in July 2004, with a deadline for scripts 30 November 2004. Further information can be found on bbc.co.uk/writersroom Previous winners: Julia Copus, Michael Stewart, Ben Tagoe, Katie Douglas.
AWARD Up to £6000 over two years and a BBC Radio Drama commission, the opportunity to develop further ideas with Radio Drama.

British Academy Small Research Grants
10 Carlton House Terrace, London SW1Y 5AH
☎020 7969 5200 Fax 020 7969 5300
www.britac.ac.uk
Contact *Assistant Secretary, Research Grants*

Award to further original academic research at postdoctoral level in the humanities and social sciences. Entrants must be resident in the UK. Final entry dates: 15 January, 15 April and 15 October.
AWARD £5000 (maximum).

Cholmondeley Awards
The Society of Authors, 84 Drayton Gardens, London SW10 9SB
☎020 7373 6642 Fax 020 7373 5768
✉ info@societyofauthors.org
www.societyofauthors.org

Founded 1965 by the late Dowager Marchioness of Cholmondeley. Annual honorary awards to recognise the achievement and distinction of individual poets. 2003 winners: Ciaran Carson, Michael Donaghy, Lavinia Greenlaw, Jackie Kay.

AWARD £8000 (total).

Olive Cook Prize
See **Tom-Gallon Trust Award**

Tony Doyle Bursary for New Writing
BBC Northern Ireland Drama, Broadcasting House, Ormeau Avenue, Belfast BT2 8HQ
☎02890 338497 Fax 02890 338408
✉ tvdrama.ni@bbc.co.uk
www.bbc.co.uk/ni/drama

Contacts *Deidre Cartmill, Stephen Wright*

This bursary is aimed at encouraging Irish writers to write for television – the medium in which Tony Doyle had his greatest successes. It also aims to inform writers of the opportunities that television affords and to nurture long-term creative links between all broadcasters and writers in Ireland. Writers must have an Irish background and must not have had a drama in English previously produced for television. Final entry date is usually 31 January each year (opens in October). Previous winners: Dominique Moloney (2003), Brian Dungan (2002). The winner receives a cash prize of £2000. The finalists are invited to a residential seminar to introduce them to the world of television drama through a series of intensive sessions with the BBC Northern Ireland Drama Development Team and experienced practitioners. Two typed copies of a 60-minute script for an original television drama should be submitted. Only one entry accepted per person. Enties must be in English. Contact the department and ask for criteria as these may change annually.

The Economist/ Richard Casement Internship
The Economist, 25 St James's Street, London SW1A 1HG
☎020 7830 7000
www.economist.com

Contact *Science Editor (re. Casement Internship)*

For an aspiring journalist under 25 to spend three months in the summer writing for *The Economist* about science and technology. Applicants should write a letter of introduction along with an article of approximately 600 words suitable for inclusion in the Science and Technology Section. Competition details normally announced in the magazine late January or early February and 4–5 weeks allowed for application.

European Jewish Publication Society
PO Box 19948, London N3 3ZJ
Fax 020 8346 1776
✉ cs@ejps.org.uk
www.ejps.org.uk
Contact *Dr Colin Shindler*

Established in 1995 to help fund the publication of books of European Jewish interest which would otherwise remain unpublished. Helps with the marketing, distribution and promotion of such books. Publishers who may be interested in publishing works of Jewish interest should approach the Society with a proposal and manuscript in the first instance. Books which have been supported in 2003/4 include: *Mordechai's First Brush with Love* ed. Laura Phillips and Marion Baraitser; *The History of Zionism* Walter Laqueur; *Photographing the Holocaust* Janina Struk; *Isaac Rosenberg: Selected Poems and Letters* ed. Jean Liddiard. Also supports the publication of poetry, and translations from and into other European languages.

GRANT £3000 (maximum).

Fulbright Awards
The Fulbright Commission, Fulbright House, 62 Doughty Street, London WC1N 2JZ
☎020 7404 6880 Fax 020 7404 6834
www.fulbright.co.uk

Contact *British Programme Manager*

The Fulbright Commission has a number of scholarships given at postgraduate level and above, open to any field (science and the arts) of study/research to be undertaken in the USA. Length of award is typically an academic year. Application deadline for postgraduate awards is usually late October/early November of preceding year of study; and mid-March/early April for distinguished scholar awards. Further details and application forms are available on the Commission's website. Alternatively, send A4 envelope with sufficient postage for 100g with a covering letter explaining which level of award is of interest.

Tony Godwin Memorial Trust
c/o 38 Lyttelton Court, Lyttelton Road, London N2 0EB
☎020 8209 1613
✉ info@tgmt.org.uk

www.tgmt.org.uk

Chairman *Iain Brown*

Biennial award established to commemorate the life of Tony Godwin, a prominent publisher in the 1960s/70s. Open to all young people (under 35 years old) who are UK nationals and working, or intending to work, in publishing. The award provides the recipient with the means to spend at least one month as the guest of an American publishing house in order to learn about international publishing. The recipient is expected to submit a report upon return to the UK. Next award: 2006; final entry date: 31 December 2005. Previous winners: George Lucas (Hodder), Clive Priddle (Fourth Estate), Richard Scrivener (Penguin), Lisa Shakespeare (Weidenfeld & Nicolson), Fiona Stewart (HarperCollins).

AWARD Bursary of approx. US$5000.

Eric Gregory Trust Fund

The Society of Authors, 84 Drayton Gardens, London SW10 9SB

☎020 7373 6642 Fax 020 7373 5768

✉ info@societyofauthors.org

www.societyofauthors.org

Annual awards of varying amounts are made for the encouragement of poets under the age of 30 on the basis of a submitted collection. Open only to British-born subjects resident in the UK. Final entry date: 31 October. Contact the **Society of Authors** for full entry details. 2003 winners: Jen Hadfield, Zoe Brigley, Paul Batchelor, Olivia Cole, Sasha Dugdale, Anna Woodford.

AWARD £24,000 (total).

The Guardian Research Fellowship

Nuffield College, Oxford OX1 1NF

☎01865 288540 Fax 01865 278676

Contact *The Administrative Officer*

One-year fellowship endowed by the Scott Trust, owner of *The Guardian*, to give someone working in the media the chance to put their experience into a new perspective, publish the outcome and give a *Guardian* lecture. Applications welcomed from journalists and management members, in newspapers, periodicals or broadcasting. Research or study proposals should be directly related to experience of working in the media. Accommodation and meals in college will be provided and a stipend. Advertised biennially in November.

Hawthornden Castle Fellowship

Hawthornden Castle, The International Retreat for Writers, Lasswade EH18 1EG

☎0131 440 2180 Fax 0131 440 1989

Contact *The Administrator*

Established 1982 to provide a peaceful setting where published writers can work without disturbance. The Retreat houses five writers at a time, who are known as Hawthornden Fellows. Writers from any part of the world may apply for the fellowships. No monetary assistance is given, nor any contribution to travelling expenses, but once arrived at Hawthornden, the writer is the guest of the Retreat. Applications on forms provided must be made by the end of September for the following calendar year. Previous winners include: Les Murray, Alasdair Gray, Helen Vendler, Olive Senior, Hilary Spurling.

Francis Head Bequest

The Society of Authors, 84 Drayton Gardens, London SW10 9SB

☎020 7373 6642 Fax 020 7373 5768

✉ info@societyofauthors.org

www.societyofauthors.org

Provides grants to published British authors over the age of 35 who need financial help during a period of illness, disablement or temporary financial crisis. Contact the **Society of Authors** for an information sheet and application form.

Jerwood Awards

See **The Royal Society of Literature/Jerwood Awards**

Ralph Lewis Award

University of Sussex Library, Brighton BN1 9QL

☎01273 678158 Fax 01273 678441

✉ p.a.ringshaw@sussex.ac.uk

Established 1985. Occasional award set up by Ralph Lewis, a Brighton author and art collector who left money to fund awards for promising manuscripts which would not otherwise be published. The award is given in the form of a grant to a UK-based publisher in respect of a publication of literary works by new authors. No direct applications from writers. Previous winners: **Peterloo Poets**; **Serpent's Tail**; **Stride Publications**.

The Elizabeth Longford Grants

The Society of Authors, 84 Drayton Gardens, London SW10 9SB

☎020 7373 6642 Fax 020 7373 5768

✉ info@societyofauthors.org

www.societyofauthors.org

Biannual grant, sponsored by Flora Fraser and Peter Soros, to a historical biographer whose publisher's advance is insufficient to cover the costs of research involved. Contact the **Society of Authors** for full details. Final entry dates: 30 April and 30 September.

GRANT £2500.

The John Masefield Memorial Trust

The Society of Authors, 84 Drayton Gardens, London SW10 9SB

☎020 7373 6642 Fax 020 7373 5768

✉ info@societyofauthors.org

www.societyofauthors.org

This trust makes occasional grants to professional poets (or their immediate dependants) who are faced with sudden financial problems. Contact the **Society of Authors** for an information sheet and application form.

Somerset Maugham Trust Fund

The Society of Authors, 84 Drayton Gardens, London SW10 9SB

☎020 7373 6642 Fax 020 7373 5768

✉ info@societyofauthors.org

www.societyofauthors.org

Annual awards designed to encourage writers under the age of 35 to travel. Given on the basis of a published work of fiction, non-fiction or poetry. Open only to British-born subjects resident in the UK. Final entry date: 20 December. 2003 winners: Hari Kunzru *The Impressionist*; William Fiennes *Snow Geese*; Jon McGregor *If Nobody Speaks of Remarkable Things*.

AWARDS £12,000 (total).

The Airey Neave Trust

PO Box 36800, 40 Bernard Street, London WC1N 1WJ

☎020 7833 4440

✉ hanthoc@aol.com

Contact *Hannah Scott*

Initiated 1989. Annual research fellowships for up to three years – towards a book or paper – for serious research connected with national and international law, and human freedom. Preferably attached to a particular university in Britain.

Newspaper Press Fund

Dickens House, 35 Wathen Road, Dorking RH4 1JY

☎01306 887511 Fax 01306 888212

✉ enquiries@pressfund.org.uk

Director/Secretary *David Ilott*

Aims to relieve distress among journalists and their dependants. Continuous and/or occasional financial grants; also retirement homes for eligible beneficiaries. Further information and subscription details available from the Director.

North East Literary Fellowship

Arts Council England, North East, Central Square, Forth Street, Newcastle upon Tyne NE1 3PJ

☎0191 255 8542 Fax 0191 230 1020

www.artscouncil.org.uk

Contact *Literature Officer*

A competitive fellowship in association with the Universities of Durham and Newcastle upon Tyne. Contact Arts Council England, North East, for details.

Northern Rock Foundation Writer's Award

New Writing North, 2 School Lane, Whickham, Newcastle upon Tyne NE16 4SL

☎0191 488 8580 Fax 0191 488 8576

✉ mail@newwritingnorth.com

www.nr-foundationwriters.com

Contact *Silvana Michelini*

Annual award established in 2002 with the aim of liberating established writers who live in the region from work other than writing. Applicants must have at least two books published by a recognised publisher and *must* live and work in Northumberland, Tyne and Wear, County Durham, Cumbria or Teesside. 2003 winner: novelist and playwright, Julia Darling.

AWARD £60,000 (£20,000 a year for three years).

Northern Writers' Awards

See **New Writing North** under *Professional Associations*

PAWS (Public Awareness of Science) Drama Fund

The PAWS Office, OMNI Communications, Chancel House, Neasden Lane, London NW10 2TU

☎020 8214 1543 Fax 020 8214 1401

✉ pawsomni@globalnet.co.uk

Contacts *Barrie Whatley, Andrew Millington*

Established 1994. Annual award aimed at encouraging television scriptwriters to include science and engineering scenarios in their work. Grants are given to selected writers to develop their script ideas into full treatments. The PAWS Fund holds science events enabling writers to meet scientists and engineers and also offers a contacts service to put writers in 'one-to-one' contact with specialists who can help them develop their ideas. See also the **Euro-PAWS Midas Prize** under *Prizes*.

Pearson Playwrights' Scheme

80 Strand, London WC2R 0RL
www.pearson.com
Administrator *Jack Andrews, MBE*

Awards four bursaries to playwrights annually, each worth £5000. Applicants must be sponsored by a theatre which then submits the play for consideration by a panel. Each award allows the playwright a twelve-month attachment. Applications invited via theatres in October each year. For up-to-date information, contact Jack Andrews (☎020 8943 8176).

Charles Pick Fellowship

School of English and American Studies, University of East Anglia, Norwich NR4 7TJ
☎01603 492810 Fax 01603 507728
✉ v.striker@uea.ac.uk
www.uea.ac.uk/eas/fellowships/pick.shtml
Contact *Val Striker*

An annual award, founded in 2001 by the Charles Pick Consultancy in memory of the publisher and literary agent who died in 2000, to support a new unpublished writer of fictional or non-fictional prose. Award of the Fellowship, which is residential from August to January, is judged on the quality of writing and reference from a literary agent, editor or accredited creative writing teacher. Previous winner: Luke Williams. Deadline for applications: 31 January each year.

AWARD £10,000 plus free campus accommodation.

Peggy Ramsay Foundation

Hanover House, 14 Hanover Square, London W1S 1HP
☎020 7667 5000 Fax 020 7667 5100
✉ laurence.harbottle@harbottle.com
www.peggyramsayfoundation.org
Contact G. *Laurence Harbottle*

Founded 1992 in accordance with the will of the late Peggy Ramsay, the well-known agent. Grants are made to writers for the stage who have some experience and who need time and resources to make writing possible. Grants are also made for writing projects by organisations connected with the theatre. The Foundation does not support production costs or any project that does not have a direct benefit to play-writing. Writers must have some record of successful writing for the stage.

GRANTS total £150,000 to £200,000 per year.

The Royal Literary Fund

3 Johnson's Court, off Fleet Street, London EC4A 3EA
☎020 7353 7150 Fax 020 7353 1350
✉ egunnrl@globalnet.co.uk
www.rlf.org.uk
Secretary *Eileen Gunn*

Grants and pensions are awarded to published authors of several works in financial need, or to their dependants. Examples of author's works are needed for assessment by Committee. Contact the Secretary for further details and application form.

The Royal Society of Literature/Jerwood Awards

The Royal Society of Literature, Somerset House, Strand, London WC2R 1LA
☎020 7845 4676 Fax 020 7845 4679
✉ rsl&jerwood@billingplace.co.uk
www.rslit.org
Submissions *Paula Johnson*

New awards offering financial assistance to authors engaged in writing their first major commissioned works of non-fiction. Three awards: one of £10,000 and two of £5000 will be offered annually in 2004, 2005 and 2006 to writers working on substantial non-fiction projects. Open to UK and Irish writers and writers who have been resident in the UK for at least three years. Applications for the first awards should be submitted by end August 2004. Further details available on the website.

Scottish Arts Council Book Awards

Scottish Arts Council, 12 Manor Place, Edinburgh EH3 7DD
☎0131 226 6051 Fax 0131 225 9833
✉ gavin.wallace@scottisharts.org.uk
www.scottisharts.org.uk
Contact *Gavin Wallace*, Literature Officer

Awards are made annually and are given in recognition of high standards in fiction, poetry, non-fiction and literary non-fiction. Authors should be Scottish or resident in Scotland, but books of Scottish interest by other authors are eligible for consideration. Applications are made by publishers only, and the closing date is

31 January for books published in the previous calendar year.

AWARDS Three shortlisted adult and three shortlisted children's writers each receive an award of £2000. The Scottish Arts Council Book of Year Award is worth a total of £10,000 and the Children's Book of the Year is a total of £5000.

Scottish Arts Council Creative Scotland Awards

Scottish Arts Council, 12 Manor Place, Edinburgh EH3 7DD
☎0131 226 6051/ Help Desk: 0845 603 6000
Fax 0131 225 9833
✉ help.desk@scottisharts.org.uk
www.scottisharts.org.uk

The details of this scheme are currently under review but substantial awards or commissions will be available to established artists based in Scotland working in any medium, including writing.

Scottish Arts Council New Writers' Bursaries

Scottish Arts Council, 12 Manor Place, Edinburgh EH3 7DD
☎0131 226 6051 Fax 0131 225 9833
✉ gavin.wallace@scottisharts.org.uk
www.scottisharts.org.uk

Contact *Gavin Wallace*, Head of Literature

Ten bursaries of £2000 awarded annually to enable previously unpublished writers of literary work more time to devote to their writing. Applicants should be based in Scotland.

Scottish Arts Council Writers' and Playwrights' Bursaries

Scottish Arts Council, 12 Manor Place, Edinburgh EH3 7DD
☎0131 226 6051 Fax 0131 225 9833
✉ gavin.wallace@scottisharts.org.uk
www.scottisharts.org.uk

Contact *Gavin Wallace*, Head of Literature

Bursaries to enable published writers of literary work and recognised playwrights to devote more time to their writing. Around 20 bursaries of up to £15,000 awarded annually; deadline for applications in July and January. Application open to writers based in Scotland.

Laurence Stern Fellowship

Department of Journalism, City University, Northampton Square, London EC1V 0HB
☎020 7040 8224 Fax 020 7040 8594

✉ B.Jones@city.ac.uk
www.city.ac.uk/journalism

Contact *Bob Jones*

Founded 1980. Awarded to a young journalist experienced enough to work on national stories. It gives them the chance to work on the national desk of the *Washington Post*. Benjamin Bradlee, the *Post*'s Vice-President-at-Large, selects from a shortlist drawn up in March/April. 2004 winner: Mary Fitzgerald of the *Belfast Telegraph*. Full details available on the website.

Tom-Gallon Trust Award and the Olive Cook Prize

The Society of Authors, 84 Drayton Gardens, London SW10 9SB
☎020 7373 6642 Fax 020 7373 5768
✉ info@societyofauthors.org
www.societyofauthors.org

An award of £1000 is made on the basis of a submitted story to fiction writers of limited means who have had at least one short story accepted for publication. Both awards are biennial and are awarded in alternate years. Contact the **Society of Authors** for an entry form. Final entry date 20 September 2005.

The Betty Trask Awards

The Society of Authors, 84 Drayton Gardens, London SW10 9SB
☎020 7373 6642 Fax 020 7373 5768
✉ info@societyofauthors.org
www.societyofauthors.org

These annual awards are for authors who are under 35 and Commonwealth citizens, awarded on the strength of a first novel (published or unpublished) of a traditional or romantic nature. The awards must be used for a period or periods of foreign travel. Final entry date: 31 January. Contact the **Society of Authors** for an entry form. 2003 winners: Jon McGregor *If Nobody Speaks of Remarkable Things*; Sarah Hall *Haweswater*; Elizabeth Garner *Nightdancing*; Zoe Strachan *Negative Space*; Adam Thirlwell *Politics*.
AWARD £25,000 (total).

The Travelling Scholarships

The Society of Authors, 84 Drayton Gardens, London SW10 9SB
☎020 7373 6642 Fax 020 7373 5768
✉ info@societyofauthors.org
www.societyofauthors.org

Annual honorary grants to established British writers. 2003 winners: Kate Chisolm, Jamie McKendrick, Aonghas MacNeacail.
AWARD £6000 (total).

UEA Writing Fellowship

School of English and American Studies,
University of East Anglia, University Plain,
Norwich NR4 7TJ
☎01603 592734   Fax 01603 593522
www.uea.ac.uk/eas/fellowships/
   writingfellow.shtml

Director of Personnel & Registry Services
J.R.L. Beck

Established 1971. Awarded to a writer of established reputation in prose fiction and poetry for
a period of six months, January to end June.
The duties of the Fellowship are discussed at an
interview. It is assumed that one activity will
be the pursuit of the Fellow's own writing. In
addition the Fellow will be expected to teach
an undergraduate creative writing workshop in
the School of English and American Studies
during the Spring semester, and to undertake a
programme of events around the county in
association with Arts Council England, East.
Office space and some limited secretarial assistance will be provided. Applications for the
Fellowship should be lodged with the Director
of Personnel & Registry Services in the autumn;
candidates should submit two examples of recent
work. Previous winner: David Flusfeder.

AWARD £7500, plus accommodation as
required.

David T.K. Wong Fellowship

School of English and American Studies,
University of East Anglia, University Plain,
Norwich NR4 7TJ
☎01603 592810   Fax 01603 507728
✉ v.striker@uea.ac.uk
www.uea.ac.uk/eas/fellowships/wong/
   wong.shtml

Contact *Val Striker*

Founded 1998. An annual endowment to
enable a writer of promise to spend a year at
the University writing a work of fiction on
some aspect of life in the Far East. Judged on
the basis of submitted written work, the award
is open to all nationalities. Final entry date:
31 October. 2003/4 winner: Lakambini Sitoy.

AWARD £25,000.

Prizes

Academi Book of the Year Awards

Academi, 3rd Floor, Mount Stuart House, Mount Stuart Square, Cardiff CF10 5FQ
☎029 2047 2266 Fax 029 2049 2930
✉ post@academi.org

Annual non-competitive prizes awarded for works of exceptional literary merit written by Welsh authors (by birth or residence), published in Welsh or English during the previous calendar year. There is one major prize in English, the Book of the Year Award, and one major prize in Welsh, Gwobr Llyfr y Flwyddyn.
PRIZES £5000 each; £1000 to each of four runners-up.

J.R. Ackerley Prize

English PEN, Lancaster House, 33 Islington High Street, London N1 9LH
☎020 7713 0023 Fax 020 7713 0005
✉ enquiries@englishpen.org
www.englishpen.org

Commemorating the novelist/autobiographer J.R. Ackerley, this prize is awarded for a literary autobiography, written in English and published in the year preceding the award. Entry restricted to nominations from the Ackerley Trustees only ('please do not submit books'). 2003 winner: Jenny Diski *Stranger on a Train*.
PRIZE £1000, plus silver pen.

Aldeburgh Poetry Festival Prize

See **Jerwood Aldeburgh First Collection Prize**

Alexander Prize

Royal Historical Society, University College London, Gower Street, London WC1E 6BT
☎020 7387 7532 Fax 020 7387 7532
✉ rhs.info@sas.ac.uk

Contact *Executive Secretary*

Awarded for a historical essay of not more than 8000 words. Competitors may choose their own subject for the essay. Closing date: 1 November.
PRIZE £250 or a silver medal.

ALPSP Awards/ALPSP/ Charlesworth Awards

ALPSP, South House, The Street, Clapham, Worthing BN13 3UU
☎01903 871686 Fax 01903 871457
✉ chief-exec@alpsp.org
www.alpsp.org

Contact *Sally Morris*

Presented in recognition of significant achievement in the field of learned and professional publishing by the **Association of Learned and Professional Society Publishers** and the Charlesworth Group. The awards were originally for excellence in design and typography in journals but since 2001 they also recognise innovation, contribution to not-for-profit publishing, library-publisher relations and service to ALPSP. The awards are international and open to publishers, organisations and individuals. Details available on the Association's website.

Hans Christian Andersen Awards

IBBY, Nonnenweg 12, Postfach, CH-4003 Basel, Switzerland
☎00 41 61 272 2917 Fax 00 41 61 272 2757
✉ ibby@ibby.org
www.ibby.org

Executive Director *Kimete Basha i Novosejt*

The highest international prizes for children's literature: The Hans Christian Andersen Award for Writing, established 1956; The Hans Christian Andersen Award for Illustration, established 1966. Candidates are nominated by National Sections of IBBY (The International Board on Books for Young People). Biennial prizes are awarded, in even-numbered years, to an author and an illustrator whose body of work has made a lasting contribution to children's literature. 2004 winners: Award for Writing: Martin Waddell (Ireland); Award for Illustration: Max Velthuijs (The Netherlands).
AWARD Gold medals.

Angus Book Award

Angus Council Cultural Services, County Buildings, Forfar DD8 3WF
☎01307 461460 Fax 01307 462590
✉ cultural.services@angus.gov.uk

Contact *Moyra Hood*, Educational Resources Librarian

Established 1995. Designed to try to help teenagers develop an interest in and enthusiasm for reading. Eligible books are read and voted on by third-year schoolchildren in all eight Angus secondary schools. 2003 winner: Keith Gray *Warehouse*.

PRIZE £250 cheque, plus trophy in the form of a replica Pictish stone.

Annual Theatre Book Prize
See **The Society for Theatre Research Annual Theatre Book Prize**

Artists' Choice Award for Art Instruction Book of the Year
PO Box 3, Huntingdon PE28 0QX
☎01832 710201 Fax 01832 710488
✉ award@acaward.com
www.acaward.com

Contact *Henry Malt*

Established 1995 by Artists' Choice Book Club to recognise the quality of books published in this specialised field. Books must have an element of art instruction and be first published in the UK. 2003 winner: *The Artist's Colour Manual*, Simon Jennings.

PRIZE Cheque presented to the author; trophy to the publisher.

Arts Council Children's Award
Arts Council England, 14 Great Peter Street, London SW1P 3NQ
☎020 7333 0100
www.artscouncil.org.uk

Contact *Theatre Writing Section*

Founded 2000. An annual award for playwrights who write for children up to the age of 12. The plays, which must have been produced professionally between 1 July 2004 and 30 June 2005, should be suitable for children up to the age of 12 and be at least 45 minutes long. The playwright must be resident in UK. Contact the Theatre Writing Section for full details and application form. 2004 winner: Charles Way *Red Red Shoes*.

AWARD £6000.

Arvon Foundation International Poetry Competition
2nd Floor, 42a Buckingham Palace Road, London SW1W 0RE
☎020 7931 7611 Fax 020 7963 0961
✉ london@arvonfoundation.org
www.arvonfoundation.org

Contact *The London Office*

Established 1980. Biennial competition (next in 2006) for poems written in English and not previously broadcast or published. There are no restrictions on the number of lines, themes, age of entrants or nationality. No limit to the number of entries. Entry fee: £5 per poem. Previous winners: Paul Farley *Laws of Gravity*; Don Paterson *A Private Bottling*.

PRIZE (1st) £5000 and £5000 worth of other prizes sponsored by Duncan Lawrie Limited.

Authors' Club First Novel Award
Authors' Club, 40 Dover Street, London W1S 4NP
☎020 7499 8581 Fax 020 7409 0913
www.authorsclub.co.uk

Contact *Lucy Jane Tetlow*

Established 1954. This award is made for the most promising work published in Britain by a British author, and is presented at a dinner held at the Authors' Club. Entries for the award are accepted from publishers from September of the year in question and must be full-length (short stories are not eligible). For further details/application form, contact *Lucy Jane Tetlow* or access the website. 2003 winner: Dan Rhodes *Timoleon Vieta Come Home*.

AWARD £1000.

Aventis Prizes for Science Books
c/o The Royal Society, 6–9 Carlton House Terrace, London SW1Y 5AG
☎020 7451 2576 Fax 020 7930 2170
✉ aventisprizes@royalsoc.ac.uk
www.aventisprizes.com

Contact *Aosaf Afzal*

Annual prizes established in 1988 to celebrate the best in popular science writing. Awarded to books that make science more accessible to readers of all ages and backgrounds. Managed by the Royal Society and sponsored by the Aventis Foundation. All entries must be written in English and their first publication in the UK must have been between 1 January and 31 December; submission by publishers only. Educational textbooks published for professional or specialist audiences are not eligible. 2003 winners: Chris McManus *Right Hand, Left Hand* (General Prize); Francis Dipper *The DK Guide to the Oceans* (Junior Prize).

PRIZES (total) £30,000: £10,000 to each winner; £1000 to each of the five shortlisted authors in each prize.

The BA/Nielson BookData Author of the Year Award
Booksellers Association Ltd, 272 Vauxhall Bridge Road, London SW1V 1BA
☎020 7802 0801 Fax 020 7802 0803

✉ anna.okane@booksellers.org.uk
www.booksellers.org.uk

Contact *Anna O'Kane*

Founded as part of the BA Annual Conference to involve authors more closely in the event. Authors must be British or Irish. Not an award open to entry but voted on by the BA's membership. 2003 winner: Sarah Waters.

AWARD £1000, plus trophy.

BAAL Book Prize

BAAL Publications Secretary, School of Education and Lifelong Learning, University of Wales Aberystwyth, Aberystwyth SY23 2AX
☎01970 622927
✉ mqm@aber.ac.uk
www.baal.org.uk

Contact *Marilyn Martin-Jones*

Annual award made by the British Association for Applied Linguistics to an outstanding book in the field of applied linguistics. Final entry at the end of October/November. Nominations from publishers only. 2003 winner: A. Wray *Formulaic Language and the Lexicon.*

Verity Bargate Award

Soho Theatre Company, 21 Dean Street, London W1D 3NE
☎020 7287 5060 Fax 020 7287 5061
✉ writers@sohotheatre.com
www.sohotheatre.com

Contact *David Lane*, Literary Assistant

The award was set up to commemorate the late Verity Bargate, co-founder and director of the **Soho Theatre Company**. This national award is presented biennially for a new and unperformed play (next in 2006). To go on the mailing list, please e-mail or send s.a.e. to *David Lane*. Previous winners include: Shan Khan, Fraser Grace, Lyndon Morgans, Adrian Pagan, Diane Samuels, Judy Upton and Toby Whithouse.

BBC Wildlife Magazine Poet of the Year Awards

PO Box 229, Bristol BS99 7JN
☎0117 973 8402 Fax 0117 946 7075

Annual award for a poem, the subject of which must be the natural world and/or our relationship with it. Entrants may submit one poem only of no more than 50 lines with the entry form which appears in the magazine. Closing date for entries varies from year to year. Contact the magazine for entry information.

PRIZES Poet of the Year: £500, publication in the magazine, plus reading of the poem on

Radio 4's *Poetry Please*; runners-up: cash prizes, plus publication in the magazine; four young poets awards.

BBC Wildlife Magazine Travel Writing Award

PO Box 229, Bristol BS99 7JN
☎0117 973 8402 Fax 0117 946 7075

Awarded to a travel essay that is a true account involving an intimate encounter with wildlife, either local or exotic. The essay should convey a strong impression of the environment and incorporate the idea of travel and discovery. Maximum 800 words. Contact the magazine for entry information.

PRIZE Publication in the magazine, plus 'holiday of a lifetime'.

The BBCFour Samuel Johnson Prize for Non-Fiction

Colman Getty PR, Middlesex House, 34–42 Cleveland Street, London W1T 4JE
☎020 7631 2666 Fax 020 7631 2699
✉ cathryn@colmangettypr.co.uk

Contact *Cathryn Summerhayes*

Established 1998. Annual prize sponsored by BBCFour. Eligible categories include the arts, autobiography, biography, business, commerce, current affairs, history, natural history, popular science, religion, sport and travel. Entries submitted by publishers only. 2003 winner: Tim Binyon *Pushkin.*

PRIZE £30,000; £1000 to each shortlisted author.

David Berry Prize

Royal Historical Society, University College London, Gower Street, London WC1E 6BT
☎020 7387 7532 Fax 020 7387 7532
✉ rhs.info@sas.ac.uk

Contact *Executive Secretary*

Annual award for an essay of not more than 10,000 words on Scottish history. Closing date: 31 October.

PRIZE £250,

Besterman/McColvin Medal

See **CILIP: The Chartered Institute of Library and Information Professionals Besterman/McColvin Medal**

The Biographers' Club Prize

17 Sutherland Street, London SW1V 4JU
☎020 7828 1274 Fax 020 7828 7608
✉ lownie@globalnet.co.uk

www.booktrust.org.uk

Contact *Andrew Lownie*

Established 1999 by literary agent, biographer and founder of the Biographers' Club, Andrew Lownie, to finance and encourage first-time writers researching a biography. Sponsored by the *Daily Mail*. Open to previously uncommissioned and unpublished writers producing a proposal of 15–20 pages, broken down by chapter with a note of author's credentials, the market for the book, sources used, competing/comparable books and sample chapter. 2003 winner: Richard Adams.

PRIZE £1000.

Birdwatch Bird Book of the Year

c/o Birdwatch Magazine, 3D/F Leroy House, 436 Essex Road, Islington N1 3QP

☎020 7704 9495

Contact *Dominic Mitchell*

Established in 1992 to acknowledge excellence in ornithological publishing – an increasingly large market with a high turnover. Annual award. Entries, from publishers, must offer an original and comprehensive treatment of their particular ornithological subject matter and must have a broad appeal to British-based readers. 2002 winner: *A Complete Guide to Antarctic Wildlife* Hadoram Shirihai.

Biscuit Poetry and Fiction Prizes

Biscuit Publishing, PO Box 123, Washington, Newcastle upon Tyne NE37 2YW

☎0191 431 1263 Fax 0191 431 1263

✉ info@biscuitpublishing.com

www.biscuitpublishing.com

Contacts *Brian Lister, Jacqui Lister*

Founded 2000. Annual award that aims to support new writers of short fiction and poetry. The 'Top Twenty' winners from each category are published in an anthology. In addition, the winning poet and fiction author will each have separate publications. Closing date: 31 May. Previous winners: Veronica Lloyd *Adrift, from Belize to Havana*; Bob Beagrie *Huginn and Muninn*; Tracey Fuller *The System Was Turned On*; Sue Vickerman *The Sensitively Thin Bill of the Shag*.

PRIZES Publication and advance royalties of £2000.

Bisto/CBI Book of the Year Awards

17 Lower Camden Street, Dublin 2, Republic of Ireland

☎00 353 1 872 5854 Fax 00 353 1 872 5854

✉ bistoawards@childrensbooksireland.com

Contact *Liz Marshall*

Founded 1990 as Bisto Book of the Decade Awards. This led to the establishment of an annual award made by the Irish Children's Book Trust, later to become Children's Books Ireland. Open to any author or illustrator of children's books born or resident in Ireland; open to English or Irish languages. Final entry date 31 January. 2003/04 winners: Marie Louise Fitzpatrick *You, Me and the Big Blue Sea*, Kate Thompson *The Alchemist's Apprentice*; Patrick Deeley *The Lost Orchard*; Matin Waddell *Ghostly Tales*; Martina Murphy *Dirt Tracks*; Eoin Colfer *The Wish List*.

PRIZES €3000 (Bisto Book of the Year); €1000 (Eilís Dillon Award); three merit awards €800 each.

James Tait Black Memorial Prizes

University of Edinburgh, David Hume Tower, George Square, Edinburgh EH8 9JX

☎0131 650 3619 Fax 0131 650 6898

www.englit.ed.ac.uk/jtbinf.hrm

Contact *Department of English Literature*

Established 1918 in memory of a partner of the publishing firm of **A.&C. Black Ltd**. Two prizes, one for biography and one for fiction. Closing date for submissions: 30 September. Each prize is awarded for a book published in Britain in the previous twelve months. 2003 winners: Andrew O'Hagan *Personality* (fiction); Janet Browne *Charles Darwin: The Power of Place* (biography).

PRIZES £3000 each.

Blue Peter Book Awards

c/o Awards Administrator, Fraser Ross Associates, 6 Wellington Place, Edinburgh EH6 7EQ

☎0131 553 2759 Fax 0131 553 2759

✉ lindsey.fraser@tiscali.co.uk

www.bbc.co.uk/bluepeter

Contacts *Lindsey Fraser, Kathryn Ross*

Established in 1999 to highlight paperback fiction, poetry and non-fiction for young people. The initial shortlist is selected by a panel of adults and the final decisions are taken by a panel of Blue Peter judges. Final entry date: mid-June. Previous winners: Nicky Singer *Feather Boy*; Philip Reeve *Mortal Engines*.

AWARD Trophy.

Boardman Tasker Award

Pound House, Llangennith, Swansea SA3 1JQ

☎01792 386215 Fax 01792 386215

✉ margaretbody@lineone.net
www.boardmantasker.com

Contact *Maggie Body*, Honorary Secretary

Established 1983, this award is given for a work of fiction, non-fiction or poetry, whose central theme is concerned with the mountain environment and which can be said to have made an outstanding contribution to mountain literature. Authors of any nationality are eligible, but the book must have been published or distributed in the UK for the first time between 1 November 2003 and 31 October 2004. Entries from publishers only. 2003 winner: Simon Mawer *The Fall*.

PRIZE £2000 (at Trustees' discretion).

Bollinger Everyman Wodehouse Prize

Everyman's Library, Northburgh House, 10 Northburgh Street, London EC1V 0AT
☎020 7566 6350 Fax 020 7490 2708
✉ dcampbell@everyman.uk.com *or* katy@everyman.uk.com
www.everyman.uk.com

Contact *Katy Moran*

Established in 2000 by Everyman's Library, Bollinger and the Hay Festival to celebrate comic writing in memory of P.G. Wodehouse. Books are nominated by readers of the *Sunday Times* and visitors to www.bol.com. 2003 winner: D.B.C. Pierre *Vernon God Little*.

The Booker Prize for Fiction
See **The Man Booker Prize for Fiction**

Booktrust Early Years Awards

Booktrust, Book House, 45 East Hill, London SW18 2QZ
☎020 8516 2972 Fax 020 8516 2978
✉ tarryn@booktrust.org.uk
www.booktrust.org.uk

Contact *Tarryn McKay*

Formerly the Sainsbury's Baby Book Award, established in 1999. Annual awards with three categories: the Baby Book Award, the Best Book for Pre-School Children (up to the age of 5), and an award for the Best New Illustrator. Books to be submitted by publishers only; authors and illustrators must be of British nationality or other nationals who have been resident in the UK for at least five years.

PRIZE £2000 for each category; in addition the Best New Illustrator receives a specially commissioned award.

Booktrust Teenage Prize

Book House, 45 East Hill, London SW18 2QZ
☎020 8516 2986 Fax 020 8516 2978
✉ hannah@booktrust.org.uk
www.bookheads.org.uk

Contact *Hannah Rutland*

Established 1993. Annual prize that recognises and celebrates the best in teenage fiction. Funded and administered by Booktrust. Open to works of fiction for young adults in the UK, the books to be published between 1 July 2004 and 30 June 2005. Final entry date in March. 2003 winner: Mark Haddon *The Curious Incident of the Dog in the Night-time*.

PRIZE £1500.

Harry Bowling Prize

c/o MBA Literary Agents, 62 Grafton Way, London W1T 5DW
☎020 7387 2076 Fax 020 7387 2042
✉ dana@mbalit.co.uk

Contact *Dana Arnott*

Established 2000 in honour of Harry Bowling, 'the king of Cockney sagas' (died 1999). Biennial award (next in 2006), sponsored by **Headline Book Publishing**, to encourage writers of adult fiction set in London. Open to anyone who has not been published previously. Final entry date: 31 March. Entry fee charged; forms from MBA Literary Agents (enclose s.a.e.). 2002 joint winners: Catherine Woodman *Waking Up*; Mark Lalbeharry *The Symian Curve*.

PRIZES Winner, £1000; five runners-up, £100 each.

The Branford Boase Award

9 Bolderwood Close, Bishopstoke, Eastleigh SO50 8TG
☎023 8060 0439
✉ anne@marleyhcl.freeserve.co.uk
www.henriettabranford.co.uk

Administrator *Anne Marley*

Established in 2000 in memory of children's novelist, Henrietta Branford and editor and publisher, Wendy Boase. To be awarded annually to encourage and celebrate the most promising novel by a new writer of children's books, while at the same time highlighting the importance of the editor in nurturing new talent. 2003 winner: Kevin Brooks *Martyn Pig* (book); Barry Cunningham, **The Chicken House** (editor).

AWARD Specially commissioned box, carved and inlaid in silver with the Branford Boase Award logo.

The Bridport Prize

Bridport Arts Centre, South Street, Bridport
DT6 3NR
☎01308 485064 Fax 01308 485120
✉ frances@poorton.demon.co.uk
www.bridportprize.org.uk

Contact *Frances Everitt*, Administrator

Annual competition for poetry and short story writing. Unpublished work only, written in English. Winning stories are read by a literary agent, the winning poems are put forward to the **Forward Prize**, and an anthology of winning entries is published. Final entry date: 30 June. Send s.a.e. for entry forms.

PRIZES £3000, £1000 & £500 in each category, plus 10 supplementary prizes of £50 each.

Katharine Briggs Folklore Award

The Folklore Society, c/o The Warburg Institute, Woburn Square, London
WC1H 0AB
☎020 7862 8564/8562
✉ enquiries@folklore-society.com
www.folklore-society.com

Contact *The Convenor*

Established 1982. An annual award in November for the book, published in Britain and Ireland between 1 June in the previous calendar year and 30 May, which has made the most distinguished non-fiction contribution to folklore studies. Intended to encourage serious research in the field which Katharine Briggs did so much to establish. The term folklore studies is interpreted broadly to include all aspects of traditional and popular culture, narrative, belief, custom and folk arts. 2003 winner: Dr Malcolm Jones *The Secret Middle Ages*.

PRIZE £50, plus engraved goblet.

The British Academy Book Prize

10 Carlton House Terrace, London
SW1Y 5AH
☎020 7969 5263 Fax 020 7969 5228
✉ m.reade@britac.ac.uk

Contact *Dr Michael Reade*

Annual award founded in 2001 to celebrate outstanding scholarly books in the humanities and social sciences that are have an appeal to the general reader. Nominations from publishers only; final entry date: mid-February. 2003 winner: Dr Elizabeth Cowling *Picasso: Style and Meaning*.

British Book Awards

Publishing News, 39 Store Street, London
WC1E 7DB
☎020 7692 2900 Fax 020 7419 2111
✉ mailbox@publishingnews.co.uk
www.britishbookawards.com

Established 1988. Viewed by the book trade as the one to win, 'The Nibbies' are presented annually. The awards are made in various categories. Each winner receives the prestigious Nibbie and the awards are presented to those who have made the most impact in the book trade during the previous year. 2003 winners included: Michael Moore, the late Roy Jenkins, Allison Pearson, Jacqueline Wilson, Michael Palin, the publishers **Canongate** and a lifetime achievement award for Alan Bennett. For further information contact: Merric Davidson, 12 Priors Heath, Goudhurst, Cranbrook TN17 2RE (☎/Fax 01580 212041; ✉ nibbies@mdla. co.uk).

British Czech & Slovak Association Prize

The BCSA Prize Administrator, 24 Ferndale, Tunbridge Wells TN2 3NS
☎01892 543206
✉ prize@bcsa.co.uk
www.bcsa.co.uk

Contact *Prize Administrator*

The British Czech & Slovak Association offers an annual prize for the best piece of original writing, in English, on the links between Britain and the Czech and Slovak Republics, or describing society in transition in those Republics since the Velvet Revolution in 1989. Entries can be fiction or factual, should not have been previously published and should be up to 2000 words in length. Submissions are invited from individuals of any age, nationality or educational background. Closing date: 30 June. Entry details for 2005 should be checked with the Prize Administrator. 2003 winner: Jonathan Gresty *The Slovak Year*.

PRIZE £300, presented at the BCSA's annual dinner in London. Second prize, £100. The winning entry is published in the *British Czech & Slovak Review*.

British Fantasy Awards

201 Reddish Road, South Reddish, Stockport
SK5 7HR
☎0161 476 5368 (after 6.00 pm)
✉ faliol@yahoo.com
www.britishfantasysociety.org.uk

Secretary *Robert Parkinson*

Awarded by the **British Fantasy Society** by members at its annual conference for Best Novel and Best Short Story categories, among others. Not an open competition. Previous winners include: Ramsey Campbell, Dan Simmons, Michael Marshall Smith, Thomas Ligotti.

British Press Awards
Press Gazette, Quantum House, 19 Scarbrook Road, Croydon CR9 1LX
☎020 8565 3056 Fax 020 8565 4395
✉ andreah@quantumbusinessmedia.com
www.britishpressawards.com

'The Oscars of British journalism.' Open to all British morning and Sunday newspapers sold nationally and news agencies. March event. Run by *Press Gazette*.

British Science Fiction Association Award
26 Northampton Road, Croydon CR0 7HA
☎020 8656 0137
✉ awards@fishlifter.demon.co.uk
www.bsfa.co.uk
Award Administrator *Claire Brialey*

Established 1966. Categories for novel, short fiction, artwork and non-fiction. The awards are announced and presented at the British Annual SF Convention every Easter. 2003 winners: Jon Courtenay *Felaheen*; Neil Gaiman and Dave McKean *The Wolves in the Wall*; Colin Odell, for the cover of *The True Knowledge of Ken MacLeod*; Farah Mendlesohn *Reading Science Fiction*.

British Sports Journalism Awards
See **Sports Writers' Association of Great Britain** under *Professional Associations*

The Caine Prize for African Writing
2 Drayson Mews, London W8 4LY
☎020 7376 0440 Fax 020 7938 3728
✉ caineprize@jftaylor.com
www.caineprize.com
Administrator *Nick Elam*
Secretary *Jan Hart*

Annual award founded in 1999 in memory of Sir Michael Caine, former chairman of Booker plc, to recognise the worth of African writing in English. Awarded for a short story by an African writer, published in English anywhere in the world. 'An African writer' is someone who was born in Africa, or who is a national of an African country, or whose parents are African, and whose work has reflected African sensibilities. Final entry date: 31 January; sub-

missions by publishers only. 2003 winner: Yvonne Adhiambo Owuor *Weight of Whispers*. PRIZE $15,000.

The Calouste Gulbenkian Prize
See **The Translators Association Awards**

James Cameron Award
City University, Department of Journalism, Northampton Square, London EC1V 0HB
☎020 7040 8221 Fax 020 7040 8594
Contact *The Administrator*

Annual award for journalism to a reporter of any nationality, working for the British media, whose work is judged to have contributed most during the year to the continuance of the Cameron tradition. Administered by the City University Department of Journalism. 2003 winner: Norma Percy.

Canadian Poetry Association Annual Poetry Contest
Box 22571, St George Postal Outlet, 264 Bloor Street West, Toronto, Ontario M5S 1V8, Canada
www.mirror.org/cpa

Annual contest open to members and non-members of the CPA worldwide. Submission fee: $5 per poem. See the website for entry details. All winning poems are published on the CPA website.

Six cash PRIZES and publication in *Poetmata*.

Canadian Poetry Association Shaunt Basmajian Award
Box 22571, St George Postal Outlet, 264 Bloor Street West, Toronto, Ontario M5S 1V8, Canada
www.mirror.org/cpa

Annual poetry contest open to members and non-members of the CPA worldwide. Entry fee: C$15; cheque or money order payable to the Canadian Poetry Association. Submit a manuscript of poems up to 24 pages in length, published or unpublished, and in any style or tradition. See the website for full details. The author of the winning manuscript receives 50 copies of the resulting chapbook as well as C$100 cash.

Cardiff International Poetry Competition
PO Box 438, Cardiff CF10 5YA
☎029 2047 2266 Fax 029 2049 2930
✉ post@academi.org

www.academi.org

Contact *Peter Finch*

Established 1986. An annual competition for unpublished poems in English of up to 50 lines. Closing date in January.

PRIZE £5000 (total).

Carey Award

Society of Indexers, Blades Enterprise Centre, John Street, Sheffield S2 4SU

☎0114 292 2350 Fax 0114 292 2351

✉ admin@indexers.org.uk

www.indexers.org.uk

Secretary *Ann Kingdom*

A private award made by the Society to a member who has given outstanding services to indexing. The recipient is selected by Council with no recommendations considered from elsewhere.

Carnegie Medal

See **CILIP: The Chartered Institute of Library and Information Professionals Carnegie Medal**

Sid Chaplin Short Story Competition

Shildon Town Council, Civic Centre Square, Shildon DL4 1AH

☎01388 772563 Fax 01388 775227

Contact *Mrs J.M. Stafford*

Established 1986. Annual themed short story competition (2003 subject was loyalty). Maximum 3000 words; £2 entrance fee (juniors free). All stories must be unpublished and not broadcast and/or performed. Application forms available from September 2004; closing date: 31 April 2005.

PRIZES £300 (1st); £150 (2nd); £75 (3rd); £50 (Junior).

Children's Book Circle Eleanor Farjeon Award

See **Eleanor Farjeon Award**

The Children's Laureate

Booktrust, Book House, 45 East Hill, London SW18 2QZ

☎020 8516 2972 Fax 020 8516 2978

www.childrenslaureate.org

Established 1998. The Laureate is awarded biennially to an eminent British writer or illustrator of children's books both in celebration of a lifetime's achievement and to highlight the role of children's book creators in inspiring,

informing and entertaining young readers. 2003 winner: Michael Morpurgo.

AWARD Medal and £10,000.

CILIP: The Chartered Institute of Library and Information Professionals Besterman/McColvin Medal

7 Ridgmount Street, London WC1E 7AE

☎020 7255 0650 Fax 020 7255 0501

www.cilip.org.uk/awards

Part of the CILIP/Nielsen BookData Reference Awards. Annual award for an outstanding reference work first published in the UK during the preceding year. Consists of two categories: printed and electronic. Works eligible for consideration include: encyclopedias, general and special dictionaries; annuals, yearbooks and directories; handbooks and compendia of data; atlases. Nominations are invited from members of **CILIP**, publishers and others. 2003 winners: *Early Printed Books Catalogue 1478–1840: Catalogue of the British Architectural Library, Early Imprints Collection Vol 5* (printed); *xreferplus www.xrefer.com* published by xrefer ltd (electronic).

AWARD Medal and cash prize for each category.

CILIP: The Chartered Institute of Library and Information Professionals Carnegie Medal

7 Ridgmount Street, London WC1E 7AE

☎020 7255 0650 Fax 020 7255 0501

www.ckg.org.uk

Established 1936. Presented for an outstanding book for children written in English and first published in the UK during the preceding year. Fiction, non-fiction and poetry are all eligible. 2002 winner (presented in 2003): Sharon Creech *Ruby Holler*.

AWARD Medal.

CILIP: The Chartered Institute of Library and Information Professionals Kate Greenaway Medal

7 Ridgmount Street, London WC1E 7AE

☎020 7255 0650 Fax 020 7255 0501

www.ckg.org.uk

Established 1955. Presented annually for the most distinguished work in the illustration of children's books first published in the UK during the preceding year. 2002 winner (presented in 2003): *Jethro Byrde–Fairy Child* by Bob Graham.

AWARD Medal. The Colin Mears Award (£5000 cash) is given annually to the winner of the Kate Greenaway Medal.

CILIP: The Chartered Institute of Library and Information Professionals Walford Award

7 Ridgmount Street, London WC1E 7AE
☎020 7255 0650 Fax 020 7255 0501
www.cilip.org.uk/awards

Part of the CILIP/Nielsen BookData Reference Awards. Awarded to an individual who has made a sustained and continual contribution to British bibliography over a period of years. The nominee need not be resident in the UK. The award is named after Dr A.J. Walford, a bibliographer of international repute. 2003 winner: Paul W. Nash.

AWARD Cash prize and certificate.

CILIP: The Chartered Institute of Library and Information Professionals Wheatley Medal

7 Ridgmount Street, London WC1E 7AE
☎020 7255 0650 Fax 020 7255 0501
www.cilip.org.uk/awards

Part of the CILIP/NielsenBookData Awards. Established 1962. Annual award for an outstanding index first published in the UK during the preceding three years. Whole work must have originated in the UK and recommendations for the award are invited from members of **CILIP**, the **Society of Indexers**, publishers and others. 2003 winner: Lisa Virgo (Merrall-Ross International) for the index to *Encyclopedia of Cognitive Sciences*, published by Nature Publishing Group.

AWARD Medal and cash prize.

Arthur C. Clarke Award for Science Fiction

60 Bournemouth Road, Folkestone CT19 5AZ
☎01303 252939
✉ arthurcclarkeaward@yahoo.com
www.clarkeaward.com

Administrator *Paul Kincaid*

Established 1986. The Arthur C. Clarke Award is given annually to the best science fiction novel with first UK publication in the previous calendar year. Both hardcover and paperback books qualify. Made possible by a generous donation from Arthur C. Clarke, this award is selected by a rotating panel of judges nominated by the

British Science Fiction Association, the **Science Fiction Foundation** and the Science Museum. 2003 winner: Christopher Priest *The Separation*.

AWARD £2004 (award increases by £1 per year), plus trophy.

David Cohen British Literature Prize

Arts Council England, 14 Great Peter Street, London SW1P 3NQ
☎020 7973 5325 Fax 020 7973 6983
✉ info.literature@artscouncil.org.uk
www.artscouncil.org.uk

Literature Director *Gary McKeone*
Literature Administrator *Jessica Ryan*

Established 1993 by the Arts Council and awarded biennially, the British Literature Prize is one of the most distinguished literary prizes in Britain. It recognises writers who use the English language and who are British citizens, encompassing dramatists as well as novelists, poets and essayists. The prize is for a lifetime's achievement and is donated by the David Cohen Family Charitable Trust. Set up in 1980 by David Cohen, general practitioner and son of a property developer, the Trust has helped composers, choreographers, dancers, poets, playwrights and actors. The Council is providing a futher £10,000 to enable the winner to commission new work, with the dual aim of encouraging young writers and readers. Previous winners: William Trevor, Dame Muriel Spark, Harold Pinter, V.S. Naipaul, Doris Lessing. The 2003 prize was shared between novelist Beryl Bainbridge and poet Thom Gunn.

AWARD £30,000, plus £10,000 towards new work.

The Commonwealth Writers Prize

Booktrust, Book House, 45 East Hill, London SW18 2QZ
☎020 8516 2972 Fax 020 8516 2978
✉ tarryn@booktrust.org.uk
www.booktrust.org.uk
www.commonwealthwriters.com

Contact *Tarryn McKay*

Established 1987. An annual award to reward and encourage the upsurge of new Commonwealth fiction. Any work of prose or fiction is eligible, i.e. a novel or collection of short stories. No drama or poetry. The work must be first written in English by a citizen of the Commonwealth and be first published in the year before its entry for the prize. Entries must be submitted by the publisher to the region of the writer's Commonwealth citizenship. The four regions are: Africa, Eurasia, S.E. Asia and South Pacific, Caribbean and Canada. 2004 winners: Caryl Phillips *A Distant Shore* (Best Book Award); Mark Haddon *The Curious Incident of the Dog in the Night-time* (Best First Book Award).

PRIZES £10,000 for Best Book; £3000 for Best First Book; 8 prizes of £1000 for each best and first best book in four regions.

The Thomas Cook Travel Book Award
Thomas Cook Publishing, PO Box 227, Peterborough PE3 8XX
☎01733 417352 Fax 01733 416688

Established in 1980 by The Thomas Cook Group. Annual award given to the author of the book, published (in the English language) in the previous year, which most inspires the reader to want to travel. Submissions by publishers only. 2003 winner: Jenny Diski *Stranger on a Train*.
AWARD £10,000.

The Duff Cooper Prize
54 St Maur Road, London SW6 4DP
☎020 7736 3729 Fax 020 7731 7638

Contact *Artemis Cooper*

An annual award for a literary work of biography, history, politics or poetry, published by a recognised publisher (member of the **Publishers Association**) during the previous 12 months. The book must be submitted by the publisher, not the author. Financed by the interest from a trust fund commemorating Duff Cooper, first Viscount Norwich (1890–1954). 2004 winner: Anne Applebaum *Gulag: A History of the Soviet Camps*.
PRIZE £3000.

Rose Mary Crawshay Prize
The British Academy, 10 Carlton House Terrace, London SW1Y 5AH
☎020 7969 5200 Fax 020 7969 5300
www.britac.ac.uk

Contact *British Academy Secretary*

Established 1888 by Rose Mary Crawshay, this prize is given for a historical or critical work by a woman of any nationality on English literature, with particular preference for a work on Keats, Byron or Shelley. The work must have been published in the preceding three years.
PRIZES Normally two of approximately £500 each.

Crime Writers' Association (Cartier Diamond Dagger)
PO Box 273, Boreham Wood WD6 2XA
✉ secretary@thecwa.co.uk
www.thecwa.co.uk

Contact *The Secretary*

Established 1986. An annual award for a lifetime's outstanding contribution to the genre. 2004 winner: Lawrence Block.

Crime Writers' Association (The Gold Dagger for Non-Fiction)
PO Box 273, Boreham Wood WD6 2XA
✉ secretary@thecwa.co.uk
www.thecwa.co.uk

Contact *The Secretary*

Annual award for the best non-fiction crime book published during the year. Nominations from publishers only. 2003 winner: Samantha Weinberg *Pointing from the Grave*.
AWARD Dagger, plus cheque (sum varies).

Crime Writers' Association (The CWA Ellis Peters Historical Dagger)
PO Box 273, Boreham Wood WD6 2XA
✉ secretary@thecwa.co.uk
www.thecwa.co.uk

Contact *The Secretary*

Established 1999. Annual award for the best historical crime novel. Nominations from publishers only. 2003 winner: Andrew Taylor *The American Boy*.
AWARD Dagger, plus cheque.

Crime Writers' Association (The Gold and Silver Daggers for Fiction)
PO Box 273, Boreham Wood WD6 2XA
✉ secretary@thecwa.co.uk
www.thecwa.co.uk

Contact *The Secretary*

Two annual awards for the best crime fiction published during the year. Nominations for Gold Dagger from publishers only. 2003 winners: Minette Walters *Fox Evil* (Gold); Morag Joss *Half Broken Things* (Silver).
AWARD Dagger, plus cheque (sum varies).

Crime Writers' Association (The Ian Fleming Steel Dagger)
PO Box 273, Boreham Wood WD6 2XA
✉ secretary@thecwa.co.uk
www.thecwa.co.uk

Contact *The Secretary*

Founded 2002. Annual award for the best thriller, adventure or spy novel. Sponsored by Ian Fleming (Glidrose) Publications Ltd to celebrate the best of contemporary thriller writing. 2003 winner: Dan Fesperman *The Small Boat of Great Sorrows*.

AWARD Dagger, plus cheque.

Crime Writers' Association (The Short Story Dagger)

PO Box 273, Boreham Wood WD6 2XA

✉ secretary@thecwa.co.uk

www.thecwa.co.uk

Contact *The Secretary*

Established 1993. An award for a published crime story. Publishers should submit three copies of the story by 30 September. 2003 winner: Jerry Sykes *Closer to the Flame*.

PRIZE Dagger, plus cheque.

Crime Writers' Association (The Creasey Dagger for Best First Crime Novel)

PO Box 273, Boreham Wood WD6 2XA

✉ secretary@thecwa.co.uk

www.thecwa.co.uk

Contact *The Secretary*

Established 1973 following the death of crime writer John Creasey, founder of the **Crime Writers' Association**. This award, sponsored by **Chivers Press**, is given annually for the best crime novel by an author who has not previously published a full-length work of fiction. Nominations from publishers only. 2003 winner: William Landay *Mission Flats*.

AWARD Dagger, plus cheque.

Crime Writers' Association (The Dagger in the Library)

PO Box 273, Boreham Wood WD6 2XA

✉ secretary@thecwa.co.uk

Contact *The Secretary*

Reinstated 2002. Annual award (sponsored by **Random House**) to the author whose work has given most pleasure to readers. Nominated and judged by librarians. 2003 winner: Stephen Booth.

AWARD Dagger, plus cheque.

Crime Writers' Association (The Debut Dagger)

New Writing Competition, P.O. Box 63, Wakefield WF2 0YW

✉ debut.dagger@thecwa.co.uk

www.thecwa.co.uk

Contact *The Secretary*

Annual competition (sponsored by **Orion**) for unpublished writers to submit the first 3000 words and 500 word outline of a crime novel (entry fee and form required). For full details see website or send s.a.e. to address above. 2003 winner: Kirsty Evans *The Cuckoo*.

AWARD Dagger, plus cheque.

Hunter Davies Prize

See **Lakeland Book of the Year Awards**

Isaac & Tamara Deutscher Memorial Prize

SML, University of Southampton, Highfield, Southampton SO17 1BJ

✉ ed2@soton.ac.uk

Contact *Dr Elizabeth Dore*

An annual award in recognition of, and as an encouragement to, outstanding research in or about the Marxist tradition. Made to the author of a published book. Final entry date: 1 May.

AWARD £250.

George Devine Award

17A South Villas, London NW1 9BS

☎020 7267 9793 (evenings only)

Contact *Christine Smith*

Annual award for a promising new playwright writing for the stage in memory of George Devine, artistic director of the **Royal Court Theatre**, who died in 1965. The play, which can be of any length, does not need to have been produced. Send two copies of the script, plus outline of work, to Christine Smith. Closing date: 1 March 2005. Send s.a.e. for the script to be returned if required. Information leaflet available from January on receipt of s.a.e.

PRIZE £10,000.

Dingle Prize

British Society for the History of Science, 5 Woodcote Green, Fleet GU51 4EY

✉ execsec@bshs.org.uk

www.bshs.org.uk

Biennial award made by the BSHS to the best book in the history of science (broadly construed) which is accessible to a wide audience of non-specialists. Next award: 2005. Previous winners: Ken Alder, *The Measure of All Things*; Deborah Cadbury *The Dinosaur Hunters*; Steven Shapin *The Scientific Revolution*.

PRIZE £300.

Drama Association of Wales Playwriting Competition

The Old Library, Singleton Road, Splott, Cardiff CF24 2ET

☎029 2045 2200 Fax 029 2045 2277

✉ aled.daw@virgin.net

Contact *Teresa Hennessy*

Annual competition held to promote the writing of one-act plays in English and Welsh of between 20 and 50 minutes' playing time. Application forms from the address above.

The Dryden Competition

British Comparative Literature Association/British Centre for Literary Translation, School of Language, Linguistics and Translation Studies, University of East Anglia, Norwich NR4 7TJ

Fax 01603 250599

✉ transcomp@uea.ac.uk

www.bcla.org

Competition Organiser *Dr Jean Boase-Beier*

Established 1983. Annual competition open to unpublished literary translations from all languages. Maximum submission: 25 pages.

PRIZES £350 (1st); £200 (2nd); £100 (3rd); plus publication for all winning entries in the Association's annual journal. Other entries may receive commendations.

The Dundee Book Prize

City of Discovery Campaign, 3 City Square, Dundee DD1 3BA

☎01382 434275 Fax 01382 434096

✉ deborah.kennedy@dundeecity.gov.uk

www.dundeecity.gov.uk/bookprize

Contact *Deborah Kennedy*

Launched in 1996, this is a biennial award. Previous winners include Andrew Murray Scott for *Tumulus* and Claire-Marie Watson for *The Curewife*. Entry qualifications are detailed in the entry form. Launch date: March 2005. Final entry date: March 2006.

PRIZE £6000, plus publication of novel.

S.T. Dupont Golden PEN Award for Lifetime Distinguished Service to Literature

English PEN, Lancaster House, 33 Islington High Street, London N1 9LH

☎020 7713 0023 Fax 020 7713 0005

✉ enquiries@englishpen.org

www.englishpen.org

Awarded to a senior writer, with a distinguished body of work over many years, who has made a significant and constructive impact on fellow writers, the reading public and the literary world. Nominations by members of English PEN only. Previous winners include: Francis King, Harold Pinter, Doris Lessing. 2003 award winner: Michael Frayn.

PRIZE £500 and a golden pen awarded by S.T. Dupont.

The Encore Award

The Society of Authors, 84 Drayton Gardens, London SW10 9SB

☎020 7373 6642 Fax 020 7373 5768

✉ info@societyofauthors.org

www.societyofauthors.org

Established 1990. Awarded for the best second published novel or novels of the year. Final entry date: 30 November. Details from the **Society of Authors**. 2003 winner: Jeremy Gavron *The Book of Israel*.

PRIZE £10,000.

Envoi Poetry Competition

Envoi, 44 Rudyard Road, Biddulph Moor, Stoke on Trent ST8 7JN

☎01782 517892

Contact *Roger Elkin*

Run by *Envoi* poetry magazine. Competitions are featured regularly, with prizes of £300, plus three annual subscriptions to *Envoi*. Winning poems along with full adjudication report are published. Send s.a.e. to Competition Secretary, 17 Millcroft, Bishops Stortford CM23 2BP.

EuroPAWS (European Public Awareness of Science) Midas Prize

The EuroPAWS Office, OMNI Communications, Chancel House, Neasden Lane, London NW10 2TU

☎020 8214 1543 Fax 020 8214 1401

✉ pawsomni@globalnet.co.uk

Contacts *Barrie Whatley, Andrew Millington*

Established 1998. Annual prize awarded to the writer and producer of the best television drama, first transmitted in the year up to the end of October, that bears in a significant way on science or engineering. The drama may be a single play or an episode of a series, serial or soap. It need not necessarily be centred on a science or engineering theme, although clearly it can be. The context and quality of the drama and the audience size all weigh alongside the science in making the Award. To enter a programme or suggest that a programme should be entered, contact the EuroPAWS office above.

PRIZE varies from year to year.

Euroscript Film Story Competitions

See **Euroscript** under *UK Writers' Courses*

Geoffrey Faber Memorial Prize

Faber & Faber Ltd, 3 Queen Square, London
WC1N 3AU
☎020 7465 0045 Fax 020 7465 0034

Established 1963 as a memorial to the founder
and first chairman of **Faber & Faber**, this prize
is awarded in alternate years for the volume of
verse and the volume of prose fiction published
in the UK in the preceding two years, which is
judged to be of greatest literary merit. Authors
must be under 40 at the time of publication
and citizens of the UK, Commonwealth,
Republic of Ireland or South Africa. 2003 winner: Justin Hill *The Drink and Dream Teahouse.*
PRIZE £1000.

Eleanor Farjeon Award

Children's Book Circle, c/o Hodder
Children's Books, 338 Euston Road, London
NW1 3BH
☎020 7873 6483

This award, named in memory of the much-
loved children's writer, is for distinguished services to children's books either in this country or
overseas, and may be given to a librarian,
teacher, publisher, bookseller, author, artist,
reviewer, television producer, etc. Nominations
from members of the **Children's Book Circle**.
2003 winner: Miriam Hodgson.
AWARD £750.

The Fish Short Story Prize

Fish Publishing, Durrus, Bantry, Republic of
Ireland
☎00 353 27 61246
✉ info@fishpublishing.com
www.fishpublishing.com
Contact *Clem Cairns*

Founded 1994. Annual international award
which aims to discover, encourage and publish
exciting new literary talent. The best 15 stories
are published in an anthology. Closing date: 30
November. PRIZE €10,000 (1st).

Also: the Very Short Story Prize (250 words)
– best 10 stories published in the *Fish Anthology*;
closing date: 14 February. PRIZE €2000. And:
the Unpublished Novel Prize. Send first chapter
and synopsis. Winning novel published, plus cash
prizes. Closing date: 30 September.

Details of entry fees, further prizes and online entry form can be found on the website.

Sir Banister Fletcher Award

Authors' Club, 40 Dover Street, London
W1S 4NP
☎020 7408 5092 Fax 020 7409 0913
✉ membership@theartsclub.co.uk
www.theartsclub.co.uk
Contact *Lucy Jane Tetlow*

This award was created by Sir Banister Fletcher,
President of the **Authors' Club** for many years,
and is presented annually. The prize alternates
between books on architecture and the fine arts.
In 2003 the prize was awarded for the best book
on architecture published during the previous
two years. Submissions to *Lucy Jane Tetlow* at the
Authors' Club. 2003 winner: Professor David
Watkins *Sir John Soane, Enlightenment, Thought
and the Royal Academy.*

The John Florio Prize

See **The Translators Association Awards**

The Forward Prizes for Poetry

Colman Getty PR, Middlesex House,
34–42 Cleveland Street, London W1T 4JE
☎020 7631 2666 Fax 020 7631 2699
✉ sophie@colmangettypr.co.uk
Contact *Sophie Rochester*

Established 1992. Three awards: the Forward
Prize for Best Collection, the Forward Prize for
Best First Collection and the Tolman Cunard
Prize for Best Single Poem which is not already
part of an anthology or collection. All entries
must be published in the UK or Republic of
Ireland and submitted by poetry publishers (collections) or newspaper and magazine editors
(single poems). Individual entries of poets' own
work are not accepted. 2003 winners: Ciaran
Carson (best collection), A.B. Jackson (best first
collection), Robert Minhinnick (best single
poem).
PRIZES £10,000 for best collection; £5000 for
best first collection; £1000 for best single poem.

The Frogmore Poetry Prize

42 Morehall Avenue, Folkestone CT19 4EF
www.frogmorepress.co.uk
Contact *Jeremy Page*

Established 1987. Awarded annually and sponsored by the Frogmore Foundation. The winning poem, runners-up and short-listed entries
are all published in the magazine. Previous winners: David Satherley, Caroline Price, Bill
Headdon, John Latham, Diane Brown, Tobias
Hill, Mario Petrucci, Gina Wilson, Ross Cogan,
Joan Benner, Ann Alexander, Gerald Watts.
PRIZE The winner receives 200 guineas and

a life subscription to the biannual literary magazine, *The Frogmore Papers*.

Martha Gellhorn Trust Prize

Rutherfords, Herbert Road, Salcombe
TQ8 8HN

Annual prize for journalism in honour of one of the twentieth century's greatest reporters. Open for journalism published in English, giving 'the view from the ground – a human story that penetrates the established version of events and illuminates an urgent issue buried by prevailing fashions of what makes news'. The subject matter can involve the UK or abroad. Six copies of each entry should be sent to the above address by 7 March. 2002 winner: Geoffrey Lean.

PRIZE £5000.

The Gladstone History Book Prize

Royal Historical Society, University College London, Gower Street, London WC1E 6BT
☎020 7387 7532 Fax 020 7387 7532
✉ rhs.info@sas.ac.uk

Contact *Executive Secretary*

Established 1998. Annual award for the best new work on any historical subject which is not primarily related to British history, published in the UK in the preceding calendar year. The book must be the author's first (solely written) history book and be an original and scholarly work of historical research. Closing date: 31 December. 2003 winner: Patrick Major *The Death of the KPD: Communism and Anti-Communism in West Germany 1945–1956*.

PRIZE £1000.

Glenfiddich Food & Drink Awards

c/o Wild Card PR, Kenilworth House, 79–80 Margaret Street, London W1W 8TA
www.glenfiddich.com/foodanddrink

Known as the 'Cooker Bookers' or the 'Oscars' of the gastronomic world, the awards aim to recognise excellence in writing, publishing and broadcasting on the subjects of food and drink. There are 11 category winners in 2004 from work published or broadcast in the UK and the Republic of Ireland. 2004 winners: Food Book: *Toast, the story of a boy's hunger* Nigel Slater; Drink Book: *Rum* Dave Broom; Food Writer: Philippa Davenport for work in the *Financial Times*; Cookery Writer: Angela Nilsen for work in *BBC Good Food*; Drink/Bar Writers: Roger Protz for work in *The Guardian* and *What's Brewing*; Wine Writer: Tim Atkin for work in *Observer Magazine* and *Observer Food Monthly*; Restaurant Critic: Guy Dimond for

work in *Time Out London*; Regional Writer: Alastair Gilmour for work in *The Journal*, Newcastle; Television Programme: *Nick Naim*, for *Nick and the Dinner Ladies*, BBC Scotland; Radio Programme: *Bombay Lunch Boxes*, *The Food Programme*, BBC Radio 4, presented by Simon Parkes; Photography: Giacomo Bretzel for work in *Telegraph Magazine*; GQ/Glenfiddich Food & Drink Personality of the Year: Heston Blumenthal, chef/owner of The Fat Duck; 2004 Glenfiddich Independent Spirit Award: Randolph Hodgson, Neal's Yard Dairy; Glenfiddich Trophy: Guy Dimond.

AWARD Overall winner (chosen from the category winners) £3000, plus the Glenfiddich Trophy (which is held for one year); category winners £1000 each, plus a case of Glenfiddich Single Malt Scotch Whisky.

The Phillip Good Memorial Prize

QWF Magazine, PO Box 1768, Rugby
CV21 4ZA
✉ jo.good@ntlworld.com
www.qwfmagazine.co.uk

Contact *Competition Secretary*

Established in 1997, the competition is run by *QWF Magazine*. The prize commemorates the memory of Phillip Good (late husband of *QWF* editor, Jo Good) and is for short stories of less than 5000 words in any style or genre (except children's). Open entry. Entrants may request in-depth critique of their stories for an extra fee. For entry forms send s.a.e. to the address above. Closing date: 21 August.

PRIZES (total) at least £525, plus free subscription to *QWF Magazine*; also book prizes and publication for winning authors.

Gourmand World Cookbook Awards

Pintor Rosales 36, 28008 Madrid, Spain
☎00 34 91 541 6768 Fax 00 34 91 541 6821
✉ icr@virtualsw.es
www.cookbookfair.com

Contact *Edouard Cointreau*

Founded in 1995 by Edouard Cointreau to reward those who 'cook with words'. The only world competition for food and wine books in all languages. Annual event. In 2003 there were 53 local or regional competitions worldwide, with the winners competing for the 'Best Book in the World' award – 2003 winner: *Family Food*, Heston Blumenthal.

Kate Greenaway Medal

See **CILIP: The Chartered Institute of**

Library and Information Professionals
Kate Greenaway Medal

The Griffin Poetry Prize

6610 Edwards Boulevard, Mississauga,
Ontario, Canada L5T 2V6
☎001 905 565 5993 Fax 001 905 564 3645
✉ info@griffinpoetryprize.com
www.griffinpoetryprize.com
Contact *Ruth Smith*, Manager

Annual award established in 2000 by Toronto-based entrepreneur, Scott Griffin, for books of poetry written in or translated into English. Trustees include Margaret Atwood and Michael Ondaatje. Submissions from publishers only.

PRIZES A total of C$80,000, divided into two categories: International and Canadian.

The Guardian Children's Fiction Award

The Guardian, 119 Farringdon Road, London
EC1R 3ER
☎020 7239 9694 Fax 020 7713 4366
Children's Book Editor *Julia Eccleshare*

Established 1967. Annual award for an outstanding work of fiction for children aged seven and over by a British or Commonwealth author, first published in the UK in the year of the award, excluding picture books. Final entry date: 1 June. No application form necessary. 2003 winner: Mark Haddon *The Curious Incident of the Dog in the Night-Time*.
AWARD £1500.

The Guardian First Book Award

The Guardian, 119 Farringdon Road, London
EC1R 3ER
☎020 7239 9694
Contact *Literary Editor*

Established 1999. Annual award for first time authors published in English in the UK. All genres of writing eligible, apart from academic, guidebooks, children's, educational, manuals, reprints and TV, radio and film tie-ins. 2003 winner: Robert MacFarlane *Mountains of the Mind*. Submissions are only received direct from publishers, not from individual authors. Self-published work is not eligible.
AWARD £10,000, plus *Guardian/Observer* advertising package.

Guild of Food Writers Awards

48 Crabtree Lane, London SW6 6LW
☎020 7610 1180 Fax 020 7610 0299
✉ awards@gfw.co.uk
www.gfw.co.uk
Contact *Christina Thomas*

Established 1985. Annual awards in recognition of outstanding achievement in all areas in which food writers work and have influence. Entry is not restricted to members of the Guild. Entry form available from the address above. 2003 winners: Derek Cooper Award: *Local Food Programme Toolkit* various authors; Michael Smith Award: Colin Spencer *British Food: An Extraordinary Thousand Years of History*; Jeremy Round Award for Best First Book of the Year: Clarissa Hyman *Cucina Siciliana*; Food Journalist of the Year: Kevin Gould for work in *Waitrose Food Illustrated*; Cookery Journalist of the Year: Annie Bell for work in *Country Living*; Food Book of the Year: David Thompson *Thai Food*; Cookery Book of the Year: Monisha Bharadwaj *Stylish Indian in Minutes*.

Gwobr Llyfr y Flwyddyn
See **Academi Book of the Year Awards**

James W. Hackett Award
See **The British Haiku Society** under *Organisations of Interest to Poets*

Hastings National Poetry Competition
See **Hastings International Poetry Festival First of All** under *Festivals*

W.H. Heinemann Award

The Royal Society of Literature, Somerset House, Strand, London WC2R 1LA
☎020 7845 4676 Fax 020 7845 4679
✉ info@rslit.org
www.rslit.org

Established 1945. This prize is most often awarded to works of non-fiction: biography, history, poetry, criticism, though novels, if of sufficient distinction, will not be overlooked. Books must be written in the English language and have been published in the previous year; translations are not eligible for consideration nor are single poems, nor collections of pieces by more than one author, nor may individuals put forward their own work. Publishers must contact the Secretary for details of how to submit works. Final entry date: 15 December. Up to three awards may be given. Previous winner: Miranda Carter *Anthony Blunt – His Lives*.
PRIZE £5000.

Hellenic Foundation Prize
See **The Translators Association Awards**

Felicia Hemans Prize for Lyrical Poetry

University of Liverpool, PO Box 147, Liverpool L69 7WZ
☎0151 794 2458 Fax 0151 794 2454
✉ wilderc@liv.ac.uk

Contact *The Sub-Dean, Faculty of Arts*

Established 1899. Annual award for published or unpublished verse. Open to past or present members and students of the University of Liverpool. One poem per entrant only. Closing date 1 May.

PRIZE £30.

The Hessell-Tiltman Prize for History

English PEN, Lancaster House, 33 Islington High Street, London N1 9LH
☎020 7713 0023 Fax 020 7713 0005
✉ enquiries@englishpen.org
www.englishpen.org

Founded 2002. Awarded for a history book, written in English (including translations) and aimed at a wide audience. Submissions by publishers only. 2003 winner: Jenny Uglow *The Lunar Men*.

PRIZE £3000 and Silver Dupont pen.

Heywood Hill Literary Prize

10 Curzon Street, London W1J 5HH
☎020 7629 0647

Contact *John Saumarez Smith*

Established 1995 by the Duke of Devonshire to reward a lifetime's contribution to the enjoyment of books. Three judges chosen annually. No applications are necessary for this award. 2003 joint winners: Hilary Spurling and Mark Amory.

PRIZE £15,000.

Hidden Brook Press International Poetry Anthology Contests

412–701 King Street West, Toronto, Ontario, Canada M5V 2W7
☎001 416 504 3966 Fax 001 801 751 1837
✉ writers@hiddenbrookpress.com
www.HiddenBrookPress.com

International poetry competitions: No Love Lost Poetry Anthology Contest; The Open Window Poetry Anthology Contest and Seeds International Poetry Chapbook Anthology Contest. Electronic and hard copy submissions are required. Closing dates and full entry details can be found on the website. Ten cash prizes, up to 12 Honourable Mentions and up to 300 runners up published in perfect bound colour-cover book.

William Hill Sports Book of the Year

Greenside House, Station Road, Wood Green, London N22 7TP
☎020 8918 3731 Fax 020 8918 3728
✉ pressoffice@williamhill.co.uk

Contact *Graham Sharpe*

Established 1989. Annual award introduced by Graham Sharpe of bookmakers William Hill. Sponsored by William Hill and thus dubbed the 'Bookie' prize, it is the first, and only, Sports Book of the Year award. Final entry date: September. 2003 winner: Tom Bower *Broken Dreams*.

PRIZE (reviewed annually) £16,000 package including £14,000 cash, hand-bound copy, £1000 free bet. Runners-up prizes.

Calvin & Rose G. Hoffman Prize

King's School, Canterbury CT1 2ES
☎01227 595501

Contact *The Headmaster*

Annual award for distinguished publication on Christopher Marlowe, established by the late Calvin Hoffman, author of *The Man Who was Shakespeare* (1955) as a memorial to himself and his wife. For unpublished works of at least 5000 words written in English for their scholarly contribution to the study of Christopher Marlowe and his relationship to William Shakespeare. Final entry date: 1 September. 2002 joint winners: Lukas Erne and Dr Peter Roberts.

Winifred Holtby Memorial Prize

See **The Royal Society of Literature Ondaatje Prize**

How do I love thee? Magazine Love Poetry Competition

Poetry Life Publishing, 1 Blue Ball Corner, Water Lane, Winchester SO23 0ER

Contact *Adrian Bishop*

Open competition for original love poems which have not been published in a book. Maximum length of 80 lines. Entry fee of £3 per poem. Send s.a.e. for details.

PRIZES £500 (1st); £100 (2nd); £50 each (3rd & 4th).

L. Ron Hubbard's
Writers of the Future Contest

PO Box 218, East Grinstead RH19 4GH
Contest Administrator *Andrea Grant-Webb*

Established 1984 by L. Ron Hubbard to encourage new and amateur writers of science fiction, fantasy and horror. Quarterly awards with an annual grand prize. Entrants must submit a short story of up to 10,000 words, or a novelette less than 17,000 words, which must not have been published previously. The contest is open only to those who have not been published professionally. Previous winners: Roge Gregory, Malcolm Twigg, Tom Brennan, Alan Smale, Janet Barron. Send s.a.e. for entry form.

PRIZES £640 (1st), £480 (2nd) and £320 (3rd) each quarter; Annual Grand Prize: £2500. All winners are awarded a trip to the annual L. Ron Hubbard Achievement Awards which include a series of professional writers' workshops, and are published in the *L. Ron Hubbard Presents Writers of the Future* anthology.

The Richard Imison
Memorial Award

The Society of Authors, 84 Drayton Gardens SW10 9SB
☎020 7373 6642 Fax 020 7373 5768
✉ info@societyofauthors.org
www.societyofauthors.org

Contact *The Secretary, The Broadcasting Committee*

Annual award established 'to perpetuate the memory of Richard Imison, to acknowledge the encouragement he gave to writers working in the medium of radio, and in memory of the support and friendship he invariably offered writers in general, and radio writers in particular'. Administered by the **Society of Authors** and generally sponsored by the **Peggy Ramsay Foundation**, the purpose is 'to encourage new talent and high standards in writing for radio by selecting the radio drama by a writer new to radio which, in the opinion of the judges, is the best of those submitted.' An adaptation for radio of a piece originally written for the stage, television or film is not eligible. Any radio drama first transmitted in the UK between 1 January and 31 December by a writer or writers new to radio, is eligible, provided the work is an original piece for radio and it is the first dramatic work by the writer(s) that has been broadcast. Submission may be made by any party to the production in the form of two copies of an audio cassette (not-returnable) accompanied by a nomination form.

2003 winners: Nell Lyshon and Steven McAanena *Milk*; Celia Bryce *The Skate Grinder*.
PRIZE £1500.

The Independent
Foreign Fiction Prize

c/o Literature Department, Arts Council of England, 14 Great Peter Street, London SW1P 3NQ
☎020 7973 5325 Fax 020 7973 6590
✉ info.literature@artscouncil.org.uk
www.artscouncil.org.uk

Awarded for translated fiction by living authors first published in Britain in the year preceding the award. 2004 winner: *Soldiers of Salamis* by Javier Cercas, translated by Anne McLean.

PRIZE £10,000 shared equally between author and translator.

The International IMPAC
Dublin Literary Award

Dublin City Library & Archive, 138–144 Pearse Street, Dublin 2, Republic of Ireland
☎00 353 1 674 4802 Fax 00 353 1 674 4879
✉ dubaward@iol.ie
www.impacdublinaward.ie

Established 1995. Sponsored by Dublin City Council and a US-based productivity improvement firm, IMPAC, this prize is awarded for a work of fiction written and published in the English language or written in a language other than English and published in English translation. Initial nominations are made by municipal public libraries in major and capital cities worldwide, each library putting forward up to three books to the international panel of judges in Dublin. 2003 winner: Orhan Pamuk *My Name is Red*.

PRIZE €100,000 (if the winning book is in English translation, the prize is shared €75,000 to the author and €25,000 to the translator).

International Reading Association
Literacy Award

International Reading Association, 800 Barksdale Road, PO Box 8139, Newark, Delaware 19714–8139, USA
☎001 302 731 1600 Fax 001 302 731 1057

Executive Director *Alan E. Farstrup*

The International Reading Association is a non-profit education organisation devoted to improving reading instruction and promoting literacy worldwide. In addition to the US $15,000 award presented each year on International Literacy Day (September 8), the organisation gives more than 25 awards in recognition of achievement in reading research, writing for children, media coverage of literacy and literacy instruction.

International Student Playscript Competition
See **University of Hull** under *UK Writers' Courses*

Jerwood Aldeburgh First Collection Prize
The Poetry Trust, The Cut, 9 New Cut, Halesworth IP19 8BY
☎01986 835950
✉ info@thepoetrytrust.org
www.thepoetrytrust.org
Contact *Naomi Jaffe*

Awarded to the author/s of what in the opinion of the panel of judges is/are the best first full collection/s of poetry published in Great Britain and Eire in the preceding twelve months. The prize, sponsored for fourteen years by the Aldeburgh Bookshop, was relaunched in 2003 with substantial new funding from the Jerwood Charitable Foundation. The winner/s will receive £2000 plus an invitation to read at the **Aldeburgh Poetry Festival** the following year. 2004 joint winners: Martha Kapos, Helena Nelson and Matthew Welton.

Jewish Quarterly Literary Prizes
PO Box 35042, London NW1 7XH
☎020 7284 1117 Fax 020 7284 1117
Contact *Gerald Don*

Formerly the H.H. Wingate Prize. Annual awards (one for fiction and one for non-fiction) for works which best stimulate an interest in and awareness of themes of Jewish interest. Books must have been published in the UK in the year of the award and be written in English by an author resident in Britain, the Commonwealth, Israel, Republic of Ireland or South Africa. 2004 winners: David Grossman *Someone to Run With* (fiction); Amos Elon *The Pity of It All* (non-fiction).
PRIZES £4000 each.

Samuel Johnson Prize for Non-Fiction
See **The BBCFour Samuel Johnson Prize for Non-Fiction**

Mary Vaughan Jones Award
Cyngor Llyfrau Cymru (Welsh Books Council), Castell Brychan, Aberystwyth SY23 2JB
☎01970 624151 Fax 01970 625385

✉ wbc.children@wbc.org.uk
www.wbc.org.uk
Contact *The Administrator*

Triennial award for distinguished services in the field of children's literature in Wales over a considerable period of time. 2003 winner: Elfyn Pritchard.
AWARD Silver trophy.

Keats–Shelley Prize
Keats–Shelley Memorial Association, 117 Cheyne Walk, London SW10 0ES
☎020 7352 2180 Fax 020 7352 6705
✉ harrietcullenuk@yahoo.com
www.keats-shelley.com
Contact *Harriet Cullen*

Established 1998. Annual award to promote the study and appreciation of Keats and Shelley, especially in the universities, and of creative writing inspired by the younger Romantic poets. Two categories: essay and poem; open to all ages and nationalities. Previous winners: Jane Draycott, Joe Francis, Leonie Rushforth, Stephen Burley, Linda Rose Parkes, Olivia McCannon, David Olshansky.
PRIZE £3000 distributed between the winners of the two categories.

The Keeley–Sherrard Translation Award
Poetry Greece, Mitropolitou Athanasiou 10, 3rd Parados, Corfu 49100, Greece
☎00 302 661 047990 Fax 00 302 661 047990
✉ wendyholborow@hotmail.com
users.otenet.gr/~wendyhol/poetry_greece/
Contact *Wendy Holborow*

Annual award in memory of the late Philip Sherrard who worked closely with Edmund Keeley translating many Greek poets into English. The award is for Greek poetry translated into English. Potential translators should contact Poetry Greece for further information.

The Petra Kenney Poetry Competition
PO Box 32, Filey YO14 9YG
✉ morgan@kenney.uk.net
www.petrapoetrycompetition.co.uk
Contact *Secretary*

Established 1995. Annual poetry award. Original, unpublished poems up to 80 lines on any theme. Closing date: 1 December. Entry fee: £3 per poem. Send s.a.e. for rules and entry form.
PRIZES £1000 (1st); £500 (2nd); £250 (3rd)

and three highly commended prizes of £125 each; plus publication in *Writers' Forum* and inscribed Royal Brierley Crystal Vase to each winner. New prizes for comic verse: £250 (1st); £124 (2nd) and Young poets (14–18): £250 (1st); £125 (2nd).

Kent & Sussex Poetry Society Open Competition

13 Ruscombe Close, Southborough, Tunbridge Wells TN4 0SG
☎01892 543862

Chairman *Clive R. Eastwood*

Annual competition. Entry fee: £3 per poem, maximum 40 lines.
PRIZES £1000 (total).

Kiriyama Pacific Rim Book Prize

Kiriyama Institute, 650 Delancy St, Suite 101, San Francisco, CA 94107, USA
☎001 415 777 1628 Fax 001 415 777 1646
✉ admin@kiriyamaprize.org
www.kiriyamaprize.org

Contact *Jeannine Cuevas*, Manager

Founded 1996 with the aim of promoting books that contribute to greater understanding and cooperation among the peoples and nations of the Pacific Rim and South Asia, this annual award takes its name from the Reverend Seiyu Kiriyama. Entry details may be obtained from the address above or from the website. 2002 winners: Shan Sa *The Girl Who Played Go* (fiction); Inga Clendinnen *Dancing With Strangers* (non-fiction).
PRIZES $30,000, divided between both winners.

Kraszna-Krausz Book Awards

122 Fawnbrake Avenue, London SE24 0BZ
☎020 7738 6701 Fax 020 7738 6701
✉ awards@k-k.org.uk
www.k-k.org.uk

Administrator *Andrea Livingstone*

Established 1985. Annual award to encourage and recognise oustanding achievements in the publishing and writing of books on the art, practice, history and technology of photography and the moving image (film, television, video and related screen media). Books in any language, published worldwide, are eligible. Entries must be submitted by publishers only. Prizes for books on still photography alternate annually with those for books on the moving image (2004: photography). 2003 winners: Giuliana Bruno *Atlas of Emotion: Journeys in*

Art, Architecture and Film; Roger Smither (ed.) and Catherine Surowiec (associate ed.) *This Film is Dangerous: A Celebration of Nitrate Film*.
PRIZES £5000 in each of the main categories; £1000 special commendations.

Lakeland Book of the Year Awards

Cumbria Tourist Board, Ashleigh, Holly Road, Windermere LA23 2AQ
☎01539 444444 Fax 01539 444041
✉ slindsay@gocumbria.org
www.golakes.co.uk

Contact *Sheila Lindsay*

Established in 1984 by local author and broadcaster Hunter Davies in conjunction with the Cumbria Tourist Board, the books entered can be about any aspect of life in the county of Cumbria, from local history books and walking guides to novels and poetry. The contest attracts entries from both new and established authors. Since the establishment of the awards they have grown in importance and popularity with the 2003 event attracting 60 entries, all competing for the Hunter Davies Prize for the Lakeland Book of the Year.

In addition to the Hunter Davies Prize there are currently five categories including Award for Guides, Walks and Places; Award for People and Social History; Award for Arts and Culture; Award for Heritage and Tradition; and the Best Illustrated Book. Sponsors include Titus Wilson and Son Ltd, the Bill Rollinson Trust, the Cumberland Building Society and Barclays. Closing date for entries is mid-March. The awards are presented at a charity luncheon in early June.
AWARDS £100 for each category together with a framed certificate. Overall winner of the Hunter Davies Prize for the Lakeland Book of the Year also receives a cheque for £100 and a framed certificate.

Lancashire County Library Children's Book of the Year Award

Lancashire County Library Headquarters, County Hall, PO Box 61, Preston PR1 8RJ
☎01772 534040 Fax 01772 264043
✉ jean.wolstenholme@lcl.lancscc.gov.uk

Manager, Young People's Service *Jean Wolstenholme*

Established 1986. Annual award, presented in June for a work of original fiction suitable for 12–14-year-olds. The winner is chosen by 13–14-year-old secondary school pupils in Lancashire. Books must have been published between 1 September and 31 August in the previous year of the award and authors must be UK and Republic of Ireland residents. Final entry date: 1 September each year. 2003 winner: Julie Bertagna *Exodus*.

PRIZE £500, plus engraved glass decanter.

Lannan Literary Award

Lannan Foundation, 313 Read Street, Santa Fe, New Mexico 87501, USA
☎001 505 986 8160
www.lannan.org

Established 1989. Annual awards given to writers of exceptional poetry, fiction and non-fiction who have made a significant contribution to English-language literature, as well as emerging writers of distinctive literary merit who have demonstrated potential for outstanding future work. On occasion, the Foundation recognises a writer for lifetime achievement. Candidates for the awards are recommended to the Foundation by a network of writers, literary scholars, publishers and editors. Applications for the awards are not accepted.

Legend Writing Award

39 Emmanuel Road, Hastings TN34 3LB
www.legendwritingaward.com
Contact *Legend Coordinator*

Established 2001. Annual award to encourage new fiction writers resident in the UK. The competition is for short stories of 2000 words maximum and there is no set theme. Closing date: 31 August. Entry fee: £4.50. Rules/entry form available from website or by sending s.a.e. to address above. The competition is organised by Hastings Writers' Group and prize-winning entries are selected by its patron, author, David Gemmell.

PRIZES £500 (1st); £250 (2nd); £100 (3rd); plus three runners-up prizes of £50.

The Library Association Awards
See **CILIP: The Chartered Institute of Library and Information Professionals** individual awards

Lichfield Prize

Lichfield Garrick, Castle Duke, Lichfield WS13 6HR
☎01543 412110
✉ lichfield-prize@lichfielddc./gov.uk

Contact *Maria Whatton*

Founded 1989. An entry must be a novel and an original work of fiction. No entered manuscript should have been previously published. The judges are looking for a quality manuscript with wide audience appeal and commercial sales potential. Short-listed authors will be invited to the Lichfield Prize presentation during the **Lichfield Festival** in July 2004. Final entry date 30 April 2004.

PRIZE £5000.

The Astrid Lindgren Memorial Award for Literature

Swedish National Council for Cultural Affairs, PO Box 8743, SE-103 98 Stockholm, Sweden
☎00 46 8 519 264 00/08
Fax 00 46 8 519 264 99
✉ anna.cokorilo@kulturradet.se
www.alma.se

Project Manager *Anna Cokorilo*

Established 2002 by the Swedish government in memory of the children's author Astrid Lindgren. Administered by the Swedish National Council for Cultural Affairs, it is an international award for children's and young people's literature given annually to one or more recipients, irrespective of language or nationality. Writing, illustrating and storytelling, as well as reading promotion activities may be awarded. Selected organisations worldwide will be invited to submit nominations; jury members may also contribute nominations. Inaugural winner: Christine Nostlinger.

AWARD SEK5 million (approx. €500,000)

The London Writers Competition

Room 224a, The Town Hall, Wandsworth High Street, London SW18 2PU
☎020 8871 8711   Fax 020 8871 7630
✉ arts@wandsworth.gov.uk
www.wandsworth.gov.uk

Contact *Wandsworth Arts Office*

Arranged by Wandsworth Borough Council in association with Roehampton, University of Surrey. An annual competition, open to all writers who live, work or study in the Greater London area. Work must not have been published previously. There are four sections: poetry, short story, play and fiction for children.

PRIZES £1000 for each section, with a first prize of £600. Poetry and story winners are published and the winning play is showcased.

The Elizabeth Longford Prize for Historical Biography

The Society of Authors, 85 Drayton Gardens, London SW10 9SB
☎020 7373 6642   Fax 020 7373 5768
✉ info@societyofauthors.org
www.societyofauthors.org

Established in 2003 in memory of Elizabeth Longford and sponsored by Flora Fraser and Peter Soros. Awarded annually for a historical biography published in the year preceding the prize. No unsolicited submissions. 2003 winner: David Gilmour *The Long Recessional*.
PRIZE £3000.

Longman-*History Today* Book of the Year Award

c/o History Today, 20 Old Compton Street, London W1D 4TW
☎020 7534 8000

Contacts *Peter Furtado, Marion Soldan*

Established 1993. Annual award set up as joint initiative between the magazine *History Today* and publisher Longman (**Pearson Education**) to mark the past links between the two organisations, to encourage new writers, and to promote a wider public understanding of, and enthusiasm for, the study and publication of history. Submissions are made by publishers only. 2004 winner: Alan Bray *The Friend*.
PRIZE £1000 (see *History Today* from July 2004).

Sir William Lyons Award

The Guild of Motoring Writers, 39 Beswick Avenue, Ensbury Park, Bournemouth BH10 4EY
☎01202 518808 Fax 01202 518808
✉ gensec@gomw.co.uk
www.guildofmotoringwriters.co.uk

Contact *Patricia Lodge*

An annual competitive award to encourage young people in automotive journalism and to foster interests in motoring and the motor industry. Entrance by two essays and interview with Awards Committee. Applicants must be British, aged 17–23 and resident in UK. Final entry date: 30 September.

McColvin Medal

See **CILIP: The Chartered Institute of Library and Information Professionals Besterman/McColvin Medal**

W.J.M. Mackenzie Book Prize

Political Studies Association, Department of Politics, University of Newcastle, Newcastle upon Tyne NE1 7RU
☎0191 222 8021 Fax 0191 222 3499
✉ psa@ncl.ac.uk
www.psa.ac.uk

PSA Executive Director *Jack Arthurs*

Established 1987. Annual award to best work of political science published in the UK during the previous year. Submissions from publishers only. Final entry date: 31 October. Prizes are judged in the year following publication and awarded the year after that. The 2001 winner was David McKay for *Designing Europe: Comparative Lessons from the Federal Experience*.

McKitterick Prize

Society of Authors, 84 Drayton Gardens, London SW10 9SB
☎020 7373 6642 Fax 020 7373 5768
✉ info@societyofauthors.org
www.societyofauthors.org

Contact *Awards Secretary*

Annual award for a full-length novel in the English language, first published in the UK or unpublished. Open to writers over 40 who have not had any novel published other than the one submitted (excluding works for children). Closing date: 20 December. 2003 winner: Mary Lawson *Crow Lake*.
PRIZE £4000.

Enid McLeod Prize

Franco-British Society, Room 227, Linen Hall, 162–168 Regent Street, London W1R 5TB
☎020 7734 0815 Fax 020 7734 0815

Executive Secretary *Kate Brayn*

Established 1982. Annual award to the author of the work of literature published in the UK which, in the opinion of the judges, has contributed most to Franco-British understanding. Any full-length work written in English by a citizen of the UK, Commonwealth, Republic of Ireland, Pakistan, Bangladesh and South Africa. No English translation of a book written originally in any other language will be considered. Nominations from publishers for books published between 1 January and 31 December of the year of the prize. Closing date: 31 December. 2003 winner: Andrea Stuart *Rose of Martinique*.
PRIZE Cheque.

Macmillan Prize for a Children's Picture Book Illustration

Macmillan Children's Books, 20 New Wharf Road, London N1 9RR
☎020 7014 6124 Fax 020 7014 6142
✉ i.blundell@macmillan.co.uk
www.panmacmillan.com

Contact *Imogen Blundell, Macmillan Children's Books*

Set up in order to stimulate new work from young illustrators in art schools, and to help them start their professional lives. Fiction or non-fiction. **Macmillan** have the option to publish any of the prize winners.

PRIZES £1000 (1st); £500 (2nd); £250 (3rd).

The Mail on Sunday Novel Competition

Postal box address changes each year (see below)

Annual award established 1983. Judges look for a story/character that springs to life in the 'tantalising opening 50–150 words of a novel'. Details of the competition, including the postal box address, are published in *The Mail on Sunday* in July/August. 2003 winner: Christine Harrison.

AWARDS (1st) £400 book tokens and a writing course at the **Arvon Foundation**; (2nd) £300 tokens; (3rd) £200 tokens; three further prizes of £150 tokens each.

The Mail on Sunday/ John Llewellyn Rhys Prize

Booktrust, Book House, 45 East Hill, London SW18 2QZ
☎020 8516 2972 Fax 020 8516 2978
✉ tarryn@booktrust.org.uk
www.booktrust.org.uk

Contact *Tarryn McKay*

Established 1942. An annual young writer's award for a memorable work of any kind. Entrants must be under the age of 35 at the time of publication; books must have been published in the UK in the year of the award. The author must be a citizen of the UK or the Commonwealth, writing in English. 2003 winner: Mary Laven *Virgins of Venice*.

PRIZE £5000 (1st); £500 for shortlisted entries.

The Man Booker Prize for Fiction

Colman Getty PR, Middlesex House,
34–42 Cleveland Street, London W1T 4JE
☎020 7631 2666 Fax 0207631 2699
✉ pr@colmangettypr.co.uk
www.themanbookerprize.com

Contact *Cathryn Summerhayes* (Submissions)

The Booker Prize for Fiction was originally set up by Booker plc in 1968 to reward merit, raise the stature of the author in the eyes of the public and encourage an interest in contemporary fiction. In April 2002 it was announced that the Man Group had been chosen by the Booker Prize Foundation as the new sponsor of the Booker Prize. The sponsorship is due to run for five years during which time the prize will be known as the Man Booker Prize for Fiction. United Kingdom publishers may enter up to two full-length novels, with scheduled publication dates between 1 October 2003 and 30 September 2004. In addition, any title by an author who has previously won the Booker or Man Booker Prize and any title by an author who has been shortlisted in the last ten years may be submitted. 2003 winner was *Vernon God Little*, D.B.C. Pierre.

PRIZE The winner receives £50,000. The six shortlisted authors each receive £2500.

Marsh Award for Children's Literature in Translation

National Centre for Research in Children's Literature, University of Surrey Roehampton, Digby Stuart College, Roehampton Lane, London SW15 5PH
☎020 8392 3008 Fax 020 8392 3819
✉ g.lathey@roehampton.ac.uk

Contact *Dr Gillian Lathey*

Established 1995 and sponsored by the Marsh Christian Trust, the award aims to encourage translation of foreign children's books into English. It is a biennial award (next award: 2005), open to British translators of books for 4–16-year-olds, published in the UK by a British publisher. Any category will be considered with the exception of encyclopedias and reference books. No electronic books. 2003 winner: Anthea Bell for her translation of *Where Were You Robert?* by Hans Magnus Enzensberger.

PRIZE £1000.

Marsh Biography Award

The English-Speaking Union, Dartmouth House, 37 Charles Street, London W1J 5ED
☎020 7529 1565 Fax 020 7495 6108
✉ tim_rolph@esu.org
www.esu.org

Contact *Tim Rolph*

A biennial award for the most significant biography published over a two-year period by a British publisher. Next award October 2005. 2003 winner: Brenda Maddox *Rosalind Franklin, The Dark Lady of DNA*.

AWARD Membership of the ESU and £4000, plus a silver trophy presented at a dinner.

Colin Mears Award

See **CILIP: The Chartered Institute of Library and Information Professionals Kate Greenaway Medal**

Medical Book Awards

The Society of Authors, 84 Drayton Gardens, London SW10 9SB
☎020 7373 6642 Fax 020 7373 5768
✉ info@society of authors.org
www.societyofauthors.org

Contact *Secretary, Medical Writers Group*

Annual awards sponsored by the Royal Society of Medicine. Nine categories for medical texts published in the twelve months preceding the deadline. Contact the **Society of Authors** for entry details. Closing date: 20 April.
PRIZES £6500 (total).

The Mercedes-Benz Award for the Montagu of Beaulieu Trophy

Guild of Motoring Writers, 39 Beswick Avenue, Ensbury Park, Bournemouth BH10 4EY
☎01202 518808 Fax 01202 518808
✉ gensec@gomw.co.uk
www.guildofmotoringwriters.co.uk

Contact *Patricia Lodge*

First presented by Lord Montagu on the occasion of the opening of the National Motor Museum at Beaulieu in 1972. Awarded annually to a member of the **Guild of Motoring Writers** who, in the opinion of the nominated jury, has made the greatest contribution to recording in the English language the history of motoring or motor cycling in a published book or article, film, television or radio script, or research manuscript available to the public. Cash PRIZE sponsored by Mercedes-Benz UK.

Mere Literary Festival Open Competition

'Lawrences', Old Hollow, Mere BA12 6EG
☎01747 860475
www.merewilts.org.uk

Contact *Mrs Adrienne Howell* (Events Organiser)

Annual open competition which alternates between short stories and poetry. The winners are announced at the **Mere Literary Festival** during the second week of October. The 2005 competition is for poetry with a closing date for entries in July. For further details, including entry fees and form, access the website or contact the address above from 1 March with s.a.e.
Cash PRIZES.

Meyer-Whitworth Award

Arts Council England, 14 Great Peter Street, London SW1P 3NQ

☎020 7333 0100
www.artscouncil.org.uk

Contact *Theatre Writing, Theatre Department*

This annual award is intended to help further the careers of UK playwrights who are not yet established, and to draw contemporary theatre writers to the public's attention. Nominations are made by directors of professional theatre companies. Plays must have been written in the English language and produced professionally in the UK in the 12 months between 1 August 2004 and 31 July 2005. Candidates will have had no more than two of their plays professionally produced. No writer who has won the award previously may re-apply and no play that has been submitted previously for the award is eligible. Further details and application form from the address above.
AWARD £8000.

MIND Book of the Year

Granta House, 15–19 Broadway E15 4BQ
☎020 8215 2305 Fax 020 8215 2269
✉ h.finch@mind.org.uk
www.mind.org.uk

Established 1981. Annual award, in memory of Sir Allen Lane, for the author of a book published in the current year (fiction or non-fiction), which furthers public understanding of mental health problems. 2003 winner: Studs Terkel *Will the Circle be Unbroken? Reflections on Death and Dignity*.

The Mitchell Prize for Art History/ The Eric Mitchell Prize

c/o The Burlington Magazine, 14–16 Duke's Road, London WC1H 9SZ
☎020 7388 8157 Fax 020 7388 1230
✉ annette.bradshaw@burlington.org.uk

Executive Director *Caroline Elam*
Contact *Annette Bradshaw*

Established 1977 by art collector, philanthropist and businessman, Jan Mitchell, to draw attention to exceptional achievements in the history of art. Consists of two prizes: The Mitchell Prize, given for an outstanding and original contribution to the study and understanding of visual arts, and The Eric Mitchell Prize, given for the outstanding exhibition catalogue of the year. The prizes are awarded to authors of books in English that have been published in the previous 12 months. Nominations should be submitted by publishers before the end of April. Previous winners: The Mitchell Prize: John Golding *Paths to the*

Absolute; The Eric Mitchell Prize: Michael Bury *The Print in Italy 1550–1620*.
PRIZES $10,000 each.

Momaya Press Short Story Writing Competition

Momaya Press, J75 Ducane Court, Balham High Road, London SW17 7JX
☎020 8673 9616
✉ infouk@momayapress.com
www.momayapress.com

Contact *Monisha Saldanha*

Established 2004. Annual competition open to writers in the English language worldwide. Entries, which should not have been published previously, can be in any style and format and on any subject, 2500 words maximum. Entry fee: £6; final entry date: 1 July 2005. Submissions via entry form on the website.

PRIZES £130 (1st); £65 (2nd), plus 8 honourable mentions; all winners are published in the *Momaya Annual Review*.

Scott Moncrieff Prize

See **The Translators Association Awards**

The Oscar Moore Screenwriting Prize

The Oscar Moore Foundation, c/o Screen International, 33–39 Bowling Green Lane, London EC1R 0DA
☎020 7505 8080 Fax 020 7505 8087
✉ sade.sharp@emap.com
www.screendaily.com

Coordinator *Sade Sharp*

Established 1997. Annual prize in honour of Oscar Moore, former *Guardian* columnist and editor-in-chief of *Screen International*, who died in 1996. The genre for the competition changes each year (thriller for 2004, comedy for 2005), as does the closing date. Contact the Foundation to obtain an entry form. 2003 winners: Ben Gooder and Philip Greenacre *A Fine Line*.

AWARD £10,000 cash, plus week-long script development course courtesy of Arista, and performance of the winning script by the Script Factory.

Shiva Naipaul Memorial Prize

The Spectator, 56 Doughty Street, London WC1N 2LL
☎020 7405 1706 Fax 020 7242 0603
✉ lucy@spectator.co.uk

Contact *Lucy Vickery*

Established 1985. Annual prize given to an English language writer of any nationality under the age of 35 for an essay of not more than 4000 words describing a culture alien to the writer. Final entry date is 30 April.
PRIZE £3000.

NASEN Special Educational Needs Book Awards

NASEN House, 4–5 Amber Business Village, Amber Close, Amington, Tamworth B77 4RP
☎01827 311 500 Fax 01827 313 005
✉ welcome@nasen.org.uk
www.nasen.org.uk

Organised by the National Association for Special Education Needs (NASEN) and the *Times Educational Supplement* (TES). Three awards: The Children's Book Award, for the book that most successfully provides a positive image of children with special educational needs; The Academic Book Award celebrates the work of authors and editors who have made an outstanding contribution to the theory and practice of special education; The Books for Teaching and Learning Award is presented for curriculum materials for pupils or teachers in early years, primary or secondary phases. Eligibility: books must have been published in the UK within the year (Academic) preceding the award.
PRIZE £500 each category.

National Poetry Anthology

United Press, Admail 3735, London EC1B 1JB
☎0870 240 6190 Fax 0870 240 6191

Contact *Peter Quinn*, Publishing Director

Free-to-enter annual poetry competition. Entrants may submit three poems (of 160 words and 20 lines maximum each) by annual closing date of 30 June. Organisers select around 200 regional winners which are published in the annual book, the *National Poetry Anthology*. The 200 winners all receive a free copy of the book and vote for one overall champion. This person receives the prize when the book is published in the spring.
PRIZE £1000, plus trophy to keep in perpetuity.

National Poetry Competition

The Poetry Society, 22 Betterton Street, London WC2H 9BX
☎020 7420 9880 Fax 020 7240 4818
✉ info@poetrysociety.org.uk
www.poetrysociety.org.uk

Contact *Competition Organiser (WH)*

One of Britain's major open poetry competitions. Closing date: 31 October. Poems on any theme, up to 40 lines. For rules and entry form send s.a.e. to the competition organiser at the address above or enter the competition via the website.

PRIZES £5000 (1st); £1000 (2nd); £500 (3rd); plus 10 commendations of £50.

National Sporting Club Sports Book Awards (in association with WHSmith)

NSC, Café Royal, 68 Regent Street, London W1B 5EL
☎020 7437 0144 Fax 020 7437 5441
✉ david@nationalsportingclub.co.uk
www.nationalsportingclub.co.uk
Chairman *David Willis*

Established 2003. Annual awards presented at a lunch at the Café Royal in London in May. In the inaugural year there were four categories of awards: autobiography, biography, best illustrator or best new writer. Books submitted must have been published in the previous calendar year. Final entry date: 15 December. 2003 winner: Leo McInstry *Bobby and Jack, Brothers in Conflict*.

Bill Naughton Short Story Competition

Box No. 2004, Aghamore, Ballyhaunis, Co. Mayo, Republic of Ireland
www.aghamoregaa.com/society/knschool.htm

Organised by the **Kenny/Naughton Society** (see entry under *Literary Societies*). Stories may be on any topic and no more than 2500 words in length. All work must be unpublished; typed scripts only with no name or address appearing on the work. Entry fee: £5 or €6 per story; three stories may be submitted for the price of two. Closing date: 1 September each year. No entry form required.

PRIZES £150 (€200) (1st); £100 (€130) (2nd); £50 (€65) (3rd). Best stories published in a collection entitled *Splinters*.

Nestlé Smarties Book Prize

Booktrust, Book House, 45 East Hill, London SW18 2QZ
☎020 8516 2972 Fax 020 8516 2978
✉ hannah@booktrust.org.uk
www.booktrusted.com
Contact *Hannah Rutland*

Established 1985 to encourage high standards and stimulate interest in books for children, this prize is given for a children's book (fiction or poetry), written in English by a citizen of the UK or an author resident in the UK, and published in the UK in the year ending 31 October. There are three age-group categories: 5 and under, 6–8 and 9–11. Uniquely, the shortlist for each age category is judged by classes of schoolchildren, who enter a competition to win a chance to be Young Judges. 50 classes from each age category judge the books, deciding who gets Gold, Silver and Bronze. The class projects entered for the judging process are then judged to see which classes will come to London for the prize presentation. 2003 Gold Award winners: Ursula Jones and Russell Ayto *The Witch's Children and the Queen* (5 and under); S.F. Said *Varjek Paws* (6–8); David Almond *The Fire-Eaters* (9–11); Sally Gardner *The Countess' Calamity* (Kids' Clubs Special Network Award).

PRIZES in each category: £2500 (gold); £1500 (silver); £500 (bronze).

The New Writer
Prose & Poetry Prizes

The New Writer, PO Box 60, Cranbrook TN17 2ZR
☎01580 212626 Fax 01580 212041
✉ admin@thenewwriter.com
www.thenewwriter.com
Contact *Merric Davidson*

Established 1997. Annual award. Open to all poets writing in the English language for an original, previously unpublished poem or collection of six to ten poems. Also open to writers of short stories and novellas/serials, features, articles, essays and interviews. Final entry date: 31 October. Previous winners: Mark Granier, Ros Barber, Celia de Fréine, John Hilton.

PRIZES (total) £2000, plus publication in annual collection published by *The New Writer*.

'The Nibbies'
See **British Book Awards**

Nielsen Gold & Platinum Book Awards

Nielsen BookScan, Woolmead House West, Bear Lane, Farnham GU9 7LG
☎01252 742555 Fax 01252 742556
✉ gold&platinumawards@nielsenbookscan. co.uk
www.nielsenbookscan.co.uk
Contact *Pamela Dodd*

Established in 2000 to award actual consumer purchases of a title through UK bookshops. Awarded to any title, in all its editions, that sells more than 500,000 copies (Gold) or one million copies (Platinum) over a period of five consecutive years.

AWARDS Commemorative plaque issued by the publisher to the author.

No Love Lost Poetry Anthology Contest

See **Hidden Brook Press International Poetry Anthology Contest**

Nobel Prize

The Nobel Foundation, PO Box 5232, 102 45 Stockholm, Sweden
☎00 46 8 663 0920 Fax 00 46 8 660 3847
www.nobel.se

Contact *Information Section*

Awarded yearly for outstanding achievement in physics, chemistry, physiology or medicine, literature and peace. Founded by Alfred Nobel, a chemist who proved his creative ability by inventing dynamite. In general, individuals cannot nominate someone for a Nobel Prize. The rules vary from prize to prize but the following are eligible to do so for Literature: members of the Swedish Academy and of other academies, institutions and societies similar to it in constitution and purpose; professors of literature and of linguistics at universities or colleges; Nobel Laureates in Literature; presidents of authors' organisations which are representative of the literary production in their respective countries. British winners of the literature prize, first granted in 1901, include Rudyard Kipling, John Galsworthy and Winston Churchill. Recent winners: Derek Walcott (St Lucia); Toni Morrison (USA); Kenzaburo Oe (Japan); Seamus Heaney (Ireland); Wislawa Szymborska (Poland); Dario Fo (Italy); José Saramago (Portugal); Günter Grass (Germany); Gao Xingjian (France); V.S. Naipaul (Great Britain); Imre Kertész (Hungary). Nobel Laureate in Literature 2003: J.M. Coetzee (South Africa).

The Noma Award for Publishing Africa

PO Box 128, Witney OX8 5XU
☎01993 775235 Fax 01993 709265
✉ maryljay@aol.com
www.nomaaward.org

Contact *Mary Jay*, Secretary to the Managing Committee

Established 1979. Annual award, founded by the late Shoichi Noma, President of Kodansha Ltd, Tokyo. The award is for an outstanding book, published in Africa by an African writer, in three categories: scholarly and academic; literature and creative writing; children's books. Entries, by publishers only, by 31 March for a title published in the previous year. Maximum number of three entries. Previous winners: Abosede Emanuel *Odun Ifa/Ifa Festival*; Hamdi Sakku *The Arabic Novel: Bibliography and Critical Introduction 1865–1995*; Elinor Sisulu *In Our Lifetime*.

PRIZE US$10,000 and presentation plaque.

C.B. Oldman Prize

Special Libraries & Archives, University of Aberdeen, King's College, Aberdeen AB24 3SW
☎01224 274266 Fax 01224 273891
✉ r.turbet@abdn.ac.uk

Contact *Richard Turbet*

Established 1989 by the International Association of Music Libraries, UK & Ireland Branch. Annual award for best book of music bibliography, librarianship or reference published the year before last (i.e. books published in 2002 considered for the 2003 prize). Previous winners: Michael Talbot, Donald Clarke, John Parkinson, John Wagstaff, Stanley Sadie, William Waterhouse, Richard Turbet, John Gillaspie, David Fallows, Arthur Searle, Graham Johnson.

PRIZE £200.

Ondaatje Prize

See **The Royal Society of Literature Ondaatje Prize**

Open Window Poetry Anthology Contest

See **Hidden Brook Press International Poetry Anthology Contests**

Orange Prize for Fiction

Booktrust, 45 East Hill, London SW18 2QZ
☎020 8516 2972 Fax 020 8516 2978
✉ tarryn@booktrust.org.uk
www.orangeprize.com

Contact *Tarryn McKay*

Established 1996. Annual award founded by a group of senior women in publishing to 'create the opportunity for more women to be rewarded for their work and to be better known by the reading public'. Awarded for a full-length novel written in English by a woman of any nationality, and published in the UK between 1 April and 31 March of the following year. 2003 winner: Valerie Martin *Property*.

PRIZE £30,000 and a work of art (a limited edition bronze figurine known as 'The Bessie' in acknowledgement of anonymous prize endowment).

A new prize, the **Orange Prize for New Writers**, will be awarded for the first time in 2005. All first works of fiction, written by women of any age or nationality, published in the UK between 1 April 2004 and 31 March 2005, will be eligible (short story collections and novellas also eligible).

The Orwell Prize

Alive Events, Fulton House, Fulton Road, Wembley Park HA9 0TF
☎020 8584 0444 Fax 020 8584 0443
✉ orwell@aliveevents.co.uk
www.aliveevents.co.uk

Contact *Sue Dowsett*

Jointly established in 1993 by the George Orwell Memorial Fund and the *Political Quarterly* to encourage and reward writing in the spirit of Orwell's 'What I have most wanted to do ... is to make political writing into an art'. Two categories: book or pamphlet; newspaper and/or articles, features, columns, or sustained reportage on a theme in non-fiction or fiction. Submissions by editors, publishers or authors. 2004 winners: Robert Cooper *The Breaking of Nations*; special award by Reuters to the family of the late Hugo Young of *The Guardian* for *Supping with the Devils* and for his 'outstanding contribution to political journalism'.
Prizes £1000 for each category.

Ottakar's and Faber National Poetry Competition

Ottakar's Plc, Brewery House, 36 Milford Street, Salisbury SP1 2AP
☎01722 428500 Fax 01722 428502
✉ enquiries@ottakars.co.uk
www.ottakars.co.uk

Contacts *Jon Howells, Jo James*

Established 1997. Annual competition in support of National Book Day and to promote poetry within Ottakar's bookshops and their local communities. Maximum 40 lines; only one poem per applicant. The poems, which must be previously unpublished, can be on any subject and in any style. 2003 winner: Josephine Walker.
Prize £500 (National winner) plus publication in a national newspaper.

The Wilfred Owen Award for Poetry

c/o 17 Belmont, Shrewsbury SY1 1TE
☎01743 460089

www.1914-18.co.uk/owen

Contact *Michael Grayer*

Established in 1988 by the **Wilfred Owen Association**. Given to a poet whose poetry reflects the spirit of Owen's work in its thinking, expression and inspiration. Applications are not sought; the decision is made by the Association's committee. Previous winner: Seamus Heaney.

Award A silver and gunmetal work of art, suitably decorated and engraved.

OWG Awards for Excellence

Outdoor Writers' Guild, PO Box 118, Twickenham TW1 2XB
☎020 8538 9468 Fax 020 8538 9468
www.owg.org.uk

Contact *Hazelle Jackson*

Established 1980. Annual awards by the **Outdoor Writers' Guild** to raise the standard of outdoor writing, journalism, broadcasting and photography. Winning categories include guidebook, outdoor book, feature (one-off), feature (regular), photography. Open to OWG members only. Final entry date: May.

The Oxford Weidenfeld Translation Prize

St Anne's College, Oxford OX2 6HS
☎01865 274820 Fax 01865 274899
✉ patrick.mcguinness@st-annes.ox.ac.uk

Contact *The Fellows' Secretary*

Established in 1996 by publisher Lord Weidenfeld to encourage good translation into English. Annual award to the translator(s) of a work of fiction, poetry or drama written in any living European language. Translations must have been published in the previous year. Submissions from publishers only. For further information, contact *Dr Patrick McGuinness* at the address above.
Prize £1000.

PEN Awards

See **J.R. Ackerley Prize**; **S.T. Dupont Golden PEN Award for Lifetime Distinguished Service to Literature**; **The Hessell-Tiltman Prize for History**

Samuel Pepys Award

Samuel Pepys Award Trust, Montreal House, Winson, Cirencester GL7 5EL

Established 2003. Biennial award (next in 2005) given by the Samuel Pepys Award Trust for a book that makes the greatest contribution to the understanding of Samuel Pepys, his times or his contemporaries. 2003 winner: Claire Tomalin *Samuel Pepys: The Unequalled Self.*

AWARD £2000 plus commemorative medal.

Peterloo Poets
Open Poetry Competition
The Old Chapel, Sand Lane, Calstock
PL18 9QX
☎01822 833473
✉ poets@peterloo.fsnet.co.uk
www.peterloopoets.co.uk

Contact *Harry Chambers*

Established 1986. Annual competition for unpublished English language poems of not more than 40 lines. Final entry date: 1 March. Send s.a.e. for rules and entry form. Previous winners: John Watts, Jem Poster, David Craig, Rodney Pybus, Debjani Chatterjee, Donald Atkinson, Romesh Gunesekera, Anna Crowe, Carol Ann Duffy, Mimi Khalvati, John Lyons, M.R. Peacocke, Alison Pryde, Carol Shergold, John Weston, Maureen Wilkinson, Chris Woods.

PRIZES £1500 (1st); £1000 (2nd); £500 (3rd); £100 (4th); plus 10 prizes of £50; 15–19 age group: 5 prizes of £100.

Poetry Business Competition
The Studio, Byram Arcade, Westgate,
Huddersfield HD1 1ND
☎01484 434840 Fax 01484 426566
✉ edit@poetrybusiness.co.uk
www.poetrybusiness.co.uk

Contact *The Competition Administrator*

Established 1986. Annual award which aims to discover and publish new writers. Entrants should submit a manuscript of poems. Winners will have their work published by the **Poetry Business** under the Smith/Doorstop imprint. Final entry date: end of October. Contact for conditions of entry. Previous winners include: Pauline Stainer, Michael Laskey, Mimi Khalvati, David Morley, Moniza Alvi, Selima Hill, Catherine Smith, Daljit Nagra.

PRIZES Publication of full collection; runners-up have pamphlets; 20 complimentary copies. Also cash prize (£1000) to be shared equally between all winners.

Poetry Life Poetry Competition
1 Blue Ball Corner, Water Lane, Winchester
SO23 0ER
freespace.virgin.net/poetry.life/
Contact *Adrian Bishop*

Established 1993. Open competition for original poems in any style which have not been pub-

lished in a book. Maximum length of 80 lines. Entry fee of £4 per poem. Send s.a.e. for details.

PRIZES £3000 (1st); £500 (2nd); £250 (3rd) plus 20 Special Commendations winning £25 book token.

The Poetry Society's National
Poetry Competition
See **National Poetry Competition**

The Portico Prize
The Portico Library, 57 Mosley Street,
Manchester M2 3HY
☎0161 236 6785 Fax 0161 236 6803
✉ librarian@theportico.org.uk
www.theportico.org.uk

Contact *Miss Emma Marigliano*

Established 1985. Administered by the Portico Library in Manchester. Biennial award for a work of fiction or non-fiction published between the two closing dates. Set wholly or mainly in the North West of England, including Cumbria and the High Peak District of Derbyshire. Next award: 2006. Previous winners include: Anthony Burgess *Any Old Iron*; Jenny Uglow *Elizabeth Gaskell: A Habit of Stories*. 2002 winner: Shelley Rhode *The Lowry Lexicon*.

PRIZE £3000.

The Dennis Potter
Screenwriting Award
BBC Broadcasting House, Whiteladies Road,
Bristol BS8 2LR
☎0117 974 7586

Editor *Jeremy Howe*

Annual award established in 1995 in memory of the late television playwright to 'nurture and encourage the work of new writers of talent and personal vision'. Submissions should be made through a BBC TV drama producer or an independent production company (no start date confirmed; contact the editor for further information).

The Premio Valle Inclán
See **The Translators Association Awards**

The Mathew Prichard Award
for Short Story Writing
Competition Secretary, 2 Rhododendron Close,
The Greenways, Cyn Coed, Cardiff CF23 7HS
www.samwaw.org.uk

Competition Organiser *Philip Beynon*
Competition Secretary *Marjorie Williams*

Established 1996 to provide sponsorship and

promote Wales and its writers. Entry fee: £5; NB scripts are not returned. Competition open to all writers in English; the final entry date is 28 February each year. Entry forms and information from website.

PRIZES A total of £2000.

V.S. Pritchett Memorial Prize

The Royal Society of Literature, Somerset House, Strand, London WC2R 1LA
☎020 7845 4676 Fax 020 7845 4679
✉ info@rslit.org
www.rslit.org

Established 1999. Awarded for a previously unpublished short story of between 2000 and 5000 words. For entry forms, please contact the Secretary. Closing date: 31 January. Entrants must be a citizen and/or resident of the UK and the Republic of Ireland.

PRIZE £1000.

Pulitzer Prizes

The Pulitzer Prize Board, 709 Journalism Building, Columbia University, 2950 Broadway, New York, NY 10027, USA
☎001 212 854 3841 Fax 001 212 854 3342
✉ pulitzer@www.pulitzer.org
www.pulitzer.org

Awards for journalism in US newspapers, and for published literature, drama and music by American nationals. 2004 winners include: Edward P. Jones *The Known World* (fiction); William Taubman *Kruschev: The Man and His Era* (biography); Franz Wright *Walking to Martha's Vineyard* (poetry).

Real Writers Short Story Awards

PO Box 170, Chesterfield S40 1FE
☎01246 238492
✉ info@real-writers.com
www.real-writers.com

Awards Coordinator *Lynne Patrick*

Established 1994. Annual award, open to anyone who writes in English. Maximum length: 5000 words; entry fee: £5. Optional full-page critique for additional fee. 2003 winner: Ginny Swart.

AWARDS £2500 (1st), plus section prizes. Prizewinners have the opportunity to pitch a novel to a leading publisher. Winning entries published in an anthology.

The Red House Children's Book Award

The Federation of Children's Book Groups, The Old Malt House, Aldbourne SN8 2DW

☎01672 540629 Fax 01672 541280
✉ marianneadey@aol.com

Coordinator *Marianne Adey*

Established 1980. Awarded annually for best book of fiction suitable for children. Unique in that it is judged by the children themselves. 2003 winner: *Skeleton Key*, Anthony Horowitz.

AWARD Portfolio of letters, drawings and comments from the children who took part in the judging. Silver bowls and trophy.

Trevor Reese Memorial Prize

Institute of Commonwealth Studies, University of London, 28 Russell Square, London WC1B 5DS
☎020 7862 8844 Fax 020 7862 8820

Contact *Events & Publicity Officer*

Established 1979 with the proceeds of contributions to a memorial fund to Dr Trevor Reese, Reader in Commonwealth Studies at the Institute and a distinguished scholar of imperial history (d.1976). Biennial award (next award 2006) for a scholarly work, usually by a single author, in the field of Imperial and Commonwealth History published in the preceding two academic years. All correspondence relating to the prize should be marked 'Trevor Reese Memorial Prize'.

PRIZE £1000.

Regional Press Awards

Press Gazette, Quantum House, 19 Scarbrook Road, Croydon CR9 1LX
☎020 8565 3056 Fax 020 8565 4462
✉ andrea@quantumbusinessmedia.com

Comprehensive range of journalist and newspaper awards for the regional press. Five newspapers of the year, by circulation and frequency, and a full list of journalism categories. Open to all regional journalists, whether freelance or staff. July event. Run by the *Press Gazette*.

Renault UK Journalist of the Year Award

Guild of Motoring Writers, 39 Beswick Avenue, Ensbury Park, Bournemouth BH10 4EY
☎01202 518808 Fax 01202 518808
✉ gensec@gomw.co.uk
www.guildofmotoringwriters.co.uk

Contact *Patricia Lodge*

Originally the Pierre Dreyfus Award and established 1977. Awarded annually by Renault UK Ltd in honour of Pierre Dreyfus, president director general of Renault 1955–75, to the member of the **Guild of Motoring Writers** who is judged to have made the most outstanding journalistic effort in any medium during the year. Particular emphasis is placed on initiative and endeavour.

John Llewellyn Rhys Prize
See **The Mail on Sunday/John Llewellyn Rhys Prize**

The Romantic Novel of the Year
57 Coniger Road, London SW6 3TB
☎020 7736 4968

Award Organiser *Mary de Laszio*

Established 1960. Annual award for the best romantic novel of the year, open to non-members as well as members of the **Romantic Novelists' Association**. Novels must be published in the UK between specified dates and authors must be based in the UK unless members of the RNA. 2004 winner: Jojo Moyes *Forbidden Fruit*. Send s.a.e. to the organiser for entry form.
AWARD £10,000.

Rooney Prize for Irish Literature
Rooney Prize, Strathin, Templecarrig, Delgany, Co. Wicklow, Republic of Ireland
☎00 353 1 287 4769/4376
Fax 00 353 1 287 2595
✉ rooneyprize@ireland.com

Contacts *Jim Sherwin, Thelma Cloake*

Established 1976. Annual award to encourage young Irish writing to develop and continue. Authors must be Irish, under 40 and published. A non-competitive award with no application procedure.
PRIZE €8000.

Royal Economic Society Prize
c/o University of York, York YO10 5DD
☎01904 433575 Fax 01904 433575

Contact *Professor Mike Wickens*

Annual award for the best article published in *The Economic Journal*. Open to members of the Royal Economic Society only. Previous winners: Professors Kip Viscusi, Mark Armstrong, Jim Heckman, Jeffrey Smith, Richard Dickens and Casey Mulligan.
PRIZE £3000.

The Royal Society of Literature Awards
W.H. Heinemann Prize, **The Royal Society of Literature Ondaatje Prize**, **V.S.**

Pritchett Memorial Prize and (under *Bursaries, Fellowships and Grants*) **The Royal Society of Literature/Jerwood Awards**

The Royal Society of Literature Ondaatje Prize
The Royal Society of Literature, Somerset House, Strand, London WC2R 1LA
☎020 7845 4676 Fax 020 7845 4679
✉ paulaj@rslit.org
www.rslit.org

Submissions *Paula Johnson*

Newly established prize, administered by the **Royal Society of Literature** and endowed by Sir Christopher Ondaatje. The prize, which replaces the Winifred Holtby Memorial Prize, will be awarded annually to a book of literary merit, fiction or non-fiction, best evoking the spirit of place. All entries must be published within the calendar year 2004 and should be submitted between 1 September and 1 December 2004. The writer must be a citizen of the UK, Commonwealth or Ireland. Further details available on the website. Inaugural winner: Louise Waugh *Hearing Birds Fly: A Year in a Mongolian Village*.
PRIZE £10,000.

Runciman Award
The Anglo-Hellenic League, c/o The Hellenic Centre, 16–18 Paddington Street, London W1U 5AS
☎020 7486 9410
Fax 020 7486 4254 (c/o Hellenic Centre)

Contact *The Administrator*

Established 1985. Annual award, sponsored by the National Bank of Greece. Founded by the Anglo-Hellenic League to promote Anglo-Greek understanding and friendship, for a work wholly or mainly about some aspect of Greece or the Hellenic scene, which has been published in its first English edition in the UK or in Greece during the previous year and listed in Whitaker's Books in Print. Named after the late Sir Steven Runciman, former chairman of the Anglo-Hellenic League. The Award may be given for a work of fiction, poetry, drama or non-fiction; concerned academically or non-academically with the history of any period; biography or autobiography, travel and topography; the arts, architecture, archaeology and the environment; the social and political sciences and current affairs; a guide book or a translation from the Greek of any period. Final entry date in late January; award presented in May/June. 2003 winner: Sir John Boardman *The Archaeology of*

Nostalgia: How the Greeks Re-created their Mythical Past.
AWARD £5000.

RUSI Westminster Medal for Military Literature

Royal United Services Institute for Defence and Security Studies, Whitehall, London SW1A 2ET
☎020 7930 2602 Fax 020 7321 0943
✉ sarahh@rusi.org
www.rusi.org

Contact *Sarah Haybittle*

Established 1997 this annual award is sponsored by the Duke of Westminster and aims to mark a notable and original contribution to the study of international or national security, or the military profession. Work must be in English, by a living author, and have been published as a book, rather than an article, in the preceding or next six months of the closing date for entries. 2003 winner: Sir Marrack Goulding.

PRIZE Silver medal, £1000. Winning author is invited to give lecture at RUSI and collect medal from the Duke of Westminster.

The Saga Award for Wit

c/o Colman Getty PR, Middlesex House, 34–42 Cleveland Street, London W1T 4JE
☎020 7631 2666 Fax 020 7631 2699
✉ pr@colmangettypr.co.uk
www.saga.co.uk

Contact *Award Administrator*

Established 2003. Annual award, dubbed 'The Silver Booker', was created by *Saga Magazine* to recognise and promote the gentle art of humorous writing. A work of fiction or non-fiction by a British author aged 50 or over on publication. Books must be submitted by the UK publisher or nominated by the judges; no submissions by authors. 2003 winner: Alexander McCall-Smith, *The Full Cupboard of Life.*

AWARDS £20,000; £1000 for each short-listed author.

Sagittarius Prize

Society of Authors, 84 Drayton Gardens, London SW10 9SB
☎020 7373 6642 Fax 020 7373 5768
✉ info@societyofauthors.org
www.societyofauthors.org

Established 1990. For first published novel by an author over the age of 60. Final entry date: 20 December. Full details available from the

Society of Authors. 2003 winner: Margaret Kaine *Ring of Clay.*
PRIZE £4000.

Sainsbury's Baby Book Award
See **Booktrust Early Years Awards**

The David St John Thomas Charitable Trust Competitions and Awards

PO Box 6055, Nairn IV12 4YB
☎01667 453351
✉ dsjtcharitynairn@fsmail.net

Competition & Awards Manager *Lorna Edwardson*

A large programme of writing competitions and awards including annual ghost story and love story competitions (each 1600–1800 words with £1000 first prize), and open poetry competition (poems up to 32 lines, total prize money £1000). Publication of winning entries is guaranteed, usually in *Writers' News/Writing Magazine* and/or annual anthology. The awards are led by the annual Self-Publishing Award, established in 1993, which is open to anyone who has self-published a book during the preceding calendar year. There are four categories each with a £250 prize; the overall winner is declared self-publisher of the year with a total award of £1000. For full details, send large s.a.e. to the address above.

The Saltire Literary Awards

Saltire Society, 9 Fountain Close, 22 High Street, Edinburgh EH1 1TF
☎0131 556 1836 Fax 0131 557 1675
✉ saltire@saltiresociety.org.uk
www.saltiresociety.org.uk

Administrator *Kathleen Munro*

Established 1982. Annual awards, one for Book of the Year, the other for Best First Book by an author publishing for the first time. Open to any author of Scottish descent or living in Scotland, or to anyone who has written a book which deals with either the work and life of a Scot or with a Scottish problem, event or situation. Nominations are invited from editors of leading newspapers, magazines and periodicals. 2003 winners: Saltire Society Scottish Book of the Year: James Robertson *Joseph Knight*; Royal Mail Group/Saltire Best First Book: Martin MacIntyre *Ath-Aithne*. The Saltire Society Research Book of the Year: Emily B. Lyle and Katherine Campbell *The Greig-Duncan Folk Song Collection.*

PRIZES £5000 (Scottish Book); £1500 (First Book).

Schlegel–Tieck Prize
See **The Translators Association Awards**

Science Writer Awards
The Daily Telegraph, 1 Canada Square, Canary Wharf, London E14 5DT
☎020 7538 6257 Fax 020 7513 2512
✉ enquiries@science-writer.co.uk
www.science-writer.co.uk

Contact *Emma Gilbert-Harris*

Established 1987, this award is designed to bridge the gap between science and writing, challenging the writer to come up with a piece of no more than 700 words that is friendly, informative and, above all, understandable. Sponsored by BASF, the award is open to two age groups: 16–19 and 20–28.

AWARD Winners and runners-up receive cash prizes and have the opportunity to have their pieces published on the science pages of *The Daily Telegraph*. The winner in each category also gets an all expenses paid trip to the USA for the meeting of the American Association for the Advancement of Science and an invitation to meet Britain's most distinguished scientists at the British Association's Festival of Science. There is also a prize for schools and a prize for teachers. To check launch date, visit the website, telephone the hotline number or e-mail for further information.

Scottish Book of the Year
See **The Saltire Literary Awards**

Scottish History Book of the Year
The Saltire Society, 9 Fountain Close, 22 High Street, Edinburgh EH1 1TF
☎0131 556 1836 Fax 0131 557 1675
✉ saltire@saltiresociety.org.uk
www.saltiresociety.org.uk

Administrator *Kathleen Munro*

Established 1965. Annual award in memory of the late Dr Agnes Mure Mackenzie for a published work of distinguished Scottish historical research of scholarly importance (including intellectual history and the history of science). Editions of texts are not eligible. Nominations are invited and should be sent to the Administrator. Previous winner: Dr Roland Tanner *The Late Medieval Scottish Parliament: Politics and the Three Estates, 1424–1488*.

PRIZE Bound and inscribed copy of the winning publication.

SEEDS International Poetry Chapbook Anthology Contest
See **Hidden Brook Press International Poetry Anthology Contests**

SES Book Prizes
University of Sunderland, School of Education & Lifelong Learning, Forster Building, Chester Road, Sunderland SR1 3SD
☎0191 515 2364 Fax 0191 515 2628
✉ gill.crozier@sunderland.ac.uk

Contact *Professor Gill Crozier*

Annual awards given by the Society for Educational Studies for the best books on education published during the preceding year. Nomination by members of the Society for Educational Studies and publishers or by individual authors based in the UK.

PRIZES £2000, £1000 and £400.

Bernard Shaw Translation Prize
See **The Translators Association Awards**

André Simon Memorial Fund Book Awards
5 Sion Hill Place, Bath BA1 5SJ
☎01225 336305 Fax 01225 421862
✉ tessa@tantraweb.co.uk

Contact *Tessa Hayward*

Established 1978. Awards given annually for the best book on drink, best on food and special commendation in either. 2003 winners: David Thompson *Thai Food*; Andrew Jefford *The New France*; Colin Spencer *British Food* (special commendation).

AWARDS £2000 (best books); £1000 (special commendation); £200 to shortlisted books.

WHSmith's 'People's Choice' Book Awards
WHSmith PLC, Nations House, 103 Wigmore Street, London W1U 1WH
☎020 7514 9623 Fax 020 7514 9635
✉ elizabeth.walker@WHSmith.co.uk
www.WHSmithbookawards.co.uk

Contact *Elizabeth Walker*, Group Event Marketing Manager

Now in their fourth year, these WHSmith book awards were the first where the winners are voted for entirely by the public. Teams of celebrity and public judges choose the shortlists but *any* book published during the calendar year can be voted for. There are nine award categories in total. Eight are voted for by the public: Fiction; Debut Novel; Lifestyle; Autobiography/

Biography; Travel Writing; Business; Factual and Teen Choice. Voting (in any WHSmith store, local library, by text message, freepost or via the website) starts in January (lasting six weeks) and winners are announced in March. Recent winners have included Jamie Oliver, Ben Elton, Sir David Attenborough and Donna Tartt. The ninth category, the long-standing WHSmith Literary Award, is not put out to public vote but is decided by a panel led by the Professor of English Literature at Merton College, Oxford, and Chief Book Reviewer for the *Sunday Times*, John Carey. Three members of the public join at shortlist stage to help decide the winner.

PRIZES Each winning author receives a trophy and £5000.

WHSmith Literary Award

See **WHSmith's 'People's Choice' Book Awards**

The Society for Theatre Research Annual Theatre Book Prize

c/o The Theatre Museum, 1e Tavistock Street, London WC2E 7PR
✉ e.cottis@btinternet.com
www.str.org.uk

Established 1997. Annual award for books, in English, of original research into any aspect of the history and technique of the British Theatre. Not restricted to authors of British nationality nor books solely from British publishers. Books must be first published in English (no translations) during the calendar year. Play texts and those treating drama as literature are not eligible. Publishers submit books directly to the independent judges and should contact the Book Prize Administrator for further details. 2003 winner: Richard Eyre *National Service*.

AWARD £400.

Sony Radio Academy Awards

Alan Zafer & Associates, 47–48 Chagford Street, London NW1 6EB
☎ 020 7723 0106 Fax 020 7724 6163
✉ secretariat@radioawards.org
www.radioawards.org
Contact *The Secretariat*

Established 1982 in association with the **Society of Authors** and Sony UK. Presented in association with the **Radio Academy**. Annual awards to recognise excellence in radio broadcasting. Entries must have been broadcast in the UK between 1 January and 31 December in the year preceding the award. The categories for the awards are reviewed each year.

Southport Writers' Circle Poetry Competition

32 Dover Road, Southport PR8 4TB
Contact *Mrs Hilary Tinsley*

For previously unpublished work. Entry fee: £2 per poem. Any subject, any form; maximum 40 lines. Closing date: end April. Poems must be entered anonymously, accompanied by a sealed envelope marked with the title of poem, containing s.a.e. Entries must be typed on A4 paper and be accompanied by the appropriate fee payable to Southport Writers' Circle. No application form is required. Envelopes should be marked 'Poetry Competition'. Postal enquiries only. No calls.

PRIZES £200 (1st); £100 (2nd); £50 (3rd); additional £25 Humour Prize.

The Spoken Word Awards

The Spoken Word Publishing Association, Macmillan Audio Books, 20 New Wharf Road, London N1 9RR
☎ 020 7014 6041
✉ z.howes@macmillan.co.uk
Contact *Zoe Howes*

Hosted by the **Spoken Word Publishing Association**, the Awards are for excellence in the spoken word industry and recognise the valuable work of all those involved with the production of audio books. There are 25 categories of award, consisting of 14 Consumer Awards (including Drama, Biography, Poetry, Children's and Comedy), four Trade Awards (including Best Retailer and Best Media Coverage) and four Performance Awards (Male and Female Performer of the Year, Publisher of the Year and Spoken Word Audio of the Year).

PRIZES Glass trophy for the 'Gold' awards; certificates for Silver and Bronze.

Bram Stoker Awards for Superior Achievement

Horror Writers Association, PO Box 50577, Palo Alto, CA 94303, USA
☎ 001 650 561 9511
✉ hwa@horror.org
www.horror.org
Contact *Nancy Etchemendy*

Founded 1988 and named in honour of Bram Stoker, author of *Dracula*. Presented annually by the **Horror Writers Association** (HWA) for works of horror first published in the English language. Works are eligible during their first year of publication. HWA members recommend works for consideration in twelve categories: novel, first novel, short fiction, long fiction, fiction collection, anthology, non-fiction, illustrated narrative, screenplay, work for young readers, poetry and other media. In addition, Lifetime Achievement Stokers are occasionally presented to individuals whose entire body of work has substantially influenced horror.

Strokestown International Poetry Prize

Strokestown Poetry Festival, Strokestown, Co. Roscommon, Republic of Ireland
☎00 353 7196 33759
✉ merrilyharpur@eircom.net
www.strokestownpoetryprize.com

Contacts *M. Harpur, Pat Compton*

Annual poetry festival and competition now in its fifth year. Established to reward excellence in poetry. Festival takes place the first weekend in May. Readings and competitions over three days. A centrepiece of the festival is the Strokestown International Poetry prize.

PRIZES €4000 (£2500); runners-up prizes of €2000 (2nd) and €1000 (3rd) with €450 reading fee for seven other shortlisted poets. Also prizes totalling €2400 for winning poems in the Irish language. There is also €1000 for a political satire in verse.

Sunday Times Writer of the Year Award

The Sunday Times, 1 Pennington Street, London E1 9XW
☎020 7782 5770   Fax 020 7782 5798
www.societyofauthors.org

Established 1987. Annual award to fiction and non-fiction writers. The panel consists of *Sunday Times* journalists and critics. Previous winners: Anthony Burgess, Seamus Heaney, Stephen Hawking, Ruth Rendell, Muriel Spark, William Trevor, Martin Amis, Margaret Atwood, Ted Hughes, Harold Pinter, Tom Wolfe, Robert Hughes. No applications; prize at the discretion of the Literary Editor.

Sunday Times Young Writer of the Year Award

The Society of Authors, 84 Drayton Gardens, London SW10 9SB
☎020 7373 6642   Fax 020 7373 5768
✉ info@societyofauthors.org

Contact *Awards Secretary*

Established 1991. Annual award given on the strength of the promise shown by a full-length published work of fiction, non-fiction, poetry or drama. Entrants must be British citizens, resident in Britain and under the age of 35. The panel consists of *Sunday Times* journalists and critics. Closing date: 31 October. The work must be by one author, in the English language, and published in Britain. Applications by publishers via the **Society of Authors**. 2003 winner: William Fiennes *The Snow Geese*.

Reginald Taylor and Lord Fletcher Essay Prize

Journal of the British Archaeological Association, Institute of Archaelogy, 36 Beaumont Street, Oxford OX1 2PG
Contact *Dr Martin Henig*

A biennial prize, in memory of the late E. Reginald Taylor and of Lord Fletcher, for the best unpublished scholarly essay, not exceeding 7500 words, on a subject of archaeological, art history or antiquarian interest within the period from the Roman era to AD 1830. The essay should show *original* research on its chosen subject, and the author will be invited to read the essay before the Association. The essay may be published in the journal of the Association if approved by the Editorial Committee. Closing date for entries is 1 June 2006. All enquiries by post, please. No phone calls. Send s.a.e. for details.

PRIZE £300 and a medal.

The Tir Na N-Og Award

Cyngor Llyfrau Cymru (Welsh Books Council), Castell Brychan, Aberystwyth SY23 2JB
☎01970 624151   Fax 01970 625385
✉ wbc.children@wbc.org.uk
www.wbc.org.uk

An annual award given to the best original book published for children in the year prior to the announcement. There are three categories: Best Welsh Fiction; Best Welsh Non-fiction; Best English Book with an authentic Welsh background.

AWARDS £1000 (each category).

TLS/Blackwells Poetry Competition

Times Literary Supplement, Admiral House, 66–68 East Smithfield, London E1W 1BX
☎020 7782 3000
www.the-tls.co.uk

Contacts *Mick Imlah (Poetry Editor, TLS), Sonia Allen*

Established 1997. Annual open competition.

Entry details published in the *TLS*. 2003 winner: Stephen Knight.

PRIZES £2000; three runners-up £500 each.

Tolman Cunard Prize
See **The Forward Prizes for Poetry**

The Translators Association Awards
The Translators Association, 84 Drayton Gardens, London SW10 9SB
☎020 7373 6642 Fax 020 7373 5768
✉ info@societyofauthors.org
www.societyofauthors.org

Contact *Awards Secretary*

Various awards for published translations into English from Dutch and Flemish (The Vondel Translation Prize), French (Scott Moncrieff Prize), German (Schlegel-Tieck Prize), Greek (Hellenic Foundation Prize), Italian (The John Florio Prize), Portuguese (The Calouste Gulbenkian Prize), Spanish (The Premio Valle Inclán) and Swedish (Bernard Shaw Translation Prize). Contact the **Translators Association** for full details.

The Betty Trask Awards
See entry under *Bursaries, Fellowships and Grants*

The Trollope Society Short Story Prize
9A North Street, London SW4 0HN
☎020 7720 6789 Fax 020 7978 1815
✉ pamela@tvdox.com
www.trollopestoryprize.org

Contacts *Pamela Neville-Sington, John Williams*

Established in 2001 to encourage interest in Trollope's novels among young people with the emphasis on reading – and writing – for fun. The competition, which is held annually, focuses on a different Trollope book each year; visit the website for details. Open to students (aged 21 and younger) of all countries. Final entry date: 15 January. The winning story will be published in the Society's quarterly journal, *Trollopiana*.

PRIZE £1000.

Sir Peter Ustinov Television Scriptwriting Award
The International TV Academy Foundation, 142 West 57th Street, New York City, NY 10019, USA
☎001 212 489 6969 Fax 001 212 489 6557

✉ ludovic@iemmys.tv
www.iemmys.tv

Contact *Ludovic Attal*

Established 1998. The International TV Academy, recognised worldwide since 1969 for its celebration of world-class international programming through its International Emmy Awards, will also recognise excellence in the writing of television programmes for a family audience. The late Sir Peter Ustinov, the quintessential writer, director and performer, gave his name to the International TV Academy Foundation's Television Scriptwriting Award. This annual competition is designed to motivate novice writers worldwide. The scriptwriter cannot be a United States citizen nor resident and must be below 30 years of age. Final date for entry: 1 September. Previous winners: 2000: Sylke Rene Meyer (Germany); 2001 Colm Mahon (Ireland); 2002 Howard Hund (UK).

PRIZE The award winner will receive US$5000 and the opportunity to work with an established writer as mentor.

Ver Poets Open Competition
Haycroft, 61–63 Chiswell Green Lane, St Albans AL2 3AL
☎01727 867005

Contact *May Badman*

Various competitions are organised by **Ver Poets**, the main one being the annual Open for unpublished poems of no more than 30 lines written in English. Entry fee: £3 per poem. Entries must be made under a pseudonym, with name and address on form or separate sheet. Two copies of poems typed on A4 white paper. *Vision On*, the anthology of winning and selected poems, and the adjudicators' report are normally available from mid-June. Final entry date: 30 April. Back numbers of the anthology are available for £4, post-free; one copy each free to those included.

PRIZES £500 (1st); £300 (2nd); two runner-up prizes of £100.

Also runs High Lights, an open competition for younger poets (aged 15–19). Entry fee: £1 per poem (3 poems for £2; 4 for £3, etc.); closing date: 31 March. PRIZES £200 (1st); £150 (2nd); two runner-up prizes of £50.

Vogue Talent Contest
Vogue, Vogue House, Hanover Square, London W1S 1JU
☎020 7152 3003 Fax 020 7408 0559

Contact *Frances Bentley*

Established 1951. Annual award for young writers and journalists (under 25 on 1 January in the year of the contest). Final entry date is in April. Entrants must write three pieces of journalism on given subjects.

PRIZES £1000, plus a month's paid work experience with *Vogue*; £500 (2nd).

The Vondel Translation Prize
See **The Translators Association Awards**

Wadsworth Prize for Business History
Business Archives Council, c/o Ms Fiona Maccoll, Records Manager, Rio Tinto plc, 6 St James Square, London SW1Y4LD
☎020 7753 2123 Fax 020 7753 2211
✉ fiona.macoll@riotinto.com

Contact *Fiona Maccoll*

Established 1978. Annual award for the best book published on British business history. 2003 winner: Martin Fransman *Telecoms in the Internet Age. From boom to bust to ...?*
PRIZE £500.

Walford Award
See **CILIP: The Chartered Institute of Library and Information Professionals Walford Award**

The David Watt Prize
Rio Tinto plc, 6 St James's Square, London SW1Y 4LD
☎020 7753 2316 Fax 020 7930 3249
✉ davidwattprize@riotinto.com

Contact *The Administrator*

Initiated in 1988 to commemorate the life and work of David Watt. Annual award, open to writers currently engaged in writing for English language newspapers and journals, on international and national affairs. The winners are judged as having made 'outstanding contributions towards the greater understanding of national, international or global issues'. Entries must have been published during the year preceding the award. Final entry date 31 March. 2003 winner: David Gardner *Democracy is Just a Mirage*.
PRIZE £7500.

The Harri Webb Prize
10 Heol Don, Whitchurch, Cardiff CF14 2AU
☎029 2062 3359

Contact *Professor Meic Stephens*

Established 1995. Annual award to commemo-

rate the Welsh poet, Harri Webb (1920–94), for a single poem in any of the categories in which he wrote: ballad, satire, song, polemic or a first collection of poems. The poems are chosen by three adjudicators; no submissions. Previous winner: Grahame Davies.
PRIZES £100/£200.

Wheatley Medal
See **CILIP: The Chartered Institute of Library and Information Professionals Wheatley Medal**

Whitbread Book Awards
The Booksellers Association, Minster House, 272 Vauxhall Bridge Road, London SW1V 1BA
☎020 7802 0802 Fax 020 7802 0803
✉ nicola.tarling@booksellers.co.uk
www.whitbread-bookawards.co.uk

Contact *Nicola Tarling*

Established 1971. The awards celebrate and promote the best contemporary British writing. They are judged in two stages and offer a total of £50,000 prize money. The awards are open to novel, first novel, biography, poetry and children's book, each judged by a panel of three judges, with two young judges joining the panel for the Whitbread Children's Book Award. The winner of each award receives £5000. The Whitbread Book of the Year (£25,000) is chosen from the category winners. Writers must have lived in Britain and Ireland for three or more years. Submissions received from publishers only. Closing date: early July. Sponsored by Whitbread PLC. 2003 winners: David Almond *The Fire-Eaters* (children's); Mark Haddon *The Curious Incident of the Dog in the Night-time* (novel & overall winner); D.B.C. Pierre *Vernon God Little* (first novel); D.J. Taylor *Orwell: The Life* (biography); Don Paterson *Landing Light* (poetry)

Whitfield Prize
Royal Historical Society, University College London, Gower Street, London WC1E 6BT
☎020 7387 7532 Fax 020 7387 7532
✉ rhs.info@sas.ac.uk

Contact *Executive Secretary*

Established 1977. An annual award for the best new work within a field of British history, published in the UK in the preceding calendar year. The book must be the author's first (solely written) history book and be an original and scholarly work of historical research. Final entry date: 31 December. Previous winners:

John Goodall *God's House at Ewelme: Life, Devotion and Architecture in a Fifteenth-Century Almshouse*; Frank Salmon *Building on Ruins: The Rediscovery of Rome and English Architecture.* PRIZE £1000.

John Whiting Award

Arts Council England, 14 Great Peter Street, London SW1P 3NQ
☎020 7333 0100
www.artscouncil.org.uk
Contact *Theatre Writing, Theatre Department*

Founded 1965. Annual award to commemorate the life and work of the playwright John Whiting (*The Devils, A Penny for a Song*). Any writer who has received during 2003 and 2004: (a) an award through the **Arts Council's Theatre Writing Schemes**; (b) a commission from a theatre company in receipt of an annual or revenue subsidy from either the Arts Council or a Regional Arts Board; or (c) a première production by a theatre company in receipt of annual subsidy is eligible to apply. The play must have been written during 2004 and/or 2005. Awarded to the writer whose play most nearly satisfies the following criteria: a play in which the writing is of special quality; a play of relevance and importance to contemporary life; a play of potential value to the British theatre. No writer who has won the award previously may reapply and no play that has been submitted for the award previously is eligible. Contact the theatre writing section for full details and application form. PRIZE £6000.

Wilkins Memorial Poetry Prize

Birmingham & Midland Institute, 9 Margaret Street, Birmingham B3 3BS
☎0121 236 3591 Fax 0121 212 4577
Administrator *Mr P.A. Fisher*

The Birmingham & Midland Institute, as organiser of the competition, is seeking new young talent and to this end has changed the structure of the next competition. Class 1 – Open Class: for anyone whose 16th birthday fell on or before 2 July 2004 (entry fee: £30); Class 2 – Student Class: open to those whose 18th birthday fell on or before 20 July 2004 or whose 22nd birthday fell on or after that date (entry fee: £1 per poem); Class 3 – Sixth-form Class: for those registered in a sixth form on 20 July 2004 (entry fee: £1 per poem). Enquire for closing dates. PRIZES Class 1: £400 (1st), £200 (2nd), £100 (3rd); Class 2: £200; Class 3: £100.

H.H. Wingate Prize
See **Jewish Quarterly Literary Prizes**

Wolfson History Prizes

Wolfson Foundation, 8 Queen Anne Street, London W1G 9LD
☎020 7323 5730 Fax 020 7323 3241
Contact *Executive Secretary*

The Wolfson History Prize, established in 1972, is awarded annually to promote and encourage standards of excellence in the writing of history for the general reading public. 2003 winners: Robert Gildea *Marianne in Chains: In Search of the German Occupation 1940–1945*; William Dalrymple *White Mughals: Seduction and Betrayal in 18th-Century India.*

The David T.K. Wong Prize for Short Fiction

International PEN, 9/10 Charterhouse Buildings, Goswell Road, London EC1M 7AT
☎020 7253 4308 Fax 020 7253 5711
✉ gvincent@dircon.co.uk
www.internatpen.org
Contact *Gilly Vincent*

Established 2000, this international prize is presented every other year to promote literary excellence in the form of the short story written in English. Unpublished stories of between 2500 words to 6000 words are welcome from writers worldwide, but entries must incorporate one or more of International PEN's ideals as set out in its Charter. *Entries should not be sent direct to International PEN but should be submitted via the entrant's local PEN Centre.* Details of closing date should be obtained from individual Centres. In those few countries without a PEN Centre, entrants can be directed to the nearest appropriate centre by International PEN. Copies of PEN's Charter, in English, French and Spanish and addresses of PEN Centres can be found on the website. 2002/3 winner: Chimamanda Ngozi Adichie *Half of a Yellow Sun.* PRIZE £7500 (1st).

The Writers Bureau Poetry and Short Story Competition

The Writers Bureau, Sevendale House, 7 Dale Street, Manchester M1 1JB
☎0161 228 2362 Fax 0161 228 3533
✉ studentservices@writersbureau.com
www.writersbureau.com
Competition Secretary *Angela Cox*

Established 1994. Annual award. Poems should be no longer than 40 lines and short stories no more than 2000 words. £5 entry fee. Closing date: 31 July 2005.

PRIZES in each category: £1000 (1st); £400 (2nd); £200 (3rd); £100 (4th); £50 (x 6).

Yorkshire Post Book of the Year Award

The Rectory, Ripley, Near Harrogate HG3 3AY
☎01423 772217   Fax 01423 772217

Contact *Margaret Brown*

An annual award for the book (either fiction or non-fiction) which, in the opinion of the judges, is the best work published in the preceding year. Closing date: 31 December. Previous winner:

Steven Pinker *The Blank State – the Modern Denial of Human Nature*.
PRIZE £1200.

Youngminds Book Award

Youngminds, 102–108 Clerkenwell Road, London EC1M 5SA
☎020 7336 8445   Fax 020 7336 8446
✉ bookaward@youngminds.org.uk
www.youngminds.org.uk/bookaward

Contacts *Richard Meigr, Tarryn Hawley*

Established 2003. This award is given to a published work of literature that throws fresh light on the ways a child takes in and makes sense of the world he or she is growing into – novels, memoirs, diaries, poetry collections which portray something of the unique subtlety of a child's experience. 2003 winner: Judy Pascoe.

Library Services

Aberdeen Central Library

Rosemount Viaduct, Aberdeen AB25 1GW
☎01224 652500 Fax 01224 641985
✉ centlib@arts-rec.aberdeen.net.uk
www.aberdeen.gov.uk

OPEN 9.00 am to 7.00 pm Monday to
Thursday; 9.00 am to 5.00 pm Friday
(Reference & Local Studies/Business &
Technical: 9.00 am to 8.00 pm); 9.00 am to
5.00 pm Saturday. Branch library opening
times vary

OPEN ACCESS
General reference and loans. Books, pamphlets, periodicals and newspapers; videos, CDs,
DVDs; arts equipment lending service; Internet
and Learning Centre for public access; photographs of the Aberdeen area; census records,
maps, newspapers; online databases, patents and
standards. The library offers special services to
housebound readers. Non-resident administrative fee.

Armitt Library

Ambleside LA22 9BL
☎015394 31212 Fax 015394 31313
✉ info@armitt.com
www.armitt.com

OPEN 10.00 am to 12.30 pm and 1.30 pm to
4.00 pm Monday to Friday

FREE ACCESS (To view original material please
give prior notice)
A small but unique reference library of rare
books, manuscripts, pictures, antiquarian prints
and museum items, mainly about the Lake
District. It includes early guidebooks and topographical works, books and papers relating to
Ruskin, H. Martineau, Charlotte Mason and
others; fine art including work by W. Green,
J.B. Pyne, John Harden, K. Schwitters, and
Victorian photographs by Herbert Bell; also a
major collection of Beatrix Potter's scientific
watercolour drawings and microscope studies.
Museum and Exhibition open seven days per
week from 10.00 am to 5.00 pm. Entry charge.

The Athenaeum, Liverpool

Church Alley, Liverpool L1 3DD
☎0151 709 7770 Fax 0151 709 0418
✉ library@athena.force9.net
www.theathenaeum.org.uk

OPEN 10.00 am to 12.30 pm and 1.30 pm to
4.00 pm Monday to Friday

ACCESS To club members; researchers by application only
General collection, with books dating from
the 15th century, now concentrated mainly on
local history with a long run of Liverpool directories and guides. SPECIAL COLLECTIONS
Liverpool playbills; Robert Gladstone; William
Roscoe; Blanco White; 18th-century plays;
19th-century economic pamphlets; the Norris
books; Bibles; Yorkshire and other genealogy.
Some original drawings, portraits, topographical
material and local maps.

Bank of England
Information Centre

Threadneedle Street, London EC2R 8AH
☎020 7601 4715 Fax 020 7601 4356
✉ informationcentre@bankofengland.co.uk
www.bankofengland.co.uk

OPEN 9.00 am to 5.30 pm Monday to Friday
ACCESS For research workers by prior
arrangement only, when material is not readily
available elsewhere
50,000 volumes of books and periodicals.
2000 periodicals taken. UK and overseas coverage of banking, finance and economics. SPECIAL
COLLECTIONS Central bank reports; UK 17th–
19th-century economic tracts; Government
reports in the field of banking.

Barbican Library

Barbican Centre, London EC2Y 8DS
☎020 7638 0569 Fax 020 7638 2249
✉ barbicanlib@corpoflondon.gov.uk
www.cityoflondon.gov.uk/libraries

OPEN 9.30 am to 5.30 pm Monday and
Wednesday; 9.30 am to 7.30 pm Tuesday
and Thursday; 9.30 am to 2.00 pm Friday;
9.30 am to 4.00 pm Saturday

OPEN ACCESS
Situated on Level 2 of the Barbican Centre,
this is the Corporation of London's largest lending library. Study facilities are available plus free
Internet access. In addition to a large general
lending department, the library seeks to reflect
the Centre's emphasis on the arts and includes

strong collections (including DVDs, videos and CD-ROMs), on painting, sculpture, theatre, cinema and ballet, as well as a large music library with books, scores and CDs (sound recording loans available at a small charge). Also houses the City's main children's library and has special collections on finance, natural resources, conservation, socialism and the history of London. Service available for housebound readers. A literature events programme is organised by the Library which supplements and provides cross-arts planning opportunities with the Barbican Centre artistic programme. Reading groups meet in the library on the first Tuesday and Thursday of every month.

Barnsley Public Library

Central Library, Shambles Street, Barnsley S70 2JF
☎01226 773930 Fax 01226 773955
✉ barnsleylibraryenquiries@barnsley.gov.uk
www.barnsley.gov.uk/service/libraries /index.asp

OPEN Lending & Reference: 9.30 am to 7.00 pm Monday and Wednesday; 9.30 am to 5.30 pm Tuesday and Friday; 9.30 am to 4.00 pm Saturday. Please telephone to check hours of other departments.

OPEN ACCESS
General library, lending and reference. Archive collection of family history and local firms; local studies: coal mining, local authors, Yorkshire and Barnsley; large junior library. (Specialist departments are closed on certain weekday evenings and Saturday afternoons.)

BBC Written Archives Centre

Peppard Road, Caversham Park, Reading RG4 8TZ
☎0118 948 6281 Fax 0118 946 1145
✉ wac.enquiries@bbc.co.uk
www.bbc.co.uk/thenandnow

Contact *Jacqueline Kavanagh*
OPEN 9.30 am to 5.30 pm Monday to Friday

ACCESS For reference, by appointment only on Wednesday to Friday

Holds the written records of the BBC, including internal papers from 1922 to 1979 and published material to date. 20th century biography, social history, popular culture and broadcasting. Charges for certain services.

Bedford Central Library

Harpur Street, Bedford MK40 1PG
☎01234 350931/270102 (Reference Library)
Fax 01234 342163

www.bedfordshire.gov.uk ·
OPEN 9.30 am to 7.00 pm Monday and Wednesday; 9.30 am to 5.30 pm Tuesday, Thursday, Friday; 9.30 am to 5.00 pm Saturday

OPEN ACCESS
Lending library with a wide range of stock, including books, music (CDs and cassettes), audio books and videos; reference and information library, children's library, local history library and Internet facilities.

Belfast Public Libraries: Central Library

Royal Avenue, Belfast BT1 1EA
☎028 9050 9150 Fax 028 9033 2819
✉ info.belb@ni-libraries.net
www.belb.org.uk
www.ni-libraries.net

OPEN 9.00 am to 8.00 pm Monday and Thursday; 9.00 am to 5.30 pm Tuesday, Wednesday, Friday; 9.00 am to 1.00 pm Saturday

OPEN ACCESS To lending libraries; reference libraries by application only

Over two million volumes for lending and reference. SPECIAL COLLECTIONS United Nations depository; complete British Patent Collection; Northern Ireland Newspaper Library; British and Irish government publications. The Central Library provides the following Reference Departments: General Reference; Belfast, Ulster and Irish Studies; Music. A Learning Gateway includes public Internet facilities and a Learndirect Centre. The Lending Library is one of over 20 branches along with a range of outreach services to hospitals, care homes and housebound readers.

BFI National Library

21 Stephen Street, London W1T 1LN
☎020 7255 1444 Fax 020 7436 2338
✉ library@bfi.org.uk
www.bfi.org.uk

OPEN 10.30 am to 5.30 pm Monday and Friday; 10.30 am to 8.00 pm Tuesday and Thursday; 1.00 pm to 8.00 pm Wednesday; Telephone Enquiry Service operates from 10.00 am to 5.00 pm

ACCESS For reference only; annual, 5-day and limited day membership available

The world's largest collection of information on film and television including periodicals, cuttings, scripts, related documentation, personal papers. Main library catalogue available via website.

Birmingham Library Services
Central Library, Chamberlain Square,
Birmingham B3 3HQ
☎0121 303 4511
✉ central.library@birmingham.gov.uk
www.birmingham.gov.uk/libraries
OPEN 9.00 am to 8.00 pm Monday to Friday;
9.00 am to 5.00 pm Saturday

Over a million volumes. RESEARCH COLLECTIONS the Shakespeare Library; War Poetry Collection; Parker Collection of Children's Books and Games; Johnson Collection; Milton Collection; Cervantes Collections; Early and Fine Printing Collection (including the William Ridler Collection of Fine Printing); Joseph Priestley Collection; Loudon Collection; Railway Collection; Wingate Bett Transport Ticket Collection; Labour, Trade Union and Co-operative Collections. PHOTOGRAPHIC ARCHIVES Sir John Benjamin Stone; Francis Bedford; Francis Frith; Warwickshire Photographic Survey; Boulton and Watt Archive. Also, Charles Parker Archive; Birmingham Repertory Theatre Archive and Sir Barry Jackson Library; Local Studies (Birmingham); Patents Collection; Song Sheets Collection; Oberammergau Festival Collection.

Birmingham and Midland Institute
9 Margaret Street, Birmingham B3 3BS
☎0121 236 3591 Fax 0121 212 4577
www.bmi.org.uk
Administrator & General Secretary *Philip Fisher*
ACCESS Members only
Established 1854. Later merged with the Birmingham Library which was founded in 1779. The Library specialises in the humanities, with approximately 100,000 volumes in stock. Founder member of the **Association of Independent Libraries**. Meeting-place of many affiliated societies devoted to poetry and literature.

Booktrust Children's Reference Library
Book House, 45 East Hill, London SW18 2QZ
☎020 8516 2985 Fax 020 8516 2978
✉ ed@booktrust.org.uk
www.booktrust.org.uk
www.booktrusted.com
Contact *Mr E. Zaghini*
OPEN 9.00 am to 5.00 pm Monday to Friday
(by appointment only)

ACCESS For reference only
A comprehensive collection of children's literature, related books and periodicals. Aims to hold most of all children's titles published within the last two years. An information service covers all aspects of children's literature, including profiles of authors and illustrators. Reading room facilities. Publishes a quarterly magazine, *Booktrust News* and *The Best Book Guide for Children and Young Adults*.

Bournemouth Library
22 The Triangle, Bournemouth BH2 5RQ
☎01202 454848 Fax 01202 454840
OPEN 10.00 am to 7.00 pm Monday; 9.30 am to 7.00 pm Tuesday, Thursday, Friday; 9.30 am to 5.00 pm Wednesday; 10.00 am to 2.00 pm Saturday
OPEN ACCESS
Main library for Bournemouth with lending, reference and music departments, plus the Heritage Zone – local and family history.

Bradford Central Library
Princes Way, Bradford BD1 1NN
☎01274 753600 Fax 01274 395108
✉ public.libraries@bradford.gov.uk
OPEN 9.00 am to 7.30 pm Monday to Friday; 9.00 am to 5.00 pm Saturday
OPEN ACCESS
Wide range of books and media loan services. Comprehensive reference and information services, including major local history collections and specialised business information service.

Brighton Central Library
Vantage Point, New England Street, Brighton BN1 2GW
☎01273 290800 Fax 01273 296951
OPEN 10.00 am to 7.00 pm Monday to Friday (closed Wednesday); 10.00 am to 4.00 pm Saturday
Brighton History Centre: Church Street, Brighton BN1 2EE ☎01273 296972
OPEN 10.00 am to 7.00 pm Tuesday; 10.00 am to 5.00 pm Wednesday to Saturday (closed Monday)
ACCESS Limited stock on open access; material for reference use and lending
Founded 1869, the library has a large stock covering most subjects. Specialisations include art and antiques, history of Brighton and Sussex, family history, local illustrations, TSO, business and large bequests of antiquarian books and ecclesiastical history.

Bristol Central Library

College Green, Bristol BS1 5TL
☎0117 903 7200 Fax 0117 922 1081
www.bristol-city.gov.uk
www.digitalbristol.org

OPEN 9.30 am to 7.30 pm Monday, Tuesday and Thursday; 9.30 am to 5.00 pm Wednesday, Friday and Saturday; 1.00 pm to 4.00 pm Sunday

OPEN ACCESS

Lending, reference, art, music, business and local studies are particularly strong. DVD, video and CD collections on site. Facilities available: PCs (large screen with Jaws and Zoomtext), Internet, printing; videophone on site; black & white and colour photocopiers.

British Architectural Library

Royal Institute of British Architects,
66 Portland Place, London W1B 1AD
☎020 7580 5533 Fax 020 7631 1802
✉ info@inst.riba.org
www.architecture.com

Members' Information Line: 020 7307 3600 (membership number required)
Public Information Line (50p per min.): 0906 302 0400

OPEN 10.00 am to 8.00 pm Tuesday; 10.00 am to 5.00 pm Wednesday to Friday; 10.00 am to 1.30 pm Saturday; Closed Sunday, Monday and any Saturday preceding a Bank Holiday; full details on the website

ACCESS Free to RIBA members; non-members must buy a day ticket (£14/£7 concessions, but on Tuesdays between 5.00 pm–8.00 pm and Saturdays £7/£3.50); subscriber membership available (write for details); loans available to RIBA and library members only

Collection of books, drawings, manuscripts, photographs and periodicals. All aspects of architecture, current and historical. Material both technical and aesthetic, covering related fields including: interior design, landscape architecture, topography, the construction industry and applied arts. Brochure available; queries by telephone, letter, e-mail or in person. Charge for research (min. charge £40 plus VAT).

The British Library

Admission to St Pancras Reading Rooms

The British Library does not provide access to all those who request admission to use its research facilities but operates an admissions policy which grants access to those who need to use the collection because they cannot find the material they require in other libraries.

Admission is by interview and applicants are required to demonstrate that they need access to the reading rooms because: (a) material they need to consult is not available elsewhere; (b) their work or studies require the facilities of a large research library; (c) they need access to the Library's public records.

For further information, contact the Reader Admissions Office, The British Library, 96 Euston Road, London NW1 2DB ☎020 7412 7677 Fax 020 7412 7794 ✉ reader-admissions @bl.uk .

British Library Asia, Pacific and Africa Collections

96 Euston Road, London NW1 2DB
☎020 7412 7873 Fax 020 7412 7641
✉ oioc-enquiries@bl.uk
www.bl.uk

OPEN 10.00 am to 5.00 pm Monday; 9.30 am to 5.00 pm Tuesday to Saturday; closed for public holidays

ACCESS By British Library reader's pass (identification required)

A comprehensive collection of printed volumes and manuscripts in the languages of North Africa, the Near and Middle East and all of Asia, plus records of the East India Company and British government in India until 1947. Also prints, drawings and paintings by British artists of India.

For information on British Library collections and services, visit the website.

To access British Library catalogues, go to the website at blpc.bl.uk

British Library Business Information Service (BIS)

96 Euston Road, London NW1 2DB
☎020 7412 7454 (free enquiry service)
Fax 020 7412 7453 (free enquiry service)
✉ business-information@bl.uk
www.bl.uk/bis

OPEN 10.00 am to 8.00 pm Monday; 9.30 am to 8.00 pm Tuesday to Thursday; 9.30 am to 5.00 pm Friday and Saturday; closed for public holidays

ACCESS Pass required for access

BIS holds the most comprehensive collection of business information literature in the UK. This includes market research reports and journals, directories, company annual reports, trade and business journals, house journals, trade literature and CD-ROM services.

British Library Early Printed Collections/Rare Book and Music Reading Room

96 Euston Road, London NW1 2DB
☎020 7412 7676 Fax 020 7412 7577
✉ rare-books@bl.uk
www.bl.uk

General enquiries about reader services &
advance reservations: ☎020 7412 7676
Fax 020 7412 7609
✉ reader-services-enquiries@bl.uk

OPEN 10.00 am to 8.00 pm Monday; 9.30 am
to 8.00 pm Tuesday to Thursday; 9.30 am
to 5.00 pm Friday and Saturday; closed for
public holidays

ACCESS By British Library reader's pass

Early Printed Collections, which is an integral
part of British Library Scholarship and Collections, selects, acquires, researches and provides
access to material printed in the British Isles to
1914 and in Western European languages before
1851. The collections are available in the Rare
Books and Music Reading Room at St Pancras
which also functions as the focus for the British
Library's extensive collection of humanities
microforms.

Further information about Early Printed
Collections can be found at the British Library
website.

British Library Humanities Reading Room

96 Euston Road, London NW1 2DB
☎020 7412 7676 Fax 020 7412 7609
✉ reader-services-enquiries@bl.uk
www.bl.uk/resources/humanities

Open 10.00 am to 8.00 pm Monday; 9.30 am
to 8.00 pm Tuesday, Wednesday, Thursday;
9.30 am to 5.00 pm Friday and Saturday;
closed for public holidays

ACCESS By British Library reader's pass

This reading room is the focus for the
Library's modern collections service in the
humanities. It is on two levels, Humanities 1 and
Humanities 2 and provides access to the Library's
comprehensive collections of books and periodicals in all subjects in the humanities and social
sciences and in all languages apart from Oriental.
These collections are not available for browsing
at the shelf. Material is held in closed access storage and needs to be identified and ordered from
store using an online catalogue. A selective open
access collection on most humanities subjects can
be found in Humanities 1 whilst in Humanities 2
there are open access reference works relating to

periodicals and theses, to recorded sound and to
librarianship and information science.

To access British Library catalogues, go to
the website.

British Library Manuscript Collections

96 Euston Road, London NW1 2DB
☎020 7412 7513 Fax 020 7412 7745
✉ mss@bl.uk
www.bl.uk

OPEN 10.00 am to 5.00 pm Monday; 9.30 am
to 5.00 pm Tuesday to Saturday; closed for
public holidays

ACCESS Reading facilities only, by British
Library reader's pass; a written letter of recommendation and advance notice is required for
certain categories of material

Two useful publications, *Index of Manuscripts
in the British Library*, Cambridge 1984–6, 10 vols,
and *The British Library: Guide to the Catalogues and
Indexes of the Department of Manuscripts* by M.A.E.
Nickson, help to guide the researcher through
this vast collection of manuscripts dating from
Ancient Greece to the present day. Approximately 300,000 mss, charters, papyri and seals are
housed here.

For information on British Library collections and services and to access British Library
catalogues, including the Manuscripts online
catalogue, visit the website.

British Library Map Collections

96 Euston Road, London NW1 2DB
☎020 7412 7702 Fax 020 7412 7780
✉ maps@bl.uk
www.bl.uk/collections/maps

OPEN 10.00 am to 5.00 pm Monday; 9.30 am
to 5.00 pm Tuesday to Saturday; closed for
public holidays

ACCESS By British Library reader's pass

A collection of about 4.5 million maps, charts
and globes, manuscript, printed and, increasingly, digital, with particular reference to the history of British cartography. Maps for all parts of
the world in a wide range of scales, formats and
dates, including the most comprehensive collection of Ordnance Survey maps and plans.
SPECIAL COLLECTIONS King George III
Topographical Collection and Maritime
Collection, the Crace Collection of maps and
plans of London and the cartographic archive of
the Ministry of Defence (i.e. GSGS).

For information on British Library collections and services, visit the website.

To access main British Library catalogues, go to the website at blpc.bl.uk

British Library Music Collections

96 Euston Road, London NW1 2DB
☎020 7412 7772 Fax 020 7412 7751
✉ music-collections@bl.uk
www.bl.uk

OPEN 10.00 am to 8.00 pm Monday; 9.30 am to 8.00 pm Tuesday to Thursday; 9.30 am to 5.00 pm Friday and Saturday; closed for public holidays

ACCESS By British Library reader's pass
SPECIAL COLLECTIONS The Royal Music Library (containing almost all Handel's surviving autograph scores), The Zweig Collection of Music & Literary Mss, The Royal Philharmonic Society Archive and the Paul Hirsch Music Library. Also a large collection (about one and a quarter million items) of printed music (UK via legal deposit) and about 100,000 items of manuscript music, both British and foreign.

The British Library website contains details of collections and services, and provides access to the catalogues.

British Library Newspapers

Colindale Avenue, London NW9 5HE
☎020 7412 7353 Fax 020 7412 7379
✉ newspaper@bl.uk
www.bl.uk/collections/newspapers.html

OPEN 10.00 am to 4.45 pm Monday to Saturday (last newspaper issue 4.15 pm); closed for public holidays

ACCESS By British Library reader's pass or Newspaper Library pass (available from and valid only for Colindale)

Major collections of English provincial, Scottish, Welsh, Irish, Commonwealth and selected overseas foreign newspapers from c.1700 are housed here. Some earlier holdings are also available. London newspapers from 1801 and many weekly and fortnightly periodicals are also in stock. (London newspapers pre-dating 1801 are housed at the new library building in St Pancras (96 Euston Road, NW1 2DB) though many are available at Colindale Avenue on microfilm.) Readers are advised to check availability of material in advance.

For information on British Library Newspapers collections and services, visit the website.

British Library Oriental and India Office Collections

See **British Library Asia, Pacific and Africa Collections**

British Library Science, Technology and Innovation

96 Euston Road, London NW1 2DB
☎020 7412 7288/7494 (General Enquiries)
Fax 020 7412 7495
✉ scitech@bl.uk
www.bl.uk

Patent enquiries: ☎020 7412 7903
Fax 020 7412 7480
✉ patents-information@bl.uk
www.bl.uk/patents

Business enquiries: ☎020 7412 7454 (Business quick enquiry line available 9.00 am to 5.00 pm Monday to Friday)

OPEN 10.00 am to 8.00 pm Monday; 9.30 am to 8.00 pm Tuesday to Thursday; 9.30 am to 5.00 pm Friday and Saturday; closed for public holidays

Engineering, business information on companies, markets and products, physical science and technologies. British, European and Patent Co-operation Treaty patents and trade marks.

For information on British Library collections and services, visit the website.

To access British Library catalogues go to the website at blpc.bl.uk

British Library Social Policy Information Service

96 Euston Road, London NW1 2DB
☎020 7412 7536 Fax 020 7412 7761
www.bl.uk/services/information/social.html

OPEN 10.00 am to 8.00 pm Monday; 9.30 am to 8.00 pm Tuesday to Thursday; 9.30 am to 5.00 pm Friday and Saturday; closed for public holidays

ACCESS By British Library reader's pass

Provides an information service on social policy, public administration, and current and international affairs, and access to current and historical official publications from all countries and intergovernmental bodies, including House of Commons sessional papers, UK legislation, UK electoral registers, up-to-date reference books on official publications and on the social sciences, a major collection of statistics and a browsing collection of recent social science books and periodicals.

To access British Library catalogues, go to the website at blpc.bl.uk/catalogues/blpc.html

British Library Sound Archive

96 Euston Road, London NW1 2DB
☎020 7412 7676 Fax 020 7412 7441
✉ sound-archive@bl.uk

www.bl.uk/soundarchive

OPEN 10.00 am to 8.00 pm Monday; 9.30 am to 8.00 pm Tuesday to Thursday; 9.30 am to 5.00 pm Friday and Saturday; closed for public holidays

Listening service (by appointment)

Northern Listening Service British Library Document Supply Centre, Boston Spa: 9.15 am to 4.30 pm Monday to Friday

OPEN ACCESS

An archive of over 1,000,000 discs and more than 200,000 hours of tape recordings, including all types of music, oral history, drama, literature, poetry, wildlife, selected BBC broadcasts and BBC Sound Archive material. Produces a twice-yearly newsletter, *Playback*.

For information on British Library Sound Archive collections and services, visit the website.

British Psychological Society Library

c/o Psychology Library, University of London Library, Senate House, Malet Street, London WC1E 7HU

☎020 7862 8451/8461 Fax 020 7862 8480

✉ enquiries@ull.ac.uk

www.ull.ac.uk

OPEN Term-time: 9.00 am to 9.00 pm Monday to Thursday; 9.00 am to 6.30 pm Friday; 9.30 am to 5.30 pm Saturday (Holidays: 9.00 am to 6.00 pm Monday to Friday; 9.30 am to 5.30 pm Saturday)

ACCESS Members only; Non-members £5 day ticket

Reference library, containing the British Psychological Society collection of periodicals – over 140 current titles housed alongside the University of London's collection of books and journals. Largely for academic research. General queries referred to **Swiss Cottage Library** in London which has a good psychology collection.

Bromley Central Library

London Borough of Bromley – Leisure & Community Services, High Street, Bromley BR1 1EX

☎020 8460 9955 Fax 020 8313 9975

✉ reference.library@bromley.gov.uk

www.bromley.gov.uk

OPEN 9.30 am to 6.00 pm Monday, Wednesday, Friday; 9.30 am to 8.00 pm Tuesday and Thursday; 9.30 am to 5.00 pm Saturday

OPEN ACCESS

A large selection of fiction and non-fiction books for loan, both adult and children's. Also DVDs, videos, CDs, cassettes, language courses, open learning packs, CD-ROM and Playstation games for hire. Other facilities include a business information service (✉ bis@bromley.gov.uk), CD-ROM, computer hire, People's Network Internet, local studies library, 'Upfront' teenage section, large reference library with photocopying, fax, microfiche and film facilities, 'Bromley Knowledge' – online community information. SPECIALIST COLLECTIONS include: H.G. Wells, Walter de la Mare, Crystal Palace, The Harlow Bequest, and the history and geography of Asia, America, Australasia and the polar regions.

Bromley House Library

Angel Row, Nottingham NG1 6HL

☎0115 947 3134

Librarian *Julia Wilson*

OPEN 9.30 am to 5.00 pm Monday to Friday; also first Saturday of each month from 10.00 am to 12.30 pm

ACCESS For members only

Founded 1816 as the Nottingham Subscription Library. Collection of 30,000 books including local history, topography, biography, travel and fiction.

CAA Library and Information Centre

Aviation House, Gatwick Airport RH6 0YR

☎01293 573725 Fax 01293 573181

www.caa.co.uk

OPEN 9.30 am to 4.30 pm Monday to Friday; 10.00 am to 4.30 pm first Wednesday of the month

OPEN ACCESS

Books, periodicals and reports on air transport, air traffic control, electronics, radar and computing.

Cambridge Central Library (Reference Library & Information Service)

7 Lion Yard, Cambridge CB2 3QD

☎0845 045 5225 Fax 01223 712036

✉ cambridge.central.library@cambridgeshire.gov.uk

www.cambridgeshire.govuk/library

OPEN 9.00 am to 7.00 pm Monday to Friday; 9.00 am to 5.30 pm Saturday

OPEN ACCESS

Large stock of books, periodicals, newspapers,

maps, plus comprehensive collection of directories and annuals covering UK, Europe and the world. Microfilm and fiche reading and printing services. Online access to news and business databases. News databases on CD-ROM; Internet access. Monochrome photocopiers.

Camomile Street Library
12–20 Camomile Street, London EC3A 7EX
☎020 7247 8895

OPEN 9.30 am to 5.30 pm Monday to Friday

OPEN ACCESS
Corporation of London lending library. Wide range of fiction and non-fiction books and language courses on cassette, foreign fiction, paperbacks, maps and guides for travel at home and abroad, children's books, a selection of large print, and collections of DVDs, videos and music CDs. Free Internet access.

Cardiff Central Library
Frederick Street, St David's Link, Cardiff CF10 2DU
☎029 2038 2116 Fax 029 2087 1599
✉ robboddy@hotmail.com
www.libraries.cardiff.gov.uk

OPEN 9.00 am to 6.00 pm Monday, Tuesday, Wednesday, Friday; 9.00 am to 7.00 pm Thursday; 9.00 am to 5.30 pm Saturday

General lending library with the following departments: leisure, music, children's, local studies, information, science and humanities.

Carmarthen Public Library
St Peter's Street, Carmarthen SA31 1LN
☎01267 224830 Fax 01267 221839
✉ wtphillips@carmarthenshire.gov.uk

OPEN 9.30 am to 7.00 pm Monday, Tuesday, Wednesday, Friday; 9.30 am to 5.00 pm Thursday and Saturday

OPEN ACCESS
Comprehensive range of fiction, non-fiction, children's books and reference works in English and in Welsh. Large local history library. Free Internet access and CD-ROM facilities. Large Print books, books on tape, CDs, CD-ROMs, cassettes and videos available for loan.

Catholic Central Library
☎020 7383 4333
✉ librarian@catholic-library.org.uk
www.catholic-library.org.uk

OPEN ACCESS For reference (non-members must sign in; loans restricted to members)
Contains books, many not readily available

elsewhere, on theology, religions worldwide, scripture and the history of churches of all denominations. The Library is in the process of moving to new premises; access the website for further information.

The Centre for the Study of Cartoons and Caricature
See entry under *Picture Libraries*

City Business Library
1 Brewers' Hall Garden, off Aldermanbury Square, London EC2V 5BX
☎020 7332 1812/3803 (Textphone)
Fax 020 7332 1847
✉ cbl@corpoflondon.gov.uk
www.cityoflondon.gov.uk/libraries

OPEN 9.30 am to 5.00 pm Monday to Friday (except public holidays)

OPEN ACCESS
Local authority free public reference library run by the Corporation of London. Books, directories, periodicals, newspapers and electronic databases of current business interest. Provided for anyone with a business informatin enquiry and is one of the leading public resource centres in Britain in its field. Large directory collection for both the UK and overseas, plus companies information, market research reports, management, banking, insurance, investment and statistics. Free public Internet access. No academic journals or textbooks.

Commonwealth Secretariat Library
Marlborough House, Pall Mall, London SW1Y 5HX
☎020 7747 6164 Fax 020 7747 6168
✉ library@commonwealth.int
www.thecommonwealth.org

Librarian *David Blake*

Open 10.00 am to 4.45 pm Monday to Friday

ACCESS For reference only, by appointment
Extensive reference source concerned with economy, development, trade, production and industry of Commonwealth countries; also human resources including women, youth, health, management and education. Includes the archives of the Secretariat.

Corporation of London Libraries
See **Barbican Library**; **Camomile Street Library**; **City Business Library**; **Guildhall Library**

Coventry Central Library

Smithford Way, Coventry CV1 1FY
☎024 7683 2314/2395 (Minicom)
Fax 024 7683 2440
✉ central.library@coventry.gov.uk
www.coventry.gov.uk

OPEN 9.00 am to 8.00 pm Monday to Friday;
9.00 am to 4.30 pm Saturday; 12.00 am to
4.00 pm Sunday

OPEN ACCESS

Located in the middle of the city's main shopping centre. Approximately 120,000 items (books, cassettes, CDs and DVDs) for loan; plus reference collection of business information and local history. SPECIAL COLLECTIONS Cycling and motor industries; George Eliot; Angela Brazil; Tom Mann Collection (trade union and labour studies); local newspapers on microfilm from 1740 onwards. Over 300 periodicals taken. 'Peoplelink' community information database available.

Department for Environment, Food and Rural Affairs

Nobel House, 17 Smith Square, London
SW1P 3JR
☎020 7238 3000 Fax 020 7238 6591

DEFRA Helpline 08459 335577 (local call rate): general contact point which can provide information on the work of DEFRA, either directly or by referring callers to appropriate contacts. Available 9.00 am to 5.00 pm Monday to Friday (excluding Bank Holidays)

OPEN 9.30 am to 5.00 pm Monday to Friday

ACCESS For reference (but at least 24 hours notice must be given for intended visits)

Large stock of volumes on temperate agriculture.

Derby Central Library

Wardwick, Derby DE1 1HS
☎01332 255398 Fax 01332 369570
www.derby.gov.uk/libraries

Open 9.30 am to 7.00 pm Monday, Tuesday, Thursday, Friday; 9.30 am to 1.00 pm Wednesday and Saturday

Local Studies Library

25B Irongate, Derby DE1 3GL
☎01332 255393 Fax 01332 255381

Open 9.30 am to 7.00 pm Monday and Tuesday; 9.30 am to 5.00 pm Wednesday, Thursday, Friday; 9.30 am to 4.00 pm Saturday

OPEN ACCESS

General library for lending, information and Children's Services. The Central Library also houses specialist private libraries: Derbyshire Archaeological Society; Derby Philatelic Society. The Local Studies Library houses the largest multimedia collection of resources in existence relating to Derby and Derbyshire. The collection includes mss deeds, family papers, business records including the Derby Canal Company, Derby Board of Guardians and the Derby China Factory. Both libraries offer Internet access for a small charge.

Devon & Exeter Institution Library

7 Cathedral Close, Exeter EX1 1EZ
☎01392 251017
✉ J.P.Gardner@exeter.ac.uk
www.devonandexeterinstitution.org.uk

OPEN 9.00 am to 5.00 pm Monday to Friday

ACCESS Members only (Temporary membership available)

Founded 1813. Under the administration of Exeter University Library. Contains over 36,000 volumes, including long runs of 19th-century journals, theology, history, topography, early science, biography and literature. A large and growing collection of books, journals, newspapers, prints and maps relating to the South West.

Doncaster Libraries and Information Services

Central Library, Waterdale, Doncaster
DN1 3JE
☎01302 734305 Fax 01302 369749
✉ Reference.Library@doncaster.gov.uk
library.doncaster.gov.uk

OPEN 9.00 am to 6.00 pm Monday; 8.30 am to 6.00 pm Tuesday and Friday; 8.30 am to 8.00 pm Wednesday and Thursday; 9.00 am to 5.00 pm Saturday

OPEN ACCESS

Books, cassettes, CDs, videos, picture loans. Reading aids unit for people with visual handicap; activities for children during school holidays, including visits by authors, etc. Also reference library.

Dorchester Library (part of Dorset County Library)

Colliton Park, Dorchester DT1 1XJ
☎01305 224440 (lending)/224448 (reference)
Fax 01305 266120
✉ Dorchesterreflibrary@dorset-cc.gov.uk

OPEN 10.00 am to 7.00 pm Monday; 9.30 am to 7.00 pm Tuesday, Wednesday, Friday; 9.30 am to 5.00 pm Thursday; 9.00 am to 4.00 pm Saturday

OPEN ACCESS

General lending and reference library, including Local Studies Collection, special collections on Thomas Hardy, the Powys Family and William Barnes. Periodicals, children's library, CD-ROMs, free Internet access. Video lending service.

Dundee Central Library

The Wellgate, Dundee DD1 1DB

☎01382 431500 Fax 01382 431558

✉ central.library@dundeecity.gov.uk

www.dundeecity.gov.uk

OPEN Lending & Local Studies Departments and General Reference: 9.30 am to 6.00 pm Monday, Tuesday, Friday; 10.00 am to 6.00 pm Wednesday; 9.30 am to 8.00 pm Thursday; 9.30 am to 5.00 pm Saturday. Commerce & Technology: 9.30 am to 9.00 pm Monday, Tuesday, Thursday, Friday; 10.00 am to 9.00 pm Wednesday; 9.30 am to 5.00 pm Saturday.

ACCESS Reference services available to all; lending services to those who live, work, study or were educated within Dundee City

Adult lending, reference and children's services. Art, music, audio, video and DVD lending services. Internet access. Schools service (Agency). Housebound and mobile services. SPECIAL COLLECTIONS The Wighton Collection of National Music; The Wighton Heritage Centre; The Wilson Photographic Collection; The Lamb Collection.

Durning-Lawrence Library

See **University of London Library**

English Nature

Northminster House, Peterborough PE1 1UA

☎01733 455000 Fax 01733 568834

✉ enquiries@english-nature.org.uk

www.english-nature.org.uk

OPEN 8.30 am to 5.00 pm Monday to Thursday; 8.30 am to 4.30 pm Friday

ACCESS *Bona fide* students only. Telephone library for appointment on 01733 455094

Information on nature conservation, nature reserves, SSSIs, planning, legislation, etc. English Nature is the government-funded body whose purpose is to promote the conservation of England's wildlife and natural features.

Equal Opportunities Commission

Arndale House, Arndale Centre, Manchester M4 3EQ

☎0845 601 5901 Fax 0161 838 8303

✉ info@eoc.org.uk

www.eoc.org.uk

The EOC is open to the public via the Helpline (0845 601 5901) 9.00 am to 5.00 pm Mondays to Fridays.

Essex County Council Libraries

County Library Headquarters, Goldlay Gardens, Chelmsford CM2 0EW

☎01245 284981 Fax 01245 492780

✉ essexlib@essexcc.gov.uk

www.essexcc.gov.uk

Essex County Council Libraries has 73 static libraries throughout Essex as well as 13 mobile libraries and three special-needs mobiles. Services to the public include books, newspapers, periodicals, CDs, cassettes, videos, pictures, CD-ROMs and Internet access as well as postal cassettes for the blind and subtitled videos. Specialist subjects and collections are listed below at the relevant library.

Chelmsford Library

PO Box 882, Market Road, Chelmsford CM1 1LH

☎01245 492758 Fax 01245 492536

✉ chelmford.library@essexcc.gov.uk

OPEN 8.30 am to 7.00 pm Monday to Friday; 8.30 am to 5.30 pm Saturday; 12.30 pm to 4.30 pm Sunday

Science and technology, business information and social sciences.

Colchester Library

Trinity Square, Colchester CO1 1JB

☎01206 245900 Fax 01206 245901

✉ colchester.library@essexcc.gov.uk

OPEN 8.30 am to 7.30 pm Monday, Tuesday, Wednesday and Friday; 8.30 am to 5.00 pm Thursday and Saturday; 1.00 pm to 4.00 pm Sunday

Local studies, music scores; Castle collection (18th-century subscription library); Cunnington collection; Margaret Lazell collection; Taylor collection.

Harlow Library

The High, Harlow CM20 1HA

☎01279 413772 Fax 01279 424612

✉ harlow.library@essexcc.gov.uk

OPEN 9.00 am to 7.00 pm Monday to Friday; 9.00 am to 5.00 pm Saturday; 1.00 pm to 4.00 pm Sunday

Sir John Newson Memorial collection; Maurice Hughes Memorial collection.

Loughton Library
Traps Hill, Loughton IG10 1HD
☎020 8502 0181 Fax 020 8508 5041
✉ loughton.library@essexcc.gov.uk
OPEN 9.00 am to 7.00 pm Monday, Tuesday, Wednesday and Friday; 9.00 am to 1.00 pm Thursday; 9.30 am to 5.30 pm Saturday; 11.00 am to 3.00 pm Sunday
National Jazz Foundation Archive.

Saffron Walden Library
2 King Street, Saffron Walden CB10 1ES
☎01799 523178 Fax 01799 513642
OPEN 9.00 am to 7.00 pm Monday, Tuesday, Thursday, Friday; 9.00 am to 5.00 pm Saturday; 1.00 pm to 4.00 pm Sunday (closed Wednesday)
Victorian studies collection.

Witham Library
18 Newland Street, Witham CM8 2AQ
☎01376 519625 Fax 01376 501913
OPEN 9.00 am to 7.00 pm Monday, Tuesday, Thursday, Friday; 9.00 am to 5.00 pm Saturday (closed Wednesday); 1.00 pm to 4.00 pm Sunday
Drama. Dorothy L. Sayers and Maskell collections.

Family Records Centre
1 Myddleton Street, London EC1R 1UW
☎020 8392 5200 Fax 020 8392 5307
✉ frc@nationalarchives.gov.uk
www.familyrecords.gov.uk/frc
OPEN 9.00 am to 5.00 pm Monday, Wednesday, Friday; 10.00 am to 7.00 pm Tuesday; 9.00 am to 7.00 pm Thursday; 9.30 am to 5.00 pm Saturday (closed public holidays)
ACCESS for reference; no i.d. required
The Centre provides a family history service to visitors, advising on how to use the wealth of genealogical records available, including births, marriages, adoptions and deaths. Part of the **National Archives** (see entry).

The Fawcett Library
See **The Women's Library**

Foreign and Commonwealth Office Library
King Charles Street, London SW1A 2AH
☎020 7008 3925 Fax 020 7008 3270

www.fco.gov.uk
ACCESS By appointment only
An extensive stock of books, pamphlets and other reference material on all aspects of historical, socio-economic and political subjects relating to countries covered by the Foreign and Commonwealth Office. Particularly strong on colonial history, early works on travel, and photograph collections, mainly of Commonwealth countries and former colonies, c.1850s–1960s.

Forestry Commission Library
Forest Research Station, Alice Holt Lodge, Wrecclesham, Farnham GU10 4LH
☎01420 22255 Fax 01420 23653
✉ library@forestry.gsi.gov.uk
www.forestry.gov.uk/forest_research
OPEN 9.00 am to 5.00 pm Monday to Thursday; 9.00 am to 4.30 pm Friday
ACCESS By appointment for personal visits
Approximately 20,000 books on forestry and arboriculture, plus 500 current journals. CD-ROMS include TREECD (1939 onwards). Offers a Research Advisory Service for advice and enquiries on forestry (☎01420 23000) with a charge for consultations and diagnosis of tree problems exceeding ten minutes.

French Institute Library
Institut français, 17 Queensberry Place, London SW7 2DT
☎020 7073 1350 Fax 020 7073 1363
✉ library@ambafrance.org.uk
www.institut-francais.org.uk
OPEN 12 noon to 7.00 pm Tuesday to Friday; 12 noon to 6.00 pm Saturday; Children's Library: 12 noon to 6.00 pm Tuesday to Saturday; closed in August; closed for one week at Christmas
OPEN ACCESS For reference and consultation (loans restricted to members)
A collection of over 55,000 volumes mainly centred on French cultural interests with special emphasis on language, literature and history. Books in French and English. Collection of videos, periodicals, CDs (French music), CD-ROMs; special collections: 'France Libre', microfilms and CD-ROMs of *Le Monde* (1944–2003). Denis Saurat MSS, recordings of lectures, press-cuttings on French current affairs. Inter-library loans; quick information service; Internet access to members. Group visits on request. Children's library (8,000 documents).

John Frost Newspapers
22b Rosemary Avenue, Enfield EN2 0SS
☎020 8366 1392/0946 Fax 020 8366 1379
✉ andrew@johnfrostnewspapers.com
www.johnfrostnewspapers.co.uk

Contacts *Andrew Frost, John Frost*
A collection of 80,000 original newspapers (1630 to the present day) and 200,000 press cuttings available, on loan, for research and rostrum/stills work (TV documentaries, book and magazine publishers and audiovisual presentations). Historic events, politics, sports, royalty, crime, wars, personalities, etc., plus many in-depth files.

Gloucestershire County Council Libraries & Information
Quayside House, Shire Hall, Gloucester GL1 2HY
☎01452 425020 Fax 01452 425042
✉ gclams@gloucestershire.gov.uk
www.gloucestershire.gov.uk

Head of Libraries & Information *David Paynter*
OPEN ACCESS
The service includes 39 local libraries and six mobile libraries. The website (GlosNet) includes library opening hours, mobile library route schedules; the library catalogue; and a book renewal/reservations facility.

Goethe-Institut Library
50 Princes Gate, Exhibition Road, London SW7 2PH
☎020 7596 4040 Fax 020 7594 0230
✉ Library@London.goethe.org
www.goethe.de/london

Librarian *Gerlinde Buck*
OPEN 12.00 am to 8.00 pm Monday to Thursday; 11.00 am to 5.00 pm Saturday

Specialises in German literature and books/audiovisual material on German culture and history: 20,000 books (4000 in English), 120 periodicals, 13 newspapers, 3700 audiovisual media (including 1200 videos/DVDs), selected press clippings on German affairs from the German and UK press, information service, photocopier, video facility. Also German language teaching material for teachers and students.

Goldsmiths' Library
See **University of London Library**

Greater London Record Office
See **London Metropolitan Archives Library Services**

Guildford Institute of the University of Surrey Library
Ward Street, Guildford GU1 4LH
☎01483 562142
✉ c.miles@surrey.ac.uk

Librarian *Clare Miles*
OPEN 10.00 am to 3.00 pm Tuesday to Friday
OPEN ACCESS To members only but open to enquirers for research purposes
Founded 1834. Some 12,000 volumes of which 7500 were printed before the First World War. The remaining stock consists of recently published works of fiction and non-fiction. Newspapers and periodicals also available. SPECIAL COLLECTIONS include an almost complete run of the *Illustrated London News* from 1843–1906, a collection of Victorian and early 20th century scrapbooks, and about 400 photos and other pictures relating to the Institute's history and the town of Guildford. Publishes Library newsletter twice-yearly.

Guildhall Library
Aldermanbury, London EC2P 2EJ
☎See below Fax 020 7600 3384
www.cityoflondon.gov.uk

ACCESS For reference (but much of the material is kept in storage areas and is supplied to readers on request; proof of identity is required for consultation of certain categories of stock). A free, *limited* enquiry service is available. There is also a fee-based service for in-depth research: ☎020 7332 1854 Fax 020 7600 3384 ✉search.guildhall @corpoflondon.gov.uk www.cityoflondon.gov. uk/search_guildhall
Part of the Corporation of London libraries., the Guildhall Library seeks to provide a basic general reference service but its major strength, acknowledged worldwide, is in its historical collections. The library is divided into three sections (printed books, manuscripts, the print & maps room), each with its own catalogues and enquiry desks.

PRINTED BOOKS
☎020 7332 1868/1870
OPEN 9.30 am to 5 pm Monday to Saturday; NB closes on Saturdays preceding Bank Holidays; check for details

Strong on all aspects of London history, with wide holdings of English history, topography and genealogy, including local directories, poll books and parish register transcripts. Also good collections of English statutes, law reports, parliamentary debates and journals, and House of Commons papers. Home of several important collections deposited by London institutions: the Marine collection of the Corporation of Lloyd's, the Stock Exchange's historical files of reports and prospectuses, the Clockmakers' Company library and museum, the Gardeners' Company, Fletchers' Company, the Institute of Masters of Wine, International Wine and Food Society and Gresham College.

MANUSCRIPTS
☎020 7332 1862/3
✉ manuscripts.guildhall@corpoflondon.gov.uk

OPEN 9.30 am to 4.45 pm Monday to Saturday (no requests for records after 4.30 pm; no manuscripts can be produced between 12 noon and 2 pm on Saturdays); NB closes on Saturdays preceding Bank Holidays; check for details

The official repository for historical records relating to the City of London (except those of the Corporation of London itself, which are housed at the Corporation Records Office). Records date from the 11th century to the present day. They include archives of most of the City's parishes, wards and livery companies, and of many individuals, families, estates, schools, societies and other institutions, notably the Diocese of London and St Paul's Cathedral, as well as the largest collection of business archives in any public repository in the UK. Although mainly of City interest, holdings include material for the London area as a whole and beyond.

PRINT & MAPS ROOM
☎020 7332 1839
✉ print&maps@corpoflondon.gov.uk

OPEN 9.30 am to 5.00 pm Monday to Friday

An unrivalled collection of prints and drawings relating to London and the adjacent counties. The emphasis is on topography, but there are strong collections of portraits and satirical prints. The map collection includes maps of the capital from the mid-16th century to the present day and various classes of Ordnance Survey maps. Other material includes photographs, theatre bills and programmes, trade cards, book plates and playing cards as well as a sizeable collection of Old Master prints. Over 30,000 items have been digitally imaged on Collage, including topographical prints, some maps, a small number of photographs and all the Guildhall Art Gallery collection.

Guille–Alles Library
Market Street, St Peter Port, Guernsey
GY1 1HB
☎01481 720392 Fax 01481 712425

✉ ga@library.gg
www.library.gg

OPEN 9.00 am to 5.00 pm Monday, Thursday, Friday, Saturday; 10.00 am to 5.00 pm Tuesday; 9.00 am to 8.00 pm Wednesday

OPEN ACCESS For residents; payment of returnable deposit by visitors. Music CD collection: £10 for two-year subscription

Lending, reference and information services. Public Internet service.

Herefordshire Libraries and Information Service
Shirehall, Hereford HR1 2HY
☎01432 359830 Fax 01432 260744
www.libraries.herefordshire.gov.uk

OPEN Opening hours vary in the libraries across the county

ACCESS Information and reference services open to anyone; loans to members only (Membership criteria: resident, being educated, working, or an elector in the county or neighbouring authorities; temporary membership to visitors. Proof of identity and address required)

Information service, reference and lending libraries. Non-fiction and fiction for all age groups, including normal and large print, spoken word cassettes, sound recordings (CD and cassette), videos, maps, local history, CD-ROMs for reference at Hereford and Leominster Libraries. Internet access at all libraries. SPECIAL COLLECTIONS Cidermaking; Beekeeping; Alfred Watkins; John Masefield; Pilley.

University of Hertfordshire Library
College Lane, Hatfield AL10 9AB
☎01707 284678 Fax 01707 284666
www.herts.ac.uk/lis

OPEN See website for term-time and vacation opening hours

ACCESS For reference use of printed collections. Appropriate ID required for Visitor's pass.

For further information please refer to the website.

Highgate Literary and Scientific Institution Library
11 South Grove, London N6 6BS
☎020 8340 3343 Fax 020 8340 5632
✉ admin@hlsi.net

OPEN 10.00 am to 5.00 pm Tuesday to Friday; 10.00 am to 4.00 pm Saturday (closed Sunday and Monday)

ANNUAL MEMBERSHIP £50 (individual); £80 (household)

25,000 volumes of general fiction and non-fiction, with a children's section and extensive local archives. SPECIAL COLLECTIONS on local history, London, and local poets Samuel Taylor Coleridge and John Betjeman.

Highland Libraries, The Highland Council, Education, Culture and Sport Service

Library Support Unit, 31a Harbour Road, Inverness IV1 1UA

☎01463 235713 Fax 01463 236986

✉ libraries@highland.gov.uk

www.highland.gov.uk

OPEN Library opening hours vary to suit local needs. Contact administration and support services for details (8.00 am to 6.00 pm Monday to Friday)

OPEN ACCESS

Comprehensive range of lending and reference stock: books, pamphlets, periodicals, newspapers, CDs, audio and video cassettes, maps, census records, genealogical records, photographs, educational materials, etc. Highland Libraries provides the public library service throughout the Highlands with a network of 43 static and 12 mobile libraries.

Holborn Library

32–38 Theobalds Road, London WC1X 8PA

☎020 7974 6345/6

OPEN 10.00 am to 7.00 pm Monday and Thursday; 10.00 am to 6.00 pm Tuesday, Wednesday and Friday; 10.00 am to 5.00 pm Saturday

OPEN ACCESS

London Borough of Camden public library. Includes a law collection and the London Borough of Camden Local Studies and Archive Centre.

Sherlock Holmes Collection (Westminster)

Marylebone Library, Marylebone Road, London NW1 5PS

☎020 7641 1206 Fax 020 7641 1019

✉ ccooke@westminster.gov.uk

www.westminster.gov.uk/libraries/special/sherlock.cfm

OPEN 9.30 am to 8.00 pm Monday, Tuesday, Thursday, Friday; 10.00 am to 8.00 pm Wednesday; Closed Saturday and Sunday (unless by prior arrangement)

ACCESS By appointment only

Located in Westminster's Marylebone Library. An extensive collection of material from all over the world, covering Sherlock Holmes and Sir Arthur Conan Doyle. Books, pamphlets, journals, newspaper cuttings and photos, much of which is otherwise unavailable in this country. Some background material.

Imperial College Central Library

See **Science Museum Library**

Imperial War Museum

Department of Printed Books, Lambeth Road, London SE1 6HZ

☎020 7416 5342 Fax 020 7416 5246

✉ books@iwm.org.uk

www.iwm.org.uk

OPEN 10.00 am to 5.00 pm Monday to Saturday (restricted service Saturday; closed on Bank Holiday Saturdays and two weeks during the year for annual stock check)

ACCESS For reference (but at least 24 hours' notice must be given for intended visits)

A large collection of material on British and Commonwealth 20th-century life with detailed coverage of the two world wars and other conflicts. Books, pamphlets and periodicals, including many produced for short periods in unlikely wartime settings; also maps, biographies and privately printed memoirs, and foreign language material. Additional research material available in the following departments: Art, Documents, Exhibits and Firearms, Film, Sound Records, Photographs. Active publishing programme based on reprints of rare books held in library. Catalogue available.

Instituto Cervantes

102 Eaton Square, London SW1W 9AN

☎020 7201 0757 Fax 020 7235 0329

✉ biblon@cervantes.es

www.cervantes.es

OPEN 12 noon to 6.30 pm Monday to Friday; 9.30 am to 2.00 pm Saturday

OPEN ACCESS For reference and lending

Spanish language and literature, history, art, philosophy. The library houses a collection of books, periodicals, videos, DVDs, slides, tapes, CDs, cassettes, CD-ROMs specialising entirely in Spain and Latin America.

Italian Institute Library

39 Belgrave Square, London SW1X 8NX

☎020 7396 4425 Fax 020 7235 4618

www.italcultur.org.uk

OPEN 10.00 am to 1.00 pm and 2.00 pm to 5.00 pm Monday to Friday

OPEN ACCESS For reference
A collection of over 21,000 volumes relating to all aspects of Italian culture. Texts are mostly in Italian, with some in English.

Jersey Library

Halkett Place, St Helier, Jersey JE2 4WH
☎01534 759991 (lending)/759992 (reference)
Fax 01534 769444
✉ library@jsylib.gov.je
www.jsylib.gov.je

OPEN 9.30 am to 5.30 pm Monday, Wednesday, Thursday, Friday; 9.30 am to 7.30 pm Tuesday; 9.30 am to 4.00 pm Saturday

OPEN ACCESS
Books, periodicals, newspapers, CDs, cassettes, CD-ROMs, videos, microfilm, specialised local studies collection, public Internet access. Branch Library at Les Quennevais School, St Brelade. Mobile library and homes services. Open Learning Centre.

Kent County Central Library

Kent Libraries and Archives, Springfield, Maidstone ME14 2LH
☎01622 696511 Fax 01622 696494
www.kent.gov.uk/libs

OPEN 9.30 am to 5.30 pm Monday, Wednesday, Friday; 9.30 am to 6.00 pm Tuesday; 9.30 am to 7.00 pm Thursday; 10.00 am to 5.00 pm Saturday

OPEN ACCESS
50,000 volumes available on the floor of the library plus 250,000 volumes of non-fiction, mostly academic, available on request to staff. English literature, poetry, classical literature, drama (including play sets), music (including music sets). Strong, too, in sociology, art history, business information and government publications. Loans to all who live or work in Kent; those who do not may consult stock for reference or arrange loans via their own local library service.

Leeds Central Library

Calverley Street, Leeds LS1 3AB
☎0113 247 8911 Fax 0113 247 8426
www.leeds.gov.uk/libraries

OPEN 9.00 am to 8.00 pm Monday, Tuesday, Wednesday; 9.30 am to 5.30 pm Thursday; 9.00 pm to 5.00 pm Friday; 10.00 am to 5.00 pm Saturday; 12.00 am to 4.00 pm Sunday

OPEN ACCESS to lending libraries; reference material on request. Free public Internet access.

Lending Library
☎0113 247 8270 Covers all subjects.

Music Library
☎0113 247 8273 Contains scores, books, video and audio.

Business & Research Library
☎0113 247 8426/8282
✉ information.for.business@leeds.gov.uk *and* research.and.studies@leeds.gov.uk

Company information, market research, statistics, directories, journals and computer-based information. Extensive files of newspapers and periodicals plus all government publications since 1960. SPECIAL COLLECTIONS include military history, Judaic, early gardening books.

Art Library
☎0113 247 8247 Major collection of material on fine and applied arts.

Local Studies Library
☎0113 247 8290
✉ local.studies@leeds.gov.uk

Extensive collection on Leeds and Yorkshire, including maps, books, pamphlets, local newspapers, illustrations and playbills. Census returns for the whole of Yorkshire also available. International Genealogical Index and parish registers.

Leeds City Libraries has an extensive network of 65 branch and mobile libraries.

Leeds Library

18 Commercial Street, Leeds LS1 6AL
☎0113 245 3071 Fax 0113 245 1191

OPEN 9.00 am to 5.00 pm Monday to Friday

ACCESS To members; research use upon application to the librarian
Founded 1768. Contains over 125,000 books and periodicals from the 15th century to the present day. SPECIAL COLLECTIONS include Reformation pamphlets, Civil War tracts, Victorian and Edwardian children's books and fiction, European language material, spiritualism and psychical research, plus local material.

Lincoln Central Library

Free School Lane, Lincoln LN2 1EZ
☎01522 510800 Fax 01522 535882
✉ lincoln.library@lincolnshire.gov.uk
www.lincolnshire.gov.uk

OPEN 9.30 am to 7.00 pm Monday to Friday; 9.30 am to 4.00 pm Saturday

OPEN ACCESS to the library; appointment required for the Tennyson Research Centre

Lending and reference library. Special collections include Lincolnshire local history (printed and published material, photographs, maps, directories and census data) and the Tennyson Research Centre (contact *Grace Timmins*: grace. timmins@lincolnshire.gov.uk).

Linen Hall Library
17 Donegall Square North, Belfast BT1 5GB
☎028 9032 1707 Fax 028 9043 8586
✉ info@linenhall.com
www.linenhall.com

Librarian *John Gray*
OPEN 9.30 am to 5.30 pm Monday to Friday; 9.30 am to 4.00 pm Saturday

OPEN ACCESS For reference (loans restricted to members)

Founded 1788. Contains about 200,000 books. Major Irish and local studies collections, including the Northern Ireland Political Collection relating to the current troubles (c. 250,000 items).

Literary & Philosophical Society of Newcastle upon Tyne
23 Westgate Road, Newcastle upon Tyne NE1 1SE
☎0191 232 0192 Fax 0191 261 4494
✉ library@litandphil.org.uk
www.litandphil.org.uk

Librarian *Kay Esson*
OPEN 9.30 am to 7.00 pm Monday, Wednesday, Thursday, Friday; 9.30 am to 8.00 pm Tuesday; 9.30 am to 1.00 pm Saturday

ACCESS Members; research facilities for *bona fide* scholars on application to the Librarian

200–year-old library of 140,000 volumes, periodicals (including 130 current titles), classical music on vinyl recordings and CD, plus a collection of scores. Free public lectures, events and recitals. Recent publications include: *The Reverend William Turner: Dissent and Reform in Georgian Newcastle upon Tyne* Stephen Harbottle; *History of the Literary and Philosophical Society of Newcastle upon Tyne, Vol. 2 (1896–1989)* Charles Parish; *Bicentenary Lectures 1993* ed. John Philipson.

Liverpool Libraries and Information Services
William Brown Street, Liverpool L3 8EW
☎0151 233 5829 Fax 0151 233 5886

✉ refbt.central.library@liverpool.gov.uk
www.liverpool.gov.uk
OPEN 9.00 am to 8.00 pm Monday to Thursday; 9.00 am to 7.00 pm Friday; 9.00 am to 5.00 pm Saturday; 12 noon to 4.00 pm Sunday

OPEN ACCESS
Humanities Reference Library A total stock in excess of 120,000 volumes and 24,000 maps, plus book plates, prints and autographed letters. SPECIAL COLLECTIONS Walter Crane and Edward Lear illustrations, Kelmscott Press, Audubon.

Business and Technology Reference Library Extensive stock dealing with all aspects of science, commerce and technology, including British and European standards and patents and trade directories.

Audio Visual Library Extensive stock relating to all aspects of music. Includes 128,000 volumes and music scores, over 3000 CDs, 2000 videos and 800 DVDs.

Record Office and Local History Department Material relating to Liverpool, Merseyside, Lancashire and Cheshire, together with archive material mainly on Liverpool. Proof of name and address required to obtain reader's ticket.

University of London Library
Senate House, Malet Street, London WC1E 7HU
☎020 7862 8461/62 (Information Centre)
Fax 020 7862 8480
✉ enquiries@ull.ac.uk (Information Centre)
www.ull.ac.uk
MEMBERSHIP DESK: ☎020 7862 8439/40
✉ userservices@ull.ac.uk

OPEN Term-time: 9.00 am to 9.00 pm Monday to Thursday; 9.00 am to 6.30 pm Friday; 9.30 am to 5.30 pm Saturday. Vacation: 9.00 am to 6.00 pm Monday to Friday; 9.30 am to 5.30 pm Saturday (closed on Sundays and at certain periods during Bank Holidays)

The University of London Library is a major academic research library predominantly based across the Humanities and Social Sciences. Housed within its 16 floors in Senate House are some two million titles including 5500 current periodicals and a wide range of electronic resources. It contains a number of outstanding research collections which, as well as supporting the scholarly activities of the University, attract researchers from throughout the United Kingdom and internationally. These include:

English (e.g. the Durning-Lawrence Library and Sterling Collection of first editions); Economic and Social History (the Goldsmiths' Library, containing 70,000 items ranging from 15th to early 19th century); Modern Languages (primarily Romance and Germanic); Palaeography (acclaimed as being the best open access collection in its field in Europe); History (complementary to the Institute of Historical Research); Music, Philosophy (acts as the Library of the Royal Institute of Philosophy); Psychology (includes the BPS library); Major area studies collections (Latin-American – including Caribbean; United States and Commonwealth Studies, British Government Publications and maps). The Library has a wide range of Special Collections holdings. Check the website for full details of collections and current access arrangements.

The London Institute – London College of Communication: Library and Learning Resources
Elephant and Castle, London SE1 6SB
☎020 7514 6527 Fax 020 7514 6597
www.linst.ac.uk/library
ACCESS By arrangement

Library and Learning Resources provides books, periodicals, slides, CD-ROMs, videos and computer software on all aspects of the art of the book, printing, management, film/photography, graphic arts, plus retailing. SPECIAL COLLECTIONS history and development of published and unpublished scripts and the art of the western book.

The London Library
14 St James's Square, London SW1Y 4LG
☎020 7930 7705 Fax 020 7766 4766
✉ membership@londonlibrary.co.uk
www.londonlibrary.co.uk
Librarian *Miss Inez Lynn*
OPEN 9.30 am to 5.30 pm Monday, Friday, Saturday; 9.30 am to 7.30 pm Tuesday, Wednesday, Thursday
ACCESS For members only (£170 p.a., 2004)

With over a million books and 8400 members, The London Library 'is the most distinguished private library in the world; probably the largest, certainly the best loved'. Founded in 1841, it is a registered charity and wholly independent of public funding. Its permanent collection embraces most European languages as well as English. Its subject range is predominantly within the humanities, with emphasis on literature, history, fine and applied art, architecture,

bibliography, philosophy, religion, and topography and travel. Some 8000–9000 titles are added yearly. Most of the stock is on open shelves to which members have free access. Members may take out up to 10 volumes; 15 if they live more than 20 miles from the Library. The comfortable Reading Room has an annexe for users of personal computers. There are photocopiers, CD-ROM workstations, free access to the Internet, and the Library also offers a postal loans service.

Prospective members are required to submit a refereed application form in advance of admission, but there is at present no waiting list for membership. The London Library Trust may make grants to those who are unable to afford the full annual fee; details on application.

London Metropolitan Archives Library Services
History Library: 40 Northampton Road, London EC1R 0HB
☎020 7332 3820/7278 8703 (Minicom)
Fax 020 7833 9136
www.cityoflondon.gov.uk/lma
Contact *The Enquiry Team*
ACCESS For reference only

This 100,000 volume library covers all aspects of the life and development of London, with strong holdings on the history and organisation of London local government. As the former Greater London Council History Library, the collection covers all subjects of London life, from architecture and biography to theatres and transport. The collection includes London directories from 1677 to the present, Acts of Parliament, statistical returns, several hundred periodical titles and public reports.

Lord Louis Library
Orchard Street, Newport PO30 1LL
☎01983 527655/823800 (Reference Library)
Fax 01983 825972
✉ reflib@postmaster.co.uk
OPEN 9.00 am to 5.30 pm Monday to Wednesday and Friday; 10.00 am to 8.00 pm Thursday; 9.00 am to 5.00 pm Saturday; 10.00 am to 4.00 pm Sunday
OPEN ACCESS

General adult and junior fiction and non-fiction collections; local history collection. Also the county's main reference library.

Manchester Central Library
St Peters Square, Manchester M2 5PD
☎0161 234 1900 Fax 0161 234 1963
✉ mclib@libraries.manchester.gov.uk

www.manchester.gov.uk/libraries

OPEN 10.00 am to 8.00 pm Monday to Thursday; 10.00 am to 5.00 pm Friday and Saturday; Commercial and European Units: 10.00 am to 6.00 pm Monday to Thursday; 10.00 am to 5.00 pm Friday and Saturday

OPEN ACCESS
One of the country's leading reference libraries with extensive collections covering all subjects. Departments include: commercial, European, technical, social sciences, arts, music, local studies, Chinese, general readers, language & literature. Large lending stock and VIP (visually impaired) service available.

Marylebone Library (Westminster)
See Sherlock Holmes Collection

The Mitchell Library
North Street, Glasgow G3 7DN
☎0141 287 2999 Fax 0141 287 2815
www.glasgowlibraries.org

OPEN 9.00 am to 8.00 pm Monday to Thursday; 9.00 am to 5.00 pm Friday and Saturday

OPEN ACCESS
One of Europe's largest public reference libraries with stock of over 1,200,000 volumes. It subscribes to 48 newspapers and more than 1200 periodicals. There are collections in microform, records, tapes and videos, as well as CD-ROMs, electronic databases, illustrations, photographs, postcards, etc.

The library contains a number of special collections, e.g. the Robert Burns Collection (5000 vols), the Scottish Poetry Collection (12,000 items) and the Scottish Drama Collection (1650 items).

Morrab Library
Morrab House, Morrab Gardens, Penzance TR18 4DA
☎01736 364474

Librarian *Annabelle Read*

OPEN 10.00 am to 4.00 pm Tuesday to Friday; 10.00 am to 1.00 pm Saturday

ACCESS Non-members may use the library for a small daily fee but may not borrow books

Formerly known as the Penzance Library. An independent subscription lending library of over 40,000 volumes covering virtually all subjects except modern science and technology, with large collections on history, literature and religion. There is a comprehensive Cornish collection of books, newspapers and manuscripts including the Borlase letters; a West Cornwall photographic archive; many runs of 18th- and 19th-century periodicals; a collection of over 2000 books published before 1800.

The National Archives
Kew, Richmond TW9 4DU
☎020 8876 3444 Fax 020 8878 8905
✉ enquiry@nationalarchives.gov.uk
www.nationalarchives.gov.uk

OPEN 9.00 am to 5.00 pm Monday, Wednesday, Friday; 10.00 am to 7.00 pm Tuesday; 9.00 am to 7.00 pm Thursday; 9.30 am to 5.00 pm Saturday (closed public holidays and 29 November to 4th December for annual stocktaking)

ACCESS for reference, by reader's ticket, available free of charge on production of proof of identity (UK citizens: banker's card or driving licence; non-UK: passport or national identity card. Telephone for further information)

Over 168 kilometres of shelving house the national repository of records of central government in the UK and law courts of England and Wales, which extend in time from the 11th–20th century. Medieval records and the records of the State Paper Office from the early 16th–late 18th century, plus the records of the Privy Council Office and the Lord Chamberlain's and Lord Steward's departments. Modern government department records, together with those of the Copyright Office dating mostly from the late 18th century. Under the Public Records Act, records are normally only open to inspection when they are 30 years old.

National Library of Scotland
George IV Bridge, Edinburgh EH1 1EW
☎0131 226 4531 Fax 0131 622 4803
✉ enquiries@nls.uk
www.nls.uk

OPEN Main Reading Room: 9.30 am to 8.30 pm Monday, Tuesday, Thursday, Friday; 10.00 am to 8.30 pm Wednesday; 9.30 am to 1.00 pm Saturday. Map Library: 9.30 am to 5.00 pm Monday, Tuesday, Thursday, Friday; 10.00 am to 5.00 pm Wednesday; 9.30 am to 1.00 pm Saturday

ACCESS To all reading rooms, for research not easily done elsewhere, by reader's ticket

Collection of over seven million volumes. The library receives all British and Irish publications. Large stock of newspapers and periodicals. Many special collections, including early Scottish books, theology, polar studies, baking, phrenology and liturgies. Also large collections of maps, music and manuscripts including personal archives of notable Scottish persons.

National Library of Wales
Aberystwyth SY23 3BU
☎01970 632800 Fax 01970 615709
www.llgc.org.uk

OPEN 9.30 am to 6.00 pm Monday to Friday; 9.30 am to 5.00 pm Saturday (closed Bank Holidays)

ACCESS To reading rooms by reader's ticket, available on application. Open acess to regular exhibition programme and to permanent exhibition 'The Treasures of the Nation'

Collection of over four million books and including large collections of periodicals, maps, manuscripts and audiovisual material. Particular emphasis on humanities in printed foreign material, and on Wales and other Celtic areas in all collections.

National Meteorological Library and Archive
FitzRoy Road, Exeter EX1 3PB
☎0870 900 0100 Fax 0870 900 5050
✉ metlib@metoffice.com
www.metoffice.com

OPEN Library & Archive: 8.30 am to 4.30 pm Monday to Friday; Archive closed between 1.00 pm and 2.00 pm

ACCESS By Visitor's Pass available from the reception desk; advance notice of a planned visit is appreciated

The major repository of most of the important literature on the subjects of meteorology, climatology and related sciences from the 16th century to the present day. The Library houses a collection of books, journals, articles and scientific papers, plus published climatological data from many parts of the world. The Technical Archive (The Scott Building, Sterling Centre, Eastern Road, Bracknell RG12 2PW ☎01344 855960; Fax 01344 855961. NB due to move to the Exeter address above at the end of 2004. Closed Fridays in 2004 only.) holds the document collection of meteorological data and charts from England, Wales and British overseas bases, including ships' weather logs. Records from Scotland are stored in Edinburgh and those from Northern Ireland in Belfast.

The Natural History Museum Library
Cromwell Road, London SW7 5BD
☎020 7942 5460 Fax 020 7942 5559
✉ library@nhm.ac.uk
www.nhm.ac.uk/library/index.html

OPEN 10.00 am to 4.30 pm Monday to Friday

ACCESS To *bona fide* researchers, by reader's ticket on presentation of identification (telephone first to make an appointment)

The library is in five sections: general; botany; zoology; entomology; earth sciences. The sub-department of ornithology is housed at the Zoological Museum, Akeman Street, Tring HP23 6AP (☎01442 834181). Resources available include books, journals, maps, manuscripts, drawings and photographs covering all aspects of natural history, including palaeontology and mineralogy, from the 14th century to the present day. Also archives and historical collection on the museum itself.

Newcastle upon Tyne City Library
Princess Square, Newcastle upon Tyne NE99 1DX
☎0191 277 4100 Fax 0191 277 4137
✉ city.information@newcastle.gov.uk *or* information@newcastle.gov.uk

LOCAL STUDIES ☎local.studies@newcastle. gov.uk

OPEN 9.00 am to 8.00 pm Monday to Thursday; 9.00 am to 5.00 pm Friday and Saturday; 12 noon to 4.00 pm Sunday

Extensive local studies collection, including newspapers, illustrations and genealogy. Also business, science, humanities and arts.

Nielsen BookData
Globe House, 1 Chertsey Road, Twickenham TW1 1LR
☎0870 777 8710 Fax 0870 777 8711
✉ sales@bookdata.co.uk
www.nielsenbookdata.com
www.nielsenbooknet.com

Contact *Sales Department*

The leading supplier of high-quality, content-rich book information and other published media to the book industry. Nielsen BookData takes information from publishers and creates a unique title record, which includes bibliographic details, text summaries, tables of contents, extensive subject-related information, market-rights details, jacket images and prize information. This bibliographic record is then available through a variety of services worldwide: as a direct feed, range of CD-ROMs or online. The company also offers order routing, order tracking, EDI and Web services.

Norfolk Library & Information Service

Norfolk and Norwich Millennium Library, The Forum, Millennium Plain, Norwich NR2 1AW

www.norfolk.gov.uk/council/departments/lis/libhome.htm

OPEN Lending Library, Reference and Information Service and Norfolk Studies: 9.00 am to 8.00 pm Monday, Wednesday, Thursday, Friday; 10.00 am to 8.00 pm Tuesday; 9.00 am to 5.00 pm Saturday. EXPRESS: 9.00 am to 9.30 pm Monday to Friday; 9.00 am to 8.30 pm Saturday; 10.30 am to 4.30 pm Sunday

OPEN ACCESS

Reference lending library (stock merged together) with wide range, including books, recorded music, music scores, plays and videos. Houses the 2nd Air Division Memorial Library and has a strong Norfolk Heritage Library. Extensive range of reference stock including business information. Online database and CD-ROM services. Public fax and colour photocopying, free access to the Internet. EXPRESS (fiction, sound & vision library within a library) – selection of popular fiction, videos, CDs and DVDs available, with extended opening hours.

Northamptonshire Libraries & Information Service

Library HQ, PO Box 216, John Dryden House, 8–10 The Lakes, Northampton NN4 7DD

☎01604 237959 Fax 01604 237937
✉ kobrien@northamptonshire.gov.uk

Since 1991, the Libraries and Information Service has offered its 'WordsWork' diary of literature events. The programme now attracts exciting literary names as well as new and locally-based writers. There are two diaries each year for an adult audience. Writers have an opportunity to read at a variety of venues. Literature workshops, activities and other events are supported. Regular book displays and dedicated notice boards in libraries support the programme across the county.

Northumberland Central Library

The Willows, Morpeth NE61 1TA
☎01670 534518/534514 Fax 01670 534513

✉ referencelibrary@northumberland.gov.uk
www.northumberland.gov.uk

Open 10.00 am to 8.00 pm Monday, Tuesday, Wednesday, Friday; 9.30 am to 12.30 pm Saturday (closed Thursday)

OPEN ACCESS

Books, periodicals, newspapers, story cassettes, CD-ROMs, DVDs, CDs, videos, Free Internet access, word processing facilities, prints, microforms, vocal scores, playsets, community resource equipment. SPECIAL COLLECTIONS Northern Poetry Library: 15,000 volumes of modern poetry (see entry under *Organisations of Interest to Poets*); Cinema: comprehensive collection of about 5000 volumes covering all aspects of the cinema; Family History.

Nottingham Central Library

Angel Row, Nottingham NG1 6HP
☎0115 915 2828 Fax 0115 915 2850
✉ arts.library@nottinghamcity.gov.co.uk
www.nottinghamcity.gov.uk

OPEN 9.30 am to 7.00 pm Monday to Friday; 9.00 am to 1.00 pm Saturday

OPEN ACCESS

General public lending library: business information, online information, the arts, local studies, religion, community languages, literature. Videos, periodicals, spoken word, recorded music, CD-ROM service – textual information on CD-ROM on public access machines. People's Network Internet, providing free public access. SPECIAL COLLECTION on D.H. Lawrence. Extensive back-up reserve stocks. Drama and music sets for loan to groups. Art gallery – contemporary exhibitions; coffee shop.

Nottingham Subscription Library Ltd

See **Bromley House Library**

Office for National Statistics, National Statistics Information and Library Service

1 Drummond Gate, London SW1V 2QQ
☎0845 601 3034/01633 812399 (Minicom)
Fax 01633 652747
✉ info@statistics.gov.uk
www.statistics.gov.uk

OPEN 9.00 am to 5.00 pm; no appointment required

Also: National Statistics Information and Library Service, Government Buildings, Cardiff Road, Newport NP9 1XG

OPEN as above

Wide range of government statistical publications and access to government Internet-based data. Census statistical data from 1801; population and health data from 1837; government social survey reports from 1941; recent international statistical data (UN, Eurostat, etc.); monograph and periodical collections of statistical methodology. The library in south Wales holds a wide range of government economic and statistical publications.

Orkney Library
44 Junction Road, Kirkwall KW15 1AG
☎01856 873166 Fax 01856 875260
✉ orkney.library@orkney.gov.uk
www.orkneylibrary.org.uk
OPEN 9.00 am to 8.00 pm Monday to
Thursday; 9.00 am to 6.00 pm Friday;
9.00 am to 5.00 pm Saturday. Archives:
9.00 am to 4.45 pm Monday, Wednesday,
Friday; 9.00 am to 7.45 pm Tuesday and
Thursday; 9.00 am to 1.00 pm and 2.00 pm
to 5.00 pm Saturday
OPEN ACCESS
Local studies collection. Archive includes sound and photographic departments.

Oxford Central Library
Westgate, Oxford OX1 1DJ
☎01865 815549 Fax 01865 721694
✉ centlib.occdla@dial.pipex.com
www.oxfordshire.gov.uk
OPEN Call 01865 815509 for details

General lending and reference library including the Centre for Oxfordshire Studies. Also periodicals, audio visual materials, music library, children's library and Business Information Point.

PA News Centre
Central Park, New Lane, Leeds LS11 5DZ
☎0870 830 6824 Fax 0870 830 6801
✉ palibrary@pa.press.net
www.pa.press.net
OPEN 8.00 am to 6.00 pm Monday to Friday;
10.00 am to 6.00 pm Saturday; 8.00 am to
4.00 pm Sunday
OPEN ACCESS
PA News, the 24-hour national news and information group, offers the PA Digital Library which holds Press Association stories. Personal callers welcome or research undertaken by in-house staff.

Penzance Library
See **Morrab Library**

City of Plymouth Library and Information Services
Central Library, Drake Circus, Plymouth
PL4 8AL
www.plymouthlibraries.info
OPEN ACCESS

CENTRAL LIBRARY LENDING DEPARTMENTS
Lending ☎01752 305912
✉ lendlib@plymouth.gov.uk

Children's Department ☎ 01752 305916
✉ childrens.library@plymouth.gov.uk

Music & Drama Department
☎01752 305914
✉ music@plymouth.gov.uk

OPEN 9.00 am to 7.00 pm Monday and
Friday; 9.00 am to 5.30 pm Tuesday,
Wednesday, Thursday; 9.00 am to 5.00 pm
Saturday

The Lending departments offer books on all subjects; language courses on cassette and foreign language books; the Holcenberg Jewish Collection; books on music and musicians, drama and theatre; music parts and sets of music parts; play sets; DVDs, videos; song index; cassettes and CDs; public Internet access.

CENTRAL LIBRARY REFERENCE DEPARTMENTS
Reference ☎01752 305907
✉ ref@plymouth.gov.uk

Business Information ☎01752 305908
✉ keyinfo@plymouth.gov.uk

Local Studies & Naval History Department
☎01752 305909
✉ localstudies@plymouth.gov.uk

OPEN 9.00 am to 7.00 pm Monday to Friday;
9.00 am to 5.00 pm Saturday

The Reference departments include an extensive collection of Ordnance Survey maps and town guides; community and census information; marketing and statistical information; Patents; books on every aspect of Plymouth; naval history; Mormon Index on microfilm; Baring Gould manuscript of 'Folk Songs of the West'; public Internet access.

Plymouth Proprietary Library
Alton Terrace, 111 North Hill, Plymouth
PL4 8JY
☎01752 660515
Librarian *John R. Smith*
OPEN Monday to Saturday from 9.30 am
(closing time varies)

ACCESS To members; visitors by appointment only

Founded 1810. The library contains approximately 17,000 volumes of mainly 20th-century work. Member of the **Association of Independent Libraries**.

The Poetry Library
See entry under *Organisations of Interest to Poets*

Polish Library
238–246 King Street, London W6 0RF
☎020 8741 0474 Fax 020 8741 7724
✉ bibliotekapolska@posklibrary.fsnet.co.uk *or* polish.library@posk.org
Librarian *Mrs Jadwiga Szmidt*

OPEN 10.00 am to 8.00 pm Monday and Wednesday; 10.00 am to 5.00 pm Friday; 10.00 am to 1.00 pm Saturday (library closed Tuesday and Thursday)

ACCESS For reference to all interested in Polish affairs; limited loans to members and *bona fide* scholars only through inter-library loans

Books, pamphlets, periodicals, maps, music, photographs on all aspects of Polish history and culture. SPECIAL COLLECTIONS Emigré publications; Joseph Conrad and related works; Polish underground publications; bookplates.

Poole Central Library
Dolphin Centre, Poole BH15 1QE
☎01202 262424 Fax 01202 262442
✉ poolelibrary@poole.gov.uk

OPEN 8.00 am to 7.00 pm Monday; 8.30 am to 6.30 pm Tuesday, Wednesday, Thursday; 8.00 am to 7.00 pm Friday; 9.00 am to 5.00 pm Saturday

OPEN ACCESS

General lending and reference library, including Healthpoint health information centre, business information, children's library, periodicals and newspapers, cafe, IT suite and meeting room.

Press Association Library
See **PA News Centre**

Public Record Office
See **The National Archives**

Reading Central Library
Abbey Square, Reading RG1 3BQ
☎0118 901 5955 Fax 0118 901 5954
✉ info@readinglibraries.org.uk

www.readinglibraries.org.uk

OPEN 9.30 am to 5.30 pm Monday and Friday; 9.30 am to 7.00 pm Tuesday and Thursday; 9.30 am to 5.00 pm Wednesday and Saturday

OPEN ACCESS

Ground Floor: Fiction, audio-visual material, children's library; First Floor: Newspapers, non-fiction – biography, business, careers, cookery, DIY, engineering, gardening, health, languages, law, mind, body & spirit, pets, science, social studies, sport, transport, travel; Second Floor: LearnDirect, non-fiction – art, music, literature, plays, computing; Third floor: Non-fiction – world history, national history, local history. Magazines and periodicals and Internet access on all floors.

Religious Society of Friends Library
Friends House, 173 Euston Road, London NW1 2BJ
☎020 7663 1135 Fax 020 7663 1001
✉ library@quaker.org.uk
www.quaker.org.uk

OPEN 1.00 pm to 5.00 pm Monday, Tuesday, Thursday, Friday; 10.00 am to 5.00 pm Wednesday

OPEN ACCESS A letter of introduction from a college/employer/publisher or Friends meeting is required for researchers who are not members of the Society (it is advisable to make an appointment before visiting)

Quaker history, thought and activities from the 17th century onwards. Supporting collections on peace, anti-slavery and other subjects in which Quakers have maintained long-standing interest. Also archives and manuscripts relating to the Society of Friends.

Richmond Central Reference Library
Old Town Hall, Whittaker Avenue, Richmond TW9 1TP
☎020 8940 5529 Fax 020 8940 6899
✉ reference.services@richmond.gov.uk
www.richmond.gov.uk

OPEN 9.30 am to 6.00 pm Monday, Thursday, Friday (Tuesday until 1.00 pm; Wednesday until 8.00 pm and Saturday until 5.00 pm)

OPEN ACCESS

General reference library serving the needs of local residents and organisations. Internet access and online databases for public use.

Royal Geographical Society Library (with the Institute of British Geographers)

1 Kensington Gore, London SW7 2AR
☎020 7591 3040 Fax 020 7591 3001
www.rgs.org

The Library and Map Room are closed for major refurbishment until Summer 2004. See website for details. For information on the Picture Library see entry under *Picture Libraries*.

Royal Institute of Philosophy

See **University of London Library**

Royal Society Library

6–9 Carlton House Terrace, London SW1Y 5AG
☎020 7451 2606 Fax 020 7930 2170
✉ library@royalsoc.ac.uk
www.royalsoc.ac.uk

OPEN 10.00 am to 5.00 pm Monday to Friday

ACCESS Open to all researchers with an interest in the history of science, the Fellowship of the Royal Society and science policy. Researchers are advised to contact the Library in advance of their first visit.

History of science, scientists' biographies, science policy reports, and publications of international scientific unions and national academies from all over the world.

RSA (Royal Society for the Encouragement of Arts, Manufactures & Commerce)

8 John Adam Street, London WC2N 6EZ
☎020 7930 5115 Fax 020 7839 5805
www.theRSA.org

OPEN Library: 8.30 am to 8.00 pm every weekday. Archive material by appointment

ACCESS to Fellows of RSA; by application and appointment to non-Fellows (Contact Librarian, ☎020 7451 6874 or ✉ library@rsa.org.uk)

Archives of the Society since 1754. A collection of approximately 10,000 volumes; international exhibition material.

Royal Society of Medicine Library

1 Wimpole Street, London W1G 0AE
☎020 7290 2940 Fax 020 7290 2939
✉ library@rsm.ac.uk
www.rsm.ac.uk

Director of Information Services *Ian Snowley*

OPEN 9.00 am to 8.30 pm Monday to Thursday; 9.00 am to 5.30 pm Friday;

10.00 am to 5.00 pm Saturday

ACCESS For reference only, on introduction by Fellow of the Society or temporary membership is available to non-members; £12 per day; £35 per week; £90 per month. Identification required.

Books, periodicals, databases on postgraduate biomedical information. Extensive historical collection dating from the fifteenth century and medical portrait collection.

Eric Frank Russell Archive

See **Science Fiction Foundation Research Library**

St Bride Printing Library

Bride Lane, London EC4Y 8EE
☎020 7353 4660 Fax 020 7583 7073
✉ library@stbrideinstitute.org
www.stbride.org

OPEN 9.30 am to 5.30 pm Monday and Friday; 12 noon to 5.30 pm Tuesday and Thursday; 12 noon to 9.00 pm Wednesday

OPEN ACCESS

A public reference library maintained by the St Bride Foundation. Appointments advisable for consultation of special collections. Every aspect of printing and related matters: publishing and bookselling, newspapers and magazines, graphic design, calligraphy and type, papermaking and bookbinding. One of the world's largest specialist collections in its field, with over 50,000 volumes, over 3000 periodicals (200 current titles), and extensive collection of drawings, manuscripts, prospectuses, patents and materials for printing and typefounding. Noted for its comprehensive holdings of historical and early technical literature.

Science Fiction Foundation Research Library

Liverpool University Library, PO Box 123, Liverpool L69 3DA
☎0151 794 3142 Fax 0151 794 3142
✉ asawyer@liverpool.ac.uk
www.liv.ac.uk/~asawyer/sffchome.html

Contact *Andy Sawyer*

ACCESS For research, by appointment only (telephone first)

This is the largest collection outside the US of science fiction and related material – including autobiographies and critical works. SPECIAL COLLECTION Runs of 'pulp' magazines dating back to the 1920s. Foreign-language material (including a large Russian collection), and the papers of the Flat Earth Society. The collection also features a growing range of archive and manuscript material, including the Eric Frank Russell archive. The University of Liverpool also holds the Olaf Stapledon and John Wyndham archives.

Science Museum Library
Imperial College Road, London SW7 5NH
☎020 7942 4242 Fax 020 7942 4243
✉ smlinfo@nmsi.ac.uk
www.nmsi.ac.uk/library

OPEN 9.30 am to 9.00 pm Monday to Friday (closes 5.30 pm outside academic terms); 9.30 am to 5.30 pm Saturday

OPEN ACCESS Reference only; no loans
National reference library for the history and public understanding of science and technology, with a large collection of source material. Operates jointly with Imperial College Central Library.

Scottish Poetry Library
See entry under *Organisations of Interest to Poets*

Sheffield Libraries, Archives and Information
Central Library, Surrey Street, Sheffield S1 1XZ
☎0114 273 4712 Fax 0114 273 5009
✉ libraries@sheffield.gov.uk
www.sheffield.gov.uk (click on 'In your area')

Central Lending Library
☎0114 273 4727 (enquiries)/4729 (book renewals)

OPEN 10.00 am to 8.00 pm Monday; 9.30 am to 5.30 pm Tuesday, Thursday and Friday; 9.30 am to 8.00 pm Wednesday; 9.30 am to 5.30 pm Saturday

Books, talking books, large print, language courses, European fiction, books in cultural languages, play sets. Writers' Resource Centre, Wednesday evenings, 5.00 pm to 7.00 pm. Proof of signature and a separate proof of address required to join.

Sheffield Archives
52 Shoreham Street, Sheffield S1 4SP
☎0114 203 9395 Fax 0114 203 9398
✉ archives@sheffield.gov.uk

OPEN 9.30 am to 5.30 pm Tuesday to Thursday; 9.30 am to 1.00 pm and 2.00 pm to 5.00 pm Saturday (documents should be ordered by 5.00 pm Thursday for Saturday); closed Monday and Friday

ACCESS By reader's pass
Holds documents relating to Sheffield and South Yorkshire, dating from the 12th century to the present day, including records of the City Council, churches, businesses, landed estates, families and individuals, institutions and societies.

Arts and Social Sciences and Sports Reference Service
☎0114 273 4747/8
✉ archives@sheffield.gov.uk

OPEN 10.00 am to 8.00 pm Monday; 9.30 am to 5.30 pm Tuesday, Thursday and Friday; 9.30 am to 8.00 pm Wednesday; 9.30 am to 5.30 pm Saturday

ACCESS For reference only
A comprehensive collection of books, newspapers and periodicals covering all aspects of arts (excluding music) and social sciences.

Music and Video Service
☎0114 273 4733
✉ music&video.library@sheffield.gov.uk

OPEN as for Arts and Social Sciences above

ACCESS For reference and lending
An extensive range of books, CDs, cassettes, scores, etc. related to music. Also a video cassette and DVD loan service.

Local Studies Service
☎0114 273 4753
✉ localstudies.library@sheffield.gov.uk

OPEN as for Arts & Social Sciences above (except Wednesday 9.30 am to 5.30 pm)

ACCESS For reference

Extensive material covering all aspects of Sheffield and its population, including maps, photos and videos. Photograph collection available on www.picturesheffield.com

Business, Science and Technology Reference Services
☎0114 273 4736/7 or 273 4742
✉ cbt.library@sheffield.gov.uk

OPEN as for Arts & Social Sciences above

ACCESS For reference only
Extensive coverage of science and technology as well as commerce and commercial law. British patents and British and European standards with emphasis on metals. Hosts the World Metal Index. The business section holds a large stock of business and trade directories, plus overseas telephone directories and reference works with business emphasis.

Sheffield Information Service
☎0114 273 4712 Fax 0114 275 7111
✉ libraries@sheffield.gov.uk

Website www.sheffieldinfo.org.uk

OPEN 10.00 am to 5.30 pm Monday; 9.30 am to 5.30 pm Tuesday to Saturday

Full local information service covering all aspects of the Sheffield community.

Children's and Young People's Library Service
☎0114 273 4734
✉ cyp.library@sheffield.gov.uk

OPEN 10.30 am to 5.00 pm Monday and Friday; 1.00 pm to 5.00 pm Tuesday, Wednesday and Thursday; 9.30 am to 5.30 pm Saturday

Books, spoken word sets, videos; under-five play area; teenage reference section; readings and promotions; storytime sessions.

Shetland Library
Lower Hillhead, Lerwick ZE1 0EL
☎01595 693868 Fax 01595 694430
✉ shetlandlibrary@sic.shetland.gov.uk
www.shetland-library.gov.uk

OPEN 10.00 am to 7.00 pm Monday, Wednesday, Thursday; 10.00 am to 5.00 pm Tuesday, Friday, Saturday

General lending and reference library; extensive local interest collection including complete set of *The Shetland Times*, *The Shetland News* and other local newspapers on microfilm and many old and rare books; audio collection including talking books/newspapers. Junior room for children. Disabled access and Housebound Readers Service (delivery to reader's home). Mobile library services to rural areas. Open Learning Service. Same day photocopying service. Publishing programme of books in dialect, history, literature. Learning centre providing access to learning opportunities including Internet.

Shoe Lane Library
Hill House, Little New Street, London EC4A 3JR
☎020 7583 7178 Fax 020 7353 0884
✉ shoelane@corpoflondon.gov.uk
www.corpoflondon.gov.uk

OPEN 9.00 am to 5.30 pm Monday, Wednesday, Thursday, Friday; 9.00 am to 6.30 pm Tuesday

OPEN ACCESS

Corporation of London general lending library, with a comprehensive stock of 50,000 volumes, most of which are on display.

Shrewsbury Library and Reference & Information Service
Castlegates, Shrewsbury SY1 2AS
☎01743 255300 Fax 01743 255309
✉ shrewsbury.library@shropshire-cc.gov.uk
www.shropshire-cc.gov.uk/library.nsf

OPEN 9.30 am to 5.00 pm Monday, Wednesday, Friday; 9.30 am to 8.00 pm Tuesday and Thursday; 9.00 am to 5.00 pm Saturday

OPEN ACCESS

The largest public library in Shropshire. Books, cassettes, CDs, talking books, DVDs, videos, language courses. Open Learning and study centre with three public use computers for word processing, CD-ROMs and Internet access. Music, literature and art book collection for lending and reference. The West Midlands Literary Heritage Collection is housed at Shrewsbury Library.

Spanish Institute Library
See **Instituto Cervantes**

Sterling Collection
See **University of London Library**

Suffolk County Council Libraries & Heritage
Endeavour House, Russell Road, Ipswich IP1 2BX
☎01473 265086 Fax 01473 216847
✉ help@libher.suffolkcc.gov.uk
www.suffolkcc.gov.uk/libraries

OPEN See website for details of individual libraries or contact Endeavour House as above. Major libraries open seven days a week; all libraries open Sunday

ACCESS A single library card gives access to the lending service of 43 libraries and resource centres across the county. Loans can be collected and/or returned at any service point. Details on website

Full range of lending and reference services, free public access to the Internet. Wide range of online services for registered library users through the Suffolk Libraries Direct pages, e.g. self-service reservations, renewals, free access to subscription services. Suffolk InfoLink Plus database gives details of local organisations throughout the county. SPECIAL COLLECTIONS include

Suffolk Archives and Local History Collection; Benjamin Britten Collection; Edward Fitzgerald Collection; Seckford Collection and Racing Collection (Newmarket). The Suffolk Infolink service gives details of local groups and societies and is available in libraries throughout the county and on the website.

Sunderland City Library and Arts Centre

28–30 Fawcett Street, Sunderland SR1 1RE
☎0191 514 1235 Fax 0191 514 8444
✉ enquiry.desk@sunderland.gov.uk
www.sunderland.gov.uk/libraries

OPEN 9.30 am to 7.30 pm Monday and Wednesday; 9.30 am to 5.00 pm Tuesday, Thursday, Friday; 9.30 am to 4.00 pm Saturday

The city's main library for lending and reference services. Local studies and children's sections, plus Sound and Vision department (CDs, DVDs, cassettes, videos, CD-ROMs, talking books). The City of Sunderland also maintains community libraries of varying size, offering a range of services, plus mobile libraries. Free Internet access is available in all libraries across the city. A Books on Wheels service is available to housebound readers; the Schools Library Service serves teachers and schools. Two writers' groups meet at the City Library and Arts Centre: Janus Writers, every Wednesday, 1.30 pm to 3.30 pm. Tuesday Writers, every Tuesday, 7.30 pm to 9.30 pm.

Swansea Central Reference Library

Alexandra Road, Swansea SA1 5DX
☎01792 516753/516757 Fax 01792 516759
✉ central.library@swansea.gov.uk
www.swansea.gov.uk/culture/libraries/library
Intro.htm

OPEN 9.00 am to 7.00 pm Monday, Tuesday, Wednesday, Friday; 9.00 am to 5.00 pm Thursday and Saturday. The library has a lending service but hours tend to be shorter – check in advance (☎01792 516750/1)

ACCESS For reference only (Local Studies closed access: items must be requested on forms provided)

General reference material; also British standards, statutes, company information, maps, European Community information. Local studies: comprehensive collections on Wales; Swansea & Gower; Dylan Thomas. Local maps, periodicals, illustrations, local newspapers from 1804. B&w and colour photocopying facilities,

free computer and Internet access available (library membership required and pre-booking recommended) and microfilm/microfiche copying facility.

Swiss Cottage Central Library

88 Avenue Road, London NW3 3HA
☎020 7974 6522 Fax 020 7974 6532

OPEN 10.00 am to 7.00 pm Monday and Thursday; 10.00 am to 6.00 pm Tuesday, Wednesday, Friday; 10.00 am to 5.00 pm Saturday

OPEN ACCESS

Over 300,000 volumes in the lending and reference libraries. Home of the London Borough of Camden's Information and Reference Services.

Theatre Museum Library & Archive

1e Tavistock Street, London WC2E 7PR
☎020 7943 4727 Fax 020 7943 4777
✉ tmenquiries@vam.ac.uk
www.theatremuseum.vam.ac.uk

OPEN 10.30 am to 4.30 pm Wednesday to Friday

ACCESS By appointment only

The Theatre Museum was founded as a separate department of the Victoria & Albert Museum in 1974 and moved to its own building in Covent Garden in 1987. The museum (open Tuesday to Sunday 10.00 am to 6.00 pm) houses permanent displays, temporary exhibitions, a studio theatre, and organises a programme of special events, performances, lectures, guided visits and workshops. The library houses the UK's largest performing arts research collections, including books, photographs, designs, engravings, programmes, press cuttings, etc. All the performing arts are covered but strengths are in the areas of theatre, dance, musical theatre and stage design. A large store in West London houses the Museum's special collections of archives; a separate reading room there provides access to them.

Thurrock Council Libraries & Cultural Services Department

Grays Library, Orsett Road, Grays RM17 5DX
☎01375 383611 Fax 01375 370806
✉ grays.library@thurrock.gov.uk

OPEN 9.00 am to 7.00 pm Monday, Tuesday, Thursday; 9.00 am to 5.00 pm Wednesday, Friday, Saturday; branch library opening times vary

OPEN ACCESS

General library lending and reference through ten libraries and a mobile library. Services include books, magazines, newspapers, audio cassettes, CDs, videos and language courses. Large collection of Thurrock materials. Internet and Microsoft Office.

Truro Library

Union Place, Truro TR1 1EP
☎01872 279205 (lending)/272702 (reference)
✉ truro.library@cornwall.gov.uk
www.cornwall.gov.uk/library
OPEN 9.00 am to 6.00 pm Monday to Friday; 9.00 am to 4.00 pm Saturday
Books, cassettes, CDs, videos and DVDs for loan through branch or mobile networks. Study centre and IT suite. Reference collection. SPECIAL COLLECTIONS on local studies.

United Nations Information Centre

The UN Library closed down in the autumn of 2003.

Western Isles Libraries

Public Library, 19 Cromwell Street, Stornoway HS1 2DA
☎01851 708631 Fax 01851 708676
www.cne-siar.gov.uk
OPEN 10.00 am to 5.00 pm Monday to Wednesday; 10.00 am to 6.00 pm Thursday and Friday; 10.00 am to 5.00 pm Saturday
OPEN ACCESS
General public library stock, plus local history and Gaelic collections including maps, videos, printed music, cassettes and CDs; census records and Council minutes; music collection (CDs and cassettes). Branch libraries on the isles of Barra, Benbecula, Harris and Lewis.

City of Westminster Archives Centre

10 St Ann's Street, London SW1P 2DE
☎020 7641 5180/4879 (Minicom)
Fax 020 7641 5179
✉ archives@westminster.gov.uk
www.westminster.gov.uk/archives
OPEN 10.00 am to 7.00 pm Tuesday Wednesday, Thursday, 10.00 am to 5.00 pm Friday and Saturday (closed Monday)
ACCESS For reference
Comprehensive coverage of the history of Westminster and selective coverage of general London history. 22,000 books, together with a large stock of maps, prints, photographs, local newspapers, theatre programmes and archives.

Westminster Music Library

Victoria Library, 160 Buckingham Palace Road, London SW1W 9UD
☎020 7641 4292 Fax 020 7641 4281
✉ musiclibrary@westminster.gov.uk
www.westminster.gov.uk/libraries/special/music
OPEN 11.00 am to 7.00 pm Monday to Friday; 10 am to 5.00 pm Saturday
OPEN ACCESS
Located at Victoria Library, this is the largest public music library in the South of England, with extensive coverage of all aspects of music, including books, periodicals and printed scores. No recorded material, notated only. Lending library includes a small collection of CDs and videos.

Westminster Reference Library

35 St Martin's Street, London WC2H 7HP
☎020 7641 4636 Fax 020 7641 4606
✉ referencelibrarywc2@westminster.gov.uk
www.westminster.gov.uk/libraries
GENERAL REFERENCE & PERFORMING ARTS:
☎020 7641 4636
ART & DESIGN: ☎020 7641 4638
BUSINESS AND OFFICIAL PUBLICATIONS: ☎020 7641 4634
Open 1.00 pm to 8.00 pm Monday to Friday; 10.00 am to 5.00 pm Saturday
ACCESS For reference only
A general reference library with emphasis on the following: Art & Design – fine and decorative arts, architecture, graphics and design; Performing Arts – theatre, cinema, radio, television and dance; Official Publications – major collection of HMSO publications from 1947, plus parliamentary papers dating back to 1906; Business – UK directories, trade directories, company and market data; Official EU Depository Library – carries official EU material; Periodicals – long files of many titles. One working day's notice is required for some government documents, some monographs and most older periodicals.

The Wiener Library

4 Devonshire Street, London W1W 5BH
☎020 7636 7247 Fax 020 7436 6428
✉ info@wienerlibrary.co.uk
wienerlibrary.co.uk
Director *Ben Barkow*
Education and Outreach Coordinator *Katherine Klinger*
OPEN 10.00 am to 5.30 pm Monday to Friday

ACCESS By letter of introduction (readers needing to use the Library for any length of time should become members)

Private library – one of the leading research centres on European history since the First World War, with special reference to the era of totalitarianism and to Jewish affairs. Founded by Dr Alfred Wiener in Amsterdam in 1933, it holds material that is not available elsewhere. Books, periodicals, press archives, documents, pamphlets, leaflets, photo archive, audiovisual material, brochures.

Vaughan Williams Memorial Library

English Folk Dance and Song Society, Cecil Sharp House, 2 Regent's Park Road, London NW1 7AY
☎020 7485 2206 ext. 18/19
Fax 020 7284 0523
✉ library@efdss.org
www.efdss.org
Contact *Elinor Pearson*
OPEN 9.30 am to 5.30 pm Tuesday to Friday; 10.00 am to 4.00 pm 1st & 3rd Saturday (sometimes closed between 1.00 pm and 2.00 pm)

ACCESS For reference to the general public, on payment of a daily fee; members may borrow books and use the library free of charge

A multimedia collection: books, periodicals, manuscripts, tapes, records, CDs, films, videos. Mostly British traditional culture and how this has developed around the world. Some foreign language material, and some books in English about foreign cultures. Also, the history of the English Folk Dance and Song Society.

Dr Williams's Library

14 Gordon Square, London WC1H 0AR
☎020 7387 3727
✉ enquiries@dwlib.co.uk
OPEN 10.00 am to 5.00 pm Monday, Wednesday, Friday; 10.00 am to 6.30 pm Tuesday and Thursday

OPEN ACCESS to reading room (loans restricted to subscribers). Visitors required to supply identification. Annual subscription £10; ministers of religion and certain students £5

Primarily a library of theology, religion and ecclesiastical history. Also philosophy, history (English and Byzantine). Particularly important for the study of English Nonconformity. Trustees of Dr William's Library manage the Congregational Library on behalf of the Memorial Hall Trustees.

Wolverhampton Central Library

Snow Hill, Wolverhampton WV1 3AX
☎01902 552025 (lending)/552026 (reference)
Fax 01902 552024
✉ wolverhampton.libraries@dial.pipex.com
www.wolverhampton.gov.uk
OPEN 9.00 am to 7.00 pm Monday to Thursday; 9.00 am to 5.00 pm Friday and Saturday

Archives & Local Studies Collection

42–50 Snow Hill, Wolverhampton WV2 4AB
☎01902 552480
OPEN 10.00 am to 5.00 pm Monday, Tuesday, Friday, 1st and 3rd Saturday of each month; 10.00 am to 7.00 pm Wednesday; closed Thursday

General lending and reference libraries, plus children's library and audiovisual library holding cassettes, CDs, videos and music scores. Internet access.

The Women's Library

London Metropolitan University, Old Castle Street, London E1 7NT
☎020 7320 2222 Fax 020 7320 2333
✉ moreinfo@thewomenslibrary.ac.uk
www.thewomenslibrary.ac.uk
Director *Antonia Byatt*
OPEN Reading Room: 9.30 am to 5.00 pm Tuesday to Friday (8.00 pm Thursday); 10.00 am to 4.00 pm Saturday
OPEN ACCESS Exhibition: 9.30 am to 5.30 pm Monday to Friday (8.00 pm Thursday); 10.00 am to 4.00 pm Saturday

The Women's Library, national research library for women's history, is the UK's oldest and most comprehensive research library on all aspects of women in society, with both historical and contemporary coverage. The Library includes materials on feminism, work, education, health, the family, law, arts, sciences, technology, language, sexuality, fashion and the home. The main emphasis is on Britain but many other countries are represented, especially the Commonwealth and the developing countries. Established in 1926 as the library of the London Society of Women's Service (formerly Suffrage), a non-militant organisation led by Millicent Fawcett. In 1953 the Society was renamed after her and the library became the Fawcett Library.

Collections include: women's suffrage, work,

education, women and the church, the law, sport, art, music, abortion, prostitution. Mostly British materials but some American, Commonwealth and European works. Books, journals, pamphlets, archives, photographs, posters, postcards, audiovisual materials, artefacts, scrapbooks, albums and press cuttings dating mainly from the 19th century although some materials date from the 17th century.

The Library's new building, which opened in February 2002, includes a reading room, exhibition space, café, education areas and a conference room, and is the cultural and research centre for anyone interested in women's lives and achievements.

Worcestershire Libraries and Information Service

Cultural Services, Worcestershire County Council, County Hall, Spetchley Road, Worcester WR5 2NP
☎01905 766231 Fax 01905 766244
✉ libraries@worcestershire.gov.uk
www.worcestershire.gov.uk/libraries

OPEN Opening hours vary in the 22 libraries, the History Centre and mobile libraries covering the county; all full-time libraries open at least one evening a week until 7.00 pm or 8.00 pm, and on Saturday until 4.00 pm; part-time libraries vary

ACCESS Information and reference services open to anyone; loans to members only (membership criteria: resident, being educated, working, or an elector in the county or neighbouring authorities; temporary membership to visitors. Proof of identity and address required. No charge for membership or for borrowing books.)

Information service, and reference and lending libraries. Non-fiction and fiction for all age groups, including normal and large print, spoken word cassettes, sound recordings (CD, cassette), videos, maps, local history, CD-ROMs for reference at main libraries, free public Internet access in all libraries. Joint Libraries Service/County Record Office History Centre with resources for local and family history. SPECIAL COLLECTIONS Carpets and Textiles; Needles & Needlemaking; Stuart Period; A.E. Housman.

John Wyndham Archive
See **Science Fiction Foundation Research Library**

York Central Library
Museum Street, York YO1 7DS
☎01904 655631 Fax 01904 611025
✉ reference.library@york.gov.uk

Lending Library
OPEN 9.30 am to 8.00 pm Monday, Tuesday, Friday; 9.30 am to 5.30 pm Wednesday and Thursday; 9.30 am to 4.00 pm Saturday

General lending library including videos, CDs, DVDs, CD-ROMs, music cassettes, audio books, children's storytapes language courses and printed music. Large print books. Photocopying, Internet and fax facilities.

Reference Library
OPEN 9.00 am to 8.00 pm Monday, Tuesday, Wednesday, Friday; 9.00 am to 5.30 pm Thursday; 9.00 am to 4.00 pm Saturday

General reference library; periodicals, newspapers, local newspaper index, EU information, organisations database; local studies library for York and surrounding area; business information service; microfilm/fiche readers for national and local newspapers; census returns and family history resource; general reference collection. Maintains strong links with other local history resource centres, namely the Borthwick Institute, York City Archive and York Minster Library. CD-ROM and Internet facilities. Room 18: IT resource centre available to the public. In addition, 14 branch libraries and one mobile, serving the City of York Council area.

Zoological Society Library
Regent's Park, London NW1 4RY
☎020 7449 6293 Fax 020 7586 5743
✉ library@zsl.org
www.zsl.org

OPEN 9.30 am to 5.30 pm Monday to Friday

ACCESS To members and staff; non-members by application and on payment of fee

160,000 volumes on zoology including 5000 journals (1300 current) and a wide range of books on animals and particular habitats. Slide collection available and many historic zoological prints.

Picture Libraries

A–Z Botanical Collection Ltd
192 Goswell Road, London EC1V 7DT
☎020 7253 0991 Fax 020 7253 0992
✉ sales@azbotanical.com
www.azbotanical.com
Contact *Anna Gibson*

300,000 transparencies, specialising in plants and related subjects.

Acme
See **Popperfoto.com**

Action Plus
54–58 Tanner Street SE1 3PH
☎020 7403 1558 Fax 020 7403 1526
✉ info@actionplus.co.uk
www.actionplus.co.uk

Founded 1986. Specialist sports and action library with a vast comprehensive collection of small-format colour and b&w images covering all aspects of over 130 professional and amateur sports from around the world. As well as personalities, events, venues, etc, also covers themes such as success, celebration, dejection, teamwork, effort and exhaustion. 35mm colour stock and online digital archive.

Lesley & Roy Adkins Picture Library
Ten Acre Wood, Whitestone, Exeter EX4 2HW
☎01392 811357 Fax 01392 811435
✉ mail@adkinsarchaeology.com
www.adkinsarchaeology.com

Colour coverage of archaeology, antiquity, heritage and related subjects in the UK, Europe, Egypt and Turkey. Subjects include towns, villages, housing, landscape and countryside, churches, temples, castles, monasteries, art and architecture, gravestones and tombs, inscriptions and antiquarian views. No service charge if pictures are used.

The Advertising Archive Limited
45 Lyndale Avenue, London NW2 2QB
☎020 7435 6540 Fax 020 7794 6584
✉ suzanne@advertisingarchives.co.uk
www.advertisingarchives.co.uk
Contacts *Suzanne Viner, Larry Viner*

With over one million images, the largest collection of British and American press ads, TV commercial stills and magazine cover illustrations in Europe. Material spans the period from 1850 to the present day. Expert in-house research; rapid service, competitive rates. On-line database and digital delivery available. Visitors by appointment.

AKG images Ltd, The Arts and History Picture Library
5 Melbray Mews, 158 Hurlingham Road, London SW6 3NS
☎020 7610 6103 Fax 020 7610 6125
✉ enquiries@akg-images.co.uk
www.akg-images.co.uk
Contact *Julia Engelhardt*

Collection of 250,000 images with direct access to ten million (more than 200,000 available as high resolution scans) kept in the Berlin AKG Library. Specialises in art, archaeology, history, topography, music, personalities and film.

Bryan & Cherry Alexander Photography
Higher Cottage, Manston, Sturminster Newton DT10 1EZ
☎01258 473006 Fax 01258 473333
✉ alexander@arcticphoto.co.uk
www.arcticphoto.co.uk
Contact *Cherry Alexander*

Arctic and Antarctic specialists; indigenous peoples, wildlife and science in polar regions; Norway, Iceland, Siberia and Alaska.

Alpine Garden Society
AGS Centre, Avon Bank, Pershore WR10 3JP
☎01386 554790 Fax 01386 554801
✉ ags@alpinegardensociety.org
www.alpinegardensociety.org
Contact *Peter Sheasby*

Over 20,000 colour transparencies (35mm) covering plants in the wild from many parts of the world; particularly strong in plants from mountain and sub-alpine regions, and from Mediterranean climates – South Africa, Australia, Patagonia, California and the Mediterranean.

Extensive coverage of show alpines in pots and in gardens and of European orchids. Full slide list available.

Alvey & Towers

The Springboard Centre, Mantle Lane, Coalville LE67 3DW
☎01530 450011 Fax 01530 450011
✉ alveytower@aol.com
www.alveyandtowers.com

Contact *Emma Rowen*

Houses one of the country's most comprehensive collections of transport images depicting not only actual transport systems but their surrounding industries as well. Also specialist modern railway image collection.

Andalucia Slide Library

Apto 499, Estepona, Malaga 29 680, Spain
☎00 34 952 793647 Fax 00 34 952 880138
✉ info@andaluciaslidelibrary.com
www.andaluciaslidelibrary.com

Library Manager *Michelle Chaplow*

Specialist library covering all aspects of Spain and Spanish life and culture. Cities, white villages, landscapes, festivals, art, gastronomy, leisure, tourism. Also images of Portugal, Madeira and Malta. Commissions undertaken.

Andes Press Agency

26 Padbury Court, London E2 7EH
☎020 7613 5417 Fax 020 7739 3159
✉ apa@andespressagency.com
www.andespressagency.com

Contacts *Val Baker, Carlos Reyes*

80,000 colour transparencies and 300,000 b&w, specialising in social documentary, world religions, Latin America and Britain.

Heather Angel/Natural Visions

Highways, 6 Vicarage Hill, Farnham GU9 8HJ
☎01252 716700 Fax 01252 727464
✉ hangel@naturalvisions.co.uk
www.naturalvisions.co.uk

Contact *Valerie West*

Constantly expanding worldwide natural history, wildlife and landscapes: polar regions, tropical rainforest flora and fauna, all species of plants and animals in natural habitats from Africa, Asia (notably China and Malaysia), Australasia, South America and USA, urban wildlife, pollution, biodiversity, global warming. Also worldwide gardens and cultivated flowers. With the new website a digital light-box can be sent to authors with an e-mail. The library then supplies either high resolution digital files or transparencies direct to the publisher.

Ansel Adams

See **Corbis Images**

Aquarius Library

PO Box 5, Hastings TN34 1HR
☎01424 721196 Fax 01424 717704
✉ aquarius.lib@clara.net
www.aquariuscollection.com

Contact *David Corkill*

Over one million images specialising in cinema past and present, television, pop music, ballet, opera, theatre, etc. The library includes various American showbiz collections. Film stills date back to the beginning of the century. Interested in film stills, the older the better.

Architectural Association Photo Library

36 Bedford Square, London WC1B 3ES
☎020 7887 4066 Fax 020 7414 0782
✉ valerie@aaschool.ac.uk
www.aaschool.ac.uk

Contacts *Valerie Bennett, Sarah Franklin, Henderson Downing*

100,000 35mm transparencies on architecture, historical and contemporary. Archive or large-format b&w negatives from the 1920s and 1930s.

ArenaPAL

Lambert House, 55 Southwark Street, London SE1 1RU
☎020 7403 8542 Fax 020 7403 8561
✉ searches@arenapal.com
www.arenapal.com

'All the entertainment pictures you'll ever need'. Continually updated specialist performing arts image collection covering classical music, opera, theatre, musicals, film, pop, rock, jazz, instruments, festivals, venues, circus, ballet and contemporary dance, props and personalities. Over two million images from late 19th century onwards. Please phone, fax or e-mail to make a selection.

Art Directors & Trip Photo Library

57 Burdon Lane, Cheam SM2 7BY
☎020 8642 3593 Fax 020 8395 7230
✉ images@artdirectors.co.uk
www.artdirectors.co.uk

Contacts *Helene Rogers, Bob Turner*

Extensive coverage, with over 750,000 images, of all countries, lifestyles, peoples, etc. with detailed coverage of all religions. Backgrounds a speciality. Catalogues available free to professionals.

Aspect Picture Library Ltd
40 Rostrevor Road, London SW6 5AD
☎020 7736 1998/7731 7362
Fax 020 7731 7362
✉ Aspect.Ldn@btinternet.com
www.aspect-picture-library.co.uk

Colour and b&w worldwide coverage of countries, events, industry and travel, with large files on art, namely paintings, space, China, the Middle East, French villages, English villages and Ireland.

Australia Pictures
28 Sheen Common Drive, Richmond TW10 5BN
☎020 7602 1989 Fax 020 7602 1989

Contact *John Miles*

Collection of 4000 transparencies covering all aspects of Australia: Aboriginal people, paintings, Ayers Rock, Kakadu, Tasmania, underwater, reefs, Arnhem Land, Sydney. Also Africa, Middle East and Asia.

Aviation Photographs International
15 Downs View Road, Swindon SN3 1NS
☎01793 497179 Fax 01793 434030

250,000 photographs comprise a comprehensive coverage of army, naval and airforce hardware ranging from early pistols to the latest ships. Extensive coverage of military and civil aviation includes modern together with many air-to-air views of vintage/warbird types. Collections available on disk. Commissions undertaken for additional photography and research. CD-ROM available of part of the library collection.

Aviation Picture Library
116 The Avenue, St Stephens, West Ealing, London W13 8JX
☎020 8566 7712/07860 670073 (mobile)
Fax 020 8566 7714
✉ avpix@aol.com
www.aviationpictures.com

Contact *Austin John Brown*

Specialists in the aviation field but also a general library which includes travel, architecture, transport, landscapes and skyscapes. SPECIAL COLLECTIONS aircraft and all aspects of the aviation industry, including the archival collection

of John Stroud; aerial obliques of Europe, USA, Caribbean and West Africa; architectural and town planning. Photographers for *Flyer* magazine in the UK. Commissions undertaken on the ground and in the air.

aviation–images.com
42B Queens Road, London SW19 8LR
☎020 8944 5225 Fax 020 8944 5335
✉ mark.wagner@aviation-images.com
www.aviation-images.com

Contacts *Mark Wagner, Mark Steele*

500,000+ aviation images, civil and military, archive and modern, from the world's best aviation photographers. Member of **BAPLA** and RAeS.

Axel Poignant Archive
115 Bedford Court Mansions, Bedford Avenue, London WC1B 3AG
☎020 7636 2555 Fax 020 7636 2555
✉ Rpoignant@aol.com

Contact *Roslyn Poignant*

Anthropological and ethnographic subjects, especially Australia and the South Pacific. Also Scandinavia (early history and mythology), Sicily and England.

Barnaby's Library
See **Mary Evans Picture Library**

Barnardo's Photographic and Film Archive
Barnardo's House, Tanners Lane, Barkingside, Ilford IG6 1QG
☎020 8498 7345 Fax 020 8498 7090
✉ stephen.pover@barnardos.org.uk
www.barnardos.org.uk

Image Librarian *Stephen Povers*

Images of social history from 1872 to 1905. Office hours: Monday to Friday, 9.30 am to 4.30 pm.

Colin Baxter Photography Limited
Woodlands Industrial Estate, Grantown-on-Spey PH26 3NA
☎01479 873999 Fax 01479 873888
✉ sales@colinbaxter.co.uk
www.colinbaxter.co.uk

Contacts *Colin B. Kirkwood* (Marketing), *Mike Rensner* (Editorial)

Over 50,000 images specialising in Scotland and Charles Rennie Mackintosh's work. Also the Lake District, Yorkshire, France and Iceland. Publishes guidebooks, books, calendars, postcards and greetings cards on landscape, cityscape and natural history using images which are primarily, but not exclusively, Colin Baxter's. Also publishes the *Worldlife Library* of natural history books.

BBC Natural History Unit Picture Library
See **Nature Picture Library**

The Photographic Library Beamish, The North of England Open Air Museum
The North of England Open Air Museum, Beamish DH9 0RG
☎0191 370 4000 Fax 0191 370 4001
✉ museum@beamish.org.uk
www.beamish.org.uk

Keeper of Resource Collections *Jim Lawson*
Comprehensive collection; images relate to the North East of England and cover agricultural, industrial, topography, advertising and shop scenes, people at work and play. Also on laser disk for rapid searching. Visitors by appointment weekdays.

Francis Bedford
See **Birmingham Library Services** under *Library Services*

Ivan J. Belcher Colour Picture Library
57 Gibson Close, Abingdon OX14 1XS
☎01235 521524 Fax 01235 521524

Extensive colour picture library specialising in top-quality medium-format transparencies depicting the British scene. Particular emphasis on tourist, holiday and heritage locations, including famous cities, towns, picturesque harbours, rivers, canals, castles, cottages, rural scenes and traditions photographed throughout the seasons. Mainly of recent origin and constantly updated.

Andrew Besley PhotoLibrary
'Trenerth Barton', Fraddam, Near Hayle TR27 5EP
☎01736 850086 Fax 01736 850086
✉ bes.pix@btinternet.com
www.andrewbesley-photolibrary.co.uk
Contact *Andrew Besley*

Specialist library of 20,000 images of West Country faces, places and moods.

Bettmann Archive
See **Corbis Images**

bfi Stills, Posters and Designs
British Film Institute, 21 Stephen Street, London W1T 1LN
☎020 7957 4797 Fax 020 7323 9260
✉ stills.films@bfi.org.uk
ww.bfi.org.uk/collections/stills/index.html

'bfi Stills, Posters and Designs is the world's most comprehensive collection of film and television images.' The collection captures on and off screen moments, portraits of the world's most famous stars – and those behind the camera who made them famous – as well as publicity posters, set designs, images of studios, cinemas, special events and early film and TV technologies. Rapid access to these images can be provided by photographic or digital reproduction. Visits by appointment only.

Blackwoods Picture Library
See **Geoslides Photography**

Anthony Blake Photo Library
20 Blades Court, Deodar Road, Putney, London SW15 2NU
☎020 8877 1123 Fax 020 8877 9787
✉ info@abpl.co.uk
www.abpl.co.uk

'Europe's premier source' of food and wine-related images, from the farm and the vineyard to the plate and the bottle. Cooking and kitchens, top chefs and restaurants, country trades and markets, worldwide travel with an extensive Italian section. Many recipes available to accompany transparencies. Free brochure available.

Peter Boardman Collection
See **Chris Bonington Picture Library**

Boating Images Photo Library
Foxes Studio, Foxes, Heath Road, Ramsden Heath CM11 1HR
☎0268 710454 Fax 01268 710353
✉ info@boating-images.com
www.boating-images.com
Contacts *Wendy Hollis, Scott Thwaites*

Comprehensive online boating image library. For marine, lifestyle, maritime heritage and inland waterways – worldwide. New images weekly. Search available.

Chris Bonington Picture Library
Badger Hill, Nether Row, Hesket Newmarket, Wigton CA7 8LA
☎016974 78286 Fax 016974 78238
✉ frances@bonington.com

www.bonington.com

Contact *Frances Daltrey*

Based on the personal collection of climber and author Chris Bonington and his extensive travels and mountaineering achievements; also work by Doug Scott and other climbers, including the Peter Boardman and Joe Tasker Collections. Full coverage of the world's mountains, from British hills to Everest, depicting expedition planning and management stages, the approach march showing inhabitants of the area, flora and fauna, local architecture and climbing action shots on some of the world's highest mountains.

Boulton and Watt Archive

See **Birmingham Library Services** under *Library Services*

The Bridgeman Art Library

17–19 Garway Road, London W2 4PH
☎020 7727 4065 Fax 020 7792 8509
✉ london@bridgeman.co.uk
www.bridgeman.co.uk

Head of Picture Research *Jenny Page*

Fine art photo archive acting as an agent to more than 1000 museums, galleries and picture owners around the world. Large-format colour transparencies of private collections, artists, paintings, sculptures, prints, manuscripts, antiquities and the decorative arts. The Library is currently expanding at the rate of 500 new images each week and has offices in Paris, New York and Berlin. Collections represented by the library include the British Library, the National Galleries of Scotland, the National Library of Australia, and the National Gallery of South Africa. Fully searchable catalogue online.

British Library Picture Library and Images Online/Reproductions

British Library, 96 Euston Road, London NW1 2DB

Images Online
☎020 7412 7614 Fax 020 7412 7771
✉ imagesonline@bl.uk
www.bl.uk/imagesonline

Reproductions
☎020 7412 7613 Fax 020 7412 7596
✉ reproductions@bl.uk
www.bl.uk/reproductions

The Picture Library holds a growing number of images from the British Library's collections of manuscripts, books, maps, music and phi-

lately. Transparencies or prints are available for hire and printouts are supplied free for selection purposes.

The fully searchable website, Images Online, includes images scanned from the Library's existing transparencies. High-resolution images are available on CD-ROM; smaller JPEGs can be purchased online and downloaded instantly. Reproductions offers high quality paper copying, microfilming, photographic and digital services to customers who require copies from the following collection areas: Maps, Music, Printed Books, Manuscripts and the Asia, Pacific and Africa Collections. There are two levels of copying service: standard 25 working days and express 10 working days. For commercial reproduction, please use the contact details.

Brooklands Museum Picture Library

Brooklands Museum, Brooklands Road, Weybridge KT13 0QN
☎01932 857381 Fax 01932 855465
✉ info@brooklandsmuseum.com
www.brooklandsmuseum.com

Contacts *John Pulford* (Curator of Collections), *Julian Temple* (Curator of Aviation)

About 40,000 b&w and colour prints and slides. Subjects include: Brooklands Motor Racing 1907–1939; British aviation and aerospace 1908–present day – particularly BAC, Hawker, Sopwith and Vickers aircraft built at Brooklands.

Hamish Brown MBE, D.Litt, FRSGS Scottish Photographic

26 Kirkcaldy Road, Burntisland KY3 9HQ
☎01592 873546

Contact *Hamish Brown*

Coverage of most topics and areas of Scotland (sites, historic, buildings, landscape, mountains), also travel, mountains, general (50,000 items) and Morocco. Commissions undertaken.

Capital Pictures

85 Randolph Avenue, London W9 1DL
☎020 7286 2212 Fax 020 7286 1218
✉ sales@capitalpictures.com
www.capitalpictures.com

Contact *Phil Loftus*

Specialises in photographs of famous people from the worlds of showbusiness, rock and pop, television, politics, royalty and film stills.

The Centre for the Study of Cartoons and Caricature

The Templeman Library, University of Kent at Canterbury, Canterbury CT2 7NU
☎01227 823127   Fax 01227 823127
✉ N.P.Hiley@kent.ac.uk *or*
J.M.Newton@kent.ac.uk
library.kent.ac.uk/cartoons/

Contacts *Dr Nicholas Hiley, Jane Newton*

A national research archive of over 85,000 twentieth century cartoons and caricatures, supported by a library of books, papers, journals, catalogues and assorted ephemera. A computer database of 110,000 cartoons provides quick and easy catalogued access via the Web. A source for exhibitions and displays as well as a picture library service. Specialises in historical, political and social cartoons from British newspapers.

Cephas Picture Library

Hurst House, 157 Walton Road, East Molesey KT8 0DX
☎020 8979 8647   Fax 020 8224 8095
✉ pictures@cephas.co.uk
www.cephas.com

The wine industry and vineyards of the world is the subject on which Cephas has made its reputation. 100,000 images, mainly original 6x7″ make this the most comprehensive and up-to-date archive in Britain. Almost all wine-producing countries and all aspects of the industry are covered in depth. Spirits, beer and cider also included. A major food and drink collection now also exists, through preparation and cooking, to eating and drinking.

Giles Chapman Library

18 Hazelwood Heights, Oxted RH8 0QQ
☎01833 723846
✉ chapman.media@virgin.net

Contact *Giles Chapman*

Around 125,000 colour and b&w images of cars and motoring, from 1945 to the present day. No research fees.

Christel Clear Marine Photography

5 Providence Place, Stoke Damerel, Plymouth PL1 5QS
☎01752 297598   Fax 07931 157717
✉ julianne@cristelclear.co.uk
www.cristelclear.co.uk

Contact *Julie-Anne Wilce*

Over 70,000 images on 35mm and 645 transparencies: yachting and boating from Grand Prix sailing to small dinghies, cruising locations and harbours. Recent additions include angling, fly fishing and travel. Visitors by appointment.

Christian Aid Photo Section

PO Box 100, London SE1 7RT
☎020 7523 2235   Fax 020 7620 0719

Contacts *J. Cabon, B. Nicholson, C. Lands*

Pictures are mainly from Africa, Asia and Latin America, relating to small-scale, community-based programmes. Mostly development themes: health, agriculture, education, urban and rural life.

Christie's Images Ltd

1 Langley Lane, London SW8 1TJ
☎020 7582 1282   Fax 020 7582 5632
✉ imageslondon@christies.com
www.christiesimages.com

Contact *Emma Strouts*

The UK's largest fine art photo library. 150,000 images of fine and decorative art. An extensive list of subjects is covered through paintings, drawings and prints of all periods as well as silver, ceramics, jewellery, sculpture, textiles and many other decorative and collectable items. Staff will search files and database to locate specific requests or supply a selection for consideration. Visits by appointment. Search fee.

Chrysalis Images

The Chrysalis Building, Bramley Road, London W10 6SP
☎020 7314 1400   Fax 020 7314 1583
✉ pictures@chrysalisbooks.co.uk

Contact *Terry Forshaw*

One million photographs and illustrations, colour and b&w, on military, history, transport, cookery, crafts, natural history, space and travel.

The Cinema Museum

The Master's House, Old Lambeth Workhouse, off Renfrew Road, London SE11 4TH
☎020 7840 2200   Fax 020 7840 2299
✉ martin@cinemamuseum.org.uk

Colour and b&w coverage (including stills) of the motion picture industry throughout its history, including the Ronald Grant Archive. Smaller collections on theatre, variety, television and popular music.

John Cleare/Mountain Camera

Hill Cottage, Fonthill Gifford, Salisbury SP3 6QW
☎01747 820320   Fax 01747 820320

✉ cleare@btinternet.com
www.mountaincamera.com

Colour and b&w coverage of mountains and wild places, climbing, ski-touring, trekking, expeditions, wilderness travel, landscapes, people and geographical features from all continents. Specialises in the Himalaya, Andes, Antarctic, Alps and the British countryside, and a range of topics from reindeer in Lapland to camels in Australia, from whitewater rafting in Utah to ski-mountaineering in China. Commissions and consultancy work undertaken. Researchers welcome by appointment. Member of **BAPLA** and the **OWG**.

Michael Cole Camerawork

The Coach House, 27 The Avenue, Beckenham BR3 2DP
☎020 8658 6120   Fax 020 8658 6120
✉ mikecole@dircon.co.uk

Contacts *Michael Cole, Derrick Bentley*

Probably the largest and most comprehensive collection of tennis pictures in the world. Over 50 years' coverage of the Wimbledon Championships. M.C.C. also incorporates the tennis archives of Le Roye Productions, established in 1945.

Collections

13 Woodberry Crescent, London N10 1PJ
☎020 8883 0083   Fax 020 8883 9215
✉ collections@btinternet.com
www.collectionspicturelibrary.com

Contact *Brian Shuel*

Extensive coverage of the British and Ireland from the Shetlands to the Channel Islands, and Connemara to East Anglia, including people, traditional customs, workers, religions and pastimes, as well as places both well known and obscure, and an extensive collection of 'things'. Includes the landscapes of Fay Godwin. Visitors are welcome but please make an appointment.

Concannon Golf History Library

See **Phil Sheldon Golf Picture Library**

Corbis Images

111 Salusbury Road, London NW6 6RG
☎020 7644 7644/7600/Freephone: 0800 731 9995   Fax 020 7644 7645
✉ sales.uk@corbis.com
www.corbis.com

Contact *Giles Howard*

A unique and comprehensive resource containing more than 65 million images, with over 2.1

million of them available online. The images come from professional photographers, museums, cultural institutions and public and private collections worldwide, including images from the Bettmann Archive, Ansel Adams, Lynn Goldsmith, the Turnley Collection and Hulton Deutsch. Subjects include history, travel, celebrities, events, science, world art and cultures. Free catalogues are available or register for a free password to search, save and order online.

Sylvia Cordaiy Photo Library

45 Rotherstone, Devizes SN10 2DD
☎01380 728327   Fax 01380 728328
✉ info@sylvia-cordaiy.com
www.sylvia-cordaiy.com

Over 170 countries on file from the obscure to main stock images – Africa, North, Central and South America, Asia, Atlantic, Indian and Pacific Ocean islands, Australasia, Europe, polar regions. Covers travel, architecture, ancient civilisations, people worldwide, environment, wildlife, natural history, Antarctica, domestic pets, livestock, marine biology, veterinary treatment, equestrian, ornithology, flowers. UK files cover cities, towns villages, coastal and rural scenes, London collection. Transport, railways, shipping and aircraft (military and civilian). Aerial photography. Backgrounds and abstracts. Also the Paul Kaye B/W archive.

Country Images Picture Library

27 Camwood, Bamber Bridge, Preston PR5 8LA
☎01772 321243   Fax 0870 137 8888
✉ terrymarsh@wpu.org.uk
www.countryimages.info

Contact *Terry Marsh*

35mm and medium format colour coverage of landscapes and countryside features generally throughout the UK (Cumbria, North Yorkshire, Lancashire, southern Scotland, Isle of Skye, Scottish islands, Wales, Cornwall), France (Alps, Pyrenees, Provence, Aube-en-Champagne, Loire valley, Somme) and Australia. Commissions undertaken.

Country Life Picture Library

King's Reach Tower, Stamford Street, London SE1 9LS
☎020 7261 6337   Fax 020 7261 6216
✉ camilla_costello@ipcmedia.com
www.clpicturelibrary.co.uk

Contact *Camilla Costello*

Over 150,000 b&w negatives dating back to 1897, and 80,000 colour transparencies. Country houses, stately homes, churches and town houses in Britain and abroad, interiors of architectural interest (ceilings, fireplaces, furniture, paintings, sculpture), and exteriors showing many landscaped gardens, sporting and social events, crafts, people and animals. Visitors by appointment. Open Tuesday to Friday.

Philip Craven Worldwide Photo-Library

Surrey Studios, 21 Nork Way, Nork, Banstead SM7 1PB
☎0870 220 2121
www.philipcraven.com

Contact *Philip Craven*

Extensive coverage of British scenes, cities, villages, countryside, gardens, historic buildings and wildlife. Worldwide travel and wildlife subjects on medium- and large-format transparencies.

CTC Picture Library

CTC Ltd, Unit 26, Woodside Park, Catteshall Lane, Guildford GU7 1LG
☎01483 419566 Fax 01483 861640
✉ mail@crightonthomascreative.com
www.crightonthomascreative.com

Contact *Vic Thomas*

One of the biggest specialist libraries in the UK with 250,000 slides covering world and UK agriculture, horticulture, and environmental subjects. Also a small section on travel.

Cumbria Picture Library
See **Eric Whitehead Photography**

Sue Cunningham Photographic

56 Chatham Road, Kingston upon Thames KT1 3AA
☎020 8541 3024 Fax 020 8541 5388
✉ pictures@scphotographic.com
www.scphotographic.com

Extensive coverage of many geographical areas: South America (especially Brazil), Eastern Europe from the Baltic to the Balkans, various African countries, Western Europe including the UK. Colour and b&w. Member of **BAPLA**.

Dalton–Watson Collection
See **The Ludvigsen Library**

James Davis Worldwide

65 Brighton Road, Shoreham BN43 6RE
☎01273 452252 Fax 01273 440116
✉ library@eyeubiquitous.com
www.eyeubiquitous.com

Travel collection: people, places, emotive scenes and tourism. Constantly updated by a team of photographers, both at home and abroad. Same-day service available.

The Defence Picture Library

1 Creykes Court, Craigie Drive, The Millfields, Plymouth PL1 3JB
☎01752 401800/01752 312061
Fax 01752 402800
✉ picdesk@defencepictures.com
www.defencepictures.com

Contacts *David Reynolds, Jessica Kelly, James Rowlands, Andrew Chittock*

Leading source of military photography covering all areas of the UK Armed Forces, supported by a research agency of facts and figures. More than 500,000 images with a significant number on CD-ROM. Latest images include British and US forces in Iraq. Specialist collections include the Chinese Armed Forces, US Special Forces, as well as military units of Italy, Spain and France. Visitors welcome by appointment.

Douglas Dickins Photo Library

2 Wessex Gardens, Golders Green, London NW11 9RT
☎020 8455 6221

Sole Proprietor *Douglas Dickins, FRPS*

Worldwide colour and b&w coverage, specialising in Asia, particularly India, Indonesia and Japan. *In Grandpa's Footsteps*, highly illustrated book of world travel published by Book Guild in 2000.

CM Dixon

The Orchard, Marley Lane, Kingston, Canterbury CT4 6JH
☎01227 830075 Fax 01227 831135
✉ cmd@cmdixon.com
www.cmdixon.com

Colour coverage of ancient civilisations, archaeology and art, ethnology, mythology, world religion, museum objects, geography, geology, meteorology, landscapes, people and places from many countries including most of Europe, former USSR, Ethiopia, Iceland, Jordan, Morocco, Sri Lanka, Tunisia, Turkey, Egypt, Uzbekistan.

Dominic Photography

4B Moore Park Road, London SW6 2JT
☎020 7381 0007 Fax 020 7381 0008

Contacts *Zoë Dominic, Catherine Ashmore*

Colour and b&w coverage of the entertainment world from 1957 onwards: dance, opera, theatre, ballet, musicals and personalities.

E&E Picture Library – Ecclesiastical and Eccentricities

Beggars Roost, Woolpack Hill, Brabourne Lees, Ashford TN25 6RR
☎01303 812608   Fax 01303 812608
✉ isobel@picture-library.freeserve.co.uk
www.picture-library.freeserve.co.uk

Contact *Isobel Sinden*

Specialises in world religions, manuscripts, buildings, artifacts, clothes, festivals, clergy, arts, culture, history, pilgrimages, ancient stones, Bible lands, symbols, carvings, death and burial worldwide, ancient to modern. Curiosities such as follies, mazes, towers, pyramids. Also wind and water.

Patrick Eagar Photography

1 Queensberry Place, Richmond TW9 1NW
☎020 8940 9269   Fax 020 8332 1229
✉ patrick@patrickeagar.com
www.patrickeagar.com

The cricket library consists of Patrick Eagar's work over the last 30 years with coverage of over 270 Test matches worldwide, unique coverage of all eight World Cups, countless one-day internationals and player action portraits of over 2000 cricketers. The wine library consists of vineyards, grapes and festivals from Argentina to New Zealand. France and Australia are specialist areas. Photographs can be supplied by e-mail, on CD, prints and transparencies.

Ecoscene

The Oasts, Passfield, Liphook GU30 7RX
☎01428 751056   Fax 01428 751057
✉ sally@ecoscene.com
www.ecoscene.com

Contact *Sally Morgan*

Expanding colour library of over 80,000 transparencies specialising in all aspects of the environment: pollution, conservation, recycling, restoration, wildlife (especially underwater), habitats, education, landscapes, industry and agriculture. All parts of the globe are covered with specialist collections covering Antarctica, Australia, North America. Sally Morgan, who runs the library, is a professional ecologist and expert source of information on all environmental topics. Photographic and writing commissions undertaken. Images delivered by post, on CD-ROM and by e-mail.

Edifice

14 Doughty Street, London WC1N 2PL
☎020 7242 0740   Fax 020 7267 3632
✉ info@edificephoto.com
www.edificephoto.com

Contacts *Philippa Lewis, Gillian Darley*

Colour coverage of architecture, buildings of all possible descriptions, gardens, urban and rural landscape. Specialises in details of ornament, period style and material. British Isles, USA, Africa, Europe and Japan all covered. Detailed list available, visits by appointment. Website is searchable on line.

Education Photos

April Cottage, Warners Lane, Albury Heath, Guildford GU5 9DE
☎01483 203846
✉ johnwalmsley@educationphotos.co.uk
www.educationphotos.co.uk

Formerly the John Walmsley Photo Library. Specialist library of learning/training/working subjects. Comprehensive coverage of learning environments such as playgroups, schools, colleges and universities. Images reflect a multiracial Britain. Commissions undertaken.

English Heritage Photo Library

23 Savile Row, London W1S 2ET
☎020 7973 3338/9   Fax 020 7973 3027
✉ photo.library@english-heritage.org.uk
www.english-heritage.org.uk

Contact *Photo Librarian*

Images of English castles, abbeys, houses, gardens, Roman remains, ancient monuments, battlefields, industrial and post-war buildings, interiors, paintings, artifacts, architectural details, conservation, archaeology, scenic views, landscapes.

Mary Evans Picture Library

59 Tranquil Vale, Blackheath, London SE3 0BS
☎020 8318 0034   Fax 020 8852 7211
✉ pictures@maryevans.com
www.maryevans.com

Historical archive of illustrations, photographs, prints and ephemera documenting all aspects of the past, from ancient times to the later decades of the 20th century. Subject areas: social and political history, portraits, events, transport, costume, trade and industry, places worldwide and natural history plus specialist material on folklore and paranormal phenomena. Notable acquisitions include the Thomas Fall Collection of historic dog photographs, the Weimar Archive documenting the Third Reich and Barnaby's Library covering social scenes and events from the '30s to the '70s. MEPL's own material is complemented by many contributors such as Sigmund Freud Copyrights, the **Women's Library** (women's rights) and the Meledin Collection of 20th century Russian history. Over 150,000 images searchable online. Brochure on request. Founder member of **BAPLA**. Compilers of the *Picture Researcher's Handbook* by Pira International.

Exile Images
1 Mill Row, West Hill Road, Brighton BN1 3SU
☎01273 208741 Fax 01273 382782
✉ pics@exileimages.co.uk
www.exileimages.co.uk
Contact *Howard Davies*

Online photo library with over 5000 pictures of refugees, conflict, asylum seekers, UK protests and Third World issues. Picture editors can search and download high resolution photographs online.

Express Newspapers Syndication
Ludgate House, 245 Blackfriars Road, London SE1 9UX
☎020 7922 7884 Fax 020 7922 7871
✉ syndication@express.co.uk
Manager *Adam Williams*

Two million images updated daily, with strong collections on personalities, royalty, showbiz, sport, fashion, nostalgia and events. Also includes the *OK! Magazine* collection. Electronic transmission available. Daily news and feature service.

Eye Ubiquitous
65 Brighton Road, Shoreham BN43 6RE
☎01273 440113 Fax 01273 440116
✉ library@eyeubiquitous.com
www.eyeubiquitous.com
Contact *Stephen Rafferty*

General stock specialising in social documentary worldwide, including the work of Tim Page, and now incorporating the **James Davis Travel** library (see entry).

Thomas Fall Collection
See **Mary Evans Picture Library**

Famous Pictures & Features Agency
13 Harwood Road, London SW6 4QP
☎020 7731 9333 Fax 020 7731 9330
✉ info@famous.uk.com
www.famous.uk.com

Celebrity features agency with a growing library of high quality celebrity interviews and digital images to accompany text. The library is supplied by a team of freelance celebrity journalists and photographers from the UK, US and around the world, keeping it up-to-date with a variety of the hottest features on a daily basis. 'We are always looking out for new writers who specialise in material dealing with *famous* people.'

ffotograff
10 Kyveilog Street, Pontcanna, Cardiff CF11 9JA
☎029 2023 6879
✉ ffotograff@easynet.co.uk
www.ffotograff.com
Contact *Patricia Aithie*

Library and agency specialising in travel, exploration, the arts, architecture, traditional culture, archaeology and landscape. Based in Wales but specialising in the Middle and Far East; Africa, Central and South America; Yemen and Wales are strong aspects of the library. Churches and cathedrals of Britain and Crusader castles.

Financial Times Pictures
One Southwark Bridge, London SE1 9HL
☎020 7873 3671 Fax 020 7873 4606
✉ photosynd@ft.com

Photographs from around the world ranging from personalities in business, politics and the arts, people at work and other human interests and activities. '*FT* Graphics are outstanding in their ability to make complex issues comprehensible.' Delivery via ISDN or e-mail.

Fine Art Photographic Library Ltd
2A Milner Street, London SW3 2PU
☎020 7589 3127 Fax 020 7584 1944
✉ info@fineartphotolibrary.com
www.fineartphotolibrary.com
Contact *Linda Hammerbeck*

Over 30,000 large-format transparencies, with a specialist collection of 19th and 20th century paintings. CD-ROM available.

Firepix International
68 Arkles Lane, Anfield, Liverpool L4 2SP
☎0151 260 0111/0777 5930419 (mobile)
Fax 0151 260 0111
✉ info@firepix.com
www.firepix.com
Contact *Tony Myers*

The UK's only fire photo library. 23,000 images of fire-related subjects, firefighters, fire equipment manufacturers. Website contains 15 categories from industrial fire, domestic, digital images and abstract flame. Member of **BAPLA**.

Fogden Wildlife Photographs
16 Locheport, North Uist, Western Isles HS6 5EU
☎01876 580245 Fax 01876 580777
✉ susan.fogden@virgin.net
www.fogdenphotos.com
Contact *Susan Fogden*

Natural history collection, with special reference to rain forests and deserts. Emphasis on quality rather than quantity; growing collection of around 15,000 images.

Food Features
Farnham Forge, 5 Upper Church Lane, Farnham GU9 7PW
☎01252 735240 Fax 01252 735242
✉ frontdesk@foodpix.co.uk
www.foodpix.co.uk
Contacts *Steve Moss, Alex Barker*

Specialised high-quality food and drink photography, features and tested recipes. Clients' specific requirements can be incorporated into regular shooting schedules.

Christine Foord
Colour Picture Library
155B City Way, Rochester ME1 2BE
☎01634 847348 Fax 01634 847348

Specialist library with over 1000 species of British and European wild flowers, plus garden flowers, trees, indoor plants, pests and diseases, mosses, lichen, cacti and the majority of larger British insects.

Forestry Commission
Picture Library
231 Corstorphine Road, Edinburgh EH12 7AT
☎0131 314 6411
✉ neill.campbell@forestry.gsi.gov.uk
www.forestry.gov.uk
Contacts *Douglas Green, Neill Campbell*

The official image bank of the Forestry Commission, the library provides a single source for all aspects of forest and woodland management. The comprehensive subject list includes tree species, scenic landscapes, employment, wildlife, flora and fauna, conservation, sport and leisure.

Werner Forman Archive Ltd
36 Camden Square, London NW1 9XA
☎020 7267 1034 Fax 020 7267 6026

✉ wfa@btinternet.com
www.werner-forman-archive.com

Colour and b&w coverage of ancient civilisations, oriental and primitive societies around the world. A number of rare collections. Searchable website.

Formula One Pictures
2013 Pomaz, Buzavirag U.6., Hungary
☎00 36 26 322 826
(Mobile +44 7905 819 555)
✉ jt@f1pictures.com
www.f1pictures.com
Contacts *John Townsend, Erika Townsend*

500,000 35mm colour slides, b&w and colour negatives of all aspects of Formula One grand prix racing including driver profiles and portraits.

Robert Forsythe Picture Library
16 Lime Grove, Prudhoe NE42 6PR
☎01661 834511 Fax 01661 834511
✉ robert@forsythe.demon.co.uk
www.forsythe.demon.co.uk
Contacts *Robert Forsythe, Fiona Forsythe*

25,000 transparencies of industrial and transport heritage; plus a unique collection of 70,000 items of related publicity ephemera from 1945. Image finding service available. Robert Forsythe is a transport/industrial heritage historian and consultant. Nationwide coverage, particularly strong on Northern Britain. A bibliography of published material is available.

Fortean Picture Library
Henblas, Mwrog Street, Ruthin LL15 1LG
☎01824 707278 Fax 01824 705324
✉ janet.bord@forteanpix.demon.co.uk
www.forteanpix.demon.co.uk
Contact *Janet Bord*

30,000 colour and 45,000 b&w images: mysteries and strange phenomena worldwide, including ghosts, UFOs, witchcraft and monsters; also antiquities, folklore and mythology. Subject list available.

The Fotomas Index
12 Pickhurst Rise, West Wickham BR4 0AL
☎020 8776 2772 Fax 020 8776 2236
✉ fotomasindex@btconnect.com
Contact *John Freeman*

General historical collection, mostly pre-1900. Subjects include London, topography, art, satirical, social and political history. Large portrait section.

The Francis Frith Collection
Frith's Barn, Teffont, Salisbury SP3 5QP
☎01722 716376 Fax 01722 716881
✉ john_buck@francisfrith.co.uk
www.francisfrith.co.uk

Contact *John Buck*

Publishers of *Frith's Photographic Memories* series of illustrated local books, all featuring nostalgic photographs from the archive, founded by Frith in 1860. The archive contains over 360,000 images of 7000 British towns.

John Frost Newspapers
See entry under *Library Services*

Andrew N. Gagg's Photo Flora
Town House Two, Fordbank Court, Henwick Road, Worcester WR2 5PF
☎01905 748515
✉ a.n.gagg@ntlworld.com
homepage.ntlworld.com/a.n.gagg/photo/photoflora.html

Specialist in British and European wild plants, flowers, ferns, grasses, trees, shrubs, etc. with colour coverage of most British and many European species (rare and common) and habitats; also travel in India, Sri Lanka, Nepal, Egypt, China, Mexico, Thailand, Tibet, Vietnam and Cambodia.

Galaxy Picture Library
34 Fennels Way, Flackwell Heath, High Wycombe HP10 9BY
☎01628 521338 Fax 01628 520132
✉ robin@galaxypix.com
www.galaxypix.com

Contact *Robin Scagell*

Specialises in astronomy, space, telescopes, observatories, the sky, clouds and sunsets. Composites of foregrounds, stars, moon and planets prepared to commission. Editorial service available.

Garden and Wildlife Matters Photo Library
'Marlham', Henley's Down, Battle TN33 9BN
☎01424 830566 Fax 01424 830224
✉ gardens@gmpix.com
www.gardenmatters.uk.com
www.gmpix.com

Contact *Dr John Feltwell*

Collection of 110,000 6x4″ and 35mm images. General gardening techniques and design; cottage gardens and USA designer gardens. 9000 species of garden plants and over 1000 species of trees. Flowers, wild and house plants, trees and crops. Environmental, ecological and conservation pictures, including sea, air, noise and freshwater pollution, SE Asian and Central and South American rainforests; Eastern Europe, Mediterranean. Recycling, agriculture, forestry, horticulture and oblique aerial habitat shots from Europe and USA. 24/7 service. Digital images supplied worldwide by ISDN.

Garden Picture Library
Unit 12, Ransome's Dock, 35 Parkgate Road, London SW11 4NP
☎020 7228 4332 Fax 020 7924 3267
✉ info@gardenpicture.com
www.gardenpicture.com

Picture Research Manager *Lorraine Shill*

'Our inspirational images of gardens, plants and gardening lifestyle offer plenty of scope for writers looking for original ideas to write about.' The collection covers all garden related subjects; everything from plant portraits to floral graphics and garden design details to whole landscapes. 'Bringing together the work of over 100 professional photographers from across the gardening globe our picture editors select the very best images from each individual portfolio, creating an outstanding range of images by photographic style as well as subject for all possible media requirements. We hold approximately 400,000 fully captioned images of which around 15,000 are available digitally.' In-house picture research can be undertaken on request or searches can be made online via keyword or subject category to create lightboxes which can be emailed or downloaded. Visitors to the library are welcome by appointment and copies of promotional literature are available on request.

Ed Geldard Photo Collection
9 Sunderland Bridge Village, Durham DH6 5HB
☎0191 378 2592
✉ ed@camera-one.freeserve.co.uk

Contact *Ed Geldard*

Approximately 20,000 colour transparencies and b&w negs, all by Ed Geldard, specialising in mountain landscapes: particularly the mountain regions of the Lake District; and the Yorkshire limestone areas, from valley to summit. Commissions undertaken. Books published: *Wainwright's Tour of the Lake District*; *Wainwright in the Limestone Dales*; *The Lake District*.

Genesis Space Photo Library
Greenbanks, Robins Hill, Raleigh, Bideford EX39 3PA

☎01237 471960   Fax 01237 472060
✉ tim@spaceport.co.uk
www.spaceport.co.uk
Contact *Tim Furniss*

Contemporary and historical colour and b&w spaceflight collection including rockets, spacecraft, spacemen, Earth, moon and planets. Catalogue of 775 images on website.

Geo Aerial Photography
4 Christian Fields, London SW16 3JZ
☎020 8764 6292/0115 981 9418
Fax 020 8764 6292/0115 981 9418
✉ geo.aerial@geo-group.co.uk
www.geo-group.co.uk
Contact *Kelly White*

Established 1990 and now a growing collection of aerial oblique photographs from the UK, Scandinavia, Asia and Africa – landscapes, buildings, industrial sites, etc. Commissions undertaken.

GeoScience Features
6 Orchard Drive, Wye TN25 5AU
☎01233 812707   Fax 01233 812707
✉ gsf@geoscience.demon.co.uk
www.geoscience.demon.co.uk

Fully computerised and comprehensive library containing the world's principal source of volcanic phenomena. Extensive collections, providing scientific detail with technical quality, of rocks, minerals, fossils, microsections of botanical and animal tissues, animals, biology, birds, botany, chemistry, earth science, ecology, environment, geology, geography, habitats, landscapes, macro/microbiology, peoples, sky, weather, wildlife and zoology. Over 300,000 original colour transparencies in medium- and 35mm-format. Subject lists and CD-ROM catalogue available. Incorporates the RIDA photolibrary.

Geoslides Photography
4 Christian Fields, London SW16 3JZ
☎020 8764 6292/0115 981 9418
Fax 020 8764 6292/0115 981 9418
✉ geoslides@geo-group.co.uk
www.geo-group.co.uk
Contact *John Douglas*

Established 1968. Landscape and human interest subjects from the Arctic, Antarctica, Scandinavia, UK, Africa (south of Sahara), Middle East, Asia (south and southeast); also Australia via Blackwoods Picture Library. Specialist collections of British India (the Raj) and Boer War.

Getty Images
101 Bayham Street, London NW1 0AG
☎020 7544 2987   Fax 020 7544 3334
✉ john.hagelin@gettyimages.com
www.gettyimages.com
Contact *Sales Department*

'Getty Images is the world's leading imagery company, creating and providing the largest collection of still and moving images to communication professionals around the globe. From sports and news photography to archival and contemporary imagery, Getty Images' products are found each day in newspapers, magazines, advertising, films, television, books and websites.' For those who wish to commission photographers to fulfil specific needs, the company maintains a full-service department for custom-shot images.

Lynn Goldsmith
See **Corbis Images**

Martin and Dorothy Grace
40 Clipstone Avenue, Mapperley, Nottingham NG3 5JZ
☎0115 920 8248   Fax 0115 962 6802
✉ graces@lineone.net

Colour coverage of Britain's natural history, specialising in trees, shrubs and wild flowers. Also ferns, birds and butterflies, habitats, landscapes, ecology.

Ronald Grant Archive
See **The Cinema Museum**

Sally and Richard Greenhill
357 Liverpool Road, London N1 1NL
☎020 7607 8549   Fax 020 7607 7151
✉ sr.greenhill@virgin.net
www.srgreenhill.co.uk
Photo Librarian *Denise Lalonde*

Social documentary photography in colour and b&w of working lives: pregnancy and birth, child development, education, work, old people, medical, urban. Also Modern China, 1971 to the present; most London statues. Some material from Borneo, USA, India, Israel, Philippines and Sri Lanka.

V.K. Guy Ltd
Silver Birches, Troutbeck, Windermere LA23 1PN
☎015394 33519   Fax 015394 32971
✉ vic@vk.guy.co.uk
www.vkguy.co.uk

Contacts *Vic Guy, Pauline Guy, Mike Guy, Paul Guy, Nicola Guy*

British landscapes and architectural heritage. 20,000 5x4" transparencies, suitable for tourism brochures, calendars, etc. Colour catalogue available.

Angela Hampton
'Family Life Picture Library'
Holly Tree House, The Street, Walberton, Arundel BN18 0PH
☎01243 555952 Fax 01243 555952
✉ enquiries@familylifepictures.co.uk
www.familylifepictures.co.uk

Contact *Angela Hampton*

Over 50,000 transparencies on all aspects of contemporary lifestyle, including pregnancy, childbirth, babies, children, parenting, behaviour, education, medical, holidays, pets, family life, relationships, teenagers, women and men's health, over-50s and retirement. Also domestic and farm animal life. Environmental and travel pictures in 35mm. Commissions undertaken. Offers fully illustrated text packages on most subjects and welcomes ideas for collaboration from writers with proven, successful background.

Tom Hanley
41 Harefield, Esher KT10 9TG
☎020 8972 9165 Fax 020 8972 9164
✉ Tomhanley31@hotmail.com

Colour and b&w coverage of London, England, Europe, Canada, India, the Philippines, Brazil, China, Japan, Korea, Taiwan, the Seychelles, Cayman Islands, USA. Also pop artists of the 1960s, First World War trenches, removal of London Bridge to America, and much more. Current preoccupation with Greece, Turkey, Spain and Egypt, ancient and modern.

Robert Harding Picture Library
58–59 Great Marlborough Street, London W1F 7JY
☎020 7478 4000 Fax 020 7631 1070
✉ info@robertharding.com
www.robertharding.com

A leading source of stock photography with over two million colour images covering a wide range of subjects – worldwide travel and culture, geography and landscapes, people and lifestyle, architecture, business and industry, medicine, sports, food and drink. Rights protected and royalty-free images. Can supply images as transparencies, on CD or ISDN.

Visitors welcome; telephone or visit the website.

Dennis Hardley Photography, Scottish Photo Library
Rosslynn, Benderloch, Oban PA37 1ST
☎01631 720434 Fax 01631 720434
✉ dennis.hardley@btinternet.com *and* info@scotphoto.com
www.scotphoto.com

Contacts *Dennis Hardley, Tony Hardley*

Established 1974. About 30,000 images (6x7, 6x9 format colour transparencies) of Scotland: castles, historic, scenic landscapes, islands, transport, etc. Also English views – Liverpool, Chester, Bath, Weston Super Mare, Sussex, Somerset and Cambridge.

Jim Henderson
Photographer & Publisher
Crooktree, Kincardine O'Neil, Aboyne AB34 4JD
☎01339 882149 Fax 01339 882149
✉ JHende7868@aol.com
www.jimhendersonphotography.com

Contact *Jim Henderson, AMPA, ARPS*

Scenic and general activity coverage of the north east Scotland/Grampian region and Highlands for tourist, holiday and activity illustration. Specialist collection of over 150 Aurora Borealis displays from 1989–2004 in Grampian and co-author of *The Aurora* (pub. 1997). Large collection of recent images of Egypt: Cairo through to Abu-Simbel. Commissions undertaken.

Heritage and Natural History
Photographic Library
37 Plainwood Close, Summersdale, Chichester PO195YB
☎01243 533822 Fax 01243 533822

Contact *Dr John B. Free*

Specialises in insects (particularly bees and beekeeping), tropical and temperate agriculture and crops, archaeology and history worldwide.

John Heseltine Archive
Mill Studio, Frogmarsh Mill, South Woodchester GL5 5ET
☎01453 873792
✉ john@heseltine.co.uk
www.heseltine.co.uk

Contact *John Heseltine*

Over 200,000 colour transparencies and digital

files of landscapes, architecture, food and travel with particular emphasis on Italy and the UK.

Christopher Hill Photographic Library

17 Clarence Street, Belfast BT2 8DY
☎028 9024 5038 Fax 028 9023 1942
✉ info@scenicireland.com
www.scenicireland.com

Contact *Christopher Hill*

A comprehensive collection of scenic landscapes of Ireland. Every aspect of Irish life is shown, concentrating on the positive. Also large miscellaneous section. The website contains over 6000 images available to buy online.

Hobbs Golf Collection

5 Winston Way, New Ridley, Stocksfield NE43 7RF
☎01661 842933 Fax 01661 842933
✉ info@hobbsgolfcollection.com
www.hobbsgolfcollection.com

Contact *Margaret Hobbs*

Specialist golf collection: players, courses, art, memorabilia and historical topics (1300 to present). 40,000+ images – mainly 35mm colour transparencies and b&w prints. Commissions undertaken. Author of 30 golf books.

David Hoffman Photo Library

c/o BAPLA, 18 Vine Hill, London EC1R 5DZ
☎020 8981 5041 Fax 020 8980 2041
✉ info@hoffmanphotos.com
www.hoffmanphotos.com

Contact *David Hoffman*

Commissioned photography and stock library with a strong emphasis on social issues built up from 35mm journalistic and documentary work dating from the late 1970s. Files on drugs and drug use, policing, disorder, riots, youth, prostitution, protest, homelessness, housing, environmental demonstrations and events, waste disposal, alternative energy, industry and pollution. Wide range of images especially from UK and Europe but also USA, Canada, Venezuela, Mexico and Thailand. General files on topical issues and current affairs plus specialist files from leisure cycling to local authority services. Many photographs available for online delivery from www.alamy.com

Holt Studios International Ltd

The Courtyard, 24 High Street, Hungerford RG17 0NF
☎01488 683523 Fax 01488 683511
✉ library@holt-studios.co.uk
www.holt-studios.co.uk

Director *Nigel Cattlin*

Specialist photo library covering world agriculture, horticulture, gardens and gardening from pictorial and technical aspects. Worldwide assignments undertaken.

Houghton's Horses/ Kit Houghton Photography

Radlet Cottage, Spaxton, Bridgwater TA5 1DE
☎01278 671362 Fax 01278 671739
✉ kit@enterprise.net
www.houghtonshorses.com

Contacts *Kit Houghton, Debbie Cook*

Specialist equestrian library of over 300,000 transparencies on all aspects of the horse world, with images ranging from the romantic to the practical, step-by-step instructional and competition pictures in all equestrian disciplines worldwide. Online picture delivery.

Chris Howes/Wild Places Photography

51 Timbers Square, Cardiff CF24 3SH
☎029 2048 6557 Fax 029 2048 6557
✉ photos@wildplaces.co.uk

Contacts *Chris Howes, Judith Calford*

Expanding collection of over 50,000 colour transparencies and b&w prints covering travel, topography and natural history worldwide, plus action sports such as climbing. SPECIALIST AREAS include caves, caving and mines (with historical coverage using engravings and early photographs), wildlife, landscapes and the environment, including pollution and conservation. Europe (including Britain), USA, Africa and Australia are all well represented within the collection. Commissions undertaken.

Hulton Deutsch
See **Corbis Images**

Huntley Film Archive

191 Wardour Street, London W1F 82E
☎020 7287 8000 Fax 020 7287 8001
✉ films@huntleyarchives.com
www.huntleyarchives.com

Contact *Amanda Huntley*

Originally a private collection, the library is now a comprehensive archive of rare and vintage documentary film dating from 1895. 30,000–35,000 films on all subjects of a documentary nature, plus 50,000 feature film stills. Hollywood and the British film studios plus a television archive of rare stills and films. On-line catalogue available.

Jacqui Hurst

66 Richford Street, Hammersmith, London
W6 7HP
☎020 8743 2315/07970 781336 (mobile)
✉ jacquih@dircon.co.uk
www.jacquihurstphotography.co.uk
Contact *Jacqui Hurst*

A specialist library of traditional and contemporary applied arts, regional food producers and markets. The photos form illustrated essays of how something is made and finish with a still life of the completed object. The collection is always being extended and a list is available on request. Commissions undertaken.

Hutchison Picture Library

65 Brighton Road, Shoreham-by-Sea
BN43 6RE
✉ library@hutchisonpictures.co.uk
www.hutchisonpictures.co.uk

Worldwide contemporary images from the straight-forward to the esoteric and quirky. With over half a million documentary colour photographs on file and more than 200 photographers continually adding new work, this is an ever-growing resource covering people, places, customs and faiths, agriculture, industry and transport. SPECIAL COLLECTIONS include the environment and climate, family life (including pregnancy and birth), ethnic minorities world-wide (including Disappearing World archive), conventional and alternative medicine, and music around the world. Search service available.

Illustrated London News Picture Library

20 Upper Ground, London SE1 9PF
☎020 7805 5585 Fax 020 7805 5905
✉ iln.pictures@ilng.co.uk
www.ilnpictures.co.uk

Engravings, photographs and illustrations from 1842 to the present day, taken from magazines published by Illustrated Newspapers: *Illustrated London News*; *Graphic*; *Sphere*; *Tatler*; *Sketch*; *Illustrated Sporting and Dramatic News*; *Illustrated War News 1914–18*; *Bystander*; *Britannia & Eve*. Social history, London, Industrial Revolution, wars, travel. Visitors by appointment.

Images of Africa Photobank

11 The Windings, Lichfield WS13 7EX
☎01543 262898 Fax 01543 417154
✉ info@imagesofafrica.co.uk
www.imagesofafrica.co.uk
Contact *Jacquie Shipton*
Owner *David Keith Jones, FRPS*

Over 135,000 images covering Botswana, Chad, Egypt, Ethiopia, Kenya, Lesotho, Madagascar, Malawi, Morocco, Namibia, Rwanda, South Africa, Swaziland, Tanzania, Uganda, Zaire, Zambia, Zanzibar and Zimbabwe. 'Probably the best collection of photographs of Kenya in Europe.' A wide range of topics are covered. Strong on African wildlife with over 80 species of mammals including many sequences showing action and behaviour. Popular animals like lions and elephants are covered in encyclopædic detail. More than 100 species of birds and many reptiles. Other strengths are National Parks and reserves, natural beauty, tourism facilities, traditional and modern people. Most work is by David Keith Jones, FRPS but several other photographers are represented. An attractive colour brochure is available: the library offers next day delivery by post or same day by e-mail when requested.

ImageState Europe

Ramillies House, 1–2 Ramillies Street,
London W1F 7LN
☎020 7734 7344 Fax 020 7434 0673
✉ sales@imagestate.co.uk
www.imagestate.com

Markets royalty free and rights protected images. Image and footage subjects include people and lifestyles, business and industry, sport, travel, nature and animals and more. Visit the website for details.

Imperial War Museum Photograph Archive

All Saints Annexe, Austral Street, London
SE11 4SJ
☎020 7416 5333 Fax 020 7416 5355
✉ photos@iwm.org.uk
www.iwm.org.uk

A national archive of over six million photographs illustrating all aspects of 20th century conflict. Emphasis on the two world wars but includes material from other conflicts involving Britain and the Commonwealth. Majority of material is b&w, although holdings of colour material increases with more recent conflicts. Visitors welcome by appointment, Monday to Friday, 10.00 am. to 5.00 pm.

Infoterra

Atlas House, Wembley Road, Leicester
LE3 1HT
☎0116 273 2315 Fax 0116 273 2400

✉ davidread@infoterra-global.com
www.infoterra-global.com

Contact *David Read*

Leading supplier of earth observation data, including satellite imagery, aerial photography and airborne remote sensing.

International Photobank

Unit D1, Roman Hill Business Park, Broadmayne DT2 8LY
☎01305 854145 Fax 01305 853065
✉ peter@internationalphotobank.co.uk
www.internationalphotobank.co.uk

Over 400,000 transparencies, partly medium-format. Colour coverage of travel subjects: places, people, folklore, events. Assignments undertaken for guide books. ISDN digital service available for newspapers, magazines and other users.

Robbie Jack Photography

45 Church Road, Hanwell, London W7 3BD
☎020 8567 9616 Fax 020 8567 9616
✉ robbie@robbiejack.com
www.robbiejack.com

Contact *Robbie Jack*

Built up over the last 20 years, the library contains over 350,000 colour images of the performing arts – theatre, dance, opera and music. Includes West End shows, the RSC and Royal National Theatre productions, English National Opera and Royal Opera. The dance section contains images of the Royal Ballet, English National Ballet, the Rambert Dance Company, plus many foreign companies. Also holds the largest selection of colour material from the Edinburgh International Festival. Researchers are welcome to visit by appointment. From 2001 began offering colour transparencies as digital images which are being added to on a daily basis.

Katz Pictures/FSP

109 Clifton Street, London EC2A 4LD
☎020 7749 6000 Fax 020 7749 6001
✉ katzpictures@katzpictures.com
www.katzpictures.com

Contact *Sarah Bennett*

Contains an extensive collection of colour and b&w material covering a multitude of subjects from around the world – business, environment, industry, travel, lifestyles, politics plus celebrity portraits from the entertainment world.

David King Collection

90 St Pauls Road, London N1 2QP
☎020 7226 0149 Fax 020 7354 8264
✉ davidkingcollection@btopenworld.com

Contact *David King*

250,000 b&w original and copy photographs and colour transparencies of historical and present-day images. Russian history and the Soviet Union from 1900 to the fall of Khrushchev; the lives of Lenin, Trotsky and Stalin; the Tzars, Russo-Japanese War, 1917 Revolution, World War I, Red Army, the Great Purges, Great Patriotic War, etc. SPECIAL COLLECTIONS on China, Eastern Europe, the Weimar Republic, John Heartfield, American labour struggles, Spanish Civil War. Open to qualified researchers by appointment, Monday to Friday, 10.00 am to 6.00 pm. Staff will undertake research; negotiable fee for long projects. David King's latest photographic books: *The Commissar Vanishes*, documents the falsification of photographs and art in Stalin's Russia, and *Ordinary Citizens*, mugshots from the archives of Stalin's secret police of victims shot without trial.

The Kobal Collection

2 The Quadrant, 135 Salusbury Road, London NW6 6RJ
☎020 7624 3300 Fax 020 7624 3311
✉ info@picture-desk.com
www.picture-desk.com

Colour and b&w coverage of Hollywood films: portraits, stills, publicity shots, posters, ephemera. Visitors by appointment.

Kos Picture Source Ltd

7 Spice Court, Ivory Square, Plantation Wharf, London SW11 3UE
☎020 7801 0044 Fax 020 7801 0055
✉ images@kospictures.com
www.kospictures.com

Specialists in water-related images including international yacht racing and cruising, classic boats and superyachts, and extensive range of watersports. Also worldwide travel including seascapes, beach scenes, underwater photography and the weather.

Ed Lacey Collection

See **Phil Sheldon Golf Picture Library**

Frank Lane Picture Agency Ltd

Pages Green House, Wetheringsett, Stowmarket IP14 5QA
☎01728 860789 Fax 01728 860222
✉ pictures@flpa-images.co.uk

www.flpa-images.co.uk

Colour coverage of natural history, environment, pets and weather. Represents Sunset from France, Foto Natura from Holland, Minden Pictures from the US and works closely with Eric and David Hosking, plus 270 freelance photographers.

Last Resort Picture Library

Manvers Studios, 12 Ollerton Road, Tuxford, Newark NG22 0LF
☎01777 870166 Fax 01777 871739
✉ LRPL@dmimaging.co.uk
www.dmimaging.co.uk

Contact *Jo Makin*

Subject areas include agriculture, architecture, computing, education, food, industry, landscape, people at work, skiing, trees, flowers. Images cover a wide variety of topics rather than specialising, ranging from the everyday to the obscure. 'Bespoke service available through our linked photographic studio. Contact us for details.'

LAT Photographic

Somerset House, Somerset Road, Teddington TW11 8RU
☎020 8251 3000 Fax 020 8251 3001
✉ lat.photo@haynet.com
www.latphoto.co.uk

Motor sport collection of over nine million images dating from 1895 to the present day.

André Laubier Picture Library

Flat 2, 1 Bishops Road, London N6 4HP
☎020 8341 2947

An extensive library of photographs from 1935 to the present day in 35mm and medium-format. Main subjects are: archaeology and architecture, art and artists (wood carving, sculptures, contemporary glass), botany, historical buildings, sites and events, landscapes, nature, leisure sports, events, experimental artwork and photography, people and travel. Substantial stock of many other subjects, including: birds, buildings and cities, folklore, food and drink, gardens, transport. SPECIAL COLLECTION Images d'Europe (Austria, Britain, France, Greece, S.W. Ireland, Italy, Spain, Turkey, Egypt – from Cairo to Abu Simbel, Norway and former Yugoslavia). Africa and Kenyan safari. PRIVATE COLLECTION World War II to D-Day. List available on request. Correspondence welcome in English, French or German.

Lebrecht Music and Arts

58b Carlton Hill, London NW8 0ES

☎020 7625 5341/7372 8233
Fax 020 7625 5341
✉ pictures@lebrecht.co.uk
www.lebrecht.co.uk

Contact *Elbie Lebrecht*

'The world's most comprehensive archive of music images from early antiquity to the present day has expanded to incorporate coverage of ballet, literature, fine art and artists, film stills, historical personalities, jazz, world music and instruments.'

The Erich Lessing Archive of Fine Art & Culture

c/o ak-images Ltd, The Arts and History Picture Library, 5 Melbray Mews, 158 Hurlingham Road, London SW6 3NS
☎020 7610 6103 Fax 020 7610 6125
✉ enquiries@akg-images.co.uk
www.akg-images.co.uk

Archive of large-format transparencies and high resolution scans depicting the contents of many of the world's finest art galleries as well as ancient archaeological and biblical sites. Represented by **AKG Images Ltd**.

Life File Photos Ltd

26 Ambleside Drive, Oxford OX3 0AQ
☎01865 422002 Fax 01865 422002

Contact *Caroline Birch*

300,000 images of people and places, lifestyles, industry, environmental issues, natural history and customs, from Afghanistan to Zimbabwe. Stocks most of the major tourist destinations throughout the world, including the UK.

Lindley Library, Royal Horticultural Society

80 Vincent Square, London SW1P 2PE
☎020 7821 3051 Fax 020 7821 3022

Contact *Picture Librarian*

20,000 original drawings and approx. 8000 books with hand-coloured plates of botanical illustrations. Appointment is absolutely essential; all photography is done by own photographer.

Link Picture Library

33 Greyhound Road, London W6 8NH
☎020 7381 2261/2433 Fax 020 7385 6244
✉ lib@linkpicturelibrary.com
www.linkpicturelibrary.com

Contact *Orde Eliason*

100,000 images of South Africa, India, China, Vietnam and Israel. A more general collection of colour transparencies from 100 countries world-wide. Link Picture Library has an international network and can source material not in its file from Japan, Scandinavia, India and South Africa. Original photographic commissions undertaken.

London Aerial Photo Library

Studio D1, Fairoaks Airport, Chobham, Woking GU24 8HU
☎01276 855997 Fax 01276 855455
✉ info@londonaerial.co.uk
www.londonaerial.co.uk

Contact *Amanda Campbell*

120,000 colour negatives of aerial photographs covering most of Britain, with particular emphasis on London and surrounding counties. Includes large library of digital images. No search fee. E-mailed library prints are supplied free of charge to enquirers. Welcomes enquiries in respect of either general subjects or specific sites and buildings.

The London Film Archive

78 Mildmay Park, London N1 4PR
☎020 7923 4074 Fax 020 7287 8000
✉ info@londonfilmarchive.org
www.londonfilmarchive.org

Contact *Robert Dewar*

Archive which concentrates on all aspects of commercial, political and social life in the City and suburbs of London. The collection is primarily a film collection but also has stills, glass plate negatives, posters, advertising and documents of London interest.

London Metropolitan Archives

40 Northampton Road, London EC1R 0HB
☎020 7332 3820/7278 8703 (Minicom)
Fax 020 7833 9136
www.cityoflondon.gov.uk/lma

Contact *The Enquiry Team*

London Metropolitan Archives (LMA) is the largest local authority record office in the UK. Holds over 32 miles of archives – an enormous amount of information about the capital and its people. These include records of London government, hospitals, charities, businesses and parish churches. Types of record range from books and manuscript documents to photographs, maps and drawings. 'Nearly 900 years of London history can be brought to life at LMA.' There is also a 100,000 volume reference library specialising in London history. See entry under *Library Services*.

London's Transport Museum Photographic Library

39 Wellington Street, London WC2E 7BB
☎020 7379 6344 Fax 020 7565 7252
www.ltmuseum.co.uk

Contacts *Hugh Robertson, Simon Murphy, Samantha Ratcliffe*

Around 100,000 b&w images from the 1860s and 20,000 colour images from c.1975. SPECIALIST COLLECTIONS Poster archive, Underground construction, corporate design and architecture, street scenes, London Transport during the war. Collection available for viewing by appointment on Monday and Tuesday. No loans system but prints and transparences can be purchased. Digital images available on CD-ROM.

Lonely Planet Images

See **Lonely Planet Publications** under *UK Publishers*

Ludvigsen Library

Scoles Gate, Hawkedon, Bury St Edmunds IP29 4AU
☎01284 789246 Fax 01284 789246
✉ library@ludvigsen.com
www.ludvigsen.com

Contact *Sam Turner*

Extensive information research facilities for writers and publishers. Approximately 400,000 images (both b&w and many colour transparencies) of automobiles and motorsport, from 1890s through 1980s. Glass plate negatives from the early 1900s; Formula One, Le Mans, motor car shows, vintage, antique and classic cars from all countries. Includes the Dalton–Watson Collection and the work of noted photographers such as John Dugdale, Edward Eves, Peter Keen, Max le Grand, Karl Ludvigsen, Rodolfo Mailander, Ove Nielsen, Stanley Rosenthall and others.

MacQuitty International Photographic Collection

7 Elm Lodge, River Gardens, Stevenage Road, London SW6 6NZ
☎020 7385 5606 Fax 020 7385 5606
✉ miranda.macquitty@btinternet.com

Contact *Dr Miranda MacQuitty*

Colour and b&w collection on aspects of life in over 70 countries: dancing, music, religion, death, archaeology, buildings, transport, food, drink, nature. Visitors by appointment.

Magnum Photos Ltd
Moreland Buildings, 2nd Floor, 5 Old Street,
London EC1V 9HL
☎020 7490 1771 Fax 020 7608 0020
✉ magnum@magnumphotos.co.uk
www.magnumphotos.com
Head of Library *Hamish Crooks*

Founded 1947 by Cartier Bresson, George
Rodger, Robert Capa and David 'Chim'
Seymour. Represents over 50 of the world's
leading photo-journalists. Coverage of all
major world events from the Spanish Civil War
to present day. Also a large collection of personalities.

The Raymond Mander &
Joe Mitchenson Theatre Collection
Jerwood Library of the Performing Arts,
Trinity College of Music, King Charles Court,
Old Royal Naval College, London SE10 9JF
☎020 8305 4426 Fax 020 8305 3993
✉ rmangan@tcm.ac.uk
www.mander-and-mitchenson.co.uk

Contact *Richard Mangan*

Enormous collection covering all aspects of the
theatre: plays, actors, dramatists, music hall,
theatres, singers, composers, etc. Visitors welcome by appointment.

The Roger Mann Collection
Wensley Court, 48 Barton Road, Torquay
TQ1 4DW
☎01803 323868 Fax 01803 616448
✉ rogermann48bart@aol.com
www.therogermanncollection.co.uk

Contact *R.F. Mann*

Comprehensive collection of cricket memorabilia covering the period 1750–1945. The photographs feature most of the first-class players,
teams, Test match action and overseas tours of
the period. Includes almost 2000 original
match scorecards, cartoons, images, prints,
postcards, cigarette cards, letters and the personal memorabilia of many of the best-known
players of the time. Also some coverage of the
period 1946–1970.

S&O Mathews Photography
Little Pitt Place, Brighstone, Isle of Wight
PO30 4DZ
☎01983 741098 Fax 01983 740592
✉ oliver@mathews-photography.com
www.mathews-photography.com

Library of colour transparencies of gardens,
plants and landscapes.

Institution of Mechanical Engineers
1 Birdcage Walk, London SW1H 9JJ
☎020 7973 1265 Fax 020 7222 8762
✉ k_moore@imeche.org.uk
www.imeche.org.uk
Head Librarian & Archivist *Keith Moore*

Historical images and archives on mechanical
engineering. Open 9.15 am to 5.30 pm, Mon.
to Fri. Telephone for appointment.

Meledin Collection
See **Mary Evans Picture Library**

The MerseySlides Collection
c/o Tropix Photo Library, 44 Woodbines
Avenue, Kingston-upon-Thames KT1 2AY
☎020 8546 0823/0151 625 4576
Fax 0870 706 1317
✉ images@tropix.co.uk
www.tropix.co.uk

Contact *Veronica Birley*

The MerseySlides Collection comes from
Tropix Photo Library and contains powerful
images of Liverpool, Merseyside, Wirral,
Cheshire and much of North West England.
Also North Wales, Scotland, other parts of
England, Ireland and some Europe. Assignment
and studio photography are regularly undertaken
for a wide range of clients, both commercial and
editorial. Photography is available in all formats
including digital and panoramic.

Lee Miller Archives
Farley Farm House, Chiddingly, Near Lewes
BN8 6HW
☎01825 872691 Fax 01825 872733
✉ archives@leemiller.co.uk
www.leemiller.co.uk

The work of Lee Miller (1907–77). As a photo-
journalist she covered the war in Europe from
early in 1941 to VE Day with further reporting
from the Balkans. Collection includes photographic portraits of prominent Surrealist artists:
Ernst, Eluard, Miró, Picasso, Penrose, Carrington, Tanning, and others. Surrealist and contemporary art, poets and writers, fashion, the Middle
East, Egypt, the Balkans in the 1930s, London
during the Blitz, war in Europe and the liberation of Dachau and Buchenwald.

Mirrorpix
22nd Floor, 1 Canada Square, Canary Wharf,
London E14 5AP
☎020 7293 3700 Fax 020 7293 2712
✉ desk@mirrorpix.com
www.mirrorpix.com

General Manager *John Churchill*

For the past 100 years the photographers of the *Daily Mirror* and its sister titles have recorded both the light and dark sides of British life in startling detail. The people, places, events and movements that have shaped modern Britain can be found in the comprehensive catalogue.

Monitor Picture Library

The Forge, Roydon, Harlow CM19 5HH
☎01279 792700 Fax 01279 792600
✉ info@monitorpicturelibrary.com
www.monitorpicturelibrary.com

Colour and b&w coverage of 1960s, '70s and '80s personalities and celebrities from: music, entertainment, sport, politics, royals, judicial, commerce etc. Specialist files on Lotus cars. Syndication to international, national and local media.

Moroccan Scapes

Seend Park, Seend SN12 6NZ
☎01380 828533 Fax 01380 828630
✉ chris@realmorocco.com
www.realmorocco.com

Contact *Chris Lawrence*

Specialist collection of Moroccan material: scenery, towns, people, markets and places, plus the Atlas Mountains. Over 18,000 images.

Motoring Picture Library

National Motor Museum, Beaulieu SO42 7ZN
☎01590 614656 Fax 01590 612655
✉ motoring.pictures@beaulieu.co.uk
www.motoringpicturelibrary.com

Contact *Jonathan Day*

Three-quarters of a million b&w images, plus 100,000 colour images covering all forms of motoring history from the 1880s to the present day. Commissions undertaken. Own studio.

Mountain Camera

See **John Cleare**

Moving Image Communications

The Maidstone Studios, Zinters Park, Maidstone ME14 5NZ
☎01622 684569 Fax 01622 687444
✉ mail@milibrary.com
www.milibrary.com

Contact *Nathalie Banaigs*

Over 11,350 hours of quality archive and contemporary footage, including: Channel X Communications; TVAM Archive 1983–92;

Leo & Mandy Dickinson Action & Adventure Sports Archive; The Lonely Planet (TV travel series); Shark Bay Films (tropical and sub-aqua); British Tourist Authority – BTA (1930 to present day); TIDA Public Information Films (BTA's predecessor); Buff Films (aviation archive/NATO planes and ships); Drummer Films (travel classics, 1950–70); Universal Newsreels (1950s-60s); The Freud Archive (1930–39); Natural World; Stockshots (time-lapse, cityscapes, land and seascapes, chroma-key); Space Exploration (NASA); Wild Islands; Flying Pictures; National Trust.

Museum of Antiquities Picture Library

University and Society of Antiquaries of Newcastle upon Tyne, Newcastle upon Tyne NE1 7RU
☎0191 222 7846 Fax 0191 222 8561
✉ m.o.antiquities@ncl.ac.uk
www.ncl.ac.uk/antiquities

Contact *Lindsay Allason-Jones*

25,000 images, mostly b&w, of special collections including: Hadrian's Wall Archive (b&ws taken over the last 100 years); Gertrude Bell Archive (during her travels in the Near East, 1900–26); and aerial photographs of archaeological sites in the North of England. Visitors welcome by appointment.

Museum of London Picture Library

150 London Wall, London EC2Y 5HN
☎020 7814 5604 Fax 020 7600 1058
✉ picturelib@museumoflondon.org.uk

The Museum of London Picture Library tells the story of London from its earliest settlers to the present day. Suffragettes: photographs and memorabilia; Museum Objects: gallery and reserve collections – Prehistoric, Roman, Saxon, Medieval, Tudor, Stuart, Georgian, Victorian, London Now; Photographs: social history of the capital – working life, East End, inter-war years, the Blitz, post-war; Prints and Caricatures: political and social satire, architecture; Paintings: dating from the 17th century, portraits, landscapes, cityscapes.

The National Archives

Ruskin Avenue, Kew, Richmond TW9 4DU
☎020 8392 5225 Fax 020 8392 5266
✉ image-library@nationalarchives.gov.uk

Contacts *Paul Johnson, Hugh Alexander*

British and colonial history from the Domesday

Book to the 1960s, shown in photography, maps, illuminations, posters, advertisements, textiles and original manuscripts. Approximately 30,000 5x4″ and 35mm colour transparencies and b&w negatives. Open: 9.00 am to 5.00 pm, Monday to Friday.

National Galleries of Scotland Picture Library

The Dean Gallery, Belford Road, Edinburgh EH4 3DS
☎0131 624 6258/6260 Fax 0131 623 7135
✉ picture.library@nationalgalleries.org

Contact *Deborah Hunter*

Over 80,000 b&w and several thousand images in colour of works of art from the Renaissance to present day. SPECIALIST SUBJECTS cover fine art (painting, sculpture, drawing), portraits, Scottish, historical, still life, photography and landscape. Colour leaflet and CD-ROM guide available on request.

National Maritime Museum Picture Library

Greenwich, London SE10 9NF
☎020 8312 6631/6704 Fax 020 8312 6533
✉ picturelibrary@nmm.ac.uk
www.nmm.ac.uk/picturelibrary

Contacts *David Taylor, Lucy Waitt*

Over 350,000 maritime-related images, including oil paintings from the 16th century to present day, prints and drawings, historic photographs, plans of ships built in the UK since the beginning of the 18th century, models, rare maps and charts, globes, manuscripts, navigation and scientific instruments, etc. Over 50,000 items within the collection are now photographed and with the Historic Photographs Collection form the basis of the picture library's stock.

National Meteorological Library and Archive

See entry under *Library Services*

National Monuments Record

National Monuments Record Centre, Kemble Drive, Great Western Village, Swindon SN2 2GZ
☎01793 414600 Fax 01793 414606
✉ nmrinfo@english-heritage.org.uk
www.english-heritage.org.uk

The National Monuments Record is the first stop for photographs and information on England's heritage. Over 10 million photographs,

documents and drawings are held. English architecture from the first days of photography to the present, air photographs covering every inch of England from the first days of flying to the present, and archaeological sites. The Record is the public archive of English Heritage (see **English Heritage Photo Library**).

National Museum of Photography, Film & Television

See **Science & Society Picture Library**

National Museum of Science & Industry (NMSI)

See **Science & Society Picture Library**

National Portrait Gallery Picture Library

St Martin's Place, London WC2H 0HE
☎020 7312 2474/5/6 Fax 020 7312 2464
✉ picturelibrary@npg.org.uk
www.npg.org.uk

Contact *Tom Morgan*

Pictures of brilliant, daring and influential characters who have made British history are available for publication. Images can be searched, viewed and ordered on the website. Copyright clearance is arranged for all images supplied.

National Railway Museum Picture Library

Leeman Road, York YO26 4XJ
☎01904 621261 Fax 01904 611112
✉ nrm@nmsi.ac.uk
www.nrm.org.uk

1.5 million images, mainly b&w, covering every aspect of railways from 1850s to the present day. Visitors by appointment.

The National Trust Photo Library

36 Queen Anne's Gate, London SW1H 9AS
☎020 7447 6788/9 Fax 020 7447 6767
✉ photolibrary@ntrust.org.uk
www.nationaltrust.org.uk/photolibrary

Contact *Chris Lacey*

Collection of mixed-format transparencies covering landscape and coastline throughout England, Wales and Northern Ireland; also architecture, interiors, gardens, paintings and conservation, plus a new collection of wildlife photographs. Award-winning brochure available on request. Profits from the picture library are reinvested in continuing the work of the Trust.

Natural History Museum Picture Library

Cromwell Road, London SW7 5BD
☎020 7942 5401/5324 Fax 020 7942 5443
✉ nhmpl@nhm.ac.uk
www.nhm.ac.uk/piclib

Contacts *Carla Penagos, Rupert Calvocoressi*

Pictures from the Museum's collections, including dinosaurs, man's evolution, extinct species and fossil remains. Also pictures of gems, minerals, birds and animals, plants and insect specimens, plus historical artworks depicting the natural world.

Natural Science Photos

33 Woodland Drive, Watford WD17 3BY
☎01923 245265 Fax 01923 246067

Colour coverage by some 150 photographers of natural history subjects worldwide. The collection includes amphibia, angling, animals, birds, fish, insects and other invertebrates, reptiles, habitats, plants, fungi, horticulture, agriculture, geography, weather, scenics, farm animals, registered dog breeds. Researched by experienced scientists, Peter and Sondra Ward. Visits by appointment. Commissions undertaken.

Nature Photographers Ltd

West Wit, New Road, Little London, Tadley RG26 5EU
☎01256 850661 Fax 01256 851157
✉ info@naturephotographers.co.uk
www.naturephotographers.co.uk

Contact *Dr Paul Sterry*

Over 150,000 images on worldwide natural history and environmental subjects. The library is run by a trained biologist and experienced author on his subject.

Nature Picture Library

BBC Broadcasting House, Whiteladies Road, Bristol BS8 2LR
☎0117 974 6720 Fax 0117 923 8166
✉ info@naturepl.com
www.naturepl.com

Contact *Helen Gilks*

A collection of 150,000 nature photos from around the world, including strong coverage of animal portraits and behaviour. Other subjects covered include plants, pets, landscapes and travel, environmental issues and wildlife filmmakers at work. Thousands of images can be viewed online and downloaded direct for reproduction.

Peter Newark's Picture Library

3 Barton Buildings, Queen Square, Bath BA1 2JR
☎01225 334213 Fax 01225 480554

Over one million images covering world history from ancient times to the present day. Includes an extensive military collection of photographs, paintings and illustrations. Also a special collection on American history covering Colonial times, exploration, social, political and the Wild West and Native-Americans in particular. Subject list available. Telephone, fax or write for further information.

Newsquest (Herald & Times) Ltd

200 Renfield Street, Glasgow G2 3QB
☎0141 302 7364 Fax 0141 302 7383
✉ piclib@glasgow.newsquest.co.uk
www.thepicturedesk.co.uk

Over six million images: b&w and colour photographs from *c*.1900 from the *Herald* (Glasgow) and *Evening Times*. Current affairs, Scotland, Glasgow, Clydeside shipbuilding and engineering, personalities, World Wars I and II, sport.

NHPA Ltd

Little Tye, 57 High Street, Ardingly RH17 6TB
☎01444 892514 Fax 01444 892168
✉ nhpa@nhpa.co.uk
www.nhpa.co.uk

Library Manager *Tim Harris*

Extensive coverage on all aspects of natural history – animals, plants, landscapes, environmental issues, gardens and pets. Over 150 photographers worldwide provide a steady input of high-quality images. SPECIALIST FILES include the unique high-speed photography of Stephen Dalton, extensive coverage of African and American wildlife, also rainforests, marine life and the polar regions. UK agents for the ANT collection of Australasian material. Loans are generally made direct to publishers; individual writers must request material via their publisher. See our website to view over 18,000 pictures.

Odhams Periodicals Library

See **Popperfoto.com**

Offshoot

See **Skishoot**

Only Horses Picture Agency

27 Greenway Gardens, Greenford UB6 9TU
☎020 8578 9047 Fax 020 8575 7244
✉ onlyhorsespics@aol.com

www.onlyhorsespictures.com

Colour and b&w coverage of all aspects of the horse. Foaling, retirement, racing, show jumping, eventing, veterinary, polo, breeds, personalities.

OSF (Oxford Scientific Films) Photo Library

Ground Floor, Network House, Station Yard, Thame OX9 3UH

☎01844 262370 Fax 01844 262380

✉ enquiries@osf.uk.com

www.osf.uk.com

Account Executives *Rebecca Marsden* (stills), *Sandra Berry* (footage)

Collection of 350,000 colour transparencies and digital files of wildlife and natural science images supplied by over 300 photographers worldwide, covering all aspects of wildlife plus landscapes, weather, seasons, plants, pets, environment, anthropology, habitats, science and industry, space, creative textures and backgrounds, and geology. Macro and micro photography. UK agents for Animals Animals, USA, Okapia, Germany and Dinodia, India. Research by experienced researchers for specialist and creative briefs. Visits welcome, by appointment.

Oxford Picture Library

15 Curtis Yard, North Hinksey Lane, Oxford OX2 0LX

☎01865 723404 Fax 01865 725294

✉ opl@cap-ox.com

www.cap-ox.co.uk

Contacts *Chris Andrews, Annabel Matthews*

Specialist collection on Oxford: the city, university and colleges, events, people, spires and shires. Also, the Cotswolds, architecture and landscape from Stratford-upon-Avon to Bath; the Thames and Chilterns, including Henley on Thames and Windsor; Channel Islands, especially Guernsey and Sark. Aerial views of all areas specified above. General collection includes wildlife, trees, plants, clouds, sun, sky, water and teddy bears. Commissions undertaken.

PA Photos

PA News Centre, 292 Vauxhall Bridge Road, London SW1V 1AE

☎020 7963 7990 Fax 020 7963 7066

✉ paphotos@pa.press.net

www.paphotos.com

PA Photos is the photographic agency of the Press Association, the national news agency of the UK and Ireland, and is the comprehensive resource for news, entertainment, celebrity and sport images from the UK and across the globe. Photographs date from 1890 to the present day.

Hugh Palmer

21 Walton Crescent, Oxford OX1 2JG

✉ hugh@hughpalmer.com

www.hughpalmer.com

Extensive collection of landscapes, rural life and architecture from Britain and Europe, as featured in *The Most Beautiful Villages* series of books published by Thames & Hudson.

Panos Pictures

Studio 3b, 38 Southwark Street, London SE1 1UN

☎020 7234 0010 Fax 020 7357 0094

✉ pics@panos.co.uk

www.panos.co.uk

Documentary colour and b&w library specialising in Third World and Eastern Europe, with emphasis on environment and development issues. Leaflet available. Fifty per cent of all profits from this library go to the Panos Institute to further its work in international sustainable development.

Charles Parker Archive

See **Birmingham Library Services** under *Library Services*

Ann & Bury Peerless Picture Library

St David's, 22 King's Avenue, Minnis Bay, Birchington-on-Sea CT7 9QL

☎01843 841428 Fax 01843 848321

www.peerlessimages.com

Contacts *Ann, Peerless, Bury Peerless*

Specialist collection on world religions: Hinduism, Buddhism, Confucianism, Taoism, Jainism, Christianity, Islam, Sikhism, Zoroastrianism (Parsees of India). Geographical areas covered: India, Afghanistan (Bamiyan Valley of the Buddhas), Pakistan, Bangladesh, Sri Lanka, Cambodia (Angkor), Java (Borobudur), Bali, Thailand, Russia, Republic of China, Spain, Poland, Uzbekistan (Samarkand and Bukhara), Vietnam. Basis of collection (35mm colour transparencies), historical, cultural, extensive coverage of art (sculpture and miniature paintings), architecture including Pharaonic Egypt.

Photo Resources

The Orchard, Marley Lane, Kingston, Canterbury CT4 6JH

☎01227 830075 Fax 01227 831135

Colour and b&w coverage of archaeology, art, ancient art, ethnology, mythology, world religion, museum objects.

Photofusion
17A Electric Lane, London SW9 8LA
☎020 7733 3500   Fax 020 7738 5509
✉ library@photofusion.org
www.photofusion.org
Contact *Liz Somerville*

Colour and b&w coverage of contemporary social and environmental UK issues including babies and children, disability, education, the elderly, environment, family, health, housing, homelessness, people and work. Brochure available.

The Photolibrary Wales
2 Bro-nant, Church Road, Pentyrch, Cardiff CF15 9QG
☎029 2089 0311   Fax 029 2089 2650
✉ info@photolibrarywales.com
www.photolibrarywales.com
Contacts *Steve Benbow, Kate Benbow*

Over 60,000 colour transparences covering all areas and subjects of Wales. Represents the work of 140 photographers, living and working in Wales.

Photos Horticultural
PO Box 105, Ipswich IP1 4PR
☎01473 257329   Fax 01473 233974
✉ library@photos.keme.co.uk
www.photos-horticultural.co.uk

Wide coverage of gardens and all aspects of gardening from library established in 1968. Illustrated features to order. Commissions undertaken. 'Extensive travelling ensures the best material from around the world is on file.'

PictureBank Photo Library Ltd
Parman House, 30–36 Fife Road, Kingston upon Thames KT1 1SY
☎020 8547 2344   Fax 020 8974 5652
✉ info@picturebank.co.uk
www.picturebank.co.uk

Over 400,000 colour transparencies covering people (girls, couples, families, children), travel and scenic (UK and world), moods (sunsets, seascapes, deserts, etc.), industry and technology, environments and general. Commissions undertaken. Visitors welcome. Member of **BAPLA**. New material on medium/large format welcome.

Pictures Colour Library
10 James Whatman Court, Turkey Mill, Ashford Road, Maidstone ME14 5SS
☎01622 609809   Fax 01622 609806
✉ Researcher@PicturesColourLibrary.co.uk
www.picturescolourlibrary.co.uk

Travel and travel-related images depicting lifestyles and cultures, people and places, attitudes and environments from around the world, including a comprehensive section on Great Britain.

H.G. Ponting
See **Popperfoto.com**

Popperfoto.com
The Old Mill, Overstone Farm, Overstone, Northampton NN6 0AB
☎01604 670670   Fax 01604 670635
✉ enquiries@popperfoto.com
www.popperfoto.com

Home to over 14 million images, covering 150 years of photographic history. Renowned for its archival material, a world-famous sports library and stock photography. Popperfoto's credit line includes Bob Thomas Sports Photography, UPI, Acme, INP, Planet, Paul Popper, Exclusive News Agency, Victory Archive, Odhams Periodicals Library, Illustrated, Harris Picture Agency, and H.G. Ponting which holds the Scott 1910–1912 Antarctic expedition. Colour from 1940, b&w from 1870 to the present. Major subjects covered worldwide include events, personalities, wars, royalty, sport, politics, transport, crime, history and social conditions. Material available on the same day to clients throughout the world. Mac-desk available. Researchers welcome by appointment.

PPL (Photo Agency) Ltd
Bookers Yard, The Street, Walberton, Arundel BN18 0PF
☎01243 555561   Fax 01243 555562
✉ ppl@mistral.co.uk
www.pplmedia.com
Contacts *Barry Pickthall, Natasha Wakefield*

Two million pictures covering watersports, sub-aqua, business and commerce, travel and tourism and a fast growing archive on Sussex and the home counties. Pictures available in high resolution directly from website.

Premaphotos Wildlife
Amberstone, 1 Kirland Road, Bodmin PL30 5JQ
☎01208 78258   Fax 01208 72302

✉ authors@premaphotos.co.uk
www.premaphotos.co.uk

Contact *Jean Preston-Mafham*, Library Manager

Natural history worldwide. Subjects include flowering and non-flowering plants, fungi, slime moulds, fruits and seeds, galls, leaf mines, seashore life, mammals, birds, reptiles, amphibians, insects, spiders, habitats, scenery and cultivated cacti. Commissions undertaken. Visitors welcome. 'Make sure your name is on our mailing list to receive regular, colourful mailers.'

Professional Sport UK Ltd

18–19 Shaftesbury Quay, Hertford SG14 1SF
☎01992 505000 Fax 01992 505020
✉ pictures@prosport.co.uk
www.professionalsport.com

Photographic coverage of tennis, soccer, athletics, golf, cricket, rugby, winter sports and many minor sports. Major international events including the Olympic Games, World Cup soccer and all Grand Slam tennis events. Also news and feature material supplied worldwide. Online photo archive; photo transmission services available for editorial and advertising.

Public Record Office
Image Library

See **The National Archives**

Punch Cartoon Library

87–135 Brompton Road, London SW1X 8XL
☎020 7225 6710/6793 Fax 020 7225 6712
✉ punch.library@harrods.com
www.punch.co.uk

Owner *Liberty Publishing*

Gives access to the 500,000 cartoons published in *Punch* magazine between 1841–1992. The library has a 500+ subject listing and can search on any topic. Social history, politics, fashion, fads, famous people and more by the world's most famous cartoonists, including Tenniel, du Maurier, Pont, Fougasse, E.H. Shepard and Emmett.

PWA International Ltd

4 Brightfield Road, Lee, London SE12 8QF
☎020 8297 3434 Fax 020 8297 0617
✉ pwaint@dircon.co.uk
www.pwainternational.com

Contact *Terry Allen*

Leading comprehensive library of story illustrations comprising work by some of the UK's best-known illustrators, including book covers and magazines.

Railfotos

Millbrook House Ltd., Unit 1, Oldbury Business Centre, Pound Road, Oldbury B68 8NA
☎0121 544 2970
Fax 0121 253 6836 (quote Millbrook House)

One of the largest specialist libraries dealing with railway subjects worldwide. Colour and b&w dating from the turn of the century to present day. Up-to-date material on UK, South America and Far East. Visitors by appointment.

Redferns Music Picture Library

7 Bramley Road, London W10 6SZ
☎020 7792 9914 Fax 020 7792 0921
✉ info@redferns.com
www.redferns.com

Picture library covering every aspect of music, from 18th century classical to present day pop. Over one million archived artists and other subjects including musical instruments, recording studios, crowd scenes, festivals, etc. Brochure available. Over 80,000 images available on the website.

Retna Pictures Ltd

Stills Road, Pinewood Studios, Pinewood Road, Iver Heath SL0 0NH
☎01753 785450 Fax 01753 785 451
✉ ukinfo@retna.com
www.retna.com

Established 1978, Retna Pictures Ltd is a leading picture agency with two libraries: celebrity and lifestyle. The former specialises in images of international and national celebrities, early and contemporary music, films and personalities. The lifestyle library specialises in people, family life, work, leisure and food. Both libraries are constantly receiving new material from established and up and coming photographers.

Rex Features Ltd

18 Vine Hill, London EC1R 5DZ
☎020 7278 7294 Fax 020 7696 0974
✉ library@rexfeatures.com
www.rexfeatures.com

Contact *Glen Marks*, Library Sales Manager

Extensive picture library established in the 1950s. Daily coverage of news, politics, personalities, showbusiness, glamour, humour, art, medicine, science, landscapes, royalty, etc.

Royal Air Force Museum

Grahame Park Way, Hendon, London NW9 5LL
☎020 8205 2266 Fax 020 8200 1751

photographic@rafmuseum.org

About a quarter of a million images, mostly b&w, with around 1500 colour in all formats, on the history of aviation. Particularly strong on the activities of the Royal Air Force from the 1870s to 1970s. Researchers are requested to enquire in writing only.

The Royal Collection, Photographic Services

Windsor Castle, Windsor SL4 1NJ
☎01753 868286   Fax 01753 620046
photoservices@royalcollection.org.uk

Contact *Shruti Patel*

Photographic material of items in the Royal Collection, particularly oil paintings, drawings and watercolours, works of art, and interiors and exteriors of royal residences. 35,000 colour transparencies, plus 25,000 b&w negatives.

Royal Geographical Society Picture Library

1 Kensington Gore, London SW7 2AR
☎020 7591 3060   Fax 020 7591 3061
pictures@rgs.org
www.rgs.org/picturelibrary

Contact *Justin Hobson*

A strong source of geographical and historical images, both archival and modern, showing the world through the eyes of photographers and explorers from the 1830s to the present day. The RGS Contempory Collection provides up-to-date transparencies from around the world, highlighting aspects of cultural activity, environmental phenomena, anthropology, architectural design, travel, mountaineering and exploration. Offers a professional and comprehensive service for both commercial and academic use.

RSPB Images

PO Box 7515, Billericay CM11 1WR
☎01268 71171   Fax 01268 710353
rspb@thatsgood.biz
www.rspb-images.com

Contact *Wendy Hollis*

Colour images of birds, butterflies, moths, mammals, reptiles and their habitats. Also colour images of all RSPB reserves. Growing selection of various habitats. Online search facility of over 30,000 digitised images.

RSPCA Photolibrary

RSPCA Trading Limited, Wilberforce Way, Southwater, Horsham RH13 9RS
☎0870 754 0150   Fax 0870 753 0150

pictures@rspcaphotolibrary.com
www.rspcaphotolibrary.com

Photolibrary Manager *Andrew Forsyth*

Over 100,000 colour transparencies and over 5000 b&w/colour prints. A comprehensive collection of natural history images whose subjects include mammals, birds, domestic and farm animals, amphibians, insects and the environment, as well as a unique photographic record of the RSPCA's work. Also includes the Wild Images collections. Catalogue available. No search fees.

Russia and Eastern Images

'Sonning', Cheapside Lane, Denham, Uxbridge UB9 5AE
☎01895 833508
easteuropix@btinternet.com
www.easteuropix.com

Architecture, cities, landscapes, people and travel images of Russia and the former Soviet Union. Considerable background knowledge available and Russian language spoken.

Peter Sanders Photography

24 Meades Lane, Chesham HP5 1ND
☎01494 773674/771372   Fax 01494 773674
photos@petersanders.com
www.petersanders.com

Contacts *Peter Sanders, Hafsa Garwatuk*

Specialises in the world of Islam in all its aspects from culture, arts, industry, lifestyles, celebrations, etc. Areas included are north, east and west Africa, the Middle East (including Saudi Arabia), China, Asia, Europe and USA. A continually expanding library.

Science & Society Picture Library

Science Museum, Exhibition Road, London SW7 2DD
☎020 7942 4400   Fax 020 7942 4401
piclib@nmsi.ac.uk
www.nmsi.ac.uk/piclib/

Contact *Angela Murphy*

Currently digitising over 50,000 of the best from the millions of images in the collections. 'Science & Society has one of the widest ranges of photographs, paintings, prints, posters and objects in the world.' The images come from the collections of the National Museum of Science & Industry (NMSI) – which includes the Science Museum, the **National Railway Museum** and the National Museum of Photography, Film & Television. Images are available as high or low resolution via e-mail or ftp; alternatively, transparency or print can be supplied.

Science Museum
See **Science & Society Picture Library**

Science Photo Library
327–329 Harrow Road, London W9 3RB
☎020 7432 1100 Fax 020 7286 8668
✉ info@sciencephoto.com
www.sciencephoto.com

Subjects include the human body, health and medicine, research, genetics, technology and industry, space exploration and astronomy, earth science, satellite imagery, environment, nature and wildlife and the history of science. The whole collection, more than 100,000 images, is available online.

Seaco Picture Library
Sea Containers House, 20 Upper Ground, London SE1 9PF
☎020 7805 5831 Fax 020 7805 5807
✉ seaco.pictures@seacontainers.com

Contact *Luci Gosling*

Approx. 250,000 images of containerisation, shipping, fast ferries, manufacturing, fruit farming, ports, hotels and leisure.

Mick Sharp Photography
Eithinog, Waun, Penisarwaun, Caernarfon LL55 3PW
☎01286 872425 Fax 01286 872425
✉ mick.jean@virgin.net

Contacts *Mick Sharp, Jean Williamson*

Colour transparencies (6x4.5cm and 35mm) and black & white prints (5x4″ and 6x4.5cm negs) of subjects connected with archaeology, ancient monuments, buildings, churches, environment, history, countryside, landscape, past cultures and topography from Britain and abroad. Photographs by Mick Sharp and Jean Williamson, plus access to other specialist collections on related subjects. Commissions undertaken.

Phil Sheldon Golf Picture Library
40 Manor Road, Barnet EN5 2JQ
☎020 8440 1986 Fax 020 8440 9348
✉ gill@philsheldongolfpics.co.uk *or* phil@philsheldongolfpics.co.uk
www.philsheldongolfpics.co.uk

An expanding collection of over 500,000 quality images of the 'world of golf'. In-depth worldwide tournament coverage including every Major championship and Ryder Cup since 1976. Instruction, portraits, trophies and over 400 golf courses from around the world. Also the Dale Concannon collection covering the period 1870 to 1940, the classic 1960s collection by photographer Sidney Harris and the Ed Lacey Collection.

Skishoot–Offshoot
Hall Place, Upper Woodcott, Whitchurch RG28 7PY
☎01635 255527 Fax 01635 255528
✉ skishootsnow@aol.com
www.skishoot.co.uk

Contacts *Kate Parker, Jo Crossley*

Skishoot ski and snowboarding picture library has 400,000 images. Offshoot travel library specialises in France.

The Skyscan Photolibrary
Oak House, Toddington, Cheltenham GL54 5BY
☎01242 621357 Fax 01242 621343
✉ info@skyscan.co.uk
www.skyscan.co.uk

As well as the Skyscan Photolibrary collection of unique balloon's-eye views of Britain, the library now includes the work of photographers from across the aviation spectrum; air to ground, aviation, aerial sports – 'in fact, anything aerial!' Links have been built with photographers across the world; photographs can be handled on an agency basis and held in house, or as a brokerage where the collection stays with the photographer; terms 50/50 for both. Commissioned photography arranged. Enquiries welcome.

Snookerimages (Eric Whitehead Photography)
25 Oak Street, Windermere LA23 1EN
☎015394 48894 Fax 015394 48294
✉ snooker@snookerimages.co.uk
www.snookerimages.co.uk

Over 30,000 images of snooker from 1982 to the present day. The agency covers local news events, PR and commercial material.

SOA Photo Library
Lovells Farm, Dark Lane, Stoke St Gregory, Taunton TA3 6EU
☎0870 333 6062 Fax 0870 333 6082
✉ info@soaphotoagency.com
www.soaphotoagency.com

Contact *Sabine Oppenlander*

85,000 colour slides, 15,000 b&w photos covering *Stern* productions, sports, travel and geographic, advertising, social subjects and funny photos. Representatives of Voller Ernst, Picture Press, Look and many freelance photographers. Free catalogues available.

Solo Syndication Ltd
17–18 Haywards Place, Clerkenwell, London EC1R 0EQ
☎020 7566 0360 Fax 020 7566 0388
Syndication Director *Trevor York*
Sales *Danny Howell, Nick York*
Online transmissions *Geoff Malyon* (☎020 7566 0370)
Three million images from the archives of the *Daily Mail, Mail on Sunday, Evening Standard* and *Evening News*. Hard prints or Mac-to-Mac delivery. 24-hour service.

Sotheby's Picture Library
34-35 New Bond Street, London W1A 2AA
☎020 7293 5383 Fax 020 7293 5062
✉ piclib.london@sothebys.com
Contacts *Joanna Ling, Sue Daly*
The library consists of over 200,000 selected transparencies of pictures sold at Sotheby's. Images from the 15th to the 20th century. Oils, drawings, watercolours, prints and decorative items. 'Happy to do searches or, alternatively, visitors are welcome by appointment.'

South American Pictures
48 Station Road, Woodbridge IP12 4AT
☎01394 383963 Fax 01394 380176
✉ morrison@southamericanpictures.com
www.southamericanpictures.com
Specialist site: www.nonesuchinfo.info
Contact *Marion Morrison*
Colour and b&w images of South/Central America, Cuba, Mexico, New Mexico (USA), Dominican Republic and Haiti, including archaeology and the Amazon. There is an archival section, with pictures and documents from most countries. Now with 40 contributing photographers.

The Special Photographers Library
236 Westbourne Park Road, London W11 1EL
☎020 7221 3489 Fax 020 7792 9112
✉ info@specialphotographers.com
www.specialphotographers.com
Contacts *Chris Kewbank*
Represents over 100 contemporary fine art photographers who are unusual in style, technique or subject matter. 'The content could be anything!'

Still Digital
8 Saxe Coburg Place, Edinburgh EH3 5BR
☎0131 332 1123
✉ info@stilldigital.co.uk
www.stilldigital.co.uk
Contact *John Hutchinson*
Fully searchable and downloadable service for thousands of Scottish images.

Still Pictures' Whole Earth Photolibrary
199 Shooters Hill Road, London SE3 8UL
☎020 8858 8307 Fax 020 8858 2049
✉ info@stillpictures.com
www.stillpictures.com
Contacts *Kate Watson, Mark Edwards*
Founded 1970, the library is a leading source of pictures illustrating the human impact on the environment, Third World development issues, industrial ecology, nature and wildlife, endangered species and habitats. 400,000 colour medium-format transparencies, 100,000 b&w prints. Over 400 leading photographers from around the world supply the library with stock pictures. Write, phone or fax for Still Pictures' environment catalogue, *Earth and People*, the UNEP (United Nations Environment Programme) catalogue, *Elements* and the *Nature and Wildlife* catalogue.

Stockfile
5 High Street, Sunningdale SL5 0LX
☎01344 872249 Fax 01344 872263
✉ info@stockfile.co.uk
www.stockfile.co.uk
Contacts *Jill Behr, Steven Behr*
Specialist cycling collection with emphasis on mountain biking. Expanding adventure sports section covering snow, land, air and water activities.

Stockscotland.com
Croft Roy, Crammond Brae, Tain IV19 1JG
☎01862 892298 Fax 01862 892298
✉ info@stockscotland.com
www.stockscotland.com
Contact *Hugh Webster*
150,000 Scottish images with 10,000 currently available online.

Sir John Benjamin Stone
See **Birmingham Library Services** under *Library Services*

Jessica Strang Photo Library
504 Brody House, Strype Street, London
E1 7LQ
☎020 7247 8982 Fax 020 7247 8982
✉ jessica@jessicastrang.plus.com

Contact *Jessica Strang*

Approximately 60,000 transparencies covering architecture, interiors (contemporary), gardens, 'obsessive and not just small but tiny, or from almost no space at all', men, women, couples and animals in architecture, and vanishing London details. Recycled ideas for the home.

Joe Tasker Collection
See **Chris Bonington Picture Library**

Tate Enterprises Picture Library
Top Floor, The Lodge, Tate Britain, Millbank, London SW1P 4RG
☎020 7887 8871 Fax 020 7887 8805
✉ picture.library@tate.org.uk
www.tate.org.uk

Contact *Alison Miles*

Around 8000 images of British art from the 16th century; international 20th century painting and sculpture. Artists include Blake, Hogarth, Turner, Rossetti, Barbara Hepworth, Henry Moore, Stanley Spencer, Picasso, Mark Rothko, Dali, Lucien Freud and David Hockney. Colour transparencies of more than half the works in the main collection are available for hire. For a fee, new photography is available depending on the location and condition of the art work. B&w prints of nearly all the works in the collection can be purchased. Colour slides and prints can be made on request provided a colour transparency exists. Picture researchers must make an appointment to visit the library:. Applications must be made by e-mail, fax or letter.

Bob Thomas Sports Photography
See **Popperfoto.com**

Thoroughbred Photography Ltd
The Hornbeams, 2 The Street, Worlington
IP28 8RU
☎01638 713944
✉ mail@thoroughbredphoto.com
www.thoroughbredphoto.com

Contacts *Trevor Jones, Gill Jones, Laura Green*

Extensive library of high-quality colour images depicting all aspects of thoroughbred horseracing dating from 1987. Major group races, English Classics, studs, stallions, mares and foals, early morning scenes, personalities, jockeys, trainers and prominent owners. Also international work: USA Breeders' Cup, Arc de Triomphe, French Classics, Irish Derby, Dubai racing scenes, Japan Cup and Hokkaido stud farms; and more unusual scenes such as racing on the sands at low tide, Ireland, and on the frozen lake at St Moritz. Visitors by appointment.

Rick Tomlinson Marine Photo Library
18 Hamble Yacht Services, Port Hamble, Hamble, Southampton SO31 4NN
☎023 8045 8450 Fax 023 8045 8350
✉ ricktom@compuserve.com
www.rick-tomlinson.com

Contacts *Rick Tomlinson*

Established 1985. Specialises in marine subjects. 100,000 35mm transparencies of yachting, racing, cruising, Whitbread Round the World Race, Volvo Ocean Race, Americas Cup, Tall Ships, RNLI Lifeboats, Antarctica, wildlife and locations.

Topham Picturepoint
PO Box 33, Edenbridge TN8 5PB
☎01732 863939 Fax 01732 860215
✉ admin@topfoto.co.uk
www.topfoto.co.uk

Contact *Alan Smith*

Eight million contemporary and historical images, ideal for advertisers, publishers and the travel trade. Delivery online.

B.M. Totterdell photography
Constable Cottage, Burlings Lane, Knockholt
TN14 7PE
☎01959 532001 Fax 01959 532001
✉ btrial@btinternet.com

Contact *Barbara Totterdell*

Specialist volleyball library covering all aspects of the sport.

Tessa Traeger Picture Library
7 Rossetti Studios, 72 Flood Street, London
SW3 5TF
☎020 7352 3641 Fax 020 7352 4846
✉ tessatraeger@solutions-inc.co.uk
www.tessatraeger.com

Food, gardens, travel and artists.

Travel Ink Photo & Feature Library
The Old Coach House, 14 High Street, Goring on Thames, Nr Reading RG8 9AR
☎01491 873011 Fax 01491 875558

✉ info@travel-ink.co.uk
www.travel-ink.co.uk

Contact *Felicity Bazell*

A collection of over 120,000 travel, tourism and lifestyle images, carefully edited and constantly updated, from countries worldwide. SPECIALIST COLLECTIONS from the UK, Greece, France, Hong Kong, Far East, Canada, USA and Caribbean. The website offers a fully captioned and searchable selection of over 20,000 images and is ideal for picture researchers.

Peter Trenchard's Image Store Ltd

The Studio, West Hill, St Helier, Jersey JE2 3HB
☎01534 769933 Fax 01534 789191
✉ peter-trenchard@jerseymail.co.uk
www.peter-trenchard.com

Contact *Peter Trenchard, FBIPP, AMPA, PPA*

Slide library of the Channel Islands – mainly tourist and financial-related. Commissions undertaken.

Tropix Photo Library

44 Woodbines Avenue, Kingston-upon-Thames KT1 2AY
☎020 8546 0823/0151 625 4576
Fax 0870 706 1317
✉ images@tropix.co.uk
www.tropix.co.uk

Contact *Veronica Birley*

Specialises in images of developing nations: travel and editorial pictures emphasising the attractive and progressive, not just the problems. Evocative photos concerning the economies, environment, culture and society of 100+ countries across Africa, Central and South America, Caribbean, Eastern Europe, Middle East, Indian subcontinent, South East Asia, CIS and Far East; also Antarctica. Also incorporating **MerseySlides Collection** (see entry). Assignment photography available worldwide. All photos supplied with detailed captions. Rapid response with one-hour digital delivery available. Established 1982. **BAPLA** member.

True North Picture Source

26 New Road, Hebden Bridge HX7 8EF
☎01422 845532
✉ john@trunorth.demon.co.uk

Contact *John Morrison*

30,000 transparencies on 35mm and 6x4.5cm format on the life and landscape of the north of England, photographed by John Morrison.

Turnley Collection

See **Corbis Images**

Ulster Museum Picture Library

Botanic Gardens, Belfast BT9 5AB
☎028 9038 3000 ext 3113 Fax 028 9038 3103
✉ patricia.mclean.um@nics.gov.uk
www.ulstermuseum.org.uk

Contact *Mrs Pat McLean*

SPECIALIST SUBJECTS art – fine and decorative, late 17th–20th century, particularly Irish art, archaeology, ethnography, treasures from the Armada shipwrecks, geology, botany, zoology, local history and industrial archaeology. Commissions welcome for objects not already photographed.

Universal Pictorial Press & Agency Ltd

29–31 Saffron Hill, London EC1N 8SW
☎020 7421 6000 Fax 020 7421 6006
✉ contact@uppa.co.uk
www.uppa.co.uk

News Editor *Peter Dare*

Photo archive dates back to 1944 and contains approximately four million pictures. Colour and b&w coverage of news, royalty, politics, sport, arts, and many other subjects. Commissions undertaken for press and public relations. Fully interactive digital photo archive accessible via ISDN or modem. Full digital scanning, retouching and transmission facilities.

UPI

See **Popperfoto.com**

V&A Images

Victoria and Albert Museum, Cromwell Road, South Kensington, London SW7 2RL
☎020 7942 2966 Fax 020 7942 2482
✉ vanda.images@vam.ac.uk
www.vandaimages.com

A vast collection of photographs from the world's largest museum of decorative and applied arts, reflecting culture and lifestyle spanning over 1000 years of history to the present time. Digital delivery of large format transparencies of contemporary and historical textiles, costumes and fashions, ceramics, furniture, metalwork, glass, sculpture, toys, and games, design and photographs from around the world. Unique photographs include 1960s fashion by John French, Harry Hammond's behind the scenes pop idols, Houston Rogers theatrical world of the 1930–70s, Lafayette's images of royalty, Cecil

Beaton, and the 19th century pioneer photographers. Images from the National Art Library, Library of Art & Design, the Theatre Museum and Museum of Childhood are readily available.

Valley Green
Barn Ley, Valley Lane, Buxhall, Stowmarket IP14 3EB
☎01449 736090 Fax 01449 736090
✉ pics@valleygreen.co.uk
Contacts *Joseph Barrere, Colette Barrere*

'Profusion of perennials – all correctly labelled.' Over 10,000 hardy plant transparencies in stock, plus watercolours and line drawings available. Commissions undertaken as well as creative copywriting.

Victory Archive
See **Popperfoto.com**

Vin Mag Archive Ltd
84–90 Digby Road, London E9 6HX
☎020 8533 7588 Fax 020 8533 7283
✉ piclib@vinmag.com
www.vinmagarchive.com

Formerly the Vintage Magazine Company. A large collection of movie stills and posters, photographs, illustrations and advertisements covering music, glamour, social history, theatre posters, ephemera, postcards.

John Walmsley Photo Library
See **Education Photos**

Christopher Ware Pictures
65 Trinity Street, Barry CF62 7EX
☎01446 420875
Contact *Christopher Ware*

Large collection of images (b&w and colour) of S.E. Wales, including Barry docks and the Steam Graveyard, railways, Vale of Glamorgan landscapes, civil and military aircraft over the last 40 years. Images available on CD-ROM or via e-mail. Digital post-production. Commissions. Other photographers' work not accepted. Also broadcast camera operation.

Warwickshire Photographic Survey
See **Birmingham Library Services** under *Library Services*

Waterways Photo Library
39 Manor Court Road, Hanwell, London W7 3EJ
☎020 8840 1659 Fax 020 8567 0605
✉ watphot39@aol.com
Contact *Derek Pratt*

A specialist photo library on all aspects of Britain's inland waterways. Top-quality 35mm and medium-format colour transparencies, plus a large collection of b&w. Rivers and canals, bridges, locks, aqueducts, tunnels and waterside buildings. Town and countryside scenes, canal art, waterway holidays, boating, fishing, windmills, watermills, watersports and wildlife.

Philip Way Photography
2 Green Moor Link, Winchmore Hill, London N21 2ND
☎020 8360 3034
✉ pwphotography1@btinternet.com
Contact *Philip Way*

Over 10,000 images of St Paul's Cathedral – historical exteriors, interiors and events (1686–2003).

Weimar Archive
See **Mary Evans Picture Library**

The Wellcome Trust Medical Photographic Library
210 Euston Road, London NW1 2BE
☎020 7611 8348 Fax 020 7611 8577
✉ photolib@wellcome.ac.uk
medphoto.wellcome.ac.uk
Contact *Michele Minto*

Approximately 180,000 images on the history of medicine and human culture worldwide, including modern clinical medicine, healthcare, family life and biomedica.

Eric Whitehead Photography
25 Oak Street, Windermere LA23 1EN
☎015394 48894 Fax 015394 48284
✉ snooker@snookerimages.co.uk
www.snookerimages.co.uk

Incorporates the Cumbria Picture Library. The agency covers local news events, PR and commercial material, also leading library of snooker images (see **Snookerimages**).

Wild Images
See **RSPCA Photolibrary**

Wild Places Photography
See **Chris Howes**

David Williams Picture Library
50 Burlington Avenue, Glasgow G12 0LH
☎0141 339 7823 Fax 0141 337 3031

✉ david@scotland-guide.co.uk

Specialises in travel photography with wide coverage of Scotland, Iceland and Spain. Many other European countries also included plus smaller collections of Western USA and Canada. The main subjects in each country are: cities, towns, villages, 'tourist haunts', buildings of architectural or historical interest, landscapes and natural features. The Scotland and Iceland collections include many pictures depicting physical geography and geology. Photographic commissions and illustrated travel articles undertaken. Catalogue available.

The Neil Williams Classical Collection

22 Avon, Hockley, Tamworth B77 5QA
☎01827 286086 Fax 01827 286086
✉ neil@classicalcollection.co.uk

Contact *Neil Williams, PGDip(Mus), BA(Hons)Hum*

Archive specialising in classical music ephemera, particularly portraits of composers, musicians, conductors and opera singers comprising of old and sometimes very rare photographs, postcards, antique prints, cigarette cards, stamps, First Day Covers, concert programmes, Victorian newspapers, etc. Also modern photos of composer references such as museums, statues, busts, paintings, monuments, memorials and graves. Other subjects covered include ballet, musical instruments, concert halls, opera houses, 'music in art', manuscripts, opera scenes, music-caricatures, bands, orchestras and other music groups. Also writer of concert programme notes and CD inserts for classical music, as well as being a commissionable composer.

Vaughan Williams Memorial Library

English Folk Dance and Song Society, Cecil Sharp House, 2 Regent's Park Road, London NW1 7AY
☎020 7485 2206 ext. 18/19
Fax 020 7284 0523
✉ library@efdss.org
www.efdss.org

Mainly b&w coverage of traditional/folk music, dance and customs worldwide, focusing on Britain and other English-speaking nations. Photographs date from the late 19th century to the present day.

The Wilson Photographic Collection

See **Dundee Central Library** under *Library Services*

Windrush Photos, Wildlife Agency

99 Noah's Ark, Kemsing, Sevenoaks
TN15 6PD
☎01732 763486 Fax 01732 763285
✉ dt@windrushphotos.demon.co.uk
www.windrushphotos.com

Contact *David Tipling*

Specialists in birds (worldwide) and British wildlife. Photographic and features commissions are regularly undertaken for publications in the UK and overseas. The agency acts as ornithological consultants for all aspects of the media. **BAPLA** member.

Woodfall Wild Images

17 Bull Lane, Denbigh LL16 3SN
☎01745 815903 Fax 01745 814581
✉ wwimages@btinternet.com
www.woodfall.com

Contacts *David Woodfall*

A comprehensive and specialist collection of wildlife, landscape and environmental photographs from both the UK and the rest of the world. Award winning photography by the world's more imaginative photographers. All formats, 35mm to panoramic. 'Personal and friendly service.' Subjects include: birds, animals, insects and marine life, trees and forests, wildflowers, all habitats worldwide and canals. Environmental issues such as pollution, conservation and habitat destruction, the weather and climate, landscapes and scenics. Suitable for advertising, editorial, calendars and design purposes.

World Pictures

25 Gosfield Street, London W1W 6HQ
☎020 7437 2121/7436 0440
Fax 020 7439 1307
✉ worldpictures@btinternet.com
www.worldpictures.co.uk

Contacts *David Brenes, Carlo Irek*

600,000 colour transparencies of travel and emotive material.

WWF UK Photolibrary

Panda House, Weyside Park, Catteshall Lane, Godalming GU7 1XR
☎01483 412336 Fax 01483 861360
✉ psunters@wwf.org.uk

Contact *Paul Sunters*

Specialist library covering natural history, endangered species, conservation, environment, forests, habitats, habitat destruction, and pollution in the UK and abroad. 25,000 colour slides (35mm).

Yemen Pictures

28 Sheen Common Drive, Richmond
TW10 5BN
☎020 7602 1989 Fax 020 7602 1989

Large collection (4000 transparencies) covering all aspects of Yemen – culture, people, architecture, dance, qat, music. Also Africa, Australia, Middle East, and Asia.

York Archaeological Trust Picture Library

Cromwell House, 13 Ogleforth, York
YO1 7FG
☎01904 663000 Fax 01904 663024

✉ enquiries@yorkarchaeology.co.uk
www.yorkarchaeology.co.uk

Specialist library of rediscovered artifacts, historic buildings and excavations, presented by the creators of the highly acclaimed Jorvik Viking Centre. The main emphasis is on the Roman, Anglo-Saxon and Viking periods.

The John Robert Young Collection

61 De Montfort Road, Lewes BN7 1SS
☎01273 475216 Fax 01273 475216
✉ johnrobert@pxvobiscum.fsnet.co.uk
johnrobertyoung.members.beeb.net

Contact *Jennifer Barrett*

50,000 transparencies and monochrome prints on religion, travel and military subjects. Major portfolios: religious communities; the French Foreign Legion; the Spanish Legion; the Royal Marines; the People's Liberation Army (China).

Settling Accounts

Ian Spring takes an expert look at the latest Budget and explains how writers can be tax wise

'No man in the country is under the smallest obligation, moral or other, to arrange his affairs as to enable the Inland Revenue to put the largest possible shovel in his stores.

The Inland Revenue is not slow, and quite rightly, to take every advantage which is open to it ... for the purpose of depleting the taxpayer's pockets. And the taxpayer is, in like manner, entitled to be astute to prevent as far as he honestly can the depletion of his means by the Inland Revenue.'

Lord Clyde, *Ayrshire Pullman v Inland Revenue Commissioners, 1929*

Income Tax

What is a professional writer for tax purposes?

Writers are professionals while they are writing regularly with the intention of making a profit; or while they are gathering material, researching or otherwise preparing a publication.

A professional freelance writer is taxed under Case II of Schedule D of the Income and Corporation Taxes Act 1988. The taxable income is the amount receivable, either directly or by an agent, on his behalf, less expenses wholly and exclusively laid out for the purpose of the profession. If expenses exceed income, the loss can either be set against other income of the same or preceding years or carried forward and set against future income from writing. If tax has been paid on that other income, a repayment can be obtained, or the sum can be offset against other tax liabilities. Special loss relief can apply in the opening years of the profession. Losses made in the first four years can be set against income of up to three earlier years.

Where a writer receives very occasional payments for isolated articles, it may not be possible to establish that these are profits arising from carrying on a continuing profession. In such circumstances these 'isolated transactions' may be assessed under Case VI of Schedule D of the Income and Corporation Taxes Act 1988. Again, expenses may be deducted in arriving at the taxable income but, if expenses exceed income, the loss can only be set against the profits from future isolated transactions, or other income assessable under Case VI.

In the tax year 1996/97 a new tax system came into effect called Self Assessment. Under Self Assessment the onus is on the individual to declare income and expenses correctly. Each writer therefore has to decide whether profits arise from a professional or occasional activity. The consequences of getting it wrong can be expensive by way of interest, penalties and surcharges on additional tax subsequently found to be due. If in any doubt the writer should seek professional advice.

Income

A writer's income includes fees, advances, royalties, commissions, sale of copyrights, reimbursed expenses, etc., from any source anywhere in the world whether or not brought to the UK (non UK resident or domiciled writers should seek professional advice).

Agents

It should be borne in mind that the agent stands in the shoes of the principal. It is not always realised that when the agent receives royalties, fees, advances, etc. on behalf of the author those receipts became the property of the author on the date of their receipt by the agent. This applies for Income Tax and Value Added Tax purposes.

Expenses

A writer can normally claim the following expenses:

(a) Secretarial, typing, proof-reading, research. Where payment for these is made to the author's wife or husband they should be recorded and entered in the spouse's tax return as earned income which is subject to the usual personal allowances. If payments reach relevant levels, PAYE should be operated.

(b) Telephone, faxes, Internet costs, computer software, postage, stationery, printing, equipment maintenance, insurance, dictation tapes, batteries, any equipment or office requisites used for the profession.

(c) Periodicals, books (including presentation copies and reference books) and other publications necessary for the profession, but amounts received from the sale of books should be deducted.

(d) Hotels, fares, car running expenses (including repairs, petrol, oil, garaging, parking, cleaning, insurance, road fund tax, depreciation), hire of cars or taxis in connection with:

   (i) business discussions with agents, publishers, co-authors, collaborators, researchers, illustrators, etc.

   (ii) travel at home and abroad to collect background material.

As an alternative to keeping details of full car running costs, a mileage rate can be claimed for business use. This is known as the Fixed Profit Car Scheme and is available to writers whose turnover does not exceed the VAT registration limit, currently £58,000.

(e) Publishing and advertising expenses, including costs of proof corrections, indexing, photographs, etc.

(f) Subscriptions to societies and associations, press cutting agencies, libraries, etc., incurred wholly for the purpose of the profession.

(g) Rent, council tax and water rates, etc., the proportion being determined by the ratio of the number of rooms used exclusively for the profession, to the total number of rooms in the residence. But see note on Capital Gains Tax below.

(h) Lighting, heating and cleaning. A carefully calculated figure of the business use of these costs can be claimed as a proportion of the total.

(i) Agent's commission, accountancy charges and legal charges incurred wholly in the course of the profession including cost of defending libel actions, damages in so far as they are not covered by insurance, and libel insurance premiums. However, where in a libel case damages are awarded to punish the author for having acted maliciously the action becomes quasi-criminal and costs and damages may not be allowed.

(j) TV and video rental (which may be apportioned for private use), and cinema or theatre tickets, if wholly for the purpose of the profession.

(k) Capital allowances for business equipment. These are now divided into three categories:

  (i) Computer equipment including printers, scanners, cabling, etc. For any such equipment purchased between 1 April 2000 and 31 March 2004 there is a First Year Allowance of 100%. Prior to that the First Year Allowance was 40% of the cost of the equipment purchased after 1 July 1998 and 50% on equipment purchased after 1 July 1997. For equipment purchased prior to 1 April 2000, after the first year there is an annual Writing Down Allowance of 25% of the reducing balance. After 31 March 2004, computer equipment is treated in the same way as other business equipment.

  (ii) On motor cars the allowance is 25% in the first year and 25% of the reducing balance in each successive year limited to £3000 each year.

  (iii) For all other business equipment, e.g. TV, radio, hi-fi sets, tape and video recorders, Dictaphones, office furniture, photographic equipment, etc. there was a First Year Allowance of 40% until 31 March 2004. For small businesses (which most authors will be), for two years from 1 April 2004 the First Year Allowance is increased to 50%. After the first year there is an annual Writing Down Allowance of 25% of the reducing balance. The allowances for all the three categories mentioned above will be reduced to exclude personal (non-professional) use where necessary.

(l) Lease rent. The cost of lease rent of equipment is allowable; also on cars, subject to restrictions for private use, and for expensive cars.

(m) Other expenses incurred wholly and exclusively for professional purposes. (Entertaining expenses are not allowable in any circumstances.)

NB It essential to keep detailed records. Diary entries of appointments, notes of fares and receipted bills are much more convincing to the Inland Revenue who are very reluctant to accept estimates.

The Self Assessment regime makes it a legal requirement for proper accounting records to be kept. These records must be sufficient to support the figures declared in the tax return.

In addition to the above, tax relief is available on:

(a) Premiums to pension schemes such as the Society of Authors Retirement Benefits Scheme. Depending on age, up to 40% of net earned income can be paid into a personal pension plan.

(b) Covenants to charities. (Deeds executed prior to 6 April 2000.)

(c) Gift Aid payments to charities. Any amount.

Capital Gains Tax

The exemption from Capital Gains Tax which applies to an individual's main residence does not apply to any part of that residence which is used exclusively for business purposes. The appropriate proportion of any increase in value of the residence, since purchase or 31 March 1982 if later, can be taxed when the residence is sold, subject to adjustment for inflation to March 1998 and subsequent length of ownership, at the individual's highest rate of tax.

Writers who own their houses should bear this in mind before claiming expenses for the use of a room for writing purposes. Arguments in favour of making such claims are that they afford some relief now, while Capital Gains Tax in its present form may not stay for ever. Also, where a new house is bought in place of an old one, the gain made on the sale of the first study may be set off against the cost of the study in the new house, thus postponing the tax payment until the final sale. For this relief to apply, each house must have a study and the author must continue his profession throughout. On death there is an exemption of the total Capital Gains of the estate.

Alternatively, writers can claim that their use is non-exclusive and restrict their claim to the cost of extra lighting, heating and cleaning to avoid any Capital Gains Tax liability.

Can a writer average out his income over a number of years for tax purposes?

The Budget in March 2001 introduced measures which will enable writers to average their profits (made wholly or mainly from creative works) over two or more consecutive years. If the profits of the lower year are less than 70% of the profits of the higher year or the profits of one year (but not both) are nil, the author will be able to claim to have the profits averaged. Where the profits of the lower year are more than 70% but less than 75% of the profits of the higher year a pro-rata adjustment is made to both years to reduce the difference between them.

The first years that can be averaged are 2000/1 and 2001/2.

It is also possible to average out income within the terms of publishers' contracts, but professional advice should be taken before signature. Where a husband and wife collaborate as writers, advice should be taken as to whether a formal partnership agreement should be made or whether the publishing agreement should be in joint names.

Is a lump sum paid for an outright sale of the copyright or part of the copyright exempt from tax?

No. All the money received from the marketing of literary work, by whatever means, is taxable. Some writers, in spite of clear judicial decisions to the contrary, still seem to think that an outright sale of, for instance, the film rights in a book is not subject to tax. The averaging relief described above should be considered.

Remaindering

To avoid remaindering authors can usually purchase copies of their own books from the publishers. Monies received from sales are subject to income tax but the cost of books sold should be deducted because tax is only payable on the profit made.

Is there any relief where old copyrights are sold?

No. There was relief available until April 2001 but was then withdrawn. The averaging relief described above should be considered.

Are royalties payable on publication of a book abroad subject to both foreign tax as well as UK tax?

Where there is a Double Taxation Agreement between the country concerned and the UK, then on the completion of certain formalities no tax is deductible at source by the foreign payer, but such income is taxable in the UK in the ordinary way. When there is no Double Taxation Agreement, credit will be given against UK tax for overseas tax paid. A complete list of countries with which the UK has conventions for the avoidance of double taxation may be obtained from FICO, Inland Revenue, St John's House, Merton Road, Bootle, Merseyside L69 9BB, or a local tax office.

Residence abroad

Writers residing abroad will, of course, be subject to the tax laws ruling in their country of residence, and as a general rule royalty income paid from the United Kingdom can be exempted from deduction of UK tax at source, providing the author is carrying on his profession abroad. A writer who is intending to go and live abroad should make early application for future royalties to be paid without deduction of tax to FICO, address as above. In certain circumstances writers resident in the Irish Republic are exempt from Irish Income Tax on their authorship earnings.

Are grants or prizes taxable?

The law is uncertain. Some Arts Council grants are now deemed to be taxable, whereas most prizes and awards are not, though it depends on the conditions in each case. When submitting the Self Assessment annual returns, such items should be excluded, but reference made to them in the 'Additional Information' box on the self-employment (or partnership) pages.

What is the item 'Class 4 N.I.C.' which appears on my Self Assessment return?

All taxpayers who are self-employed pay an additional national insurance contribution if their earned income exceeds a figure which varies each year. This contribution is described as Class 4 and is calculated when preparing the return. It is additional to the self-employed Class 2 contribution but confers no additional benefits and is a form of levy. It applies to men aged under 65 and women under 60.

Should an author use a limited company?

Changes in the tax regime has made the incorporation of businesses more and more attractive and there are advantages in so doing for businesses with relatively low levels of profit although these advantages were reduced in the 2004 Budget. However, there are disadvantages in all cases and particular considerations for authors. The advice of an accountant, knowledgeable about the affairs of authors, should be sought if incorporation is contemplated.

Value Added Tax

Value Added Tax (VAT) is a tax currently levied at 17.5% on:

(a) the total value of taxable goods and services supplied to consumers,
(b) the importation of goods into the UK,
(c) certain services or goods from abroad if a taxable person receives them in the UK for the purpose of their business.

Who is taxable?

A writer resident in the UK whose turnover from writing and any other business, craft or art on a self-employed basis is greater than £58,000 annually, before deducting agent's commission, must register with HM Customs & Excise as a taxable person. Turnover includes fees, royalties, advances, commissions, sale of copyright, reimbursed expenses, etc. A business is required to register:

● at the end of any month if the value of taxable supplies in the past twelve months has exceeded the annual threshold; or
● if there are reasonable grounds for believing that the value of taxable supplies in the next twelve months will exceed the annual threshold.

Penalties will be claimed in the case of late registration. A writer whose turnover is below these limits is exempt from the requirements to register for VAT but may apply for voluntary registration and this will be allowed at the discretion of HM Customs & Excise.

A taxable person collects VAT on outputs (turnover) and deducts VAT paid on inputs (taxable expenses) and where VAT collected exceeds VAT paid, must remit the difference to HM Customs & Excise. In the event that input exceeds output, the difference will be refunded by HM Customs & Excise.

Outputs (Turnover)

A writer's outputs are taxable services supplied to publishers, broadcasting organisations, theatre managements, film companies, educational institutions, etc. A taxable writer must invoice, i.e. collect from, all the persons (either individuals or organisations) in the UK for whom supplies have been made, for fees, royalties or other considerations plus VAT. An unregistered writer cannot and

Inputs

Taxable at the standard rate if supplier is registered	Taxable at the zero or special rate	Not liable to VAT
Rent of certain commercial premises	Books (zero)	Rent of non-commercial premises
Advertisements in newspapers, magazines, journals and periodicals	Coach, rail and air travel (zero)	Postage
Agent's commission (unless it relates to monies from overseas)	Agent's commission (on monies from overseas)	Services supplied by unregistered persons
Accountant's and solicitor's fees for business matters	Domestic gas and electricity (5%)	Subscriptions to the Society of Authors, PEN, NUJ, etc.
Agency services (typing, copying, etc.)		Insurance
Word processors, typewriters and stationery		
Artists' materials		
Photographic equipment		
Tape recorders and tapes		
Hotel accommodation		*Outside the scope of VAT*
Taxi fares		
Motorcar expenses		PLR (Public Lending Right)
Telephone		Profit shares
Theatres and concerts		Investment income
NB This list is not exhaustive		

must not invoice for VAT. A taxable writer is not obliged to collect VAT on royalties or other fees paid by publishers or others overseas. In practice, agents usually collect VAT for the registered author.

Remit to Customs
The taxable writer adds up the VAT which has been paid on taxable inputs, deducts it from the VAT received and remits the balance to Customs. Business with HM Customs is conducted through the local VAT offices of HM Customs which are listed in local telephone directories, except for VAT returns which are sent direct to the Customs & Excise VAT Central Unit, Alexander House, 21 Victoria Avenue, Southend on Sea, Essex SS99 1AA.

Accounting
A taxable writer is obliged to account to HM Customs & Excise at quarterly intervals. Returns must be completed and sent to VAT Central Unit by the dates shown on the return. Penalties can be charged if the returns are late.

It is possible to account for the VAT liability under the Cash Accounting Scheme (leaflet 731), whereby the author accounts for the output tax when the invoice is paid or royalties, etc., are received. The same applies to the input tax, but as most purchases are probably on a 'cash basis', this will not make a considerable difference to the author's input tax. This scheme is only applicable to those with a taxable turnover of less than £660,000 and, therefore, is available to the majority of authors. The advantage of this scheme is that the author does not have to account for VAT before receiving payments, thereby relieving the author of a cash flow problem.

If turnover is less than £150,000 it is also possible to pay VAT by nine estimated direct debits, with a final balance at the end of the year (see leaflet 732). This annual accounting method also means that only one VAT return is submitted.

Flat Rate Scheme
Small businesses can elect to pay VAT under a flat rate scheme (FRS). This is open to businesses with business income up to £150,000 a year. Under the normal VAT accounting rules, each item of turnover and every claimed expense must be recorded and supported by evidence, e.g. invoices, receipts, etc. Under the FRS, detailed records of sales and purchases do not have to be kept. A record of gross income (including zero rated and exempt income) is maintained and a flat rate percentage is applied to the total. This percentage is then paid over to HM Customs. The percentage varies from one profession or business to another but for authors is 11%. In the first year of registration this percentage is reduced by 1%. The aim of the scheme is to reduce the amount of time and money spent in complying with VAT regulations and this is to be welcomed. However, there are disadvantages:

- The detailed records of income and expenses are still going to be required for taxation purposes.

- Invoices on sales are issued in the normal way.
- The percentage is applied to all business income. So 11% VAT will effectively be paid on income from abroad, zero rated under the normal basis, and PLR, otherwise exempt.

For many authors, normal VAT accounting has imposed a good, timely discipline for dealing with accounting and taxation matters.

Registration
A writer will be given a VAT registration number which must be quoted on all VAT correspondence. It is the responsibility of those registered to inform those to whom they make supplies of their registration number. The taxable turnover limit which determines whether a person who is registered for VAT may apply for cancellation of registration is £56,000.

Voluntary registration
A writer whose turnover is below the limits may apply to register. If the writer is paying a relatively large amount of VAT on taxable inputs – agent's commission, accountant's fees, equipment, materials, or agency services, etc. – it may make a significant improvement in the net income to be able to offset the VAT on these inputs. A writer who pays relatively little VAT may find it easier, and no more expensive, to remain unregistered.

Fees and royalties
A taxable writer must notify those to whom he makes supplies of the VAT Registration Number at the first opportunity. One method of accounting for and paying VAT on fees and royalties is the use of multiple stationery for 'self-billing', one copy of the royalty statement being used by the author as the VAT invoice. A second method is for the recipient of taxable outputs to pay fees, including authors' royalties, without VAT. The taxable writer then renders a tax invoice for the VAT element and a second payment, of the VAT element, will be made. This scheme is cumbersome but will involve only taxable authors. Fees and royalties from abroad will count as payments for exported services and will accordingly be zero-rated.

Agents and accountants
A writer is responsible to HM Customs for making VAT returns and payments. Neither an agent nor an accountant nor a solicitor can remove the responsibility, although they can be helpful in preparing and keeping VAT returns and accounts. Their professional fees or commission will, except in rare cases where the adviser or agent is himself unregistered, be taxable at the standard rate and will represent some of a writer's taxable inputs.

Income Tax – Schedule D
An unregistered writer can claim some of the VAT paid on taxable inputs as a

business expense allowable against income tax. However, certain taxable inputs fall into categories which cannot be claimed under the income tax regulations. A taxable writer, who has already claimed VAT on inputs, cannot charge it as a business expense for the purposes of income tax.

Certain services from abroad

A taxable author who resides in the United Kingdom and who receives certain services from abroad must account for VAT on those services at the appropriate tax rate on the sum paid for them. Examples of the type of services concerned include: services of lawyers, accountants, consultants, provision of information and copyright permissions.

Inheritance Tax

Inheritance Tax was introduced in 1984 to replace Capital Transfer Tax, which had in turn replaced Estate Duty, the first of the death taxes of recent times. Paradoxically, Inheritance Tax has reintroduced a number of principles present under the old Estate Duty.

The general principle now is that all assets owned at death are chargeable to tax (currently 40%) except the first £263,000 of the estate and any assets passed to a surviving spouse or a charity. Gifts made more than seven years before death are exempt, but those made within this period may be taxed on a sliding scale. No tax is payable at the time of making the gift.

In addition, each individual may currently make gifts of up to £3000 in any year and these will be considered to be exempt. A further exemption covers any number of annual gifts not exceeding £250 to any one person.

If the £3000 is not fully utilised in one year, any unused balance can be carried forward to the following year (but no later). Gifts out of income, which do not reduce one's living standards, are also exempt if they are part of normal expenditure.

At death all assets are valued; they will include any property, investments, life policies, furniture and personal possessions, bank balances and, in the case of authors, the value of copyrights. All, with the sole exception of copyrights, are capable (as assets) of accurate valuation and, if necessary, can be turned into cash. The valuation of copyright is, of course, complicated and frequently gives rise to difficulty. Except where they are bequeathed to the owner's husband or wife, very real problems can be left behind by the author.

Experience has shown that a figure based on two to three years' past royalties may be proposed by the Inland Revenue in their valuation of copyright. However, this may not be reasonable and may require negotiation. If a book is running out of print or if, as in the case of educational books, it may need revision at the next reprint, these factors must be taken into account. In many cases the fact that the author is no longer alive and able to make personal appearances, or provide publicity, or write further works, will result in lower or slower sales. Obviously, this is an area in which help can be given by the publishers, and in particular one needs to know what their future intentions are, what stocks of the books remain, and what likelihood there will be of reprinting.

There is a further relief available to authors who have established that they have been carrying on a business, normally assessable under Case II of Schedule D, for at least two years prior to death. It has been possible to establish that copyrights are treated as business property and in these circumstances, Inheritance Tax 'business property relief' is available. This relief at present is 100% so that the tax saving can be quite substantial. The Inland Revenue may wish to be assured that the business is continuing and consideration should therefore be given to the appointment, in the author's will, of a literary executor who should be a qualified business person or, in certain circumstances, the formation of partnership between the author and spouse, or other relative, to ensure that it is established the business is continuing after the author's death.

If the author has sufficient income, consideration should be given to building up a fund to cover future Inheritance Tax liabilities. One of a number of ways would be to take out a whole life assurance policy which is assigned to the children, or other beneficiaries, the premiums on which are within the annual exemption of £3000. The capital sum payable on the death of the assured is exempt from inheritance tax.

Anyone wondering how best to order his affairs for tax purposes should consult an accountant with specialised knowledge in this field. Experience shows that a good accountant is well worth his fee which, incidentally, so far as it relates to professional matters, is an allowable expense.

The information contained in this section has been prepared by Ian Spring of Moore Stephens, Chartered Accountants, who will be pleased to answer questions on tax problems. Please write to Ian Spring, c/o The Writer's Handbook, 34 Ufton Road, London N1 5BX.

Company Index

Subject Index